Environmental Regulation

Environmental Regulation

Law, Science, and Policy

Fifth Edition

Robert V. Percival

Robert F. Stanton Professor of Law
Director, Environmental Law Program
University of Maryland School of Law

Christopher H. Schroeder

Charles F. Murphy Professor of Law and Public Policy Studies
Director, Program in Public Law
Duke University School of Law

Alan S. Miller

GEF and Climate Change Coordinator
The International Finance Corporation

James P. Leape

Director General
World Wildlife Fund International

ASPEN

PUBLISHERS

76 Ninth Avenue, New York, NY 10011
http://lawschool.aspenpublishers.com

Aspen Publishers
Attn: Permissions Department
76 Ninth Avenue, 7th Floor
New York, NY 10011

Printed in the United States of America.

1 2 3 4 5 6 7 8 9 0

ISBN 0-7355-5785-3

Library of Congress Cataloging-in-Publication Data

Environmental regulation : law, science, and policy / Robert V.
Percival . . . [et al.]. – 5th ed.
     p. cm.
   Includes index.
   ISBN 0-7355-5785-3
 1. Environmental law—United States.   2. Environmental law—United
States—Cases.   3. Environmental policy—United States.   4. Environmental
protection.   I. Percival, Robert V.

KF3775.E548 2006
344.7304'6—dc22   2006020579

About Aspen Publishers

Aspen Publishers, headquartered in New York City, is a leading information provider for attorneys, business professionals, and law students. Written by preeminent authorities, our products consist of analytical and practical information covering both U.S. and international topics. We publish in the full range of formats, including updated manuals, books, periodicals, CDs, and online products.

Our proprietary content is complemented by 2,500 legal databases, containing over 11 million documents, available through our Loislaw division. Aspen Publishers also offers a wide range of topical legal and business databases linked to Loislaw's primary material. Our mission is to provide accurate, timely, and authoritative content in easily accessible formats, supported by unmatched customer care.

To order any Aspen Publishers title, go to *http://lawschool.aspenpublishers.com* or call 1-800-638-8437.

To reinstate your manual update service, call 1-800-638-8437.

For more information on Loislaw products, go to *www.loislaw.com* or call 1-800-364-2512.

For Customer Care issues, e-mail *CustomerCare@aspenpublishers.com*; call 1-800-234-1660; or fax 1-800-901-9075.

Aspen Publishers
a Wolters Kluwer business

To my international family,
Barbara, Marita, and Richard.

R.V.P.

To Kate, Emily, Ted, and Lily,
and to my parents, Jane and Herb,
for their unqualified support
and love.

C.H.S.

To Sue, Joanna, and my parents,
Ruth and Ralph Miller.

A.S.M.

To Suki, Benjamin, and Jonathan.

J.P.L.

Summary of Contents

Contents

— 3 —

‖ *Preventing Harm in the Face of Uncertainty* ‖   *165*

— 7 —

‖ *Land Use Regulation and Regulatory Takings* ‖   *709*

— 8 —
‖ *Environmental Impact Assessment* ‖   795

— 9 —

‖ *Preservation of Biodiversity* ‖   863

— 11 —

Protection of the Global Environment   *1039*

— **12** —

║ *Environmental Progress and Prospects* ║   *1127*

— **APPENDIX A** —

‖ *Glossary* ‖   *1155*

— **APPENDIX B** —

‖ *List of Acronyms* ‖   *1175*

Preface

Public concern for the environment has been a catalyst for profound changes in American law. During the past four decades, environmental law has grown from sparse common law roots into a vast system of public law that lies at the heart of the modern regulatory state. Environmental law has generated an immense and fiercely complex web of regulations that affects the way we live, work, and do business. Environmental regulation now affects many other areas of legal practice, including real estate and commercial transactions, corporate law, criminal law, and bankruptcy. This book seeks to provide a comprehensive introduction to environmental law.

The fifth edition of this book goes to press at a time of considerable introspection in the environmental field. After decades of rapid growth, environmental regulation now faces serious challenges from those who believe it has gone too far, become too intrusive, or accomplished too little. Others believe that burgeoning global environmental problems require much more aggressive action than taken to date. Congress remains in gridlock on most environmental legislation and some members of the judiciary are highly critical of federal regulation. In a decision issued just before this edition goes to press, the U.S. Supreme Court split 4-1-4 with four Justices joining an opinion harshly critical of federal wetlands regulation, while four dissenters and a Justice concurring in the judgment extolled its importance (see Rapanos v. United States in Chapter 6).

The fifth edition provides a comprehensive updating of the casebook, which retains most of the basic structure of the fourth edition. The only significant organizational change is that the order of appearance of Chapters 3 and 4 has been reversed. In this fifth edition, Chapter 3 (formerly called "Regulation of Toxic Substances") is now called "Preventing Harm in the Face of Uncertainty." Material on "Waste Management and Pollution Prevention," which previously was in Chapter 3, now appears as Chapter 4.

As in the previous editions, the text seeks to broaden students' vision by inviting them to explore how law relates to the larger problems society seeks to solve through collective action. It approaches environmental law through a regulatory policy focus that explores the full range of forces that shape the way law affects human behavior. By focusing on regulation—viewed expansively as embracing all forms of collective action to protect the environment—the text seeks to enhance understanding of the way law affects the behavior of institutions and individuals. This requires far more than mastery of "black letter" law; it also demands an appreciation of the complex processes by which political, economic, and ethical concerns shape regulatory policy. Thus, the text consistently focuses not only on the substance of environmental statutes, but also on how they are translated into regulations and on the factors that affect how they influence real-world behavior.

Despite its comprehensiveness, the book seeks at every turn to make environmental law and policy accessible to the nonspecialist. Among the key features it employs to accomplish this goal are charts and diagrams mapping the structure of each of the major environmental statutes; problems and questions based largely on real-world environmental controversies; "pathfinders," explaining where to find crucial source materials for every major subject area; an extensive glossary of environmental terms; and a list of environmental acronyms. The book also has its own website located at *www.law.umaryland.edu/ environment/casebook.* The site provides chapter-by-chapter updates of material in the casebook and links to the rich array of environmental information available through the Internet. Teachers using the text also will have access to the most detailed Teacher's Manual in the field. Each year a statutory and case supplement to the text is published (Environmental Law: Statutory and Case Supplement with Internet Guide), which provides both the updated text of the principal environmental statutes and new judicial decisions in the field.

The chapters are organized in a manner that gives teachers considerable flexibility in deciding what to cover and in what order. Because each chapter is designed to be self-contained, the material may be covered in a variety of sequences, depending on the length of the course and the teacher's desired areas of emphasis. The teacher's manual identifies several alternative coverage options.

The authors appreciate the numerous comments received from faculty and students who have used the previous editions of this text. These comments and suggestions have been invaluable in helping us improve the fifth edition, as we hope you will notice. We hope you will continue to give us such useful feedback on this edition as well.

Robert V. Percival
Christopher H. Schroeder
Alan S. Miller
James P. Leape

July 2006

‖ Acknowledgments ‖

The authors are grateful to the many people who have assisted us during preparation of the fifth edition of this casebook. Bob Percival would like to thank the Maryland law students who assisted him with research, including April Birnbaum and Khushi Desai, as well as Lauren Charney, Amalia Fenton, Lewis Taylor, and Ian Ullman for assistance with proofreading and revising the index and table of cases. Chris Schroeder wishes to thank Johnathan Hammond, Duke Law 2007, for his extensive assistance in preparing the fifth edition.

We remain immensely grateful to the remarkable professionals employed by Aspen Publishers. We especially wish to thank Carol McGeehan, Melody Davies, Troy Froebe, and Barbara Roth.

The authors are forever indebted to Laura Mrozek, Administrator of Maryland's Environmental Law Program, for her continued extraordinary assistance with all aspects of the project.

The authors gratefully acknowledge the permissions granted to reproduce the following materials.

A New Way of Living with Nature (editorial), N.Y. Times, December 19, 1999. Copyright 1999 by The New York Times Company. Reprinted with permission.

Botkin, Adjusting Law to Nature's Discordant Harmonies, 7 Duke Envt'l L. & Policy Forum 25 (1996). Copyright 1996. Duke University School of Law. Reprinted with permission.

Center for Progressive Reform, Perspective on Environmental Justice. Reprinted with permission.

Dreher, NEPA Under Siege (2005). Reprinted with permission of the author and the Georgetown Environmental Law and Policy Institute.

Easterbook, A Moment on the Earth: The Coming Age of Environmental Optimism (1995). Reprinted with permission.

Environmental Defense Fund, A Moment of Truth: Correcting the Scientific Errors in Gregg Easterbrook's *A Moment on the Earth* (1995). Reprinted with permission.

EPA's Assessment of Top Environmental Concerns and the Public's Ranking (chart), in Counting on Science at EPA, 249 Science 616 (1990). Copyright © 1990 by the AAAS. Reprinted with permission of Science.

Stoll, Coping with the RCRA Hazardous Waste System: A Few Practical Points for Fun and Profit, 1 Envtl. Hazards 6 (July 1989). Reprinted with permission from Prentice Hall and the author.

Titus, Rising Seas, Coastal Erosion, and the Takings Clause: How To Save Wetlands and Beaches Without Hurting Property Owners, 57 Maryland Law Review 1279 (1998). Reprinted with permission.

Toles, Motors, Inc. (cartoon). Tom Toles in the Buffalo News, Oct. 4, 1989. Reprinted with permission.

Toles, The Unwritten Contract (cartoon). Tom Toles in the Buffalo News. Copyright © 1995. Reprinted with permission of Universal Press Syndicate. All rights reserved.

Turner and Rylander, Land Use, Thinking Ecologically, The Next Generation of Environmental Policy (1997). Copyright 1997 by the Yale University Press. Reprinted by permission.

Weiss and H. Jacobson, Getting Countries to Comply with International Agreements, Environment, July/August, 1999. Reprinted by permission of Heldref Publications.

Wilson, Biophilia. Reprinted by permission of the publishers from Biophilia by Edward Wilson, Cambridge, Mass.: Harvard University Press. Copyright © 1984 by the President and Fellows of Harvard College.

World Wildlife Fund and The Conservation Foundation, excerpt from comments made by Donald Kennedy on December 5, 1978, when Kennedy was Commissioner of the Food and Drug Administration. Reprinted from Risk Assessment and Risk Control, Washington, D.C.: The Conservation Foundation (1987).

Zaelke, Stilwell, and Young, What Reason Demands: Making Laws Work for Sustainable Development in Making Law Work: Environmental Compliance & Sustainable Development (Zaelke, Kaniaru, and Kruzikova eds., 2005). Reprinted with permission.

Environmental Regulation

=1=

Environmental Values and Policies: An Introduction

Humanity faces an unprecedented challenge as our numbers grow, while Earth and its capacity to support us do not. People across the United States and around the world aspire to better lives for themselves and for their children: food, shelter, a safe and healthy environment, education, jobs, and other material needs and conveniences. Industries strive to produce more goods, farmers to grow more crops; and human demands on forests, fields, rivers, and oceans increase. Our challenge is to create a future in which prosperity and opportunity increase while life flourishes and pressures on oceans, earth, and atmosphere—the biosphere— diminish; to create, as the Council's vision suggests, "a life sustaining Earth" that supports "a dignified, peaceful, and equitable existence."*

—*President's Council on Sustainable Development*

If we listen to environmental debate, it will appear that there is even some kind of consensus regarding values. Yet when you scratch the surface, when individuals—executives, labor officials, factory workers, teachers, professional workers, farmers, traveling salesmen—begin to tell you their own life stories, their hopes, needs, feelings, and opinions, you get a glimpse of the complexity of the problem of values. Very often the same person holds contradictory attitudes. Values seem to arise from economic interests, yet many of the oldest and most deeply imbedded ones, like those prevalent for centuries in religious thought, enjoy an existence virtually independent of economic conditions. Attitudes toward [the environment] can be understood as only a small cluster in the vast constellation of values coming from hundreds of cultural sources— family, religion, economic beliefs, even personality and character.**

—*Joseph Petulla*

The desire to ensure that present and future generations enjoy the benefits of both a prosperous economy and a healthy environment has become a universal aspiration that can provide common ground between remarkably diverse interests. The path for achieving this goal is often referred to as "sustainable development," a concept that has broad public support, despite sharp disagreements over specific policies for pursuing it.

Since the late 1960s, spectacular growth in public concern for the environment has had a profound impact on the development of American law. During this period, U.S. environmental law has grown from a sparse set of common

---

*Towards a Sustainable America: Advancing Prosperity, Opportunity and a Healthy Environment for the 21st Century i (1999).
**American Environmentalism 3 (1980).

1

law precedents and local ordinances to encompass a vast body of national legislation. Numerous federal and state agencies now implement these laws through complex regulations that affect virtually every aspect of our lives. In addition, as environmental concerns increasingly transcend national boundaries, environmental law has now become an urgent priority around the globe.

U.S. environmental law has roots in many traditional fields of law, including torts, property, and constitutional law. Much of its continued evolution has been a response to perceived deficiencies of the common law as a vehicle for responding to new problems and new knowledge about the environmental effects of human activity. Chapter 2 explores the major sources of environmental law and provides an overview of the contemporary structure of the field. Throughout its development, environmental law has faced continual criticisms for not changing quickly enough. Such criticism comes both from those who think environmental law responds too weakly and too slowly to environmental problems as well as from those who think its requirements are unnecessarily burdensome and restrictive, forcing the public and private sectors to devote resources to problems that are either imaginary or overstated.

Those who consider environmental law already too burdensome and restrictive make a variety of proposals to reform its present structure. These include (a) devolving substantial authorities away from the federal government to states and localities; (b) rethinking basic approaches to preserving biodiversity and protecting wilderness and habitat; (c) suspending further regulatory action until science answers more of our questions about the impact of human action on the environment; (d) increasing protections for private property by requiring government to compensate for reductions in property values caused by environmental regulation; (e) subjecting all proposed regulatory action to a rigorous cost-benefit test; and (f) replacing traditional regulation with markets in which polluters can trade rights to emit pollutants, as well as with other "new generation" forms of regulation that emphasize making environmental law more flexible, more cost-effective, or more reliant on voluntary behavior. These ideas are not newly minted, although the widespread end-of-the-century urge to reassess produced a spate of studies aimed at taking stock of our environmental progress and prospects. See, e.g., National Academy of Public Administration's environment.gov: Transforming Environmental Protection for the 21st Century (2000); J. Clarence Davies and Jan Mazurek, Pollution Control in the United States: Evaluating the System (1999); Mary Graham, The Morning After Earth Day (1999); Enterprise for the Environment, The Environmental Protection System in Transition: Toward a More Desirable Future (1998). A comprehensive summary and analysis of reform proposals, together with thorough references to other studies, is Richard Stewart, A New Generation of Environmental Regulation?, 29 Cap. U. L. Rev. 21 (2001). Throughout the book, we will address many of the reforms proposed by these studies in the course of examining specific environmental problems.

For those who think environmental law has been too weak and too slow, swifter implementation and more vigorous enforcement of existing laws are often demanded, but it is also recognized that existing laws can be improved, and often times must be, if further environmental progress is to be made. For this group, policy makers and implementers need to be more aggressive in regulating toxic releases into the environment, in reevaluating the registration of pesticides, in cleaning up hazardous waste sites and groundwater contamination, and in addressing global environmental problems such as global warming. So their crucial issue is the design of regulatory instruments that achieve greater environmental quality protection and improvement. Accordingly, if a scheme that permits polluters to trade the right to emit pollutants achieves genuine pollution reductions, for instance, they are usually willing to entertain such an idea. That said, there is today a good deal of suspicion in such quarters that most calls from polluters for regulatory reform are actually efforts to obtain regulatory relief.

This casebook introduces you to the modern environmental law and policy regimes that have prompted these diverse reactions. It will enable you to develop a competence in understanding and interpreting the law as it currently exists, and will provide you with some of the perspective and analytical tools necessary to evaluate calls for change and reform. This chapter begins this dual project by exploring some of the fundamental traditions of thought and attitude that form contemporary views regarding the environment. There are areas of broad agreement that some forms of collective action are necessary to address environmental problems. At the same time, the diversity of diagnoses about how environmental law needs to change intimates that there are also areas of fundamental disagreement about the concrete form such collective action should take.

A. ENVIRONMENTAL PROBLEMS AND PROGRESS

The domain of environmental law and policy extends to any place where the earth is modified by human action. Some of today's environmental problems have been around for centuries. Lead poisoning from wine goblets affected the Roman Empire. The Ancestral Pueblo peoples of the American Southwest intensively used and eventually depleted the natural resources of the mesas upon which they built their cliff dwellings.

Others are new. Synthetic organic compounds and nuclear power did not exist prior to World War II. Still others are old problems with new consequences caused by great increases in scale. In the past 50 years we have added more people and more pollutants to the planet than in the preceding 10,000 years. As just one illustration, carbon emissions from fossil fuel burning—a major contributor to global warming—has grown from practically nothing at the start of the Industrial Revolution to 500 million tons at the turn of the last century to 1.6 billion in 1950 to 6.3 billion in 2000. The Energy Information Administration estimates that number will grow to 8.89 billion by 2025. EIA, Annual Energy Outlook 2005—Market Trends, Carbon Dioxide Emissions (2005).

John Holdren and Paul Ehrlich are credited with first suggesting that the impact (I) that human behavior has on the environment results from the combined effect of population size (P), the level of affluence (A), and the type of technologies (T) that enhance our abilities to consume resources. Paul Ehrlich & John Holdren, Impact of Population Growth, 171 Science 1212-1217 (1971). This I = PAT formula ignores interdependencies and other complicating factors, but it does identify three significant elements that give rise to environmental issues.

The global population has increased from 3.85 billion in 1972 to 6.50 billion in 2005, U.S. Bureau of the Census, International Data Base, electronic database, updated February 22, 2006, *http://www.census.gov/ipc/www/world.html*, and the United Nations Population Division estimates it is growing at the rate of

77 million people per year. Increases in population change land use patterns, consume more nonrenewable natural resources such as fossil fuels, intensify land uses such as agriculture, and produce more pollution. The group of individuals adversely affected by health-related environmental factors also increases as total population increases. For example, despite the fact that the percentage of the world's population served with water supplies that have been treated or improved grew from 79 percent in 1972 to 82 percent in 2000, over 1.1 billion people now lack access to safe drinking water, and 2.4 billion lack adequate sanitation. As a consequence, more than 5 million people die every year from water-related diseases. UNEP, Global Environmental Outlook-3 152 (2002) (GEO-3).

The impacts of technological change on the environment have been substantial. The automobile, which barely existed at the turn of the century, now contributes about one-third of global greenhouse gases and is a major source of some of the most harmful air pollutants. Technological improvements such as sonar and vast drift nets give fishing fleets the ability to wipe out ocean fisheries—a real concern in light of the fact that two-thirds of the world's marine fisheries are currently considered over-exploited by the FAO. The development of plastics has facilitated growth in the throw-away economy, increasing per capita waste generation significantly.

The role of affluence can be illustrated through the idea of an Ecological Footprint. Developed by the World Wildlife Fund and others, the Ecological Footprint provides a measure of the human pressures being placed on global ecosystems. It estimates how much productive land is required to produce food and wood, to build and maintain human infrastructure, and to absorb the carbon dioxide people generate from energy production, expressing that estimate in terms of a "global hectare," or a hectare of land with biological productivity equal to the global average. The per capita Footprint for high income countries was 6.48 in 1999, compared to only 0.83 for low income countries. The United States' footprint was 9.6. Each American uses more than 12 times the ecological resources as does a citizen in Eritrea or Mozambique. Regional variations are shown in Figure 1.1. World Wildlife Fund, Living Planet Report 2004, Table 2.

Society and government have not been silent in the face of increasing human pressures on the global ecosystem. Since the early 1970s national, international, state, and local governments have been responding to the increased human pressure on the environment in a wide variety of ways. At the international level, agreements and programs aimed at reducing adverse environmental impacts of human activity have proliferated. Beginning in 1972, a series of once-a-decade environment summits have provided a focal point for these efforts. These summits began with the United Nations Conference on the Human Environment in Stockholm in 1972 and now extend through to the World Summit on Sustainable Development in Johannesburg in August and September 2002.

National and local environmental efforts have been equally impressive. Again, the early 1970s were a catalytic period, with the first Earth Day, April 22, 1970, symbolically marking the beginning of the modern environmental era. In the United States, a structure of national legislation sprang into place in a remarkably short period of time, and the Environmental Protection Agency was established to administer many of the new laws and regulations. For an overview of these developments, see Mary Graham, The Morning After Earth Day (1999). Today, we have a complex array of rules and regulations aimed at mitigating adverse environmental effects, the implementation of which now annually costs the private sector approximately $200 billion per year.

FIGURE 1.1
Ecological Footprint by Region, 2001

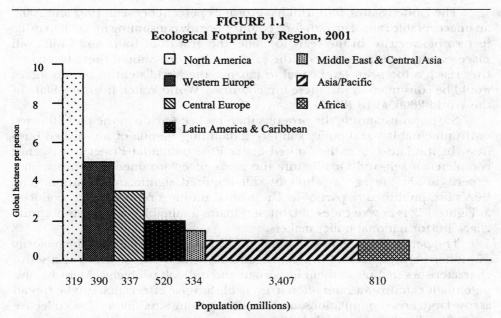

Source: World Wide Fund for Nature (WWF), United Nations Environment Programme World Conservation Monitoring Centre, Living Planet Report 2004. Gland, Switzerland: World Wide Fund for Nature.

The world's policy responses have had positive effects. For example, air quality in the United States has generally improved, notwithstanding increases in population and Gross National Product. EPA reports that emissions of carbon monoxide, 60 percent of which come from automobiles, have fallen by 61 percent from 1981 to 2000 (and by 41 percent between 1991 and 2000), even though vehicle miles traveled increased by 24 percent during the 1991–2000 time period. EPA, Air Quality Trends Report 14 (2002). Controls on the use of lead additives have been even more successful: Emissions of lead fell 94 percent between 1981 and 2000. Id. at 15. Internationally, global average life expectancy has been extended by eight years since 1972, with some of this improvement clearly due to reduction in environmental health risks. UNEP, GEO-3 at 32.

The Ecological Footprint proves a helpful summary statistic for our current environmental situation. The good news is that the global per capita Footprint is now growing at a slower rate than population growth—1.6 percent per year since 1985 versus 1.8 percent per year. We have begun, it would seem, to take steps to reduce the pressures that population growth puts on the global ecosystem. More disturbing, however, is news that the World Wildlife Fund (WWF) and others believe that our present levels of use exceed the maximum Footprint that the earth can sustain indefinitely, which they estimate to be 1.9 global hectares per capita, based on 2001 population figures. According to WWF, we have been overshooting the capacity of the world to sustain existing population levels since 1980. In 2001, we overshot the earth's biological capacity by 21 percent. World Wildlife Fund, Living Planet Report 2004, at 10. Continued ecological deficits of this kind will lead to a gradual depletion of the earth's capital stock, and is inconsistent with the objective of sustainable development that is now embraced in one form or another by almost all environmental organizations.

The United States' footprint has grown 21 percent between 1992 and 2002, an unacceptable rate of growth for a country already consuming more than twice its own biocapacity. In the years to come, the growth of India and China will place even greater pressures on the earth's resources. Should these two countries reach a footprint level equal to Japan's, the world's entire bio resources would be consumed by just these two countries. World Watch Institute, State of the World 2006, at 18 (2006).

So, notwithstanding the progress that has been made in the past 30 years, environmental law and policy still face a daunting agenda of unfinished business. In the late 1980s, the United States Environmental Protection Agency completed a self-study to identify the areas of environmental concern that experts inside the agency thought still required significant attention. The EPA's list, published as part of its Unfinished Business report and reproduced as Figure 1.2, is now decades old, but it remains a valuable and largely accurate check list for national policy makers.

The persistent problems on the Unfinished Business list, and the majority of modern environmental problems generally, share one or more of a set of characteristics that make them important and difficult problems. Many involve potentially catastrophic and often irreversible adverse effects that can be spread across large areas, populations, and time periods in ways that makes collective action to solve them essential. At the same time, there is great uncertainty about the mechanisms and effects of actions affecting the environment, so that debate over whether or not activities are actually causing substantial harm is often intense. There is also great resistance to actions aimed at solving them, sometimes because the economic costs are concentrated among a powerful few, sometimes because the costs involve life style changes among the many.

One imperative of the modern environmental era has been to improve our understanding of the environment and the effects of human action on it, so as to chip away at the uncertainties just mentioned. As we learn more about such cause and effect relationships, we sometimes conclude that adverse effects are worse than supposed, in some cases meaning that even substantial gains in addressing a problem need to be pushed further. Lead concentrations in the environment are an outstanding example. Despite the elimination of lead from gasoline, and the ban on lead in paint and plumbing, which have drastically reduced new sources of lead pollution, nearly half a million children still have lead levels high enough to be of medical concern. A major reason for this is our improved understanding of the adverse effects of low levels of lead exposure on neurodevelopment, which has prompted the Centers for Disease Control to lower its action levels for lead several times since the 1970s.

There are reasons to think that further environmental progress will be increasingly difficult. For one thing, we have taken a number of steps that lay along the path of least resistance, going after obvious environmental problems where remedial steps were relatively manageable. Rivers literally on fire because of the oil and chemical film on their surface, lakes suffocating from massive algae blooms, dense clouds of smog over cities, and odors from open solid waste dumps cried out for attention. Improving environmental quality by picking off such "low-hanging" fruit was clearly the correct first step, but by and large the actions taken to redress such obvious problems have proven insufficient to bring the quality of our environment to where we wish it to be. Progress from here on confronts tougher problems.

FIGURE 1.2
Agenda of "Unfinished Business" Identified by EPA

Inactive hazardous waste sites
Active hazardous waste sites
Accidental releases of toxics from chemical plants
Pesticide applications in farming
Other pesticide risks
Discharges of point sources directly into water systems
Indirect discharges of point sources into water systems
Nonpoint source (irrigation runoff, stormwater runoff, etc.) discharge into
    water systems
Criteria air pollutants (including acid rain)
Hazardous air pollutants
Other air pollutants
Occupational exposure to chemicals
Pesticide residues in food
Drinking water contamination
Genetic engineering
Mining wastes
Radon—indoor air pollution
Indoor air pollution other than radon
Indoor air pollution from consumer products
The greenhouse effect
Stratospheric ozone depletion
Contaminated sludge disposal
Wetlands preservation
Nonhazardous waste sites—municipal
Nonhazardous waste sites—industrial
New toxic chemicals
Releases from storage tanks
Other groundwater contamination
Accidental releases from oil tankers
Non-nuclear radiation
Estuaries, coastal waters, and oceans
Source: EPA, Unfinished Business (1987).

The same trend of increasingly stubborn problems has also been noted on the international front. Speaking of environmental health management issues, a World Bank report concludes:

> Many of the easiest gains from introducing better water management, providing clean water and sanitation, encouraging the use of cleaner fuels, and reducing the impact of floods and droughts have already been captured. Yet millions of children still die each year, and many families lose their assets and sources of income, as a result of diseases and disasters that are linked to the quality of their environment. There are indications that progress in the 1990s was much slower than in previous decades.

World Bank, Making Sustainable Commitments—An Environment Strategy for the World Bank 6 (2001).

Lead pollution illustrates this dynamic. Lead has been removed from U.S. gasoline, lead paint has been banned, and new lead plumbing is no longer being installed. However, existing houses containing lead paint and relying upon lead plumbing and fixtures will continue to be part of the housing stock for decades. The problems of reducing human exposure from these existing sources of lead pollution are much less tractable than the problems associated with eliminating new sources. In addressing the problem of lead in drinking water, the Environmental Protection Agency has struggled to find the right strategy. See Chapter 3, pages 251-252, for further discussion.

Environmental policy has become a much more partisan political issue than it was in the 1970s, when the major environmental laws passed Congress with wide bipartisan support. Republicans in Congress are now much less likely to support environmental initiatives than Democrats. This was even more true after the election of 1994, which brought in a more conservative cadre of Republican House members. Mathews, Scorched Earth: Why the Hill Has Become an Environmental Disaster Area, Wash. Post, Oct. 18, 1994, at A17. This is a reflection of the fact that further actions to improve the environment are more difficult and more costly, and it is also a contributing element to the difficulty of making further progress, as legislative compromises are frequently elusive.

The increasingly partisan nature of environmental debate marks the current political landscape despite the fact that public opinion surveys throughout the modern environmental era have registered strong support for environmental quality, to such a degree that public opinion analysts label the environment "a consensual issue." Dunlop, Public Opinion and Environmental Policy, in Environmental Politics and Policy 87, 98 (J. Lester ed., 1990). This remained true throughout the 1990s and into the twenty-first century. "The expectation of a clean environment has evolved into a virtual norm—a near universal belief in the country that this is the right way to organize society." Greenberg Research Memorandum to League of Conservation Voters and Sierra Club, Jan. 30, 1997.

So partisanship over the environment does not typically express itself as disagreement about whether or not environmental quality is an important goal. Instead, the battles over further environmental initiatives focus on whether they are effective, as well as whether or not they come at too high a cost to other values, including private property rights, economic growth, and individual freedom. The costs and benefits of environmentally damaging behavior frequently fall on quite distinct groups of people; the beneficiaries of a cement factory's production and profits are typically distinct from the downwind communities affected by the plant's air pollution, for example. Similarly, the costs and benefits of environmental improvements typically create different groups of winners and losers. This makes for difficult political decision making, especially as proposals for further improvement become more and more expensive.

B.　AMERICAN ENVIRONMENTALISM: SOURCES AND VALUES

Samuel Hays has argued that changes in environmental values are part of a still larger complex of changes in social attitudes and values:

> [Changes in environmental attitudes] are but one aspect of massive social changes that include television and the computer, new realms of production

beyond manufacturing, new attitudes about the relationships between men and women, new levels of income and education, and new intensities of information acquisition and exchange. . . .

While one could easily focus on the crisis aspect of pollution problems (and this usually was the tone of media coverage), on a more fundamental level the notion of pollution as a problem arose far more from new attitudes that valued both smoothly functioning ecosystems and higher levels of human health. . . .

While preventive medicine had made impressive accomplishments in vaccination against infectious diseases, it now seemed to be less interested in the limitations on optimum health that might come from environmental causes. . . . Hence, a major aspect of the public's concern for chemical pollution was either to take matters into their own hands and avoid contaminants by means of new personal lifestyles, or to demand public action to prevent exposure. [S. Hays, Three Decades of Environmental Politics, in Government and Environmental Politics 19, 20, 25, 35 (M. J. Lacey ed., 1989).]

Expanding on Hays, is it fair to conclude that the concept of "adverse environmental impact" is to an important degree a matter of perceptions, informed by some set of values, and not purely a feature of the physical world? For instance, is it right to think that when some people affirm wilderness preservation and see great environmental harm from cutting down trees, while others affirm forest land as a productive human resource and see little environmental harm from cutting (perhaps followed by reforestation), their disagreement rests in part on a disagreement about values?

Physical alterations of the world are not matters of perception alone, of course. Still, humans interact with the world in two ways relevant to environmental policy. Their physical actions alter the world in measurable ways, and they also organize, categorize, and evaluate that world through the conceptual schemes and value perspectives they inhabit. This understanding of the role of values in interpreting the world suggests that terms like "adverse environmental impacts" and "environmental problems" are concepts constructed by and of human beings. Different value perspectives may construct a term differently, and hence different worldly phenomena may be included within it.

Indeed, American environmentalism comprises a mix of value systems, beliefs, and perspectives, and draws on a complex of historical, philosophical, and religious traditions. This diversity will not always be apparent: In the policy context, differences in perspective may often be masked from view by a shared consensus that a certain state of affairs deserves attention. After proposals to dam the Grand Canyon surfaced in the 1960s, for example, opposition to the idea was waged on economic grounds, on conservationist grounds, on cultural-historical grounds, on Deep Ecological grounds, as well as others. Because consensus existed at the programmatic level of opposition to the dam, dissecting differences in the underlying rationale for that opposition was superfluous to the process of building a political coalition to fight the project; indeed, such dissection might actually inhibit such coalition-building.

Such consensus will not always exist, however. The economic perspective on environmental value, the conservationist perspective, and the Deep Ecological perspective strenuously disagree about the nature of the environmental problem posed by logging old-growth forest in the Pacific Northwest, for instance. Consensus among environmentalists often falls apart over the question of remedy: Should the country's response to toxic air pollutants consist of efforts to reduce emissions to their optimal level—the point at which further reduction costs more than the human health and welfare gains from such reduction—or should it consist of strategies aimed at achieving zero emissions, and if the latter, how quickly? Should animal experimentation be permitted when the information gained will serve human needs, only when it will serve vital human needs, or not at all? Remedial questions often expose underlying value disagreements because they press advocates to articulate their vision of a properly functioning economy or society. Many of the issues joined in this text can be better understood by seeing how different perspectives within environmentalism urge different solutions to problems.

Environmental values can be distinguished in many ways. One fundamental division separates perspectives depending on whether their main object of moral or ethical concern is humankind, living things (with a further division between approaches that place high value on all living things versus some smaller set of living things, such as all mammals or all animals capable of experiencing pain), or entire ecosystems. These are referred to as human-centered (or anthropocentric), bio-centered, and eco-centered, respectively. Economics supplies the human-centered perspective most influential in contemporary policy debates. The scientific discipline of ecology provides the intellectual framework for some of the most influential bio-centered and eco-centered approaches. We will return to each of these in more detail after canvassing the large landscape of values influencing environmental thinking today.

A great deal of writing about environmental philosophy views all human-centered approaches to ethics or morals as seriously insufficient. Some rule out classifying a human-centered ethic as an environmental ethic at all, preferring to reserve the latter name for any "ethic which holds that natural entities and/or states of affairs are intrinsically valuable, and thus deserve to be the object of our moral concern," irrespective of whether they are useful or valuable to us in meeting our needs. Thompson, A Refutation of Environmental Ethics, 12 Envtl. Ethics 147, 148 (1990). Defined this way, only bio-centered or eco-centered ethics qualify.

Consider, for example, Aldo Leopold's land ethic. Building on an understanding of humanity as but one part of a dynamic ecosystem, Leopold wrote that "a thing is right when it tends to preserve the integrity, stability, and beauty of the biotic community. It is wrong when it tends otherwise." A. Leopold, A Sand County Almanac 201, 224-225 (1968). Much of Leopold's work was devoted to expressing the value of aspects of the environment that had no obvious economic value. "To sum up," he wrote, "a system of conservation based solely on economic self-interest is hopelessly lopsided. It tends to ignore, and thus eventually to eliminate, many elements in the land community that lack commercial value, but that are (as far as we know) essential to its healthy functioning. It assumes, falsely, I think, that the economic parts of the biotic clock will function without the uneconomic parts." Id. at 213. Leopold plainly thought that polluting discharges may "tend otherwise" at levels well below those that are optimum from the economic perspective. For Leopoldians, the environmental problem of pollution can arise in situations in which the economic perspective would see no problem.

In particular, Leopold and other ecologists tend to believe that the scale of man's actions constitutes its most destructive quality. "The combined evidence of history and ecology seems to support one general deduction: the less violent the man-made changes, the greater the probability of successful readjustment in the [ecosystem]. Violence, in turn, varies with human population density; a dense population requires a more violent conversion. In this respect, North

America has a better chance for permanence than Europe, if she can contrive to limit her density." Id. at 220. From the economic perspective, in contrast, large-scale disruptions of natural order are not necessarily to be avoided; it all depends on what costs and benefits to human beings are associated with those disruptions.

In recent years, the science of ecology has had an influence on both human-centered and bio-centered systems of environmental values. NEPA's call for "systematic, interdisciplinary" analysis of "the profound impact of man's activity on the interrelationships of all components of the natural environment" is very much a call with ecological origins. Ecology's central orientation is to view "living organisms and this nonliving (abiotic) environment [as] inseparably interrelated and interact [ing] upon each other." E. Odum, Fundamentals of Ecology 10 (2d ed. 1959). Ecological study provides a warning that if humans want to retain the relatively hospitable surroundings the earth has so far provided, we must become much more cognizant of the ecological ramifications of our actions. Leopold's land ethic evolved from his reflections as an applied ecologist studying the diversity and resilience of local ecosystems.

Perhaps most significant, seen as a way of understanding the human-environment relationship, ecology serves as a unifying thread for a number of different biocentric and ecocentric points of view. Its stress on relationships among mutually dependent components lends itself to an emphasis on harmony and cooperation that a variety of perspectives have found congenial. Leopold's land ethic is the starting point for many contemporary efforts to develop a picture of ethical behavior that is not centered on humans. For an investigation of the land ethic's meaning and its influence, see Companion to A Sand County Almanac (J.B. Callicott ed., 1987).

Religious values also play significant roles in environmental perspectives. The relationship between Western religions and the environment has been particularly controversial. In 1967, Lynn White wrote an influential essay in which he argued that much of the blame for our current situation rests with the biblical account of the Creation, in which God set humankind apart from the rest of creation, gave men and women dominion over creation, and instructed them to subdue it. White, The Historical Roots of Our Ecological Crisis, 155 Science 1203 (Mar. 10, 1967). White's analysis was supported soon thereafter in John Passmore's Man's Responsibility for Nature (1974).

Among the world's religions, the Judeo-Christian tradition has often seemed to fare the worst in terms of its alleged association with beliefs inhospitable to environmental protection. The dominion tradition, however, has been responded to by others who retrieve the biblical tradition of stewardship as a counterweight to the views of White and Passmore. In January 1990, for example, Pope John Paul II issued a message entitled "Peace with All Creation." In it he explained that alongside the arms race, regional conflicts, and domestic injustice, world peace is threatened "by a lack of due respect for nature, by the plundering of natural resources and by a progressive decline in the quality of life." Throughout the message, the Pope employed the vocabulary of ecology.

> [A] new ecological awareness is beginning to emerge which, rather than being downplayed, ought to be encouraged to develop into concrete programs and initiatives. . . . The profound sense that the earth is "suffering" is shared by those who do not profess our faith in God. Indeed, the increasing devastation of

the world of nature is apparent to all. It results from the behavior of people who show a callous disregard for the hidden, yet perceivable requirements of the order and harmony which govern nature itself.

People are asking anxiously if it is still possible to remedy the damage which has been done. Clearly, an adequate solution cannot be found merely in a better management or more rational use of the earth's resources, as important as these may be. Rather, we must go to the source of the problem and face in its entirety that profound moral crisis of which the destruction of the environment is only one troubling aspect, . . . Theology, philosophy and science all speak of a harmonious universe, of a "cosmos" endowed with its own integrity, its own internal, dynamic balance. This order must be respected. The human race is called to explore this order, to examine it with due care and to make use of it while safeguarding its integrity.

More recently, Christian evangelicals concerned about the environment have begun organizing under the banner of "creation care," which they state "will be rooted in their faith in a divine creator, driven by their concern for the health of families and children, and tempered by the traditional evangelical skepticism of liberal, big-government solutions." John Cochran, New Heaven, New Earth, CQ Weekly, p. 2768 (Oct. 17, 2005). In 2004, the Evangelical Environmental Network published an Evangelical Declaration on the Care of Creation, which states:

> Because we worship and honor the Creator, we seek to cherish and care for the creation. . . . Because we await the time when even the groaning creation will be restored to wholeness, we commit ourselves to work vigorously to protect and heal that creation for the honor and glory of the Creator—whom we know dimly through creation, but meet fully through Scripture and in Christ. We and our children face a growing crisis in the health of the creation in which we are embedded, and through which, by God's grace, we are sustained. Yet we continue to degrade that creation.
>
> These degradations of creation can be summed up as 1) land degradation; 2) deforestation; 3) species extinction; 4) water degradation; 5) global toxification; 6) the alteration of atmosphere; 7) human and cultural degradation. Many of these degradations are signs that we are pressing against the finite limits God has set for creation. With continued population growth, these degradations will become more severe. Our responsibility is not only to bear and nurture children, but to nurture their home on earth. We respect the institution of marriage as the way God has given to insure thoughtful procreation of children and their nurture to the glory of God. We recognize that human poverty is both a cause and a consequence of environmental degradation. *http://www.creationcare.org/.*

In 2005, leaders of the National Association of Evangelicals (NAE) undertook to develop a consensus statement specifically on climate change. This effort revealed fissures within the Christian conservative community, with some supporting a strong statement calling for policy change to reduce greenhouse gases and others endorsing the skepticism of the Bush Administration toward the issue and its approach of urging voluntary actions to reduce those gases. In early 2006, the president of the NAE retreated from the goal of a consensus statement because of the "wide divergence" of views within the Christian conservative movement. Some Evangelicals Plow Ahead On Climate Amid Conservative Opposition, Inside EPA, Feb. 7, 2006. Ultimately 86 evangelical leaders, but not the NAE itself, endorsed an "Evangelical Climate Initiative" calling for federal regulations to reduce emissions of greenhouse gases. Laurie Goodstein, Evangelical Leaders Join Global Warming Initiative, N.Y. Times, Feb. 7, 2006. They signed a statement arguing that "millions of people could die in this century because of climate change, most of them our poorest global neighbors." Climate Change: An Evangelical Call to Action, available at *http://www.christiansandclimate.org/statement.*

A good examination of the relationship between ecology and the major religions of the world, including a review of the dominion/stewardship debate, can be found in D. Kinsley, Ecology and Religion (1995).

Another distinctive value system whose influence you will see in American policy and law is that of the preservationist. Preservationists may emphasize historical continuity, within our culture, our traditions, and our relationships with the natural environment. They may, however, also demand the preservation of certain places because they provide the context and catalyst for contemporary revelation and self-understanding. "Why should we not also enjoy an original relation with the universe?" asks Emerson.

> Why should not we have a poetry and philosophy of insight and not of tradition, and a religion by revelation to us, and not the history of theirs? Embosomed for a season in nature, whose floods of life stream around and through us, and invite us, by the powers they supply, to action proportioned to nature, why should we grope among the dry bones of the past . . . ? The sun shines today also. There is more wool and flax in the fields. There are new lands, new men, new thoughts. Let us demand our own works and law and worship.

Where are these insights found? By communing with nature itself, for "[undoubtedly, we have no questions to ask which are unanswerable."

> We must trust the perfection of creation so far as to believe that whatever curiosity the order of things has awakened in our minds, the order to things can satisfy. . . . [N]ature is already, in its forms and tendencies, describing its own design. Let us interrogate the great apparition that shines so peacefully around us. Let us inquire, to what end is nature? . . . In the woods, we return to reason and faith. There I feel that nothing can befall me in life—no disgrace, no calamity (leaving me my eyes), which nature cannot repair. Standing on the bare ground—my head bathed by the blithe air and uplifted into infinite space—all mean egotism vanishes. I become a transparent eyeball; I am nothing; I see all; the current of the Universal Being circulates through me; I am part or parcel of God. [R.W. Emerson, "Nature" (1836), reprinted in New World Metaphysics 171, 171-174 (G. Gunn ed., 1981).]

The writings of Emerson, Thoreau, and other Transcendentalists firmly graft into American literary history the connection between spiritual renewal and nature, so that one recurring argument for wilderness preservation urges doing so "because our lives and our conception of ourselves will be enhanced—in a spiritual sense—if we learn to appreciate [nature] for what it is and we learn how to live in harmony with it." J. Thompson, Preservation of Wilderness and the Good Life, in Environmental Philosophy (R. Elliot and A. Gare eds., 1983).

These thoughts may misleadingly suggest that preservationists are necessarily human-centered thinkers, valuing nature for what it provides for the human spirit. For many in this tradition, nature is to be valued first for itself; it then turns out that human contemplation of nature proves a source of inspiration as well. This biocentric idea is well expressed by the naturalist John Muir, founder of the Sierra Club:

> The world, as we are told, was made especially for man—a presumption not supported by the facts. . . . Now it never seems to occur to [many

people] . . . that Nature's object in making animals and plants might possibly be first of all the happiness of each of them, not the creation of all for the happiness of one. Why should man value himself as more than a small part of the one great unit of creation?

Some argue that the kind of intrinsic value Muir attributes to nonhumankind supports the conclusion that those nonhumans possess rights that environmental policy ought to respect. David Brower, when he was chairman of the Sierra Club, expressed his agreement with Muir by announcing, "I believe in the rights of creatures other than man." However, animal rights advocates disagree over the precise source of those rights. Peter Singer and others argue for an animal welfare ethic, basing their views on the capacity of animals to experience pleasure and pain, and on that basis extending a human-centered ethic, Benthamite utilitarianism, to cover nonhuman species. See P. Singer, Animal Liberation (2d ed. 1990). Tom Regan, on the other hand, rejects the utilitarian approach and instead finds support for animal rights in the idea that living beings who have the capacity to experience life in certain qualitative ways (including having beliefs and desires, perceptions, memory, and a sense of the future) possess inherent value that gives them a right to respect, independent of the pleasures or pains they may experience. See T. Regan, The Case for Animal Rights (1983).

However wide the internal disagreements among these and other bio-centered or eco-centered ethics, they remain distinguishable from economics and other human-centered views in that they seek to articulate "not an ethic for the *use* of the environment, a 'management ethic,' but an ethic *of the* environment." J.B. Callicott; The Case Against Moral Pluralism, 12 Envtl. Ethics 99, 99 (1990).

ENVIRONMENTAL PHILOSOPHY: A PATHFINDER

For those wishing to explore more of the historical development and diversity of American environmental thought, see S.P. Hays, Conservation and the Gospel of Efficiency: The Progressive Conservation Movement, 1890-1920 (1959); R. Nash, Wilderness and the American Mind (1967); J. Petulla, American Environmental History (2d ed. 1988); R. Nash, The Rights of Nature (1989), which contains an excellent annotated bibliography; and P. Shabecoff, A Fierce Green Fire: The American Environmental Movement (1993).

A classic statement of the economic perspective on environmental issues is J.H. Dales, Pollution, Property, and Prices (1968). This perspective is also outlined in simplified form in W. Baxter, People or Penguins: The Case for Optimal Pollution (1974); R. Posner, The Economics of Law (1987); and A.M. Polinsky, An Introduction to Law and Economics (1983). Mark Sagoff has done some of the most interesting work critiquing the economic perspective on environmental issues. Much of his work is summarized in M. Sagoff, The Economy of the Earth (1988). J. Baird Callicott is the leading expositor of Leopold's land ethic. See his In Defense of the Land Ethic (1989) as well as his edited collection of essays, Companion to a Sand County Almanac: Interpretive and Critical Essays (1987).

Useful collections of essays in environmental philosophy include: D. Scherer ed., Upstream/Downstream: Issues in Environmental Ethics (1990); F. Ferre & P. Hartel eds., Ethics and Environmental Policy (1994); R. Attfield & A. Belsey eds., Philosophy and the Natural Environment (1994); M. Zimmerman et al., Environmental Philosophy (1998); M. Smith, Thinking Through the Environment (1989). Bill McKibben's books stress the significance of the loss of nature on the human spirit as well as on nature itself. B. McKibben, The End of Nature (1990); Enough (2004).

Many scholars have put forward their own approach to environmental philosophy. For good reviews and extensive bibliographies, see R. Attfield, The Ethics of Environmental Concern (2d ed. 1991); A. Dobson, Green Political Thought, ch. 1 & 2 (1998); N. Carter, The Politics of the Environment, ch. 2 (2001).

Much of the important literature in this rapidly developing field is contained in Environmental Ethics, a journal published quarterly by the Center for Environmental Philosophy at the University of North Texas. The center maintains a website devoted to environmental ethics at *www.cep.unt.edu*, which contains an excellent collection of resources. For additional web-based resources as well as links to bioethics discussion groups, see *http://ethics.acusd.edu/Applied/Environment/*.

General values that are not exclusively environmental in their focus play significant roles in the debate over environmental policy. A prominent characteristic of many environmental issues is that they impose costs or risks on individuals that are not of those individuals' choosing. The residents of Love Canal did not choose to be exposed to toxic substances; citizens all over the world did not choose to run the risks of global warming. Undisclosed trace elements of carcinogens in food create risks to consumers that they did not choose. In a society such as ours, it is possible to argue that "the principal value informing public law for the workplace and the environment—as well as private behavior—may be *autonomy*, not *efficiency*," as Mark Sagoff has written:

> An efficient society promotes the ability of the individuals in it to satisfy their wants and desires; it promotes freedom in the sense that refers to an individual's welfare. This sense of freedom—"negative" freedom or freedom from interference in one's pursuit of happiness—has no necessary connection with autonomy. Freedom, in this sense, has to do with getting what you want or doing what you like; autonomy, on the other hand, consists in your ability to get or to do these things on your own, without being beholden to any other person, without accepting favors, and without having the important background decisions made by somebody else. . . . [T]he public's primary goal . . . may not be efficiency; it may be autonomy. People want to determine the background level of risk; they do not want the working conditions of their lives to be determined by others. It does not matter how cost-beneficial risks are; it is a question, rather, of who controls them. [Sagoff, On Markets for Risks, 41 Md. L. Rev. 755, 761-762, 764 (1982).]

The most important new current within the environmental movement is the environmental justice movement. The environmental justice movement challenges current environmental policy to shift to a new paradigm that would emphasize preventing vulnerable populations from being exposed to environmental risks, rather than simply managing, regulating and distributing such risks. Connecting environmental issues to a larger agenda of social justice, this movement focuses on the connections between discrimination, poverty, and the distribution of environmental risks. It argues that "low-income communities and communities of color bear a disproportionate burden of the nation's pollution problem" because the "environmental laws, regulations, and policies have not been applied fairly across all segments of the population." R. Bullard, Unequal Protection: Environmental Justice and Communities of Color xv (1994). In a relatively short period of time, environmental justice concerns have had a profound effect on the entire environmental movement. Sierra Club Executive Director Carl Pope has written that "the two major ethical streams in modern environmentalism are deep ecology and environmental justice." Pope, An In-Depth Response to "The Death of Environmentalism," Jan. 15, 2005, even though the environmental justice movement was unknown until the 1990s. *http://www.grist.org/news/maindish/2005/01/13/pope-reprint/*.

Center for Progressive Reform: Perspective on Environmental Justice (2005)
http://www.progressiveregulation.org/ perspectives/environJustice.cfm

Although communities of color and the poor have been heavily and disproportionately affected by noxious and risk-producing environmental practices for decades, the issue of environmental racism did not gain national prominence until the 1980s. Several high-profile events brought national attention to the issue, including a demonstration against the siting of a hazardous waste landfill in a predominantly African-American county in North Carolina; a General Accounting Office report finding that, in one U.S. region, large, commercial hazardous waste facilities were more likely to be sited in African-American communities; and a national study finding a positive correlation between minority racial status and proximity to commercial hazardous waste facilities and uncontrolled waste sites. . . . [A] National Law Journal investigation also found racial disparities in the enforcement of federal environmental laws. Subsequent studies, mostly regional in scope, tend to reinforce many of the findings of this early research. . . .

Conclusive judgments about the reasons for all of the disproportionate environmental burdens borne by communities of color remain elusive. At the same time, researchers' fixation on causation . . . has deflected attention away from the more fundamental questions of whether, regardless of the cause, such marked inequality in risk distribution is to be condoned, and assuming it is not, what is to be done about existing disparities. These disparities persist not just in the siting of undesirable facilities but in a wide range of decisions affecting the environment, including standard setting, program design, enforcement, the cleanup of contaminated properties, and exclusionary regulatory processes. In the last 15 to 20 years, communities of color and poor communities, and organizations representing them, have persistently challenged disparities resulting from the current system. Numerous failings of the environmental regulatory system have been identified and challenged in recent years.

In the area of standard setting, EPA and other agencies employ scientific risk assessments to support environmental standards that often do not take into account the special characteristics of communities of color and low-income communities. For example, in developing water quality criteria, environmental agencies estimate an average fish consumption that ignores the higher rates of fish consumption among Native Americans and other ethnic minorities. . . . As a result of such inappropriate assumptions, agencies fail to propose standards that are sufficiently protective of vulnerable ethnic and racial groups. This lack of regulatory protection is then compounded by these groups' inadequate access to health care. . . .

[B]ecause pollutants may have cumulative and even synergistic effects that are not captured when risks are assessed one pollutant at a time, the current regulatory approach may badly underestimate overall pollution problems in minority communities.

In the area of program design, gushing enthusiasm for pollution trading has often overlooked the potential of trading programs to cause or exacerbate toxic "hot spots." Most of the older, larger, and dirtiest facilities—such as power plants, oil refineries, and chemical plants—are located in communities where people of color and poor people live. These facilities are more likely than newer facilities to buy credits to pollute in lieu of controlling their own pollution because of the high costs of retrofitting existing plants. The result is that a trading scheme can result in higher concentrations of dangerous pollution—"hot spots"—in poor areas and where persons of color live than in the rest of the area covered by the trading program. . . .

Enforcement is another area in which people of color and the poor fare worse than the general population. . . . Although empirical evidence in this area is scarce, several factors might contribute to enforcement disparities. The states are often the front-line enforcers of federal environmental law, yet they differ significantly in their ability and willingness to do this job. And some of the states with poor enforcement track records have large African-American, Latino, and/ or low-income populations.

Because of the degree of discretion regulatory agencies have to prosecute violations or impose penalties, people of color and poor persons can do little in the face of lax enforcement by public officials. For these communities, even private citizen lawsuits are no panacea. Such litigation can be complicated and resource-intensive, making it difficult for financially strapped community groups to underwrite the sophisticated monitoring, sampling, and analysis—let alone the sophisticated legal work—required to detect and challenge permit violations.

The cleanup of contaminated properties also raises several environmental justice issues. The divestment and blight that accompanies areas with more than their share of contaminated sites leaves people of color and poor persons who live nearby in a difficult situation. The first problem is that these areas have to compete with other contaminated sites for government cleanup resources. . . . [E]nvironmental justice advocates [claim] that sites in their communities are often neglected or receive less effective cleanups than sites in wealthier, predominantly white areas. . . . EPA-sponsored "brownfield" initiatives have offered some improvement by promoting community involvement in cleanup decisions. However, many contaminated sites are relegated to state brownfield programs because, although still dangerous, they are not contaminated enough to qualify for a federally sponsored cleanup. State brownfield programs vary widely in the degree of community involvement and cleanup. Moreover, because brownfield redevelopment projects often allow less stringent cleanup standards in light of anticipated industrial re-use, they have a tendency to lock in the legacy of industrial development in areas where people of color and poor persons live. Although there is typically a serious attempt to control the exposure to remaining hazardous wastes through physical means such as capping and through legal means such as deed restrictions, surrounding communities are left with the risk that these controls will fail. . . .

Finally, environmental justice advocates have consistently raised issues about environmental decision making and public participation. Environmental decision makers traditionally have heard the views of industry giants, conventional environmental organizations, state and local governments, and federal land managers, but not the people who actually live in the most affected areas. Gaining access to the fora where important environmental decisions are being resolved has been a large priority of environmental justice communities and organizations. Even where access is allowed, meaningful participation can be difficult; conventional stakeholders have significantly more time, money, and other resources to participate in these processes and influence agency policy and implementation. Environmental justice advocates often lack the resources to participate as effectively in such a highly technical arena, and this fundamentally tilted playing field significantly compounds the problems explained above, producing bad decisions that harm public health.

NOTES AND QUESTIONS

1. **Subject Overview.** For a history and analysis of the environmental justice movement, see C. Rechtschaffen & E. Gauna, Environmental Justice: Law, Policy and Regulation (2002).

2. **LULU Siting Patterns and Other Concerns.** Most specific environmental justice disputes so far have involved the locating of undesirable polluting facilities, often referred to as LULUs (for locally undesirable land uses). A number of studies have now documented that more LULUs are located in areas with significant minority populations than a random distribution of those facilities would explain. The academic debate about causation noted in the Center for Progressive Reform's Perspective focuses on identifying the cause of this observable pattern. Several scholars have questioned whether this pattern can be best explained as the result of facility locators choosing to locate in areas with disproportionate minority populations.

> Employing an original analysis of data from the St. Louis metropolitan area to separate out the possible causes of environmental disparities, this Article concludes that, to the degree that environmental disparities exist, it is economic factors—not siting discrimination—that are behind many claims of environmental racism. Industrial facilities that were originally sited in white areas often became surrounded by minority residents who are attracted to these neighborhoods by falling housing prices. . . .
>
> Between 1970 and 1990, concentrations of poor and minority individuals increased disproportionately around the St. Louis area's CERCLA sites, TSDFs, and nonhazardous landfills and incinerators. . . . While the concentration of minority residents in a given census tract in the overall St. Louis area increased, on average, by 29%, concentration of minority residents in tracts containing industrial facilities increased by 67%. . . .
>
> From 1970 to 1990, the average census tract in the St. Louis area experienced a 10% net increase in its poverty rate, compared to a 53% increase in tracts containing industrial and waste facilities. While St. Louis's mean family income rose 5.6%, in real terms, from 1970 to 1990, this figure actually fell 1.4%

around industrial and waste sites. Relative increases in poverty rates and decreases in family incomes indicate that a higher percentage of low-income families were moving to (or remaining in) these areas from 1970 to 1990. [T. Lambert & C. Boerner, Environmental Inequity: Economic Causes, Economic Solutions, 14 Yale J. on Reg. 196, 197, 206-207 (1997).]

Professor Vicki Been has also questioned whether discriminatory purpose is the best single explanation for the pattern:

> [M]y research team conducted a nationwide study of the demographics of the 544 communities that in 1994 hosted active commercial hazardous waste treatment storage and disposal facilities. . . .
> [W]e found no substantial evidence that the facilities that began operating between 1970 and 1990 were sited in areas that were disproportionately African American. Nor did we find any evidence that these facilities were sited in areas with high concentrations of the poor; indeed, the evidence indicates that poverty is negatively correlated with sitings. We did find evidence that the facilities were sited in areas that were predominantly Hispanic at the time of the siting. The analysis produced little evidence that the siting of a facility was followed by substantial changes in a neighborhood's socioeconomic status or racial or ethnic composition. Finally, the analysis shows that the areas surrounding [hazardous waste facilities] currently are disproportionately populated by African Americans and Hispanics. [V. Been & F. Gupta, Coming to the Barrios? A Longitudinal Analysis of Environmental Justice Claims, 24 Ecology L.Q. 1, 9 (1997).]

Others have found that a better predictor of LULU location than either race or class is the degree to which a local community is politically organized.

> Communities facing identical potential losses from the location of a noxious facility may nevertheless differ in the effective opposition they offer to the siting because of differences in their rates of political participation. The greater an area's potential for participation in collective action, the higher the firm's expected costs of litigation, lobbying, and compensation, and thus the less likely it will be to locate there. [Jay Hamilton, Politics and Social Costs: Estimating the Impact of Collective Action on Hazardous Waste Facilities, 24 Rand. J. of Econ. 101, 104-105 (1993).]

3. **Administrative Action.** At the federal level, responses to the environmental justice movement have been predominantly from the executive branch so far. President Clinton took a significant step in 1994, when he issued Executive Order 12,898, 59 Fed. Reg. 7,629 (1994), which directs each federal agency to

> make achieving environmental justice part of its mission by identifying and addressing, as appropriate, disproportionately high and adverse human health or environmental effects of its programs, policies and activities on minority populations and low-income populations.

EPA itself has been widely criticized for failure to implement Executive Order 12,898 as vigorously as it might. Organizationally, the agency's Office of Environmental Justice (OEJ) is a component of the Office of Enforcement and Compliance Assurance (OECA). Lacking a separate appropriation from the Congress, its budget depends entirely upon agency priorities. In fiscal year 2002, the OEJ's budget was $4.4 million, or less than 1 percent of OECA's total. EPA, Office of Inspector General, EPA Needs to Consistently Implement the Intent of the Executive Order on Environment Justice, p. 4 (March 1, 2004).

EPA's Inspector General (IG) has criticized the agency for issuing a strategic plan for environmental justice that defines environmental justice as "the *fair treatment* of people of all races, cultures and incomes with respect to the development, implementation, and enforcement of environmental laws and policies. . . ." Memorandum from Administrator Whitman, Aug. 9, 2001 (emphasis in original). As a consequence of this "fair treatment of all" approach, the IG concluded that EPA is refusing to provide program officers and regional offices "the definitions or attributes necessary to determine what constitutes minority, low-income, a minority or low-income community, or a definition of disproportionality" thus impairing their ability to carry forward the mandate of the Executive Order. IG Report at 7.

The Government Accountability Office similarly concluded that EPA was failing to take environmental justice considerations adequately into account when developing rules under the Clean Air Act. For instance, in developing a rule to reduce the sulfur content of gasoline, EPA analysis determined that pollution near oil refineries would be increased as a result of the rule, because the process of removing the sulfur generates some air emissions, while the amount of pollution being emitted by automobiles would be decreased. This raises potential environmental justice issues, because minority and low-income communities are disproportionately located near such facilities. Yet in responding to comments that raised this environmental justice concern, "specifically, EPA did not publish its estimate that potentially harmful emissions would increase in 26 of the 86 counties with refineries affected by the rule." GAO, EPA Should Devote More Attention to Environmental Justice When Developing Clean Air Rules, p. 4 (July 2005).

Executive Order 12,898 prompted all federal agencies to undertake a review of their internal decision-making procedures to incorporate consideration of environmental justice issues into those procedures, pursuant to guidance published by EPA's Environmental Justice Office in 1995. The Nuclear Regulatory Commission was among the agencies who revised its procedures accordingly. (As an independent agency, the NRC is not directly covered by Executive Order 12,898, but it voluntarily promulgated an environmental justice strategy for internal decisions.)

A license application by Louisiana Energy Services (LES) to build a uranium enrichment plant in Homer, Louisiana, an almost entirely African-American town located in economically depressed northern Louisiana, provided a major test of the NRC's strategy. The draft environmental impact statement (EIS) for the application, issued prior to the executive order, did not include an analysis of environmental equity, but the final one, issued after the order, did. It described the neighborhoods surrounding the proposed facility, the site selection process, possible discrimination, and possible disproportionate impacts. The EIS concluded that there was no evidence of discrimination and no significant disproportionate impacts.

In May 1997, the NRC's Atomic Safety and Licensing Board (ASLB) rejected LES's permit application on environmental justice grounds. The Board found that NRC staff had failed to comply with the executive order by conducting only a cursory review of the site selection process. On appeal, the full NRC Board agreed that NRC staff had failed to delve sufficiently into disparate impacts that might be caused by the new facility, but it rejected the ASLB's additional instructions to the staff to inquire into whether racial discrimination influenced the process, ruling that the National Environmental Policy Act was not a tool for addressing racial discrimination. LES subsequently abandoned its plans and terminated the licensing process. The LES application is discussed further in Chapter 8.

A non-environmental statute, Section 601 of Title VI of the Civil Rights Act of 1964, prohibits discrimination on the basis of race, color, or national origin under any program or activity receiving federal funding. Section 602 authorizes agencies to issue implementing regulations tailored to agencies' individual programs. Administrative complaints under these Title VI regulations have become a main avenue for environmental justice advocates to challenge agency decisions they claim impose disproportionate burdens on disadvantaged communities. Under these regulations, complainants do not have to prove a discriminatory intent, which would be their burden if they sued in court claiming a violation of Section 601. The Supreme Court has ruled that Section 602 authorizes regulations designed to avoid disparate impact alone. Guardians Ass'n v. Civil Serv. Comm'n, 463 U.S. 582 (1983).

EPA has issued such disparate impact regulations, and on February 5, 1998, it issued further Interim Guidance describing how it would investigate environmental justice complaints in order to "accommodate the increasing number of Title VI complaints that allege discrimination in the environmental permitting context." Industry, state, and local governments, and environmental groups have all criticized the Guidance as vague, but they disagree on the proper clarifications. The EPA's Interim Guidance, as well as draft documents subsequently issued in response to criticisms, can be found at *http://www.epa.gov/civilrights/extcom.htm.*

Title VI complaints based on environmental justice concerns are handled by EPA's Office of Civil Rights (OCR), which has been receiving complaints regarding siting of facilities, such as hazardous waste facilities, under programs administered by EPA. Under the cooperative federalism design of many of our environmental laws, qualifying states actually administer the day-to-day decisions of many of our federal statutes, and the Title VI complaint process extends to state decisions under those statutes. Environmental justice advocates have used the Title VI complaint process to challenge the state of Michigan's issuance of an air pollution permit to a proposed steel mill in Flint, Michigan. EPA ultimately dismissed the complaint, relying primarily on evidence that the facility would not violate any health-based ambient air quality standard. The text of OCR's denial of the complaint is available at *http://www.epa.gov/civilrights/docs/ssdec_ir.pdf.* Environmental justice organizations appealed to EPA for reconsideration, but in April 1999 the company elected to build near Lansing, at a site on which the company already held the necessary permits.

4. **Litigation.** Private parties can seek declaratory or injunctive relief under Section 601 of Title VI. Cannon v. University of Chicago, 441 U.S. 677 (1979). Success in such actions requires proof of discriminatory intent. In situations where such intent is absent or difficult to prove, environmental justice advocates have sought to establish a similar private right of action to enforce agency implementing regulations issued under Section 602, which would only require proof of disparate impact. In a non-environmental case, the Supreme Court has now foreclosed that option by denying an implied right of action to enforce agency regulations issued to implement Title VI. Alexander v. Sandoval, 121 S. Ct. 1511 (2001).

A dissent by Justice Stevens in *Sandoval* invited litigants to avoid the consequences of the denial of a private right of action under Title VI itself by utilizing the protections of 42 U.S.C. §1983, which establishes liability against any "person, who, under color of [state law] . . . [deprives any citizen of the United States] of any rights, privileges, or immunities secured by the Constitution and laws of the [United States]." In the Title VI context, the Section 1983 claim would be that agency implementing regulations prohibiting the administration of federal programs in ways that had a disparate impact create a right secured by a law of the United States. A New Jersey district court judge adopted this interpretation of Section 1983, ruling that a preliminary injunction preventing issuance of a permit under the Clean Air Act, entered just five days prior to *Sandoval* based on an implied right of action under EPA's implementing regulations, would remain in effect under a Section 1983 theory. South Camden Citizens in Action v. New Jersey Dept. of Envt'l Protection, 145 F. Supp. 505 (D.N.J. 2001). On appeal, however, the Third Circuit reversed, holding that Section 1983 is satisfied only by regulations that "merely further define[] or flesh[] out the content of [a right conferred on the plaintiff by the statute itself]." South Camden Citizens in Action v. New Jersey Dept. of Envt'l Protection, 274 F.3d 771, 786-787 (3d Cir. 2001). Because Section 601 covered only intentional discrimination and Section 602 was not by itself clear and unambiguous in establishing a federal right by itself, plaintiffs could not use the Title VI regulations as the basis for a Section 1983 lawsuit. This setback did not end the South Camden litigation, however. Subsequently, the district court held that plaintiffs had alleged sufficient facts to state a claim for intentional discrimination directly under Title VI and the Fourteenth Amendment. 254 F. Supp. 2d 486 (D.N.J. 2003).

There is now a split in the circuit courts regarding the availability of Section 1983 to raise environmental justice challenges under Section 601, with the Fourth, Ninth, and Eleventh Circuits agreeing with the Third that there is not, and the District of Columbia and the Sixth Circuits concluding that there is. See Save Our Valley v. Sound Transit, 335 F.3d 932 (9th Cir. 2003) (collecting cases). Each of the circuits recognizing a cause of action, however, did so in cases decided prior to the Supreme Court opinion in Gonzaga Univ. v. Doe, 536 U.S. 273 (2002), which ruled that Section 1983 protects federal rights, not laws, and which has been read to support the more restrictive interpretation of Section 1983.

Despite the general lack of success in Title VI and Section 1983 litigation, environmental justice claims do occasionally become the object of litigation when agencies incorporate EJ considerations into their normal administrative procedures, as instructed by the executive order. For example, environmental justice analysis has been held subject to judicial review under NEPA and the APA when an agency has included such analysis in its environmental impact statement. E.g., Communities Against Runway Expansion, Inc. v. FAA, 355 F.3d 678 (D.C. Cir. 2004).

5. **Environmental Justice and Democratic Decision Making.** In addition to being concerned with outcomes, environmental justice stresses the existence of procedural inequities inconsistent with the ideals of participatory democracy, whereby communities should be involved in decisions that affect their lives. Environmental justice advocates "demand[] the right to participate as equal partners at every level of decision making, including needs assessment, planning, implementation, enforcement and evaluation." First National People of Color Environmental Leadership Summit, Principles of Environmental Justice (1991).

Along with problems that raise the other environmental values reviewed in this introduction, environmental justice issues will come up and be reviewed in more detail in subsequent chapters of this text that deal with siting controversies, the exposure of sensitive populations to toxic substances, regulatory priority-setting, enforcement, and environmental impact statements. The pathfinder below provides a guide to the rapidly expanding literature on environmental justice.

6. **Success Stories.** Although environmental policy development, execution, and enforcement still falls well short of what advocates of environmental justice seek, the issue of environmental justice now clearly occupies a central place in many environmental policy debates, as the earlier quotation from Carl Pope suggests. To one degree or another, environmental justice concerns undoubtedly influence a good number of government decisions being made today. In itself, that is a success story for environmental justice. Smaller successes can also be found. In 2004, for example, the state of North Carolina completed detoxification of the PCB landfill in Warren County that had become an early symbol of the lack of class- and race-related justice in environmental policy. "State and federal sources spent $18 million to detoxify or neutralize contaminated soil stored at the Warren County PCB landfill. A private contractor hired by the state dug up and burned 81,500 tons of oil-laced soil in a kiln that reached more than 800 degrees Fahrenheit to remove the PCBs (polychlorinated biphenyls). The soil was put back in a football-size pit, re-covered to form a mound, graded, and seeded with grass." Robert Bullard, Environmental Racism PCB Landfill Finally Remedied But No Reparations for Residents, see World News and Press Releases at *http://www.ejrc.cau.edu/.* Throughout the casebook, you will be confronted with policy controversies that have environmental justice dimensions.

ENVIRONMENTAL JUSTICE: A PATHFINDER

C. Rechtschaffen and E. Gauna, Environmental Justice: Law, Policy and Regulation (2002) is a wonderful resource on environmental justice issues, with extensive references to the rapidly expanding literature. The websites identified in the environmental philosophy pathfinder also contain links to web-based resources on environmental justice. Robert Bullard, one of the pioneers in studying the disparate impact of environmental risks, maintains an environmental justice resource center at Clark University, with a website at *http://www.ejrc.cau.edu/,* including extensive links to other web resources. R. Bullard, Dumping in Dixie: Race, Class and Environmental Quality (1990), and Unequal Protection, Environmental Justice and Communities of Color (1994) are classics in the field. His most recent book is Highway Robbery: Transportation Racism and New Routes to Equity (South End Press, 2004).

Environmental justice issues have been the subject of many law review articles, including: Foster, Justice from the Ground Up: Distributive Inequalities, Grassroots Resistance, and the Transformative Politics of the Environmental Justice Movement, 86 Cal. L. Rev. 775 (1998); Schnell & Davies, Environmental Justice, 29 Env. Rep. (BNA) 528 (1998); Been & Gupta, Coming to the Nuisance or Going to the

---

Barrios? A Longitudinal Analysis of Environmental Justice Claims, 24 Ecol. L.Q. 1 (1997); Mank, Environmental Justice and Discriminatory Siting: Risk-Based Representation and Equitable Compensation, 56 Ohio St. L.J. 329 (1995); Been, Locally Undesirable Land Uses in Minority Neighborhoods: Disproportionate Siting or Market Dynamics? 103 Yale L.J. 1383 (1994); Williams, Environmental Law and Democratic Legitimacy, 4 Duke Envtl. L. & Pol'y F. 1 (1994); Lazarus, Pursuing "Environmental Justice": The Distributional Effects of Environmental Protection, 87 Nw. U. L. Rev. 101 (1993); Foster, Race(ial) Matters: The Quest for Environmental Justice, 20 Ecol. L.Q. 721 (1993). Several symposia have addressed environmental justice issues, including: Environmental Justice: Mobilizing for the 21st Century, 23 Vt. L. Rev. 451 (1999); The Nexus Between Environmental Justice and Sustainable Development, 9 Duke Envtl. L. & Pol'y F. 147 (1999); Environmental Justice: The New Wave, 14 Va. Envtl. L.J. 567 (1995); Environmental Justice, 5 Md. J. Cont. L. Issues 1 (1993-1994); Symposium: Race, Class, and Environmental Regulation, 63 U. Colo. L. Rev. 839 (1992).

President Clinton's Executive Order 12,898, Federal Actions to Address Environmental Justice in Minority Populations and Low-Income Communities, appeared at 59 Fed. Reg. 7,629 (1994). Regulations issued by EPA to implement Title VI of the Civil Rights Act of 1964, 42 U.S.C. §2000d, can be found at 40 C.F.R. §7.35. EPA's Office of Civil Rights web page contains copies of key executive branch and EPA documents regarding implementation of the agency's Title VI compliance program, *http://www.epa.gov/civilrights/*. Information on other aspects of EPA's environmental justice program, including reports by the National Environmental Justice Advisory Committee, can be found at *http://www.epa.gov/compliance/environmentaljustice/index.html*.

PROBLEM EXERCISE: MERCURY CONTAMINATION

For centuries, mercury, or quicksilver, has been known to be a nerve toxin. In the last several decades, scientists have gained greater awareness of how mercury enters the human body. Of particular concern, mercury emitted from smokestacks of coal-fired power plants and incinerators, or released by chlor-alkali plants have been identified as specific causes of mercury contamination. These mercury emissions eventually are deposited on land or water and then, either directly or through leaching of the soil, enter water bodies where the mercury is consumed by living organisms. Mercury then bioaccumulates as larger organisms consume smaller ones, eventually becoming quite concentrated in a wide number of fish species.

EPA now recognizes fish consumption as the major source of human exposure to mercury. That exposure is considerable. A recent Centers for Disease Control study estimates that 6 percent of women of child-bearing age have blood levels of mercury higher than that considered safe by the EPA, with a consequence that around 630,000 children per year are born with elevated levels of mercury in their umbilical cord blood.

Based on a United States Department of Agriculture Continuing Survey of Food Intakes by Individuals conducted from 1994 through 1996, the EPA currently recommends that water quality standards for mercury be set based on the assumption that individuals consume 17.5 g of fish per day or two 8-oz. fish meals per month. This rate is far lower than what is actually consumed by many subsections of the population. In particular, "members of fishing tribes and indigenous peoples and members of other communities of color are among the highest consumers." Catherine A. O'Neill, Mercury, Risk, and Justice, 34 Envtl. L. Rep. 11070, 11077 (2004). For instance, members of Ojibwe tribes of the Great Lakes were consuming fish at rates raging from 115.8 g/day to 240.7 g/day in the fall and 189.6 g/day to 393.8 g/day in the spring. Id. One reason that fishing tribes, indigenous peoples, and members of other communities of color consume far more fish than the national average, of course, is that many of these communities rely upon a fish catch as part of their subsistence living patterns. Others who are sensitive to mercury may eat the recommended amount and still be adversely affected. Body weight and age can affect the amount of fish a person is able to eat safely.

Question One.   Does the problem of reducing mercury contamination from fish raise environmental justice concerns? How ought EPA respond to them? Should the water quality standards be set based on an assumption of much higher levels of consumption than EPA currently employs, even though the current standards, if met, would protect the vast majority of Americans and even though achieving more stringent water quality standards will be very costly?

One strategy that federal and state agencies have employed in their attempts to reduce fish consumption and the mercury contamination that can accompany it is to issue fish advisories that notify communities of the hazards of fish consumption and urge reductions in that consumption when tests reveal too much fish contamination in a watershed. While fish advisories can be given for a variety of reasons, in fact mercury accounts for 76 percent of all U.S. advisories, encompassing roughly 32 percent of the nation's lakes and 100 percent of Lakes Superior, Michigan, Huron, and Erie.

Question Two.   Does the use of fish advisories as a strategy for lowering mercury contamination in human beings raise environmental justice concerns? How might those concerns be addressed?

In deliberating about strategies for reducing the man-made contribution to the mercury problem, the EPA has considered two different approaches. One would require each major source of mercury pollution to install maximum available control technology, thereby reducing each source's emissions by 90 percent or more. The other would employ a market system for mercury abatement, which would set a national cap on mercury emissions, assign an initial allocation of permissible mercury emissions to each source, and then let the sources trade permits to emit emissions with one another. Under such an approach, reductions would not be uniform, presumably, as one source might find it cheaper to purchase emissions permits from another source rather than abate. (See Chapter 5, pages 553-555, for a discussion of how such a system works.)

Question Three.   Does the choice between these two approaches raise environmental justice concerns? The effect of a market approach on a particular source or sources emissions is difficult to predict because it depends upon decisions made by firms after the market system is implemented. Nonetheless, one study has projected the impact of EPA's market alternative compared to the maximum available control technology approach. It predicts that "every source in the upper Great Lakes states of Michigan, Minnesota and Wisconsin but one" will emit more mercury under the market approach than under the technology approach, and that several sources there will actually emit more under the market approach than they do now. O'Neill, at 11100. Does this information affect your answer? How would you decide which approach to use?

(Mercury is also the subject of a Case Study in Chapter 3, as well—pages 216-223. See that Case Study for more information on mercury as well as for further citations documenting the contents of this one.)

Question Four.   In 1999 U.S. coal-fired power plants emitted approximately 120 tons of mercury into the air, while coal-fired power plants in China emitted 600 tons of mercury. Because of long-distance, atmospheric transport of these pollutants, it is estimated that 30 percent or more of the mercury found in the United States originates in China. Matt Pottinger, Steve Stecklow & John J. Fialka, Invisible Export—A Hidden Cost of China's Growth: Mercury Migration, Wall St. J., Dec. 20, 2004, at A1. By the year 2020, China is expected to double its electric power production, primarily by constructing new coal-fired power plants. Unless China acts to reduce mercury emissions from these new power plants, increases in mercury emissions from China that reach the United States will vastly offset any reductions from U.S. sources. What effect, if any, should mercury emissions from China have on U.S. mercury control policy? If China refuses to act to control these emissions, is it futile for the U.S. to try to reduce emissions from its own power plants?

C. ECONOMICS AND THE ENVIRONMENT

Each of the value systems we have briefly canvassed has associated with it a distinctive discourse and set of concepts within which its problems are formulated and debated. In recent years, economics has become increasingly the lingua franca in government policy discussions about the environment. The late William Baxter, writing in the language of economics, argued that "to assert that there is a pollution problem or an environmental problem is to assert, at least implicitly, that one or more resources is not being used so as to maximize human satisfactions. Environmental problems are economic problems, and better insight can be gained by the application of economic analysis." W. Baxter, People or Penguins: The Case for Optimal Pollution 17 (1974).

Users of other value systems relevant to environmental policy disagree with this statement. They object to the value premises implicit in the economic approach, they reformulate environmental problems in their own discourses, and they engage in technical criticisms of economic methods to show that those methods are incomplete, misleading, or inaccurate. Because economic concepts and terminology are so prevalent in this field, it is vital that everyone approaching environmental law be conversant with those concepts and terminology—if only so that criticism of them can be informed and astute.

The readings in this section serve to introduce the economic approach to environmental problems.

1. *The Role of Prices and Markets*

|| *Eban S. Goodstein, Economics and the Environment* 33-39 (1995) ||

From an economist's point of view, market systems generate pollution because many natural inputs into the production of goods and services such as air and water are "underpriced." Because no one owns these resources, in the absence of government regulation or legal protection for pollution victims, businesses will use them up freely, neglecting the external costs imposed on others. For example, suppose the Stinky Paper Co. discharges polluted water into a stream, which kills the fish that downstream people enjoy eating. If Stinky were forced to compensate these people for the damages it imposed (**internalize the externality**), the firm would in effect be paying for the water it used up. Water would no longer be "underpriced." As a result, Stinky would conserve its use of water and would seek out ways to clean up its discharge. This, in turn, would raise the production costs of the firm. . . .

Because the river water is commonly owned and thus a "free" good, Stinky overexploits it and the fisherfolk downstream are exposed to a negative externality of the paper production process. From an economic point of view, many pollution problems arise because by their nature environmental resources such as water and air are commonly owned. . . .

Because all resources in an economy cannot be privately owned, market systems will generate too much pollution by either of the standards considered in this book—efficiency or safety. There are two related reasons for this. The first is the **free-access problem** which can arise when property is commonly held. The free-access problem can be stated simply: If people weigh private benefits against private (as opposed to social) costs, they will overexploit common resources when given free access. This idea was popularized in the late 1960s by a social ecologist named Garrett Hardin, who called it "The Tragedy of the Commons." [See pages 49-51.] . . .

The free-access problem may explain why there is a tendency for commonly held resources such as clean air and water or fisheries to be overexploited. But why does the government have to decide what to do about it? Instead, why don't the victims of negative externalities simply band together on their own to prevent pollution? As we noted earlier, this was the response to environmental degradation of common grazing and fishing grounds in traditional societies. Informal social pressure and tradition were relied on to prevent overexploitation. The modern American equivalent would be to sue an offending company or individual for damages. Indeed, a few so-called **free-market environmentalists** have advocated eliminating many environmental regulations, then relying on lawsuits by injured parties to "internalize" externalities.

Such private remedies to environmental degradation run into what economists call the **public goods problem**. Public goods are goods which are enjoyed in common. The provision of public goods is a problem for the free market due to the existence of two factors: free-riding and transactions costs. To illustrate, consider a good that is enjoyed in common such as, for example, the noise level after 11 o'clock at night in Axl's neighborhood. Now suppose that neighbor Tipper cranks her sound system. Axl could go to the considerable trouble of obtaining signatures from all of his neighbors, getting money from them to hire a lawyer, file a lawsuit, and possibly obtain a legal injunction requiring her to turn the music down. The costs of undertaking this action are known as **transaction costs**, and they are particularly high because of the public nature of the injury.

If Axl does undertake the effort, he will benefit not only himself but also the entire neighborhood. Some of the neighbors might refuse to help out and instead **free-ride** on Axl's provision of the public good. Instead, Axl decides it's not really worth organizing a lawsuit and tosses and turns in bed, hoping that someone else will make the effort. The result is that although there may be considerable total demand for a quiet evening in the neighborhood, it doesn't get expressed. It is not worth it to any one individual to overcome the transaction costs and the possibility of free-riding required to provide the public good of the lawsuit though, if he did, the social benefits might far outweigh the cost.

In most towns, the response to noise pollution is a government regulation called a nuisance law. With such a regulation in place, Axl can just call the police, greatly reducing the costs associated with stopping the noise. The general principle is that without government intervention, public goods—in this case, a quiet evening—will be undersupplied. . . .

To summarize . . . , in contrast to private goods, public goods are goods which are consumed in common. The true demand for public goods will not be satisfied in pure market economies due to high transaction costs and free-riding. Free-market environmentalists who advocate relying solely on the court system to internalize environmental externalities recognize these twin hurdles. But they believe these obstacles are not really that large, especially considering the costs associated with regulation. Most economists, however, argue that as a result of transaction costs and free-riding, public goods such as clean air or water, rain forests, wilderness parks, and other environmental amenities will be undersupplied in a laissez-faire market system.

NOTES AND QUESTIONS

1. **Polluter Pays Principle.** Markets limit resource use to activities valued in the market more highly than its value when used in other ways. If the resource, e.g., clean air, is not sold in a market, it will be used for waste disposal (polluted) even if clean air is valued more. Having the polluter pay for the externalities or damages caused by its pollution ensures that the costs of production reflect the costs of environmental damage. If this "polluter pays" principle were carried through to all factors of production, the result would be an efficient allocation of resources. The difficulties of internalizing externalities by implementing the "polluter pays" principle are well explored in F. Anderson et al., Environmental Improvement Through Economic Incentives (1982).

2. **Beneficiary Pays Principle.** Some situations do not lend themselves to implementation of the polluter pays principle. Especially significant, international environment problems, such as global warming, do not, because international agreements operate under a rule of voluntary assent by nation-states. If treaties sought to impose net costs on a country because that country imposed more pollution costs on other countries than they imposed on it, the country "will simply decline to participate. . . . Under the rules of international law,

where each country must give consent, regulatory instruments must instead follow a 'Beneficiary Pays Principle.' The beneficiaries of global environmental protection must attract non-beneficiary sources to participate, because the former cannot compel the latter to comply." Wiener, Global Environmental Regulation: Instrument Choice in Legal Context, 108 Yale L.J. 677, 752 (1999).

3. **The Coase Theorem.** In an important article, Ronald Coase argued that polluter pays and beneficiary pays would, if bargaining were costless, each lead to efficient allocation of resources. Under either approach, the pollution will be abated only if controlling it is cheaper than the damage it causes its victims. For example, if the peace of mind of the residents who live near a nuclear reactor currently shut down for repairs was worth more than the value of operating the plant, then the plant would not have been restarted either because the residents could gain by paying the plant not to operate (under beneficiary pays) or because it would not be economical for the plant to compensate residents for their fears (under polluter pays). In principle, either solution will result in solving the environmental problem, economically viewed, because it will eliminate the undesirable externality aspects of the situation. See Coase, The Problem of Social Cost, 3 J.L. & Econ. 1 (1960).

Coase's views have been particularly influential in the privatization movement, because one application of Coase's argument is to urge that sometimes pollution problems can be left to private market solutions, where polluter and pollutee can bargain for the appropriate level of polluting activity relatively free from governmental interference. See, e.g., T.L. Anderson & D.R. Leal, Free Market Environmentalism (revised ed. 2001). One of the earliest, and still among the most valuable, essays on the advantages of markets for pollution rights is H. Dales, Pollution. Property and Prices (1968).

4. **Are the Two Really Equivalent?** Whether polluter pays or beneficiary pays can be viewed as a question of who has been assigned an initial entitlement. If the polluter can continue polluting until she is paid to stop, she has a right to pollute; if the polluter must pay the beneficiaries (who you might think of as victims, were the pollution not stopped), they have a right to be free of pollution. In addition to noting the obvious unreality of the zero-transaction-cost assumption, critics of Coase's Theorem are quick to point out that the initial allocation of such rights can have a significant impact on the distribution of income. The distribution of income in turn affects tastes and alters the ultimate outcomes produced by market economies. In addition, one's thinking about the initial allocation may be affected by ethical or moral considerations.

While extolling the importance of efficiency, economists have tried to dismiss distributional concerns by arguing that they should be dealt with by general tax and welfare policies or by assuming that winners and losers are approximately the same when more efficient policies are pursued. Noting that Coase himself emphasized that all market transactions have costs (Coase argued that the very existence of firms illustrated that nonmarket mechanisms can be cheaper in some circumstances than market ones), Judge Guido Calabresi maintains that "distributional issues cannot, even in theory, be avoided." Calabresi, The Pointlessness of Pareto: Carrying Coase Further, 100 Yale L.J. 1211, 1215 (1991). Calabresi argues that transaction costs, "no less than existing technology, define the limits of what is currently achievable in society," id. at 1212, and that "there is no difference, in theory or in practice, between the reduction or elimination of these impediments and any other innovation in knowledge or organization which might make us all better off." Id. at 1218.

Thus, he maintains that the real challenge for social policy is to decide which impediments to invest in removing, which inevitably requires explicit consideration of distributional concerns.

5. **Economic Efficiency as a Policy Objective.** The economic approach to environmental problems treats the environment as a resource that is underpriced. Were it priced properly, markets would ensure it was used by whoever valued it most, as measured by persons' willingness to pay for it. Ideally, markets produce efficient outcomes—resources move to the users who value them most highly, and no voluntary exchange among potential users is left unexecuted. Many of the value systems introduced earlier in this chapter challenge whether this is the appropriate way to approach environmental issues. Some have questioned whether efficiency in the sense just described has any justification as a public policy objective.

> If the efficiency criterion had a normative basis in the ethical theory of utilitarianism, it would have a demonstrable connection with happiness or a related normative conception of the good, and it would judge the value of actions and decisions according to their consequences. The efficiency criterion and the theory of welfare economics from which it is developed possess neither of these attributes, however, and they therefore have no justification in the ethical theory of utilitarianism.
>
> Sophisticated economic analysts do not try to connect the efficiency norm with the classical [utilitarian goal] of maximizing pleasure or happiness. . . . As Richard Posner correctly points out, "The most important thing to bear in mind about the concept of value in the welfare economist's sense is that it is based on what people are willing to pay for something rather than the happiness they would derive from it."
>
> Some policy analysts, however, believe that the satisfaction of consumer and other personal preferences has a moral foundation as a policy goal because it leads to or produces satisfaction in the sense of pleasure or happiness. This belief rests on nothing more than a pun on the word "satisfaction." Preferences are *satisfied* in the sense of "met" or "fulfilled"; this is also the sense in which conditions and equations are satisfied. "Satisfaction" of this sort has no necessary connection with "satisfaction" in the sense of pleasure or happiness.
>
> The evidence indicates, in fact, that the satisfaction of preferences does not promote or cause satisfaction in the sense of happiness. Empirical research confirms what ordinary wisdom suggests: happiness depends more on the quality and pursuit of preferences than on the degree to which they are satisfied.
>
> It is useful to recognize, moreover, that the contemporary "utilitarianism" represented by current welfare economic theory is not concerned with what happens to people as a result of their choices. Instead, it is concerned with the beliefs and expectations revealed in those choices. The focus is on the amount people are willing to pay for things rather than on the consequences of those decisions, except insofar as those consequences are defined tautologically in terms of willingness to pay. [M. Sagoff, The Principles of Federal Pollution Control Law, 71 Minn. L. Rev. 19, 55-57 (1986).]

Is the economic approach to environmental issues a sound one? How would you defend it or criticize it?

2. Cost-Benefit Analysis

When markets for environmental resources do not exist, welfare economics suggests that government can sometimes legitimately intervene. In order to test whether any proposed governmental policy actually improves overall welfare, welfare economics recommends that such policy be subjected to a

FIGURE 1.3
Costs and Benefits of Reducing Lead in Gasoline
(Figures in 1983 dollars)

COSTS	Low-lead	No-lead
Manufacturing costs	$503 million	$691 million
Nonmonetized valve damage to engines	$0	D
TOTAL COSTS	$503 million	$691 million + D
BENEFITS		
Maintenance benefits	$660 million	$755 million
Environmental and health benefits		
<u>Conventional Pollutants</u>		
Reduced damage by eliminating misfueling	$404 million	$404 million
Nonmonetized health benefits	H1	H1
<u>Lead</u>		
Reduced medical care costs	$41 million	$43 million
Reduced cognitive damage	$184 million	$193 million
Nonmonetized health benefits	H2	H3
TOTAL BENEFITS	$1.289 billion + H1 + H2	$1.395 billion + H1 + H3
NET BENEFITS	$786 million + H1 + H2	$704 million + H1 + H3 − D

Source: EPA, Costs and Benefits of Reducing Lead in Gasoline (Mar. 1984).

cost-benefit analysis (CBA), which seeks to compare the "social benefit" of the policy to its "opportunity cost—the social value foregone when the resources in question are moved away from alternative economic activities into the specific project" contemplated by the policy. E.J. Mishan, Cost-Benefit Analysis xii (1976).

Cost-benefit and risk-benefit analyses have become a standard part of environmental policy discussions. They are at the heart of the controversy surrounding EPA's decisions to ban certain products that contain asbestos, for example. See *Corrosion Proof Fittings*, page 235. EPA's significant decision to phase down the amount of lead in gasoline (see page 181) also relied in part on a cost-benefit analysis. In 1984 EPA prepared a preliminary CBA, ultimately focusing on two options: a "low-lead" option, in which gasoline with a low-lead content (.10 grams per gallon) would continue to be marketed to ease fears that older cars would suffer valve damage from unleaded gasoline; and a "no-lead" option, which would ban all lead additives in gasoline by 1988. The results of its calculations of costs and benefits are shown in Figure 1.3.

NOTES AND QUESTIONS

1. A major source of costs in the lead phasedown CBA, as in a great many CBAs of proposed environmental regulations, comes from the capital and operating costs associated with installing and running new plant equipment. How can an agency like EPA estimate those costs? Might they sometimes be based on cost estimates for technologies that are not yet widely in use? What would the sources of EPA's information on manufacturing costs be? In a few cases, the estimates of costs used in the CBA have been compared with actual costs once

the regulation has been implemented. Would you guess that the actual costs typically exceed or are less than the estimated costs?

2. Some costs and benefits can be harder to estimate in dollars than others. How do you place a value on lost recreational opportunities, for example? In Figure 1.3, notice the benefit items labeled "Reduced medical care costs," and "Reduced cognitive damage." In calculating the latter, EPA referred to studies showing that elevated concentrations of lead in blood have an effect on cognitive abilities. Reducing these cognitive deficits by lowering blood lead levels was valued by estimating the costs of remedial education that would otherwise be necessary to remediate the deficits—an amount that came out to $4,000 per child benefited, using Department of Education estimates. More recent estimates by EPA have been as high as $8,300. It has been fairly standard practice in recent years to estimate benefits according to an estimate of what people would be willing to pay for the benefit, "because the amount people are willing to pay for a good or service is the best measure of its value to them." Executive Office of the President, Regulatory Program of the United States, xix (1987). Is the $4,000 figure consistent with that approach? Using a willingness-to-pay approach, an economist, Randall Lutter, attempted to estimate how much parents are willing to spend to treat their children when warned that their blood lead levels are too high. He used chelation therapy, which is effective for high levels of exposure, but less so for low levels. Most of the costs of such therapy in his calculations were the value of the mother's time in taking her child to and from the treatment location. Lutter's estimate is that an IQ point is worth $1,100. Randall Lutter, Valuing Children's Health: A Reassessment of Benefits of Lower Lead Levels, AEI-Brookings Joint Center for Regulatory Studies, Working Paper 00-02 (2000). The various techniques for determining what people would be willing to pay for goods that are not traded in regular markets (or "shadow prices") are discussed in I. Pearce & R. Turner, Economics of Natural Resources and the Environment 141-158 (1990).

3. Special controversies surround the willingness-to-pay principle when it is applied to benefits that save lives. What objections might be made to the exercise of "placing a value on human life" in a cost-benefit assessment? See W.K. Viscusi, Strategic and Ethical Issues in the Valuation of Life, in Strategy and Choice (R. Zeckhauser ed., 1991). However controversial the idea might be, the Administrative Conference of the United States has recommended that, except where costs and benefits are "highly conjectural" or unquantifiable, agencies should "disclose the dollar value per statistical life" used to reach determinations that the costs of regulations are cost-benefit justified. ACUS, Valuation of Human Life in Regulatory Decision-making, 1 C.F.R. §305, 88-7. Using some of the shadow price methodologies, economists have estimated people's willingness to pay to save a human life at anywhere from $200,000 to $7 million, in 1990 dollars.

4. Even when reliable market prices exist and are readily available for EPA's use, some estimates will remain uncertain. A large item of benefits in EPA's CBA for lead came from reduced maintenance cost to exhaust systems (whose life would be prolonged by low-lead or no-lead gasoline), to spark plugs (same reason), and from longer periods between oil changes. For the low-lead case, these savings were estimated at $341 million, $80 million, and $239 million, respectively. Why might these amounts be uncertain?

5. Although monetizing all costs and benefits can be difficult, and the estimates uncertain, it can be an important exercise. If some of the costs and

FIGURE 1.4
Costs and Monetized Benefits of Lead Regulation, Assuming Partial Misfueling, 1986
(millions of 1984 dollars)

Benefit Category	$
Children's health care effects	623
Adult blood pressure	6,124
Conventional pollutants	231
Maintenance	949
Fuel economy	194
Total monetized benefits	8,121
Total refining costs	631
Net benefits	7,490
Net benefits excluding blood pressure	1,366

Source: Office of Policy Analysis. Environmental Protection Agency, Costs and Benefits of Reducing Lead in Gasoline, Report no. EPA-230-05-85-006 (Feb. 1985), p. E-12. Reprinted from: P. Portney, Air Pollution Policy, in Public Policies for Environmental Protection 64 (P. Portney ed., 1990).

benefits are simply presented in a descriptive fashion, the elements of the analysis "tend to be 'less concrete,' and more 'soft' than market-place benefits [or costs], [and] [t]he temptation is to downgrade them by comparison." Pearce & Turner at 123. Why were some of the health benefits for the lead phasedown represented as "nonmonetized"?

6. When EPA adopted the lead phasedown regulation in 1985, it prepared a final cost-benefit analysis. Figure 1.4 summarizes EPA's final estimates. Note the enormous benefits from reducing adult blood pressure, a health benefit not monetized in EPA's proposal because it had only recently been discovered through epidemiological data. Because of uncertainty concerning the blood pressure studies, the final cost-benefit analysis also calculated net benefits excluding blood pressure benefits.

7. Data from the Third National Health and Nutrition Examination Survey released in 1994 found that, due largely to EPA's phasedown of lead additives in gasoline, average levels of lead in children's blood had declined sharply from 12.8 micrograms (µg) per deciliter during the 1976-1980 survey period to 2.8 µg during the 1988-1991 survey. Brody et al., Blood Lead Levels in the U.S. Population, 272 JAMA 277, 281 (1994). See Figure 1.5. A study by an EPA economist now estimates that each 1 microgram reduction in average blood lead concentrations yields monetized net benefits of $17.2 billion per year. Schwartz, Societal Benefits of Reducing Lead Exposure, 66 Env. Health 105, 119 (1994). What do these figures suggest about the accuracy of EPA's initial CBA?

8. Two scholars have written that

> The basic problem with narrow economic analysis of health and environmental protection is that human life, health, and nature cannot be meaningfully described in monetary terms; they are priceless. When the question is whether to allow one person to hurt another, or to destroy a natural resource . . . when harms stretch out over decades or even generations . . . — then we are in the realm of the priceless, where market values tell us little about the social values at stake.
>
> There are hard questions to be answered about protection of human health and the environment, and there are many useful insights about these questions from the field of economics. But there is no reason to think that the

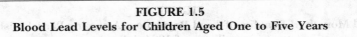

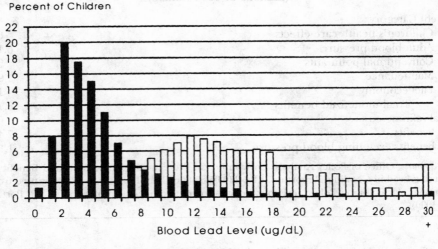

FIGURE 1.5
Blood Lead Levels for Children Aged One to Five Years

□ NHANES II (Second Survey, 1976-1980)
■ NHANES III Phase 1 (Third Survey, Phase 1, 1988-1991)

Source: National Health and Nutrition Examination Surveys (NHANES).

right answers will emerge from the strange process of assigning dollar values to human life, human health, and nature itself, and then crunching the numbers. [Frank Ackerman & Lisa Heinzerling, Priceless: On Knowing the Price of Everything and the Value of Nothing 8 (2004).]

Cost-benefit analysis has become a staple of environmental policy analysis. As you encounter it in various settings throughout the book, consider whether it is an appropriate basis for deciding what to do—because it supplies the "right answer"—or whether the elements that make it up—rigorous efforts to estimate the costs of correcting some harmful environmental stressor and to identify the magnitude of the health or environmental benefits to be gained—are better considered "useful insights" for a decision that cannot in the final analysis be made solely on economic grounds.

3. Valuing Ecosystem Services

In recent years, ecologists have been attempting to place monetary values on the services that entire ecosystems perform for the benefit of humankind. One of their premises is that hard-to-quantify values of such services, as well as benefits that emerge from the interaction and interdependency of ecosystems, may be lost when project-specific cost-benefit analyses are being performed. See, e.g., Gretchen Daily ed., Nature's Services: Societal Dependence on Natural Ecosystems (1997). One controversial attempt to place a global value on everything that the world's ecosystems do for humans came up with a central estimate of $33 trillion per year. Costanza et al., The Value of the World's Ecosystem Services and Natural Capital, 387 Nature 253 (May 1997). That figure compares to an estimate of total world gross national product of $18 trillion per year.

This "value of everything" project has attracted a great deal of criticism, in part because it is meaningless to develop a global estimate of all ecosystem services when the relevant questions almost always relate to more specifically defined ecosystems and more narrowly defined capital projects that might compete with leaving ecosystems in place. A greater appreciation of the value of ecosystems services has been working its way into the smaller, but considerably more realistic, analyses as well, as the following excerpt describes.

James Salzman, Creating Markets for Ecosystem Services
80 N.Y.U. L. Rev. 870 (2005)

Largely taken for granted, healthy ecosystems provide a variety of such critical services. Created by the interactions of living organisms with their environment, these "ecosystem services" provide both the conditions and processes that sustain human life—purifying air and water, detoxifying and decomposing waste, renewing soil fertility, regulating climate, mitigating droughts and floods, controlling pests, and pollinating plants. Although awareness of ecosystem services is certainly not new, efforts to identify and calculate these services' valuable contributions to social welfare are. Recent research by ecologists and economists has demonstrated the extremely high costs of replacing many of these services if they were to fail, on the order of many billions of dollars in the United States for pollination alone. Such estimates are inherently uncertain, of course, but the extraordinary costs required to substitute for many important services by artificial means are beyond dispute.

One cannot begin to understand flood control, for example, without realizing the impact that widespread wetland destruction has had on the ecosystem service of water retention; nor can one understand water quality without recognizing how development in forested watersheds has degraded the service of water purification. The costs from degradation of these services are high, and suffered in rich and poor countries alike. One might therefore expect that ecosystem services would be prized by markets and explicitly protected by the law. Despite their economic value and central role in provision of important public benefits, however, ecosystem services are only rarely considered in cost-benefit analyses, preparation of environmental impact assessments, or wetlands mitigation. Nor, in the past, have significant markets arisen that capitalize on the commercial value of these services. This is starting to change, however. From their origins as an obscure phrase just nine years ago, "ecosystem services" have gone mainstream, with new initiatives and markets for provision of services blossoming around the world. The United States Environmental Protection Agency (EPA), for example, has created a Science Advisory Board on Valuing the Protection of Ecological Systems and Services. In Australia, a high-level advisory body, known as the Wentworth Group, has called for a new approach to environmental protection that focuses on provision of ecosystem services. In Costa Rica, the government is administering a nationwide scheme of payments for services. The international climate change negotiations are closely focusing on policy instruments that encourage carbon sequestration. And this is just the tip of the iceberg. A recent study documented 287 cases of payments for forest ecosystem services from around the world and an international marketplace website for services has just been launched (available at *http://www.ecosystemmarketplace.com*). . . .

The first insight of an ecosystem services perspective is that investing in natural capital can prove more efficient than using built capital to deliver key services. . . . A well-known example in the water quality field makes the point in a concrete setting. In the early 1990s, a combination of federal regulation and cost realities drove New York City to reconsider its water supply strategy. New York City's water system provides about 1.5 billion tons of drinking water to almost nine million New Yorkers every day. Ninety percent of the water is drawn from the Catskill/Delaware watershed, which extends 125 miles north and west of the city. Under amendments to the federal Safe Drinking Water Act, municipal and other water suppliers were required to filter their surface water supplies unless they could demonstrate that they had taken other steps, including watershed protection measures, to protect their customers from harmful water contamination.

Presented with a choice between provision of clean water through building a filtration plant or managing the watershed, New York City easily concluded that the latter was more cost effective. It was estimated that a filtration plant would cost between $6 billion and $8 billion to build. By contrast, watershed protection efforts, which would include not only the acquisition of critical watershed lands but also a variety of other programs designed to reduce contamination sources in the watershed, would cost only about $1.5 billion. Acting on behalf of the beneficiaries of the Catskills' water purification services, New York City chose to invest in natural rather than built capital. Nor is New York City alone. As of 1996, the EPA had indicated that over 140 municipalities qualified to use watershed conservation as a means of ensuring high drinking water quality. . . .

If ecosystem services clearly provide valuable services, then why don't more payment schemes exist? Why are markets so hard to set up? The answer is threefold—ignorance, institutional inadequacy, and the problems inherent in public goods.

Perhaps the most basic reason we do not pay more attention to the provision of ecosystem services is that we take them for granted. . . . This lack of knowledge is due both to the lack of relevant data and to the multivariate complexity of the task. Analysis of how ecosystems provide services has proceeded slowly not only because ecosystem level experiments are difficult and lengthy, but also because research to date has focused much more on understanding ecosystem processes than determining ecosystem services. And how an ecosystem works is not the same as the services it provides. . . .

[It] is [also] fair to say that our laws were not designed with ecosystem services in mind. Legal protection of ecosystems was not a primary objective when the relevant laws were drafted over two decades ago. Generally speaking, our pollution laws (e.g., the Clean Air Act and Clean Water Act) rely on human health-based standards. Our conservation laws (e.g., the Endangered Species Act and Marine Mammal Protection Act) are species-specific. And planning under our resource management laws (e.g., the National Forest Management Act and Federal Land Policy and Management Act) must accommodate multiple and conflicting uses. Of course, parts of these laws, such as the Clean Water Act's Section 404 wetlands permit program and use of water quality standards, the Endangered Species Act's critical habitat provisions, and the National Forest Management Act's use of indicator species such as the spotted owl, clearly can help to conserve ecosystem services. The point, though, is that these laws were not primarily intended to provide legal standards for conservation of natural capital and the services that flow from it and, as many authors have pointed out, in practice they usually don't. . . .

The last reason there are so few markets, and perhaps the most important, concerns the role of markets and public goods. . . . We have no shortage of markets for most ecosystem goods (such as clean water and apples), but the ecosystem services underpinning these goods (such as water purification and pollination) are free. The services themselves have no market value for the simple reason that no markets exist in which they can be bought or sold. As a result, there are no direct price mechanisms to signal the scarcity or degradation of these public goods until they fail (at which point their hidden value becomes obvious because of the costs to restore or replace them). This might not be critically important if most lands providing services were public property that could be set aside for conservation, but they are not. Private lands are vital not only for biodiversity conservation, but also for provision of most other services. . . .

Such circumstances make ecosystem services easy to take for granted. Because it is difficult to prevent someone who did not pay for an ecosystem service from benefiting from it, it is equally difficult to get such people to pay for provision of these services. Why pay for something when you have always gotten it for free? As a result, a key challenge in implementing an ecosystem services approach lies in creating a market where none exists—in capturing the value of the service by compensating the providers. This approach, notably unlike that of traditional regulatory or tax instruments, views environmental protection much as a business transaction between willing parties.

NOTES AND QUESTIONS

1. The "value of everything" project derived its total value for ecosystem services by using data from studies of discrete resource allocation issues such as those discussed in the Salzman excerpt and then extrapolating to a world scale. Economists have criticized this extrapolation as "a serious error." "Values estimated at one scale cannot be expanded by a convenient [multiplier] to another scale, nor can two separate value estimates simply be added together. When we estimate a compensation measure of one element of an ecosystem, we assume that other aspects of the constraints influencing human well-being are unchanged. For example, we might compute a compensation measure for the elimination of a specific wetland. In another analysis, a compensation measure for the elimination of a different wetland might have been estimated, holding the first at its initial level. But the two compensation measures are *not* additive. . . ." Bockstael, Freeman et al., On Valuing Nature, 34 Env. Sci. & Tech. 1384 (2000).

2. There is rapidly growing interest in incorporating the value of ecosystem services into an increasing variety of environmental programs, from wetlands loss mitigation programs to emissions trading programs and beyond. See, e.g., J. Salzman and J.B. Ruhl, Apples for Oranges: The Role of Currencies in Environmental Trading Markets, 31 Envtl. L. Rep. 11438 (2001); J. Boyd et al., Compensation for Lost Ecosystem Services: The Need for Benefit-Based Transfer Ratios and Restoration Criteria, 20 Stan. Envtl. L. Rev. 393 (2001); J.B. Ruhl & J. Gregg, Integrating Ecosystem Services into Environmental Law: A Case Study of Wetlands Mitigation Banking, 20 Stan. Envtl. L. Rev. 365 (2001); Salzman & Ruhl, Protecting Ecosystem Services: Science, Economics and Law, 20 Stan. Envtl. L. Rev. 309 (2001). See also the special issue of

Environmental Science & Technology on Economic Valuation of the Environment, Vol. 34, no. 8.

3. Using incentive- or market-based plans to maintain or preserve ecosystems services has become a hot topic in natural resource management circles. For instance, an environmentally conscious entrepreneur, John Forgach, has proposed selling 25-year bonds to provide the financing for a major effort by Panama to reforest the watershed around the canal, thus providing a more regular flow of fresh water into the canal to prevent the seasonal drying up of the water supply that is slowing the flow of cargo ships through the canal. He anticipates that big shipping clients, such as Wal-Mart or Asian car makers, who rely upon the Canal, and who currently insure against the huge losses they could suffer if the Canal were closed, would pay a reduced premium if they invested in the forest bonds. Are You Being Served?, The Economist pp. 76-78 (April 23, 2005). Ecosystem services cannot be marketed, however, until the functional linkages between different elements of the environment and valuable services are well enough understood so that realistic values can be assigned to them with sufficient reliability to give investors confidence that they are getting their money's worth. New York's decision to preserve rural lands in the Catskills is evidence that this is sometimes possible, but much more will need to be learned about other ecologies in order to achieve the amount of reliability necessary. The ecosystem services idea is stimulating significant progress in ecological studies to fill these gaps. See the National Resources Council, Valuing Ecosystem Services 2 (2004).

4. Using markets to improve the environment is a topic discussed in more detail in Chapter 5, which deals with air quality, where the idea of using markets for pollution permits to achieve air quality objectives is being used extensively by the Environmental Protection Agency.

D. ECOLOGICAL PERSPECTIVES

The science of ecology seeks to understand the functioning of ecosystems, both on a small scale (such as the ecosystem of a small freshwater wetland) and on a grand scale (such as the global oxygen-carbon dioxide-water cycle, which plays a vital role in world climate and climate changes). Through studying ecosystems, ecologists seek knowledge about the entire process of life by synthesizing chemical, geological, and meteorological information about the environment and biological and chemical information about living organisms and combining them into a single system.

This drive to comprehensiveness derives from the overarching idea of interdependence, which is further reflected in such ecological slogans as "you can never do just one thing" and "everything is connected to everything else." This idea lies close to the heart of many bio-centered or eco-centered philosophies. Aldo Leopold, for instance, wrote that "all ethics rest upon a single premise: that the individual is a member of a community of interdependent parts. . . . The land ethic simply enlarges the boundaries of the community to include soils, plants, and animals, or collectively: the land." A Sand County Almanac 203 (1968). A major portion of the ecological research agenda concerns tracing the consequences of actions through successively widening sequences of effects.

The first generation of ecologists believed that most ecosystems will exhibit *homeostasis,* or the quality of returning to a self-sustaining equilibrium after being disturbed, unless the disturbance is too great. Homeostasis, which is often referred to as the balance of nature, is a dynamic equilibrium, with prey and predator, competition and coexistence within the system; nevertheless, over the system as a whole and over time, the diversity and complexity of functioning ecosystems produce a stability, or balance. In any ecosystem, the "presence and success of an organism depend upon the completeness of a complex of conditions, while in turn individual organisms contribute to the stability of the system itself by occupying an ecological 'niche'—performing a function that contributes to the stability of the system." See E. Odum, Fundamentals of Ecology (3d ed. 1971). This traditional homeostatic understanding has recently been challenged by the "new," or "nonequilibrium" ecology. See the excerpt from Daniel Botkin, page 43, below.

The extent of disruption an ecosystem could absorb and still maintain homeostasis was defined as its "carrying capacity," and this concept played an important role in debates surrounding the environmental laws passed in the early 1970s.

Because ecosystem interconnections can be complex and multifarious, an ecological rule of thumb is that seemingly simple actions typically will have non-obvious and unintended consequences that may culminate in a threat to ecosystem stability. Introduce a new organism into an ecosystem and it may function as a virulent pathogen, like the measles that decimated the Eskimos and South Sea Islanders following their first contacts with Western civilization. Bioaccumulation provides another mechanism through which seemingly discrete actions can have unintended consequences. Chemicals, such as the pesticide DDT, accumulate in the tissue of animals that consume other animals, plants, or water containing the chemical. When these animals are consumed in their turn by still others, the chemicals can continue to accumulate or concentrate until they reach dangerous, even fatal proportions. Both the American condor and the bald eagle populations have suffered because plants and insects sprayed with pesticides were consumed by rodents and snakes that were then consumed by the predator birds, eventually producing pesticide contamination in them sufficient to weaken their egg membranes so that their young died before birth.

A second rule of thumb for ecologists is that smaller actions have less drastic consequences on functioning ecosystems than do larger actions. As Leopold expressed it: "The combined evidence of history and ecology seems to support one general deduction: the less violent the man-made changes, the greater the probability of successful readjustment in the [ecosystem]. Violence, in turn, varies with human population density; a dense population requires a more violent conversion: In this respect, North America has a better chance for permanence than Europe, if she can contrive to limit her density." A Sand County Almanac, at 220.

One of the first pieces of modern-era environmental legislation, the National Environmental Policy Act, was partly premised on the idea that interdisciplinary ecological study ought to precede major federal actions in order that the unintended environmental effects of actions could be better represented in an overall cost-benefit assessment of the action. See, for example, Section 102(2)(A)-(B), requiring federal agencies to "utilize a systematic, interdisciplinary approach which will insure the integrated use of the natural and social sciences and the environmental design arts in planning [and to] insure that presently unquantified environmental amenities and values may be given appropriate consideration in decision-making. . . ."

Preferring small actions to large ones combines a counsel of caution with an underlying judgment that the ways of nature ought to be respected. The methodological principle of ecology, seeing humans as one constituent member of ecosystems composed of many interdependent parts rather than as a dominant, qualitatively distinct member, combines with an admiration for the homeostatic qualities of "natural" systems to produce a prescription for humans: Live in harmony with nature, not at odds with it. Do not maximize, but rather harmonize. The natural equilibrations of functioning ecosystems come to constitute a norm, and to provide a sense of normality, that humans are urged to respect. A good collection of essays touching on some of ecology's broader implications is The Subversive Science: Essays Toward an Ecology of Man (P. Shepard & D. McKinley eds., 1969).

The preference for smallness blossomed into an entire worldview in the late 1960s and 1970s, stimulated by the publication of E.F. Schumacher's Small Is Beautiful (1973) and I. Illich's Tools for Conviviality (1973). As described by Schumacher,

> To strive for smallness means to try to bring organizations and units of production back to a human scale. . . . There are many reasons for favoring smallness. Small units of production can use small resources—a very important point when concentrated, large resources are becoming scarce or inaccessible. Small units are ecologically sounder than big ones: the pollution or damage they may cause has a better chance of fitting into nature's tolerance margins. Small units can be used for decentralized production, leading to a more even distribution of the population, a better use of space, the avoidance of congestion and of monster transport. Most important of all: small units, of which there can be a great number, enable more people "to do their own thing" than large units of which there can only be a few. Smallness is also conductive to simplicity. Simplicity . . . is a value in itself. [E.F. Schumacher, The Age of Plenty: A Christian View, in Economics, Ecology and Ethics 126, 133 (H. Daly ed., 1980).]

The following reading illustrates how the principles of ecology have been combined with ecocentric strands of environmental ethics to produce a distinctive approach to organizing society to respond to environmental problems.

Robert Paehlke, Environmentalism and the Future of Progressive Politics
117-119, 137-145 (1989)

Environmentalism can be seen as a political movement that seeks to impose upon the physical sciences and engineering restraints based on the findings and judgments of the social and life sciences. . . .

Environmentalism involves, in effect, a scientific revolution, a paradigm shift, in the sense developed by Thomas Kuhn. Science can never again be an activity solely devoted to removing humanity from nature, lifting us out of natural limits—for centuries, if not millennia, its implicit goal. . . . But environmentalism fundamentally shifts the purpose of science. The new science can continue to advance productive efficiency, but that efficiency must also be seen in organic and ecological rather than merely in mechanistic terms. Productivity must be measured by its long-term sustainability rather than by short-term increases in output.

Environmental science assumes that every new technology introduces undesirable and commonly unanticipated impacts. . . . An expanding research emphasis on the negative impacts of science and technology need not diminish our appreciation of their benefits. We must simply acknowledge that every benefit carries costs. . . .

The balance reasonable environmentalists seek involves reminding society that unanticipated costs of negative impacts can be severe, even irreversible. This has happened so often that environmentalists seek to reverse the burden of proof regarding safety of new technologies. Proponents of new technologies and substances should be required to demonstrate their safety. In our court system, people are innocent until proven guilty. But new technologies should be seen as guilty until proven innocent.

On the other hand, environmentalists should grant that nothing is absolutely safe, and that technological decisions must involve consideration of benefits as well as costs. Environmentalists would like such decision-making to be more conscious and democratic than it has been. Someone must speak for other species and for future generations, and we all must be willing to accept less economically desirable options when necessary.

Economics is at the heart of decisions regarding the application and evolution of science, and it is central also to the gulf within science. Scientists have been urged toward economic considerations by both private interests andgovernments of every ideological perspective. Much of humankind has been freed from resource scarcity by a science guided largely by conventional notions of economic progress. This scientific optimism need not now be rejected, but it does need to be guided by a more complex understanding of progress. . . .

Two other attempts were made to summarize the key characteristics of society and economy anticipated and/or advocated by environmentalists. . . .

The concept of the conserver society was popularized by the Science Council of Canada in its all-time best-selling publication, *Canada as a Conserver Society: Resource Uncertainties and the Need for New Technologies.* The best summary of this concept is the carefully developed definition contained in the report:

> A Conserver Society is on principle against waste and pollution. Therefore it is a society which
>
> —promotes economy of design of all systems, i.e., "doing more with less";
> —favours re-use or recycling and, wherever possible, reduction at source;
> —questions the ever-growing per capita demand for consumer goods, artificially encouraged by modern marketing techniques; and
> —recognizes that a diversity of solutions in many systems, such as energy and transportation, might in effect increase their overall economy, stability, and resiliency.
>
> In a Conserver Society, the pricing mechanism should reflect not just the private cost, but as much as possible the total cost to society, including energy and materials used, ecological impact and social considerations. This will permit the market system to allocate resources in a manner that more closely reflects societal needs, both immediate and long term.

This definition includes many of the goals of environmentalism and many of the findings of environmental science, and it also suggests means by which these goals might be achieved, such as full-cost market pricing and restraints on modern marketing techniques.

The fact of nonrenewability stands at the center of the last conception of environmentalism and environmental science that we will discuss: the sustainable society. The cover of Lester Brown's book [Building a Sustainable Society] summarizes this perspective: "We have not inherited the earth from our fathers, we are borrowing it from our children." Rather than building his concept of environmentalism around avoidance of waste and depletion, Brown chose to emphasize the notion of sustainability, the maintenance and use of the earth's renewable resource base. He stressed the protection of land and soil quality, sustaining biological resources against the pressures of over-population and industrialization, the use of renewable energy sources, and the need for population stabilization. In combination, Building a Sustainable Society and Canada as a Conserver Society convey virtually all the major themes rooted in the findings of the environmental sciences. The two concepts of sustainable and conserver societies together capture the essence of moderate environmentalism. . . .

Some environmentalists, particularly in the mid-1970s, felt obliged to deny that environmental values had a significant political dimension. Political solutions were rejected in favor of personal changes, particularly in one's habits as a consumer. Achieving environmental goals solely in this way is only marginally more plausible than achieving socialism through large-scale voluntary charity. Nonetheless, environmentalism as a set of values has an autonomous logical validity apart from the political process, and it ought to be set out separately from environmentalism as an ideology. More important, since politics itself rests on values—it has been defined as "the authoritative allocation of values"—one cannot see clearly the political implications of environmentalism without delineating first its value priorities.

What, then, are the central value assertions of environmentalism? The following have consistently been emphasized in the writing of environmentalists and are implicit in their actions.

1. An appreciation of all life forms and a view that the complexities of the ecological web of life are politically salient.
2. A sense of humility regarding the human species in relation to other species and to the global ecosystem.
3. A concern with the quality of human life and health, including an emphasis on the importance of preventative medicine, diet, and exercise to the maintenance and enhancement of human health.
4. A global rather than a nationalist or isolationist view.
5. Some preference for political and/or population decentralization.
6. An extended time horizon—a concern about the long-term future of the world and its life.
7. A sense of urgency regarding the survival of life on earth, both long-term and short-term.
8. A belief that human societies ought to be reestablished on a more sustainable technical and physical basis. An appreciation that many aspects of our present way of life are fundamentally transitory.

9. A revulsion toward waste in the face of human need (in more extreme forms, this may appear as asceticism).
10. A love of simplicity, although this does not include rejection of technology or "modernity."
11. An aesthetic appreciation for season, setting, climate, and natural materials.
12. A measurement of esteem, including self-esteem and social merit, in terms of such nonmaterial values as skill, artistry, effort, or integrity.
13. An attraction to autonomy and self-management in human endeavors and, generally, an inclination to more democratic and participatory political processes and administrative structures.

Needless to say, not all environmentalists accept all of these values. Most environmentalists find many of these values central to their outlook on life, but the list is not a catechism.

Paehlke sketches a distinctive approach to environmental problems rooted in the ecological sciences. How much of that approach would change if the balance of nature, as understood by traditional ecology, were a myth, as the following excerpt suggests?

|| *Daniel Botkin, Adjusting Law to Nature's Discordant Harmonies* 7 Duke Envtl. Law & Pol'y F. 25-37 (1996) ||

I. THE MYTH OF THE BALANCE OF NATURE

There has been a revolution in environmental sciences. At the heart of this revolution is a shift from the old idea of the constancy of Nature which is part of the ancient myth of the Balance of Nature. Briefly stated, the Balance of Nature myth has three basic features: First, Nature, undisturbed by human influences, achieves a permanency of form and structure that persists indefinitely. Second, this permanent condition is the best condition for Nature: best for other creatures, best for the environment, and best for humans. Third, when disturbed from this perfect state, Nature is capable of returning to it. The idea of the Balance of Nature is deeply rooted in our history, civilization, and religions. . . .

Unfortunately, the Balance of Nature myth is not true. During the past 30 years, this has been demonstrated as part of the revolution in environmental sciences. One of the central findings of this scientific revolution is that Nature is characterized by change, not constancy. The environment has always changed, and species have adapted to those changes. If we are to conserve and manage our living resources, then we must understand the naturalness of change, and this requires that we move away from the ancient and pervading myth of the Balance of Nature. . . .

[An] example which demonstrates the dominance of the Balance of Nature myth is the story of Hutchinson Memorial Forest, a nature preserve near to and managed by Rutgers University. . . .

[The Forest was established in the 1950s to preserve the only nevercut Oak-Hickory forest in New Jersey.] Life magazine ran an article showing a drawing of the forest that looked right out of a Walt Disney movie with all the forest creatures happily living together. All the popular articles and advertisements emphasized the idea that here, in Hutchinson Forest, was a natural ecosystem that had taken thousands of years to develop and, if left free from human disturbances, it would persist indefinitely in the beautiful state imagined by Life magazine. . . .

[Records from the 1750s showed] that this area was filled with large trees so widely spaced that [someone] could easily drive a horse and carriage through the forest. So, at that time the area was a picture book idea of an old-growth virgin forest. Today, and when I was a caretaker, the forest had some old trees, but it was primarily a dense thicket of small stems of shrubs and saplings, very hard to walk through, and, as I mentioned before, with the young trees primarily Maple, not Oak.

So Nature was not playing fair by not staying the way it was supposed to stay. It was not remaining a forest of huge, old Oaks and Hickories. It was not the open forest of huge trees. . . . That is one of the problems with studying natural ecological systems, Nature does not play fair in the sense that it does not do what we expect it to do, and therefore want it to do, according to our myths and beliefs.

What was going on here? Why was the forest not remaining in a constant condition and in the specific constant condition people had imagined it should have been in? [By examining tree rings, you can tell how frequently a tree has been scarred by fire. Study of trees felled by a hurricane showed that] there had been fires on the average of every ten years until 1701, and then there had been no fires since that time.

The fires that were common before European settlement were primarily lit by the Indians. The early European explorers, such as Henry Hudson, reported seeing many fires and attributed them to the Indians. There were many different reasons given as to why the Indians lit fires or let them burn once they were started, including: to drive game and to make travel easier. Whatever the reason, these fires were predominately Indian lit. It turns out that Oak and Hickory are more resistant to fire than Sugar Maple. Therefore, the reason Hutchinson Forest was predominately an Oak and Hickory forest was because the Native Americans burned it. It was also an open forest because of the fire. If you do not burn this kind of forest, it becomes a dense thicket dominated by Sugar Maple. So with the suppression of fire, Hutchinson Memorial Forest was becoming a forest that nobody had predicted, and I do not think anybody really wanted. It was becoming a scientific experiment, not the conservation of old-growth as originally intended.

What this suggests is that often what we really admire and appreciate about Nature, and think of as natural, has been heavily influenced by human beings. But the old Balance of Nature paradigm assumes that Nature remains in a single, constant condition which is the most desirable. This implies that people should leave Nature alone if we want Nature to attain its most desirable condition. Nature is perfect without human influence. Therefore, we have no place within Nature.

As I stated earlier, the new findings in ecology show that natural ecological systems are dynamic—always changing—and, as illustrated by Hutchinson Memorial Forest, sometimes the changes that are desirable are those induced through human action. In these ways, a nature preserve is different from a jar of strawberry preserves. However, we have acted as if the two were much the same: as with strawberry preserves, a nature preserve merely needed to be set aside and left alone.

Hutchinson Forest is not unique. The more that we study the history of natural areas, the more that we find that pre-industrial societies have altered the environment, often in ways that we like and that we think of as natural. As a result, we have to rethink how people and civilization fit with Nature.

II.   IMPLICATIONS OF THE PARADIGM SHIFT

What are the implications of these changes in our understanding of natural ecological systems and the relationship between people and Nature for laws and policy? I will illustrate some implications by way of another example. I was asked by the State of Oregon to direct a study about salmon and their habitat. The central questions to be answered were: (1) what was the relative effect of forest practices on salmon; and (2) what could be done to better improve the conservation and management of salmon? We were asked to study Western Oregon south of Columbia River to the Klammath River in California, an area that includes 26 rivers that reach the Pacific Ocean.

There are five important species of salmonids in this area: chum, coho, chinook, steelhead trout, and cutthroat trout. They spawn, hatch, and rear in the streams and rivers. The young fish stay in fresh water for about a year—the time varies with the species. During this early phase of their lives, the salmon are subject to short-term environmental variations such as annual variations of water flow and changes in the seasons which affect the vegetation along the streams. They are also subject to gradual, long-term changes in the condition of the forest. When the salmon swim out to the ocean where they typically remain for two to six years, depending on the species, they are affected by other kinds of environmental variations. These variations include changes in the ocean currents.

Moreover, salmon are fish of northern waters, so over centuries they have had to adapt to existing in rivers which freeze in the winter yet thaw in the summer, allowing the fish to spawn. In addition, in the Pacific Northwest, rivers and streams are subjected to volcanic eruptions, mud slides, forest fires, and other environmental variations that affect the stream habitats over significant periods of time.

The standard story about salmon is that they always return to the stream where they were spawned. But this is not quite the case. About fifteen percent of the adults return to a different stream from the one in which they were spawned. Given the variations in the environment, the ability to find new streams for spawning is essential to the survival of the species. The ability of individual salmon to adapt is essential to the existence of the species because it allows salmon to adapt to very slow environmental changes.

There is a common set of beliefs about salmon in Oregon that needs to be addressed. The important beliefs for our purposes are: (1) prior to European settlement, there was a superabundance of salmon; (2) the number was constant from year to year; (3) old-growth forests covered the entire area; (4) the great abundance of salmon was due to the existence of the continuous cover of old-growth forests. Here, among the common beliefs about salmon, we find a reassertion of the myth of the Balance of Nature.

One would think the state of Oregon would have a lot of information about this subject since they were paying for the project, but in actuality the state did not. . . . It was difficult to find data, but once some were obtained, even the simplest analyses yielded useful results. . . . We found that salmon were counted on only two of those rivers in a statistically valid way: the Rogue and the Umpqua Rivers.

Upon commencing the study, it was discovered that the number of adult salmon returning to spawn varied tremendously. Variation, rather than constancy, was the rule. But how have the salmon been managed? It is generally assumed that, without human harvest, the number of returning salmon would be the same year after year, unaffected by changes in the environment. This assumption is set forth mathematically in standard fishery harvest models. However, major fisheries relying on such harvest models have failed to maintain their fish levels. These failures call into question the validity of the assumption that without human intervention the salmon population would remain constant year after year.

Therefore, while conducting the study, we decided to avoid assumptions accepted prior to the examination of the facts. We also searched for available data, analyzed that data, and let new generalizations emerge from the data analysis. . . .

Attributes of our approach were openness and democracy. We listened to public, national, and local interest groups, and both nongovernmental and governmental organizations. We also held open meetings because we wanted to learn from the public and to relay information to the public as we uncovered it. . . .

We performed statistical analysis on [water flow data on the Rogue and Umpqua Rivers] and discovered that water flow accounted for a large percentage in the variation in fish returns during the past 20 years on the Rogue River.

What we had done was to turn the standard beliefs upside down. Instead of avoiding environmental variation and assuming that it did not exist, we used environmental variation as the basis for prediction and therefore as a basis for policy. Using [the fact that water flow in the year the fish were hatched bore a strong relationship to the number of adults returning three and four years later,] we developed a new tool that allowed an estimate to be made three years in advance about whether a year was likely to be a good one for salmon harvests. . . . Under the old methods, the allowable harvest is set during the present year sometimes close to the harvest time which allowed fishermen little time to plan and little flexibility. . . .

By learning to understand the dynamic of these systems, we can make better forecasts and make better laws and policies than we ever could previously. It is not clear if the people in management will actually use these new ideas, because they may still be locked in the old way of thinking. Policy-makers, and we as scientists, need to move away from the old beliefs about nature.

It may seem quite strange that there is such lack of interest in using data. Part of the reason for this, I believe, can be traced back to the myth of the Balance of Nature. As I have tried to make clear, this myth involves the idea that Nature knows best and will always move itself to a perfect, constant state. If this were true, then you would not have to know anything about Nature in order to manage it, data would have no importance. Nature would take care of itself; knowledge would not be important. This produces a strange irony in the late twentieth century "information age." The failure to use the data about adult fish returns, or to seek to obtain such data in a statistically valid way, is typical. Whenever I have been asked to examine an environmental problem, I have found that key information is lacking. . . .

Not only do we tend to formulate policy from myths about Nature, we also formulate policy based on what appears plausible, whether or not there are facts to support it. As an example from Oregon, in the 1940s people watching salmon swimming up stream noticed that in drought years the fish had trouble going over logs that had fallen across the streams. Many of these logs were large and, because they were submerged in water, decayed slowly. The logs had considerable value, especially during World War II. So a plan was devised to harvest all these logs on many streams throughout the state. The negative effect of the log debris in the streams on salmon seemed plausible. Both salmon and the war effort could be helped at the same time. No one conducted a test study to determine if the removal was actually beneficial. The result was a disaster for salmon. Those logs were fundamental to the structure of salmon breeding habitat. Thus, by removing the logs, the salmon habitat was destroyed. To correct for this past mistake, the Oregon Department of Fish and Wildlife is spending over $30,000 a mile to put logs back into the streams and anchor them. But are they doing tests to see if this works? No. I went out with some of the Department's staff and asked whether they counted the returning fish before they started putting logs back in the streams. No. I asked if they were counting the fish now. No. Were they doing any comparative studies? No. So the action had changed, but the approach was the same: do what seems plausible.

CONCLUSION

I have discussed some of the implications of new ideas in ecology upon environmental laws and policies. There has been a revolution in ecology, in fact in all environmental sciences, during the last 30 years. However, our laws and policies are still based on old, now outmoded, concepts, especially on the myth of the Balance of Nature. That myth not only tells us that Nature, undisturbed by human actions, will remain constant, but also that this constant state is the most desirable. Thus, Nature knows best. A corollary of this belief is that to manage our natural resources we do not need any information, we need only to leave Nature alone and it will find the correct state. Laws and policies based on this belief have dominated natural resource management in the twentieth century. As a result, there has been little emphasis on data. In addition to a dependency on outmoded concepts, environmental laws suffer from a dependency on what I have referred to as arguments from plausibility rather than arguments based on scientific information.

NOTES AND QUESTIONS

1. What are the implications of the "new ecology" for environmental policy and hence environmental law? Several scholars have begun to address this question. See, e.g., Tarlock, Slouching Toward Eden: The Eco-Pragmatic Challenges of Ecosystem Revival, 87 Minn. L. Rev. 1173 (2003); Wiener, Law and the New Ecology: Evolution, Categories, and Consequences, 22 Ecol. L.Q. 325 (1995); Meyer, The Dance of Nature: New Concepts in Ecology, 69 Chi.-Kent L. Rev. 875 (1994). The notes that follow raise some of the considerations.

2. Those views of environmental ethics that draw on ecology stress that humans are but one element in a complex, interrelated system of elements,

each of which is entitled to respect. Adherents of such ecocentric perspectives contrast their views with the human-centered principle that actions are good or bad insofar as they benefit or harm humans alone. How, if at all, do you think the "new ecology" as described in the preceding article might affect ecocentric perspectives on environmental ethics?

3. In his book Ecology and the Politics of Scarcity, William Ophuls provides the following statement of "the essential message of ecology."

> [A]lthough it is possible in principle to exploit nature rationally and reasonably for human ends, man has not done so. Because he has not been content with the portion naturally allotted him, man has invaded the biological capital built up by evolution. Moreover, due to man's ignorance of nature's workings, he has done so in a peculiarly destructive fashion. . . . We must learn to work with nature and to accept the basic ecological trade-offs between protection and production, optimum and maximum, quality and quantity. This will necessarily require major changes in our life, for the essential message of ecology is limitation: there is only so much the biosphere can take and only so much it can give, and this may be less than we desire. [Ecology and the Politics of Scarcity 43 (1977).]

How must Ophuls's "essential message" be modified, if at all, if the new ecology is sound?

4. How will ecology's contribution to the assessment of the consequences of human actions be affected by the new ecology? Has the science of ecology been made less relevant or more relevant to a careful evaluation of costs and benefits of large-scale human action? If there are no "natural" states to use as benchmarks, does calculating harm and benefit become more difficult, less difficult, or remain the same? How about deciding what is a harm or a benefit in the first place?

5. For over a decade, a controversy has raged over whether scientists should deliberately destroy the last remaining samples of variola, the virus that causes smallpox. An intense, worldwide effort to eradicate the disease ultimately was successful in 1977, and throughout the 1990s the only remaining variola samples were being held in tightly guarded research laboratories, one at the Centers for Disease Control and Prevention in Atlanta, the other at the Russian State Centre for Research on Virology and Biotechnology, Koltsovo, Novosibirsk Region, Russian Federation. Siebert, Smallpox Is Dead, Long Live Smallpox, N.Y. Times, Aug. 21, 1994, Magazine at 31. Some scientists argued that the molecular structure of the virus had been thoroughly studied and documented, while other virologists maintained that through further study the world could accrue additional knowledge. If you had had a vote prior to the terrorist attacks of September 11, 2001, how would you have voted on the issue of the irreversible destruction of the virus? After September 11? The World Health Organization (WHO) has three times decided that the samples should be destroyed (in 1993, 1996, and 1999), and three times has granted the virus a stay of execution, most recently in May 2002. Fowler, UN Group Voids Smallpox Deadline: Bioterrorism Fears Prompt Ruling to Retain Virus Stocks, Chicago Trib., May 19, 2002. Would the world have been better off had the WHO gone ahead with variola destruction earlier?

6. Is the ultimate objective of environmental policy to answer the question Christopher Stone poses: What sort of planet will this be? Stone argues that while technology and resource constraints define the range of future options that we

realistically can seek, environmental ethics seek to tell us which of these alternative futures we ought to select. Environmental law, then, seeks to determine how we can arrange our social institutions in order to achieve the future that we want. C. Stone, Earth and Other Ethics 15-16 (1987). What obligation do we have toward future generations when making choices concerning what sort of planet this will be? Do we have an obligation to leave future generations at least the same range of choices that we have? Or do we owe them some lesser obligation because they depend on us for their existence and their values will be influenced by the state of the world we choose to leave them? How would proponents of the economic perspective approach these questions? The ecological perspective?

E. COMMON POOL RESOURCES

Previous discussions have already explained how we tend to overuse our environmental resources because they are available without cost to us, so that the price mechanism does not make us aware of the harm we are causing to other humans or the environment. That harm is thus external to our private calculations concerning how much of the resource we should use. A good many environmental issues present this problem of external costs in ways that share a common structure. The essence of that structure is captured in this classic article.

|| *Garrett Hardin, The Tragedy of the Commons* ||
168 Science 1243 (1968)

The tragedy of the commons develops in this way. Picture a pasture open to all. It is to be expected that each herdsman will try to keep as many cattle as possible on the commons. Such an arrangement may work reasonably satisfactorily for centuries because tribal wars, poaching, and disease keep the numbers of both man and beast well below the carrying capacity of the land. Finally, however, comes the day of reckoning, that is, the day when the long-desired goal of social stability becomes a reality. At this point, the inherent logic of the commons remorselessly generates tragedy.

As a rational being, each herdsman seeks to maximize his gain. Explicitly or implicitly, more or less consciously, he asks, "What is the utility to me of adding one more animal to my herd?" This utility has one negative and one positive component.

(1) The positive component is a function of the increment of one animal. Since the herdsman receives all the proceeds from the sale of the additional animal, the positive utility is nearly +1.

(2) The negative component is a function of the additional overgrazing created by one more animal. Since, however, the effects of overgrazing are shared by all the herdsmen, the negative utility for any particular decision-making herdsman is only a fraction of −1.

Adding together the component partial utilities, the rational herdsman concludes that the only sensible course for him to pursue is to add another animal to his herd. And another, and another. . . . But this is the conclusion reached by each and every rational herdsman sharing a commons. Therein is the tragedy. Each man is locked into a system that compels him to increase his herd without limit in a world that is limited. Ruin is the destination toward which all men rush, each pursuing his own best interest in a society that believes in the freedom of the commons. Freedom in a commons brings ruin to all. . . .

In an approximate way, the logic of the commons has been understood for a long time, perhaps since the discovery of agriculture or the invention of private property in real estate. But it is understood mostly only in special cases which are not sufficiently generalized. Even at this late date, cattlemen leasing national land on the western ranges demonstrate no more than an ambivalent understanding, in constantly pressuring federal authorities to increase the head count to the point where overgrazing produces erosion and weed-dominance. Likewise, the oceans of the world continue to suffer from the survival of the philosophy of the commons. Maritime nations still respond automatically to the shibboleth of the "freedom of the seas." Professing to believe in the "inexhaustible resources of the oceans," they bring species after species of fish and whales closer to extinction.

The National Parks present another instance of the working out of the tragedy of the commons. At present, they are open to all, without limit. The parks themselves are limited in extent—there is only one Yosemite Valley—whereas population seems to grow without limit. The values that visitors seek in the parks are steadily eroded. Plainly, we must soon cease to treat the parks as commons or they will be of no value to anyone.

What shall we do? We have several options. We might sell them off as private property. We might keep them as public property, but allocate the right to enter them. The allocation might be on the basis of wealth, by the use of an auction system. It might be on the basis of merit, as defined by some agreed-upon standards. It might be by lottery. Or it might be on a first-come, first-serve basis, administered to long queues. These, I think, are all the reasonable possibilities. They are all objectionable. But we must choose—or acquiesce in the destruction of the commons that we call our National Parks. . . .

In a reverse way, the tragedy of the commons reappears in problems of pollution. Here it is not a question of taking something out of the commons, but of putting something in—sewage, or chemical, radioactive, and heat wastes into water, noxious and dangerous fumes into the air; and distracting and unpleasant advertising signs into the line of sight. The calculations of utility are much the same as before. The rational man finds that his share of the cost of the wastes he discharges into the commons is less than the cost of purifying his wastes before releasing them. Since this is true for everyone, we are locked into a system of "fouling our own nest," so long as we behave only as independent, rational, free-enterprisers.

The tragedy of the commons as a food basket is averted by private property, or something formally like it. But the air and waters surrounding us cannot readily be fenced, and so the tragedy of the commons as a cesspool must be prevented by different means, by coercive laws or taxing devices that make it cheaper for the polluter to treat his pollutants than to discharge them untreated. We have not progressed as far with the solution of this problem as we have with the first. Indeed, our particular concept of private property, which deters us from exhausting the positive resources of the earth, favors pollution. The owner of a factory on the bank of a stream—whose property extends to the middle of the stream—often has difficulty seeing why it is not his natural right to muddy the waters flowing past his door. The law, always behind the times, requires elaborate stitching and fitting to adapt it to this newly perceived aspect of the commons.

NOTES AND QUESTIONS

1. Hardin's story of the commons is a "tragedy" because a dynamic is at work within the story that is leading to eventual disaster, disaster for all. What is that dynamic?

Insofar as the dynamic relates to the desire of "each herdsman to maximize his gain," is the tragedy unavoidable? Many who disagree with the economic approach to environmental problems do so because they believe humans ought not, and need not, pursue their own "gain" single-mindedly. Aldo Leopold, for one, claimed that anyone approaching the environment as exclusively an object for personal gain in effect treated it as a piece of property, "entailing privileges but not obligations." In arguing for a "land ethic," he argued for a change in humanity's disposition toward the environment, one that "changes the role of Homo sapiens from conqueror of the land-community to plain member and citizen of it. [This] implies respect for his fellow-members, and also respect for the community as such." A. Leopold, A Sand County Almanac 204 (1968). This idea has been widely influential among environmentalists. For summaries and appraisals, see Meyers, An Introduction to Environmental Thought: Some Sources and Some Criticisms, 50 Ind. L.J. 426 (1975); Heffernan, The Land Ethic: A Critical Appraisal, 4 Envtl. Ethics 235 (1982); C. Stone, Earth and Other Ethics (1987).

2. Surely the tragedy of commons is not inevitable, as other studies have shown, because some commons have existed for centuries, and continue to exist. E. Ostrom, Governing the Commons: The Evolution of Institutions for Collective Action (1990). As one study suggests, "Perhaps what existed in fact was not a 'tragedy of the commons' but rather a triumph: that for hundreds of years—and perhaps thousands, although written records do not exist to prove the longer era—land was managed successfully by communities." Cox, No Tragedy of the Commons, 7 Envtl. Ethics 49, 60 (1985). Small communities are likely to be more successful at avoiding the tragedy through informal controls so long as there are no external markets for the resources. Cultural anthropologists, including especially students of Native American cultures, have identified cultural and ideological explanations for husbanding commons resources. Moreover, as Carol Rose points out, the tragedy occurs only when use of the commons reaches a level where congestion develops or where the resources are used so intensively that it exceeds the carrying capacity of the commons. Rose, Rethinking Environmental Controls: Management Strategies for Common Resources, 1991 Duke L.J. 1.

3. The type of situation exemplified by Hardin's article is often called a "common pool resource" problem (CPR). CPRs are sometimes analyzed through a model of behavior known as the Prisoner's Dilemma, named for the story used to illustrate the behavior. In that story, two persons suspected of a serious crime are isolated from each other and told that if either testifies against her colleague she will go free, so long as the other suspect doesn't also turn state's evidence, in which case each will receive a moderate sentence. If neither suspect testifies, then each will be convicted of a lesser crime, for which there already is sufficient evidence. Each will then receive a light sentence for the lesser crime. However, if one suspect keeps quiet while the other testifies, the silent suspect will receive a harsh sentence.

From the perspective of any single suspect, each gets a shorter sentence by testifying against the other, regardless of what the other one does. Thus the strategy of testifying "dominates" any other strategy that the suspect could choose, and any suspect interested in minimizing his or her sentence should adopt it. However, the final result of both actors following this strategy is that they each get moderate sentences, which is worse for each than if they had both kept silent, in which case each would have received a light sentence.

The result of the prisoner's dilemma is an outcome that is "individually rational and collectively deficient." B. Barry & R. Hardin, Rational Man and Irrational Society? 25 (1982). It is individually rational because each player chooses her dominant strategy, which is the rational thing to do. It is collectively deficient because there exists another outcome that would leave each suspect better off than the all-testify outcome. This individual rationality and collective deficiency identifies the problem of collective action, namely that "it may be in everyone's individual interest not to cooperate in a collective effort even though everyone would be better off if everyone cooperated." Id.

4. Some have urged that organizing collective action to prevent tragedies of the commons should constitute a primary function of government. The late Mancur Olson, for instance, wrote that "[a] state is first of all an organization that provides public goods for its members, the citizens." M. Olson, The Logic of Collective Action 15 (1965). Long before the problem of collective action became identified as such, theorists had observed that such cases were ones in which government might legitimately intervene, and even writers not otherwise associated with interventionist views about government have concluded that prisoner's dilemma cases provide a legitimate occasion for intervention. For example, John Stuart Mill wrote:

> There are matters in which interference of law is required, not to overrule the judgment of individuals respecting their own interest, but to give effect to that judgment; they being unable to give effect to it except by concert, which concert again cannot be effectual unless it receives validity and sanction from the law. [J.S. Mill, Principles of Political Economy, Bk. V., Chap. XI, Sec. 12.]

Mill suggested that "I would rather cooperate than welch, but only if you cooperate" is an individually rational judgment in some circumstances, and that it may require legal sanction to ensure universal cooperation, which all seem to desire.

5. Others have argued that privatizing the commons by creating property rights in common resources is a solution superior to government regulation of access. Jim Krier cautions that there are difficulties with either approach. Given that the root of the tragedy of the commons is the difficulty of coordinating human behavior, Krier questions whether proponents of these approaches are "implicitly arguing that a community plagued by noncooperation can improve its condition by cooperating." Krier, The Tragedy of the Commons, Part Two, 15 Harv. J.L. & Pub. Pol'y 325, 338 (1992). Krier claims that because the public must organize in order to get the government to intervene to protect the commons, the problems of free riders and factional influence persist. Because "markets themselves depend on an active governmental role," Krier finds no reason to believe that the same governmental failures that plague regulatory programs will not plague the establishment and oversight of new natural resources markets. Id. at 341-342.

PROBLEM EXERCISE: SHOULD THE ARCTIC
NATIONAL WILDLIFE REFUGE BE OPENED TO OIL
EXPLORATION AND DEVELOPMENT?

Along the northeast coast of Alaska, 200 miles north of the Arctic Circle, lies a pristine wilderness area. Sometimes called North America's Serengeti, the area is home to a vast herd of porcupine caribou whose migratory range extends over 96,000 square miles. It is the kind of place most Americans encounter only in the pages of National Geographic, which describes it as "a land of mountains and broad, lake-filled plains, where caribou have worn trails in rock and geese have traced paths in the sky over millennia of rhythmic wandering; where ice holds the sea and frost the land until a brief, glorious burst of flowering summer; . . . a roadless land, a part of the North little touched by the 20th century, or the 19th, or the first." Lee, Oil in the Wilderness: An Arctic Dilemma, National Geographic, Dec. 1988, at 858. More recently, former President Jimmy Carter described the visit he and Mrs. Carter took to the area as "a profoundly humbling experience. We were reminded of our human dependence on the natural world." Jimmy Carter, Make This Natural Treasure a National Monument, N.Y. Times, Dec. 29, 2000.

To an oil company geologist the area is inspirational for a very different reason. Located 40 miles east of North America's largest oil field at Prudhoe Bay, the area represents "the chance of a lifetime to search for 'elephants'—oil fields with more than a hundred million barrels of producible reserves—in perhaps the last major hunting ground on North America's mainland." Lee, supra at 863.

Since 1960, Congress has taken steps to preserve the special wilderness qualities of Alaska's northeastern coastal plan while continuing to study oil exploration as an option. Congress has now set aside 19 million acres as the Arctic National Wildlife Refuge (ANWR), half of it as wilderness area, and 1.5 million acres along the coast ("section 1002 lands," named after the section of the statute creating the category) for further study as to the possibility of oil exploration on them. Ever since then, the issue has indeed been studied. The U.S. Geological Survey has issued two comprehensive reports on the amount of recoverable oil in the ANWR (1987 and 1998). The most recent one reports a likely range of 5.7 to 16 billion barrels of oil (BBO), with a mean value of 10.4 BBO, higher figures than the 1987 study. The Department of the Interior (DOI) has performed numerous environmental studies. The Fish and Wildlife Service performed one retrospective study on the environmental effects of oil exploration in Prudhoe Bay, an adjacent site of oil drilling (1988), and numerous assessments of environmental impacts on wildlife have been produced over the years. These studies vary in their assessment of the environmental consequences of drilling, and the assessments of environmental organizations differ with the government reports even more widely.

The draft of a 1987 DOI assessment concluded that "[l]ong-term losses in fish and wildlife resources, subsistence uses, and wilderness values would be the inevitable consequences" of development, which "will result in widespread, long-term changes in wildlife habitats, wilderness environment, and Native community activities," and possibly a "major population decline" in the caribou herd. DOI Secretary Hodel disagreed with those conclusions, and the final report conceded only that "there is a risk that a decline could occur" in the caribou population, but anticipated "no appreciable population decline."

Following the release of the Interior Department report, the U.S. Fish and Wildlife Service was asked by a member of Congress to evaluate whether the environmental impact of oil development in nearby Prudhoe Bay had been as benign as predicted in the government's environmental impact statement. A draft of their report was leaked to Congress in May 1988. The draft report found that the environmental impact of oil drilling in Prudhoe Bay had been far greater than estimated in the environmental impact statements prepared 15 years earlier. It noted that 11,000 acres of wildlife habitat had been destroyed, nearly twice what had been predicted, and that the populations of bears, wolves and other predators, and most bird species had declined. Although caribou had increased in number, the report attributed this increase to a decline in the numbers of bears and other caribou predators. It noted that more than 200 million gallons of fresh water unexpectedly were being withdrawn from lakes and streams by oil operations each year and that erosion, sedimentation, and oil spills had done far more damage to water quality than anticipated.

These reports had been done prior to the first congressional vote on whether to open the section 1002 lands. Shortly before that vote, the New York Times editorialized about the ANWR.

Risks Worth Taking for Oil
N.Y. Times, June 2, 1988, at A26

Can Big Oil and its Government regulators be trusted with the fragile environment of Alaska's Arctic Wildlife Refuge? . . . Last month, opponents' skepticism was heightened by a leaked report from the Fish and Wildlife Service saying that environmental disruption in the nearby North Slope oil fields is far worse than originally believed.

The North Slope development has been America's biggest test by far of the proposition that it is possible to balance energy needs with sensitivity for the environment. The public therefore deserves an independent assessment of the ecological risks and an honest assessment of the energy rewards.

No one wants to ruin a wilderness for small gain. But in this case, the potential is enormous and the environmental risks are modest. Even if the report's findings are confirmed, the likely value of the oil far exceeds plausible estimates of the environmental cost.

The amount of oil that could be recovered from the Wildlife Refuge is not known. But it seems likely that the coastal plain, representing a small part of the acreage in the refuge, contains several billion barrels, worth tens of billions of dollars. But drilling is certain to disrupt the delicate ecology of the Arctic tundra. . . .

According to the authors [of the Fish and Wildlife study], development [in Prudhoe Bay] used more land, damaged more habitat acreage, and generated more effluent than originally predicted. The authors also argue that Government monitoring efforts and assessment of long-term effects have been inadequate.

It's important to find out whether these interpretations are sensible and how environmental oversight could be improved. . . . But even taken at face value, the report's findings hardly justify putting oil exploration on hold.

No species is reported to be endangered. No dramatic permanent changes in ecology are forecast. Much of the unpredicted damage has arisen because more oil has been produced than originally predicted. Even so, the total acreage affected by development represents only a fraction of 1 percent of the North Slope wilderness.

The trade-off between energy and ecology seems unchanged. If another oil field on the scale of Prudhoe Bay is discovered, developing it will damage the environment. That damage is worth minimizing. But it is hard to see why absolutely pristine preservation of this remote wilderness should take precedence over the nation's energy needs.

Question One. The editorial argues in favor of opening ANWR to drilling. Do you find its arguments to be persuasive? The editorial does not favor drilling for oil in all circumstances. When would the editorial writers be opposed to drilling in a wilderness area? Do you agree? Are there additional circumstances in which you would oppose drilling? The editorial suggests that anyone supporting "absolutely pristine preservation" of the Wildlife Refuge mistakenly gives wilderness "precedence over the nation's energy needs." Is that correct? For someone concerned about endangered species or ecological damage, is it sufficient that "no species is reported to be endangered" and that "[n]o dramatic permanent changes in ecology are forecast"?

Question Two. Once a wilderness area has been developed, it will never again be wilderness, or at least not for a very, very long time. So the decision to develop cannot be reversed. On the other hand, a decision to place an area off limits can later be reversed. Following Iraq's invasion of Kuwait in August 1990, Alaska's congressional delegation argued that the ANWR should be opened for drilling to reduce American dependence on foreign oil. In 2001 and 2002, President Bush and his administration have made the same argument as a result of tensions with Iraq. His National Energy Plan (NEP) reports that "ANWR production could equal 46 years of current oil imports from Iraq." NEP 5-9 (2001). How should the apparent irreversibility of a decision to open a wilderness area to development be factored into the decision-making process?

Question Three. Scientists have continually emphasized the uncertainty of projections concerning the environmental impact of development at ANWR. Faced with this uncertainty, both sides in the debate over ANWR offer sharply different projections based largely on the same data. For example, proponents of opening ANWR to drilling argue that the growth of the Central Arctic caribou herd in the vicinity of the Prudhoe Bay oil field from 5,000 to 18,000 head during the past 15 years demonstrates that drilling will not cause unacceptable harm to the environment. In the Clinton Administration, which opposed drilling, DOI forecast more environmental damage than had either previous DOI report, concluding that drilling would result "in a major, adverse impact on the [caribou] herd" and damage to water supplies and fragile tundra vegetation. Kenworthy, Study Condemns Arctic Oil Drilling, Wash. Post, Aug. 27, 1995, at A4. Opponents argue that caribou herds have grown worldwide in the past decade as part of a cyclical increase that scientists do not fully understand. Noting that calving has fallen sharply within a half mile of the roads and facilities at Prudhoe Bay, they argue that drilling at ANWR would threaten its much larger 150,000-head porcupine caribou herd, which is dependent on a much smaller area of land. In response to this, proponents of drilling now argue that new drilling technologies permit drilling to be done with a "dramatically reduced . . . footprint on the tundra, minimiz[ing] waste produced, and protect[ing] the land for resident and migratory wildlife. . . . Estimates indicate that no more than 2,000 will be disturbed." NEP 5-9 (2001). Scientists emphasize that the long-term, cumulative impacts of development at Prudhoe Bay will take decades to assess. How much confidence in projections of environmental impact should be required before a decision concerning a major development project is based on them? Should it depend on the likely magnitude of the consequences? On their reversibility?

Question Four.   Does the battle over ANWR raise environmental justice concerns? Native Americans living in remote villages near ANWR have a very different perception of what the ANWR battle is about. To Sarah James, a Gwich'in from Arctic Village, Alaska, it "is not just an environmental issue." Rather,

> [i]t is about the survival of the ancient culture that depends on the caribou. It is about the basic tribal and human rights to continue [our] way of life. For thousands of years we have lived with the caribou right where we are today. We are talking about an Indian nation that still lives on the land and depends on the herd. In my village 75 percent of protein comes from caribou. It's not just what we eat. It is who we are. Caribou are our life. It's in our stories and songs and the whole way of the world. [Sarah James, Testimony before a Subcomm. of the Senate Environment and Public Works Comm. (Mar. 1991).]

How should Ms. James's concerns be factored into the ANWR decision? Should preservation of a way of life be an important goal of environmental policy? Ms. James notes her tribe always protected the habitat of the caribou "[e]ven during hard times." They feel a moral "responsibility to keep this land pure and pass it on to our children, grandchildren, and so on for generations yet to come."

In contrast to the Gwich'in, Inupiat Eskimos argue that ANWR should be opened to oil exploration because of the economic benefits development will provide. The Arctic Slope Regional Corporation, which represents the Inupiat of the North Slope, owns 92,000 acres of land that they wish the oil companies to develop. An Inupiat representative argues that as a result of development at Prudhoe Bay,

> [r]evenues from the only economy we have—the oil industry—have provided high schools in each of our eight villages for the first time in our history. We now have health clinics, utilities, a local senior citizens' home and other basic public services that most Americans take for granted. [Letter from Brenda Itta-Lee, Vice President for Human Resources, Arctic Slope Regional Corporation, to the editors, Wash. Post, Aug. 28, 1991.]

How would you respond to her concerns?

Question Five.   As already indicated, a strong stimulus for drilling in the ANWR has always been reducing the nation's dependence on foreign oil. After the events of September 11, 2001, the national security advantages of greater domestic oil drilling have been stressed heavily by supporters of opening the ANWR. What role should the possibility of reducing dependence on foreign oil in other ways play in the debate? President Bush's NEP includes provisions for energy conservation and alternative energy sources, but it has been criticized for not going far enough with these approaches to satisfy energy demand before turning to the ANWR. When the latest proposal to open section 1002 lands for oil exploration was before the House and the Senate, conservation and alternative energy sources were among the points stressed by opponents to drilling. Public Citizen argued, for example, that "a more forward-looking national energy security act should be developed that actively promotes and funds cutting-edge renewable and sustainable energy sources. A comprehensive plan would include conservation measures and research, development and implementation of green energy production." Public Citizen, Oppose Drilling in the National Arctic Wildlife Refuge (May 14, 2001). On August 1, 2001, the House voted to open ANWR for exploration. The matter came before the Senate in the spring of 2002, prior to which the New York Times once again editorialized.

The Missing Energy Strategy
N.Y. Times, April 10, 2002, at A26

The events of the past year—prominently, a power crisis in California and the terrorist attacks on Sept. 11—gave the nation many reasons to re-examine its energy strategy. . . .

Mr. Hussein's [ceasing export of oil to the United States] draws attention once again to America's dependence on imported oil. . . . It also points to Washington's sorry failure to devise a balanced strategy to reduce America's reliance on gulf imports and give itself greater maneuvering room in the war on terrorism and other foreign policy issues as well.

[To produce a respectable bill, Senators must] defeat any amendment aimed at opening the Arctic refuge to drilling. Such an amendment is almost certain to be offered by Frank Murkowski of Alaska, but the facts are not on his side. Every available calculation—including those that accept Mr. Murkowski's inflated estimates of the amount of oil underneath the refuge—show that much more oil can be saved by fuel efficiency than by drilling.

Next, they must resist efforts to weaken the renewable energy provision, while defending energy efficiency measures that have yet to be voted on—chiefly a provision that would increase efficiency standards for air-conditioners by 30 percent. The Senate should also preserve a useful provision that would require companies to give a public accounting of their production of carbon dioxide and other so-called greenhouse gases. On the supply side, it can take steps to improve the reliability of the nationwide electricity grid, while increasing incentives for smaller and potentially more efficient producers of power.

Estimates of recoverable oil were generally higher in 2002 than they were in 1988, while assessments of environmental impacts were arguably lower, and national security issues loomed larger. What explains the N.Y. Times change? As a United States Senator, how would you vote?

Section 1002 lands can only be opened to exploration through a congressional vote, and the question has been the subject of periodic controversies in

Congress ever since the lands were established. In recent years, advocates of opening the ANWR to drilling have used the budget authorization process as means of ensuring that a vote is taken on the question. In 2002, drilling supporters included a provision approving drilling in the Senate's budget resolution, but this approval was stripped from the resolution by a vote of 52-48 on the Senate floor. However, after the 2004 elections gave the Republicans a greater majority in the Senate, a vote taken on March 16, 2005, to strip a similar authorization failed by 49-51. For this drilling approval to become law, however, it also needed to be included in one of the spending, or authorization, bills that the Senate passes reflecting the decisions made in the budget resolution. Accordingly, the drilling approval was subsequently included in the defense authorization bill, with supporters of drilling thinking that including it in this "must-pass" measure would help ensure passage. However, on December 21, 2005, the Senate was unable to stop a filibuster on the defense authorization bill. The vote was 56-44 to end debate, but it takes 60 affirmative votes to succeed. Earlier, protectors of ANWR had also succeeded in stripping a drilling approval provision from the budget reconciliation bill. With the defense authorization also blocked from final passage, Senator Ted Stevens (R-AL) agreed to remove the ANWR provision from it. When President Bush submitted his request for funding for the Interior Department in early 2006, however, he once again included a call to open the ANWR to drilling. Govindaraian and Duncan, ANWR Redux; Jump in Leasing Revenues Predicted, CQ Today, Feb. 6, 2006. Additional congressional votes on the issue are certain to come.

Question Six.   Is the ANWR controversy primarily a dispute over values (between adherents of the economic and ecological perspectives) or a factual dispute that turns on differing predictions of the likely consequences of drilling? Consider the following contrasting descriptions of ANWR offered by opponents and proponents of drilling during March 1991 congressional hearings. Brooks Yeager, vice president of the National Audubon Society, described ANWR as "one of the earth's last great dynamic ecosystems." Accusing environmentalists of distorting the facts about ANWR, Walter Hickel, governor of Alaska, described it as "a barren, marshy wilderness in the summer, infested with uncountable mosquitoes, and locked in temperatures of 60 and 70 degrees below zero for up to nine months of the year." What explains these sharply contrasting descriptions of ANWR? Are they the product of differences in values or of different views concerning what "the facts" are? Do our values inevitably influence our willingness to accept certain propositions as "facts" and to draw certain conclusions from them? In thinking about these questions, consider the views of an Alaskan writing to his newspaper shortly before the 2002 Senate vote.

	Gary Rolf, Stick with the Science and Keep	
	the Emotionalism Out of ANWR	
	Anchorage Daily News, April 10, 2002, at B8	

Kiss the scientific process goodbye! Last week the U.S. Geological Survey published an Arctic National Wildlife Refuge report suggesting possible harm to the refuge from oil operations. But wait, do the conditions causing the harm reflect reality in the actual proposed plan to mitigate environmental concerns? I predicted Sen. Joe Lieberman's response that a request to answer that question would be politically motivated. It was so predictable! The environmentalist movement rarely wins using sound scientific principles. Instead they resort to tactics that are meant to confuse the general public, causing a stir, discrediting any attempts to keep the scientific principle pure, with the intention of making issues like these purely political. I saw it in college 23 years ago in a debate about nuclear power. The anti-nuke guy said, if you have two opposing scientific opinions we should vote on it! Nonsense! Science is science. There are answers. If we could just keep the emotionalism and "Chicken Little" rhetoric out of the discussion. . . .

Question Seven.   In March 2003, a committee of the National Research Council of the National Academy of Sciences released a report on the "Cumulative Effects of Oil and Gas Activities on Alaska's North Slope" (available at *www.nap.edu*). The report, which had been requested by congressional proponents of opening ANWR, confirmed that oil companies have reduced the "footprint" of their drilling technologies, but it also found that oil exploration in Alaska has produced "a steady accumulation of harmful environmental and social effects that will probably grow as exploration expands." Andrew C. Revkin, Experts Conclude Oil Drilling Has Hurt Alaska's North Slope, N.Y. Times, March 5, 2003, at A15. The report states:

> Northern Alaska's environment and culture have already been significantly affected by oil infrastructure and activities. There have been many benefits to North Slope residents including more jobs and improved hospitals and schools. These economic benefits have been accompanied by environmental and social consequences, including effects of the roads, infrastructure and activities of oil exploration and production on the terrain, plants, animals and peoples of the North Slope and the adjacent marine environment. [National Research Council, Cumulative Environmental Effects of Oil and Gas Activities on Alaska's North Slope (2003).]

The report notes that fewer than 1 percent of dormant drilling areas had been restored and that "the effects of abandoned structures and unrestored landscapes could persist for centuries and accumulate." It also warns that recent warming trends in the area may jeopardize the use of technologies, such as ice roads, to reduce the footprint left by drilling.

The NRC committee was careful not to make any judgment concerning "whether the benefits derived from oil and gas production justify the accompanying undesirable environmental consequences." It concludes that "[s]ociety as a whole must debate and decide that issue." Opponents of opening ANWR hailed the report as confirmation that drilling would cause substantial, irreversible environmental damage there. Proponents of drilling emphasized the report's confirmation that new drilling technologies leave a smaller environmental footprint. After reading a summary of the report, which is available online at *www.nap.edu*, how, if at all, should it affect one's judgment concerning the merits of the ANWR policy debate? Does the report provide the kind of "scientific answers" Gary Rolf calls for in Question Six above?

=2=
Environmental Law: A Structural Overview

Most of today's environmental law violates the basic principles of ecology. Nature teaches the connectedness of all activities, but most current-generation law regulates separate pollutants with little consideration of ecosystems as a whole. The continuums of nature generally adapt gradually, but today's environmental law makes sharp distinctions between safe and unsafe, attainment versus nonattainment areas, permissible versus impermissible levels of pollution.*

—*Donald Elliott*

If you have traveled in the remote parts of the Deep South, I am sure you have seen the architecture of Tobacco Road—shacks built of whatever materials were available at the time, often by a series of owners. Maybe the roof is corrugated tin, but one wall is made from a billboard and the door step is a cinder block. No part matches any other part, and there are holes here and there. Still, it provides a measure of basic shelter, and there comes a point where it is easier to tack a new board over a gap that appears than to redesign the entire structure.**

—*Ronald Outen*

Although U.S. environmental law often is portrayed as if it were invented by Congress during the 1970s, its roots run much deeper. Environmental law is an outgrowth of centuries of common law doctrines that seek to protect people and property from harm caused by the actions of others. Its common law roots help explain both the complexity of environmental law and the difficulties it confronts in seeking to preserve natural resources and to prevent harm that often is far removed in space and time from the actions that cause it.

Environmental law's structural complexity is a product of centuries of evolving common law doctrine, federal and state statutes that direct agencies to issue a vast array of regulations, and even agreements between sovereign states. Most environmental statutes respond to particularly visible manifestations of broader ecological problems. Considered together, environmental statutes and common law principles provide regulatory authority that is at once piecemeal and overlapping. Thus, even though the environmental law articulates some of society's noblest aspirations, its legal architecture may resemble more closely a shack on Tobacco Road than a Gothic cathedral.

---

*Toward Ecological Law and Policy, in Thinking Ecologically (M.R. Chertow & D.C. Esty eds., 1997).

**Environmental Pollution Laws and the Architecture of Tobacco Road, in National Research Council, Multimedia Approaches to Pollution Control: Symposium Proceedings 139 (1987).

61

The complex architecture of environmental law reflects not only the circumstances of its birth, but also the complexity of the problems it addresses and the difficulty of reconciling the competing values environmental policy implicates. Although there is a remarkable cross-disciplinary consensus in favor of collective action to address problems caused by "individually rational but collectively deficient" behavior, often there is sharp disagreement concerning the precise form that action should take. The diverse philosophies that animate environmental concerns and the immense uncertainties that surround forecasts of likely policy outcomes provide ample opportunity for controversy.

This chapter is designed to introduce the "big picture" of environmental law by providing a roadmap of sorts to help you navigate this legal labyrinth. After reviewing the roots of environmental law, it explores the principal federal environmental statutes and the wide range of alternative regulatory strategies they employ. The chapter concludes with a brief introduction to the process by which statutes are translated into regulations.

A. SOURCES OF ENVIRONMENTAL LAW

What is environmental law? Dan Tarlock argues that environmental law, "as now defined, is primarily a synthesis of pre-environmental era common law rules, principles from other areas of law, and post-environmental era statutes which are lightly influenced by the application of concepts derived from ecology and other areas of science, economics, and ethics." A. Dan Tarlock, "Is There A There There in Environmental Law?" 19 J. Land Use & Envtl. L. 213, 222 (2004). Tarlock notes that environmental law lacks not only an internal set of rules, but also a clear constitutional foundation. He acknowledges that environmental law "looks like and is positive law." However, Tarlock argues that it actually could be viewed as representing "a radical break with the Western legal tradition," including both the common law and constitutionalism, because much of it seeks to protect natural systems and future generations that traditionally are not recognized as having legal personalities. Id. at 235. Dean James Huffman agrees that environmental law has radical roots, but he notes that "[w]hat was once the exclusive cause of radicals is now the day-to-day work of legions of button-down lawyers from Wall Street to San Francisco." James L. Huffman, The Past and Future of Environmental Law, 30 Envtl. L. 23 (2000). Richard Lazarus observes that environmental law "has evolved from a radical intruder into an essential element of a mature legal system in a democratic society." Richard J. Lazarus, The Making of Environmental Law 253 (2004).

There is broad agreement that environmental law cannot be reduced to a simple set of decision rules that can dictate how policy makers should act in the face of uncertainty. Tarlock maintains that "for the foreseeable future, environmental law will be a law about the process of decision rather than a process of evolving decision rules." Id. at 219-220. It will "be a messy process of adapting the contingencies and limitations of science to 'wicked' problems informed by rebuttable principles." Id. at 253-254. Continued controversy over environmental policy seems a given, even as the environmental law field has matured to the point where it is possible to outline fundamental principles described in this chapter. Because environmental regulation inevitably creates winners and losers, it always will provide ample incentive for pushback by regulatory targets. While Dean Huffman assures us that "[e]nvironmental law is here to stay," he foresees growing tensions between decentralization and internationalization, the ascendance of market mechanisms, and the rise of "unexpected political alliances," fueled in part by the environmental justice movement. 30 Envtl. L. at 24. Professor Lazarus questions "whether environmental law can maintain the passion and commitment needed to rebuff the never-ending efforts to make it more responsive to the concerns of the here and now at the expense of those in seemingly distant places and future times." Lazarus, The Making of Environmental Law 254.

Environmental law today is a complex combination of common law, legislation, regulations, and international agreements. After centuries of wrestling with environmental conflicts, the common law now has been supplemented, and in some cases supplanted, by regulatory statutes that declare broad environmental goals while delegating to administrative agencies responsibility for developing specific policies to achieve them. Despite the ascendance of regulatory legislation, understanding of the common law roots of environmental law remains important for several reasons. The common law articulates foundational principles that have shaped the development of regulatory programs and it retains considerable vitality as a safety net when unregulated activities cause environmental harm. Common law notions also retain considerable influence, for better or worse, on courts reviewing environmental regulations and efforts to enforce compliance with them.

1. Common Law Roots

Prior to the explosion of environmental legislation in the 1970s, the common law was the legal system's primary vehicle for responding to environmental problems. For centuries common law courts had wrestled with what is perhaps the quintessential question of environmental law: how to harmonize conflicts that inevitably occur when human activity interferes with the interests of others in the quality of their physical surroundings. The common law relied largely on nuisance law doctrines to resolve environmental controversies, although conduct that resulted in a physical invasion of property could be addressed as a trespass. Nuisance law is designed to protect against invasions of interests in the use and enjoyment of land, while trespass protects against invasions of interests in the exclusive possession of land.

A leading treatise's declaration that nuisance law is an "impenetrable jungle," W. Prosser, Handbook of the Law of Torts §86, at 571 (4th ed. 1971), no doubt reflects, in some respects, the difficulties courts face in attempting to harmonize the competing interests at stake in environmental controversies. The history of nuisance law illustrates the tension between competing perspectives on environmental problems that can be characterized as "moral outrage" and "cool analysis." The early common law of nuisance held actors strictly liable when their actions interfered with property rights held by others. This common law version of moral outrage focused largely on whether certain interests had been invaded, not on the utility of the conduct that produced the invasion. As the Industrial Revolution intensified environmental conflicts, the common law more frequently employed balancing approaches, reflecting the cool analysis perspective, that considered not only the nature of the interference with property rights but also the nature and utility of the conduct that generated the interference.

While applicable to related problems, private and public nuisance actions have distinct legal roots. Private nuisance actions focus on invasions of interests in the private use and enjoyment of land. Public nuisances were common law crimes that involved offenses against the state arising from actions that interfered with public property (e.g., obstruction of the king's highway, encroachment on the royal domain) or that endangered the health or property of large numbers of people. Actions to abate private nuisances could be brought by private parties damaged by them. Public nuisances were subject to abatement actions by governmental authorities or by private parties who suffered special injury.

A.   PRIVATE NUISANCE

Nontrespassory invasions of another's interest in the private use and enjoyment of land are actionable as *private nuisances*. Unlike intentional trespass, where liability attaches even in the absence of a showing of harm, private nuisance liability requires a showing of significant harm. Moreover, the interference with property rights must be intentional and unreasonable or actionable under rules imposing strict liability on those engaging in abnormally dangerous activities as in Fletcher v. Rylands, L.R. 3 H.L. 330 (1868). As the Restatement of Torts explains, these requirements reflect a recognition that some conflicts are inevitable in a modern society:

> Life in organized society, and especially in populous communities, involves an unavoidable clash of individual interests. Practically all human activities unless carried on in a wilderness, interfere to some extent with others or involve some risk of interference, and these interferences range from the mere trifling annoyances to serious harms. It is an obvious truth that each individual in a community must put up with a certain amount of risk in order that all may get together. The very existence of an organized society depends upon the principle of "give and take, live and let live," and therefore the law of torts does not attempt to impose liability or shift the loss in every case where one person's conduct has some detrimental effect on another. Liability is imposed only in those cases where the harm or risk to one is greater than he ought to be required to bear under the circumstances at least without compensation. [Restatement of Torts (Second) §822 comment g (1978).]

Nuisance law has long wrestled with the difficult question of how to determine the level of harm or risk that requires compensation.

Actions for private nuisance evolved from the ancient assize of nuisance, which was designed to secure the free enjoyment of property. In the early fifteenth century the assize of nuisance was displaced by an action on the case for nuisance. While procedurally simpler than the assize, actions on the case provided only a damages remedy. Suits in equity were necessary in order to obtain injunctions ordering the abatement of private nuisances; such actions were rarely brought prior to the mid-nineteenth century.

An influential early case in the development of nuisance law was a seventeenth-century decision involving a pig sty built adjacent to William Aldred's property. In Aldred's Case, 77 Eng. Rep. 816 (1611), the pig sty was held to be a private nuisance because the wretched stench that it generated interfered with Aldred's enjoyment of his property. While the decision did not imply that all unpleasant odors emanating from the property of others were actionable, it established that if a nontrespassory invasion of property rights was sufficiently great, air pollution was actionable as a private nuisance. As Lord Holt explained in declaring the failure to repair a wall separating a privy from a neighbor's property to be a nuisance, "every man must so use his own as not to damnify another." Tenant v. Goldwin, 92 Eng. Rep. 222 (1702). This principle—that no one has the right to use their property in a manner that causes harm to another—has come to be known as the "sic utere" principle because it is derived from a Roman law maxim ("sic utere tuo ut alienum non laedas").

Early nuisance law performed a kind of zoning function by initially encouraging noxious activities to move away from populated areas. As the Industrial Revolution progressed, environmental insults became more difficult to avoid simply by relocating noxious activities. This created a tension between common law notions of strict liability and approaches that would balance the value of activities that generated pollution against the rights of victims. The clearest example of this tension is the 1858 decision of the Court of Common Pleas in Hole v. Barlow, 4 C.B.N.S. 334 (1858). Citing fears that nuisance actions could bring industry to a halt in England's great manufacturing towns, the court refused to hold a brickmaking operation liable as a private nuisance despite the pollution it produced. The court upheld a jury instruction that "no action lies for the use, the reasonable use, of a lawful trade in a convenient and proper place even though some one may suffer annoyance from its being carried on." While this sharp departure from precedent threatened to eviscerate private nuisance doctrine, it was soon overruled. The decision in Bamford v. Turnley, 122 Eng. Rep. 27 (1862), returned to the strict liability premise that private property may not be used to cause harm to another. The court held that pollution from a brick kiln erected by a defendant while constructing a house was actionable as a nuisance. The court rejected the defendant's argument that operation of the brick kiln was justified because of its convenience for the defendant. But it left open the prospect that pollution caused by factories might not be held to a similarly strict standard.

While not deviating from the black-letter principle of Aldred's Case, the common law gradually tempered private nuisance doctrines by increasing the severity of harm required and by adjusting notions of reasonableness. As industrialization changed the conditions of urban environments, courts expected individuals to become more tolerant of discomfort produced by industrial activity. To qualify as a private nuisance, the degree of interference with a plaintiff's "comfortable and convenient enjoyment" of land had to be substantial. Because the standards of substantiality and reasonableness could vary with the location and circumstances of the pollution, nuisance law became a kind of zoning device. As Lord Thesiger explained in Sturges v. Bridgman, L.R. 11 Ch. D. 852 (1879): "What would be a nuisance in Belgrave Square would not necessarily be one in Bermondsey." Judges observed that plaintiffs were not entitled to pollution-free air, but rather to "air not rendered to an important degree less compatible, or at least not rendered incompatible, with the physical comfort of human existence." Walter v. Selfe, 4 De G. & Sm. 315, 322 (1851).

In St. Helens Smelting Co. v. Tipping, 11 H.L.C. 642 (1865), the owner of a large estate one and one-half miles from a copper smelter alleged that the smelter's emissions had damaged his trees, crops, and animals and caused him substantial personal discomfort. The area around the smelter had been singled out in a report by the Lords Select Committee on Noxious Vapors in 1863 as a "scene of desolation" caused by pollution from heavy industry. The report had stated that "[f]arms recently well-wooded, and with hedges in good condition, have now neither tree nor hedge left alive; whole fields of corn are destroyed in a single night, especially when the vapours fall upon them while in bloom; orchards and gardens, . . . have not a fruit tree left alive. . . ." Brenner, Nuisance Law and the Industrial Revolution, 3 J. Legal Stud. 403, 416 (1974). The court rejected the company's argument that smelting may be carried on with impunity if the smelter is in a suitable location. As the lord chancellor explained: "The word 'suitable' unquestionably cannot carry with it this conse-quence, that a trade may be carried on in a particular locality, the consequence of which trade may be injury and destruction to the neighboring property." The court held the company liable only for damage to the property that could be shown "visibly to diminish [its] value," and not for mere personal discomfort that the pollution may have caused Tipping.

American courts followed the English common law's rejection of the notion, reflected in Hole v. Barlow, that activities causing substantial harm can be tolerated if they are conducted in a lawful and convenient place. Like the British courts, many American courts rejected the "coming to the nuisance" doctrine, which would have barred recovery to victims who complained about conditions that existed prior to their moving into an area. Relying on the prin-ciple that any unreasonable use of property to the injury of others is a nuisance, the Maryland Court of Appeals in 1890 explained its rejection of balancing approaches in the following terms:

> The law, in cases of this kind, will not undertake to balance the conve-niences, or estimate the difference between the injury sustained by the plaintiff and the loss that may result to the defendant from having its trade and business, as now carried on, found to be a nuisance. No one has a right to erect works which are a nuisance to a neighboring owner, and then say he has expended large sums of money in the erection of his works, while the neighboring prop-erty is comparatively of little value. The neighboring owner is entitled to the reasonable and comfortable enjoyment of his property, and, if his rights in this respect are invaded, he is entitled to the protection of the law, let the conse-quences be what they may. [Susquehanna Fertilizer Co. v. Malone, 73 Md. 268, 20 A. 900, 902 (1890).]

Thus, Maryland's highest court upheld a judgment that noxious vapors from a large fertilizer factory that damaged the health and property of a neighboring family were actionable as a nuisance, even though several other fertilizer plants were located in the area.

This did not mean that U.S. courts would issue injunctions to shut down nuisances caused by economically important activities, particularly if they could afford to compensate their victims. In determining what relief to award, American courts generally were more inclined to balance environmental dam-age against the value of polluting activities than English courts. This has been interpreted by some legal historians as reflecting the American legal system's efforts to promote industrial growth in the nineteenth century, L. Friedman, A History of American Law (1973); M. Horwitz, The Transformation of American Law, 1780-1860 (1977), though others have found a more mixed picture. Schwartz, Tort Law and the Economy in Nineteenth-Century America: A Rein-terpretation, 90 Yale L.J. 1717 (1981). In any event, it is clear that courts increasingly were confronted by conflicts caused by the environmental impact of industrial activity.

In a society that encouraged industrial growth, many courts were reluctant to award injunctions against private nuisances if they involved activities that had considerable economic value, as indicated in the decision below. The case arose from a series of lawsuits brought by landowners who lived in the vicinity of two copper smelters located in Ducktown, Tennessee, near the Georgia-Tennessee border. Copper had been discovered near Ducktown in 1843 by a prospector disappointed in the search for gold. Copper mines were developed in the early 1850s, and the area thrived for a time. An economic downturn and the absence of a rail link for transporting the ore caused the mines to close in 1879. After the bankruptcy of the Union Consolidated Mining Company, thousands abandoned Ducktown, leaving it a virtual ghost town. A remarkable engineering feat permitted construction of a railroad spur to Ducktown, and in 1891 the Ducktown Sulphur, Copper & Iron Company, a British corporation, purchased the assets of Union and reopened the mines. In 1893 and 1894 it opened copper smelters. In 1899 a group of New York investors formed the Tennessee Copper Company which began smelting copper in the Ducktown area in 1901. Charging that the smelters were private nuisances, nearby landowners filed three lawsuits against the companies seeking damages and an injunction to stop pollution from the smelters. In each case, the court of chancery appeals had directed that operation of the smelters be enjoined, reversing the trial court's refusal to issue an injunction. Appeals were then heard by the Tennessee Supreme Court.

Madison v. Ducktown Sulphur, Copper & Iron Co.
113 Tenn. 331, 83 S.W. 658 (1904)

MR. JUSTICE NEIL delivered the opinion of the Court.

The bills are all based on the ground of nuisance, in that the two companies, in the operation of their plants at and near Ducktown, in Polk county, in the course of reducing copper ore, cause large volumes of smoke to issue from their roast piles, which smoke descends upon the surrounding lands, and injures trees and crops, and renders the homes of complainants less comfortable and their lands less profitable than before. The purpose of all the bills is to enjoin the further operation of these plants. . . .

Ducktown is in a basin of the mountains of Polk county, in this State, not far from the State line of the States of Georgia and North Carolina. This basin is six or eight miles wide. The complainants are the owners of small farms situated in the mountains around Ducktown.

The method used by the defendants in reducing their copper ores is to place the green ore, broken up, on layers of wood, making large open-air piles, called "roast piles," and these roast piles are ignited for the purpose of expelling from the ore certain foreign matters called "sulphurets." In burning, these roast piles emit large volumes of smoke. This smoke, rising in the air, is carried off by air currents around and over adjoining land. . . .

The general effect produced by the smoke upon the possessions and families of the complainants is as follows, viz.:

Their timber and crop interests have been badly injured, and they have been annoyed and discommoded by the smoke so that the complainants are prevented from using and enjoying their farms and homes as they did prior to the inauguration of these enterprises. The smoke makes it impossible for the owners of farms within the area of the smoke zone to subsist their families thereon with the degree of comfort they enjoyed before. They cannot raise and harvest their customary crops, and their timber is largely destroyed. . . .

The court of chancery appeals finds that the defendants are conducting and have been conducting their business in a lawful way, without any purpose or desire to injure any of the complainants; that they have been and are pursuing the only known method by which these plants can be operated and their business successfully carried on; that the open-air roast-heap is the only method known to the business or to science by means of which copper ore of the character mined by the defendants can be reduced; that the defendants have made every effort to get rid of the smoke and noxious vapors, one of the defendants having spent $200,000 in experiments to this end, but without result.

It is to be inferred from the description of the locality that there is no place more remote to which the operations referred to could be transferred.

It is found, in substance, that, if the injunctive relief sought be granted, the defendants will be compelled to stop operations and their property will become practically worthless, the immense business conducted by them will cease, and they will be compelled to withdraw from the State. It is a necessary deduction from the foregoing that a great and increasing industry in the State will be destroyed, and all of the valuable copper properties of the State become worthless. . . .

While there can be no doubt that the facts stated make out a case of nuisance, for which the complainants in actions at law would be entitled to recover damages, yet the remedy in equity is not a matter of course. Not only must the bill state a proper case, but the right must be clear, and the injury must be clearly established, as in doubtful cases the party will be turned over to his legal remedy; and, if there is a reasonable doubt as to the cause of the injury, the benefit of the doubt will be given to the defendant, if his trade is a lawful one, and the injury is not the necessary and natural consequence of the act; and, if the injury can be adequately compensated at law by a judgment for damages, equity will not interfere. . . .

A judgment for damages in this class of cases is a matter of absolute right, where injury is shown. A decree for an injunction is a matter of sound legal discretion, to be granted or withheld as that discretion shall dictate, after a full and careful consideration of every element appertaining to the injury. . . .

The question now to be considered is, what is the proper exercise of discretion, under the facts appearing in the present case? Shall the complainants be granted, in the way of damages, the full measure of relief to which their injuries entitle them, or shall we go further, and grant their request to blot out two great mining and manufacturing enterprises, destroy half of the taxable values of a county, and drive more than 10,000 people from their homes? We think there can be no doubt as to what the true answer to this question should be.

In order to protect by injunction several small tracts of land, aggregating in value less than $1,000, we are asked to destroy other property worth nearly $2,000,000, and wreck two great mining and manufacturing enterprises, that are engaged in work of very great importance, not only to their owners, but to the State, and to the whole country as well, to depopulate a large town, and deprive thousands of working people of their homes and livelihood, and scatter them broadcast. The result would be practically a confiscation of the property of the defendants for the benefit of the complainants—an appropriation without compensation. The defendants cannot reduce their ores in a manner different from that they are now employing, and there is no more remote place to which they can remove. The decree asked for would deprive them of all of their rights. We appreciate the argument based on the fact that the homes of the complainants who live on the small tracts of land referred to are not so comfortable and useful to their owners as they were before they were affected by the smoke complained of, and we are deeply sensible of the truth of the proposition that no man is entitled to any more rights than another on the ground that he has or owns more property than that other. But in a case of conflicting rights, where neither party can enjoy his own without in some measure restricting the liberty of the other in the use of property, the law must make the best arrangement it can between the contending parties, with a view to preserving to each one the largest measure of liberty possible under the circumstances. We see no escape from the conclusion in the present case that the only proper decree is to allow the complainants a reference for the ascertainment of damages, and that the injunction must be denied to them. . . .

NOTES AND QUESTIONS

1. Despite the damage caused by the smelters, the Tennessee Supreme Court in *Madison* refused to issue an injunction to control their harmful emissions because they had considerable economic value to the community. Is this tantamount to allowing the smelters to condemn the plaintiffs' property? How can you reconcile the court's refusal to enjoin the emissions with the conclusion by Maryland's highest court in Susquehanna Fertilizer Co. v. Malone that a property owner is "entitled to the reasonable and comfortable enjoyment of his property, and, if his rights in this respect are invaded, he is entitled to the protection of the law, let the consequences be what they may"?

2. The Tennessee Supreme Court's decision in *Madison* demonstrates that landowners at least could recover damages in private nuisance actions when pollution caused sufficient harm to their property. In *Madison* there was virtually no discussion of the issue that has proved to be the most substantial obstacle to common law recovery in modern environmental cases today: proof of causal injury. Why was the causation issue not litigated more vigorously by the defendants in *Madison*?

3. While private nuisance actions offered some prospect of redress for pollution damage, their promise had been largely illusory at the time of the *Madison* litigation, particularly when the damage was caused by substantial industrial establishments. A study of private nuisance actions in late nineteenth-century England concluded that the law simply "was not being applied in industrial towns." Brenner, Nuisance Law and the Industrial Revolution, 3 J. Legal Stud. 403, 419 (1974). Several factors diminished the practical value of nuisance law. Recovery generally was only permitted for actual, physical damage to property that caused a decline in its market value. Property values generally increased with industrialization even in contaminated areas, making recovery difficult. Lawsuits were prohibitively expensive for the average British worker. Environmental conditions in most factory towns were so bad that the requirement that nuisances be evaluated in light of the "state of the neighborhood" actually "militated against the recognition by the common law of

minimum standards of comfort and health." Id. at 420. Fearful of discouraging industrialization, courts held factories liable only in rare cases where the pollution was so devastating that it produced a "scene of desolation" for miles around, as in Tipping's Case. Id. at 416. Moreover, many of the largest polluters were public or quasipublic enterprises that were protected from liability because their actions were authorized by statute.

4. There is evidence that nuisance actions against polluting facilities were much more common in the United States than in Britain in the late nineteenth and early twentieth centuries. In addition to the *Madison* litigation, dozens of other private nuisances actions were filed against the Ducktown smelters during this period. While courts in the United States often awarded damages, instead of issuing injunction to shut down polluting facilities, private parties occasionally succeeded in shutting down polluters in cases where environmental damage was quite severe. See, e.g., McClung v. North Bend Coal & Coke Co., 1 Ohio Dec. 187 (C.P. Hamilton 1892), aff'd, 9 Ohio C.C. 259 (1895) (injunction obtained against coking operations that destroyed more than 200 evergreen trees and impaired the health of persons on the ancestral estate of President William Henry Harrison).

5. The early common law did not provide much protection against pollution of groundwater. Only in the rare cases where landowners could prove that a specific source of pollution caused groundwater to reach their land in a polluted condition were nuisance principles applied. Ballard v. Tomlinson, 29 Ch. D. 115 (1885) (common law liability for sewage discharged into well that resulted in pollution of the well of another). For similar reasons, the common law has not proved adequate for redressing nonpoint source pollution. See Columbia Avenue Saving Fund Co. v. Prison Commission of Georgia, 92 F. 801 (W.D. Ga. 1899) and cases cited therein (refusing to enjoin prison construction because the damage it would cause to nearby streams would be the product of nonpoint source pollution); United States v. Brazoria County Drainage District No. 3, 2 F.2d 861 (S.D. Tex. 1925) (drainage ditch that contributed to erosion not a common law nuisance).

6. The Restatement of Torts (Second) defines private nuisance as "a non-trespassory invasion of another's interest in the private use and enjoyment of land." Restatement of Torts (Second) §821D (1978). Only those who have property rights and privileges with respect to the use and enjoyment of the land may recover, and only if the harm they suffer is significant. Why does nuisance law require a showing of significant harm, while trespass law does not? The Restatement provides that to constitute a private nuisance the invasion of property rights must be either "intentional and unreasonable; or unintentional and otherwise actionable under the rules governing liability for negligent, reckless or ultrahazardous conduct." §822. Why do intentional invasions of property rights that cause significant harm have to be unreasonable in order to be actionable as a private nuisance?

7. The traditional common law requirement for a private nuisance is a substantial and unreasonable interference with the private use and enjoyment of land. Is a decline in property values caused by proximity to a polluted site actionable at common law even if there is no proof that the pollution has seeped onto plaintiffs' property? In Adkins v. Thomas Solvent Company, 487 N.W.2d 715 (Mich. 1992), the Michigan Supreme Court held that 22 property owners who lived near a contaminated site could not recover for the diminution of their property values because no contaminants actually had migrated to their

property and a hydrogeological barrier precluded such migration in the future. The court reasoned that

> [i]f any property owner in the vicinity of the numerous hazardous-waste sites that have been identified can advance a claim seeking damages when unfounded public fears of exposure cause property depreciation, the ultimate effect might be a reordering of the polluter's resources for the benefit of persons who have suffered no cognizable harm at the expense of those claimants who have been subjected to a substantial and unreasonable interference in the use and enjoyment of property. [Adkins v. Thomas Solvent Company, 487 N.W.2d 715, 727 (Mich. 1992).]

Two dissenting justices argued that depreciation of property values can constitute an actionable interference with the use and enjoyment of property when it can be shown to be the normal consequence of a defendant's conduct. Cf. Livingston v. Jefferson County Board of Equalization, 640 N.W. 2d 426, 10 Neb. App. 934 (2002) (proximity to a confined animal feed operation (CAFO) should be considered when assessing the value of property for tax purposes).

8. When pollutants do physically invade the property of another, liability also may be premised on a theory of trespass. In Martin v. Reynolds Metals Co., 221 Ore. 86, 342 P.2d 790 (Ore. 1959), the Oregon Supreme Court affirmed an award of $91,500 in damages to farmland due to fluoride emissions from a nearby aluminum plant that settled on the land and poisoned cattle. The court held that the intrusion of fluoride particles constituted a trespass because the particles invaded the property owner's interest in exclusive possession. In *Martin* the plaintiffs opted to pursue a trespass theory because the statute of limitations for trespass was more favorable than that applicable in nuisance actions. See also Borland v. Sanders Lead Co., Inc., 369 So. 2d 523 (Ala. 1979) (lead pollution constituting a trespass) and Bradley v. American Smelting & Refining Co., 104 Wash. 2d 677, 709 P.2d 782 (1985) (allowing a trespass claim based on the deposit of airborne pollutants from a copper smelter but only where "actual and substantial damage" can be shown).

9. In defining what constitutes an intentional invasion of property rights, the Restatement focuses on the foreseeability of harm. For certain kinds of activities that result in environmental harm, this may have important consequences. For example, the Restatement deems pollution of groundwater to be far less foreseeable than surface water pollution. It notes that invasions of property rights that result from discharges to lakes, streams, and surface waters ordinarily should be considered intentional, because such discharges are substantially certain to cause such an invasion, particularly if the pollution is continued for any length of time. However, invasions resulting from the pollution of groundwater "are ordinarily not intentional since the course of such waters is usually unknown and the actor can thus foresee no more than a risk of harm in most cases." Restatement of Torts (Second), §832 comment f.

10. While groundwater contamination is more readily foreseeable than in the past, the foreseeability requirement can be a formidable obstacle to using the common law to recover for contamination caused by past dumping practices. In Cambridge Water v. Eastern Counties Leather, 1 All ER H.L. 53 (1994), a British leather company's repeated spillage of perchloroethene (PCE) over a period of several decades resulted in contamination of an aquifer used by Cambridge Water to supply drinking water. Due to the contamination, the water company had to discontinue use of the aquifer and develop an alternative

water supply. The water company sued and was awarded a judgment of approximately £1 million by a court of appeal. The court held the leather company strictly liable for the damage it had caused. Citing Ballard v. Tomlinson, 29 Ch. D. 115 (1885), the court deemed it unimportant whether the leather company could foresee that its accidental spillages would cause groundwater contamination in violation of modern water quality standards. The House of Lords then allowed an appeal and reversed the court of appeal's decision. After noting that Ballard v. Tomlinson involved harm that was foreseeable (sewage discharged into a well polluted another well), Lord Goff concluded that "foreseeability of harm is indeed a prerequisite of the recovery of damages in private nuisance, as in the case of public nuisance." Id. at 72. He then considered whether the leather company could be held liable under the rule in Rylands v. Fletcher, 3 H.L. 330 (1868), imposing strict liability for harm caused by abnormally dangerous activities. However, he found that "foreseeability of damage of the relevant type should be regarded as a prerequisite of liability in damages under the rule" in *Rylands*. 1 All ER H.L., at 76 (1994). Finding that the leather company could not reasonably have foreseen the damage that it caused the water company, Lord Goff concluded that the leather company could not be held liable. Although Cambridge Water argued that the leather company should at least be held liable for releases of PCE that continued after the discovery of the aquifer contamination, Lord Goff rejected this argument, noting that the PCE that actually had reached the groundwater probably had been released at a time when the contamination was not foreseeable.

Harmonizing Conflicting Interests: To Balance or Not to Balance in Fashioning Remedies for Nuisances?

The early common law assessed nuisance claims by focusing almost exclusively on the nature of the interference pollution caused to the property rights of its victims. Yet defendants continued to press courts to balance the hardship of pollution abatement against the damage to victims when considering requests for equitable relief. By 1927, this debate had reached the point where Judge Learned Hand described the state of nuisance law as one of "great confusion" with U.S. courts split over whether or not to balance comparative hardships between polluters and victims. Smith v. Staso Milling Co., 18 F.2d 736 (2d Cir. 1927). In *Staso Milling*, Judge Hand explained why he believed that the balancing approach was reasonable, particularly when courts were considering whether to grant injunctions against private nuisances:

> The very right on which the injured party stands in such cases is a quantitative compromise between two conflicting interests. What may be an entirely tolerable adjustment, when the result is only to award damages for the injury done, may become no better than a means of extortion if the result is absolutely to curtail the defendant's enjoyment of his land. Even though the defendant has no power to condemn, at times it may be proper to require of him no more than to make good the whole injury once and for all. [Id. at 738.]

Yet a balancing approach does not necessarily preclude injunctions against nuisances. In *Staso Milling*, Judge Hand affirmed an injunction barring a slate processing mill from polluting a stream. Even though construction of the plant had altered "the balance of convenience" in a manner that might normally preclude an injunction, Hand noted that prior to building the plant the plant's owners specifically had promised nearby property owners that it would not pollute the stream. Noting that no similar promise had been made with respect to air pollution, Hand indicated that an injunction barring the plant from releasing dust could be modified if the plant could demonstrate that no better technology was available for controlling emissions of dust.

While many American courts have enthusiastically embraced the balancing approach, some tension between strict liability and balancing has persisted in private nuisance cases. The evolution of the Restatement of Torts' position illustrates this tension. The First Restatement adopted an explicit balancing approach for determining whether an interference with property rights was unreasonable. Section 826 of the First Restatement provided that intentional invasions of another's interest in the use or enjoyment of land are unreasonable unless the utility of the actor's conduct outweighs the gravity of the harm. This encouraged courts to balance the social value of a polluting activity against the damage it caused. After criticism of the First Restatement's formulation, the Second Restatement added an alternative criterion of unreasonableness in section 826(b). It states that an intentional invasion is unreasonable if *either* the gravity of the harm outweighs the utility of the actor's conduct *or* "the harm caused by the conduct is serious and the financial burden of compensating for this and similar harm to others would not make the continuation of the conduct not feasible." This has supplemented what appeared to be a kind of risk-benefit calculus of reasonableness with an alternative test focusing on the financial feasibility of damages. A further embellishment was added by section 829 of the Second Restatement. It states that even in cases where compensation is beyond the financial capacity of an enterprise, an invasion should be deemed unreasonable if the harm it causes "is severe and greater than the other should be required to bear without compensation." As a result, the Second Restatement's definition of unreasonableness now embraces notions of fairness or moral outrage as well as feasibility and risk-benefit balancing. Each of these three notions is represented in current regulatory approaches for controlling pollution, as we will see in subsequent chapters.

Economists emphasize that because environmental problems involve interactions between polluters and victims, efficient solutions to nuisance problems involve remedies that minimize the joint costs or maximize the joint value of the interacting activities. If only the polluters determine the extent of harm, then a rule holding polluters strictly liable for the damages they cause is efficient because it will induce them to take the efficient amount of care while ensuring that the prices of their goods reflect their full social costs. However, if the victim's behavior can affect the extent of damage (e.g., by moving away or by investing in measures that shield her from the effects of pollution), economists argue that strict liability is only efficient if a defense of contributory negligence is recognized, because victims otherwise will have no incentive to take actions that can avoid damage more cheaply. These arguments are explained in clear and nontechnical terms for the noneconomist in A.M. Polinsky, An Introduction to Law and Economics 92-93 (1983).

William Landes and Judge Richard Posner argue that the common law is best understood as an attempt by judges to promote efficient resource allocation. They argue that efficiency dictates that liability for private nuisances be imposed only "where the nuisance causes substantial damage that exceeds the cost of eliminating it and where, moreover, the defendant (injurer) can eliminate the nuisance at a lower cost than the plaintiff (victim)." W. Landes & R. Posner, The Economic Structure of Tort Law 49 (1987). Landes and Posner conclude that nuisance law generally, but not always, conforms to this principle, particularly now that courts frequently balance the value of competing land uses, the suitability of the conduct to the character of the locality, and the relative costs of avoiding harm. They note that the requirement that harm be substantial serves to screen out cases in which damage is too small to warrant resort to the legal system for abating the nuisance. Id. at 49. Landes and Posner criticize as inefficient the alternative test of unreasonableness articulated in section 826(b) of the Second Restatement, but they note that few American courts have adopted it.

As noted in Chapter 1, the Coase Theorem states that if bargaining is costless and cooperative then any choice of an entitlement or remedy will lead to an efficient outcome. This observation is premised on the notion that parties can engage in exchanges that will lead to efficient outcomes. Ours, however, is not a world of zero transaction costs; imperfect information and strategic behavior make it difficult to reach efficient outcomes. Estimates of the damages caused by pollution, the benefits of polluting activity, and the costs of control alternatives are fraught with uncertainty. Polluters and their victims can gain strategic advantages by misrepresenting these parameters or by providing estimates that fall at different ends of the range of uncertainty. Moreover, as Judge Hand noted in *Staso Milling*, if victims always are entitled to injunctions against pollution they could use this entitlement as "a means of extortion" to hold out for more than the efficient level of compensation. In theory the common law offers a flexible, case-by-case assessment of liability that could permit courts to overcome some of the problems of strategic behavior. Economists argue that the common law can promote efficient outcomes by placing liability on the party that is the cheapest cost avoider. See Michelman, Pollution as a Tort: A Non-Accidental Perspective on Calabresi's Costs, 80 Yale L.J. 647 (1971). This approach, however, may require courts to obtain accurate estimates of the damages and benefits of polluting activities, information that is not always readily available. For suggestions concerning how courts can minimize the impact of such uncertainty, see A.M. Polinsky, An Introduction to Law and Economics 24 (1983).

One approach for coping with imperfect information is for courts to structure flexible remedies that take advantage of market forces to determine which party can control pollution most efficiently. See Calabresi & Melamed, Property Rules, Liability Rules and Inalienability: One View of the Cathedral, 85 Harv. L. Rev. 1089 (1972); Rabin, Nuisance Law: Rethinking Fundamental Assumptions, 63 Va. L. Rev. 1209 (1977). The conditional injunction approach has been recommended on these grounds. It was used by the New York Court of Appeals in the famous decision of Boomer v. Atlantic Cement Co., 26 N.Y.2d 219, 257 N.E.2d 870 (1970). The court in *Boomer* issued a conditional injunction barring the operation of a cement plant whose air emissions had caused substantial damage to nearby property until the plant paid surrounding residents the full value of their permanent damages if the plant continued operation. The theory behind this approach was that the plant would opt to continue operations only if the operations had more economic value than the cost of the damage they produced. Further background information on the *Boomer* case can be found in Daniel A. Farber, The Story of Boomer: Pollution and the Common Law in Environmental Law Stories 7 (R. Lazarus & O. Houck eds., 2005). Farber reports that the plaintiff landowners ultimately recovered substantially more in damages than would have been expected from the appellate decision and that the plant remains the second largest cement facility in the United States. Id., at 21, 25.

The notion that rights and liabilities should be allocated in a manner that promotes efficiency can be controversial because of its distributional consequences. Viewed from the moral outrage perspective, the Tennessee Supreme Court's refusal to enjoin the Ducktown smelter's emissions and the New York court's decision to permit the cement plant in *Boomer* to purchase the right to continue operation may seem outrageous to the victims of the pollution, even though they ultimately may receive damages. After all, as Judge Hand noted in *Staso Milling*, the polluter "has no power to condemn" the victim's property, but a damage award that allows the pollution to continue produces virtually the same result. Despite courts' concern for achieving efficient outcomes, distributional concerns also play a significant role in shaping environmental policy, as we will see throughout this casebook.

While the common law is most useful for addressing conflicts between a single source of pollution and a few neighbors, there is wide agreement that private nuisance actions alone are grossly inadequate for resolving the more typical pollution problems faced by modern industrialized societies. When numerous and diverse pollutants emanating from widely dispersed sources affect large populations, the common law is a poor vehicle for providing redress, as even staunch advocates of the economic perspective concede. See, e.g., R. Posner, Economic Analysis of Law 46-47 (2d ed. 1977). But see The Common Law and the Environment: Rethinking the Statutory Basis for Modern Environmental Law (R. Meiners & A. Morriss eds., 2000) (arguing that common law institutions are more capable of protecting the environment than is commonly believed and that they may be superior to reliance on regulatory statutes). The difficulty plaintiffs face is well described in the Report of the Lords Select Committee on Noxious Vapors in 1862, which noted that "partly in consequence of the expense such actions occasion, partly from the fact that where several works are in immediate juxtaposition, the difficulty of tracing the damage to any one, or of apportioning it among several, is [so] great as to be all but insuperable." H.L. Select Committee on Noxious Vapours at v, quoted in Brenner, Nuisance Law and the Industrial Revolution, 3 J. Legal Stud. 403, 425 (1974). Even when the *aggregate* damage caused by pollution is quite large, the damage to any individual victim may be insufficient to make a lawsuit worthwhile. While the class action device provides a mechanism for dealing with such problems, it has not played a significant role in redressing environmental damage. In cases where pollution interferes with rights held in common by the public, the common law's response has been to rely on public nuisance actions, to which we now turn.

B.   Public Nuisance

The common law offers somewhat greater promise for protecting the environment when used by governmental entities to protect their citizens against *public* nuisances. The Second Restatement defines a public nuisance as "an unreasonable interference with a right common to the general public." Restatement of Torts (Second) §821B (1978). As with the doctrine of private nuisance, with public nuisance not all invasions of rights are actionable, only unreasonable ones. In determining whether interference with a public right is unreasonable, the Restatement directs courts to consider whether the conduct: (1) involves a significant interference with the public health, safety, comfort, or convenience; (2) is illegal; or (3) is of a continuing nature or has produced a long-lasting effect on the public right that the actor has reason to know will be significant.

The doctrine of public nuisance was used most frequently in the early common law to prosecute those who obstructed public highways or encroached on the royal domain. The doctrine later expanded to embrace actions against those who fouled public waters or emitted noxious fumes. Following the Industrial Revolution, public nuisance actions were rarely prosecuted to abate pollution. When such actions were brought, courts were not "eager to find large enterprises guilty of public nuisances, because they feared the economic consequences of a policy of strict enforcement." Brenner, Nuisance Law and the Industrial Revolution, 3 J. Legal Stud. 403, 421 (1974). It is not surprising that many of the public nuisance actions that were brought by governmental authorities targeted nonresident polluters, as illustrated in the decisions below.

Two early Supreme Court decisions involved public nuisance actions brought by state authorities against out-of-state polluters. The first grew out of the burgeoning sewage disposal problem faced by many rapidly expanding American cities. In the late nineteenth century, most cities disposed of their sewage by simply dumping it untreated into the nearest lake or stream. As one American court had noted, "the history of sewers shows that from time immemorial the right to connect them with navigable streams has been regarded as part of the jus publicum." Newark v. Sayre Co., 60 N.J. Eq. 361, 45 A. 985 (1900). Not surprisingly, with rapid urbanization, sewage disposal became a major source of environmental conflict among cities and states that shared public waterways.

Chicago disposed of its raw sewage by dumping it into the Chicago River, which flowed into Lake Michigan, the source of the city's drinking water. When a cholera epidemic killed more than 1,400 Chicago residents in 1854 (more than 2 percent of the city's population), polluted drinking water was viewed as a likely culprit. To improve the quality of its drinking water, Chicago in 1867 built a water tunnel two miles out into Lake Michigan. However, this provided only temporary relief, as the lake became more contaminated with the city's sewage and diseases believed to be associated with contaminated drinking water increased to frightening levels. In 1891, the death rate from typhoid fever in Chicago reached 174 per 100,000 persons.

To resolve the city's sewage disposal problem, in 1892 the Illinois Drainage and Water Supply Commission began construction of a 28-mile canal to reverse the flow of the Chicago River. This ambitious project would link the river with the Des Plaines River, which drained into the Mississippi River. Chicago's raw sewage no longer would flow into Lake Michigan; it would empty into the Mississippi River instead.

Though hundreds of miles away, residents of St. Louis, Missouri became upset when they learned that the Mississippi River, their source of drinking water, would now become the recipient of the raw sewage from more than one million Chicago residents. Missouri filed a common law nuisance action against Illinois in the United States Supreme Court. Arguing that the sewage would endanger the health of its citizens, Missouri asked the Supreme Court to enjoin Illinois and the Sanitary District of Chicago from discharging sewage through the canal.

Illinois tried to have the case dismissed on jurisdictional grounds, arguing that it was not really a dispute between states subject to the Supreme Court's original jurisdiction. The Supreme Court rejected Illinois's arguments and held that it had jurisdiction. Missouri v. Illinois, 180 U.S. 208 (1901). As Justice Holmes later explained:

> The nuisance set forth in the bill was one which would be of international importance—a visible change of a great river from a pure stream into a polluted and poisoned ditch. The only question presented was whether as between the States of the Union this court was competent to deal with a situation which, if it arose between independent sovereignties, might lead to war. Whatever differences of opinion there might be upon matters of detail, the jurisdiction and authority of this court to deal with such a case is not now open to doubt. Missouri v. Illinois, 200 U.S. 496, 518 (1906).

The Supreme Court appointed a special commissioner to hear evidence in the case, which dragged on for years as Chicago's sewage poured through the canal and on to the Mississippi. Missouri's lawyers argued that disease-producing bacteria contained in Chicago's sewage had caused a 77 percent increase in typhoid fever deaths in St. Louis after the canal was opened in January 1900. Illinois argued that any increase in deaths from typhoid fever was an artifact of a change in reporting practices that for the first time had consolidated a host of fever-related deaths under the classification of typhoid fever. Illinois's lawyers argued that the drainage canal actually had improved water quality in the Mississippi's tributaries by increasing their volume and rate of flow. They maintained that any injury caused by bacteria in the Mississippi was the product of sewage dumped by other Missouri cities upriver from St. Louis. Missouri responded that any increase in the volume or rate of flow of the river's tributaries served only to hasten the delivery of Chicago's sewage and its accompanying bacteria.

Missouri v. Illinois
200 U.S. 496 (1906)

MR. JUSTICE HOLMES delivered the opinion of the court.

This is a suit brought by the State of Missouri to restrain the discharge of the sewage of Chicago through an artificial channel into the Desplaines River, in the State of Illinois. That river empties into the Illinois River, and the latter empties into the Mississippi at a point about forty-three miles above the city of St. Louis. It was alleged in the bill that the result of the threatened discharge would be to send fifteen hundred tons of poisonous filth daily into the Mississippi, to deposit great quantities of the same upon the part of the bed of the last-named river belonging to the plaintiff, and so to poison the water of that river, upon which various of the plaintiff's cities, towns, and inhabitants depended, as to make it unfit for drinking, agricultural, or manufacturing, purposes. . . .

Before this court ought to intervene the case should be of serious magnitude, clearly and fully proved, and the principle to be applied should be one which the court is prepared deliberately to maintain against all considerations on the other side. See Kansas v. Colorado, 185 U.S. 125.

As to the principle to be laid down the caution necessary is manifest. It is a question of the first magnitude whether the destiny of the great rivers is to be the sewers of the cities along their banks or to be protected against everything which threatens their purity. To decide the whole matter at one blow by an irrevocable fiat would be at least premature. If we are to judge by what the plaintiff itself permits, the discharge of sewage into the Mississippi by cities and towns is to be expected. We believe that the practice of discharging into the river is general along its banks, except where the levees of Louisiana have led to a different course. The argument for the plaintiff asserts it to be proper within certain limits. These are facts to be considered. Even in cases between individuals some consideration is given to the practical course of events. In the back country of England parties would not be expected to stand upon extreme rights. St. Helen's Smelting Co. v. Tipping, 11 H.L.C. 642. See Boston Ferrule Co. v. Hills, 159 Massachusetts, 147, 150. Where, as here, the plaintiff has sovereign powers and deliberately permits discharges similar to those of which it complains, it not only offers a standard to which the defendant has the right to appeal, but, as some of those discharges are above the intake of St. Louis, it warrants the defendant in demanding the strictest proof that the plaintiff's own conduct does not produce the result, or at least so conduce to it that courts should not be curious to apportion the blame.

We have studied the plaintiff's statement of the facts in detail and have perused the evidence, but it is unnecessary for the purposes of decision to do more than give the general result in a very simple way. At the outset we cannot but be struck by the consideration that if this suit had been brought fifty years ago it almost necessarily would have failed. There is no pretence that there is a nuisance of the simple kind that was known to the older common law. There is nothing which can be detected by the unassisted senses—no visible increase of filth, no new smell. On the contrary, it is proved that the great volume of pure water from Lake Michigan which is mixed with the sewage at the start has improved the Illinois River in these respects to a noticeable extent. Formerly it was sluggish and ill smelling. Now it is a comparatively clear stream to which edible fish have returned. Its water is drunk by the fishermen, it is said, without evil results. The plaintiff's case depends upon an inference of the unseen. It draws the inference from two propositions. First, that typhoid fever has increased considerably since the change and that other explanations have been disproved, and second, that the bacillus of typhoid can and does survive the journey and reach the intake of St. Louis in the Mississippi.

We assume the now prevailing scientific explanation of typhoid fever to be correct. But when we go beyond that assumption everything is involved in doubt. The data upon which an increase in the deaths from typhoid fever in St. Louis is alleged are disputed. The elimination of other causes is denied. The experts differ as to the time and distance within which a stream would purify itself. No case of an epidemic caused by infection at so remote a source is brought forward, and the cases which are produced are controverted. The plaintiff obviously must be cautious upon this point, for if this suit should succeed many others would follow, and it not improbably would find itself a defendant to a bill by one or more of the States lower down upon the Mississippi. The distance which the sewage has to travel (357 miles) is not open to debate, but the time of transit to be inferred from experiments with floats is estimated at varying from eight to eighteen and a half days, with forty-eight hours more from intake to distribution, and when corrected by observations of bacteria is greatly prolonged by the defendants. The experiments of the defendants' experts lead them to the opinion that a typhoid bacillus could not survive the journey, while those on the other side maintain that it might live and keep its power for twenty-five days or more, and arrive at St. Louis. Upon the question at issue, whether the new discharge from Chicago hurts St. Louis, there is a categorical contradiction between the experts on the two sides.

The Chicago drainage canal was opened on January 17, 1900. The deaths from typhoid fever in St. Louis, before and after that date, are stated somewhat differently in different places. We give them mainly from the plaintiff's brief: 1890, 140; 1891, 165; 1892, 441; 1893, 215; 1894, 171; 1895, 106; 1896, 106; 1897, 125; 1898, 95; 1899, 131; 1900, 154; 1901, 181; 1902, 216; 1903, 281. It is argued for the defendant that the numbers for the later years have been enlarged by carrying over cases which in earlier years would have been put into a miscellaneous column (intermittent, remittent, typho-malaria, etc., etc.), but we assume that the increase is real. Nevertheless, comparing the last four years with the earlier ones, it is obvious that the ground for a specific inference is very narrow, if we stopped at this point. The plaintiff argues that the increase must be due to Chicago, since there is nothing corresponding to it in the watersheds of the Missouri or Mississippi. On the other hand, the defendant points out that there has been no such enhanced rate of typhoid on the banks of the Illinois as would have been found if the opening of the drainage canal were the true cause.

Both sides agree that the detection of the typhoid bacillus in the water is not to be expected. But the plaintiff relies upon proof that such bacilli are discharged into the Chicago sewage in considerable quantities; that the number of bacilli in the water of the Illinois is much increased, including the *bacillus coli communis*, which is admitted to be an index of contamination, and that the chemical analyses lead to the same inference. To prove that the typhoid bacillus could make the journey, an experiment was tried with the *bacillus prodigiosus*, which seems to have been unknown, or nearly unknown, in these waters. After preliminary trials, in which these bacilli emptied into the Mississippi near the mouth of the Illinois were found near the St. Louis intake and in St. Louis in times varying from three days to a month, one hundred and seven barrels of the same, said to contain one thousand million bacilli to the cubic centimeter, were put into the drainage canal near the starting point on November 6, and on December 4 an example was found at the St. Louis intake tower. Four others were found on the three following days, two at the tower and two at the mouth of the Illinois. As this bacillus is asserted to have about the same length of life in sunlight in living waters as the *bacillus typhosus*, although it is a little more hardy, the experiment is thought to prove one element of the plaintiff's case, although the very small number found in many samples of water is thought by the other side to indicate that practically no typhoid germs would get through. It seems to be conceded that the purification of the Illinois by the large dilution from Lake Michigan (nine parts or more in ten) would increase the danger, as it now generally is believed that the bacteria of decay, the saprophytes, which flourish in stagnant pools, destroy the pathogenic germs. Of course the addition of so much water to the Illinois also increases its speed.

On the other hand, the defendant's evidence shows a reduction in the chemical and bacterial accompaniments of pollution in a given quantity of water, which would be natural in view of the mixture of nine parts to one from Lake Michigan. It affirms that the Illinois is no better or no worse at its mouth than it was before, and makes it at least uncertain how much of the present pollution is due to Chicago and how much to sources further down, not complained of in the bill. It contends that if any bacilli should get through they would be scattered and enfeebled and would do no harm. The defendant also sets against the experiment with the *bacillus prodigiosus* a no less striking experiment with typhoid germs suspended in the Illinois River in permeable sacs. According to this the duration of the life of these germs has been much exaggerated, and in that water would not be more than three or four days. It is suggested, by way of criticism, that the germs may not have been of normal strength, that the conditions were less favorable than if they had floated down in a comparatively unchanging body of water, and that the germs may have escaped, but the experiment raises at least a serious doubt. Further, it hardly is denied that there is no parallelism in detail between the increase and decrease of typhoid fever in Chicago and St. Louis. The defendants' experts maintain that the water of the Missouri is worse than that of the Illinois, while it contributes a much larger proportion to the intake. The evidence is very strong that it is necessary for St. Louis to take preventive measures, by filtration or otherwise, against the dangers of the plaintiff's own creation or from other sources than Illinois. What will protect against one will protect against another. The presence of causes of infection from the plaintiff's action makes the case weaker in principle as well as harder to prove than one in which all came from a single source. . . .

We might go more into detail, but we believe that we have said enough to explain our point of view and our opinion of the evidence as it stands. What the future may develop of course we cannot tell. But our conclusion upon the present evidence is that the case proved falls so far below the allegations of the bill that it is not brought within the principles heretofore established in the cause.

NOTES AND QUESTIONS

1. Why did Missouri fail to convince the Supreme Court that Chicago's sewage discharges constituted a public nuisance? Did the discharge of raw sewage into a canal that eventually flows into the Mississippi affect the quality of drinking water in St. Louis? If so, was it an unreasonable interference with the rights of Missouri's citizens? Should it make any difference that Chicago's sewage would not have reached the Mississippi but for construction of the canal?

2. What is the relevance of Justice Holmes's statement that "[e]ven in cases between individuals some consideration is given to the practical course of events. In the back country of England parties would not be expected to stand upon extreme rights"? Does this suggest that some balancing of interests is appropriate in public nuisance cases?

3. Following the opening of the canal, the death rate from typhoid fever in Chicago fell from more than 80 per 100,000 to less than 10 per 100,000. But Missouri claimed that the canal had improved public health in Chicago only at the expense of citizens of St. Louis. How persuasive was the statistical evidence Missouri presented to demonstrate that the sewage discharges had caused a substantial increase in typhoid fever deaths in St. Louis? What other evidence could Missouri have presented to demonstrate that the sewage discharges had harmed its residents? Suppose that Missouri had been successful in proving that the opening of the canal had caused a substantial increase in the incidence of typhoid fever in St. Louis, but that Illinois was able to prove that it produced an even larger decrease in typhoid fever deaths in Chicago. Would Missouri be entitled to the injunction that it sought?

4. As Chicago continued to grow, it had to divert ever larger amounts of water from Lake Michigan to flush out the increased volumes of sewage in the drainage canal. In 1924, Wisconsin, Michigan, and New York invoked the Supreme Court's original jurisdiction to sue Illinois and the Sanitary District for diverting too much water from Lake Michigan. They successfully argued that Illinois's diversions had lowered the levels of Lakes Michigan, Huron, Erie, and Ontario, their connecting waterways, and the St. Lawrence River more than six inches, causing serious injury to their citizens and property. Ironically, Illinois was joined as a defendant by the state of Missouri, which intervened because of its interest in keeping as much water as possible flowing through the drainage canal to the Mississippi River. Former Justice Charles Evans Hughes, who had just finished serving as Secretary of State in the Harding and Coolidge administrations, was appointed by the Court to serve as special master. Based on his findings confirming the allegations of the upstream states, the Court ruled against Illinois in January 1929. The Court concluded that the upstream states were entitled to equitable relief, Wisconsin v. Illinois, 278 U.S. 367 (1929), and it ultimately issued an injunction requiring Chicago to build sewage treatment plants to reduce its need to divert water from Lake Michigan. Wisconsin v. Illinois, 281 U.S. 179 (1930) and 281 U.S. 696 (1930).

5. Justice Holmes notes that Missouri's own cities, including cities upstream of St. Louis, routinely discharged raw sewage into the Mississippi. What is the significance of this observation? Would the outcome of this case have been any different if Missouri had required its cities to employ more sophisticated treatment technology to protect the Mississippi from pollution? Thomas Merrill describes the decision in Missouri v. Illinois as an endorsement of "the reverse golden rule: in a transboundary pollution case, the affected state cannot demand that the source state adhere to a higher standard than the affected state applies to its own citizens." Thomas W. Merrill, Golden Rules for Transboundary Pollution, 46 Duke L.J. 931, 1000 (1997).

6. In a subsequent case, the Court denied relief to New York when it sought an injunction to prevent New Jersey from discharging raw sewage into New York Bay. The Court declared that before it would act "to control the conduct of one state at the suit of another, the threatened invasion must be of serious magnitude and it must be established by clear and convincing evidence." New York v. New Jersey, 256 U.S. 296, 309 (1921). The Court emphasized that New York had failed to prove that there were visible suspended particles, odors, or a reduction in the dissolved oxygen content of the Bay sufficient to interfere with aquatic life. It also observed that New York itself discharged sewage from 450 sewers directly into adjacent waters.

7. New Jersey was more successful when it sued to stop New York City from ocean dumping of garbage. A special master found that New York City had caused enough garbage to wash upon New Jersey shores to fill 50 trucks, damaging fish nets and making swimming impracticable. The Supreme Court issued an injunction prohibiting the city from dumping garbage off the coast of New Jersey effective June 1, 1933. New Jersey v. City of New York, 284 U.S. 585 (1931). The Court subsequently extended this deadline for a year to give the city more time to build garbage incinerators. New Jersey v. City of New York, 290 U.S. 237 (1933).

8. Is the judiciary an appropriate institution for formulating pollution control policy, or is such a task better left to administrative agencies with more specialized expertise? As we will see, a major obstacle to effective pollution control has been the reluctance of politically accountable officials to implement

policies that may adversely affect local industries. Could judges, who are more insulated from political forces, do a more effective job of formulating environmental policy?

9. Governmental entities have themselves been among the most persistent violators of environmental regulations. Efforts to force them to comply with the environmental laws perennially come up against the argument that there isn't enough money to do so. Confronted with this argument in a public nuisance action in 1858, a British court said of local authorities: "If they have not funds enough to make further experiments, they must apply to Parliament for power to raise more money. If, after all possible experiments, they cannot [dispose of their sewage] without invading the Plaintiff's rights, they must apply to Parliament for power to invade his rights." A.G. v. Birmingham Borough Council, 70 Eng. Rep. 220, 4 K. J. 528, 541 (Vice Ch. Ct. 1858). See also Wisconsin v. Illinois, 289 U.S. 395, 406 (1933) (holding the state of Illinois responsible for providing the necessary funds to complete construction of sewage treatment works for Chicago).

10. A year after it decided Missouri v. Illinois, the Supreme Court was again confronted with a common law nuisance action involving interstate pollution. This time the controversy involved a source of pollution already familiar to us—sulfur dioxide emissions from the very Ducktown, Tennessee copper smelters involved in Madison v. Ducktown Sulphur, Copper & Iron Co. Invoking the Court's original jurisdiction, the state of Georgia brought a common law nuisance action against the smelters, which, as you may recall, were located directly across the Georgia-Tennessee border. In 1904, the year that the Tennessee Supreme Court had decided not to enjoin operation of the smelters, Georgia filed suit in the Supreme Court, complaining that the smelters' emissions crossed the border and caused considerable property damage in Georgia. Georgia asked the Supreme Court to enjoin operation of the smelters. In response to Georgia's lawsuit, the companies pledged to change their method of operation to reduce their emissions. Georgia then agreed to dismiss its lawsuit without prejudice. But after the smelters installed tall smokestacks that simply transported the pollution across a wider swath of territory, Georgia again filed suit.

Georgia v. Tennessee Copper Co.
206 U.S. 230 (1907)

MR. JUSTICE HOLMES delivered the opinion of the court.

This is a bill in equity filed in this court by the State of Georgia in pursuance of a resolution of the legislature and by direction of the Governor of the State, to enjoin the defendant Copper Companies from discharging noxious gas from their works in Tennessee over the plaintiff's territory. It alleges that in consequence of such a discharge a wholesale destruction of forests, orchards, and crops is going on, and other injuries are done and threatened in five counties of the State. It alleges also a vain application to the State of Tennessee for relief. A preliminary injunction was denied, but, as there was ground to fear that great and irreparable damage might be done, an early day was fixed for the final hearing and the parties were given leave, if so minded, to try the case on affidavits. This has been done without objection, and, although the method would be unsatisfactory if our decision turned on any nice question of fact, in the view that we take we think it unlikely that either party has suffered harm.

The case has been argued largely as if it were one between two private parties; but it is not. The very elements that would be relied upon in a suit between fellow-citizens as a ground for equitable relief are wanting here. The State owns very little of the territory alleged to be affected, and the damage to it capable of estimate in money, possibly, at least, is small. This is a suit by a State for an injury to it in its capacity of quasi-sovereign. In that capacity the State has an interest independent of and behind the titles of its citizens, in all the earth and air within its domain. It has the last word as to whether its mountains shall be stripped of their forests and its inhabitants shall breathe pure air. It might have to pay individuals before it could utter that word, but with it remains the final power. The alleged damage to the State as a private owner is merely a make-weight, and we may lay on one side the dispute as to whether the destruction of forests has led to the gullying of its roads.

The caution with which demands of this sort, on the part of a State, for relief from injuries analogous to torts, must be examined, is dwelt upon in Missouri v. Illinois, 200 U.S. 496, 520, 521. But it is plain that some such demands must be recognized, if the grounds alleged are proved. When the States by their union made the forcible abatement of outside nuisances impossible to each, they did not thereby agree to submit to whatever might be done. They did not renounce the possibility of making reasonable demands on the ground of their still remaining quasi-sovereign interests; and the alternative to force is a suit in this court. Missouri v. Illinois, 180 U.S. 208, 241.

Some peculiarities necessarily mark a suit of this kind. If the State has a case at all, it is somewhat more certainly entitled to specific relief than a private party might be. It is not lightly to be required to give up quasi-sovereign rights for pay; and, apart from the difficulty of valuing such rights in money, if that be its choice it may insist that an infraction of them shall be stopped. The States by entering the Union did not sink to the position of private owners subject to one system of private law. This court has not quite the same freedom to balance the harm that will be done by an injunction against that of which the plaintiff complains, that it would have in deciding between two subjects of a single political power. Without excluding the considerations that equity always takes into account, we cannot give the weight that was given them in argument to a comparison between the damage threatened to the plaintiff and the calamity of a possible stop to the defendants' business, the question of health, the character of the forests as a first or second growth, the commercial possibility of reducing the fumes to sulphuric acid, the special adaption of the business to the place.

It is a fair and reasonable demand on the part of a sovereign that the air over its territory should not be polluted on a great scale by sulphurous acid gas, that the forests on its mountains, be they better or worse, and whatever domestic destruction they have suffered, should not be further destroyed or threatened by the act of persons beyond its control, that the crops and orchards on its hills should not be endangered from the same source. If any such demand is to be enforced this must be, notwithstanding the hesitation that we might feel if the suit were between private parties, and the doubt whether for the injuries which they might be suffering to their property they should not be left to an action at law.

The proof requires but a few words. It is not denied that the defendants generate in their works near the Georgia line large quantities of sulphur dioxid[e] which becomes sulphurous acid by its mixture with the air. It hardly is denied and cannot be denied with success that this gas often is carried by the wind great distances and over great tracts of Georgia land. On the evidence the pollution of the air and the magnitude of that pollution are not open to dispute. Without any attempt to go into details immaterial to the suit, it is proper to add that we are satisfied by a preponderance of evidence that the sulphurous fumes cause and threaten damage on so considerable a scale to the forests and vegetable life, if not to health, within the plaintiff State as to make out a case within the requirements of Missouri v. Illinois, 200 U.S. 496. Whether Georgia by insisting upon this claim is doing more harm than good to her own citizens is for her to determine. The possible disaster to those outside the State must be accepted as a consequence of her standing upon her extreme rights.

It is argued that the State has been guilty of laches. We deem it unnecessary to consider how far such a defense would be available in a suit of this sort, since, in our opinion, due diligence has been shown. The conditions have been different until recent years. After the evil had grown greater in 1904 the State brought a bill in this court. The defendants, however, already were abandoning the old method of roasting ore in open heaps and it was hoped that the change would stop the trouble. They were ready to agree not to return to that method, and upon such an agreement being made the bill was dismissed without prejudice. But the plaintiff now finds, or thinks that it finds, that the tall chimneys in present use cause the poisonous gases to be carried to greater distances than ever before and that the evil has not been helped.

If the State of Georgia adheres to its determination, there is no alternative to issuing an injunction, after allowing a reasonable time to the defendants to complete the structures that they now are building, and the efforts that they are making, to stop the fumes. The plaintiff may submit a form of decree on the coming in of this court in October next.

Injunction to issue.

NOTES AND QUESTIONS

1. Why did Georgia succeed in getting an injunction from the United States Supreme Court when plaintiffs in Madison v. Ducktown Sulphur, Copper & Iron Co. had been refused such relief by the Tennessee Supreme Court? Justice Holmes suggests that in fashioning a remedy for a public nuisance, the Court has less latitude to balance the equities because the plaintiff is a sovereign state. What is his rationale for this conclusion? Is this why the Court ultimately held that Georgia was entitled to an injunction?

2. Why did Georgia succeed in the *Tennessee Copper* case when Missouri failed to get the Supreme Court to enjoin Chicago's discharge of sewage in Missouri v. Illinois? Did Georgia simply have better evidence than Missouri that the pollution had caused damage to its citizens? Did it make any difference that the defendants in *Tennessee Copper* were two private companies rather than another sovereign state?

3. In *Tennessee Copper,* Justice Holmes warned: "Whether Georgia by insisting upon this claim is doing more harm than good to her own citizens is for her to determine. The possible disaster to those outside the State must be accepted as a consequence of her standing upon her extreme rights." What did he mean by this? Recall Justice Holmes's comment in Missouri v. Illinois that if Missouri had won the case many other suits would follow and Missouri might find itself a defendant in cases brought by downstream states.

4. In a separate opinion, Justice John Marshall Harlan argued that the Court should apply the same standard in nuisance cases brought by public authorities as it would in private nuisance actions. He wrote: "If this were a suit between private parties, and if, under the evidence, a court of equity would not give the plaintiff an injunction, then it ought not to grant relief, under like circumstances, to the plaintiff, because it happens to be a state, possessing some powers of sovereignty." However, he concurred in the majority's decision, explaining that "Georgia is entitled to the relief sought, not because it is a state, but because it is a party, which has established its right to such relief by proof." Do you agree that courts should apply the same standard in deciding nuisance cases regardless of whether or not the plaintiff is a public entity? Why do you think the common law developed different standards to govern public and private nuisances?

5. In addition to actions by governmental authorities, public nuisance actions can be brought by private parties if they can demonstrate that the nuisance has harmed them in a manner not shared with the general public. William Prosser notes that the traditional "special injury" requirement for private actions derived from the ancient notion that private parties should not be able to vindicate the rights of the sovereign and from a desire to prevent a multitude of actions to redress the same nuisance. Prosser, Private Action for Public Nuisance, 52 Va. L. Rev. 997 (1966). As courts and legislatures broadened citizen rights of action to redress environmental damage, the special injury requirement has come under fire. As Professor Denise Antolini notes, the "traditional doctrine presents a paradox: the broader the injury to the community and the more the plaintiff's injury resembles an injury also suffered by other members of the public, the less likely the plaintiff can bring a public nuisance lawsuit." Denise E. Antolini, Modernizing Public Nuisance: Solving the Paradox of the Special Injury Rule, 28 Ecol. L.Q. 755, 761 (2001). While the Restatement (Second) of Torts suggested that the special injury requirement should not bar actions seeking equitable relief or class actions brought against public nuisances by private individuals, Restatement (Second) of Torts §821C and comment j (1978), this approach has not been embraced by courts. "Although courts still struggle with application of the different-in-kind test (often bending the rule to avoid unfair results), the traditional doctrine is nonetheless repeated like a mantra in virtually every public nuisance case." Antolini, 28 Ecol. L.Q. at 861. Professor Antolini argues that courts should adopt an "actual community injury" standard that would permit recovery of damages or injunctive relief in a private action for a public nuisance, if the plaintiff "suffered an actual or threatened injury in common with the community that was the subject of the nuisance," with "injury" defined as "substantial interference with community values," which would not be limited to pecuniary loss and could include environmental and aesthetic injury. Id. at 862-863.

6. Faced with the threat of an injunction, the Tennessee Copper Company eventually settled with the state of Georgia by setting up a fund to compensate those injured by its emissions and by agreeing to restrict its operations during the growing season (April to October). The other smelting company, the Ducktown Sulphur, Copper & Iron Company, refused to restrict its operations, claiming that it already had spent $600,000 constructing "purifying works" to reduce the percentage of sulfur emitted from the ores from 85.5 percent to 41.5 percent. Despite this investment, Ducktown released more than 13,000 tons of sulfur emissions in 1913. In 1914 Georgia applied to the Supreme Court for

a final injunction against Ducktown. While noting that it could not determine precisely how much of a reduction in Ducktown's emissions would be necessary to prevent harm to property in Georgia, the Court issued a final injunction on June 1, 1915. Georgia v. Tennessee Copper Co., 237 U.S. 474 (1915). The Court specified that no more than 20 tons of sulfur per day could be emitted during the period from April to October and no more than 40 tons per day during the rest of the year. 237 U.S. at 678. The Court appointed an inspector to monitor Ducktown's operations. A year later, in response to the inspector's report, the Court modified the injunction to permit releases of 25 tons of sulfur per day from April to October, and 50 tons per day during the rest of the year. 240 U.S. 650 (1916). In light of the Court's conclusion that it could not determine what level of emissions reduction would prevent harm to property in Georgia, what basis do you think it had for specifying emissions limits in its injunction?

7. Both the Tennessee Copper and Ducktown companies ultimately settled with the State of Georgia by agreeing to participate in an administrative compensation system where a board of arbitrators would rule on claims of damage caused by the smelters' emissions. The companies and the State each appointed one arbitrator to rule on claims of injury, with an umpire designated by the two arbitrators to resolve disagreements between the other two. While the companies posted bonds to ensure that they could provide $25,000 per year in compensation, review of the records of the arbitral tribunal reveals that it actually awarded only a tiny amount of compensation. Between 1921 and 1928 it approved 140 out of 203 claims filed (approximately 69 percent), but it awarded only an average of $189 per year in damages, approximately 10 percent of the total amount of claims made annually. Percival, *Resolución de Conflictos Ambientales: Lecciones Aprendidas de la Historia de la Contaminación de las Fundiciones de Minerales*, in *Prevención y Solución de Conflictos Ambientales: Vías Administrativas, Jurisdiccionales y Alternativas* 399 (Lexis Nexis 2004).

8. Causation was not a significant issue in the litigation because the environmental effects of the open roast-heap smelting process were strikingly visible. The smelter emissions destroyed virtually all vegetation over a vast swath of land, transforming the Ducktown area into a bizarre moonscape of barren red hills that is apparent even today after decades of intensive reforestation efforts. Although the Supreme Court's injunction ultimately was relaxed in 1918 with Georgia's consent due to unusual demand for copper during World War I, fear of liability helped advance the development of a new pollution control technology, the lead chamber process, that permits sulfur to be reclaimed and used to produce sulfuric acid. Indeed, the technology proved so successful that the production of sulfuric acid eventually replaced copper as the area's major product. While all copper mining in the area ceased in 1987, the area's largest employer today is a Swiss chemical company that continues to use the old Tennessee Copper production facilities to produce sulfuric acid.

9. Interstate pollution remains a serious problem, but the Supreme Court no longer is in the business of establishing emissions limits in federal common law nuisance actions. Why would the Supreme Court be reluctant to hear such actions? Consider the following comment by the Court in refusing the injunction sought by New York against New Jersey's sewage disposal practices:

> We cannot withhold the suggestion, inspired by the consideration of this case, that the grave problem of sewage disposed presented by the large and growing populations living on the shores of New York Bay is one more likely to

be wisely solved by cooperative study and by conference and mutual concession on the part of the representatives of the States so vitally interested in it than by proceedings in any court however constituted. [New York v. New Jersey, 256 U.S. 296, 313 (1921).]

Do you agree with the Court's conclusion?

10. In Illinois v. City of Milwaukee, 406 U.S. 91 (1972) (*Milwaukee I*), the Supreme Court confirmed that federal common law nuisance actions could be brought against polluting governmental entities, but it reversed its previous willingness to hear such actions under its original jurisdiction. The Court held that the federal district courts were the proper forum for hearing a nuisance action by Illinois charging four Wisconsin cities with polluting Lake Michigan. While rejecting the argument that new federal environmental legislation had preempted federal common law, the Court noted:

> It may happen that new federal laws and new federal regulations may in time pre-empt the field of federal common law of nuisance. But until that comes to pass, federal courts will be empowered to appraise the equities of the suits alleging creation of a public nuisance by water pollution. While federal law governs, consideration of state standards may be relevant. Thus, a State with high water-quality standards may well ask that its strict standards be honored and that it not be compelled to lower itself to the more degrading standards of a neighbor. There are no fixed rules that govern; these will be equity suits in which the informed judgment of the chancellor will largely govern. [406 U.S. at 107-108.]

Not long after this decision, the explosion of federal environmental protection legislation led the Court to slam the door on most federal common law actions, as we will see below.

11. Even in cases of public nuisance, the common law has proved to be a crude mechanism at best for controlling the onslaught of modern-day pollution. An excellent account of the history and shortcomings of common law actions to redress air pollution problems is provided by Noga Morag-Levine, Chasing the Wind: Regulating Air Pollution in the Common Law State (2003). Most of what we study today as environmental law consists of federal and state statutes, which often create elaborate regulatory schemes implemented by administrative agencies. Common law principles, however, have had an important impact on many current regulatory programs. And as scientific advances make it easier to measure pollutants and to trace their impacts on the environment, common law actions may become more popular (as already seems to be occurring in certain areas). Thus, although most of our attention will be focused on the large and complex body of environmental statutes, it is important not to lose sight of the big picture that includes the common law, which can still serve as an important tool for addressing regulatory gaps left by public law. For example, in February 2006, a Rhode Island jury found former manufacturers of lead paint liable, decades after their product has been banned, for the continuing harm caused by the presence of lead paint in the housing stock. Charles Forelle, Rhode Island Wins Lead-Paint Suit, Wall St. J., Feb. 23, 2006, at D7. Theories of anticipatory nuisance also have been used in an effort to forestall the introduction of genetically modified corn seeds because of the difficulty of controlling the unauthorized spread of genetically modified organisms through the food chain. Molly McDonough, Growing Use of Nuisance, ABA J., Aug. 2003, at 16. See also Donald G. Gifford, Public Nuisance as a Mass Products Liability Tort, 71 U. Cin. L. Rev. 741 (2003).

2. Regulatory Legislation

A. ENVIRONMENTAL STATUTES: A HISTORICAL PERSPECTIVE

The federal statutes that dominate environmental law today are the product of a remarkable burst of legislative activity that began in 1970, the year of the first Earth Day celebration. But, as noted above, the historical roots of environmental law extend much further back in time. The historical evolution of environmental law in the United States can be divided into roughly six major phases, as indicated below.

SIX STAGES IN THE HISTORY OF U.S. ENVIRONMENTAL LAW

1. The Common Law and Conservation Era: Pre-1945
2. Federal Assistance for State Problems: 1945-1962
3. The Rise of the Modern Environmental Movement: 1962-1970
4. Erecting the Federal Regulatory Infrastructure: 1970-1980
5. Extending and Refining Regulatory Strategies: 1980-1990
6. Regulatory Recoil and Reinvention: 1991-present

Until the end of World War II, environmental law was largely a product of common law, as discussed above, with federal legislative efforts concentrated on the development and later the conservation of public resources. We call this period the *Common Law and Conservation Era.*

In nineteenth-century America, regulatory legislation was left largely to state and local governments. State laws and local ordinances to protect public health and to require the abatement or segregation of public nuisances were common, although they were poorly coordinated and rarely enforced in the absence of a professional civil service. Like the early English antipollution laws, American smoke abatement ordinances did not clearly specify what levels of emissions were proscribed. See, e.g., Sigler v. Cleveland, 4 Ohio Dec. 166 (C.P. Cuyahoga 1896) (holding that an ordinance outlawing "dense smoke" was unconstitutionally overbroad because it was so vague that it could ban all smoke).

Most federal legislation that affected the environment did so by promoting development of natural resources. The Homestead Act of 1862 and the Mining Act of 1872 unabashedly encouraged rapid development of public resources by authorizing private parties to lay claim to public land and the mineral resources on it. Land grants to encourage railroad construction turned over up to 180 million acres of public lands to private developers. R. Robbins, Our Landed Heritage: The Public Domain, 1776-1970 (1976). While the concerns of preservationists and conservationists helped spur establishment of the first national park in 1872, support also came from the railroads, which were seeking to promote tourism and to further the development of western lands. The establishment of the national forest system in 1891 marked a turning point of sorts, for it withdrew forest lands from development under the Homestead Act.

During this period, Congress did adopt some regulatory legislation, including the Rivers and Harbors Act of 1899 and the Pure Food and Drug Act of 1906. However, these statutes were not motivated primarily by concern over public health or environmental protection, but rather by a desire to promote commerce. Congress banned discharges of refuse to navigable waters not out of concern for water quality, but rather to prevent obstructions to the free flow of commerce, which at that time was largely conducted on waterways. When it enacted the Pure Food and Drug Act in 1906 and the Federal Insecticide Act of 1910, Congress's primary concern was not to protect public health, but rather to prevent consumers from being defrauded by products that were not what they were advertised to be.

Congress was not entirely oblivious to public health concerns during this period. In an unusual case when a public health problem was particularly visible and obvious, Congress was capable of acting. For example, in 1838 Congress acted to impose safety regulations to prevent steamship boilers from exploding. Several decades later, when it was discovered that the use of white phosphorus in match manufacturing caused many workers to be inflicted with a horribly disfiguring disease called phossy-jaw, because it literally ate away that area of the face, Congress acted again. The Esch-Hughes Act of 1912 sought to eliminate the use of white phosphorus in match manufacturing to prevent this disease. Because Congress did not believe at the time that it had the constitutional authority to directly prohibit such an activity, it imposed a federal excise tax to make it prohibitively expensive to use white phosphorus in match manufacturing.

The period from 1945-1962 coincides with the second phase in the history of U.S. environmental law, the period of *Federal Assistance for State Problems.* Although federal law imposed few regulations on private industry that were animated by environmental concerns, after World War II the federal government became involved in encouraging the states to adopt pollution control measures of their own. The Water Quality Act of 1948 provided grants to states for water pollution control. In 1956, over President Eisenhower's veto, Congress provided funding for the construction of sewage treatment plants by munici- palities. This funding was premised on the notion that cities otherwise would be reluctant to build sewage treatment plants that would primarily benefit down- stream cities. While this eventually became a major program of federal financial assistance, it did not create any system of federal regulation. Instead, the federal government sought to encourage the states to regulate on their own.

The federal programs in the 1950s and 1960s were premised on the notion that environmental problems were the responsibility of state and local govern- ments. The primary federal role was to assist with research and funding while letting the states decide how to control pollution. With expanding economic activity in the post-World War II era, the interstate character of pollution became increasingly apparent. The notion that pollutants do not respect state or even national boundaries was brought home by scientists' warnings that the entire planet was being dangerously poisoned by radiation from nuclear tests in the atmosphere. The premise that the federal role in pollution control should be a nonregulatory one became increasingly tenuous.

When Congress adopted legislation in 1955 directing the Department of Health, Education, and Welfare (HEW) to conduct a five-year program of research on the effects of air pollution, it continued to emphasize that pollution control was primarily a state responsibility. By 1960 Congress had begun to appreciate the national dimensions of the air pollution problem. Recognizing that a large percentage of the pollution came from products marketed nation- wide, Congress mandated a federal study to determine what levels of automobile emissions were safe. In 1963, when it enacted an early version of the Clean Air Act, Congress acknowledged the need for federal involvement in efforts to pro- tect interstate air quality. The Act directed HEW to publish national air quality criteria, and it also authorized a cumbersome conference procedure for dealing with interstate air pollution problems.

The third phase in the history of U.S. environmental law, the period from 1962-1970, constitutes the *Rise of the Modern Environmental Movement*. This is often traced from the publication of Rachel Carson's *Silent Spring*, which alerted the public to the possibility that pesticides could be accumulating in the food chain in a way that could cause severe, long-term environmental damage. In 1967, the Environmental Defense Fund was formed by a group of scientists who sought to have DDT banned on the ground that it was precisely that kind of pesticide. Another group, the Natural Resources Defense Council, was the product of efforts to force the Federal Power Commission to consider environmental concerns when licensing an electric power project that would have destroyed a particularly scenic and historic stretch of the Hudson River at Storm King Mountain. At the time, no federal agencies shouldered primary responsibility for responding to concerns about environmental protection. The new environmental groups went to court to try to require government agencies to be more responsive to environmental concerns.

The growing popularity of outdoor recreation and increased concern over the environmental impact of public works produced landmark legislation during this period. In 1960, Congress adopted the Multiple-Use Sustained Yield Act, which directs federal agencies to manage the national forests to serve the multiple uses of "recreation, range, timber, watershed, and wildlife and fish purposes." Growing concern for the preservation of natural areas was reflected in the subsequent enactment of the Wilderness Act in 1964 and the Wild and Scenic Rivers Act in 1968. Other federal laws reflected public interest in protecting social and cultural values from the impact of public works programs. For example, section 4(f) of the Department of Transportation Act of 1966 required that special effort be made to prevent federally funded construction projects from damaging parks, recreation areas, wildlife refuges, and historic sites.

To the extent that federal law was regulatory in character prior to 1970, most targets of environmental regulation were government agencies rather than private industry. In legislation like the National Historic Preservation Act of 1966, Congress sought to ensure that government agencies respected social and cultural values when pursuing development projects. These laws laid the groundwork for the subsequent enactment of the landmark National Environmental Policy Act (NEPA), which was signed into law on January 1, 1970. NEPA required federal agencies to take environmental concerns into account when taking any action with a significant impact on the environment. This served as a catalyst for forcing federal agencies that previously had been unresponsive to environmental concerns to incorporate them in their decision-making processes.

The fourth phase of the history of U.S. environmental law encompasses the decade of the 1970s, which has been called "the environmental decade" because it marked the period when virtually all the major federal regulatory legislation to protect the environment was first enacted. While environmental issues had hardly been mentioned by either candidate during the 1968 presidential campaign, by 1970 "the environment[al] cause had swollen into the favorite sacred issue of all politicians, all TV networks, all goodwilled people of any party." Theodore White, The Making of the President 45 (1973). President Nixon's embrace of environmental causes may have been motivated more by political opportunism than genuine environmental concern, but his administration's environmental accomplishments were considerable, including the creation of EPA and the establishment of major federal regulatory programs, including the Clean Air Act and Clean Water Act. For a description of this history, see Richard J. Lazarus, The Making of Environmental Law 67-97 (2005). Further perspective on this extraordinary period is provided in an entertaining memoir by Russell Train, who served as the second administrator of EPA. Russell E. Train, Politics, Pollution, and Pandas (2003).

We call this fourth phase in the history of U.S. environmental law *Erecting the Federal Regulatory Infrastructure* because it featured an explosion of federal regulatory legislation adopted between 1970 and 1980. These statutes established the ground rules for environmental protection efforts by mandating that environmental impacts be considered explicitly by federal agencies, by prohibiting actions that jeopardize endangered species, and by requiring the establishment of the first comprehensive controls on air and water pollution, toxic substances, and hazardous waste. The rapid growth of environmental legislation in the 1970s was accompanied by a parallel opening up of the courts to judicial review of agency decisions that affected the environment and to citizen suits to force implementation and enforcement of the new laws. This gave concerned citizens sorely needed tools for challenging agency action and for ensuring that previously unresponsive agencies implemented the ambitious new legislative directives.

A chronology of the major federal environmental statutes is presented below. While the statutes listed are among the principal statutes covered in this casebook, they are by no means a comprehensive catalog of all federal environmental legislation.

CHRONOLOGY OF SIGNIFICANT FEDERAL ENVIRONMENTAL LEGISLATION

1. *National Environmental Policy Act* (NEPA): Signed into law on January 1, 1970; establishes broad national environmental policy goals; requires federal agencies to assess environmental impacts of significant actions; establishes Council on Environmental Quality.

2. *Clean Air Act.* Clean Air Amendments of 1970 establish basic framework for federal regulation of air pollution; replace Clean Air Act of 1963 and Air Quality Act of 1967, which had authorized HEW to publish air quality criteria to be used by states in setting standards; set deadlines for EPA to promulgate national ambient air quality standards to be implemented by the states, national emission standards for hazardous air pollutants, and auto emission standards; authorized citizen suits. The Act was substantially amended in 1977 and 1990 to require implementation of more stringent controls in areas that had failed to attain national standards, to address the acid rain problem (in 1990), and to make other substantial changes in the framework for federal regulation of air pollution.

3. *Federal Water Pollution Control Act* (Clean Water Act): Enacted in 1972, it bans the unpermitted discharge of pollutants into surface waters, requires application of technology-based controls on dischargers, and establishes a national permit program, the National

Pollutant Discharge Elimination System (NPDES), which is implemented by states subject to EPA supervision; authorized grants for construction of sewage treatment plants; authorizes citizen suits. Reauthorized and substantially amended by the Clean Water Act Amendments of 1977 and the Water Quality Act of 1987.

4. Federal Insecticide, Fungicide, and Rodenticide Act (FIFRA): 1972 Federal Environmental Pesticide Control Act, which amended 1947 legislation, establishes basic framework for pesticide regulation; requires registration of pesticides and authorizes EPA to ban unreasonably dangerous pesticides. Amended in 1988 to require more expeditious review of pesticides previously registered and in 1996 by the Food Quality Protection Act to strengthen protections against pesticide residues on food.

5. Marine Protection, Research, and Sanctuaries Act of 1972 (Ocean Dumping Act): Prohibits ocean dumping of wastes except with a permit at sites designated by EPA.

6. Endangered Species Act (ESA): Enacted in December 1973, this legislation prohibits federal action that jeopardizes the habitat of species in danger of extinction and prohibits the taking of any such species by any person.

7. Safe Drinking Water Act (SDWA): Enacted in 1974; requires EPA to set limits for maximum allowable levels of contaminants in public drinking water systems. Amended in 1986 to require more expeditious promulgation of standards and in 1996 to provide more flexibility in standard-setting.

8. Toxic Substances Control Act of 1976 (TSCA): Provides EPA with comprehensive authority to regulate or prohibit the manufacture, distribution, or use of chemical substances that pose unreasonable risks; requires premanufacture notification of EPA for new chemicals or significant new uses of existing chemicals.

9. Resource Conservation and Recovery Act of 1976 (RCRA): Directs EPA to establish regulations ensuring the safe management of hazardous waste from cradle to grave. Reauthorized and substantially amended by the Hazardous and Solid Waste Amendments of 1984 (HSWA), which impose new technology-based standards on landfills handling hazardous wastes, require phaseout of land disposal for certain untreated hazardous wastes, and increase federal authority over disposal of nonhazardous solid wastes.

10. Comprehensive Environmental Response, Compensation, and Liability Act of 1980 (CERCLA): Establishes strict liability system for releases of hazardous substances and creates a "Superfund" to finance actions to clean up such releases. Amended in 1986 to increase the size of the Superfund, impose numerical goals and deadlines for cleanup of Superfund sites, and specify standards and procedures to be followed in determining the level and scope of cleanup actions, and in 2002 to encourage redevelopment of brownfields sites.

11. Emergency Planning and Community Right-to-Know Act (EPCRA): Enacted in 1986, this statute requires corporations to provide local authorities with detailed information concerning their use of any of several hundred toxic substances and to report annually the quantities of such chemicals released into the environment.

The federalizing of environmental law began with President Nixon signing the National Environmental Policy Act (NEPA), 42 U.S.C. §§4321-4370a, on national television on January 1, 1970. Declaring that "each person should enjoy a healthful environment," the statute established as "the continuing policy of the Federal Government . . . to use all practicable means and measures . . . to create conditions under which man and nature can exist in harmony. . . ." NEPA revolutionized environmental policy making not by imposing any substantive environmental controls, but rather by mandating changes in the decision-making process of federal agencies. The statute requires agencies to incorporate environmental concerns into their decision making by requiring them to perform detailed assessments of the environmental impacts of, and to consider alternatives to, any "major Federal actions significantly affecting the quality of the human environment." While NEPA only mandated *consideration* of environmental impacts, Congress soon declared certain impacts to be presumptively unacceptable when it forbade the taking of endangered species of fish, wildlife, or plants by enacting the Endangered Species Act in 1973. Once it became clear that citizens could enforce these requirements in court, they became a powerful new tool for challenging development projects.

Following the enactment of NEPA, Congress launched a succession of far-reaching regulatory programs to control pollution. In December 1970, Congress adopted the Clean Air Act, 42 U.S.C. §§7401-7642, and in October 1972 the Federal Water Pollution Control Act, 33 U.S.C. §§1251-1376, subsequently renamed the Clean Water Act. These statutes replaced what had been relatively modest federal research and financial assistance programs with comprehensive regulatory schemes to control air and water pollution throughout the nation. The Environmental Protection Agency (EPA), established by executive order in 1970, was directed to identify air pollutants that threatened public health or welfare and to establish national ambient air quality standards to be implemented by the states. In the Clean Water Act, Congress prohibited all unpermitted discharges of pollutants into the waters of the United States, it required EPA to implement technology-based effluent limits on dischargers, and it established a national permit system to be implemented by EPA or states subject to EPA supervision. Both acts spawned breathtakingly complex national regulatory programs. These programs have grown even more complicated over time as Congress, EPA, and state regulators have made adjustments in them in response to problems with their implementation.

While the first federal environmental statutes focused on control of conventional pollutants, growing public concern over toxic substances spurred enactment of a series of additional statutes that focused on protection of public health. Congress enacted the Safe Drinking Water Act (SDWA) in 1974, and in 1976 it enacted both the Toxic Substances Control Act (TSCA), 15 U.S.C. §§2601-2629, and the Resource Conservation and Recovery Act (RCRA), 42 U.S.C. §§6901-6987. The Safe Drinking Water Act requires EPA to establish regulations to protect public health from contaminants in public water supplies. TSCA authorizes the most explicitly far-reaching regulatory controls, which can be imposed on any chemical substance found by EPA to present an unreasonable risk to health or the environment. RCRA (which is a part of legislation also known as the Solid Waste Disposal Act) requires EPA to establish controls ensuring the safe management of hazardous waste from "cradle to grave."

Although EPA was formed in 1970 to consolidate environmental protection responsibilities in a single federal agency, EPA is not the only regulatory agency with substantial responsibilities for protecting public health and the environment. The Food and Drug Administration, which is now under the direction of the Department of Health and Human Services, has long been responsible for ensuring the safety of food, drugs, and cosmetics under the federal Food, Drug, and Cosmetic Act. In 1970 Congress created the Occupational Safety and Health Administration as part of the Department of Labor and charged it with ensuring the safety of the workplace. The Nuclear Regulatory Commission and the Department of Energy are responsible for protecting the public from risks posed by atomic material under the Atomic Energy Act. While the laws administered by these agencies usually are referred to as health and safety laws rather than environmental legislation, they are extremely important for the control of substances, products, and activities that pose environmental risks. Other agencies with substantial environmental responsibilities include the Department of the Interior, which is responsible for managing most public lands; the Department of Transportation, which regulates the transport of hazardous materials under the Hazardous Materials Transportation Act; the Council on Environmental Quality, charged with coordinating federal environmental policy and assisting federal agencies with NEPA compliance; the U.S. Army Corps of Engineers, which operates a permit program for dredge and fill activities under section 404 of the Clean Water Act; and the Department of Energy, which administers the National Energy Policy and Conservation Act.

Perhaps the final chapter in the erection of the federal regulatory infrastructure was the enactment in 1980 of the Comprehensive Environmental Response, Compensation, and Liability Act, known as CERCLA or the Superfund law. This legislation went beyond the traditional command-and-control regulatory approach to controlling pollution and established a system of strict joint, and several liability for broad classes of parties associated with the release of hazardous substances. CERCLA creates powerful incentives for businesses to prevent releases of hazardous substances to avoid future liability.

Figure 2.1 provides a crude illustration of the jurisdictional reach of the major federal environmental laws. It illustrates that the regulatory authorities available for responding to an environmental problem generally depend on its location or the medium affected by the problem or the characteristics of the pollutant or product thought to be the source of the problem. For example, the Occupational Safety and Health Administration has jurisdiction over workplace hazards; the Consumer Product Safety Commission has authority to regulate hazards in consumer products; foods, drugs, and cosmetics are regulated by the federal Food and Drug Administration (FDA).

The regulatory authorities available to EPA to control pollution are largely dependent on where pollutants are discharged and the nature and source of each pollutant. The Clean Air Act authorizes the use of ambient air quality standards to control pollutants that come from numerous or diverse sources and that threaten public health or welfare. The types of controls that can be imposed depend on whether the source is a mobile or a stationary source of pollution; more stringent controls are imposed on new sources than on existing sources. EPA's jurisdiction under the Clean Water Act covers virtually all discharges of pollutants into the "waters of the United States," although the Army Corps of Engineers is given jurisdiction under the Act over the discharge of dredged or fill material into navigable waters. The Ocean Dumping Act gives EPA jurisdiction over the transport and dumping in ocean waters of materials other than dredged material. The Safe Drinking Water Act gives EPA

FIGURE 2.1
Legislative Authorities Affecting the Life Cycle of a Chemical

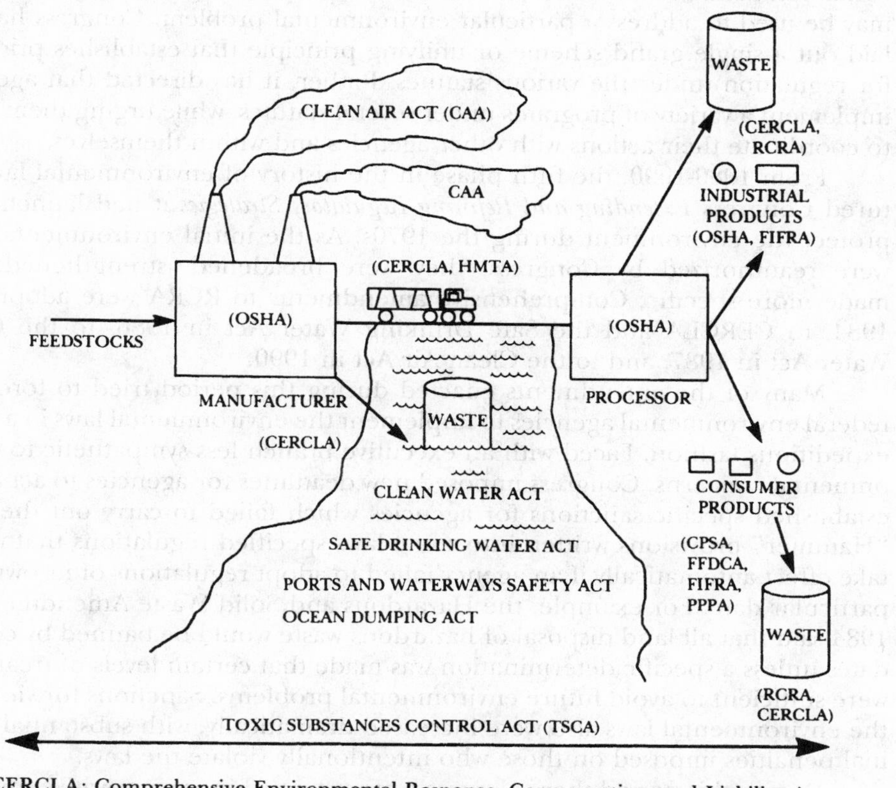

CERCLA: Comprehensive Environmental Response, Compensation, and Liability Act
FFDCA: Federal Food, Drug, and Cosmetic Act
RCRA: Resource Conservation and Recovery Act
FIFRA: Federal Insecticide, Fungicide, and Rodenticide Act
CPSA: Consumer Product Safety Act
OSHA: Occupational Safety and Health Act
HMTA: Hazardous Materials Transportation Act
PPPA: Poison Prevention Packaging Act

jurisdiction over contaminants in public water supply systems, while FIFRA allows EPA to regulate the licensing and use of pesticides.

In theory, the Toxic Substances Control Act (TSCA) is the broadest source of EPA's regulatory authority because it authorizes EPA to ban or to restrict the manufacture, marketing, use, or disposal of any "chemical substance or mixture" (with the exception of pesticides and products regulated by the FDA). TSCA thus authorizes EPA to regulate chemicals through all phases of their "life cycle," from manufacture through use and disposal in any environmental medium. Thus it appears to cover all of the activities shown in the diagram. While RCRA's coverage is somewhat more narrowly confined to solid wastes that are deemed hazardous by EPA, it too authorizes extensive controls. RCRA mandates regulation of hazardous wastes from "cradle to grave," including controls on disposal of it in any environmental medium (e.g., land disposal, incineration).

Complaints are often heard that the fragmented structure of environmental law makes it difficult to pursue coordinated regulatory responses to cross-media contamination. Often there is considerable overlap among the various laws that may be used to address a particular environmental problem. Congress has not laid out a single grand scheme or unifying principle that establishes priorities for regulation under the various statutes. Rather, it has directed that agencies implement a variety of programs under several statutes, while urging them to try to coordinate their actions with other agencies and within themselves.

From 1980-1990, the fifth phase in the history of environmental law featured Congress *Extending and Refining Regulatory Strategies* it had launched to protect the environment during the 1970s. As the initial environmental laws were reauthorized by Congress, they were broadened, strengthened, and made more specific. Comprehensive amendments to RCRA were adopted in 1984, to CERCLA and the Safe Drinking Water Act in 1986, to the Clean Water Act in 1987, and to the Clean Air Act in 1990.

Many of the amendments enacted during this period tried to force the federal environmental agencies to implement the environmental laws in a more expeditious fashion. Faced with an executive branch less sympathetic to environmental concerns, Congress imposed new deadlines for agencies to act and it established specific sanctions for agencies which failed to carry out the laws. "Hammer" provisions written into some laws specified regulations that would take effect automatically if an agency failed to adopt regulations of its own by a particular date. For example, the Hazardous and Solid Waste Amendments of 1984 said that all land disposal of hazardous waste would be banned by certain dates unless a specific determination was made that certain levels of treatment were sufficient to avoid future environmental problems. Sanctions for violating the environmental laws also were increased dramatically, with substantial criminal penalties imposed on those who intentionally violate the laws.

During this period there also was a move toward more innovative forms of regulation. The Emergency Planning and Community Right-to-Know Act, 42 U.S.C. §§11001-11050, enacted in 1986, requires industries to report annually the volume of their releases of hundreds of toxic substances. The Act creates a national inventory of toxic releases that must be made accessible to the public, using information as a tool for mobilizing public pressure to reduce toxic emissions. The Clean Air Act Amendments of 1990 provide the first large-scale experiment with emissions trading approaches long advocated by economists as a more efficient means for reducing pollution. While mandating significant reductions in sulfur dioxide emissions, the law creates emissions allowances that may be bought and sold to ensure that the reductions are obtained in the cheapest manner possible. During this period Congress also amended several environmental statutes to broaden the role of Native American tribes in environmental policy. EPA is now authorized to treat tribes in the same manner as it treats states under the Clean Air Act, the Clean Water Act, the Comprehensive Environmental Response, Compensation and Liability Act, and the Safe Drinking Water Act.

Beginning around 1991, the pendulum that swung so powerfully toward environmental protection during the 1970s and 1980s appeared to be moving in the other direction with a Congress and a judiciary decidedly more skeptical about environmental regulation. We call this a period of *Regulatory Recoil and Reinvention.*

The 1994 congressional elections gave the Republicans control of both houses of Congress under a leadership decidedly antagonistic toward

FIGURE 2.2

environmental regulation. However, their aggressive efforts to repeal major provisions of the federal environmental statutes backfired, as demonstrated in 1995 when legislation to dramatically weaken the Clean Water Act passed the House but was killed because of public outcry and President Clinton's veto threat.

Unable to directly repeal the environmental statutes, the congressional leadership concentrated on measures to make it more difficult to adopt new regulations or to enforce existing laws. These included appropriations riders that temporarily prevented the listing of new endangered species and that suspended environmental safeguards for timber harvesting on federal lands. They also included legislation to make it more difficult to regulate state and local governments and small businesses. In March 1995 Congress enacted the Unfunded Mandates Reform Act, which makes it procedurally more difficult to impose new regulatory requirements on state and local governments in the absence of federal funding for compliance. In March 1996 Congress enacted the Small Business Regulatory Enforcement Fairness Act (SBREFA), which makes it more difficult for EPA to issue regulations that affect small businesses.

To defuse pressures to weaken the environmental laws, the Clinton administration launched a series of initiatives to "reinvent regulation" to make it more flexible and less costly. Efforts to find common ground between industry and environmental groups over legislative reforms were successful in August 1996 when food safety reform legislation (the Food Quality Protection Act of 1996) and legislation to reauthorize the Safe Drinking Water Act were enacted by overwhelming margins in Congress. Each piece of legislation was the product of significant compromises between industrial and environmental interests that produced consensus legislation with broad support from traditionally antagonistic groups.

Significant amendments to CERCLA to encourage cleanup and redevelopment of brownfields were adopted unanimously by Congress in 2001 and signed into law by President George W. Bush in January 2002. Small Business Liability Relief and Brownfields Revitalization Act, Pub. L. No. 107-118. Because the two major political parties remain sharply divided on many environmental issues, the ability of Congress to enact comprehensive legislation in the future may turn on the success of similar consensus-building approaches. With Republicans regaining control of both houses of Congress after the 2002 elections, environmental groups have concentrated their efforts on blocking environmentally damaging legislation by Senate filibusters, if necessary, to stop measures to open ANWR to oil drilling (discussed in Chapter 1) or legislation weakening the Endangered Species Act, which passed the House of Representatives in 2005.

B.   THE IMPACT OF REGULATORY LEGISLATION ON COMMON LAW ACTIONS

With the advent of comprehensive federal regulatory statutes, courts soon faced questions concerning the impact of public law on common law actions. While statutes may supplant common law if legislative bodies so intend, legislative intent is often deliberately left murky because legislators are loath to disturb the products of decades of judicially developed doctrine. Thus, the relationship between environmental statutes and the common law can be a complicated one.

As noted above, the Supreme Court in Illinois v. City of Milwaukee, 406 U.S. 91 (1972) (*Milwaukee I*) delegated jurisdiction over federal common law nuisance actions between states to the federal district courts. Thus, following the Supreme Court's decision in *Milwaukee I*, Illinois pursued its common law nuisance action in federal district court. While this action was pending, the federal Clean Water Act was enacted. This legislation established a comprehensive regulatory scheme to control water pollution by requiring all dischargers of pollutants into surface waters to obtain a permit, usually from a state environmental agency operating under federal oversight. Milwaukee ultimately obtained a permit limiting the discharges from its sewage treatment plants. While Milwaukee argued that the permit precluded Illinois's nuisance action, Illinois maintained that the permit limits were too lax and that the discharges remained a nuisance at common law.

In 1977, the district court rejected Milwaukee's defense, ruling that Milwaukee's discharge of inadequately treated sewage was a nuisance under federal common law and ordering the city to control its discharges more stringently than required by its Clean Water Act permit. The Seventh Circuit affirmed the district court's holding that the Clean Water Act had not preempted the federal common law of nuisance, but it held that the district court should not have required more stringent limits on discharges of treated sewage than required by the city's permit. The case then returned to the Supreme Court, which addressed the impact of the Clean Water Act's regulatory scheme on federal common law nuisance actions in City of Milwaukee v. Illinois, 451 U.S. 304 (1981) (*Milwaukee II*).

In *Milwaukee II* the Supreme Court held that Illinois's federal common law nuisance action had been preempted by the federal Clean Water Act. Writing for the Court, Justice Rehnquist noted that legislative preemption of *federal* common law did not implicate the same federalism concerns that require clear expressions of congressional intent before state law may be preempted. Illinois had argued that there was clear evidence that Congress had not intended to preempt federal common law based on the savings clause in the citizen suit provision of section 505(e) of the Clean Water Act, which provides: "Nothing in this section shall restrict any right which any person (or class of persons) may have under any statute or common law to seek enforcement of any effluent standard or limitation or to seek any other relief (including relief against the Administrator or a State agency)." However, the Supreme Court read this language narrowly to mean "that nothing *in §505*, the citizen-suit provision, should be read as limiting any other remedies which might exist. . . . [I]t means only that the provision of such suit does not revoke other remedies. It most assuredly cannot be read to mean that the Act as a whole does not supplant formerly available federal common-law actions but only that the particular section authorizing citizen suits does not do so." 451 U.S. at 328-329 (emphasis in original).

Citing the comprehensive nature of the Clean Water Act's regulatory scheme and the technical complexities courts would have to confront to formulate pollution control standards, Justice Rehnquist concluded that Congress implicitly had supplanted federal common law by adopting a comprehensive regulatory scheme for water pollution control. "Congress' intent in enacting the Amendments was clearly to establish an all-encompassing program of water pollution regulation. *Every* point source discharge is prohibited unless covered by a permit, which directly subjects the discharger to the administrative apparatus established by Congress to achieve its goals." Justice Rehnquist concluded that "[t]he establishment of such a self-consciously comprehensive program by Congress, which certainly did not exist when Illinois v. Milwaukee was decided, strongly suggests that there is no room for courts to attempt to improve on that program with federal common law." *Milwaukee II*, 451 U.S. at 318-319 (emphasis in original). He went on to note that application of federal common law would be "peculiarly inappropriate in areas as complex as water pollution control. . . . Not only are the technical problems difficult—doubtless the reason Congress vested authority to administer the Act in administrative agencies possessing the necessary expertise—but the general area is particularly unsuited to the approach inevitable under a regime of federal common law. Congress criticized past approaches to water pollution control as being 'sporadic' and 'ad hoc,' S. Rep. No. 92-414, p. 95 (1971), 2 Leg. Hist. 1511, apt characterizations of any judicial approach applying federal common law, see Wilburn Boat Co. v. Fireman's Fund Ins. Co., 348 U.S. 310, 319 (1955)." *Milwaukee II*, 451 U.S. at 325.

Justice Rehnquist noted that Illinois was free to pursue its case for more stringent controls on Milwaukee's discharges before the Wisconsin state agency responsible for issuing Milwaukee a permit under the Clean Water Act. But he maintained that "[i]t would be quite inconsistent with this scheme if federal courts were in effect to 'write their own ticket' under the guise of federal common law after permits have already been issued and permittees have been planning and operating in reliance on them."

The Court soon confronted the question whether the Clean Water Act preempted *state* common law actions in International Paper Company v. Ouellette, 479 U.S. 481 (1987). The *Ouellette* litigation commenced when Harmel Ouellette, a Vermont resident, appeared in the office of Peter Langrock, a country lawyer in a two-person firm. Ouelette complained that he and his wife, who owned property in Vermont fronting on Lake Champlain, no longer could tolerate the stench generated by pollution from a paper mill located across the lake in New York. Langrock filed a private nuisance action in Vermont state court on behalf of 150 lakeshore property owners. The defendant, International Paper Company (IPC), removed the action to federal court, where it maintained that the Clean Water Act preempted state common law in light of the Supreme Court's *Milwaukee II* decision. The case ultimately went to the U.S. Supreme Court, which rendered the following decision.

|| *International Paper Co. v. Ouellette* ||
|| 479 U.S. 481 (1987) ||

JUSTICE POWELL delivered the opinion of the court. . . .

[W]e turn to the question presented: whether the Act pre-empts Vermont common law to the extent that law may impose liability on a New York point source. We begin the analysis by noting that it is not necessary for a federal statute to provide explicitly that particular state laws are pre-empted. Hillsborough County v. Automated Medical Laboratories, Inc., 471 U.S. 707, 713 (1985). Although courts should not lightly infer pre-emption, it may be presumed when the federal legislation is "sufficiently comprehensive to make reasonable the inference that Congress 'left no room' for supplementary state regulation." Ibid. In addition to express or implied pre-emption, a state law also is invalid to the extent that it "actually conflicts with a . . . federal statute." Ray v. Atlantic Richfield Co., 435 U.S. 151, 158 (1978). Such a conflict will be found when the state law "stands as an obstacle to the accomplishment and execution of the full purposes and objectives of Congress." Hillsborough County v. Automated Medical Laboratories, Inc., supra, at 713. . . .

Given that the Act itself does not speak directly to the issue, the Court must be guided by the goals and policies of the Act in determining whether it in fact preempts an action based on the law of an affected State. After examining the CWA as a whole, its purposes and its history, we are convinced that if affected States were allowed to impose separate discharge standards on a single point source, the inevitable result would be a serious interference with the achievement of the "full purposes and objectives of Congress." See Hillsborough County v. Automated Medical Laboratories, Inc., supra, at 713. Because we do not believe Congress intended to undermine this carefully drawn statute through a general saving clause, we conclude that the CWA precludes a court from applying the law of an affected State against an out-of-state source.

. . . In this case the application of Vermont law against IPC would allow respondents to circumvent the NPDES permit system, thereby upsetting the balance of public and private interests so carefully addressed by the Act. . . .

An interpretation of the saving clause that preserved actions brought under an affected State's law would disrupt this balance of interests. If a New York source were liable for violations of Vermont law, that law could effectively override both the permit requirements and the policy choices made by the source State. The affected State's nuisance laws would subject the point source to the threat of legal and equitable penalties if the permit standards were less stringent than those imposed by the affected State. Such penalties would compel the source to adopt different control standards and a different compliance schedule from those approved by the EPA, even though the affected State had not engaged in the same weighing of the costs and benefits.

Our conclusion that Vermont nuisance law is inapplicable to a New York point source does not leave respondents without a remedy. The CWA precludes only those suits that may require standards of effluent control that are incompatible with those established by the procedures set forth in the Act. The saving clause specifically preserves other state actions, and therefore nothing in the Act bars aggrieved individuals from bringing a nuisance claim pursuant to the law of the source State. By its terms the CWA allows States such as New York to impose higher standards on their own point sources, and in *Milwaukee II* we recognized that this authority may include the right to impose higher common-law as well as higher statutory restrictions. 451 U.S., at 328 (suggesting that "States may adopt more stringent limitations . . . through state nuisance law, and apply them to in-state dischargers").

An action brought against IPC under New York nuisance law would not frustrate the goals of the CWA as would a suit governed by Vermont law. First, application of the source State's law does not disturb the balance among federal, source-state, and affected-state interests. Because the Act specifically allows source States to impose stricter standards, the imposition of source-state law does not disrupt the regulatory partnership established by the permit system. Second, the restriction of suits to those brought under source-state nuisance law prevents a source from being subject to an indeterminate number of potential regulations. Although New York nuisance law may impose separate standards and thus create some tension with the permit system, a source only is required to look to a single additional authority, whose rules should be relatively predictable. Moreover, States can be expected to take into account their own nuisance laws in setting permit requirements.

NOTES AND QUESTIONS

1. *Ouellette* preserves the ability of plaintiffs to bring state common law actions against polluters so long as the law of the source state, rather than the receiving state, is applied. As Dan Farber observes in discussing *Ouellette*, "after hanging by its fingernails from a cliff in *Milwaukee II*, the common law came roaring back in the final episode." Farber, The Story of Boomer, Environmental Law Stories 40 (2005). Preemption of state common law remedies by state regulatory statutes remains extremely rare.

2. The requirement that the state common law of the source state be applied did not significantly disadvantage the plaintiffs in *Ouellette*. On remand, New York nuisance law proved no more favorable to the paper company than Vermont's would have been. International Paper hired an engineering firm, which conducted extensive "smell test" experiments in an effort to show that the plant's air emissions were not a nuisance. Langrock countered with the testimony of tolltakers working at the Crown Point Bridge who said out-of-state drivers persistently asked, "What the hell is that awful smell?" when they arrived at the tollbooth. With evidence showing that International Paper had violated its air and water permits more than 1,000 times, plaintiffs pressed for punitive damages. The company ultimately settled with the plaintiffs for $5 million, including the establishment of a trust fund for environmental projects in the Lake Champlain area. The colorful story of this litigation is

recounted by Peter Langrock, the plaintiffs' lawyer, in P. Langrock, Addison County Justice: Tales from a Vermont Courthouse (1997).

3. For a discussion of the difficulty the Court had in developing a defensible rationale for the result in *Ouellette*, as revealed in the papers of the late Justice Thurgood Marshall, see Percival, Environmental Law in the Supreme Court: Highlights from the Marshall Papers, 23 Envtl. L. Rep. 10606, 10618 (1993). The history of the interstate nuisance litigation over water pollution is described in more detail in Percival, The Clean Water Act and the Demise of the Federal Common Law of Interstate Nuisance, 55 Ala. L. Rev. 717 (2004).

4. An important part of the rationale for preemption in *Milwaukee II* was the pervasive regulatory scheme provided by the Clean Water Act's NPDES permit program. The Act requires permits for all discharges of pollutants to surface waters from point sources. The Ninth Circuit in National Audubon Society v. Department of Water, 869 F.2d 1196 (9th Cir. 1989), held that the Clean Water Act preempts a federal common law nuisance action against the Los Angeles Department of Water and Power for damage it caused by diverting water from Mono Lake. The court, however, reserved judgment on the question whether the federal Clean Air Act would preempt a federal common law nuisance action against the Department for air pollution. The Ninth Circuit held that a federal common law action was not available under the facts of the case because, unlike the situation in Georgia v. Tennessee Copper Co., there was no interstate dispute involved. A dissenting judge argued that there is a uniquely federal interest in preserving air quality even in intrastate disputes. Plaintiffs had argued that a federal common law nuisance action for interstate water pollution should be available to them because the Clean Water Act does not apply to the action they challenged since no NPDES permit was required for the water diversions they challenged.

5. The Supreme Court has not determined whether the federal Clean Air Act preempts federal common law nuisance actions for interstate air pollution, though some lower courts have suggested that it might. See U.S. v. Kin-Buc, Inc., 532 F. Supp. 699 (D.C.N.J 1982). In New England Legal Foundation v. Costle, 666 F.2d 30, 32 n. 2 (2d Cir. 1981), the Second Circuit reserved judgment on this question while noting that the Clean Air Act, unlike the Clean Water Act, did not regulate pollution from all sources. Prior to enactment of the 1990 Amendments, the Clean Air Act did not employ a federal permit program. Now that it does, is it likely that a court would find that it preempts federal common law?

6. In July 2004 eight states (Connecticut, New York, California, Iowa, New Jersey, Rhode Island, Vermont, and Wisconsin) and the City of New York filed a federal and state common law nuisance action against six of the largest electric utilities in the United States. The suit alleges that power plants operated by the defendant utilities contribute 10 percent of U.S. emissions of carbon dioxide (CO_2), a greenhouse gas that contributes to global warming and climate change. The plaintiff states claim that global warming already has begun to alter the climate of the United States and that it will cause significant harm to them. They seek to hold defendants jointly and severally liable for contributing to global warming and an injunction ordering them to cap their emissions of CO_2 and then to reduce them by a specified percentage each year for at least a decade. The case raises the question whether the Clean Air Act preempts the federal common law of nuisance for interstate air pollution. While the Act now has a comprehensive permit program like that of the Clean Water Act, the Clean Air Act has not been used to regulate emissions of CO_2 and during the Bush

administration EPA's general counsel has taken the position that the agency has no authority to regulate CO_2 emissions under the Clean Air Act. On September 15, 2005, federal district judge Loretta Preska dismissed the states' lawsuit without reaching the preemption issue. Connecticut v. American Electric Power Co., 406 F. Supp. 2d 265 (S.D.N.Y. 2005). Judge Preska held that the case presented nonjusticiable political questions. She distinguished previous interstate nuisance cases like Georgia v. Tennessee Copper and New Jersey v. New York City, by noting that none "has touched on so many areas of national and international policy" as the climate change litigation. 406 F. Supp. 2d at 272. Judge Preska concluded that the "explicit statements of Congress and the Executive on the issue of global climate change in general and their specific refusal to impose the limits on carbon dioxide emissions Plaintiffs now seek to impose by judicial fiat confirm that making the 'initial policy determination[s]' addressing global climate change is an undertaking for the political branches." Id. at 274. "Because resolution of the issues presented here requires identification and balancing of economic, environmental, foreign policy, and national security interests," she concluded that the cases "present non-justiciable political questions that are consigned to the political branches, not the Judiciary." Id.

C.   ENVIRONMENTAL FEDERALISM: THREE MODELS OF FEDERAL-STATE RELATIONS

While the growth of environmental regulation largely has been driven by federal legislation, states and Native American tribes continue to play an important role in the development and implementation of environmental policy. Even though the federal environmental laws often require states to meet minimum national standards, they generally do not preempt state law except in narrowly defined circumstances. State common law remains an important tool for seeking compensation for environmental damage. Some of the most innovative environmental protection measures are the product of state legislation, such as California's Proposition 65 (see Chapter 4), New Jersey's Environmental Cleanup and Responsibility Act (discussed in Chapter 3), and Michigan's Environmental Protection Act.

The federalization of environmental law was a product of the concern that state and local authorities lacked the resources and political capability to control problems that were becoming national in scope. Congress has employed three general approaches for accomplishing its environmental protection objectives. The first approach is to *provide federal financial assistance* to encourage states to adopt environmental standards on their own. While this approach proved largely ineffective for controlling air and water pollution, it remains the principal federal approach to issues such as land use management where political opposition to federal regulation is particularly acute. Federal programs encourage state and local planning for land use and solid waste management under the Coastal Zone Management Act, the Clean Water Act, and Subtitle D of the Resource Conservation and Recovery Act. The power of this tool for motivating states to act depends largely on the amount of federal financial assistance involved. As federal funding for such programs has declined, this approach has become a less significant vehicle for promoting state action.

The second model, which currently is the predominant approach to federal-state relations under the environmental statutes, can be called a *"cooperative federalism" approach.* Under this model, federal agencies establish national environmental standards and states may opt to assume responsibility for administering them or to leave implementation to federal authorities. The Clean Air Act, the Clean Water Act, RCRA, and the Safe Drinking Water Act require EPA to establish minimum national standards, while authorizing delegation of authority to implement and administer the programs to states that demonstrate that they can meet minimum federal requirements. In states that choose not to seek program delegation, the programs are operated and enforced by federal authorities. Federally recognized Native American tribes also may qualify for EPA approval to be treated "in the same manner as a state" to manage delegated programs under the Clean Air Act, Clean Water Act, and Safe Drinking Water Act, but not under the Resource Conservation and Recovery Act. See D. Pingaro, Tribal Environmental Protection Activity Under EPA-Administered Programs, 8 Env. L. News 11 (Summer 1999).

Statutes requiring the establishment of minimum federal standards have long been thought to be necessary to prevent regulatory competition among states from undermining environmental quality. Professor Richard Revesz has presented a powerful challenge to this "race-to-the-bottom" rationale in Revesz, Rehabilitating Interstate Competition: Rethinking the "Race-to-the-Bottom" Rationale for Federal Environmental Regulation, 67 N.Y.U. L. Rev. 1210 (1992). Based on economic models positing that state regulatory standards would be set at levels where the benefits of increased employment would at least offset the costs of increased environmental degradation, Revesz argues that there is no theoretical basis for believing that regulatory competition would induce states to set suboptimally low standards. He also notes that there is little empirical support for the notion that environmental standards have a substantial effect on industry location decisions. Revesz, "Federalism and Regulation: Some Generalizations" in Regulatory Competition and Economic Integration: Comparative Perspectives (D. Esty & D. Geradin eds., 2000). Professor Kirsten Engel responds that even if regulatory standards have little effect on industrial location, a "race-to-the-bottom" would occur because state officials believe that they do based on the results of a survey of state regulators. K. Engel, State Environmental Standard-Setting: Is There a "Race" and Is It "To the Bottom"?, 48 Hastings L.J. 271 (1997).

A third approach to environmental federalism eschews state administration of federal standards in favor of federal control. *Preemption of state law* has been employed sparingly in the federal environmental laws. It usually is reserved for regulation of products that are distributed nationally, as businesses favor nationally uniform regulation to avoid having to comply with balkanized regulatory standards. Examples include regulation of chemicals under the Toxic Substances Control Act (TSCA), pesticide registration under the Federal Insecticide, Fungicide, and Rodenticide Act (FIFRA), provisions of the Clean Air Act governing vehicle emissions, regulation of nuclear materials under the Atomic Energy Act, and regulation of hazardous materials transportation under the Hazardous Materials Transportation Act. While these laws generally provide that federal regulation preempts inconsistent state standards, the question of whether state standards are inconsistent with federal regulations can be a difficult one. See, e.g., Silkwood v. Kerr-McGee Corp., 464 U.S. 238 (1984) (holding that award of punitive damages under state law for exposure to nuclear material not preempted by the Atomic Energy Act); Cippollone v. Liggett Group, Inc., 505 U.S. 504 (1992) (Federal Cigarette Labeling and Advertising Act preempted only claims based on failure to warn and neutralization of federally mandated warnings but not claims based on express warranty, intentional fraud and mis-representation, or conspiracy); Huron Portland Cement Co. v. Detroit, 352 U.S. 440 (1960) (upholding municipality's smoke abatement ordinance as applied to ships on the Great Lakes against claims it interfered with interstate commerce and was preempted by federal safety regulation of seagoing vessels); Burbank v. Lockheed Air Terminal, Inc., 411 U.S. 624 (1973) (holding that Noise Control Act and Federal Aviation Act preempted a local noise abatement ordinance that effectively barred jet aircraft from taking off at night); Pacific Gas & Elec. v. California Energy Comm'n, 461 U.S. 190 (1983) (upholding California state initiative that blocked licensing of new nuclear power plants pending develop-ment of facility for disposal of high-level nuclear waste on ground that it is an economic measure rather than a safety regulation in conflict with Atomic Energy Act); Gade v. National Solid Waste Management Assn., 505 U.S. 88 (1992) (Occupational Safety and Health Act preempted state hazardous waste licensing in certain circumstances); United States v. Locke, 529 U.S. 89 (2000) (federal Ports and Waterways Safety Act preempts Washington state regulations that imposed training, English proficiency, navigation watch, and casualty reporting requirements on oil tanker crews operating in state waters). See also D. Spence & P. Murray, The Law, Economics, and Politics of Federal Preemption Jurisprudence: A Quantitative Analysis, 87 Cal. L. Rev. 1125 (1999) (arguing that judges have been too predisposed to preempt state and local environmental regulations because they have failed to distinguish between those that seek to internalize locally generated costs and those that seek to shift costs to other jurisdictions).

In Engine Manufacturers Association v. South Coast Air Quality Manage-ment District, 541 U.S. 246 (2004), the Court reversed a Ninth Circuit decision that had rejected an industry challenge to regulations requiring operators of public and private fleets of more than 15 vehicles to buy only low-emission or alternative fuel vehicles. By an 8-to-1 vote the Court agreed with the claim of diesel engine manufacturers and oil companies that the regulations issued by the South Coast Air Quality Management District are preempted by the federal Clean Air Act. In 2005 the Court decided another preemption case, Bates v. Dow Agrosciences, LLP, 544 U.S. 431 (2005). The case involved the question whether the Federal Insecticide, Fungicide and Rodenticide Act (FIFRA) preempts state tort claims against the manufacturer of the "Strongarm" herbicide that alleged-ly damaged the crops of 29 Texas peanut farmers. The farmers argued that FIFRA should not be held to preempt state law claims premised on the manu-facture of a defective herbicide, while the manufacturer argued that the claims are based on a failure to warn, which should be preempted by FIFRA's labeling requirements. The farmers claimed that Dow had not disclosed that the herbi-cide in question damaged crops planted in soil with pH content above a certain level, in violation of the Texas Deceptive Trade Practices Act (DTPA). Both the district court and the U.S. Court of Appeals for the Fifth Circuit held that Bates's claims for breach of warranty, fraud, violation of the DTPA, and failure to warn were all preempted by FIFRA's express preemption clause. The Supreme Court reversed and remanded. The Court held that section 136v(b) of FIFRA pre-empts only those statutory or common law rules "that would impose a labeling requirement that diverges from those set out in FIFRA and its implementing regulations. It does not, however, pre-empt any state rules that are fully consist-ent with federal requirements." The Court remanded the case to the Court of

Appeals to determine whether the plaintiffs' fraud and failure-to-warn claims were preempted.

Claims that federal environmental regulation has been too intrusive on state and local prerogatives have become a prominent part of the current political ferment over federalism. Recently there has been considerable debate over how responsibility for environmental protection should be divided in our federal system and how to improve relations between federal agencies and the states. State officials have lobbied for devolution of greater authority from federal to state authorities. EPA has sought to be more responsive to state concerns, but it finds itself in a difficult position. As the National Academy of Public Administration describes the problem: "EPA's paradox is that it must maintain national programs and seek national consistency while simultaneously attempting to make its programs and standards fit an incredibly diverse and dynamic nation." Resolving the Paradox of Environmental Protection: An Agenda for Congress, EPA & the States xii-xiii (1997).

Those who challenge calls to devolve more responsibility for environmental protection to the states cite several reasons for their opposition. First, there are economies of scale in having national regulatory programs. Professor Daniel Esty questions whether "we really want every state or hamlet to determine for itself whether polychlorinate biphenyls create additional cancer risks greater than 10^{-6}, and if so, at what cost these risks are worth worrying about." Esty, Revitalizing Environmental Federalism 95 Mich. L. Rev. 570, 573 (1996). Second, national programs are better able to deal with transboundary pollution. "[I]nsofar as the central reason for environmental regulation is to mitigate the impact of market failures that emerge from uninternalized externalities, drawing more lines on the map only multiplies the potential for transboundary spillovers." Id. Third, fairness and equal protection concerns may support "the establishment of baseline national standards so that Americans are not exposed to fundamentally unequal levels of environmental risk." Steinzor, Unfunded Environmental Mandates and the "New (New) Federalism": Devolution, Revolution, or Reform? 81 Minn. L. Rev. 101, 172 (1996). Professor Peter Swire notes that it may be easier to focus public attention on environmental problems and enact legislation at the national level so that citizen preferences can overcome the concentrated interests of regulated industry. Swire, The Race to Laxity and the Race to Undesirability: Explaining Failures in Competition Among Jurisdictions in Environmental Law, 14 Yale L. & Policy Rev./Yale J. Reg. 167 (1996).

State and local officials have become increasingly upset about the cost of implementing federal requirements, such as regulations implementing the Safe Drinking Water Act. Arguing that it is unfair for the federal government to impose "unfunded mandates," state and local officials lobbied Congress to restrict this practice. In March 1995, Congress overwhelmingly approved legislation making it more difficult to impose federal mandates on state and local governments. The legislation, known as the Unfunded Mandate Reform Act of 1995, Pub. L. No. 104-4, 109 Stat. 48 (1995), requires that more detailed cost estimates be provided for federal mandates and makes it easier for opponents of such provisions to defeat them in Congress. The law requires the Congressional Budget Office (CBO) to provide estimates of the future cost of legislative mandates if they may exceed $50 million annually for state or local governments or the private sector. Any member of Congress can raise a point of order demanding that mandates estimated to cost state or local governments more than $50 million annually be stricken from legislation unless federal funding is provided or the mandate is specifically approved by a majority vote. Mandates for which future federal funding is promised are to expire if the funding is not subsequently provided.

The legislation also imposes new requirements on agencies issuing regulations that impose federal mandates. The law requires federal agencies, prior to publishing a notice of proposed rulemaking, to prepare assessments of the anticipated costs and benefits of any mandate that may cost state or local governments or the private sector more than $100 million annually. It also prohibits federal agencies from issuing regulations containing federal mandates that do not employ the least costly method or that do not have the least burdensome effect on governments or the private sector unless the agency publishes an explanation of why the more costly or burdensome method was adopted. These provisions are subject to judicial review if the underlying agency action already is reviewable in court.

States have become more aggressive at challenging federal mandates in court. In the case that follows, the state of New York argued that the federal government infringed on its Tenth Amendment rights when it directed in the Low-Level Radioactive Waste Policy Act that states that failed to make arrangements to dispose of low-level radioactive wastes by January 1, 1993, must "take title" to all such waste generated within their borders.

New York v. United States
505 U.S. 144 (1992)

JUSTICE O'CONNOR delivered the opinion of the Court.

. . . Petitioners do not contend that Congress lacks the power to regulate the disposal of low level radioactive waste. Space for radioactive waste disposal sites is frequently sold by residents of one State to residents of another. Regulation of the resulting interstate market in waste disposal is therefore well within Congress' authority under the Commerce Clause. Cf. Philadelphia v. New Jersey, 437 U.S. 617, 621-623 (1978). Petitioners likewise do not dispute that under the Supremacy Clause Congress could, if it wished, preempt state radioactive waste regulation. Petitioners contend only that the Tenth Amendment limits the power of Congress to regulate in the way it has chosen. Rather than addressing the problem of waste disposal by directly regulating the generators and disposers of waste, petitioners argue, Congress has impermissibly directed the States to regulate in this field.

1

As an initial matter, Congress may not simply "commandee[r] the legislative processes of the States by directly compelling them to enact and enforce a federal regulatory program." Hodel v. Virginia Surface Mining & Reclamation Assn., Inc., 452 U.S. 264, 288 (1981). In *Hodel*, the Court upheld the Surface Mining Control and Reclamation Act of 1977 precisely because it did not "commandeer" the States into regulating mining. The Court found that "the States are not compelled to enforce the steep-slope standards, to expend any state funds, or to participate in the federal regulatory program in any manner whatsoever. If a State does not wish to submit a proposed permanent program that complies with the Act and implementing regulations, the full regulatory burden will be borne by the federal Government." Ibid. . . .

While Congress has substantial powers to govern the Nation directly, including in areas of intimate concern to the States, the Constitution has never been understood to confer upon Congress the ability to require the States to govern according to Congress' instructions. . . .

In providing for a stronger central government . . . the Framers explicitly chose a Constitution that confers upon Congress the power to regulate individuals, not States. As we have seen, the Court has consistently respected this choice. We have always understood that even where Congress has the authority under the Constitution to pass laws requiring or prohibiting certain acts, it lacks the power directly to compel the States to require or prohibit those acts. The allocation of power contained in the Commerce Clause, for example, authorizes Congress to regulate interstate commerce directly; it does not authorize Congress to regulate state governments' regulation of interstate commerce.

2

This is not to say that Congress lacks the ability to encourage a State to regulate in a particular way, or that Congress may not hold out incentives to the States as a method of influencing a State's policy choices. Our cases have identified a variety of methods, short of outright coercion, by which Congress may urge a State to adopt a legislative program consistent with federal interests. Two of these methods are of particular relevance here.

First, under Congress' spending power, "Congress may attach conditions on the receipt of federal funds." South Dakota v. Dole, 483 U.S., at 206. Such conditions must (among other requirements) bear some relationship to the purpose of the federal spending, id., at 207-208, and n.3; otherwise, of course, the spending power could render academic the Constitution's other grants and limits of federal authority. Where the recipient of federal funds is a State, as is not unusual today, the conditions attached to the funds by Congress may influence a State's legislative choices. Dole was one such case: The Court found no constitutional flaw in a federal statute directing the Secretary of Transportation to withhold federal highway funds from States failing to adopt Congress' choice of a minimum drinking age.

Second, where Congress has the authority to regulate private activity under the Commerce Clause, we have recognized Congress' power to offer States the choice of regulating that activity according to federal standards or having state law preempted by federal regulation. Hodel v. Virginia Surface Mining & Reclamation Assn., Inc., supra, 452 U.S., at 288. This arrangement, which has been termed "a program of cooperative federalism," Hodel, supra, 452 U.S., at 289, is replicated in numerous federal statutory schemes. These include the Clean Water Act, the Occupational Safety and Health Act of 1970, the Resource Conservation and Recovery Act of 1976, and the Alaska National Interest Lands Conservation Act.

By either of these two methods, as by any other permissible method of encouraging a State to conform to federal policy choices, the residents of the State retain the ultimate decision as to whether or not the State will comply. If a State's citizens view federal policy as sufficiently contrary to local interests, they may elect to decline a federal grant. If state residents would prefer their government to devote its attention and resources to problems other than those deemed important by Congress, they may choose to have the Federal Government rather than the State bear the expense of a federally mandated regulatory program, and they may continue to supplement that program to the extent state law is not preempted. Where Congress encourages state regulation rather than compelling it, state governments remain responsive to the local electorate's preferences; state officials remain accountable to the people.

By contrast, where the Federal Government compels States to regulate, the accountability of both state and federal officials is diminished. If the citizens of New York, for example, do not consider that making provision for the disposal of radioactive waste is in their best interest, they may elect state officials who share their view. That view can always be preempted under the Supremacy Clause if it is contrary to the national view, but in such a case it is the Federal Government that makes the decision in full view of the public, and it will be federal officials that suffer the consequences if the decision turns out to be detrimental or unpopular. But where the Federal Government directs the States to regulate, it may be state officials who will bear the brunt of public disapproval, while the federal officials who devised the regulatory program may remain insulated from the electoral ramifications of their decision. Accountability is thus diminished when, due to federal coercion, elected state officials cannot regulate in accordance with the views of the local electorate in matters not preempted by federal regulation. . . .

With these principles in mind, we turn to the three challenged provisions of the Low-Level Radioactive Waste Policy Amendments Act of 1985. . . .

Construed as a whole, the Act comprises three sets of "incentives" for the States to provide for the disposal of low-level radioactive waste generated within their borders. We consider each in turn.

[The Court then concluded that the portions of the Act which authorized states to impose surcharges on radioactive waste received from other states, and eventually to deny access to such waste altogether, were within Congress's power to authorize states to burden interstate commerce.]

C

The take title provision is of a different character. This third so-called "incentive" offers States, as an alternative to regulating pursuant to Congress' direction, the option of taking title to and possession of the low-level radioactive waste generated within their borders and becoming liable for all damages waste generators suffer as a result of the States' failure to do so promptly. In this provision, Congress has crossed the line distinguishing encouragement from coercion. . . .

The take title provision offers state governments a "choice" of either accepting ownership of waste or regulating according to the instructions of Congress. Respondents do not claim that the Constitution would authorize Congress to impose either option as a freestanding requirement. On one hand, the Constitution would not permit Congress simply to transfer radioactive waste from generators to state governments. Such a forced transfer, standing alone, would in principle be no different than a congressionally compelled subsidy from state governments to radioactive waste producers. The same is true of the provision requiring the States to become liable for the generators' damages. Standing alone, this provision would be indistinguishable from an Act of Congress directing the States to assume the liabilities of certain state residents. Either type of federal action would "commandeer" state governments into the service of federal regulatory purposes, and would for this reason be inconsistent with the Constitution's division of authority between federal and state governments. On the other hand, the second alternative held out to state governments—regulating pursuant to Congress' direction—would, standing alone, present a simple command to state governments to implement legislation enacted by Congress. As we have seen, the Constitution does not empower Congress to subject state governments to this type of instruction.

Because an instruction to state governments to take title to waste, standing alone, would be beyond the authority of Congress, and because a direct order to regulate, standing alone, would also be beyond the authority of Congress, it follows that Congress lacks the power to offer the States a choice between the two. Unlike the first two sets of incentives, the take title incentive does not represent the conditional exercise of any congressional power enumerated in the Constitution. In this provision, Congress has not held out the threat of exercising its spending power or its commerce power, it has instead held out the threat, should the States not regulate according to one federal instruction, of simply forcing the States to submit to another federal instruction. A choice between two unconstitutionally coercive regulatory techniques is no choice at all. Either way, "the Act commandeers the legislative processes of the States by directly compelling them to enact and enforce a federal regulatory program." Hodel v. Virginia Surface Mining & Reclamation Assn., Inc., supra, 452 U.S., at 288, an outcome that has never been understood to lie within the authority conferred upon Congress by the Constitution.

Respondents emphasize the latitude given to the States to implement Congress' plan. The Act enables the States to regulate pursuant to Congress' instructions in any number of different ways. States may avoid taking title by contracting with sited regional compacts, by building a disposal site alone or as part of a compact, or by permitting private parties to build a disposal site. States that host sites may employ a wide range of designs and disposal methods, subject only to broad federal regulatory limits. This line of reasoning, however, only underscores the critical alternative a State lacks: A State may not decline to administer the federal program. No matter which path the State chooses, it must follow the direction of Congress.

The take title provision appears to be unique. No other federal statute has been cited which offers a state government no option other than that of implementing legislation enacted by Congress. Whether one views the take title provision as lying outside Congress' enumerated powers, or as infringing upon the core of state sovereignty reserved by the Tenth Amendment, the provision is inconsistent with the federal structure of our Government established by the Constitution.

NOTES AND QUESTIONS

1. Justice O'Connor's analysis appears founded on concern about maintaining political accountability. Do you agree with her analysis that while direct federal regulation leaves the federal government politically accountable, "where

the Federal Government directs the states to regulate, it may be state officials who will bear the brunt of public disapproval, while the Federal officials who devised the regulatory program may remain insulated from the electoral ramifications of their decision"?

2. In dissent, Justice White argued that it was ironic for the Court to invalidate part of the LLRWPA on grounds of federalism when enactment of the statute was "Very much the product of cooperative federalism" because it "reflected hard-fought agreements among states as refereed by Congress." Is he right when he argues that the majority's decision "gives Congress fewer incentives to defer to the wishes of state officials in achieving local solutions to local problems"?

3. The papers of the late Justice Harry A. Blackmun revealed for the first time information concerning the Court's deliberations in New York v. United States. They confirm how strongly Justices O'Connor, Kennedy, and Scalia felt about the "take title" provision's affront to state sovereignty and an interesting debate between O'Connor and Kennedy concerning whether the Tenth Amendment is but a mirror image of the commerce clause or rather an independent limit on federal authority. See Robert V. Percival, Environmental Law in the Supreme Court: Highlights from the Blackmun Papers, 35 Envtl. L. Rep. 10637, 10650 (2005).

4. The Court's decision has not had a major impact on the federal environmental laws because they usually offer states a choice between regulating according to federal standards or having state standards preempted by federal ones. One rare exception was the subject of ACORN v. Edwards, 81 F.3d 1387 (5th Cir. 1996), a case in which the Fifth Circuit held that a provision in the Safe Drinking Water Act requiring states to establish programs for removal of lead contamination from school and day care drinking water systems violated the Tenth Amendment principles outlined in New York v. United States. The court held that the requirement "is an attempt by Congress to force States to regulate according to Congressional direction." 81 F.3d at 1394. While noting that Congress is free to regulate directly drinking water coolers that move in interstate commerce, the court held that it could not force the states to establish a regulatory program under penalty of civil sanctions without violating the Tenth Amendment.

5. In Printz v. United States, 521 U.S. 898 (1997), the Supreme Court, by a 5-to-4 vote, held that the Brady Handgun Violence Protection Act's requirements that state and local law enforcement officers conduct background checks of handgun purchasers was unconstitutional. Citing New York v. United States, the Court majority reiterated the notion that the federal government may not compel the states to enact or administer a federal regulatory program. While the four dissenters attempted to distinguish the Brady law as not requiring state or local officials to make policy, the Court majority concluded that the entire object of the law was to direct the functioning of the state executive, which would compromise the dual sovereignty structure of federalism established by the Constitution.

6. Which environmental problems are appropriate subjects for federal regulation and which should be left to state, tribal, or local authorities? Economist Wallace Oates argues that responsibility "should be assigned to the smallest jurisdiction whose geographical scope encompasses the relevant benefits and costs" of the problem. W. Oates, Thinking About Environmental Federalism, 130 Resources 14 (Winter 1998). Do you agree? Because ecosystem boundaries

rarely conform to political boundaries, problems that involve interstate externalities clearly warrant federal intervention. How strong is the federal interest in establishing minimum national standards for the quality of drinking water municipalities provide, as Congress has done in the Safe Drinking Water Act? In June 2003, the D.C. Circuit rejected arguments that the Safe Drinking Water Act exceeded Congress's constitutional authority under the Commerce Clause. The state of Nebraska challenged EPA's regulations setting maximum contaminant levels for arsenic in drinking water by arguing that Congress had no authority to regulate intrastate distribution and sale of drinking water. Noting that this was a facial challenge to the Act, the court stated that to succeed it would require a showing that under "no set of circumstances" could the Act be constitutional. Because a number of water utilities sell substantial volumes of drinking water across state lines, the court concluded that "the Act is a valid exercise of power under the Commerce Clause," without addressing whether intrastate sales of drinking water had a sufficiently substantial impact on interstate commerce to justify federal regulation. Nebraska v. EPA, 331 F.3d 995 (D.C. Cir. 2003).

The Commerce Clause and Congressional Authority to Protect the Environment

In 1995, the Supreme Court for the first time in nearly 60 years overturned a federal law for exceeding Congress's authority under the Commerce Clause. In United States v. Lopez, 514 U.S. 549 (1995), the Court held, by a bare 5-to-4 majority, that Congress does not have the authority under the Commerce Clause to prohibit the possession of firearms in the vicinity of schools. The Court stated that Congress has the authority to regulate three broad classes of activities under the Commerce Clause: (1) "the use of the channels of interstate commerce"; (2) intrastate activities that threaten "the instrumentalities of interstate commerce, or persons or things in interstate commerce"; and (3) "activities having a substantial relation to interstate commerce." The Court added that the "proper test" for the third category is "whether the regulated activity 'substantially affects' interstate commerce." Id. at 558-559.

While it now has become routine to raise *Lopez* challenges whenever federal regulatory authority is asserted, the decision has had scant impact on environmental law. The *Lopez* majority emphasized that the Gun-Free School Zones Act had "nothing to do with 'commerce' or any sort of economic enterprise, however broadly one might define those terms." Id. at 561. Citing with approval Hodel v. Virginia Surface Mining & Reclamation Association, Inc., 452 U.S. 264 (1981), which upheld federal regulation of intrastate coal mining under the Surface Mining Control and Reclamation Act, the Chief Justice stated that "[w]here economic activity substantially affects interstate commerce, legislation regulating that activity will be sustained." 514 U.S. at 560. Significantly, the Chief Justice did not question the validity of even Wickard v. Filburn, 317 U.S. 111 (1942), which he described as "the most far reaching example of Commerce Clause authority over intrastate activity," because it "involved economic activity in a way that the possession of a gun in a school zone does not." Id. In *Wickard*, the Court upheld federal regulation of the production and consumption of home-grown wheat because of its effect on the price and market for wheat sold in interstate commerce. Because *Wickard* remains good law, *Lopez* should not significantly restrict federal authority to regulate businesses or individuals when they engage in virtually any activity that can be deemed economic. For an analysis of the likely implications of *Lopez* and *Morrison* on the environmental laws, see Schroeder, Environmental Law, Congress and the Court's New Federalism, 78 Indiana L.J. 413-457 (2003).

Lopez has generated several challenges to other federal environmental laws. A challenge to the constitutionality of the federal Superfund legislation (the Comprehensive Environmental Response, Compensation and Liability Act, also known as CERCLA) on *Lopez* grounds was rejected in United States v. Olin Corp., 107 F.3d 1506 (11th Cir. 1997). The Eleventh Circuit reversed a district court decision declaring that CERCLA exceeded Congress's authority under the Commerce Clause. The court found that regulation of intrastate, on-site waste disposal was an appropriate element of a broader attempt by Congress to protect interstate commerce from pollution. In National Association of Home Builders v. Babbitt, 130 F.3d 1041 (D.C. Cir. 1997) (pages 877-885), a divided panel of the D.C. Circuit rejected a *Lopez*-based challenge to Congress's constitutional authority to apply section 9 of the Endangered Species Act to prohibit the taking of an endangered fly that was located entirely within a small area.

Since *Lopez* had cited Wickard v. Filburn with approval, most observers assumed that cumulative effects analysis could continue to be used to meet the substantially affects test. This assumption was called into question when the Court struck down a portion of the Violence Against Women Act in Morrison v. United States, 529 U.S. 598 (2000). By the same 5-to-4 lineup as in the previous cases, the Court held that Congress exceeded the limits of its commerce power when it created a private cause of action in federal courts for victims of gender-motivated violence. Unlike the situation in *Lopez*, Congress had made extensive findings concerning the impact of gender-motivated violence on interstate commerce, including lost days of work and women refraining from taking certain kinds of jobs or from working particular hours. However, in his majority opinion for the Court, Chief Justice Rehnquist rejected these findings as based on a line of "but for" causation that would allow Congress to regulate virtually anything, including "family law and other areas of traditional state regulation since the aggregate effect of marriage, divorce, and childrearing on the national economy is undoubtedly significant." Arguing that Congress's commerce power is far broader when economic activity is regulated, the Chief Justice noted that "[g]ender-motivated crimes of violence are not, in any sense of the phrase, economic activity." While declining to hold expressly that the effects of noneconomic activity cannot be aggregated for purposes of Commerce Clause analysis, Rehnquist noted that "thus far in our Nation's history our cases have upheld Commerce Clause regulation of intrastate activity only where that activity is economic in nature." *Morrison* thus raises the prospect that Congress cannot constitutionally regulate intrastate activity that the Court deems noneconomic in character. The difficulty of distinguishing between economic and noneconomic activity is illustrated by Gibbs v. Babbitt, 214 F.3d 483 (4th Cir. 2000), where a divided panel of the Fourth Circuit upheld the authority of Congress to protect an experimental population of endangered red wolves from being harmed on private land. Construing the taking of red wolves by farmers as economic activity to protect farms, the majority concluded that the cumulative effect of individual takings would substantially affect interstate commerce. The court noted that many tourists and scientists cross state lines to view the wolves and that efforts to protect them ultimately might permit a renewed market to develop for wolf pelts. A dissenting judge argued that Congress did not have the power to regulate a handful of animals in one small region of one state because the activity had no economic character.

In March 2003 the U.S. Court of Appeals for the Fifth Circuit upheld the ESA's prohibition on taking endangered species as applied to six species of invertebrates found only in caves in two counties in Texas. The court concluded that most of the activities the ESA seeks to prohibit to protect species are commercial in nature, thus allowing Wickard v. Filburn cumulative effects aggregation for the purposes of assessing how substantial an activity's effects on interstate commerce are. It explained that the "ESA is an economic regulatory scheme; the regulation of intrastate takes of the Cave Species is an essential part of it. Therefore, Cave Species takes may be aggregated with all other ESA takes" and "such aggregation substantially affects interstate commerce." GDF Realty Investments, Ltd. v. Norton, 326 F.3d 622, 640-641 (5th Cir. 2003). In a concurring opinion, Judge Dennis noted that the ESA is "a comprehensive program for the conservation of endangered and threatened species and the ecosystems upon which they depend." As a result, he concluded that "Congress has the authority to make a rational determination to conserve such non-commercial, intrastate species as an essential or integral part of the comprehensive ESA program that regulates activities having a substantial impact on interstate commerce." 326 F.3d at 641 (Dennis, J., concurring).

In April 2003 the D.C. Circuit rejected a developer's challenge to the constitutionality of the ESA's protection of the arroyo southwestern toad, holding that the case was governed by its previous decision upholding protection of the Delhi sands flower-loving fly (NAHB v. Babbitt, pages 877-885). The court rejected the developer's argument that Morrison v. United States had undermined NAHB v. Babbitt. The court stated that the regulated activity for purposes of Commerce Clause analysis was the developer's planned commercial housing development, rather than the toad, and that the ESA was designed in large part to preserve the commercial benefits of biodiversity. Rancho Viejo, LLC. v. Norton, 323 F.3d 1062 (D.C. Cir. 2003). In a concurring opinion, Chief Judge Douglas Ginsburg sought to qualify the court's holding by questioning whether a lone hiker could be prohibited from taking an endangered species in a non-commercial context. "Our rationale is that, with respect to a species that is not an article in interstate commerce and does not affect interstate commerce, a take can be regulated if—but only if—the take itself substantially affects interstate commerce. Just as important, however, the lone hiker in the woods, or the homeowner who moves dirt in order to landscape his property, though he takes the toad, does not affect interstate commerce." 323 F.3d at 1080 (Ginsburg, C.J., concurring). In July 2003, the D.C. Circuit denied a rehearing en banc in the *Rancho Viejo* case over the dissents of two of the nine judges, 334 F.3d 1158. Judge David Sentelle argued in dissent that "protecting a toad from a land owner pinning a fence on its own property" is not the kind of commercial activity that could be regulated under Congress's power to regulate interstate commerce. Judge John Roberts, who subsequently became Chief Justice of the United States in 2005, also dissented. He argued that by focusing on "whether the challenged regulation substantially affects interstate commerce, rather than whether the activity being regulated does so," the panel had adopted a rationale inconsistent with that employed by the Fifth Circuit in the *GDF Realty* case. "The panel's approach in this case leads to the result that regulating the taking of a hapless toad that, for reasons of its own, lives its entire life in California constitutes regulating 'Commerce . . . among the several States.'" While conceding that the panel's decision was consistent with National Association of Home

Builders v. Babbitt, Roberts argued that it was inconsistent with the rationale of *GDF Realty* and that en banc review "would also afford the opportunity to consider alternative grounds for sustaining application of the Act that may be more consistent with Supreme Court precedent."

The one area in which the Court has addressed the effect of *Lopez* on environmental law, albeit somewhat obliquely, is with respect to the jurisdictional reach of the Clean Water Act. Solid Waste Agency of Northern Cook County v. U.S. Army Corps of Engineers (*SWANCC*), 531 U.S. 159 (2001), which is discussed in Chapter 6, raised the question whether Congress has the constitutional authority to regulate isolated wetlands because they are used by migratory birds. Relying on *Lopez*, a county agency argued that Congress could not require it to obtain a federal permit under section 404(a) of the Clean Water Act to fill wetlands in an abandoned sand and gravel pit. Deciding *SWANCC* by the same 5-to-4 lineup that prevailed in *Lopez*, the Court ducked the constitutional issue by construing section 404(a) narrowly. The Court found that Congress had not expressed a clear intent to apply section 404(a) to isolated wetlands visited by migratory birds, which "would result in a significant impingement of the states' traditional and primary power over lands and water use." To avoid what it described as "significant constitutional and federalism questions," the Court held that section 404(a)'s jurisdictional predicate—"waters of the United States"—did not include isolated wetlands where migratory birds are present. Thus, *SWANCC* narrows the jurisdictional reach of the Clean Water Act, while leaving the ultimate effect of *Lopez* on federal constitutional authority to protect the environment unresolved.

In June 2005, the Supreme Court decided Gonzales v. Raich, 545 U.S. 1 (2005), which upheld federal authority to prohibit the cultivation and use of marijuana for medical purposes. In an opinion by Justice Stevens that was joined by four other Justices, the Court held that Congress had a rational basis for concluding that the personal cultivation and use of marijuana would substantially affect interstate commerce because failure to regulate intrastate cultivation and use would leave a gaping hole in the comprehensive federal scheme for regulating illicit drugs. The Court majority emphasized that Congress clearly acted rationally in deciding that regulation of intrastate cultivation and use of marijuana was an essential part of the larger regulatory scheme. Justice Scalia, who did not join the majority opinion, filed a separate opinion concurring in the judgment. Scalia argued that Congress's authority to regulate intrastate activities that substantially affect interstate commerce derives from the Necessary and Proper Clause. "Where necessary to make a regulation of interstate commerce effective, Congress may regulate even those intrastate activities that do not themselves substantially affect interstate commerce," Scalia stated. One week after it decided Gonzales v. Raich, the Supreme Court denied review in the *GDF Realty* case, which it had held pending its decision concerning federal authority to prohibit cultivation and use of medical marijuana.

NOTES AND QUESTIONS

1. While no federal environmental law has been found to exceed Congress's authority to regulate activities that substantially affect interstate commerce, there has been considerable uncertainty concerning the proper rationale for upholding federal authority under the Commerce Clause to protect endangered species. One source of confusion is the uncertainty concerning

the proper focus for analyzing whether interstate commerce is substantially affected. Should the focus be on: (1) the commercial value of the resource or species sought to be protected—in which case the more endangered a species is the lesser may be the federal authority to protect it, or (2) the commercial nature of the prohibited activity that threatens the species—which would make it possible to ban commercial construction that threatens a species, but perhaps not actions by hikers or dirt-bikers, or (3) the effect of the overall regulatory program on interstate commerce—which would permit consideration of the potentially enormous economic benefits of protecting biodiversity? Which of these is the proper focus for analyzing the constitutional authority of Congress to protect the environment under the Commerce Clause?

2. Does Gonzales v. Raich, 545 U.S. 1 (2005), effectively lay to rest any doubt concerning the constitutionality of individual applications of the Endangered Species Act to noneconomic, intrastate activity because they can be viewed as necessary to preserve the integrity of a larger regulatory program that clearly satisfies Commerce Clause requirements?

3. The *Lopez* and *Morrison* decisions have spawned numerous challenges to federal regulatory authority based on the argument that Congress has exceeded the bounds of its Commerce Clause authority. Virtually all of these challenges have failed, though a few arsonists have been released from prison because of the Supreme Court's decision in Jones v. United States, 529 U.S. 848 (2000), construing the federal arson statute as not applying to residential properties. This may suggest that the Court's efforts to revive limits on federal authority have been primarily a symbolic "shot across the bow" to encourage Congress to articulate more clearly the connection between activities it seeks to regulate and interstate commerce. For a discussion of how Congress's Commerce Clause authorities can be harnessed to protect environmental values, see Robert V. Percival, "Greening" the Constitution—Harmonizing Environmental and Constitutional Values, 32 Env. L. 809 (2002).

B. APPROACHES TO REGULATION: ASSESSING THE OPTIONS

1. Regulation and Its Alternatives

Regardless of the philosophic perspective one brings to environmental policy, there is broad agreement that some form of collective action should be undertaken to address environmental problems for reasons explored in Chapter 1. While this can provide a powerful rationale for government regulation, it is important to bear in mind that collective action can assume a wide variety of forms, not all of which involve centralized action by government. Some communities are able to avoid the depletion of common resources without government involvement by using informal and private means to discourage overuse. These may include efforts to discourage outsiders from using the commons, see, e.g., To Protect Resources, Many Communities Use Informal Regulations, Wash. Post, July 17, 1989, at A2 (noting that lobster trappers avoid depletion of the lobster stock by using surreptitious violence to keep outsiders away), or community norms that regulate its use by neighbors. See Ellickson, Of

Coase and Cattle: Dispute Resolution Among Neighbors in Shasta County, 38 Stan. L. Rev. 623 (1986) (study of cattle grazing patterns). Natural resources also can be protected from environmental damage by privatizing them—by creating enforceable property rights owned by someone with an incentive to protect the resource. The Nature Conservancy, for example, has been enormously success- ful in buying environmentally significant properties in order to preserve them.

Informal, community-based controls are most likely to protect common resources where such resources are concentrated in a small area and there is strong community support for limiting exploitation. If entry into the commons is difficult to control or community support is lacking, informal controls are unlikely to work. See, e.g., Ingrassia, Overfishing Threatens to Wipe Out Species and Crush Industry, Wall St. J., July 16, 1991, at Al (failure of informal controls to halt the depletion of fish stocks in the North Atlantic); Kerr, Geothermal Tra- gedy of the Commons, 253 Science 134 (July 12, 1991) (depletion of northern California geothermal resources). Privatization is more likely to succeed in pro- tecting resources such as land (in which property rights can be easily defined) than in protecting the quality of air or water.

Thus, one should be cautious about drawing the simplistic conclusion that government regulation is always the appropriate response to the circumstances described by Hardin's "Tragedy of the Commons." One need not quarrel with the problem Hardin identifies—that truly unrestricted use of the commons will tend to deplete common resources—to appreciate the diversity of approaches, both governmental and nongovernmental, that can be used to combat it.

Kip Viscusi has identified four institutional mechanisms that may be used to control environmental risk: market forces, government regulation, liability, and social insurance. Viscusi, Toward a Diminished Role for Tort Liability: Social Insurance, Government Regulation, and Contemporary Risks to Health and Safety, 6 Yale J. on Reg. 65 (1989). These categories provide a useful frame- work for organizing our discussion of society's options for responding to envir- onmental problems when informal controls fail. Each of the institutions Viscusi identifies plays a role in environmental policy with varying emphasis depending on the nature of the problem to be addressed.

While most of the focus of environmental policy has been on government regulation, nonregulatory alternatives are becoming increasingly important complements to regulatory policy. Indeed, government now frequently uses regulation to enhance the effectiveness of the other institutional mechanisms for protecting the environment. For example, some regulatory legislation now requires information disclosure to harness the market power of informed con- sumers as a means to prevent environmental damage. Other regulations require that insurance be purchased by those engaging in activities that create environ- mental risk to ensure that the liability system can provide compensation for environmental damage. Thus, these four institutional mechanisms are best viewed not as discrete alternatives, but rather as part of a web of societal responses to environmental problems.

As illustrated in Figure 2.3, each of the four institutions has its own strengths and weaknesses as a vehicle for controlling environmental risks. Mar- ket forces can respond more quickly and flexibly than government regulation to discourage consumption of products that cause environmental damage, but markets are likely to be effective only when consumers are sufficiently well- informed about the link between a product and environmental damage to induce the marketing of less damaging substitutes. Unlike regulation, the

FIGURE 2.3
Comparison of Institutional Mechanisms for Controlling
Environmental Risks

Institutional mechanism	*Advantages*	*Drawbacks*
Market Forces	Can control risks rapidly and efficiently when consumers are well informed and have a choice of alternatives	Inadequate incentives to generate and disclose accurate information to consumers; many risks not tradeable in markets due to absence of transferable property rights
Common Law Liability	Can provide compensation to victims of environmental damage; more efficient than regulation when private parties have better information than government about nature of risks and how to control them	Inadequate incentives to control risks due to difficulties of proving causal injury and recovering for harm that is widely dispersed or in excess of source's capacity to provide compensation
Government Regulation	Can efficiently prevent environmental harm by internalizing external costs of risky activity; can be used to respond to equity concerns by altering the distribution of risks and benefits; can be used to generate better information about risks	Does not provide compensation to victims of environmental damage; difficult to tailor regulation to take into account relevant differences within classes of regulatory targets; can be counterproductive in the absence of accurate information about the nature of risks and control options
Insurance	Helps ensure that compensation will be available for victims of environmental damage	Can reduce incentives to prevent environmental damage

liability system can provide compensation to victims of environmental damage. This provides an incentive for potentially liable parties to prevent harm, the goal regulation seeks to pursue more directly by requiring or prohibiting certain conduct. The effectiveness of the liability system, both in providing compensation and deterring harm, is limited by the financial capability of parties, which can be expanded through the purchase of insurance. The availability of insurance may tend to reduce the insured's incentives to prevent harm, though premiums priced to reflect differences in the riskiness of insured activity provide some incentive for investments in preventive measures.

When consumers are well-informed and free to choose, market forces can generate remarkably effective pressure to stop practices that cause

FIGURE 2.4
Tuna Label Logo

environmental damage. For example, although the Marine Mammal Protection Act limits the number of dolphins that tuna fishers can kill each year, environmentalists had long complained that the law was poorly enforced, particularly on foreign boats. They launched a boycott of tuna that succeeded when major seafood processors announced that they would no longer purchase tuna that had been captured using fishing practices that result in harm to dolphins.

In the absence of informed consumers, seafood processors who used "dolphin-safe" methods would be placed at a competitive disadvantage because it is more expensive to catch tuna using methods that avoid harm to dolphins who swim nearby. Indeed, the company that first announced the new policy stated that tuna prices would rise by 2 to 10 cents a can because of the higher costs of purchasing tuna caught using dolphin-safe methods. Because of their higher cost, companies could not be expected to employ dolphin-safe fishing methods in the absence of consumer pressure. To attract environmentally conscious consumers, firms that purchase only dolphin-safe tuna began labeling their products as dolphin-safe (see Figure 2.4).

Monitoring compliance with corporate pledges of voluntary action can be difficult when highly visible practices are not involved. To monitor compliance with "dolphin-safe" claims, an international monitoring program inspects tuna facilities and sends monitors out with fishing vessels. Congress has enacted the Dolphin Consumer Protection Information Act, 16 U.S.C. §1385, which prohibits companies from making false "dolphin-safe" claims. Concerned that some "green advertising" has been deceptive, the Federal Trade Commission (FTC) has adopted guidelines governing the use of environmental claims in advertising and marketing. The guidelines, which apply to any claims about the environmental attributes of products or packaging, are designed to offer guidance to companies and are not enforceable regulations. 57 Fed. Reg. 36,363 (1992).

Many states have laws that regulate "green marketing" claims. California's statute is the most detailed. The law prohibits the use of terms such as "recycled," "ozone friendly," and "biodegradable" unless products meet certain specifications. For example, to be identified as "recycled," a product must contain at least 10 percent of post-consumer material. Advertisers challenged the California law on grounds that it violated their First Amendment rights. But an appellate court held that the state's interests in preventing deceptive advertising sufficed to justify the burden on commercial speech rights. Association of National Advertisers v. Lungren, 44 F.3d 726 (9th Cir. 1994).

Several countries now have government-sponsored eco-labeling programs. Germany's Blue Angel program awards environmental seals of approval to products based on life-cycle analysis of their environmental impacts. The European Union has established an ambitious eco-labeling program modeled on the German approach. Products deemed environmentally superior are identified with a flower logo containing an "E" in the flower's pistil. In the United States, private organizations, including Green Seal, Inc. and Scientific Certification Systems, have established environmental certification programs. For a critique of government involvement in eco-labeling, see Menell, Structuring a Market-Oriented Federal Eco-Information Policy, 54 Md. L. Rev. 1435 (1995).

Common law liability has been the principal alternative to government regulation for protecting the environment. Even the staunchest supporters of market mechanisms for controlling risk, who describe themselves as "free market environmentalists," emphasize the importance of liability standards for defending property rights against environmental insults. As discussed at the beginning of this chapter, the difficulties involved in proving a causal link between a particular action and damage to a particular plaintiff have limited the effectiveness of common law liability as a mechanism for controlling environmental risk. One strength of liability approaches is that they offer some prospect of compensating victims after damage is done, which the regulatory system does not. And the prospect of having to pay compensation can serve as a powerful deterrent to spur investment in efforts to prevent environmental harm.

Economists argue that the decision concerning the relative emphasis to place on liability and regulation is analogous to a choice between letting the market regulate the price of outputs and organizing a firm to control inputs into the production process. Liability rules establish the price of environmental damage (the output), while regulations seek to control the activities (inputs) that create such damage. While the former approach might seem more appealing to market enthusiasts, regulation of inputs is not as unusual as it might seem. Indeed, the very reason why firms are organized is that resort to markets has its own costs, and companies find it is cheaper to control inputs into the production process by resorting to a nonmarket substitute, the formation of firms. Calabresi, The Pointlessness of Pareto: Carrying Coase Further, 100 Yale L.J. 1211 (1991). In some circumstances it is simply more efficient to resort to nonmarket mechanisms to achieve our goals. Of course, in the environmental arena the choice is not really between free markets and government regulation. Instead, as Judge Richard Posner notes, "the choice is between two methods of public control, the common law system of privately enforced rights and the administrative system of direct public control." R.A. Posner, Economic Analysis of Law 271 (2d ed. 1977). The question of how to find the proper mix of liability and regulation is one of the fundamental challenges facing environmental policy makers.

Economist Steven Shavell argues that four factors should be considered in assessing the relative efficiency of liability and regulation as mechanisms for controlling risk. Shavell, Liability for Harm Versus Regulation of Safety, 13 J. Legal Stud. 357 (1984). The first is the *relative knowledge of private parties and the public* concerning the benefits of risky activities and the costs of reducing risks. Shavell argues that liability tends to be more efficient than regulation in controlling risk when a private actor is in a better position than the government to assess the risks of an activity and to determine the level of care to exercise. Regulation is favored when the government is in a better position than a private actor to assess risks and to determine what precautions to employ.

The second factor Shavell identifies is *the capacity of private parties to provide compensation* for the full amount of harm their actions produce. If an activity can cause more damage than the actor is capable of repaying, fear of liability will not provide sufficient incentive for private investment in an efficient level of precautions. Shavell's third consideration is the *chance that some private parties will escape suit* for the harm that they cause. Parties unlikely to be held liable for harm they produce, such as those who cause harm that is widely dispersed or difficult to trace, will not have adequate incentive to reduce risks to an efficient level in the absence of regulation.

The fourth consideration Shavell identifies is the *relative administrative costs* of the tort system and of direct regulation. Despite complaints about the administrative costs of the tort system, he notes that the liability system's administrative costs usually are incurred only if harm occurs, while the administrative costs of regulation are incurred regardless of the occurrence of harm. Applying these factors, Shavell advocates using regulation to prevent environmental harms where the government has a superior capability to assess risks and private parties are likely to escape liability for the harm their actions cause. He also suggests liability may be superior to regulation where private parties have better access to information about the true costs of prevention and neither governmental nor private parties are systematically better at estimating harm. Kaplow and Shavell, Property Rules Versus Liability Rules: An Economic Analysis, 109 Harv. L. Rev. 713, 750 (1996).

We now turn to a contemporary case study to illustrate the choices available to policy makers in determining the relative emphases to place on liability and regulation in preventing environmental damage.

Case Study: Liability, Regulation, and the Prevention and Remediation of Oil Spills

Until 1990, liability for oil spills in U.S. waters was governed by a confusing patchwork of five federal laws, three international conventions, three private international agreements, and dozens of state laws. The federal laws and international agreements were designed largely to limit the liability of shipowners in the event of a major spill, with the precise liability limits depending on where the oil came from (e.g., the Trans-Alaska Pipeline Act) or where it was spilled (e.g., the Deepwater Port Act, the Outer Continental Shelf Lands Act). The most extreme of these acts, the aptly named Limitation of Liability Act of 1851, limited liability to the value of the vessel after the casualty occurred. Courts strained to interpret this pre-Civil War relic expansively because of its potentially extreme consequences. For example, in the case of the wreck of the *Torrey Canyon*, which spilled 100,000 tons of crude oil into the English Channel in 1967, liability under this statute would have been just $50—the value of the sole lifeboat that survived the wreck.

Proposals to rationalize this patchwork of oil spill laws were bottled up in Congress for nearly two decades. This legislative gridlock finally was overcome only after the *Exxon Valdez* disaster. Consider the issues that confronted Congress in determining what mix of liability and regulation to impose when it enacted the Oil Pollution Act of 1990 (OPA 90), 33 U.S.C. §§2701-2761.

Question One: Who Should Be Held Liable for Oil Spills? Environmentalists argued that both shipowners and the oil companies that own the cargo should be held strictly liable for oil spills to deter oil companies from shipping their oil in "rust buckets" manned by untrained crews. (Because Exxon happened to be the owner of the *Exxon Valdez,* this would not have made any difference with respect to liability for that spill.) Oil companies argued that only the owners and operators of vessels should be held strictly liable for spills. The oil companies maintained that holding cargo owners liable for oil spills would be akin to making persons who ship something by Federal Express responsible for damages in the event a Federal Express cargo plane crashed. With whom do you agree? Is the Federal Express analogy an apt one? Should the nature of the cargo make any difference?

During the debate leading to enactment of OPA 90, the Royal Dutch/Shell Group announced that it would stop using its own tankers to carry oil to the United States except for an offshore terminal near Louisiana. The company explained that it took this move because a "shipowner who is involved in a pollution incident in the U.S.A., even when he has behaved properly, responsibly and without negligence, may face claims which far outweigh the potential commercial reward from such trade." Wald, Oil Companies Rethink Risk of Having Tankers, N.Y. Times, June 13, 1990, at A26. Does this reinforce the case for extending liability to cargo owners? By contrast, Arco Marine, a subsidiary of Atlantic Richfield, announced that it will ship oil only in its own ships. "We think we have better control that way, and therefore, have some control over the liability," explained Jerry Aspland, president of Arco Marine. Id. Which decision is more likely to expose the company to liability—Royal Dutch/Shell's or Arco Marine's? Which decision is likely to reduce the chances that the company's oil would be involved in a spill?

Question Two: Should Liability Be Limited?   Liability limits, such as that embodied in the Limitation of Liability Act of 1851, were designed originally to facilitate the rapid development of shipping trade by reducing the risks facing shipping companies. Critics argue that liability limits unfairly subsidize large oil companies by relieving them of responsibility for paying the full costs of the environmental damage they cause. They maintain that the liability limits that existed prior to enactment of OPA 90 were absurdly low in light of the enormous damage that can be done by a large oil spill. For example, section 311 of the Clean Water Act, 33 U.S.C. §1321, limited liability to $150 per gross ton per vessel, which would have limited the liability of the *Exxon Valdez* to between $15 and $31 million for a spill that cost billions to clean up. (The Act makes liability unlimited if the spill results from "willful negligence.")

Oil companies argue that unlimited liability creates an uninsurable risk that makes doing business extremely risky. Noting that the cost of the *Valdez* cleanup exceeded the net worth of many oil companies, the president of the American Petroleum Institute asks, "Could you afford to risk your whole company every time you move a ship?" Wald, Oil Companies Rethink Risk of Having Tankers, N.Y. Times, June 13, 1990, at A26. Is there any justification for a liability cap? If so, how would you determine at what level the cap should be set?

Question Three: Should State Oil Spill Liability Laws Be Preempted?   At the time OPA 90 was enacted, two dozen states had their own oil spill liability laws, including 19 coastal states with laws that provide for unlimited liability. Disagreement over whether Congress should preempt these laws was largely responsible for the legislative gridlock that blocked enactment of new oil spill liability legislation for nearly two decades. The oil industry and the Bush Administration argued that the United States should join the most recent international protocol, which would limit a shipowner's liability to $61 million and preempt state laws providing for greater liability. The administration argued that foreign shippers would simply stop shipping to U.S. ports if state laws providing for unlimited liability were not preempted. Opponents of preemption argued that the shippers were bluffing, noting that oil had been shipped for years to states with unlimited liability laws. Proponents of preemption responded that the *Exxon Valdez* spill has changed everything because now shippers realize that cleanup costs from a single spill could be several billion dollars. Should state laws providing for unlimited liability be preempted?

   Question Four: What Role Should Regulation Play in Prevention of Oil Spills?   Regulation seeks to prevent damage that fear of liability alone will not deter. What mix of regulation and liability should be employed to ensure that the appropriate amount of care is exercised? Liability will not be much of a deterrent for those who believe they can escape liability for their actions because of the difficulty of proving causation under the common law. Large oil spills are another matter, however, because their source is usually obvious, although precise assessments of the damage they wreak can be difficult. Professor Shavell notes that regulation is more efficient than liability for deterring accidents that cause more damage than responsible parties are capable of repaying. Except in circumstances where major multinational oil companies are the responsible parties, large oil spills certainly are capable of causing damage that exceeds the capacity of private parties to provide compensation. Indeed, arguments in favor of limited liability are premised on the notion that spills may be so expensive to clean up that it will be impossible to get adequate insurance to pay the full costs of a spill. In these circumstances, what regulations, if any, should be imposed to prevent oil spills or to minimize the damage they cause? From an economist's perspective, regulation should be used to stimulate investment in safety to the point where further investment would cost more than the reduction in damage it would produce. See, e.g., Stigler, What an Oil Spill Is Worth, Wall St. J., April 17, 1990, at A22. How would you apply this principle to regulations designed to prevent oil spills?

   Question Five: Should Oil Tankers Be Required to Have Double Hulls? Congress previously had directed the Secretary of Transportation to consider whether or not to require oil tankers operating in U.S. waters to have double hulls. The oil and shipping industries fiercely resisted a double hull requirement, and no action was taken to impose one. Proponents of a double hull requirement argued that had the *Exxon Valdez* been equipped with a double hull, far less oil would have been spilled. Shipowners argued that the cost of outfitting ships with double hulls would be prohibitive, particularly if existing ships had to be retrofitted. Understandably more enthusiastic, the Shipbuilders Council of America claimed that double bottoms could be added to the entire American fleet for less than $2 billion, less than the amount Exxon spent cleaning up the Alaskan spill. They admitted that retrofitting existing ships with double hulls would be far more expensive than installing them on new vessels. Lowey, In '88, 6 Oil Spills Every 7 Days, N.Y. Times, June 22, 1990, at A27. In the wake of the *Valdez* spill, one major oil company stunned the industry by announcing that it was ordering double hulls for all its new tankers. Should double hulls be required? If so, should they be required only on new ships, or should existing ships be retrofitted?

   After a long and bitter legislative struggle, Congress ultimately addressed these issues when it enacted OPA 90, whose provisions are outlined below.

PROVISIONS OF THE OIL POLLUTION PREVENTION, RESPONSE, LIABILITY, AND COMPENSATION ACT OF 1990 (OPA 90)

Parties Liable. OPA 90 makes owners and operators of vessels or facilities that discharge oil strictly liable for cleanup costs and damages caused by such discharges. Liability was not extended to cargo owners. §1002, 33 U.S.C. §2702.

Limitation of Liability. Section 1004 of OPA 90 increases the federal liability limit to $1,200 per gross ton, an eight-fold increase over the cap formerly provided in section 311 of the Clean Water Act. OPA 90 also creates a new $1 billion Oil Spill Liability Trust Fund, funded by a five-cent-per-barrel tax on oil, to pay for cleanup costs in excess of the liability limit. The entire $1 billion fund can be paid out for a single spill, with up to $500 million available for payments for damage to natural resources. (Section 311 of the Clean Water Act formerly had authorized a $35 million compensation fund, but the fund contained only $4 million at the time of the *Exxon Valdez* spill.)

State Liability Laws. OPA 90 expressly disavows any intent to preempt state liability requirements with respect to oil spills and removal activities. §1018, 33 U.S.C. §2718.

Regulations to Prevent Oil Spills. Congress ultimately opted to impose a double hull requirement on virtually all oil tankers operating in U.S. waters. For existing ships, the double hull requirement is to be phased in over the next 20 years on a schedule that varies based on tankers' size and age. The older and larger the ship, the sooner the requirement phases in. For example, beginning on January 1, 1995, single-hull tankers of at least 30,000 gross tons that were at least 28 years old had to be retrofitted or retired, as did smaller tankers that were at least 40 years old. Barges of less than 5,000 tons operating on inland waterways and ships that transfer their oil to smaller ships more than 60 miles offshore are exempt from the requirements.

NOTES AND QUESTIONS

1. The Oil Pollution Act of 1990 is widely viewed as an enormous success. It is credited with improving the safety of oil tankers operating in U.S. waters and its double hull requirement has now been adopted internationally. Two years after the legislation was enacted, a study by the Petroleum Industry Research Foundation found a "sea change" in the shipping industry's safety practices, including improved operational procedures and new inspection regimes. Solomon, U.S. Oil Spills Have Declined Sharply, Study Says; Suffer Federal Law Is Cited, Wall St. J., Aug. 24, 1992, at A5A. A 1998 study by the National Research Council (NRC) of the National Academy of Sciences noted

that there has been a substantial reduction in the amount of oil spilled in U.S. waters. The study concluded that this decline

> was the result of a number of actions that are in process or emerging, notably: an increased awareness among vessel owners and operators of the financial consequences of oil spills and a resulting increase in attention to policies and procedures aimed at eliminating vessel accidents; actions by port states to ensure the safety of vessels using their ports; increased efforts by ship classification societies to ensure that vessels under their classification meet or exceed existing requirements; improved audit and inspection programs by charterers and terminals; and the increased liability, financial responsibility, and other provisions of OPA 90.

National Research Council, Double-Hull Tanker Legislation: An Assessment of the Oil Pollution Act of 1990 (1998). The NRC study concluded that "complete conversion of the maritime oil transportation fleet to double hulls will significantly improve protection of the marine environment." The committee estimated that the cost of this conversion worldwide will total approximately $30 billion over a 20-year period. This represents an additional cost of approximately 10 cents per barrel of oil transported. The capital costs of double hull tankers are estimated to be 9 to 17 percent higher than single hulls' and their operating and maintenance costs are expected to be 5 to 13 percent greater.

2. As noted above, it had been argued that because OPA 90 does not extend liability to cargo owners "there is no incentive to charter safer, but perhaps more expensive tankers," Anderson, Oil Pollution Act Fouls the Regulatory Waters, Wall St. J., Feb. 20, 1992, at A14. Thus, many predicted that the market would not support investments in safer tankers and that OPA 90 could prove counterproductive. The NRC study found that there has been a decline in the percentage of oil shipped in tankers owned by oil companies, a trend it attributed to "a decision by some major oil companies to leave the tanker business, in large part to avoid high-liability exposure as well as for other economic reasons." Greenpeace International was sharply critical of the decision by Exxon Mobil in January 2001 to charter two single hulled tankers for five years each despite the availability of double hulled alternatives. A London tanker broker expressed surprise at Exxon Mobil's decision. "I find it strange that such a profitable company can't afford a double-hulled tanker," given their record profits. The broker noted that double hull tankers cost only a few thousand dollars more per day to charter. Pete Harrison, Galapagos Oil Spill Renews Tanker Safety Debate, Reuters News Wire, Jan. 26, 2001.

3. The regulatory provisions of OPA 90 have been influential throughout the world. The International Maritime Organization adopted regulations that required all new oil tankers to have double hulls or equivalent safety features beginning in July 1993. The regulations were adopted after the organization released a study showing that double hulls would prevent any oil spillage in 80 percent of cases where tankers ran aground. Hudson, Tanker Safety Plans Are Mulled as Oil Spill Threatens Shetlands, Wall St. J., Jan. 8, 1993, at A7B. The international community has generally adopted the MARPOL regulations, which also require all existing oil tankers to be double hulled (or to use some approved alternative) by no later than 2023. As double hull requirements are gradually being phased in, the percentage of tankers in the world fleet with double hulls increased from 4 percent in 1990 to 10 percent in 1994, and 30 percent in 2001. More than 50 percent of very large crude oil carriers (VLCCs) (carriers of 200,000 tons or more) now have double hulls.

4. Is the key to the success of OPA's double hull requirement the fact that it was phased in on a strict schedule over time? Contrast the success of the Oil Pollution Act's scheduled phase-in of the double hull requirement with the sorry record of the Clean Air Act's new source review program. In the Clean Air Act Congress did not specify a schedule for phasing in new pollution control technology, it simply required all new sources (or old sources making major modifications) to install the new pollution control technology. This created an incentive to continue to operate older, much dirtier sources far longer than initially anticipated and to try to disguise major modifications of those sources as routine maintenance activities that would not trigger new source review. See the discussion at page 532.

5. Despite increasing interest in nonregulatory strategies, there is wide agreement that some form of regulation is essential to prevent environmental degradation. We now turn to the question of what form that regulation should take. This has become a topic of considerable controversy in recent years as proponents of regulatory approaches that employ economic incentives harshly criticize command-and-control regulation.

2.   *The Regulatory Options*

Environmental regulations have become so complicated that the field is beginning to resemble tax law, where practitioners must be specialists to comprehend fully the meaning of regulations. Before examining any particular scheme of environmental regulation, it is useful to try to identify some essential components of regulation, even if in highly idealized form, to provide a framework for comparing alternative options.

Figure 2.5 illustrates some of the essential elements of environmental regulation. Regulation usually is undertaken in response to a perception that a problem exists that requires a collective response. How societies become aware of problems and decide to initiate regulatory action is a very important, but poorly understood, part of the process. Regulatory action often is initiated in response to highly visible incidents of harm or widely publicized problems. For example, in 1954 public concern over unidentified flying objects inspired the French wine village of Chateauneuf-du-Pape to pass an ordinance prohibiting flying saucers from landing within the village limits.* While the goal of this ordinance apparently has been achieved—no flying saucers have landed in the village—this incident illustrates why there is concern that regulation often is not directed to the problems most deserving of attention. Regulatory priorities often are established in a seemingly ad hoc fashion as agencies respond to whatever issues command public attention at the time.

Once it has been determined that a problem deserves some form of collective response, three important issues must be confronted: (1) What conduct or activity should be targeted for collective action? (2) On what basis should judgments be made about how that conduct should be altered? (3) What form of collective action should be employed in an effort to alter that conduct? These issues are not an exhaustive catalog of all the components of regulation, and

---

*This incident has been made famous by a California winery, Bonny Doon Vineyards, which has named one of its wines "Le Cigare Volant" (The Flying Cigar) because it is based on the traditional grape blend that comprises Chateauneuf-du-Pape wine.

FIGURE 2.5
The Components of Regulation

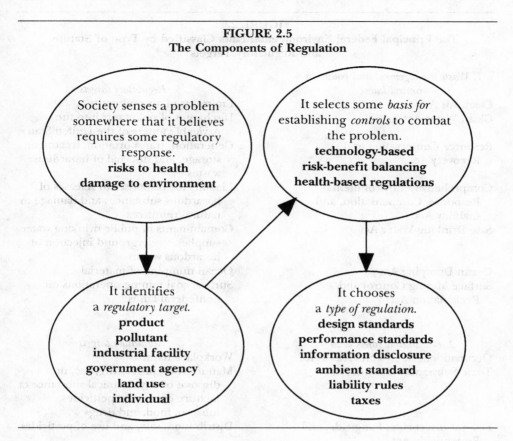

decisions concerning them need not be made in any particular sequence. But the classifications can serve as a useful starting point for study of environmental regulation by isolating some of the major points of dispute over the strengths and weaknesses of various regulatory alternatives. Thus, for present purposes we can think of an environmental regulation as a government directive given to a particular *regulatory target* based on some finding (*basis for controls*) that prohibits or requires some type of action (depending on the *type of regulation* employed).

Regulation can assume many forms, and it can be implemented through a wide array of instrumentalities. To understand how environmental regulation works it is useful to outline the range of possible options for each of the three components of regulation identified above.

A. REGULATORY TARGETS

The environmental statutes generally define what activities, products, pollutants, or entities (industrial facilities, individuals, government agencies) can be regulated. The categories listed below are all well-represented within the current universe of environmental regulation, as shown in Figure 2.6.

Products. Legislation aimed at products ranges from the very broad, such as the Toxic Substances Control Act (TSCA), under which EPA can regulate virtually any aspect of the life cycle of "any chemical substance or mixture"

FIGURE 2.6
The Principal Federal Environmental Laws Classified by Type of Statute and Regulatory Targets

1. Waste management and pollution control laws

	Regulatory targets
Clean Air Act	Emissions of air pollutants
Clean Water Act	Discharges of pollutants into the navigable waters of the United States
Resource Conservation and Recovery Act	Generation, transportation, treatment, storage, and disposal of hazardous wastes
Comprehensive Environmental Response, Compensation, and Liability Act	Liability for responses to releases of hazardous substances and damage to natural resources
Safe Drinking Water Act	Contaminants in public drinking water supplies, underground injection of hazardous wastes
Ocean Dumping Act	Ocean dumping of material
Surface Mining Control and Reclamation Act	Surface coal mining operations on nonfederal lands

2. Health and safety laws

	Regulatory targets
Occupational Safety and Health Act	Workplace hazards
Toxic Substances Control Act	Manufacture, processing, use, or disposal of any chemical substance or mixture except for pesticides, tobacco, food, and drugs
Federal Insecticide, Fungicide, and Rodenticide Act	Distribution, sale, and use of pesticides
Emergency Planning and Community Right-to-Know Act	Storage and release of hazardous substances
Hazardous Materials Transportation Act	Transportation of hazardous materials
Consumer Product Safety Act	Dangerous consumer products
Food, Drug, and Cosmetic Act	Food additives, drugs, and cosmetics
Atomic Energy Act	Atomic materials

3. Resource management laws

	Regulatory targets
National Environmental Policy Act	Major federal actions significantly affecting the environment
Endangered Species Act	Actions that threaten endangered species
Federal Land Policy and Management Act	Management of federal lands
Coastal Zone Management Act	Development in coastal zones
Multiple-Use Sustained-Yield Act	Management of national forests
Wild and Scenic Rivers Act	Wild and scenic rivers
Wilderness Act of 1964	Wilderness areas

(manufacture, processing, distribution, use, or disposal); to the rather specific, such as the Federal Insecticide, Fungicide, and Rodenticide Act (FIFRA), governing just the substances mentioned in the Act's title; to the very specific, such as the Lead-Based Paint Poisoning Prevention Act or the provisions of TSCA directed at particular substances (e.g., asbestos or PCBs).

Pollutants. Virtually all damaging residuals from industrial, commercial, and some domestic activities fall within the jurisdiction of some federal environmental statute, although it also seems that regulation never quite covers the entire universe of residuals, as illustrated by periodic outcries when a heretofore unregulated substance or activity causes widely publicized environmental damage.

Industrial Facilities. Federal regulation targeted at industrial facilities is perhaps the best known, and seemingly the easiest, form of regulation to enforce, for facilities are fewer in number than individuals. Consider the difference, for example, between the EPA's requirement that the automobile industry install emission control devices at the factory and a regulation imposing no obligation on automobile manufacturers but requiring each car owner to install a comparable device. Industrial facilities may be a more attractive target for federal regulators because enforcement against them raises none of the federalism concerns that arise when the federal government tries to coerce state and local government into action. As environmental regulation becomes more comprehensive, small businesses frequently are becoming regulatory targets (e.g., gas station owners whose underground storage tanks are now regulated by RCRA subtitle I, dry cleaners affected by both RCRA and the 1990 Clean Air Act Amendments).

Government Agencies. In some cases government entities are regulated because they own certain kinds of facilities that have become part of the pollution problem (e.g., public water supply systems, sewage treatment plants, nuclear weapons production plants, schools with asbestos-containing materials). Regulations aimed at government *qua* government are best represented by NEPA, which requires federal agencies to change their decision-making processes to incorporate environmental concerns.

Individuals. There are few extant examples of federal regulation of private individuals who are not doing business as firms. Among the important exceptions are federal prohibitions generally applicable to all persons, such as the ban on unpermitted dredging and filling of wetlands and the federal prohibition on the taking of endangered species. Regulation of individual conduct is less popular than regulation of corporations for both political and practical reasons. Early attempts by EPA to solve some of the air pollution problem by imposing transportation control plans on cities in ways that would directly affect individual driving habits were barred by Congress after vehement protests. For a strong argument that environmental law needs to rethink its aversion to regulating the behavior of individuals, who now contribute a substantial share of many pollution problems, see Michael P. Vandenbergh, From Smokestack to SUV: The Individual as Regulated Entity in the New Era of Environmental Law, 57 Vand. L. Rev. 515 (2004).

Land Uses. The major pieces of federal lands legislation establish rules governing the management of public lands. While most private land use decisions are regulated only at the local level, some of the federal environmental laws contain provisions that affect land use decisions, such as the Clean Water Act's requirements that permits be obtained before dredge-and-fill operations are conducted in wetlands.

The choice of regulatory target can be a crucial determinant of the success of a regulatory scheme. A program that seeks to regulate a few easily identified targets will be much easier to implement and to enforce than one that attempts to regulate numerous, poorly identified, or widely dispersed entities. Environmental regulation inevitably creates winners and losers based on how the costs and benefits of regulation are distributed. This has important political and practical consequences. Politically powerful regulatory targets are more likely to be successful in lobbying against environmental regulation that will affect them.

B.   BASES FOR CONTROLS

Although environmental regulations ultimately are aimed at improving environmental quality, the terms of each specific regulation are founded on methodologies that have different starting points, or bases. The environmental statutes employ three major approaches for determining how far to go in controlling a regulatory target.

Health (or Environment). Some statutes direct that controls be established on the basis of what is required to achieve a goal stated exclusively in health- or environment-related terms. For example, §109 of the Clean Air Act instructs EPA to set ambient air quality standards at a level requisite to protect human health with an "adequate margin of safety." At least the first part of that instruction—requisite to protect human health—takes EPA on a search for a level of ambient air quality based on a medical assessment of the effects of air pollution on human health. In setting that level, EPA is not supposed to examine other issues that might be germane to setting a standard, such as how much it will cost to achieve that level of control or whether technology exists to do so. The Delaney Clauses of the federal Food, Drug, and Cosmetic Act also impose controls on a purely health-related basis by directing that no food or color additives be approved if they have been found to induce cancer in man or in animals.

Technology (or Feasibility). Other statutes tie the ultimate regulatory standard to the capabilities of technology. These might be viewed as the opposite of health-based standards, because instead of asking what is needed to protect health they ask what it is possible to do. For example, under the Clean Air Act (CAA), EPA issues performance standards for new sources that are based on the best control technology that has been adequately demonstrated (CAA §111(a)(1)(C)). Other statutes employ a hybrid approach that directs that health be protected to the extent feasible. For example, the Occupational Safety and Health Act directs OSHA to ensure "to the extent feasible" that no worker "will suffer material impairment of health or functional capacity." Since it limits health-based regulation to what is feasible, this approach is best described as a feasibility-limited, health-based approach.

Balancing. While this category can capture a variety of values that may serve as bases for controls, they all share the common attribute of requiring some

FIGURE 2.7
Bases for Controls: Health-Based, Technology-Based,
and Balancing Approaches

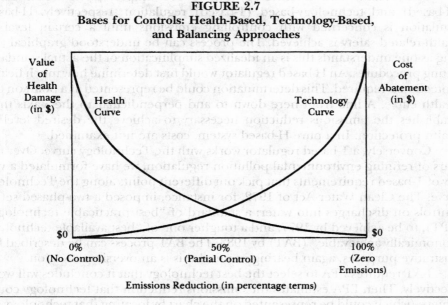

comparison of the gains of a proposed standard with its costs. For example, the Toxic Substances Control Act requires EPA to protect against "unreasonable risks" to be determined by balancing the environmental and health effects of chemicals against the economic consequences of regulation.

Consider how the three bases for controls relate to one another. Figure 2.7 supplies a rough schematic representation that facilitates comparison of how each of the three options operates when used to control a pollutant that harms human health.

The figure shows two graphs, the right-hand one of which has been flipped on its y-axis so that the two curves drawn can be shown intersecting. The line descending from left to right is the Health curve. It indicates that the adverse health effects of pollution generally decline as emissions are reduced. A line from any point on the Health curve to the left-hand y- axis identifies the monetary value of the "marginal" health benefits, those gained by further emissions controls. The shape of the curve as drawn is suggestive only; many other configurations are possible. In the toxics field, one particular aspect of the curve as drawn is, however, salient. Current federal policy assumes that there is no safe level of exposure to most toxic air pollutants. Accordingly, you cannot get to zero health effects until you get to zero emissions.

In depictions of this kind, the line emanating from the left-hand origin, labeled "Technology," is frequently designated "Costs of Abatement." Costs are determined by the underlying technologies available for abating, so it is fair to designate this the Technology curve. Each point on this curve implies an underlying technology, which produces the incremental pollution reduction at that point on the curve, and at the marginal cost indicated by extending a line to the right-hand y-axis, but the same technology need not underlie each point. A rudimentary and inexpensive technology may suffice to eliminate 80 percent of emissions, for example, but after that point this becomes ineffective and another must be selected.

The Health and Technology curves are employed in health-based (H-based) and technology-based (T-based) regulation, respectively. H-based regulation is concerned with controlling emissions until a certain level of health-related safety is achieved. The process can be understood graphically as long as one understands this is an idealized simplification of the actual standard-setting procedures. An H-based regulator would first determine how much health protection is required. This determination could be represented as a point on the Health curve. A line from here down to and perpendicular to the *x*-axis then establishes the emissions reduction necessary to achieve the desired level of health protection. In a pure H-based system, costs are not examined.

Conversely, a T-based regulator works with the Technology curve. Over the years of refining environmental pollution regulation, we have formulated a variety of T-based requirements that pick out different points along the Technology curve. The Clean Water Act of 1972, for instance, imposed a two-phased set of controls on discharges into water: a standard of "best practicable technology" (BPT), to be achieved by 1977, and a tougher one of "best available technology economically achievable" (BAT) by 1983. The BAT process can be described for illustrative purposes, again bearing in mind this is an oversimplification.

BAT requires EPA to select the best technology that it concludes will work effectively. Then EPA estimates the emissions reduction that technology could achieve (which could be represented on the chart by locating that technology on the Technology curve and finding the level of emissions reduction associated with it). Finally, the Agency determines whether bearing those costs is "economically achievable" by industry. If they are, the level of control corresponding to the chosen technology (represented, again, by extending a line through the correct point on the technology curve, perpendicular to the horizontal axis) becomes the regulatory standard; if not, EPA must proceed leftward along the technology curve until an economically achievable point is reached.

Other T-based regulations use the Technology curve in different ways, but they all share the essential feature of ignoring the Health curve, just as H-based regulations ignore the Technology curve. In contrast, regulations based on balancing approaches are concerned with both curves, particularly where they intersect. The central idea behind balancing approaches is to determine, at least approximately, where to set emission controls so that any stricter control is not justified, because the incremental costs of control are greater than the incremental value of the health gains, and any more lenient controls are likewise unjustified, because the health losses would be greater than the savings in control costs. This point can be represented as the point where the two curves intersect.

C. Types of Regulation

Regulations must be expressed in directives that are specifically understandable by the regulatory target and enforceable by subsequent government intervention, if necessary. Among the major types of regulation (not all of them germane to all the categories of regulated activity) are:

Design Standards or Technology Specifications. These specify how a certain plant, piece of machinery, or pollution control apparatus should be designed. OSHA has written numerous design standards, such as the standard of 36 inches' clearance between library shelves in law libraries. EPA writes fewer of them, although some of its performance standards become de facto technology specifications. This can occur when EPA has written a regulation on the assumption that a particular technology exists whose performance can meet the regulation. A regulatory target may prudently decide its safest course to compliance is to install that technology. Then, should the target fail to comply, it can defend by attempting to place responsibility on EPA.

Performance Standards or Emission Limits. These set an objective, or performance level, for the regulatory target to meet, without specifying how. These include emission limits that specify the rate, amount, and kind of pollutants that may be emitted from a given source over a specific period of time. EPA's new-source performance standards under the Clean Air Act and its various effluent limitations under the Clean Water Act are simply a few of the many environmental regulations that are nominally performance standards—but bear in mind that some of these routinely devolve into de facto design standards.

Ambient or Harm-based Standards. A very different type of performance standard than emissions limits, these play a significant enough role in regulatory decision making to merit separate mention. These establish a level of environmental quality to be achieved or maintained in some environment, be it a lake or stream, an airshed or an underground aquifer. As such, ambient standards are incomplete, because they are not directed at a particular regulatory target. Typically, federal ambient standards are contained in legislation that instructs the states to achieve those levels within a certain time period, but without specifying how the states are to do this—this is why ambient standards can be viewed as performance standards (whose target is the states). Of course, under New York v. United States, such legislation cannot compel states to comply, but states frequently do cooperate with such legislation. The option in case of noncompliance is for the federal government to make choices of pollution levels for individual sources, choices that states themselves prefer to make.

Product Bans or Use Limitations. These prohibit a product or activity or limit its use. They typically involve products such as chemicals, pesticides, or food additives. They also may include a land use strategy, as when the National Park Service bans autos in Yosemite National Park during certain times or bans off-road vehicles from specified wilderness areas. In occupational settings, use limits can be directed at workers.

Marketable Allowances. Economists have long advocated marketable allowances, which permit companies to buy and sell emission rights, using market forces to ensure that pollution is reduced in the least costly manner. The 1990 Amendments to the Clean Air Act embrace this approach by providing electric utilities with tradeable allowances to emit sulfur dioxide. These allowances are based on the theory that companies that can reduce emissions most cheaply will do so and sell their allowances to companies for whom such reductions would be more expensive.

Challenge Regulation or Environmental Contracting. While not widely employed in the United States yet, there is considerable interest in these tools. With challenge regulation, the government establishes a clear environmental performance target, while the regulated community designs and implements a program for achieving it. Unlike purely voluntary programs, such as EPA's 33/50 program, specific regulatory responses take effect if the target is not met. Environmental contracting, used in EPA's Project XL, involves an agreement between a government agency and a source to waive certain regulatory requirements in return for an enforceable commitment to achieve superior performance.

Pollution Taxes or Emissions Charges. Economists also have supported pollution taxes or emissions charges to internalize the social costs of activities damaging public health or the environment. One early example was the Esch-Hughes Act of 1912, which imposed a tax on white phosphorus to induce manufacturers of matches to use a safer, but more expensive, substitute. Congress in 1989 imposed an escalating tax on CFC production to accelerate both the phaseout of these chemicals and the development of substitutes. Emissions charges are based on the polluter-pays principle, to provide added incentive for emissions reductions. For example, the 1990 Clean Air Act Amendments finance a new national permit program by imposing an emissions charge of at least $25 per ton on sources needing permits.

Subsidies. Subsidies are the converse of taxes. Corporate investments beneficial to the environment can be encouraged by providing companies with public funds, tax breaks, or other benefits to subsidize such activity. In the past, subsidies frequently promoted environmentally destructive activities, such as the development of wetlands or logging on public lands. Elimination of such subsidies can be a means to promote environmental protection.

Deposit-Refund Schemes. Combining elements of both taxes and subsidies, deposit-refund schemes impose a fee that later can be refunded when a product is returned for recycling or disposal in an environmentally responsible manner. Several states have enacted "bottle bills" that impose a refundable deposit on beverage containers. Deposit-refund schemes help reduce litter and can serve as a disincentive for "midnight dumping," which taxes on waste disposal otherwise might encourage.

Liability Rules and Insurance Requirements. Some statutes strengthen common law rules imposing liability for environmental damage. CERCLA imposes strict, joint, and several liability for environmental cleanup costs and natural resource damages. Regulations issued under other statutes seek to increase the effectiveness of liability rules by requiring that facilities seeking permits to handle hazardous materials have sufficient insurance or other resources to pay for potential damage caused by their activities. In return for limiting liability for nuclear accidents, the Price Anderson Act requires utilities to purchase $150 million of private insurance per reactor and to contribute to a second-tier federal compensation fund totaling $7 billion.

Planning or Analysis Requirements. Beginning with NEPA's directive that federal agencies prepare environmental impact statements, environmental regulation occasionally requires that certain information be gathered and analyzed or that certain plans be prepared prior to undertaking environmentally significant decisions. Efforts to encourage states to control nonpoint source pollution and to improve the management of nonhazardous solid waste have relied largely on requirements for more comprehensive planning.

Information Disclosure (Labeling) Requirements. These require the regulatory target to disseminate information. Their usual objective has been to inform persons of hazards they can avoid through proper conduct, such as wearing ear protection in noisy areas or avoiding foods containing sodium when on a low-sodium diet. Disclosure requirements may be subdivided into design and performance categories. Congress has specified the precise wording of cigarette warning labels (a design standard). California's Proposition 65 requires businesses employing toxic chemicals to give "clear and reasonable warning" to exposed individuals (a performance standard). Informational regulation also is being used to generate public pressure for emissions reductions, as illustrated by the EPCRA's requirement that facilities report annual releases of toxic substances.

The choice of what mix of controls to employ is likely to be influenced by the nature of the regulatory targets and the chosen basis for control. Some types of controls are better suited for certain regulatory targets and bases for control than are others. For example, information disclosure and labeling requirements are more likely to be effective when the regulatory target is a product that informed consumers can decline to purchase than when it is widely dispersed sources of air pollution. Statutes that require that controls be based on the capabilities of a certain level of technology leave little room for choice concerning the type of control to employ. While regulators can set performance standards that reflect the capabilities of a given level of technology, regulatory targets may play it safe by simply installing the particular technology used to derive the standard. Unless regulators are extraordinarily prescient in determining appropriate levels of emissions charges or environmental taxes, they cannot ensure that pollution will be limited to any specific level, such as that required by health-based standards.

Like the choice of regulatory targets, the choice of which type of control to impose will create winners and losers because it will not affect every member of the regulated community in the same way. By requiring companies to pay for emissions they previously could discharge for free, emissions charges may transfer wealth from polluters to regulators. Yet these same polluters may be winners under a marketable permit scheme because the scheme would allow them to sell rights to pollute that previously were not transferable. Advocates of marketable permits claim this is a virtue because it creates an incentive for emission reductions beyond what otherwise would be required by regulation. Opponents note that because the source of this incentive is the ability to transfer rights to pollute, aggregate levels of pollution will not be any lower and pollution actually may increase around facilities purchasing pollution rights.

3.   Comparing Regulatory Strategies

The choice of which regulatory strategy to employ usually is a matter for Congress. The environmental statutes generally identify regulatory targets by defining the jurisdictional reach of the authorities they delegate to agencies. Congress also usually specifies the bases for control and types of regulation agencies may employ to implement the environmental laws. For example, when air pollution became politically salient, Congress chose to regulate by establishing *health-based performance standards,* the national, uniform *ambient air standards* (see sections 108 and 109 of the Clean Air Act), through an instruction *targeted at the states* instructing each state to develop a plan outlining how it would achieve those standards. When it enacted the Clean Water Act, Congress required EPA to impose *technology-based effluent standards* targeted directly at the *industrial facilities* that discharge pollutants into surface waters.

Dissatisfaction with the performance of executive agencies in implementing the environmental laws has encouraged Congress to write regulatory legislation with increasing specificity. Congress now often specifies deadlines for implementing action by agencies, and occasionally it spells out precise regulatory consequences should an agency fail to meet a deadline. For example, the 1984 amendments to the Resource Conservation and Recovery Act (RCRA) provided that the land disposal of broad classes of hazardous wastes would be banned automatically after certain deadlines unless EPA specified levels of treatment that would render such disposal safe.

Despite the increasing specificity with which Congress writes the environmental statutes, executive agencies inevitably have considerable discretion in defining the precise contours of the regulatory strategy used to implement statutory commands. Thus, both legislators and executive officials face important choices in choosing among the available regulatory options. Given the high stakes of these choices (for both the regulated community and the environment) and the rich mix of available options, it is not surprising that assessments of regulatory alternatives can be highly controversial. Indeed, dissatisfaction with existing regulatory strategies has ignited a lively debate between proponents of approaches that rely on economic incentives and defenders of the traditional command-and-control approach. Before exploring this debate, it is important to identify the various criteria available for assessing regulatory options.

Many criteria can be used to evaluate alternative regulatory strategies. Professor Thomas McGarity suggests six such criteria: (1) administrative feasibility, (2) survivability (under existing conditions of judicial and political review), (3) enforceability, (4) efficiency, (5) fairness and equity, and (6) ability to encourage technological advance. McGarity, Media-Quality, Technology, and Cost-Benefit Balancing Strategies for Health and Environmental Regulation, 46 Law & Contemp. Probs. 159 (Summer 1983). McGarity concludes that each regulatory strategy scores high under some of these six criteria but not under others. Similar conclusions were reached in an OTA report, Environmental Policy Tools: A User's Guide 23 (1995). OTA found that the best mix of regulatory tools depends on the relative importance of each criterion. For example, because efficiency is enormously important to most economists, they are harshly critical of command-and-control regulations that generally do not vary regulatory standards to take into account differences in compliance costs. Proponents of command-and-control regulation may recognize its inefficiency, but believe that it scores high on administrative simplicity, enforceability, and equity, which they may view as more important values than efficiency.

Given the pervasive uncertainty that surrounds environmental problems and the enormous diversity of regulatory targets encompassed by the environmental laws, the task confronting regulators is indeed a difficult one. The legal system seeks to formulate general rules to be applied to certain classes of activities and enterprises. Yet the diversity of regulatory targets implies that it will be virtually impossible to design regulations that take into account relevant differences between individual targets.

There are several strategies available for adjusting regulations to account for the diversity of regulated entities. Consider the following possibilities. Uniform regulations can be issued with a procedure for granting variances. Regulations can be designed to apply to a smaller class of activities or entities that have similar characteristics or regulations can rely on case-by-case decision making to permit consideration of individual circumstances. While case-by-case review can be valuable if the number of regulatory targets is small, it is likely to prove extremely cumbersome if there are large numbers of regulated firms. Another possibility is enforced self-regulation, which directs individual firms to draft their own rules, subject to some form of certification. See I. Ayres and J. Braithwaite, Responsive Regulation: Transcending the Deregulation Debate (1992). These privately written rules can then be publicly enforced, e.g., under the Clean Water Act EPA can penalize firms for violating their privately drafted oil spill prevention rules. In an effort to increase regulatory flexibility, EPA has begun experimenting with environmental contracting through its Project XL. The project gives selected companies more flexibility to meet environmental standards if they enter into contracts with EPA that promise greater reductions in pollutant discharges than would be achieved through existing standards.

The tension between flexibility and complexity and its implications for enforcement of environmental regulations is explored in the following case study.

Case Study: Oil Spill Liability and Section 311 of the Clean Water Act

The tradeoff between regulatory flexibility and complexity is well illustrated by the history of federal regulation of discharges of oil spills and hazardous substances under section 311 of the Clean Water Act. This experience, on which the strict liability provisions of the Superfund legislation (CERCLA) are modeled, began in 1970 with the precursor of today's Clean Water Act. In 1970 Congress established a national policy that "there should be no discharges of oil or hazardous substances into or upon the navigable waters of the United States." As originally written, section 311 of this Act prohibited and required the reporting of all discharges of "harmful quantities" of oil. While this sounds like a relatively straightforward prohibition, it required the Secretary of the Interior, who at the time administered the statute, to determine what constituted "harmful quantities" of oil. Given the enormous uncertainties that surround assessments of the impact of pollutants on aquatic life, any regulation that required actual proof of harm would be extremely difficult to enforce. For small discharges of oil or hazardous substances, the costs of demonstrating harm surely would exceed any likely recovery. As a result, the Secretary of the Interior opted for a simpler, but less flexible, interpretation of section 311. He promulgated what came to be known as the "sheen test" for oil discharges. Under that test, any oil spill that caused "a film or sheen upon or discoloration of the surface of the water or adjoining shorelines" was deemed a harmful quantity prohibited by the statute.

The sheen test was challenged by dischargers, who argued that section 311 required evidence that small spills actually had caused harm. In United States v. Boyd, 491 F.2d 1163 (9th Cir. 1973), the Ninth Circuit held that the "harmful quantities" language in the statute meant that de minimis discharges were not illegal if they were not actually harmful. As a result, defendants charged with spilling oil could contest whether the discharges actually had caused harm. In a subsequent case, United States v. Chevron Oil Co., 583 F.2d 1357 (5th Cir. 1978), the Fifth Circuit held that the sheen test was only a rebuttable presumption of harm to the environment. The court emphasized that Congress had not chosen to prohibit *all* discharges of oil, but rather only discharges in "harmful quantities." Under the Fifth Circuit's approach, defendants were free to contest whether their discharges had caused harm, but they bore the burden of showing that the discharge had not actually been harmful.

In 1978, Congress amended section 311 to provide that environmental officials could prohibit any discharge of oil or hazardous substances that they found "may be harmful to the public health or welfare of the United States." After extensively considering alternative approaches for determining what discharges may be harmful, EPA in 1987 again promulgated the sheen test. The sheen test again came under judicial scrutiny when challenged by defendants charged with releasing oil. After the Coast Guard assessed civil penalties ranging from $250 to $1,000 against Chevron for 12 discharges of oil that created oil sheens, the company successfully argued in court that the discharges were not illegal under section 311 because any impact of the spills on the ecosystem was de minimis. On appeal, the Fifth Circuit reversed. The court held that the 1978 amendments had authorized EPA to prohibit spills that "may be harmful" regardless of whether or not they caused actual harm. In holding that spills that violated the sheen test violated the statute regardless of whether or not they caused harm, the court explained that EPA could adopt a less flexible approach to regulation in order to avoid the administrative expense of a more complicated inquiry: "In sum, the agency may both proscribe incipient injury and measure its presence by a test that avoids elaborated inquiry. While it is apparent that such an approach sometimes overregulates, it is equally apparent that this imprecision is a trade-off for the administrative burden of case-by-case proceedings." Chevron U.S.A., Inc. v. Yost, 919 F.2d 27 (5th Cir. 1990).

NOTES AND QUESTIONS

1. Why do you suppose that Congress did not simply prohibit *all* discharges of oil in section 311? What was to be gained by prohibiting only discharges in harmful quantities? Does the use of the sheen test effectively sacrifice these ends by prohibiting even discharges that may not be harmful?

2. If you determined that only discharges of oil or hazardous substances that are harmful should be prohibited, who should bear the burden of proof concerning the impact of the discharge: the discharger or enforcement officials? What effect is the allocation of the burden of proof likely to have on the enforceability of the prohibition?

3. Should it matter whether the discharger believed that the discharge would be harmful? Criminal prohibitions generally require some element of intentional conduct, though it need not necessarily be an intent to cause harm to the environment. By contrast, strict liability provisions impose liability without regard to fault. What impact would an intent requirement have on incentives to prevent discharges? What impact would a strict liability standard have on such incentives?

4. In April 1994, the Coast Guard announced a pilot program to issue "tickets" to dischargers who spill less than 100 gallons of oil. The tickets can be served on violators immediately by Coast Guard officials. The alleged violators then have the option of paying the fine within 30 days or seeking an administrative hearing to contest the charges. 59 Fed. Reg. 16,558 (1994).

Assessing Regulatory Strategies and Their Effect on Technological Innovation

Each regulatory strategy places its own informational demands on regulators and each has its own practical and political consequences. Uniform, technology-based controls initially were thought to be easier to develop and monitor. Thus, it is not surprising that some form of nationally uniform, technology-based controls are an essential feature of the regulatory approach employed in the Clean Air Act, the Clean Water Act, and RCRA. Risk-balancing and health-based standards were thought to be more difficult to implement and administer because they require considerable information about health effects and economic impacts that are difficult to assess with precision.

Critics of technology-based approaches have emphasized their inefficiencies. See, e.g., Ackerman & Stewart, Reforming Environmental Law: The Democratic Case for Market Incentives, 13 Colum. J. Envtl. L. 171, 173-175 (1988). Others disagree. Howard Latin argues that proposals for more flexible regulatory approaches are based on "an excessive preoccupation with theoretical efficiency" that ignores "actual decisionmaking costs and implementation constraints." Latin, Ideal Versus Real Regulatory Efficiency: Implementation of Uniform Standards and "Fine-Tuning" Regulatory Reforms, 37 Stan. L. Rev. 1267, 1270 (1985). He maintains that because "[a]ny system for environmental regulation must function despite the presence of pervasive uncertainty, high decision-making costs, and manipulative strategic behavior resulting from conflicting private and public interests," the "indisputable fact that uniform standards are inefficient does not prove that any other approach would necessarily perform better."

Professor Carol Rose has proposed a hierarchy of efficient management strategies for common resources. She argues that the strategy with the least net costs depends upon the level of pressure on the resources. Rose, Rethinking Environmental Controls: Management Strategies for Common Resources, 1991 Duke L.J. 1. When there is little pressure on congestible resources, no regulation is needed (what she calls a DO NOTHING strategy, as illustrated in Figure 2.8).

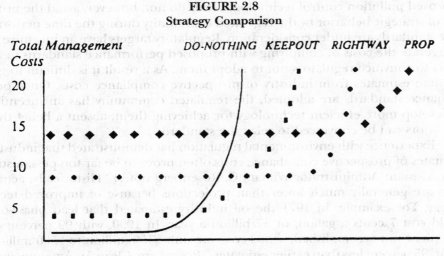

FIGURE 2.8
Strategy Comparison

Pressure on Resource
Source: 1991 Duke L.J. 1, 24.

As resource use increases, a zoning approach that excludes certain uses from certain areas (KEEPOUT) has the least net costs. At still greater levels of pressure on common resources, regulations that prescribe the ways in which the resources can be used (RIGHTWAY) have the lowest management costs. Finally, at very high levels of pressure on congestible resources, a strategy that creates transferable property rights (PROP) that will promote their efficient use has the least net costs.

Professor Rose argues that environmental policy is currently making a partial transition from RIGHTWAY to PROP in the air pollution area. Implicit in her model is the notion that the outcome of the debate over the future of regulatory policy should turn on how far to the right we are along the horizontal axis of pressure on resources in her model. If her hypothesis about the relative shape of the cost curves is accurate, then critics of technology-based regulation have the better of the argument if resource pressures have grown beyond the point where RIGHTWAY has greater costs than PROP, while its defenders are right if we are to the left of this point, where RIGHTWAY has lower costs than PROP. Professor Rose also notes that much of the criticism of PROP is based on concern for its distributional impact and fears that it may sacrifice some of the moral force of RIGHTWAY by promoting the notion of "rights to pollute." While she suggests some approaches for addressing these problems, Professor Rose emphasizes that more attention must be paid to the norm-formation impact of environmental management strategies.

Our discussion so far has assumed that the balance of costs and benefits represents an inflexible tradeoff: Greater environmental protection can only be achieved at the expense of greater costs. However, costs are not in fact fixed but reflect the technology available for pollution control. Improving technology can increase the level of reductions achievable *and* lower costs. Technological innovation that expands the menu, increases the capability, or reduces the cost of available pollution control technology is commonly viewed as a desirable goal. The impact of regulation on technological innovation and the potential for regulation to stimulate such innovation are crucial issues that must be considered in designing any regulatory scheme.

Regulations that establish performance standards without specifying the technology to be used to meet them preserve incentives for the development of improved pollution control technology. They do not, however, avoid the problem of strategic behavior by the regulated community during the time performance standards are under consideration. Regulatory targets have an incentive to exaggerate the costs of complying with proposed performance standards in an effort to convince regulators not to adopt them. As a result it is difficult to get accurate estimates from industry of prospective compliance costs. Once performance standards are adopted, the regulated community has an incentive to develop more efficient technology for achieving them, absent a belief that regulators can be convinced to relax the standards.

Experience with environmental regulation has demonstrated that industry estimates of prospective compliance costs often prove to be far too pessimistic. EPA Assistant Administrator William G. Rosenberg notes: "Historically, actual costs are generally much lower than projections because of improved technology. For example, in 1971 the oil industry estimated that lead phase-out would cost 7 cents a gallon, or $7 billion a year. In 1990, with 99 percent of lead phase-out accomplished, actual costs are only $150 million to $500 million a year, 95 percent less than earlier estimates." Rosenberg, Clean Air Amendments, 251 Science 1546, 1547 (1991).

Industry estimates of the costs of complying with the acid rain control program in the 1990 Clean Air Act Amendments quickly proved to be substantially overstated. By 1992, EPA had reduced its cost estimate of the acid rain control program to $3 billion per year from the $4 to $5 billion it employed when the legislation was adopted. EPA then estimated that emissions allowances would trade for only $275 per ton instead of its previous estimates of $500 to $750 per ton and industry estimates of as much as $1,500 per ton. EPA Issues Final Rules for Utilities on Acid Rain, Wall St. J., Oct. 27, 1992, at A18. In fact, allowances have sold for far less, at prices ranging from $75 to $225 per ton between 1997 and 1999.

Several studies have confirmed that pollution control regulations tend to be substantially less costly than expected before regulations are adopted. One reason for this phenomenon is that new technologies that lower control costs are developed in response to regulation. Goodstein & Hodges, Polluted Data, 35 The American Prospect 64 (1997). Another factor may be that regulations do not achieve as much pollution control as expected. See Harrington, Morgenstern & Nelson, Predicting the Costs of Environmental Regulations, 41 Environment 10 (Sept. 1999).

The question of how regulatory policy best can incorporate incentives for technological innovation is becoming an increasingly important issue. See Miller, Environmental Regulation, Technological Innovation, and Technology-Forcing, 10 Nat. Res. & Env. 64 (Fall 1995). The Clinton administration actively promoted the development of environmental technologies. EPA's Golden Carrot program, funded by a consortium of electric utilities, offered $30 million to the appliance manufacturer who won a contest to develop a refrigerator 50 percent more efficient than 1990 models. The program was funded by contributions from electric utilities based upon calculations of the financial savings they would enjoy by avoiding costly investments in new power plants due to the efficiency gains the refrigerator would provide. In June 1992, the Whirlpool Corporation won the competition, which generated 14 competing proposals. The product Whirlpool began marketing in 1994 is the most energy-efficient refrigerator in the world. C. Moore & A. Miller, Green Gold 207-208 (1994).

Based on analysis of the development of technology to control sulfur dioxide pollution, Margaret R. Taylor, Edward L. Rubin, and David A. Hounshell argue that regulation and the anticipation of regulation played a particularly important role in stimulating technological innovation. Regulation as the Mother of Innovation: The Case of SO_2 Control, 27 Law & Policy 348 (2005). They demonstrate that there was a huge surge in patent applications for new pollution control technology at the time of enactment of the Clean Air Act in 1970 and whenever other measures to strengthen regulation were imminent.

NOTES AND QUESTIONS

1. Technology has proved to be remarkably adaptable once regulation has created the proper incentives. The chemical industry publicly denied the availability of reasonable substitutes for chlorofluorocarbons (CFCs), chemicals that damage the ozone layer, until regulation became imminent after the discovery of the Antarctic ozone hole and the development of an international consensus that CFCs should be phased out. Since regulations were announced, substitutes

have become available at a remarkable rate. Miller, Policy Responses to Global Warming, 14 So. Ill. L. Rev. 187 (1990).

2. The economic and political risks are such that Congress has only rarely chosen to threaten the shutdown of an entire industry should emissions standards prove unachievable. The issue is more often what form of regulation is most conducive to innovation. In particular, fixed emissions standards based on current assessments of technology are widely faulted for the absence of incentives for further innovation. An industry regulated by a "best available technology" standard may rightly question the benefits of research on new pollution control methods knowing that the costs could increase. Moreover, once the required level of emissions reduction has been achieved, there is no remaining incentive for efforts to go still further. See Dudek & Palmisano, Emissions Trading: Why Is This Thoroughbred Hobbled?, 13 Colum. J. Envtl. L. 217, 234-236 (1988).

3. Is there any way to judge the innovation potential in particular industries in advance of technology-forcing requirements? Some technologies appear to be mature, in the sense that they have been in use for decades and improvements over time might readily be expected to approach theoretical limits. Consider, for example, the relative potential for improving computers and the gasoline combustion engine. On the other hand, technology forcing may lead to a necessary examination of alternative fuels that offer significant opportunities for improvement. See, e.g., The Greening of Detroit, Business Week, April 8, 1991, at 54-60. Another example is steelmaking, an industry that goes back more than 200 years. Dramatic reductions have been achieved in the energy requirements and emissions associated with conventional steelmaking. Nevertheless, much more advanced methods of steelmaking are now being developed that would produce better-quality steel using lower-quality (and less expensive) coal, while also reducing energy needs and emissions. J. Goldemberg, Energy for a Sustainable World 67-69 (1987).

4. Advocates of increased reliance on economic incentive approaches to regulation argue that they are better suited for stimulating technological innovation than the "game of chicken" approach Congress employed in dealing with the auto industry in the early 1970s. Pollution taxes and emissions trading schemes create a continuous incentive for innovations that reduce emissions while giving companies flexibility to meet emissions limits however they can, including process changes and other alternatives to conventional end-of-pipe technology. Others are more skeptical of the impact of economic incentive approaches on technological innovation. They argue that such approaches are best suited for stimulating cost savings rather than improvements in pollution control. Should this matter? A study of emissions trading under the Clean Air Act suggests that flexibility has led to innovation in the form of cost-saving modifications as opposed to new hardware or exotic technologies. Dudek & Palmisano, supra at 235-236.

5. While renewed interest in economic incentive approaches to environmental regulation makes them appear to be a recent invention, they actually have been the subject of high-level debate from the start of the federalization of environmental law. In 1965 the Economic Pollution Panel of the President's Science Advisory Committee discussed pollution taxes in their report Restoring the Quality of the Environment. In 1966, the President's Council of Economic Advisers (CEA) proposed the use of effluent charges to create incentives for dischargers to reduce pollution, with the revenue raised to be used to pay for municipal treatment plants. CEA, Economic Report of the President, 1966, at

FIGURE 2.9
Comparison of Uniform, National Regulatory Approaches with
Incentive-based Approaches to Regulation

	Pros	Cons
1. *Uniform, National Regulation*	Arguably easier to establish	Inefficient since ignores differences in marginal control costs
	Assures protection of health	Provides no incentive to reduce emissions beyond maximum permitted
	Precludes relocation to avoid controls	
2. *Effluent Charges*	Creates incentives for dischargers to reduce emissions in the most cost-effective manner	No guarantee sufficiently protective levels of control will be achieved
	Provides funds to cover social costs of pollution	Difficult to determine socially efficient level of such charges
		Increases cost of production
		Creates incentive for midnight dumping
3. *Marketable Permits*	Creates incentives for dischargers to reduce emissions in the most cost-effective manner	Can result in less equitable distributions of pollutants
	Overall allowable level of pollution can be determined in advance by allocation of permit rights	Some believe it is unfair to permit polluters to profit from sale of rights to pollute
4. *Deposit-Refund Schemes*	Reduces incentive for midnight dumping	Administrative costs of collecting and refunding deposits reduce attractiveness
5. *Provision of Subsidies for Investments in Pollution Controls*	Assists small and less profitable firms in bearing costs of compliance	Penalizes firms that already have invested in compliance technology
		Redistributes income from taxpayers to polluting activities

Source: Adapted from Congressional Research Service, Pollution Taxes, Effluent Charges and Other Alternatives for Pollution Control 2-8 (May 1977).

124 (1966). In his Environmental Message of 1971, President Nixon proposed that Congress impose a charge on sulfur dioxide emissions, and he pushed for a stiff tax on gasoline lead additives to encourage their rapid phaseout. These proposals were not given serious consideration by Congress.

6. One of the most important reasons why Congress did not quickly embrace incentive-based approaches to regulation was its awareness that a shift to such policies would create losers as well as winners. As Figure 2.9 indicates, each of the principal incentive-based approaches has advantages and drawbacks that reflect, at least in part, how they alter the distribution of the costs and benefits of regulation. In addition, a study of congressional staff discovered that neither proponents nor opponents of effluent charges really understood the theory behind them. S. Kelman, What Price Incentives? Economists and the Environment 100-101 (1981).

7. A report issued by the World Resources Institute (WRI) estimates that a strategy of shifting the revenue burden of taxation from economic "goods" to environmental "bads" could raise between $100 to $180 billion per year. "Congestion tolls on urban highways could generate $40 to $100 billion, carbon taxes would yield $30 to $50 billion, and solid-waste charges could raise another $5 to $10 billion." R. Repetto, R. Dower, R. Jenkins & J. Geoghegan, Green Fees: How a Tax Shift Can Work for the Environment and the Economy 11 (1992). These additional revenues could permit the government to reduce marginal tax rates on economically productive activities like labor, producing $45 to $80 billion in net economic benefits annually. Id. The WRI estimated that effluent charges, charges on environmentally damaging activities or products, and the reduction of tax benefits and subsidies for resource exploitation could generate nearly $40 billion in extra revenue each year. Id. at 83.

C. THE REGULATORY PROCESS

The regulatory process is the arena in which law is translated into policy. This occurs in large part through the actions of administrative agencies operating under the watchful eye of the judiciary. By increasing the authority of administrative agencies, regulatory legislation has helped transform "the system of shared powers created by the constitution" into "a system of shared influence over bureaucratic decision-making." Strauss, Legislative Theory and the Rule of Law, 89 Colum. L. Rev. 427, 428 (1989), quoting M. McCubbins & T. Sullivan eds., Congress: Structure and Policy 403 (1987). A wide range of interests seek to influence how agencies implement the environmental statutes, including environmental groups, regulated industries, powerful congressional committees, and the Executive Office of the President. The umpire lurking in the background is the judiciary, whose intervention routinely is sought by parties disappointed by agency decisions.

1. Law, Policy, and Agency Decision Making

Whenever Congress decides to confront an environmental issue, its options can be visualized as a "policy space," in the parlance of our policy sciences colleagues. Each point within that space represents a discrete, defined program for action, including the action of doing nothing. The statutes Congress enacts seldom point to a single unique location within the policy space, however. Instead, Congress identifies a target area, a subset of all the available options, and instructs an administrative agency to implement the statute by resolving all the remaining issues necessary to produce a definitive governmental decision.

To translate the environmental laws into regulations, administrative agencies must choose a regulatory alternative within the policy space established by law and develop, propose, and promulgate regulations. The Administrative Procedure Act and the environmental laws under whose authority the agency acts outline the ground rules for agency action, but agencies generally have considerable discretion over both the substance of regulatory policy and the procedures used to formulate it. How agency discretion is exercised within the policy space identified by the environmental statutes determines the precise contours of environmental policy and, presumably, the level of environmental protection the laws actually provide. Thus, study of the rulemaking process and agency decision making is critical to understanding environmental policy.

Dissatisfied with administrative implementation of the environmental laws, Congress has incorporated increasingly detailed regulatory directives into the environmental laws, coupled with provisions designed to force agencies to act. The classic agency-forcing device is a provision that authorizes a citizen suit against agency officials who fail to take certain action.

Virtually all of the major federal environmental statutes authorize citizens to bring action-forcing litigation against EPA when the EPA administrator has failed to perform a nondiscretionary duty. Most citizen suit provisions are patterned on section 304(a)(2) of the Clean Air Act, which authorizes "any person" to sue the administrator of EPA "where there is alleged a failure of the Administrator to perform any act or duty under this chapter which is not discretionary with the Administrator." 42 U.S.C. §7604(a)(2). Virtually identical provisions are contained in the Clean Water Act (§504(a)(2)), 33 U.S.C. §1365, the Resource Conservation and Recovery Act (§7002(a)(2)), 42 U.S.C. §6972(a)(2), the Safe Drinking Water Act (§1449), 42 U.S.C. §300j-8, the Toxic Substances Control Act (§20(a)(2)), 15 U.S.C. §2619, the Comprehensive Environmental Response, Compensation, and Liability Act (§310), 42 U.S.C. §9654, and other statutes. Because these statutes also authorize court awards of attorneys' fees to prevailing parties, plaintiffs can recover their legal costs when they successfully sue officials who fail to act.

During the 1980s Congress often amended the environmental statutes to require agencies to issue regulations by certain deadlines. Agencies who missed these deadlines usually became the targets of citizen suits, called "deadline litigation," alleging that the agency had failed to perform a nondiscretionary duty. While such lawsuits are not the only avenue for persuading agencies to initiate regulatory proceedings, they have been one of the most effective ones. The Administrative Procedure Act and most federal environmental laws require agencies to give citizens the right to petition for the initiation of rulemaking proceedings. See 5 U.S.C. §553(e). A study performed for the Administrative Conference of the United States found that citizen petitions were used relatively infrequently. Most administrative practitioners indicated that there "were more effective ways to influence agency action, such as informal contacts or litigation, and that they would be loath to file a petition for rulemaking because of the delay they expect in the final disposition of their requests." Luneberg,

Petitions for Rulemaking: Federal Agency Practice and Recommendations for Improvement 140 (1986).

Although agencies generally are not required to respond to citizen petitions by a certain date, one unusual exception to this rule is provided by section 21 of the Toxic Substances Control Act, 15 U.S.C. §2620. Section 21 of TSCA requires EPA within 90 days to grant or deny citizen petitions to initiate rulemaking actions under TSCA to control chemicals that may present "unreasonable risks" to public health or the environment. If EPA fails to act on such a petition within 90 days, or denies the petition, the petitioners may file suit in federal district court seeking de novo review of such failure or denial. If a court determines that the action sought by the petition meets the requisite statutory standard, "the court shall order the [EPA] Administrator to initiate the action requested by the petitioner." 15 U.S.C. §2620(b)(4)(B). The combination of a tight deadline for EPA to respond to petitions and a cause of action to challenge petition denials in court provides petitioners with a potentially significant tool to stimulate agency action.

2.   *Rulemaking Procedures*

In the late 1960s, when the fledgling environmental movement launched an assault on the use of DDT, a formal adjudicatory hearing was held to consider cancelling the registration of DDT. The hearing took more than 7 months and produced more than 9,000 pages of testimony from 125 expert witnesses. After environmental concerns stimulated an avalanche of federal environmental legislation in the early 1970s, agencies relied increasingly on informal rulemaking proceedings to make regulatory decisions. Today most environmental regulations are promulgated through informal rulemaking, although pesticide cancellation proceedings under FIFRA still involve formal adjudicatory hearings.

The procedural requirements for informal rulemaking are relatively straightforward. Informal rulemaking proceedings are governed by section 4 of the Administrative Procedure Act (APA), 5 U.S.C. §553, which requires that agencies provide (1) public notice in the Federal Register of proposed rulemaking actions, (2) an opportunity for the public to submit written comments, and (3) publication of final rules in the Federal Register accompanied by a concise statement of their basis and purpose. Agencies are permitted to formulate rules through informal rulemaking unless an enabling statute requires that hearings be conducted on the record.

Agencies undertake to develop rulemaking proposals prior to issuing a notice of proposed rulemaking. In some cases agencies may publish an advance notice of proposed rulemaking (ANPR) to solicit input from the public when the agency need not act quickly or to defuse pressure for faster action by indicating that the agency is considering the issue.

For EPA rulemaking proceedings, draft rulemaking documents usually are prepared by a work group of EPA staff who represent offices likely to be affected by the initiative. Draft notices of proposed rulemaking and supporting documents, which may be prepared with the help of outside consulting firms in more complex rulemakings, generally are reviewed by a steering committee composed of representatives from the major EPA offices. The final step in EPA's internal review procedures is "red border" review by top-level management and the EPA administrator.

Some of the federal environmental laws specify additional rulemaking procedures, but these procedures generally are consistent with those of the informal rulemaking model. For example, section 307(d) of the Clean Air Act, 42 U.S.C. §7607(d), provides extensive requirements for maintenance of a rulemaking docket by EPA for rulemakings under the Clean Air Act. It also specifies a standard for judicial review of agency action, which generally tracks the judicial review provisions of APA section 706 (although it provides that courts may invalidate rules for procedural errors only if the errors were so serious that "there is a substantial likelihood that the rule would have been significantly changed if such errors had not been made").

Other environmental statutes require that public hearings be held before certain major regulatory decisions are made (see, e.g., §§3001(a) and 3004(a) of RCRA, 42 U.S.C. §§6921(a) and §6924(a), which also require "consultation with appropriate Federal and State agencies"). Section 6(c) of the Toxic Substances Control Act, 15 U.S.C. §2605(c), specifies detailed procedures for informal rule making under section 6(a) of TSCA. It requires that EPA provide an opportunity for oral testimony and authorizes the submission of rebuttal testimony and cross-examination if the EPA administrator determines that it is necessary to resolve disputed issues of material fact. The Occupational Safety and Health Act also requires OSHA to hold a public hearing if written objections are filed to a proposed rule by any interested parties, and it gives such parties the right to conduct cross-examination when it conducts hearings on proposed rules.

THE REGULATORY PROCESS: A PATHFINDER

The Administrative Procedure Act (APA), 5 U.S.C. §§551 et seq., establishes the basic procedural requirements agencies must follow in conducting informal rulemaking. Its basic requirements—that agencies provide public notice and an opportunity to comment prior to promulgating regulations—are implemented through notices published daily in the Federal Register describing agency actions and how to comment on them. The Federal Register can be accessed online at *www.archives.gov/federal_register/*. Public comments and background documentation for agency actions are usually kept in rulemaking dockets referenced in the Federal Register notices. Information concerning EPA's rule-making dockets is available online at *www.epa.gov/epahome/dockets.htm* and comments on rules proposed by any federal agency may be submitted electronically at *www.regulations.gov*.

Some environmental statutes supplement the APA by specifying additional procedures agencies must follow before taking certain actions. See, e.g., §6(c) of TSCA or §307(d) of the Clean Air Act. The Negotiated Rulemaking Act of 1990 generally codifies agency practices for conducting negotiated rulemaking. The Freedom of Information Act, 5 U.S.C. §552, provides an important tool for obtaining information from agencies that may assist citizens in participating in rulemaking proceedings.

Other statutes require agencies to consider certain factors when undertaking rulemaking. The Regulatory Flexibility Act (RFA) 5 U.S.C. §601, requires agencies to consider the impact of regulations on small businesses, and the Small Business Regulatory Enforcement Fairness Act (SBREFA) authorizes judicial review of an agency's compliance with the RFA.

Executive Order 12,866 requires federal agencies to submit significant rulemaking actions to OMB's Office of Information and Regulatory Affairs (OIRA) for review prior to publication in the Federal Register. Each agency publishes a summary of its rulemaking plans and a description of the status of existing rulemakings in an Agenda of Regulatory and Deregulatory Actions that appears in the Federal Register at the end of April and October. See, e.g., 67 Fed. Reg. 33,724 (2002).

A useful introduction to the regulatory process that highlights important legal and procedural issues is Jeffrey S. Lubbers, A Guide to Federal Agency Rulemaking (3d ed. 1998). The Administrative Law Review, published by the ABA's Section of Administrative Law and Regulatory Practice, features articles on the regulatory process and an annual review of administrative law cases.

Despite the relatively minimal procedural requirements imposed by the APA, it has become enormously difficult for regulatory agencies to issue regulations through informal rulemaking. Agencies face several constraints on their ability to complete complex rulemakings efficiently and expeditiously. These include budgets that rarely provide sufficient resources to conduct more than a handful of major rulemakings in any given year, frequent turnover of technical staff, and the difficulty of obtaining critical information that typically is more readily available to the regulated community than to the regulators. As a result of these and other constraints, "[n]o health and safety agency has been able to promulgate regulations for more than three controversial chemicals in any given year." Shapiro & McGarity, Reorienting OSHA: Regulatory Alternatives and Legislative Reform, 6 Yale J. on Reg. 1, 6-7 (1989).

Although the procedural requirements for informal rulemaking remain remarkably simple, fear of judicial reversal has caused agencies to bend over backwards to supply detailed justifications for their actions. For example, Thomas McGarity notes that when EPA issued the initial national ambient air quality standards in 1971, the APA-required "concise general statement of basis and purpose" for the rules occupied a single page in the Federal Register. By 1987, "revision of a single primary standard consumed 36 pages in the Federal Register and was supported by a 100-plus-page staff paper, a lengthy Regulatory Impact Analysis that cost the agency millions of dollars, and a multi-volume criteria document." Id. at 1387. T. McGarity, Some Thoughts on "Deossifying" the Rulemaking Process, 1992 Duke L.J. 1385, 1386.

The seemingly innocuous requirement of a concise statement of basis and purpose "has blossomed into a requirement that agencies provide a 'reasoned explanation' for rules and that they rationally respond to outside comments passing a 'threshold requirement of materiality.'" Id. at 1400. As McGarity notes, while these additional analytic requirements are "not especially burdensome in theory," in practice they "invite abuse by regulatees who hire consultants and lawyers to pick apart the agencies' preambles and background documents and launch blunderbuss attacks on every detail of the legal and technical bases for the agencies' rules." Id. As a result, agencies seeking to avoid judicial reversals must go to great lengths to provide exceedingly thorough responses to comments.

Agencies also must comply with requirements for presidential and congressional review of rulemaking actions, as discussed below. These include the provisions of Executive Order 12,866, which specifies that significant regulatory actions must be reviewed by the Office of Management and Budget before they can be published in the Federal Register, and the Small Business Regulatory Enforcement Fairness Act (SBREFA), Pub. L. 104-121. SBREFA requires EPA and OSHA to give representatives of small businesses an opportunity to review and comment on certain rules that may affect them before the rules are even proposed publicly. SBREFA also authorizes judicial review of agency compliance with the Regulatory Flexibility Act (RFA), 5 U.S.C. §§601 et seq. The RFA requires agencies to prepare "regulatory flexibility analyses" when proposed or final rules are issued that "have a significant economic impact on a substantial number of small entities." Modeled on NEPA's environmental impact statement requirement, regulatory flexibility analyses require EPA to analyze alternatives to any regulatory action likely to have a substantial effect on small entities. SBREFA also requires that all rules issued by federal agencies be sent first to Congress for review before taking effect. The legislation creates special fast-track procedures for Congress to enact a resolution disapproving the rules. This provision, known as the Congressional Review Act, 5 U.S.C. §§801 to 808, provides that if Congress enacts a joint resolution disapproving a regulation, the regulation shall not take effect or continue in effect. If a regulation is disapproved by Congress, the Act prohibits the agency that issued it from issuing any new rule that is "substantially the same as" the disapproved rule unless specifically authorized by subsequent legislation. 5 U.S.C. §801(b)(2).

In Immigration and Naturalization Service v. Chadha, 462 U.S. 919 (1983), the Supreme Court held that a legislative veto of regulations is unconstitutional because it bypassed the President's role in approving or disapproving legislation. The Congressional Review Act avoids this constitutional problem by providing that joint resolutions of disapproval must be signed by the President or enacted over his veto. In March 2001 Congress used the Congressional Review Act for the first time to repeal a regulation. The regulation repealed by Congress was the Occupational Health and Safety Administration's ergonomics standard to protect workers from repetitive stress injuries. The regulation, which had been under development by OSHA for a decade, finally had been issued in the closing days of the Clinton administration. OSHA expected that the rule would prevent 500,000 worker injuries per year from carpal tunnel syndrome, back strains, and other ailments. OSHA acknowledged that the rule would be expensive for businesses, estimating that it ultimately could cost $4.5 billion to implement, but it projected that it would save $9 billion per year by reducing worker injuries. On March 1, Congressional Republicans introduced a resolution of disapproval, which was approved by the Senate on March 6, 2001, by a vote of 56-44. On March 7, the House of Representatives adopted the joint resolution by a vote of 223-206. Using the fast-track procedures of the Congressional Review Act, the joint resolution was adopted without any hearings or committee action, with no opportunities for amendments, and with floor debate limited to ten hours. President Bush endorsed the disapproval effort and signed the joint resolution repealing the rule.

In December 2000, Congress enacted the Information Quality Act (IQA), §515 of Title V of Pub. L. 106-554, also sometimes called the Data Quality Act, as part of the FY 2001 Treasury and General Government Appropriations Act. The IQA requires the Office of Management and Budget (OMB) to issue "guidelines ensuring and maximizing the quality, objectivity, utility, and integrity of information (including statistical information) disseminated by Federal agencies." The OMB published government-wide guidelines for complying with the IQA in February 2002—67 FR 8452. These and other requirements piled by the executive branch on top of the APA's seemingly simple statutory provisions have contributed to ossification of the regulatory process and the ability of regulated industries to successfully forestall the adoption of new regulatory standards. See McGarity, Shapiro & Bollick, Sophisticated Sabotage (2004) for a description of how regulatory targets are able to use procedural gambits to sabotage the adoption of regulations.

3. Reforming Rulemaking

Using advances in electronic communication, EPA and other regulatory agencies are attempting to make it easier for the public to participate in rulemaking proceedings and to retrieve information from the agencies. EPA's World Wide Web site (*http://www.epa.gov*) provides detailed information on the agency's activities and access to agency reports and databases. EPA and other agencies are now allowing comments on proposed rules to be submitted electronically. In 2003 the federal government launched a website (*www.regulations.gov*) that permits the public to submit comments online on any rule proposed by a federal agency.

While improvements in technology may make it easier to communicate with government agencies, they are unlikely to serve as a vaccine for regulatory ossification. Indeed, if easier access is not accompanied by fundamental reforms in the process, the slow pace and contentious nature of rulemaking may be exacerbated. Efforts to improve the rulemaking process have spawned a variety of initiatives. These include regulatory negotiation, generic rulemaking, and the latest efforts to "reinvent regulation."

A. NEGOTIATED RULEMAKING

Negotiated rulemaking has become increasingly popular in recent years. In 1982 the Administrative Conference of the United States recommended that federal agencies experiment with negotiated rulemaking procedures. Congress explicitly endorsed negotiated rulemaking in 1990 when it adopted the Negotiated Rulemaking Act, Pub. L. No. 101648, 104 Stat. 4969, 5 U.S.C. §581. The Act confirms federal agencies' authority to conduct negotiated rulemaking, but does not require that it be employed.

In a negotiated rulemaking, the major groups interested in a prospective rulemaking action attempt to resolve their differences through negotiations prior to issuance of a proposed rule. Pursuant to the Federal Advisory Committee Act, the participants in a negotiated rulemaking are appointed to a negotiating committee by the agency responsible for the rule. Negotiations among the interest groups then take place with the assistance of an agency-appointed mediator. Agency staff responsible for developing the proposed rule also may participate. If the negotiations are successful, the parties agree on the substance of a proposed rule, which is then issued by the agency for public comment. The agency then follows the standard notice-and-comment procedures of informal rulemaking and the parties to the negotiation participate in the rulemaking.

If successful, negotiated rulemaking should reduce the chances that conflicts among interest groups will result in legal challenges to the regulation ultimately adopted. Once a consensus rule has been proposed, the rulemaking should be able to proceed relatively quickly because contentious issues presumably will have been resolved during the pre-proposal negotiations.

Not all rules are good candidates for negotiated rulemaking. Indeed, the procedure probably works well only in certain narrowly defined circumstances. Philip Harter has identified certain criteria for a successful regulatory negotiation. These include the following:

(1) The parties should have power to affect the decision and an incentive to bargain.
(2) The number of parties should be small enough to permit bargaining.
(3) The issue must be ready for decision and a firm deadline for decision should be set.
(4) Negotiation must have the potential to benefit all parties.
(5) The issue should not center on a fundamental value conflict between parties.
(6) More than one issue should be involved to allow tradeoffs across issues.
(7) The agency should commit to propose the product of the negotiations.

Harter, Negotiating Regulations: A Cure for Malaise, 71 Geo. L.J. 1 (1982).

The Negotiated Rulemaking Act of 1990 endorses some of these criteria, as reflected in the factors that it requires agencies to consider before embarking on a negotiated rulemaking. The Act specifies that agencies should consider whether there are a limited number of significantly affected interests that can be adequately represented in a negotiation and whether there is a reasonable likelihood of reaching consensus within a fixed period of time. The Act essentially codifies what had been existing agency procedures for conducting negotiated rulemakings.

Regulatory negotiation is becoming an accepted alternative for developing proposed rules, although it is doubtful that it can be used successfully in the most controversial rulemakings, which rarely will meet the criteria outlined above. Only regulations that involve a small number of issues, that affect a limited number of interests, and that have firm deadlines requiring that some action be taken are likely to be successful candidates for regulatory negotiation.

B. GENERIC APPROACHES TO RULEMAKING

Agencies have tried several alternative approaches for speeding up the glacial progress of standard-setting. One approach has been to permit agencies to adopt interim standards based on substantially reduced information thresholds while the agency gathers the necessary data to determine at what levels final standards should be set. When OSHA was created, Congress realized that the Agency faced a mammoth task in promulgating regulations to protect workers from exposure to a plethora of workplace hazards. To ensure that workers were rapidly provided with at least a modicum of protection, Congress directed OSHA to adopt as interim standards, without conducting rulemaking under the Administrative Procedure Act, national consensus standards already established by a national standard-setting organization or any health or safety standards already adopted by other federal agencies. 5 U.S.C. §655(a). In 1971 OSHA adopted exposure limits for approximately 400 chemicals based largely on the Threshold Limit Values (TLVs) adopted by the American Conference of Governmental Industrial Hygienists (ACGIH) in 1968.

While this approach allowed OSHA to promulgate relatively comprehensive regulations rapidly, it did not address the problem the Agency would face in enforcing such standards. Moreover, "interim" standards have a way of acquiring a life of their own. Although Congress contemplated that OSHA would revise the interim standards to provide more protection to workers through normal rulemaking proceedings, OSHA did not attempt to revise the standards to keep them up to date with changes in the ACGIH TLVs until 1989, long after the TLVs had been lowered for hundreds of the chemicals. When it finally got around to updating the standards, OSHA employed a generic rulemaking approach that considered health, risk, and feasibility evidence for 428 substances in one massive rulemaking. On June 7, 1988, OSHA proposed to amend the permissible exposure limits (PELs) covering air contaminants and to add new PELs to address substances not previously regulated. OSHA adopted a final regulation in January 1989. The 650-page final rule occupied an entire volume of the Federal Register. It strengthened 212 permissible exposure limits while setting new PELs for 164 substances that had not been regulated by OSHA. 54 Fed. Reg. 2332 (1989). However, OSHA's rule ultimately was struck down by the Eleventh Circuit in the *Air Contaminants* decision, AFL-CIO v. OSHA, 965 F.2d 962 (11th Cir. 1992). The court held that OSHA needed to make more individualized findings concerning the risks of the chemicals regulated and the feasibility of controls on various industries in order to justify such a rule. As a result of the court's decision, the problems OSHA faces in just updating old standards will be compounded dramatically. Indeed it was not until February 2006 that OSHA issued its first significant occupational exposure standard during the more than 5 years that President Bush had then been in office. 71 FR 10349 (Feb. 28, 2006) (PEL to control occupational exposure to hexavalent chromium).

C. REINVENTING REGULATION

Faced with legislative proposals to drastically alter the regulatory process, President Clinton announced his own regulatory reform program in March 1995. The President directed agencies to intensify their efforts to identify and eliminate unnecessary regulations. As part of this "reinventing regulation" initiative, the Clinton administration launched Project XL. The project, whose acronym stands for Excellence and Leadership, is designed to give greater flexibility to businesses and state and local governments in deciding how to meet environmental standards. Participants in Project XL enter into comprehensive contracts with EPA that promise greater, multi-faceted reductions in pollutant discharges than would be achieved through existing standards in return for waiving application of some of those standards. While this effort to "reinvent regulation" has been widely endorsed by projects examining ways to improve future environmental policy, see, e.g., NAPA, Resolving the Paradox of Environmental Protection: An Agenda for Congress, EPA & the States 75 (1997), it is not without its critics. See Rena Steinzor, Reinventing Environmental Regulation: The Dangerous Journey from Command to Self-Control, 22 Harv. Envtl. L. Rev. 103 (1998). One concern is the difficulty of defining and measuring what constitutes improved environmental performance. EPA's legal authority to waive existing standards also has been questioned. EPA staff reportedly have developed the motto, "If it isn't illegal, it isn't XL." What's Up With Project XL—Week of 3/11/96, Project XL Update. For a discussion of the prospects for greater use of collaborative process for developing regulations, see Jody Freeman, Collaborative Governance in the Administrative State, 45 U.C.L.A. L. Rev. 1 (1997). Freeman notes that the limited resources of public interest and community groups restrict their ability to participate in the collaborative development of regulations.

EPA's reinvention efforts have sought to promote five principles: (1) offering regulatory flexibility in return for better results; (2) building stronger partnerships with state and local governments, tribes, community leaders, businesses, and private citizens; (3) facilitating compliance by making regulatory information easier to obtain and to understand; (4) cutting red tape associated with environmental regulations; and (5) making it easier to report, obtain, and understand information about the environment. EPA is seeking to measure its progress through a strategic planning process with objective goals, as required by the Government Performance and Results Act.

4. Presidential Oversight of Rulemaking

When decisions are being made about environmental regulations that affect important constituencies, few government officials are purely disinterested observers of the rulemaking process. No official has more clout with executive agencies than the president, who appoints agency officials who serve at the president's pleasure. In the exercise of this "clout" over executive agencies, the president is supposed to be guided by a constitutional duty to "take Care that the Laws be faithfully executed." U.S. Const., art. II, §3.

Every president since Richard Nixon has established some sort of regulatory review program. The programs operated during the Reagan and Bush administrations were the targets of harsh criticism by environmentalists who argued that they were used to block implementation of the laws. President Clinton's regulatory review program was established by Executive Order 12,866, which provides that only significant regulatory actions are subject to OMB review. Executive Order 12,866 also establishes time limits on OMB review and it provides for public disclosure of information concerning the review process.

The Clinton administration also sought to use its executive oversight authority to require agencies to incorporate environmental justice concerns in their actions. In 1994, President Clinton issued Executive Order 12,898, 59 Fed. Reg. 7,629 (1994). The executive order directs each federal agency to "make achieving environmental justice part of its mission by identifying and addressing, as appropriate, disproportionately high and adverse human health or environmental effects of its programs, policies, and activities on minority and low-income populations." The executive order directs agencies to consider the impact of environmental and human health risks on minority and poor communities. Each agency is required to develop an environmental justice strategy and to revise agency rules or policies to promote environmental justice. Other executive orders require agencies to consult and coordinate with Indian Tribal Governments (E.O. 13,084) and to respect principles of federalism (E.O. 13,132).

The president is not the only source of pressure exerted on agencies. Its lawmaking and appropriations powers give Congress formidable tools for influencing agency decision making. Although the Supreme Court's decision in INS v. Chadha, 462 U.S. 919 (1983), removed the "legislative veto" from Congress's arsenal, Congress has not hesitated to exercise other oversight authority to influence agency action and to contest presidential efforts to exert greater control over regulatory decisions. As noted above, congressional dissatisfaction with EPA's performance has resulted in the enactment of increasingly specific statutory directives designed to serve as agency-forcing mechanisms. These provisions effectively dictate what agency priorities should be and establish timetables for agency action enforceable in court.

Congress has been far more than a disinterested observer of the regulatory process. Members of Congress often seek to influence agency decisions, and congressional pressure can have a significant impact on agency decision making.

The legal bounds on executive and congressional oversight of the rule-making process were addressed in the case that follows. The D.C. Circuit was faced with a challenge to EPA's promulgation of new source performance standards for coal-fired power plants. The court rejected a variety of challenges to the regulation from utilities and environmental groups. An important procedural question in the case centered around the environmentalists' claim that the standards had been weakened significantly at the eleventh hour due to the personal intervention of President Carter, a key member of Congress, and the White House staff.

Sierra Club v. Costle
657 F.2d 298 (D.C. Cir. 1981)

WALD, Circuit Judge:

We have already held that a blanket prohibition against meetings during the post-comment period with individuals outside EPA is unwarranted, and this perforce applies to meetings with White House officials. We have not yet addressed, however, the issue whether such oral communications with White House staff, or the President himself, must be docketed on the rulemaking record, and we now turn to that issue. The facts, as noted earlier, present us with a single undocketed meeting held on April 30, 1979, at 10:00 A.M., attended by the President, White House staff, other high ranking members of the Executive Branch, as well as EPA officials, and which concerned the issues and options presented by the rulemaking.

We note initially that section 307 makes specific provision for including in the rulemaking docket "written comments" of other executive agencies along with accompanying documents on any proposed draft rules circulated in advance of the rulemaking proceeding. Drafts of the final rule submitted to an executive review process prior to promulgation, as well as all "written comments," "documents," and "written responses" resulting from such interagency review process, are also to be put in the docket prior to promulgation. This specific requirement does not mention informal meetings or conversations concerning the rule which are not part of the initial or final review processes, nor does it refer to oral comments of any sort. Yet it is hard to believe Congress was unaware that intra-executive meetings and oral comments would occur throughout the rulemaking process. We assume, therefore, that unless expressly forbidden by Congress, such intra-executive contacts may take place, both during and after the public comment period; the only real issue is whether they must be noted and summarized in the docket.

The court recognizes the basic need of the President and his White House staff to monitor the consistency of executive agency regulations with Administration policy. He and his White House advisers surely must be briefed fully and frequently about rules in the making, and their contributions to policymaking considered. The executive power under our Constitution, after all, is not shared—it rests exclusively with the President. The idea of a "plural executive," or a President with a council of state, was considered and rejected by the Constitutional Convention. Instead the Founders chose to risk the potential for tyranny inherent in placing power in one person, in order to gain the advantages of accountability fixed on a single source. To ensure the President's control and supervision over the Executive Branch, the Constitution—and its judicial gloss—vests him with the powers of appointment and removal, the power to demand written opinions from executive officers, and the right to invoke executive privilege to protect consultative privacy. In the particular case of EPA, Presidential authority is clear since it has never been considered an "independent agency" but always part of the Executive Branch.

The authority of the President to control and supervise executive policy-making is derived from the Constitution; the desirability of such control is demonstrable from the practical realities of administrative rulemaking. Regulations such as those involved here demand a careful weighing of cost, environmental, and energy considerations. They also have broad implications for national economic policy. Our form of government simply could not function effectively or rationally if key executive policymakers were isolated from each other and from the Chief Executive. Single mission agencies do not always have the answers to complex regulatory problems. An overworked administrator exposed on a 24-hour basis to a dedicated but zealous staff needs to know the arguments and ideas of policymakers in other agencies as well as in the White House.

We recognize, however, that there may be instances where the docketing of conversations between the President or his staff and other Executive Branch officers or rulemakers may be necessary to ensure due process. This may be true, for example, where such conversations directly concern the outcome of adjudications or quasi-adjudicatory proceedings; there is no inherent executive power to control the rights of individuals in such settings. Docketing may also be necessary in some circumstances where a statute like this one *specifically requires* that essential "information or data" upon which a rule is based be docketed. But in the absence of any further Congressional requirements, we hold that it was not unlawful in this case for EPA not to docket a face-to-face policy session involving the President and EPA officials during the post-comment period, since EPA makes no effort to base the rule on any "information or data" arising from that meeting. Where the President himself is directly involved in oral communications with Executive Branch officials, Article II considerations—combined with the strictures of *Vermont Yankee* [where the Supreme Court held that courts may not require agencies to employ additional rule-making procedures not required by Congress]—require that courts tread with extraordinary caution in mandating disclosure beyond that already required by statute.

The purposes of full-record review which underlie the need for disclosing ex parte conversations in some settings do not require that courts know the details of every White House contact, including a Presidential one, in this informal rulemaking setting. After all, any rule issued here with or without White House assistance must have the requisite *factual support* in the rulemaking record, and under this particular statute the Administrator may not base the rule in whole or in part on any "*information or data*" which is not in the record, no matter what the source. The courts will monitor all this, but they need not be omniscient to perform their role effectively. Of course, it is always possible that undisclosed Presidential prodding may direct an outcome that *is* factually based on the record, but different from the outcome that it would have obtained in the absence of Presidential involvement. In such a case, it would be true that the political process did affect the outcome in a way the courts could not police. But we do not believe that Congress intended that the courts convert informal rulemaking into a rarified technocratic process, unaffected by political considerations or the presence of Presidential power. In sum, we find that the existence of intra-Executive Branch meetings during the post-comment period, and the failure to docket one such meeting involving the President, violated neither the procedures mandated by the Clean Air Act nor due process.

NOTES AND QUESTIONS

1. Does Sierra Club v. Costle lay to rest any questions concerning the legality of regulatory review? Does it suggest that the president can lawfully dictate to an agency head the substance of a regulatory decision Congress has directed the agency to make?

2. In subsequent litigation, plaintiffs argued that President Reagan's regulatory review program had allowed OMB unlawfully to usurp decision-making authority delegated by Congress to executive agencies. In Public Citizen Health Research Group v. Tyson, 796 F.2d 1479 (D.C. Cir. 1986), Public Citizen charged that OMB had illegally forced OSHA to delete a short-term exposure limit (STEL) from regulations controlling occupational exposures to ethylene oxide (EtO). Faced with vigorous OMB opposition to a STEL and a court-ordered deadline for promulgating the EtO standard, OSHA had simply crossed out all reference to the STEL in the final regulation that was sent to the Federal Register for publication. The regulations were then published without any explanation of why the STEL had been deleted. The D.C. Circuit struck down the decision to delete the STEL as unsupported by the administrative record. The court noted that "OMB's participation in the EtO rulemaking presents difficult constitutional questions concerning the executive's proper role in administrative proceedings and the appropriate scope of delegated power from Congress to certain executive agencies." However, the court found it unnecessary to reach this issue in light of its decision that deletion of the STEL was unsupported by the record.

3. The result in Public Citizen Health Research Group v. Tyson confirms that, regardless of who ultimately is responsible for an administrative decision, that decision must conform to applicable requirements of the underlying regulatory statute and the Administrative Procedure Act in order to withstand judicial review. If OMB directs agencies to make decisions arbitrarily or capriciously or to base them on factors inconsistent with the requirements of the underlying

regulatory statute, such decisions are likely to be reversed. Suppose, however, that the administrative record and the appropriate statutory criteria would support *either* a decision favored by the agency or a different decision favored by OMB. Does Sierra Club v. Costle suggest that a decision directed by the president might be upheld in these circumstances even if it differs from that which the agency would have reached independent of presidential input? Would this present the "difficult constitutional questions" to which the *Public Citizen* court referred?

4. Some statutory limits on executive oversight may be inferred from the environmental statutes themselves. In Environmental Defense Fund v. Thomas, 627 F. Supp. 566 (D.D.C. 1986), OMB blocked EPA from issuing regulations governing the storage of hazardous waste in underground tanks, even though the statutory deadline for issuing such regulations had passed. EDF filed a deadline suit against EPA, but it took the unusual step of also joining OMB as a defendant. The court held that OMB had no authority to block EPA from promulgating regulations beyond the date of a statutory deadline. While noting that "[a] certain degree of deference must be given to the authority of the President to control and supervise executive policymaking," the court declared that efforts by OMB to block regulations after deadlines have expired are "incompatible with the will of Congress and cannot be sustained as a valid exercise of the President's Article II powers." 627 F. Supp. at 570. "Thus, if a deadline already has expired, OMB has no authority to delay regulations subject to the deadline in order to review them under the executive order." Id. at 571. Does this decision mean that EPA effectively could avoid OMB's regulatory review simply by waiting until after a statutory deadline had expired before issuing proposed regulations?

5. Elena Kagan notes that President Clinton assumed directive authority over agency heads by issuing an unprecedented 107 presidential directives to them. She argues that the president should be viewed as having the authority to direct decision making by agency heads, not as a result of a constitutional imperative, but rather as an appropriate rule of interpretation in circumstances where Congress has not expressly indicated to the contrary. Elena Kagan, Presidential Administration, 114 Harv. L. Rev. 2245 (2001). Robert Percival notes that this interpretive rule would be contrary to the understanding of Congress at the time it adopted the regulatory statutes, an understanding reinforced by the pre-Clinton regulatory review programs that expressly disavowed such directive authority. Percival, Presidential Management of the Administrative State: The Not-So-Unitary Executive, 51 Duke L.J. 963 (2001). Percival argues that such authority cannot be derived from the president's appointment and removal powers, even though as a practical matter they give him considerable ability to influence decisions by executive officers. He argues that the constitutionally required confirmation process envisions that agency heads will have some degree of independence from the president and that the political cost of the president firing an agency head serves as an important check on abuses of presidential power.

5. *Judicial Review and the Regulatory Process*

The major federal environmental statutes specifically authorize judicial review of agency action taken pursuant to them, and they also specify the procedures for obtaining judicial review. See, e.g., RCRA §7006(a), 42 U.S.C. §6976; TSCA §19, 15 U.S.C. §2618; CWA §509(b), 33 U.S.C. §1369(b); CAA §307(b), 42 U.S.C. §7607(b). These statutes, coupled with the judicial review provisions of the APA, 5 U.S.C. §§701-706, lay out the ground rules for challenging agency decisions in the federal courts. They generally permit suits challenging final agency action (as distinguished from "preliminary, procedural, or intermediate agency action," which may be reviewed only when the final action is taken, APA §704) as long as it is not "committed to agency discretion by law" (such as a decision whether or not to initiate enforcement action, Heckler v. Chancy, 470 U.S. 821 (1985)), §701(a)(2). Plaintiffs seeking judicial review also must have exhausted administrative remedies by raising objections in the rulemaking proceeding before the agency. The agency's action also must be deemed sufficiently "ripe for review" by courts, who seek to avoid premature adjudication of issues that have not crystallized to the point at which they are having more than a hypothetical impact on prospective litigants.

Virtually all of the federal environmental statutes also authorize *citizen suits* (FIFRA is the principal exception) against governmental agencies who fail to perform their statutory duties and against those who violate the statutes. It is important not to confuse the citizen suit provisions of the environmental statutes with the statutes' judicial review provisions. The citizen suit provisions generally authorize two types of lawsuits: action-forcing lawsuits against the agency for failure to perform a nondiscretionary duty and citizen suits against anyone who violates the environmental laws. The *judicial review* provisions of the environmental statutes authorize courts to review agency actions, such as the issuance or repeal of environmental regulations. We now turn to a brief history of judicial review and its impact on the regulatory process.

When the Supreme Court in Citizens to Preserve Overton Park v. Volpe, 401 U.S. 402 (1971), reversed a decision to authorize the expenditure of federal funds to build an interstate highway through a park, the decision was a surprise for two reasons: it indicated that courts were willing to review a wider range of agency actions and to scrutinize more carefully the rationale behind agency decisions. The plaintiffs in *Overton Park* alleged that the Secretary of Transportation had violated a provision of the Department of Transportation Act of 1966 that prohibited him from approving any project that required public parkland unless he determined that no feasible and prudent alternative to the use of the land existed and that all possible planning had been done to minimize harm to the park from such use. Relying on the judicial review provisions of section 706 of the APA, the plaintiffs argued that the Secretary's decision was an abuse of discretion and contrary to law.

In response to the lawsuit, the government argued that the Secretary's decision was not reviewable by a court because it was "committed to agency discretion by law" and thus exempt from review pursuant to the judicial review provisions of the APA, 5 U.S.C. §701(a). Because the Secretary had not made any specific findings at the time he made the decision, the Agency submitted affidavits to the court to support the Secretary's claim that he had indeed balanced the cost of other routes and safety considerations against the environmental impacts of the project. Although the court held that the Secretary did not need to make formal findings, it remanded the case to the district court for review based on reconstruction of the record actually before the Secretary at the time the decision was made. The court indicated that the Secretary had an obligation under the statute to do more than simply articulate a universally applicable rationale (i.e., that considerations of costs, the directness of the route, and community disruption favor use of the parkland) and that courts had an obligation to ensure that agency officials exercise their discretion properly.

With the enactment of the National Environmental Policy Act, which declared the importance of environmental values in national policy and required agencies to prepare environmental impact statements, environmentalists gained a powerful tool for challenging agency decisions. Courts began a period of greater scrutiny of agency actions characterized as the "hard look" doctrine, as Judge Leventhal referred to it in Greater Boston Television Corp. v. FCC, 444 F.2d 841, 851 (D.C. Cir. 1970), cert. denied, 403 U.S. 923 (1971).

This burst of judicial activism featured greater scrutiny of agency actions not only at the behest of environmentalists, but also in response to challenges by regulated industries. The courts struck down several EPA regulations in response to lawsuits by affected industries, even after the Agency began to develop detailed administrative records to support its rules. See, e.g., Kennecott Copper Corp. v. EPA, 462 F.2d 846 (D.C. Cir. 1972) (national secondary air quality standard for sulfur dioxide struck down as inadequately justified by agency); International Harvester Co. v. Ruckelshaus, 478 F.2d 615 (D.C. Cir. 1973) (denial of waiver for new motor vehicle emissions reduction standards invalidated); Portland Cement Association v. Ruckelshaus, 486 F.2d 375 (D.C. Cir. 1973) (new source performance standard for Portland cement plants struck down).

The movement by reviewing courts to require agencies to go beyond the minimum procedures required by the APA was brought to an abrupt halt by the Supreme Court in Vermont Yankee Nuclear Power Corp. v. Natural Resources Defense Council, 435 U.S. 519 (1978). *Vermont Yankee* involved a challenge to a decision by the Atomic Energy Commission to grant a license to a nuclear power plant. Although the license had been granted only after extensive licensing hearings, the hearings did not consider the environmental effects of the uranium fuel cycle, deferring that issue for a subsequent informal rulemaking proceeding. NRDC argued that NEPA required the AEC to employ additional factfinding procedures when considering the environmental impact of nuclear waste disposal, beyond those explicitly required by the APA. The D.C. Circuit agreed and held that such issues must be considered in individual licensing proceedings employing more formalized factfinding procedures. Natural Resources Defense Council v. Nuclear Regulatory Commission, 547 F.2d 633, 653 (D.C. Cir. 1976). The Supreme Court then reversed.

In an opinion by Justice Rehnquist, the Court held that the APA "established the maximum procedural requirements which Congress was willing to have the courts impose upon agencies in conducting rulemaking procedures." While noting that "[a]gencies are free to grant additional procedural rights in the exercise of their discretion," the Court held that "reviewing courts are generally not free to impose them if the agencies have not chosen to grant them." Vermont Yankee Nuclear Power Corp. v. Natural Resources Defense Council, 435 U.S. 519 (1978). Sternly admonishing the lower courts that "our cases could hardly be more explicit in this regard," Justice Rehnquist warned:

> [I]f courts continually review agency proceedings to determine whether the agency employed procedures which were, in the court's opinion, perfectly tailored to reach what the court perceives to be the "best" or "correct" result, judicial review would be totally unpredictable. And the agencies, operating under this vague injunction to employ the "best" procedures and facing the threat of reversal if they did not, would undoubtedly adopt full adjudicatory

procedures in every instance. Not only would this totally disrupt the statutory scheme, through which Congress enacted "a formula upon which opposing social and political forces have come to rest," Wong Yang Sung v. McGrath, 339 U.S., at 40, but all the inherent advantages of informal rulemaking would be totally lost. [435 U.S. at 546-547.]

Vermont Yankee repudiated attempts by reviewing courts to require agencies to provide more complete rulemaking records encompassing a wider range of issues that might be deemed relevant on judicial review. The decision had important implications for judicial review of agency compliance with the procedural obligations established by the National Environmental Policy Act (NEPA), an issue we will examine when we study NEPA in Chapter 8. But it had even broader implications, sending the lower courts a message that they should be more deferential to agency rulemaking procedures.

While *Vermont Yankee* mandated greater judicial deference to agency procedural decisions, the Court did not abandon judicial review as a check on the substance of agency decisions. Even though the APA specifies a relatively deferential standard of review (section 706 provides that courts are to overturn agency action only if it is "arbitrary, capricious, an abuse of discretion, or otherwise not in accordance with law"), the Court has not made the standard a toothless one. In Motor Vehicle Manufacturers Association v. State Farm Mutual Auto Insurance Co., 463 U.S. 29 (1983), the Supreme Court affirmed a D.C. Circuit decision striking down the Reagan administration's rescission of a regulation requiring automobile manufacturers to install passive restraint systems in cars. The Court held that the agency had failed to offer an adequate explanation of its decision in light of the extensive evidence in the record that passive restraint systems could prevent substantial numbers of deaths in automobile accidents.

Shortly after the *State Farm* decision, the Supreme Court substantially expanded judicial deference to agency decisions in the case that follows. The case involved a challenge to another agency effort to change policy abruptly.

Chevron U.S.A. v. Natural Resources Defense Council
467 U.S. 837 (1984)

Justice Stevens delivered the opinion of the Court.

In the Clean Air Act Amendments of 1977, Pub. L. 95-95, 91 Stat. 685, Congress enacted certain requirements applicable to States that had not achieved the national air quality standards established by the Environmental Protection Agency (EPA) pursuant to earlier legislation. The amended Clean Air Act required these "nonattainment" States to establish a permit program regulating "new or modified major stationary sources" of air pollution. Generally, a permit may not be issued for a new or modified major stationary source unless several stringent conditions are met. The EPA regulation promulgated to implement this permit requirement allows a State to adopt a plantwide definition of the term "stationary source." Under this definition, an existing plant that contains several pollution-emitting devices may install or modify one piece of equipment without meeting the permit conditions if the alternative will not increase the total emissions from the plant. The question presented by these cases is whether EPA's decision to allow States to treat all of the pollution-emitting devices within the same industrial grouping as though they were encased within a single "bubble" is based on a reasonable construction of the statutory term "stationary source."

The EPA regulations containing the plantwide definition of the term stationary source were promulgated on October 14, 1981. 46 Fed. Reg. 50766. Respondents filed a timely petition for review in the United States Court of Appeals for the District of Columbia Circuit pursuant to 42 U.S.C. §7607(b)(1). The Court of Appeals set aside the regulations. National Resources Defense Council, Inc. v. Gorsuch, 222 U.S. App. D.C. 268, 685 F.2d 718 (1982).

The court observed that the relevant part of the amended Clean Air Act "does not explicitly define what Congress envisioned as a 'stationary source,' to which the permit program . . . should apply," and further stated that the precise issue was not "squarely addressed in the legislative history." Id., at 273, 685 F.2d, at 723. In light of its conclusion that the legislative history bearing on the question was "at best contradictory," it reasoned that "the purposes of the nonattainment program should guide our decision here." Id., at 276, n.39, 685 F.2d, at 726, n.39. Based on two of its precedents concerning the applicability of the bubble concept to certain Clean Air Act programs, the court stated that the bubble concept was "mandatory" in programs designed merely to maintain existing air quality, but held that it was "inappropriate" in programs enacted to improve air quality. Id., at 276, 685 F.2d, at 726. Since the purpose of the permit program—its "raison d'etre," in the court's view—was to improve air quality, the court held that the bubble concept was inapplicable in these cases under its prior precedents. Ibid. It therefore set aside the regulations embodying the bubble concept as contrary to law. We granted certiorari to review that judgment, 461 U.S. 956 (1983), and we now reverse.

The basic legal error of the Court of Appeals was to adopt a static judicial definition of the term "stationary source" when it had decided that Congress itself had not commanded that definition. Respondents do not defend the legal reasoning of the Court of Appeals. Nevertheless, since this Court reviews judgments, not opinions, we must determine whether the Court of Appeals' legal error resulted in an erroneous judgment on the validity of the regulations.

When a court reviews an agency's construction of the statute which it administers, it is confronted with two questions. First, always, is the question whether Congress has directly spoken to the precise question at issue. If the intent of Congress is clear, that is the end of the matter; for the court as well as the agency must give effect to the unambiguously expressed intent of Congress. If, however, the court determines Congress has not directly addressed the precise question at issue, the court does not simply impose its own construction on the statute, as would be necessary in the absence of an administrative interpretation. Rather, if the statute is silent or ambiguous with respect to the specific issue, the question for the court is whether the agency's answer is based on a permissible construction of the statute.

"The power of an administrative agency to administer a congressionally created . . . program necessarily requires the formulation of policy and the making of rules to fill any gap left, implicitly or explicitly, by Congress." Morton v. Ruiz, 415 U.S. 199 (1974). If Congress has explicitly left a gap for the agency to fill, there is an express delegation of authority to the agency to elucidate a specific provision of the statute by regulation. Such legislative regulations are given controlling weight unless they are arbitrary, capricious, or manifestly contrary to the statute. Sometimes the legislative delegation to an agency on a particular question is implicit rather than explicit. In such a case, a court may not substitute its own construction of a statutory provision for a reasonable interpretation made by the administrator of an agency . . . .

In light of these well-settled principles it is clear that the Court of Appeals misconceived the nature of its role in reviewing the regulations at issue. Once it determined, after its own examination of the legislation, that Congress did not actually have an intent regarding the applicability of the bubble concept to the permit program, the question before it was not whether in its view the concept is "inappropriate" in the general context of a program designed to improve air quality, but whether the Administrator's view that it is appropriate in the context of this particular program is a reasonable one. Based on the examination of the legislation and its history, which follows, we agree with the Court of Appeals that Congress did not have a specific intention on the applicability of the bubble concept in these cases, and conclude that the EPA's use of that concept here is a reasonable policy choice for the agency to make. . . .

In these cases, the Administrator's interpretation represents a reasonable accommodation of manifestly competing interests and is entitled to deference: the regulatory scheme is technical and complex, the agency considered the matter in a detailed and reasoned fashion, and the decision involves reconciling conflicting policies. Congress intended to accommodate both interests, but did not do so itself on the level of specificity presented by these cases. Perhaps that body consciously desired the Administrator to strike the balance at this level, thinking that those with great expertise and charged with responsibility for administering the provision would be in a better position to do so; perhaps it simply did not consider the question at this level; and perhaps Congress was unable to forge a coalition on either side of the question, and those on each side decided to take their chances with the scheme devised by the agency. For judicial purposes, it matters not which of these things occurred.

Judges are not experts in the field, and are not part of either political branch of the Government. Courts must, in some cases, reconcile competing political interests, but not on the basis of the judges' personal policy preferences. In contrast, an agency to which Congress has delegated policymaking responsibilities may, within the limits of that delegation, properly rely upon the incumbent administration's views of wise policy to inform its judgments. While agencies are not directly accountable to the people, the Chief Executive is, and it is entirely appropriate for this political branch of the Government to make such policy choices—resolving the competing interests which Congress itself either inadvertently did not resolve, or intentionally left to be resolved by the agency charged with the administration of the statute in light of everyday realities . . . .

We hold that the EPA's definition of the term "source" is a permissible construction of the statute which seeks to accommodate progress in reducing air pollution with economic growth. "The Regulations which the Administrator has adopted provide what the agency could allowably view as . . . [an] effective reconciliation of these twofold ends. . . ." United States v. Shinier, 367 U.S., at 383.

The judgment of the Court of Appeals is reversed.

NOTES AND QUESTIONS

1. The judicial review provisions of the Administrative Procedure Act provide that reviewing courts are to "decide all relevant questions of law, interpret constitutional and statutory provisions, and determine the meaning or

applicability of the terms of an agency action." 5 U.S.C. §706. Is this consistent with the notion that courts should defer to agency interpretations of statutes?

2. Judicial deference to the decisions of administrative agencies stems in part from notions of agency expertise. To what extent are such notions relevant when the agency is not making complicated technical or scientific judgments, but rather is engaging in statutory interpretation? Who should be more "expert" at divining the intent of Congress—courts or agencies?

3. *Chevron* was decided by a unanimous Supreme Court, though only six justices participated in the decision. The papers of the late Justice Thurgood Marshall provided no evidence that the six justices appreciated that *Chevron* would work any significant change in administrative law. Within a week of its initial circulation, Justice Stevens's first draft opinion was joined by the other five justices without any substantive comment or suggested changes. Percival, Environmental Law in the Supreme Court: Highlights from the Marshall Papers, 23 Envtl. L. Rep. 10606, 10613 (1993). Release of the papers of the late Justice Harry A. Blackmun shed further light on this mystery because they contained notes taken by Justice Blackmun during conference. These notes indicate that the Justices initially were badly split when they voted in conference. Justice Stevens, who ultimately authored the unanimous opinion for the six Justices who participated in the final vote is recorded as stating, "When I am so confused, I go with the Agency." His statement appeared to reflect frustration expressed by several Justices at the difficulty of understanding the workings of complex, new regulatory programs like the Clean Air Act, which may have influenced their ultimate directive to afford agencies greater deference. See Robert V. Percival, Environmental Law in the Supreme Court: Highlights from the Blackmun Papers, 35 ELR 10637, 10644 (2005). Further background information on the *Chevron* litigation is provided in Jody Freeman, The Story of *Chevron*: Environmental Law and Administrative Discretion, in Environmental Law Stories 171 (Lazarus & Houck, eds. 2005).

4. *Chevron*'s two-step framework leaves reviewing courts considerable wiggle room because they still must determine whether a statute is ambiguous (Step 1)—and statutory ambiguity often is in the eye of the beholder, as decisions subsequent to *Chevron* quickly made clear. In Chemical Manufacturers Association v. Natural Resources Defense Council, 470 U.S. 116 (1985), the Supreme Court split 5-4 on the question whether or not the word "modified" in the Clean Water Act was ambiguous. In Board of Governors v. Dimension Financial Corp., 474 U.S. 361 (1986), the Supreme Court unanimously rejected the Federal Reserve Board's interpretation of the term "bank" by concluding that the term was clear and unambiguous.

5. How, if at all, do you think *Chevron* has affected judicial review of decisions by administrative agencies? *Chevron* must be the most frequently cited decision in administrative law cases. Shortly after its sixth birthday *Chevron* had been cited more than 1,000 times, with the number of citations to it continuing to increase rapidly. Sunstein, Law and Administration After *Chevron*, 90 Colum. L. Rev. 2071, 2074-2075 (1990). Yet *Chevron* does not seem to have insulated agency interpretations of statutes from effective judicial review. In the first four years after *Chevron* was decided, the Supreme Court rejected an administrative agency's interpretation of a statutory provision in six cases. See, e.g., Immigration and Naturalization Service v. Cardoza-Fonseca, 408 U.S. 421 (1988) (rejecting INS's interpretation of the term "well founded fear" of persecution for purposes of determining when asylum may be granted to refugees).

6. In a study of the Supreme Court's use of *Chevron,* Thomas Merrill finds it "clear that *Chevron* is often ignored by the Supreme Court." Merrill, Judicial Deference to Executive Precedent, 101 Yale L.J. 969, 970 (1992). Statistics compiled by Professor Merrill indicate that *Chevron*'s two-step framework has been used in only about half of the cases in which the Court has recognized that a question of deference to an agency interpretation is presented. In contrast to the Supreme Court itself, the Courts of Appeals have treated *Chevron*'s two-step approach as controlling whenever the agency is entitled to heightened deference, as in cases of agency rulemaking. In a study of all the courts of appeals decisions in the 1990s involving EPA rulemaking, Schroeder and Glicksman found *Chevron* to be universally applied. The agency prevailed in 75% of those challenges. Interestingly, when the court concluded that the Congress had clearly spoken (Chevron Step One), the agency success rate was much lower: 41%. When the agency was able to get past Step One to Step Two, where the question is whether the agency's construction of the statute was reasonable, it prevailed in 93% of the case. Schroeder & Glicksman, Chevron, State Farm and the EPA in the Courts of Appeals During the 1990s. 31 Envtl. L. Rep. 10371 (2001).

7. *Chevron*'s scope has been further diminished by the Supreme Court's decision in United States v. Mead Corp., 533 U.S. 218 (2001). In *Mead,* the Court held, over a lone, but vigorous dissent by Justice Scalia, that "administrative implementation of a particular statutory provision qualifies for *Chevron* deference when it appears that Congress delegated authority to the agency generally to make rules carrying the force of law, and that the agency interpretation claiming deference was promulgated in the exercise of that authority." 533 U.S. at 226-227. *Mead* moves judicial review of agency interpretations in the direction of Skidmore v. Swift & Co., 323 U.S. 134 (1944), which stated that the degree of deference owed an agency interpretation of a statute should depend on several factors, including the thoroughness of the agency's deliberations and the persuasiveness of its reasoning. *Mead* has clarified that the *Chevron* doctrine is grounded in congressional intent, rather than notions of separation of powers. To determine when *Chevron* deference is due, *Mead* makes the threshold questions whether Congress intended to give the agency authority to make rules with the force of law and whether the agency interpretation in question was issued in the exercise of such authority. As Professor Thomas Merrill observes, the post-*Mead* landscape of judicial review now encompasses three different degrees of deference to agency interpretations:

> *Chevron,*— a rule-like doctrine that requires courts to accept reasonable agency interpretations of ambiguous statutes; *Skidmore*—a standard that requires courts to consider agency interpretations under multiple factors and defer to the interpretation if it is persuasive; and no deference—a rule that applies when independent judicial review is required, for example, where the agency action is alleged to violate the Constitution, or where statutes designed to constrain agency discretion like the Administrative Procedure Act (APA) are at issue.

Thomas W. Merrill, The *Mead* Doctrine: Rules and Standards, Meta-Rules and Meta-Standards, 54 Admin. L. Rev. 807, 812-813 (2002). Although Professor Merrill criticizes the Court for leaving unclear how to determine when Congress has given an agency the power to act with force of law, he concludes that *Mead* actually will strengthen *Chevron,* by diminishing the need to water it down in cases that fall within its now-narrower scope.

=3=

Preventing Harm in the Face of Uncertainty

Some risks are plainly acceptable and others are plainly unacceptable. If, for example, the odds are one in a billion that a person will die from cancer by taking a drink of chlorinated water, the risk clearly could not be considered significant. On the other hand, if the odds are one in a thousand that regular inhalation of gasoline vapors that are 2% benzene will be fatal, a reasonable person might well consider the risk significant and take appropriate steps to decrease or eliminate it.

—*Industrial Union Dept., AFL-CIO v. American Petroleum Institute,*
448 U.S. 607, 655 (1980) (Stevens, J., plurality opinion)

SEN. BIDEN: . . . As you well know . . . the law is not merely logic, it's a reflection of societal values. . . . And we up here legislate and attempt to reflect societal values, which don't always lend themselves to easy weighing and computation.

. . . [O]ne quarter of all the health care costs in the United States of America are spent on the last three months of a person's life. . . . Rather than take a quarter of that almost trillion dollars we spend and spend it . . . on the young and immunization, which might very well, if you were looking purely from a utilitarian standpoint, provide for the greater good for a greater number . . . , we as a society have decided we do not have the view that has been expressed in some early cultures [that] when you get old enough your requirement is to crawl off into the bushes and die so . . . you don't impact on . . . society. We consciously made a decision, . . . we're willing to do the economically imprudent thing, spend one quarter of all our resources on the last three months of a life. . . .

JUDGE BREYER: . . . [T]hat's the kind of decision—my goodness, . . . it's health. It's safety. There is no economics that tells you the right result in that kind of area. There is no economics that tells . . . us how much we're prepared to spend . . . on the life of another person. . . . [T]hat's . . . a decision that people will make through their elected representatives. . . .

—*The Confirmation Hearings of Judge Stephen Breyer to be Associate*
Justice of the United States Supreme Court before the
Senate Judiciary Committee, July 15, 1994

The contemporary approach to environmental contamination rests on two central premises. First, some of the consequences of human activity that harm human health, the environment, or the health of other living things are unacceptable. Second, unacceptable harm ought to be prevented rather than compensated for after the fact. Each premise forms a part of "the expectation of a clean environment [that] has evolved into a virtual norm," Greenberg Research Memorandum, Chapter 1, page 8. But what is the cash value of these premises? What harms are unacceptable, how are they best prevented, and how does one know what actions to prevent if actual harm has not yet occurred?

As one moves from statute to statute and from problem area to problem area—air pollution, water pollution, hazardous waste, pesticides, drinking water contaminants, commercially produced chemicals, and other sub-compartments of environmental harm-causing activities—these difficult questions receive different answers. They vary according to the nature of the particular medium or product being addressed, the history of regulation in a certain field, the structure of the industries being regulated, the nature of the environmental problem, the politics of the Congress at the moments when crucial legislation was being drafted, and other context-dependent factors. While these contextual elements need to be given their due, these questions also pose some universally relevant challenges, due to the fact that the same competing values are present in most of the debates over specific programs, that all decisions must be made in the face of great uncertainties, and that the evaluation of risk under modern environmental regulation increasingly employs a common set of techniques, so that questions raised by those techniques can have implications throughout the entire regulatory network.

This chapter takes up the central generic issues raised by the ambition to prevent unacceptable harm under conditions of uncertainty. Logically, the preventative ambition prompts two lines of inquiry—one focuses on human activity and attempts to characterize the potential of that activity for causing harm; the other focuses on the issue of acceptability, and attempts to determine how much of that harm-causing potential ought to be eliminated. We refer to the latter question as the question of "how safe is safe?" It implicates questions of "risk management," and is the subject of section C. The first question implicates techniques for characterizing an activity's harm-causing potential that are subsumed under the general label of "risk assessment." Section B focuses on questions raised by the evolving modern techniques of risk assessment.

Toxic substances are characterized by the potential of causing serious harm or death at relatively low exposure levels, levels at which further preventative action can sometimes be very costly. The harm that low exposures will cause is also very hard to predict, and impossible to predict with certainty. Thus the regulation of toxic substances vividly exposes some of the hardest problems in risk assessment and risk management, when the harm-causing potentials of human activities are shrouded in uncertainty, difficult to assess, and expensive to reduce. Accordingly, this chapter relies heavily on illustrations drawn from experiences under a number of toxic substances statutes, including the Toxic Substances Control Act (TSCA), the Federal Insecticide Fungicide and Rodenticide Act (FIFRA), the Safe Drinking Water Act (SDWA), and the Occupational Safety and Health Act (OSHA). None of these statutes will be examined in the detail found in other chapters of this casebook that address specific laws like the Clean Air Act, the Clean Water Act, RCRA, or Superfund. Nonetheless, the illustrations will expose you to some of the context-dependent considerations as well as to the generic regulatory techniques and questions of values and priorities raised by the preventative ambition.

We begin with a look at several of the early, foundational environmental and legal decisions.

A. PRECURSORS OF MODERN REGULATORY APPROACHES

Even before the "precautionary principle" rose to prominence, the wisdom of preventing harm before it occurs spawned instances of precautionary regulation in the face of uncertainty. Long before the regulatory system became as elaborate and complex as it currently is, courts, legislatures, and agencies were grappling with risk assessment and risk management issues. This is because these two lines of inquiry—what activities warrant regulation and what constitutes acceptable risk—are embedded in any system of preventative regulation. For instance, courts asked to enjoin some activity as a nuisance due to its harm-causing potential must engage in a form of risk assessment, aimed at determining whether the defendant's activity poses risks (or causes harms) that warrant judicial intervention. If intervention of some kind seems warranted, the court must then address risk management issues when it sets the terms of an injunction. For illustrations, see the nuisance cases studied in Chapter 2, pages 81-86.

The direction these two lines of inquiry have taken in the modern regulatory state has been heavily influenced by several court decisions rendered during the Rise of the Modern Environmental Movement, before the risk assessment/ management apparatus became as elaborate and complex as it currently is. Two of these, Reserve Mining v. EPA and Ethyl Corp. v. EPA, highlight in stark and understandable ways the uncertainties and critical decisions to be found in much environmental decision making, uncomplicated by much of the modern esoterica. The third case, Industrial Union Dept. AFL-CIO v. American Petroleum Institute (Benzene), helped marshal in the modern era of regulatory analysis.

1. Identifying Activities Subject to Regulation

Before an agency or court is authorized to regulate any substance or product, typically some threshold finding must be made, and typically that finding relates to the harmful potential of the substance or product to be regulated. For instance, the agency implementing a statute might be instructed to issue a preventative regulation only when it has definitive proof that a substance or product will in fact cause harm if exposure continues. Section 108 of the Clean Air Act, for example, originally ordered EPA to issue ambient air quality standards for certain pollutants "which, in [the] judgment [of the administrator], [have] an adverse effect on public health or welfare." This language was interpreted to require proof of actual harm before agency action could be taken. Ethyl Corp. v. EPA, 541 F.2d 1, 14 (D.C. Cir. 1976) (en banc). One implication of such a threshold requirement when dealing with toxic substances is that the regulatory process may end up waiting until it is possible to "count the dead bodies," because definitive evidence of harm to humans typically comes only when actual deaths or serious illnesses can be linked to past exposures.

A striking characteristic of modern statutes regulating toxic substances is precisely their unwillingness to wait for such definitive proof. Instead they instruct agencies and courts to act in advance of such proof; in other words, when either the harmful nature of a substance or the magnitude of the harm that it will cause, or both, are still doubtful. The crucial question then is: Short of certainty of serious harm, what must be known before it is appropriate to regulate?

Historical experience—as opposed to regulatory theory—indicates that even though the manifest language of modern statutes has authorized regulation prior to definitive proof of harm, the regulatory system still frequently continues to wait for such proof before implementing strict regulation because of the enormous pressures to avoid imposing regulatory burdens in doubtful cases. Most of the chemicals that have been stringently regulated became the focus of regulatory attention only after highly publicized incidents in which high-level, acute exposures caused visible and substantial harm. See E. Silbergeld & R. Percival, The Organometals: Impact of Accidental Exposures and Experimental Data on Regulatory Policies, in Neurotoxicants and Neurobiological Function: Effects of Organoheavy Metals 328 (H. Tilson & S. Sparber eds., 1987). For example, early regulatory action to restrict mercury discharges was undertaken only after the discovery that children in Minimata, Japan, had suffered severe birth defects from mercury that had accumulated in fish from waste discharges between 1953 and 1960. (For more about mercury, see the Case Study on Mercury, page 216, in this chapter.)

In other cases opportunities to prevent significant, chronic health damage were missed even though there had been highly publicized incidents involving acute exposures. In October 1924 the use of lead additives in gasoline became a source of considerable public controversy after several workers in a tetraethyl lead processing plant in Elizabeth, New Jersey, died from acute lead poisoning. Some cities banned the use of tetraethyl lead, which was taken off the market while a panel convened by the Surgeon General studied the health effects of lead additives. After a study was quickly prepared showing that gas station attendants where leaded gasoline was sold did not have higher levels of lead in their blood, tetraethyl lead returned to the market. The Surgeon General recognized that the study was inadequate for assessing the long-term effect of lead additives on human health and recommended follow-up studies that never were undertaken. It was not until several decades later that regulatory attention focused on the effects of lead emissions on children's health. The early story of lead (non)regulation is told in Gerald Markowitz & David Rosner, Deceit and Denial 12-138 (2002). For the connection between children's health and lead, see pages 175-178.

One of the early, important cases addressing the issue of how much must be known before regulatory action is justified is Reserve Mining Co. v. EPA, 514 F.2d 492 (8th Cir. 1975) (en banc). In that case, a mining company was discharging 67,000 tons of taconite tailings daily into the pristine water of Lake Superior, the source of drinking water for the city of Duluth, Minnesota. The federal government, joined by Minnesota, Wisconsin, Michigan, and several environmental groups, brought suit under the Clean Water Act, the Rivers and Harbors Act, and the federal common law of nuisance against the Reserve Mining Company for discharging the tailings. The district court entered an order, later stayed by an Eighth Circuit panel, that required the company immediately to cease discharging tailings into the water and air around its iron ore processing plant. Reserve Mining Co. v. United States, 498 F.2d 1073 (8th Cir. 1974). The district court had found that both air and water discharges were "substantially endanger[ing]" the surrounding population, despite the inconclusiveness of evidence concerning their effects on human health. Although it was known that the taconite tailings contained asbestiform fibers similar in structure to asbestos fibers known to cause diseases in occupational settings, there was no evidence that ingestion of the fibers in drinking water would increase the incidence of such diseases. Sitting en banc, the Eighth Circuit addressed Reserve's claim that its discharges posed no legally cognizable risk to public health in the decision below.

Reserve Mining Company v. EPA
514 F.2d 492 (8th Cir. 1975) (en banc)

BRIGHT, Circuit Judge:

[On appeal from the district court's injunction of further discharges by Reserve Mining into Lake Superior, the Eighth Circuit addressed] first, whether the ingestion of fibers, as compared with their inhalation, poses any danger whatsoever; and second, should ingestion pose a danger, whether the exposure resulting from Reserve's discharge may be said to present a legally cognizable risk to health.

1. Ingestion of Fibers as a Danger to Health

All epidemiological studies which associate asbestos fibers with harm to health are based upon inhalation of these fibers by humans. Thus, although medical opinion agrees that fibers entering the respiratory tract can interact with body tissues and produce disease, it is unknown whether the same can be said of fibers entering the digestive tract. If asbestos fibers do not interact with digestive tissue, they are presumably eliminated as waste without harmful effect upon the body.

The evidence bearing upon possible harm from ingestion of fibers falls into three areas: first, the court-sponsored tissue study, designed to measure whether asbestos fibers are present in the tissues of long-time Duluth residents; second, animal experiments designed to measure whether, as a biological phenomenon, fibers can penetrate the gastrointestinal mucosa and thus interact with body tissues; third, the increased incidence of gastrointestinal cancer among workers occupationally exposed to asbestos, and the hypothesis that this increase may be due to the ingestion of fibers initially inhaled.

a. The Tissue Study

Recognizing the complete lack of any direct evidence (epidemiological or otherwise) on the issue of whether the ingestion of fibers poses a risk, the trial court directed that a tissue study be conducted to determine whether the tissues of long-time Duluth residents contain any residue of asbestoslike fibers.

The study sought to analyze by electron microscope the tissues of recently deceased Duluth residents who had ingested Duluth water for at least 15 years; that is, approximately since the beginning of Reserve's operations. As a "control" check on results, tissue samples were obtained from the deceased residents of Houston, Texas, where the water is free of asbestos fibers. Although this study was necessarily expedited, plaintiffs' principal medical witness, Dr. Selikoff, testified to the sound design of the study and expressed his belief that it would yield significant information.

One of the court-appointed experts, Dr. Frederick Pooley, in explaining the results of the study, stated that he found that the tissues of the Duluth residents were virtually free of any fibers which could be attributed to the Reserve discharge. Dr. Brown said of this study:

> It is my conclusion, from the tissue study, that residents of Duluth have not been found to have asbestiform fibers in their tissues when compared with Houston . . .

[P]laintiffs argued, and the district court agreed, that because the specimens of tissue represented only a microscopically minute body area, the actual presence of fibers may have been overlooked.*

We note that this limitation had not seemed dispositive prior to the study when Dr. Selikoff commented:

> I would think we should find some fibers there. We're looking for needles in a haystack, but that's all right, we should find needles in the haystack with all the difficulties of the study, the technical difficulties, if we examine sufficiently large numbers of samples in some instances we should find some fibers there.

The district court decided, and we agree, that the study cannot be deemed conclusive in exonerating the ingestion of fibers in Lake Superior water as a hazard. The negative results must, however, be given some weight in assessing the probabilities of harm from Reserve's discharge into water. The results also weigh heavily in indicating that no emergency or imminent hazard to health exists. Thus, while this study crucially bears on the determination of whether it is necessary to close Reserve down immediately, the negative results do not dispose of the broader issue of whether the ingestion of fibers poses some danger to public health justifying abatement on less immediate terms.

b. Animal Studies and Penetration of the Gastrointestinal Mucosa

At a somewhat more theoretical level, the determination of whether ingested fibers can penetrate the gastrointestinal mucosa bears on the issue of harm through ingestion. If penetration is biologically impossible, then presumably the interaction of the fibers with body tissues will not occur.

This medical issue has been investigated through experiments with animals which, unfortunately, have produced conflicting results. For example, Reserve witness Dr. Davis reported on his experiment in feeding crocidolite and chrysotile asbestos to rats for varying periods of up to six months. He killed the rats at the end of the period and examined their gastrointestinal tissues for evidence of fibers. At the time of trial, light and electron microscopy had so far revealed no evidence of fibers in the tissues.

---

*[Editor's Note: The electron microscope techniques used in the study could only observe a minute area at any one time. Even a Reserve witness conceded on cross-examination that reviewing a single cubic centimeter of tissue would require 9,000 years, assuming the microscope was in use 24 hours a day, 7 days a week. See Applegate, The Story of Reserve Mining: Managing Scientific Uncertainty in Environmental Regulation in Environmental Law Stories 44 (Houck & Lazarus eds., 2005).]

Plaintiffs, however, cited contrary studies. Research by George Westlake, in which rats were fed a diet including chrysotile fibers, indicated that fibers had traveled through the colon wall and accumulated in the area of the mesothelium. Pontrefact, who injected chrysotile fibers into the stomachs of rats, found that fibers had dispersed throughout the body tissues.

On this conflicting scientific evidence, Dr. Brown testified that the Westlake and Pontrefact studies provide some support for the hypothesis that asbestos fibers can penetrate the gastrointestinal mucosa.

c.   Excess Gastrointestinal Cancer Among the Occupationally Exposed

The affirmative evidence supporting the proposition that the ingestion of fibers poses a danger to health focuses on the increased rate of gastrointestinal cancer among workers occupationally exposed to asbestos dust. Plaintiffs' experts attribute this excess incidence of gastrointestinal cancer to a theory that the asbestos workers first inhaled the asbestos dust and thereafter coughed up and swallowed the asbestos particles.

The attribution of health harm from ingestion rests upon a theoretical basis. As Dr. Selikoff explained, there are several possible explanations for the increased evidence of gastrointestinal cancer, some of which do not involve ingestion. Moreover, as noted previously, the excess rates of gastrointestinal cancer are generally "modest," and substantially lower than the excess rates of mesothelioma and lung cancer associated with inhalation of asbestos dust. Also, the experts advised that an analysis of a small exposed population may produce statistically "unstable" results.

The existence of an excess rate of gastrointestinal cancer among asbestos workers is a matter of concern. The theory that excess cancers may be attributed to the ingestion of asbestos fibers rests on a tenable medical hypothesis. Indeed, Dr. Selikoff testified that ingestion is the "probable" route accounting for the excess in gastrointestinal cancer. The occupational studies support the proposition that the ingestion of asbestos fibers can result in harm to health.

2.   Level of Exposure Via Ingestion

The second primary uncertainty with respect to ingestion involves the attempt to assess whether the level of exposure from drinking water is hazardous. Of course, this inquiry is handicapped by the great variation in fiber counts, and Dr. Brown's admonition that only a qualitative, and not a quantitative, statement can be made about the presence of fibers.

In spite of these difficulties, the district court found that the level of exposure resulting from the drinking of Duluth water was "comparable" to that found to cause gastrointestinal cancer in asbestos workers. 380 F. Supp. at 48. The court drew this finding from an elaborate calculation by Dr. Nicholson in which he attempted to make a statistical comparison between the fibers probably ingested by an asbestos worker subject to an excess risk of gastrointestinal cancer with the probable number of amphibole fibers ingested by a Duluth resident over a period of 18 years. To make this calculation, Dr. Nicholson computed what he believed to be the level of exposure in a typical occupational environment and multiplied this figure by the total amount of air inhaled by the worker over a four-year period (taken to be the relevant period in which a risk of excess gastrointestinal cancer was posed), thereby obtaining total fibers inhaled. A percentage reduction was then applied to obtain the number of fibers brought up the respiratory tract and swallowed. For Duluth residents, Dr. Nicholson calculated the number of fibers ingested over an 18-year period, assuming a daily intake of two liters of water and a fiber concentration of 25 million fibers/liter. From these assumptions, Dr. Nicholson opined that a Duluth resident over a period of 18 years ingested about two-thirds of the amount of asbestos fibers swallowed by an asbestos worker in four years. As is evident, this calculation is beset by several uncertainties. The assumptions as to fiber concentration in occupational settings and the resulting percentage of fibers ingested involve margins of error. Furthermore, in assuming that the relevant fiber concentration in Duluth water was 25 million fibers/liter, Dr. Nicholson used a figure twice that found by the court as the mean concentration of *all* amphibole fibers. Reserve witness Dr. Gross performed a calculation similar to Dr. Nicholson's, but using somewhat different assumptions, and concluded that Duluth water would have to contain several hundred million fibers/liter and be ingested for 60 years before an exposure comparable with occupational levels would be reached.

The comparison has other weaknesses, for without regard to the comparability of the gross exposure levels, the dynamics of the exposure process are markedly different. The vagaries attendant to the use of assumptions rather than facts result in comparisons which are of dubious accuracy. Thus, Dr. Brown testified that, if Nicholson's calculations were correct, he would conclude only that the risk was non-negligible.

The Nicholson comparison, although evidentially weak, must be considered with other evidence. The record does show that the ingestion of asbestos fibers poses some risk to health, but to an undetermined degree. Given these circumstances, Dr. Brown testified that the possibility of a future excess incidence of cancer attributable to the discharge cannot be ignored:

> I would say that it is conceivable that gastrointestinal cancers can develop from the ingestion of asbestos, and what I don't know, your Honor, is just how low that level of ingestion must be before the likelihood of GI cancer becomes so remote as to be, for all intents and purposes, ignored as a real live possibility. . . .

C.   Conclusion

The preceding extensive discussion of the evidence demonstrates that the medical and scientific conclusions here in dispute clearly lie "on the frontiers of scientific knowledge." The trial court, not having any proof of actual harm, was faced with a consideration of 1) the probabilities of any harm and 2) the consequences, if any, should the harm actually occur. . . .

In assessing probabilities in this case, it cannot be said that the probability of harm is more likely than not. Moreover, the level of probability does not readily convert into a prediction of consequences. On this record it cannot be forecast that the rates of cancer will increase from drinking Lake Superior water or breathing Silver Bay air. The best that can be said is that the existence of this asbestos contaminant in air and water gives rise to a reasonable medical concern for the public health. The public's exposure to asbestos fibers in air and water creates some health risk. Such a contaminant should be removed.

As we demonstrate in the following sections of the opinion, the existence of this risk to the public justifies an injunction decree requiring abatement of the health hazard on reasonable terms as a precautionary and preventive measure to protect the public health. . . .

The district court found that Reserve's discharge into Lake Superior violated §§1160(c)(5) and (g)(1) of the Federal Water Pollution Control Act. (FWPCA). These two provisions authorize an action by the United States to secure abatement of water discharges in interstate waters where the discharges violate state water quality standards and "endanger . . . the health or welfare of persons." §1160(g)(1). . . .

In the context of this environmental legislation, we believe that Congress used the term "endangering" in a precautionary or preventive sense, and, therefore, evidence of potential harm as well as actual harm comes within the purview of that term. We are fortified in this view by the flexible provisions for injunctive relief which permit a court "to enter such judgment and orders enforcing such judgment as the public interest and the equities of the case may require." 33 U.S.C. §1160(c)(5). . . . The record shows that Reserve is discharging a substance into Lake Superior waters which under an acceptable but unproved medical theory may be considered as carcinogenic.

Concededly, the trial court considered many appropriate factors in arriving at a remedy, such as a) the nature of the anticipated harm, b) the burden on Reserve and its employees from the issuance of the injunction, c) the financial ability of Reserve to convert to other methods of waste disposal, and d) a margin of safety for the public.

An additional crucial element necessary for a proper assessment of the health hazard rests upon a proper analysis of the probabilities of harm.

With respect to the water, these probabilities must be deemed low for they do not rest on a history of past health harm attributable to ingestion but on a medical theory implicating the ingestion of asbestos fibers as a causative factor in increasing the rates of gastrointestinal cancer among asbestos workers. With respect to air, the assessment of the risk of harm rests on a higher degree of proof, a correlation between inhalation of asbestos dust and subsequent illness. But here, too, the hazard cannot be measured in terms of predictability, but the assessment must be made without direct proof. But, the hazard in both the air and water can be measured in only the most general terms as a concern for the public health resting upon a reasonable medical theory. Serious consequences could result if the hypothesis on which it is based should ultimately prove true.

A court is not powerless to act in these circumstances. But an immediate injunction cannot be justified in striking a balance between unpredictable health effects and the clearly predictable social and economic consequences that would follow the plant closing.

In addition to the health risk posed by Reserve's discharges, the district court premised its immediate termination of the discharges upon Reserve's persistent refusal to implement a reasonable alternative plan for on-land disposal of tailings. . . .

During these appeal proceedings, Reserve has indicated its willingness to deposit its tailings on land and to properly filter its air emissions. At oral argument, Reserve advised us of a willingness to spend 243 million dollars in plant alterations and construction to halt its pollution of air and water. Reserve's offer to continue operations and proceed to construction of land disposal facilities for its tailings, if permitted to do so by the State of Minnesota, when viewed in conjunction with the uncertain quality of the health risk created by Reserve's discharges, weighs heavily against a ruling which closes Reserve's plant immediately.

Indeed, the intervening union argues, with some persuasiveness, that ill health effects resulting from the prolonged unemployment of the head of the family on a closing of the Reserve facility may be more certain than the harm from drinking Lake Superior water or breathing Silver Bay air.

Furthermore, Congress has generally geared its national environmental policy to allowing polluting industries a reasonable period of time to make adjustments in their efforts to conform to federal standards. . . .

We believe that on this record the district court abused its discretion by immediately closing this major industrial plant. In this case, the risk of harm to the public is potential, not imminent or certain, and Reserve says it earnestly seeks a practical way to abate the pollution. A remedy should be fashioned which will serve the ultimate public weal by insuring clean air, clean water, and continued jobs in an industry vital to the nation's welfare. . . .

Reserve must be given a reasonable opportunity and a reasonable time to construct facilities to accomplish an abatement of its pollution of air and water and the health risk created thereby. In this way, hardship to employees and great economic loss incident to an immediate plant closing maybe avoided. See Georgia v. Tennessee Copper Co. [pages 82-84].

Reserve shall be given a reasonable time to stop discharging its wastes into Lake Superior. A reasonable time includes the time necessary for Minnesota to act on Reserve's present application to dispose of its tailings at Milepost 7 . . . or to come to agreement on some other site acceptable to both Reserve and the state. Assuming agreement and designation of an appropriate land disposal site, Reserve is entitled to a reasonable turn-around time to construct the necessary facilities and accomplish a changeover in the means of disposing of its taconite wastes.

NOTES AND QUESTIONS

1. In announcing its initial stay, the three-judge panel had stated:

> The discharges may or may not result in detrimental health effects, but, for the present, that is simply unknown. The relevant legal question is thus what manner of judicial cognizance may be taken of the unknown.
> We do not think that a bare risk of the unknown can amount to proof in this case. Plaintiffs have failed to prove that a demonstrable health hazard exists. This failure, we hasten to add, is not reflective of any weakness which it is within their power to cure, but rather, given the current state of medical and scientific knowledge, plaintiffs' case is based only on medical hypothesis and is simply beyond proof. [498 F.2d at 1083-1084.]

Did the en banc opinion reverse course on this point?

2. The en banc court concluded that the negative results of the effort to find asbestiform fibers in Duluth residents could not be "deemed conclusive in exonerating the ingestion of fibers in Lake Superior as a hazard," but that it had

to be "weigh[ed] heavily in indicating that no emergency or imminent hazard to health exists." See page 170. Do you agree with the latter conclusion? If fibers were there that the study simply failed to identify because of its small scope, how does the failure to find them suggest the absence of an imminent hazard?

3. Federal and state environmental officials responded to this decision with alarm. A bill was introduced in Congress to shift the burden of proof to polluters to prove the safety of their discharges once it was shown that they presented "a reasonable risk of being a threat to public health." Supporting this proposed legislation, then-CEQ chairman Russell W. Peterson explained the problem in the following terms:

> Because of the latent health effects of carcinogens it will be more than 10 years before the magnitude of the health risk to the people of Duluth and Silver Bay will be fully realized, and unfortunately it will be based upon the fate of over 200,000 people. Even a few more days of additional exposure pose an unnecessary and unacceptable risk to the residents of the area. [Peterson, letter to Hon. Wallace H. Johnson, reprinted in Burdens of Proof in Environmental Litigation, Hearing before the Subcomm. on Environment of the Senate Commerce Comm., 93d Cong., 2d Sess. 8 (1974).]

4. The full story of the battle and litigation over Reverse Mining's taconite dumping has proven so compelling that it has been the subject of a number of books and articles exploring the case's background, the colorful characters involved, and its implications. The most recent is John Applegate, The Story of Reserve Mining: Managing Scientific Uncertainty in Environmental Regulation in Environmental Law Stories 44 (Houck & Lazarus eds., 2005). Applegate's footnote 3 identifies other important books and articles, as well as identifying the prior allegiances and financial arrangements of other persons who have written about the incident, so as to inform interested readers of the possible biases of various authors.

5. A second influential early decision was Ethyl Corp. v. EPA, 541 F.2d 1 (D.C. Cir. 1976) (en banc). *Ethyl Corp.* involved part of the Clean Air Act that at the time of the decision authorized EPA to regulate gasoline additives if their emissions "will endanger the public health or welfare" (§211(c)(1)(A)). The EPA reviewed a number of suggestive, but inconclusive, studies on the effects of lead emissions from gasoline exhausts on urban populations, especially children. The administrator concluded that lead in gasoline presented "a substantial risk of harm," and on that basis ordered reductions in the lead content of gasoline.

Like *Reserve, Ethyl Corp.* also highlights the uncertainty that dogs risk analyses. It was impossible for the EPA to demonstrate conclusively that lead was harmful at the levels being considered for regulation; nor could EPA determine precisely the probability that lead at such levels was harmful.

The lead additive manufacturers sought judicial review of EPA's decision. They claimed the statute required EPA to have "proof of actual harm" from auto emissions of lead before it could order limits on the amount of lead in gasoline. In December 1974, a three-judge panel of the D.C. Circuit, with one dissent, struck down the regulations. The panel held that there was insufficient evidence to prove that lead emissions "will endanger the public health or welfare," as required by the Clean Air Act. Emphasizing that EPA could not prove that specific cases of lead poisoning had been caused by gasoline emissions, despite the fact that leaded gasoline had been on the market for 50 years, the majority concluded that "the case against auto lead emissions is a speculative and inconclusive one at best."

EPA sought a rehearing en banc, and the full court agreed to hear the case. In March 1976, the court reversed the panel decision in a 5-4 decision. The majority's decision was written by the late Judge J. Skelly Wright, the dissenting judge in the panel decision. The en banc opinion is over 100 pages long. The following brief excerpt addresses the question of whether the "will endanger" standard of the statute required the EPA to demonstrate that actual harm would occur if the lead content of gasoline was not reduced.

Ethyl Corp. v. EPA
541 F.2d 1 (D.C. Cir. 1976) (en banc)

WRIGHT, Circuit Judge:

... Case law and dictionary definition agree that endanger means something less than actual harm. When one is endangered, harm is *threatened*; no actual injury need ever occur. Thus, for example, a town may be "endangered" by a threatening plague or hurricane and yet emerge from the danger completely unscathed. A statute allowing for regulation in the face of danger is, necessarily, a precautionary statute. Regulatory action may be taken before the threatened harm occurs: indeed, the very existence of such precautionary legislation would seem to *demand* that regulatory action precede, and, optimally, prevent, the perceived threat. ...

The Administrator read [§211(c)(l)(A)] [as a precautionary statute], interpreting "will endanger" to mean "presents a significant risk of harm." We agree with the Administrator's interpretation. ...

While the dictionary admittedly settles on "probable" as its measure of danger, we believe a more sophisticated case-by-case analysis is appropriate. Danger, the Administrator recognized, is not set by a fixed probability of harm, but rather is composed of reciprocal elements of risk and harm, or probability and severity. ... That is to say, the public health may properly be found endangered both by a lesser risk of a greater harm and by a greater risk of a lesser harm. Danger depends upon the relation between the risk and harm presented by each case, and cannot legitimately be pegged to "probable" harm, regardless of whether that harm be great or small. ...

Where a statute is precautionary in nature, the evidence difficult to come by, uncertain, or conflicting because it is on the frontiers of scientific knowledge, the regulations designed to protect the public health, and the decision that of an expert administrator, we will not demand rigorous step-by-step proof of cause and effect. Such proof may be impossible to obtain if the precautionary purpose of the statute is to be served. Of course, we are not suggesting that the Administrator has the power to act on hunches or wild guesses. ... [H]is conclusions must be rationally justified. ... However, we do hold that in such cases the Administrator may assess risks. He must take account of available facts, of course, but his inquiry does not end there. The Administrator may apply his expertise to draw conclusions from suspected, but not completely substantiated, relationships between facts, from trends among facts, from theoretical projections from imperfect data, from probative preliminary data not yet certifiable as "fact," and the like. We believe that a conclusion so drawn—a risk assessment—may, if rational, form the basis for health-related regulations under the "will endanger" language of Section 211.[58]

NOTES AND QUESTIONS

1. *Reserve* and *Ethyl Corp.* differ in several respects. For one thing, in *Reserve* a federal court was asked in the first instance to regulate potentially harmful behavior, while in *Ethyl Corp.* an administrative agency had taken the initial step, which then came before the court for judicial review.

Second, *Reserve* involved a substance, taconite mill tailings, that had not yet been shown to cause adverse health effects, although it was judged physically indistinguishable at the fiber level from asbestos fibers, which had been. The medical concern in *Reserve* was based on a medical opinion, found by the district court to be "reasonable," that such similarity was enough to raise a public health concern. *Ethyl Corp.*, in contrast, involved lead, an element known to be "toxic, causing anemia, severe intestinal cramps, paralysis of nerves, fatigue, and even death." 541 F.2d at 8. The question for the EPA administrator, however, was not whether lead was toxic; rather it was whether "the automotive emissions caused by leaded gasoline present 'a significant risk of harm' to the public health." 541 F.2d at 7. The answer to this question was much less clear than the question of whether lead was toxic, because inhalation of airborne lead was only one of several significant sources of lead exposure for urban children (diet, ingestion of lead-based paint, ingestion of lead in dirt and dust were others), because it was unclear how much inhaled lead contributed to the total body burden of lead,

---

58. It bears emphasis that what is herein described as "assessment of risk" is neither unprecedented nor unique to this area of law. To the contrary, assessment of risk is a normal part of judicial and administrative fact-finding. Thus EPA is not attempting to expand its powers; rather, petitioners seek to constrict the usual flexibility of the fact-finding process. Petitioners argue that the Administrator must decide that lead emissions "will endanger" the public health solely on "facts," or, in the words of the division majority, by a "chain of scientific facts or reasoning leading [the administrator] ineluctably to this conclusion. . . ." Petitioners demand sole reliance on *scientific* facts, on evidence that reputable scientific techniques certify as certain. Typically, a scientist will not so certify evidence unless the probability of error, by standard statistical measurement, is less than 5%. That is, scientific fact is at least 95% certain.

Such certainty has never characterized the judicial or the administrative process. It may be that the "beyond a reasonable doubt" standard of criminal law demands 95% certainty. But the standard of ordinary civil litigation, a preponderance of the evidence, demands only 51% certainty. A jury may weigh conflicting evidence and certify as adjudicative (although not scientific) fact that which it believes is more likely than not. . . . Inherently, such a standard is flexible; inherently, it allows the fact-finder to assess risks, to measure probabilities, to make subjective judgments. Nonetheless, the ultimate finding will be treated, at law, as fact and will be affirmed if based on substantial evidence, or, if made to a judge, not clearly erroneous.

The standard before administrative agencies is no less flexible. . . . Thus, as a matter of administrative law, the Administrator found as *fact* that lead emissions "will endanger" the public health. That in so doing he did not have to rely solely on proved scientific fact is inherent in the requirements of legal fact-finding. Petitioners' assertions of the need to rely on "fact" confuse the two terminologies. We must deal with the terminology of law, not science. At law, unless the administrative or judicial task is peculiarly factual in nature, or Congress expressly commands a more rigorous finding, assessment of risks as herein described typifies both the administrative and the judicial fact-finding function, and is not the novel or unprecedented theory that petitioners contend.

and because it was uncertain at what level of total body burden it became appropriate to conclude lead was having an adverse health effect.

2. In *Ethyl*, EPA had based its decision to require reductions in lead additives on three conclusions: (1) based on a preliminary determination that a level of 40 μg/dl of lead in blood is indicative of a danger to health, a significant part of the population was currently experiencing a dangerous condition because blood lead levels in excess of 40 μg/dl existed to a small but significant extent in the general adult population and to a very great extent among children; (2) airborne lead is directly absorbed in the body through respiration to a degree that constitutes a significant risk to public health; and (3) airborne lead falls to the ground, where it mixes with dust and poses a significant risk to the health of urban children. The court observed that while no specific blood lead level could be identified as the threshold for danger, the 40 μg/dl level was a conservative standard, and that studies of the blood lead levels of workers who work outside and whose only exposure to lead is through the ambient air justified EPA's second conclusion. The court found that theoretical, epidemiological, and clinical studies also supported the second conclusion, and it upheld the third conclusion as a hypothesis consistent with known information about the behavior of children and the presence of high lead concentrations in urban soil and dust.

3. By comparison, consider the government's case in *Reserve*:

> The government's case . . . had several steps, virtually all of which were debatable. The first step was to show that Reserve's tailings were in fact present in Duluth's water supply. The second was to demonstrate that [the taconite tailing] were asbestos or its functional equivalent. . . . Third, while the carcinogenicity of inhaled asbestos was well known, the effects of the ingestion of asbestos were unknown. Lacking direct evidence, the government sought to infer a hazard from epidemiological studies of asbestos workers, animal studies on the movement of fibers within mammalian bodies, and a study of number of fibers found in residents of Duluth. . . . Epidemiological studies of gastrointestinal cancer among Duluth residents did not show a higher than expected rate, however, given the long latency of the disease, the worst effects could have been yet to come. Finally, the government had to show that there were enough asbestos fibers in Duluth's water to have toxic effects. [Applegate at 60-61.]

If you were a young government attorney at the time, would you have thought your chances were better in defending EPA's lead decision in *Ethyl Corp.* or in prosecuting the case in *Reserve*?

4. Shortly after the *Ethyl Corp.* decision, Congress amended the Clean Air Act to change the standard for regulating fuel additives from "will endanger public health or welfare" to "may reasonably be anticipated to endanger the public health or welfare." Is the new statutory standard more consistent with what the EPA administrator actually found in support of the lead phasedown decision than the "will endanger" standard is?

5. The idea that danger or risk is a composite of the probability of harm occurring and the magnitude of the harm that might occur has proved widely influential. Did *Reserve* and *Ethyl Corp.* properly employ this concept in reaching their respective decisions?

As explained earlier, a federal agency must make some threshold finding about a toxic substance before regulation is appropriate. Very often that finding will be related to the danger posed by the substance—sometimes that the substance poses a "significant risk" or an "unreasonable risk," sometimes that the substance "will endanger public health," as in *Ethyl Corp.*, sometimes that the substance "may reasonably be anticipated to endanger public health," as section 211 was subsequently amended to read. (We will return to explore the differences between these and other formulations in Part C of this chapter.)

6. Whatever the threshold level of risk happens to be, the idea that danger is composed of reciprocal elements of probability and severity has the implication that two exposures might both satisfy the threshold finding, even though the probability of one causing harm is much less than the probability of the other one causing harm, as long as the severity of the harm associated with the first is correspondingly greater than that associated with the second. In an article published shortly after *Ethyl Corp.*, Talbot Page employed the image of a seesaw to depict the underlying concept. See Page, A Generic View of Toxic Chemicals and Similar Risks, 7 Ecology L.Q. 207 (1978). We will adopt the same imagery here.

In Figure 3.1, the Threshold Finding can represent some level of risk, whether it be a "will endanger" standard, a "may reasonably be anticipated to endanger" standard, or some other formulation. What *Ethyl Corp.* acknowledges is that the concept of risk gives us at least two variables, magnitude of harm and probability of it occurring. In Figure 3.1, the other rectangular figure represents the probability that a substance under review will actually cause harm, and the distance the rectangle is from the fulcrum, "O," represents the magnitude of that harm, should it occur. The regulator's initial task is to decide whether risk associated with the substance under review exceeds that threshold level of concern or, in seesaw terms, whether the left side pushes the right side down because the left side weighs more. Because there are two variables, the threshold finding might be satisfied either by a high probability of a lesser harm occurring (the seesaw on the left) or by a lower probability of a greater harm occurring (the seesaw on the right).

FIGURE 3.1
Threshold Finding

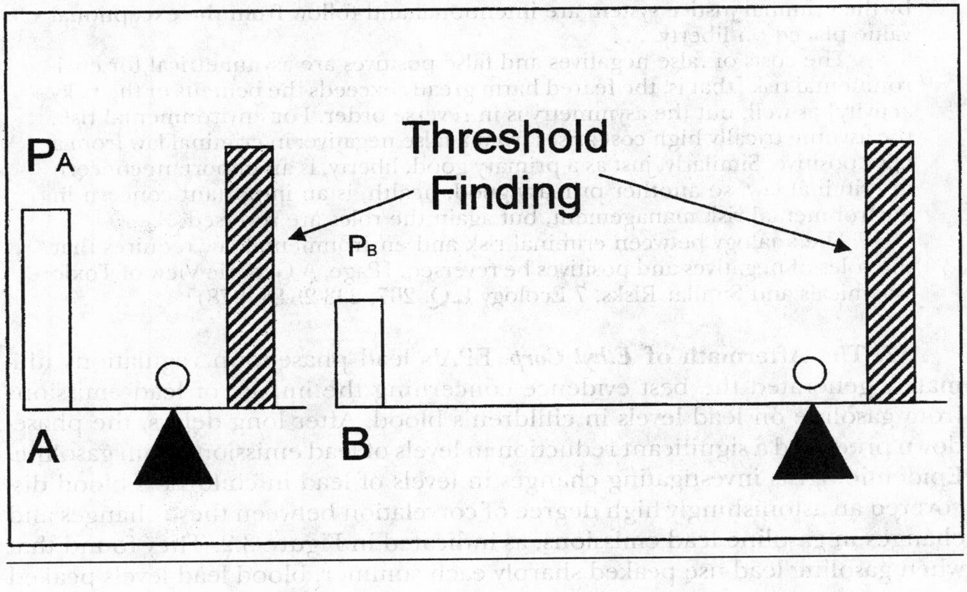

Straightforward as this idea may initially seem, it has powerful implications. One of the most dramatic arises with substances that exceed the relevant threshold even though they have fairly low probabilities of causing harm, because that harm would be catastrophic should it occur. Suppose, for example, that the harm that might occur because of some exposure was 10 times greater than a harm that we would want to prevent if we were certain the smaller harm would occur. Then the seesaw concept of risk or danger would urge us to regulate that exposure even though we thought it only 10 percent likely that the harm would actually occur, because the lower probability of harm occurring would be offset by the greater magnitude of that harm, should it occur.

Now suppose that we have a number of substances that may cause substantial harm, but as to which we are relatively uncertain whether they will. Will following the advice of the seesaw make sensible policy? In terms statisticians (and environmental lawyers) use, this policy tolerates a number of "false positives," chemicals regulated that turn out not to cause the anticipated harm, in order to reduce "false negatives," chemicals not regulated that turn out to cause harm. This is so because the policy regulates such substances when there is only a small chance that the exposure will prove harmful in the feared way. Using the numbers from our example, regulating when there is a 10 percent chance the harm will occur means that over a number of different regulatory decisions we will actually expect to be wrong 90 percent of the time. Over time, in other words, the ratio of "guilty" chemicals to "innocent" chemicals should approach 1 to 9.

This is just the opposite of the criminal law, where many believe that it is better that 10 guilty persons go free (false negatives) than to have a single innocent person convicted (a false positive). Talbot Page argues that these contrasting policies are justified by the different values at stake in each case:

> Limiting false positives is the guiding principle of criminal law. The objective is to limit the chance of a false conviction. . . . A principal reason for this is that liberty is a primary good, i.e., a good for the deprivation of which there is no adequate compensation. The asymmetrical results achieved by the criminal justice system are intentional and follow from the exceptional value placed on liberty. . . .
>
> The costs of false negatives and false positives are asymmetrical for environmental risk [that is, the feared harm greatly exceeds the benefits of the risky activity] as well, but the asymmetry is in reverse order. For environmental risk, the asymmetrically high cost arises from a false negative: in criminal law from a false positive. Similarly, just as a primary good, liberty, is an important concern in criminal law, so another primary good, health, is an important concern in environmental risk management, but again the roles are reversed.
>
> The analogy between criminal risk and environmental law requires that the roles of negatives and positives be reversed. [Page, A Generic View of Toxic Chemicals and Similar Risks, 7 Ecology L.Q. 207, 233-234 (1978)]

7. The Aftermath of *Ethyl Corp*. EPA's lead phasedown regulations ultimately generated the best evidence concerning the impact of lead emissions from gasoline on lead levels in children's blood. After long delays, the phasedown produced a significant reduction in levels of lead emissions from gasoline. Epidemiologists investigating changes in levels of lead in children's blood discovered an astonishingly high degree of correlation between these changes and changes in gasoline lead emissions, as indicated in Figure 3.2. They found that when gasoline lead use peaked sharply each summer, blood lead levels peaked

FIGURE 3.2
Lead Used in Gasoline Production and Average NHANES II
Blood Lead Levels (Feb. 1976-Feb. 1980)

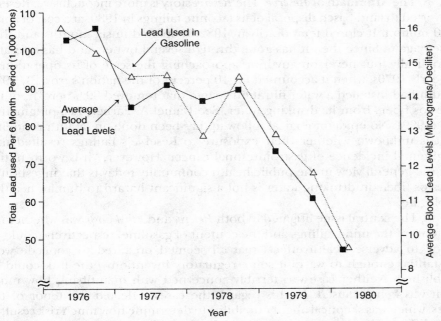

Source: Small Refiner Lead Phasedown Task Force v. EPA, 705 F.2d 506, 528 (D.C. Cir. 1983).

sharply as well. They concluded that this could only be explained by changes in the levels of lead emissions from gasoline because other major sources of lead (lead paint and food) are roughly constant year-round. This and other evidence that had developed subsequent to the *Ethyl Corp.* decision proved so striking that the D.C. Circuit subsequently stated, in a case reviewing even stricter lead limits imposed by EPA in 1982, that "the demonstrated connection between gasoline lead and blood lead, the demonstrated health effects of blood lead levels of 30 µg/dl or above, and the significant risk of adverse health effects from blood lead levels as low as 10-15 µg/dl, would justify EPA in banning lead from gasoline entirely." Small Refiner Lead Phasedown Task Force v. EPA, 705 F.2d 506, 531 (D.C. Cir. 1983). In 1985, EPA went almost that far by requiring reductions in levels of lead in gasoline to one-fifteenth the level upheld in the *Ethyl Corp.* decision. EPA's decision virtually to eliminate lead additives from gasoline relied heavily on the results of a cost-benefit analysis made possible by the initial precautionary action upheld in *Ethyl Corp.* This is one of the reasons that the case "is considered a landmark in U.S. environmental law because it established that EPA could act in a precautionary fashion rather than wait for scientific certainty about the harmfulness of a substance before acting." Ackerman & Heinzerling, Priceless—On Knowing the Price of Everything and the Value of Nothing 4 (2004).

The 1990 Amendments to the Clean Air Act completed the phaseout of gasoline lead additives by entirely prohibiting the sale of leaded gasoline for highway use, effective January 1, 1996. CAA §211(n). The phaseout of lead additives has produced a dramatic reduction in average levels of lead in children's blood. See Figure 1.5, page 34. Thus, it is widely viewed as one of the greatest environmental success stories, even by those otherwise critical of environmental regulation.

8. **The Aftermath of *Reserve*.** The *Reserve* story is more inconclusive. Reserve converted to land-based disposal of its taconite tailings in 1980, at a cost of about $200 million. It closed temporarily in 1982, reopened in six months and then closed again. Since then it has gone through several owners and has operated sporadically, but never on anything approaching the scale of its operation in the early 1970s, when it accounted for 10 percent of the nation's iron. By 1977, Duluth had installed a water filtration system that removed 99.9 percent of the asbestos fibers from its drinking water. See Daniel A. Farber, Eco-pragmatism 124 (1999). No epidemiological follow-up has been done on Duluth residents, so it is unknown whether their exposure to Reserve's tailings resulted in a heightened incidence of gastrointestinal cancer. However, "it is worth noting that the general view in the public health community today is that ingestion of asbestos fibers in drinking water is not a significant hazard to human health." Applegate, 74.

9. The central issue litigated in both *Reserve* and *Ethyl Corp.* was whether the contents of the mine tailings and the content of gasoline, respectively, could be linked to adverse health effects that all seemed prepared to concede were substantial enough to warrant some regulatory invention *if* the link could be established. Neither case was terribly concerned with quantifying how much harm was being caused. In this regard, the cases reflected the tenor of the times, which was skeptical about our ability to determine how much risk resulted from different levels of exposure to environmental hazards such as these. In the mid-1970s, for instance, committees of both the House and the Senate examined approaches to quantifying environmental risk. One concluded that "the number of unknowns contributing to the measurement of risk make the measurements . . . only a rough indication of effects. [In particular, efforts] to precisely measure risk posed by individual cancer-causing agents currently involve so many obstacles that they are an essentially useless exercise . . ." Report of the Subcomm. on Oversight and Investigations of the Comm. on Interstate and Foreign Commerce, H.R., 94th Cong., 2d Sess. 510-511, 515 (1976). The other reasoned that when regulation addresses "health, safety and environmental" issues, "it is extremely difficult to quantify benefits since they are subject to great uncertainty and often become apparent only with the passage of time. . . . [In particular,] there is the question of how the value of risks to human life, injury and suffering are computed. At present, there is no generally accepted method for evaluating such losses." Study of Federal Regulation, Vol. VI, Committee on Governmental Affairs, S., 96th Cong., 1st Sess. xxiv (1978).

Notwithstanding this skepticism, the use of risk assessments that quantify the amount of risk associated with different environmental exposures has become routine in the modern regulatory state. The next section examines the ascendancy of quantitative risk assessment techniques.

2. *Quantifying Risks Subject to Regulation*

While the *Ethyl Corp.* decision stands as a powerful endorsement of the concept of precautionary regulation, neither it nor the "precautionary principle" provide a ready answer for the question of how precautionary regulatory policy should be. See Percival, Who Is Afraid of the Precautionary Principle?, 23 Pace Envtl. L. Rev. 801, 808 (2006). The *Ethyl Corp.* majority stated that regulations could not be based "on hunches or wild guesses," and it expressly endorsed the notion that regulators should engage in risk assessment. Four years later an influential Supreme Court decision provided even greater momentum toward development and use of quantitative risk assessment techniques. The decision reviewed regulation of toxic exposures in the workplace by the Occupational Health and Safety Administration (OSHA) of the Department of Labor.

The Occupational Safety and Health Act requires OSHA to establish standards to control workplace exposures to toxic substances. Section 6(b) of the OSH Act directs OSHA to "set the standard which most adequately assures, to the extent feasible, on the basis of the best available evidence, that no employee will suffer material impairment of health or functional capacity even if such employee has regular exposure to the hazard dealt with by such standard for the period of his working life," 29 U.S.C. §655(b)(5). The OSH Act initially authorized OSHA to set exposure limits based on previously established national consensus standards. Thus, in 1971 OSHA adopted the threshold limit values (TLVs) recognized by the American Council of Government Industrial Hygienists (ACGIH) and approximately 20 consensus standards established by the American National Standards Institute (ANSI). To assist OSHA in promulgating permanent exposure limits, the OSH Act established the National Institute for Occupational Safety and Health (NIOSH), a research agency charged with recommending occupational safety and health standards to OSHA.

In October 1976 NIOSH strongly recommended that OSHA promulgate an emergency temporary standard (ETS) to protect employees from "grave danger" from exposure to benzene. NIOSH based this recommendation on epidemiological studies showing that workers exposed to benzene were suffering an unusually high incidence of cases of leukemia. After OSHA issued an ETS of 1 ppm effective May 1977, the standard was invalidated by the U.S. Court of Appeals for the Fifth Circuit. OSHA then conducted a rulemaking to promulgate a permanent permissible exposure limit (PEL) for benzene of 1 ppm, which again was struck down by the Fifth Circuit.

The Fifth Circuit held that OSHA had not demonstrated that the costs of the standard bore a reasonable relationship to its benefits. OSHA sought Supreme Court review to consider whether such cost-benefit balancing was required under the OSH Act. A badly divided Supreme Court then surprised the parties by deciding the case on other grounds.

	Industrial Union Dept., AFL-CIO v.	
	American Petroleum Institute	
	448 U.S. 607 (1980) (the Benzene decision)	

MR. JUSTICE STEVENS announced the judgment of the Court and delivered an opinion, in which THE CHIEF JUSTICE and MR. JUSTICE STEWART joined and in Parts I, II, III-A, III-B, III-C and III-E of which MR. JUSTICE POWELL joined.

[Justice Stevens set forth the facts of the case at some length, reciting the studies upon which OSHA had relied, and the industries' criticisms of them.

Although studies associated benzene with a variety of adverse health effects, including nonmalignant blood disorders, chromosomal aberrations, and leukemia, all studies were at levels of exposure higher than 10 ppm. The Court found the record evidence of adverse effects at that level "sketchy at best."]

In the end, OSHA's rationale for lowering the permissible exposure limit to 1 ppm was based, not on any finding that leukemia has ever been caused by exposure to 10 ppm of benzene and that it will *not* be caused at 1 ppm, but rather on a series of assumptions indicating that some leukemias might result from exposure to 10 ppm and that the number of cases would probably be reduced by reducing the exposure level to 1 ppm. In reaching this result, the Agency first unequivocally concluded that benzene is a human carcinogen. Second, it concluded that industry had failed to prove that there is a safe threshold level of exposure to benzene.

[Having made these findings and conclusions, OSHA determined that 1 ppm was the lowest feasible level of exposure that could be achieved. Estimated compliance costs included $266 million in capital investments, $200 million in first-year, startup costs, and $34 million in annual costs. About 35,000 employees would benefit from the regulation.

As Justice Stevens framed the issues, there were two arguably relevant sections of the Occupational Safety and Health Act, section 3(8), which defines an "occupational safety and health standard," and section 6(b)(5), which instructs the Secretary to set a standard based on feasibility. The two provisions read as follows:

> The term "occupational safety and health standard" means a standard which requires conditions, or the adoption or use of one or more practices, means, methods, operations, or processes, reasonably necessary or appropriate to provide safe or healthful employment and places of employment. §3(8), 29 U.S.C. §652(8).
>
> The Secretary, in promulgating standards dealing with toxic materials or harmful physical agents under this subsection, shall set the standard which most adequately assures, to the extent feasible, on the basis of the best available evidence, that no employee will suffer material impairment of health or functional capacity even if such employee has regular exposure to the hazard dealt with by such standard for the period of his working life. Development of standards under this subsection shall be based upon research, demonstrations, experiments, and such other information as may be appropriate. In addition to the attainment of the highest degree of health and safety protection for the employee, other considerations shall be the latest available scientific data in the field, the feasibility of the standards, and experience gained under this and other health and safety laws. §6(b)(5), 29 U.S.C. §655(b)(5).]

III

. . . In the Government's view, §3(8)'s definition of the term "standard" has no legal significance or at best merely requires that a standard not be totally irrational. It takes the position that §6(b)(5) is controlling and that it requires OSHA to promulgate a standard that either gives an absolute assurance of safety for each and every worker or reduces exposures to the lowest level feasible. The Government interprets "feasible" as meaning technologically achievable at a cost that would not impair the viability of the industries subject to the regulation. The respondent industry representatives, on the other hand, argue that the Court of Appeals was correct in holding that the "reasonably necessary and appropriate" language of §3(8), along with the feasibility requirement of §6(b)(5), requires the Agency to quantify both the costs and the benefits of a proposed rule and to conclude that they are roughly commensurate.

In our view, it is not necessary to decide whether either the Government or industry is entirely correct. For we think it is clear that §3(8) does apply to all permanent standards promulgated under the Act and that it requires the Secretary, before issuing any standard, to determine that it is reasonably necessary and appropriate to remedy a significant risk of material health impairment. Only after the Secretary has made the threshold determination that such a risk exists with respect to a toxic substance would it be necessary to decide whether §6(b)(5) requires him to select the most protective standard he can consistent with economic and technological feasibility, or whether, as respondents argue, the benefits of the regulation must be commensurate with the costs of its implementation. Because the Secretary did not make the required threshold finding in these cases, we have no occasion to determine whether costs must be weighed against benefits in an appropriate case.

Under the Government's view, §3(8), if it has any substantive content at all, merely requires OSHA to issue standards that are reasonably calculated to produce a safer or more healthy work environment. Apart from this minimal requirement of rationality, the Government argues that §3(8) imposes no limits on the Agency's power, and thus would not prevent it from requiring employers to do whatever would be "reasonably necessary" to eliminate all risks of any harm from their workplaces. With respect to toxic substances and harmful physical agents, the Government takes an even more extreme position. Relying on §6(b)(5)'s direction to set a standard "which most adequately assures . . . that no employee will suffer material impairment of health or functional capacity," the Government contends that the Secretary is required to impose standards that either guarantee workplaces that are free from any risk of material health impairment, however small, or that come as close as possible to doing so without ruining entire industries.

If the purpose of the statute were to eliminate completely and with absolute certainty any risk of serious harm, we would agree that it would be proper for the Secretary to interpret §§3(8) and 6(b)(5) in this fashion. But we think it is clear that the statute was not designed to require employers to provide absolutely risk-free workplaces whenever it is technologically feasible to do so, so long as the cost is not great enough to destroy an entire industry. Rather, both the language and structure of the Act, as well as its legislative history, indicate that it was intended to require the elimination, as far as feasible, of significant risks of harm.

B

By empowering the Secretary to promulgate standards that are "reasonably necessary or appropriate to provide safe or healthful employment and places of employment," the Act implies that, before promulgating any standard, the Secretary must make a finding that the workplaces in question are not safe. But "safe" is not the equivalent of "risk-free." There are many activities that we engage in every day—such as driving a car or even breathing city air—that entail some risk of accident or material health impairment; nevertheless, few people would consider these activities "unsafe." Similarly, a workplace can hardly be considered "unsafe" unless it threatens the workers with a significant risk of harm.

Therefore, before he can promulgate *any* permanent health or safety standard, the Secretary is required to make a threshold finding that a place of employment is unsafe—in the sense that significant risks are present and can be eliminated or lessened by a change in practices. This requirement applies to permanent standards promulgated pursuant to §6(b)(5), as well as to other types of permanent standards. For there is no reason why §3(8)'s definition of a standard should not be incorporated by reference into §6(b)(5). . . .

This interpretation of §§3(8) and 6(b)(5) is supported by the other provisions of the Act. Thus, for example, §6(g) provides in part that

> [i]n determining the priority for establishing standards under this section, the Secretary shall give due regard to the urgency of the need for mandatory safety and health standards for particular industries, trades, crafts, occupations, businesses, workplaces or work environments.

The Government has expressly acknowledged that this section requires the Secretary to undertake some cost-benefit analysis before he promulgates any standard, requiring the elimination of the most serious hazards first. If such an analysis must precede the promulgation of any standard, it seems manifest that Congress intended, at a bare minimum, that the Secretary find a significant risk of harm and therefore a probability of significant benefits before establishing a new standard.

Section 6(b)(8) lends additional support to this analysis. That subsection requires that, when the Secretary substantially alters an existing consensus standard, he must explain how the new rule will "better effectuate" the purpose of the Act. If this requirement was intended to be more than a meaningless formality, it must be read to impose upon the Secretary the duty to find that an existing national consensus standard is not adequate to protect workers from a continuing and significant risk of harm. Thus, in this case, the Secretary was required to find that exposures at the current permissible exposure level of 10 ppm present a significant risk of harm in the workplace.

In the absence of a clear mandate in the Act, it is unreasonable to assume that Congress intended to give the Secretary the unprecedented power over American industry that would result from the Government's view of §§3(8) and 6(b)(5), coupled with OSHA's cancer policy. Expert testimony that a substance is probably a human carcinogen—either because it has caused cancer in animals or because individuals have contracted cancer following extremely high exposures—would justify the conclusion that the substance poses some risk of serious harm no matter how minute the exposure and no matter how many experts testified that they regarded the risk as insignificant. That conclusion would in turn justify pervasive regulation limited only by the constraint of feasibility. In light of the fact that there are literally thousands of substances used in the workplace that have been identified as carcinogens or suspect carcinogens, the Government's theory would give OSHA power to impose enormous costs that might produce little, if any, discernible benefit.

If the Government were correct in arguing that neither §3(8) nor §6(b)(5) requires that the risk from a toxic substance be quantified sufficiently to enable the Secretary to characterize it as significant in an understandable way, the statute would make such a "sweeping delegation of legislative power" that it might be unconstitutional under the Court's reasoning in A.L.A. Schechter Poultry Corp. v. United States, 295 U.S. 495, 539, and Panama Refining Co. v. Ryan, 293 U.S. 388. A construction of the statute that avoids this kind of open-ended grant should certainly be favored.

The legislative history also supports the conclusion that Congress was concerned, not with absolute safety, but with the elimination of significant harm. The examples of industrial hazards referred to in the Committee hearings and debates all involved situations in which the risk was unquestionably significant. For example, the Senate Committee on Labor and Public Welfare noted that byssinosis, a disabling lung disease caused by breathing cotton dust, affected as many as 30% of the workers in carding or spinning rooms in some American cotton mills and that as many as 100,000 active or retired workers were then suffering from the disease. It also noted that statistics indicated that 20,000 out of 50,000 workers who had performed insulation work were likely to die of asbestosis, lung cancer, or mesothelioma as a result of breathing asbestos fibers. . . .

D

Given the conclusion that the Act empowers the Secretary to promulgate health and safety standards only where a significant risk of harm exists, the critical issue becomes how to define and allocate the burden of proving the significance of the risk in a case such as this, where scientific knowledge is imperfect and the precise quantification of risks is therefore impossible. The Agency's position is that there is substantial evidence in the record to support its conclusion that there is no absolutely safe level for a carcinogen and that, therefore, the burden is properly on industry to prove, apparently beyond a shadow of a doubt, that there *is* a safe level for benzene exposure. The Agency argues that, because of the uncertainties in this area, any other approach would render it helpless, forcing it to wait for the leukemia deaths that it believes are likely to occur before taking any regulatory action.

We disagree. As we read the statute, the burden was on the Agency to show, on the basis of substantial evidence, that it is at least more likely than not that long-term exposure to 10 ppm of benzene presents a significant risk of material health impairment. Ordinarily, it is the proponent of a rule or order who has the burden of proof in administrative proceedings. See 5 U.S.C. §556(d). In some cases involving toxic substances, Congress has shifted the burden of proving that a particular substance is safe onto the party opposing the proposed rule.[61] The fact that Congress did not follow this course in enacting the Occupational Safety and Health Act indicates that it intended the Agency to bear the normal burden of establishing the need for a proposed standard.

In this case OSHA did not even attempt to carry its burden of proof. The closest it came to making a finding that benzene presented a significant risk of harm in the workplace was its statement that the benefits to be derived from

---

61. See Environmental Defense Fund, Inc. v. EPA, 548 F.2d 998, 1004, 1012-1018 (1977), cert. denied, 431 U.S. 925, where the court rejected the argument that the EPA has the burden of proving that a pesticide is unsafe in order to suspend its registration under the Federal Insecticide, Fungicide, and Rodenticide Act. The court noted that Congress has deliberately shifted the ordinary burden of proof under the APA, requiring manufacturers to establish the continued safety of their products.

lowering the permissible exposure level from 10 to 1 ppm were "likely" to be "appreciable." The Court of Appeals held that this finding was not supported by substantial evidence. Of greater importance, even if it were supported by substantial evidence, such a finding would not be sufficient to satisfy the Agency's obligations under the Act.

The inadequacy of the Agency's findings can perhaps be illustrated best by its rejection of industry testimony that a dose-response curve can be formulated on the basis of current epidemiological evidence and that, even under the most conservative extrapolation theory, current exposure levels would cause at most two deaths out of a population of about 30,000 workers every six years. In rejecting this testimony, OSHA made the following statement:

> In the face of the record evidence of numerous actual deaths attributable to benzene-induced leukemia and other fatal blood diseases, OSHA is unwilling to rely on the hypothesis that at most two cancers every six years would be prevented by the proposed standard. By way of example, the Infante study disclosed seven excess leukemia deaths in a population of about 600 people over a 25-year period. While the Infante study involved higher exposures than those currently encountered, the incidence rates found by Infante, together with the numerous other cases reported in the literature of benzene leukemia and other fatal blood diseases, make it difficult for OSHA to rely on the [witness's] hypothesis to assure the statutorily mandated protection of employees. In any event, due to the fact that there is no safe level of exposure to benzene and that it is impossible to precisely quantify the anticipated benefits, OSHA must select the level of exposure which is most protective of exposed employees. 43 Fed. Reg. 5941 (1978).

There are three possible interpretations of OSHA's stated reason for rejecting the witness' testimony: (1) OSHA considered it probable that a greater number of lives would be saved by lowering the standard from 10 ppm; (2) OSHA thought that saving two lives every six years in a work force of 30,000 persons is a significant savings that makes it reasonable and appropriate to adopt a new standard; or (3) even if the small number is not significant and even if the savings may be even smaller, the Agency nevertheless believed it had a statutory duty to select the level of exposure that is most protective of the exposed employees if it is economically and technologically feasible to do so. Even if the Secretary did not intend to rely entirely on this third theory, his construction of the statute would make it proper for him to do so. Moreover, he made no express findings of fact that would support his 1 ppm standard on any less drastic theory. Under these circumstances, we can hardly agree with the Government that OSHA discharged its duty under the Act.

Contrary to the Government's contentions, imposing a burden on the Agency of demonstrating a significant risk of harm will not strip it of its ability to regulate carcinogens, nor will it require the Agency to wait for deaths to occur before taking any action. First, the requirement that a "significant" risk be identified is not a mathematical straitjacket. It is the Agency's responsibility to determine, in the first instance, what it considers to be a "significant" risk. Some risks are plainly acceptable and others are plainly unacceptable. If, for example, the odds are one in a billion that a person will die from cancer by taking a drink of chlorinated water, the risk clearly could not be considered significant. On the other hand, if the odds are one in a thousand that regular inhalation of gasoline vapors that are 2% benzene will be fatal, a reasonable person might well consider the risk significant and take appropriate steps to decrease or eliminate it. Although the Agency has no duty to calculate the exact probability of harm, it does have an obligation to find that a significant risk is present before it can characterize a place of employment as "unsafe."

Second, OSHA is not required to support its finding that a significant risk exists with anything approaching scientific certainty. Although the Agency's findings must be supported by substantial evidence, 29 U.S.C. §655(f), §6(b)(5) specifically allows the Secretary to regulate on the basis of the "best available evidence." As several Courts of Appeals have held, this provision requires a reviewing court to give OSHA some leeway where its findings must be made on the frontiers of scientific knowledge. Thus, so long as they are supported by a body of reputable scientific thought, the Agency is free to use conservative assumptions in interpreting the data with respect to carcinogens, risking error on the side of overprotection rather than underprotection.

Finally, the record in this case and OSHA's own rulings on other carcinogens indicate that there are a number of ways in which the Agency can make a rational judgment about the relative significance of the risks associated with exposure to a particular carcinogen.[64]

[In a concurring opinion, Justice Powell indicated that although he would not rule out the possibility that OSHA's regulation of benzene could have been upheld on the basis of a properly promulgated generic cancer policy, OSHA had not adopted such a policy at the time it established its revised PEL for benzene. Justice Powell indicated that he agreed with the Fifth Circuit's decision below that the "reasonably necessary" language of §3(8) required OSHA to establish that the costs of its regulations were not disproportionate to their benefits.]

MR. JUSTICE REHNQUIST, concurring in the judgment.

. . . I believe that this litigation presents the Court with what has to be one of the most difficult issues that could confront a decision-maker: whether the statistical possibility of future deaths should ever be disregarded in light of the economic costs of preventing those deaths. I would also suggest that the widely varying positions advanced in the briefs of the parties and in the opinions of Mr. Justice Stevens, the Chief Justice, Mr. Justice Powell, and Mr. Justice Marshall demonstrate, perhaps better than any other fact, that Congress, the governmental body best suited and most obligated to make the choice confronting us in this litigation, has improperly delegated that choice to the Secretary of Labor and, derivatively, to this Court. . . .

Read literally, the relevant portion of §6(b)(5) is completely precatory, admonishing the Secretary to adopt the most protective standard if he can, but excusing him from that duty if he cannot. In the case of a hazardous substance for which a "safe" level is either unknown or impractical, the language of §6(b)(5) gives the Secretary absolutely no indication where on the continuum of relative safety he should draw his line. Especially in light of the importance of the

---

64. In other proceedings, the Agency has had a good deal of data from animal experiments on which it could base a conclusion on the significance of the risk. . . .

In this case the Agency did not have the benefit of animal studies, because scientists have been unable as yet to induce leukemia in experimental animals as a result of benzene exposure. It did, however, have a fair amount of epidemiological evidence, including both positive and negative studies. Although the Agency stated that this evidence was insufficient to construct a precise correlation between exposure levels and cancer risks, it would at least be helpful in determining whether it is more likely than not that there is a significant risk at 10 ppm.

interests at stake, I have no doubt that the provision at issue, standing alone, would violate the doctrine against uncanalized delegations of legislative power. . . .

[Justice Rehnquist then discussed why he believed that additional constraints on OSHA's authority cannot be ascertained from the legislative history or context of §6(b)(5). He termed that section's feasibility requirement "a legislative mirage" that could assume "any form desired by the beholder." He then concluded that this was not a question of whether such an unconstrained delegation was necessary.]

. . . It is difficult to imagine a more obvious example of Congress simply avoiding a choice which was both fundamental for purposes of the statute and yet politically so divisive that the necessary decision or compromise was difficult, if not impossible, to hammer out in the legislative forge. Far from detracting from the substantive authority of Congress, a declaration that the first sentence of §6(b)(5) of the Occupational Safety and Health Act constitutes an invalid delegation to the Secretary of Labor would preserve the authority of Congress. If Congress wishes to legislate in an area in which it has not previously sought to enter, it will in today's political world undoubtedly run into opposition no matter how the legislation is formulated. But that is the very essence of legislative authority under our system. It is the hard choices, and not the filling in of the blanks, which must be made by the elected representatives of the people. When fundamental policy decisions underlying important legislation about to be enacted are to be made, the buck stops with Congress and the President insofar as he exercises his constitutional role in the legislative process. . . .

Accordingly, for the reasons stated above, I concur in the judgment of the Court affirming the judgment of the Court of Appeals.

MR. JUSTICE MARSHALL, with whom MR. JUSTICE BRENNAN, MR. JUSTICE WHITE, and MR. JUSTICE BLACKMUN join, dissenting. . . .

[T]oday's decision represents a usurpation of decision making authority that has been exercised by and properly belongs with Congress and its authorized representatives. The plurality's construction has no support in the statute's language, structure, or legislative history. The threshold finding that the plurality requires is the plurality's own invention. It bears no relationship to the acts or intentions of Congress, and it can be understood only as reflecting the personal views of the plurality as to the proper allocation of resources for safety in the American workplace.

The plurality is obviously more interested in the consequences of its decision than in discerning the intention of Congress. But since the language and legislative history of the Act are plain, there is no need for conjecture about the effects of today's decision. "It is not for us to speculate, much less act, on whether Congress would have altered its stance had the specific events of this case been anticipated." TVA v. Hill, 437 U.S., at 185. I do not pretend to know whether the test the plurality erects today is, as a matter of policy, preferable to that created by Congress and its delegates: the area is too fraught with scientific uncertainty, and too dependent on considerations of policy, for a court to be able to determine whether it is desirable to require identification of a "significant" risk before allowing an administrative agency to take regulatory action. But in light of the tenor of the plurality opinion, it is necessary to point out that the question is not one-sided, and that Congress' decision to authorize the Secretary to promulgate the regulation at issue here was a reasonable one.

In this case the Secretary found that exposure to benzene at levels [of] about 1 ppm posed a definite, albeit unquantifiable, risk of chromosomal damage, nonmalignant blood disorders, and leukemia. The existing evidence was sufficient to justify the conclusion that such a risk was presented, but it did not permit even rough quantification of that risk. Discounting for the various scientific uncertainties, the Secretary gave "careful consideration to the question of whether th[e] substantial costs" of the standard "are justified in light of the hazards of exposure to benzene," and concluded that "these costs are necessary in order to effectuate the statutory purpose . . . and to adequately protect employees from the hazards of exposure to benzene," 43 Fed. Reg. 5941 (1978).

In these circumstances it seems clear that the Secretary found a risk that is "significant" in the sense that the word is normally used. There was some direct evidence of chromosomal damage, nonmalignant blood disorders, and leukemia at exposures at or near 10 ppm and below. In addition, expert after expert testified that the recorded effects of benzene exposure at higher levels justified an inference that an exposure level above 1 ppm was dangerous. The plurality's extraordinarily searching scrutiny of this factual record reveals no basis for a conclusion that quantification is, on the basis of "the best available evidence," possible at the present time. If the Secretary decided to wait until definitive information was available, American workers would be subjected for the indefinite future to a possibly substantial risk of benzene-induced leukemia and other illnesses. It is unsurprising, at least to me, that he concluded that the statute authorized him to take regulatory action now.

Under these circumstances, the plurality's requirement of identification of a "significant" risk will have one of two consequences. If the plurality means to require the Secretary realistically to "quantify" the risk in order to satisfy a court that it is "significant," the record shows that the plurality means to require him to do the impossible. But regulatory inaction has very significant costs of its own. The adoption of such a test would subject American workers to a continuing risk of cancer and other serious diseases; it would disable the Secretary from regulating a wide variety of carcinogens for which quantification simply cannot be undertaken at the present time.

There are encouraging signs that today's decision does not extend that far. My Brother POWELL concludes that the Secretary is not prevented from taking regulatory action "when reasonable quantification cannot be accomplished by any known methods." The plurality also indicates that it would not prohibit the Secretary from promulgating safety standards when quantification of the benefits is impossible. The Court might thus allow the Secretary to attempt to make a very rough quantification of the risk imposed by a carcinogenic substance, and give considerable deference to his finding that the risk was significant. If so, the Court would permit the Secretary to promulgate precisely the same regulation involved in these cases if he had not relied on a carcinogen "policy," but undertaken a review of the evidence and the expert testimony and concluded, on the basis of conservative assumptions, that the risk addressed is a significant one. Any other interpretation of the plurality's approach would allow a court to displace the agency's judgment with its own subjective conception of "significance," a duty to be performed without statutory guidance.

The consequences of this second approach would hardly be disastrous; indeed, it differs from my own principally in its assessment of the basis for the Secretary's decision in these cases. It is objectionable, however, for three reasons. First, the requirement of identification of a "significant" risk simply has no relationship to the statute that the Court today purports to construe. Second, if the "threshold finding" requirement means only that the Secretary must find "that there is a need for such a standard," the requirement was plainly satisfied by the Secretary's express statement that the standard's costs "are necessary in order to effectuate the statutory purpose . . . and to adequately protect employees from the hazards of exposure to benzene." 43 Fed. Reg. 5941 (1978). Third, the record amply demonstrates that in light of existing scientific knowledge, no purpose would be served by requiring the Secretary to take steps to quantify the risk of exposure to benzene at low levels. Any such quantification would be based not on scientific "knowledge" as that term is normally understood, but on considerations of policy. For carcinogens like benzene, the assumptions on which a dose-response curve must be based are necessarily arbitrary. To require a quantitative showing of a "significant" risk, therefore, would either paralyze the Secretary into inaction or force him to deceive the public by acting on the basis of assumptions that must be considered too speculative to support any realistic assessment of the relevant risk. See McGarity, Substantive and Procedural Discretion in Administrative Resolution of Science Policy Questions: Regulating Carcinogens in EPA and OSHA, 67 Geo. L.J. 729, 806 (1979). It is encouraging that the Court appears willing not to require quantification when it is not fairly possible.

Though it is difficult to see how a future Congress could be any more explicit on the matter than was the Congress that passed the Act in 1970, it is important to remember that today's decision is subject to legislative reversal. Congress may continue to believe that the Secretary should not be prevented from protecting American workers from cancer and other fatal diseases until scientific evidence has progressed to a point where he can convince a federal court that the risk is "significant." Today's decision is objectionable not because it is final, but because it places the burden of legislative inertia on the beneficiaries of the safety and health legislation in question in these cases. By allocating the burden in this fashion, the Court requires the American worker to return to the political arena and to win a victory that he won once before in 1970. I am unable to discern any justification for that result. . . .

In passing the Occupational Safety and Health Act of 1970, Congress was aware that it was authorizing the Secretary to regulate in areas of scientific uncertainty. But it intended to require stringent regulation even when definitive information was unavailable. In reducing the permissible level of exposure to benzene, the Secretary applied proper legal standards. His determinations are supported by substantial evidence. The Secretary's decision was one, then, which the governing legislation authorized him to make.

In recent years there has been increasing recognition that the products of technological development may have harmful effects whose incidence and severity cannot be predicted with certainty. The responsibility to regulate such products has fallen to administrative agencies. Their task is not an enviable one. Frequently no clear causal link can be established between the regulated substance and the harm to be averted. Risks of harm are often uncertain, but inaction has considerable costs of its own. The agency must decide whether to take regulatory action against possibly substantial risks or to wait until more definitive information becomes available—a judgment which by its very nature cannot be based solely on determinations of fact.

Those delegations, in turn, have been made on the understanding that judicial review would be available to ensure that the agency's determinations are supported by substantial evidence and that its actions do not exceed the limits set by Congress. In the Occupational Safety and Health Act, Congress expressed confidence that the courts would carry out this important responsibility. But in these cases the plurality has far exceeded its authority. The plurality's "threshold finding" requirement is nowhere to be found in the Act and is antithetical to its basic purposes. "The fundamental policy questions appropriately resolved in Congress . . . are *not* subject to re-examination in the federal courts under the guise of judicial review of agency action." Vermont Yankee Nuclear Power Corp. v. NRDC, 435 U.S. at 558 (emphasis in original). Surely this is no less true of the decision to ensure safety for the American worker than the decision to proceed with nuclear power. See ibid.

Because the approach taken by the plurality is so plainly irreconcilable with the Court's proper institutional role, I am certain that it will not stand the test of time. In all likelihood, today's decision will come to be regarded as an extreme reaction to a regulatory scheme that, as the Members of the plurality perceived it, imposed an unduly harsh burden on regulated industries. But as the Constitution "does not enact Mr. Herbert Spencer's Social Statics," Lochner v. New York, 198 U.S. 45, 75 (1905) (Holmes, J., dissenting), so the responsibility to scrutinize federal administrative action does not authorize this Court to strike its own balance between the costs and benefits of occupational safety standards. I am confident that the approach taken by the plurality today, like that in *Lochner* itself, will eventually be abandoned, and that the representative branches of government will once again be allowed to determine the level of safety and health protection to be accorded to the American worker.

NOTES AND QUESTIONS

1. What did OSHA fail to do in promulgating a revised PEL for benzene that in the Court's view was necessary for the regulation to withstand judicial review? As a result of the Court's decision, what must OSHA do differently in the future?

2. In light of the *Benzene* decision, who bears the burden of proving that the risk to be regulated is "significant"? How does Justice Stevens justify this allocation of the burden of proof? How can this burden be discharged?

3. Why did OSHA fail to prepare quantified dose-response estimates for benzene prior to promulgating the revised PEL? Did OSHA believe that its revised PEL for benzene would have significant benefits? Must OSHA prepare quantitative dose-response estimates in the future?

4. In most cases involving the regulation of potentially toxic substances there is considerable uncertainty over the magnitude and nature of the substance's impact on health. One means of coping with uncertainty is to use default assumptions or a "safety factor" approach that errs on the side of caution to protect health. Is OSHA free to use such conservative assumptions after *Benzene?* How much confidence must OSHA have in its finding that a risk is significant before it will withstand judicial review?

5. What is the principal point of disagreement between Justice Stevens's plurality opinion and Justice Marshall's dissent? In cases in which a substance is known to pose a risk but it is impossible to quantify the *magnitude* of the risk, what would happen under Justice Stevens's approach? Under Justice Marshall's?

6. How "significant" must a risk be in order to satisfy Justice Stevens? His plurality opinion notes that "safe" does not mean "risk free." He later states that a risk of one in a billion of dying from drinking chlorinated water is "clearly not significant," while a risk of one in a thousand that benzene inhalation might be fatal might well lead a reasonable person to consider the risk "significant." Where is the line between "significant" and "insignificant" risks to be drawn and by whom? Does Justice Marshall advocate a zero risk approach? Would he permit OSHA to regulate truly trivial risks? We will return to the question of "how safe is safe" in section C of this chapter.

7. Only three other Justices (Chief Justice Burger, Justice Stewart, and Justice Powell) joined in Justice Stevens's plurality opinion. Justice Powell did not join Part III-D of Justice Stevens's opinion, which discussed how to define and allocate the burden of proving the significance of a risk. In a concurring opinion, Justice Powell noted that he "would not rule out the possibility that the necessary findings [of significant risk] could rest in part on generic policies properly adopted by OSHA." Justice Powell, however, also expressed the view that OSHA was required "to determine that the economic effects of its standard bear a reasonable relationship to the expected benefits." As a result of the unusual 4-4-1 split, what is the actual "holding" in this case?

8. Justice Stevens's plurality opinion bases the requirement that OSHA determine that risks to be regulated are "significant" on an interpretation of section 3(8) of the OSH Act, 29 U.S.C. §652, which defines the term "occupational safety and health standard." What impact, if any, is the Court's decision likely to have on the regulation of toxic substances by EPA and other agencies operating under different statutory authorities?

9. Justice Rehnquist argues that section 6(b)(5) of the OSH Act is an unconstitutional delegation of legislative power to OSHA, a position that is not accepted by any other member of the Court. What do you think Congress would have to do to satisfy his concern? Compare Justice Rehnquist's position with that of the Court in Whitman v. American Trucking Ass'ns, 531 U.S. 457 (2001), discussed in Chapter 5, page 486.

10. The Fifth Circuit had struck down OSHA's benzene PEL largely because OSHA had failed to demonstrate that the benefits of the standard bore a reasonable relationship to its costs. When the case was briefed and argued in the Supreme Court, it was widely expected that the Court would determine whether or not some form of cost-benefit balancing was required by the OSH Act. Why did the Supreme Court refuse to decide this issue? One year after the *Benzene* decision the Court again was faced with the question whether the OSH Act required some balancing of costs and benefits. In American Textile Manufacturers Institute, Inc. v. Donovan, 452 U.S. 488 (1981) (the *Cotton Dust* case), the Court held that the OSH Act did not require cost-benefit balancing. The case was argued the day after the Reagan administration assumed office. The Justice Department asked the Court for a voluntary remand because the Reagan administration disagreed with OSHA's former position that cost-benefit balancing was not required. The Court refused, and decided the case in favor of OSHA. The vote was 5-3, with Justice Stevens joining the four *Benzene* dissenters. For an account of this case and the court's unusual efforts to muster a majority in *Benzene*, see Percival, Environmental Law in the Supreme Court: Highlights from the Marshall Papers, 23 Envtl. L. Rep. 10606, 10614-10616 (1993).

11. For an in-depth discussion of the *Benzene* story, see Thomas O. McGarity, The Story of the Benzene Case: Judicially Imposed Regulatory Reform

Through Risk Assessment, in Environmental Law Stories 141 (Houck & Lazarus eds., 2005).

A Note on Regulation of Benzene by OSHA Following the *Benzene* Decision

Justice Marshall's prediction that the plurality decision would "eventually be abandoned" proved inaccurate. In fact, Justice Stevens's opinion provided considerable further impetus to a direction in which federal agencies were already heading—toward greater use of quantitative risk assessment as part of an overall approach to rulemaking. In a retrospective of OSHA's regulation of asbestos (on which see *Corrosion Proof Fittings* and accompanying notes, pages 235-247), several OSHA veterans observed that "quantitative assessment of risk was a result of the Supreme Court's 1980 benzene decision requiring OSHA to perform an analysis when appropriate data are available." John F. Martonik et al., The History of OSHA's Asbestos Rulemakings and Some Distinctive Approaches that They Introduced for Regulating Occupational Exposure to Toxic Substances, 62 A.I.H.A. J. 208, 213 (2001). For a discussion of the various factors influencing agency use of Quantitative Risk Assessment (QRA) and cost-benefit analysis, see McGarity, pages 145-154. As a result of *Benzene* and the other forces, QRAs became part of the standard procedures for toxics regulation. OSHA itself already had completed a risk assessment for the cotton dust standard, which meant that it did not have to be withdrawn following the *Benzene* decision.

Justice Marshall's dissent was prescient in one respect. He argued that the outcome in the *Benzene* decision could subject American workers to continuing exposure to substances that increased risks of cancer and other serious diseases. In the years that followed, OSHA performed several assessments of the risks of benzene exposure to humans. These assessments, which were based on a wealth of new epidemiological data, confirmed that benzene posed extremely serious risks to workers. In 1982, the International Agency for Research on Cancer concluded that workers exposed to 10 to 100 ppm of benzene faced excess leukemia risks of 170 per 1,000. Based on the results of five risk assessments, OSHA eventually concluded that workers exposed to 10 ppm of benzene faced excess leukemia risks ranging from 44 to 152 per 1,000, and that even workers exposed to 1 ppm of benzene faced excess leukemia risks ranging from 5 to 16 per 1,000.

OSHA noted that these estimates were among the most conservative of the estimates that could be derived from studies of benzene exposure. Studies performed by the Chemical Manufacturers Association, Dow Chemical, and NIOSH all found substantial excess leukemia risks from benzene exposure (88 per 1,000 at 10 ppm and 9.5 per 1,000 at 1 ppm). Experimental bioassays also revealed that benzene induces multiple site cancers in both sexes of two species of rodents, evidence that had not been available when the *Benzene* decision was decided. New studies showed that benzene was associated with chromosomal aberrations in exposed workers.

Despite all this data, OSHA took several years to promulgate a new PEL for benzene. In April 1983, a group of unions petitioned OSHA to issue an emergency temporary standard of 1 ppm for benzene. OSHA denied this petition, claiming that the risk assessments needed additional review and that no emergency existed because 90 percent of workers were believed to be exposed to less than 1 ppm of benzene. After an abortive effort by OSHA at regulatory negotiation between the unions and the affected industry, the United Steelworkers of America sought a writ of mandamus in December 1984 to compel OSHA to regulate benzene on an expedited basis.

Fully a year later, when oral argument was heard on the union lawsuit, OSHA lawyers told the court that a proposed rule had just been sent to the Federal Register. Holding that OSHA's issuance of a notice of proposed rule-making had made the case moot, the court subsequently dismissed the union's lawsuit.

OSHA held hearings on its proposed PEL in March and April 1986 and compiled a 36,000-page record prior to promulgating a new PEL in September 1987. The new standard, effective December 1987, lowered the benzene PEL from 10 ppm to 1 ppm as an 8-hour average, while lowering the short-term exposure limit (STEL) from 25 ppm to 5 ppm as a 10-minute average.

OSHA based its new PEL on risk assessments showing that exposure to 10 ppm of benzene posed a risk of 95 additional leukemia deaths per 1,000 workers, a level greatly in excess of both other toxic substance risks OSHA had deemed significant (including arsenic, ethylene oxide, and ethylene dibromide) and the risk of accidental death in high- and average-risk industries (where death risks ranged from 30 to 3 in 1,000). OSHA estimated that the new PEL would prevent at least 326 deaths from leukemia and other blood diseases and that the actual number of deaths prevented would be considerably greater. What OSHA left unsaid was that, due to judicial intervention, it had taken ten years to lower the benzene PEL to the very levels the Agency had sought to adopt on an emergency basis in May 1977. (That ETS had been abandoned by OSHA after it had been struck down by the U.S. Court of Appeals for the Fifth Circuit.) The PEL ultimately promulgated by OSHA was at the same level as the PEL vacated by the Supreme Court in 1980 in the *Benzene* decision. Thus, if OSHA's risk assessments are accurate, by delaying promulgation of the stricter PEL judicial intervention allowed thousands of workers to be exposed to significant risks that will result in scores of additional deaths.

3.   *What We Know about Toxics Exposures*

Aided by the impetus of *Benzene,* modern regulation of toxics has come to rely increasingly on quantitative risk assessments (QRAs) as important ingredients to any regulatory decision. All Presidents since Jimmy Carter have issued an executive order requiring agencies wishing to promulgate major rules to perform a regulatory impact analysis (RIA) that includes quantification of the benefits of the regulation, to the extent possible, as well as a comparison of those benefits to the costs of regulation. See Chapter 2, pages 153-154. One reason Presidents have issued these executive orders is to give the Office of Management and Budget (OMB), which has the responsibility of reviewing the RIAs, significant authority over agency rules and regulations. OMB's Office of Information and Regulatory Analysis (OIRA) reviews RIAs and benefit-cost analyses for adequacy, and can return these analyses to the agency, requesting that the regulations be reconsidered. While having some mechanism for the President to exercise some central authority over agency action is surely desirable, the process and the analytic requirements of risk assessments also slow and complicate agency rulemakings considerably, because they are time consuming and resource intensive and because they provide fertile grounds for petitioners to challenge the sufficiency of the justification for new regulations. See Chapter 2, pages 148-150.

Assessing the risk of particular sources of any environmental risk is a multi-step process necessarily involving many scientific disciplines and a great deal of data in order to develop even the imprecise estimates that are the staple of decision making under conditions of uncertainty. The exact scientific disciplines and subdisciplines will vary from context to context, but the object of the exercise varies little. The aim of a risk assessment is to provide an adequate understanding of how human beings react to exposure to a substance as well as an adequate understanding of how much human exposure is occurring or likely to occur. Given their crucial importance to the risk assessment enterprise, it is perhaps surprising to realize just how little information we have about either exposures or their effects.

A.   INFORMATION ABOUT CHEMICAL RISKS

In 1987, the Conservation Foundation published a report that identified major deficiencies in our knowledge base in several areas. "Distressingly little is known about the toxic effects of many chemicals. . . . If little is known about the toxicity of chemical substantives, even less is known about the extent of human and environmental exposure." Conservation Foundation, State of the Environment: A View Toward the Nineties 136-138 (1987).

Industrialized society produces a large quantity and a large number of chemicals. EPA now carries 75,000 chemicals in its Toxic Substances Control Act (TSCA) inventory as having some toxic effects, but little remains known about many of them. TSCA requires manufacturers to submit whatever toxicity data they have when filing a premanufacture notice (PMN), but it does not require any certification of safety or any mandatory battery of tests prior to manufacture. Only 6 percent of the PMNs received annually by EPA have any toxicity test data at all. While TSCA gives EPA authority to order additional testing under limited circumstances, this authority has produced little information because it requires EPA to have individualized information suggesting that a chemical may pose an unreasonable risk before it can order testing. GAO, Toxic Substances Control Act: EPA's Limited Progress in Regulating Toxic Chemicals, May 17, 1994. In this regard, TSCA differs markedly from the Food, Drug and Cosmetic Act (FDCA), which places the burden of proof on the manufacturer to demonstrate safety and requires extensive testing, as well as express approval, before food additives and therapeutic drugs can be placed on the market. It also differs from the approach to commercial toxics being developed by the European Union. Similar to the FDCA, the EU's REACH program adopts a policy of "no data, no market." For more about REACH, see note 4, page 199.

While the number of chemicals used in the economy is vast, a more limited number are used in high quantities. Approximately 3,000 organic chemicals have been classified as high production volume (HPV) chemicals because they are produced or imported in quantities greater than one million pounds per year in the United States. Perhaps the knowledge base for such HPV chemicals is better than for those that are less used. Unfortunately, in 1997, the Environmental Defense Fund (EDF) (EDF has subsequently changed its name to Environmental Defense (ED)) issued a report casting doubt on that proposition. EDF, Toxic Ignorance (1997). EDF charged that in a random sample of 100 of the HPV chemicals, it had found very little toxicity data. After the EDF report, EPA undertook its own review, part of which is excerpted below.

|| **EPA, Chemical Hazard Data**
Availability Study
(1998) ||

The US produces or imports close to 3,000 chemicals (excluding polymers and inorganic chemicals) at over 1 million pounds per year. A fundamental question concerns whether, and to what extent, basic toxicity information is available to the public on these major commercial chemicals in the United States. One might assume that basic toxicity information is available for these chemicals so that producers, users, workers, and consumers could be aware and be able to evaluate the hazards and risks posed by the chemicals they encounter in their daily lives. Based on results from a recent analysis done by EPA, this is not a prudent assumption. EPA's analysis found that *no basic toxicity information, i.e., neither human health nor environmental toxicity, is publicly available for 43% of the high volume chemicals manufactured in the US and that a full set of basic toxicity information is available for only 7% of these chemicals.* . . .

International authorities agree that testing in six basic endpoint areas (known as "basic tests" in this report) is necessary for a minimum understanding of a chemical's toxicity. These tests cover: acute toxicity; chronic toxicity; developmental and reproductive toxicity; mutagenicity; ecotoxicity; and environmental fate. [Developed by the Organization for Economic Cooperation and Development (OECD)], [t]his basic level of testing and other information is called the Screening Information Data Set, or SIDS. The SIDS includes information on the identity of the chemical, its physical and chemical properties, uses, sources and extent of exposure. The testing required is designed to answer basic questions about the chemical. For instance, fate testing can indicate whether the chemical degrades quickly in the environment and how it is distributed throughout the environment. Acute toxicity testing is designed to measure how toxic the chemical is from acute or one-time exposures, such as from accidental ingestion or skin contact. Other tests measure the effects from longer exposures as might be encountered in the workplace or in communities near production facilities, such as subchronic toxicity testing and mutagenicity tests (which could indicate a potential to cause cancer). Tests are also required that measure the chemical's ability to interfere with reproduction (fertility) and fetal development. Finally, a number of studies are required to indicate the potential for environmental effects such as to fish, invertebrates, and aquatic plants should the chemical be released to water from production and wastewater treatment facilities. While these tests do not fully measure a chemical's toxicity, they do provide a minimum set of information that can be used to determine the relative hazards of chemicals and to judge if additional testing is necessary. . . .

Last year (1997), the Environmental Defense Fund reported in "Toxic Ignorance" the results of its analysis of the availability of basic health test data on HPV chemicals and concluded that only 29% of the HPV chemicals in the US met the minimum data requirements for health hazard screening established by the OECD/SIDS program. . . . The Chemical Manufacturers Association (CMA) conducted its own analysis of the sample of 100 HPV chemicals and concluded that 47% of the chemicals had full SIDS health data sets—a conclusion which, although quantitatively different from EDF's, is consistent with the view that significant basic testing requirements remain to be filled for the HPV chemicals.

With regard to industry response to the EDF challenge, CMA, its member companies, and others in the US chemical industry have expressed an interest and willingness to engage both EDF and EPA in a constructive dialogue to address the significant issues raised in the "Toxic Ignorance" report.

NOTES AND QUESTIONS

1. In the same report, EPA estimates that the full battery of basic SIDS screening tests costs about $205,000 per chemical. It further estimates that "it would cost the chemical industry approximately 0.2% of the total annual sales of the top 100 US chemical companies to fill all of the basic screening gaps" for the entire set of HPV chemicals, or approximately $427 million compared with 1996 industry sales figures of $231 billion. The basic screens could produce data prompting more elaborate testing, however, so that the total cost of assembling satisfactory toxicity data would be higher than this. Why isn't testing required?

2. By 2004, EPA had commitments from over 400 companies to voluntarily test approximately 2,150 chemicals for potential health and environmental effects. This High Production Volume Chemical Challenge Program is expected to provide the public with basic toxicity information about chemicals manufactured or imported in quantities greater than one million pounds per year. The Program uses the six tests that form the SIDS as a guideline and asks companies to sponsor specific chemicals, determine whether there are data gaps, and to fill those gaps. The HPV chemicals list currently contains approximately 2,900 chemicals. Approximately 600 of those on the list have subsequently been exempted for various reasons, although they are still eligible for being sponsored by a manufacturer or other entity, and so remain on the complete list. By the beginning of 2005, EPA had accepted complete data sets for 550 chemicals, and was expecting to receive the remainder by the end of 2005. At the same time, more than 600 "emerging" HPVs—chemicals newly qualified for the HPV list—had been identified. Industry has agreed to extend the voluntary testing program to approximately 500 of these. As of the beginning of 2005, there were still approximately 300 "orphan" chemicals—chemicals that satisfied the HPV volume threshold but for which no one had volunteered to provide testing information.

So far, costs have proven to be much lower than industry and EPA originally projected, because chemical companies have been able to rely substantially on already existing data instead of original testing.

3. In December 2000, EPA launched a Voluntary Children's Chemical Evaluation Program to obtain health effects and exposure information on 23 pilot chemicals to which children are believed to be disproportionately exposed. If no companies agree to sponsor voluntary Tier I testing for a particular chemical, EPA will consider issuing a test rule for the chemical under Section 4 of TSCA.

4. The European Union (EU) has decided to take a different approach to the problem of improving our knowledge of the hazards associated with commercial chemicals. Through the Registration, Evaluation and Authorization of Chemicals (REACH) program, the EU is pursuing a "no data, no market,"

approach. Approved by European Commission vote on October 29, 2003, the full details required prior to implementation are still under review in the EU's consultation process. See *http://europa.eu.int/comm/enterprise/reach/index_en.htm*. In the European Commission's words, REACH is "based on the principle that it is up to manufacturers, importers and down-stream users of substances to ensure that they manufacture, place on the market, import or use such substances that do not adversely affect human health or the environment." Under REACH, all manufacturers, importers, and exporters of chemicals will be required to register such chemicals and to supply basic toxicological information about those chemicals as a precondition to registration. Applicable to chemicals with sales over 1 ton/year (by comparison, the HPV Challenge Program's 1 million pounds per year is equivalent to 5,000 tons/year), REACH is anticipated to affect some 30,000 chemicals, and its informational requirements are anticipated to run between $200,000 to $2.2 million per chemical (the requirements are tiered by tons sold per year, as well as by the toxicity of the chemical).

B.   INFORMATION ABOUT ENVIRONMENTAL RELEASES OF TOXIC SUBSTANCES

The second deficiency noted by the 1987 Conservation Foundation was information about human or environmental exposures. Here, we have since learned some useful information due to provisions of the Emergency Planning and Community Right to Know Act (EPCRA), 42 U.S.C. §§11001-11050, enacted in 1986, which requires firms annually to report chemical releases into the environment, initially of some 329 chemicals and, by 2000, more than 650 chemicals. While the amount released into the environment and the amount to which humans are exposed are two quite different things, information about releases can be pivotal in helping to determine the extent to which controls of human-generated environmental risks might be able to ameliorate an identified exposure problem.

The first Toxics Release Inventory (TRI) reports, published in 1989, stunned EPA officials. The 18,500 companies that reported disclosed that they had released 10.4 billion pounds of the listed toxic chemicals in 1987: 3.9 billion pounds into landfills, 3.3 billion pounds were sent to treatment and disposal facilities, 2.7 billion pounds into the air, and 550 million pounds discharged into surface waters. EPA Assistant Administrator Linda Fisher described the totals as "startling," "unacceptably high," and "far beyond" EPA's expectations. Weisskopf, EPA Finds Pollution "Unacceptably High," Wash. Post, April 13, 1989, at A33. Corrections to the data, including eliminating some reports filed by companies not required to do so, lowered the total figure to 7 billion pounds.

Releases went down in 1988 to 4.5 billion pounds, then up to 5.7 billion in 1989. Some viewed this as progress compared with 1987, because the number of firms reporting had increased to 22,650, and industrial production had risen 7 percent. Release of Toxic Chemicals in 1989 Reached 5.7 Billion Pounds, EPA Reports, 22 Env. Rep. 223 (1991). Environmental organizations disagreed, arguing that the chemicals reported under the TRI omitted 95 percent of the actual total, due to noncompliance and limitations of the types of chemicals and facilities that must report. NRDC, The Right to Know More (1991).

TRI reporting requirements have evolved over the years. Major additions to the list of industries who must report were made effective in 1998, including mining, utilities operating coal-fired power plants, RCRA Subtitle C facilities, and solvent recovery services. Chemicals also have been added to the list, including a major addition of persistent bioaccumulative toxics (PBTs), which became effective in 2000. In addition, minimum threshold reporting amounts have changed. For these reasons, year-to-year comparisons are complicated. In addition to providing current year data with regard to all the current reporting requirements, EPA's annual reports also provide some data for comparative purposes that pertain just to the "original" industries and chemicals—those required to report and to be reported in 1988. For this original grouping, total releases of TRI chemicals stood at 1.901 billion pounds in 1995, 2.067 in 1997, 1.636 in 2000, and 1.281 in 2003. EPA, 2003 TRI Public Data Release Report, Figure 4 (2005). Total releases in 2003 for all reporting industries stood at 4.439 billion pounds, a reduction of 6 percent from 2002. 2003 TRI Public Data Release Report, Table 1 (2005). For more about TRI, see pages 300-308.

NOTES AND QUESTIONS

1. Is it surprising to you that such a large volume of toxic materials continues to be released into the environment despite nearly two decades of rapid growth in federal environmental legislation?

2. Compare the pros and cons of the EPA's HPV Challenge Program and the EU's REACH program. Why has the United States chosen not to adopt a program similar to REACH? Will the REACH program provide any benefits in the United States?

3. Is it surprising that we still know so little about the adverse health effects of so many toxic chemicals? If TSCA had been written to require the provision of a certain set of health effects data as a condition to marketing approval, would the situation be different? What explains the difference between the form of regulation established by FDCA compared to TSCA?

4. How would you characterize the seriousness of the toxics "problem"? Is it a result of society's fear of the unknown, is it the product of unpleasant surprises that have been discovered only after substantial damage has been done or something else? What additional information would you wish to obtain before deciding whether or how to allocate additional resources to toxic chemical regulation?

B. MODERN APPROACHES TO ASSESSING RISK

In 1983, the National Research Council issued an influential study, Risk Assessment in the Federal Government: Managing the Process (1983), that continues to feature prominently in how government and others approach the risk assessment process. The NRC Report identified four principal steps in the risk assessment process:

- *Hazard identification:* Is the item under study (e.g., a chemical) causally linked to particular health (or public welfare) effects?

- *Dose-response assessment:* What is the relationship between the magnitude of exposure and the probability that the health (or public welfare) effects will occur?
- *Exposure assessment:* What is the level of exposure of humans (or the environment) to the hazard?
- *Risk characterization:* What is the overall magnitude of the risk?

Each of the first three steps in the risk assessment process requires the use of research data to estimate the types of hazard posed (hazard identification), the probability a hazard will occur (dose-response assessment), and the number of people exposed and their levels of exposure (exposure assessment). These three elements are then combined in the process of risk characterization.

Hazard Identification Then and Now: Exploding Boilers versus Cancer-Causing Substances

The following is an excerpt from comments made by Donald Kennedy, then the commissioner of the Food and Drug Administration, on December 5, 1978.

> The way we regulate the complex and refractory must, unfortunately, differ from the way in which we regulate the comparatively straightforward. To show you what I mean, let me refer you to the very first federal regulatory agency. That agency—the Steamboat Inspection Service—was founded in 1836. It was called into being to address a specific problem: exploding boilers on steamboats. This was what one might call an unequivocal problem. Boilers exploded, or they did not. Given the explicit nature of explosion, the results were inescapable; there was noise, fire, usually followed quite rapidly by the lapping of water around one's ankles. I hope you don't take it as an extreme statement if I say that people detested having the boilers on their steamboat explode. There was no constituency that favored, let's say from motives of overwhelming ennui, the excitement that followed your run-of-the-mill boiler explosion. No one had organized the survivors into a committee for freedom of choice. And the causes of these unfortunate occurrences were well understood. . . . Even private enterprise saw [the profit advantages in being able to offer safer travel to passengers]. So, there we have the father of federal regulation, just oozing common sense. Today, people fear cancer more than, I imagine, our floating ancestors feared boiler explosions. But we do not have a single agency dealing in a comparatively straightforward way with the problem. Nor are we aware of the initiation of the carcinogenic process; we are not really certain how it happens; we do not by any means have a complete inventory of the environmental causes; we do not understand the matrix of reactions between outer and inner environment; we understand practically nothing about interaction among carcinogens and co-carcinogens, potentiation of carcinogens by other substances, and a host of other complex problems of this nature; nor do we have any real proof about threshold or linearity, and if we did we could not be sure that your threshold was the same as mine due to differences in genetic background and our inventory of habits, bad and good. [The Conservation Foundation, Risk Assessment and Control 3 (1985).]

Risks can be characterized in either quantitative or qualitative terms. *Quantitative* risk assessments generally specify either the total numbers of people likely to experience the adverse effect or the likelihood that any one individual exposed to the hazard would suffer the adverse effect. The former is referred to as "population risk" (e.g., 100 additional cases of cancer in the exposed population), the latter "individual risk" (e.g., an exposed individual faces a 1-in-10,000 chance of developing cancer). *Qualitative* risk assessments characterize risks in nonquantitative terms (e.g., the risk is small or large). They are used occasionally to provide rough rank orderings of the seriousness of different risks, a practice referred to as *comparative* risk assessment (which also is used at times to compare quantitative estimates to assess their significance).

An excellent nontechnical introduction to risk assessment is Conservation Foundation, Risk Assessment, and Control (1985). Also useful is a joint report by the American Chemical Society and Resources for the Future, Understanding Risk Analysis (1998). See *http://www.rff.org/rff/Publications/ReferenceMaterials.cfm.* As one might expect from the previous material on the paucity of toxics information that is available, the Conservation Foundation study, at page 4, notes that "almost all risk assessments are plagued by inadequate data." The joint ACS/RFF study, at page 7, concludes that "the current state of scientific understanding has often been found to be incomplete, indecisive and controversial."

> Virtually all elements of risk assessment are clouded with uncertainty, basically of two kinds. First, the various scientific disciplines involved in assessing risk are not sufficiently developed either to explain the mechanisms by which particular causes produce particular effects or to provide good quantitative estimates of cause-and-effect relationships. Second, the data needed to analyze particular risks are usually not available. [Conservation Foundation at 5.]

The difficulties of using existing data and techniques for performing risk assessments were highlighted in 1987 when EPA asked its staff to assess the Agency's priorities by performing rough risk assessments of the 31 environmental problems listed in Figure 1.2, page 7. EPA sought to compare the seriousness of these problems by assessing the risks they posed in four areas: cancer risks, noncancer health effects, damage to public welfare (economic damage), and ecological risks. This exercise produced a study, entitled Unfinished Business, describing some of the obstacles to performing risk assessments:

> The best information available is for cancer risk. Even there, however, it was not nearly as good as one might expect.
> The data and methods available for assessing noncancer health effects are poor. Exposure data are surprisingly poor, even on chemicals that are objects of major regulatory efforts.
> There is no general methodology for assessing noncancer health risks. There is no generally applicable methodology for ecological risk assessment. The number of different types of ecological systems, the relative scarcity of ecosystem exposure data and methods, and scientific uncertainties compound the problem. Moreover, the extraordinary complexity of ecological systems prohibits objective assessment of ecological risks.
> While there are generally accepted methods for assessing welfare effects, there is a general scarcity of data and analysis in this area. [EPA, Unfinished Business 98-99 (1987).]

Consider some of the reasons that uncertainty affects the various steps in the risk assessment process.

Hazard identification. Regulatory agencies today have a far more difficult task than the first federal safety agency, the Steamboat Inspection Service (see page 202), which was charged with preventing boilers on steamships from exploding. Exploding boilers are a clearly identifiable problem, and the causes of such are reasonably amenable to investigation and discovery. Not so with respect to many modern environmental hazards. Cancer, far and away the most studied and feared health hazard, is better understood than when Donald Kennedy wrote in 1978, but there remain significant gaps in knowledge, especially as they relate to the important issue of whether any specific carcinogen has a safe, or "no effects" threshold. Furthermore, it is sometimes difficult even to tell whether a given chemical is actually a human carcinogen. All the potential sources of information have their deficiencies and uncertainties, as described below.

Epidemiologic data. After incidences of disease are noted in a given segment of the population, well-conducted epidemiologic studies of that segment can sometimes find an association between a causative agent and that disease. Because epidemiology would provide direct evidence in human beings of the hazard, in theory this would be a most valuable source of reliable information. Such evidence, however, is extremely limited. Except in occupational exposure settings, it is extremely difficult to identify population subgroups whose characteristics are virtually identical save for their exposure to a substance being investigated. Even when such groups can be identified, historic levels of exposure actually experienced by each group are difficult to determine with precision. High background levels of common diseases like cancer mask all but the most catastrophic associations between diseases and particular causative agents. There may simply be too many variables—potential causes of the disease—in the population's history to sort out relative influences. Epidemiologic analysis, furthermore, requires that a disease manifest itself, yet the ideal function of environmental protection is to prevent disease.

Experimental data. Experimental data have significant advantages over epidemiologic data in that they permit scientists to assess environmental hazards in carefully controlled circumstances before widespread human exposure has occurred. Because ethical considerations preclude human exposure to substances that threaten health, most experimental data are derived from short-term tests or animal bioassays.

Short-term studies and molecular comparisons. Certain short-term tests of chemicals (e.g., for mutagenicity) have been shown to be highly correlative to carcinogenicity; thus performing such tests can provide some evidence of whether the suspected hazard is a carcinogen. However, scientists now know that not all mutagens are carcinogens and that many nonmutagenic substances may play an important role in the complex process by which cancer develops. Short-term screening tests thus have proved more useful for identifying cancer initiators than for screening cancer promoters or receptors. Scientists also have sought to infer that certain chemicals may be carcinogens by analyzing their molecular structure to determine if it is similar to that of known carcinogens. This is called inference from structure-activity relationships and has been used for limited purposes such as determining whether to require additional testing of certain chemicals for carcinogenicity. Neither of these sources of information assists in estimating the potency of the hazard.

Toxicological experiments on laboratory animals. Exposure of animals under controlled conditions to a suspected hazard allows researchers to control for other variables and thus isolate the hazard potential of the suspect chemical. Bioassay data are necessarily skimpy, however, because of the enormous sample sizes that are required to detect the risks posed by low-level exposures to toxic substances. Hazard identification frequently relies on just one or two experiments in a single species of rodent. Furthermore, while the validity of translating animal findings into conjectures of human reactions is widely accepted (indeed, fundamental to the entire toxicological research effort), the precise formulae for translating such findings remain disputed and depend on inferences that cannot be scientifically validated. Moreover, there are occasions when observations in animals are of very limited relevance to humans. Still, such studies remain the backbone of governmental and industry research in hazard identification. They are expensive and time-consuming—two years and $2.5 million is typical for a single rodent bioassay—so we should expect such data to be limited.

The Screening Information Data Set compiled under the High Production Chemical Challenge Program on a voluntary basis and under the EU's REACH program on a mandatory basis are primarily aimed at providing a standard set of hazard identification information, to determine whether the chemical is associated with one or more adverse health effects, such as cancer, birth defects, neuro-developmental abnormalities, and the like.

Dose-response assessment. Experimental or epidemiologic data very seldom exist for the relatively low levels of exposure that must be examined when regulatory intervention is being considered. Scientists therefore must extrapolate from the available data the relationship between the doses relevant to regulation and the human health or environmental effects (the response) to assess the potency of a hazard.

Uncertainties in dose-response assessment come from a variety of sources. With epidemiologic data, the population as a whole typically contains subpopulations that are likely to be more susceptible to disease than the population studied, for instance, children, pregnant women, fetuses, and the elderly. It is often unclear how to translate epidemiologic data to predict the effects of exposure on such groups.

Toxicological studies present further problems, as noted above. There is no scientific consensus on how to transfer information about animal reactions to suspected hazards and human reactions, even holding the dose constant. Because body weight, body metabolism, differences in immune systems, and other variables are thought to be relevant to the study of how an organism responds to exposures, responses of humans and laboratory animals are likely to differ, but scientists are unsure as to how.

Toxicological studies also present the problem of extrapolating from higher doses to regulation-relevant, lower doses. In order to induce laboratory responses, animals are exposed to extremely high doses. There is disagreement about whether high-dose responses in animals provide an accurate basis for predicting low-dose response even in the same animals, let alone a basis for drawing conclusions about humans exposed to low levels. Cancer-causing substances cause special problems, because the precise mechanisms through which specific carcinogens operate are still not completely understood, and therefore what effect extremely low levels of exposure will have cannot be known and hence must be estimated.

A number of competing models for low-dose responses to carcinogens have been developed, each plausible under different hypotheses about carcinogenesis. Figure 3.3 illustrates some of the competing predictions. The upper graph shows how three commonly used models of cancer causation predict roughly identical response rates for doses of DDT within the ranges of dosage that laboratory animals receive in toxicological tests. The differences are so small that each model fits the data fairly well, and hence the laboratory findings do not permit any of them to be rejected. However, the implications of each of the models for risk estimates at much lower levels of exposure—the region relevant to much

FIGURE 3.3
Low-Dose Extrapolations for DDT

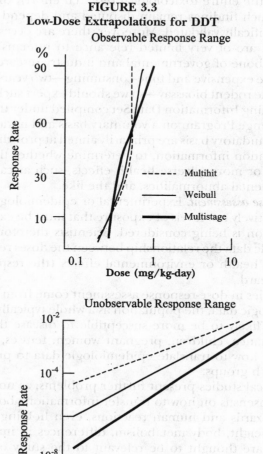

Observable Response Range

Unobservable Response Range

Source: Based on Paustenbach, D.J. Retrospective on U.S. Health Risk Assessment: How Others Can Benefit, *Risk* 1995, 6, 283-332.

regulation—are substantially different. The graph on the bottom illustrates that these three models predict response to the dosages to which people may typically be exposed that disagree by a factor of roughly 10,000.

When dealing with noncancer effects, one of the most common purposes of dose-response assessment is to locate the level of exposure which if experienced daily is "likely to be without an appreciable risk of deleterious health effects during a lifetime." This so-called reference dose or reference concentration (RfD or RfC) is calculated through a multi-step process. First, a specific health effect, or endpoint, is selected. Then all available studies are examined in an attempt to find the highest level of exposure at which no such adverse effect is

---

Figure 3.4
Uncertainty Factors in Reference Dose Calculations

Standard Uncertainty Factors (UFs)

Use a 10-fold factor when extrapolating from valid experimental results from studies using prolonged exposure to average healthy humans. This factor is intended to account for the variation in sensitivity among the members of the human population.

Use an additional 10-fold factor when extrapolating from valid results of long-term studies on experimental animals when results of studies of human exposure are not available or are inadequate. This factor is intended to account for the uncertainty in extrapolating animal data to risks for humans. 3-fold uncertainty factor is used for extrapolating from inhalation studies on experimental animals to humans for the derivation of an inhalation Rfc. . . .

Use an additional 10-fold factor when extrapolating from less than chronic results on experimental animals when there are no useful long-term human data. This factor is intended to account for the uncertainty in extrapolating from less than chronic NOAELs to chronic NOAELs. Use an additional 10-fold factor when deriving an RfD from a LOAEL instead of a NOAEL. This factor is intended to account for the uncertainty in extrapolating from LOAELs to NOAELs.

Modifying Factor (MF)

Use professional judgment to determine another uncertainty factor (MF) that is greater than zero and less than or equal to 10. The magnitude of the MF depends upon the professional assessment of scientific uncertainties of the study and data base not explicitly treated above, e.g., the completeness of the overall data base and the number of species tested. The default value for the MF is 1.

Source: Mercury Study Report to Congress, EPA-452/R-97-007 (Dec. 1997).

---

observed. If found, this is the No Observed Adverse Effects Level, or NOAEL. If no NOAEL can be found, then the lowest level at which effects are observed (or LOAEL) is located. Finally, the NOAEL or LOAEL is divided by one or more uncertainty factors to provide a margin of safety. These uncertainty factors can vary in magnitude. A "10-fold factor" divides the NOAEL or LOAEL by ten; a "three-fold factor" by three, and so on.

Exposure assessment. Often the weakest data link in the chain of steps in the risk assessment process is meaningful exposure data. Samples of the concentrations of a chemical in the blood or other organs can be taken, but this does not answer the question of the extent to which individuals have been exposed to that chemical because of environmental factors. Exposure assessments usually require the use of fate and transport models, which attempt to predict concentrations in the ambient air or water by starting with some estimates of the amount of chemicals being put into the environment by human and other sources. These models then take into account weather patterns, movements of water bodies, and any other environmental features that affect the transport of those chemicals. These models, needless to say, are imperfect. They also must take into account the fact that many chemicals interact with other chemicals in the presence of sunlight or other catalysts, forming new chemicals. These parts of the models also are imperfect because neither the precise quantities of other chemicals, nor the identity of all the chemicals present, nor the precise environmental conditions can be known, and chemical reactions can be significantly affected by these factors. Multiple pathways (e.g., the concentration of the chemicals in the air, in the water, in the soil, in products or foods consumed by the public) may sometimes need to be estimated. Finally, the characteristics of population groups potentially exposed to certain substances also may have a significant impact on risk assessment because some types of people are more susceptible than others to certain hazards.

NOTES AND QUESTIONS

1. Hazard identification and dose-response assessment attempt to answer the questions of whether a substance is hazardous and, if so, how hazardous it is. Gaps in scientific knowledge with which to determine the answers to these questions must be bridged by assumptions or default conclusions. Consider eight common assumptions of the hazard and dose-response assessment processes:

1. In general, data from studies in humans are preferred to animal data for purposes of hazard and dose-response identification.
2. In the absence of human data, or when the available human data are insufficiently quantitative or are insufficiently sensitive to rule out risks, animal data will be used for hazard and dose-response evaluation.
3. In the absence of information to demonstrate that such a selection is incorrect, data from the animal species, strain, and sex showing the greatest sensitivity to a chemical's toxic properties will be selected as the basis for human risk assessment.
4. Animal toxicity data collected by the same route of exposure as that experienced by humans are preferred for risk assessments, but if the toxic effect is a systemic one, then data from other routes can be used.
5. For all toxic effects other than carcinogenicity, a threshold in the dose-response curve is assumed. The lowest NOEL (no observed effects level) from all available studies is assumed to be the threshold for the groups of subjects (humans or animals) in which toxicity data were collected.
6. The threshold for the human population is estimated by dividing the NOEL by a safety factor, the size of which depends upon the nature and quality of the toxicity data and the characteristics of the human population.
7. For carcinogens a linear, no-threshold dose-response model is assumed to apply at low doses. . . .
8. Generally, human exposures and resulting doses and risks are estimated for those members of the population experiencing the highest intensity and rate of contact with the chemical, although other, less-exposed subgroups and people experiencing average exposures will frequently be included. [J. Rodricks, Calculated Risks 188-189 (1992).]

These eight assumptions are only the tip of the iceberg. The NAS Report identifies 50 data gaps that quantitative risk assessments can face, at which point assumptions or "inferential bridges" must be employed to complete the quantitative risk assessment or QRA. National Research Council, Risk Assessment in the Federal Government: Managing the Process 33-37 (1983).

2. In its work leading up to the *Benzene* litigation, OSHA concluded that the gaps that needed to be bridged in producing a quantitative risk assessment argued against trying to generate a QRA at all. The tendency in the post-*Benzene* era, in contrast, has been to adopt sufficient assumptions to generate quantitative conclusions. These QRAs have had an enormous impact on how agencies attempt to discharge their statutory responsibilities. The scientific work, the analytical tools employed, and the assumptions necessarily made all create points of contention that can be challenged by the regulated community. Much of the controversy over whether agencies are employing "sound science" in their work focuses on disputes over QRAs and especially over whether new scientific findings counsel in favor of revising some of the assumptions agencies employ. Those who wish to see government being more preventative in its approach to exposures to toxic materials, on the other hand, worry that QRAs contribute to the problem of "paralysis by analysis" that agencies increasingly confront. See pages 148-150.

Agencies are caught in a squeeze by these opposing forces. They know they cannot act precipitously because the courts will strike down rules and regulations that lack an adequate evidentiary basis. Yet they also know that, however much they analyze and refine, the realities of science and the available evidence dictate that they will never eliminate all the major assumptions and judgments from their decision making, either. As much as regulatory foes assert that we can never achieve a risk-free society, so it also seems that an agency can never write an assumption- and judgment-free regulation.

3. When all is said and done, agencies appear to be doing their work carefully enough so that courts have generally deferred to agency decisions regarding how to fill in the analytical gaps in risk assessments. In International Fabricare Institute v. EPA, 972 F.2d 384 (D.C. Cir. 1992), representatives of a group of chemical companies raised what the court termed "a general challenge to the EPA policy of rejecting the existence of safe threshold levels for carcinogens in the absence of contrary evidence." 972 F.2d at 387. The court rejected their claim that it was arbitrary and capricious for EPA not to consider "new scientific evidence" questioning the appropriateness of assuming no safe thresholds of exposure to carcinogens.

The court concluded that new evidence offered amounted to "the opinion of a few scientists who, however qualified, are in their own words at odds with what is 'generally thought' about the subject." Id. at 391. EPA had previously considered these and other dissenting views, and had declined to change its working assumptions. The court concluded that the agency need not "undertake a more detailed re-justification of its prior position" simply because of the "submission of comments consisting of little more than assertions that in the opinion of the commenters the agency got it wrong." Id. See also Synthetic Organic Chem. Mfrs. Assn. v. Secretary, Dept. of Health & Human Servs., 720 F. Supp. 1244 (W.D. La. 1989) (rejecting claims that risk assessment methodologies are arbitrary and capricious). A study of court cases challenging EPA selection among conflicting scientific findings or among different modeling assumptions or other choices of inferential bridges found that EPA had never been reversed when addressing these questions, which stand on "the frontiers of scientific knowledge." Christopher H. Schroeder & Robert L. Glicksman, Chevron, State Farm, and EPA in the Courts of Appeals During the 1990s, 31 Envtl. L. Rep. 10371 (2001).

4. Risk assessments involving cancer-causing materials have sparked a particularly significant number of disputes, because agencies have invested

considerable resources in identifying and regulating carcinogens, and because the assumptions employed in QRAs for carcinogens employ cautious default assumptions, such as the assumption that there is no safe level of exposure to a carcinogen (embodied in Rodricks' assumption number seven, above), as well as the assumption that toxicological studies on laboratory animals that have been given massive doses of a chemical provide valid bases for extrapolating to effects in humans who are exposed to much lower doses of the chemical. The experimental approach that employs animals who are given such a Maximum Tolerated Dose (MTD) is the standard experimental technique in the animal studies referenced in Rodricks' assumptions two and three, above.

One focal point of the "sound science" criticisms of QRAs rests on the opinion of some scientists that we have acquired enough knowledge about the mechanisms of cancer causation in humans to question the relevance of the MTD and no-safe-threshold assumptions, at least in some cases. The challenge to EPA's approach that was rejected in the *International Fabricare* decision, note 3, above, was a broad-scale attack on EPA's approach. Theories and evidence about mechanisms of action, and about pharmacokinetics (the analysis of how an organism processes a toxic substance—the rate of uptake, distribution within the body, excretion, metabolites formed in response) form the basis of such criticisms.

Numerous studies and commissions have examined these and other risk assessment methods and assumptions, some enpaneled by provisions in enacted laws, such as the Clean Air Act Amendments of 1990. After a three-year study mandated by those Amendments, a committee of the National Academy of Sciences (NAS) refused to endorse the notion that the MTD animal studies and no-safe-threshold should be abandoned. National Academy of Science Issues in Risk Assessment 61-64 (1993). Dr. Bernard Goldstein, chairman of the committee, noted that although 6 of the 17 committee members had favored such a shift, the "science isn't there yet," Racz, Science Panel Splits Over Chemical Dose Given to Animals, Wall St. J., Jan. 28, 1993, at B7. While urging additional refinements in the risk assessment process, the National Research Council (NRC) of the NAS similarly concluded that EPA's general approach, relying upon MTD tests, should be retained. "It is prudent and reasonable to use animal models to predict potential carcinogenicity. . . ." National Research Council, Science and Judgment in Risk Assessment 140 (1994). At the same time, the NRC urged EPA to devote more resources to improving knowledge of pharmacokinetics and mechanisms of action, and to incorporating those results into EPA's modeling, permitting departures from the default assumptions where warranted. Id. at 141-142. See also Presidential/Congressional Commission on Risk Assessment and Risk Management, Risk Assessment and Risk Management in Regulatory Decision-Making (1997).

5. EPA has heeded the advice of the NAS and others, and in formulating policy, has continued to monitor and analyze advances in the scientific understanding of how particular substances cause or promote cancer. In incorporating new science, EPA's challenge is to define what must be shown when and by whom to warrant deviation from the default assumptions about the relevance of animal test data. For example, water is deliberately chlorinated by public health authorities to eliminate microbial pathogens (germs). Chloroform is a chemical byproduct of the chlorination of water. In regulating chloroform under the Safe Drinking Water Act, EPA acknowledged and credited studies providing reason to believe that chloroform did exhibit a no-effects threshold below which it did not pose a cancer risk to humans, and hence was unnecessary to remove the substance

from drinking water. Yet, EPA nonetheless issued a standard of zero when it regulated chloroform in drinking water pursuant to a provision of the Safe Drinking Water Act (SDWA) requiring maximum contaminant level goals to be set on the basis of the "best available . . . science." 42 U.S.C. §300g-l(b)(3)(A). (The entire SDWA statutory scheme is described at pages 249-264.) Litigation challenging EPA's decision produced one of the infrequent cases in which a court has reversed an EPA choice among different scientific conclusions.

|| *Chlorine Chemistry Council v. EPA* ||
|| **206 F.3d 1286 (D.C. Cir. 2000)** ||

STEPHEN F. WILLIAMS, Circuit Judge:

The Safe Drinking Water Act ("SDWA" or the "Act") directs the Environmental Protection Agency to set standards for the regulation of covered drinking water contaminants. For each EPA sets a "maximum contaminant level goal" ("MCLG"), defined as "the level at which no known or anticipated adverse effects on the health of persons occur and which allows an adequate margin of safety." 42 U.S.C. §300g-l(b)(4)(A). The MCLG is somewhat aspirational. After having set it, EPA is to promulgate an enforceable standard, known as a maximum contaminant level ("MCL"), which takes practical considerations into account while remaining "as close to the [MCLG] as is feasible." *Id.*

In March 1998 EPA concluded that chloroform, a drinking water contaminant, exhibits a "nonlinear mode of carcinogenic action." Notice of Data Availability: National Primary Drinking Water Regulations: Disinfectants and Disinfection Byproducts, 63 Fed. Reg. 15,674, 15,686/1 (1998). In other words, exposures to chloroform below some threshold level pose no risk of cancer. But in promulgating the MCLG it retained the existing standard of zero, which was based on the previously held assumption that there was no safe threshold. Final Rule: National Primary Drinking Water Regulations: Disinfectants and Disinfection Byproducts, 63 Fed. Reg. 69,390, 69,398/3 (1998) ("Final Rule"). EPA justified its action on a variety of grounds, including an alleged need to consult the report of its Science Advisory Board ("SAB"), which would not be available until after the statutory deadline for rulemaking had expired. Petitioners, including the Chlorine Chemistry Council, a trade association comprised of chlorine and chlorine product manufacturers, petitioned this court for review, arguing that EPA violated its statutory mandate to use the "best available" evidence when implementing the provisions of the Safe Drinking Water Act. 42 U.S.C. §300g-l(b)(3)(A). We agree. . . .

On July 29, 1994 EPA issued a proposed rule on disinfectants and disinfection byproducts in water. This included a zero MCLG for chloroform, based on EPA's finding of an absence of data to suggest a threshold level below which there would be no potential carcinogenic effects. Id. The Agency's default method of inferring risk at exposure levels for which it has no adequate data is linear extrapolation from cancer incidence inferred at exposures for which it does have data. See EPA's Proposed Guidelines for Carcinogen Risk Assessment, 61 Fed. Reg. 17,960, 17,968/3 (1996). Thus, either if the evidence supports linearity, or if there is "insufficient" evidence of nonlinearity, EPA assumes that if a substance causes cancer at any exposure it will do so at every nonzero exposure (though with cancer incidence declining with exposure). But

EPA acknowledges its authority "to establish nonzero MCLGs for carcinogens if the scientific evidence" indicates that a "safe threshold" exists. See Final Rule, 63 Fed. Reg. at 69,401/2. And petitioners here assume the validity of the linear default assumption. . . .

On the basis of [a Scientific Advisory Board (SAB) convened pursuant to SDWA] findings and recommendations, EPA in November 1997 published a Notice of Data Availability ("NODA"). . . . Among the findings it discussed were those arrived at by a panel of experts organized by the International Life Sciences Institute. The panel whose work was subject to independent peer review and was convened under the auspices of the EPA, concluded on the basis of chloroform's mode of action that although it was "a likely carcinogen to humans above a certain dose range, [it was] unlikely to be carcinogenic below a certain dose range." Id. at 15,685/1. The panel recommended "the nonlinear[] or margin of exposure approach [as] the preferred approach to quantifying the cancer risk associated with chloroform exposure." Id. at 15,686/1.

EPA agreed. It said that "although the precise mechanism of chloroform carcinogenicity is not established," nevertheless "the chloroform dose-response should be considered nonlinear." Id. at 15,685/3. Rather than operating through effects on DNA, which is consistent with linearity, chloroform evidently works through "cytotoxicity" (i.e., damage to the cells) followed by regenerative cell proliferation. Id. Employing the threshold approach that it found was entailed by chloroform's mode of action, EPA then calculated an MCLG of 600 parts per billion ("ppb"), based solely on carcinogenicity. Id. at 15,686/2. This level built in a 1000-fold margin of error in relation to the maximum safe dosage implied from the animal studies used by EPA. Id. But because even lower chlorine doses cause liver toxicity (a non-cancer effect), EPA proposed an MCLG of 300 ppb. Id.

When EPA came to promulgate its final rule in December 1998, however, its MCLG was again zero. Final Rule, 63 Fed. Reg. at 69,398/3. It stuck with 1994's zero level despite its explicit statement that it now "believe[d] that the underlying science for using a nonlinear extrapolation approach to evaluate the carcinogenic risk from chloroform is well founded." Id. at 69,401/1. It justified the action on the basis that "additional deliberations with the Agency's SAB on the analytical approach used" and on the underlying scientific evidence were needed "prior to departing from a long-held EPA policy." Id. at 69,399-69,401. It could not complete such additional deliberations by the November 1998 statutory deadline, and, moreover, the rulemaking would not affect the enforceable MCL for TTHMs.

After briefing on the petition for review at issue here, but before oral argument, EPA moved for a voluntary remand to consider the SAB report on chloroform that would soon be available. But EPA made no offer to vacate the rule; thus EPA's proposal would have left petitioners subject to a rule they claimed was invalid. We denied the motion.

On February 11, 2000, the day of oral argument, EPA released a draft report by the SAB on chloroform. The report concluded that chloroform exhibits a "cytotoxic" mode of action. Such a mode of action (unlike a "genotoxic" mechanism, which acts directly on a cell's DNA) involves no carcinogenic effects at low doses; thus a nonlinear approach is "scientifically reasonable." After consideration of the draft SAB report, EPA stated that it "no longer believes that it should continue to defend its original decision," and moved that this court vacate the MCLG.

[The court denied EPA's motion to vacate, and proceeded to the merits, because in its motion EPA had not committed itself to promulgate a nonzero MCLG for chloroform, which was the specific relief sought by petitioners.]

Petitioners argue that EPA's decision to adopt a zero MCLG in the face of scientific evidence establishing that chloroform is a threshold carcinogen was inconsistent with the Safe Drinking Water Act. Section 300g-l(b)(3)(A) of the Act states unequivocally that "to the degree that an Agency action is based on science, the Administrator shall use . . . the best available, peer-reviewed science and supporting studies conducted in accordance with sound and objective scientific practices." In promulgating a zero MCLG for chloroform EPA openly overrode the "best available" scientific evidence, which suggested that chloroform is a threshold carcinogen.

EPA provides several arguments in defense of its action. First, it argues that to establish a non-zero MCLG would be a "precedential step," that represents "a major change in the substance of regulatory decisions related to chloroform." EPA's Br. at 28-29. We do not doubt that adopting a nonzero MCLG is a significant step, one which departs from previous practice. But this is a change in result, not in policy. The change in outcome occurs simply as a result of steadfast application of the relevant rules: first, the statutory mandate to set MCLGs at "the level at which no known or anticipated adverse effect on the health of persons occur," 42 U.S.C. §300g-l(b)(4)(A), as determined on the basis of the "best available" evidence; and second, EPA's Carcinogen Risk Assessment guidelines, stating that when "adequate data on mode of action show that linearity is not the most reasonable working judgment and provide sufficient evidence to support a nonlinear mode of action," the default assumption of linearity drops out. Proposed Guidelines for Carcinogen Risk Assessment, 61 Fed. Reg. at 17,969/1. The fact that EPA has arrived at a novel, even politically charged, outcome is of no significance either for its statutory obligation or for fulfillment of its adopted policy.

Second, and similarly, EPA supports its action on the basis that "it could not complete the deliberations with the SAB" before the November 1998 deadline. But however desirable it may be for EPA to consult an SAB and even to revise its conclusion in the future, that is no reason for acting against its own scientific findings in the meantime. The statute requires the agency to take into account the "best available" evidence. EPA cannot reject the "best available" evidence simply because of the possibility of contradiction in the future by evidence unavailable at the time of action—a possibility that will always be present. . . .

[W]e vacate the rule.

NOTES AND QUESTIONS

1. *Chlorine Chemistry Council* arose in unusual circumstances. EPA had reached a fairly firm conclusion that the best available science justified concluding that chloroform had a no-effects threshold and yet it declined to use that science in issuing a regulation under a statute requiring the use of the best available science. The more typical disputes over "sound science" involve cases in which scientific findings are less conclusive, some pointing in one direction, others in different directions, and EPA resolves the disagreement and draws inferences that industry or other challengers argue to be unjustified. How applicable is the holding in *Chlorine Chemistry Council* to these situations?

2. Regulators are acutely aware of the uncertainties of risk assessments. Nonetheless, in justifying decisions regarding toxic exposures, EPA and other health agencies rely heavily upon such risk assessment. Science has such a powerful influence in modern society that Wendy Wagner suggests agencies engage in a "pervasive 'science charade,'" where [they] exaggerate the contributions made by science in setting toxic standards in order to avoid accountability for the underlying policy decisions." Wagner, The Science Charade in Toxic Risk Regulation, 95 Colum. L. Rev. 1613, 1617 (1995).

3. Disputes over cancer mechanisms dominate debate over what constitutes good science in regulatory proceedings, but there are numerous other complicating factors. Analysts grow increasingly aware of the interactive, or synergistic, effects of multiple numbers of chemicals. Nonetheless, EPA has developed very little capability to assess synergistic effects. Likewise, non-carcinogenic effects have received less attention than cancer effects have, and yet these effects are increasingly a primary object of concern. When California performed a statewide comparative risk analysis, for example, its human health valuation committee concluded that many of its final rankings

> were driven by the extent and severity of noncancer impacts. The relative importance of noncancer impacts suggests that comparative risk projects must be cautious about rankings based on assessment methods that provide quantitative risk estimates for carcinogens and that the development and validation of non-cancer risk assessment methods should be a higher priority. [California Comparative Risk Project, Toward the 21st Century: Planning for the Protection of California's Environment 85 (1994).]

4. Environmental health officials are increasingly concerned about chemicals that affect the expression of hormones in the human body, interfering with the endocrine system in a variety of ways, including by impairing sexual development and function. The presence of persistent organic pollutants (POPs) in the environment seems to be linked to a global decline in human sperm counts, a disturbing increase in the rate of testicular cancer, and declines in the reproductive success of many species of wildlife. Stone, Environmental Estrogens Stir Debate, 265 Science 308 (1994); Colborn et al., Developmental Effects of Endocrine-Disrupting Chemicals in Wildlife and Humans, 101 Envtl. Health Persp. 378 (1993). While dozens of chemicals are known to be capable of disturbing the endocrine system by binding to the estrogen receptor, some scientists argue that the risks are low because most of these chemicals have only a very weak effect on estrogen. However, exposure to POPs is so ubiquitous that Our Stolen Future (T. Colborn et al.), which warns about the problem, was heralded by some as the next Silent Spring. Mathews, Overlooking the "POPs Problem," Wash. Post, Mar. 11, 1996, at A19. EPA has struggled to formulate testing protocols for endocrine-disrupting chemicals in part because much remains unknown about how their mechanisms of action work. E.g., Comm. on Hormonally Active Agents in the Env't, Nat'l Research Council, Hormonally Active Agents in the Environment (2000) (identifying scientific unknowns for hormonally active agents, including mechanisms of action, and identifying several major areas for needed future research); see John P. Myers et al., Endocrine Disruptors—A Controversy in Science and Policy: Session III Summary and Research Needs, 22 NeuroToxicology 557, 557-558 (2001) (discussing the new discoveries and resulting research needs that flow from research on endocrine disrupters). Recently, EPA began sponsoring low-dose animal study experiments

for several suspected endocrine disrupters, including perchlorate, which is commonly found in drinking water supplies. See EPA Studies Could Spark New Risk Levels for Endocrine Disruptors, Inside EPA, Dec. 24, 2004.

5. The ability of some toxins to interfere with the development of neurological systems is also an area of increasing environmental health concern. Here, the timing of exposure becomes as critical as the amount of exposure, because neurotoxins have their greatest adverse effects early in life, when the neurological system is not fully developed and hence is most vulnerable.

> Evidence from numerous sources demonstrates that neural development extends from the embryonic period through adolescence. In general, the sequence of events is comparable among species, although the time scales are considerably different. Developmental exposure of animals or humans to numerous agents (e.g., X-ray irradiation, methylazoxymethanol, ethanol, lead, methyl mercury, or chlorpyrifos) demonstrates that interference with one or more of these developmental processes can lead to developmental neurotoxicity. Different behavioral domains (e.g., sensory, motor, and various cognitive functions) are subserved by different brain areas. . . . Furthermore, various clinical disorders in humans (e.g., schizophrenia, dyslexia, epilepsy, and autism) may also be the result of interference with normal ontogeny of developmental processes in the nervous system. Of critical concern is the possibility that developmental exposure to neurotoxicants may result in an acceleration of age-related decline in function. This concern is compounded by the fact that developmental neurotoxicity that results in small effects can have a profound societal impact when amortized across the entire population and across the life span of humans. [Rice & Barone, Envtl. Health Persp. 108 (Supp. 3): 511-533 (2000).]

6. Concerns about the potential health effects of electromagnetic radiation also have commanded attention. Humans are exposed to extremely low-frequency electric and magnetic fields (EMF) from a variety of sources, including power lines, video display terminals, and household appliances. Some early studies found statistically significant associations between the risk of some cancers and presumed measures of EMF exposure; a few others found a relationship between such measures and noncancer health effects. Florig, Containing the Costs of the EMF Problem, 257 Science 468 (1992). However, the exposure estimates used by these studies are subject to considerable uncertainty, and there are many potentially confounding factors that may account for these relationships. Even as studies with more refined measures of exposure are being conducted, inconsistent findings seem to be the only constant. See, e.g., Major EMF Report Warns of Health Risks, 269 Science 911 (1995); Taubes, Another Blow Weakens EMF-Cancer Link, 269 Science 1816 (1995); Bishop, Link Between EMF, Brain Cancer Is Suggested by Study at Five Utilities, Wall St. J., Jan. 11, 1995, at B6. Concerns over EMF were eased somewhat in 1996 when a major National Research Council study found that there was scant evidence of a link between EMFs and adverse health effects. A comprehensive review of existing epidemiological studies by the Standing Committee on Epidemiology of the International Commission for Non-Ionizing Radiation Protection in 2004 found "no consistent or convincing evidence of a causal relation between RF exposure and any adverse health effect." Ahblom et al., Epidemiology of Health Effects of Radiofrequency Exposure, 112 Envtl. Health Persp. 1741 (2004). However, it noted that "the studies have too many deficiencies to rule out an association."

7. Amidst growing concern over noncancer health effects, carcinogenicity still continues to receive the lion's share of attention. As suggested by EPA's stance in *Chlorine Chemistry Council*, federal environmental health regulators take seriously our growing knowledge of the causal mechanisms of carcinogenic chemicals. Over the years, EPA's policies with respect to its fundamental premises for assessing risk from carcinogens have been embodied in Agency Guidelines and draft Guidelines. *Chlorine Chemistry Council* references EPA's 1996 Proposed Guidelines for Carcinogen Risk Assessment, which were intended to update Guidelines that had been issued in 1986. In March 2005, the Agency finalized the process begun in 1996 by issuing new Guidelines for Carcinogen Risk Assessment, EPA/630/P-03/001B (March 2005), 70 Fed. Reg. 17,765 (April 7, 2005). These Guidelines signal a greater Agency willingness to accept pharmacokinetic and mechanism of action evidence for nonlinearity than the prior Guidelines had:

> As an increasing understanding of carcinogenesis is becoming available, these cancer guidelines adopt a view of default options that is consistent with EPA's mission to protect human health while adhering to the tenets of sound science. Rather than viewing default options as the starting point from which departures may be justified by new scientific information, *these cancer guidelines view a critical analysis of all of the available information that is relevant to assessing the carcinogenic risk as the starting point from which a default option may be invoked if needed to address uncertainty or the absence of critical information.* [U.S. EPA, Guidelines for Carcinogen Risk Assessment, §1.3.1., EPA/630/P-03/001B (April 2005) (emphasis in original), 70 Fed. Reg. at 17,771.]

To what extent do these Guidelines change EPA's approach to evidence of nonlinearity that the court discusses in *Chlorine Chemistry Council*?

8. Initial hazard characterization and dose-response assessments are often the most visible and widely publicized features of a controversial risk assessment. Yet the components of a QRA that estimate the amount of human and environmental exposure are equally critical in determining how much harm an activity is actually causing. A chemical can be the most toxic in the world, but if it is also being completely contained it may not warrant further regulation. Even if exposure is occurring, in order to justify regulating an activity there must be some reason to believe that the activity is contributing to that exposure. High degrees of exposure may not justify regulating an activity if the exposure is coming from somewhere else. So exposure assessment is critical to a risk assessment, as are the hazard identification and dose-response assessment components, and such assessments similarly raise the issue of how much one needs to know about these exposure-related questions before regulation is justified. In *Ethyl Corp.*, for instance, there were gaps in the exposure assessment because the relationship between the lead that was being emitted from auto exhausts and the lead content in human blood was not well understood.

The following case study highlights some of the difficulties in developing an adequate understanding of human exposure in the course of producing a QRA.

‖ *Case Study: Mercury from Power Plants* ‖

The only metal that is a liquid at room temperature in its pure, or elemental, form, mercury (Hg) has been known to be toxic for centuries.

Romans using slave labor in mercury mines noticed an unusually high death rate. Hatters in England used mercury to soften animal hair, and many became mentally unstable, probably inspiring the character of the Mad Hatter in Lewis Carroll's *Alice's Adventures in Wonderland.* The hazards of mercury in its methylated form (MeHg) have only recently become known. When a fishing village in Japan, Minimata, began to experience neurological effects and their newborns had severe birth defects in the 1970s, the source of the problem was traced to an upstream chemical plant that was dumping methylmercury into the river. As the toxin bioaccumulated in the fish that the villagers ate, the villagers began to get sick. The Minimata tragedy stimulated research confirming that even at low doses, methylmercury, or MeHg, is a damaging neurotoxin.

Minimata illustrates the dominant source of human exposure to methylmercury—fish consumption. As mercury gets deposited in oceans, lakes, and rivers, it is converted to its methylated form by microorganisms. Fish consume those organisms and bioaccumulation increases the concentration of MeHg. By the time humans eat the fish, the concentration can be great.

Human consumption rates vary widely across the population, but people have often been encouraged to add more fish to their diet because fish provide many dietary benefits. Subsistence fishermen (those who live off of fish almost exclusively at certain times of the year) consume an even greater amount and are exposed to more MeHg as a result. In the United States, Native American tribes around the Great Lakes are among the highest consumers. Catherine A. O'Neill, *Mercury, Risk, and Justice,* 34 Envtl. L. Rep. 11070, 11077 (2004).

Dose-Response Assessment—Setting the Reference Dose.   After an exposure incident in Iraq in 1995, the EPA established a reference dose (RfD) for MeHg of 0.1 micrograms per kilogram (µg/kg) of body weight per day. EPA defines a reference dose as "an estimate of daily exposure to the human population (including sensitive subpopulations) that is likely to be without a risk of adverse effects when experienced over a lifetime." National Research Council, National Academy of Sciences (NAS), Toxicological Effects of Methyl Mercury 2 (2000). In this case, the RfD is intended to correspond to a blood lead level of 5.8 µg per liter or 5.8 parts per billion (ppb). As is often the case with dose-response assessments, in setting this RfD EPA had to evaluate a diverse array of scientific findings. Industry argued that the science did not support as low an RfD as EPA's. Seeking a respected second opinion, EPA referred the issue to an NAS advisory committee. Such referrals have been increasingly common when the agency is performing controversial risk assessments. Other recent examples include the arsenic and perchlorate risk assessments, both performed under the Safe Drinking Water Act. On arsenic, see pages 253-264.

The NAS committee examined the entire body of available evidence. The committee used 30 years of animal studies to determine that "[o]verall, data from animal studies, including studies on nonhuman primates, indicate that the developing nervous system is a sensitive target organ for low-dose MeHg exposure. Results from animal studies have reported effects on cognitive, motor, and sensory functions." The committee also examined nine human studies. Three of those studies were major epidemiological studies. Two of those studies, one conducted in the Faroe Islands and one in New Zealand, found associations between prenatal consumption of mercury-contaminated fish and neurological defects in children. The third study, conducted in the Seychelles Islands, did not find such associations. Despite the conflicting studies, the committee determined that since "there is a large body of scientific evidence showing adverse neurodevelopmental effects, including well-designed epidemiological studies, . . . an RfD should not be derived from a study, such as the Seychelles study, that did not observe any associations with MeHg." After its review, the NAS committee concluded that on the basis of the entire "body of evidence from human and animal studies" regarding neurological effects that the proposed RfD was "scientifically justifiable." 2000 NAS Report at 11.

Working independently of EPA's proceedings, in 2003 the World Health Organization decided to cut its Provisional Tolerable Weekly Intake of MeHg in half, down to a level of 1.6 µg/kg body weight per week. The PTWI amounts to an allowable level of mercury that is approximately twice as high as EPA's RfD. The sensitive subpopulation with whose health EPA, WHO, and other public health experts who study mercury contamination are most concerned are young children and women of child-bearing age, as the neurological systems that are most actively developing in fetuses are typically the most sensitive to the effects of neurotoxins. Exposure to mercury *in utero* can severely damage the neurological development of fetuses. Recently, studies also have linked mercury to cardiac abnormalities in children that may result in an increase in the risk of heart attack in adults. James K. Hammitt, Is the EPA Low-Balling the Mercury Risk?, L.A. Times, Apr. 14, 2005, at 1. A 2000 statistical analysis conducted by the Centers for Disease Control (CDC) concluded that approximately 8 percent of women of child-bearing age, or 5.5 million women, had blood lead levels in excess of reference dose exposure. See EPA, America's Children and the Environment, EPA 240-F-03-001 (2003).

Sources of Mercury in the Environment. Mercury enters the environment from a variety of sources. Mercury is found in volcanic emissions and it occurs naturally in rock formation and in fossil fuels. From rocks, it can be released into the environment naturally by weathering, but its release from fossil fuels comes primarily when humans burn those fuels. Other human sources include the incineration of waste containing mercury and some industrial processes employing mercury. Once released from whatever source, mercury enters a global cycle. Mercury that is released into the atmosphere is typically gaseous elemental mercury (Hg) also known as mercury zero. It can travel great distances before weather patterns like wind and rain deposit it on land or in surface waters. This means that some of the mercury deposited in the United States actually comes from foreign sources. American sources contribute about 107 tons each year to the global mercury cycle and we receive about 35 tons from outside the country. While mercury emissions from U.S. sources comprise a small percentage of global emissions (about 3 percent), EPA estimates that roughly 60 percent (about 52 tons per year) of mercury deposited in the United States comes from anthropogenic sources inside the country.

Ten years ago, there were three major sources of anthropogenic mercury: medical waste incinerators, municipal waste combustors, and coal-fired electrical utility power plants. Mid-nineties regulations issued by EPA reduced mercury emissions by 90 percent for the incinerators and combustors. Standards of Performance for New Stationary Sources and Emission Guidelines for Existing Sources: Hospital/Medical/Infectious Waste Incinerators, 62 Fed. Reg. 48,348 (Sept. 15, 1997); Standards of Performance for New Stationary Sources and Emission Guidelines for Existing Sources Municipal Waste Combustors, 60 Fed. Reg. 65387 (Dec. 19, 1995). A growing number of states are enacting legislation to reduce mercury contained in consumer products like thermo-meters, batteries, and fluorescent lights. For other state efforts, see *http://www.epa.gov/epaoswer/hazwaste/mercury/index.htm*. The largest contributors of U.S. emissions are now coal power plants which account for almost 40 percent of U.S. anthropogenic emissions. Industrial boilers contribute about 10 percent; burning of hazardous waste about 5 percent and chlorine production (about 5 percent). 1999 National Emissions Inventory.

Coal power plants have been under review for further regulation ever since the enactment of the 1990 Clean Air Act Amendments. American power plants are much cleaner than those abroad. Deciding whether and how stringently to regulate mercury emissions from these sources has proven just as complex and controversial as was establishing the RfD:

> However complex the science underlying MeHg's implications for public health, it is at least equaled by intense debate over the fate and transport of mercury through the environment. Millions of dollars have been spent on studies of the various facets of this puzzle: how much and what species of mercury are emitted by global sources, either natural or anthropogenic; what is the breakdown between global, natural, regional and local sources; how far and how fast do air emissions travel before they are deposited on the land; how does air deposition become methylated, entering the food chain and threatening public health; which specific categories of sources contribute the species of mercury most likely to become methylated; and—given the uncertainty that plagues the monitoring and modeling necessary to answer these questions—will regulation do any good? [Lisa Heinzerling & Rena I. Steinzor, A Perfect Storm: Mercury and the Bush Administration, 34 Envtl. L. Rep. 10297, 10303 (2004).]

Modeling the deposition of mercury has proved to be very challenging for scientists. In its Mercury Study Report to Congress, EPA modeling predicted the highest concentrations of mercury would be found in the Northeast and around the Ohio River Valley. U.S. EPA Mercury Study Report to Congress O-2 (1997) (EPA 452/R-97-003). However, the National Atmospheric Deposition Program/Mercury Deposition Network measured much higher concentrations in the South, especially in Louisiana and Florida. This illustrates the complexity and uncertainty of air quality modeling. These models must account not only for anthropogenic sources of mercury, but also changing weather patterns, existing environmental mercury, and deposition from foreign sources. The amount of mercury deposition attributable to U.S. sources varies by state due to weather patterns; for example, prevailing winds cause more mercury to be deposited locally in the Northeast and around the Great Lakes and Ohio River Valley than in the West.

Different Types of Mercury. Mercury released from a coal-fired utility comes in two forms besides mercury zero. Oxidized mercury (Hg^{++}) and particulate-bound mercury ($Hg(p)$) have relatively short atmospheric residence times compared to elemental mercury. These two are deposited in a matter of days and accumulate more locally than elemental mercury. On average, power plants emit roughly 50 percent Hg, 40 percent Hg^{++}, and 10 percent $Hg(p)$, but these are only averages. These numbers can vary widely depending on the specific power plant and meteorological and climate conditions. All of the species emitted from power plants can be converted to any number of organic and inorganic compounds, each with its own hazards and toxicity.

Many factors may contribute to the amount of mercury deposited in any one locality. In general, concentrations will be greater near areas that produce more Hg^{++} and $Hg(p)$ due to their shorter travel times. Hot spots can develop near power plants with high volumes of locally deposited mercury. When hot spots form near sensitive members of the population, severe damage can occur. Fate, transport, and transformation models try to predict how mercury gets from the smokestack to the water bodies where fish then consume the mercury. Once released into the atmosphere, oxidized and particulate-bound mercury can be deposited in both wet and dry forms. Winds cause dry deposition while precipitation like rain and snow cause wet deposition. Both oxidized and particulate-bound mercury are readily soluble in water making wet deposition via precipitation very common. This can occur in a matter of hours. Elemental mercury is not soluble in water and as a result has a longer life span in the atmosphere. It can spend a year or more in the atmosphere before depositing. Elemental mercury contributes heavily to the global mercury cycle, while oxidized and particulate-bound mercury significantly affect local and regional mercury cycles. Several complex reactions can change elemental mercury into one of the other two species allowing quicker deposition.

Deposition is heavily dependent on weather, which adds to the difficulties of prediction. If a local meteorologist often cannot reliably predict if it is going to rain within the next 24 hours, imagine predicting where and when it will rain across the country over a long range of time. Then add in our imperfect understanding of the many complex chemical reactions involved.

In its Mercury Study Report to Congress, EPA acknowledged the uncertainty of predicted exposure values. Discussing modeling mercury emissions from different sources, the agency noted "that a complete discussion is not practical for all facilities; there are 144 possible combinations: 12 model plants, 2 sites, 3 distances, and two possible RELMAP values (50th percentile or 90th percentile)." (RELMAP is one of the many available fate and transport models for air emissions.) U.S. EPA, Mercury Study Report to Congress 3-1 (1997) (EPA 452/R-97-006).

How Mercury Gets into Fish. Still other models are necessary to estimate the journey of mercury to the fish. U.S. EPA, Mercury Study Report to Congress 2-14 (1997) (EPA 452/R-97-005). Even within specific water bodies, only general information is known about the methylation process. Generally, microbes convert deposited mercury into MeHg. The rate of methylation depends heavily on site-specific environmental factors like the number of available microbes as well as the present vegetation and wildlife. In its Mercury Study Report to Congress, EPA acknowledged that there is "a large degree of scientific uncertainty and variability among water bodies concerning the processes that methylate mercury."

Once converted into MeHg, low-level predators consume the contaminated microbes. They are in turn consumed by higher-level predators. As MeHg rises up the food chain, it bioaccumulates and becomes more concentrated. When one predator consumes ten contaminated prey, it now contains ten times the concentration of MeHg. When a higher predator consumes ten of the first, it now contains 100 times the concentration of MeHg. By the time humans eat the contaminated fish, the dose of MeHg can reach toxic levels.

Different fish species accumulate MeHg at different rates. Freshwater fish like catfish, smallmouth bass, and northern pike tend to have higher mercury concentration than saltwater fish like tuna, pollack, and shrimp. Even among the same species, fish can have varying levels of MeHg contamination. Age and trophic level can affect the amount of MeHg found in fish. Older fish which are higher on the food chain can be expected to have higher levels of MeHg.

To further complicate the issue, total methylmercury concentrations in the environment are not always indicative of the concentration in fish. No one is certain about the exact connection between mercury emissions and fish contamination, prompting EPA to note, "We recognize that it is difficult to quantify with precision how a specific change in air deposition of Hg leads to a change in fish tissue levels." 70 Fed. Reg. 15,994 at 16,012. Compounding the problem is the fact that decreasing mercury emissions will cause an immediate decrease in mercury deposition but not in methylmercury concentrations in fish. There is a lag time for these concentrations to reach a steady state. That time can be as little as 5 years or as great as 50 years or more. In short, mercury poses challenges to scientists along every step of the way from power plant emission to human consumption.

Despite concerns over the many variables involved in the mercury problem, EPA ultimately concluded:

> The EPA's 1997 Mercury Study Report to Congress suggests a plausible link between anthropogenic releases of Hg from industrial and combustion sources in the U.S. and methylmercury in fish in the U.S. However, other sources of Hg emissions, including Hg from natural sources (such as volcanos [sic]) and anthropogenic emissions in other countries, contribute to the levels of methylmercury observed in fish in the U.S. Our current understanding of the global Hg cycle and the impact of the anthropogenic sources allow us to make estimates on a global, continental, or regional scale of their relative importance. It is more difficult to make accurate predictions of the fluxes on a local scale given our current understanding. [70 Fed. Reg. 15,994 at 16,012.]

Uncertainties and Variabilities in Fish Consumption. See the Problem Exercise on mercury in Chapter 1, pages 24-26.

Putting the Pieces Together. EPA's regulations reducing mercury emissions from medical waste incinerators and municipal waste combustors were issued under the provisions for hazardous air pollutants (HAPs), section 112 of the Clean Air Act, which was extensively rewritten by the 1990 Clean Air Act Amendments. In those Amendments, Congress listed 189 priority HAPs, and instructed EPA to issue technology-based standards for them that achieved "maximum degree of reduction in emissions" (MACT). The stringency of these technology-based regulations for incinerators and combustors resulted in a 90 percent reduction in mercury emissions from those sources in a matter of just a few years.

The Amendments treated coal power plants differently. They required EPA first to study the relationship between these plants and mercury and then to make a finding that regulation under section 112 was "appropriate and necessary" before proceeding further. 42 U.S.C. §7412(n)(1)(A). EPA made such a finding in December 2000. 65 Fed. Reg. 79,825. EPA then began work on regulation of those emissions. EPA then began to develop a maximum available control technology standard. The standard was expected to reduce emissions of mercury by 90 percent in as little as three years.

Plans changed, however, when a new administration took control of the White House. EPA revisited its initial finding that regulation of mercury emissions from coal-fired utilities was "appropriate and necessary." The agency concluded that its December 2000 decision relied too heavily on risks posed to the environment rather than focusing exclusively on the threat to public health. The March 2005 announcement states, "EPA erred in its December 2000 'appropriate' finding to the extent that it hinged on the environmental effects of HAP, including Hg." 70 Fed. Reg. 15,994. In addition, the March 2005 announcement concluded that the December 2000 decision did not consider reductions of mercury that incidentally resulted from other regulations like the Clean Air Interstate Rule (CAIR) that reduced air pollutants like SO_2 and NO_X, but which would have "co-benefits" of reducing mercury emissions as well.

The Agency also concluded it had authority to regulate new sources under the New Source Performance Standards of section 111 and on that basis concluded that regulation of mercury under the section 112 program was not "necessary." Acting under section 111(d), EPA then created a cap-and-trade emissions program for mercury. An overall cap on emissions would be set, and utilities would be allowed to trade emissions, banking presently unused credits so that they could emit more in the future. They could also buy credits in an unlimited amount from a future bank of credits. The gradually decreasing cap is set at an amount high enough so that utilities need not do anything to comply with the new emissions standard other than comply with other air quality laws, at least until 2018. For discussion of how cap-and-trade works, see pages 550-553.

Question One. In light of the uncertainty about the relationship between particular sources of mercury and adverse human health effects, should the EPA not regulate mercury now, but await the development of further information?

Question Two. In his article *EPA: Shoot First, Ask Later,* Patrick Michaels of the Cato Institute points out "The United States, with about 25 percent of the world's total economic activity, should logically emit about 1000 megagrams [of mercury]. But we only throw out, according to the EPA, 144 megagrams, or 3.6 percent of the world's total. That's a pretty good bang for your mercury buck." Not only are U.S. sources already responsible for less than their proportionate share of anthropogenic mercury emissions, approximately 40 percent of the U.S. mercury deposition comes from foreign sources. If that is so, why should utilities be required to clean up further until the "dirtier" sources in other countries improve their performance? What do considerations of proportionality say in the area of climate change, where the U.S. is responsible for far more than its fair share of greenhouse gas emissions?

Question Three. In the same article, Michaels notes that emissions regulations will increase the cost of electrical power which could cause the deaths of those unable to afford heat in the winter or air conditioning in the summer. Reducing fish intake can be harmful, too. How ought these considerations be weighed in the risk management decision regarding mercury?

Question Four. Should EPA be concerned about sensitive members of the population once the average fish consumer is being protected? If so, what should it do about those populations? Most states and some tribes have issued fish advisories for areas with contaminated fish. Mercury is responsible for 76 percent of all advisories issued which cover 32 percent of the nation's lake acreage. Catherine A. O'Neill, Mercury, Risk, and Justice, 34 Envtl. L. Rep.

11070, 11079 (2004). See also the Problem Exercise on mercury in Chapter 1. Rather than lower emissions of mercury, why can't people just avoid eating fish that are contaminated?

C. HOW SAFE IS SAFE?—MODERN APPROACHES TO MANAGING RISK

Up to this point, this chapter has focused on the issues raised by the first line of inquiry prompted by the preventative ambition—trying to determine what activities warrant regulatory attention due to their potential to cause harm. The second line of inquiry asks just "how safe is safe?" What constitutes acceptable risk, what should be done to reduce the harm causing potential? The issues raised are no less complex or controversial.

This section focuses on the issues raised by this second line of inquiry. It is often said that the question of "how safe is safe" raises primarily questions of social policy, as a society must negotiate the conflict between the values served by preventing harm and the values served by the harmful activity, which often advance social interests as well. This is then contrasted with the nature of the first line of inquiry, which is characterized as primarily scientific. It is largely due to this difference that the influential National Academy of Sciences report on risk regulation urged federal agencies to segregate these two activities as much as possible, assigning the resolution of risk assessment issues to science panels and the resolution of risk management issues to the regulatory agencies. National Research Council, Risk Assessment in the Federal Government: Managing the Process 5-8 (1983). The preceding section has suggested some of the ways in which this distinction is misleading. Risk assessment involves heavy elements of social policy and cannot be considered a matter of "pure science," especially when inferential bridges are required to fill gaps or where science is uncertain; see pages 203-210 and 280-284. The NAS Report urges explicit identification of the options available at each point where an assumption must be made or an inferential bridge built to span a data gap so that the policy makers can address those questions. However, critics doubt that such complete explicitness can ever be achieved in practice; thus, isolating the risk assessment process from the policy-making process inevitably will result in some, possibly important, policy decisions being made by scientists and other "experts" without public scrutiny. See Latin, Good Science, Bad Regulations, and Toxic Risk Assessment, 5 Yale J. on Reg. 89 (1988).

The question of how much information we need to have before it is appropriate to manage risk at all is also a question of assessing risk that is heavily policy-laden. For instance, in issuing the regulation that lead up to the *Ethyl Corp.* litigation, EPA decided to regulate the lead content of gasoline even though the harm that the lead was causing was "impossible to forecast." Thus EPA "assessed" the risk of lead without performing a quantitative risk assessment at all. The decision that lead posed enough of a public health concern to justify regulation was an assessment based on policy, not pure science, even though of course science informed the decision. EPA in effect was operating on a version of the Precautionary Principle. That Principle, which is much more frequently invoked in international environmental disputes than it is domestically, has become a lightning rod because it endorses regulatory intervention based on less information than those who wish to avoid regulation would prefer. See pages 208-214. The *Reserve* court necessarily answered similar policy questions, and also adopted a precautionary stance.

So long as the interpenetration of science and policy into both risk assessment and risk management issues is not forgotten, there is value in distinguishing the two for analytical purposes because it enables exploration of the issues that Congress and regulatory agencies frequently face in choosing among the different regulatory responses to potentially harmful activity.

1. *Introduction: Remedial Approaches in* Reserve *and* Ethyl Corp.

As they did with the first line of inquiry, the early *Reserve* and *Ethyl Corp.* decisions provide useful introductions into the issues raised in determining "how safe is safe."

First, *Reserve.* After finding that the air and water pollution from Reserve's plant posed a reasonable medical concern, the district court had ordered the facility closed immediately. The Eighth Circuit first stayed the injunction and then modified it. The court concluded "the evidence is insufficient to support the kind of demonstrable danger to the public health that would justify the immediate closing of Reserve's operations." Reserve Mining Co. v. EPA, 514 F.2d 492, 507 (8th Cir. 1975). While the appellate court referred approvingly to Judge Wright's analysis of risk in *Ethyl Corp.*, the court also concluded that "it cannot be said that the probability of harm is more likely than not" and that "it cannot be forecast that the rates of cancer will increase" as a result of the air and water pollution. 514 F.2d at 520. The court continued:

> In fashioning relief in a case such as this involving a possibility of future harm, a court should strike a proper balance between the benefits conferred and the hazards created by Reserve's facility. In its pleadings Reserve directs our attention to the benefits arising from its operations. [Reserve represented a $350 million capital investment with an annual payroll of $32 million, which supported 3,367 employees. Its production of taconite was 12 percent of the U.S. total.]
>
> [On the other side], the hazard in both the air and water can be measured in only the most general terms as a concern for the public health resting on a reasonable medical theory. Serious consequences could result if the hypothesis on which it is based should ultimately prove true. [514 F.2d at 535-536.]

In speaking of the need to balance "the benefits conferred and the hazards created" by Reserve, did the court explain how to strike such a balance? How can one strike a balance if one "cannot . . . forecast" the amount of harm that might occur? In fact, what did the court mean when it said that an increase in cancer rates cannot be forecast? Does it imply that a court must be *certain* that harm will occur before it can enjoin? Would that be consistent with Judge Wright's approach assessing and responding to risk? What is the implication of the court's conclusion that harm was less than likely? Is it that the probability of harm must be greater than 50 percent before a court should enjoin? Would that be consistent with Judge Wright's approach to assessing and responding to risk?

Suppose villagers living in a valley below an earthen dam convince a court that there is a one-in-ten chance that the dam would fail. Would the court be justified in enjoining the dam owner *either* to drain the dam completely *or* to reinforce the dam, and to do so immediately? Is your answer consistent with *Reserve?* With *Ethyl Corp.?* Suppose the dam operator complained that fixing or draining the dam immediately would cause it grievous financial loss, whereas a phased, three-year improvement and reinforcement plan could be accomplished at much lower costs. Would that influence your answer?

Next, *Ethyl Corp.* EPA's rule had ordered a graduated phasedown of the lead content in gasoline, beginning with a refinery average of 1.7 grams per gallon as of January 1, 1975, down through five steps to a final average of 0.5 grams after January 1, 1979. 38 Fed. Reg. 33,734 (1973). The court upheld EPA's phasedown order without closely examining its details or the agency rationale for choosing this particular phasedown instead of any of the counterproposals of industry. (Industry protested the rule's use of a refinery average instead of a company average; they also protested EPA's requirement that averages be computed quarterly, preferring semiannual or annual averaging.) Not only did the court not scrutinize the details of the phasedown, it did not deliberate over the final target figure, 0.5 grams per gallon, that EPA issued. In its proposal for the phasedown rule, EPA had stated:

> Based on the available evidence, the Administrator has concluded that airborne lead levels exceeding 2 micrograms per cubic meter, averaged over a period of 3 months or longer, are associated with a sufficient risk of adverse physiologic effects to constitute endangerment of public health. . . . [A]ttainment of a 2-microgram level will require a 60 to 65 percent reduction in lead from motor vehicles. [37 Fed. Reg. 3,882 (1972).]

Does EPA seem to be saying here that 2 micrograms or less is not an "endangering" level of exposure? If so, it was initially justifying the phasedown from 0.7 to 0.5 (a 70 percent reduction) as necessary to achieve nonendangering exposure.

In issuing its final rule, EPA appeared to shift ground:

> [I]t is difficult, if not impossible, to establish a precise level of airborne lead as an acceptable basis for a control strategy. . . . [However,] [s]trong evidence existed which supported the view that through these routes [air and dust] airborne lead contributes to excessive lead exposure in urban adults and children. In light of this evidence of health risks, the Administrator concluded that it would be prudent to reduce preventable lead exposure. [38 Fed. Reg. 33,734 (1973).]

To buttress its determination that a 70 percent reduction in the amount of lead used in gasoline was possible, EPA lengthened its initial reduction schedule from 4 to 5 years, so as to "moderate the economic and technological impacts of the regulations during the period over which the reduction would be accomplished." That done, EPA wrote that "though the benefits associated with the . . . lead reductions have not been quantified, the Administrator has concluded that this approach is not unreasonably costly and will prudently prevent unnecessary exposure to airborne lead." Costs, in fact, were projected to be less than 0.1 cent per gallon refined, adding only between $82 million and $133 million to the total of $1.5 billion the industry was to invest in refining capacity through the year 1980. 38 Fed. Reg. 33,734, 33,739 (1973).

Thus, EPA appeared to switch from justifying its decision on the basis of achieving a level of exposure that would not pose an endangering risk to one based on what technology and economic considerations would "prudently" permit. What considerations could have contributed to the shift? If 70 percent were "preventable," would 80 or 90 percent have been? EPA did not examine this question. Instead, it expressed the aim of determining the most cost-effective approach to the reduction of lead exposure from any source, whether airborne or not. Unfortunately, EPA had previously conceded that because the relative contribution of lead exposure from any one source could not be precisely quantified, "the most cost-effective approach to the aggregate prevention of excessive lead exposure has not been defined." 38 Fed. Reg. 1,258, 1,259 (1973). EPA continued, "the lead in gasoline issue presents particular difficulties regarding the cost-effectiveness of reducing lead contents below the level of 0.5 grams per gallon." So apparently EPA used its misgivings about whether removing lead from gasoline below 0.5 grams was cost-effective, when compared to other techniques for reducing the total body burden of lead, as a reason to stop at that point. Under its regulatory statutes, cost-effectiveness is occasionally a requirement, such as in the case of CERCLA's requirement that remedial measures be "cost-effective," 42 U.S.C. §9621(b) but more often it is not.

If EPA thought it "difficult, if not impossible" to determine an acceptable level of airborne lead, should it have ordered an immediate removal of all lead from gasoline? This would have been akin to the district court injunction in *Reserve,* whereas what EPA actually did more nearly resembled the court of appeals's decision there. If EPA had ordered immediate removal, should the court of appeals have reversed?

Recall, finally, that the decision to phase down lead content in gasoline that was sustained by *Ethyl Corp.* subsequently assisted EPA in both demonstrating the connection between lead exposure and adverse health effects and in quantifying those effects. Subsequently, EPA's decision to eliminate lead from gasoline entirely was supported by a risk assessment and then a cost benefit analysis—based on data available because the decision to phase down lead had permitted scientists to understand the health effects of removing lead from the atmosphere. See pages 31-34, and pages 230-242.

2.   *Statutory Authorities for Regulating Risks*

A complex array of statutory authorities addresses the risks presented by toxic chemicals. The Toxic Substances Control Act (TSCA), which gives EPA authority over any chemical substance or mixture (other than pesticides regulated by FIFRA and food products, drugs, and cosmetics, regulated by the Food and Drug Administration), appears to provide the most comprehensive regulatory authority, although the procedural and evidentiary demands of the statute sap it of much of its effectiveness. See pages 230-242. The Federal Insecticide, Fungicide, and Rodenticide Act (FIFRA) governs EPA's regulation of pesticides; the Safe Drinking Water Act (SDWA) governs EPA regulation of contaminants in public drinking water systems; section 112 of the Clean Air Act requires EPA to regulate emissions of hazardous air pollutants; and sections 304(l) and 307 of the Clean Water Act require EPA to regulate toxic water pollutants. Agencies other than EPA also have significant authority to regulate toxic substances. The Food and Drug Administration (FDA), which is part of the Department of

Health and Human Services, has jurisdiction over foods, drugs, cosmetics, and medical devices under the federal Food, Drug, and Cosmetic Act (FDCA). The Labor Department's Occupational Safety and Health Administration (OSHA) is responsible for protecting workers against toxic chemical hazards in the workplace pursuant to the Occupational Safety and Health Act (OSH Act). Workers in mines are protected separately under the federal Mine Safety and Health Act (MSHA), which is administered by the Department of Labor and its National Institute of Occupational Safety and Health. The Consumer Product Safety Commission (CPSC) regulates hazardous consumer products pursuant to the Consumer Product Safety Act (CPSA) and it also administers the Federal Hazardous Substances Act and the Poison Prevention Packaging Act, which require labeling of hazardous and poisonous substances. The Nuclear Regulatory Commission is responsible for regulating radioactive substances under the Atomic Energy Act.

This is by no means an exhaustive list. Several other statutes address specific aspects of the toxic substances problem. In 1985, the Office of Science and Technology Policy identified 21 different statutes that may be used by 12 different agencies just to regulate carcinogens.

Statutory authorities for regulating toxics differ greatly in the extent to which they require review or approval prior to the manufacture or use of such substances. The federal Food, Drug, and Cosmetic Act requires FDA approval prior to the marketing of new food additives, drugs, and cosmetics. EPA similarly must approve the registration of new pesticides under FIFRA prior to marketing. TSCA, however, is not a licensing statute. Under it, EPA must be notified 90 days prior to the manufacture of a new chemical or the application of an old chemical to a significant new use, and the EPA can intervene to require further information, but no specific approval is required unless EPA does intervene. Another class of statutes, "standard-setting laws," requires agencies to establish standards limiting toxic emissions, controlling worker exposure to toxics, or mandating warning labels on products. These include the OSH Act, the Safe Drinking Water Act, the Consumer Product Safely Act, TSCA, and the provisions of the Clean Air and Clean Water Acts that deal with toxic substances.

The early EPA actions regarding lead, as well as the various judicial opinions in *Ethyl Corp.* and *Reserve*, took differing approaches to the "how safe is safe" question, and these modern statutes regulating toxic substances do so as well. Three general types, mirroring the three bases for regulatory controls discussed in Chapter 2, pages 130-132, capture most of the statutory approaches. Some statutes (e.g., TSCA and FIFRA) require that regulators balance the threat to public health against the cost of regulation when setting regulatory standards—thus, they are risk-benefit balancing statutes. Others (e.g., the OSH Act and the Safe Drinking Water Act) direct that threats to health be regulated as stringently as is feasible. Such statutes are a special case of technology-based standards. Because the concern with toxics exposure at any level is so great that Congress frequently expresses the desire to eliminate exposure if only it were feasible, such standards as those of the OSH Act and the SDWA can be termed *feasibility-limited* standards. A third approach, which is embodied in the national ambient air quality standards of the Clean Air Act as well as in the original toxic air pollutants provisions of the Clean Air Act and the Delaney Clauses of the FDCA, requires that standards be based exclusively on concerns for protecting public health (health-based statutes). As amended in 1990,

FIGURE 3.5
Summary of Federal Laws Authorizing Regulation of Toxic Substances

BALANCING STATUTES

Law	Type of controls	Threshold finding	Basis for controls
Food, Drug, and Cosmetic Act (FDCA)	controls levels of natural components of foods	"poisonous or deleterious . . . unless the quantity does not ordinarily render it injurious to health"	balances risk against need for plentiful and affordable food
FDCA	controls levels of environmental contaminants in foods	"poisonous or deleterious . . . unless the quantity does not ordinarily render it injurious to health"	balances risk against whether required, unavoidable, or measurable
FDCA	regulates introduction of new drugs and biologics	"substantial evidence that [it is] safe and effective"; "no imminent hazard to public health"	balances risk against efficacy and impact on health
Federal Insecticide, Fungicide, and Rodenticide Act	prohibits use of pesticides unless registered by EPA; EPA may restrict or condition usage	"will not generally cause any unreasonable risk to man or the environment"	balances adverse impacts of pesticide on human health and the environment against benefits of pesticide
Toxic Substances Control Act	can ban or restrict production, use, or disposal of existing chemicals (§6); can require testing of chemicals where data are inadequate to assess risk (§4); requires 90-day notice to EPA before introduction into commerce of new chemicals (§5)	"reasonable basis to believe presents or will present an unreasonable risk of injury to human health or the environment"	balances risk posed by chemicals against economic consequences of regulation
Consumer Product Safety Act	authorizes bans of unreasonably dangerous consumer products	"an unreasonable risk of injury"	balances risk against product utility, cost, and availability

TECHNOLOGY- or FEASIBLITY-LIMITED STATUTES

Law	Type of controls	Threshold finding	Basis for controls
Occupational Safety and Health Act	can limit worker exposure to toxic substances in the workplace	existence of a significant risk that can be reduced appreciably by regulation	ensure that no worker suffers material impairment of health or functional capacity to the extent feasible
Safe Drinking Water Act	limits contaminants in public drinking water supplies	"may have an adverse effect on the health of persons"	reduces contaminants as closely as feasible to levels where no adverse health effects will occur and which allow an adequate margin of safety

FIGURE 3.5
Continued

Law	Type of controls	Threshold finding	Basis for controls
Clean Water Act	sets effluent standards for discharges of toxic pollutants into surface waters	"identifiable effects on health and welfare"	uses best available technology to control discharges with health-based water quality standards as backstop

HEALTH-BASED STATUTES

Law	Type of controls	Threshold finding	Basis for controls
§112 of the Clean Air Act	establishes emission standards for hazardous air pollutants	substance is one of 189 chemicals on initial list specified in statute or added to list on finding that it may present "a threat of adverse human health effects"	sets limits that "provide an ample margin of safety to protect the public health" if technology-based controls fail to do so after 8 years
FDCA	controls levels of added substances in food	"any poisonous or deleterious substance which may render it injurious to health"	reasonable certainty of no harm
FDCA	controls levels of added substances in food	"induce[s] cancer in laboratory animals"	reasonable certainty of no harm

section 112 now requires that technology-based controls (reflecting the maximum achievable control technology, or MACT) be applied initially to control hazardous air pollutants, supplemented with purely health-based controls if the "residual risk" remaining after MACT has been applied is sufficiently great.

Sometimes specific types of risk-creating activities have been singled out for distinctive treatment within a broader regulatory regime. For instance, the Delaney clause applies a health-based standard of zero to food additives, originally including pesticide residues in raw or processed foods, and to color additives if the additives caused cancer in laboratory animals. See pages 266-271. The Food Quality Protection Act (FQPA) of 1996 now exempts pesticide residues from the food additives covered by Delaney and makes them subject to a standard of "reasonable certainty of no harm." The legislative history of the Act suggests that many members of Congress anticipated this being interpreted as exposing individuals to no greater than a 1-in-1-million risk of cancer, but the degree of certainty required under FQPA is undefined in the statute itself.

These statutes also differ in the amount and kind of evidence that must be shown before a substance can be regulated and in the type of controls that they authorize regulators to impose. Some laws authorize outright prohibitions on the manufacture or use of certain chemicals (e.g., TSCA, FIFRA, FDCA), while others authorize the establishment of emission standards or ambient concentration limits (CAA, CWA, OSH Act), restrictions on use, and labeling, warning, or reporting requirements (TSCA). Figure 3.5 offers a rough comparison of the statutory authorities for regulating toxics.

3.   Risk-Benefit Balancing Approaches*

A.   INTRODUCTION

Risk-benefit balancing is cost-benefit analysis applied to policy decisions involving risks. See Chapter 1, pages 31-34. Quantitative risk assessments are the backbone of modern risk-benefit balancing. To the maximum extent possible, benefits from a proposed rule reducing exposure to toxic substances are evaluated through a QRA that estimates anticipated adverse health effects and, where applicable, environmental effects in terms of their dollar values. Costs of achieving those benefits are then also calculated by estimating capital and operating expenditures that the regulated community would incur if the rule were adopted.

Implementing a risk-balancing statute for toxics is almost always controversial and difficult. All the problems and uncertainties of QRAs discussed in the previous section—uncertainties of data, the necessity of making assumptions linking data to policy-related conclusions, and decision making on the "frontiers of scientific knowledge"—make toxics-related decision making difficult. In fact, one student of environmental regulatory policy has remarked that these difficulties have created regulatory structures that "eat up heroic amounts of money, remain information-starved, feature shameless manipulation of the data, face crippling political pressure, and produce little abatement." Oliver A. Houck, Tales from a Troubled Marriage: Science and Law in Environmental Policy 163, 169-170 (2003).

B.   EXAMPLE: THE TOXIC SUBSTANCES CONTROL ACT

Perhaps the best way to appreciate the pros and cons of risk-benefit analysis is to consider specific instances where agencies employed this approach to regulation writing. In this regard, the Toxic Substances Control Act is a classic example of a risk-benefit balancing statute. In fact, the term "unreasonable risk" appears 35 times in 33 pages of the statute. Rodgers, The Lesson of the Owls and the Crows: The Role of Deception in the Evolution of the Environmental Statutes, 4 J. Land Use & Envtl. L. 377, 379 (1989). TSCA grants EPA broad authority to regulate the manufacture, processing, distribution, use, or disposal of any chemical substance on a finding that there is a "reasonable basis to conclude" that such an activity "presents or will present an unreasonable risk of injury to health or the environment," TSCA §6(a), 15 U.S.C. §2605(a). In determining whether a substance poses an "unreasonable risk," TSCA explicitly requires EPA to make findings concerning not only health and environmental effects, but also the benefits of various uses of the substance, the availability of substitutes for it, and "the reasonably ascertainable economic consequences" of regulation. TSCA§6(c)(1), 15 U.S.C. §2605(c)(1).

---

*While the terms "risk-benefit balancing" and "cost-benefit balancing" can almost be used interchangeably, it is easy to get confused by them because they place the word "benefit" on different sides of the balancing equation—the "benefits" in "risk-benefit balancing" are the benefits provided by the substance to be regulated (which are the "costs" in "cost-benefit balancing"); the "benefits" in "cost-benefit balancing" are the gains to health or the environment from regulating the risks (the "risk" in "risk-benefit balancing").

Although TSCA does not specify how this risk-benefit balancing is to be performed, it directs EPA to regulate "to the extent necessary to protect adequately against such risk using the least burdensome requirements." TSCA §6(a), 15 U.S.C. §2605(a). This suggests that EPA is to determine what constitutes adequate protection and then to determine the least burdensome means of achieving it. While TSCA explicitly requires EPA to consider the economic impact of regulation and the benefits of the substance to be regulated, the legislative history of TSCA indicates that Congress did not envision that EPA would be required to perform quantitative risk assessments followed by formal cost-benefit analyses. The House Committee report on the legislation explained that the balancing required by section 6 "does not require a formal benefit-cost analysis" because "such an analysis would not be very useful" given the difficulty of assigning monetary values to benefits and costs of chemical regulation. Toxic Substances Control Act, Report by the Comm. on Interstate and Foreign Commerce, U.S. House of Representatives, H.R. Rep. 94-1341, 94th Cong., 2d Sess. 14 (1976). The Senate Committee report emphasized that while section 6(c) required some balancing, "it is not feasible to reach a decision just on the basis of quantitative comparisons" because "[i]n comparing risks, costs, and benefits . . . one is weighing noncommensurates." It stressed that EPA also must give "full consideration" to the extraordinary "burdens of human suffering and premature death." Toxic Substances Control Act, Report of the Senate Comm. on Commerce, S. Rep. 94-698, 94th Cong., 2d Sess. 13 (1976).

After TSCA's enactment, however, QRAs became routine under all statutes, even if they are not risk-benefit balancing statutes. Presidential Executive Orders have for decades required QRAs to be performed for all major rules, regardless of whether or not the statute under which the rule is to be issued requires risk-benefit balancing. See pages 153-154. The *Benzene* decision pushed threshold findings of significant risk in the direction of QRAs, too. See pages 182-196. In such a regulatory environment, it was inevitable that statutes requiring risks to be weighed against benefits would end up relying upon QRAs.

PRINCIPAL PROVISIONS OF THE TOXIC SUBSTANCES CONTROL ACT

Section 4 authorizes the EPA administrator to require the testing of any chemical substance or mixture on finding that such testing is necessary because there are insufficient data from which the chemical's effects can be predicted and the chemical either "may present an unreasonable risk of injury to health or the environment" or the chemical is produced in substantial quantities or may result in substantial human exposure.

Section 5 prohibits any person from manufacturing any new chemical substance or from processing any chemical substance for a significant new use unless the person notifies the EPA administrator at least 90 days in advance and submits any data that the person believes show that the chemical will not present an unreasonable risk. The EPA administrator may prohibit or limit the manufacturing, processing, distribution, use, or disposal of any chemical if he or she determines that the information is insufficient to permit a reasoned evaluation of the effects of the chemical and that it either may present an unreasonable risk or that it may result in significant human exposure.

Section 6 authorizes the EPA administrator, to the extent necessary to protect adequately against such risk using the least burdensome requirements, to prohibit the manufacture, processing, or distribution in commerce of a chemical substance; to limit the amounts, concentrations, or uses of it; to require labeling or record-keeping concerning it; or to prohibit or otherwise regulate any manner or method of disposal of it, on a finding that there is a reasonable basis to conclude that the chemical "presents or will present an unreasonable risk of injury to health or the environment."

Section 7 authorizes the EPA administrator to sue to seize or to obtain other relief to protect against imminently hazardous chemical substances.

Section 8 authorizes the EPA administrator to require record-keeping or the submission of reports concerning the manufacture or processing of chemical substances.

Section 9 requires the EPA administrator to refer chemicals to other federal agencies for regulation or to use other laws administered by EPA to regulate the chemical if he or she determines that the risks posed by the chemical may be sufficiently prevented or reduced by action taken under other laws.

Section 19 authorizes judicial review of EPA regulations issued under TSCA.

Section 20 authorizes citizen suits against any person alleged to be in violation of TSCA or against the EPA administrator for failure to perform nondiscretionary duties.

Section 21 authorizes citizen petitions for the commencement of rulemaking proceedings.

The best illustration of how EPA performs risk-benefit analysis is the story of the Agency's efforts to regulate asbestos risks under section 6 of TSCA. Acutely aware of the enormous difficulty of protecting the public from asbestos in schools and buildings, EPA announced in 1979 that it would consider banning all remaining uses of asbestos. 44 Fed. Reg. 60,061 (1979). It took EPA nearly ten years to promulgate such a rule, after developing a 45,000-page record. EPA's rationale for the rule is described in the following excerpt from the Federal Register notice that accompanied it.

EPA, Asbestos: Manufacture, Importation, Processing, and Distribution in Commerce Prohibitions
54 Fed. Reg. 29,460 (1989)

EPA is issuing this final rule under section 6 of the Toxic Substance Control Act (TSCA) to prohibit, at staged intervals, the future manufacture, importation, processing, and distribution in commerce of asbestos in almost all products, as identified in this rule. EPA is issuing this rule to reduce the unreasonable risks presented to human health by exposure to asbestos during activities involving these products. . . .

Section 6 of TSCA authorizes EPA to promulgate a rule prohibiting or limiting the amount of a chemical substance that may be manufactured, processed, or distributed in commerce in the U.S. if EPA finds that there is a reasonable basis to conclude that the manufacture, processing, distribution in commerce, use, or disposal of the chemical substance, or any combination of these activities, presents or will present an unreasonable risk of injury to human health or the environment. . . .

To determine whether a risk from activities involving asbestos-containing products presents an unreasonable risk, EPA must balance the probability that harm will occur from the activities against the effects of the proposed regulatory action on the availability to society of the benefits of asbestos. EPA has considered these factors in conjunction with the extensive record gathered in the development of this rule. EPA has concluded that the continued manufacture, importation, processing, and distribution in commerce of most asbestos-containing products poses an unreasonable risk to human health. This conclusion is based on information summarized [below].

EPA has concluded that exposure to asbestos during the life cycles of many asbestos-containing products poses an unreasonable risk of injury to human health. EPA has also concluded that section 6 of TSCA is the ideal statutory authority to regulate the risks posed by asbestos exposure. This rule's pollution prevention actions under TSCA are both the preferable and the least burdensome means of controlling the exposure risks posed throughout the life cycle of asbestos-containing products. Findings supporting this conclusion include the following:

1. Exposure to asbestos causes many painful, premature deaths due to mesothelioma and lung, gastrointestinal, and other cancers, as well as asbestosis and other diseases. Risks attributable to asbestos exposure and addressed by this rule are serious and are calculated for this rule using direct evidence from numerous human epidemiological studies. Studies show that asbestos is a highly potent carcinogen and that severe health effects occur after even short-term, high-level or longer-term, low-level exposures to asbestos. Asbestos exposure is compatible with a linear, no-threshold dose-response model for lung cancer. In addition, there is no undisputed evidence of quantitative differences in potency based on fiber size or type.

For the quantitative risk assessment performed as part of this rule-making, EPA used dose-response constants for lung cancer and mesothelioma that were the geometric means of the "best estimates" from a number of epidemiological studies. If EPA had instead used an upper bound estimate, as is normally done by the scientific community and in EPA regulatory risk assessment when only data from animal studies is available to extrapolate human health risk, predicted lung cancer deaths could increase by a factor of 10 and mesothelioma deaths could increase by a factor of 20.

2. People are frequently unknowingly exposed to asbestos and are rarely in a position to protect themselves. Asbestos is generally invisible, odorless, very durable, and highly aerodynamic. It can travel long distances and exist in the environment for extended periods. Therefore, exposure can take place long after the release of asbestos and at a distant location from the source of the release.

3. Additions to the current stock of asbestos-containing products would contribute to the environmental loading of asbestos. This poses the potential for an increased risk to the general population of asbestos-related disease and an increased risk to future generations because of asbestos' longevity.

4. Asbestos fibers are released to the air at many stages of the commercial life of the products that are subject to this rule. Activities that might lead to the release of asbestos include mining of the substance, processing asbestos fibers into products, and transport, installation, use, maintenance, repair, removal, and disposal of asbestos-containing products. EPA has found that the occupational and nonoccupational exposure existing over the entire life cycles of each of the banned asbestos-containing products poses a high level of individual risk. EPA has determined that thousands of persons involved in the manufacture, processing, transport, installation, use, repair, removal, and disposal of the asbestos-containing products affected by this rule are exposed to a serious lifetime asbestos exposure risk, despite OSHA's relatively low workplace PEL. In addition, according to the EPA Asbestos Modeling Study, millions of members of the general U.S. population are exposed to elevated levels of lifetime risk due to asbestos released throughout the life cycle of asbestos-containing products. EPA believes that the exposures quantified for the analyses supporting this rule represent an understatement of actual exposure.

5. Release of asbestos fibers from many products during life cycle activities can be substantial. OSHA stated in setting its PEL of 0.2 f/cc that remaining exposures pose a serious risk because of limitations on available control technologies. Even with OSHA's controls, thousands of workers involved in the manufacture and processing of asbestos-containing products are exposed to a lifetime risk of 1 in 1,000 of developing cancer. Many other exposures addressed by this rule are not affected by engineering controls required by OSHA's PEL or by other government regulation. Because asbestos is a highly potent carcinogen, the uncontrolled high peak episodic exposures that are faced by large populations pose a significant risk.

6. Because of the life cycle or "cradle-to-grave" nature of the risk posed by asbestos, attempts by OSHA, the Consumer Product Safety Commission (CPSC), and other EPA offices to regulate the continued commercial use of asbestos still leave many persons unprotected from the hazards of asbestos exposure. Technological limitations inhibit the effectiveness of existing or possible exposure control actions under non-TSCA authorities. Many routes of asbestos exposure posed by the products subject to this rule are outside the jurisdiction of regulatory authorities other than TSCA. EPA has determined that the residual exposure to asbestos that exists despite the actions taken under other authorities poses a serious health risk throughout the life cycle of many asbestos-containing products. This residual exposure can only be adequately controlled by the exposure prevention actions taken in this rule.

7. Despite the proven risks of asbestos exposure and the current or imminent existence of suitable substitutes for most uses of asbestos, asbestos continues to be used in large quantities in the U.S. in the manufacture or processing of a wide variety of commercial products. Total annual U.S. consumption of asbestos dropped from a 1984 total of about 240,000 metric tons to less than 85,000 metric tons in 1987, according to the U.S. Department of Interior, Bureau of Mines data. This change suggests that the use of substitutes has increased markedly since the proposal. However, the 1987 consumption total indicates that significant exposure due to the commercial use of asbestos and the resultant risks would continue for the foreseeable future absent the actions taken in this rule.

Evidence supports the conclusion that substitutes already exist or will soon exist for each of the products that are subject to the rule's bans. In scheduling products for the different stages of the bans, EPA has analyzed the probable availability of nonasbestos substitutes. In the rule, the various asbestos products are scheduled to be banned at times when it is likely that suitable nonasbestos substitutes will be available. However, the rule also includes an exemption provision to account for instances in which technology might not have advanced sufficiently by the time of a ban to produce substitutes for certain specialized or limited uses of asbestos.

8. EPA has calculated that the product bans in this rule will result in the avoidance of 202 quantifiable cancer cases, if benefits are not discounted, and 148 cases, if benefits are discounted at 3 percent. The figures decrease to 164 cases, if benefits are not discounted, and 120 cases, if benefits are discounted at 3 percent, if analogous exposures are not included in the analysis. In all likelihood, the rule will result in the avoidance of a large number of other cancer cases that cannot be quantified, as well as many cases of asbestos-related diseases. Estimates of benefits resulting from the action taken in this rule are limited to mesothelioma and lung and gastrointestinal cancer cases avoided, and do not include cases of asbestosis and other diseases avoided and avoided costs from treating asbestos diseases, lost productivity, or other factors.

EPA has estimated that the cost of this rule, for the 13-year period of the analyses performed, will be approximately $456.89 million, or $806.51 million if a 1 percent annual decline in the price of substitutes is not assumed. This cost will be spread over time and a large population so that the cost to any person is likely to be negligible. In addition, the rule's exemption provision is a qualitative factor that supports the actions taken in this rule. EPA has concluded that the quantifiable and unquantifiable benefits of the rule's staged ban of the identified asbestos-containing products will outweigh the resultant economic consequences to consumers, producers, and users of the products.

9. EPA has determined that, within the findings required by section 6 of TSCA, only the staged-ban approach employed in this final rule will adequately control the asbestos exposure risk posed by the product categories affected by this rule. Other options either fail to address significant portions of the life cycle risk posed by products subject to the rule or are unreasonably burdensome. EPA has, therefore, concluded that the actions taken in this rule represent the least burdensome means of reducing the risk posed by exposure to asbestos during the life cycles of the products that are subject to the bans.

10. Based on the reasons summarized in this preamble, this rule bans most asbestos-containing products in the U.S. because they pose an unreasonable risk to human health. These banned products account for approximately 94 percent of U.S. asbestos consumption, based on 1985 consumption figures. The actions taken will result in a substantial reduction in the unreasonable risk caused by asbestos exposure in the U.S.

The asbestos industry challenged EPA's asbestos ban in the following case.

Corrosion Proof Fittings v. EPA
947 F.2d 1201 (5th Cir. 1991)

JERRY E. SMITH, Circuit Judge:

The Environmental Protection Agency (EPA) issued a final rule under section 6 of the Toxic Substances Control Act (TSCA) to prohibit the future manufacture, importation, processing, and distribution of asbestos in almost all products. Petitioners claim that the EPA's rule-making procedure was flawed and that the rule was not promulgated on the basis of substantial evidence. . . .

[The court recited the facts and procedural history of the rulemaking and disposed of several procedural issues, including a challenge to the standing of several of the petitioners. It then proceeded to analyze the statutory requirements that the administrator have a "reasonable basis" to conclude that asbestos presents an "unreasonable risk" and that he or she choose the "least burdensome" regulations "to protect adequately against such risk." TSCA §6(a).]

1.   LEAST BURDENSOME AND REASONABLE

TSCA requires that the EPA use the least burdensome regulation to achieve its goals of minimum reasonable risk. This statutory requirement can create problems in evaluating just what is a "reasonable risk." Congress' rejection of a no-risk policy, however, also means that in certain cases, the least burdensome yet still adequate solution may entail somewhat more risk than would other, known regulations that are far more burdensome on the industry and the economy. The very language of TSCA requires that the EPA, once it has determined what an acceptable level of non-zero risk is, choose the least burdensome method of reaching that level.

In this case, the EPA banned, for all practical purposes, all present and future uses of asbestos—a position the petitioners characterize as the "death penalty alternative," as this is the *most* burdensome of all possible alternatives listed as open to the EPA under TSCA. TSCA not only provides the EPA with a list of alternative actions, but also provides those alternatives in order of how burdensome they are. [TSCA §6(a)(1)-(7); 15 U.S.C. §2605a(1)-(7).] Total bans head the list as the most burdensome regulatory option.

By choosing the harshest remedy given to it under TSCA, the EPA assigned to itself the toughest burden in satisfying TSCA's requirement that its alternative be the least burdensome of all those offered to it. . . . [T]he EPA's regulation cannot stand if there is any other regulation that would achieve an acceptable level of risk as mandated by TSCA. . . .

The EPA considered, and rejected, such options as labeling asbestos products, thereby warning users and workers involved in the manufacture of asbestos-containing products of the chemical's dangers, and stricter workplace rules. EPA also rejected controlled use of asbestos in the workplace and deferral to other government agencies charged with worker and consumer exposure to industrial and product hazards, such as OSHA, the CPSC, and the Mine Safety and Health Administration (MSHA). The EPA determined that deferral to these other agencies was inappropriate because no one other authority could address all the risks posed "throughout the life cycle" by asbestos, and any action by one or more of the other agencies still would leave an unacceptable residual risk.

Much of the EPA's analysis is correct, and the EPA's basic decision to use TSCA as a comprehensive statute designed to fight a multi-industry problem was a proper one that we uphold today on review. What concerns us, however, is the manner in which the EPA conducted some of its analysis. TSCA requires the EPA to consider, along with the effect of toxic substances on human health and the environment, "the benefits of such substance[s] or mixture[s] for various uses and the availability of substitutes for such uses," as well as "the reasonably ascertainable economic consequences of the rule, after consideration for the effect on the national economy, small business, technological innovation, the environment, and public health." Id. §2605(c)(1)(C-D).

The EPA presented two comparisons in the record: a world with no further regulation under TSCA, and a world in which no manufacture of asbestos takes place. The EPA rejected calculating how many lives a less burdensome regulation would save, and at what cost. Furthermore the EPA, when calculating the benefits of its ban, explicitly refused to compare it to an improved workplace in which currently available control technology is utilized. See 54 Fed. Reg. at 29,474. This decision artificially inflated the purported benefits of the rule by using a baseline comparison substantially lower than what currently available technology could yield. . . .

This comparison of two static worlds is insufficient to satisfy the dictates of TSCA. While the EPA may have shown that a world with a complete ban of asbestos might be preferable to one in which there is only the current amount of regulation, the EPA has failed to show that there is not some intermediate state of regulation that would be superior to both the currently-regulated and the completely-banned world. Without showing that asbestos regulation would be ineffective, the EPA cannot discharge its TSCA burden of showing that its regulation is the least burdensome available to it.

Upon an initial showing of product danger, the proper course for the EPA to follow is to consider each regulatory option, beginning with the least burdensome, and the costs and benefits of regulation under each option. The EPA cannot simply skip several rungs, as it did in this case, for in doing so, it may skip a less-burdensome alternative mandated by TSCA. Here, although the EPA mentions the problems posed by intermediate levels of regulation, it takes no steps to calculate the costs and benefits of these intermediate levels. See 54 Fed. Reg. at 29,462, 29,474. Without doing this it is impossible, both for the EPA and for this court on review, to know that none of these alternatives was less burdensome than the ban in fact chosen by the agency. . . .

2. THE EPA'S CALCULATIONS

Furthermore, we are concerned about some of the methodology employed by the EPA in making various of the calculations that it did perform. In order to aid the EPA's reconsideration of this and other cases, we present our concerns here.

First, we note that there was some dispute in the record regarding the appropriateness of discounting the perceived benefits of the EPA's rule. . . .

Although various commentators dispute whether it ever is appropriate to discount benefits when they are measured in human lives, we note that it would skew the results to discount only costs without according similar treatment to the benefits side of the equation. Adopting the position of the commentators who advocate not discounting benefits would force the EPA similarly not to calculate costs in present discounted real terms, making comparisons difficult. Furthermore, in evaluating situations in which different options incur costs at varying time intervals, the EPA would not be able to take into account that soon-to-be-incurred costs are more harmful than postponable costs. Because the EPA must discount costs to perform its evaluations properly, the EPA also should discount benefits to preserve an apples-to-apples comparison, even if this entails discounting benefits of a non-monetary nature. See What Price Posterity?, The Economist, March 23, 1991, at 73 (explaining use of discount rates for non-monetary goods). . . .

Of more concern to us is the failure of the EPA to compute the costs and benefits of its proposed rule past the year 2000, and its double-counting of the costs of asbestos use. In performing its calculus, the EPA only included the number of lives saved over the next thirteen years, and counted any additional lives saved as simply "unquantified benefits." 54 Fed. Reg. at 29,486. The EPA and intervenors now seek to use these unquantified lives saved to justify calculations as to which the benefits seem far outweighed by the astronomical costs. For example, the EPA plans to save about three lives with its ban of asbestos pipe, at a cost of $128-227 million (i.e., approximately $43-76 million per life saved). Although the EPA admits that the price tag is high, it claims that the lives saved past the year 2000 justify the price. See generally id. at 29,473 (explaining use of unquantified benefits).

Such calculations not only lessen the value of the EPA's cost analysis, but also make any meaningful judicial review impossible. While TSCA contemplates a useful place for unquantified benefits beyond the EPA's calculation, unquantified benefits never were intended as a trump card allowing the EPA to justify any cost calculus, no matter how high.

The concept of unquantified benefits, rather, is intended to allow the EPA to provide a rightful place for any remaining benefits that are impossible to quantify after the EPA's best attempt, but which still are of some concern. But the allowance for unquantified costs is not intended to allow the EPA to perform its calculations over an arbitrarily short period so as to preserve a large unquantified portion.

Unquantified benefits can, at times, permissibly tip the balance in close cases. They cannot, however, be used to effect a wholesale shift on the balance beam. Such a use makes a mockery of the requirements of TSCA that the EPA weigh the costs of its actions before it chooses the least burdensome alternatives.[20]

We do not today determine what an appropriate period for the EPA's calculations would be, as this is a matter better left for agency discretion. See *Motor Vehicle Mfrs. Ass'n,* 463 U.S. at 53. We do note, however, that the choice of a thirteen-year period is so short as to make the unquantified period so unreasonably large that any EPA reliance upon it must be displaced. . . .

3. REASONABLE BASIS

In addition to showing that its regulation is the least burdensome one necessary to protect the environment adequately, the EPA also must show that it has a reasonable basis for the regulation, 15 U.S.C. §2605(a). . . .

Most problematical to us is the EPA's ban of products for which no substitutes presently are available. In these cases, the EPA bears a tough burden indeed to show that under TSCA a ban is the least burdensome alternative, as

---

20. . . . By not using such concerns in its quantitative analysis, even where doing so was not difficult, and reserving them as additional factors to buttress the ban, the EPA improperly transformed permissible considerations into determinative factors.

TSCA explicitly instructs the EPA to consider "the benefits of such substance or mixture for various uses and the availability of substitutes for such uses." [15 U.S.C. §2605(c)(1)(C). These words are particularly appropriate where the EPA actually has decided to ban a product, rather than simply restrict its use, for it is in these cases that the lack of an adequate substitute is most troubling under TSCA.

As the EPA itself states, "[w]hen no information is available for a product indicating that cost-effective substitutes exist, the estimated cost of a product ban is very high." 54 Fed. Reg. at 29,468. Because of this, the EPA did not ban certain uses of asbestos, such as its use in rocket engines and battery separators. The EPA, however, in several other instances, ignores its own arguments and attempts to justify its ban by stating that the ban itself will cause the development of low-cost, adequate substitute products.

As a general matter, we agree with the EPA that a product ban can lead to great innovation, and it is true that an agency under TSCA, as under other regulatory statutes, "is empowered to issue safety standards which require improvements in existing technology or which require the development of new technology." Chrysler Corp. v. Department of Transp., 472 F.2d 659, 673 (6th Cir. 1972). As even the EPA acknowledges, however, when no adequate substitutes currently exist, the EPA cannot fail to consider this lack when formulating its own guidelines. Under TSCA, therefore, the EPA must present a stronger case to justify the ban, as opposed to regulation, of products with no substitutes.

We note that the EPA does provide a waiver provision for industries where the hoped-for substitutes fail to materialize in time. See 54 Fed. Reg. at 29,464. Under this provision, if no adequate substitutes develop, the EPA temporarily may extend the planned phase-out.

The EPA uses this provision to argue that it can ban any product, regardless of whether it has an adequate substitute, because inventive companies soon will develop good substitutes. The EPA contends that if they do not, the waiver provision will allow the continued use of asbestos in these areas, just as if the ban had not occurred at all.

The EPA errs, however, in asserting that the waiver provision will allow a continuation of the status quo in those cases in which no substitutes materialize. By its own terms, the exemption shifts the burden onto the waiver proponent to convince the EPA that the waiver is justified. See id. As even the EPA acknowledges, the waiver only "may be granted by [the] EPA in very limited circumstances." Id. at 29,460.

The EPA thus cannot use the waiver provision to lessen its burden when justifying banning products without existing substitutes. . . .

We also are concerned with the EPA's evaluation of substitutes even in those instances in which the record shows that they are available. The EPA explicitly rejects considering the harm that may flow from the increased use of products designed to substitute for asbestos, even where the probable substitutes themselves are known carcinogens. Id. at 29,481-83. The EPA justifies this by stating that it has "more concern about the continued use and exposure to asbestos than it has for the future replacement of asbestos in the products subject to this rule with other fibrous substitutes." Id. at 29,481. The agency thus concludes that any "[r]egulatory decisions about asbestos[,] which poses well-recognized, serious risks[,] should not be delayed until the risks of all replacement materials are fully quantified." Id. at 29,483.

This presents two problems. First, TSCA instructs the EPA to consider the relative merits of its ban, as compared to the economic effects of its actions. The EPA cannot make this calculation if it fails to consider the effects that alternate substitutes will pose after a ban.

Second, the EPA cannot say with any assurance that its regulation will increase workplace safety when it refuses to evaluate the harm that will result from the increased use of substitute products. While the EPA may be correct in its conclusion that the alternate materials pose less risk than asbestos, we cannot say with any more assurance than that flowing from an educated guess that this conclusion is true.

Considering that many of the substitutes that the EPA itself concedes will be used in the place of asbestos have known carcinogenic effects, the EPA not only cannot assure this court that it has taken the least burdensome alternative, but cannot even prove that its regulations will increase workplace safety. Eager to douse the dangers of asbestos, the agency inadvertently actually may increase the risk of injury Americans face. The EPA's explicit failure to consider the toxicity of likely substitutes thus deprives its order of a reasonable basis.

Our opinion should not be construed to state that the EPA has an affirmative duty to seek out and test every workplace substitute for any product it seeks to regulate. TSCA does not place such a burden upon the agency. We do not think it unreasonable, however, once interested parties introduce credible studies and evidence showing the toxicity of workplace substitutes, or the decreased effectiveness of safety alternatives such as non-asbestos brakes, that the EPA then consider whether its regulations are even increasing workplace safety, and whether the increased risk occasioned by dangerous substitutes makes the proposed regulation no longer reasonable. In the words of the EPA's own release that initiated the asbestos rulemaking, we direct that the agency consider the adverse health effects of asbestos substitutes "for comparison with the known hazards of asbestos," so that it can conduct, as it promised in 1979, a "balanced consideration of the environmental, economic, and social impact of any action taken by the agency." 44 Fed. Reg. at 60,065 (1979).

In short, a death is a death, whether occasioned by asbestos or by a toxic substitute product, and the EPA's decision not to evaluate the toxicity of known carcinogenic substitutes is not a reasonable action under TSCA. Once an interested party brings forth credible evidence suggesting the toxicity of the probable or only alternatives to a substance, the EPA must consider the comparative toxic costs of each. Its failure to do so in this case thus deprived its regulation of a reasonable basis, at least in regard to those products as to which petitioners introduced credible evidence of the dangers of the likely substitutes.[22]

---

22. We note that at least part of the EPA's arguments rest on the assumption that regulation will not work because the federal government will not adequately enforce any workplace standards that the EPA might promulgate. This is an improper assumption. The EPA should assume reasonable efforts by the government to implement its own regulations. A governmental agency cannot point to how poorly the government will implement regulations as a reason to reject regulation. Rather, the solution to poor enforcement of regulations is better enforcement, not more burdensome alternative solutions under TSCA.

4. Unreasonable Risk of Injury

The final requirement the EPA must satisfy before engaging in any TSCA rulemaking is that it only take steps designed to prevent "unreasonable" risks. . . .

That the EPA must balance the costs of its regulations against their benefits further is reinforced by the requirement that it seek the least burdensome regulation. While Congress did not dictate that the EPA engage in an exhaustive, full-scale cost-benefit analysis, it did require the EPA to consider both sides of the regulatory equation, and it rejected the notion that the EPA should pursue the reduction of workplace risk at any cost. See *American Textile Mfrs. Inst.*, 452 U.S. at 510 n.30 ("unreasonable risk" statutes require "a generalized balancing of costs and benefits"). Thus, "Congress also plainly intended the EPA to consider the economic impact of any actions taken by it under . . . TSCA." *Chemical Mfrs. Ass'n*, 899 F.2d at 348.

Even taking all of the EPA's figures as true, and evaluating them in the light most favorable to the agency's decision . . . the agency's analysis results in figures as high as $74 million per life saved. For example, the EPA states that its ban of asbestos pipe will save three lives over the next thirteen years, at a cost of $128-277 million ($43-76 million per life saved), depending upon the price of substitutes; that its ban of asbestos shingles will cost $23-34 million to save 0.32 statistical lives ($72-106 million per life saved); that its ban of asbestos coatings will cost $46-181 million to save 3.33 lives ($14-54 million per life saved); and that its ban of asbestos paper products will save 0.60 lives at a cost of $4-5 million ($7-8 million per life saved). See 54 Fed. Reg. at 29,484-85. . . .

While we do not sit as a regulatory agency that must make the difficult decision as to what an appropriate expenditure is to prevent someone from incurring the risk of an asbestos-related death, we do note that the EPA, in its zeal to ban any and all asbestos products, basically ignored the cost side of the TSCA equation. The EPA would have this court believe that Congress, when it enacted its requirement that the EPA consider the economic impacts of its regulations, thought that spending $200-300 million to save approximately seven lives (approximately $30-40 million per life) over thirteen years is reasonable.

As we stated in the OSHA context, until an agency "can provide substantial evidence that the benefits to be achieved by [a regulation] bear a reasonable relationship to the costs imposed by the reduction, it cannot show that the standard is reasonably necessary to provide safe or healthful workplaces." Although the OSHA statute differs in major respects from TSCA, the statute does require substantial evidence to support the EPA's contentions that its regulations both have a reasonable basis and are the least burdensome means to a reasonably safe workplace.

The EPA's willingness to argue that spending $23.7 million to save less than one-third of a life reveals that its economic review of its regulations, as required by TSCA, was meaningless. As the petitioners' brief and our review of EPA case-law reveals, such high costs are rarely, if ever, used to support a safety regulation.

[The court then reviewed each of four subcategories of product bans included in the rulemaking—friction products (where EPA had determined that three-fourths of the anticipated asbestos-related cancer benefits would be achieved); asbestos-cement pipe products; gaskets, roofing, shingles, and paper products; and products produced outside the United States—and found each of them legally unjustified, in each case substantially on the basis of the general deficiencies reviewed in the first part of the opinion. However, the court upheld EPA's decision to ban products that once were, but no longer are, being produced in the United States, noting that "sections 5 and 6 of TSCA allow the EPA to ban a product that presents or will present a *significant* risk" (emphasis the court's).]

We regret that this matter must continue to take up the valuable time of the agency, parties and, undoubtedly, future courts. The requirements of TSCA, however, are plain, and the EPA cannot deviate from them to reach its desired result. We therefore GRANT the petition for review, VACATE the EPA's proposed regulation, and REMAND to the EPA for further proceedings in light of this opinion.

NOTES AND QUESTIONS

1. TSCA and Multimedia Regulation. Why did the court strike down the asbestos ban? What impact will the court's decision have on EPA's ability to use TSCA as a comprehensive approach for reducing multimedia exposures to highly toxic substances? Note that the court states that "EPA's basic decision to use TSCA as a comprehensive statute designed to fight a multi-industry problem was a proper one that we uphold today on review." What then was wrong with EPA's decision to ban asbestos?

2. Sufficiency of Evidence. The court held that EPA had presented insufficient evidence to justify its asbestos ban. In what respects was EPA's evidence lacking? Note that EPA's decision to ban asbestos had not been undertaken lightly. It was the product of ten years of Agency activity that included an advance notice of proposed rulemaking in 1979 and a data collection rule promulgated under section 8(a) of TSCA in 1982. EPA had held 22 days of public hearings, taken thousands of pages of testimony, and received 13,000 pages of comments from more than 250 interested parties. The Agency and its contractors had prepared ten major regulatory analysis documents in support of the rule. What additional information would EPA need and what additional analysis would it have to undertake to justify an asbestos ban?

3. The "Least Burdensome" Requirement. Why did EPA believe that a ban was the "least burdensome" means "to protect adequately against" the risks posed throughout the life cycle of asbestos use? How does the court interpret section 6(a)(1)'s "least burdensome" requirement? What findings must EPA make before banning a product under the court's interpretation?

4. Reasonableness of Risk. Did the court believe that the risks posed by asbestos were not unreasonable in light of the cost of the asbestos ban? EPA had estimated that the quantifiable benefits from the rule included the prevention of at least 202 cases of cancer at a total cost of $459 million over 13 years. 54 Fed. Reg. 29,484-29,485 (1989). Did the court think that this was too much for society to "spend" to prevent asbestos risks, did it simply disagree with EPA's calculations of costs and benefits, or both? Do you think that a risk that costs more than $2 million per life saved to eliminate is reasonable?

5. How Much Is a Life Worth? While the Fifth Circuit did not specify what dollar value it would place on preventing deaths from asbestos exposure, the court noted in a footnote that

the EPA regularly rejects, as unjustified, regulations that would save more lives at less cost. For example, over the next 13 years, we can expect more than a dozen deaths from ingested *toothpicks*—a death toll more than twice what the EPA predicts will flow from the quarter-billion-dollar bans of asbestos pipe, shingles, and roof coatings. See L. Budnick, Toothpick-Related Injuries in the United States, 1979 Through 1982, 252 J. Am. Med. Ass'n, Aug. 10, 1984, at 796 (study showing that toothpick-related deaths average approximately one per year). [947 F.2d at 1223 n.23 (emphasis in original).]

What is the relevance of the toothpick data?

6. **Comparing Costs and Benefits.** EPA estimated that the most likely costs of its decision were $459 million and its quantified benefits were estimated at 202 deaths avoided (148 if benefits are discounted). That is between $2.4 and $3.1 million per death avoided. Yet the court criticizes parts of EPA's rule for costing as much as $74 million per death avoided. Why did the court disaggregate EPA's data by product?

7. **Discounting Lives.** The debate over whether benefits of health and safety regulation should be discounted when those benefits include saving lives is considerably more intense, with many more twists and turns, than the court's treatment suggests. Among other arguments, those opposed to discounting argue that the obligation to save life is a moral obligation owed equally to everyone, including future generations, so that a life saved 20, 40, or 100 years from now should be as highly valued as a life saved tomorrow. Some also argue that the avoidance of an irreversible course of events that culminates in death should be considered a present benefit.

Those favoring discounting remind us that dollars expended today to save a life in the future are actually more expensive than dollars expended to save a life tomorrow, because by spending now for future benefits we are deprived of the stream of benefits that would otherwise flow from those dollars between now and the future time when they will save a life. In that period of time, we might find ways to prevent the future loss of life more cheaply. Richard Revesz has urged a distinction between the problems of discounting raised by programs that mitigate latent harms to existing persons and those raised by programs designed to benefit future generations. "The reason for discounting in the case of latent harms," he writes, "is not that a regulator . . . determines that life in the future is less valuable than life in the present. Instead, discounting simply reflects the fact that the individual who is valuing her own life derives less utility from living a year in the future than in the present. Discounting is therefore necessary to provide an accurate value of the utility that the individual loses in the present as a result of a premature death that might occur in the future." Revesz, Environmental Regulation, Cost-Benefit Analysis, and the Discounting of Human Lives, 99 Colum. L. Rev. 941, 984 (1999). Revesz endorses discounting as appropriate in such cases, but only if significant adjustments to current regulatory practices are made, which would tend to raise the value of future benefits compared to methodologies such as those endorsed in *Corrosion Proof Fittings*. Id.

As for problems of intergenerational equity raised by issues such as global warming, Revesz argues that whereas "intragenerational discounting affects the timing with which a particular individual decides to expend a fixed amount of resources [and thus reflects that individual's preferences] . . . intergenerational discounting affects the quantity of resources available to each individual . . . [so that] in an intergenerational context, one must initially decide how to allocate resources to individuals in different generations—a societal decision with ethical underpinnings." Id. at 999.

In addition to employing a 3 percent discount rate in its asbestos decision, EPA discounted benefits from the date of exposure rather than the date of illness. What impact did this decision have on the apparent reasonableness of the asbestos ban? Was EPA justified in making that decision? The court did not think so; "[EPA] chose an unreasonable time upon which to base its discount calculation. . . . The EPA's approach implicitly assumes that the day on which the risk of injury occurs is the same day the injury actually occurs." Do you agree? On remand, what impact will this aspect of the court's decision have on the reasonableness of the asbestos ban? In its comments on EPA's Regulatory Impact Analysis, OMB had observed that "a life saved 40 years from now [the latency period for asbestos-related cancers is 30-40 years] is worth roughly only one forty-fifth as much as a life saved this year." An outraged congressional oversight committee calculated that such discounting would mean that it would be worth only $22,094.93 to OMB to save a life in these circumstances. EPA's Asbestos Regulations, Report of the Subcomm. on Oversight and Investigations of the House Comm. on Energy and Commerce, 99th Cong., 1st Sess. 79 (Oct. 1985). Lisa Heinzerling argues that mitigation of latent harms has substantial present benefits that are ignored by a pure discounting approach. In her view, "life-saving environmental regulation produces benefits from the very moment it takes effect." Heinzerling, Environmental Law and the Present Future, 87 Geo. L.J. 2025, 2026 (1999). These benefits include reducing the dread people have of involuntary, long-term risk exposure, bolstering trust in institutions undermined by potentially misleading statements their representatives may make about the significance of an unmitigated risk, the reduction in risk itself, which can be treated as an immediate benefit, as well as avoiding the adverse physiological effects that occur contemporaneously with exposure to some latent harms such as chemical agents. She argues that these considerations "cast[] a shadow over [the] analytic technique[] . . . [of] discounting." Id. at 2078.

8. The Discount Rate. Whatever the merits of the debate over discounting various types of life-saving environmental measures, the Office of Management and Budget requires discounting. When the value of future lives saved is being discounted, the rate at which the value is discounted is vitally important. For an illustration of the effect of discounting, the Center for Progressive Reform has posted on the Web a "future lives calculator." Go to its Perspective on cost-benefit analysis and click on the link to "Honey I shrunk the future" at the bottom of the second paragraph. The calculator shows the impact of various discount rates. *http://www.progressivereform.org/perspectives/costbenefit.cfm.* In a footnote the court found that EPA's use of a 3 percent discount rate was reasonable. 947 F.2d at 1218 n.19. For years, the OMB and EPA had disagreed over various aspects of the asbestos ban rule. For one thing, OMB had urged that a 10 percent discount rate be applied to asbestos-related cancers. The dispute is documented in EPA's Asbestos Regulations, Report of the Subcomm. on Oversight and Investigations of the House Comm. on Energy and Commerce, 99th Cong., 1st Sess. 78-82 (Oct. 1985).

In 1992, OMB revised its discount rate for cost-benefit analyses downward to 7 percent. 57 Fed. Reg. 53,519, 53,522 (1992). This rate is still higher than the current views of the majority of economists, who have concluded that the most appropriate discount rate for government projects is the "real return on long-term government debt—the interest rate on long-term government bonds minus the rate of inflation," Revesz, Environmental Regulation, Cost-Benefit Analysis, and the Discounting of Human Lives, 99 Colum. L. Rev. 941, 978

(1999). In recent years this rate has been between 2 and 3 percent, id. at 979, roughly the same rate that EPA used in the asbestos rule struck down in *Corrosion Proof Fittings.*

9. Nonquantified Benefits. EPA's benefit estimates did not attempt to quantify certain benefits including the prevention of asbestosis and certain other diseases and the avoided costs of treating asbestos diseases and lost productivity. EPA also stated that if it had followed the normal practice of using "upper bound" estimates, its risk assessment could have projected 10 times more lung cancer deaths and 20 times more mesothelioma deaths due to asbestos exposure. Recall the concern that cost-benefit analysis exhibits a tendency to "downgrade" unquantified benefits. How does the court of appeals treat the unquantified benefits of EPA's ban? Is its treatment appropriate? Do you believe that unquantified benefits should only be used as a "tie-breaker" in cost-benefit analyses?

10. The Risks of Substitutes. The data available to EPA concerning the health risks posed by asbestos were far better than the data available for virtually any other toxic substance. Unlike many other substances, scientific understanding of the dangers of asbestos is based on the results of numerous epidemiological studies that have documented scores of thousands of deaths from asbestos exposure. The court faulted EPA for not giving more serious consideration to the potential risks posed by other substances that might be substituted for asbestos. For example, vinyl chloride is used to make PVC pipe, a likely substitute for asbestos-cement pipe. Under what circumstances did the court think EPA must assess the risk of substitutes? How extensively must EPA analyze such products?

Inquiry into the riskiness of substitutes as a desirable prerequisite to regulation involves a special case of risk-benefit analysis that has come to be called "risk-tradeoff" analysis. It arises in numerous regulatory contexts, and is exacerbated in the eyes of some by the perceived tendency of environmental statutes to impose higher standards of safety on new products than on old, already marketed products. What do you think the explanation for that practice might be? The result of the practice can be the inability of a new product or use to be authorized because it fails an agency's risk requirements for new products, whereas allowing its use would actually reduce overall risks because the new product would replace an already established product that was riskier.

There are circumstances in which risk-tradeoff analysis seems a sensible regulatory approach and yet in others it raises significant questions. In a concurring opinion in International Union, UAW v. OSHA, 938 F.2d 1310 (D.C. Cir. 1991), Judge Williams carried the logic of risk-tradeoff analysis to one of its logical extremes. Citing studies finding that higher incomes correlate with improved health (why might that be so?), Judge Williams referred in particular to one economist's study suggesting that each $7.5 million of costs generated by a new regulation depresses workers' incomes sufficiently to induce one fatality. Judge Williams suggested that OSHA ought to conduct risk-risk analysis whenever its regulatory initiatives generated significant compliance costs. 938 F.2d at 1326-1327. OMB subsequently followed up on Judge Williams's suggestion by blocking an OSHA regulation on the ground that its $163 million in compliance costs would cause 22 additional deaths, more than the 8 to 13 lives OSHA estimated would be saved. Swoboda, OMB's Logic: Less Protection Saves Lives, Wash. Post, Mar. 17, 1992, at A15. After the controversy received publicity, OMB withdrew its objection, although it continued to insist that "richer is safer" ought to be considered in rulemaking. For an opinion rejecting an effort to require OSHA to conduct risk-tradeoff analysis, see American Dental Association v. Martin, 984 F.2d 823 (7th Cir. 1993). For an argument that risk-tradeoff analysis has been systematically biased by focusing only on regulation's ancillary risks and not its ancillary benefits see Rascoff & Revesz, The Biases of Risk Trade-off Analysis: Toward Parity in Environmental and Health-and-Safety Regulation, 69 U. Chi. L. Rev. 1763 (2002).

11. Technology-Forcing Regulation. The court criticized EPA's assumption that the availability of a waiver would reduce the costs of replacing products for which no adequate substitutes for asbestos currently were available. Is the court suggesting that EPA should not be able to use TSCA to force the development of safer technology? Would a better approach for forcing technology be to impose a tax on asbestos products that increases over time?

12. Marginal Analysis. The court appears to require that EPA calculate the costs and benefits of the product ban compared to the costs and benefits of the next less burdensome regulatory alternative. In this way, the Agency can assess the incremental, or marginal, costs and benefits of the final regulatory step. Suppose the next less burdensome alternative were found to save 128 (discounted) lives at a cost of $125 million. Then the incremental benefits and costs of the product ban would be 20 lives and $334 million. If the Agency had made such a determination as this, would TSCA permit it to go ahead with the product ban?

13. Risk Disaggregation. EPA had found that 102 (or 144, if benefits are not discounted) of the deaths avoided came from its ban of asbestos in friction products—primarily brake drums. The cost of this ban was estimated to be between $31 million and $85 million. The court indicated that it might have been inclined to uphold this part of the asbestos to ban if that had been the only part of the rule challenged. As long as the court was remanding, however, it found that it was "impossible to ignore" EPA's failure to study the effect of nonasbestos brakes on automotive safety, "despite credible evidence that non-asbestos brakes could increase significantly the number of highway fatalities." Was EPA's failure to conduct further study of the highway fatality issue justified? To what extent does the court's decision hinge on disaggregation of the overall risks posed by asbestos by following analysis on risk and cost estimates for each type of product containing it?

Compare the approach in *Corrosion Proof Fittings* to that in American Dental Association v. Martin, 984 F.2d 823 (7th Cir. 1993). There, the Seventh Circuit refused to require OSHA to disaggregate risks in more detail when making the "significant risk" findings required by the *Benzene* decision. The court explained that

> OSHA cannot impose onerous requirements on an industry that does not pose substantial hazards to the safety or health of its workers merely because the industry is a part of some larger sector or grouping and the agency has decided to regulate it wholesale. That would be an irrational way to proceed. But neither is the agency required to proceed workplace by workplace, which in the case of bloodborne pathogens would require it to promulgate hundreds of thousands of separate rules. It is not our business to pick the happy medium between these extremes. It is OSHA's business. If it provides a rational explanation for its choice, we are bound. [984 F.2d at 827.]

The court found that OSHA's explanation that the risks of infection from blood-borne pathogens do not vary in a readily determinable fashion from industry to industry was sufficiently rational so as not to require an industry-by-industry disaggregation of risk estimates. OSHA had found that infection risks vary with practices, rather than industries, and it had issued regulations designed to control these practices.

14. "Cleanup" Ban on Future Products. The one aspect of the asbestos ban that the court upheld was a ban on asbestos products not currently being produced. How could EPA determine that the benefits of such a ban would outweigh its costs? Such products pose no current risks. The court stated that although "EPA cannot possibly evaluate the costs and benefits of banning unknown, uninvented products, we hold that the nebulousness of these future products, combined with TSCA's language authorizing the EPA to ban products that 'will' create a public risk, allows the EPA to ban future uses of asbestos even in products not yet on the market."

15. International Developments. While the *Corrosion Proof Fittings* decision derailed EPA's efforts to ban asbestos in the United States, a growing number of countries throughout the world are enacting asbestos bans. In September 2000, the World Trade Organization (WTO) rejected a challenge by Canada to France's decision to ban imports of chrysotile asbestos. As of January 1, 2005, 37 countries had adopted national asbestos bans, including the 22 members of the European Union and Australia, Argentina, Chile, and Saudi Arabia. Japan has severely restricted asbestos use, reducing Japanese consumption by more than 90 percent. In 2004 South Africa announced a five-year phaseout of asbestos use and Brazilian cities and states accounting for 70 percent of Brazil's market also have banned asbestos use. In the United States, Senator Patty Murray (D-WA) has since 2003 sponsored the Ban Asbestos in America Act, which would accomplish through legislation what EPA attempted to do under its TSCA authority. The measure has yet to come to a vote in either chamber of the Congress.

4. (Technology-Based) Feasibility-Limited Regulation

In most of the environmental statutes regulating toxic substances, Congress has not explicitly endorsed cost-benefit or risk-benefit balancing in setting standards to control pollution or to protect public health. Rather, it has instructed agencies to control potentially dangerous substances by using technology-based standards (as in parts of the Clean Water Act and the Clean Air Act), usually up to the point at which further reductions in exposures are no longer "feasible" (as in the OSH Act, see below), or sometimes simply to regulate so as to "protect the public health," often with a "margin of safety" (as in the Clean Air Act, which requires provision of an "adequate margin of safety" from conventional air pollutants, CAA §109, and an "ample margin of safety" from hazardous air pollutants, CAA §112(f)).

This section discusses several feasibility-limited approaches to risk management. These statutes direct regulators to protect against certain health risks to the extent feasible. They are a species of technology-based approaches because the state of existing technology ultimately determines what is technologically feasible.

Not all technology-based approaches to regulation impose pollution controls that are as stringent as those required by a strict feasibility-limited standard. For example, the "best practicable technology" controls established by the Clean

Water Act are less stringent than standards that require control of health risks to the limits of feasibility. Because of the nature of the adverse health effects associated with toxics, when Congress employs a technology-based approach to risk management, it generally mandates that technology be used up to the point at which it becomes infeasible to reduce emissions any further. At least, that is the theory. This feasibility-limited type of technology-based approach bases the level of control on the capabilities of technology rather than on the degree of risk or the results of risk-benefit balancing. The degree of risk is not entirely irrelevant to feasibility-limited statutes, for they require that some threshold level of risk, sufficient to satisfy the statute's regulatory trigger, be found, as illustrated by the interpretation of OSHA in *Benzene*, requiring OSHA to make a "significant risk" determination prior to issuing a regulation. Once that trigger has been satisfied, feasibility-limited approaches to regulation then instruct the agency to eliminate as much of the health risk as can feasibly be done.

Feasibility has two components: the technological and the economic. Something may be strictly possible given the current state of technology, e.g., a trip to the moon or to Mars, but so expensive that it could force an entire industry to shut down if mandated by regulators. Most feasibility-limited regulation is so limited precisely to avoid causing such massive dislocations. Thus, regulatory authorities implementing feasibility-limited standards have had to give consideration to both technological and economic factors, as we will see below.

A.   First Example: The OSH Act

You have already encountered an important decision dealing with a feasibility-limited, health-based regime: the OSH Act. In the *Benzene* decision, Justice Rehnquist argued that the term "feasible" in the statute was unconstitutionally vague. Subsequent decisions, however, have given the standard greater definition. In the only other Supreme Court decision addressing the authority of OSHA to regulate toxics in the workplace, the Court held that feasible meant "capable of being done, executed, or effected," both technologically and economically. American Textile Manufacturers Institute, Inc. v. Donovan, 452 U.S. 490, 508-509 (1981). To show that a standard is technologically feasible, OSHA must demonstrate by substantial evidence "that modern technology has at least conceived some industrial strategies which are likely to be capable of meeting the PEL, and which the industries are generally capable of adopting." AFL-CIO v. OSHA, 965 F.2d 962, 980 (11 Cir. 1992). Economic feasibility requires a showing, again by substantial evidence, of a "reasonable likelihood that the[] costs [of implementation] will not threaten the existence or competitive structure of an industry, even if it does portend disaster for some marginal firms." Id. at 982.

NOTES AND QUESTIONS

1. In light of the court's interpretation of feasibility in AFL-CIO v. OSHA, is the Occupational Safety and Health Act a "technology-forcing" statute? What meaning would you give to the concept of technology-forcing under the Act?

2. Will statutes that regulate to the limits of feasibility always be more protective of the safety of the exposed population than statutes that regulate

on the basis of a risk-benefit balance? Usually? What factors contribute to making feasibility-limited regulations more stringent than risk-benefit based regulations? If you are a union member, do you prefer the OSH Act's approach to the sort of risk-benefit regulatory regime established by TSCA?

3. Some U.S. industries are in economic decline as a result of market forces or a failure to invest in research and development and capital improvements. If investments in modern engineering controls to protect workers from exposure to toxic substances are far more economically damaging to declining industries, does feasibility-limited regulation imply that workers in such industries must be exposed to greater risks?

4. Other industries are growing rapidly due to market forces but face stiff foreign competition (e.g., the nickel cadmium industry, which is growing rapidly, but in which Japanese producers are making substantial inroads). They argue that requirements that they invest in expensive engineering controls will cause them substantial economic harm. How would you respond to these concerns in the context of the OSH Act's definition of feasibility?

5. One of the major difficulties with implementing feasibility-based regulation is that it can require complicated engineering assessments that are difficult and expensive to make, particularly when most relevant information is controlled by the regulated industry. OSHA notes that it "spends an average of $500,000 and takes one year of study to determine the lowest feasible level for a *single* substance" and that it "does not have the resources to engage in that kind of analysis for more than a few substances." 54 Fed. Reg. 2,363 (1989).

6. Industry has a clear incentive to engage in strategic behavior to convince OSHA that stringent standards are infeasible. Because industry has better access to cost data, it sometimes has convinced OSHA that certain standards are far more expensive than they actually prove to be. For example:

> OSHA predicted the cotton dust standard would cost $500 million in 1977 dollars whereas industry predicted twice the cost and anticipated substantial technical problems. As a matter of fact, a later detailed study indicated that the standard cost only $250 million in 1983 dollars, improved industry competitiveness and productivity as well, and improved health more than predicted. See 50 FR 51,121, 51,164-67 (Dec. 13, 1985).
>
> OSHA's contractor predicted that the OSHA vinyl chloride standard could not generally be achieved with engineering controls and the attempt would cost $1.5 billion. As a matter of fact, compliance was achieved within three years at a cost of less than 10% of that predicted. See 49 FR 5,001, 5,253 (Jan. 22, 1980). [54 Fed. Reg. 2,366 (1989).]

Should this evidence of strategic behavior by industry lead regulatory agencies in the future to discount industry cost estimates by some factor?

B.   SECOND EXAMPLE: THE SAFE DRINKING WATER ACT

The Safe Drinking Water Act authorizes EPA to limit contaminants in public drinking water supply systems that have at least 15 service connections or that regularly serve at least 25 individuals. The principal provisions of the Act are described below.

As amended in 1996, the SDWA incorporates the most recent refinements in the development of a feasibility limited regulatory regime. The *Chlorine Chemistry Council* opinion, pages 211-213, describes how part of the statute works. The statute sets up a three-step process that EPA must complete. The EPA is instructed to establish health-protective goals for contaminants in drinking water, which are termed maximum contaminant level goals (MCLGs). These are to be set at the level at which "no known or anticipated adverse effects on the health of persons occur and which allows an adequate margin of safety." MCLGs are not enforceable standards, however. EPA next determines the level that is as close "as is feasible" to the MCLGs. 42 U.S.C. §300g-l(b)(4)(B). This "maximum contaminant level" (MCL) becomes the enforceable standard unless EPA analyzes the "quantifiable and nonquantifiable" costs and benefits with respect to any MCL it proposes, 42 U.S.C. §300g-l(b)(3)(C), and determines that the strictest feasible standard "would not justify the costs of complying with the level," in which case EPA can back away from the maximum feasible standard to a lesser standard.

The Act defines "feasible" to mean "feasible with the use of the best technology, treatment techniques and other means which the Administrator finds, after examination for efficacy under field conditions and not solely under laboratory conditions, are available (taking cost into consideration)." 42 U.S.C. §300g-l(b)(5).

The 1996 Amendments contain refinements designed to improve upon EPA's slow record of implementation. As enacted in 1974, the SDWA directed EPA to establish national interim primary drinking water standards within 90 days, and to revise those standards after a National Academy of Sciences study recommended MCLs for various substances. EPA promulgated 16 interim standards, based on the recommendations of a 1962 U.S. Public Health Service study. Although the NAS issued its report, Drinking Water and Health, in 1977, by 1986 EPA had proposed final MCLs for only 8 chemicals, all volatile organic compounds. Amendments in 1986 instructed EPA to regulate 83 chemicals by 1989 and to add 25 chemicals to the list every 3 years after 1989. These same Amendments contained a statutory stipulation that any MCL set for synthetic organic chemicals had to be at least as stringent as the levels achieved by granulated activated carbon filtration. By January 1991, EPA had promulgated MCLs for 67 of the 83 mandated chemicals and pledged to set new standards for 108 contaminants by 1995, 56 Fed. Reg. 3,526, 3,528 (1991), a goal it did not meet. The 1996 Amendments rescind the provision for regulating 25 chemicals every 3 years. In its place, EPA is now directed to publish a list of contaminants not now subject to regulation but that are known to occur in public water systems. Every 5 years thereafter, EPA is required to decide whether or not to regulate at least 5 contaminants on the list. Once EPA decides to regulate, it has 24 months to propose an MCLG and an MCL, and 18 months from then to promulgate the proposal. MCLs must be reviewed every 5 years. The 1996 Amendments also required EPA to review the 68 standards that it had issued prior to 1997. On July 1, 2003, the EPA announced completion of that review. 68 Fed. Reg. 42,907.

PRINCIPAL PROVISIONS OF THE SAFE DRINKING WATER ACT

Section 300g-1 requires EPA to promulgate national drinking water regulations (MCLGs and MCLs) for public water systems. Regulations are to be issued for each contaminant that may have any adverse effect on health and that is known or anticipated to occur in such systems. MCLGs are to be set "at the level at which no known or anticipated adverse effects on the health of persons occur and which allows an adequate margin of safety." MCLs are to be set as close to the MCLGs "as is feasible," unless after weighing the "quantifiable and nonquantifiable costs and benefits," the EPA determines that the benefits of that level would not justify the costs, in which case the MCL is to be set to "maximize[] health risk reduction benefits at a cost that is justified by the benefits."

Section 300g-2 authorizes states to assume primary enforcement responsibility under the Act.

Section 300g-3 requires EPA to notify states of violations of national primary drinking water regulations and to take enforcement action against public water systems if the states fail to do so. Owners or operators of public water systems are required to notify customers of violations.

Sections 300g-4 & 5 authorize states to grant variances and exemptions under certain conditions.

Section 300g-6 prohibits the use of lead in pipes, solder, or flux in public water systems or in plumbing used to provide water for human consumption that is connected to such a system.

Section 300h-1 requires EPA to establish minimum requirements for state underground injection control programs.

Section 300i grants EPA emergency powers to act against contamination of drinking water that may present an imminent and substantial endangerment to public health.

Section 300j-4 directs EPA to promulgate regulations requiring monitoring of drinking water and authorizes EPA to establish recordkeeping requirements.

Section 300j-7 authorizes judicial review of national primary drinking water regulations in the D.C. Circuit and of any other EPA action under the Act in the U.S. Courts of Appeal where the petitioner resides or transacts business.

Section 300j-8 authorizes citizen suits against any person alleged to be in violation of the Act and against the EPA administrator for failure to perform any nondiscretionary duty.

Sections 300j-21 to 26 codify the Lead Contamination Control Act of 1988, which requires recall of drinking water coolers with lead-lined tanks.

Like the OSH Act, the SDWA requires feasibility-limited reductions in risk. In implementing these statutes, costs must be given some consideration in determining the limits of feasibility.

Difficulties that EPA faced in regulating lead in drinking water under SDWA's feasibility standard as originally formulated played a role in the proviso added in 1996 that authorizes EPA to set the MCL at the level that "maximizes health risk reduction benefits at a cost that is justified by the benefits," if the EPA concludes that the "quantifiable and nonquantifiable benefits" of the feasibility-limited level do not justify the "quantifiable and nonquantifiable costs" of that level.

In 1991 EPA promulgated standards for controlling lead in drinking water, 56 Fed. Reg. 26,460 (1991). Because of its potentially severe health effects at even low levels of exposure, EPA established an MCLG of zero for lead. In order to promulgate the MCL for lead, EPA had to determine how close to zero the standard could feasibly be set. Although the use of lead pipes and lead solder in drinking water systems was prohibited in the 1986 Amendments to the SDWA, an enormous number of homes have such plumbing or are served by water distribution systems with such plumbing. While it would be technologically possible to reduce levels of lead in drinking water to "safe" levels, it could cost tens of billions of dollars to remove all lead service pipes.

Although the SDWA then appeared to require EPA to establish MCLs if "it is economically and technologically feasible to ascertain the level" of contaminants in water, §300f(1)(C), 42 U.S.C. §1401(1)(C), EPA decided not to promulgate an MCL for lead. The Agency argued that Congress had not anticipated the problem of drinking water contamination occurring as a byproduct of pipe corrosion and that public water systems should not be responsible for contamination from portions of the distribution system beyond their control. 56 Fed. Reg. 26,460, 26,476 (1991).

Because of the source of the lead, measurements of lead in water at the tap vary widely within a single system. Compounding the issue of regulatory solutions, chemicals that might be added to the water system to reduce corrosion have the deleterious effect of increasing the levels of other chemicals subject to their own MCLs. EPA therefore adopted a "treatment technique" approach that requires water suppliers to employ corrosion control measures if more than 10 percent of water samples exceed 15 ppb lead at the tap. Corrosion control requirements took effect between 1996 and 1999 depending on the size of the water supply system. If corrosion control fails to reduce the percentage of samples exceeding this action level, water suppliers eventually may have to replace lead service lines on a schedule that stretches to the year 2014.

EPA's lead regulations were attacked by environmental groups as well as state and local officials. Environmentalists argued that the absence of an MCL, the 90th percentile action level approach, and the lengthy compliance deadlines made the regulations virtually impossible to enforce while leaving hundreds of thousands of children exposed to high levels of lead in drinking water. Arguing that section 300f(1)(C) required EPA to establish an MCL because it is feasible to measure lead levels in water, environmental groups sued EPA. EPA countered by asserting that the term "feasible" encompasses the concept of "capable of being accomplished in a manner consistent with the Act." In EPA's view, the SDWA permitted EPA to decide that it could eschew a fixed MCL where the monitoring for and achievement of that MCL would not be conducive to overall water quality, because the levels of other controlled contaminants would be raised in the process. On review before the D.C. Circuit, this interpretation was sustained. American Water Works Ass'n v. EPA, 40 F.3d 1266 (D.C. Cir. 1994).

Notwithstanding EPA's efforts to temper the level of lead reduction measures required, compliance costs remained a source of resistance. For instance, California officials maintained that they cannot afford to implement the regulations, despite state legislation imposing fees on water suppliers to defray the costs of regulation. California Says 'No' to New Lead Rules, Calls Cost Too High for State to Implement, 22 Envtl. Rep. 2052 (1991).

Financially strapped localities also expressed concern that they lack the resources to implement other SDWA regulations that are beginning to take effect. EPA regulations now require thousands of communities with unfiltered drinking water to install filtration systems unless EPA approves an alternative watershed protection program. EPA estimates that about one-half of all such communities will have to install filtration. New York City officials claim that a filtration system would cost the city $4 billion. As a result, the city is pursuing an alternative program that relies on purchases of open space and strict controls on land use to prevent contamination of the city's watershed.

In the 1996 Amendments, Congress provided some flexibility for EPA to address cost concerns of small water distribution systems, by permitting variances to such systems if they cannot afford to comply with the MCL and if they otherwise comply with "treatment technology, treatment technique[s] or other means" that the Administrator finds "ensure adequate protection of human health." 42 U.S.C. §300g-4(e)(2), (3). MCLs promulgated prior to 1986, and MCLs for microbial contamination are excluded from the variance provisions.

Enforcement of the SDWA has been a chronic problem, particularly because the Act's regulatory targets usually are agencies of state and local government. To enhance enforcement Congress in 1996 added provisions that require water systems to notify their customers within 24 hours if violations are discovered that have potentially serious health effects. For other violations, the supplier must notify its customers within one year of the violation. Water suppliers also must provide the public with an annual report of the levels of various contaminants found in their system. These reports, which are to be called "Consumer Confidence Reports," must explain in layperson's terms the health concerns that resulted in the regulation of each regulated contaminant and they must provide a toll-free hotline number for consumers to use to seek more information.

|| *Case Study: Regulation of Arsenic in Drinking Water* ||

Inorganic arsenic is a naturally occurring element in the Earth's crust. Arsenic is released into ground water that travels through underground rocks and soil. Erosion can deposit arsenic in water bodies and the metal also can be absorbed by animals and plants. Consumption of food and water are the major sources of arsenic exposure for the majority of U.S. citizens. People also may be exposed from industrial sources, as arsenic is used in semiconductor manufacturing, petroleum refining, wood preservatives, animal feed additives, and herbicides.

Arsenic can combine with other elements to form inorganic and organic arsenicals. In general, inorganic derivatives are regarded as more toxic than the organic forms. While food contains both inorganic and organic arsenicals, primarily inorganic forms are present in water. Exposure to arsenic at high levels poses serious health effects as it is a known human carcinogen. In addition, it has been reported to affect the vascular system in humans and has been associated with the development of diabetes. Water from wells often has higher concentrations of arsenic than does surface water such as lakes and streams. Arsenic also can be found in plants, fish, and shellfish. Serious health problems associated with very high levels of arsenic in drinking water have surfaced in India and Bangladesh.

The World Health Organization's International Standards for Drinking-Water for arsenic were established in 1958, initially at 200 micrograms per liter ($\mu g/L$), or parts per billion (ppb), and lowered to 50 ppb in 1963. In 1993, WHO again lowered its guideline for arsenic in drinking water to 10 ppb. The WHO noted the fact that inorganic arsenic compounds are classified by the International Agency for Research on Cancer (IARC) in Group 1 (carcinogenic to humans) on the basis of sufficient evidence for carcinogenicity in humans and limited evidence for carcinogenicity in animals. Based on data from Taiwan and using an EPA risk assessment, WHO estimated the lifetime risk of skin cancer to be greater than 1 in 100,000 even in a population ingesting far less than 10 ppb of arsenic. However, because 10 ppb was deemed the practical quantification limit for arsenic in drinking water, it was selected as the guideline level even though skin cancer risks at this level of exposure were estimated to be 6 in 10,000.

In a number of countries, the WHO provisional guideline of 10 ppb has been adopted as the standard. Japan adopted this standard in 1993. The European Union endorsed it in 1998. Australia has a standard of 7 ppb. Many other countries have retained the earlier WHO guideline of 50 ppb as their national standard, including China, India, and Bangladesh. Canada's standard is 25 ppb.

In the United States, EPA established the current maximum contaminant level (MCL) for arsenic in drinking water at 50 ppb as an interim standard in 1975, following enactment of the Safe Drinking Water Act (SDWA). This initial standard was set at the level recommended by the Public Health Service in 1943. While EPA in 1985 proposed to adopt 50 ppb as a permanent standard, it had not taken final action on this proposal when the 1986 Amendments to the Safe Drinking Water Act converted the interim standard into a national primary drinking water regulation, which was to be revised within three years. EPA missed the 1989 deadline for revising the arsenic standard, in part due to disagreements over agency risk assessments for arsenic. A citizen suit, which was filed to require EPA to revise the standard, was settled by consent decree, which extended the deadline to 1995 as controversy continued over EPA's assessments of arsenic risks.

The Wall Street Journal reports that mining companies made extensive efforts to influence scientific assessments of arsenic risks during the 1990s. Peter Waldman, All Agree Arsenic Kills; The Question Is How Much It Takes To Do So, Wall St. J., April 19, 2001, at A1. Faced with billions of dollars in cleanup costs under the Superfund program, the mining industry hired numerous scientists in an effort to demonstrate that there was a safe threshold for human exposure to arsenic. In 1990 Professor Richard Wilson of Harvard was hired by Atlantic Richfield (ARCO), owner of the Anaconda mining complex, to demonstrate that low levels of arsenic were not carcinogenic to humans. However, after he encountered epidemiological data linking arsenic exposures to lung, bladder, and kidney cancers, he recommended that EPA set more stringent limits on arsenic. ARCO then canceled the research project and barred Wilson and others from publishing their results. Id. at A8. Corporate interests then helped fund an arsenic task force within the Society of Environmental Geochemistry and Health, which sponsored biannual international conferences on arsenic beginning in 1993. Although EPA co-sponsored the task force, some independent scientists viewed it as an industry effort to disrupt the regulatory process. Id. In an effort to counter epidemiological data from Taiwan, an industry consultant published a paper in 1995 ostensibly co-authored by the author of the previous Taiwanese studies. Dr. Chien-Jen Chen, the author of the Taiwanese studies "was shocked . . . to learn that his data had been improperly manipulated in a paper under his own name," id. In 1996 after new epidemiological data from Chile showed high risks from human exposure to arsenic, ARCO sought unsuccessfully to hire the Chilean researchers "to do research to show the EPA that the impact of arsenic was not as high as was claimed." Id.

The 1996 SDWA Amendments required EPA to propose a national primary drinking water regulation for arsenic by January 1, 2000, and to promulgate final regulations by January 1, 2001 after consulting with the National Academy of Sciences (NAS) to "reduce the uncertainty in assessing health risks" at low levels of exposure.

On March 23, 1999, the NAS's National Research Council released its report. National Research Council, Arsenic in Drinking Water (1999). The report recommended that EPA develop a stricter standard for allowable levels of arsenic in the nation's drinking water as soon as possible. The report noted that while arsenic in drinking water has been associated with skin cancer and other disorders, recent studies suggest that it also can lead to bladder and lung cancer, which are more likely to be fatal.

The committee examined clinical studies and epidemiological data from several international studies, including research from Taiwan, Argentina, and Chile. These studies show that in addition to causing skin, bladder, and lung cancer, consuming arsenic in drinking water also can cause skin lesions, anemia, nerve damage, and circulatory problems. Studies examining males who daily consume water that contains 50 micrograms of arsenic per liter show that they have about a 1 in 1,000 risk of developing bladder cancer. However, the choice of models used to estimate risks posed by arsenic can significantly affect risk estimates. See page 206. Linear dose-response models assume that there is some risk at every level of exposure, but some scientists believe that small amounts of arsenic actually could be beneficial to humans. However, the NRC report noted that arsenic has not been tested as an essential nutrient for humans, and no evidence suggests that arsenic is required for any human biochemical processes.

Arsenic is readily absorbed from the gastrointestinal tract to the blood. The mechanisms through which arsenic causes cancer are not well-understood, but data suggest that arsenic probably causes chromosomal abnormalities that lead to cancer. Sensitivity to arsenic's toxic effects—including carcinogenic effects—varies with each individual and appears to be influenced by such factors as nutrition and genetic susceptibility. No human studies of sufficient scope in the United States have directly examined whether regular consumption of arsenic in drinking water at EPA's current standard increases the risk of cancer or other adverse health effects. Rather, the NRC committee's characterization of risk was based on findings from the international studies, experimental data on the mechanisms through which arsenic causes cancer, and available information on human susceptibility.

However, the committee noted that there were problems in applying the data from the international studies. The studies measured exposure to arsenic in drinking water regionally, rather than assessing the amount of arsenic to which each individual was exposed. Moreover, most people in these studies were exposed to concentrations of more than 100 micrograms of arsenic per liter of water. While the committee concluded that more research is needed to assess how exposure to very small amounts of arsenic affects human health, these uncertainties did not change its finding that exposure to arsenic in drinking water increases risks for developing bladder and lung cancer.

Long before the NRC report was issued, EPA had begun holding a series of public meetings with states, tribes, local governments, water utilities, and the public to solicit their views on how to develop a new standard for arsenic in drinking water. These included several "stakeholder meetings" in 1997 and 1998. Following the issuance of the NRC report, EPA convened another two-day stakeholder meeting to discuss development of the arsenic standard. EPA explained that it was scheduled to propose the arsenic rule by January 1, 2000, and to promulgate the final rule by January 1, 2001.

EPA missed the January 2000 deadline for proposing a new arsenic standard. In February 2000, the Natural Resources Defense Council issued a report entitled "Arsenic and Old Laws: A Scientific and Public Health Analysis of Arsenic Occurrence in Drinking Water, Its Health Effects, and EPA's Outdated Arsenic Tap Water Standard." The report, which is available at *http:// www.nrdc. org/water/drinking/arsenic/aolinx.asp*, estimated that more than 34 million Americans drink tap water supplied by systems containing average levels of arsenic that pose unacceptable cancer risks. While noting that drinking water provided by most water utility companies meets or falls below the current 50 ppb standard, NRDC argued that the standard was outdated because it was established in 1942, before health officials knew that arsenic causes cancer. Based on data in the NRC report, NRDC estimated the lifetime risks of dying of cancer from arsenic in tap water as indicated in Figure 3.6.

EPA worked extensively with the U.S. Geological Survey (USGS) to gather data on levels of arsenic in ground water. Arsenic analyses were collected from approximately 18,500 sites throughout the United States, including wells used for public supply, research, agriculture, industry and domestic supply (which are not necessarily current sources of drinking water). Approximately 12 percent of the samples were taken from public supplies as defined by USGS to include wells used for bottling, commercial, medicinal, or institutional purposes, as well as individual homeowners' and public water utility wells. In May 2000, the USGS released a report analyzing the concentrations of arsenic in groundwater throughout the United States. U.S. Geological Survey, A Retrospective Analysis on the Occurrence of Arsenic in Ground-Water Resources of the United States and Limitations in Drinking-Water-Supply Characterizations (2000). The report found that while the large majority of groundwater samples contained less than the WHO guideline level of 10 ppb arsenic, approximately 10 percent of the samples exceeded this level. The highest concentrations of arsenic were found throughout the West and in parts of the Midwest and Northeast.

On June 22, 2000, EPA proposed to establish the aspirational maximum contaminant level goal (MCLG) for arsenic in drinking water at zero and to set the enforceable maximum contaminant level (MCL) for it at 5 ppb. The agency requested comment on alternative MCL options of 3 ppb, 10 ppb, and 20 ppb. 65 Fed. Reg. 38,887 (2000). EPA explained that 3 ppb was the lowest technically feasible level, but that the agency did not believe that the benefits of regulating arsenic at this level would justify the costs. In August 2000, the agency convened another stakeholder meeting, attended by more than 140 people in person and 40 people who joined the meeting by conference call. In response to its proposed rule, EPA received more than 6,500 pages of comments from 1,100 commenters.

FIGURE 3.6
NRDC's Estimates of Lifetime Risks of Dying of Cancer from Ingesting Arsenic in Drinking Water Based on Data in National Research Council Report

Arsenic Level in Tap Water	Approximate Total Cancer Risk
0.5 ppb	1 in 10,000
1 ppb	1 in 5,000
3 ppb	1 in 1,667
4 ppb	1 in 1,250
5 ppb	1 in 1,000
10 ppb	1 in 500
20 ppb	1 in 250
25 ppb	1 in 200
50 ppb	1 in 100

Although the Safe Drinking Water Act Amendments of 1996 had required EPA to issue a final arsenic rule by January 1, 2001, Congress extended the deadline until June 22, 2001, the date one year after EPA proposed its regulations. The vehicle for this extension was language inserted into the conference report on the VA-HUD appropriations bill for Fiscal Year 2001. In January 2001, days before the Clinton administration left office, outgoing EPA Administrator Carol Browner adopted final regulations for arsenic in drinking water. The regulations set the MCLG at zero and the MCL at 10 ppb, a less stringent level than the 5 ppb the agency had proposed. 66 Fed. Reg. 6,976 (2001). While EPA had proposed to give small public water suppliers (those serving 10,000 people or less) five years to meet the new standard and large suppliers three years, the final rule gave all water supply systems five years (until January 23, 2006) to comply.

EPA's decision to set the MCLG at zero was based on its conclusion that any level of exposure to arsenic in drinking water could cause harm to health. While some commenters had argued that there may be a safe threshold level of human exposure to arsenic, EPA concluded that the most scientifically valid approach, given the lack of critical data, was to use a linear approach to assessing the risks of arsenic. EPA noted that because the available data point to several potential carcinogenic modes of action for arsenic, the dose-response relationship may be sublinear. However, because the data do not provide any basis upon which EPA could reasonably construct a dose-response curve exhibiting a zero risk threshold, EPA concluded that it could not depart from its no-threshold assumption. The agency cited that the NRC report's findings that available data that could help determine the shape of dose-response curve are inconclusive and do not meet EPA's stated criteria for departure from its default assumption of linearity.

Recall that EPA's decision to set a zero MCLG for chloroform was struck down in *Chlorine Chemistry Council* (pages 211-213) as contrary to the SDWA's mandate to use the best available evidence. In its final arsenic rule, EPA distinguished arsenic from chloroform in the following manner:

> In the case of chloroform, there was sufficient information to describe key events and undertake mode of action analysis. In the case of arsenic, the postulated mode of action cannot be specifically described, the key events are

unknown, and no analysis of the remaining elements of the mode of action framework can be made. Several possible influences of arsenic on the carcinogenic process have been postulated, but there are insufficient experimental data either to show that any one of the possible modes is the influence actually at work or to test the dimensions of its influence as the framework requires.

For chloroform there are extensive data on metabolism that identify the likely active metabolite. The key events—cell toxicity followed by sustained cell proliferation and eventually tumor effects—have been extensively studied in many experiments. The key events have been empirically demonstrated to precede and consistently be associated with tumor effects. In sum, a very large number of studies have satisfied the requirements of the framework analysis. By contrast, the arsenic database fails to even be able to satisfy the first element of the framework; the key events are unknown. While there are a number of possible modes of action implied by existing data, none of them has been sufficiently studied to be analyzed under the Agency's framework. For this reason the comparison of the "best available, peer reviewed data" for arsenic and chloroform shows quite different results. There are not sufficient data on arsenic to describe a mode of action as there were for chloroform. This was also the conclusion of the SAB review of arsenic. 66 Fed. Reg. 6,976 (2001).

In its final regulations, EPA justified its choice of a 10 ppb MCL based on its discretionary authority under 42 U.S.C. §300g-1(b)(6)(A) to set the standard at a level that "maximizes health risk reduction benefits at a cost that is justified by the benefits." EPA estimated that its MCL of 10 ppb for arsenic would prevent between 37.4 and 55.7 cases of bladder and lung cancer per year, as indicated in Figure 3.7. EPA also estimated that the standard would produce significant nonquantified benefits by reducing cancers affecting other parts of the body, including skin, kidney, liver, prostate, and nasal passages.

EPA estimated that the quantified benefits of the 10 ppb MCL in reducing lung and bladder cancers would range from $140 million to $198 million annually, as indicated in Figure 3.8. It constructed this estimate by applying a value of $6.1 million to each death prevented and a value of $607,000 to each nonfatal cancer case prevented. The $607,000 figure was derived from surveys showing that this is the average amount people would pay to avoid a case of chronic bronchitis, which the agency acknowledged might understate the value of avoiding a nonfatal cancer. The $6.1 million figure is the current "value of a statistical life" employed by the agency in performing cost-benefit analyses (in 1999 dollars)—a figure EPA now indicates should be increased to $6.77 million

---

FIGURE 3.7
Estimated Annual Total Quantified Cancer Cases (Lung & Bladder Cancer) Prevented by 10 ppb MCL

Arsenic Level (ppb)	Reduced Mortality Cases	Reduced Morbidity Cases	Total Lung/Bladder Cancers Avoided
3 ppb	32.6 to 74.1	24.6 to 64.2	57.2 to 138.3
5 ppb	29.1 to 53.7	22.0 to 46.5	51.1 to 100.2
10 ppb	21.3 to 29.8	16.1 to 25.9	37.4 to 55.7
20 ppb	10.2 to 11.3	8.5 to 8.8	19.0 to 19.8

Source: 66 Fed. Reg. 7009.

FIGURE 3.8
EPA's Estimates of the Quantified and Potential Non-Quantified Health Benefits from Reducing Arsenic in Drinking Water
[$ in millions, 1999]

MCL Level (ppb)	Total Quantified Health Benefits	Potential Non-Quantified Health Benefits
3	$213.8-$490.9	Reductions in Skin Cancer, Kidney
5	$191.1-$355.6	Cancer, Cancer of Nasal Passages,
10	$139.6-$197.7	Liver Cancer, Prostate Cancer
20	$66.2-$75.3	Cardiovascular Effects, Pulmonary
		Effects, Immunological Effects,
		Neurological Effects, Endocrine Effects

in light of the growth in real income over time. Figure 3.8 shows EPA's summary of the monetized benefits of each of the alternative standards.

EPA estimates that the overall cost of complying with its 10 ppb MCL would be approximately $200 million annually. This estimate includes total annual costs for community water systems (CWSs) of $172.3 million and total annual compliance costs for nontransient, noncommunity water systems of $8.1 million, as indicated in Figure 3.9.

For alternative arsenic MCLs, EPA estimated the annual cost per cancer case avoided using two different discount rates. The agency's upper-bound and lower-bound estimates are shown in Figure 3.10.

The costs of complying with the new standard are not evenly distributed across the country. EPA estimates that roughly 5 percent, or 3,000, of community water systems, serving 11 million people, would have to take corrective action to lower their current levels of arsenic in drinking water. Five percent, or 1,100, of the water supply systems in schools, nursing homes, and factories, serving approximately 2 million people, also will need to take measures to meet the new arsenic standard. Of all the systems affected by the new rule, 97 percent are small systems that serve fewer than 10,000 people each.

EPA estimates that for small community water systems (those serving fewer than 10,000 people), the new regulations would increase costs per customer between $38 and $327. For community water systems that serve greater than 10,000 people, annual household costs for water were expected to increase from $0.86 to $32. EPA offered to provide financial assistance for these systems through its drinking-water state revolving program, which had funded $3.6 billion in projects to improve the infrastructure of drinking water systems. EPA also offered to give compliance period extensions of up to 9 years (resulting in a total compliance period of 14 years) to small systems through an exemption process. After analyzing the costs and benefits of alternative MCLs, EPA concluded "that, based on comparisons of cost and benefits (using the various benefit-cost comparison tools discussed), the monetized benefits of a regulatory level of 10 µg/L best justify the costs." EPA noted that "strict parity of monetized costs and monetized benefits is not required to find that the benefits of a particular MCL option are justified under the [SDWA]."

On March 20, 2001, the Bush administration stunned the environmental community when it announced that it would delay the effective date of EPA's new standard for arsenic in drinking water. EPA published a notice in the Federal Register delaying the effective date of the regulation from March 23,

FIGURE 3.9
Total Annual National System and State Compliance Costs for Various Arsenic MCLs
[$ in millions, 1999]

MCL = 3 µg/L	CWS Discount Rate		NTNCWS Discount Rate		Total Discount Rate	
	3%	7%	3%	7%	3%	7%
System Costs	$668.1	$759.5	$28.2	$31.0	$696.3	$790.4
Treatment	665.9	756.5	27.2	29.6	693.1	786.0
Monitoring/Administrative	2.2	3.0	1.0	1.4	3.2	4.4
State Costs	1.4	1.6	0.1	0.2	1.5	1.7
Total	$669.4	761.0	28.3	31.1	697.8	792.1
MCL = 5 µg/L						
System Costs	396.4	451.1	17.3	18.9	413.5	470.2
Treatment	394.4	448.3	16.3	17.6	410.6	466.1
Monitoring/Administrative	2.0	2.8	1.0	1.3	2.9	4.1
State Costs	1.1	1.3	0.1	0.2	1.2	1.4
Total	$397.5	452.5	17.3	19.1	414.8	471.7
Final MCL = 10 µg/L						
System Costs	171.4	195.5	7.9	8.9	179.4	204.4
Treatment	169.6	193.0	7.0	7.6	176.7	200.6
Monitoring/Administrative	1.8	2.5	0.9	1.3	2.7	3.8
State Costs	0.9	1.0	0.1	0.2	1.0	1.2
Total	$172.3	196.6	8.1	9.1	180.4	205.6
MCL = 20 µg/L						
System Costs	62.4	71.4	3.5	4.1	65.9	75.5
Treatment	60.7	69.0	2.6	2.8	63.3	71.8
Monitoring/Administrative	1.7	2.4	0.9	1.3	2.6	3.7
State Costs	0.7	0.8	0.1	0.2	0.9	1.0
Total	$63.2	72.3	3.6	4.2	66.8	76.5

Source: 66 Fed. Reg. 7011.

2001, until May 22, 2001, in order to give the administration an opportunity to reconsider the standard. EPA did not seek public comment prior to suspending the regulations. The Agency stated that "seeking public comment is impracticable, unnecessary, and contrary to the public interest."

Both EPA Administrator Christine Whitman and President George W. Bush described the decision to suspend the new arsenic standard as an effort to ensure that the regulation is based on "sound science." Douglas Jehl, EPA to Abandon New Arsenic Limits for Water Supply, N.Y. Times, March 21, 2001, at A1. Peter Waldman, All Agree Arsenic Kills; The Question Is How Much It Takes to Do So, Wall St. J., April 19, 2001, at A1. The Bush administration had been heavily lobbied to block the new arsenic standard by the National Mining Association, Republican Senator Pete Domenici of New Mexico, and Utah Governor Mike Leavitt, who personally lobbied Administrator Whitman at a reception during inaugural weekend. Jeanne Cummings & John Harwood, Arsenic Issue May Poison Bush's "Compassionate Conservatism," Wall St. J., April 20, 2001, at A16. In a letter to Administrator Whitman, which argued that the

FIGURE 3.10
Estimated Annual Cost per Cancer Case Avoided for Various Arsenic MCLs
(Combined Bladder and Lung Cancer Cases)
[$ in millions, 1999]

Arsenic Level (ppb)	Lower-Bound Estimate	Upper-Bound Estimate
3% Discount Rate		
3	$12.2	$5.0
5	8.1	4.1
10	4.8	3.2
20	3.5	3.4
7% Discount Rate		
3	$13.8	$5.7
5	9.2	4.7
10	5.5	3.7
20	4.0	3.9

Source: 66 Fed. Reg. 7018.

regulation would place an "excruciating financial burden" on water users in New Mexico, Sen. Domenici added a hand-written postscript: "No benefits, huge costs." Id.

The decision to reconsider the arsenic rule provoked considerable public outrage. Public opinion polls showed that it was intensely unpopular. Editorial writers harshly denounced it. The Democratic Party quickly filmed a television commercial attacking the decision by having a small child ask her mother for more arsenic. The former EPA official responsible for the rule during the Clinton administration denounced the decision as an "action [that] will jeopardize the health of millions of Americans" and that "compromises literally a decade's worth of work on behalf of developing a public health standard." Douglas Jehl, EPA to Abandon New Arsenic Limits for Water Supply, N.Y. Times, March 21, 2001, p. A1.

Representatives of water suppliers and the mining and wood preserving industries had a very different reaction. Nebraska Attorney General Don Stenberg praised the decision, noting that it could have cost nearly $100 million for Nebraska communities to comply with the new regulations. "People in these communities have been drinking the exact same water for 50 to 100 years, and we're not aware of any health problems as a result." Peter Waldman & John Fialka, EPA's Move to Rescind Arsenic Standard Is Welcomed by Those Facing the Cleanup," Wall St. J., March 22, 2001, at A2. A spokesperson for the National Mining Association also praised the decision: "The Clinton administration rushed this out in the midnight hour. We felt all along that it was really a political decision unsupported by the science." Id. A spokesperson for the American Wood Preservers Institute expressed "delight" at the decision to block the new regulations. Id.

Responding to public criticism, the Bush administration explained that it only had instructed EPA to review the new standard to ensure that it was based on sound science and accurate cost and benefit estimates. However, moderate Republicans in the U.S. House of Representatives later joined Democrats in adopting an appropriations rider to bar EPA from spending any funds to block the Clinton administration's arsenic standard from going into effect. This action represented a stunning legislative defeat for the Bush administration, and it placed more pressure on the administration to reverse its efforts to reconsider the arsenic regulation.

On April 23, EPA requested public comment on a proposal to delay the effective date of the rule until February 22, 2002. On May 22, 2001, EPA announced that it would delay the effective date for the rule until February 22, 2002 to give it time to complete its reassessment process and to afford the public a full opportunity to provide further input. On July 19, 2001, EPA issued a proposal to request comment on whether the data and technical analyses associated with the January 2001 arsenic rule support setting the arsenic standard at 3 ppb, 5 ppb, 10 ppb, or 20 ppb. In addition, the Agency asked commenters to submit new information for review.

After the June 22, 2001 statutory deadline for issuing a new arsenic standard expired, the Natural Resources Defense Council filed suit against EPA in federal district court in Washington, D.C. The suit charged that the EPA has failed to perform a non-discretionary duty required by law. EPA's National Drinking Water Advisory Council, which was asked to reexamine EPA's analysis of the cost of implementing the arsenic rule, completed its reassessment on August 21. The working group concluded that EPA's previous estimate of compliance costs was credible given the constraints the agency was operating under. While noting that there are considerable uncertainties in the development of national cost estimates, the working group made a number of recommendations to improve future cost estimates.

On October 31, 2001, EPA announced that it had decided to retain the same 10 ppb standard effective in 2006 that the Clinton administration had adopted. Although EPA Administrator Christie Todd Whitman had initially questioned whether the 10 ppb standard was based on "sound science," she ultimately concluded that additional study and consultation "has reinforced the basis for the decision." Announcing EPA's decision, Whitman stated that she was "reassured by all of the data that significant reductions are necessary. As required by the Safe Drinking Water Act, a standard of 10 ppb protects public health based on the best available science and ensures that the cost of the standard is achievable." EPA Announces Arsenic Standard for Drinking Water of 10 Parts Per Billion, October 31, 2001, a press release which can be found on the Agency's website at *http://www.epa.gov/newsroom.*

NOTES AND QUESTIONS

1. Should the Bush administration have suspended the Clinton administration's stricter standard for arsenic in drinking water? Now that the standard is being reconsidered by the Bush administration, at what level should the MCL for arsenic be set?

2. Is it fair to characterize the Clinton administration's arsenic standard as a "midnight regulation"? The regulation had been under development for several years, but Congress has extended the deadline for promulgating it until June 22, 2001.

3. Would NRDC have been likely to win its lawsuit against EPA for failure to promulgate a new arsenic standard by the statutory deadline? Could EPA argue successfully that it did in fact meet the statutory deadline by promulgating a new regulation, but that it was then free to reconsider the regulation since there is nothing in the statute that would prohibit such a reconsideration?

4. One of the major difficulties faced by EPA in assessing the risks of arsenic is the problem of gathering reliable epidemiological information on the health effects of low levels of exposure. How reassuring is the comment by the Attorney General of Nebraska that: "People in these communities have been drinking the exact same water for 50 to 100 years, and we're not aware of any health problems as a result"?

5. Did the public overreact to the Bush administration's decision to suspend the new regulation because it involved a substance widely known to be poisonous at high levels of exposure? In a paper analyzing the dispute over the arsenic standard, Professor Cass Sunstein observes that people are "intuitive toxicologists" who tend to believe that substances that cause cancer are unsafe and should simply be banned. This reaction, according to Sunstein, "does not accommodate the judgment that low levels of admittedly carcinogenic substances should sometimes be tolerated, because the risks are low and the costs of eliminating them are high." Sunstein, The Arithmetic of Arsenic (Aug. 2001) (Working Paper 01-10 of the AEI/Brookings Joint Center for Regulatory Studies). Sunstein argues that cost-benefit analysis should be understood as a way of moving beyond this "intuitive toxicology" to one based on data.

6. After analyzing the cost-benefit analyses performed by EPA and industry groups attacking the arsenic standard, Professor Sunstein concludes that plausible alternative assumptions can lead to cost-benefit analyses findings that the arsenic regulation has net costs of $210 million or net benefits of $3.15 billion. Id., at 35. Sunstein notes that this demonstrates the wide range of uncertainty that can prevail when costs and benefits of difficult regulatory policy choices are estimated. However, he concludes that cost-benefit analysis can play a highly useful role in regulatory decisions and he argues that courts should be highly deferential to agencies' estimates of costs and benefits.

7. Consider the uncertainties in extrapolating from the Taiwanese epidemiological studies of arsenic risks. Both the NRC and EPA's Science Advisory Board endorsed the use of the Taiwanese studies, citing the following advantages: "mortality data were drawn from a cancer registry; arsenic well water concentrations were measured for each of the 42 villages; there was a large, relatively stable study population that had life-time exposures to arsenic; there are limited measured data for the food intake of arsenic in this population; age- and dose-dependent responses with respect to arsenic in the drinking water were demonstrated; the collection of pathology data was unusually thorough; and the populations were quite homogeneous in terms of lifestyle." But the data also had the following problems: "the use of median exposure data at the village level; the low income and relatively poor diet of the Taiwanese study population (high levels of carbohydrates, low levels of protein, selenium and other essential nutrients); high exposure to arsenic via food and cooking water, . . . confounding factors that may have contributed to risk may not be adequately accounted for."

8. An epidemiological study often cited by opponents of stricter regulation of arsenic focused on Utah residents and was published in 1999. It did not find any excess bladder or lung cancer risks after exposure to arsenic at concentrations ranging from 14 to 166 ppm. The study estimated excess risk by comparing cancer rates among the study population, in Millard County, Utah, to background rates in all of Utah. Here is why EPA did not find the data persuasive:

> the cancer rates observed among the study population, even those who consumed the highest levels of arsenic, were lower, in many cases significantly

lower, than in all of Utah. This is evidence that there are important differences between the study and comparison populations besides their consumption of arsenic. One such difference is that Millard County is mostly rural, while Utah as a whole contains some large urban populations. Another difference is that the subjects of the Utah study were all members of the Church of Jesus Christ of Latter Day Saints, who for religious reasons have relatively low rates of tobacco and alcohol use. For these reasons, the Agency believes that the comparison of the study population to all of Utah is not appropriate for estimating excess risks.

9. Why did EPA decide that the benefits of its proposed MCL of 5 ppb would not 'justify" the costs of complying with that standard? Why did the agency find that the 10 ppb MCL would "best justify the costs"? Does EPA's decision reflect an implicit judgment concerning how much it is worth to save a human life?

5. *Health-Based Regulation*

A third approach to the "how safe is safe" question is provided by statutes requiring that regulations be based solely on assessments of public health effects. These are generally referred to as "health-based" regulations. Different statutes mandate different health-based objectives. In a few rare instances, Congress has mandated that risks of a certain kind be reduced to zero. A more common health-based approach is to require that the risks of certain kinds be reduced enough to "protect" the public health or to eliminate "significant risk." Some of the most important environmental statutes in terms of the adverse health effects they reduce as well as the magnitude of compliance costs are the national ambient air quality standards of the Clean Air Act. You will study these in more detail in Chapter 5. The EPA is instructed to set the NAAQS at a level adequate to "protect the public health" "with an adequate margin of safety." See pages 475-480.

A.   DE MINIMIS RISK AND COMPARATIVE RISK ASSESSMENT

Some statutes, like the Safe Drinking Water Act, do not use purely health-based approaches to standard-setting, but they do require that purely health-based goals, or MCLGs, be established as an initial matter. See pages 249-253. As you will recall from the previous section, in setting those goals, EPA is told to set them at a level at which "no known or anticipated adverse effects on the health of persons occur and which allows an adequate margin of safety." Under this standard, EPA has quite often set the MCLG at zero. This is especially true when the contaminant under review is a known or suspected carcinogen. Consequently, SDWA goal-setting has become one of the frequent battle grounds over whether EPA is justified in using this no-threshold default assumption.

EPA has also set nonzero MCLGs for suspected carcinogens when the evidence of carcinogenicity is considered to be rather weak. For example, in November 1985 EPA established final recommended maximum contaminant levels (the term for MCLGs prior to the 1986 Amendments) for eight volatile organic compounds. While EPA established zero as the health-based goal for those compounds that were known or probable carcinogens, it established a nonzero goal for vinylidene chloride because the evidence of its carcinogenicity was weak. To take into account the possibility that vinylidene chloride was a carcinogen, EPA reduced the level of its nonzero health-based goal by a factor of ten from the level that it would have set based solely on consideration of noncancer health effects. This approach was upheld in NRDC v. EPA, 824 F.2d 1211 (D.C. Cir. 1987). The court described EPA's decision to compromise in the face of uncertainty as "neither an unreasonable interpretation of the statute nor an unwise choice of policy." The court rejected the argument that EPA had violated its obligation to resolve uncertainty on the side of protecting public health with the following explanation:

> If the evidence established, for example, a 40% probability that a compound was carcinogenic, the agency's decision not to regulate would be difficult to square with the Drinking Water Act's instruction to the agency to establish a recommended level for each contaminant which, in its judgment, may have any adverse effect on health. Such a decision might well constitute an abuse of the discretion the agency is granted under the Drinking Water Act. But that situation in no way describes the instant case, and certainly there is no indication in the final rule that the agency has adopted a general policy not to establish a recommended level for a VOC unless a preponderance of the evidence demonstrates that it is a carcinogen. NRDC perhaps has taken too much to heart the agency's use of the word "possible" in its categorization of different VOCs. Although that label on its face could augur a preponderance-of-the-evidence test, the agency's explication of the Category II—compounds for which there is *some equivocal evidence* of carcinogenicity—makes it clear that the EPA has no such test in mind. Nor does the EPA's treatment of vinylidene chloride suggest that the agency employed a threshold preponderance-of-the-evidence test. The EPA here reasonably concluded that the evidence of vinylidene chloride's carcinogenicity was not even close to being in equipoise. The agency pointed out that no fewer than a dozen long-term animal studies had not demonstrated that vinylidene chloride has any carcinogenic effect. See 50 Fed. Reg. 46,888. Against this data EPA weighed two studies that revealed a possibility of carcinogenic or protocarcinogenic effects, and it noted that the results in both of these studies had limitations that made their applicability to humans highly questionable. The agency therefore had adequate support for its conclusion that the evidence of TCE's carcinogenicity was sparse and equivocal. [824 F.2d at 1217 (emphasis in original).]

The court also rejected industry arguments that it was improper for EPA to establish a goal of zero for all known or probable carcinogens. Industry had argued that the *Benzene* decision required EPA first to determine that the risks were significant at all nonzero levels before adopting zero as a goal. The court rejected this argument by noting that Congress had expressly directed EPA to regulate these substances in the 1986 Amendments to the SDWA and that the *Benzene* decision therefore did not apply in this different statutory context.

The SDWA's regulatory regime also permits the relaxation of its standards if the benefits to be achieved from regulating as much as feasible cannot justify the costs of regulating that stringently. See pages 249-253. Such a provision acknowledges that the primary objective of all toxics statutes is to advance public health, in this case by employing an assessment of adverse health effects to relax a regulatory standard. Most statutes are not structured in this way, but even when they are not, health-based considerations have sometimes been raised as an argument for relaxing a regulatory standard or not regulating at all. Suppose, for example, that a particular application of a feasibility-based or even a health-based standard resulted in extremely low levels of remaining risk, so low as to be in some sense almost unnoticeable, and a less stringent regulation would still result in extremely low risk. Even if risk-benefit balancing is not required by statute, should the agencies relax regulations in such cases? Achieving the final small degrees of pollution reduction is often very expensive, so that substantial economic consequences can turn on whether the agency imposes the strict demands of a statute or whether it recognizes the "common sense" proposition that an activity poses risks "too small to be regulated."

In a number of regulatory settings, the regulated community has promoted the notion that regulators should recognize the concept of a de minimis risk level in establishing health-based standards. The idea of de minimis risk differs from risk-benefit balancing because risks are not compared with benefits. Instead, an activity's risks are compared with a relatively low level of risk, the de minimis level. The notion is that de minimis levels pose risks that ought to be acceptable to society; thus the idea of de minimis risk is also sometimes advanced as one way to interpret the objective of statutes that seek to "protect public health" or to ensure that a substance is "safe."

For advocates of the de minimis risk principle, how small is too small to be regulated? To answer this question, de minimis risk advocates typically employ a *comparative risk assessment,* arguing that the de minimis level for regulatory purposes should correspond to, or be slightly lower than, the risk associated with some general activity commonly thought to be "safe" (or at least thought to pose trivial risks). De minimis determinations at EPA and the Nuclear Regulatory Commission have been described this way:

> EPA and the Nuclear Regulatory Commission (NRC) . . . have proposed to set federal radiation standards using as a yardstick the fatality rates prevalent in industries commonly considered to be relatively safe. In its radiation protection proposal, EPA noted that "the risk of job-related accidental death in the safest of all major occupational categories, retail trades, [was] an annual death rate [of] 60 per million workers in 1975." This risk equates to a 45-year worklife risk of 2.7 in 1,000. The Agency based its proposed radiation protection guidelines on its finding that radiation risks of a magnitude similar to 3 in 1,000 "do not appear unreasonably high" because "they are comparable to risk of accidental death in the least hazardous occupations." In a similar vein, NRC's recent radiation protection proposal follows the approach recommended by the International Commission on Radiological Protection[.] . . . which developed its guidelines by "comparing [radiation] risk with that of workers in industries . . . which are recognized as having high standards of safety." As NRC pointed out, "in such '[s]afe' industries . . . average annual mortality due to occupational hazards does not exceed 10^{-4}. . . ." This annual rate amounts to a 45-year lifetime risk in excess of 4 in 1,000. Like EPA, NRC proposed standards on the basis that occupational mortality risks due to radiation are "acceptable" if kept at or below this "safe industry" risk level. [Rodricks et al., Significant Risk Decisions in Federal Regulatory Agencies, 7 Regulatory Toxicol. and Pharmacol. 307 (1987).]

The de minimis principle has been litigated in a variety of contexts, including the Delaney Clauses. Enacted in the 1950s and 1960s, these provisions, all named after Congressman James Delaney (D-NY) who introduced them, prohibit the marketing or use of any food additive, color additive, or animal drug that is "found . . . to induce cancer in man or animal." 21 U.S.C. §376(b)(5)(B) (color additives), regardless of how small that risk of cancer might be. When the FDA sought to authorize the marketing of two color additives, Orange No. 17 and Red No. 19 (for use in cosmetics) on the grounds that the risk of cancer they posed was de minimis, Public Citizen sued to enforce the Delaney Clause's absolute bar. Public Citizen v. FDA, 831 F.2d 1108 (D.C. Cir. 1987).

Using QRAs, the FDA had estimated the risk of cancer from Orange No. 17 to be one in 19 billion at worst, and for Red No. 19 one in 9 million at worst. The FDA explained that [it] had used conservative assumptions in deriving these figures, and it characterized the risks as "so trivial as to be effectively no risk." It concluded that the two dyes were safe. 51 Fed. Reg. at 28,344, 28,360. The court of appeals agreed with the FDA that the risks were extremely small, relying in part on comparative risk assessments:

> Assuming that the quantitative risk assessments are accurate, as we do for these purposes, it seems altogether correct to characterize these risks as trivial. . . . A consumer would run a one-in-a-million lifetime risk of cancer if he or she ate one peanut with the FDA-permitted level of aflatoxins once every 250 days (liver cancer). . . . Another activity posing a one-in-a-million lifetime risk is spending 1,000 minutes (less than 17 hours) every year in the city of Denver—with its high elevation and cosmic radiation levels—rather than in the District of Columbia. Most of us would not regard these as high-risk activities. Those who indulge in them can hardly be thought of as living dangerously. Indeed, they are risks taken without a second thought by persons whose economic position allows them a broad range of choice.
>
> According to the risk assessments here, the riskier dye poses one ninth as much risk as the peanut or Colorado hypothetical; the less risky one poses only one 19,000th as much.
>
> It may help put the one-in-a-million lifetime risk in perspective to compare it with a concededly dangerous activity, in which millions nonetheless engage, cigarette smoking. Each one-in-a-million risk amounts to less than one 200,000th the lifetime risk incurred by the average male smoker. J.A. 536, citing E. Crouch & R. Wilson, "Inter-Risk Comparisons," in J. Rodricks & R. Tardiff, eds., Assessment and Management of Chemical Risks 97, 105, 108 (1984). Thus, a person would have to be exposed to more than 2,000 chemicals bearing the one-in-a-million lifetime risk, at the rates assumed in the risk assessment, in order to reach 100th the risk involved in smoking. To reach that level of risk with chemicals equivalent to the less risky dye (Orange No. 17), he would have to be exposed to more than 40 million such chemicals. [831 F.2d 1108, 1111]

The court went on to note that the law does recognize as a general principle the idea of "the de minimis doctrine, shorthand for *de minimis non curat lex* ('the law does not concern itself with trifles')":

> The doctrine . . . serves a number of purposes. One is to spare agency resources for more important matters. But that is a goal of dubious relevance here. The finding of trivial risk necessarily followed not only the elaborate animal testing, but also the quantitative risk assessment process itself; indeed, application of the doctrine required additional expenditure of agency resources.
>
> More relevant is the concept that "notwithstanding the 'plain meaning' of a statute, a court must look beyond the words to the purpose of the act where its literal terms lead to 'absurd or futile results.'". . . . Imposition of pointless burdens on regulated entities is obviously to be avoided if possible, especially as burdens on them almost invariably entail losses for their customers: here, obviously, loss of access to the colors made possible by a broad range of dyes. We have employed the concept in construing the Clean Air Act's mandate to the Environmental Protection Agency to set standards providing "an ample margin of safety to protect the public health," 42 U.S.C. §7412(b)(1) (1982). That does not, we said, require limits assuring a "risk-free" environment. Rather, the agency must decide "what risks are acceptable in the world in which we live" and set limits accordingly. . . .
>
> Moreover, failure to employ a de minimis doctrine may lead to regulation that not only is "absurd or futile" in some general cost-benefit sense but also is directly contrary to the primary legislative goal. In a certain sense, precisely

that may be the effect here. The primary goal of the Act is human safety, but literal application of the Delaney Clause may in some instances increase risk. No one contends that the color additive Amendments impose a zero-risk standard for noncarcinogenic substances; if they did, the number of dyes passing muster might prove minuscule. As a result, makers of drugs and cosmetics who are barred from using a carcinogenic dye carrying a one-in-20-million lifetime risk may use instead a noncarcinogenic, but toxic, dye carrying, say, a one-in-10-million lifetime risk. The substitution appears to be a clear loss for safety. Judge Leventhal articulated the standard for application of de minimis as virtually a presumption in its favor: "Unless Congress has been extraordinarily rigid, there is likely a basis for an implication of de minimis authority to provide [an] exemption when the burdens of regulation yield a gain of trivial or no value." But the doctrine obviously is not available to thwart a statutory command; it must be interpreted with a view to "implementing the legislative design." Nor is an agency to apply it on a finding merely that regulatory costs exceed regulatory benefits. 831.F.2d 1108, 1112.

Notwithstanding these considerations, the court invalidated FDA's decision, finding that the Delaney Clause permitted no de minimis exception. The question, said the court, is ultimately one of what Congress meant in the statute. The language of the Delaney Clauses did not acknowledge any exception and was absolute in its language. The legislative history also supported the idea that Congress intended an absolute bar. "[S]hort of an explicit declaration in the statute barring use of a de minimis exception, this is perhaps as strong as it is likely to get. Facing [during congressional debate over the Clause] the explicit claim that the Clause was "extraordinarily rigid," . . . "Congress persevered."

> Moreover, our reading of the legislative history suggests some possible explanations for Congress' apparent rigidity. One is that Congress, and the nation in general (at least as perceived by Congress), appear to have been truly alarmed about the risks of cancer. . . . This concern resulted in a close focus on substances increasing cancer threats and a willingness to take extreme steps to lessen even small risks. . . .
> A second possible explanation for Congress' failure to authorize greater administrative discretion is that it perceived color additives as lacking any great value. For example, Congressman Delaney remarked, "color additives provide no nutrient value. They have no value at all, except so-called eye appeal." Color Additives Hearings at 108. Representative Sullivan said, "we like the bright and light [lipstick] shades but if they cannot safely be produced, then we prefer to do without these particular shades." . . . [T]here is evidence that Congress thought the public could get along without carcinogenic colors, especially in view of the existence of safer substitutes. Thus the legislators may have estimated the costs of an overly protective rule as trivial.
> So far as we can determine, no one drew the legislators' attention to the way in which the Delaney Clause, interacting with the flexible standard for determining safety of noncarcinogens, might cause manufacturers to substitute more dangerous toxic chemicals for less dangerous carcinogens. . . . But the obviously more stringent standard for carcinogens may rest on a view that cancer deaths are in some way more to be feared than others.
> Finally, as we have already noted, the House committee (or its amanuenses) considered the possibility that its no-threshold assumption might prove false and contemplated a solution: renewed consideration by Congress. Considering these circumstances—great concern over a specific health risk, the apparently low cost of protection, and the possibility of remedying any mistakes— Congress' enactment of an absolute rule seems less surprising. . . . 831 F.2d at 1117-1118.

NOTES AND QUESTIONS

1. The FDA's de minimis policy is but one of a variety of measures that the Agency has taken through the years, in an effort to breathe some flexibility into an extremely rigid piece of legislation. Richard Merrill has depicted the policy as part of the "FDA's decade-long efforts to reconcile Congress's language with circumstances Congress may not have foreseen and for which it surely did not provide." He summarizes the factors that have induced FDA to seek escape from Delaney's literal meaning:

> Improvements in analytic chemistry have enlarged the universe of compounds that FDA regulates as food (and color) additives. More extensive testing of chemicals and more sensitive protocols have enhanced toxicologists' ability to identify substances capable of producing tumors, including several substances adopted for food use years ago [e.g., saccharin, which had been in use since the early 1900s, but was not found to be carcinogenic in animals until the early 1970s]. Some of these substances gained market acceptance long before their carcinogenicity was discovered. In addition to these science-driven pressures on regulators, the public health community's concerns about the relationship between diet and cancer have shifted focus. A consensus has emerged that dietary patterns influence cancer incidence. Investigators have also revealed that the human food supply is full of substances (most occurring naturally) that have been, or may be, shown to cause cancer in laboratory animals. [Merrill, FDA's Implementation of the Delaney Clause: Repudiation of Congressional Choice or Reasoned Adaptation to Scientific Progress?, 5 Yale J. on Reg. 1, 2-3 (1988).]

2. What is the relevance of the last two points Professor Merrill makes? On these points, see also Gold, Slone, Stern, Manley & Ames, Rodent Carcinogens: Setting Priorities, 258 Science 261 (1992); Ames, Dietary Carcinogens and Anticarcinogens: Oxygen Radicals and Degenerative Diseases, 221 Science 1256 (1983); Committee on Diet, Nutrition, and Cancer, Commission on Life Sciences, National Research Council, National Academy of Sciences, Diet, Nutrition and Cancer: Directions for Research (1982). Professor Bruce Ames has argued that it is a serious mistake to focus regulatory attention and economic resources on removing extremely low risks of cancer associated with man-made chemicals because humans are exposed to much greater cancer risks from their dietary patterns and the consumption of natural carcinogens and anticarcinogens. See Ames, Ranking Possible Carcinogenic Hazards, 236 Science 271 (1987). How did Public Citizen v. Young address these comparative risk considerations?

3. Ames's suggestion that naturally occurring substances are consistently riskier than man-made substances has been challenged by some researchers. Two researchers from the Columbia University School of Public Health reexamined Ames's data by including allegedly more representative examples of synthetic chemicals and more consistent measures of exposure. Their results suggest that risks ranging from large to small are presented by both natural and synthetic substances. See Perera & Boffetta, Perspectives of Comparing Risks of Environmental Carcinogens, 80 J. Nat'l Cancer Inst. 1282 (1988). They argue that few natural substances have been tested for carcinogenesis and that Ames has exaggerated the risks of exposure to naturally occurring carcinogens.

4. Public Citizen v. Young dealt only with the Delaney Clause applicable to color additives in section 706 of the FDCA, 21 U.S.C. §376(B)(5)(B), and not

with the separate Delaney Clause applicable to food additives in section 409, 21 U.S.C. §348(c)(3)(A). The court noted that while "the clauses have almost identical wording, the context is clearly different" given the potentially greater social costs of banning certain food additives. 831 F.2d at 1117. Do you agree? Citing this statement, EPA interpreted the food additives Delaney Clause to permit a de minimis exception when it establishes tolerances for pesticide residues on processed foods under section 409. 56 Fed. Reg. 7,750 (1991). EPA argued that since FIFRA contains no Delaney Clause and no Delaney Clause applies to pesticide residues on nonprocessed foods under section 408 of the FDCA, it would be irrational to apply the Clause strictly to processed foods. The Ninth Circuit rejected EPA's argument. It held that the interpretation of the color additives Delaney Clause in Public Citizen v. Young was "equally applicable" to the statutory language in section 409. Les v. Reilly, 968 F.2d 985, 989 (9th Cir. 1992). Finding the statutory language to be "clear and mandatory," the court explained that the legislative history indicates that "Congress intended the very rigidity that the language it chose commands." Id. at 988, 989. The court refused EPA's invitation to distinguish between the color additives Delaney Clause and the clause governing food additives. It found that "Congress intended to ban all carcinogenic food additives, regardless of amount or significance of risk, as the only safe alternative." Id. at 989. Yet the court recognized that strict application of the Delaney Clause might not accomplish Congress's goal. It noted that consumers might switch to raw foods with pesticide residues that actually pose greater risks than the residues on processed foods that were at issue in the case.

5. The Clinton administration announced in May 1993 that it would seek to develop new food safety legislation in response to the *Les* decision. In June 1993, EPA, FDA, and the Department of Agriculture announced a major policy shift to promote reduced use of pesticides in food production. The agencies pledged a coordinated effort to remove high-risk pesticides from the market, and they endorsed integrated pest management, which emphasizes nonchemical pest-control alternatives. The new policy coincided with the release of a National Academy of Sciences report finding that existing regulatory policies failed to protect children adequately in light of their greater sensitivity to pesticide risks. NRC, Pesticides in the Diets of Infants and Children (1993). EPA had begun to consider reforms in the process for registering pesticides under FIFRA in July 1992 when the Agency requested public comment on how to structure regulatory incentives to encourage the development of safer pesticides. 57 Fed. Reg. 32,140 (1992). EPA indicated that it was considering accelerating the registration process for lower-risk pesticides and the possible restriction or removal of higher-risk pesticides for which safer substitutes become available. EPA policy that prohibits safety claims for pesticides also could be reconsidered in order to harness market forces to encourage the development of safer alternatives.

6. Concerned that EPA was not implementing the *Les* decision, NRDC subsequently sued EPA to force the elimination of carcinogenic residues on processed foods. In October 1994, EPA settled the lawsuit by agreeing to conduct an expedited review of previously approved uses for 36 pesticides believed to contain carcinogens. Cushman, EPA Settles Suit and Agrees to Move Against 36 Pesticides, N.Y. Times, Oct. 13, 1994, at A24. In February 1995, EPA announced that it would require that 34 pesticides be phased out of processed foods within two years and that it would review data on 87 other pesticides during the next five years. EPA's decision increased pressure in Congress to

reform the Delaney Clause. McCoy, EPA Agrees to Ban Pesticides, Comply with Rule in Food Act, Wall St. J., Feb. 9, 1995, at B16.

7. In deciding Les v. Reilly, the court noted the cogency of the arguments for the EPA's position but held that the Delaney Clause was clear, categorical, and dispositive. "If there is to be a change," the court added, "it is for Congress to direct." 968 F.2d at 990. The prospect that numerous high-volume pesticides would be removed from the market prompted the consensus enactment of the Food Quality Protection Act (FQPA) in 1996. The FQPA amended the food additives Delaney Clause to specify that it does not include pesticide chemical residues in raw or processed foods. 21 U.S.C. §321(s). Such residues are now governed by a new, health-based standard of "reasonable certainty of no harm," and this standard is extended to raw foods on which a much wider range of pesticides typically are used than the 80 to 100 chemicals used on processed foods. Advocates of strict tolerances for pesticides on foods were willing to forego the application of Delaney to pesticide residues on processed foods in return for the application of the new standard for pesticide residues on both raw and processed foods. The new standard requires "a reasonable certainty that no harm will result from aggregate exposure to the pesticide chemical residue, including all dietary exposures and all other exposures for which there is reliable information." Language in the legislative history, but not in the statute, suggests this reflects a policy to limit individual cancer risks to the exposed population to no greater than 1-in-1-million additional lifetime risk, although industry representatives are urging a more flexible interpretation. The FQPA also provides for a less onerous, expedited registration process for "minor use" pesticides, defined as those that are used on commercial crops where the crop is smaller than 300,000 acres, for which no alternative pesticides are available, and where other requirements are met. It also establishes some tolerance setting flexibility for such pesticides, which expose a smaller population to risk than higher-volume pesticides do. As of August 2002, the EPA had reassessed 6,493 tolerances out of a total of 9,721. The product of these reviews has been to raise 334 tolerances, leave 3,544 unchanged, lower 286, and revoke 2,238. EPA Tolerance Reassessment Status, *http://www.epa.gov/pesticides/tolerance/tolerance_statistics* (last viewed Sept. 9, 2005).

8. How persuasive were the reasons for applying the Delaney Clause to food additives, as opposed to color additives, in the first place? Is the FQPA an improvement over the Delaney Clause approach to carcinogens in food additives?

9. In addition to the de minimis argument to which the court devoted most of its attention in Public Citizen v. Young, the Justice Department also argued that the two color additives did not "induce cancer within the meaning of the Delaney Clause," despite the FDA's previous finding to the contrary. This position, which "is difficult to reconcile with FDA's historical view, shared by other agencies, that high-dose animal tests are a reliable means for identifying human cancer hazards," Merrill, FDA's Implementation of the Delaney Clause: Repudiation of Congressional Choice or Reasoned Adaptation to Scientific Progress?, 5 Yale J. on Reg. 1, 85 (1988), was not taken seriously by the court.

B. ACCEPTABLE RISK AND SECTION 112 OF THE CLEAN AIR ACT

The Delaney Clauses administered by the FDA are rare instances of a "zero-risk" regulatory scheme under current environmental laws. Until the Clean Air

Act was amended in 1990, the section of the Clean Air Act regulating hazardous air pollutants, section 112, had been interpreted as another example of a zero-risk statute because it required EPA to provide an "ample margin of safety to protect the public health."

In Natural Resources Defense Council v. EPA, 824 F.2d 1146 (D.C. Cir. 1987) *(Vinyl Chloride)*, a unanimous U.S. Court of Appeals sitting en banc addressed the meaning of section 112. It held that to determine what constitutes an "ample margin of safety" the EPA "Administrator [must] make an initial determination of what is 'safe.' This determination must be based exclusively upon the Administrator's determination of the risk to health at a particular emission level." The court emphasized that "the Administrator's decision does not require a finding that 'safe' means 'risk-free,'" citing Justice Stevens' observation in the *Benzene* decision that few people consider many daily activities that entail risk (such as driving a car or breathing city air) to be unsafe. Instead, the court found only that "the Administrator's decision must be based upon an expert judgment with regard to the level of emission that will result in an 'acceptable' risk to health" and that "[t]his determination must be based solely upon the risk to health."

The *Vinyl Chloride* case indicated that EPA must decide what constitutes an "ample margin of safety" through a two-step process. In the first step, EPA must determine what is a safe level of emissions without considering costs or techno-logical feasibility. In the second step, EPA may then consider costs and feasibility in determining how far to go beyond mere "safety" in providing an "ample margin" of same. Because EPA had not applied this two-step approach in two other pending regulations involving hazardous air pollutants—a standard for radionuclides promulgated only after EPA had been held in contempt of court and a standard for benzene emissions—it withdrew them as well as the vinyl chloride standard. EPA's first opportunity to respond to the *Vinyl Chloride* decision came when it reproposed the benzene standard in July 1988.

The D.C. Circuit's *Vinyl Chloride* decision forced EPA to confront the "how safe is safe" question head on, and when it announced its reproposed benzene standard it requested public comment on four possible approaches for deter-mining what constitutes an "acceptable risk." 53 Fed. Reg. 28,496 (1988). Approach A, called the "Case-by-Case Approach," proposed to base acceptable risk decisions on case-by-case consideration of levels of individual risk (proba-bility of an exposed individual's getting cancer), population risk (number of predicted cases of cancer when average individual risk is multiplied by the number of exposed individuals), the distribution of risks among exposed popu-lations, and the uncertainties involved, without establishing any hard-and-fast rules. Approach B, called the "Incidence" or "Population Risk Approach," would deem acceptable one case of cancer per year per source category. Approach C would deem an individual risk of 1 in 10,000 to be acceptable, while Approach D would accept an individual risk of 1 in 1 million.

Three of these four approaches are represented in Figure 3.11, which is adapted from a figure in EPA's Federal Register notice. The x-axis represents the size of the exposed population (ranging from 1 to 70 million); levels of individual risk (ranging from 1 in 1 million to 1 in one thousand) appear on the y-axis. The one-cancer-per-year "Incidence" or "Population Risk" approach (Approach B) appears as the line descending from left to right, while the "Individual Risk" approaches of 1 in 10,000 (Approach C) and 1 in 1 million (Approach D) appear as the horizontal lines.

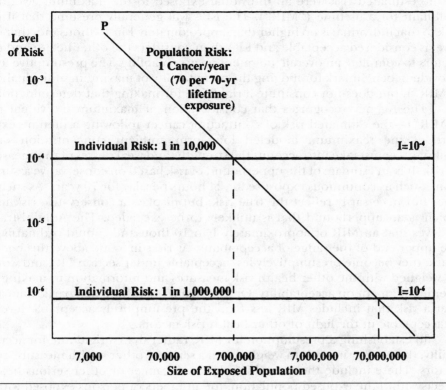

FIGURE 3.11
Approaches for Determining Acceptable Risk:
Population Risk & Individual Risk

In 1989, EPA reached a final decision on its proposed standards for controlling benzene emissions under section 112, which it announced in the following Federal Register notice. The General Counsel of EPA at the time described the contents of the final rule as representing the state-of-the-art thinking on how to determine acceptable or significant risk. What follows is an excerpt from EPA's final rule.

║ *EPA, National Emission Standards for Hazardous*
║ *Air Pollutants; Benzene Emissions from Maleic*
║ *Anhydride Plants, Ethylbenzene/Styrene Plants, Benzene*
║ *Storage Vessels, Benzene Equipment Leaks,*
║ *and Coke By-Product Recovery Plants*
║ **54 Fed. Reg. 38,044 (1989)**

SELECTION OF APPROACH

Based on the comments and the record developed in the rulemaking. EPA has selected an approach, based on Approaches A and C but also incorporating consideration of incidence from Approach B and consideration of health protection for the general population on the order of 1 in 1 million from Approach D. Thus, in the first step of the *Vinyl Chloride* inquiry, EPA will consider the extent of the estimated risk were an individual exposed to the maximum level of a pollutant for a lifetime ("MIR"). The EPA will generally presume that if the risk to that individual is no higher than approximately 1 in 10 thousand, that risk level is considered acceptable and EPA then considers the other health and risk factors to complete an overall judgment on acceptability. The presumptive level provides a benchmark for judging the acceptability of maximum individual risk ("MIR"), but does not constitute a rigid line for making that determination.

The Agency recognizes that consideration of maximum individual risk ("MIR")—the estimated risk of contracting cancer following a lifetime exposure at the maximum, modeled long-term ambient concentration of a pollutant—must take into account the strengths and weaknesses of this measure of risk. It is an estimate of the upperbound of risk based on conservative assumptions, such as continuous exposure for 24 hours per day for 70 years. As such, it does not necessarily reflect the true risk, but displays a conservative risk level which is an upperbound that is unlikely to be exceeded. The Administrator believes that an MIR of approximately 1 in 10 thousand should ordinarily be the upper end of the range of acceptability. As risks increase above this benchmark, they become presumptively less acceptable under section 112, and would be weighed with the other health risk measures and information in making an overall judgment on acceptability. Or, the Agency may find, in a particular case, that a risk that includes MIR less than the presumptively acceptable level is unacceptable in the light of other health risk factors.

In establishing a presumption for MIR, rather than a rigid line for acceptability, the Agency intends to weigh it with a series of other health measures and factors. These include the overall incidence of cancer or other serious health effects within the exposed population, the numbers of persons exposed within each individual lifetime risk range and associated incidence within, typically, a 50 km exposure radius around facilities, the science policy assumptions and estimation uncertainties associated with the risk measures, weight of the scientific evidence for human health effects, other quantified or unquantified health effects, effects due to co-location of facilities, and co-emission of pollutants.

The EPA also considers incidence (the numbers of persons estimated to suffer cancer or other serious health effects as a result of exposure to a pollutant) to be an important measure of the health risk to the exposed population. Incidence measures the extent of health risk to the exposed population as a whole, by providing an estimate of the occurrence of cancer or other serious health effects in the exposed population. The EPA believes that even if the MIR is low, the overall risk may be unacceptable if significant numbers of persons are exposed to a hazardous air pollutant, resulting in a significant estimated incidence. Consideration of this factor would not be reduced to a specific limit or range, such as the 1 case/ year limit included in proposed Approach B, but estimated incidence would be weighed along with other health risk information in judging acceptability.

The limitations of MIR and incidence are put into perspective by considering how these risks are distributed within the exposed population. This information includes both individual risk, including the number of persons exposed within each risk range, as well as the incidence associated with the persons exposed within each risk range. In this manner, the distribution provides an array of information on individual risk and incidence for the exposed population.

Particular attention will also be accorded to the weight of evidence presented in the risk assessment of potential human carcinogenicity or other health effects of a pollutant. While the same numerical risk may be estimated for an exposure to a pollutant judged to be a known human carcinogen, and to a pollutant considered a possible human carcinogen based on limited animal test data, the same weight cannot be accorded to both estimates. In considering the potential public health effects of the two pollutants, the Agency's judgment on acceptability, including the MIR, will be influenced by the greater weight of evidence for the known human carcinogen.

In the *Vinyl Chloride* decision, the Administrator is directed to determine a "safe" or "acceptable" risk level, based on a judgment of "what risks are acceptable in the world in which we live." 824 F.2d at 1165. To aid in this inquiry, the Agency compiled and presented a "Survey of Societal Risk" in its July 1988 proposal (53 FR 28512-28513). As described there, the survey developed information to place risk estimates in perspective, and to provide background and context for the Administrator's judgment on the acceptability of risks "in the world in which we live." Individual risk levels in the survey ranged from 10^{-1} to 10^{-7} (that is, the lifetime risk of premature death ranged from 1 in 10 to 1 in 10 million), and incidence levels ranged from less than 1 case/year to estimates as high as 5,000 to 20,000 cases/year. The EPA concluded from the survey that no specific factor in isolation could be identified as defining acceptability under all circumstances, and that the acceptability of a risk depends on consideration of a variety of factors and conditions. However, the presumptive levels established for MIR of approximately 1 in 10 thousand is within the range for individual risk in the survey, and provides health protection at a level lower than many other risks common "in the world in which we live." And, this presumptive level also comports with many previous health risk decisions by EPA premised on controlling maximum individual risks to approximately 1 in 10 thousand and below.

In today's decision, EPA has selected an approach based on the judgment that the first step judgment on acceptability cannot be reduced to any single factor. The EPA believes that the level of the MIR, the distribution of risks in the exposed population, incidence, the science policy assumptions and uncertainties associated with the risk measures, and the weight of evidence that a pollutant is harmful to health are all important factors to be considered in the acceptability judgment. The EPA concludes that the approach selected best incorporates all of this vital health information, and enables it to weigh them appropriately in making a judgment. In contrast, the single measure Approaches B, C, and D, while providing simple decisionmaking criteria, provide an incomplete set of health information for decisions under section 112. The Administrator believes that the acceptability of risk under section 112 is best judged on the basis of a broad set of health risk measures and information. As applied in practice, the EPA's approach is more protective of public health than any single factor approach. In the case of the benzene sources regulated here, more than 99 percent of the population living within 50 km would be exposed to risks no greater than approximately 1 in 1 million; and, the total number of cases of death or disease estimated to result would be kept low.

Under the two-step process specified in the *Vinyl Chloride* decision, the second step determines an "ample margin of safety," the level at which the standard is set. This is the important step of the standard-setting process of which the actual level of public health protection is established. The first step consideration of acceptability is only a starting point for the analysis, in which a floor for the ultimate standard is set. The standard set at the second step is the legally enforceable limit that must be met by a regulated facility.

Even though the risks judged "acceptable" by EPA in the first step of the *Vinyl Chloride* inquiry are already low, the second step of the inquiry, determining an "ample margin of safety," again includes consideration of all of the health factors, and whether to reduce the risks even further. In the second step, EPA strives to provide protection to the greatest number of persons possible to an individual lifetime risk level no higher than approximately 1 in 1 million. In the ample margin decision, the Agency again considers all of the health risks and other health information considered in the first step. Beyond that information, additional factors relating to the appropriate level of control will also be considered, including costs and economic impacts of controls, technological feasibility, uncertainties, and any other relevant factors. Considering all of these factors, the Agency will establish the standard at a level that provides an ample margin of safety to protect the public health, as required by section 112.

NOTES AND QUESTIONS

1. Recall the four approaches to answering the "how safe is safe" question that EPA initially had proposed. Which of these approaches do you think the public favored? Which approach would be favored by industry? By regulators? Why?

2. One result of employing the Incidence Approach (Approach B) would be that the level of protection for any individual would depend on how densely populated the surrounding area is. As can be seen from Figure 3.11, very high levels of individual risk (e.g., 1 in 1,000) could be tolerated for (e.g., a community of 70,000) while far lower levels (e.g., less than 1 in 100,000) would be required in large metropolitan areas (e.g., New York City). Would this approach unfairly discriminate against individuals living in rural areas?

3. Why do you think EPA chose a combination of the four approaches for making "ample margin of safety" determinations rather than adhering to a single approach? Does EPA's policy provide adequate guidance concerning how the Agency will make ample margin of safety determinations in the future, or does it simply confirm existing ad hoc practices? Would it be desirable for EPA to follow a less flexible, but more certain, policy for making such decisions?

4. How flexible do you think EPA will be in determining what levels of individual risk constitute an "ample margin of safety"? In applying its new approach to regulation of benzene source categories, EPA determined not to tighten controls on ethylbenzene-styrene process vents. EPA's decision left some individuals exposed to a maximum individual risk of 1 in 50,000 from this source, because the total numbers of such people were small enough that the incidence of cancer produced by this source category was estimated to be 1 case of cancer every 300 years. 54 Fed. Reg. 38,046. EPA decided to reduce emissions from benzene storage vessels by 20 to 60 percent to lower the estimated maximum individual risk from this source from a range of 1 in 2,500 to 1 in 25,000 to a level of 1 in 33,000, reducing the estimated incidence of cancer from this source from 1 case every 10 to 20 years to 1 case every 25 years. Id. at 38,047. For coke by-product recovery plants, EPA promulgated a standard that it estimated would reduce benzene emissions from this source by 97 percent. However, even at this reduced level the maximum individual risk would be

1 in 5,000, a risk greater than the 1 in 10,000 benchmark of EPA's overall approach. EPA sought to justify this decision by noting that it reflected a significant reduction in MIR from current levels and by stressing uncertainties in emissions estimates. EPA noted that the standard for coke byproduct recovery plants would reduce MIR from an estimated current level of 7 in 1,000 (which is estimated to be responsible for 2 cases of cancer per year) to 1 in 5,000 and a cancer incidence of 1 case every 20 years. The Agency described this as "comparable" to the 1 in 10,000 benchmark in light of "estimating uncertainties in this case," which it believed to have resulted in an overestimation of actual levels of benzene emissions from this source. Id. EPA also determined not to tighten controls on benzene equipment leaks, despite previous estimates that emissions from this source category presented an MIR of 6 in 10,000 and 1 case of cancer every five years. EPA concluded that actual emissions levels were substantially lower than its previous estimates. Although the Agency was not able to calculate actual emissions levels, it expressed the view that "the resulting MIR would be comparable to the benchmark of approximately 1 in 10,000." Id. at 38,048.

5. More recently, when EPA interpreted the food additives Delaney Clause of section 409 of the FDCA to contain a de minimis exception, see page 270, the Agency stated that it would consider three factors in deciding what constitutes a "trivial risk": "the weight of the evidence regarding carcinogenicity, the size of the population exposed to the risk, and the level of the risk." 56 Fed. Reg. 7,750, 7,754 (1991). EPA stated that "the risk comparisons most relevant to such an exercise are the prior decisions of the regulatory agencies" because they are the products of a public process. Id. at 7,757. After reviewing how the "how safe is safe" issue had been addressed in other contexts, EPA concluded that when the entire U.S. population is exposed to a probable human carcinogen, "the agency consensus appears to be that risks less than 1 in 1 million generally can be found to be acceptable without consideration of other factors while risks greater than that level require further analysis as to their acceptability." Id. Is this approach consistent with the policy articulated in EPA's NESHAP for benzene?

6. In 1990, Congress substantially revised section 112. The 1990 Amendments require EPA to establish technology-based controls on an initial list of 189 toxic air pollutants specified in section 112(b)(1). These standards are to reflect use of the maximum achievable control technology (MACT). Congress gave EPA ten years to write all the MACT standards. By the fall of 2003, EPA had issued nearly 100 standards—nearly 10 a year—a far greater rate of success than it had had under the health-based predecessor statute. Still, EPA fell behind the strict statutory deadlines early on, and this triggered section 112's "hammer" provision, requiring any source emitting a section 112 toxic for which a categorical MACT had not been issued to apply to its state air quality agency for a "case-by-case" MACT determination by May 15, 2002. §112(j). Industrial groups challenged EPA's interpretation of the hammer provision, and EPA entered into a settlement agreement with industry groups that divided the case-by-case submission process into two parts, and effectively extended the section 112(j) deadline until May, 2004—the date by which EPA anticipated finishing the categorical MACT rules—by making that the deadline for the second and more burdensome part of the submission. 67 Fed. Reg. 16,582 (April 5, 2002). The Sierra Club then challenged these rules as inconsistent with the plain language of the Act and EPA, fearful that its 2002 rules might be vacated, entered into a series of complex negotiations and settlement agreements with the Sierra

Club. These agreements covered issues in MACT implementation beyond the deadline issues. One of the more contentious of these issues has been how to interpret the so-called "MACT floor" provisions of section 112. Those provisions provide that the technology-based standard EPA issues for existing sources in any industrial category cannot be less stringent than the "best performing 12%" of that category, and that the standard for new sources cannot be less stringent than the control achieved in practice by the single best-controlled similar plant. While EPA is close to complying with the negotiated deadlines for MACTs, some of the last to be issued, for industrial boilers, hazardous waste combustors, and electric utilities, have been delayed due to lawsuits that have successfully challenged how EPA has interpreted the MACT floor provisions. A second point of contention has been EPA's decision to exempt some categories from MACT if they can be shown to be causing minimal risk. EPA has incorporated this risk-based exemption into its final rule for industrial boilers, and environmental groups are challenging the exemption, claiming that it violates the statute, which requires technology-based controls to be installed regardless of risk levels, allowing such risk considerations to come into play only when EPA moves to the second stage of hazardous air pollutant controls. See Environmentalists Question EPA Review of Risk-Based Air Toxics Rule, Inside EPA (Aug. 19, 2005). In that second phase, EPA must examine whether the "residual risk" that remains after MACT standards have been met warrants still stricter controls, in order to ensure the "ample margin of safety" required by the pre-1990 version of section 112. By statute, EPA must apply further controls on emissions of any toxic air pollutant if the most exposed individual faces more than a one-in-one-million lifetime cancer risk. What is the relevance of EPA's 1989 rule after the 1990 Amendments? See section 112(f)(2).

7. EPA's track record in implementing health-based standards is not encouraging. EPA promulgated national emissions standards for only seven hazardous air pollutants in the first 20 years after enactment of section 112. One interpretation of this history is that EPA's difficulties were the result of its reluctance to implement what is perceived to be an unreasonably stringent statutory standard. EPA argues that some balancing of cost and economic considerations against protection of public health is inevitable in making regulatory decisions for controlling toxic substances.

While EPA would prefer statutory authorities that permit a more explicit balancing of risks against costs, EPA's track record for implementing TSCA, which requires such balancing, is no better than its record for implementing section 112. EPA regulated only a few toxic substances under section 6 of TSCA, just as under section 112 of the Clean Air Act. EPA's most comprehensive regulation under section 6 of TSCA—the phaseout of commercial uses of asbestos—took a decade for EPA to complete and then was struck down by the Fifth Circuit in *Corrosion Proof Fittings.*

8. Why has EPA had such a dismal track record in implementing statutes to control toxic substances? Does the problem lie with the way EPA's statutory authorities are structured, or is it simply a result of the way EPA has chosen to implement these authorities? Do the statutes that EPA must implement place impossible informational demands on the Agency? Wendy Wagner calculates that EPA and OSHA issued less than 15 percent of the standards Congress required them to promulgate during the 1970s and 1980s under science-based statutory mandates. Wagner, The Science Charade in Toxic Risk Regulation, 95 Colum. L. Rev. 1613, 1614-1615 (1995).

9. Health-based standards are largely a product of the notion that life is too precious to compromise for economic gain. When Senator Mitchell articulated this principle during the debate on the 1990 Clean Air Act Amendments, George Will wrote a column describing it as "useful nonsense." Will explains that "[i]t is useful to talk that way, thereby inclining our minds to place high value on life, precisely because we constantly must act in ways that cause that value to be jostled and compromised by competing values." George Will, Suddenly: The American Idea Abroad and at Home, 1986-1990 206 (1990).

10. When EPA chose to adopt a multi-factor approach to acceptable risk, it might have drawn on the field of cognitive psychology to have identified even more relevant factors. Research in this area suggests that when people think about risk, many qualitative factors are relevant to their evaluation, in addition to the quantitative measures that are the exclusive focus of QRAs. Among the important distinctions, people have been found to accept voluntary risks more readily than involuntarily imposed risks, dispersed risks more readily than concentrated risks, and risks that have received little media coverage more than risks that have been heavily covered in the news. Figure 3.12 captures some of the significant risk traits that influence people's evaluations of risk.

The fact that people incorporate these qualitative elements of risk into their assessments of risk situations is undeniable, and it sets up a tension

FIGURE 3.12
Qualitative Elements of Risk

Risk Traits	Aggravating	Mitigating
Familiarity	New	Old
Personal control	Uncontrollable	Controllable
Voluntariness	Involuntary	Voluntary
Media attention	Heavy media coverage	No media coverage
Equity	Unevenly distributed	Evenly distributed
Impact on children	Children at special risk	Children not at risk
Impact on future generations	Future generations at risk	Future generations not at risk
Reversibility	Irreversible	Reversible
Identifiability of victims	Victims known	Victims unknown
Accompanying benefits	Benefits invisible	Benefits clear
Source	Human-generated	Natural origins
Trust in relevant institutions	Low trust in institutions	High trust in institutions
Immediacy of adverse effects	Adverse effects immediate	Adverse effects delayed
Understanding	Mechanisms poorly understood	Mechanisms well understood
Precedents	History of accidents	No past accidents

Note: The first column lists certain important risk traits. The second lists the conditions that make the risk more threatening and, hence, less acceptable, holding all else constant. The third lists the conditions that reduce the threat of the risk, making it more tolerable.

Source: Timur Kuran and Cass Sunstein, Availability Heuristics and Risk Regulation, 51 Stanford Law Review 683, 709 (1999).

between the way experts tend to view risk and the way laypersons do. "To the experts, risk means expected annual mortality. But to the public . . . risk means much more than that. Let's redefine terms. Call [population risk] 'hazard.' Call all the other factors, collectively, 'outrage.' Risk, then, is the sum of hazard and outrage. . . . We have two decades of data indicating that voluntariness, control, fairness, and the rest are important components of our society's definition of risk. When a risk manager continues to ignore these factors—and continues to be surprised by the public's response of outrage—it is worth asking whose behavior is irrational." Sandman, Risk Communication: Facing Public Outrage, EPA J. 21-22 (Nov. 1987).

Do these considerations help explain why EPA refused to settle on a one-dimensional definition of risk? Do they help explain some of the reactions to risk and risk regulation decisions discussed in this chapter?

PROBLEM EXERCISE: REGULATION OF TOXIC SUBSTANCES

Assume that the U.S. Department of Health and Human Services determines on the basis of the results of animal bioassays that chemical X is a probable human carcinogen. HHS lists the chemical as a substance reasonably anticipated to be a carcinogen in its Annual Report on Carcinogens.

Question One. Under what statutory authority could chemical X be regulated when it is used as: (a) an industrial solvent, (b) a pesticide, (c) a food or color additive, (d) a contaminant in drinking water, and (e) an air pollutant?

Question Two. What additional information, if any, would EPA, OSHA, or PDA need in order to be able to regulate chemical X under each of the statutes that authorize regulation of it for each of the five uses listed above? Why?

Question Three. How stringently could chemical X be regulated under each of the statutes that authorize regulation of it?

The "Sound Science" Debates

Science has become heavily embedded in the regulatory and policy processes. With respect to regulatory toxic substances, scientific conclusions are critical to the modern process of quantitative risk assessment. Yet as the examples in this chapter and elsewhere in the casebook illustrate, science seldom if ever can provide a definitive answer to significant questions that arise at each stage of the risk assessment process. If the lack of a definitive answer can be used to cast the scientific basis of a regulatory action into enough doubt, the action may have to be delayed or even abandoned. One way to question science is to ask whether scientific conclusions are based on the best available research techniques and the best available scientific theories. Another is to take advantage of the inevitable disagreements in science about important conclusions to argue that an insufficient consensus exists to justify government action. Because such opportunities present themselves frequently in regulatory decision making, it cannot be too surprising that "science itself has increasingly become the battleground of choice for determining what regulatory actions the government will take." Chris Mooney, Interrogations—Thanks to a Little-Known

Piece of Legislation, Scientists at the EPA and Other Agencies Find Their Work Questioned Not Only by Industry, But by Their Own Government, Boston Globe, Aug. 28, 2005.

Both the regulated community and the environmental community have raised challenges to regulatory decisions through arguments about science. On the environmental side, when the White House instructed EPA to delete from a 2003 report on the environment references to a study showing sharp increases in global temperature and to replace them with a study financed by the American Petroleum Institute that questioned those increases, environmentalists were quick to charge the White House with ignoring the virtual consensus within the scientific community that global warming is occurring. Andrew C. Revkin & Katharine Q. Seelye, Report by EPA Leaves Out Data on Climate Change, June 19, 2003. Similarly, a group of state attorneys general charged that EPA was ignoring evidence that established a scientific basis for regulating carbon dioxide as a greenhouse gas. EPA responded both with statutory and policy arguments for not regulating carbon dioxide and by citing a National Research Council study concluding that "a causal linkage" between carbon dioxide and other greenhouse gas emissions and global warming "cannot be unequivocally established." Massachusetts v. EPA, 415 F.3d 50 (D.C. Cir. 2005).

On the other hand, the regulated community often contends that EPA manipulates or ignores science to justify decisions they are making for primarily political reasons. See, e.g, Michael Gough, Politicizing Science (2003) (eleven case studies). Frequently the objections of the regulated community proceed under the banner of the call for "sound science." "The difficulty of allocating limited resources for maximizing risk reduction is compounded," they argue, "by the common failure of agencies to base their analyses on the most advanced scientific principles. Without sound science, risks cannot be accurately assessed and effectively compared." The Business Roundtable, Toward Smarter Regulation 14 (1994). The regulated community's most consistent criticism of risk assessment is the notion that it employs assumptions that are too conservative, resulting in unreasonably stringent regulation. This argument was made most vociferously by the Office of Management and Budget during the G.H.W. Bush administration. OMB made three general arguments:

1. The continued reliance on conservative (worst-case) assumptions distorts risk assessment, yielding estimates that may overstate likely risks by several orders of magnitude. . . .
2. Conservative biases embedded in risk assessment impart a substantial "margin of safety." The choice of an appropriate margin of safety should remain the province of responsible risk-management officials, and should not be preempted through biased risk assessments. . . .
3. Conservatism in risk assessment distorts the regulatory priorities of the Federal Government, directing societal resources to reduce what are often trivial carcinogenic risks while failing to address more substantial threats to life and health. [OMB, Regulatory Program of the United States Government for Fiscal Year 1991 14 (1990).]

After reviewing OMB's critique, the Center for Risk Analysis at the Harvard School of Public Health concluded that it "does not present a balanced, accurate critique" of actual risk assessment practices by federal agencies. They noted that although OMB emphasizes the use of "worst case" assumptions, it does not mention the many factors that may cause risk assessments to seriously underestimate actual risks. Most risk assessments do not consider all exposure pathways, all hazard endpoints, or the possible synergistic effects of the multiple pollutants to which humans are exposed. Some human subpopulations may be more sensitive to the toxic effects of certain substances than the animal species typically tested in bioassays. Moreover, in arguing for the use of "most likely" estimates of risk, the OMB report confuses this concept with "expected value" estimates, which generally are not equivalent. Center for Risk Analysis, Comments on OMB, Current Regulatory Issues in Risk Assessment and Management (Dec. 17, 1990).

The notion that risk assessment is inherently too cautious has been contradicted in several instances by discoveries that certain substances pose substantially greater risks than originally thought. For example, as indicated in Figure 3.13, scientists' definition of lead poisoning has been ratcheted downward substantially over the last three decades as new information has revealed that levels previously thought to be safe posed significant risks to health. Moreover, because individual variability in susceptibility to risks is high, if risks associated with chemical exposure are relative, rather than simply additive, as data suggest for radiation-induced tumors, Storer, Mitchell & Mitchell, Extrapolation of the Relative Risk of Radiogenic Neoplasms Across Mouse Strains to Man, 114 Radiation Res. 331 (1988), then susceptible individuals face much greater

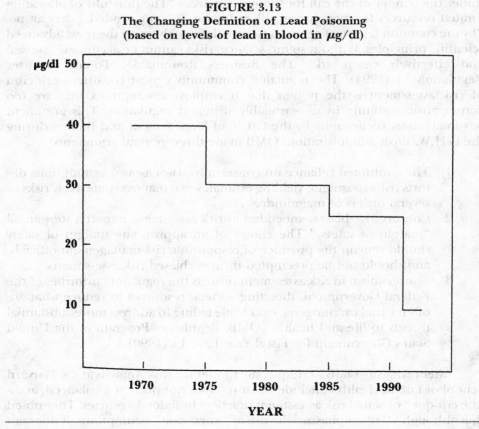

FIGURE 3.13
The Changing Definition of Lead Poisoning
(based on levels of lead in blood in μg/dl)

additional risks from chemical exposure than are reflected in current risk assessments. Hoel, A Balanced Approach to Risk Assessment, 7 Toxicology & Indus. Health 305, 310 (1991).

More generally, when the regulated community insists on "sound science," it often is asserting or implying that agencies like EPA are simply not using the best science, the latest theories, or the most recent studies. One venue where this claim has been raised repeatedly has been the regulation of human carcinogens, where EPA and other agencies almost always rely upon laboratory experiments of the effects of those substances on animals, followed by the use of mathematical models to extrapolate from high-dose responses to low-dose responses. Each of the default assumptions or inferential bridges found in the risk-assessment process constitutes a point of potential vulnerability inviting the charge that science has now advanced to the point that the default ought to be replaced by scientific findings. See the discussion of default assumptions, pages 205-211. The regulated community has persistently contested the validity of the translation of animal data to humans, so far without success. It has also regularly argued that the use of extrapolation models that assume there is no safe threshold of exposure to a carcinogen ought to be abandoned, asserting that studies of the ways in which carcinogens contribute to the process of carcinogenesis can demonstrate threshold levels. See the *Chlorine Chemistry Council* decision and the accompanying discussion of EPA's evolving acceptance of a no-effects threshold for a carcinogen. Pages 211-213. The regulated community generally disfavors relying upon animal studies whether dealing with carcinogens or noncarcinogens, because of the practice of adding an uncertainty factor of 10 when extrapolating from animal data to humans. See page 207. The regulated community tends to prefer epidemiological studies that examine defined human populations that have already been exposed to a substance, rather than animal studies, for this reason. Failure to adopt models that employ no-effects thresholds or failure to give priority to epidemiological studies will often be challenged as a failure to adopt sound science.

One illustration of how much is at stake in some sound science debates comes from the EPA's continual reevaluation of the risks of dioxin. Dioxin is a by-product from the manufacture of chlorophenoxyacetic acids, which revolutionized agriculture after WW II because they are wide-spectrum and yet selective herbicides. Two of these herbicides were used extensively in the Vietnam War as a forest defoliant, in a combination called Agent Orange. In 1973, it was discovered that a contractor had used waste oil containing dioxin as a dust suppressant on the roadways of Times Beach, Missouri. Following a number of horse deaths in the area, the CDC traced the cause to the presence of dioxin. Eventually, the town was evacuated and the federal government purchased the properties. In 1976, an industrial accident in Seveso, Italy was followed by cases of acute chemical burns that were also traced to dioxin. These events stimulated efforts to describe the risks associated with dioxin. A number of studies were done, almost all of which have been disregarded as the years have gone by, because their research designs are no longer considered adequate to provide reliable findings. One two-year study, however, sponsored by Dow Chemical (the manufacturer of Agent Orange), was designed so well that it effectively became a gold standard for animal bioassays.

EPA has now been struggling with dioxin risk assessments and reassessments for about two decades, and is now on its third revision of its dioxin risk reassessment (2003 draft). In each of these reassessments, the original Dow study continues to be relied upon as the best empirical evidence available. The reassessments have been prompted entirely because of challenges to the *interpretation* of that study's data, which depends upon modeling. Scientists regularly reappraise the circumstances in which one of the 15 or so different models is the best to use in describing low-dose human health effects. "In the case of dioxin, applying the data from the [Dow] study, both the multistage model used by EPA and the quadratic model, which fits the data equally well, produces a difference in [estimate of risk] of over one thousand-fold [at low levels]. Obviously, the choice of the model becomes a factor, if not the critical factor, in identifying a dose associated with an acceptable level of risk. . . . The practical implications of [decisions to use various models] in assessing dioxin risks can be seen when the various regulatory decisions and interpretations between 1984 and 2000 regarding the daily dioxin dose required to increase the estimated lifetime risk of contracting cancer by one in 1 million ranges from .001 to 10.0 picograms/kg. These various standards and guidelines span three [sic] orders of magnitude over nearly three decades despite the fact that these values are based on the same data set and use many of the same assumptions." Wright, Long & Aylward, Twenty Five Years of Dioxin Cancer Risk Assessment, 19 SPG Nat. Resources & Env't 31, 33, 35 (2005). Each of those reinterpretations have come about because of controversies over which model to use, with the weight of scientific opinion changing from time to time.

In addition to attacks made on regulatory actions based on sound science concerns, such concerns have been used extensively by the G.W. Bush administration itself as reasons for not regulating—see the discussion of carbon dioxide regulation above—or for reevaluating regulatory actions—see the arsenic case study, pages 253-262. By and large, however, close analysis of EPA decisions has found that "[a]fter more than [30] years of vigorous public health and safety regulation . . . there are surprisingly few examples of EPA using unreliable science or using science inappropriately to support a final regulation." Wendy Wagner, The "Bad Science" Fiction: Reclaiming the Debate Over the Role of Science in Public Health and Environmental Regulation, 66 L. & C. P. 63, 72 (2003). This suggests that the point of contention in sound science debates is more frequently a policy or political disagreement. Sometimes it is prompted by wanting to impose a higher burden of proof on government to demonstrate a clear causal connection between exposure and human health effects. This essentially recapitulates the debate over a precautionary approach to regulatory action embodied in decisions like *Ethyl Corp.*, pages 175-177. Sometimes it is prompted by the belief that giving a different priority to different scientific methods or recognizing different scientific theories will systematically produce better regulatory outcomes for the regulated community. None of these disagreements can be resolved purely as a matter of science, but science is the battlefield upon which they are often fought.

Reducing Risk through Comparative Risk Assessment?: The Case of Radon

Some have argued that protection of public health and the environment could be improved by using comparative risk assessment to readjust regulatory priorities to focus on problems posing the greatest risks. In 1990, EPA's Science Advisory Board (SAB) completed its own comparative risk assessment that found that the "environmental risks considered most serious by the general public today are different from those considered most serious by the technical professionals charged with reducing environmental risks." EPA Science Advisory Board, Reducing Risk: Setting Priorities and Strategies for Environmental Protection 12 (1990). As indicated in Figure 3.14, the SAB found that the public's top environmental concerns do not correspond well with the problems identified as most serious by EPA's experts. The SAB found that EPA's current priorities were more in line with the public's ranking of risk than with the results of its experts' comparative risk assessment.

For example, the SAB determined that radon in indoor air poses one of the most significant risks to public health, even though it is near the bottom of the public's concerns (see Figure 3.14). Radon is a naturally occurring radioactive gas that is a known human carcinogen. It enters people's homes through two routes: from rocks and soils beneath foundations, and through tap water drawn from groundwater contaminated by radon. Based on epidemiological studies of uranium miners, EPA estimated that between 6,700 and 30,600 Americans die each year from lung cancer caused by radon, making it the second leading cause of lung cancer next to smoking. The vast majority of these deaths are the result of breathing radon in indoor air, which EPA does not believe it has the authority to regulate directly. EPA's risk assessments estimate that only 1 to 2 percent of radon exposures come from drinking water, which causes 40 to 408 cancer deaths per year.

The Safe Drinking Water Act (SDWA) requires EPA to regulate radon in public drinking water supplies. In 1991 EPA proposed a maximum contamination level (MCL) of 300 picoCuries of radon per liter (pCi/L) of water, which it estimated would save 84 lives per year. Because 27,000 public water systems would have to build towers to aerate their water to meet the standard, EPA estimated it would cost $272 million, or $3.2 million per life saved. Water suppliers, who claimed the MCL could cost $2.5 billion, argued that it was irrational to spend so much money reducing radon in drinking water when far more lives could be saved more cheaply if homeowners acted to reduce radon levels in indoor air. It was estimated that sealing basements or ventilating houses could save lives at a cost of only $700,000 per life saved.

Responding to these complaints, the Safe Drinking Water Act Amendments of 1996, 42 U.S.C. §300g-1(b)(13), directed EPA to adopt an unusual strategy for responding to radon risks. They required EPA to withdraw its proposed 300 pCi/L MCL pending a new risk assessment conducted by the National Academy of Sciences (NAS). Following the NAS study, EPA is required to promulgate both a new MCL and a more relaxed, alternative MCL (AMCL). The AMCL is to be set at the level that would reduce drinking water's contribution to indoor radon only to levels equivalent to average concentrations of radon in outdoor air. States are given the option of electing to adopt the AMCL if they develop a "multimedia radon mitigation program" (MMM program), approved by EPA, to encourage homeowners to reduce radon in indoor air. MMM programs can encompass "public education, testing, training, technical assistance," and other measures. The Amendments require EPA to approve state MMM programs if the benefits they are expected to achieve equal or exceed those the much stricter MCL would achieve.

In 1998 the NAS released its risk assessment on radon in drinking water. Based on this report, EPA estimated that radon from soil causes 15,000 to 22,000 lung cancer deaths each year and that radon from drinking water causes 168

FIGURE 3.14
EPA's Assessment of Top Environmental Concerns and the Public's Ranking

EPA's TOP CONCERNS
(not in rank order)*
  Ecological risks
Global climate change
Stratospheric ozone depletion
Habitat alteration
Species extinction and loss of
  biodiversity

  Health risks
Criteria air pollutants (e.g., smog)
Toxic air pollutants (e.g.,
  benzene)
Radon
Indoor air pollution
Drinking water contamination
Occupational exposure to
  chemicals
Application of pesticides
Stratospheric ozone depletion

PUBLIC'S TOP CONCERNS
(in rank order)**
1. Active hazardous waste sites (67%)
2. Abandoned hazardous waste sites (65%)
3. Water pollution from industrial wastes (63%)
4. Occupational exposure to toxic chemicals (63%)
5. Oil spills (60%)
6. Destruction of the ozone layer (60%)
7. Nuclear power plant accidents (60%)
8. Industrial accidents releasing pollutants (58%)
9. Radiation from radioactive wastes (58%)
10. Air pollutions from factories (56%)
11. Leaking underground storage tanks (55%)
12. Coastal water contamination (45%)
13. Solid waste and litter (53%)
14. Pesticide risk to farm workers (52%)
15. Water pollution from agricultural runoff (51%)
16. Water pollution from sewage plants (50%)
17. Air pollution from vehicles (50%)
18. Pesticide residues in foods (49%)
19. Greenhouse effect (48%)
20. Drinking water contamination (46%)
21. Destruction of wetlands (42%)
22. Acid rain (40%)
23. Water pollution from city runoff (35%)
24. Nonhazardous waste sites (31%)
25. Biotechnology (30%)
26. Indoor air pollution (22%)
27. Radiation from x-rays (21%)
28. Radon in homes (17%)
29. Radiation from microwave ovens (13%)

*EPA Science Advisory Board, Reducing Risk (1990)
**March 1990 Roper Poll (% rating each problem "very serious")
Source: Counting on Science at EPA, 249 Science 616 (1990).

deaths annually. In October 1999, EPA reproposed national primary drinking water regulations for radon, 64 Fed. Reg. 59,245 (1999). The Agency proposed a maximum contaminant level goal (MCLG) of zero, an MCL of 300 pCi/L, and an AMCL of 4,000 pCi/L. States that develop approved MMM programs addressing health risks from radon in indoor air may adopt the more relaxed AMCL.

Question One. Is it surprising that EPA's priorities are more closely aligned with the public's ranking of risks than with the results of comparative risk assessment? Why is the public not as concerned with radon risks as EPA's experts are?

Question Two. Is it irrational or inefficient for EPA to try to regulate radon in drinking water when radon in indoor air poses a greater health risk? Will the multimedia radon mitigation approach employed by the 1996 SDWA Amendments provide greater protection to public health at lower cost? EPA estimates that existing federal and state programs to encourage reduction of indoor radon risks already will save more than 2,500 lives through the year 2000. Will new MMM programs guarantee additional risk reduction greater than or equal to compliance with the MCL?

Question Three. Why should states with approved MMM programs be allowed to adopt much looser limits on radon in drinking water? Is this fair to people who do not have a radon problem in their household air, but who are exposed to radon in their drinking water? EPA estimates that the AMCL of 4,000 pCi/L will prevent less than three cancer deaths while leaving individuals exposed at this level facing cancer risks greater than 1 in 400; the MCL of 300 pCi/L would prevent 62 cancer deaths while reducing individual cancer risks to 1 in 5,000.

Question Four. Should EPA be given authority to regulate radon levels in household air? Could it enforce such regulations when the regulatory target would be individual homeowners?

REGULATION OF TOXIC SUBSTANCES: A PATHFINDER

Risk assessment is explained in several useful studies. An influential early report is the National Research Council study, Risk Assessment in the Federal Government: Managing the Process (1983). A helpful introduction to risk assessment for nonscientists is the Conservation Foundation's 1985 monograph Risk Assessment and Control. The National Academy of Sciences' comprehensive review of EPA's use of risk assessment is National Research Council, Science and Judgment in Risk Assessment (1994). Also useful are the reports of the Presidential/Congressional Commission on Risk Assessment and Risk Management, Framework for Environmental Health Risk Management (1997) and Risk Assessment and Risk Management in Regulatory Decision-Making (1997), which are available from the Government Printing Office. Before disbanding, the Commission, which was created by the Clean Air Act Amendments of 1990, made scores of recommendations for improving the use of risk assessment in regulatory decision making.

Regulations implementing TSCA are found at 40 C.F.R. pts. 700-799. FIFRA regulations appear at 40 C.F.R. pts. 150-189, and regulations implementing EPCRA are at 40 C.F.R. pts. 355-372. FDA regulations appear at 21 C.F.R. pts. 1-1299. OSHA's occupational safety and health standards can be found at 29 C.F.R. pt. 1910.

A comprehensive *practitioner's guide* to the Toxic Substances Control Act is published by the Environmental Law Institute. E. Brown et al., TSCA Deskbook (1999). Clark Boardman publishes an excellent *treatise* on regulation of toxic substances, which also covers hazardous waste issues. D. Stever, Law of Chemical Regulation and Hazardous Waste.

EPA's Office of Prevention, Pesticides and Toxic Substances makes *chemical release data* from the agency's Toxics Release Inventory (TRI) available to the public on its website at *www.epa.gov/tri*. Environmental Defense has created a website that enables visitors to use the TRI and other data to examine data on pollutant releases and their sources by zip code at *www.scorecard.org*.

An excellent source of online news on developments in risk assessment and risk management is Riskworld's website, which can be found at *www.riskworld.com*. The site also includes an online casebook of materials relating to risk, science and law, and the reports of the Presidential/Congressional Commission on Risk Assessment and Risk Management.

D. REGULATION THROUGH REVELATION

People voluntarily engage in many activities—driving a car, skiing, mountain climbing—that subject them to risks, sometimes significant ones. Yet people resent being exposed involuntarily to even relatively modest risks and demand that society act to minimize such exposure. See Sagoff, On Markets for Risk, 41 Md. L. Rev. 755 (1982). If the goal of toxic substance regulation is to minimize involuntary exposure to risks, it can be pursued not only by regulations that reduce toxic emissions, but also by providing individuals with information that will enable them to choose to avoid certain risks. Even when the incidence of toxics exposure does not directly affect them, consumers may desire to avoid purchasing products that have environmental or human health effects that they consider undesirable.

> [A]t least with regard to some areas of choice . . . consumer preferences may be heavily influenced by information regarding the manner in which goods are produced. Such information . . . can include the labor conditions of workers who produce a consumer good, the environmental effects of a good's production, the use of controversial engineering techniques such as genetic modification to create a good, or any number of other social, economic, or environmental circumstances that are related causally to a consumer product, but that do not necessarily manifest themselves in the product itself. [A]lthough

such factors generally do not bear on the functioning, performance, or safety of the product, they nevertheless can, and often do, influence the willingness of consumers to purchase the product. Douglas Kysar, Preferences for Processes: The Process/Production Distinction and the Regulation of Consumer Choice, 118 Harv. L. Rev. 525, 529 (2004).

Either or both of these mechanisms that inform consumers of risks associated with products can provide incentives to producers to reduce those risks.

The distinction between risks borne voluntarily and those borne involuntarily is not always an easy one to make. Some risks are easier to avoid than others, and some individuals are more capable than others of taking steps to avoid risks. We have no choice about breathing, although in theory we could all wear space suits that filter toxic pollutants out of the air we breathe. But few would be comfortable with the notion that this makes such exposures a risk that we bear voluntarily, even if we were provided with comprehensive information about what pollutants were in each batch of air we encounter. Opportunities for voluntary avoidance of risks are greater when the risks involve products that informed consumers can choose not to purchase. Thus, as discussed in Chapter 2, when individuals are informed and have choices, market forces can serve as a powerful complement to regulation to prevent environmental damage.

But it is not easy to keep consumers with limited attention spans informed of the risks they may choose to avoid. Information is not gathered and distributed without cost. Yet approaches that inform consumers of risks may often be far cheaper than traditional regulatory approaches for controlling risks. The latter often place significant burdens on regulators to demonstrate that certain substances or activities pose risks worth regulating in the face of scientific uncertainty. Thus, considerable effort is being devoted to develop new informational approaches to regulation as well as approaches that shift the burden of gathering information to respond to uncertainty.

Some federal environmental regulations already require the disclosure of risk information to workers and consumers. For example, OSHA has required that workers be informed of the presence of hazardous chemicals in the workplace through a regulation called the hazard communication standard. As a result of a decision by the U.S. Court of Appeals for the Third Circuit, OSHA has expanded its initial hazard communication standard to cover all industries it regulates. United Steelworkers of America v. Auchter, 763 F.2d 728 (3d Cir. 1985). The federal Emergency Planning and Community Right-to-Know Act, discussed below, is designed to provide the public with information on the presence of toxic chemicals in their communities. It requires that companies publicly disclose their annual emissions of more than 600 different toxic chemicals and that local authorities be notified about hazardous substances stored or used by the companies.

Informational approaches also may assist in the enforcement of environmental laws. For example, the Safe Drinking Water Act requires that public water suppliers inform their customers when they violate the Act either by failing to monitor drinking water or by detecting contaminants in it at levels that exceed the maximum contaminant levels promulgated under the Act. By requiring that potential victims be informed of violations, this kind of informational regulation can contribute to public pressure to correct violations. For example, the editor of a small newspaper in Washington, North Carolina, became curious when he noticed a cryptic sentence on the back of his water bill. When he inquired further, he discovered information that led to his writing a Pulitzer Prize–winning series of articles. The articles revealed that for eight years local authorities had sought to conceal the fact that enormously high levels of carcinogenic chemicals had contaminated the town's drinking water. Within a month of the first article informing residents of the danger, the town's water supply system was shut down and the incumbent mayor was defeated in a bid for reelection. A new filtration system ultimately was installed to remove the chemicals from the drinking water. Pitt, City Gets Clean Water; Its Paper Gets a Pulitzer, N.Y Times, April 16, 1990, at A10.

Informational regulations have not always proved successful. In 1983, EPA decided an informational approach was the best way to respond to the widespread presence of asbestos hazards in schools. Rather than issuing regulations requiring that asbestos hazards be abated, EPA required school authorities to undertake a one-time inspection of their buildings to determine if friable asbestos was present and to inform parents and school employees if such materials were found. EPA officials believed that if parents were informed that their children were exposed to a potential hazard, they would ensure that action would promptly be taken to abate it. The regulation, however, proved to have unfortunate consequences. Despite EPA's efforts to provide guidance, school officials generally had a poor understanding of asbestos hazards and the proper means for abating them. Many inspections were poorly performed. Discoveries of asbestos often produced panicked reactions from parents and school authorities that actually may have exacerbated the risks to children. In 1987, Congress responded to this debacle by requiring EPA to issue regulations requiring periodic inspections for asbestos and specifying abatement actions that must be undertaken when asbestos hazards are found.

Providing information in ways that are most accessible to consumers can require the standardization of terms, and government efforts to define terms or set conditions on permissible claims about products are often highly controversial. In 1997, the USDA proposed a rule that would define the conditions of food processing and production that would permit a marketed food to be labeled "organic." 62 Fed. Reg. 65,850, 65,893 (1997). Organic farmers complained about a number of USDA's restrictions, as well as about practices that the rule permitted. For instance, treated municipal sewage sludge was a permissible fertilizer under the proposal. In early 1999, after receiving more than 275,000 written comments, more than it had ever received on any public issue, the agency withdrew the proposal for further consideration. New regulations, proposed in March 2000, eventually were adopted by USDA. They became effective in 2002.

Responding to consumer interest in process information can occasionally raise constitutional issues. In the 1990s, the FDA determined that the use of synthetic bovine growth hormone in milk-producing cattle did not require milk manufacturers to label products to disclose they contained the growth hormone because milk from SBGH-treated cows was indistinguishable from milk from untreated cows. When Vermont initiated its own mandatory labeling program, Monsanto, the maker of the leading synthetic hormone, sued. The Second Circuit ruled that Vermont's law violated the First Amendment. Because of FDA's determination that treated and untreated products were undistinguishable, said the court, the only remaining state interest in the labeling requirement was "mere consumer concern" about "production methods." In the court's view this was insufficient to justify the state law. International Dairy Foods Ass'n v. Amestoy, 92 F.2d 67 (2d Cir. 1996).

As regulatory agencies place greater emphasis on alternatives to command-and-control methods to reduce risk, their research needs are likely to change. The late EPA Deputy Administrator Al Alm argued that informational approaches will "require much more sophistication than choosing a regulatory limit or designating a technology." Instead, such approaches will require agencies to consider social science data to obtain "a basic understanding of how decisions are made in the private sector, what stimuli would change private sector behavior, and how public sector activities could make a difference." Alm, Science, Social Science, and the New Paradigm, 26 Envtl. Sci. Tech. 1123 (1992). Alm noted that when Congress enacted the EPCRA the debate focused not on how industry would react to disclosures of their chemical releases, but rather on how the public would react to such information. Yet it now has become clear that the most significant effect of the legislation has been to encourage companies to voluntarily reduce emissions of toxic substances. See pages 300-308.

Even though information disclosure strategies are generally much less expensive than traditional regulation, cost-related arguments have sometimes been made against them. OMB, for instance, has argued that the application of "right-to-know" legislation to food labeling would constitute an unfair subsidy of the rich by the poor. Because the costs of providing information will be passed on to all consumers, poor people who do not care about risk information will have to pay for ensuring that wealthier people who are more likely to value such information are kept informed, according to OMB. OMB, Regulatory Program of the U.S. Government April 1, 1990-March 31, 1991, at 29 (1990). Id. Do you agree with these criticisms?

As we have seen, a critical issue environmental regulation attempts to address is how to respond to uncertainty. Regulations that increase incentives for gathering and disseminating information may help improve society's response to environmental risk by reducing uncertainties concerning the presence and significance of risks. While regulatory authorities generally bear the burden of proving that risks are significant enough to warrant regulation, some new approaches to regulation have sought to shift this burden by requiring persons who generate risks to demonstrate that the risks are significant enough to warrant regulation. Licensing schemes such as FIFRA and the Food, Drug, and Cosmetic Act already shift the burden to the manufacturers of pesticides, therapeutic drugs, and food additives to demonstrate the safety of their products. But society generally has not required that manufacturers of other products or dischargers of toxic pollutants make similar demonstrations, perhaps because they would be deemed too burdensome. A California citizens' initiative called Proposition 65, which was adopted in 1986, represents the most innovative effort to change the traditional burden of proof in a manner that would generate incentives for reducing public exposure to involuntary risk.

1. California's Proposition 65: A Burden-Shifting Approach to the Information Problem

On November 4, 1986, California voters overwhelmingly approved an innovative new approach to regulation of toxic substances. The law, adopted as voter initiative Proposition 65, is titled the "Safe Drinking Water and Toxic

Enforcement Act of 1986." It combines a duty-to-warn approach with a shifting of the burden of demonstrating the safety of exposures to carcinogens and reproductive toxins. The simple concept articulated in Proposition 65 is that no one should knowingly expose another without warning to chemicals known to cause cancer or reproductive toxicity unless the discharger can demonstrate that the risk is not significant. This concept had so much political appeal that the initiative's opponents thought it could be defeated only by convincing voters that it had too many loopholes. Noting that Proposition 65 did not apply to pollution from government agencies, oil companies and agribusinesses waged a $5.7 million advertising campaign against the initiative with the official slogan: "No on 65. It's Full of Exemptions." Proponents responded that they would be happy to work to remove any loopholes after Proposition 65 was approved. Voters approved the initiative by nearly a 2-1 margin. (Ironically, a subsequent voter initiative to extend Proposition 65 to government agencies was narrowly defeated in 1990 after fierce opposition from local governments concerned that it would require extensive warnings about drinking water contamination.)

The operative provisions of Proposition 65 are remarkably simple. First, the law prohibits the discharge into sources of drinking water of any chemical that is a carcinogen or reproductive toxin except in amounts that the discharger can prove are insignificant. The law states:

> No person in the course of doing business shall knowingly discharge or release a chemical known to the state to cause cancer or reproductive toxicity into water or onto or into land where such chemical passes or probably will pass into any source of drinking water, notwithstanding any other provisions of authorization of law except as provided in Section 25249.9. [Ch. 6.6 Cal. Health & Safety Code §25249.5.]

Section 25249.9 exempts discharges that the discharger shows "will not cause any significant amount of the discharged or released chemical to enter any source of drinking water" and that also are in compliance with all applicable regulations.

The second major provision of Proposition 65 is a prohibition on exposing anyone to carcinogens or reproductive toxins without warning unless the person responsible for the exposure can show that it poses no significant risk assuming lifetime exposure. The law provides:

> No person in the course of doing business shall knowingly and intentionally expose any individual to a chemical known to the state to cause cancer or reproductive toxicity without first giving a clear and reasonable warning to such individual, except as provided in Section 25249.10. [Ch. 6.6 Cal. Health & Safety Code §25249.6.]

Section 25249.10 exempts both exposures "for which federal law governs warning in a manner that preempts state authority" and:

> [a]n exposure for which the person responsible can show that the exposure poses no significant risk assuming lifetime exposure at the level in question for substances known to the state to cause cancer, and that the exposure will have no observable effect assuming exposure at one thousand (1,000) times the level in question for substances known to the state to cause reproductive toxicity, based on evidence and standards of comparable scientific validity to the evidence and standards which form the scientific basis for the listing of such

chemical [as a substance known to cause cancer or reproductive toxicity]. [Ch. 6.6 Cal. Health & Safety Code §25249.10.]

Not surprisingly, the initial implementation of Proposition 65 created considerable controversy. Bowing to industry pressure, California governor George Deukmejian placed only substances that had been demonstrated to cause cancer and reproductive toxicity in *humans* on the list of chemicals "known to the state to cause cancer." Thus, the state's original list of carcinogens and reproductive toxins subject to the law contained only 29 substances. Arguing that the law also required the listing of all substances that cause cancer or reproductive damage in animal tests, the supporters of Proposition 65 sued the governor. In AFL-CIO v. Deukmejian, 260 Cal. Rptr. 479 (Cal. App. 1989), the California Court of Appeals held that chemicals found to be carcinogens or reproductive toxins as a result of animal testing had to be included in the minimum list of chemicals "known to the state to cause cancer or reproductive toxicity" as defined by Proposition 65.

Following the decision in AFL-CIO v. Deukmejian, the list of chemicals known to the state of California to cause cancer or reproductive toxicity has been substantially expanded beyond the governor's initial list. By 1995, 542 chemicals were on the list. Some products containing these substances have been exempted by regulation.

In response to a petition from the Grocery Manufacturers of America, the California Health and Welfare Agency, the agency designated by the governor to implement Proposition 65, exempted food products containing naturally occurring carcinogens and reproductive toxins from the requirements of the legislation. The exemption applies to chemicals that are natural constituents of food or that can be shown to be present "solely as a result of absorption or accumulation of the chemical" from "the environment in which the food is raised, or grown, or obtained." 22 Cal. Code Reg. §12501. However, producers and distributors of food are required to use quality control measures that reduce natural chemical contaminants to the "lowest level currently feasible." In Nicolle-Wagner v. Deukmejian, 230 Cal. App. 3d 652, 281 Cal. Rptr. 494 (1991), this exemption was upheld by a California court of appeals which found that Proposition 65 was directed only at controlling exposure to toxics added to the environment by human activity.

While Proposition 65 does not specify what constitutes a "significant risk" for purposes of exposure to substances subject to the law, the law authorizes the California Health and Welfare Agency to issue regulations implementing its provisions. Because Proposition 65 placed the burden of disproving that a risk was significant on the discharger, California businesses discharging listed substances pressed for swift enactment of regulations specifying what exposure levels posed "significant risk." The shift in the burden of proof reversed the normal incentive for the regulated community to seek delay in the issuance of implementing regulations. Toxicologists from all over the country swarmed to California to participate in regulatory proceedings implementing the Act. Acting far more rapidly than federal regulators ever had, the Health and Welfare Agency issued regulations specifying "significant risk" levels for nearly 300 carcinogens, defining "significant risk" for carcinogens as a risk greater than 1 in 100,000. For reproductive toxins, Proposition 65 specifies that exposure at a level of one-thousandth the no-observed-effects level or above constitutes a "significant risk."

The key to its rapid and comprehensive regulatory implementation was that Proposition 65 reversed the usual incentive for industry to prolong the regulatory process with endless debates over "how safe is safe." As David Roe, a co-author of the law, observes, "California managed to draw bright lines for more chemicals in the first twelve months of the Proposition 65 era than the federal government had managed to accomplish, under the supposedly omnibus Toxic Substances Control Act, in the previous twelve years." Roe notes that "much of the scientific information on which the California lines were based came directly from federal regulatory agencies, which had long since completed their assessment of the relevant research results; the difference was that, for once, there was a premium on getting to the bottom line." Roe, An Incentive-Conscious Approach to Toxic Chemical Controls, 3 Econ. Dev. Q. 179, 181 (1989).

Businesses that discharge a listed substance at levels in excess of those defined to constitute a "significant risk" can escape liability (unless the substance passes into a source of drinking water) by providing a "clear and reasonable warning" to persons exposed. The question of what constitutes such a warning has been a subject of some dispute. A trade association of grocers initially responded to Proposition 65 by establishing a toll-free telephone number that consumers could call to find out if certain products contained carcinogens or reproductive toxins in significant amounts. Callers were not permitted to request a list of products containing carcinogens or reproductive toxins, but were warned if they happened to ask about a specific product that did. Although the hotline received 28,000 calls in the first 14 months, only 488 warning messages were issued. Grocers maintained that the availability of the toll-free number made it unnecessary for warning labels to be displayed in their stores. Proponents of Proposition 65, who dubbed the system "800-BALONEY," filed suit, maintaining that the toll-free number was an attempt to circumvent the law. In August 1989 a California Superior Court ruled that the toll-free number "does not provide clear and reasonable warnings" as required by the law.

This decision was affirmed on appeal. Ingredient Communication Council, Inc. v. Lungren, 4 Cal. Rptr. 2d 216 (1992). The court explained why the use of a toll-free number was insufficient to meet the law's requirement to provide "a clear and reasonable warning":

> The major conceptual problem was that the system proceeded on the assumption [that] most consumers before shopping sit down with the food section of the newspaper each week, see the advertised 800 number, make a list of the specific brand names of products they intend to buy, and then call to check whether these products carry a warning. This assumption is contradicted by the fact that about two-thirds of the buying decisions made by grocery consumers are made in the store on impulse. In addition, few consumers are willing to spend time researching and calling about those relatively inexpensive products they frequently buy in a grocery store; such purchases differ from those of automobiles or computers. [Id. at 225.]

California repealed a regulation that had exempted from Proposition 65 products regulated under the federal Food, Drug, and Cosmetic Act. However, a court ruled that Proposition 65's warning requirements could not be applied to dental mercury because they were preempted by the Medical Devices Amendments to the federal act. Committee of Dental Amalgam Alloy Mfrs. v. Henry, 871 F. Supp. 1278 (S.D. Cal. 1994).

Regulations implementing Proposition 65 initially created a safe harbor for companies discharging airborne carcinogens if they took out a small newspaper ad stating: "WARNING: This area contains a chemical known to the state of California to cause cancer." 22 Cal. Code Reg. §12601. After a successful court challenge to this regulation, a new warning requirement was proposed that would include signs stating: "WARNING: Emissions or effluents from this facility will expose you to chemicals known to the state of California to cause cancer, including the following. . . ." Pease, Chemical Hazards and the Public's Right to Know: How Effective Is California's Proposition 65?, 33 Environment 13 (Dec. 1991).

Shortly after enactment of Proposition 65, the chairman of the Chemical Manufacturer's Association predicted that the law would have "a significant and detrimental effect on the agricultural and manufacturing business in the state." CMA Chairman Urges Renewal of Clean Air Act. Voluntary Steps on Air Toxics by Industry 17 Envtl. L. Rep. 220 (1986). Yet little evidence has developed to suggest that the Act has had such an impact. Fear of adverse consumer reactions to warning labels has encouraged some manufacturers to reformulate their products to remove carcinogens and reproductive toxins. Kiwi Brands, Inc., a division of Sara Lee, removed a carcinogenic chemical from its Kiwi water-proofing spray for shoes. Pet, Inc. accelerated the removal of lead solder from cans used for several of its products including Old El Paso tamale/chili gravy and Progresso tomatoes. It is impossible to tell how frequently products have been reformulated. While some companies have released products with "new formulas they can now tout as safer—and sometimes even more effective, . . . [o]ther companies are reformulating quietly to avoid calling attention to chemicals in their old products." Smith, California Spurs Reformulated Products, Wall St. J., Nov. 1, 1990, at B1. Sears, Roebuck and Company reports that several of its suppliers have reformulated scores of products including carburetor cleaners and car wax.

One concern voiced by critics of Proposition 65 is that products containing weak carcinogens will be replaced with more dangerous substances that have not been identified as carcinogens or reproductive toxins because they have not been fully tested. When threatened with a lawsuit in September 1989, the Gillette Company removed Liquid Paper correction fluid from the California market because it contained trichloroediylene (TCE), a carcinogenic substance. Four months later it introduced a "New Improved" Liquid Paper reformulated with the solvent 1,1,1-trichloroethane (TCA) instead of TCE. Yet an official of the Consumer Product Safety Commission has expressed "great concern" that TCA could be carcinogenic because of its structural similarity to the solvents it replaced. Smith, above, at B7. In fact, Liquid Paper's leading competitor, Wite-Out Products, Inc., which originally had switched to TCA, has introduced a new correction fluid without TCA because of concern that TCA is toxic and likely to be banned as an ozone-depleting chemical.

Significant lawsuits continue to be brought from time to time under Proposition 65, although litigation has not played a prominent role in implementing the proposition, as many firms who have received notice of an intention to sue have chosen to alter their practices so as to avoid the need to produce warning labels. Recently, the California Attorney General and environmental groups did bring suit against McDonalds, Frito-Lay, and other manufacturers or sellers of French fries or potato chips, on the basis of acrylamide being found in those foods. Acrylamide has been shown to cause cancer in laboratory animals and has been on California's Prop. 65 list since 1990, but was only found in food in 2002. It is a byproduct of cooking starchy foods, high in trans-fats, at high temperatures. Firms, including McDonalds, are investigating means of altering the production processes. Press Release, Attorney General Lockyer Files Lawsuit to Require Consumer Warnings About Cancer-Causing Chemical in Potato Chips and French Fries (Aug. 26, 2005).

The following excerpt describes the success of Proposition 65 in reducing the exposure of Californians to lead.

Rechtschaffen, How to Reduce Lead Exposures with One Simple Statute: The Experience of Proposition 65
29 Envtl. L. Rep. 10581 (1999)

Since 1988, California's Proposition 65, a right-to-know initiative, has achieved some noteworthy successes in reducing public exposures to lead in media as diverse as calcium supplements, brass kitchen faucets, water well pumps, ceramicware, hair dyes, wine capsules, and factory emissions. These sources all were subject to regulation by the federal government, but Proposition 65 has spurred faster and more significant lead reductions than federal law by prompting companies to reformulate products and change their manufacturing processes. . . . Thus, the success of Proposition 65, in particular its technology-forcing character, provides important lessons for the ongoing national debate about how best to reform environmental regulation. . . .

Federal law . . . has left significant gaps with respect to important sources of lead exposure. . . . Federal regulation . . . has been slow to address exposures from lead in drinking water from faucets and other plumbing hardware, lead in ceramicware, and lead in calcium supplements, among other products. These sources also can contribute significant, unhealthy levels of lead to the public. For example, in 1991, EPA found that lead in drinking water contributes 20 percent of total lead exposure for an average person, and possibly as much as 85 percent of lead for infants whose diets consist mainly of formula. Researchers estimated that approximately 30 percent of this drinking water contamination was due to lead leaching from brass faucets. Lead-glazed ceramicware is the largest source of lead in the diet. In the early 1990s, the ceramicware industry itself estimated that ceramicware could be the source of up to one-quarter of the "acceptable" lead exposure for adults in this country. Similarly, calcium supplements are widely used by the public to meet dietary requirements; over 50 percent of pregnant and lactating women regularly take calcium supplements. Until recently, almost all calcium supplements contained lead at levels of concern to public health officials. . . .

Proposition 65 has had . . . a striking effect on some of these . . . important gaps left by federal law. . . . In part, Proposition 65 prohibits a person in the course of doing business from "knowingly" discharging or releasing any listed chemical "into water or onto or into land where such chemical passes or will probably pass into any source of drinking water." . . . The statute also imposes a far-reaching warning requirement: businesses must provide a "clear and reasonable" warning prior to "knowingly and intentionally" exposing any individual to a listed chemical. This includes consumer product exposures, occupational exposures, and environmental exposures.

Proposition 65 only exempts exposures or discharges below a de minimis level, defined by the statute as exposures or discharges that pose "no significant risk" of cancer or that are below 1/1,000th of the no observable effect level (NOEL) for reproductive toxicants. The state has set a de minimis level for lead of 0.5 micrograms/day.

Proposition 65 has caused substantial reductions in public exposures to lead by triggering fundamental shifts in long-standing means of production to avoid or minimize the use of lead. In the case of consumer goods, most companies have reformulated their products nationwide, giving Proposition 65 a national effect. . . .

[Pipes, solder, faucets, valves, and other fittings in household plumbing all can contain lead that dissolves into water coming through a building's plumbing system. The Safe Drinking Water Act only requires the public water system to deliver water of a certain quality up to the household; lead that is added to the water after it enters the house is not regulated.] Thus, the best efforts of public drinking water systems can be completely undermined by lead leaching at the very last points of the distribution system. . . .

In 1992, the California Attorney General's office along with two environmental organizations, the Environmental Law Foundation and the Natural Resources Defense Council (NRDC), sued 14 major faucet manufacturers for violating Proposition 65's warning and discharge provisions. Five years earlier, the plumbing industry had begun working with EPA and NSF International, an industry standard-setting organization, to develop a voluntary standard for lead leaching from faucets. The Proposition 65 litigation quickened what had been a protracted negotiation process, and NSF established a voluntary standard in 1994. In 1995, the plumbing manufacturers settled the Proposition 65 suit, agreeing to manufacture faucets that are close to lead-free. Under the agreement, kitchen faucets must leach less than 5 micrograms/liter/day of lead, which is the level the state of California determined that the Proposition 65 exposure limits translates into when normalized to 1 liter. Bathroom and other faucets must meet the less stringent, voluntary NSF standard of 11 micrograms of lead/liter. The companies have until the end of 1999 to bring 95 percent of their products into compliance. (The voluntary NSF standard for faucets was made mandatory by the 1996 amendments to the SDWA.)

The Proposition 65 litigation, as well as the new NSF standard, has prompted significant changes in how faucets are made. Faucets are manufactured by three general methods, used alone or in combination: (1) fabrication, a technique in which extruded and drawn brass rod is machined into component parts, which are then welded together; (2) permanent mold casting (employed far less in the United States than in Europe), in which brass is poured into metal molds or dies; and (3) sand casting, in which brass is poured into sand molds. [Compliance with the Proposition 65 settlement has caused substantial modifications in all three production techniques, with some manufacturers dropping the sand casting technique, which required the most fundamental alterations, in favor of mold casting and fabrication. Similar manufacturing modifications are occurring for submersible water pumps, water meters, ceramicware (china), calcium dietary supplements, and lead foil capsules on wine bottles—all of which can contribute noticeable amounts of lead to a person's total blood lead levels. Used in conjunction with TRI data,

Proposition 65 has also enabled environmental organizations to sue a number of existing sources of lead air emissions, obtaining a number of significant settlements on terms that have produced significant reductions in lead air emissions in California.] . . .

In contrast to the fragmented approach of federal law, Proposition 65 covers a very broad range of activities and environmental media with a single law. The warning requirement applies without limitation to any exposure to a listed chemical, encompassing everything from kitchen faucets, ceramicware, water coolers, food and wine, lead-based paint, miniblinds, crystal decanters, water niters, hair dyes, bullets, and galvanized nails to factory emissions and workplace exposures. The discharge provision proscribes discharges to a "source of drinking water," but this applies broadly to surface water, groundwater, and tap water, and includes direct releases to water bodies or indirect releases onto land likely to migrate to sources of drinking water.

Second, unlike federal law, Proposition 65 is self-executing. Once a chemical is listed by the state as causing cancer or reproductive harm and the relevant statutory grace periods expire, Proposition 65's provisions take effect without specific administrative standards that specify acceptable levels of exposure. This contrasts with federal statutes, where private activity causing lead exposures is permitted until and unless the government sets a restrictive standard. Proposition 65 also is more "enforcement-friendly" than federal provisions. The statute can be enforced by public prosecutors or citizen groups acting in the public interest. There are extremely limited defenses available under the statute; the most important is that an exposure or discharge is below the de minimis level. Moreover, in an enforcement action, the defendant bears the burden of proving this. Violations of the statute result in penalties of up to $25,000 per day per violation, and 25 percent of the penalties go to the plaintiff initiating the enforcement action. Thus, enforcement actions are relatively easy to bring, face few defenses, and can result in enormous penalties—creating considerable incentives for groups outside of the government to search for violations. Moreover, both the California Attorney General's office and many environmental groups and private parties bringing cases have been willing to forego civil fines on defendant companies in exchange for product reformulations. Faced with the prospect of large penalties, many companies have consented to reformulate their products in order to reduce their potential liability; other manufacturers have done so to avoid the possibility of a lawsuit entirely. As a result, enforcement actions have prompted many product reformulations over the past 10 years.

Third, the Proposition 65 de minimis lead standard of 0.5 micrograms is stricter than federal requirements. The state health and welfare agency derived this standard by using OSHA's permissible exposure limit for daily exposure to airborne lead of 500 micrograms/day as the NOEL for lead. The use of this OSHA standard as the NOEL, as well as the conservative requirement in Proposition 65 of a thousand-fold safety factor for reproductive toxicants such as lead, has been heavily criticized by industry. This standard was never challenged, however, almost certainly because given the emergent consensus that there is no safe level of exposure to lead, the standard is scientifically justifiable.

Federal regulatory standards for lead exposure vary depending on the context, but no enforceable federal limits are as stringent as the state standard. As noted, EPA has set an MCLG of zero for lead in drinking water, but this is a nonenforceable health goal. In some cases, the federal government has set specific limits that exceed the Proposition 65 levels, such as action levels set by the FDA for ceramicware. In other contexts, such as calcium supplements, leaded crystal, and other products, there are no specifically enforceable limits on human exposure to lead.

Finally, Proposition 65 differs from most federal requirements by primarily relying on information disclosure to prompt lead reductions. This approach has been especially effective in the consumer marketplace. Because consumer demand can be extremely sensitive to disclosure of adverse health and safety information, particularly with respect to food products, many businesses have elected to reformulate their products rather than provide warnings and risk significant sales losses. By contrast, federal regulation largely relies on traditional, direct regulatory approaches, such as setting lead limits in a particular product. While more prescriptive, these federal requirements trigger far less consumer demand for product changes than information disclosure mandates. . . .

Proposition 65 has been able to quickly and efficiently fill in important gaps in the regulation of lead exposures left by federal law. In 10 short years, the statute's stringent lead limits have forced the development of new technology and substantially reduced pollution across a wide range of media and products. In the plumbing industry, Proposition 65 accelerated the search for new brass alloys, new production methods, and better manufacturing processes. Proposition 65 also prompted the ceramic industry to develop new lead-free glazes and improve its firing techniques, and calcium suppliers to find cleaner sources of calcium deposits. These and other experiences over the past decade illustrate that a simple, multimedia, self-executing statute like Proposition 65 can be more powerful than a host of complex regulatory programs in achieving actual reductions of pollutants in our environment.

NOTES AND QUESTIONS

1. Apparently Proposition 65 is not having the dire economic impact forecast by those who opposed its adoption. Does this suggest that companies can readily find noncarcinogenic substitutes for substances subject to the Act, or could it indicate that the legislation has had little impact except on products targeted in lawsuits?

2. How do the levels that define "significant risk" for purposes of Proposition 65 compare with EPA's answer to the "how safe is safe" question under section 112 of the Clean Air Act?

3. An unusual provision of the law is section 25180.7, which requires government employees to report within 72 hours to local health officers and to the local Board of Supervisors any information they receive about the illegal discharge of hazardous waste that is likely to cause injury to public health. Why do you think such a provision was included in the law?

4. Critics of Proposition 65 note that it does not distinguish between the relative levels of risk posed by different products that contain substances subject to the law. Concerns have been expressed that Proposition 65 could saturate consumers with warnings about a bewildering array of relatively minor risks, overwarning consumers to the point that they will abandon risk-avoidance efforts. Proposition 65's impact could be severely diluted if industry groups

include warning labels on virtually all products to avoid any potential liability under Proposition 65. How realistic is this fear?

5. The California wine industry has now discontinued the use of lead foil wrappers. If lead continues to be found in wine, will the industry have any reason to fear liability under Proposition 65?

6. Rechtschaffen notes that some of the effects of Proposition 65 are being felt nationwide, because the adjustments that manufacturers make in order to reduce or eliminate chemicals covered by its requirements apply to a manufacturer's goods produced by that adjusted process, wherever they are sold. Is this because of the size of the California market? Would a Proposition 65–type law in the state of Montana, for example, have the same impact?

2.   The Emergency Planning and Community Right-to-Know Act (EPCRA)

In December 1984 an accidental release of methyl isocynate at a chemical plant owned by the Union Carbide Corporation in Bhopal, India killed more than 3,000 people and severely injured scores of thousands of others. In response to this tragedy, several bills were introduced into Congress to strengthen regulation of toxic air pollutants. While arguing that a similar accident could not happen in the United States, the chemical industry pledged to reexamine its safety practices. On August 11, 1985, an accidental release of aldicarboxime at a Union Carbide plant in Institute, West Virginia, resulted in the brief hospitalization of scores of residents, severely damaging the credibility of the industry shortly after it had assured the public that such accidents could not happen here.

Congress ultimately responded not by enacting new controls on toxic emissions, but rather by adopting legislation requiring comprehensive emergency planning and the reporting of chemical releases. This legislation, which was adopted at the same time as the Superfund Amendments and Reauthorization Act of 1986, is known as the Emergency Planning and Community Right-to-Know Act of 1986 (EPCRA), Pub. L. 99-499, 100 Stat. 1613 (1986), 42 U.S.C. §§11001-11050. The principal provisions of the Act are outlined below. Section 301 of EPCRA requires the establishment of state emergency response commissions and local emergency planning committees, which must develop comprehensive emergency response plans required by section 303. Section 304 of EPCRA requires companies to notify these officials if any chemicals placed by EPA on a list of extremely hazardous substances pursuant to section 302 are released in amounts greater than certain designated thresholds.

PRINCIPAL PROVISIONS OF THE EMERGENCY PLANNING AND COMMUNITY RIGHT-TO-KNOW ACT

Section 301 requires the establishment of state emergency response commissions and local emergency planning committees.

Section 302 requires EPA to publish a list of extremely hazardous substances and threshold planning quantities for these substances. Requires facilities where substances on the list are present in an amount in excess of the threshold quantities to notify the state emergency response commission and the local emergency planning committees.

Section 303 requires local emergency planning committees to prepare a comprehensive emergency response plan and specifies minimum requirements for such plans.

Section 304 requires owners and operators of facilities to notify community emergency response coordinators of releases of extremely hazardous substances.

Sections 311 and 312 require owners and operators of facilities required by OSHA to prepare material safety data sheets (MSDSs) to submit MSDSs and an emergency and hazardous chemical inventory form to the local emergency planning committee, the state emergency response commission, and the local fire department.

Section 313 requires owners and operators of facilities that have ten or more full-time employees and that were in SIC Codes 20 through 39 as of July 1, 1985 to complete a toxic chemical release form reporting the releases of each of more than 650 toxic chemicals used in quantities that exceed established threshold quantities during the preceding calendar year. These forms must be submitted to EPA and state officials by July 1 of each year to report data reflecting releases during the preceding calendar year. EPA is required to establish and maintain in a computer database a national toxic release inventory (TRI), based on data submitted on these forms, which must be accessible by the public through computer telecommunication.

Section 325 provides for civil, administrative, and criminal penalties for certain violations of the Act and authorizes enforcement actions by EPA.

Section 326 authorizes citizen suits against owners and operators of facilities that fail to comply with the Act and against the EPA administrator and state officials for failure to perform certain duties required by the Act.

To facilitate emergency planning, sections 311 and 312 of EPCRA require companies to report annually to local emergency planning authorities information concerning the identities, locations, and amounts of hazardous chemicals used at the facilities. Perhaps the most significant new requirement added by EPCRA is contained in section 313, which requires for the first time annual reporting of releases of toxic chemicals. This provision covers companies that employ ten or more full-time employees in a wide variety of industries if they manufacture, process, or otherwise use more than certain threshold quantities of listed chemicals. These companies must file Toxic Chemical Release Forms or Emissions Inventories with EPA and the states by July 1 of every year. The reports must include estimates of the "annual quantity of the toxic chemicals entering each environmental medium." The reports are to be based on readily ascertainable data; no additional monitoring or measurement requirements are imposed. Citizen suits can be brought under section 326 of EPCRA against companies that fail to comply with the reporting requirements imposed by the legislation.

Results of the first Toxic Release Inventory (TRI) were summarized earlier in this chapter. See page 201. EPA was shocked by the large volume of reported releases. Community organizations and environmental groups used the data to support calls for stronger regulation. During the first week after the TRI became available through the National Library of Medicine, the Library received 225 requests for subscriptions, most from community groups and ordinary citizens. Suro, Grass-Roots Groups Show Power Battling Pollution Close to Home, N.Y. Times, July 2, 1989, at 1. On August 1, 1989, USA Today published a two-page list of "The Toxic 500," the U.S. counties with the most pollution from industrial chemicals as reported in the TRI. The National Wildlife Federation published a book identifying the 500 largest dischargers, who released more than 7.5 billion pounds of toxics, including 39 known or probable carcinogens. See G. Poje, The Toxic 500 (1988). NRDC used the data to prepare "A Who's Who of American Toxic Air Polluters," identifying more than 1,500 major sources of toxic air emissions. Subsequent updates of the TRI have continued to receive wide publicity, Holusha, The Nation's Pollution: Who Emits What, and Where, N.Y. Times, Oct. 13, 1991, at F10, and many community groups have used the TRI to issue reports publicizing local polluters. Schneider, For Communities, Knowledge of Polluters Is Power, N.Y. Times, Mar. 14, 1991, at D5. Environmental Defense maintains an interactive pollution locator that uses TRI data to permit individuals to obtain information on the Internet (*www.scorecard.org*) about sources of pollution in their communities. By entering their zip code, individuals can find out what chemicals are being released by what sources in their neighborhoods, information about what is known concerning the potential health effects of the chemicals, and how the emissions rank relative to facilities in other parts of the country. By clicking on a link on the website, citizens can send free faxes complaining about the emissions to facilities whose releases are among the highest 20 percent in the nation.

The TRI has proven invaluable in providing information to inform public policy and public debate over those policies. For instance, Congress relied heavily on TRI data in specifying the 189 toxic chemicals required to be regulated as hazardous air pollutants in the 1990 Clean Air Act Amendments. EPA has used the TRI as the cornerstone of its pollution prevention strategy and as a means for improving the effectiveness of existing regulatory programs. Based on data from the TRI, EPA asked 600 dischargers to reduce voluntarily their emissions of 17 of the most dangerous toxics by 1995. The TRI has helped EPA adjust its regulatory priorities by revealing that some chemicals are released in far greater quantities than the Agency had anticipated. For example, epichlorohydrin, a chemical used in the production of epoxy resins, solvents, plastics, and other products, is classified as a probable human carcinogen, but EPA had not considered regulating it until the TRI revealed that 70 facilities in 24 states discharged 363,000 pounds of it in 1987. EPA previously had only been aware of 20 sources of epichlorohydrin emissions. Elkins, EPA Has Varied Plans for Use of Toxic Release Inventory Database, Hazardous Waste Management 42 (Aug. 1989). Congress subsequently placed this chemical on the list of 189 substances that must be regulated as hazardous air pollutants. EPA's Water Office has used the TRI data to identify potential violations of NPDES permits, to help in reviewing permit requests, and to establish water quality standards. The Agency's Office of Toxic Substances has screened TRI data to determine what existing chemicals should be subjected to regulatory investigations and to verify production estimates for regulated chemicals.

TRI data also assists efforts to study the impact of other policy instruments. For instance, TRI data on chlorinated solvent wastes from 1987 to 1990 has been used to analyze the impact of state taxes on the generation or management of hazardous wastes. Sigman, The Effect of Hazardous Waste Taxes on Waste Generation and Disposal, 30 J. Envtl. Econ. & Mgmt. 199 (1996). TRI data also has figured prominently in the debates over environmental justice, helping researchers employ an array of tools to identify the extent to which environmental exposures may be visited in a disproportionate fashion on certain segments of the population.

These benefits from TRI are above and beyond the main reason that advocates pushed for enacting TRI in the wake of Bhopal. TRI backers believed first, that providing information about toxics releases from facilities to the communities nearby those facilities was a good in itself and second, that the disclosure of this information would promptly firms to change their behavior in ways that reduced the amount of those releases. The evidence to date bears out this latter expectation. TRI has been extensively studied, with many studies concentrating on the years 1988 through 1992, when TRI was producing heretofore unavailable information on releases and hence might be anticipated to have its greatest effect on firm behavior. Beyond its initial impacts, however, there continues to be evidence that the annual TRI reports affect firm behavior. Of course, TRI reports also continue to inform public debate and provide a valuable source of information against which to evaluate the impact of other environmental policies. Many of the research results are summarized in a recent book by James Hamilton, an excerpt of which is presented below.

|| *Hamilton, Regulation through Revelation* ||
|| *208-256 (2005)* ||

[One group of researchers] views some firm voluntary actions to reduce emissions as strategic efforts to preempt more costly regulations. They analyzed changes in . . . TRI releases between 1988 and 1992 and conclude "that states with higher initial levels of toxic emissions and larger environmental group membership [in the neighboring communities] reduced toxic emissions more rapidly. . . . Since the threat of mandatory regulation is high while the marginal cost of self-regulation is relatively low, it makes good sense for firms to engage in voluntary emissions reductions." . . . [Other researchers] find that states with higher conservation group membership per 1,000 residents and states with less ideologically polarized politics had higher ratios of plants reducing toxic releases. This would be consistent with plants in these states facing (or anticipating) more pressure from environmentalists to reduce their TRI releases. . . .

[Investors are influenced by TRI data.] [O]n the first day the TRI data were released by the EPA to the public (June 19, 1989), the average abnormal return in the stock market for companies with TRI reports was negative and statistically significant. Companies listed in the TRI lost on average $4.1 million in stock value on the first day the data were released. . . . [Other researchers] point out that stock prices may drop upon the release of TRI data if relatively high emissions per dollar of firm revenue signal inefficient production, attract the attention of community activists, drive away green consumers, or generate scrutiny (and potential fines) from regulators. . . . [Still others] show that repeated provision of the TRI can provide new information to investors each year, because comparisons across years allow investors to see how firms change over time and relative to each other. . . . They find that "repeated provisions of the TRI information causes . . . negative returns to be statistically significant in the years 1990-1994, particularly for firms whose environmental performance worsened over time and relative to other firms."

[Community groups use TRI data to engage in environmental politics.] [Researchers] conduct a survey of active TRI users that included 67 responses from public interest groups. Among the citizen groups, 85% reported using the data to exert public pressure on facilities, 79% to educate affected residents, and 75% to lobby for legislative or regulatory changes. . . . 87% of the citizen group respondents [in a different survey] said their efforts had generated media coverage. Fifty-eight percent of the citizen groups indicated that "source reduction efforts were effected at plants" because of their work. . . .

An unanticipated and growing impact of the U.S. TRI is the adoption of pollution disclosure programs by other countries. After the initial years of the TRI demonstrated how emissions inventories and public data provision could work, in 1992 the United Nations Conference on Environment and Development (UNCED) developed an action plan that encouraged countries to create emission inventories and to allow the public access to the data. . . . Countries with versions of a [TRI-like program] include Australia, Canada, Japan, Mexico, Norway, the United Kingdom, and the United States. [Other countries such as Indonesia, also have variants of information disclosure programs.] . . .

The list of what we do not know about the impact of the TRI is . . . long. How accurate are the estimates reported by the facilities? Do plants lower their TRI figures by switching to chemicals not tracked on the list, and what impact on risks might this have? What are the exact mechanisms of information transmission in firms and communities that lead to changes in decision making? What percentage of reductions in reported TRI emissions is the result of information provision alone, and what percentages are the result of factors such as the impact of traditional command-and-control regulations or changes in firms' output levels? What factors are most important in amplifying or diminishing the influence of TRI on facility-level decisions?

[As TRI was being implemented, EPA] could not tell how widely the information would be used. Yet the first 15 years of public data releases (1989-2004) show that the TRI did bring new information to the public, did generate learning in many quarters, did change behavior in the private and public sectors, and did alter many policy debates.

NOTES AND QUESTIONS

1. Numerous anecdotal reports also attest to TRI's impact. After Monsanto Corporation found that its 35 plants released more than 374 million pounds of toxic substances, more than 20 million of which went into the air, Monsanto's chairman pledged to reduce air emissions of hazardous chemicals by 90 percent by the end of 1992. Elkins, Toxic Chemicals, the Right Response, N.Y. Times, Nov. 13, 1988, at F3. As Monsanto worked toward this goal, it updated the press on its progress, announcing in July 1991 that it had cut TRI air emissions by 58 percent from the 1987 TRI baseline. Hamilton, Regulation Through Revelation

225 (2005) In July, 1993, Monsanto declared that it had met its goal by reducing emissions by 92 percent. Id. Some environmental groups worried that much of these were phantom reductions, but a U.S. Public Interest Research Group researcher said, "They have done some truly good things." Id.

2. A 2003 EPA study, How Are the Toxics Release Inventory Data Used? Government, Business, Academic and Citizen Uses, collects a large and diverse list of case studies of TRI uses. It summarizes its findings:

> Communities use TRI data to begin dialogues with local facilities and to encourage them to reduce their emissions, develop pollution prevent[tion] (P2) plans, and improve safety measures. Public interest groups, government, academicians, and others use TRI data to educate the public about toxic chemical emissions and potential risk. Industry uses TRI data to identify P2 opportunities, set goals for toxic chemical release reduction, and demonstrate its commitment to and progress in reducing emissions. Federal, state, and local governments use TRI data to set priorities and allocate environmental protection resources to the most pressing problems. Regulators use TRI data to set permit limits, measure compliance with those limits, and target facilities for enforcement activities. Public interest groups use TRI data to demonstrate the need for new environmental regulations or improved implementation and enforcement of existing regulations. Investment analysts use TRI data to provide recommendations to clients seeking to make environmentally sound investments. Insurance companies use TRI data as one indication of potential environmental liabilities. Governments use TRI data to assess or modify taxes and fees based on toxic emissions or overall environmental performance. Consultants and others use TRI data to identify business opportunities, such as marketing P2 and control technologies to TRI reporting facilities. Id. at 1.

3. Concern about the accuracy of the TRI data has been ongoing. The first year's data is generally considered quite unreliable. Annual data quality reports generated by EPA in the mid-1990s suggest that "facilities generally determine thresholds correctly over 90 percent of the time," and hence are reporting the chemical releases that they should be. "Analyzing the EPA's data studies, Susan Dudley of the Mercatus Center noted they suggest that, 'while in the aggregate, the TRI reflects the number of pounds of listed chemicals released, releases reported on a facility basis may contain such large errors that make them unreliable for site-specific analysis.' " Hamilton, at 221. A 1998 paper reports results from a phone survey aimed at determining the cause of a substantial reduction in TRI figures for one chemical between 1991 and 1994. It found that "one type of paper change [in reporting requirements] redefining on-site recycling activities as in-process recovery, which does not have to be reported, accounted for more than half of these facilities' 1991-1994 reported reductions." . . . Id. at 222.

4. TRI reporting has been significantly expanded three times, each through EPA-initiated action. In 1994, EPA added 286 chemicals to the reporting requirements. In April 1997, EPA expanded the number of facilities required to file annual TRI reports by nearly 25 percent by subjecting to EPCRA's requirements seven additional industries—metal and coal mining, electric utilities, petroleum bulk terminals, chemical wholesalers, solvent recovery services, and commercial hazardous waste treatment operations. As a result of this decision, more than 31,000 facilities are now covered by EPCRA. In 1999, it lowered the size of the releases that trigger the reporting requirement for 18 chemicals, including aldrin, mercury, chloradan, and dioxin, out of a concern that these chemicals are persistent in the environment and bioaccumulate. Hamilton, at 136-142. In one of the last actions of the Clinton EPA, the Agency

also lowered the reporting threshold for lead on January 17, 2001, something that it had been studying for years and proposed formally in August 1999.

5. Notwithstanding that information disclosure is less expensive than regulation, it is still costly to firms. Just the revisions in reporting lead releases were estimated to generate a first year cost of $80 million and a subsequent annual expense of $40 million, as some 9,800 plants would be required to submit new TRI forms for lead. The effect of these costs, especially as they impact small businesses, together with the pressures they place on firms to change behavior, has made each expansion of TRI reporting politically divisive. There also have been efforts to reduce reporting requirements in response to those same forces. In 1995, the Congress debated omnibus regulatory reform. One of the leading bills, the Dole-Johnston proposal, would have rolled back EPA's 1994 addition of 286 chemicals unless EPA could establish that rollback "presents a foreseeable significant risk to human health or the environment." The regulatory reform bills failed to pass, in large part due to public concern over the impact they would have on environmental protection.

6. Other restrictions to TRI have been successfully implemented. In the late 1990s, hearings on the possible misuse of TRI information—the reporting of "worst case" scenarios for reporting facilities—were used as a vehicle to restrict some TRI information disclosure. U.S. House of Representatives, Committee on Commerce, Subcommittee on Health and Environment and Subcommittee on Oversight and Investigations, Joint Hearings on Internet Posting of Chemical "Worst Case" Scenarios: A Roadmap for Terrorists. Responding to concern over terrorism, Congress enacted the Chemical Safety Information, Site Security and Fuels Regulatory Relief Act, Pub. L. 106-40. Information about possible "worst case" chemical accidents is now available to the public only in limited-access reading rooms where it is easier to monitor who is accessing the information and for what purpose. The legislation also removes flammable fuels used as fuel from coverage under the RMP program.

As a result of the September 11th terrorist attacks, several federal agencies voluntarily have removed information about hazardous chemicals from their websites. EPA removed information about general risk management plans from its website and the Department of Transportation removed maps of pipelines and a study describing risk profiles for certain chemicals. The U.S. Centers for Disease Control removed a "Report on Chemical Terrorism" that described the chemical industry's vulnerabilities to a terrorist attack. The reading rooms that contain information about "worst case" chemical accidents did not experience any suspicious activity in the months immediately following September 11th. Guy Gugliotta, Agencies Scrub Web Sites of Sensitive Chemical Data, Wash. Post, Oct. 4, 2001, at A29.

7. The President G.W. Bush administration has not proposed legislative changes to TRI, but it reflected its general approach to TRI in the early days after the administration. On the first day of the new administration, January 20, 2001, the White House issued a stay of the lead reporting rule announced by the outgoing administration just a few days earlier. Perhaps stung by criticisms of this and other such actions, including revisiting of the safe drinking water standards for arsenic, pages 253-262, it ultimately decided not to make the stay permanent. See Hamilton, at 163-164. In other respects, however, it has been more successful in reducing the role of TRI. OMB has been particularly vigilant in reviewing the reporting requirements, under OMB's authority pursuant to the Paperwork Reduction Act. In 2003, Chemical Week reported that "EPA says

it is working on changes to the TRI that would reduce the burden on industry—a mandate from the White House's OMB." EPA Submits Plan for Easier TRI Reporting, Chemical Week 15 (Oct. 15, 2003). As this casebook goes to press, the EPA seems to be focusing on a proposal that "would exempt companies whose toxics emissions have not significantly changed from a prior year from reporting actual emissions in alternate years. Instead, it would allow companies to declare that there has been 'no significant change' in releases. . . . The proposal will also ease facilities' ability to use a less-detailed TRI form, known as Form A, by raising the emissions threshold from 500 to 5,000 pounds for the form." Inside EPA, Imminent EPA TRI Reforms May Dramatically Reduce Reporting (September 16, 2005). The proposed reforms prompted one environmentalist familiar with the proposal to say that "EPA's plans 'equate reducing burden with reducing information.'" Id.

8. EPCRA does not require that any warning labels be placed on products or that the public be informed prior to toxics discharges. Data on toxic releases are reported once a year, after the releases have occurred. Thus, unlike Proposition 65, which has the potential to mobilize the market forces of consumer purchasing decisions, EPCRA's effectiveness will turn on the extent to which the public uses the TRI to lobby for emissions reductions. Which approach do you think is more effective in reducing exposures to toxics, Proposition 65 or EPCRA—or are the two approaches more properly viewed as complementary? How could the TRI data help plaintiffs seeking to enforce Proposition 65's requirements?

9. NRDC has criticized EPA's pollution prevention strategy for focusing on reducing toxic *releases* rather than reducing the *generation* of toxic wastes. The group has recommended that EPCRA's reporting requirements be expanded to require accounting for quantities of chemicals used, produced, or generated as waste per unit of production. This would enable authorities to develop more effective source reduction strategies that focus on inefficient users and producers of toxics. NRDC Proposes Strategy to Reduce Inefficient Use of Toxic Chemicals, 22 Envtl. L. Rep. 2055 (1991).

10. Industry groups have sought unsuccessfully to repeal some of the reporting requirements of EPCRA and to make it more difficult for EPA to expand the lists of chemicals and facilities subject to EPCRA reporting. Among their proposals were requirements that EPA would have to demonstrate that releases of particular chemicals had caused injury to specific individuals before reporting could be required or to perform cost-benefit analyses demonstrating that the benefits of reporting would exceed its costs. Fearful that Congress might repeal TRI reporting requirements, President Clinton signed Executive Order 12,969 on August 8, 1995. The executive order requires that all federal contractors certify that they "report in a public manner on toxic chemicals released to the environment" in order to be eligible to obtain federal contracts worth $100,000 or more. As a result of the executive order and EPA regulations implementing it, 60 Fed. Reg. 55,306 (1995), even if TRI reporting requirements in EPCRA were repealed by Congress, federal contractors would remain subject to TRI reporting obligations.

11. Fears that they could be targets of terrorist attacks have led some facilities to reduce their use of hazardous chemicals. Following the September 11 terrorist attacks, the Blue Plains Wastewater Treatment Plant that serves Washington, D.C. discontinued its use of liquid chlorine that had been stored in 90-ton tanker cars at its plant located only four miles from the U.S. Capitol. Carol D.

Leonnig and Spencer S. Hsu, Fearing Attack, Blue Plains Ceases Toxic Chemical Use, Wash. Post, Nov. 20, 2001, at A1. This action was taken because a rupture of a chlorine tanker could quickly spread a toxic cloud killing thousands of people within a 10-mile radius. Some environmental groups are citing terrorism concerns as further justification to push industry to shift production processes to use inherently safer chemicals.

=4=

Waste Management and Pollution Prevention

The Congress hereby declares it to be the national policy of the United States that pollution should be prevented or reduced at the source whenever feasible; pollution that cannot be prevented should be recycled in an environmentally safe manner, whenever feasible; pollution that cannot be prevented or recycled should be treated in an environmentally safe manner whenever feasible; and disposal or other release into the environment should be employed only as a last resort and should be conducted in an environmentally safe manner.

—*Pollution Prevention Act of 1990, 42 U.S.C. §13101(b)*

CERCLA's liability provisions have caused a virtual revolution in industry's approach to hazardous waste, providing a strong incentive for pollution prevention and waste minimization efforts that have reduced dramatically the amount of hazardous waste that is generated in this country. The effectiveness of the liability and enforcement provisions of the Superfund statute is no doubt a primary cause of the attack that is now being made upon it.*

—*Assistant Attorney General Lois J. Schiffer*

Because all pollution is a form of waste, whatever affects the generation and management of waste affects the nature and scope of pollution problems. This chapter examines how regulatory policy has sought to influence waste management practices and to remediate environmental contamination. It begins by reviewing the sources of waste management and pollution problems and the broad array of regulatory authorities that have been enacted to respond to them. It then focuses on two federal laws—the Resource Conservation and Recovery Act (RCRA), which regulates how hazardous wastes are managed, and the Comprehensive Environmental Response, Compensation and Liability Act (CERCLA), often referred to as "the Superfund program," which governs remediation of hazardous substance contamination. The chapter concludes by examining constitutional limits on measures restricting interstate waste disposal and environmental justice concerns raised by the siting of waste disposal facilities.

A.   WASTE MANAGEMENT AND POLLUTION PROBLEMS

Waste is generated by virtually every entity at nearly every stage of extraction, production, and consumption processes. EPA has reported that more than 6 billion tons of agricultural, commercial, industrial, and domestic waste is generated in the United States each year. EPA, Environmental Progress and Challenges: EPA's Update 79 (1988). Much of this waste poses little environmental concern—nearly half is agricultural waste, primarily crop residues that are simply plowed under. Other waste streams can be highly dangerous. Chemical wastes that contain carcinogens and other toxic substances can harm human health when they seep through the ground and contaminate underground aquifers that supply drinking water. Mining and ore processing operations cause other environmental problems because they generate enormous quantities of overburden (soil and rock cleared away) and mineral tailings that may severely pollute streams with acidic runoff. Even common household wastes contain some dangerous constituents, though in concentrations much lower than industrial waste. Household garbage also contains organic matter that can form methane gas when decomposing in landfills.

Waste streams have changed over time in response to changes in production techniques, transportation technologies, consumption patterns, and energy use. In nineteenth-century America, horse droppings were a major part of the municipal waste stream. In 1840 New York was able to sell its street sweepings for $38,711 because they were two-thirds horse manure. The other third was dirt and dust. By 1860, better sources of fertilizer had become available and the city received less than $18,000 for its street sweepings; shortly after that it had to begin paying to dispose of them. Ash from domestic coal burning was a significant part of the early twentieth-century municipal waste stream. Manhattan alone produced nearly 1.2 million tons of coal ash in 1910.

The volume and composition of domestic waste streams have changed dramatically over time. In 1910, Americans produced about a half-pound of municipal garbage per person per day, twice the per capita amount produced in Europe. By 1960, the volume of municipal waste in the United States had grown to more than 88 million tons per year, 2.7 pounds of waste per person per day. Waste volumes continued to grow during the next four decades, reaching approximately 236 million tons in 2003, 4.5 pounds per person per day. Paper and paper products are the largest elements in the municipal waste stream today (35.2%) followed by yard waste (12.1%) and food waste (11.7%); plastics (11.3%), metals (8.0%), wood (5.8%), and glass (5.3%) also occupy prominent portions of the waste stream.

Waste management practices have changed substantially over time. In the nineteenth century valuable products were reclaimed from domestic waste where possible, whether it was horse droppings used for fertilizer, uncombusted coal in ash, scrap metal, rubber, paper, or glass collected by junk cart men. Some coastal cities dumped their garbage at sea, a practice that is prohibited today; other cities built incinerators or sent their garbage to landfills.

Today most municipal solid waste (56%) is sent to landfills. As environmental standards have tightened, the number of operating landfills that dispose of municipal waste has declined sharply from 8,000 in 1988 to only 1,767 in 2002.

Approximately 14.5 percent of the municipal waste stream is incinerated, a substantial decline from the 30 percent of the waste stream combusted in 1960. A total of 97 municipal incinerators have the capacity to generate electricity, while burning a total of up to 95,000 tons of municipal solid waste each day. In recent years there has been a substantial resurgence of recycling and composting of waste. Only 6.4 percent of the municipal waste stream was recycled or composted in 1960, but this number increased to 16.8 percent in 1990 and 30.6 percent in 2003. A total of 72 million tons of waste was either recycled or composted in 2003, more than double the 34 million tons recycled in 1990. Batteries were the materials recycled most regularly (93%), followed by yard trimmings (56%) and paper and paperboard (48%).

Concern over the rising volume of municipal solid waste helped persuade Congress to adopt the Solid Waste Disposal Act of 1965 (SWDA). This legislation funded federal research and provided financial assistance to states to improve their waste management planning. It was not until more than a decade later, in 1976, that Congress responded to the growing problem of hazardous waste management by adopting the Resource Conservation and Recovery Act (RCRA) as an amendment to the SWDA. With the expansion of the petrochemical industry after World War II, the volume and toxicity of industrial waste streams had increased dramatically. At the end of World War II, U.S. industry was generating approximately 500,000 tons of hazardous waste per year. During the next 50 years the volume of this waste increased more than 500-fold. Despite the highly toxic compounds contained in this waste, much of it simply was dumped on land with virtually no concern for its potential to cause long-term environmental harm.

Many people may have assumed that the ground could act as a kind of bottomless sponge, absorbing without consequences any chemical compounds poured into it. The prevailing philosophy throughout the 1950s and 1960s was "out of sight, out of mind." This mentality was irrevocably jarred in 1978 by the discovery of a toxic soup bubbling up into the basements of homes in the community of Love Canal, New York, following heavy rains. The homes had been constructed on the site of a former industrial dump that had been deeded to the city for $1. While Love Canal became the focus of national attention, similar problems were being discovered throughout the nation. A childhood leukemia cluster was discovered in Woburn, Massachusetts, where the municipal drinking water wells were found to be heavily contaminated with industrial toxins.

In 1979 alone, more than 300 incidents of groundwater contamination were discovered; private and public water supply wells were capped in 25 states. House Comm. on Govt. Operations, Interim Report on Groundwater Contamination: Environmental Protection Agency Oversight, H.R. No. 96-1440, 3 (1980). EPA determined that 50 billion gallons of liquid wastes were placed in industrial surface impoundments every day; 70 percent of these impoundments were unlined and 2,600 of these were sitting directly on top of groundwater sources within one mile of a water supply well. Id. at 6 (as corrected by errata sheet). This put new pressure on EPA to implement the "cradle-to-grave" regulatory program for hazardous wastes mandated by RCRA. While RCRA authorized EPA to bring lawsuits against anyone contributing to conditions that "may present an imminent and substantial endangerment to health or the environment," its primary purpose was not to remediate past contamination. Congress addressed this problem in 1980 when it created the Superfund program in the Comprehensive Environmental Response, Compensation, and Liability Act (CERCLA).

While the Superfund program concentrates on remediating contamination problems caused by past waste management practices, contemporary management of hazardous waste is regulated under RCRA. A total of 17,694 entities reported that they generated more than 30.1 million tons of RCRA hazardous waste in 2003. EPA, The National Biennial RCRA Hazardous Waste Report, at 1-1 (2004). In 2003, 1,726 facilities managed RCRA hazardous wastes, 566 were treatment, storage, or disposal facilities (TSDs); most of these were storage-only facilities. More than 36 percent of this waste was managed by facilities in two states— Texas and Louisiana. Most waste was managed by generators on site. A total of 7.3 million tons of hazardous waste were shipped offsite; 4.3 million tons of this crossed state lines. Id. at 3-3.

Deepwell or underground injection is the principal method for managing hazardous waste, accounting for more than 34 percent of waste management in 2003. Only 1.7 million tons of hazardous waste were managed in landfills or surface impoundments in 2003, id. at 2-5; 1.3 million tons were incinerated. Id.

Not all discarded toxics are regulated as hazardous waste. Household waste is exempt from federal hazardous waste regulations even though it may contain toxic constituents such as those found in paint, cleaners, oils, batteries, and pesticides. Several industries also have succeeded in winning special treatment for their wastes. The mining and petroleum industries generally have not been subjected to federal hazardous waste regulations despite the fact that their wastes have contributed to numerous incidents of environmental damage. Surface mining operations are regulated under the Surface Mining Control and Reclamation Act (SMCRA), while underground storage tanks that contain hazardous substances are regulated under RCRA.

Pollution controls imposed by the Clean Air Act and the Clean Water Act generate their own wastes including sludges from wastewater treatment plants and air pollution control equipment. As end-of-the-pipe pollution controls shifted some pollution from one medium to another, Congress recognized the importance of controlling pollution at its source. There is now broad agreement, reflected in the Pollution Prevention Act of 1990, that environmental policy should shift its focus from controlling discharges at the end of the pipe to encouraging process changes that prevent pollution by reducing the volume and toxicity of waste streams. Source reduction is now the preferred strategy, followed by recycling, and then treatment.

Following the enactment of the Pollution Prevention Act in 1990, EPA developed a national waste minimization plan as required by the Act. This plan established a national goal of reducing the presence of the most persistent, bioaccumulative toxic chemicals in hazardous wastes by 50 percent by the year 2005. After announcing a list of 53 such chemicals in 1998, EPA's Office of Solid Waste later shifted its focus to a new goal of reducing the quantity of 23 "priority chemicals" in hazardous and nonhazardous waste by 10 percent below 2001 levels by the year 2008.

Regulations raising the cost of waste disposal are one means for encouraging source reduction and recycling. EPA also has sought to use non-regulatory strategies to promote these ends. Federal procurement policies have been changed to encourage the development of markets for products containing recycled materials. In May 1995 EPA issued updated and expanded Guidelines for Procurement of Products Containing Recovered Materials. These guidelines apply to all federal, state, and local agencies and their contractors who receive federal funds and who purchase more than $10,000 worth of covered items annually. The guidelines require these agencies to develop affirmative programs to ensure that 24 types of products purchased by these agencies have a minimum recycled content specified in the guidelines. EPA expanded the range of items covered by these guidelines in a final rule adopted in 2000. 65 FR 3070 (2000).

EPA also is promoting the concept of extended product responsibility (EPR) or product stewardship. The concept, which has become popular in Europe, emphasizes principles of industrial ecology, a growing discipline that analyzes how product design and process technology affect the environment by changing energy use and waste generation patterns. EPR seeks to reduce the "environmental footprint" of products by emphasizing that all actors along the product chain should share responsibility for their life-cycle environmental impact from the impacts of material selection to those of the manufacturing process to downstream impacts from product use and disposal patterns.

As the volume of discarded electronic products escalates, concern has grown over the environmental impact of toxic materials contained in this "e-waste." It is estimated that more than 2.2 million tons of e-waste was generated in the United States in 2000 and that only about 9 percent of such waste was recovered for reuse or recycling. In 2002 the European Commission issued a Waste Electrical and Electronic Equipment directive that makes the manufacturers of electronic products responsible for their disposal. In 2003 California adopted the Electronic Waste Recycling Act creating a point-of-sale fee collection program to fund the state's efforts to recycle materials in discarded electronics. While EPA does not have any regulations specifically covering e-waste, it has encouraged manufacturers of electronic products to establish "take-back" programs to recycle used electronics.

These and other policy initiatives reflect the evolution of waste management policy from end-of-the-pipe controls to measures that create incentives for source reduction and recycling. For a description of EPA's vision for the future of waste management policy, see EPA, Beyond RCRA: Waste and Materials Management in the Year 2020 (Oct. 2002), available online at *http://www.epa.gov/epaoswer/osw/vision.pdf.*

NOTES AND QUESTIONS

1. Even the most severe incidents of environmental contamination caused by mismanagement of hazardous waste, such as Love Canal and the dioxin contamination that led to the evacuation of the town of Times Beach, Missouri, rarely cause harm that crosses state boundaries. In light of the highly localized nature of most harm caused by hazardous waste, what is the rationale for federal regulation of waste management?

2. The task of gathering data on waste generation and management is complicated by the difficulty of defining what material should be considered "waste." Are materials that are generated by production and extraction processes waste if they are not immediately used for some purpose? Are they wastes if they may be used at some time in the future as material inputs into other production processes?

3. Average per capita generation of municipal solid waste remains about twice as high in the United States as in Europe. Why is substantially more waste per capita generated by residents of the United States than by residents of other developed countries?

4. While RCRA and CERCLA are the most comprehensive statutory responses to the waste management problem, they are not the only laws that affect waste disposal practices. Before we examine the RCRA and CERCLA programs, it is useful to consider briefly the wide variety of other statutes that are used to regulate waste management practices.

B. STATUTORY AUTHORITIES AFFECTING WASTE MANAGEMENT

Congress has long recognized that the best strategy for preventing pollution is to reduce the generation of waste while encouraging recycling. Yet environmental regulations have focused almost exclusively on waste *disposal* practices, influencing waste *reduction* only indirectly by raising disposal costs. Wastes are generated at many stages in the production process by the extraction of raw materials as well as during refining and fabrication. Some wastes generated during manufacturing are recycled as scrap that is fed back into the crude materials refining process to be transformed into a form usable in further product manufacturing. The rest become industrial waste. Manufactured products are themselves sources of waste when capital goods are demolished and when consumer goods and packaging are discarded as litter or household and commercial wastes. Although the design of production processes and finished products determines the volume and composition of waste streams, waste disposal considerations often have not been incorporated into product design decisions.

The variety and complexity of activities that generate and dispose of wastes are reflected in the patchwork way in which the environmental laws control various waste management activities. Nearly a dozen major federal statutes control some aspect of waste disposal. These include not only the principal pollution control laws, listed previously, but also other statutes designed to control radioactive wastes and uranium mill tailings. These statutes are summarized below in Figue 4.1, which lists the pollutants or wastes covered by each law (what we have called "regulatory targets"), the type of regulations they impose, and the basis for imposing controls. The chart also identifies how each law may produce cross-media transfers of wastes (e.g., air pollution controls may generate sludge and incinerator residues that are disposed of on land).

As the chart confirms, the environmental statutes focus on diverse regulatory targets. The extent of regulatory authority over waste management practices varies depending on the activity or product that generates the waste, the characteristics of the waste, and the location or method of waste disposal. For example, wastes burned or vented into the air may be subject to regulation under the Clean Air Act. Wastes discharged into inland or coastal waters are regulated under the Clean Water Act, while wastes dumped into the open ocean are controlled by the Marine Protection, Research, and Sanctuaries Act (MPRSA, also known as the Ocean Dumping Act). Radioactive wastes and uranium mill tailings are covered by their own separate statutes: the Nuclear Waste Policy Act regulates the most highly radioactive wastes generated by nuclear power plants; the Low Level Radioactive Waste Policy Act controls other radioactive wastes, such as those generated by hospitals and laboratories; the Uranium Mill Tailings Radiation Control Act sets standards for the cleanup of wastes

FIGURE 4.1
Major Federal Laws Regarding Waste

Statute	Waste management objective	Pollutants/wastes covered	Regulatory approach†	Basis for controls	Primary transfers to another medium
Clean Water Act: 33 U.S.C. §1251 et seq.	Protect and improve surface water quality	All discharges to surface waters, including 126 priority toxic pollutants	Performance standards (emissions limits); ambient standards	Technology with health-based backup*	Sludge to land; air emissions from treatment plant and sludge incineration
Marine Protection Research and Sanctuaries Act: 16 U.S.C. §1401 et seq.	Limit dumping into ocean	All wastes except oil and sewage in the ocean	Use restrictions (prohibited unless done with permit)	Balancing, with health-based backup	
Safe Drinking Water Act: 40 U.S.C. §§300f-300j-10	Protect public drinking water supply	Contaminants found in drinking water and wastes injected into deep wells	Ambient standards, design and performance standards	Technology*	
Clean Air Act: 42 U.S.C. §7401 et seq.	Protect and improve air quality	All emissions to air	Ambient standards; performance standards (emissions limits)	Health; technology*	Sludge and incinerator residues to land
Resource Conservation and Recovery Act: 42 U.S.C. §6901 et seq.	Control hazardous and solid wastes; encourage waste reduction and recycling	Hazardous and solid wastes	Use restrictions, design and performance standards; information disclosure	Health	Air through incineration; water through sewage treatment plants

FIGURE 4.1
Continued

Comprehensive Environmental Response, Compensation, and Liability Act: 42 U.S.C. §9601 et seq.	Cleanup of abandoned hazardous waste sites; emergency response	Release or threatened release of hazardous substance	Performance and design standards	Health, with cost-effectiveness constraint	Air through volatilization, incineration, and dust
Surface Mining Control and Reclamation Act: 30 U.S.C. §1201 et seq.	Control pollution from surface coal mines	Surface coal mining wastes	Performance standards	Health (or environment)	Releases to water
Nuclear Waste Policy Act: 42 U.S.C. §10101 et seq.	Control disposal of high-level radioactive wastes	Commercial high-level radioactive waste	Use restrictions	Health (or environment)	
Low Level Radioactive Waste Policy Act: 42 U.S.C. §2021b et seq.	Control disposal of low-level radioactive waste	Commercial low-level radioactive waste	Use restrictions, performance and design standards	Health (or environment)	
Uranium Mill Tailings Radiation Control Act: 42 U.S.C. §7901 et seq.	Manage uranium mill tailings	Uranium mill tailings	Performance standards	Health (or environment)	Air from dust
Toxic Substances Control Act: 15 U.S.C. §2601 et seq.	Prevent unreasonable risk from chemical substances	Wastes from production or use of industrial chemical substances	Use restrictions	Balancing	

†Lists the major approaches for each statute. Some statutes use nearly all the approaches identified in Chapter 2B2.

*Some or all of these are feasibility-limited technology standards.

Source: Adapted from Conservation Foundation, State of the Environment: A View Toward the Nineties 426-427 (1987).

from uranium mines. The Safe Drinking Water Act regulates contaminants that are found in public drinking water supplies as well as hazardous wastes disposed of through underground injection in deep wells.

The nature of the activity that generates a waste also may have a significant influence on the way the waste is regulated. For example, wastes generated by households have been exempted from RCRA's hazardous waste regulations because of concern over the difficulty of extending the federal regulatory system into everyone's backyard. Because mineral extraction operations generate wastes in such large volumes, Congress temporarily exempted them from federal hazardous waste regulations pending further study. Recycling activities also have been exempted from hazardous waste regulation in order to encourage efforts to reduce the volume and toxicity of waste streams.

Although Figure 4.1 might give one the impression that federal regulation has long dominated the waste management field, solid waste disposal was not regulated at the federal level until relatively recently. Garbage disposal and other forms of waste management have traditionally been the exclusive concern of local and state governments, especially municipalities. Indeed, virtually all of the other major federal environmental legislation antedates the enactment of the principal federal laws regulating waste disposal. But concern over the environmental damage caused by improper waste disposal has rapidly produced in RCRA and CERCLA two of the most far-reaching federal environmental laws. RCRA provides for cradle-to-grave regulation of hazardous waste, while CERCLA imposes strict liability for the cleanup of releases of hazardous substances. While the two statutes have complementary objectives—RCRA to prevent releases of hazardous wastes and CERCIA to clean up releases of a broader class of hazardous substances—they each employ very different means to pursue their goal. RCRA employs a regulatory approach, while CERCLA is founded on a strict liability scheme.

REGULATION OF WASTE MANAGEMENT:
A PATHFINDER

The principal statutory authorities that regulate waste management practices are contained in the Resource Conservation and Recovery Act (RCRA), codified at 42 U.S.C. §§6901-6992k, and the Comprehensive Environmental Response, Compensation, and Liability Act (CERCLA), codified at 42 U.S.C. §§9601-9675. Because RCRA was originally enacted as an amendment to the largely non-regulatory Solid Waste Disposal Act, it is sometimes referred to by that name, though practitioners and courts generally use the RCRA acronym. Because CERCLA creates the federal Superfund, it is often referred to as the Superfund legislation. RCRA was substantially revised in 1984 by the Hazardous and Solid Waste Amendments (HSWA). Minor revisions were made in 1992 by the Federal Facility Compliance Act and in 1996 by the Land Disposal Program Flexibility Act. CERCLA was substantially amended in 1986 by the Superfund Amendments and Reauthorization Act (SARA). Amendments were added to CERCLA in 1996 by the Asset Conservation, Lender Liability and Deposit Insurance Protection Act (ACLLDIPA), in 1999 by the

Superfund Recycling Equity Act, and in 2002 by the Small Business Liability Relief and Brownfields Revitalization Act (SBLRBRA). Because disposal of nonhazardous solid waste is largely governed by state law and municipal ordinances, it is important to consult sources of such law and to pay attention to the policies of state (and local) environmental officials.

EPA waste management regulations are codified at 40 C.F.R. pts. 239-282. Regulations governing management of hazardous waste begin at 40 C.F.R. pt. 260. Regulations covering underground storage tanks are found at 40 C.F.R. pts. 280-282. While CERCLA has largely been a non-regulatory program, it is beginning to generate a substantial body of regulations contained in 40 C.F.R. pts. 300-312. The list of reportable quantities of CERCLA hazardous substances appears at 40 C.F.R. pt. 302. Significant regulatory interpretations often are found in EPA guidance documents rather than in the Federal Register, which makes it difficult to monitor significant changes in EPA policy. The American Bar Association regularly sponsors satellite seminars to update practitioners on RCRA and CERCLA developments.

EPA maintains dockets containing important information about sites eligible for cleanup under CERCLA. These include a Federal Facilities Docket, a National Priority List (NPL) Docket, and Superfund Administrative Records, which include Records of Decision (RODs) concerning site cleanups. EPA also maintains a toll-free hotline that can provide answers to questions about CERCLA and EPCRA programs (it discontinued telephone support for RCRA in 2005). Outside of the Washington, D.C. area the number for the Superfund/EPCRA Call Center is (800) 424-9346. In the D.C. area the hotline number is (703) 412-9810. EPA maintains a Pollution Prevention Information Clearinghouse accessible online (*http:// www.epa.gov/opptintr/ppic*) and a "RCRA Online" database at *www. epa.gov/rcraonline* which enables users to locate documents covering a wide range of RCRA topics. A particularly useful guide to RCRA is EPA's RCRA Orientation Manual (Jan. 2003), available online at *http://www.epa.gov/epaoswer/general/orientat/r02016.pdf.*

Despite differences in their initial purposes and approaches, the RCRA and CERCLA programs are closely linked. Section 7003 of RCRA, 42 U.S.C. §6973, authorizes government actions to enjoin anyone who has contributed to waste-handling practices that may present an "imminent and substantial endangerment to health or the environment." This authority foreshadowed the enactment in 1980 of CERCLA's cleanup authorities. As congressional dissatisfaction with EPA's implementation of these programs produced major legislative revisions of each program (RCRA in 1984 and CERCLA in 1986), their interrelationship has become more important. Congress has recognized that the success or failure of RCRA's preventative regulations could have a major effect on the number of dump sites that the CERCLA program will have to clean up in the future. Thus Congress directed that RCRA's regulatory program be used to phase out the most dangerous land disposal practices while requiring operating RCRA facilities to clean up prior releases of hazardous substances as a condition for obtaining an RCRA permit.

In addition to the regulatory authorities mentioned above, Congress has acted to encourage voluntary efforts to reduce the generation of waste. The Pollution Prevention Act of 1990 represents a step in this direction.

The Act declares it "to be the national policy of the United States that pollution should be prevented at the source whenever feasible." In cases where pollution cannot feasibly be prevented, it declares recycling to be the preferred alternative, followed by treatment, and only then disposal. The Act requires EPA to establish a Pollution Prevention Office and a Source Reduction Clearinghouse to facilitate source reduction. The Act also required EPA to develop a Pollution Prevention Strategy, which EPA announced in January 1991. As part of this strategy, EPA targeted 17 high-risk chemicals, and it established a voluntary goal of reducing total environmental releases of these chemicals by 33 percent by the end of 1992 and by 50 percent by the end of 1995. EPA, Pollution Prevention Strategy (Jan. 1991). The 33/50 program was highly successful. More than 1,300 companies participated in the program, which reached its interim 33 percent reduction goal a year ahead of schedule. The 1995 goal of 50 percent reduction actually was achieved by 1994 when reductions totaled 757 million pounds. As noted above, EPA has now refocused its pollution prevention strategy from efforts to reduce the presence of 53 of the most persistent, bioaccumulative, and toxic chemicals in hazardous waste by 50 percent by the year 2005 to a new goal of reducing the quantity of 23 "priority chemicals" in hazardous and nonhazardous waste by 10 percent below 2001 levels by the year 2008.

EPA has emphasized that voluntary pollution prevention programs are not intended to substitute for strong regulatory and enforcement programs. Indeed, the Agency has indicated that it is investigating more creative use of its existing regulatory authorities to encourage source reduction, and it has used the adoption of source reduction plans as a means for settling some enforcement cases.

The Pollution Prevention Act is designed mainly to create an improved information base that can facilitate future decisions about regulatory action to prevent pollution. The Act requires companies that already must file annual reports on environmental releases pursuant to the Emergency Planning and Community Right-to-Know Act to include in these reports descriptions of their source reduction and recycling activities. This information, which is made available to the public, includes estimates of the amount of source reduction each company expects to achieve during the next two years.

C.   THE RCRA REGULATORY PROGRAM

1.   RCRA: An Introduction

A.   HISTORY OF THE RCRA PROGRAM

The Solid Waste Disposal Act of 1965 had established a modest program of research on solid waste management centered in the old Department of Health, Education, and Welfare. In 1970 this legislation was expanded to authorize federal grants to support the development of new technology for solid waste management. Congress concluded that solid waste management was primarily a local responsibility, and it continued to define the federal role as a non-regulatory one.

By 1976, this had changed. RCRA was enacted after congressional committees had received estimates that the volume of solid waste generated in the United States was much greater than previously imagined. An estimated 3 to 4 billion tons of solid waste were reportedly being generated annually, and the amount was growing at an estimated 8 percent per year. The House committee report accompanying the legislation noted that each year Americans discarded 71 billion cans, 38 billion jars and bottles, 35 million tons of paper, 7.6 million televisions, 7 million cars and trucks, and 4 million tons of plastics. H.R. Rep. 94-1491, 94th Cong., 2d Sess., at 10-11 (1976).

After 1980, the history of RCRA became tightly intertwined with that of CERCLA. Mounting evidence of lax disposal practices prompted Congress to become actively involved in cleaning up the mistakes of the past and preventing their recurrence. By and large, RCRA has become the locus of Congress's prevention concerns, while CERCLA tackles the problems of cleaning up past mistakes, although there are important areas of overlapping responsibility. Under section 7003 of RCRA, for instance, the government can sue to enjoin activities causing "imminent and substantial endangerment," and thus can compel some cleanups. In addition, RCRA's "corrective action" requirements impose cleanup responsibilities as a condition for maintaining a current operating permit. In this section we concentrate on the predominant prevention aspects of the statute. RCRA's corrective action authorities are found in §§3004(u) & (v), 42 U.S.C. §§6924(u) & (v).

The 1976 Act established a basic statutory structure, which continues to the present: a system for identifying and listing hazardous wastes, a cradle-to-grave tracking system, standards for generators and transporters of hazardous wastes and for operators of treatment, storage, and disposal (TSD) facilities, a permit system to enforce these standards, and a procedure for delegating to states the administration of the permitting program. This complicated structure reflects RCRA's distinct, though interrelated, objectives.

First, RCRA aimed at making land disposal of wastes far safer than it had been previously. The "overriding concern" of Congress in enacting RCRA, as expressed in the House committee report accompanying the legislation, was "the effect on the population and the environment of the disposal of discarded hazardous wastes—those which by virtue of their composition or longevity are harmful, toxic, or lethal." The report noted that "[w]ithout a regulatory framework, such hazardous waste will continue to be disposed of in ponds or on the ground in a manner that results in substantial and sometimes irreversible pollution of the environment."

The RCRA structure provided such a regulatory framework. The identification and listing system would notify generators, transporters, and operators as to which wastes came under the Act's safeguards for hazardous wastes; the tracking system would ensure that compliance could be monitored and responsibility for future problems fixed; the standards, especially for TSD operators, would minimize the environmental costs of disposal, while the permitting system would put operators on clear notice of those standards.

RCRA represented a significant departure from the approach of end-of-the-pipe pollution control statutes such as the Clean Air Act and Clean Water Act by regulating the entire life cycle of hazardous waste management activities. Congress recognized that environmental regulations should do more than simply transfer pollution from one medium to another. As the House committee that reported out the RCRA legislation explained:

> At present the federal government is spending billions of dollars to remove pollutants from the air and water, only to dispose of such pollutants on the land in an environmentally unsound manner. The existing methods of land disposal often result in air pollution, subsurface leachate, and surface run-off, which affect air and water quality. This legislation will eliminate this problem and permit the environmental laws to function in a coordinated and effective way.

Indeed, the committee optimistically declared that RCRA "eliminates the last remaining loophole in environmental law, that of unregulated land disposal of discarded materials and hazardous wastes." H.R. Rep. 94-1491, 94th Cong., 2d Sess., at 4 (1976). While the RCRA regulatory program has focused on protecting groundwater from contamination by hazardous wastes leaching from land disposal facilities, RCRA requires regulation of all avenues for treatment, storage, and disposal of hazardous waste, including incinerators and air emissions from hazardous waste landfills.

Second, RCRA aimed at technology forcing. The statute, through the regulations that EPA was instructed to promulgate, requires TSD operators to employ technologies for landfill disposal "as may be necessary to protect human health." §3004(a). Beyond this, however, RCRA evinces a concern that landfills were being used excessively because they were far cheaper than alternative disposal techniques. As one analyst notes: "It is not difficult to see why firms and others faced with the costs of incineration to render wastes less harmful (estimated to range from $300 to $1,000 per ton) or of burying the wastes in landfills (perhaps as little as $50 per ton) would choose the latter." R. Dower, Hazardous Wastes, in Public Policies for Environment Protection 154 (P. Portney ed., 1990). Imposing stricter safety requirements on landfills would raise the costs of such disposal; Congress believed that this would force the development of superior alternative technologies.

The desire to promote alternative disposal techniques became even more apparent as Congress has revisited the 1976 legislation, first in 1980 and again in 1984. For instance, as the late Senator John Chafee (R-RI) explained during debate on the 1984 Amendments:

> [L]and disposal is extremely cheap when compared with the available alternatives such as incineration or chemical-physical treatment. Therefore, we should not be surprised to find that land disposal and treatment in land disposal facilities such as surface impoundments are being utilized much more frequently than the newer, high-tech options. . . . What we do not have, and will not have as long as cheap land disposal options are available, is a viable market to support the development and expansion of new, safer treatment and disposal technologies. [130 Cong. Rec. S30697 (daily ed. Oct. 5, 1984).]

The 1984 Amendments reflected a new level of congressional effort to force technological change because Congress was no longer relying on market forces to express the increased costs of land disposal and hence to stimulate that change. As Representative Lent (R-NY) said, "I believe it is appropriate for the Congress to intervene at this time and to establish a new policy which calls for a review of known hazardous wastes and a determination whether these wastes are appropriate for land disposal." 130 Cong. Rec. H29490 (daily ed. Oct. 3, 1984). The most dramatic such interventions are the 1984 Amendments' land disposal ban provisions, analyzed later in this section.

Third, RCRA aimed at waste reduction. "Waste reduction" encompasses any techniques that adjust basic manufacturing processes so that waste is not generated in the first place. One incentive for waste reduction is provided by increasing the costs of waste disposal. Beyond this, initial elements of a waste reduction program were rudimentary at best and, in the process of implementing the regulatory aspects of RCRA, essentially ignored. There are signs this situation is changing following enactment of the Pollution Prevention Act of 1990.

One reason waste reduction was not more directly addressed by the 1976 statute involves the fourth objective of RCRA: Congress wanted to minimize direct regulation of American production processes. As the committee report accompanying the House version of the 1976 Act explained the provisions applicable to generators of hazardous wastes, "rather than place restrictions on the generation of hazardous waste, which in many instances would amount to interference with the production process itself, the committee has limited the responsibility of the generator for hazardous waste to one of providing information." H.R. Rep. No. 94-1491, 94th Cong., 2d Sess., at 26 (1976). The jurisdictional trigger of the statute reflects this intention, in that the statute defines "solid wastes" as "discarded material." §1004(27).

American Mining Congress v. EPA, excerpted below, involves some of the interpretational and implementational issues created by the desire of Congress to steer EPA away from direct regulation of normal production processes. As that decision suggests, some of the most significant problems arise with respect to the fifth objective of the statute: encouraging recycling. As a method for addressing the solid waste problem, recycling or resource recovery can be seen as standing between waste reduction and treatment, storage, and disposal. While waste reduction adjusts primary production processes so that waste is eliminated before it is generated, and TSD facilities dispose of or otherwise care for the generated wastes that remain, recycling takes generated wastes and returns all or part of them to primary production processes. Congress understood that increased recycling was yet another way to minimize environmental and public health damage from waste disposal and meant to encourage it. As the House report said, "an increase in reclamation and reuse practices is a major objective of the Resource Conservation and Recovery Act." H.R. Rep. No. 94-1491 at 2.

Although the desire to encourage recycling has been clear from the beginning, the status of recycling activities under RCRA's regulatory authorities has been problematic. Many of the problems relate to the distinction between "the production process itself" and "discarded material." If they are awaiting processing through a recycling facility, are piles of industrial residue from manufacturing "discarded materials" or are they part of "the production process itself"? Does it matter whether or not the recycling processes actually employed were being employed as part of production processes before RCRA was enacted (even if not employed as extensively as we would like)? From time to time, EPA has said that it "did not believe [its] authority extends to certain types of recycling activities that are shown to be similar to normal production processes. . . ." 50 Fed. Reg. at 614. In other places, however, it has been more aggressive, interpreting RCRA as "providing authority over hazardous wastes being used, reused, recycled, or reclaimed." 48 Fed. Reg. at 14,502. The line-drawing exercise here is important, because regulated firms have a substantial interest in being exempt from governmental regulation. This is precisely what was at stake in *American Mining Congress.* That litigation is also typical of a fair amount of litigation under RCRA. Because being caught by the RCRA regulatory net is financially onerous, and because the statute contains so many definitions and exemptions, we have witnessed considerable litigation about its jurisdictional boundaries.

Finally, RCRA sought to maintain substantial state responsibility for the solid waste problem. The legislation explicitly acknowledged that "the collection of solid wastes should continue to be primarily the function of State, regional and local agencies," §1002(a)(4). While it mandated comprehensive federal regulation of "hazardous wastes," it provided for the delegation of permitting responsibilities to qualifying state agencies. Thus, RCRA reflected the tendency of 1970s environmental legislation to leave politically divisive implementation of federal substantive legislation to the states. Some of this divisiveness emerges during controversies surrounding the siting of hazardous waste–related facilities.

While keeping the basic structure of the 1976 Act intact, Congress revisited RCRA with major amendments in 1984 called the Hazardous and Solid Waste Amendments (HSWA). HSWA sought to strengthen EPA's regulatory hand in accomplishing RCRA's primary objectives. Congress made more apparent its conviction that land disposal should be the disposal option of last resort and expressed its dissatisfaction with the slow pace of RCRA implementation.

Defining which of the myriad chemical waste streams are hazardous and what management practices will ensure that no damage is done to the environment proved to be far more difficult than anyone had imagined. These inherent difficulties were exacerbated in 1981 when the Reagan administration's regulatory relief program brought RCRA implementation to a temporary standstill. EPA's promulgation of final permitting standards for TSDs was delayed for years while existing TSDs were allowed to continue in operation as RCRA "interim status" facilities with minimal environmental controls. To qualify for "interim status," facilities were only required to notify EPA of their existence and to conduct minimal groundwater monitoring.

The 1984 Amendments mandated a major shift in the philosophy behind RCRA regulation. EPA previously had recognized that all landfills eventually leak, but it had focused most of its regulatory attention on measures to contain such leakage. The 1984 Amendments sought not only to speed EPA's development of regulatory standards and to close certain loopholes in EPA's existing regulations, but also to fundamentally change waste disposal practices by phasing out land disposal and by forcing the development and use of improved technology to detoxify hazardous wastes.

To speed EPA's implementation of RCRA, Congress imposed scores of new statutory deadlines for the promulgation of regulations by EPA. EPA had failed to meet most such deadlines in the original RCRA legislation. Indeed, most of the significant RCRA regulations, such as permitting standards for TSDs, were issued under court orders as a result of citizen suits brought by environmental groups. To ensure that the most significant new deadlines established by the 1984 Amendments were met, Congress coupled them with "hammer" provisions specifying what regulations would automatically take effect if EPA failed to act.

The principal thrust of the 1984 Amendments was to shift hazardous waste disposal away from the land and to encourage the development of more sophisticated treatment technologies. To minimize the land disposal of untreated wastes, Congress directed that such disposal be banned in stages unless EPA determined that there would be "no migration" of hazardous constituents as long as the waste remains hazardous. Recognizing that severe contamination already had occurred at many TSDs, Congress required facilities obtaining RCRA permits to take corrective action to clean up all prior releases of hazardous wastes and their constituents. To hasten the closing of interim status facilities that would not qualify for final permits, Congress required all TSDs to apply for final RCRA permits by October 1986 and to certify compliance with groundwater monitoring and financial responsibility requirements. As a result of these provisions, a majority of the existing treatment and storage facilities and incinerators opted to close, as did the vast majority of land disposal facilities. By 1990 EPA reported that 1,273 RCRA land disposal facilities were closing, while only 194 were either applying for, or had received, permits; 1,559 RCRA treatment and storage facilities were closing, while 1,251 were either applying for, or had received, permits; and 130 RCRA incinerators were closing, while 120 were seeking permits. EPA, The Nation's Hazardous Waste Management Program at a Crossroads 43 (July 1990).

Congress made minor amendments to RCRA in both 1992 and 1996. In 1992 it enacted the Federal Facility Compliance Act, which made it easier to enforce RCRA at federal facilities. In 1996 Congress enacted the Land Disposal Program Flexibility Act that amended RCRA to provide EPA with more flexibility in regulating the land disposal of certain wastes.

B.   Structure of the RCRA Program

To understand how the RCRA program operates, it is useful to begin by sketching in greater detail the basic structure of the regulatory scheme the statute creates, rather than plunging headlong into what one court has called a "mind-numbing journey" (American Mining Congress v. EPA, 824 F.2d 1177, 1189 (D.C. Cir. 1987)) through EPA's complicated RCRA regulations. The structure of RCRA is outlined below. When studying RCRA, bear in mind what targets EPA generally may regulate under the statute (those who generate, transport, treat, store, or dispose of hazardous solid waste) and the basis for controls specified in the statute ("as may be necessary to protect human health or the environment").

STRUCTURE OF THE RESOURCE
CONSERVATION AND RECOVERY ACT

§1002. Goals: outlines statutory goals, including the principle that land disposal should be the least favored method for managing hazardous wastes.

Subtitle C: Hazardous Waste Management (§§3001-3020)
§3001: Identification and Listing of Hazardous Waste: requires EPA to develop criteria for determining what is a hazardous waste and to list wastes determined to be hazardous.
§3002: Regulation of Generators of Hazardous Waste: requires EPA to establish recordkeeping requirements and a manifest system to be used to track shipments of hazardous waste from point of generation.

§3003: *Regulation of Transporters of Hazardous Waste:* requires transporters of hazardous waste to use the manifest system.

§3004: *Regulation of Facilities that Treat, Store, or Dispose of Hazardous Waste (TSDs):* requires EPA to set standards for TSDs to ensure safe handling of hazardous waste, sets minimum requirements for such standards, prohibits the land disposal of untreated wastes unless EPA specifically determines that such disposal is protective of human health and the environment, establishes minimum technology requirements for certain facilities, and requires corrective action for all releases of hazardous wastes or constituents.

§3005: *Permit Requirements for TSDs:* requires TSDs to obtain a permit from EPA or states that incorporates the requirements of section 3004.

Subtitle D: State or Regional Solid Waste Plans

§§4001-4010: require EPA to establish guidelines for state solid waste management plans and to set minimum requirements for state plans including a ban on new open dumps, require EPA to establish criteria for classifying facilities as sanitary landfills, prohibit open dumping of solid waste except in sanitary landfills, and require EPA to establish minimum regulatory standards for municipal landfills to be implemented by the states.

Enforcement, Citizen Suit, and Judicial Review Provisions

§3008: provides federal enforcement authorities including criminal, civil, and administrative penalties.

§7002: authorizes citizen suits against those who violate RCRA regulations or permits, against anyone who has contributed or is contributing to the past or present handling of any solid or hazardous waste that may present an imminent and substantial endangerment to health or the environment, and against the EPA administrator for failure to perform any nondiscretionary duty.

§7003: authorizes suits by EPA to restrain anyone who has contributed or is contributing to the past or present handling of any solid or hazardous waste that may present an imminent and substantial endangerment to health or the environment.

§7006: authorizes judicial review of RCRA regulations in the D.C. Circuit.

Subtitle I: Regulation of Underground Storage Tanks

§9002: requires owners of underground storage tanks to notify state authorities.

§9003: requires EPA to issue regulations governing detection, prevention, and correction of leaks from underground storage tanks, including financial responsibility requirements and new tank performance standards.

As you can see, RCRA is divided into two major parts: (1) subtitle C, a regulatory program covering *hazardous* solid wastes, and (2) subtitle D, a largely non-regulatory program to encourage states to improve their management of *nonhazardous* solid waste. Subtitle C of RCRA requires EPA to regulate generators of hazardous waste (§3002), transporters (§3003), and facilities that treat, store, or dispose of hazardous waste (§3004). Operating standards for TSD facilities are to be implemented through a permit system (§3005).

RCRA's subtitle C regulations are contained in 40 C.F.R. pts. 260-272. While they are too complicated to be reviewed in detail here, some idea of the general types of requirements they impose on generators, transporters, and TSD facilities is provided in Figure 4.2. Generators are responsible for determining if their wastes are hazardous. Those who accumulate more than 100 kilograms of hazardous waste per month—an estimated 200,000 firms—are subject to regulation under subtitle C. These generators must obtain an identification number for their hazardous waste. To ensure that shipments of hazardous waste can be traced, generators must complete a multiple-copy manifest form to accompany the waste to its ultimate destination at a licensed TSD. The generator must notify authorities if a copy of the manifest form is not returned certifying that the waste reached its intended destination. 40 C.F.R. pt. 262.

Transporters also must use the manifest system, and they must mark and label their shipments of hazardous waste. 40 C.F.R. pt. 263. Transporters of hazardous waste must comply not only with EPA's manifest requirements, but also with regulations on hazardous materials transportation established by the Department of Transportation pursuant to the Hazardous Materials Transportation Act.

Facilities that treat, store, or dispose of hazardous waste must obtain a permit that incorporates minimum national standards established in EPA's regulations. 40 C.F.R. pt. 270. See Figure 4.3. These include not only general administrative requirements for recordkeeping, personnel training, and emergency preparedness, but also specific design, performance, and operating requirements for each category of facility. New units, replacement units, and lateral expansions of existing landfills and surface impoundments must meet certain minimum technology requirements. (For example, landfills must have double liners and a leachate collection system.) Facilities also must prepare closure plans describing how the facilities ultimately will be closed, and they must demonstrate that they have sufficient financial resources to compensate third parties for damages as well as to undertake safe closure and to conduct postclosure monitoring and maintenance.

Another significant requirement of the 1984 Amendments is that RCRA permits now must require facilities to take "corrective action for all releases of hazardous waste or constituents from any solid waste management unit" at the facility. Thus, TSD facilities that wish to continue operation must clean up any prior contamination at their facility regardless of when or where it occurred. TSDs also must conduct regular groundwater monitoring and take corrective action if contamination is detected. When closing, TSDs must take precautions designed to ensure that their facilities will not leak in the decades to come, and they must ensure their financial responsibility to clean up releases that occur during postclosure care. Generators, transporters, and TSDs must all train their personnel in waste management and emergency response procedures, and they must notify the authorities of releases of hazardous substances.

The regulatory program established by RCRA can be viewed as essentially a two-tiered scheme: "hazardous wastes" are to be regulated stringently under

FIGURE 4.2

Summary of RCRA Subtitle C Regulations Applicable to Hazardous Waste Generators, Transporters, and Treatment, Storage, and Disposal Facilities

RCRA requirements	Generators	Transporters	Treatment, storage, disposal facilities[a]
Determine if wastes are hazardous	X		X
Notify EPA if RCRA hazardous waste handler and obtain identification number	X	X	X
Train personnel in waste management procedures and emergency response	X		X
Preparedness and prevention measures and notification of releases	X	X	X
Contingency planning and emergency procedures	X		X
Inspect facility operations periodically	X		X
Track waste with manifest system	X	X	X
Recordkeeping and reporting	X	X	X
Package, marking, labeling, and transport vehicle placarding	X		
Physical security			X
Use and manage containers, landfills, and other operating areas properly			X
Design and operate waste handling areas adequately[b]			X
Groundwater monitoring			X
Closure and postclosure care			X
Ensure financial responsibility for closure and postclosure care			X

[a] Treatment, storage, or disposal facilities in operation on or before November 19, 1980, could continue operating under "interim status" until a hazardous waste permit was issued, at which time the facility must be in compliance with the final permit regulations.

[b] This includes the design and operation of tanks, surface impoundments, waste piles, land treatment facilities, landfills, incinerators, and injection wells.

Source: GAO, New Approach Needed to Manage the Resource Conservation and Recovery Act, July 1988, at 24.

FIGURE 4.3
A Capsule Description of RCRA's Subtitle C Program

EPA and the states share the responsibility for regulating newly generated hazardous waste under RCRA. RCRA was created to minimize the risks from hazardous wastes at all points in their life cycle, from their generation to their disposal. It was also designed to require safeguards; to encourage the proper disposal of municipal, commercial, and industrial waste; to eliminate or reduce waste; and to conserve energy and natural resources.

Hazardous Waste and "Cradle to Grave" Management

RCRA involves a "cradle to grave" effort covering the generation, transportation, storage, treatment, and disposal of newly generated hazardous waste. EPA's system includes five basic elements:

- **Identification**—Generators and the types of waste that they produce must be initially identified.
- **Tracking**—A uniform "manifest" describing the waste, its quantity, the generator, and receiver, must accompany transported hazardous waste from the point at which it is generated to its final off-site destination and disposal.
- **Permitting**—All hazardous waste treatment, storage, and disposal facilities will be issued permits to allow EPA and the states to ensure their safe operation. There are about 7,000 facilities that must receive permits in order to continue operating.

- **Restrictions and controls**—Hazardous waste facilities must follow EPA's rules and guidance specifying acceptable conditions for disposal, treatment, and storage of hazardous wastes.
- **Enforcement and compliance**—Generators, transporters, and facilities are penalized if they do not comply with the regulations.

The cradle to grave system works through requirements for hazardous waste treatment, storage, and disposal facilties. Key to this system are RCRA operating permits. Basic operating permits identify administrative and technical standards with which facilities must comply. For example, the permits require operators of hazardous waste landfills to keep thorough records of the types and quantities of wastes they manage.

Hazardous Waste Manifest Trail

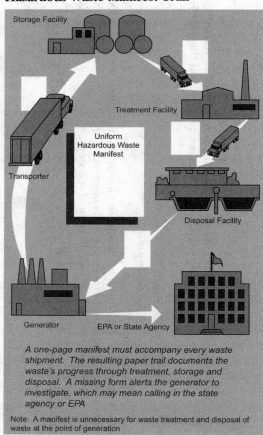

A one-page manifest must accompany every waste shipment. The resulting paper trail documents the waste's progress through treatment, storage and disposal. A missing form alerts the generator to investigate, which may mean calling in the state agency or EPA

Note: A manifest is unnecessary for waste treatment and disposal of waste at the point of generation

Source: EPA, Environmental Progress and Challenges: EPA's Update 88 (Aug. 1988).

subtitle C (from generation through transport to disposal), while all other solid wastes are subject to subtitle D and left largely untouched by federal regulation (although municipal solid waste landfills are now subject to minimum federal standards under subtitle D). Rather than attempting to vary the degree of regulation to match the degree of hazard posed by a particular waste, the RCRA program with few exceptions leaves only two regulatory options: comprehensive regulation with little regard for cost considerations, or no federal regulation at all. If a facility is found to be treating, storing, or disposing of a hazardous waste, it generally must comply with all permit requirements regardless of the degree of hazard its waste poses. Thus, RCRA properly can be viewed as mandating a form of health-based regulation, but one that does not vary once the regulatory threshold of "hazardousness" has been crossed.

To be sure, there is another provision in RCRA that gives EPA more discretion to tailor the extent of regulation to the degree of hazard involved. Section 7003 of RCRA authorizes EPA to sue to enjoin any person who has contributed to, or is contributing to, any solid or hazardous waste management practices that "may present an imminent and substantial endangerment to health or the environment." This was used extensively by the government to address the need to clean up abandoned dump sites prior to the enactment of CERCLA in 1980.

EPA's implementation of the land disposal ban provisions of the 1984 Amendments to RCRA has now moved the RCRA program much closer to technology-based regulation. While the land ban appears to be a health-based standard on paper (it prohibits the disposal of untreated hazardous wastes unless it can be shown with a reasonable degree of certainty that there will be no migration of the waste as long as it remains hazardous), EPA has chosen to implement it by requiring that facilities use the best demonstrated available treatment technology (BDAT) before disposing of wastes on land.

Most of the dump site cleanup problem is a legacy of the inadequacy of controls on waste disposal practices in the past. But few people are confident that even new, tougher controls on hazardous waste disposal can ensure that existing facilities regulated under subtitle C of RCRA will not eventually become Superfund sites. This lack of confidence stems not only from the fact that a certain amount of illegal dumping undoubtedly occurs, but also from gaps in subtitle C's coverage. As a result, HSWA amended subtitle D of RCRA, which covers nonhazardous solid wastes, to require EPA to establish minimum regulatory standards to be used by the states in regulating municipal landfills. While these regulations subjected management practices for nonhazardous solid wastes to their first significant dose of regulation, subtitle C's regulations remain far stricter, particularly in light of the land disposal ban.

In the sections that follow we consider how far RCRA's jurisdiction extends by exploring the meaning of the terms that are the crucial jurisdictional triggers for RCRA regulation: "solid waste" and "hazardous waste." To be regulated under RCRA a substance must be a *solid waste;* only solid wastes that are *hazardous* are subject to regulation under the onerous subtitle C.

2. What Substances Are "Solid Wastes"?

RCRA's jurisdiction extends to "solid waste." A waste does not have to be in solid form in order to be considered a "solid waste" for purposes of RCRA

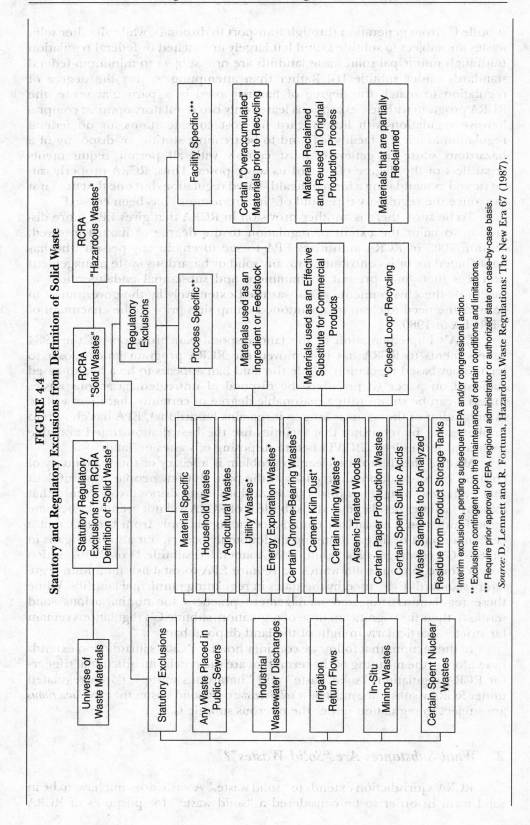

FIGURE 4.4
Statutory and Regulatory Exclusions from Definition of Solid Waste

Universe of Waste Materials

Statutory Regulatory Exclusions from RCRA Definition of "Solid Waste"

RCRA "Solid Wastes"

RCRA "Hazardous Wastes"

Statutory Exclusions
- Any Waste Placed in Public Sewers
- Industrial Wastewater Discharges
- Irrigation Return Flows
- In-Situ Mining Wastes
- Certain Spent Nuclear Wastes

Regulatory Exclusions

Material Specific
- Household Wastes
- Agricultural Wastes
- Utility Wastes*
- Energy Exploration Wastes*
- Certain Chrome-Bearing Wastes*
- Cement Kiln Dust*
- Certain Mining Wastes*
- Arsenic Treated Woods
- Certain Paper Production Wastes
- Certain Spent Sulfuric Acids
- Waste Samples to be Analyzed
- Residue from Product Storage Tanks

Process Specific**
- Materials used as an Ingredient or Feedstock
- Materials used as an Effective Substitute for Commercial Products
- "Closed Loop" Recycling

Facility Specific***
- Certain "Overaccumulated" Materials prior to Recycling
- Materials Reclaimed and Reused in Original Production Process
- Materials that are partially Reclaimed

* Interim exclusions, pending subsequent EPA and/or congressional action.
** Exclusions contingent upon the maintenance of certain conditions and limitations.
*** Require prior approval of EPA regional administrator or authorized state on case-by-case basis.

Source: D. Lennett and R. Fortuna, Hazardous Waste Regulations: The New Era 67 (1987).

jurisdiction. Section 1004(27) of RCRA defines "solid waste" as including "any garbage, refuse, sludge from a waste treatment plant, water supply treatment plant, or air pollution control facility and other discarded material, including solid, liquid, semisolid or contained gaseous material, resulting from industrial, commercial, mining, and agricultural operations, and from community activities." 42 U.S.C. §6903(27).

Certain categories of waste have been exempted from RCRA by EPA or Congress by excluding them from the definition of solid waste. As illustrated in Figure 4.4 on page 330, Congress has exempted domestic sewage, industrial wastewater discharges that are subject to regulation as point sources under section 402 of the Clean Water Act, irrigation return flows, mining wastes not removed from the ground, and certain nuclear materials covered by the Atomic Energy Act. EPA by regulation also has exempted other categories of waste including household wastes (i.e., the garbage we generate at home), fertilizer used in agricultural operations, and certain categories of high-volume wastes that Congress had directed EPA to study (e.g., certain mining wastes). These exclusions can have significant environmental consequences because the wastes removed from the RCRA regulatory program include millions of gallons of hazardous materials whose disposal is largely unregulated.

A particularly troublesome issue for EPA has been the extent to which RCRA covers recycled materials. If material that otherwise would be discarded is recycled, can it be considered a solid waste? If a generator maintains that materials that otherwise would be considered wastes are being stored for future recycling, should the materials be covered by RCRA's regulations?

On January 4, 1985, EPA issued a definition of "solid waste" that required 54 pages of explanation in the Federal Register, 50 Fed. Reg. 614. Under EPA's definition, materials are considered solid wastes if they are abandoned by being disposed of, burned, or incinerated; or stored, treated, or accumulated before or in lieu of those activities. EPA determined that certain materials used in recycling also might fall within RCRA's jurisdiction depending on the nature of the material and the recycling activity involved. This resulted in a legal challenge by representatives of the mining and petroleum industries. They argued that EPA's jurisdiction under RCRA could not extend to materials that eventually would be reused because such materials were not wastes. The D.C. Circuit decided this challenge to EPA's definition of solid waste in the case that follows.

|| *American Mining Congress v. EPA* ||
|| 824 F.2d 1177 (D.C. Cir. 1987) ||

Before STARR and MIKVA, Circuit Judges, and MCGOWAN, Senior Circuit Judge. STARR, Circuit Judge:

These consolidated cases arise out of EPA's regulation of hazardous wastes under the Resource Conservation and Recovery Act of 1976 ("RCRA"), as amended, 42 U.S.C. §§6901-6933 (1982 & Supp. III 1985). Petitioners, trade associations representing mining and oil refining interests, challenge regulations promulgated by EPA that amend the definition of "solid waste" to establish and define the agency's authority to regulate secondary materials reused within an industry's ongoing production process. In plain English, petitioners maintain that EPA has exceeded its regulatory authority in seeking to bring materials that are not discarded or otherwise disposed of within the compass of "waste."

I

RCRA is a comprehensive environmental statute under which EPA is granted authority to regulate solid and hazardous wastes. . . .

Congress' "overriding concern" in enacting RCRA was to establish the framework for a national system to insure the safe management of hazardous waste. H.R. Rep. No. 1491, 94th Cong., 2d Sess. 3 (1976), U.S. Code Cong. & Admin. News 1976, pp. 6238, 6240, 6241. . . .

RCRA includes two major parts: one deals with nonhazardous solid waste management and the other with hazardous waste management. Under the latter, EPA is directed to promulgate regulations establishing a comprehensive management system. Id. §6921. EPA's authority, however, extends only to the regulation of "hazardous waste." Because "hazardous waste" is defined as a subset of "solid waste," id. §6903(5), the scope of EPA's jurisdiction is limited to those materials that constitute "solid waste." That pivotal term is defined by RCRA as

> any garbage, refuse, sludge from a waste treatment plant, water supply treat-ment plant, or air pollution control facility *and other discarded material*, includ-ing solid, liquid, semisolid or contained gaseous material, resulting from industrial, commercial, mining, and agricultural operations, and from com-munity activities. . . .

42 U.S.C. §6903(27) (emphasis added). As will become evident, this case turns on the meaning of the phrase, "and other discarded material," contained in the statute's definitional provisions.

EPA's interpretation of "solid waste" has evolved over time. On May 19, 1980, EPA issued interim regulations defining "solid waste" to include a material that is "a manufacturing or mining by-product and sometimes is dis-carded." 45 Fed. Reg. 33,119 (1980). This definition contained two terms need-ing elucidation: "by-product" and "sometimes discarded." In its definition of "a manufacturing or mining by-product," EPA expressly *excluded* "an interme-diate manufacturing or mining product which results from one of the steps in a manufacturing or mining process and is typically processed through the next step of the process within a short time." Id.

In 1983, the agency proposed narrowing amendments to the 1980 interim rule. 48 Fed. Reg. 14,472 (1983). The agency showed especial concern over *recycling* activities. In the preamble to the amendments, the agency observed that, in light of RCRA's legislative history, it was clear that "Congress indeed intended that materials being recycled or held for recycling can be wastes, and if hazardous, hazardous wastes." Id. at 14,473. The agency also asserted that "not only can materials destined for recycling or being recycled be solid and hazard-ous wastes, but the Agency clearly has the authority to regulate recycling activ-ities as hazardous waste management." Id.

While asserting its interest in recycling activities (and materials being held for recycling), EPA's discussion left unclear whether the agency in fact believed its jurisdiction extended to materials recycled in an industry's on-going produc-tion processes, or only to materials disposed of and recycled as part of a waste management program. In its preamble, EPA stated that "the revised definition of solid waste sets out the Agency's view of its jurisdiction over the recycling of hazardous waste. . . . Proposed section 261.6 then contains exemptions from regulations for those hazardous waste recycling activities that we do not think require regulation." Id. at 14,476. The amended regulatory description of "solid waste" itself, then, did not include materials "used or reused as effective substitutes for raw materials in processes, using raw materials as principal feedstocks." Id. at 14,508. EPA explained the exclusion as follows:

> [These] materials are being used essentially as raw materials and so ordinarily are not appropriate candidates for regulatory control. Moreover, when these materials are used to manufacture new products, the processes generally are normal manufacturing operations. . . . The Agency is reluctant to read the statute as regulating actual manufacturing processes.

Id. at 14,488. This, then, seemed clear: EPA was drawing a line between discarding and ultimate recycling, on the one hand, and a continuous or ongoing manufacturing process with one-site "recycling," on the other. If the activity fell within the latter category, then the materials were not deemed to be "discarded."

After receiving extensive comments, EPA issued its final rule on January 4, 1985. 50 Fed. Reg. 614 (1985). Under the final rule, materials are considered "solid waste" if they are abandoned by being disposed of, burned, or incinerated; or stored, treated, or accumulated before or in lieu of those activities. In addition, certain recycling activities fall within EPA's definition. EPA determines whether a material is an RCRA solid waste when it is recycled by examining both the material or substance itself and the recycling activity involved. The final rule identifies five categories of "secondary materials" (spent materials, sludges, by-products, commercial chemical products, and scrap metal). These "secondary materials" constitute "solid waste" when they are disposed of; burned for energy recovery or used to produce a fuel; reclaimed; or accumulated speculatively. Id. at 618-19, 664.[1] Under the final rule, if a material constitutes "solid waste," it is subject to RCRA regulation *unless* it is directly reused as an ingredient or as an effective substitute for a commercial product, or is returned as a raw material substitute to its original manufacturing process.[2] Id. In the jargon of the trade, the latter category is known as the "closed-loop" exception. In either case, the material must not first be "reclaimed" (processed to recover a usable product or regenerated). Id. EPA exempts these activities "because they are like ordinary usage of commercial products." Id. at 619.

---

1. Under the final rule, a "use constituting disposal" is defined as direct placement on land of wastes or products containing or derived from wastes. A material is "accumulated speculatively" if it is accumulated prior to being recycled. If the accumulator can show that the materials feasibly can be recycled, and that during a one-year calendar period the amount of material recycled or transferred for recycling is 75% or more of the amount present at the beginning of the year, the materials are not considered solid wastes. A material is "reclaimed" if it is processed to recover a usable product, or if it is regenerated. Id.

2. Specifically, the final rule excludes materials recycled by being: "(1) [u]sed or reused as ingredients in an industrial process to make a product, *provided the materials are not being reclaimed*; or (2) [u]sed or reused as effective substitutes for commercial products; or (3) [r]eturned to the original process from which they are generated, without first being reclaimed." Id. (emphasis added). In the third category, the material must be returned to the original manufacturing process as a substitute for raw material feedstock, and the process must use raw materials as principal feedstocks.

II

Petitioners, American Mining Congress ("AMC") and American Petroleum Institute ("API"), challenge the scope of EPA's final rule. Relying upon the statutory definition of "solid waste," petitioners contend that EPA's authority under RCRA is limited to controlling materials that are *discarded or intended for discard.* They argue that EPA's reuse and recycle rules, as applied to in-process secondary materials, regulate materials that have not been discarded, and therefore exceed EPA's jurisdiction.

[The court then describes how petroleum refineries use a complex retrieval system to recapture escaping hydrocarbons and return them to appropriate parts of the refining process. The court also states that mining facilities reprocess ore and recapture for reuse in the production process metal- and mineral-bearing dusts released during processing. The court notes that the materials recaptured by petroleum refineries and mining facilities are considered "solid waste" under EPA's rule.]

III

Because the issue is one of statutory interpretation, the principles enunciated in Chevron, U.S.A., Inc. v. NRDC, 467 U.S. 837 (1984), and its progeny guide our inquiry. In *Chevron,* a unanimous Supreme Court laid out a now familiar, general framework for analyzing agency interpretations of statutes. First, the reviewing court is to consider whether Congress "has directly spoken to the precise question at issue." Id. at 842. This inquiry focuses first on the language and structure of the statute itself. If the answer is not yielded by the statute, then the court is to look to secondary indicia of intent, such as the measure's legislative history. As the *Chevron* court emphatically declared: "[I]f the intent of Congress is clear, that is the end of the matter; for the court, as well as the agency, must give effect to the unambiguously expressed intent of Congress." Id. at 842-43.

. . . Congress, it will be recalled, granted EPA power to regulate "solid waste." Congress specifically defined "solid waste" as "discarded material." EPA then defined "discarded material" to include materials destined for reuse in an industry's *ongoing* production processes. The challenge to EPA's jurisdictional reach is founded, again, on the proposition that in-process secondary materials are outside the bounds of EPA's lawful authority. Nothing has been *discarded,* the argument goes, and thus RCRA jurisdiction remains untriggered.

The first step in statutory interpretation is, of course, an analysis of the language itself. In pursuit of Congress' intent, we "start with the assumption that the legislative purpose is expressed by the ordinary meaning of the words used." Securities Industry Ass'n v. Board of Governors, 468 U.S. 137, 149 (1984). These sound principles governing the reading of statutes seem especially forceful in the context of the present case. Here, Congress defined "solid waste" as "discarded material." The ordinary plain-English meaning of the word "discarded" is "disposed of," "thrown away," or "abandoned." Encompassing materials retained for immediate reuse within the scope of "discarded material" strains, to say the least, the everyday usage of that term. . . .

. . . [A] complete analysis of the statutory term "discarded" calls for more than resorting to the ordinary, everyday meaning of the specific language at hand. For, "the sense in which [a term] is used in a statute must be determined by reference to the purpose of the particular legislation." Burnet v. Chicago Portrait Co., 285 U.S. 1, 6 (1932). . . .

. . . RCRA was enacted in response to Congressional findings that the "rising tide of scrap, discarded, and waste materials" generated by consumers and increased industrial production had presented heavily populated urban communities with "serious financial, management, intergovernmental, and technical problems in the disposal of solid wastes." Id. §6901(a). . . .

The question we face, then, is whether, in light of the National Legislature's expressly stated objectives and the underlying problems that motivated it to enact RCRA in the first instance, Congress was using the term "discarded" in its ordinary sense—"disposed of" or "abandoned"—or whether Congress was using it in a much more open-ended way, so as to encompass materials no longer useful in their original capacity though destined for immediate reuse in another phase of the industry's ongoing production process.

For the following reasons, we believe the former to be the case. RCRA was enacted, as the Congressional objectives and findings make clear, in an effort to help States deal with the ever-increasing problem of solid waste *disposal* by encouraging the search for and use of alternatives to existing methods of disposal (including recycling) and protecting health and the environment by regulating hazardous wastes. To fulfill these purposes, it seems clear that EPA need not regulate "spent" materials that are recycled and reused in an *ongoing* manufacturing or industrial process. These materials have not yet become part of the waste disposal problem; rather, *they are destined for beneficial reuse or recycling in a continuous process by the generating industry itself.*

The situation in this case thus stands in sharp contrast to that in *Riverside Bayview,* another post-*Chevron* case. There, the Corps of Engineers had defined "the waters of the United States" within the meaning of the Clean Water Act, 33 U.S.C. §§1311, 1362 (1972), to include "wetlands." Recognizing that it strained common sense to conclude that "Congress intended to abandon traditional notions of 'waters' and include in that term 'wetlands' as well," the Court performed a close and searching analysis of Congress' intent to determine if this counterintuitive result was nonetheless what Congress had in mind. Id. at 461-65. The Court based its holding (that the agency's expansive definition of "waters of the United States" was reasonable) on several factors: Congress' acquiescence in the agency's interpretation; provisions of the statute expressly including "wetlands" in the definition of "waters"; and, importantly, the danger that forbidding the Corps to regulate "wetlands" would defeat Congress' purpose since pollutants in "wetlands" water might well flow into "waters" that were indisputably jurisdictional. Id. at 465. Thus, due to the nature of the water system, the very evil that Congress sought to interdict—the befouling of the "waters of the United States"—would likely occur were the Corps of Engineers' jurisdiction to stop short of wetlands. *Riverside Bayview,* 106 S. Ct. at 463. . . .

. . . EPA's regulation of in-process materials . . . seems to us an effort to get at the same evil (albeit, very broadly defined) that Congress had identified by extending the agency's regulatory compass, rather than, as with the regulation of wetlands, an attempt to reach activities that if left unregulated would sabotage the agency's regulatory mission. We are thus not presented with a situation in which Congress likely intended that the pivotal jurisdictional term be read in its broadest sense, detached from everyday parlance; instead, we have a situation in which Congress, perhaps through the process of legislative compromise which courts must be loathe to tear asunder, employed a term with a widely accepted meaning to define the materials that EPA could regulate under RCRA. See *Dimension Financial*, 106 S. Ct. at 689. And it was that term which the Congress of the United States passed and the President ultimately signed into law. . . .

IV

We are constrained to conclude that, in light of the language and structure of RCRA, the problems animating Congress to enact it, and the relevant portions of the legislative history, Congress clearly and unambiguously expressed its intent that "solid waste" (and therefore EPA's regulatory authority) be limited to materials that are "discarded" by virtue of being disposed of, abandoned, or thrown away. While we do not lightly overturn an agency's reading of its own statute, we are persuaded that by regulating in-process secondary materials, EPA has acted in contravention of Congress' intent. Accordingly, the petition for review is granted.

MIKVA, Circuit Judge, dissenting:
. . . In my opinion, the EPA's interpretation of solid waste is completely reasonable in light of the language, policies, and legislative history of RCRA. See United States v. Riverside Bayview Homes, 474 U.S. 121 (1986). Congress had broad remedial objectives in mind when it enacted RCRA, most notably to "regulat[e] the treatment, storage, transportation, and disposal of hazardous wastes which have adverse effects on the environment." 42 U.S.C. §6902(4). The disposal problem Congress was combatting encompassed more than just abandoned materials. RCRA makes this clear with its definition of the central statutory term "disposal":

> the discharge, deposit, injection, dumping, spilling, leaking, or placing of any solid waste or hazardous waste into or on any land or water so that such solid waste or hazardous waste or any constituent thereof may enter the environment or be emitted into the air or discharged into any waters, including ground-waters.

42 U.S.C. §6903(3). This definition clearly encompasses more than the everyday meaning of disposal, which is a "discarding or throwing away." Webster's Third International Dictionary 654 (2d ed. 1981). The definition is *functional*: waste is disposed under this provision if it is put into contact with land or water in such a way as to pose the risks to health and the environment that animated Congress to pass RCRA. Whether the manufacturer subjectively intends to put the material to additional use is irrelevant to this definition, as indeed it should be, because the manufacturer's state of mind bears no necessary relation to the hazards of the industrial processes he employs.

Faithful to RCRA's functional approach, EPA reasonably concluded that regulation of certain in-process secondary materials was necessary to carry out its mandate. The materials at issue in this case can pose the same risks as abandoned wastes, whether or not the manufacturer intends eventually to put them to further beneficial use. As the agency explained, "[s]imply because a waste is likely to be recycled will not ensure that it will not be spilled or leaked before recycling occurs." The storage, transportation, and even recycling of in-process secondary materials can cause severe environmental harm. Indeed, the EPA documented environmental disasters caused by the handling or storage of such materials. It also pointed out the risk of damage from spills or leaks when certain in-process secondary materials are placed on land or in underground product storage. . . .

. . . [I]n this case the EPA has interpreted solid waste in a manner that seems to expand the everyday usage of the word "discarded." Its conclusion, however, is fully supportable in light of the statutory scheme and legislative history of RCRA. The agency concluded that certain on-site recycled materials constitute an integral part of the waste disposal problem. This judgment is grounded in the EPA's technical expertise and is adequately supported by evidence in the record. The majority nevertheless reverses the agency because it believes that the materials at issue "have not yet become part of the waste disposal problem." Maj. op. at 1186. This declaration is nothing more than a substitution of the majority's own conclusions for the sound technical judgment of the EPA. The EPA's interpretation is a reasonable construction of an ambiguous statutory provision and should be upheld.

NOTES AND QUESTIONS

1. Do you agree with EPA that the definition of "solid waste" should employ a functional approach that focuses on whether or not a substance poses a risk warranting regulation? If such judgments are relevant for definitional purposes, who should make them—EPA or the courts? Note that in his dissent Judge Mikva challenged the majority's statement that materials stored on-site for possible future reclamation "have not yet become part of the waste disposal problem." What basis did he have for questioning their statement? Did the majority give sufficient deference to EPA's conclusion that such materials are an integral part of the waste disposal problem? Should EPA's judgment on this factual issue make any difference to a court reviewing the scope of EPA's regulatory authority? Is the court's decision consistent with *Chevron* (p. 160)?

2. Should EPA be able to define "solid waste" broadly to encompass materials that it believes need to be regulated to prevent deliberate evasion of RCRA regulations? Consider, for example, whether gaseous materials can be regulated under RCRA. Congress defined "solid waste" in section 1004(27) of RCRA to include "solid, liquid semisolid or *contained gaseous material*," 42 U.S.C. §6903(27) (emphasis supplied). While this language suggests that RCRA extends only to gases in containers, EPA has expressed concern that "a plant could evade regulation by designing a [production] process to keep the process emissions in a gaseous state." 54 Fed. Reg. 50,973 (1989). EPA notes that the Bhopal tragedy occurred when a volatile liquid (methyl isocyanate) was released as a gas. Thus, EPA initially declared that only "true gases," defined as "those which are not capable of being condensed and which remain gaseous at standard temperature and pressure," were exempt from RCRA when released in uncontained form. Under this interpretation gases capable of being condensed and materials that are not gases at standard temperature or pressure would be subject to subtitle C of RCRA when released in uncontained form. Is this position consistent with the statutory definition of "solid waste"? EPA subsequently reconsidered its position and now states that its RCRA authority "is limited to containerized or condensed gases." 54 Fed. Reg. 50,973 (1989). Which interpretation is more consistent with the statutory language? Which is more consistent with the goals of RCRA? If a facility deliberately heats a solid waste until it

becomes a gas and is released into the air, can EPA regulate this activity under subtitle C? See 54 Fed. Reg. 50,973 (col. 2). Why or why not? If a facility designs its production process so that this occurs, can an RCRA permit be required? See id.

3. Five months after the D.C. Circuit's *AMC* decision, EPA proposed a new definition of "solid waste" in response to the court's decision. 53 Fed. Reg. 519 (Jan. 8, 1988). While EPA proposed to exclude from the definition materials reclaimed in a "closed loop," it concluded that the court's decision did not affect its authority to regulate materials "recycled in ways where the recycling activity itself is characterized by discarding," 53 Fed. Reg. at 520. Thus, EPA indicated that it would consider several factors in deciding whether materials recycled without passing through "a continuous, ongoing manufacturing process" were solid wastes. These factors include: (1) whether the material is typically discarded on an industry-wide basis, (2) whether the material replaces a raw material when it is recycled and the degree to which its composition is similar to that of the raw material, (3) the relation of the recovery practice to the principal activity of the facility, (4) whether the material is handled prior to reclamation in a secure manner that minimizes loss and prevents releases to the environment, and (5) other factors, such as the length of time the material is accumulated. 53 Fed. Reg. 35,415. How are each of these factors relevant to the question whether a material should be considered a solid waste?

4. As a result of the *AMC* decision, industry representatives argued that a number of substances that EPA has regulated under subtitle C of RCRA are not "solid wastes." For example, can EPA regulate sludge from wastewater stored in a surface impoundment if the sludge may at some time in the future be reprocessed for metals recovery? EPA said yes because it is the product of wastewater and it is stored in an impoundment that can threaten harm to the environment. The D.C. Circuit agreed in American Mining Congress v. EPA (*AMC II*), 907 F.2d 1179 (D.C. Cir. 1990). The court distinguished *AMC* in the following terms:

> *AMC*'s holding concerned only materials that are "destined for *immediate reuse* in another phase of the industry's ongoing production process," id. at 1185 (emphasis added), and that "have not yet become part of the waste disposal problem," id. at 1186. Nothing in *AMC* prevents the agency from treating as "discarded" the wastes at issue in this case, which are managed in land disposal units that *are* part of wastewater treatment systems, which *have* therefore become "part of the waste disposal problem," and which are *not* part of ongoing industrial processes. Indeed, [we have] explicitly rejected the very claim that petitioners assert in this case, . . . namely, that under RCRA, potential reuse of a material prevents the agency from classifying it as "discarded." [907 F.2d at 1186 (emphasis in original).]

5. Can materials that are in fact recycled be considered wastes at the time of recycling? Citing *AMC*, EPA determined that materials inserted into a metals reclamation process cease to be solid wastes for purposes of RCRA regulation at the time they arrive at a reclamation facility because they are no longer "discarded materials." 53 Fed. Reg. 11,753 (1988). The materials involved were wastes that EPA had required to be treated through metals reclamation. Environmentalists successfully challenged this interpretation in American Petroleum Institute v. EPA, 906 F.2d 729 (D.C. Cir. 1990). The court explained that

> *AMC* is by no means dispositive of EPA's authority to regulate [such waste]. Unlike the materials in question in *AMC*, [the waste] is indisputably "discarded" *before* being subject to metals reclamation. Consequently, it *has* "become part of

the waste disposal problem"; that is why EPA has the power to require that [it] be subject to mandatory metals reclamation. See 53 Fed. Reg. 11,752-53 (recognizing this point). Nor does anything in *AMC* require EPA to cease treating [the material] as "solid waste" once it reaches the metals reclamation facility. [The material] is delivered to the facility not as part of an "*ongoing* manufacturing or industrial process" within "the generating industry," but as part of a mandatory waste treatment plan prescribed by EPA. [906 F.2d at 741 (emphasis in original).]

Noting that Congress consciously had decided not to regulate the *generation* of waste when it adopted RCRA due to concerns about interfering with production processes, EPA had maintained that it could not regulate material undergoing metals reclamation because that would interfere with an ongoing production process. Regulating furnaces used to recover metals from zinc-laden waste "would be like directly regulating the industrial production of zinc from ore," EPA argued. Rejecting this argument, the court explained: "The two forms of regulation might be 'like' each other, but they are by no means one and the same." 906 F.2d at 741 n.15. The court emphasized that even if the treatment process produced something of value—reclaimed metals—the important distinction for purposes of RCRA jurisdiction was whether the material being processed had been discarded, not whether the process extracted valuable products from the discarded material. 906 F.2d at 741 n.16.

6. In Chapter 2 we discussed the problem of defining regulatory targets given the regulated community's incentive to escape regulation. This is nowhere better illustrated than by the problem of defining "solid waste." Because *AMC* created uncertainty concerning a key jurisdictional term—the definition of "solid waste"—the regulated community sought to embrace it as a major loophole for avoiding RCRA regulation. Under the most extreme interpretation of *AMC*, a company might escape RCRA regulation simply by asserting that it eventually would recycle waste material that otherwise would be regulated. However, in light of the decisions in *American Petroleum Institute* and *AMC II*, EPA staff now believe that *AMC*'s holding has been sharply limited. Do you agree?

7. Two ex-EPA officials formerly in charge of solid waste programs have commented:

> [T]he regulatory distinction between wastes and products has led to discrepancies that are not defensible from an environmental standpoint. For example, certain pesticides that can be applied directly to the land at high concentrations cannot be legally disposed in state-of-the-art hazardous waste landfills until they have been pretreated. . . . Similarly, chemical treatment processes that are part of chemical production are relatively unregulated compared with chemical waste processes that are part of waste disposal. . . .
> [These discrepancies] grow even more problematic as recycling becomes a desirable component of waste management.
> Historically, a facility performing "legitimate" recycling has been exempt from many of the environmental management standards that apply to facilities deemed to be managing hazardous waste. . . . Yet a long list of recycling facilities, including oil refiners, battery recyclers, and scrap metal recyclers, have ended up as Superfund sites. Moreover, some facilities that claimed the recycling exemption (e.g., certain thermal facilities) look amazingly similar to hazardous waste treatment facilities, yet the same recycling facilities are allowed to reuse their ash as product while the hazardous waste incinerator must continue to treat it as hazardous waste, regardless of how clean that ash is. [Williams & Cannon, Rethinking RCRA for the 1990s, 21 Envtl. L. Rep. 10,063, 10,067 (1991).]

Are there any legitimate justifications for these discrepancies?

8. Courts also have continued to wrestle with the definition of solid waste. In United States v. Ilco, Inc., 996 F.2d 1126 (11th Cir. 1993), the Eleventh Circuit held that lead parts reclaimed from spent car and truck batteries for recycling purposes are solid wastes subject to regulation under RCRA. While the recycler argued that it had never discarded the lead plates and groups removed from old batteries it had purchased, the court emphasized that the fact that "*[s]omebody* has discarded the battery in which these components are found . . . does not change just because a reclaimer has purchased or finds value in the components." 996 F.2d at 1131 (emphasis in original). In Owen Electric Steel Company v. Browner, 37 F.3d 146 (4th Cir. 1994), the Fourth Circuit held that slag produced by a steel mill which is "cured" on the ground for six months prior to being sold for use as a road base material is, despite its ultimate reuse, "discarded material" subject to regulation under RCRA. The court observed that "the fundamental inquiry in determining whether a by-product has been 'discarded' is whether the by-product is *immediately* recycled for use in the same industry; if not, then the by-product is justifiably seen as 'part of the waste disposal problem,'" *AMC I,* 824 F.2d at 1186, and therefore as a "solid waste." 37 F.3d at 150 (emphasis in original).

9. In 2000, the U.S. Court of Appeals for the D.C. Circuit issued two decisions that focused on the question whether material had been "discarded," subjecting it to regulation as waste under RCRA. In Association of Battery Recyclers v. EPA, 208 F.3d 1047 (D.C. Cir. 2000), the court held that EPA improperly classified secondary and residual materials generated in mining and mineral processing operations as solid waste for purposes of RCRA. The agency had done so when it promulgated Phase IV of its regulations limiting land disposal of hazardous waste. EPA argued that the materials could be regulated as wastes because they were not immediately reintroduced into the production process. However, the court rejected the notion that temporary storage of the materials even "for a few minutes" subjected them to regulation as solid waste. Referring to its 1987 decision in *AMC I,* the court asserted that "[l]ater cases in this court do not limit AMC," noting that none of the decisions subsequent to *AMC I* undermined the notion that material must be discarded before it can be regulated as a waste. The court distinguished American Petroleum Institute v. EPA, 906 F.2d 729 (D.C. Cir. 1990), as involving the taking of waste from one industry for reclamation in another. It distinguished *AMC II* as involving a situation where it was not clear whether or not the waste ultimately would be recycled because the defendants had asserted only that they "may" reclaim the material at some time in the future. In American Petroleum Institute v. EPA, 216 F.3d 50 (D.C. Cir. 2000), the court vacated part of an RCRA regulation that sought to subject oil-bearing wastewaters generated by the petroleum refining industry to regulation as a solid waste. While recognizing that wastewaters eventually become waste as they progress through later phases of treatment, the court held that EPA had not adequately explained why it had determined that wastewaters should be considered discarded even before they had received primary treatment.

These decisions suggest that secondary materials that are stored for beneficial reuse may not be considered to be solid waste even if they are not immediately reused. However, it still is probably the case that secondary materials accumulated for excessive periods of time can be regulated as solid wastes. EPA has taken the position that material "accumulated speculatively" for possible reuse may be regulated as a solid waste—the agency's regulations require that 75 percent of the secondary material be reused within a calendar year.

A more difficult issue involves material that is accumulated for reuse by another company at another site in another industry. *Association of Battery Recyclers* dealt with "closely related" materials intended for reuse at the same site where they were generated. While there are indications that EPA believes the impact of the decision is limited to such materials, others disagree. See Donald J. Paterson, Jr., The Definition of Solid Waste: Discerning the "Intelligible Principle," in Proceedings of the ABA 30th Annual Conference on Environmental Law, March 2001, at 99, 106.

10. One proposal for determining whether a material is a waste would focus on its market value. Recycled material would be considered a waste if a producer had to pay someone to dispose of it. But if a recycler would pay the producer for the material, it would not be considered a waste. EPA believes that such an approach would not be enforceable because of frequent shifts in market prices and the ability of parties to finance materials transfers in ways that disguise their true value. 50 Fed. Reg. 614, 617 (1985). For an argument that EPA should reconsider this decision, despite the difficulties of applying a value-based standard, see Smith, The Solid Waste Definitional Dilemma, 9 Natural Resources & Env't 3 (Fall 1994).

11. In October 2003, EPA proposed to revise the RCRA definition of "solid waste" to exclude hazardous secondary materials when they are generated and reclaimed in a continuous process within the same industry. 68 Fed. Reg. 61,557 (Oct. 28, 2003). The proposed rules offer different options for defining what constitutes a "continuous process" within the same industry—one would allow reclamation in multiple processing steps at different physical locations, while the other would not allow it to occur at facilities that also recycle hazardous materials from other industries. EPA's proposed exclusion would apply only to materials that produce a product or ingredient that can be used without any further reclamation. EPA also proposes to establish the first specific criteria for distinguishing "sham recycling" from legitimate recycling practices. It is estimated that EPA's proposal would exclude 1.5 million tons of hazardous waste annually from RCRA regulation. EPA's proposal, which has generated strong opposition from environmental groups, is analyzed in Joseph Kraft, How to Take Recycling One Step Forward, Two Steps Back: The EPA's Proposal to Revise the Definition of Solid Waste Under RCRA, 18 Tul. Envtl. L.J. 385 (2005).

In order to be subject to the cradle-to-grave regulations of RCRA's subtitle C, a material must be not only a "solid waste" but also a "hazardous" one. We now turn to the question of what solid wastes are hazardous for purposes of RCRA.

3.   Identifying "Hazardous Waste"

Although Congress required EPA to regulate hazardous waste under subtitle C of RCRA, it did not specify how the agency was to determine what wastes were hazardous. "Hazardous waste" is defined by section 1004(5) of RCRA as

> a solid waste, or combination of solid wastes, which because of its quantity, concentration, or physical, chemical, or infectious characteristics may—
> (A) cause or significantly contribute to an increase in mortality or an increase in serious irreversible, or incapacitating reversible, illness; or
> (B) pose a substantial present or potential hazard to human health or the environment when improperly treated, stored, transported, or disposed of, or otherwise managed.

Section 3001 of RCRA requires EPA to promulgate regulations identifying the characteristics of hazardous waste and listing particular wastes as hazardous "taking into account toxicity, persistence, and degradability in nature, potential for accumulation in tissue, and other related factors such as flammability, corrosiveness, and other hazardous characteristics."

EPA has implemented these provisions (40 C.F.R. pt. 261) by establishing two principal avenues for solid waste to be deemed "hazardous": by exhibiting one of four hazardous characteristics ("characteristic wastes") or by being specifically listed as a hazardous waste in EPA's regulations ("listed wastes"). Waste streams can be specifically listed as hazardous if EPA determines that they routinely contain hazardous constituents or exhibit hazardous characteristics. As indicated in Figure 4.5, EPA has established four general categories of listed wastes (the "F," "K," "P," and "U" lists). By the end of 1999, EPA had listed more than 860 types of wastes as hazardous by placing them in one of these four categories.

To prevent generators from evading hazardous waste regulations by diluting or otherwise changing the composition of listed waste streams, EPA in 1980 adopted two important rules: the "mixture rule" and the "derived-from" rule. The mixture rule provides that any mixture of a listed waste with another solid waste is itself considered to be a hazardous waste. The derived-from rule provides that wastes derived from the treatment, storage, or disposal of a listed waste (such as the ash residue from incineration of a listed waste) are deemed to be hazardous wastes. 40 C.F.R. §261.3(c)(2)(i). Thus, listed wastes are deemed to remain hazardous unless they are specifically "delisted" by EPA.

Although some industry groups maintained that the mixture and derived-from rules unlawfully expanded EPA's jurisdiction under RCRA, the rules became an important part of the RCRA program while legal challenges to the rules were held in abeyance for more than a decade. When the D.C. Circuit finally addressed the issue in December 1991, it struck down the mixture and derived-from rules without deciding whether they exceeded EPA's authority. Surprisingly, the court held that EPA had not provided adequate notice and opportunity for comment when it proposed the rules in 1978. Shell Oil Co. v. EPA, 950 F.2d 741 (D.C. Cir. 1991). The court rejected EPA's argument that industry had suffered no prejudice from this 13-year-old procedural defect, even though the Agency maintained that it had considered and rejected the very criticisms industry would have made had adequate notice been provided. Noting "the dangers that may be posed by a discontinuity in the regulation of hazardous wastes," the court suggested that EPA reenact the rules on an interim basis under the "good cause" exception to the Administrative Procedure Act, 5 U.S.C. §553(b)(3)(B). EPA then reinstated the rules, 57 Fed. Reg. 7,628 (1992), and it ultimately adopted a final rule that largely retains them while expanding certain exclusions. 66 Fed. Reg. 27,266 (May 16, 2001). The Agency expanded an exclusion for mixtures and/or derivatives of wastes listed solely for the ignitability, corrosivity, and/or reactivity characteristics and it established a new conditional exemption for mixed wastes (that is, wastes that are both hazardous and radioactive).

Figure 4.6 identifies the different classifications of hazardous waste and the places where EPA regulations pertaining to them appear in the Federal Register. Wastes not specifically listed as hazardous must be managed as hazardous wastes if they exhibit one of the four hazardous characteristics (ignitability, corrosivity,

FIGURE 4.5
RCRA Hazardous Waste Classifications

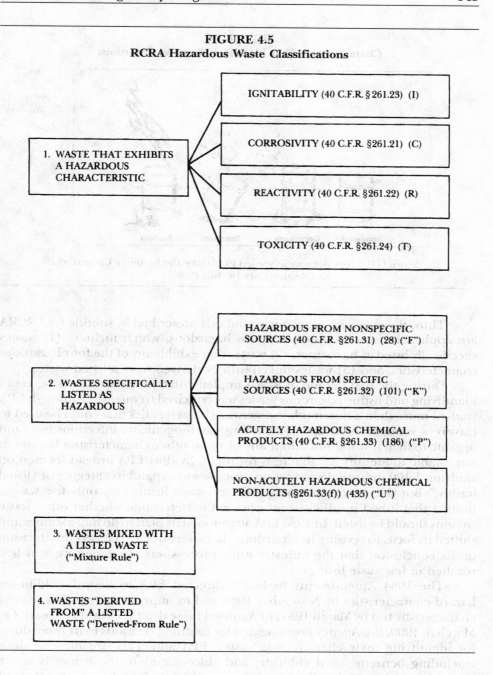

reactivity, or toxicity) that are illustrated in Figure 4.6. These "characteristic wastes" are considered hazardous only until they no longer exhibit the hazardous characteristic. Unlike listed wastes, characteristic wastes are not subject to the mixture or derived-from rules. If they are mixed with a substance other than a listed waste they need to be managed as a hazardous waste only as long as they continue to exhibit a hazardous characteristic. Substances derived from a characteristic waste are considered hazardous only if they continue to exhibit a hazardous characteristic.

FIGURE 4.6
Characteristics That Identify a Waste as Hazardous

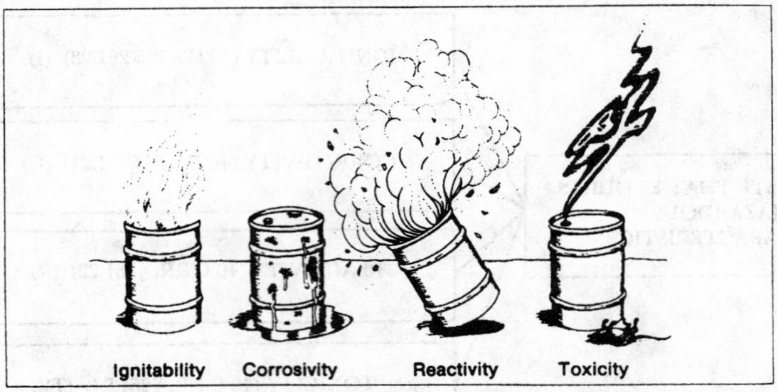

Source: GAO, New Approach Needed to Manage the Resource Conservation
and Recovery Act 18 (July 1988).

Thus, the extensive regulatory standards prescribed by subtitle C of RCRA are applicable to solid wastes that are hazardous, which include: (1) wastes specifically listed as hazardous, (2) wastes that exhibit any of the four hazardous characteristics, and (3) wastes mixed with or derived from a listed waste.

During the first decade of RCRA implementation, EPA's slow progress in identifying and listing hazardous wastes was criticized frequently. Although EPA studied more than a dozen other potential characteristics that could be used to classify a waste as hazardous (including carcinogenicity, infectiousness, and organic toxicity), it did not adopt any of these other characteristics because it was unable to identify suitable tests for them. In 1981 EPA instead focused on studying 1,100 industrial production processes to expand its category of "listed wastes." But the Agency promulgated new waste listings for only five wastes, finding that it had insufficient information to determine whether other waste streams should be listed. In 1986 EPA abandoned its plan to do more studies and shifted its focus to revising its hazardous characteristics. EPA based this decision on its conclusion that the industry study process was too expensive and had resulted in few waste listings.

The 1984 Amendments to RCRA directed EPA to identify additional hazard characteristics by November 1986 and to improve the existing toxicity characteristic test by March 1987. EPA missed these deadlines by three years. On March 5, 1990, the Agency promulgated far-reaching revisions to its procedures for identifying toxic characteristic wastes. EPA added 25 organic chemicals (including benzene, vinyl chloride, and chloroform) to the 8 metals and 6 pesticides on its existing list of substances which if found as constituents in waste in certain concentrations render the waste hazardous under the toxicity characteristic. EPA also promulgated a new, more sensitive test, known as the toxicity characteristic leaching procedure, or TCLP, to be used to determine whether a solid waste contains these hazardous constituents. It estimated that these changes subjected more than 17,000 additional waste generators to regulation under subtitle C of RCRA, including many companies in the pulp and paper, petroleum refining and marketing, organic chemicals, pharmaceuticals, plastics, rubber, lumber, and textile industries. EPA estimated that the cost of complying with the new rules would range from $250 to $400 million per year, largely because the rules increased the volume of material considered to be hazardous waste by some 1.8 million metric tons. 55 Fed. Reg. 11,798 (1990).

Former EPA staffer William Pedersen has argued that the RCRA system is both overinclusive and underinclusive. Pedersen argues that RCRA is overinclusive because the mixture and derived-from rules result in the regulation of many wastes that are far less toxic than wastes excluded from the system. Pedersen, The Future of Federal Solid Waste Regulation, 16 Colum. J. Envtl. L. 109, 120 (1991). While EPA has acknowledged problems with the mixture and derived-from rules, prior to the *Shell Oil* decision it had been reluctant to propose any de minimis exception for fear that this would simply encourage dilution of wastes. See Gaba, The Mixture and Derived-from Rules Under RCRA: Once a Hazardous Waste Always a Hazardous Waste?, 21 Envtl. L. Rep. 10,033 (1991). Pederson maintains that RCRA is underinclusive because more truly hazardous waste is excluded from the RCRA system than is included. He notes that while data on hazardous waste generation are notoriously unreliable, only a small fraction of the waste that is generated is listed as hazardous and that special exemptions (such as those for mining waste, household waste, and waste placed in public sewers) exclude more waste that possesses a hazardous characteristic than is included in the RCRA system. Id. at 118-119.

Pedersen maintains that the RCRA program's failure to provide more comprehensive coverage of hazardous waste is a result of the "stigma and drastic regulatory burden that attend listing a waste." Although the D.C. Circuit has held that concern over the stigma attached to a waste's being listed as hazardous is an insufficient basis for refusing to list an otherwise hazardous waste, Hazardous Waste Treatment Council v. EPA, 861 F.2d 270 (D.C. Cir. 1988) (rejecting argument that used oil should not be listed as a hazardous waste because it would discourage recycling), EPA has resisted efforts to expand the coverage of RCRA listings except when expressly required by Congress.

NOTES AND QUESTIONS

1. Despite the decision in Hazardous Waste Treatment Council v. EPA, 861 F.2d 270 (D.C. Cir. 1988), EPA ultimately decided not to list used oil as a hazardous waste. 57 Fed. Reg. 21,524 (1992). The Agency based its decision on the conclusion that gasoline-powered engine oils already are subject to regulation under subtitle C as characteristic wastes and that other oils are not hazardous with sufficient frequency to warrant listing. In Natural Resource Defense Council v. EPA, 25 F.3d 1063 (D.C. Cir. 1994), EPA's decision was upheld by the D.C. Circuit. The court stated that "Congress intended the agency to have substantial room to exercise its independent expertise in determining the appropriate grounds for listing." It concluded that RCRA did not require "EPA to promulgate its [listing] criteria in a manner that would trigger automatic listing whenever certain technical conditions are met." 25 F.3d at 1070.

2. EPA's derived-from rule provides that "any solid waste generated from the treatment, storage, or disposal of a hazardous waste, including any sludge, spill residue, ash, emission control dust, or leachate (but not including precipitation run-off) is a hazardous waste." 40 C.F.R. §261.3(c)(2)(i). Why do you think EPA promulgated this regulation? As a result of the derived-from rule, would the residue left over after hazardous waste is treated to reduce its

toxicity itself be a hazardous waste? Would soil, groundwater, or any other environmental medium become a hazardous waste when it comes into contact with a listed waste? See Chemical Waste Management, Inc. v. EPA, 869 F.2d 1526 (D.C. Cir. 1989).

3. Do you agree with Pedersen that the mixture and derived-from rules are likely to require that many nonhazardous materials be managed as a hazardous waste? How could EPA narrow the scope of these rules without encouraging dilution? Should EPA exempt waste that does not have a certain threshold concentration of hazardous constituents?

4. EPA has struggled mightily to develop a new Hazardous Waste Identification Rule (HWIR) that would tailor regulatory requirements more closely to the degree of hazard posed by a waste without creating the kind of loopholes the mixture and derived-from rules are designed to avoid. In 1992, EPA proposed two alternative approaches that quickly were withdrawn after a flurry of criticism. 57 Fed. Reg. 21,450 (1992). After EPA's action temporarily reinstating the mixture and derived-from rules was upheld in Mobil Oil Corp. v. EPA, 35 F.3d 579 (D.C. Cir. 1994), EPA convened a federal advisory committee of industry and environmental representatives in an effort to seek consensus concerning how to revise the rules. This effort failed after 18 months of negotiations, and EPA missed a statutory deadline for proposing a new HWIR. Faced with lawsuits over its failure to meet the deadline, EPA signed a consent decree requiring the Agency to propose a new HWIR.

5. In December 1995, EPA proposed a new HWIR that would allow listed wastes and wastes subject to the mixture or derived-from rules to escape Subtitle C regulation when the specific hazardous constituents they contain fall below certain levels. 60 Fed. Reg. 66,344 (1995). EPA proposed "exit levels" for 376 chemical constituents based on risk assessments evaluating potential exposure pathways from a variety of sources. The exit levels were set at levels where risk assessments indicated that humans would not be exposed to toxic constituents increasing individual cancer risks by more than one in a million or that would produce other observable toxic effects. One option proposed by EPA would permit higher, less stringent exit levels for waste that is not disposed on land or that is managed in a disposal unit that meets protective design standards, though less stringent than those required by subtitle C regulations. The HWIR would be "self-implementing," meaning that generators could exit subtitle C without any advance approval so long as they tested their wastes periodically to determine that levels of hazardous constituents did not exceed exit levels. EPA's proposal represented a major step toward replacing RCRA's rigid, two-tier approach to regulation with one that more closely tailors the degree of regulation to the degree of risk posed by the waste. For an analysis of EPA's proposed rule, see Kastner and Goldman, HWIR Could Allow Low-Risk Listed Hazardous Waste to Escape RCRA Regulation, 26 Envtl. Rep. 1,623 (1996).

EPA's Science Advisory Board and industry groups heavily criticized the risk assessments the agency had been using to develop the HWIR proposal. Municipalities also were very concerned that the proposed rule might result in much larger volumes of hazardous materials ending up in municipal landfills subject only to Subtitle D. As a result of the controversy surrounding its HWIR proposal, EPA reconsidered its proposal.

6. In 2001 the agency adopted a final rule retaining the mixture and derived-from rules with revisions that expanded an exemption for mixtures and/or derivatives of characteristic waste that was hazardous solely for exhibiting a

characteristic other than toxicity. 66 Fed. Reg. 27,266 (May 16, 2001). EPA also indicated that it would continue to work on developing a concentration-based HWIR. EPA's repromulgation of the mixture and derived-from rules was upheld in American Chemistry Council v. EPA, 337 F.3d 1060 (D.C. Cir. 2003).

7. Note that the derived-from rule includes leachate (except for precipitation runoff). Leachate is produced when liquids (including rainwater) seep through wastes buried in landfills, producing a fluid that contains constituents of the original waste. State-of-the-art landfills have liners and leachate collection systems to keep hazardous constituents from escaping in the form of leachate. Would leachate collected from a hazardous waste landfill have to be managed as a hazardous waste under the derived-from rule? See Chemical Waste Management, Inc. v. EPA, 869 F.2d 1526 (D.C. Cir. 1989). What about rainwater runoff?

Incinerator Ash and the Household Waste Exclusion

Wastes that have been listed as hazardous must be managed in accordance with subtitle C unless EPA grants a petition to delist a waste generated at a particular facility pursuant to §3001(f) of RCRA. Wastes that are not listed as hazardous are subject to subtitle C regulation only when they exhibit a hazardous characteristic, which usually requires some form of testing, as with the TCLP.

As landfill space tightened, many cities built incinerators to dispose of municipal garbage. In the year 2000 approximately 160 municipal waste incinerators burnt about 16 percent of the more than 200 million tons of garbage generated in the United States that year. These incinerators generated more than 8 million tons of ash (approximately 25 percent by volume of the original waste stream). Ash residues include fly ash captured by emission control equipment, bottom ash, and the products of incomplete combustion. Heavy metals are present in the ash residues, and occur in particularly large quantities in the fly ash.

As noted above, one of the four characteristics that can make a waste "hazardous" for purposes of subtitle C regulation is toxicity. Toxicity is determined by a procedure designed to measure the potential for a waste to leach hazardous constituents. The test procedure, formerly called the "extraction procedure" and now called the "toxicity characteristic leaching procedure" (TCLP), analyzes the extract from a sample of the waste for any of 40 chemical contaminants. If the extract has any of these substances in concentrations above specified levels (generally 100 times greater than levels allowed under the Safe Drinking Water Act), the waste is considered to be toxic and must be managed as a hazardous waste.

EPA's regulations require a person who generates a solid waste to "determine if that waste is a hazardous waste," 40 C.F.R. §262.11. If a waste is not a hazardous waste specifically listed in subpart D of 40 C.F.R. pt. 261, the person must determine whether the waste is hazardous because of its characteristics by either testing the waste or "[a]pplying knowledge of the hazard characteristic of the waste in light of the materials or the processes used." 40 C.F.R. §262.11(c)(2).

In 1987, the Environmental Defense Fund (EDF), a private environmental group, reviewed the results of tests performed on ash residues from more than 20 incinerators around the country. EDF discovered that fly ash and bottom ash from municipal waste incinerators often "flunked" EPA's toxicity test by leaching lead and cadmium at concentrations greater than the 5 and 1 milligram per liter cutoff levels for the toxicity characteristic. Fly ash failed the test 80 to 90 percent of the time, bottom ash failed 20 to 25 percent of the time, and combined ash failed about 50 percent of the time. At the time, few municipal incineration facilities tested their ash regularly.

Representatives of incinerator owners and operators argued that incinerator ash should be exempt from subtitle C of RCRA pursuant to section 3001(i), which had been added by the 1984 Amendments. Section 3001(i) provides that a "facility recovering energy from the mass burning of municipal solid waste shall not be deemed to be treating, storing, disposing of, or otherwise managing hazardous wastes for the purposes of regulation under [subtitle C]" if the facility (1) receives and burns only household waste and nonhazardous waste from commercial and industrial sources, (2) does not accept hazardous waste identified or listed under subtitle C, and (3) "has established contractual requirements or other appropriate notification or inspection procedures to assure that hazardous wastes are not received at or burned in such facility."

EPA did not agree with municipalities that ash from municipal incinerators is automatically exempt from subtitle C of RCRA due to section 3001(i). In July 1985 EPA had stated that it interpreted section 3001(i) to mean that incinerators were not managing hazardous waste when they incinerated municipal solid waste, but that ash or other by-products generated by the incineration process were not exempt from subtitle C. Although EPA noted that it did not have evidence "to indicate that these ash residues are hazardous under existing rules," it concluded that such residues "would be hazardous under present EPA regulations if they exhibited a [hazardous waste] characteristic." 50 Fed. Reg. 28,725. Citing the enormous cost of managing ash as a hazardous waste, owners and operators of incinerators vigorously lobbied EPA to reinterpret section 3001(i) to exempt ash from subtitle C. EPA initially refused to do so.

EDF eventually filed suit against two incineration facilities, arguing that their failure to manage their ash in accordance with subtitle C violated RCRA. Confronted with the argument that management of incinerator ash as a hazardous waste would be enormously costly, each district court held that the ash is exempt if facilities comply with the requirements of section 3001(i). On appeal the Second Circuit affirmed, Environmental Defense Fund v. Wheelabrator Technologies, Inc., 931 F.2d 211 (2d Cir. 1991), while the Seventh Circuit reversed, Environmental Defense Fund v. City of Chicago, 948 F.2d 345 (7th Cir. 1991).

While the city of Chicago sought Supreme Court review of the Seventh Circuit's decision, EPA Administrator William Reilly issued a new memorandum determining that section 3001(i) of RCRA exempts incinerator ash from regulation under subtitle C. Although EPA previously had taken the position that section 3001(i) was not intended to affect whether ash should be considered a hazardous waste, the memorandum issued on September 18, 1992, stated that section 3001(i) "arguably extended the regulatory exclusion for ash derived from the incineration of household waste to similar residues generated by resource recovery facilities from the incineration of household waste *and* non-hazardous commercial and industrial solid waste." Noting that section 3001(i) specifies that certain resource recovery facilities are not considered to be "treating, storing, disposing of, or otherwise managing" hazardous waste, the memorandum states that

> Nothing ordinarily is "disposed of when a resource recovery facility receives or stores a nonhazardous solid waste, and the burning of such waste generally is regarded as a type of treatment under RCRA. As a result, since MWC [municipal

waste combustion] ash ordinarily is the only waste "disposed of" by such a facility, Congress arguably intended that MWC ash not be regarded as a hazardous waste. [W. Reilly, Exemption for Municipal Waste Combustion Ash from Hazardous Waste Regulation Under RCRA Section 3001(i), Sept. 18, 1992.]

In November 1992, the Supreme Court then vacated the Seventh Circuit's decision and remanded the case for reconsideration in light of the EPA Administrator's new interpretation of section 3001(i). On remand, the Seventh Circuit reaffirmed its previous finding that the ash was not exempt. The Supreme Court then granted review and reached the following decision.

City of Chicago v. Environmental Defense Fund
511 U.S. 328 (1994)

JUSTICE SCALIA delivered the opinion of the Court.

We are called upon to decide whether, pursuant to §3000(i) of the Solid Waste Disposal Act (Resource Conservation and Recovery Act of 1976 (RCRA)), as added, 98 Stat. 3252, 42 U.S.C. §6921(i), the ash generated by a resource recovery facility's incineration of municipal solid waste is exempt from regulation as a hazardous waste under Subtitle C of RCRA. . . .

II

RCRA is a comprehensive environmental statute that empowers EPA to regulate hazardous wastes from cradle to grave, in accordance with the rigorous safeguards and waste management procedures of Subtitle C, 42 U.S.C. §§6921-6934. (Nonhazardous wastes are regulated much more loosely under Subtitle D, 42 U.S.C. §§6941-6949.) . . .

RCRA does not identify which wastes are hazardous and therefore subject to Subtitle C regulation; it leaves that designation to EPA. 42 U.S.C. §6921(a). When EPA's hazardous waste designations for solid wastes appeared in 1980, see 45 Fed. Reg. 33084, they contained certain exceptions from normal coverage, including an exclusion for "household waste," defined as "any waste material . . . derived from households (including single and multiple residences, hotels and motels)," id., at 33120, codified as amended at 40 CFR §261.4(b)(1) (1992). Although most household waste is harmless, a small portion—such as cleaning fluids and batteries—would have qualified as hazardous waste. The regulation declared, however, that "[h]ousehold waste, including household waste that has been collected, transported, stored, treated, disposed, recovered (e.g., refuse derived fuel) or reused" is not hazardous waste. Ibid. Moreover, the preamble to the 1980 regulations stated that "residues remaining after treatment (e.g., incineration, thermal treatment) [of household waste] are not subject to regulation as a hazardous waste." 45 Fed. Reg. 33099. By reason of these provisions, an incinerator that burned only household waste would not be considered a Subtitle C TSDF, since it processed only nonhazardous (i.e., household) waste, and it would not be considered a Subtitle C generator of hazardous waste and would be free to dispose of its ash in a Subtitle D landfill.

The 1980 regulations thus provided what is known as a "waste stream" exemption for household waste, ibid., i.e., an exemption covering that category of waste from generation through treatment to final disposal of residues. The regulation did not, however, exempt MWC ash from Subtitle C coverage if the incinerator that produced the ash burned anything *in addition to* household waste, such as what petitioner's facility burns: nonhazardous industrial waste. Thus, a facility like petitioner's would qualify as a Subtitle C hazardous waste generator if the MWC ash it produced was sufficiently toxic, see 40 CFR §§261.3, 261.24 (1993), though it would still not qualify as a Subtitle C TSDF, since all the waste it took in would be characterized as nonhazardous. (An ash can be hazardous, even though the product from which it is generated is not, because in the new medium the contaminants are more concentrated and more readily leachable, see 40 CFR §§261.3, 261.24, and pt. 261, App. II (1993).)

Four years after these regulations were issued, Congress enacted the Hazardous and Solid Waste Amendments of 1984, Pub. L. 98-616, 98 Stat. 3221, which added to RCRA the "Clarification of Household Waste Exclusion" as §3001(i), §223, 98 Stat., at 3252. The essence of our task in this case is to determine whether, under that provision, the MWC ash generated by petitioner's facility—a facility that would have been considered a Subtitle C generator under the 1980 regulations—is subject to regulation as hazardous waste under Subtitle C. We conclude that it is.

Section 3001(i), 42 U.S.C. §6921 (i), entitled "Clarification of household waste exclusion," provides:

> A resource recovery facility recovering energy from the mass burning of municipal solid waste shall not be deemed to be treating, storing, disposing of, or otherwise managing hazardous wastes for the purposes of regulation under this subchapter, if—
>> (1) such facility—
>>> (A) receives and burns only—
>>>> (i) household waste (from single and multiple dwellings, hotels, motels and other residential sources), and
>>>> (ii) solid waste from commercial or industrial sources that does not contain hazardous waste identified or listed under this section, and
>>> (B) does not accept hazardous wastes identified or listed under this section, and
>> (2) the owner or operator of such facility has established contractual requirements or other appropriate notification or inspection procedures to assure that hazardous wastes are not received at or burned in such facility.

The plain meaning of this language is that so long as a facility recovers energy by incineration of the appropriate wastes, *it* (the *facility*) is not subject to Subtitle C regulation as a facility that treats, stores, disposes of, or manages hazardous waste. The provision quite clearly does not contain any exclusion for the *ash itself*. Indeed, the waste the facility produces (as opposed to that which it receives) is not even mentioned. There is thus no express support for petitioners' claim of a waste-stream exemption.[1]

---

1. The dissent is able to describe the provision as exempting the ash itself only by resorting to what might be called imaginative use of ellipsis: "even though the material being treated and disposed of contains hazardous components before, during, and after its treatment[,] that material shall not be deemed to be . . . hazardous." In the full text, quoted above, the subject of the phrase "shall not be deemed . . . hazardous" is *not* the material, but the *resource recovery facility,* and the complete phrase, including (italicized) ellipsis, reads "shall not be deemed to be *treating, storing, disposing of, or otherwise managing* hazardous *wastes.*" Deeming a facility not to be engaged in these activities with respect to hazardous wastes is of course quite different from deeming the output of that facility not to be hazardous.

Petitioners contend, however, that the practical effect of the statutory language is to exempt the ash by virtue of exempting the facility. If, they argue, the facility is not deemed to be treating, storing, or disposing of hazardous waste, then the ash that it treats, stores, or disposes of must itself be considered non-hazardous. There are several problems with this argument. First, as we have explained, the only exemption provided by the terms of the statute is for the *facility*. It is the facility, *not the ash*, that "shall not be deemed" to be subject to regulation under Subtitle C. *Unlike* the preamble to the 1980 regulations, which had been in existence for four years by the time §3001(i) was enacted, §3001(i) does not explicitly exempt MWC ash generated by a resource recovery facility from regulation as a hazardous waste. In light of that difference, and given the statute's express declaration of national policy that "[w]aste that is . . . generated should be treated, stored, or disposed of so as to minimize the present and future threat to human health and the environment," 42 U.S.C. §6902(b), we cannot interpret the statute to permit MWC ash sufficiently toxic to qualify as hazardous to be disposed of in ordinary landfills.

Moreover, as the Court of Appeals observed, the statutory language does not even exempt *the facility* in its capacity as a *generator* of hazardous waste. RCRA defines "generation" as "the act or process of producing hazardous waste." 42 U.S.C. §6903(6). There can be no question that the creation of ash by incinerating municipal waste constitutes "generation" of hazardous waste (assuming, of course, that the ash qualifies as hazardous under 42 U.S.C. §6921 and its implementing regulations, 40 CFR pt. 261 (1993)). Yet although §3001(i) states that the exempted facility "shall not be deemed to be treating, storing, disposing of, or otherwise managing hazardous wastes," it significantly omits from the catalogue the word "generating." Petitioners say that because the activities listed as exempt encompass the full scope of the facility's operation, the failure to mention the activity of generating is insignificant. But the statute itself refutes this. Each of the three specific terms used in §3000(i)—"treating," "storing," and "disposing of"—is separately defined by RCRA, and none covers the production of hazardous waste. The fourth and less specific term ("otherwise managing") is also defined, to mean "collection, source separation, storage, transportation, processing, treatment, recovery, and disposal," 42 U.S.C. §6903(7)—just about every hazardous waste-related activity *except* generation. We think it follows from the carefully constructed text of §3001(i) that while a resource recovery facility's management activities are excluded from Subtitle C regulation, its generation of toxic ash is not. . . .

Petitioners contend that our interpretation of §3001(i) turns the provision into an "empty gesture," since even under the pre-existing regime an incinerator burning household waste and nonhazardous industrial waste was exempt from the Subtitle C TSDF provisions. If §3001(i) did not extend the waste-stream exemption to the product of such a combined household/nonhazardous industrial treatment facility, petitioners argue, it did nothing at all. But it is not nothing to codify a household waste exemption that had previously been subject to agency revision; nor is it nothing (though petitioners may value it as less than nothing) to *restrict* the exemption that the agency previously provided which is what the provision here achieved, by withholding all waste-stream exemption for waste processed by resource recovery facilities, even for the waste stream passing through an exclusively household-waste facility.

We also do not agree with petitioners' contention that our construction renders §3001(i) ineffective for its intended purpose of promoting household/

nonhazardous-industrial resource recovery facilities, see 42 U.S.C. §§6902(a)(1), (10), (11), by subjecting them "to the potentially enormous expense of managing ash residue as a hazardous waste." It is simply not true that a facility which is (as our interpretation says these facilities are) a hazardous waste "generator," is also deemed to be "managing" hazardous waste under RCRA. Section 3001(i) clearly exempts these facilities from Subtitle C TSDF regulations, thus enabling them to avoid the "full brunt of EPA's enforcement effort under RCRA." Practice Guide §29.05(1). . . .

RCRA's twin goals of encouraging resource recovery and protecting against contamination sometimes conflict. It is not unusual for legislation to contain diverse purposes that must be reconciled, and the most reliable guide for that task is the enacted text. Here that requires us to reject the Solicitor General's plea for deference to the EPA's interpretation, cf. Chevron U.S.A., Inc. v. Natural Resources Defense Council, Inc., 467 U.S. 837, 843-844 (1984), which goes beyond the scope of whatever ambiguity §3001(i) contains. Section 3000(i) simply cannot be read to contain the cost-saving waste stream exemption petitioners seek.

For the foregoing reasons, the judgment of the Court of Appeals for the Seventh Circuit is *Affirmed.*

JUSTICE STEVENS, with whom JUSTICE O'CONNOR joins, dissenting.

The statutory provision in question is a 1984 amendment entitled "Clarification of Household Waste Exclusion." To understand that clarification, we must first examine the "waste exclusion" that the amendment clarified and, more particularly, the ambiguity that needed clarification. . . .

I

When Congress enacted the Resource Conservation and Recovery Act of 1976 (RCRA), it delegated to the Environmental Protection Agency (EPA) vast regulatory authority over the mountains of garbage that our society generates. The statute directed the EPA to classify waste as hazardous or nonhazardous and to establish regulatory controls over the disposition of the two categories of waste pursuant to Subtitles C and D of the Act. 42 U.S.C. §6921(a). To that end, the EPA in 1980 promulgated detailed regulations establishing a federal hazardous waste management system pursuant to Subtitle C.

Generally, though not always, the EPA regulations assume that waste is properly characterized as hazardous or nonhazardous when it first becomes waste. Based on that characterization, the waste is regulated under either Subtitle C or D. Household waste is regarded as nonhazardous when it is first discarded and, as long as it is not mixed with hazardous waste, it retains that characterization during and after its treatment and disposal. Even though it contains some materials that would be classified as hazardous in other contexts, and even though its treatment may produce a residue that contains a higher concentration of hazardous matter than when the garbage was originally discarded, such waste is regulated as nonhazardous waste under Subtitle D. Thus, an incinerator that burns nothing but household waste might "generate" tons of hazardous residue, but as a statutory matter it still is deemed to be processing nonhazardous waste and is regulated as a Subtitle D, rather than Subtitle C, facility.

Section 261.4(b)(1) of the EPA's 1980 regulations first established the household waste exclusion. See 45 Fed. Reg. 33120 (1980). The relevant text of that regulation simply provided that solid wastes derived from households (including single and multiple residences, hotels and motels) were "not hazardous wastes." The regulation itself said nothing about the status of the residue that remains after the incineration of such household waste. An accompanying comment, however, unambiguously explained that "residues remaining after treatment (e.g., incineration, thermal treatment) are not subject to regulation as hazardous waste." Id., at 33099. Thus, the administrative history of the 1980 regulation, rather than its text, revealed why a municipal incinerator burning household waste was not treated as a generator of hazardous waste.

The EPA's explanatory comment contained an important warning: If household waste was "mixed with other hazardous wastes," the entire mixture would be deemed hazardous. Yet neither the comment nor the regulation itself identified the consequences of mixing household waste with other wastes that are entirely *nonhazardous*. Presumably such a mixture would contain a lower percentage of hazardous material than pure household waste, and therefore should also be classified as nonhazardous—assumptions that are not inconsistent with the EPA's warning that mixing household waste "with other *hazardous* wastes" would terminate the household waste exemption. The EPA's failure to comment expressly on the significance of adding 100 percent nonhazardous commercial or industrial waste nevertheless warranted further clarification.

Congress enacted that clarification in 1984. Elaborating upon the EPA's warning in 1980, the text of the 1984 amendment—§3001(i) of RCRA, 42 U.S.C. §6921(i)—made clear that a facility treating a mixture of household waste and "solid waste from commercial or industrial sources that does not contain hazardous waste," §6921(i)(1)(A)(ii), shall not be deemed to be treating hazardous waste. In other words, the addition of nonhazardous waste derived from other sources does not extinguish the household waste exclusion.

The parallel between the 1980 regulation and the 1984 statutory amendment is striking. In 1980 the EPA referred to the exclusion of household waste "in all phases of its management." Similarly, the 1984 statute lists *all phases* of the incinerator's management when it states that a facility recovering energy from the mass burning of a mixture of household waste and other solid waste that does not contain hazardous waste "shall not be deemed to be treating, storing, disposing of, or otherwise managing hazardous wastes." See 42 U.S.C. §6921(i). Even though that text only refers to the exemption of the facility that burns the waste, the title of the section significantly characterizes it as a *waste* exclusion. Moreover, the title's description of the amendment as a "clarification" identifies an intent to codify its counterpart in the 1980 regulation. . . .

II

The relevant statutory text is not as unambiguous as the Court asserts. There is substantial tension between the broad definition of the term "hazardous waste generation" in §1004(6) of the Act and the household waste exclusion codified by the 1984 amendment: both provisions can be read to describe the same activity. The former "means the act or process of producing hazardous waste." 90 Stat. 2799; 42 U.S.C. §6903(6). Read literally, that definition is broad enough to encompass the burning of pure household waste that produces some hazardous residue. The only statutory escape from that conclusion is the 1984 amendment that provides an exemption for the activity of burning household waste. Yet that exemption does not distinguish between pure household waste, on the one hand, and a mixture of household and other nonhazardous wastes, on the other. It either exempts both the pure stream and the mixture, or it exempts neither.

Indeed, commercial and industrial waste is by definition nonhazardous: in order for it to fall within the exclusion created by the 1984 amendment, it must not contain hazardous components. As a consequence, the only aspect of this waste stream that would ordinarily be regulated by Subtitle C of RCRA is the ash residue. EPA could reasonably conclude, therefore, that to give any content to the statute with respect to this component of the waste stream, the incinerator ash must be exempted from Subtitle C regulation.

The exemption states that a facility burning solid waste "shall not be deemed to be treating, storing, disposing of, or otherwise managing hazardous wastes for the purposes of regulation under this subchapter" if two conditions are satisfied. As long as the two conditions are met—even though the material being treated and disposed of contains hazardous components before, during, and after its treatment—that material "shall not be deemed to be . . . hazardous." By characterizing both the input and the output as not hazardous, the 1984 amendment excludes the activity from the definition of hazardous waste generation that would otherwise apply. For it is obvious that the same activity cannot both subject a facility to regulation because its residue is hazardous and exempt the facility from regulation because the statute deems the same residue to be nonhazardous.[8]

Thus, if we are to be guided only by the literal meaning of the statutory text, we must either give effect to the broad definition of hazardous waste generation and subject all municipal incinerators that generate hazardous ash to Subtitle C regulation (including those that burn pure household waste) or give effect to the exclusion that applies equally to pure household waste and mixtures that include other nonhazardous wastes. For several reasons the latter is the proper choice. It effectuates the narrower and more recently enacted provision rather than the earlier more general definition. It respects the title of the 1984 amendment by treating what follows as a "clarification" rather than a repeal or a modification. It avoids the Court's rather surprising (and uninvited) decision to invalidate the household waste exclusion that the EPA adopted in 1980,[9] on which municipalities throughout the Nation have reasonably relied for over a

---

8. The Court characterizes my reading of the text as "imaginative use of ellipsis," because the subject of the predicate "shall not be deemed to be . . . hazardous" is the recovery facility rather than the residue that is disposed of after the waste is burned. That is true, but the reason the facility is exempted is because it is not "deemed to be . . . disposing of . . . hazardous wastes." Thus it is the statutorily deemed nonhazardous character of the object of the sentence—wastes—that effectively exempts from Subtitle C regulation the activity and the facility engaged in that activity. If, as the statute provides, a facility is not deemed to be disposing of hazardous wastes when it disposes of the output of the facility, it must be true that the output is deemed nonhazardous.

9. Although the first nine pages of the Court's opinion give the reader the impression that the 1980 regulatory exclusion for pure household waste was valid, the Court ultimately acknowledges that its construction of the statute has the effect of "withholding all waste-stream exemption for waste processed by resource recovery facilities, even for the waste stream passing through an exclusively household-waste facility." Of course, it is not the 1984 amendment that casts doubt on the validity of the regulation, but the Court's rigid reading of §1004(6)'s definition of the term "hazardous waste generation" that has achieved that result. Since that definition has been in the Act since 1976, the Court utterly fails to explain how the 1984 amendment made any change in the law.

decade. It explains why the legislative history fails to mention an intent to impose significant new burdens on the operation of municipal incinerators. Finally, it is the construction that the EPA has adopted and that reasonable jurists have accepted.

The majority's decision today may represent sound policy. Requiring cities to spend the necessary funds to dispose of their incinerator residues in accordance with the strict requirements of Subtitle C will provide additional protections to the environment. It is also true, however, that the conservation of scarce landfill space and the encouragement of the recovery of energy and valuable materials in municipal wastes were major concerns motivating RCRA's enactment. Whether those purposes will be disserved by regulating municipal incinerators under Subtitle C and, if so, whether environmental benefits may nevertheless justify the costs of such additional regulation are questions of policy that we are not competent to resolve. Those questions are precisely the kind that Congress has directed the EPA to answer. The EPA's position, first adopted unambiguously in 1980 and still maintained today, was and remains a correct and permissible interpretation of the Agency's broad congressional mandate.

NOTES AND QUESTIONS

1. When Administrator Reilly issued his new interpretation of the effect of section 3001(i) on incinerator ash, the president of the Integrated Waste Management Association hailed it as "a major breakthrough for solid waste managers in communities nationwide." He declared that the Administrator's decision "confirms what the scientific evidence has revealed for the past decade—namely that MWC ash is not hazardous and can be safely managed in [municipal] landfills." Ash from Combustion of Municipal Waste to Be Considered Non-Hazardous, EPA Says, 23 Envtl. Rep. 1459, 1460 (1992). Is this an accurate characterization of the Administrator's memorandum?

2. If household waste can contain hazardous constituents, why would EPA have sought to grant it a waste-stream exemption from regulation as hazardous waste under subtitle C?

3. In light of the Court's decision, would ash produced by an incinerator that burned *only* household waste and *no* other materials be exempt from subtitle C regulation? Would it have been prior to the 1984 amendment that added section 3001(i) to RCRA? What did the addition of section 3001(i) accomplish, according to Justice Scalia?

4. Justice Scalia notes that municipal incinerators whose ash becomes a hazardous waste will be subject only to the subtitle C regulations applicable to generators and not to subtitle C's more onerous requirements for TSDs. Does this mean that the Court's decision will not impose substantial additional costs on incinerators?

5. In May 1994, EPA issued guidance stating that incinerator ash be tested for hazardous constituents four times a year beginning in August 1994, using the Toxicity Characteristic Leaching Procedure (TCLP). In January 1995, EPA announced that incinerator operators could combine fly ash and bottom ash prior to testing to determine if the waste exhibits a hazardous characteristic. The agency based this decision on the notion that ash does not become a waste until it leaves the combustion facility. Because bottom ash usually is less toxic than fly ash, the decision is expected to mean that most incinerator ash will not exhibit a

hazardous characteristic when tested. EPA Says Municipal Incinerator Owners Can Combine Fly, Bottom Ash for Testing, 25 Envtl. Rep. 1841 (1995). If ash does not become a waste until it leaves the combustion facility, could incinerator operators treat ash that flunks the TCLP to render it nonhazardous prior to shipping it off-site without having to comply with subtitle C of RCRA?

4.   Avoiding TSD Status

The regulated community perceives RCRA's subtitle C regulations to be extremely burdensome, particularly for TSDs. Thus, companies go to great lengths to avoid being caught in the subtitle C net. Despite the breadth of its coverage, subtitle C leaves many avenues for escape. Consider the following advice from an industry lawyer well versed in the subtleties of RCRA. As you read this excerpt, recall the difficulties EPA faced in defining "solid waste" as reflected in American Mining Congress v. EPA, 824 F.2d 1177 (D.C. Cir. 1987) and subsequent litigation.

> ### Stoll, Coping with the RCRA Hazardous Waste System: A Few Practical Points for Fun and Profit
> #### 1 Envtl. Hazards 6 (July 1989)

Subtitle C of the federal Resource Conservation and Recovery Act (RCRA) establishes the famous "cradle to grave" framework for managing today's hazardous waste activities. Along with EPA's ever-changing and ever-expanding regulations, Subtitle C has probably expedited the trip from cradle to grave for more than one environmental manager.

It is fashionable to write and talk about how horrible the Subtitle C system has become. Words and phrases like "corrective action," "criminal convictions," "land bans," "financial assurance," "hammers," "post-closure care," and—perhaps the most spine-chilling of all—"permitting" are thrown about to scare poor readers and audiences.

In truth, the system can be horrible and most of the fear-mongering is fair. There are paths in the regulations, however, through which manufacturing companies may greatly reduce the pain and save lots of money. I would like to pass on a few hypothetical examples and pointers.

One key theme is that a reasonably logical reading of EPA's regulation might cause one to reject an otherwise attractive option. In some situations, however, happy results and great cost savings can be achieved through a more careful reading of EPA's regulations, an awareness of EPA's rulings (often unpublished), and creative thinking. Before turning to the examples, a few Subtitle C fundamentals should be reviewed.

Exclusions.   Statutory and/or regulatory provisions exclude certain materials or practices from Subtitle C jurisdiction. A few of the more notable are materials disposed into a public sewer system; industrial discharges subject to Clean Water Act permits; residues from fossil fuel combustion; and certain "mining" wastes.

Definitions of "Solid Waste" and "Hazardous Waste." A material may be hazardous but not a "waste" or a material may be a waste but not "hazardous." In either case, there would be no Subtitle C jurisdiction. A material must be *both* a waste and hazardous to trigger Subtitle C jurisdiction.

EPA's regulations for determining what is a "waste" contain some of the most puzzling English word patterns ever devised. The regulations endeavor to prescribe tests—based on the type of material and on the type of management activity—for determining whether a material is a product (and therefore exempt from RCRA) or a waste (and therefore covered). 40 C.F.R. §§260.22 et seq.; 261.1; 261.2; 261.4.

EPA's regulations for determining whether a waste is "hazardous" are somewhat simpler. A waste may be hazardous either because it is on a "list" or because—when tested—it fails one of several hazard "characteristic" protocols. 40 C.F.R. §261.3(a).

Vast Differences in Coverage Among Types of Waste Management. The "cradle-to-grave" system regulates the following types of parties involved with hazardous waste: (a) generators; (b) transporters; and (c) owners/operators of treatment, storage, or disposal facilities ("TSD" facilities). One point cannot be overemphasized: *by several orders of magnitude, the system is much harsher on TSD facilities.* Permits, corrective action, post-closure, financial assurance, and many other burdens are part of the TSD game and do not apply to those who only generate and/or transport.

HYPOTHETICAL EXAMPLES

Below are examples where a plant manager seeks ways to cut costs and/or increase revenues and avoid onerous RCRA burdens. One central theme is a follow-up to the third point above: It is often acceptable to stay in the Subtitle C system so long as TSD status can be avoided, and there are several ways (generally unpublicized) to accomplish this. Another key theme is that important RCRA interpretations appear in strange places.

1. Obtaining Useful Feedstock from Others' Wastes. Alpha Company buys Chemical A at $5.00 per pound for use as a degreasing and cleaning solvent. Once used, their "spent" solvent is a listed RCRA hazardous waste.

The Alpha plant manager develops a plan to save millions of dollars. He would buy others' spent solvents, "regenerate" or "reclaim" the solvents to make virgin-quality Chemical A, and use the reclaimed material as a feedstock. He figures he can obtain spent Chemical A at $1.00 per pound.

He runs this by his environmental people, who find the RCRA regulations quite discouraging for two reasons. (a) The spent Chemical A is a "waste." While EPA's regulations provide that certain types of materials are not wastes if they are "reclaimed," they specify that *spent* materials are wastes even if reclaimed. 40 C.F.R. §261.2(c). (b) The reclamation at Alpha's facility would trigger TSD status because (i) the reclamation is "treatment" of hazardous waste, and (ii) storage of the spent Chemical A prior to reclamation would independently trigger TSD status.

The plant manager, upon checking with corporate management, is glum. Management has concluded that even the millions in savings are not worth TSD status.

Unfortunately these people do not realize that Alpha can have its cake and eat it too. While part (a) of the foregoing analysis is correct (the spent Chemical A must be regarded as a hazardous waste), part (b) is based upon a misunderstanding of the regulations and an unnecessary factual assumption. *Even though the spent Chemical A will be a hazardous waste when generated and transported, Alpha may be able to reclaim it without triggering TSD status.*

First, even though the reclamation may be "treatment," it is also "recycling." EPA's regulations specify: "The recycling process itself is exempt from RCRA." 40 C.F.R. §261.6(c)(1). (EPA buried this fundamental in a parenthetical near the end of a paragraph dealing with storage.)

Second, Alpha might recycle the spent Chemical A *without first storing it.* EPA's regulations contemplate this, and make clear that engaging in this practice will avoid TSD status. 40 C.F.R. §261.6(c)(2). For example, Alpha may arrange a system by which trucks enter its facility, park at the reclamation device, and off-load the spent Chemical A through hoses connected directly from the truck to the reclamation device. EPA has on several occasions affirmed that in such a situation, no "storage" is involved.

If Alpha could accomplish this recycling without storage, it would avoid all of the permitting and other horrors of TSD status. It would only need to file a "notification" of its hazardous waste activity and comply with the manifesting (paper trail) requirements. 40 C.F.R. §261.6(c)(2).

2. Reclaiming Feedstock from One's Own Wastes Without a "Closed Loop" System. Beta Company uses Chemical A as a feedstock, and a secondary material from Beta's process is "spent" Chemical A. Spent Chemical A is a listed hazardous waste. Beta must pay $5.00 per pound to purchase virgin Chemical A. Beta has been paying $2.00 per pound to have a commercial incinerator destroy spent Chemical A.

The plant manager would like to save millions of dollars by devising a system to reclaim and reuse her spent Chemical A. With a recycling system, she could both drastically reduce the volume of virgin Chemical A she has to buy and eliminate her off-site disposal costs entirely.

Her environmental people tell her that in EPA's definition of solid waste, there is a "closed loop" exemption which such a recycling practice might fit. If spent material is reclaimed and returned to the original process and the entire process is "closed" through interconnected tubes and pipes, the material will not be an RCRA "waste" at all. 40 C.F.R. §261.4(a)(8).

The plant manager is glum. There is only one suitable location on her property for the reclamation process, and it is thousands of yards from the place where the spent Chemical A is generated. Because of the layout of the facility, the costs of such a "closed loop" system would be prohibitive.

Here again, the analysis has been correct, as far as it goes, but the plant people have been overlooking some basic points. Even though Beta cannot avoid being a generator, it can still avoid TSD status.

Beta may be able to collect the spent Chemical A in drums, and, *always within 90 days* of the date of generation, recycle the spent Chemical A. In this manner, no TSD status is triggered. First, as described in [the first example], the recycling process is exempt. Second, EPA's regulations have long provided that a generator may accumulate its own hazardous wastes in tanks or containers for up to 90 days without triggering TSD status. 40 C.F.R. §262.34. Thus, so long as

Beta keeps "rotating" drummed waste so that no drum is stored more than 90 days before it is recycled, TSD status can be avoided.

Caution: This result can only be achieved if the storage takes place at the same facility where the waste was generated. For instance, if Beta installed its reclamation device on a nearby but separate parcel of land, it could not store drums at all on the separate parcel without triggering TSD. The 90-day exemption applies only to the generating facility; once off-site, storage of hazardous waste for *any* period of time will trigger TSD. If the reclamation device were on a separate parcel, Beta could avoid TSD only by some form of direct off-loading from transport vehicles as described in [the first example].

**3.   *Other Treatment Avoiding TSD.*   Gamma Company generates a hazardous waste and sends it off-site for treatment at a cost of $2.00 per gallon. The plant manager learns that there is a simple and inexpensive treatment process he could use in tanks at his facility which would render the waste nonhazardous. If he could do this, he could save millions of dollars per year in off-site transport and treatment costs.

His environmental people look for regulatory exemptions under which "treatment" would not trigger TSD status. They find three: (1) where wastes which are hazardous only because they are "corrosive" are being neutralized; (2) where waste waters are being treated as part of a Clean Water Act discharge; and (3) where the treatment is part of a "totally enclosed" recycling system. 40 C.F.R. §270.1(c)(2).

The plant manager is glum. His proposal would not fit any of these three narrow exemptions. He drops his idea, because the millions in cost savings will not justify TSD status.

Unfortunately for Gamma, its people missed a paragraph in the middle of a long EPA Federal Register preamble on an unrelated topic and were unaware of an EPA letter to a Wisconsin consulting firm. With such inimitable administrative procedure, EPA has ruled that generators may "treat" hazardous waste in containers or tanks for no more than 90 days at the generating facility and not trigger TSD status. Thus, so long as treatment occurs on-site in tanks that are emptied at least every 90 days, millions in off-site disposal costs can be saved and TSD status can be avoided.

**4.   *Recycling One's Own Hazardous Wastewater.*   Delta Company plans to conduct a chemical tank steam-cleaning operation, and will need a million gallons of water a month. The plant manager would like to save money by reusing the same water after treating it, but does not want to trigger TSD status. She is told by her environmental people that the wastewater would clearly be an RCRA hazardous waste (as it will be mixed with commercial chemicals on EPA's RCRA "lists").

But they read the first three hypotheticals in this article and are now thinking creatively. They develop the following logic: (i) always store the hazardous waste in tanks or containers for less than 90 days so "storage" will not trigger TSD, then (ii) reclaim the wastewater through treatment into reusable water and this "recycling" of hazardous waste will be exempt from RCRA.

They are further comforted by language in EPA's regulations which says that materials reclaimed beneficially are not thereafter RCRA wastes (unless burned for energy recovery or placed in or on the land). 40 C.F.R. §261.3(c)(2)(i). Certainly the reclaimed wastewater fits this description.

At this point, however, a lawyer throws cold water on the idea. She discovers language in EPA's 1985 Federal Register preamble to the foregoing regulation which strongly suggests that EPA did not intend for wastewater to be protected by it. ["We caution, though, as we did in the proposal, that this principle does not apply to reclaimed materials that are not ordinarily considered to be commercial products, such as wastewaters or stabilized wastes." 50 Fed. Reg. 634 (Jan. 4, 1985).] At this point, the plant manager is glum.

But then the lawyer uses her head. She figures anything that EPA published as far back as 1985 could be suspect, and phones some EPA people. Lo and behold, she finds that EPA headquarters recently sent a memo to one of EPA's regional offices ruling that wastewater can be protected by the regulatory language. [Memorandum from Sylvia K. Lowrance, EPA Office of Solid Waste Director, to David A. Wagoner (Region VII) (Oct. 27, 1988).]

Again, TSD could be avoided and millions of dollars saved only if one were aware of an unpublished EPA interpretation. EPA's last Federal Register words on the subject would in fact have tended to squelch the idea.

QUICK POINTERS

Here are a few other quick pointers for avoiding or curtailing Subtitle C exposure:

Redirect Stream to POTW or NPDES.   You may be able to redirect certain RCRA waste streams to a public sewer system and/or a point source discharge to the navigable waters. While this may trigger additional Clean Water Act pretreatment and/or NPDES requirements, such requirements may not be nearly as costly and onerous as RCRA requirements.

Change Manufacturing Process.   If you generate a waste that is hazardous because it fails a characteristic (i.e., non-"listed"), you may be able to alter your manufacturing process (through chemical and/or engineering changes) to produce a material that does not fail the characteristic and is therefore no longer hazardous. (This approach would not work for a "listed" waste.)

Delisting.   If you generate a "listed" waste, you may be able to secure a "delisting" if you can show EPA that at your particular facility the waste is not truly hazardous. The delisting process is expensive, time consuming, and involves notice-and-comment rulemaking in the Federal Register. Nevertheless, many facilities have successfully utilized this process. While serious delays were prevalent a few years ago, EPA is now usually able to process a delisting petition in about a year.

Export.   Many companies have found that they can reduce costs by shipping their wastes to Canada or other countries for ultimate treatment and disposal. EPA regulations expressly allow for such "exports" of hazardous waste. In fact, Canada and the U.S. have a bilateral agreement under which many U.S. companies are now shipping their wastes to Canada.

Reclaim Non-Listed Sludges and By-Products.   EPA's "waste" definition draws major distinctions among "spent materials," "sludges," and "by-products." If you generate a spent material, it will always be a "waste" (even if reclaimed). But if you generate a "sludge" or "by-product," *and* it is not a "listed" waste, then it will *not* be a waste if it is reclaimed. 40 C.F.R. §261.2(c).

Thus, assume a facility in Maine generates a hazardous by-product which is not "listed." If the by-product were disposed of a mile away it would be an RCRA hazardous waste. If, however, it were shipped to Arizona for reclamation it would be totally outside RCRA jurisdiction and no generator, transporter, manifesting and/or T/S/D requirements would apply.

NOTES AND QUESTIONS

1. While some of the strategies cited by Stoll would subject TSDs to other, presumably less onerous, forms of federal regulation (e.g., the Clean Water Act's permit program if waste is discharged into surface waters or the Act's pretreatment program if it is discharged into sewers), in other cases the consequences of escaping subtitle C are avoidance of federal regulation altogether. Stoll believes that the strategies he identifies for escaping subtitle C "are not really suggestive of 'loopholes' in the RCRA system." He argues instead that "they show that recycling is something that is generally encouraged by RCRA" and that his strategies should result in "a national reduction in potential health and environmental risks." Do you agree that the strategies Stoll recommends will result in greater protection of the environment than management of hazardous waste in facilities with RCRA permits?

2. Why, do you suppose, has EPA exempted from TSD status large generators who accumulate hazardous waste in tanks or containers for no more than 90 days? Even if each batch of hazardous waste in the containers is emptied at least once every 90 days, the containers can contain hazardous waste almost continuously. Does it make any difference from the standpoint of environmental risk whether each batch of waste has been there for no more than 90 days?

3. Stoll emphasizes that surprising avenues for avoiding subtitle C regulations are buried in obscure places: cryptic statements in unrelated Federal Register notices, unpublished correspondence with EPA, or memoranda from EPA officials. For example, the solution to Gamma Company's problem appeared in a Federal Register notice concerning rules for small-quantity generators. 51 Fed. Reg. 10,146 (1986). As Stoll explains:

> Half-way through a lengthy preamble discussion labelled "Part 264/265 Facility Standard Issues," EPA explained that generators could treat (if accumulating less than 90 days) without triggering T/S/D. Id. at 10168, col. 3. EPA based this surprising ruling on 40 C.F.R. §262.34, which says that accumulation for more than 90 days would trigger storage (not "treatment" requirements). RCRA practitioners had always assumed that the 90-day rule protected storage only. A Wisconsin consultant wrote to EPA to seek confirmation and a clarification as to whether the ruling applied to all generators (not just "small quantity," which the rule specifically addressed). EPA's Solid Waste Director responded by confirming that preamble position and clarifying that it applied to all generators. [Letter from Marcia E. Williams to Kevin A. Lehner (July 25, 1986).]

Is this an appropriate procedure for informing the public about an interpretation of such potential importance to the regulated community? What should practitioners do to keep abreast of future EPA interpretations of subtitle

C regulations? In August 1990 EPA's general counsel announced that he would attempt to issue written legal opinions to make the agency's interpretations of regulations more accessible to the public. EPA's Office of General Counsel had not issued any opinions since 1985.

4. The RCRA program's heavy reliance on guidance documents is criticized in Tabler & Shere, The EPA's Practice of Regulation by Memorandum, in The Environmental Law Manual 32 (T. Garrett ed., 1992). An illustration of the practice is provided by Beazer East, Inc. v. EPA, Region III, 963 F.2d 603 (3d Cir. 1992). In *Beazer East* a company argued that its eighty-foot wide, concrete-lined aeration basins should be considered tanks rather than surface impoundments subject to more stringent regulation under RCRA. EPA's regulations define "tank" as "a stationary device, designed to contain an accumulation of hazardous waste, which is constructed primarily of non-earthen materials (e.g., wood, concrete, steel, plastic) which provide structural support." 40 C.F.R. §260.10. In an effort to clarify this definition for EPA enforcement personnel, an acting director of the agency's Office of Solid Waste issued a memorandum, known as the "Weddle memorandum," that interprets the definition to require that a device be able to support itself when removed from the ground and filled to capacity with the material it was intended to contain and that non-earthen materials provide the primary structural support. In *Beazer East* the owner of the concrete-lined basin conceded that it could not meet the test outlined in the Weddle memorandum. However, the company argued that it had been deprived of adequate notice because this interpretation was contained in a guidance document that had not been published in the Federal Register. Noting that EPA's interpretation was reasonable and consistent with the language of the regulation, the Third Circuit rejected the company's argument and affirmed the penalties that had been imposed. However, the D.C. Circuit has held that in some circumstances the issuance of guidance documents is agency action requiring public notice. In Appalachian Power Co. v. EPA, 208 F.3d 1015 (D.C. Cir. 2000), industry petitioners successfully argued that EPA's "Periodic Monitoring Guidance" for permits issued under Title V of the Clean Air Act required notice because it effectively amended regulations issued by EPA in 1992 to implement the Title V permit program. EPA claimed that the guidance was not binding, final agency action and thus did not require the Agency to conduct notice-and-comment rulemaking. See also Barrick Goldstrike Mines v. Browner, 215 F.3d 45 (D.C. Cir. 2000), where the D.C. Circuit reversed a district court's decision dismissing another challenge to EPA guidance.

5. As Stoll mentions, wastes listed as hazardous can be delisted if a generator can demonstrate to EPA's satisfaction that the waste stream is not in fact hazardous at a particular facility. To obtain a delisting, a generator must petition EPA. To correct perceived abuses in the delisting process, section 3001(f) was added to RCRA by the 1984 Amendments. This section requires EPA, when evaluating delisting petitions, to consider any other factors that could cause the waste to be hazardous in addition to those for which the waste originally was listed. EPA must publish in the Federal Register a proposal to grant or deny a delisting petition within a year of receiving the petition; final action must be taken within two years.

6. Exports of hazardous waste to another country are regulated under section 3017 of RCRA, which was added by the 1984 Amendments. This section prohibits the export of hazardous waste unless the consent of the receiving country's government has been obtained. Persons who intend to export

hazardous waste must give EPA advance notice. The Secretary of State then must inform the government of the recipient country and request its consent to accept the waste. Canada has entered into an agreement with the United States that governs the export of hazardous waste. What impact does this agreement have on exporters' obligations under section 3017 of RCRA? See §3017(f).

5. Subtitle D and the Regulation of "Nonhazardous" Waste Disposal

Subtitle D of RCRA, which addresses solid wastes that are not considered hazardous, encompasses a far broader volume of waste than subtitle C. While nearly 280 million tons of wastes are regulated as hazardous under subtitle C each year, more than 20 times more solid waste falls under the jurisdiction of subtitle D. As discussed above, responsibility for controlling the management of these wastes has remained largely the province of state and local governments. Mining waste, garbage generated by households, nonhazardous industrial waste, and waste from small generators of hazardous waste has not been regulated under subtitle C of RCRA. These wastes instead are subject only to subtitle D's prohibition of "open dumping" of waste at sites that are not classified as sanitary landfills under EPA's subtitle D criteria. With the exception of its "open dumping" ban and EPA's minimum standards for municipal landfills, subtitle D of RCRA has not been a federal regulatory program, but rather a modest program of financial assistance to encourage states to engage in area-wide waste management planning.

Soon after the enactment of RCRA, it became apparent that even landfills that had not received wastes classified as hazardous under subtitle C could pose a substantial threat to groundwater. In 1984, EPA estimated that there were approximately 93,000 such landfills in the United States. Approximately 75,000 of these were located at industrial sites and another 18,500 served as municipal dumps. EPA, A Ground-Water Protection Strategy for the Environmental Protection Agency 14 (1984). Very little was known about these sites, and only a handful of states required any regular groundwater monitoring even though most dumps were located near aquifers.

When EPA conducted a Surface Impoundment Assessment in 1984, it identified more than 180,000 surface impoundments, most of which were un-lined. About 40 percent of municipal and industrial impoundments were found to be "located in areas of thin or permeable soils, over aquifers currently used for drinking or that could be used for drinking." Id. at 38.

There are several reasons why nonhazardous waste landfills can pose substantial threats to human health and the environment. Prior to enactment of RCRA, hazardous wastes from industrial operations were often sent to municipal landfills. With the growth of the synthetic chemical industry after World War II, many highly toxic and persistent chemicals were added to this waste disposal stream. Most landfills were located at wherever seemed at the time to be the most convenient site, with little or no concern given to long-term environmental consequences. There was scant investment in technology for treating or containing wastes. Society simply assumed that nature would take care of any problems and that wastes that were placed out of sight were best left out of mind.

Even after RCRA was enacted, a considerable amount of hazardous waste continued to be sent to municipal landfills. In 1985 the Congressional Budget

Office estimated that more than 26 million tons of hazardous wastes was placed in nonhazardous waste landfills in the United States in 1983. Office of Technology Assessment, Superfund Strategy 126 (1985). A considerable portion of this waste consisted of hazardous waste from households and small-quantity generators, which were exempt from regulation under subtitle C. While these exemptions may make good sense from the standpoint of administrative convenience, they make less sense from an ecological standpoint. Households and small-quantity generators generate hazardous wastes in small quantities, but these quantities add up. While it may take longer for such wastes to cause environmental problems, eventually they will.

Another reason why nonhazardous waste disposal sites pose environmental threats is the problem of midnight dumping. In addition to receiving wastes dumped surreptitiously, many landfills have not done a thorough job of inspecting incoming waste, and it is often difficult to determine the precise chemical composition of wastes sent to landfills. As subtitle C regulations have increased the cost of hazardous waste disposal, the incentive for midnight dumping has increased.

When Congress adopted the 1984 Amendments to RCRA, it recognized that even municipal dumps that managed solid waste not regulated under subtitle C could pose serious environmental hazards. Thus the 1984 Amendments made an important change in the federal role regarding solid waste management under subtitle D. They took the first steps toward a federal regulatory role. The Amendment added section 4010(c), which required EPA to revise its subtitle D criteria for facilities that may receive hazardous household wastes or hazardous wastes from small-quantity generators. The revised criteria must require that such facilities at least perform groundwater monitoring and undertake corrective action as appropriate. Congress also required states to adopt "a permit program or other system of prior approval and conditions" to assure compliance with EPA's revised subtitle D criteria. RCRA §4005(c). In states that do not adopt adequate programs, EPA is authorized to enforce its own criteria.

The final rule adopted by EPA establishes standards for siting, design, operation, and closure of municipal landfills. Landfills are required within five years to conduct regular groundwater monitoring and to take corrective action to clean up contamination. The rules provide a flexible menu of design standards that states may elect based on their hydrogeological and other characteristics. For example, while the criteria base compliance monitoring on contamination detected at landfill boundaries, they authorize states to adopt alternative compliance points up to 150 meters from facility boundaries. The rules exempt small landfills (those receiving less than 20 tons of garbage per day) from design standards, groundwater monitoring, and corrective action requirements if they are located in regions where rainfall is light (less than 25 inches per year). 56 Fed. Reg. 50,978 (1991).

States are required to establish permit programs to incorporate the subtitle D standards. If a state approves a landfill that has less stringent design standards than required by the federal criteria, the regulation gives EPA only 30 days in which to object. EPA is authorized to impose federal standards directly in states that fail to submit acceptable state programs.

When it issued the subtitle D standards in October 1991, EPA estimated that there were approximately 6,000 nonhazardous waste landfills then operating. These landfills handle the vast majority of the more than 200 million tons of municipal solid waste generated each year. Because most of these landfills do not have adequate environmental protection measures, EPA estimated that the subtitle D regulations would cost municipalities approximately $330 million per year to implement and that approximately 3,000 landfills would close within five years. By 1996 the number of operating landfills had declined to 2,400.

EPA's subtitle D standards for municipal landfills were generally upheld by the D.C. Circuit in Sierra Club v. EPA, 992 F.2d 337 (D.C. Cir. 1993). By a 2-1 margin, over Judge Mikva's dissent, the court held that EPA had the discretion not to set numeric limits for toxics in sewage sludge when it is co-disposed with municipal waste even though the Clean Water Act imposes such limits when sludge alone is disposed. But the court agreed with environmental groups that RCRA required all municipal landfills, regardless of their size or location, to conduct groundwater monitoring. This part of the decision was partially overturned by legislation adopted in 1996. The Land Disposal Program Flexibility Act, Pub. L. 104-119, provides EPA with express statutory authority to exempt certain small municipal solid waste landfills from groundwater monitoring requirements. The exemption applies to landfills that dispose of less than 20 tons of municipal solid waste daily, provided there is no evidence of groundwater contamination from the municipal waste unit. It applies to such landfills only if they serve a community that has no practicable waste management alternative and that receives less than 25 inches of precipitation a year or that does not have year-round access to a regional waste management facility.

The legislation gives states the option to forgo the exemption and require groundwater monitoring by such landfills if necessary. It also authorizes states to suspend groundwater monitoring requirements for landfills upon a demonstration that there is no potential for migration of hazardous constituents into the uppermost aquifer during the landfill's operating life and its post-closure care period.

NOTES AND QUESTIONS

1. Many states have eschewed RCRA's all-or-nothing approach by subjecting broad classes of "nonhazardous" industrial waste to an intermediate tier of regulation more stringent than under subtitle D, but less stringent than subtitle C's standards. For example, after ten years of effort, Pennsylvania adopted comprehensive regulations governing the management of industrial wastes not considered hazardous under RCRA's federal standards. These regulations require disposal facilities to use liners and to conduct groundwater monitoring, and they direct waste generators to analyze source reduction strategies. Dernbach, The Other Ninety-Six Percent, Envtl. Forum, Jan./Feb. 1993, at 10. New York, Connecticut, and Maine require landfills to have double liners, a requirement not included in EPA's regulations.

2. Subtitle D's evolution from a modest financial assistance program to a program establishing minimum federal standards for municipal landfills follows what has become a relatively consistent pattern for federal environmental programs. As national awareness of environmental problems grows, federal programs to encourage state planning gradually evolve into national regulatory programs. Because waste management has been viewed as almost a quintessential state and local responsibility, subtitle D took longer to follow this path. The recognition that solid waste management is a significant problem that requires national regulation reflects the increasingly tenuous nature of RCRA's attempt to distinguish between hazardous and nonhazardous waste. RCRA's two-tier system

of imposing subtitle C's onerous regulatory requirements on waste deemed hazardous while allowing all other forms of solid waste to escape significant federal regulation is now eroding and seems destined to erode further. What do you think accounts for this development? Can one infer from it that EPA's efforts to identify the universe of truly hazardous wastes have not been successful?

3. In addition to municipal solid waste, a considerable amount of industrial waste is not regulated under subtitle C because it is deemed nonhazardous or because it is generated in such small quantities that the entities that generate it are conditionally exempt from subtitle C as small quantity generators. In July 1996, EPA issued regulations under subtitle D for facilities that accept conditionally exempt small quantity generator (CESQG) waste. The regulations require groundwater monitoring and corrective action at landfills accepting CESQG waste. 61 Fed. Reg. 34,252 (1996). EPA has not regulated facilities that receive nonmunicipal, nonhazardous industrial waste, but in June 1999 it issued draft guidance describing preferred approaches for managing such waste. EPA, Guide for Industrial Waste Management (1999). For a description of this guidance see J. Greenberg, The U.S. EPA Draft Guide for Industrial Waste Management—Too Little, Too Late?, 29 Envtl. L. Rep. 10764 (1999).

D.   CERCLA LIABILITY

1. CERCLA's Basic Principles

The Comprehensive Environmental Response, Compensation and Liability Act (CERCLA) was enacted four short years after Congress thought it had closed the "last remaining loophole" in environmental law through the passage of RCRA. The reconsideration was prompted by the Love Canal disaster, which came to light shortly after RCRA was enacted. In 1953, the Hooker Chemical and Plastics Corporation had transferred title to a 16-acre site to the Niagara Falls Board of Education for the sum of one dollar. The company acknowledged that it had buried chemicals on the site, which it had covered with a layer of clay, and the deed of sale stated that the company would not be responsible for any injuries that might occur. A school and 100 homes were built on the site. Following heavy rains in 1978, a chemical soup began seeping into residential basements. More than 80 chemical compounds were found, including many known carcinogens. Ultimately, 1,000 families were relocated and homes along the canal were demolished.

Love Canal became a national media event that crystallized a festering problem in terms that provoked an emotional response from the public. Love Canal highlighted the consequences of decades of poor waste management. Evidence began to appear that suggested billions of tons of hazardous waste had been dumped onto the land, into lakes, ponds, and lagoons, and scattered in 55-gallon drums that were slowly leaking contaminants or being ignited and causing toxic fires.

The public response contributed to a political climate that produced CERCLA, the most comprehensive new federal approach to environmental protection since the enactment of NEPA. Even though the story of Love Canal will forever be associated with CERCLA, it is important to understand that in many respects

CERCLA represents a natural adaptation of centuries of common law developments as extended by modern environmental statutes.

CERCLA is a direct extension of common law principles of strict liability for abnormally dangerous activities, and was modeled on a prior extension of those principles contained in the 1972 Clean Water Act's oil spill liability program. As discussed in Chapter 2, page 137, section 311 of the Clean Water Act applies the principle of strict liability to persons responsible for releases of "harmful quantities" of oil. This provision, coupled with emergency response authorities contained in section 504(b) of the Act, established a national oil spill response program that made persons responsible for the spills strictly liable for response costs. In 1978, Congress broadened section 311 to encompass not only oil spills, but also releases of other hazardous substances in navigable waters. Congress also made dischargers liable not only for cleanup costs but also for damages to natural resources.

The core of CERCLA is its liability provisions and its authorization to EPA to spend monies from the Superfund for *removal* operations—short-term action to address immediate hazards—and for *remediation* operations—targeted at longer-term solutions, including decontamination. EPA is authorized to incur expenses responding to imminent threats to health and the environment under its removal authorities, but it can only spend money on remediation for sites that it has placed on the *National Priority List*. §§104, 105. Section 105 instructs EPA to place at least 400 sites needing cleanup on the initial NPL and also to prepare a *National Contingency Plan* for dealing with hazardous waste cleanup. State governments and federal authorities can engage in joint cleanup operations. EPA also has authority to order private parties to undertake actions to abate actual or potential releases of hazardous substances in order to prevent imminent and substantial endangerment. §106.

For its response and remediation costs, the federal government draws on the Superfund, which was funded initially through a tax on chemical feedstocks, and later amended to include a small tax on petroleum. §111. This tax expired in 1995 and has not been reauthorized, requiring that greater and greater portions of the Superfund program be funded out of general revenues, appropriated annually by the Congress. The lack of reauthorization of the tax has been slowly starving the program for funds for cleanups that are not paid for by potentially responsible parties. See section D.6 for more discussion.

Section 107 identifies four classes of potentially responsible parties who bear cleanup liability under Superfund's cost recovery provisions: current owners and operators, owners and operators at the time waste was disposed of at the facility, generators of the waste, and persons who transported waste to the facility. These liability provisions are the engine driving Superfund, and the vast bulk of the substantial volume of litigation under the statute has involved the scope and implications of the Act's cost recovery provisions. In studying this comprehensive liability scheme, bear in mind that imposing liability has forward-looking deterrent effects in addition to its providing a method to finance cleanup of existing sites. Philip Cummings, the chief counsel of the Senate Environment Committee when CERCLA was drafted, has written that this deterrent effect is at the heart of the reasons for passage: "CERCLA," he writes, "is not primarily an abandoned dump cleanup program, although that is included in its purposes." Instead,

> The main purpose of CERCLA is to make spills or dumping of hazardous substances less likely through liability, enlisting business and commercial instincts

for the bottom line in place of traditional regulation. It was a conscious intention of the law's authors to draw lenders and insurers into this new army of quasi-regulators, along with corporate risk managers and boards of directors. [Cummings, Completing the Circle, Envtl. Forum 11 (Nov./Dec. 1990).]

The enormous publicity directed at CERCLA's remediation provisions (examined below) has obscured the fact that CERCLA's liability provisions also are designed to serve preventive ends. While some have argued that the CERCLA cleanup process is so bureaucratic as to make the program resemble a traditional command-and-control regulatory program, Coalition on Superfund, Coalition on Superfund Research Report ix (1989), CERCLA's liability provisions remain the heart of the statute. By imposing strict liability on broad classes of parties, Congress intended to create a powerful new incentive for waste reduction and more careful management of waste. As the Senate committee report on the original CERCLA legislation stated, "By holding the factually responsible person liable, [the bill] encourages that person—whether a generator, transporter, or disposer of hazardous substances—to eliminate as many risks as possible." S. Rep. No. 848, 96th Cong., 2d Sess. 33 (1980).

Thus, CERCLA pursues dual goals: to prevent environmental contamination and to ensure that it is cleaned up when it occurs. While some argue that CERCLA's liability scheme has delayed the cleanup of dump sites and wasted resources on litigation, any evaluation of CERCLA's liability provisions should be done in the context of the Act's dual objectives. Regardless of how rapidly EPA proceeds with dump site cleanups, the CERCLA program could still be a success if its liability provisions are effective in deterring environmental releases. Fear of CERCLA liability is likely to stimulate reductions in the volume and toxicity of waste, an increase in recycling, and an increase in the care with which waste is managed. As a report for the Rand Corporation noted:

> By exposing firms to unlimited liability for prior waste handling, Superfund sets up strong signals that equally stringent regulations will operate in the future as well. This should lead to more conservative waste-handling practices both today and in the future and may lead business to reduce its use of toxic materials—and to increase recycling of these substances. [Acton, Understanding Superfund: A Progress Report 19 (1989).]

What is not known is precisely how significant CERCLA's liability provisions have been in stimulating such behavior. In the sections that follow we consider how CERCLA's liability provisions operate.

PRINCIPAL PROVISIONS OF CERCLA

§101. *Definitions:* the term "hazardous substance" is defined in section 101(14); "release" is defined in section 101(22).

§103. *Notification Requirements:* requires reporting of releases of hazardous substances to the National Response Center.

§104. *Response Authorities:* authorizes the president to undertake removals or remedial actions consistent with the National Contingency Plan to respond to actual or potential releases of hazardous substances.

§105. *National Contingency Plan:* requires establishment of a National Priorities List (NPL) of facilities presenting the greatest danger to health, welfare, or the environment based on a hazard ranking system (HRS) and requires revision of National Contingency Plan (NCP).

§106. Abatement Orders: authorizes issuance of administrative orders requiring the abatement of actual or potential releases that may create imminent and substantial endangerment to health, welfare, or the environment.

§107. Liability: imposes liability on (1) current owners and operators of facilities where hazardous substances are released or threatened to be released, (2) owners and operators of facilities at the time substances were disposed, (3) persons who arranged for disposal or treatment of such substances, and (4) persons who accepted such substances for transport for disposal or treatment. These parties are liable for: (a) all costs of removal or remedial action incurred by the federal government not inconsistent with the NCP, (b) any other necessary costs of response incurred by any person consistent with the NCP, (c) damages for injury to natural resources, and (d) costs of health assessments. Creates exemptions for innocent purchasers, bona fide prospective purchasers and de micromis contributors.

§111. Superfund: creates a Superfund which can be used to finance governmental response actions and to reimburse private parties for costs incurred in carrying out the NCP.

§113. Judicial Review and Contribution: bars pre-enforcement judicial review of response actions and abatement orders, and authorizes private actions for contribution against potentially responsible parties.

§116. Cleanup Schedules: establishes schedules for evaluating and listing sites on NPL, commencement of remedial investigation and feasibility studies (RI/FSs), and commencement of remedial action.

§121. Cleanup Standards: establishes preference for remedial actions that permanently and significantly reduce the volume, toxicity, or mobility of hazardous substances and requires selection of remedial actions that are protective of health and the environment and cost effective, using permanent solutions to the maximum extent practicable; requires cleanups to attain level of "legally applicable or relevant and appropriate standard, requirement, criteria or limitation" contained under any federal environmental law or more stringent state law.

§122. Settlements: sets standards for settlements with potentially responsible parties.

---

2. Liability Provisions of CERCLA

CERCLA makes a broad class of parties liable for the costs of responding to the release, or the substantial threat of a release, of "any hazardous substance." It authorizes responses to such releases (or to releases of "any pollutant or contaminant which may present an imminent and substantial danger to the public health or welfare") in section 104, and then specifies in section 107 the parties liable for the costs of responding to hazardous substance releases.

The term "hazardous substance" is broadly defined by section 101(14) to include hazardous wastes subject to regulation under subtitle C of RCRA, toxic water pollutants regulated under section 307 of the Clean Water Act, hazardous air pollutants listed under section 112 of the Clean Air Act, imminently hazardous chemicals regulated under section 7 of TSCA, substances other than oil that have been designated as hazardous pursuant to section 311(b)(2)(A) of the Clean Water Act (governing oil and hazardous substance spills in navigable waters), and additional substances designated by EPA. Thus, it is considerably broader than the universe of hazardous wastes regulated under subtitle C of RCRA. Petroleum, including crude oil, and natural gas, are specifically exempted from CERCLA's definition of hazardous substances, ostensibly because oil spills already were governed by section 311 of the Clean Water Act. As a result, CERCLA could not be used to respond to the problem of leaking underground storage tanks at gasoline stations. (In 1986, Congress created a separate program to control leaking underground storage tanks by adding subtitle I to the Resource Conservation and Recovery Act).

While the definition of "hazardous substance" encompasses just about any toxic substance other than petroleum, section 104 also provides CERCLA jurisdiction over substances not listed in any of the categories of "hazardous substances" if it is a "pollutant or contaminant which may present an imminent and substantial danger to the public health or welfare." Thus, the release of a substance that does not happen to fall within CERCLA's broad definition of "hazardous substances" can still generate a CERCLA response if it presents "an imminent and substantial danger."

"Release" is broadly defined in section 101(22) to mean:

> any spilling, leaking, pumping, pouring, emitting, emptying, discharging, injecting, escaping, leaching, dumping, or disposing into the environment (including the abandonment or discarding of barrels, containers, and other closed receptacles containing any hazardous substance or pollutant or contaminant). [§101(22).]

Not all releases of hazardous substances fall within CERCLA's broad jurisdiction. Section 107(i) of CERCLA exempts the application of pesticides registered under FIFRA, and section 107(j) exempts "federally permitted releases." The latter are defined in section 101(10) to include discharges authorized by permits issued under the Clean Water Act, RCRA, the Ocean Dumping Act, the Safe Drinking Water Act, the Clean Air Act, and the Atomic Energy Act, and certain fluid injection practices for producing oil or natural gas.

As a threshold matter, consider several constitutional challenges to CERCLA. In the years after CERCLA's enactment, litigants fighting its liability provisions routinely attacked the legislation on constitutional grounds, principally because it imposed tough liability standards for cleaning up hazardous wastes that had often been deposited many years before the statute was enacted. CERCLA thus raised an issue of impermissible retroactive legislation. One court summarized the challenges and its replies:

> The generator defendants raise numerous constitutional challenges to the district court's interpretation and application of CERCLA. They contend that the imposition of "disproportionate" liability without proof of causation

violated constitutional limitations on retroactive statutory application and that it converted CERCLA into a bill of attainder and an *ex post facto* law. They further assert, along with the site-owners, that the trial court's construction of CERCLA infringed their substantive due process rights.

The district court held that CERCLA does not create retroactive liability, but imposes a prospective obligation for the post-enactment environmental consequences of the defendants' past acts. Alternatively, the court held that even if CERCLA is understood to operate retroactively, it nonetheless satisfies the dictates of due process because its liability scheme is rationally related to a valid legislative purpose. We agree with the court's latter holding, and we find no merit to the generator defendants' bill of attainder and *ex post facto* arguments. . . . While the generator defendants profited from inexpensive waste disposal methods that may have been technically "legal" prior to CERCLA's enactment, it was certainly foreseeable at the time that improper disposal could cause enormous damage to the environment. CERCLA operates remedially to spread the costs of responding to improper waste disposal among all parties that played a role in creating the hazardous conditions. Where those conditions are indivisible, joint and several liability is logical, and it works to ensure complete cost recovery. We do not think these consequences are "particularly harsh and oppressive," *United States Trust Co. v. New Jersey*, 431 U.S. 1, 17 (1977) (retrospective civil liability not unconstitutional unless it is particularly harsh and oppressive), and we agree with the Eighth Circuit that retroactive application of CERCLA does not violate due process.

U.S. v. Monsanto Co. 858 F.2d 160, 173-174 (4th Cir. 1988) (citations omitted). The various constitutional challenges were uniformly unsuccessful in other courts as well. See, e.g., United States v. Northeastern Pharmaceutical & Chemical Co., Inc., 810 F.2d 726, 732-734 (8th Cir. 1986); United States v. Hooker Chemicals & Plastics Corp., 680 F. Supp. 546 (W.D.N.Y. 1988); United States v. Shell Oil Co., 605 F. Supp. 1064, 1069-1073 (D. Colo. 1985). Constitutional challenges gradually subsided, and litigation concentrated on questions of statutory interpretation.

Then in 1995, the Supreme Court decided United States v. Lopez, 514 U.S. 549 (1995), finding that the Gun-Free School Zones Act exceeded Congress's authority under the Commerce Clause. This decision (and several subsequent Supreme Court decisions, see discussion pages 112-116) signalled that the Court was reinterpreting the limits on Congress's Commerce Clause authority and, consequently, stimulated a renewed interest in testing the constitutionality of various environmental laws, including Superfund, against those limits. One such challenge reached the Eleventh Circuit in the following case.

|| *United States v. Olin Corp.* ||
107 F.3d 1506 (11th Cir. 1997)

KRAVITCH, Senior Circuit Judge:

[Olin and the United States entered into a consent decree in which Olin agreed to pay for all response costs associated with a site designated OU-1, which assigned Olin financial responsibility for cleanup from disposal activity that occurred prior to CERCLA's effective date of December 11, 1980.]

When the parties presented the consent decree to the district court, it sua sponte ordered them to address the impact of the Supreme Court's decision in Lopez on the legality of their proposal. Olin complied with that order by answering the original complaint. It asserted that the *Lopez* Court's construction of the Commerce Clause precluded constitutional application of CERCLA in this case. . . .

III

We review de novo the constitutional challenge to CERCLA . . .

A.

The district court found that the enforcement of CERCLA against Olin violated the Commerce Clause as interpreted by the Supreme Court in *Lopez*. The *Lopez* Court held that the Commerce Clause empowers Congress to regulate: (1) channels of interstate commerce; (2) instrumentalities of and persons or things in interstate commerce; and (3) intrastate activities that substantially affect interstate commerce. . . . This case, like *Lopez*, concerns the third category.

Lopez did not alter the constitutional standard for federal statutes regulating intrastate activities. . . . Simply stated, "the proper test requires an analysis of whether the regulated activity 'substantially affects' interstate commerce." Congress can maintain the constitutionality of its statutes under this standard by including in each a "jurisdictional element which would ensure, through case-by-case inquiry, that the [regulated activity] in question affects interstate commerce." In addition, Congress, or a committee thereof, can make legislative findings indicating that a statute regulates activities with a substantial effect on interstate commerce. If Congress does so, a court may not override these findings unless they lack a rational basis. . . .

When Congress fails to ensure a statute's compliance with the Commerce Clause, however, courts must determine independently whether the statute regulates "activities that arise out of or are connected with a commercial transaction, which viewed in the aggregate, substantially affect[ ] interstate commerce." *Lopez*, 115 S. Ct. at 1631. This determination turns on whether the statute constitutes "an essential part of a larger regulation of economic activity, in which the regulatory scheme could be undercut unless the intrastate activity were regulated." Id. A court's focus, thus, cannot be excessively narrow; if the statute regulates a "class of activities . . . and that class is within the reach of the federal power, the courts have no power 'to excise, as trivial, individual instances' of the class." Perez v. United States, 402 U.S. 146, 154 (1971). . . .

The district court's Commerce Clause analysis conflicts with the foregoing standard in two main respects. First, the district court indicated that under *Lopez* a statute must regulate economic activity directly to satisfy the Commerce Clause. See Olin Corp., 927 F. Supp. at 1532. Actually, as noted above, *Lopez* reiterates that a statute will pass constitutional muster if it regulates an activity, whatever its nature, "that arise[s] out of or [is] connected with a commercial transaction, which viewed in the aggregate, substantially affects interstate commerce." The district court also concluded that *Lopez* requires every statute enacted pursuant to Congress' Commerce Clause authority to contain a jurisdictional element. See Olin Corp., 927 F. Supp. at 1532. In fact, the *Lopez* Court recognized that a statute without a jurisdictional element still would stand under the Commerce Clause, if the law satisfied the substantial effects test.

Our evaluation of CERCLA under the foregoing framework leads us to reject Olin's constitutional challenge. Specifically, we conclude that although Congress did not include in CERCLA either legislative findings or a jurisdictional element, the statute remains valid as applied in this case because it regulates a class of activities that substantially affects interstate commerce. The proper analysis first requires identification of the "class of activities" involved in the case. The class always "could be defined so narrowly as to cover only those activities that do not have a substantial impact on interstate commerce." Proyect v. United States, 101 F.3d 11, 14 (2d Cir. 1996) (ruling that class of activities covered by drug control law was not "cultivation and personal consumption of marijuana," but rather "manufacture of controlled substances"). The government contends this suit involves regulation of releases of hazardous substances generally; Olin objects to this broad classification. In our view, the disposal of hazardous waste at the site of production, or "on-site," constitutes the narrowest possible class.

In light of this understanding, we must assess whether on-site waste disposal substantially affects interstate commerce. Because the legislative history of CERCLA documents how the unregulated management of hazardous substances, even strictly within individual states, significantly impacts interstate commerce, we conclude the statute can be applied constitutionally under the circumstances of this case.

When the Senate considered S. 1480, a bill containing cleanup liability provisions later substantially incorporated into CERCLA, its Committee on Environment and Public Works ("the Committee") took notice of many facts that show a nexus between all forms of improper waste disposal and interstate commerce. First, the Committee noted the growth of the chemical industry and the concomitant costs of handling its waste. It also cited a 1980 report by the Office of Technology Assessment which gauged agricultural losses from chemical contamination in six states at $283 million. The Committee reported that the commercial damages resulting from unregulated waste management were not attributable solely to interstate trafficking in hazardous materials for disposal, but also arose from accidents associated with purely intrastate, on-site disposal activities, such as improper waste storage in tanks, lagoons, and chemical plants. Thus, CERCLA reflects Congress' recognition that both on-site and off-site disposal of hazardous waste threaten interstate commerce.

Olin notes that the record contains no evidence that its on-site disposal has caused off-site damage, much less harmed interstate commerce. This argument is analogous to, and as unpersuasive as, the drug possessor's plea for an exemption from federal narcotics laws because his individual actions have no substantial effect upon interstate commerce. See *Proyect*, 101 F.3d at 14. Olin's claim fails because, as the foregoing discussion documents, the regulation of intrastate, on-site waste disposal constitutes an appropriate element of Congress' broader scheme to protect interstate commerce and industries thereof from pollution. See *Lopez*, 115 S. Ct. at 1631.

Olin also objects to enforcement of CERCLA in this case because it contends its disposal activities are not economic in nature. As stated above, the Commerce Clause conditions congressional authority not upon the qualities of the regulated activity, but rather the degree to which that activity affects interstate commerce. Further, to the extent a chemical plant can dispose of its waste on-site free of regulation, it would have a market advantage over chemical companies that lack on-site disposal options; Olin's actions, therefore, have an economic character. For these reasons, we hold that, as applied in this case, CERCLA constitutes a permissible exercise of Congress' authority under the Commerce Clause. . . .

NOTES AND QUESTIONS

1. The district court thought that under the Supreme Court's ruling in *Lopez* the activities regulated under the authority to regulate "intrastate activities that substantially affect commerce" must themselves be economic activities. The Eleventh Circuit disagreed. A subsequent opinion by the Supreme Court strongly suggests that the Eleventh Circuit was wrong and the district court correct on this issue. United States v. Morrison, 529 U.S. 598 (2000). Does this change the correct outcome of the case?

2. As noted in Chapter 2, page 115 , in 2005, the Court decided that Congress could regulate under the Controlled Substances Act the cultivation and possession of home grown marijuana used for medicinal purposes and not sold in any market. Gonzales v. Raich 545 U.S. 1 (2005). The Court found *Gonzalez* to be consistent with *Lopez* because Congress had concluded that medicinal marijuana could substantially affect the interstate market for marijuana because, as a fungible commodity, it could easily slip into that market once grown and available. Citing the same passage from *Perez* as relied upon in *Olin*, the Supreme Court said that the fact that any single intrastate activity had only a trivial impact on interstate commerce did not preclude federal regulation. Does *Gonzales* support the result in *Olin*?

3. If the district court's position had prevailed, how would EPA and PRPs have determined which facilities were subject to the jurisdictional reach of CERCLA?

4. On the basis of the Eleventh Circuit opinion, how would you describe what is necessary for the connection between interstate commerce and intrastate activities to be sufficient to give Congress authority to regulate the intrastate activities?

3.   Responsible Parties

CERCLA embodies a liability approach to regulation. Rather than directing EPA to specify through regulations what actions persons must take to prevent environmental damage, CERCLA specifies the potential consequences if hazardous substances are released or if conditions posing a substantial threat of such a release are created. CERCLA's approach is intended not only to provide a means for financing the cleanup of environmental damage, but also to deter mismanagement of hazardous substances. Crucial to CERCLA's value as a deterrent is how the Act defines potentially liable parties. Section 107 of CERCLA broadly defines the parties potentially liable for response costs.

A.   OWNERS

The case that follows is an early interpretation of CERCLA's liability provisions that has proven very influential. As you read it, consider what impact it is likely to have on incentives to prevent releases of hazardous substances in the future. Consider also whether its strict interpretation of CERCLA could lead to unfair results in other circumstances.

|| *New York v. Shore Realty Corp.* ||
|| 759 F.2d 1032 (2d Cir. 1985) ||

Before FEINBERG, Chief Judge, OAKES and NEWMAN, Circuit Judges.

OAKES, Circuit Judge: . . .

On February 29, 1984, the State of New York brought suit against Shore Realty Corp. ("Shore") and Donald LeoGrande, its officer and stockholder, to clean up a hazardous waste disposal site at One Shore Road, Glenwood Landing, New York, which Shore had acquired for land development purposes. At the time of the acquisition, LeoGrande knew that hazardous waste was stored on the site and that cleanup would be expensive, though neither Shore nor LeoGrande had participated in the generation or transportation of the nearly 700,000 gallons of hazardous waste now on the premises. . . .

[LeoGrande controlled, directed, and made all decisions for Shore.] By contract dated July 14, 1983, Shore agreed to purchase the 3.2 acre site, a small peninsula surrounded on three sides by the waters of Hempstead Harbor and Mott Cove, for condominium development. Five large tanks in a field in the center of the site hold most of some 700,000 gallons of hazardous chemicals located there, though there are six smaller tanks both above and below ground containing hazardous waste, as well as some empty tanks on the property. The tanks are connected by pipe to a tank truck loading rack and dockage facilities for loading by barge. Four roll-on/roll-off containers and one tank truck trailer hold additional waste. And before June 15, 1984, one of the two dilapidated masonry warehouses on the site contained over 400 drums of chemicals and contaminated solids, many of which were corroded and leaking.

It is beyond dispute that the tanks and drums contain "hazardous substances" within the meaning of CERCLA. 42 U.S.C. §9601 (14). The substances involved—including benzene, dichlorobenzenes, ethyl benzene, tetrachloroethylene, trichloroethylene, 1,1,1-trichloroethylene chlordane, polychlorinated biphenyls (commonly known as PCBs) and bis (2-ethylhexyl) phthalate—are toxic, in some cases carcinogenic, and dangerous by way of contact, inhalation, or ingestion. . . . The purchase agreement provided that it could be voided by Shore without penalty if after conducting an environmental study Shore had decided not to proceed. LeoGrande was fully aware that the tenants, Applied Environmental Services, Inc., and Hazardous Waste Disposal, Inc., were then operating—illegally, it may be noted—a hazardous waste storage facility on the site. Shore's environmental consultant, WTM Management Corporation ("WTM") . . . found that there had been several spills of hazardous waste at the site, including at least one large spill in 1978. Though there had been some attempts at cleanup, the WTM testing revealed that hazardous substances, such as benzene, were still leaching into the groundwater and the waters of the bay immediately adjacent to the bulkhead abutting Hempstead Harbor. . . . The report concluded that if the current tenants "close up the operation and leave the material at the site," the owners would be left with a "potential time bomb." WTM estimated that the cost of environmental cleanup and monitoring would range from $650,000 to over $1 million before development could begin. After receiving this report Shore sought a waiver from the State Department of Environmental Conservation ("DEC") of liability as landowners for the disposal of the hazardous waste stored at the site. Although the DEC denied the waiver, Shore took title on October 13, 1983, and obtained certain rights over against the tenants, whom it subsequently evicted on January 5, 1984.

Nevertheless, between October 13, 1983, and January 5, 1984, nearly 90,000 gallons of hazardous chemicals were added to the tanks. And during a state inspection on January 3, 1984, it became evident that the deteriorating and leaking drums of chemicals referred to above had also been brought onto the site. Needless to say, the tenants did not clean up the site before they left. Thus, conditions when Shore employees first entered the site were as bad as or worse than those described in the WTM report. As LeoGrande admitted by affidavit, "the various storage tanks, pipe lines and connections between these storage facilities were in a bad state of repair." While Shore claims to have made some improvements, such as sealing all the pipes and valves and continuing the cleanup of the damage from earlier spills, Shore did nothing about the hundreds of thousands of gallons of hazardous waste standing in deteriorating tanks. In addition, although a growing number of drums were leaking hazardous substances, Shore essentially ignored the problem until June, 1984. [In October 1984 the district court held Shore liable under CERCLA for the state's response costs and issued an injunction under state nuisance law directing that Shore and LeoGrande remove the remaining hazardous waste stored on the property]

CERCLA

. . . CERCLA was designed "to bring order to the array of partly redundant, partly inadequate federal hazardous substances cleanup and compensation laws." It applies "primarily to the cleanup of leaking inactive or abandoned sites and to emergency responses to spills." And it distinguishes between two kinds of response: remedial actions—generally long-term or permanent containment or disposal programs—and removal efforts—typically short-term cleanup arrangements.

CERCLA authorizes the federal government to respond in several ways. EPA can use Superfund resources to clean up hazardous waste sites and spills. 42 U.S.C. §9611. The National Contingency Plan ("NCP"), prepared by EPA pursuant to CERCLA, id. §9605, governs cleanup efforts by "establish[ing] procedures and standards for responding to releases of hazardous substances." At the same time, EPA can sue for reimbursement of cleanup costs from any responsible parties it can locate, id. §9607, allowing the federal government to respond immediately while later trying to shift financial responsibility to others. Thus, Superfund covers cleanup costs if the site has been abandoned, if the responsible parties elude detection, or if private resources are inadequate. . . . In addition, CERCLA authorizes EPA to seek an injunction in federal district court to force a responsible party to clean up any site or spill that presents an imminent and substantial danger to public health or welfare or the environment. 42 U.S.C. §9606(a). In sum, CERCLA is not a regulatory standard-setting statute such as the Clean Air Act. Id. §§7401-7642. Rather, the government generally undertakes pollution abatement, and polluters pay for such abatement through tax and reimbursement liability. . . .

Congress intended that responsible parties be held strictly liable, even though an explicit provision for strict liability was not included in the compromise. Section 9601(32) provides that "liability" under CERCLA "shall be construed to be the standard of liability" under section 311 of the Clean Water Act, 33 U.S.C. §1321, which courts have held to be strict liability, see, e.g., Steuart Transportation Co. v. Allied Towing Corp., 596 F.2d 609, 613 (4th Cir. 1979), and which Congress understood to impose such liability, see S. Rep. No. 848, 96th Cong., 2d Sess. 34 (1980) [hereinafter cited as Senate Report], reprinted in 1 CERCLA Legislative History, supra, at 308, 341. Moreover, the sponsors of the compromise expressly stated that section 9607 provides for strict liability. . . . Strict liability under CERCLA, however, is not absolute; there are defenses for causation solely by an act of God, an act of war, or acts or omissions of a third party other than an employee or agent of the defendant or one whose act or omission occurs in connection with a contractual relationship with the defendant. 42 U.S.C. §9607(b). . . .

Covered Persons. CERCLA holds liable four classes of persons:

(1) the owner and operator of a vessel (otherwise subject to the jurisdiction of the United States) or a facility,

(2) any person who at the time of disposal of any hazardous substance owned or operated any facility at which such hazardous substances were disposed of,

(3) any person who by contract, agreement, or otherwise arranged for disposal or treatment, or arranged with a transporter for transport for disposal or treatment, of hazardous substances owned or possessed by such person, by any other party or entity, at any facility owned or operated by another party or entity and containing such hazardous substances, and

(4) any person who accepts or accepted any hazardous substances for transport to disposal or treatment facilities or sites selected by such person.

42 U.S.C. §9607(a). As noted above, section 9607 makes these persons liable, if "there is a release, or a threatened release which causes the incurrence of response costs, of a hazardous substance" from the facility, for, among other things, "all costs of removal or remedial action incurred by the United States Government or a State not inconsistent with the national contingency plan."

Shore argues that it is not covered by section 9607(a)(1) because it neither owned the site at the time of disposal nor caused the presence or the release of the hazardous waste at the facility. While section 9607(a)(1) appears to cover Shore, Shore attempts to infuse ambiguity into the statutory scheme, claiming that section 9607(a)(1) could not have been intended to include all owners, because the word "owned" in section 9607(a)(2) would be unnecessary since an owner "at the time of disposal" would necessarily be included in section 9607(a)(1). Shore claims that Congress intended that the scope of section 9607(a)(1) be no greater than that of section 9607(a)(2) and that both should be limited by the "at the time of disposal" language. By extension, Shore argues that both provisions should be interpreted as requiring a showing of causation. We agree with the State, however, that section 9607(a)(1) unequivocally imposes strict liability on the current owner of a facility from which there is a release or threat of release, without regard to causation.

Shore's claims of ambiguity are illusory; section 9607(a)'s structure is clear. Congress intended to cover different classes of persons differently. Section 9607(a)(1) applies to all current owners and operators, while section 9607(a)(2) primarily covers prior owners and operators. Moreover, section 9607(a)(2)'s scope is more limited than that of section 9607(a)(1). Prior owners and operators are liable only if they owned or operated the facility "at the time of disposal of any hazardous substance"; this limitation does not apply to current owners, like Shore. . . .

Shore's causation argument is also at odds with the structure of the statute. Interpreting section 9607(a)(1) as including a causation requirement makes superfluous the affirmative defenses provided in section 9607(b), each of which carves out from liability an exception based on causation. Without a clear congressional command otherwise, we will not construe a statute in any way that makes some of its provisions surplusage. . . .

Furthermore, as the state points out, accepting Shore's arguments would open a huge loophole in CERCLA's coverage. It is quite clear that if the current owner of a site could avoid liability merely by having purchased the site after chemical dumping had ceased, waste sites certainly would be sold, following the cessation of dumping, to new owners who could avoid the liability otherwise required by CERCLA. Congress had well in mind that persons who dump or store hazardous waste sometimes cannot be located or may be deceased or judgment-proof. See, e.g., Senate Report, supra, at 16, reprinted in 1 CERCLA Legislative History, supra, at 323. We will not interpret section 9607(a) in any way that apparently frustrates the statute's goals, in the absence of a specific congressional intention otherwise. . . .

Release or Threat of Release.   We reject Shore's repeated claims that it has put in dispute whether there has been a release or threat of release at the Shore Road site. The state has established that it was responding to "a release or a threatened release" when it incurred its response costs. We hold that the leaking tanks and pipelines, the continuing leaching and seepage from the earlier spills, and the leaking drums all constitute "releases." 42 U.S.C. §9601(22). Moreover, the corroding and deteriorating tanks, Shore's lack of expertise in handling hazardous waste, and even the failure to license the facility, amount to a threat of release. . . .

Affirmative Defense.   Shore also claims that it can assert an affirmative defense under CERCLA, which provides a limited exception to liability for a release or threat of release caused solely by

> an act or omission of a third party other than an employee or agent of the defendant, or than one whose act or omission occurs in connection with a contractual relationship, existing directly or indirectly, with the defendant (except where the sole contractual arrangement arises from a published tariff and acceptance for carriage by a common carrier by rail), if the defendant establishes by a preponderance of the evidence that (a) he exercised due care with respect to the hazardous substance concerned, taking into consideration the characteristics of such hazardous substance, in light of all relevant facts and circumstances, and (b) he took precautions against foreseeable acts or omissions of any such third party and the consequences that could foreseeably result from such acts or omissions.

42 U.S.C. §9607(b)(3).

We disagree. Shore argues that it had nothing to do with the transportation of the hazardous substances and that it has exercised due care since taking control of the site. Who the "third part(ies)" Shore claims were responsible are difficult to fathom. It is doubtful that a prior owner could be such, especially the prior owner here, since the acts or omissions referred to in the statute are doubtless those occurring during the ownership or operation of the defendant. Similarly, many of the acts and omissions of the prior tenants/operators fall outside the scope of section 9607(b)(3), because they occurred before Shore owned the property. In addition, we find that Shore cannot rely on the affirmative defense even with respect to the tenants' conduct during the period after Shore closed on the property and when Shore evicted the tenants. Shore was aware of the nature of the tenants' activities before the closing and could readily have foreseen that they would continue to dump hazardous waste at the site. In light of this knowledge, we cannot say that the releases and threats of release resulting from these activities were "caused solely" by the tenants or that Shore "took precautions" against these "foreseeable acts or omissions."

NOTES AND QUESTIONS

1. Why do you think Congress chose to extend CERCLA liability to current owners and operators of facilities where hazardous substances had been deposited? If the court had accepted Shore's argument that section 107(a)(1) covered only owners and operators at the time of disposal, what impact would it have had on the government's ability to obtain reimbursement for Superfund response costs? What impact is the court's decision likely to have on future purchasers of property containing hazardous substances?

2. *Shore Realty* rejected Shore's efforts to take advantage of the defense to liability provided by section 107(b)(3). Which of the conditions for eligibility for that defense did Shore fail to meet?

3. At the time Shore Realty purchased the property at issue in this case, Shore was aware that the tanks and drums on the site contained hazardous substances. Suppose Shore had known only that there were tanks and drums on the site, but not that they contained hazardous substances. Would this have made any difference for Shore's liability under CERCLA? Would it have made any difference if the tanks and drums had been buried on the property and Shore had not even been aware of their existence? Is it fair to hold persons who were not involved in the creation of environmental hazards liable for the costs of cleaning them up? Should innocent purchasers be absolved from CERCLA liability? If they are, what impact would this have on incentives for investigating potential contamination of property?

4. After the passage of CERCLA and decisions like *Shore Realty*, owners of properties where improper disposal had occurred in the past continued to press for relief from liability, primarily on grounds of fairness. In 1986, when Congress enacted extensive amendments to CERCLA in the Superfund Amendments and Reauthorization Act (SARA), it responded to some of these fairness concerns. The SARA revisions created a defense for so-called innocent land purchasers. Congress did this by amending the third-party defense of section 107(b)(3) to make it available to innocent purchasers of contaminated property who can establish (1) they did not have actual or constructive knowledge of the presence of hazardous substances at the time the land was acquired, (2) they are government

entities acquiring the property through involuntary transfer, or (3) they acquired the land by inheritance or bequest. To establish lack of constructive knowledge of the presence of hazardous substances, SARA further provided that a purchaser "must have undertaken at the time of acquisition, all appropriate inquiry into the previous ownership and uses of the property consistent with good commercial or customary practice in an effort to minimize liability." §101(35)(B).

In determining whether a purchaser had made "all appropriate inquiry," courts were directed to consider the purchaser's specialized knowledge or experience, the relationship of the purchase price to the value of uncontaminated property, reasonably ascertainable information about the property, the obviousness of the likely presence of contamination, and the ability to detect such contamination by inspection. By creating a defense to liability for purchasers who undertake the appropriate inquiry, these provisions encourage more thorough inspections of property at the time of purchase.

This innocent purchaser defense, set forth in section 101(35)(B), has been difficult to satisfy. The defense has been rejected by courts for a variety of reasons, including a landowner's failure to inquire about the disposal practices of a business that previously operated on the property, United States v. A & N Cleaners & Launderers Inc., 854 F. Supp. 229 (S.D.N.Y. 1994), actual knowledge that a lessor discharged waste on the property; United States v. Broderick Investment Co., 862 F. Supp. 272 (D. Colo. 1994), and failure to take precautions to prevent damage from hazardous substances known to be present on the site; Kerr-McGee Chem. Corp. v. Lefton Iron & Metal Co., 14 F.3d 321 (7th Cir. 1994).

Although a number of cases have found that on the facts presented the defendant failed to make an appropriate inquiry, no appellate decision to date has provided clear rules on what the provision requires. In 2002, Congress responded to requests for greater specificity regarding the pre-acquisition steps an owner must take to ensure compliance. The Small Business Liability Relief and Brownfields Revitalization Act (SBLRBRA), Pub. L. 107-118 (2002), required EPA to issue regulations defining standards for pre-acquisition site assessment within two years. In the interim, the Act provided that for property purchased after May 31, 1997, the all-appropriate inquiry condition is satisfied if the purchaser has complied with the requirements of a Phase I environmental site assessment as set forth in the 1997 standards issued by the American Society for Testing and Materials (ASTM), a respected organization that develops many different kinds of standards for different industries. For property purchased prior to that date, the statute sets a list of criteria courts are to examine in determining compliance. See §101(35)(B).

In November 2005 EPA published a final rule establishing standards and practices for conducting all-appropriate inquiries to satisfy sections 101(35)(B)(ii) & (iii). 70 Fed. Reg. 66,070 (2005). EPA developed these standards, which are codified at 40 C.F.R. §312, after conducting a negotiated rulemaking. A key element of the rules is that purchasers typically will need to retain the services of an "environmental professional," an individual with training in conducting environmental audits (the regulations specify a variety of alternative combinations of education and experience that may qualify some as an environmental professional). They also require interviews with past and present owners, and a number of other due diligence measures. The environmental professional must summit a written report of his or her findings.

5. If *Shore Realty* had been decided after the innocent purchaser exemption had been added, what would have been the result in the case?

6. In SBLRBRA, Congress also revisited the issue of holding liable owners who purchase the property after all disposal has occurred. In the most fundamental change in liability since CERCLA was originally enacted, a new section 107(r) now exempts bona fide prospective purchasers from owner or operator liability, if they satisfy all the requirements of section 107(r). Review those requirements and compare them to the requirements for innocent purchaser status. The earlier innocent purchaser exemption has generally been argued for on the basis of fairness, but can such fairness reasons apply to purchasers who know the property is contaminated before purchasing? What other reasons might Congress have had in mind in enacting section 107(r)? See the discussion of the brownfields problem, pages 413-414. If section 107(r) had been in place when *Share Realty* was decided, what result? Have the concerns expressed by the court in *Shore Realty* about the undesirable consequences of exempting such current owners been adequately addressed in section 107(r)?

7. In addition to current owners and operators, CERCLA imposes liability on owners and operators "at the time of disposal." CERCLA defines disposal very broadly, to include "the discharge, deposit, injection, dumping, spilling, leaking, or placing of any solid waste or hazardous waste into or on any land or water" §101(29). PRPs and EPA have disagreed over whether this language sweeps in owners who engaged in no active conduct relating to disposal themselves but who owned the land at a time when wastes deposited on the land before their ownership continued to leak or spill onto the land. The leading case upholding so-called passive interim owner liability is Nurad v. William E. Hooper & Sons, 966 F.2d 837 (4th Cir. 1992). The leading case rejecting such liability is United States v. CDMG Realty, 96 F.3d 706 (3rd Cir. 1996). *Nurad* stressed that not recognizing passive owner liability would mean that "an owner could avoid liability simply by standing idle while an environmental hazard festers on his property." 966 F.2d at 845. *CDMG* claimed that its contrary interpretation made more sense in light of the active words used to define disposal and that to acknowledge passive owner liability would vitiate the innocent purchaser defense that only applies to purchases occurring *after* disposal, 96 F.3d at 715-716. More courts have followed *CDMG*. See ABB Indus. Sys. Inc. v. Prime Tech., 120 F.3d 351 (2d Cir. 1997); United States v. 150 Acres of Land, 204 F.3d 698 (6th Cir. 2000); Carson Harbor Village, Ltd. v. Unocal Corp., 270 F.3d 863 (9th Cir. 2001) ("disposal" does not include passive soil migration, but it may include other passive migration, such as from leaking tanks). But see United States v. Waste Industries, 734 F.2d 159 (4th Cir. 1984) (in a RCRA §7003 action, passive current owner can be "contributing to . . . [the] disposal" of hazardous wastes).

A Note on Property Transfer Statutes

Some states have pursued a different strategy than the innocent purchaser defense to assist purchasers who do not wish to acquire contaminated property. Instead, they have required sellers to disclose the status of the property or to certify that it is free of contamination. Indeed, the federal government has also used this approach in specific circumstances. For instance, in order to ensure that the federal government did not itself dupe innocent purchasers, SARA added section 120(h) to CERCLA. Section 120(h) requires federal agencies to notify purchasers of federal property of the type and quantity of any hazardous substance known to have been stored (for one year or more), released, or disposed on the property. Federal agencies are required to disclose such information to the extent that it is "available on the basis of a complete search of agency files." Notice must be included not only in the contract for the sale, but also in the deed to the property. Section 120(h), however, provides even more protection to purchasers than simply disclosing environmental hazards. It also requires federal agencies to enter into covenants warranting that remedial action has been taken to clean up the property and promising that the government will undertake further remedial action if necessary after the property is transferred.

In 1990, EPA promulgated regulations applying section 120(h)'s notice requirements only to properties on which hazardous substances were stored, released, or disposed when the property was owned by the federal government. EPA believed that Congress had enacted section 120(h) largely out of concern for property, such as former military facilities, on which the government itself had placed hazardous substances, and it sought to "avoid imposing unfair and unmanageable obligations on federal agencies that had no role" in bringing the hazardous substances to the property. 55 Fed. Reg. 14,210. In Hercules, Inc. v. EPA, 938 F.2d 276 (D.C. Cir. 1991), the D.C. Circuit held that EPA's interpretation was contrary to the express terms of the statute, which requires that the federal government disclose what it knows about hazardous substances on the property regardless of when the substances were placed there. The court dismissed EPA's concern about imposing unfair and unmanageable obligations on federal agencies by noting:

> CERCLA explicitly supports the imposition of remediation obligations on parties who were not responsible for contamination and who have no experience in the handling or remediation of hazardous substances, as when it imposes liability on the sole basis that a party is the current owner or operator of a site contaminated by some previous owner or operator. [938 F.2d at 281.]

Moreover, the court observed that section 120(h) limits agencies' obligations to the disclosure of information contained in agency files.

In 1992, Congress enacted two laws that expand required environmental disclosures when property is transferred. The Community Environmental Response Facilitation Act, Pub. L. No. 102-426, amends section 120(h) of CERCLA to require federal agencies to identify uncontaminated portions of federal property that is for sale in order to facilitate transfers to private parties. While retaining the requirement that the federal government remediate environmental contamination on such properties, the Act provides that property transfers may occur before the completion of long-term remedial action once cleanup plans have been approved and initiated.

The Residential Lead-Based Paint Hazard Reduction Act, Pub. L. No. 102-550, enacted as Title X of the Housing and Community Development Act of 1992, requires sellers or lessors of residential property to disclose to purchasers or lessees "the presence of any known lead-based paint" on the property. Sellers and lessors also have to provide purchasers with an informational pamphlet on lead paint hazards and give them up to ten days to conduct a lead paint inspection.

Several states, including Illinois, California, and Indiana, have statutes requiring sellers to disclose information about known or suspected contamination on property being sold. Connecticut requires that sellers certify that any hazardous wastes discharged on the property have been cleaned up. New Jersey's statute is the most far-reaching because it requires both an environmental assessment and, if necessary, a cleanup as conditions for property transfer. New Jersey's Environmental Cleanup Responsibility Act (ECRA) took effect on December 31, 1984. ECRA requires that an environmental assessment be made when industrial property is being sold and that a cleanup plan be implemented if the property is found to be contaminated. The Act requires that the seller transfer to the buyer either (1) a "No Further Action" letter from the state Department of Environmental Protection that declares either that no hazardous substances have been released on the site or that any discharge has been cleaned up or (2) an approved cleanup plan accompanied by financial assurances that the plan will be implemented. If a seller fails to comply with ECRA, the buyer may void the transaction, and the seller is strictly liable for response costs and damages for failure to implement the cleanup.

When ECRA was first implemented, New Jersey authorities discovered far more contaminated properties than they had anticipated. This resulted in lengthy delays in property transfers and considerable criticism of ECRA from industry. In response to this criticism, New Jersey environmental officials wrote new regulations authorizing the completion of transactions prior to cleanup and permitting the sale of uncontaminated portions of a larger property without full ECRA review.

New Jersey officials maintain that ECRA produced significant environmental benefits, including far more dump site cleanups in that state than the Superfund program produced. By the end of 1991, a total of 1,759 remedial actions costing more than $478 million had been undertaken pursuant to New Jersey's Environmental Cleanup Responsibility Act (ECRA). New Jersey officials attribute ECRA's success to the fact that it avoids expensive disputes over who is at fault for contamination by internalizing the cost of cleanup in the property transfer transaction. As the New Jersey Supreme Court noted, "the statute focuses on the environmental wrong, not the wrongdoer. Identification of the polluter plays no part in the ECRA process, which imposes a 'self-executing duty to remediate.'" In re Adoption of N.J.A.C. 7:26B, 608 A.2d 288, 291 (N.J. 1992).

The New Jersey Supreme Court upheld ECRA regulations that require the cleanup of off-site contamination emanating from a property being transferred and that include within ECRA's coverage contiguous parcels of vacant land controlled by the same owner or operator. The latter was necessary, the court explained, because otherwise "exemption of vacant land contiguous to a plant would provide owners with an incentive to move hazardous wastes from the plant site to that land. Such an exemption would allow owners to sell off the uncontaminated part of the property and abandon the part that is contaminated." Id. at 297. Two dissenting justices argued that requiring cleanup of off-site contamination "converts ECRA's quick and simple determination of liability into a time-consuming and controversial analysis about the source of off-site contamination." Id. at 303 (Garibaldi, J., concurring in part and dissenting in part). The dissenters maintained this actually will delay cleanup by inviting disputes over whether or not the source of contamination is located on the property being sold.

In 1993, New Jersey amended ECRA to relax cleanup standards, streamline the remediation process required by the Act, and codify the administrative rules that allowed remediation to take place after transfer. The new legislation, the Industrial Site Recovery Act (ISRA), allows parties to defer remediation of industrial property if the new owner plans to use it for substantially the same purpose. It permits soil cleanups to proceed without prior state approval in most cases and authorizes transfers of partial interests in property without requiring cleanup of an entire site. The law permits the use of substantially lower exposure estimates in calculating cleanup levels required to reduce residual risk, depending upon the expected future use of the land, and it authorizes the use of institutional controls that restrict access to a site as an alternative to permanent remediation. The new legislation responds to concerns that ECRA was so stringent that it made old industrial properties almost impossible to sell.

ISRA applies only to certain industrial properties where hazardous substances have been deposited. See N.J.S.A. 13:1K-8. Buyer and seller are permitted to transfer the property prior to remediation, in which case the parties would enter into an agreement specifying how remediation would be completed and a "No Further Action" letter obtained from the New Jersey Department of Environmental Protection. In the absence of contractual arrangements, however, when the seller and buyer enter into a contract with the knowledge that ISRA applies, the statute imposes absolute liability for cleanup upon the seller. E.g., Racioppo v. Hunterdon Holdings, LLC, 2005 WL 2077214 (N.J. Super. Ch. 2005).

NOTES AND QUESTIONS

1. If you were a prospective purchaser of property, which approach to property transfer laws would you prefer—a pure disclosure approach or ECRA/ISRA's mandatory cleanup approach? Which would you prefer if you owned contaminated property that you wished to sell? Which if you owned property that you were certain was free of contamination?

2. Which approach is more likely to protect truly innocent purchasers—CERCLA's or ECRA's? If you are purchasing property in a state without any of the kinds of property transfer laws described above, how much investigation do you need to undertake to ensure that you will escape future CERCLA liability? Who bears the cost of this investigation? If you are purchasing property in New Jersey, how much investigation do you need to undertake? Who bears the cost?

3. The U.S. Defense Department has complained that the requirement that it clean up toxic contamination before selling federal property makes it difficult to close military bases. Schneider, Toxic Cleanup Stalls Transfer of Military Sites, N.Y. Times, June 30, 1991, at A1. In 2005 Defense Department officials estimated that more than $940 million had been spent on remediation of contamination at the 33 military bases recommended for closure in 2005 and that more than $1.54 billion in additional costs would be necessary to complete the cleanup. Congressional Research Service, Military Base Closures: Role and Costs of Environmental Cleanups, June 27, 2005, p. 6.

B. OPERATORS

Even a party who does not own a facility can be held liable as an "operator" under CERCLA section 107. In FMC Corp. v. United States Dept. of Commerce, 29 F.3d 833 (3d Cir. 1994), the U.S. government was held liable for contamination caused by a rayon manufacturing plant that had been operated during World War II at the direction of the government's War Production Board. The Third Circuit, sitting en banc, decided by an 8 to 4 vote that the government was liable as an "operator" of the facility under CERCLA. The court noted that it previously had adopted a "substantial control" test to determine when a corporation should be held liable for the environmental violations of another.

In *FMC,* the en banc court found that the government clearly had exercised substantial control over FMC's rayon plant "as the government determined what product the facility would produce, the level of production, the price of the product, and to whom the product would be sold." 29 F.3d at 843. The court distinguished this situation from cases involving "governmental regulatory activities undertaken solely with the purpose of cleaning up hazardous materials. . . ." 29 F.3d at 841. But it rejected the government's argument that regulatory activities can never constitute the basis for CERCLA liability, finding that "the government can be liable when it engages in regulatory activities extensive enough to make it an operator of a facility or an arranger of the disposal of hazardous wastes even though no private party could engage in the regulatory activities at issue." 29 F.3d at 840. The dissenting judges argued that the company that profited from production of the rayon should bear the costs of cleanup, rather than "society as the ultimate beneficiary of the war effort. . . ." 29 F.3d 854 (Sloviter, C.J., dissenting).

In United States v. Brighton, 153 F.3d 308 (6th Cir. 1998), the court held that a township must have exercised "actual control" over the activities at a privately owned dump as opposed to merely possessing the "ability to control." "[M]ere regulation does not suffice, but actual operation does." The court instructed the trial court to consider "the government's expertise and knowledge of the environmental dangers posed by hazardous waste, establishment and design of the facility, participation in the opening and closing of the facility, hiring or supervising employees involved in activities related to pollution, determination of the facility's operational plan, monitoring of and control over hazardous waste disposal, and public declarations of responsibility over the facility and/or hazardous waste disposal." 153 F.3d at 327.

In United States v. Gurley, 43 F.3d 1188 (8th Cir. 1994), the Eighth Circuit also adopted an actual control test for determining when individuals can be held liable as operators under section 107(a)(2) of CERCLA. The court held that two elements were required for such liability: (1) that the individual "had the authority to determine whether hazardous wastes would be disposed of and to determine the method of disposal and (2) actually exercised that authority, either by personally performing the tasks necessary to dispose of the hazardous wastes or by directing others to perform those tasks." 43 F.3d at 1193.

One of the most frequently litigated operator liability issues concerns the liability of a parent corporation for a facility owned by a subsidiary, an issue the Supreme Court addressed in the following case.

|| *United States v. Bestfoods* ||
|| **524 U.S. 51 (1998)** ||

JUSTICE SOUTER delivered the opinion of the Court.

The United States brought this action for the costs of cleaning up industrial waste generated by a chemical plant. The issue before us, under the Comprehensive Environmental Response, Compensation, and Liability Act of 1980 (CERCLA), is whether a parent corporation that actively participated in, and exercised control over, the operations of a subsidiary may, without more, be held liable as an operator of a polluting facility owned or operated by the subsidiary. We answer no, unless the corporate veil may be pierced. But a corporate parent that actively participated in, and exercised control over, the operations of the facility itself may be held directly liable in its own right as an operator of the facility. . . .

In 1957, Ott Chemical Co. (Ott I) began manufacturing chemicals at a plant near Muskegon, Michigan, and its intentional and unintentional dumping of hazardous substances significantly polluted the soil and ground water at the site. In 1965, respondent CPC International Inc. [which recently changed its name to Bestfoods] incorporated a wholly owned subsidiary to buy Ott I's assets in exchange for CPC stock. The new company, also dubbed Ott Chemical Co. (Ott II), continued chemical manufacturing at the site, and continued to pollute its surroundings. CPC kept the managers of Ott I, including its founder, president, and principal shareholder, Arnold Ott, on board as officers of Ott II. Arnold Ott and several other Ott II officers and directors were also given positions at CPC, and they performed duties for both corporations.

In 1972, CPC sold Ott II to Story Chemical Company, which operated the Muskegon plant until its bankruptcy in 1977. Shortly thereafter, when respondent Michigan Department of Natural Resources (MDNR) examined the site for environmental damage, it found the land littered with thousands of leaking and even exploding drums of waste, and the soil and water saturated with noxious chemicals. . . .

By 1981, the federal Environmental Protection Agency had undertaken to see the site cleaned up, and its long-term remedial plan called for expenditures well into the tens of millions of dollars. To recover some of that money, the United States filed this action under §107 in 1989, naming [CPC and Arnold Ott as two of the defendants]. . . . Because the parties stipulated that the Muskegon plant was a "facility" within the meaning of 42 U.S.C. §9601(9), that hazardous substances had been released at the facility, and that the United States had incurred reimbursable response costs to clean up the site, the trial focused on the issues of whether CPC . . . as the parent corporation[] of Ott II . . . , had "owned or operated" the facility within the meaning of §107(a)(2).

It is a general principle of corporate law deeply "ingrained in our economic and legal systems" that a parent corporation (so-called because of control through ownership of another corporation's stock) is not liable for the acts of its subsidiaries. Thus it is hornbook law that "the exercise of the 'control' which stock ownership gives to the stock-holders . . . will not create liability beyond the assets of the subsidiary. That 'control' includes the election of directors, the making of by-laws . . . and the doing of all other acts incident to the legal status of stock-holders. Nor will a duplication of some or all of the directors or executive officers be fatal." Douglas & Shanks, Insulation from Liability Through Subsidiary Corporations, 39 Yale L.J. 193 (1929) (hereinafter Douglas) 196 (footnotes omitted). Although this respect for corporate distinctions when the subsidiary is a polluter has been severely criticized in the literature, . . . nothing in CERCLA purports to reject this bedrock principle, and against this venerable common-law backdrop, the congressional silence is audible. The Government has indeed made no claim that a corporate parent is liable as an owner or an operator under §107 simply because its subsidiary is subject to liability for owing or operating a polluting facility.

But there is an equally fundamental principle of corporate law, applicable to the parent-subsidiary relationship as well as generally, that the corporate veil may be pierced and the shareholder held liable for the corporation's conduct when, inter alia, the corporate form would otherwise be misused to accomplish certain wrongful purposes, most notably fraud, on the shareholder's behalf. Nothing in CERCLA purports to rewrite this well-settled rule, either. CERCLA is thus like many another congressional enactments in giving no indication "that the entire corpus of state corporation law is to be replaced simply because a plaintiff's cause of action is based upon a federal statute," . . . and the failure of the statute to speak to a matter as fundamental as the liability implications of corporate ownership demands application of the rule that "[i]n order to abrogate a common-law principle, the statute must speak directly to the question addressed by the common law." . . . The Court of Appeals was accordingly correct in holding that when (but only when) the corporate veil may be pierced may a parent corporation be charged with derivative CERCLA liability for its subsidiary's actions. . . .

If the act rested liability entirely on ownership of a polluting facility, this opinion might end here; but CERCLA liability may turn on operation as well as ownership, and nothing in the statute's terms bars a parent corporation from direct liability for its own actions in operating a facility owned by its subsidiary. As Justice (then-Professor) Douglas noted almost 70 years ago, derivative liability cases are to be distinguished from those in which "the alleged wrong can seemingly be traced to the parent through the conduit of its own personnel and management" and "the parent is directly a participant in the wrong complained of." Douglas 207, 208. In such instances, the parent is directly liable for its own actions. The fact that a corporate subsidiary happens to own a polluting facility operated by its parent does nothing, then, to displace the rule that the parent "corporation is [itself] responsible for the wrongs committed by its agents in the course of its business," . . . and whereas the rules of veil-piercing limit derivative liability for the actions of another corporation, CERCLA's "operator" provision is concerned primarily with direct liability for one's own actions. . . . It is this direct liability that is properly seen as being at issue here.

Under the plain language of the statute, any person who operates a polluting facility is directly liable for the costs of cleaning up the pollution. See 42 U.S.C. §9607(a)(2). This is so regardless of whether that person is the facility's owner, the owner's parent corporation or business partner, or even a saboteur who sneaks into the facility at night to discharge its poisons out of malice. If any such act of operating a corporate subsidiary's facility is done on behalf of a parent corporation, the existence of the parent-subsidiary relationship under state corporate law is simply irrelevant to the issue of direct liability. . . .

This much is easy to say; the difficulty comes in defining actions sufficient to constitute direct parental "operation." Here of course we may again rue the uselessness of CERCLA's definition of a facility's "operator" as "any person . . . operating" the facility, 42 U.S.C. §9601(20)(A)(ii), which leaves us to do the best we can to give the term its "ordinary or natural meaning." . . . In a mechanical sense, to "operate" ordinarily means "[t]o control the functioning of; run: operate a sewing machine." American Heritage Dictionary 1268 (3d ed. 1992). . . . And in the organizational sense more obviously intended by CERCLA, the word ordinarily means "[t]o conduct the affairs of; manage: operate a business." . . . So, under CERCLA, an operator is simply someone who directs the workings of, manages, or conducts the affairs of a facility. To sharpen the definition for purposes of CERCLA's concern with environmental contamination, an operator must manage, direct, or conduct operations specifically related to pollution, that is, operations having to do with the leakage or disposal of hazardous waste, or decisions about compliance with environmental regulations.

By emphasizing that "CPC is directly liable under section 107(a)(2) as an operator because CPC actively participated in and exerted significant control over Ott II's business and decision-making," 777 F. Supp., at 574, the District Court applied the "actual control" test of whether the parent "actually operated the business of its subsidiary." . . .

The well-taken objection to the actual control test, however, is its fusion of direct and indirect liability; the test is administered by asking a question about the relationship between the two corporations (an issue going to indirect liability) instead of a question about the parent's interaction with the subsidiary's facility (the source of any direct liability). If, however, direct liability for the parent's operation of the facility is to be kept distinct from derivative liability for the subsidiary's own operation, the focus of the enquiry must necessarily be different under the two tests. "The question is not whether the parent operates the subsidiary, but rather whether it operates the facility, and that operation is evidenced by participation in the activities of the facility, not the subsidiary." . . . The analysis should . . . have rested on the relationship between CPC and the Muskegon facility itself. . . .

In imposing direct liability on [the basis of the actions of dual officers of CPC and Ott II], the District Court failed to recognize that "it is entirely appropriate for directors of a parent corporation to serve as directors of its subsidiary, and that fact alone may not serve to expose the parent corporation to liability for its subsidiary's acts." . . .

This recognition that the corporate personalities remain distinct has its corollary in the "well established principle [of corporate law] that directors and officers holding positions with a parent and its subsidiary can and do 'change hats' to represent the two corporations separately, despite their common ownership." . . . The Government would have to show that, despite the general presumption to the contrary, the officers and directors were acting in their capacities as CPC officers and directors, and not as Ott II officers and directors, when they committed those acts. The District Court made no such enquiry here, however, disregarding entirely this time-honored common law rule.

In sum, the District Court's focus on the relationship between parent and subsidiary (rather than parent and facility), combined with its automatic attribution of the actions of dual officers and directors to the corporate parent, erroneously, even if unintentionally, treated CERCLA as though it displaced or fundamentally altered common law standards of limited liability. Indeed, if the evidence of common corporate personnel acting at management and directorial levels were enough to support a finding of a parent corporation's direct operator liability under CERCLA, then the possibility of resort to veil piercing to establish indirect, derivative liability for the subsidiary's violations would be academic. There would in essence be a relaxed, CERCLA-specific rule of derivative liability that would banish traditional standards and expectations from the law of CERCLA liability. But, as we have said, such a rule does not arise from congressional silence, and CERCLA's silence is dispositive.

We accordingly agree with the Court of Appeals that a participation-and-control test looking to the parent's supervision over the subsidiary, especially one that assumes that dual officers always act on behalf of the parent, cannot be used to identify operation of a facility resulting in direct parental liability. Nonetheless, a return to the ordinary meaning of the word "operate" in the organizational sense will indicate why we think that the Sixth Circuit stopped short when it confined its examples of direct parental operation to exclusive or joint ventures, and declined to find at least the possibility of direct operation by CPC in this case.

In our enquiry into the meaning Congress presumably had in mind when it used the verb "to operate," we recognized that the statute obviously meant something more than mere mechanical activation of pumps and valves, and must be read to contemplate "operation" as including the exercise of direction over the facility's activities. The Court of Appeals recognized this by indicating that a parent can be held directly liable when the parent operates the facility in the stead of its subsidiary or alongside the subsidiary in some sort of a joint venture. See 113 F.3d, at 579. We anticipated a further possibility above, however, when we observed that a dual officer or director might depart so far from the norms of parental influence exercised through dual office-holding as to serve the parent, even when ostensibly acting on behalf of the subsidiary in operating the facility. Yet another possibility, suggested by the facts of this case, is that an agent of the parent with no hat to wear but the parent's hat might manage or direct activities at the facility.

Identifying such an occurrence calls for line drawing yet again, since the acts of direct operation that give rise to parental liability must necessarily be distinguished from the interference that stems from the normal relationship between parent and subsidiary. Again norms of corporate behavior (undisturbed by any CERCLA provisions) are crucial reference points. Just as we may look to such norms in identifying the limits of the presumption that a dual officeholder acts in his ostensible capacity, so here we may refer to them in distinguishing a parental officer's oversight of a subsidiary from such an officer's control over the operation of the subsidiary's facility. "[A]ctivities that involve the facility but which are consistent with the parent's investor status, such as monitoring of the subsidiary's performance, supervision of the subsidiary's finance and capital budget decisions, and articulation of general policies and procedures, should not give rise to direct liability." Oswald[, 72 Wash. U. L.Q. 223,] 282. The critical question is whether, in degree and detail, actions directed to the facility by an agent of the parent alone are eccentric under accepted norms of parental oversight of a subsidiary's facility.

[The Court then remanded the case for a determination of whether CPC might be an operator through the direct actions of its own employee.]

NOTES AND QUESTIONS

1. **Federal or State Law?** In holding that a parent corporation could be held liable for the acts of its subsidiary under ordinary rules for piercing the corporate veil, the Supreme Court declined to decide whether the courts should look to state law standards for veil piercing, or to a uniform federal standard, because the issue had not been briefed and argued by the parties. 524 U.S. 63 n.9. The Court of Appeals below had split on this question. Compare United States v. Cordova Chemical Company, 113 F.3d 562, 580 (6th Cir. 1997) (veil piercing a state law issue) with 113 F.3d 584-586 (Merritt, J. dissenting) (veil piercing to be determined under a uniform federal standard, which was met in this case). See also, U.S. v. General Battery Corp., Inc. (3rd Cir. 2005) (veil piercing a matter of uniform federal law). Does the logic of the Supreme Court's decision suggest how that court would decide the issue?

2. **What Constitutes Operating a Facility?** On the issue of what acts of the parent with respect to the facility would subject it to operator liability, how illuminating is the Court's opinion? Suppose a parent corporation wants to continue monitoring a subsidiary's activities but wishes to avoid operator liability. Based on the Court's opinion, what advice can you provide?

3. **Perverse Incentives?** Does the opinion create perverse incentives for a parent corporation who becomes knowledgeable of a potential problem at a subsidiary's facility to back away from intervening, in order to avoid exposure to liability? If so, is that desirable and consistent with CERCLA's objectives?

4. **Secured Lenders.** Secured lenders are another class whose exposure to PRP liability as owner or operator has evolved over the life of CERCLA. Section 101(20)(A) of CERCLA exempts from owner or operator status lenders who "hold indicia of ownership primarily to protect a security interest" without "participating in management." So long as a loan is not in trouble, interpreting this exemption caused little difficulty. However, whenever a lender undertook negotiations with a borrower in distress in an effort to avoid an outright default by altering the terms of the loan, the lender risked crossing the line of participating in management. In United States v. Fleet Factors, 901 F.2d 1550 (11th Cir. 1990), the court adopted an "ability to control" approach to the question of participating in management, saying that a lender loses the protection of the secured lender exemption "by participating in the financial management of a facility to a degree indicating a capacity to influence the corporation's treatment of hazardous wastes." 901 F.2d at 1557. After *Fleet Factors*, EPA attempted to provide guidance to lenders by issuing a rule interpreting the "participating in management" language of CERCLA, but in Kelley v. EPA, 15 F.3d 1100 (D.C. Cir. 1994), in a rare ruling of its type, the court held that the Congress had not given EPA rulemaking authority over the liability provisions of CERCLA, instead leaving those to judicial supervision under "evolving principles of the common law."

Finally, in 1996, the Congress enacted the Asset Conservation, Lender Liability, and Deposit Insurance Protection Act of 1996 (ACLLDIPA), adding to the statute section 101(20)(F), which sets forth standards for participating in management. That section defines participation to mean "actually participating in the management or operational affairs . . . and does not include merely having the capacity to influence, or the unexercised right to control . . . facility operations."

5. **State and Municipal Liability.** State and municipal governments are among the entities potentially subject to liability as owners or operators. (On liability as generators, see pages 399-401.) Courts have typically held that issuing regulations governing land use activities is insufficient to subject cities or counties to owner or operator liability. E.g., United States v. Dart Industries, 847 F.2d 144 (4th Cir. 1988). On the other hand, in United States v. Stringfellow, 31 E.R.C. 1315 (C.D. Cal. 1990), the state of California was found to be liable as a result of its actions in selecting a site for hazardous waste dumping and controlling all the actions at the site.

The constitutional issues raised by holding states liable were first broached in Pennsylvania v. Union Gas Co., 491 U.S. 1 (1989), which held that the Eleventh Amendment did not prohibit states from being held liable to private parties under CERCLA. However, in Seminole Tribe v. Florida, 517 U.S. 44 (1996), the Court reversed itself, holding that Congress has no power under the Commerce Clause to abrogate states' Eleventh Amendment immunity from private suit in federal court. Individuals may still obtain injunctive relief against ongoing violations by state officials under the theory of Ex parte Young, 209 U.S. 123 (1908), but private damage actions are only available if the state waives sovereign immunity. In Alden v. Maine, 527 U.S. 706 (1999), the Court amplified states' protections against imposition of monetary liability by federal statute, holding that under the Constitution the states retain a "residuary and inviolable sovereignty" that prohibits suits for money damages against them in state court as well, absent a waiver of sovereign immunity.

While *Seminole Tribe* and *Alden* reshape constitutional principles of federalism, their effect on CERCLA will be limited because counties and municipalities, which enjoy no sovereign immunity protection, are sued for contribution most frequently. Going forward, though, these cases might produce a shift of ownership and operation of sites to the state level.

6. **Transporters.** Section 107(a)(4) of CERCLA makes anyone who accept "hazardous substances for transport to disposal or treatment facilities . . . or sites selected by such person" liable for their releases. Note that transporter liability is premised on transporters playing some role in the selection of the site where the hazardous substances are to be taken. In Tippins, Inc. v. USX Corp., 37 F.3d 87 (3d Cir. 1994), the Third Circuit held that even if a transporter did not make the final decision concerning site selection, section 107(a)(4) "applies if the transporter's advice was a substantial contributing factor in the decision" to dispose of the waste at a particular facility. 37 F.3d at 90. The court determined that "a transporter selects the disposal facility when it actively and substantially participates in the decision-making process which ultimately identifies a facility for disposal." Id. The transporter held liable in *Tippins* was a company that specialized in the transport and disposal of hazardous substances. The transporter surveyed alternative disposal sites, identified two candidate landfills that would accept the waste, and provided the generator with information concerning disposal costs at each. Although the generator made the ultimate choice between the two sites, the court held the transporter liable because of its substantial participation in the site selection process.

In Kaiser Aluminum & Chemical Corp. v. Catellus Development Corp., 976 F.2d 1338 (9th Cir. 1992), a contractor who excavated contaminated soil and spread it over uncontaminated portions of a site was held liable as a transporter of hazardous substances under section 107(a)(4) of CERCLA. The court rejected arguments that transporter liability could not attach unless the substances were taken to another site. "Whether a transporter moves hazardous material from one parcel of land to another, or whether he simply takes the material from a contaminated area of the same parcel, he has spread the contamination." 976 F.2d at 1343. The court found "no logical basis" for transporter liability "to hinge solely on whether he moves hazardous substances across a recognized property boundary." Id.

C.   GENERATORS

Perhaps CERCLA's most substantial modification of common law liability is the imposition of liability on the nonnegligent generators of hazardous substances. By reaching back to the persons who produced the hazardous waste, CERCLA created powerful new incentives for such persons to ensure that wastes are managed carefully. Generators who formerly were delighted to let the cheapest waste hauler relieve them of their hazardous residues now must select treatment and disposal options, and monitor their implementation, with care. For if the generator's hazardous substances are sent to a site where a release occurs or is threatened, the generator could be held strictly, jointly, and severally liable for response costs and natural resource damages.

Generator liability is covered in section 107(a)(3) of CERCLA, which imposes liability on

> any person who by contract, agreement, or otherwise arranged for disposal or treatment, or arranged with a transporter for transport for disposal or treatment, of hazardous substances owned or possessed by such person, by any other party or entity, at any facility or incineration vessel owned or operated by another party or entity and containing such hazardous substances. [CERCLA §107(a)(3), 42 U.S.C. §9607(a)(3).]

Notice that the statutory language is not limited to producers of hazardous waste. By targeting persons who "arrange for" disposal, the Act seeks to put responsibility on persons who are in a position to take care regarding the disposal. Very often, these persons will be the entities that produce or generate the waste as byproducts to some industrial or manufacturing process.

The statutory language provides little guidance to courts seeking to apply liability to specific entities. Although it may be possible to tie generators directly to waste contained in marked drums, it is virtually impossible to prove which generator's waste comprises which part of the chemical soup typically formed under the surface of a hazardous waste dump site. Because the language of section 107(a)(3) refers to "any facility . . . containing *such* hazardous substances" (emphasis supplied), the statute suggests that the government has some obligation to prove that the generator's waste is at a facility where releases occur. But it initially was unclear if this obligation required the government to prove that the generator's wastes were part of the release in question.

Recognizing the difficulty the government would face if required to prove whose wastes are physically present in a given release, courts have interpreted section 107(a)(3) broadly to promote the remedial purposes of Congress. One circuit court opinion that has been widely cited held that the government's case was satisfied once it had proved that "(1) [a generator] shipped hazardous substances to the . . . facility; (2) hazardous substances 'like' those present in the generator's waste . . . were found at the facility; and (3) there had been a release of hazardous substances at the site." United States v. Monsanto, 858 F.2d 160, 166 (4th Cir. 1988).

The potentially expansive nature of generator liability and its larger ramifications for waste management policy are illustrated by the following unusual case.

United States v. Aceto Agricultural Chemicals Corp.
872 F.2d 1373 (8th Cir. 1989)

LARSON, Senior District Judge:

This case arises from efforts by the Environmental Protection Agency (EPA) and the State of Iowa to recover over $10 million in response costs incurred in the cleanup of a pesticide formulation facility operated by the Aidex Corporation in Mills County, Iowa. Aidex operated the facility from

1974 through 1981, when it was declared bankrupt. Investigations by the EPA in the early 1980s revealed a highly contaminated site. Hazardous substances were found in deteriorating containers, in the surface soil, in fauna samples, and in the shallow zone of the groundwater, threatening the source of irrigation and drinking water for area residents. Using funds from the "Hazardous Substance Superfund," see 26 U.S.C. §9507, the EPA, in cooperation with the State of Iowa, undertook various remedial actions to clean up the site.

The EPA now seeks to recover its response costs from eight pesticide manufacturers who did business with Aidex, in particular, who hired Aidex to formulate their technical grade pesticides into commercial grade pesticides. The complaint alleges it is a common practice in the pesticide industry for manufacturers of active pesticide ingredients to contract with formulators such as Aidex to produce a commercial grade product which may then be sold to farmers and other consumers. Formulators mix the manufacturer's active ingredients with inert materials using the specifications provided by the manufacturer. The resulting commercial grade product is then packaged by the formulator and either shipped back to the manufacturer or shipped directly to customers of the manufacturer.

The complaint alleges that although Aidex performed the actual mixing or formulation process, the defendants owned the technical grade pesticide, the work in process, and the commercial grade pesticide while the pesticide was in Aidex's possession. The complaint also alleges the generation of pesticide-containing wastes through spills, cleaning of equipment, mixing and grinding operations, and production of batches which do not meet specifications is an "inherent" part of the formulation process. . . . Plaintiffs . . . allege that six of the eight companies are liable under section 9607(a)(3) of the Comprehensive Environmental Response, Compensation, and Liability Act (CERCLA), because by virtue of their relationships with Aidex they "arranged for" the disposal of hazardous substances. See 42 U.S.C. §9607(a)(3).

The defendants have moved to dismiss the action under Fed. R. Civ. P. 12(b)(6), arguing that they contracted with Aidex for the processing of a valuable product, not the disposal of a waste, and that Aidex alone controlled the processes used in formulating their technical grade pesticides into commercial grade pesticides, as well as any waste disposal that resulted therefrom. . . . The court denied the motion under CERCLA, . . . holding that principles of common law in conjunction with the liberal construction required under CERCLA could support liability under section 9607(a)(3). 699 F. Supp. 1384. . . .

LIABILITY UNDER CERCLA

To establish a prima facie case of liability under CERCLA, plaintiff must establish

(1)   the Aidex site is a "facility";
(2)   a "release" or "threatened release" of a "hazardous substance" from the Aidex site has occurred;
(3)   the release or threatened release has caused the United States to incur response costs; and
(4)   the defendants fall within at least one of the four classes of responsible persons described in section 9607(a).

The complaint adequately alleges facts which would establish the first three elements, and defendants do not challenge these allegations for purposes of this appeal. At issue in this appeal is whether the defendants "arranged for" the disposal of hazardous substances under the Act, and thus fall within the class of responsible persons described in section 9607(a)(3). In finding plaintiffs' allegations sufficient to hold defendants liable as responsible persons, the district court relied on the principle that CERCLA should be broadly interpreted and took guidance from common law rules regarding vicarious liability. In particular, the district court found that defendants could be liable under common law for the abnormally dangerous activities of Aidex acting as an independent contractor, see Restatement (Second) of Torts §427A (1965), holding that the common law was an appropriate source of guidance when the statutory language and legislative history of CERCLA prove inconclusive. . . .

"Arrange for" is not defined by the statute, but "disposal" is. "Disposal" includes "the discharge, deposit, injection, dumping, spilling, leaking, or placing" of any hazardous substance such that the substance "may enter the environment." 42 U.S.C. §6903(3). See 42 U.S.C. §9601(29).

Citing dictionary definitions of the word "arrange," defendants argue they can be liable under section 9607(a)(3) only if they intended to dispose of a waste. Defendants argue further the complaint alleges only an intent to arrange for formulation of a valuable product, and no intent to arrange for the disposal of a waste can be inferred from these allegations. We reject defendants' narrow reading of both the complaint and the statute.

Congress used broad language in providing for liability for persons who "by contract, agreement, or otherwise arranged for" the disposal of hazardous substances. While the legislative history of CERCLA sheds little light on the intended meaning of this phrase, courts have concluded that a liberal judicial interpretation is consistent with CERCLA's "overwhelmingly remedial" statutory scheme.

Both the First and Second Circuits have declared they "will not interpret section 9607(a) in any way that apparently frustrates the statute's goals, in the absence of a specific congressional intent otherwise." Dedham Water Co. v. Cumberland Farms Dairy, Inc., 805 F.2d at 1081; New York v. Shore Realty Corp., 759 F.2d 1032, 1045 (2d Cir. 1985). We thus interpret the phrase "otherwise arranged for" in view of the two essential purposes of CERCLA:

> First, Congress intended that the federal government be immediately given the tools necessary for a prompt and effective response to the problems of national magnitude resulting from hazardous waste disposal. Second, Congress intended that those responsible for problems caused by the disposal of chemical poisons bear the costs and responsibility for remedying the harmful conditions they created.

Dedham Water Co., 805 F.2d at 1081.

The second goal—that those responsible should pay for cleanup—would be thwarted by acceptance of defendants' argument that the allegations in plaintiffs' complaint do not sufficiently allege they "arranged for" disposal of their hazardous substances. While defendants characterize their relationship with Aidex as pertaining solely to formulation of a useful product, courts have not hesitated to look beyond defendants' characterizations to determine whether a transaction in fact involves an arrangement for the disposal of a hazardous substance. In *Conservation Chemical,* for example, the court found defendants' sale of lime slurry and fly ash by-products to neutralize and treat other hazardous substances at a hazardous waste site could constitute "arranging for disposal" of the lime slurry and fly ash. 619 F. Supp. at 237-41. Denying defendants' motions for summary judgment, the court reasoned that defendants contracted with the owner of the site "for deposit or placement" of their hazardous substances on the site, and thus could be found liable under the statute. Id. at 241.

Other courts have imposed CERCLA liability where defendants sought to characterize their arrangement with another party who disposed of their hazardous substances as a "sale" rather than a "disposal." See New York v. General Electric Co., 592 F. Supp. 291, 297 (N.D.N.Y. 1984); United States v. A & F Materials, 582 F. Supp. at 845. In the *G.E.* case, General Electric had sold used transformer oil to a dragstrip, which used the oil for dust control. The oil contained PCBs and other hazardous substances, and the State of New York sought to recover costs for cleanup of the site from G.E. *G.E.,* 592 F. Supp. at 293-94. In denying G.E.'s motion to dismiss, the court emphasized G.E. allegedly arranged for the dragstrip to take away its used transformer oil with "knowledge or imputed knowledge" that the oil would be deposited on the land surrounding the dragstrip. Id. at 297. Stating that CERCLA liability could not be "facilely circumvented" by characterizing arrangements as "sales," the *G.E.* court cited CERCLA's legislative history: "[P]ersons cannot escape liability by 'contracting away' their responsibility or alleging that the incident was caused by the act or omission of a third party." Id. at 297 (and authorities cited therein). See *A & F Materials,* 582 F. Supp. at 845.

Courts have also held defendants "arranged for" disposal of wastes at a particular site even when defendants did not know the substances would be deposited at that site or in fact believed they would be deposited elsewhere.

Courts have, however, refused to impose liability where a "useful" substance is sold to another party, who then incorporates it into a product, which is later disposed of. E.g., Florida Power & Light Co. v. Allis Chalmers Corp., 27 Env't Rep. Gas. (BNA) 1558 (S.D. Fla. 1988). Defendants attempt to analogize the present case to those cited above, but the analogy fails. Not only is there no transfer of ownership of the hazardous substances in this case (defendants retain ownership throughout), but the activity undertaken by Aidex is significantly different from the activity undertaken by, for example, Florida Power & Light. Aidex is performing a process on products owned by defendants for defendants' benefit and at their direction; waste is generated and disposed of contemporaneously with the process. Florida Power & Light, on the other hand, purchased electrical transformers containing mineral oil with PCBs from defendant Allis Chalmers, used the transformers for approximately 40 years, and then made the decision to dispose of them at the site in question. *Florida Power & Light,* 27 Env't Rep. Gas. (BNA) at 1558-60. Allis Chalmers was thus far more removed from the disposal than the defendants are in this case. . . .

Finally, defendants' contention that the district court erred in looking to the common law must also be rejected. As the Seventh Circuit has recently held, the sponsors of CERCLA anticipated that the common law would provide guidance in interpreting CERCLA. Edward Hines Lumber Co. v. Vulcan Materials Co., 861 F.2d 155, 157 (7th Cir. 1988). While the *Edward Hines* court refused to find a company was an "operator" of a facility when the common law did not provide for liability, 861 F.2d at 157-58, in this case, the common law supports the imposition of liability on defendants. See Restatement (Second) of Torts §§413, 416, 427, and 427A (1965).

For all of the reasons discussed above, accepting plaintiffs' allegations in this case as true and giving them the benefit of all reasonable inferences therefrom, we agree with the district court that the complaint states a claim upon which relief can be granted under CERCLA. Any other decision, under the circumstances of this case, would allow defendants to simply "close their eyes" to the method of disposal of their hazardous substances, a result contrary to the policies underlying CERCLA.

NOTES AND QUESTIONS

1. What is the crucial factor permitting the court to impose "arranged for" liability on the pesticide manufacturers? Is it that they had the capacity to control Aidex's disposal practices? That they knew Aidex would have to dispose of hazardous byproducts or waste? That the products Aidex produced were sold or shipped to customers of the pesticide manufacturers rather than to independent customers of Aidex? That the defendants used Aidex as an independent contractor?

2. What impact will this decision have on efforts by pesticide manufacturers to ensure that their products do not create environmental contamination? The defense attorney in *Aceto* wrote an article criticizing the decision. Garrett, The Aceto Case: CERCLA Liability for Products?, 20 Envtl. Rep. 704 (1989). He argues that CERCLA liability should be limited to parties intentionally disposing of wastes because these are the only parties in a position to control the risks of environmental contamination. Do you agree? What could the pesticide manufacturers do to control the risks of contamination of the sort that occurred in *Aceto*?

3. Mr. Garrett argues that a decision in favor of his client would "have no adverse environmental effects; it would simply leave liability with the company that generated the wastes and controlled their disposal." Id. at 704, 706. Do you agree? How would a decision in favor of the defendant pesticide manufacturers in the *Aceto* case have affected cleanup efforts at the site? What impact would it have had on the manufacturers' incentives for ensuring that in the future their products do not contaminate the environment during the formulation process?

4. The Seventh Circuit has taken the approach urged by Mr. Garrett. Amcast Industrial Corp. v. Detrex Corp., 2 F.3d 746 (7th Cir. 1993), involved a facility run by Elkhart Products Corp., a subsidiary of Amcast, for the manufacture of copper fittings. The manufacturing process involved the use of trichloroethylene (TCE), which Elkhart purchased from Detrex. Some 800 gallons of TCE were discovered in the groundwater adjacent to Elkhart's plant, and investigation revealed that the truck drivers accidentally spilled TCE on Elkhart's premises while filling Elkhart's tanks. Holding that the words "arranged for" "imply intentional action," the court held that Detrex was not liable because it did not hire the trucker for the purpose of spilling TCE. 3 F.3d at 751.

5. A number of courts, including *Aceto* in dicta, have recognized that the seller of a "useful product" is not subject to arranger liability, although they will look through "sham" transactions. In addition to the cases cited in *Aceto*, see South Florida Water Management Dist. v. Montalvo, 84 F.3d 402 (11th Cir. 1996). Even bona fide sales of spent materials can subject the seller to liability, however. Noting that "all that is necessary is that the [disposal or] treatment be

inherent in the particular arrangement, even though the arranger does not retain control over its details," the Ninth Circuit held liable a seller of spent automotive batteries to a lead reclamation plant. Catellus Development Corp. v. United States, 34 F.3d 748, 753 (9th Cir. 1994).

6. *Montalvo* itself adopted a "totality of the circumstances" approach to arranger liability. It stated that "while factors such as a party's knowledge (or lack thereof) of the disposal, ownership of the hazardous substances, and intent are relevant to determining whether there has been an 'arrangement' for disposal, they are not necessarily determinative of liability in every case." 84 F.3d at 407. More recently, the Third Circuit canvassed the cases on arranger liability and noted that there was wide agreement that the liability determination was fact-sensitive and not dependent upon the defendant's characterization of the arrangement or transaction—but little agreement beyond these two points. In the end, the Third Circuit concluded: "After carefully examining the language of the statute and considering the standards adopted by other courts, we conclude that the most important factors in determining "arranger liability" are: (1) ownership or possession; and (2) knowledge; or (3) control. Ownership or possession of the hazardous substance must be demonstrated, but this factor alone will not suffice to establish liability. A plaintiff must also demonstrate either control over the process that results in a release of hazardous waste *or* knowledge that such a release will occur during the process." Morton Intern., Inc. v. A.E. Staley Mfg. Co. 343 F.3d 669, 677-678 (3rd Cir. 2003).

7. In Edward Hines Lumber Co. v. Vulcan Materials Co., 685 F. Supp. 651 (N.D. Ill.), aff'd on other grounds, 861 F.2d 155 (7th Cir. 1988), Hines owned a wood products facility in which he treated wood with various toxic chemicals supplied by Vulcan. Hines was notified by the government that his property was contaminated and ordered to clean up the site. Hines sued Vulcan, claiming Vulcan was a PRP too. Vulcan had assisted in designing and building Hines's facility, had trained the employees, and had licensed Hines to use Vulcan's trademark, and Vulcan's employees had full access to the Hines facility. The court dismissed the complaint against Vulcan, holding that liability for arranging for disposal "attaches only to parties who transact in a hazardous substance in order to dispose of or treat the substance." 685 F. Supp. at 654. "[Vulcan] did not decide how the hazardous substance would be disposed of after its use in the wood treatment process. That [it] knew . . . that Hines stored the process runoff in a holding pond . . . [is not enough to establish] liability." Id. at 656.

Is *Hines* consistent with *Aceto*? How about with *Amcast* or with *Morton*? Does the requirement that an arranger be someone who transacts in a hazardous substance "in order to dispose of the substance" mean that courts must examine the party's subjective state of mind? If so, is that consistent with CERCLA's being a strict liability statute?

8. Consider the following hypothetical: A private individual took his car to a service station to have the brakes checked. The mechanic examined the brakes and decided that, in connection with brake repairs, the brake fluid needed to be replaced. The old fluid was removed and placed into a leaky tank at the service station, along with hazardous substances from other sources, eventually resulting in federal cleanup expenditures. Would the automobile owner be liable under section 107(a)(3)? See Garrett, The Aceto Case: CERCLA Liability for Products?, 21 Envtl. Rep. 704 (1989). Would it matter whether the auto owner had taken this environmental law course?

9. In recent years, Congress has amended CERCLA to include several statutory exemptions from arranger liability, often modeling these statutory provisions on settlement policies established earlier by EPA to deal with certain special circumstances. The Superfund Recycling Equity Act, 42 U.S.C. §127, exempts from CERCLA liability arrangers (and transporters) who arrange for "recycling of recyclable materials." Recyclable materials include "scrap paper, scrap plastic, scrap glass, scrap textiles, scrap rubber (other than whole tires), scrap metal, or spent lead-acid, spent nickel-cadmium, and other spent batteries. . . ." §127(b). Qualifying for the exemption requires proving a number of conditions have been met, and is denied anyone who had an objectively reasonable basis to believe that the materials would not be recycled. It is only an arranger exemption, and does not affect liability as an owner or operator, past or present.

The Small Business Liability Relief and Brownfields Revitalization Act (SBLRBRA) added an exemption for "de micromis" generators or transporters, persons who contributed or transported less than 110 gallons of liquid materials or 200 pounds of solid materials to a facility, at least part of which had to occur before April 1, 2001. §107(o). Section 107(o)(2) does not apply if the President determines that the hazardous substances contributed significantly to response costs or if the person seeking to qualify for the exemption impeded the response action or committed a crime by generating or transporting the substance. Liability as owner or operator is once again unaffected. Does the de micromis exemption affect your analysis of the problem in note 8, above?

The SBLRBRA also added section 107(p), which exempts homeowners, certain small businesses, and certain nonprofit organizations from liability for their generation of municipal solid waste (MSW). These exemptions are discussed in the note on Shrinking the Net of CERCLA Liability, page 399.

10. Should suppliers of raw materials who have no reason to know that their materials will produce hazardous substance releases be treated like innocent purchasers of contaminated land? Note that section 107(b)(3) provides a defense to a party exercising due care who took precautions against foreseeable acts or omissions of third parties if the defendant can show that a release was caused solely by "an act or omission of a third party other than an employee or agent of the defendant." However, the defense expressly does not apply if the "act or omission occurs in connection with a contractual relationship," foreclosing this defense to most generators. Recall that the potential liability of innocent purchasers of contaminated land under section 107(a)(1) led Congress to clarify the circumstances under which the section 107(b)(3) defense can be invoked by innocent purchasers when it enacted SARA in 1986. Consider section 101(35). Should a similar provision be enacted to protect truly innocent generators?

11. In *Aceto*, the United States also charged the defendants under section 7003 of RCRA, which imposes liability on anyone who has "contributed to" the handling, storage, treatment, or disposal of hazardous wastes that pose an imminent and substantial endangerment to health or the environment. The court found the facts were sufficient to sustain liability under this remedial statute as well. Although it did not decide the issue, the court found it at least arguable that "contributed to" liability under RCRA required less involvement in the acts of disposal than "arranged for" liability under CERCLA. In Meghrig v. RFC Western, Inc., 516 U.S. 479 (1996), the Supreme Court unanimously held that section 7002(a) does not authorize a private cause of action under RCRA

to recover the costs of past efforts to clean up a petroleum leak because the "may present" and "imminent" language clearly excludes waste that already has been cleaned up. Does *Meghrig* call into question the *Aceto* court's conclusion concerning section 7003? Could the *Meghrig* plaintiff recover cleanup costs under the contribution provisions of section 113(f) of CERCLA?

12. In General Electric Co. v. AAMCO Transmissions, Inc., 962 F.2d 281 (2d Cir. 1992), the Second Circuit refused to hold major oil companies liable under section 107(a)(3) as "arrangers" for the disposal of waste oil collected by the lessees of their service stations. The court rejected the argument that "arranger" liability should turn on whether a company has the ability or authority to control the waste disposal practices of another even if this authority has not been exercised. While noting that arranger liability can attach even to parties who do not have active involvement in "the timing, manner or location of disposal," the court stated that "there must be some nexus between the potentially responsible party and the disposal of the hazardous substance" that "is premised upon the potentially liable party's conduct with respect to the disposal or transport of hazardous wastes." Finding that "Congress employed traditional notions of duty and obligation in deciding which entities would be liable under CERCLA as arrangers for the disposal of hazardous substances," the court concluded that "it is the *obligation* to exercise control over hazardous waste disposal, and not the mere ability or opportunity to control the disposal of hazardous substances that makes an entity an arranger under CERCLA's liability provision." 962 F.2d at 286. The Second Circuit distinguished *Aceto* by noting that "the oil companies did not own the hazardous substance, nor did they control the process by which waste motor oil was generated." While noting that the oil companies may have encouraged dealers to buy virgin motor oil from them, the court found it significant that they did not require dealers to perform oil changes. A federal district court has held that even an oil company that did require its dealers to perform oil changes is not liable as an "arranger" under CERCLA so long as it did not attempt to control their disposal practices. United States v. Arrowhead Refining Co., 35 E.R.C. 2065 (D. Minn. 1992).

A Note on Shrinking the Net of CERCLA Liability

Anyone found to be a PRP under sections 107(a)(1)-(4) will be potentially liable for paying for the entire costs of cleanup because of CERCLA's use of strict, joint and several liability, which is discussed in the next section. This makes the scope-of-coverage of the PRP provisions an issue of enormous importance. Deciding the issue has always pitted the statute's broad remedial goal of seeing to it "that those responsible should pay for clean up" against objections that extending liability to this or that class of persons is unfair. Over the years, EPA has responded to some of these objections administratively, by establishing settlement policies or interpretations of the statute that removed or mitigated the full effects of liability for particular persons who would otherwise be PRPs. Groups benefited in this way have included residential property owners, de micromis contributors, lending institutions that do not actively participate in their debtor's waste management decisions, persons offering to buy brownfield sites, and generators of municipal solid waste (MSW).

Enacting any legislation that makes truly substantial changes in CERCLA's statutory scheme has proven extremely divisive in the Congress ever since the

1986 SARA legislation. However, much like the EPA's development of targeted policies to address specific scope-of-coverage issues, Congress has enacted several targeted amendments aimed at scope-of-coverage questions, many times building on prior administrative decisions by EPA. Thus, in SARA in 1986, Congress enacted the innocent purchaser provisions, pages 379-380; in ACLLDIPA in 1996, the lending institutions provisions, page 390; in SREA in 1999, the recycling provisions, page 398; and in SBLRBRA in 2002, the bona fide prospective purchaser provisions, page 381, the de micromis provisions §107(o), page 398, the municipal solid waste exemption §107(p), see below, and provisions for owners of properties contiguous to a CERCLA facility (see §107(q)).

The municipal solid waste (MSW) exemption applies to the generators of MSW—including you, us, and all households throughout the United States. MSW is present at 25 percent of the sites on the NPL, and while EPA estimates that only 1 percent by weight is hazardous, its volume is so great that this 1 percent can generate significant problems (which is one reason RCRA addresses MSW as well as hazardous waste disposal). Besides, under the strict, joint and several liability scheme, MSW would not itself have to be very hazardous in order to provide a basis for private parties to seek contribution from generators of MSW.

Although EPA announced a municipal settlement policy in 1989, stating that EPA would generally not identify generators and transporters of MSW as PRPs, private parties are not so constrained. Not only have they sought to sue the municipalities who ultimately dispose of MSW, some also have sought to bring in homeowners and small private businesses whose wastes were among those picked up by municipal garbage services. In B.F. Goodrich v. Murtha, 840 F. Supp. 180 (D. Conn. 1993), the court refused to permit inclusion of some 1,100 homeowners and small business operators, because the allegation that each of them arranged for the disposal of hazardous substances was based solely on generic statistical studies showing the likely presence of hazardous substances in the homeowners' waste, rather than individualized proof. The 24 small Connecticut cities named as PRPs could be sued, however. B.F. Goodrich v. Murtha, 958 F.2d 1192 (2d Cir. 1992). See also B.F. Goodrich v. Betkoski, 99 F.3d 505 (2nd Cir. 1996) (holding that generators of even minuscule or nominal amounts of CERCLA hazardous substances can be held liable).

When it adopted the SBLRBRA in 2002, Congress restricted such actions by adding sections 107(o) & (p) to CERCLA. As noted above, section 107(o) adds a de micromis exemption that exempts generators of less than 110 gallons of liquid materials or 200 pounds of solid materials whose waste was disposed before April 1, 2001. Nongovernmental plaintiffs bringing contribution actions have the burden of proving that defendants do not qualify for this exemption. For wastes disposed after April 1, 2001, section 107(p) provides a blanket exemption for MSW generators who are residential property owners or small businesses or nonprofit organizations with no more than 100 full-time employees. This exemption includes protection from private party actions, and entitles exempt entities to recover attorneys' fees and other costs of defense should they be sued and the plaintiff be unable to prove the exemption does not apply. As with the de micromis exemption, the exemption does not apply if the President determines that the waste could contribute significantly to the cost of response actions or if the defendant impeded performance of a response action. In August 2003 EPA and the U.S. Department of Justice issued Interim Guidance on the Municipal Solid Waste

Exemption, available online at *http://www.epa.gov/compliance/resources/policies/ cleanup/superfund/interim-msw-exempt.pdf.*

For those who seek more sweeping changes to CERCLA, these modifications may be a distinctly mixed blessing because they seem to have defused pressure to further restrict CERCLA liability. As Professor Joel Mintz notes: "the SBLRBRA has left the key liability structure of CERCLA substantially intact. The new exemptions it establishes are, in general, only available to classes of parties with a relatively compelling equitable basis for liability relief. Moreover, these exemptions are crafted and conditioned in a way that provides an ample margin of safety for protecting the environment and human health." Joel A. Mintz, New Loopholes or Minor Adjustments?: A Summary and Evaluation of the Small Business Liability Relief and Brownfields Revitalization Act, 20 Pace Envtl. L. Rev. 405, 422 (2002).

PROBLEM EXERCISE: CERCLA LIABILITY

Chemspray is a pesticide formulator. Its wholly owned subsidiary is Chemairspray, an aerial spraying company. Both are controlled by Chemspray's sole stockholder, Jones. Fruitgrowers (Growers) contract with Chemairspray for aerial application of various pesticides, which Chemspray supplies. Chemspray buys its raw materials from large chemical companies, including Monsanto. Under the terms of their contracts, the Growers become owners of the pesticides to be applied to their farmland as soon as they contract for Chemairspray's services.

The airstrip used by Chemairspray and the adjoining land become a Superfund site because employees of Chemairspray sometimes spill pesticides on the runway and surrounding land while mixing and loading them onto the planes. They also rinse out the airplane's tanks after each flight to prepare for different pesticide runs. Hosing down the runways, or rain, then washes the pesticides onto the land and eventually into the groundwater near the airstrip.

Question One: The United States incurs response costs for cleaning up the contamination at the Superfund site. It brings an action under section 107 of CERCLA to recover its response costs against Chemairspray, Chemspray, and Jones. Discuss the liability of each of these defendants.

Question Two: After paying response costs, Chemairspray brings a contribution action against Growers and Monsanto. (On contribution actions, see section 113(f) and pages 416-434 below.) Chemairspray asserts that (a) Growers owned the pesticides that were spilled; and (b) Growers, some of whom visited the airstrip prior to planes taking off to spray their properties, were aware of Chemairspray's mixing, loading, and rinsing practices. Growers and Monsanto both move to dismiss the suit on the ground that they are not liable under section 107. What result?

Question Three: In order to hold Monsanto liable, what additional facts must Chemairspray prove as a result of the addition of section 107(o) to CERCLA?

4. Strict, Joint, and Several Liability

References to "strict, joint, and several liability" are nowhere to be found in CERCLA. Yet courts almost uniformly have found that CERCLA imposes strict, joint, and several liability on responsible parties. This result seems odd to some, particularly since express references to strict, joint, and several liability were deleted from the Senate bill that became CERCLA shortly before the Senate floor vote.

The only reference to a standard of liability is in the definitional section of CERCLA. Section 101(32) states that the "term 'liable' or 'liability' under this subchapter shall be construed to be the standard of liability which obtains under section 1321 of Title 33 [§311 of the federal Clean Water Act]." Philip C. Cummings, who was then chief counsel of the Senate Environment and Public Works Committee, explains that this was the final compromise prior to Senate passage of CERCLA. He tells the following story:

> The committee staff had argued that strict, joint, and several liability, explicitly referred to in S. 1480 and the November 18 substitute, was not radical but was the standard of liability under §311 of the CWA. Alan Simpson (R-Wyoming) was skeptical; if that were so, he countered, why not just say that. The committee staff agreed to put in the reference to the standard of liability under §311 that is now §101(32) of CERCLA. [Cummings, Completing the Circle, Envtl. Forum 11, 15 (Nov.-Dec. 1990).]

Early decisions interpreting section 101(32) found that it authorized imposition of strict, joint, and several liability unless a defendant could demonstrate that the harm caused by its wastes is divisible. United States v. Chem-Dyne Corp., 572 F. Supp. 802 (S.D. Ohio 1983); United States v. Bliss, 667 F. Supp. 1298 (E.D. Mo. 1987). This was the approach that had been followed by courts interpreting section 311 of the Clean Water Act and it is grounded in common law principles reflected in the Second Restatement of Torts.

Strict liability relieves the government of the obligation to prove that hazardous substances were released as the result of negligence or that the defendant's conduct was intentional and unreasonable. As experience with oil spill liability had demonstrated, strict liability was necessary if the government was to have a realistic chance of recovering response costs. Section 311's oil spill liability program provided for strict liability, premised on the notion that the burden of environmental injuries of this sort should be placed on the industry that created the risk.

While oil spills typically come from a single source, hazardous substances released at dump sites can be a complex mixture of wastes from many sources. The application of joint and several liability is designed to avoid disputes over apportionment of CERCLA liability from delaying the cleanup of environmental contamination. Recognizing that many dump sites had been abandoned or were owned by companies that were bankrupt or insolvent, Congress broadened the class of potentially liable parties in section 107 of CERCLA.

To ensure that those whose actions generated the hazardous substances would contribute to the costs of cleaning them up, and to prevent the government from having to bear the lion's share of cleanup expenses, section 107 extended strict, joint, and several liability to generators of hazardous substances. This has been one of the most controversial aspects of CERCLA. While the courts had been uncertain whether the government's abatement authority for cases of "imminent and substantial endangerment" under section 7003 of RCRA extended to generators of hazardous waste, section 107 of CERCLA imposed joint and several liability on generators who arranged for disposal of their waste. The question whether liability should be apportioned among generators was addressed in the following influential decision.

|| *O'Neil v. Picillo* ||
|| 883 F.2d 176 (1st Cir. 1989) ||

COFFIN, Senior Circuit Judge:

In July of 1977, the Picillos agreed to allow part of their pig farm in Coventry, Rhode Island, to be used as a disposal site for drummed and bulk waste. That decision proved to be disastrous. Thousands of barrels of hazardous waste were dumped on the farm, culminating later that year in a monstrous fire ripping through the site. In 1979, the state and the Environmental Protection Agency (EPA) jointly undertook to clean up the area. What they found, in the words of the district court, were massive trenches and pits "filled with free-flowing, multi-colored, pungent liquid wastes" and thousands of "dented and corroded drums containing a veritable potpourri of toxic fluids." O'Neil v. Picillo, 682 F. Supp. 706, 709, 725 (D.R.I. 1988).

This case involves the State of Rhode Island's attempt to recover the cleanup costs it incurred between 1979 and 1982 and to hold responsible parties liable for all future costs associated with the site. The state's complaint originally named thirty-five defendants, all but five of whom eventually entered into settlements totaling $5.8 million, the money to be shared by the state and EPA. After a month-long bench trial, the district court . . . found three of the remaining five companies jointly and severally liable [for costs already incurred plus any future costs].

Two of the three companies held liable at trial, American Cyanamid and Rohm and Haas, have taken this appeal. Both are so-called "generators" of waste, as opposed to transporters or site owners. See §107(a)(3), 42 U.S.C. §9607. Neither takes issue with the district court's finding that some of their waste made its way to the Picillo site. Rather, they contend that their contribution to the disaster was insubstantial and that it was, therefore, unfair to hold them jointly and severally liable for all of the state's past expenses not covered by settlements. They further contend that it was error to hold them liable for all future remedial work because the state has not demonstrated that such work ever will be necessary. . . .

. . . We . . . confine our discussion to appellants' arguments concerning the unfairness of holding them jointly and severally liable for the government's past and future cleanup costs.

JOINT AND SEVERAL LIABILITY

Statutory Background

It is by now well settled that Congress intended that the federal courts develop a uniform approach governing the use of joint and several liability in CERCLA actions. The rule adopted by the majority of courts, and the one we adopt, is based on the Restatement (Second) of Torts: Damages should be apportioned only if the *defendant* can demonstrate that the harm is divisible.

The practical effect of placing the burden on defendants has been that responsible parties rarely escape joint and several liability, courts regularly finding that where wastes of varying (and unknown) degrees of toxicity and migratory potential commingle, it simply is impossible to determine the amount of environmental harm caused by each party. It has not gone unnoticed that holding defendants jointly and severally liable in such situations may often result in defendants paying for more than their share of the harm. Nevertheless, courts have continued to impose joint and several liability on a regular basis, reasoning that where all of the contributing causes cannot fairly be traced, Congress intended for those proven at least partially culpable to bear the cost of the uncertainty.

In enacting the Superfund Amendments and Reauthorization Act of 1986 ("SARA"), Congress had occasion to examine this case law. Rather than add a provision dealing explicitly with joint and several liability, it chose to leave the issue with the courts, to be resolved as it had been—on a case-by-case basis according to the predominant "divisibility" rule first enunciated by the *Chem-Dyne* court. Congress did, however, add two important provisions designed to mitigate the harshness of joint and several liability. First, the 1986 Amendments direct the EPA to offer early settlements to defendants who the Agency believes are responsible for only a small portion of the harm, so-called de minimis settlements. See §122(g). Second, the Amendments provide for a statutory cause of action in contribution, codifying what most courts had concluded was implicit in the 1980 Act. See §113(f)(1). Under this section, courts "may allocate response costs among liable parties using such equitable factors as the court determines are appropriate." We note that appellants already have initiated a contribution action against seven parties before the same district court judge who heard this case.

While a right of contribution undoubtedly softens the blow where parties cannot prove that the harm is divisible, it is not a complete panacea since it frequently will be difficult for defendants to locate a sufficient number of additional, solvent parties. Moreover, there are significant transaction costs involved in bringing other responsible parties to court. If it were possible to locate all responsible parties and to do so with little cost, the issue of joint and several liability obviously would be of only marginal significance. We, therefore, must examine carefully appellants' claim that they have met their burden of showing that the harm in this case is divisible.

Divisibility

The district court issued two rulings on joint and several liability. First, the court held appellants jointly and severally liable for all of the state's past costs not covered by settlements, roughly $1.4 million including prejudgment interest. According to appellants, this money was spent exclusively on "removal" costs or "surface cleanup" (e.g., sampling the waste, contacting responsible parties, and ultimately, removing the barrels and contaminated soil), and not on remedying the alleged damage to groundwater and other natural resources ("remedial" costs). Second, the district court held appellants jointly and severally liable for all future removal costs to be incurred by the state, as well as for all cost-efficient remedial action the state (and EPA) may deem necessary after conducting further tests. The parties discuss the two holdings separately and we shall do likewise.

I. Past Costs

Appellants begin by stressing that the state's past costs involved only surface cleanup. They then argue that because it was possible to determine how many barrels of waste they contributed to the site, it is also possible to determine what proportion of the state's removal expenses are attributable to each of them simply by estimating the cost of excavating a single barrel. The EPA advances two reasons why this approach is incorrect. First, it claims that it was not possible to determine how many barrels were traceable to appellants, nor was it possible to determine how much of the contaminated soil removed by the state was attributable to each appellant, and therefore, that it is impossible to apportion the state's removal costs. Second, it argues that even if it were possible to determine what proportion of the state's removal costs are attributable to appellants, joint and several liability still would have been proper because the "harm to be apportioned is not the cost but the environmental contamination that prompts the response action." We shall discuss the EPA's two arguments in reverse order.

We state at the outset that we have some trouble with the EPA's second argument. Assuming the government ultimately undertakes remedial action to clean the groundwater in the area and then seeks to recover the costs of doing so, it will have in effect submitted two separate bills, one for the cost of removing the barrels and soil, and one for cleaning the water. We think it likely that the harm to the water will be indivisible, and therefore, that appellants could properly be held jointly and severally liable for the cost of this remedial action. But simply because the costs associated with cleaning the groundwater cannot be apportioned does not mean that we should decline to apportion the costs of removing the barrels and soil if those costs are in fact divisible. This would seem to follow from the basic common law principle that defendants not be held responsible for those costs traceable to others. We think that the EPA would have to accept as much. Nonetheless, the Agency adheres to the position that it is irrelevant whether or not the costs of removal can be apportioned.

The reason the Agency takes this position is not because the environmental harm that *actually occurred* was indivisible, but because the additional environmental harm that the government averted would have been indivisible had it occurred. This argument gives us pause because it appears to contravene the basic tort law principle that one pays only for the harm that was, and not for the harm that might have been.

Assume that it costs the government $1 million to remove all of the barrels from a site, but of this million, only $300,000 were spent removing the defendant's barrels. Also assume that had the barrels not been removed, the additional damage to the environment would have been $5 million and that this five million would not have been divisible. The government certainly would not take the position that it could recover $5 million in such a situation. Instead, it would ask only for the $1 million that it actually spent. Yet when it comes to apportioning that million, the Agency argues that we should look to whether the $5 million of averted harm would be divisible.

If we were to accept the EPA's "averted harm" argument, it appears that apportionment would be appropriate only in the highly unlikely event that (1) all of the barrels were empty and no further environmental harm was possible; (2) the individual barrels were sufficiently far apart that even if further spillage occurred, there would be no commingling of wastes and thus no difficulty determining whose waste caused what damage; or (3) every barrel contained precisely the same type of waste so that even if there was further spillage and commingling, the environmental harm could be apportioned according to the volumetric contribution of each defendant. As the EPA undoubtedly recognizes, it rarely, if ever, will be the case that one of these three conditions is present. As a practical matter, then, joint and several liability will be imposed in *every* case.

Because we believe Congress did not intend for joint and several liability to be imposed without exception, we are troubled by the practical implications of the Agency's argument, the more so because it seems to find no support in common law tort principles, which were to be one of our benchmarks in developing a uniform approach to govern the imposition of joint and several liability. At oral argument, the Agency did not claim, however, that its theory fit within the common law framework of joint and several liability, but instead, took the position that these CERCLA cases are not standard tort suits. Although we recognize that Congress deviated from certain tort principles, see New York v. Shore Realty Corp., 759 F.2d 1032, 1044 (2d Cir. 1985), we had thought that on the issue of joint and several liability we were to take our lead from evolving principles of common law. It would seem incumbent upon the Agency, then, to demonstrate that on this *particular* question of joint and several liability, Congress intended for us to abandon the common law.

Having said all that, we choose not to resolve the issue in this case. Had appellants met their burden of showing that the costs *actually incurred* by the state were capable of apportionment, we would have had no choice but to address the EPA's theory. But because we do not believe appellants have done so, we can, and do, choose to leave the question for another day. We turn now to the EPA's first contention that the state's removal costs are not capable of apportionment.

Removal Costs.   The state's removal efforts proceeded in four phases (0-3), each phase corresponding roughly to the cleanup of a different trench. The trenches were located in different areas of the site, but neither party has told us the distance between trenches. Appellants contend that it is possible to apportion the state's removal costs because there was evidence detailing (1) the total number of barrels excavated in each phase, (2) the number of barrels in each phase attributable to them, and (3) the total cost associated with each phase. In support of their argument, they point us to a few portions of the record, but for the most part are content to rest on statements in the district court's opinion. Specifically, appellants point to the following two sentences in the opinion: (1) "I find that [American Cyanamid] is responsible for ten drums of toxic hazardous material found at the site"; and (2) as to Rohm and Haas, "I accept the state's estimate [of 49 drums and 303 five-gallon pails]." Appellants then add, without opposition from the government, that the ten barrels of American Cyanamid waste discussed by the district court were found exclusively in Phase II, and that the 303 pails and 49 drums of Rohm and Haas waste mentioned by the court were found exclusively in Phase III. They conclude, therefore, that American Cyanamid should bear only a minute percentage of the $995,697.30 expended by the state during Phase II in excavating approximately 4,500 barrels and no share of the other phases, and that Rohm and Haas should be accountable for only a small portion of the $58,237 spent during Phase III in removing roughly 3,300 barrels and no share of the other phases. We disagree.

The district court's statements concerning the waste attributable to each appellant were based on the testimony of John Leo, an engineer hired by the state to oversee the cleanup. We have reviewed Mr. Leo's testimony carefully. Having done so, we think it inescapably clear that the district court did not mean to suggest that appellants had contributed only 49 and 10 barrels respectively, but rather, that those amounts were all that could be *positively* attributed to appellants.

Mr. Leo testified that out of the approximately 10,000 barrels that were excavated during the four phases, only "three to four hundred of the drums contained markings which could potentially be traced." This is not surprising considering that there had been an enormous fire at the site, that the barrels had been exposed to the elements for a number of years, and that a substantial amount of liquid waste had leaked and eaten away at the outsides of the barrels. Mr. Leo also testified that it was not simply the absence of legible markings that prevented the state from identifying the overwhelming majority of barrels, but also the danger involved in handling the barrels. Ironically, it was appellants themselves who, in an effort to induce Mr. Leo to lower his estimate of the number of barrels attributable to each defendant, elicited much of the testimony concerning the impossibility of accurately identifying all of the waste.

In light of the fact that most of the waste could not be identified, and that the appellants, and not the government, had the burden to account for all of this uncertainty, we think it plain that the district court did not err in holding them jointly and severally liable for the state's past removal costs. Perhaps in this situation the only way appellants could have demonstrated that they were limited contributors would have been to present specific evidence documenting the whereabouts of their waste at all times after it left their facilities. But far from doing so, appellants deny all knowledge of how their waste made its way to the site. Moreover, the government presented evidence that much of Rohm and Haas' waste found at the site came from its laboratory in Spring House, Pennsylvania and that during the relevant years, this lab generated over 2,000 drums of waste, all of which were consigned to a single transporter. Under these circumstances, where Rohm and Haas was entrusting substantial amounts of waste to a single transporter who ultimately proved unreliable, we simply cannot conclude, absent evidence to the contrary, that only a handful of the 2,000 or more barrels reached the site.

II. Future Liability

The district court held appellants jointly and severally liable for all further removal costs taken by the state, as well as for all necessary remedial actions. . . .

[A]ppellants contend that it was improper to hold them liable for future remedial action because the state has not shown that such work will ever be needed. They do not claim, however, that if remedial action is shown to be necessary, it would be a mistake to assume that their waste contributed to the damage. We see no problem with the court giving the state (and EPA) time to conduct further tests. If after conducting the necessary tests, the government concludes that there was in fact no harm to the area's groundwater, then appellants will have nothing to worry about. Moreover, the district court ruled that under section 107 of the Act, the state may take only such measures as are cost-efficient. Appellants, therefore, will have an opportunity to challenge the state's chosen remedial measures at the appropriate time.

Appellants have argued ably that they should not have been held jointly and severally liable. In the end, however, we think they have not satisfied the stringent burden placed on them by Congress. As to all other issues, we affirm substantially for the reasons set out by the district court. Appellants should now move on to their contribution action where their burden will be reduced and the district court will be free to allocate responsibility according to any combination of equitable factors it deems appropriate. Indeed, there might be no reason for the district court to place any burden on appellants. If the defendants in that action also cannot demonstrate that they were limited contributors, it is not apparent why all of the parties could not be held jointly and severally liable. However, we leave this judgment to the district court. See, e.g., Developments, Toxic Waste Litigation, 99 Harv. L. Rev. 1458, 1535-43 (1986).

Affirmed.

NOTES AND QUESTIONS

1. Although the court criticized EPA's "averted harm" theory of apportionment for the removal costs, it did not reach this issue because it held that the defendants had not met their burden of "showing that the costs actually incurred were capable of apportionment." Why was the court so reluctant to rule on this issue? What would American Cyanamid and Rohm and Haas have had to show in order to demonstrate that the removal costs actually incurred were capable of apportionment? Would the outcome in this case have been any different if the companies could prove that they had made arrangements to ship only 10 and 49 drums, respectively, to the site? What if they could prove they had only generated a total of 10 and 49 such drums, respectively?

2. As the court notes in *Picillo*, Congress did seek to ease the burden of joint and several liability when it amended CERCLA in 1986 by enacting a de minimis settlement provision in section 122(g) and by providing a statutory cause of action for contribution in section 113(f)(1). Suppose the 30 other responsible parties in this case had settled pursuant to the de minimis contributor provisions of section 122(g). What impact would this have had on the ability of American Cyanamid and Rohm and Haas, the appellants in *Picillo,* to recover in a contribution suit against the other responsible parties? See section 122(g).

3. The 30 other responsible parties in *Picillo* entered into settlements totaling $5.8 million, for an average of less than $200,000 per party. Do you think that the defendants American Cyanamid and Rohm and Haas were being penalized for their unwillingness to enter into settlements? What impact is joint and several liability likely to have on the willingness of defendants to settle? Will it make them more disposed to settlement for fear of being held liable for all the costs and damages or will it make them fight harder to avoid any liability?

4. Is it fair to hold a defendant responsible for all response costs in circumstances where it is not possible to demonstrate that the harm is divisible? Would it be reasonable to require the government to bear the burden of showing that the harm is not divisible? What impact would this have on the government's ability to recover CERCLA response costs and damages? If joint and several liability were abolished in CERCLA cases what would the government have to demonstrate in order to recover response costs?

5. During the debates over CERCLA reauthorization that culminated in 1986 with the enactment of SARA, the insurance industry and others lobbied for repeal of strict, joint, and several liability. Citing studies indicating that a great deal of money was being spent on CERCLA litigation, these companies argued that administrative costs would be lower and more funds would be available for actual cleanup if strict, joint, and several liability were abolished. How would you

respond to these arguments? What additional information, if any, would you like to have to evaluate them? Although the Reagan administration was not sympathetic to environmental regulation, its Justice Department successfully opposed efforts to repeal CERCLA's liability standard.

6. When provisions for victim compensation were dropped from the legislation that eventually became CERCLA, Congress added section 301(e)'s directive that a study be made of the adequacy of existing common law and statutory remedies. This study, known not surprisingly as the "section 301(e) study," identified three major barriers to recovery of personal injuries for exposure to hazardous substances: (1) the difficulty of proving causation, (2) statutes of limitations that may operate to bar suits before damage is discovered, and (3) the difficulty of apportioning damages among multiple tortfeasors. Senate Committee on Environment and Public Works, Injuries and Damages from Hazardous Wastes—Analysis and Improvement of Legal Remedies, Serial No. 97-12, 97th Cong., 2d Sess. (Sept. 1982). How does CERCLA's liability standard address these factors in the context of recovering response costs? Congress has been concerned that application of CERCLA's liability standard to recovery of damages for personal injury would open up the floodgates to enormous numbers of claims, many of which would be meritless. Thus, when it enacted SARA in 1986, Congress narrowly rejected a proposal for a pilot program to provide administrative compensation to victims of exposure to hazardous substances. It did, however, deal with the statute of limitations problem by adding section 309, which tolls state statutes of limitations in cases involving exposures to hazardous substances until injury is or should have been discovered.

7. The section 301(e) study concluded that strict liability standards were a useful mechanism for transferring the costs of environmental damage to those in the best position to reduce or eliminate environmental risks. The study found that strict liability would help ensure that those who engage in activities that inevitably create some environmental damage would bear the costs of such damage through insurance premiums and higher disposal costs. Considerable debate has continued concerning the question of how broadly the liability net should be cast.

8. Although there is broad support for Congress's judgment that parties involved in the creation and handling of toxic wastes should be held strictly liable for the costs of remediating the damage they cause, joint and several liability is far more controversial. In addition to expressing concerns about its fairness, Richard Epstein argues that joint and several liability actually dilutes the incentives for those handling toxic waste to take precautions to prevent releases because they know that ultimately liability may be broadly shared. Epstein, The Principles of Environmental Protection: The Case of Superfund, 2 Cato J. 9 (1982). Epstein notes that efforts by any one party to take greater precautions reduce the ultimate liability of all parties, while careless actions that result in additional releases only increase the damage that ultimately may be shared by all. Epstein, Two Fallacies in the Law of Joint Torts 73 Geo. L.J. 1377 (1985). How would you respond to these concerns?

9. In theory, joint and several liability should tend to reduce the transaction costs of CERCLA cleanups by reducing the importance of arguments over the relative degree of fault among PRPs. Some have argued, however, that by making any PRP potentially liable for the total costs of cleanup, joint and several liability actually increases transaction costs by making PRPs more resistant to settlement. During the reauthorization process that culminated in the enactment of SARA,

a number of industry lobbyists cited the transaction costs of early CERCLA litigation and the potential unfairness of joint and several liability in support of proposals to abolish it. What impact would abolition of joint and several liability have on EPA's ability to recover response costs from PRPs?

10. PRPs have continued to search for ways to avoid what they perceive to be the unfairness of joint and several liability. Having had little success in court, they have sought to appeal to the court of public opinion by publicizing cases in which small firms have been forced to shoulder heavy liabilities. See, e.g., Hamilton, Shouldering Toxic Waste Cleanup Costs, Wash. Post, Jan. 18, 1993, at D1.

11. As *Picillo* indicates, CERCLA does not preclude finding harm to be divisible, and thus apportioning it at the liability phase, but the statute places the burden of proving that apportionment is appropriate on the PRPs. This has proven to be a hard burden to meet because the same uncertainties about specifically whose waste has been involved in a release and the contribution of each PRP's waste to the harm that led to relaxing the evidentiary burden placed on the government in bringing a cleanup action now impairs any particular defendant's ability to show divisible harm. As for the showing that any PRP must make, CERCLA cases typically refer to section 433A of the Restatement (Second) of Torts, which states:

> 1. Damages for harm are to be apportioned among two or more causes where
>> (a) there are distinct harms, or
>> (b) there is a reasonable basis for determining the contribution of each cause to a single harm.
> 2. Damages for any other harm cannot be apportioned among two or more causes.

As one example of the effort to prove divisibility, consider a series of cases in which Alcan Aluminum Co. sought to show that the emulsion of water and oil that it had shipped to a site where a release subsequently occurred did not contribute at all to the cleanup costs, and thus that Alcan's liability was divisible at a level of zero. Alcan initially argued that the trace elements of metals and other substances in its emulsion were present at levels lower than the background levels already present in the environment. The federal court of appeals agreed that if Alcan could sustain this showing, its liability would be divisible. On remand, however, Alcan was unable to make this showing because some of the suspended substances in its emulsion, such as PCBs, were judged dangerous at whatever concentration they were present. In addition, the district court reasoned that even if the suspended materials in the emulsion were not hazardous, the emulsion itself "was a more aggressive solvent than either water . . . or oil . . . because [it had] a greater capacity to absorb contaminants than either water or oil alone. Alcan's emulsion, therefore, absorbed the contaminants at the site[] and facilitated their transport throughout [the release]. . . . " In other words, even if the hazardous substances in Alcan's emulsion themselves did not contribute to response costs at the sites (which the PCB and nickel did), the emulsion as a whole contributed to both the release and response costs. U.S. v. Alcan Aluminum Corp., 97 F. Supp. 2d 248, 270 (N.D.N.Y. 2000), aff'd, 315 F.3d 179 (2d Cir. 2003).

PRPs arguing for nonzero shares of liability have also found it difficult to meet the substantial burden of proof. For instance, at another site, a PRP argued that its waste had been dumped into a distinct area of the site and that a division based on volume of wastes at that location was appropriate. The district court, however, found the PRP had not sustained its burden on proving the first claim, because there just was not sufficient affirmative evidence to confirm it. It failed to sustain its burden on division by volume being appropriate because it had introduced no evidence of the "relative toxicity, migratory potential, degree of migration, and synergistic capacity" of the wastes at the site. New York v. Panex, 2004 WL 3008733 (W.D.N.Y. 2004).

5. Liability: Amount and Allocation

A. STANDARDS AND COSTS OF REMOVAL AND REMEDIATION

The cost of cleaning up facilities where there has been a release or threat of release of a hazardous substance ultimately determines the liability that must be allocated. Before addressing how the final bill for cleanup gets divided among all PRPs and others, this section provides an overview of how EPA and other parties determine what costs to incur.

The EPA has prepared general guidelines and protocols for dealing with CERCLA facilities. As required by statute, its National Contingency Plan (NCP) recognizes two kinds of responses: (1) short-term removal actions designed to alleviate immediate dangers to public health or the environment; and (2) longer-term remedial actions designed to provide a permanent remedy to the maximum extent practicable. §104. The government can order cleanups under section 106, or it can conduct the cleanup and then recover costs "not inconsistent with the NCP" from PRPs under section 107. Private parties also can clean up facilities and then recover costs "consistent with the NCP." §107(a)(4)(B).

Short-term emergency response costs averaged approximately $500,000 per incident as of 1998, and that figure probably has not changed very much. Hamilton & Viscusi, Calculating Risks 8 (1999). Estimates of per site expenditures for site cleanup range from $15 to $30 million, but EPA is increasingly concentrating on so-called megasites, where cost estimates exceed $100 million. In fiscal year 2005, for instance, EPA obligated 52 percent of its Superfund monies for cleanup efforts at just nine sites. EPA, FY 2004 Superfund Annual Report at A-1 (Sept. 2005). For the past 5 years, Congress has appropriated $1.3 billion for the Superfund program annually and EPA has obtained private commitments for response and remediation costs totaling another $0.9 billion. Id. at 8. EPA can take or compel these more expensive remedial actions only on sites that have been listed on the National Priority List (NPL). Citizens or state authorities can notify EPA of a site, which then receives a preliminary assessment to see if the site warrants further investigation. Those that do are inspected, and the most serious ones are then scored on EPA's Hazard Ranking System (HRS), an omnibus risk scale that EPA constructed for this purpose. Sites above an HRS cut-off level are placed on the NPL. As summarized by EPA, "[a]t the end of [fiscal year] 2004, 1,237 sites remained on the National Priorities List. Through [fiscal year] 2004, EPA had listed a total 1,529 sites (including 158 Federal facilities); proposed but not yet finalized 68 sites (including seven Federal facilities); and deleted 292 sites (including 13 Federal facilities). For a variety of reasons, sites may remain on the National Priorities List awaiting deletion (e.g., community interest, continued monitoring), well after cleanup construction has been completed. EPA has completed construction at more than 900 National Priorities List sites." Id. at 3.

Since the 1986 SARA amendments, section 121(a) has provided that:

> Remedial actions in which treatment [that] permanently and significantly reduces the volume, toxicity or mobility of the hazardous substances, pollutants and contaminants as a principal element are to be preferred over remedial actions not involving such treatment. The offsite transport and disposal of hazardous substances or contaminated materials without such treatment should be the least favored alternative remedial action where practicable treatment technologies are available.

The Act also instructs EPA to "select a remedial action that is protective of human health and the environment, that is cost-effective, and that utilizes permanent solutions and alternative treatment technologies to the maximum extent practicable." §121(b).

Section 121(d) specifies that the degree of cleanup to be required should be partially based on consideration of other environmental standards. It provides that remedial actions under CERCLA must assure "protection of human health and the environment" and "be relevant and appropriate under the circumstances." Remedial actions must also provide a level of cleanup that attains that required by any "legally applicable or relevant and appropriate . . . standard, requirement, criteri[on], or limitation under any Federal environmental law" and "any promulgated standard, requirement, criteri[on], or limitation under a State environmental or facility siting law that is more stringent than any Federal" provisions when identified by the state in a timely manner. §121(d)(2). Collectively, these standards are commonly referred to as ARARs.

Section 121(d) provides a number of exceptions to cleanup according to ARARs, but it also gives states the opportunity to challenge in federal court EPA decisions to deviate from them. In any event, if the state agrees to pay the incremental costs, it has the right to insist on cleanup that is more extensive than the option chosen by EPA. §121(f).

In 1990, EPA issued guidelines indicating that two principal criteria will drive cleanup decisions: protecting human health and the environment, and meeting ARARs. It stated that:

> [w]here ARARs do not exist or where the baseline risk assessment indicates that cumulative risks—due to additive or synergistic effects from multiple contaminants or multiple exposure pathways—make ARARs nonprotective, EPA will modify preliminary remediation goals, as appropriate, to be protective of human health and the environment. For cumulative risks due to noncarcinogens, EPA will set the remediation goals at levels for individual chemicals such that the cumulative effects of exposure to multiple chemicals will not result in adverse health effects. . . . EPA will set remediation goals for total risk due to carcinogens that represent an excess upperbound lifetime cancer risk to an individual to between 10^{-4} to 10^{-6} lifetime excess cancer risk. A cancer risk of 10^{-6} will serve as the point of departure for these remediation goals. . . . [A]ll preliminary remediation goals will be set so that they are protective for sensitive subpopulations, such as pregnant women and children. [55 Fed. Reg. 8666, 8713 (March 8, 1990).]

Remediation techniques to be used on the site are determined after an extensive analysis known as a Remedial Investigation/Feasibility Study (RI/FS) conducted by a government agency or a PRP. Once the RI/FS is complete, EPA conducts a hearing that produces a Record of Decision (ROD), embodying the data collected concerning the site, the evaluation of remedial options, submissions by PRPs, as well as the public, and the final remediation design. After the ROD, contracting for and constructing the remediation technologies can begin, which may lead ultimately to delisting the site.

The early execution of the statute was snarled in legal challenges, start-up difficulties, and hostility toward the program on the part of the executive branch. That hostility led to several confrontations between the Congress and EPA under President Reagan. EPA Administrator Anne Gorsuch Burford eventually resigned under a cloud of accusations that EPA was settling Superfund cases for low amounts. Clashes between Congress and EPA over access to documents concerning specific sites eventually produced the Supreme Court decision in Morrison v. Olson, 487 U.S. 654 (1988), which was based on the claim that Justice Department official Ted Olson had lied to Congress regarding advice he had given concerning the assertion of executive privilege as to some of those documents.

EPA's cleanup pace accelerated significantly in the 1990s. In July 2001, a major report commissioned by Congress found that EPA had designated 57 percent of the private sites on the NPL as "construction complete," indicating that threats to humans for toxic exposure had been removed. Resources for the Future, Superfund's Future: What Will It Cost? (July 2001). As of September, 2005, EPA reports 900 sites to be "construction complete." FY 2004 Superfund Annual Report at 18.

Private cost recovery has historically covered about 70 percent of total program costs, with the rest being covered by general appropriations and the Superfund tax. That tax expired in 1995, however. That fact plus a slow decline in private cost recovery has been drawing down program reserves and starving the program. From 1999 to 2003, EPA's inflation-adjusted Superfund expenditures declined about 11 percent, from $1.71 billion in 1999 to $1.52 billion in 2003. EPA Office of Inspector General Annual Superfund Report to Congress for Fiscal 2004 (Aug. 3, 2005). This has resulted in a scaling back of the pace of cleanup. Completed cleanups went from an average of about 75 a year from 1992 to 2000, to 47 in 2001, and estimates of 40 in 2004. Margaret Kriz, Superfund Slowdown, National Journal 1623, 1624 (June 1, 2002); EPA, FY 2004 Superfund Annual Report (Sept. 2005). The public/private balance in the program seems to be shifting somewhat as well. In fiscal year 2004, EPA reported spending $775 million on site cleanup, investigations, design of cleanup plans, and support for community, state, and local involvement while receiving private commitments of $680 million directed to future cleanup commitments and current cost recoveries. Superfund Annual Report at ii-iii. These figures compare current EPA expenditures to a mix of current and future private expenditures, but they may be showing a shift toward the public shouldering a larger share of the burden.

In recent years, the brownfields issue has been receiving a great deal of attention. Cities, developers, and the EPA have been searching for ways to facilitate the acquisition of less severely contaminated properties that are in locations suitable for redevelopment or in-filling. Use of previously contaminated urban sites have the potential for slowing urban sprawl, placing fewer demands on construction of new infrastructure, and accruing tax revenues to financially straped cities. The U.S. Conference of Mayors has estimated that developing the nation's brownfields could bring in between $880 million and $2.4 billion in tax revenues to cities, and also could generate nearly 550,000 new jobs, many of which would be filled by city dwellers. Hope Whitney, Cities and Superfund: Encouraging Brownfields Development, 30 Ecol. L.Q. 59, 65 (2003). Acquisition and development of these brownfields sites is slowed by several factors. Such sites tend to be more expensive to develop because of space constraints. Significant as well are the worries of potential purchasers that they face an uncertain cleanup liability. EPA initially responded administratively to try to reduce these uncertainties. In 1995, it announced that it would encourage greater use of "comfort letters," assuring owners that their properties would not be targets of further CERCLA actions. Noah, EPA Plans Rules to Limit Liability of Superfund Sites, Wall St. J., Jan. 26, 1995, at A5. The Agency also expressed willingness to enter into "prospective purchaser agreements," which provide similar assurances to potential buyers, contingent on performing specific cleanup tasks.

In 2002, Congress responded with legislation codifying a bona fide purchaser exemption from CERCLA liability. §107(r). See page 381, above. Under it, purchasers who undertake appropriate inquiry to discover the extent of contamination, who take steps to stop any continuing release and prevent future releases, and who cooperate fully with government and others undertaking response actions are exempted from PRP liability. If as a result of cleanup the property increases in value above the purchase price, the statute provides the government with a windfall profits lien in the amount of unrecouped cleanup costs, so that the bona fide purchaser does not profit at the expense of the taxpayers. The SBLRBRA also up a program of federal grants for brownfields development and provides other incentives for states, localities, and Indian tribes to revitalize brownfields.

In the normal course of events, the Superfund program will make some sites available for reuse simply through the results of the cleanup program. As of September 2005, EPA estimates that "244,000 acres of land [are] in use or made ready for reuse at non-Federal facility Superfund sites. Other Federal agencies identified over 400,000 acres as available for reuse. Twenty-one percent of this land is ready for residential use, and 79 percent is ready for nonresidential use. EPA also identified 420 sites with land ready for reuse, of which 226 sites are already in use." FY 2004 Superfund Annual Report, at 18. The EPA Inspector General says that the estimated number of brownfields sites ranges from 450,000 to 1 million. EPA Office of Inspector General Annual Superfund Report to Congress for Fiscal 2004 (Aug. 12, 2005).

As for sites that are subjected to removal and remediation, debate continues over the appropriate cleanup standards and the reasonable costs of remediation. One locus of debate concerns whether standards should vary according to expectations regarding how the facility and surrounding land will be used in the future. Analyzing a sample of 150 RODs involving nonfederal facilities, Jay Hamilton and Kip Viscusi calculated that 95 percent of the cancer risks found in facility risk assessments were generated by conservative assumptions that non-residential land use on and near sites would change to residential land uses in the future, with 63 percent of that risk coming from future on-site residential use. Hamilton & Viscusi, Calculating Risks 47 (1999). Findings such as these provide ammunition to those who urge consideration of other options, including future use restrictions, where residential use seems unlikely or undesirable, instead of expensive permanent remediation. Institutional controls such as fences and building restrictions in deeds have limitations, however. Richard Revesz and Richard Stewart have argued that such measures may not always be effective in restricting future access. Without permanent cleanup, expensive containment measures might have to continue indefinitely. Communities with disproportionate concentrations of poor or minority populations will suffer from the presence of contaminated sites that remain vacant, raising environmental justice concerns. Revesz & Stewart, The Superfund Debate in Analyzing Superfund: Economics, Science and Law 15 (R. Revesz & R. Stewart eds., 1995).

The Hamilton and Viscusi study also made estimates of the cost per cancer case avoided at CERCLA sites. They found that

> [o]verall, at the 150 sites for which there are both risk and cost information . . . the mean cost per cancer case averted is $3.0 million. . . . Yet the concentration of risks and costs makes this mean figure potentially misleading. The median cost per cancer case averted is $388 million, without factoring in likely cost growth at sites. The cost per cancer case averted ranges widely from less than $20,000 to over $1 billion. . . . Overall, 101 out of the 145 sites with [cost data] had costs per cancer case averted above $100 million. [Hamilton & Viscusi, Calculating Risks 16 (1999).]

Among the widely shared frustrations with CERCLA has been the realization that remediation technologies that truly restore contaminated groundwater to a condition suitable for beneficial use are much more elusive than supposed. Many of the difficulties are attributable to nonaqueous phase liquids that are heavier than water and can be absorbed into solid layers surrounding underground aquifers, where they remain highly resistant to removal and yet capable of continuing to contaminate those aquifers through molecular absorption back into the aquifers. Ferris & Rees, CERCLA Remedy Selection: Abandoning the Quick Fix Mentality, 21 Ecology L.Q. 785, 829-835 (1994). An EPA study of 19 sites where groundwater has been subject to continuous pumping and treating for up to a decade found that although considerable quantities of contaminants had been removed, there had been "little success in reducing concentrations to target levels." Abelson, Inefficient Remediation of Ground-Water Pollution, 250 Science 733 (1990).

Another study by the National Research Council found that it might take 100 to 200 years of pumping and treating to restore water quality to acceptable levels in certain aquifers. NRC, Groundwater and Soil Contamination: Toward Compatible Science, Policy and Public Perceptions (1990). Philip Abelson points out that a large portion of the more than 14 billion pounds of perchloroethylene (PCE) and 12 billion pounds of trichloroethylene (TCE) that were used by dry cleaners and machine shops between 1945 and 1984 may be contaminating groundwater. Noting that just one barrel of TCE could contaminate 10 billion gallons of water at the level of 5 ppb (the MCL under the Safe Drinking Water Act), Abelson suggests that the "present practical solution for water supplies may be to treat water at the time it enters the supply system." Abelson, supra. Others hold out hope that advances in treatment technology will make remediation of contaminated groundwater more effective and less expensive in the future. E.g., Roush, Building a Wall Against Toxic Waste, 269 Science 473 (1995) (reporting experimental use of a "reactive wall" of iron filings that is expected to react with TCE, PCE, and other chemicals to break down contamination plumes).

B. ALLOCATION OF LIABILITY

As already noted, Congress sought to ease the burden of joint and several liability when it amended CERCLA in 1986 by adding a de minimis settlement provision in section 122(g) and by providing a statutory cause of action for contribution in section 113(f). Section 122(g) seeks to encourage prompt settlements between the government and PRPs that contributed small amounts of substances whose toxic or other hazardous effects are minimal in comparison with the contributions of others. EPA's settlement policy presumes that de minimis contributors should pay some premium over and above what their proportionate contribution to the site would dictate in return for receiving an early settlement that absolves them of liability for cost overruns or potential future response costs. In United States v. Cannons Engineering Corporation, 899 F.2d 79 (1st Cir. 1990), the First Circuit approved a de minimis settlement reached between EPA and 300 generators who agreed to pay 160 percent of their projected share of all past and future response costs based on calculations of the amount of waste by volume each had contributed to a site. The court rejected the argument of nonsettling PRPs that EPA should have based its apportionment of liability on the relative toxicity of the wastes rather than on each party's volumetric share. The court also approved EPA's policy of encouraging prompt settlements by seeking greater contributions from parties who refuse initial settlement offers.

Following the enactment of section 122(g), EPA did not move quickly to pursue settlements with de minimis contributors. See Kornhauser & Revesz, De Minimis Settlements under Superfund: An Empirical Study, in Analyzing Superfund: Economics, Science, and Law 187 (Revesz & Stewart eds., 1995) (study finding that EPA had underutilized de minimis settlements prior to 1992).

More recently, EPA has taken steps to settle more quickly with de minimis PRPs. During the first 13 years of CERCLA administration, EPA had settled with approximately 6,000 de minimis PRPs. In 1994, EPA announced it would expand its efforts to reach de minimis settlements. Through the end of 1998, it had settled an additional 12,000 de minimis shares. EPA, Superfund Reforms Annual Report 20 (1999). In the 2002 SBLRBRA legislation, Congress authorized expedited and reduced settlements to people who lack the ability to pay or who have limited ability to pay.

In addition, EPA has announced new policies to pick up part of the so-called orphan shares, the liabilities of entities who are insolvent or unidentifiable. Through the end of FY 2003, EPA had made 160 offers of orphan share contribution totaling approximately $235 million. EPA, Superfund Reforms Round 3-11: Orphan Share Compensation. EPA has also been trying to speed up the cost allocation process by experimenting with neutral parties establishing nonbinding allocations of responsibility among PRPs. EPA then offers settlements to PRPs according to the terms of the neutral allocation. These are all measures designed to reduce the transaction costs of making final determinations of liability shares.

Section 113(f) of CERCLA now authorizes private parties to seek contribution from other PRPs, but it bars contribution from parties who have settled with the government for matters addressed in the settlement. This not only provides a degree of liability certainty for settling PRPs, but it also further enhances EPA's leverage in negotiating settlements by diminishing the number of PRPs subject to later contribution actions by the nonsettlers. For those PRPs who have incurred liability and who are not protected from contribution actions, the contribution action under section 113(f) constitutes the last act of the CERCLA drama, as a PRP who believes it has paid a greater than fair share of the cleanup costs brings suit to shift some of those costs to others. A court hearing such a contribution suit is authorized to "allocate response costs among liable parties using such equitable factors as the court determines are appropriate." Consequently, contribution actions are as much about what equitable formula will be used to distribute costs as they are about the facts.

As the Superfund program has matured, the nature of the litigation it has spawned has matured as well. Early on, litigation concentrated on the front-end issues—the program's constitutionality, the nature of joint and several liability, the scope of defenses to PRP status, and the consistency of the costs incurred with the national contingency plan. While these front-end issues still are being litigated, many have been resolved and the parties have moved onto the back end of the process—the allocation of responsibility among the numerous PRPs associated with many of the complicated Superfund sites. As we have seen, the Superfund statute throws a broad joint and several liability net over PRPs, but after cleanup costs have been incurred, section 113(f) does provide the PRPs the opportunity to allocate responsibility among themselves. In recent years, unresolved issues concerning these actions for contribution among the jointly liable PRPs have been producing the next wave of Superfund litigation. See Williams D. Evans, Jr., Turn Out the Lights, The Party's Over: The Emerging Consensus on CERCLA Salvage Litigation Issues, 29 Envtl. L. Rep. 10203 (1999) (noting the relative shift from litigation over the liability of PRPs to the secondary suits for contribution among liable PRPs).

As litigation resolved more and more of the front-end responsibilities of PRPs, an increasing number of site cleanups have been performed on a voluntary basis. Typically, a coalition of the willing PRPs—understanding that they would not escape liability—band together to remediate the site in compliance with EPA guidelines, sometimes after EPA or a state agency has issued an administrative order finding the site to be in violation, but prior to any lawsuit having been commenced, and prior to EPA or the state having incurred any cleanup costs themselves. Once significant costs have been incurred by the "volunteer" PRPs, these coalitions then institute a section 113(f) action against nonparticipating PRPs to allocate final cost responsibility according to a loose set of equitable principles the courts have been articulating and applying on a case-by-case basis. (For more on the allocation process, see the *Vertac* decision and notes following, pages 423-430.) While this pattern of voluntary cleanup followed by a contribution action has been used many times since section 113(f) has been written into Superfund in 1986, in 2004 the Supreme Court caught many Superfund observers by surprise when it issued the following decision.

Cooper Industries, Inc. v. Aviall Services, Inc.
543 U.S. 157 (2004)

JUSTICE THOMAS delivered the opinion of the Court.

Section 113(f)(1) of the Comprehensive Environmental Response, Compensation, and Liability Act of 1980 (CERCLA) allows persons who have undertaken efforts to clean up properties contaminated by hazardous substances to seek contribution from other parties liable under CERCLA. Section 113(f)(1) specifies that a party may obtain contribution "during or following any civil action" under CERCLA §106 or §107(a). The issue we must decide is whether a private party who has not been sued under §106 or §107(a) may nevertheless obtain contribution under §113(f)(1) from other liable parties. We hold that it may not.

I

Under CERCLA the Federal Government may clean up a contaminated area itself, see §104, or it may compel responsible parties to perform the cleanup, see §106(a). In either case, the Government may recover its response costs under §107, the "cost recovery" section of CERCLA. . . .

After CERCLA's passage, litigation also ensued over the separate question whether a private entity that had been sued in a cost recovery action (by the Government or by another PRP) could obtain contribution from other PRPs. As originally enacted in 1980, CERCLA contained no provision expressly providing for a right of action for contribution . . .

Congress subsequently amended CERCLA in the Superfund Amendments and Reauthorization Act of 1986 (SARA), 100 Stat. 1613, to provide an express cause of action for contribution, codified as CERCLA §113(f)(1):

> "Any person may seek contribution from any other person who is liable or potentially liable under section 9607(a) of this title, during or following any civil action under section 9606 of this title or under section 9607(a) of this title. Such claims shall be brought in accordance with this section and the Federal Rules of Civil Procedure, and shall be governed by Federal law. In resolving contribution claims, the court may allocate response costs among liable parties using such equitable factors as the court determines are appropriate. Nothing in this subsection shall diminish the right of any person to bring an action for contribution in the absence of a civil action under section 9606 of this title or section 9607 of this title."

SARA also created a separate express right of contribution, §113(f)(3)(B), for "[a] person who has resolved its liability to the United States or a State for some or all of a response action or for some or all of the costs of such action in an administrative or judicially approved settlement." In short, after SARA, CERCLA provided for a right to cost recovery in certain circumstances, §107(a), and separate rights to contribution in other circumstances, §§113(f)(1), 113(f)(3)(B).

II

This case concerns four contaminated aircraft engine maintenance sites in Texas. Cooper Industries, Inc., owned and operated those sites until 1981, when it sold them to Aviall Services, Inc. Aviall operated the four sites for a number of years. Ultimately, Aviall discovered that both it and Cooper had contaminated the facilities when petroleum and other hazardous substances leaked into the ground and ground water through underground storage tanks and spills.

Aviall notified the Texas Natural Resource Conservation Commission (Commission) of the contamination. The Commission informed Aviall that it was violating state environmental laws, directed Aviall to clean up the site, and threatened to pursue an enforcement action if Aviall failed to undertake remediation. Neither the Commission nor the EPA, however, took judicial or administrative measures to compel cleanup.

Aviall cleaned up the properties under the State's supervision, beginning in 1984. Aviall sold the properties to a third party in 1995 and 1996, but remains contractually responsible for the cleanup. Aviall has incurred approximately $5 million in cleanup costs; the total costs may be even greater. In August 1997, Aviall filed this action against Cooper in the United States District Court for the Northern District of Texas, seeking to recover cleanup costs. The original complaint asserted a claim for cost recovery under CERCLA §107(a), a separate claim for contribution under CERCLA §113(f)(1), and state-law claims. Aviall later amended the complaint, combining its two CERCLA claims into a single, joint CERCLA claim. That claim alleged that, pursuant to §113(f)(1), Aviall was entitled to seek contribution from Cooper, as a PRP under §107(a), for response costs and other liability Aviall incurred in connection with the Texas facilities. Aviall continued to assert state-law claims as well.

Both parties moved for summary judgment, and the District Court granted Cooper's motion. The court held that Aviall, having abandoned its §107 claim, sought contribution only under §113(f)(1). The court held that §113(f)(1) relief was unavailable to Aviall because it had not been sued under CERCLA §106 or §107. Having dismissed Aviall's federal claim, the court declined to exercise jurisdiction over the state-law claims.

A divided panel of the Court of Appeals for the Fifth Circuit affirmed. The majority, relying principally on the "during or following" language in the first sentence of §113(f)(1), held that "a PRP seeking contribution from other PRPs under §113(f)(1) must have a pending or adjudged §106 administrative order or §107(a) cost recovery action against it." The dissent reasoned that the final sentence of §113(f)(1), the saving clause, clarified that the federal common-law right to contribution survived the enactment of §113(f)(1), even absent a §106 or §107(a) civil action.

On rehearing en banc, the Fifth Circuit reversed by a divided vote, holding that §113(f)(1) allows a PRP to obtain contribution from other PRPs regardless of whether the PRP has been sued under §106 or §107. The court held that "[s]ection 113(f)(1) authorizes suits against PRPs in both its first and last sentence[,] which states without qualification that 'nothing' in the section shall 'diminish' any person's right to bring a contribution action in the absence of a section 106 or section 107(a) action." The court reasoned in part that "may" in §113(f)(1) did not mean "may only." Three members of the en banc court dissented for essentially the reasons given by the panel majority.

III

A

Section 113(f)(1) does not authorize Aviall's suit. The first sentence, the enabling clause that establishes the right of contribution, provides: "Any person *may* seek contribution . . . *during or following* any civil action under section 9606 of this title or under section 9607(a) of this title," 42 U.S.C. §9613(f)(1) (emphasis added). The natural meaning of this sentence is that contribution may only be sought subject to the specified conditions, namely, "during or following" a specified civil action.

Aviall answers that "may" should be read permissively, such that "during or following" a civil action is one, but not the exclusive, instance in which a person may seek contribution. We disagree. First, as just noted, the natural meaning of "may" in the context of the enabling clause is that it authorizes certain contribution actions—ones that satisfy the subsequent specified condition—and no others.

Second, and relatedly, if §113(f)(1) were read to authorize contribution actions at any time, regardless of the existence of a §106 or §107(a) civil action, then Congress need not have included the explicit "during or following" condition. In other words, Aviall's reading would render part of the statute entirely superfluous, something we are loath to do. Likewise, if §113(f)(1) authorizes contribution actions at any time, §113(f)(3)(B), which permits contribution actions after settlement, is equally superfluous. There is no reason why Congress would bother to specify conditions under which a person may bring a contribution claim, and at the same time allow contribution actions absent those conditions.

The last sentence of §113(f)(1), the saving clause, does not change our conclusion. That sentence provides: "Nothing in this subsection shall diminish the right of any person to bring an action for contribution in the absence of a civil action under section 9606 of this title or section 9607 of this title." 42 U.S.C. §9613(f)(1). The sole function of the sentence is to clarify that §113(f)(1) does nothing to "diminish" any cause(s) of action for contribution that may exist independently of §113(f)(1). In other words, the sentence rebuts any presumption that the express right of contribution provided by the enabling clause is the exclusive cause of action for contribution available to a PRP. The sentence, however, does not itself establish a cause of action; nor does it expand §113(f)(1) to authorize contribution actions not brought "during or following" a §106 or §107(a) civil action; nor does it specify what causes of action for contribution, if any, exist outside §113(f)(1). Reading the saving clause to authorize §113(f)(1) contribution actions not just "during or following" a civil action, but also before such an action, would again violate the settled rule that we must, if possible, construe a statute to give every word some operative effect.

Our conclusion follows not simply from §113(f)(1) itself, but also from the whole of §113. As noted above, §113 provides two express avenues for contribution: §113(f)(1) ("during or following" specified civil actions) and §113(f)(3)(B) (after an administrative or judicially approved settlement that resolves liability to the United States or a State). Section 113(g)(3) then provides two corresponding 3-year limitations periods for contribution actions, one beginning at the date of judgment, §113(g)(3)(A), and one beginning at the date of settlement, §113(g)(3)(B). Notably absent from §113(g)(3) is any provision for starting the limitations period if a judgment or settlement never occurs, as is the case with a purely voluntary cleanup. The lack of such a provision supports the conclusion that, to assert a contribution claim under §113(f), a party must satisfy the conditions of either §113(f)(1) or §113(f)(3)(B).

Each side insists that the purpose of CERCLA bolsters its reading of §113(f)(1). Given the clear meaning of the text, there is no need to resolve this dispute or to consult the purpose of CERCLA at all. As we have said: "[I]t is ultimately the provisions of our laws rather than the principal concerns of our legislators by which we are governed." Oncale v. Sundowner Offshore

Services, Inc., 523 U.S. 75, 79 (1998). Section 113(f)(1), 100 Stat. 1647, authorizes contribution claims only "during or following" a civil action under §106 or §107(a), and it is undisputed that Aviall has never been subject to such an action. Aviall therefore has no §113(f)(1) claim.

B

[The Court then declines to address the dissent's suggestion that Aviall may recover costs under §107(a)(4)(B) even though it is a PRP, because this issue was not addressed in the court below. It also declines to decide whether Aviall has an implied right to contribution under §107 or whether a §107 cost recovery action by Aviall may seek some form of liability other than joint and several].

NOTES AND QUESTIONS

1. How will this decision affect incentives for voluntary action to remediate contaminated properties? Aviall argued strenuously that it would discourage such cleanups by foreclosing section 113 contribution actions by parties who have not been subject to formal cleanup orders and perhaps even the filing of a law suit. In his opinion for the Court, Justice Thomas refuses to discuss how the decision comports with CERCLA's goal of encouraging remediation because he feels that the text of the statute compels the result he reaches.

2. This decision will have a much smaller impact on the practical functioning of Superfund cleanups if the problem turns out simply to be that Aviall prematurely dropped its claim to bring an action under section 107 rather than section 113. Section 107(a)(4)(B) provides that PRPs "shall be liable for . . . any . . . necessary costs of response incurred by any other person consistent with the national contingency plan . . ." Prior to the SARA Amendments, courts had interpreted this provision to authorize a right of contribution when one or some PRPs incur cleanup costs and then seek contribution from the remaining PRPs. In fact, in dissent in *Aviall,* Justice Ginsburg, joined by Justice Stevens, argued that the Supreme Court in Key Tronic v. United States, 511 U.S. 809 (1994), had found an implied right of contribution that a PRP may use to bring a cost recovery action under section 107(a)(4)(B). In *Key Tronic,* the Court rejected a PRP's efforts to obtain reimbursement of attorney's fees by holding that they were not "necessary costs of response" within the meaning of section 107(a)(4)(B). Justice Thomas, however, views *Key Tronic* differently, noting that it failed to address "the relevance, if any, of Key Tronic's status as a PRP or confront the relationship between sections 107 and 113." In Justice Ginsburg's view, section 107 impliedly authorizes a cause of action for contribution and section 113(f) provides the standard for allocating response costs among liable parties using such equitable factors as the court determines are appropriate.

In declining to reach this issue, Justice Thomas noted that the First, Second, Third, Fourth, Sixth, Seventh, Tenth, and Eleventh Circuit Courts of Appeals decisions have held that a private party that is itself a PRP may not pursue a section 107(a) action against other PRPs for joint and several liability. One reason for these results is that section 107(a)(4)(B) apparently authorizes a PRP who has incurred costs to recover all of them from the other PRPs, rather than being expressly limited to some appropriate share of those costs. Section 107 actions in these circuits have been allowed only when brought by an innocent party who has incurred response costs. At the same time, however, these decisions all ruled against the use of section 107 as the basis for a contribution action when section 113(f) was being read more broadly than the decision in *Aviall*, and thus that section provided a basis for the contribution action that almost everyone thinks is appropriate.

A post-*Aviall* decision addressing the scope of section 107 is Vine Street LLC v. Keeling, 362 F. Supp. 2d 754, 764 (E.D. Tex. 2005). In *Vine Street*, the district court distinguished cases that prevented PRPs from bringing suit under section 107 on the grounds that in those cases, the PRPs were bringing section 107 and 113 suits concurrently. They had all been sued under section 106 or 107, making their section 113 claim valid. By suing under section 107, the PRPs were trying to take advantage of more favorable statutory terms (more cost recovery and longer statute of limitations). The PRP in *Vine Street* had not been sued under section 106 or 107 and therefore could not bring a section 113 suit, just like Aviall. The court ruled that the defendant was akin to an innocent defendant because neither had been sued under section 106 or 107.

3. Another situation that after *Aviall* may present PRPs with problems in pursuing contribution arises when EPA elects to remediate sites under RCRA's corrective action program rather than under CERCLA. In that case, there is never any question of a Superfund action under section 106 or 107 being brought. RCRA, however, contains no contribution provisions at all, see Meghrig v. KFC Western, Inc., 516 U.S. 479 (1996), so the sole recourse of the party subject to the corrective action order will be to attempt to sue PRPs under section 107 for cost recovery. How should the lower courts now resolve the question of whether a PRP who is acting pursuant to an RCRA correction action order can utilize section 107 to seek contribution?

4. These are not the only questions that *Aviall* has generated. One industry attorney has commented that "the Supreme Court opened up a slew of niggling issues" with its decision. District Court Allows Settling Polluter Group Suits Under *Aviall* Ruling, Inside EPA 4 (July 29, 2005). One such issue was whether all of the PRPs in a group that is settling its Superfund liability had to be sued in order to then be able to use section 113(f)'s contribution action, or if it suffices that only some of them had been sued. In Boarhead Farm Agreement Group v. Advanced Environmental Technology Corp., 381 F. Supp. 2d 427 (E.D. Pa. 2005), the first district court to face the issue ruled that only some of the PRPs need to have been sued. Another unanswered question is whether an administrative action by EPA under section 106 qualifies as a "civil action" for purposes of section 113(f). In note 5 of the opinion, the *Aviall* court declined to answer that question.

5. In cases where contribution actions do go forward, the court faces the task of determining an appropriate allocation of response costs among the numerous PRPs, some of whom are generators, some past land owners or operators, some transporters, and some present owners and operators, each with very different equitable considerations arguably appropriate. In the case that follows, the district court was trying to bring down the curtain on one of the oldest pieces of Superfund litigation, a case which had actually been begun by the government under RCRA and the CWA prior to CERCLA's enactment. The CERCLA counts were added soon after the bill became law. There are now roughly a dozen reported decisions in the district court and the Eighth Circuit Court of Appeals involving *Vertac*. Together, they trace the trajectory of CERCLA

litigation as the statute and practice under it have matured over the years. *Vertac*'s reaching the allocation of liability stage provides a good signal that the part of the CERCLA cleanup and liability scheme under the most intense litigation pressure has moved from initial questions of constitutionality, retroactivity, and definitions of PRPs to the final allocation-of-liability issues.

Although the decision below was vacated, U.S. v. Hercules, Inc., 247 F.3d 706 (8th Cir. 2001), because the court of appeals ruled the district court judge had misapplied the law regarding divisibility of harm, an issue for the liability phase of the case, its discussion of contribution remains an excellent example of this last phase of CERCLA litigation. In reading the following excerpt, note the many different considerations each party uses to urge adoption of an allocation favorable to it.

United States v. Vertac Chemical Corp.
79 F. Supp. 2d 1034 (E.D. Ark. 1999)

GEORGE HOWARD, JR., District Judge.

. . . As can be expected, Hercules and Uniroyal each advance different arguments. On the one hand, Uniroyal relies primarily on the relative involvement of the liable parties. It contends that its role as an arranger was minimal. It asserts that the Court should use a volumetric calculation, which can be calculated based on the evidence presented at the hearing. Based on Uniroyal's calculations, a volumetric calculation would result in an initial allocation of 1.58% to Uniroyal and 98.42% to Hercules. In addition to its volumetric calculation, Uniroyal argues that it is then entitled to a "downward departure." Hercules, on the other hand, attempts to divvy up the site, so that it ends up with an allocation in which Uniroyal would be about 70 percent liable. In particular, Hercules advances a division in which it has no connection with the drummed waste, the EPA's single largest expenditure.

Hercules' attempt to limit its responsibility for response costs to about 30 percent is, on its face, absurd. Hercules operated or owned the plant from 1961 to 1976. It had the greatest presence, by far, of any of the responsible parties. The problem is that Uniroyal and Hercules are left "holding the bag" for Vertac, who at least arguably caused the greatest amount of harm.

Resolution of contribution claims under CERCLA is governed by 42 U.S.C. §9613(f). It provides: "In resolving contribution claims, the court may allocate response costs among liable parties using such equitable factors as the court determines are appropriate." 42 U.S.C. §9613(f)(1). The statute does not limit the courts to any particular factors, but grants the court "broad discretion to balance the equities in the interest of justice." Bedford Affiliates v. Sills, 156 F.3d 416, 429 (2d Cir. 1998). In an attempt to find an equitable resolution to what is at times a complex problem, the courts have employed a number of approaches. See David G. Mandelbaum, Toward a Superfund Cost Allocation Principle, 3 Envtl. Law. 117, 124 (1996) (noting the difficulty in allocating costs). Most have looked to what are referred to as the "Gore factors," proposed by then Senator Albert Gore as a method to apportion joint and several liability. These factors are:

(1)   the ability of the parties to demonstrate that their contribution to a discharge, release, or disposal of a hazardous waste can be distinguished;

(2)   the amount of hazardous waste involved;
(3)   the degree of toxicity of the hazardous waste;
(4)   the degree of involvement of the parties in the generation, transportation, treatment, storage, or disposal of the hazardous waste;
(5)   the degree of care exercised by the parties with respect to the hazardous waste concerned, taking into account the characteristics of such hazardous waste; and
(6)   the degree of cooperation by the parties with Federal, State, or local officials to prevent any harm to the public health or the environment.

The factors are neither an exhaustive nor exclusive list. . . . The primary emphasis is placed on the harm each party causes the environment and care on the part of the parties. . . .

Divisibility of harm is not a defense to a contribution action under §113(f), although the Court may consider separate harms caused by different parties in allocating costs. . . . But see Acushnet Co. v. Mohasco Corp., 191 F.3d 69, 77 (1st Cir. 1999) (party may avoid liability for response costs in contribution action "if it demonstrates that its share of hazardous waste deposited at the site constitutes no more than background amounts of such substances in the environment and cannot concentrate with other wastes to produce higher amounts.")

Hercules seeks to divide the Site into various areas, or "harms." The Court has previously rejected Hercules' attempt to divide the Site into "mini-sites." The Court, however, is not persuaded that the "mini-sites" represent "distinct" harms on which the Court can allocate costs. The history of this site reveals a commingling of the wastes. Furthermore, Hercules' proposed division is, at best, arbitrary, and couched in terms to reduce Hercules' liability. As the First Circuit recently noted in rejecting a quantitative minimum at which a party could be held responsible, the task of tracing chemical waste to particular sources in particular amounts "is often technologically infeasible due to the fluctuating quantity and varied nature of the pollution at a site over the course of many years." Acushnet Co. v. Mohasco Corp., 191 F.3d at 77.

The problem noted in Acushnet is illustrated by Hercules' argument regarding the costs associated with the incineration of the drummed wastes. When the State ordered Vertac to shut down in the summer of 1979, there were approximately 2700 drums of 2,4,5-T still bottoms stored on-site. Workers spent much of the summer placing those 55-gallon drums into larger drums, shoveling up contaminated soil, and placing that soil into the larger overpack drums. When Vertac resumed production in the fall of 1979, it produced only 2,4-D and eventually accumulated about 26,000 drums of 2,4-D waste. This waste was accumulated between 1979 and 1986, when Hercules had no involvement or presence at the Site.

Hercules argues that no dioxin is produced in the 2,4-D manufacturing process. Thus, according to Hercules, none of the 2,4-D waste drums should have contained dioxin. Furthermore, Hercules presented expert testimony to demonstrate that there should not have been cross contamination of the 2,4-D waste with the 2,4,5-T wastes. According to Hercules, none of the 2,4-D wastes should have had any detectable concentration of dioxin from the fall of 1979 onward, when Vertac ceased manufacturing 2,4,5-T.

Hercules states that it had no involvement in management of the drummed wastes and should not be responsible for the costs of incineration of the drummed waste. Of course, Uniroyal, as an arranger, also did not have any involvement.

The Court has previously found that there was cross-contamination and commingling of the wastes at the entire Site. During the years Hercules operated the plant, Hercules generated hazardous substances which were disposed of at the Site through "leaks, spills, drum burial, and other releases into the environment. . . . The Hercules operation resulted in contamination of soil, ground-water, equipment, tanks, sewer lines, the sewage treatment plants, and sediments and flood plains in Rocky Branch Creek and Bayou Meto." United States v. Vertac Chemical Corp., 966 F. Supp. 1491, 1494-95 (E.D. Ark. 1997).

Furthermore, as noted in previous decisions, dioxin was found in the 2,4-D wastes. See United States v. Vertac Chemical Corp., 33 F. Supp. 2d at 780. The Court will not second guess the studies and find that they are incorrect or unreliable, as requested by Hercules. Additionally, Hercules admitted that some degree of dioxin contamination found in the 2,4-D drums could have come from contaminated soil being placed in the drums. That soil was contaminated by years of production.

Thus, the Court is not persuaded that Hercules has established "separate harms" on which to allocate responsibility.

The Court has considered carefully the arguments of the parties, the voluminous record and reviewed a large number of decisions and articles in an attempt to reach an equitable resolution to the problem. Allocation of costs between the two remaining parties is difficult, given the particular circumstances of this case where one of the major polluters is insolvent, a number of parties have settled, and the remaining parties' involvement at the site are quite different. See Browning-Ferris Industries of Ill. v. Ter Maat, 13 F. Supp. 2d 756, 777-78 (N.D. Ill. 1998), rev'd on other grounds, 195 F.3d 953 (7th Cir. 1999) (discussing difficulty in allocating response costs and stating that allocation in the case would be a "best guess" proposition).

At first glance, Uniroyal's argument that it is responsible for about 1 percent of the costs seems inequitable. It would amount to less than $1 million dollars, when the overall cleanup effort for which Uniroyal was held jointly and severally liable was almost $90 million. Nevertheless, it is clear that Hercules' "responsibility as an owner and operator, who was deeply involved in the daily operations of the waste-producing enterprise," should far exceed that of Uniroyal, whose involvement with the Vertac Site was indirect and for a limited time. See Bedford Affiliates, 156 F.3d at 430. The question, of course, is how much responsibility to assign in light of the circumstances.

As discussed above, Uniroyal argues for strictly a volumetric approach. In this instance, the Court is persuaded that volumetrics is the most significant factor and should be the starting point at which to assess each party's contribution. However, the Court is not persuaded that volume alone should be the measure of allocation.

Uniroyal presented evidence of the volumes of product produced at the plant during the various ownership periods. The rates of production were based on production records and other documents. Hercules does not dispute the production rates presented by Uniroyal's expert, Steven Michael Quigley. Reasor-Hill was estimated to have produced 6,240,000 pounds of 2,4-D and 2,4,5-T. Hercules produced about 33,231,400 pounds of 2,4-D, 2,4,5-T and 2,4,5-TP during the time it owned and operated the site. During the time Transvaal leased the Site from Hercules (1971-1976), it produced approximately 43,004,255 pounds of 2,4,-D, 2,4,5-T and 2,4,5-TP. Vertac produced 71,183,140 pounds of 2,4-D, 2,4,5-T, and 2,4,5-TP between 1976 and 1987. Of that, Vertac produced 1,344,000 pounds of 2,4,5-T for sale to Uniroyal. In all, about 153,658,795 pounds of 2,4-D, 2,4,5-T and 2,4,5-TP were produced at the plant site during its years of operation.

If Uniroyal's share of the total production was considered, it would amount to 0.87 percent. The more equitable approach, however, is to calculate the amount of Uniroyal's share in comparison to that of Hercules. Production during the years Hercules owned or operated the plant was 76,235,655 pounds of 2,4-D, 2,4,5-T and 2,4,5-TP. Uniroyal's production is 1.76 percent of that of Hercules.

Hercules argues that the volumes of the parties cannot be compared because Hercules produced the majority of its 2,4-D and 2,4,5-T to fulfill Agent Orange contracts during the 1960's. According to Hercules, only 2 million pounds of 2,4-D and 1 million pounds of 2,4,5-T or 2,4,5-TP were produced for "commercial customers." Uniroyal, by comparison, produced 1.34 million pounds of 2,4,5-T for commercial customers through its tolling arrangement with Vertac.

The Court has already discussed the Agent Orange contracts in United States v. Vertac Chemical Corp., 841 F. Supp. 884 (E.D. Ark. 1993), aff'd, 46 F.3d 803 (8th Cir. 1995), cert. denied, 515 U.S. 1158 (1995). In that decision, the Court noted that Hercules bid on the contracts, and profited from them. 841 F. Supp. at 890. The Court cannot find that Hercules' production of Agent Orange which was used as part of the country's military effort in Vietnam should be given any consideration.

Hercules also argues that Uniroyal's predecessor developed a process that led to the creation of the 2,4,5-T still bottoms which should be considered in determining each party's contribution. This argument requires the Court to find causation based on a tenuous thread. The Court refuses to impose greater costs on Uniroyal based on a process developed in the 1960's which Hercules purchased and used.

As stated above, production volume is the most significant factor in allocating the costs in this case. The volumetric approach takes into account the relative involvement of the parties at the Site and their contribution to the harm created. Uniroyal argues that it is entitled to a "downward departure" because of its limited involvement. Uniroyal was neither an operator nor owner. Hercules was an operator of the Site for nine years, an owner of the plant for fourteen years and a lessor for five years, during which it had the authority to control the lessee's operations. The Court is not persuaded, however, that Uniroyal's "lack of involvement" warrants a downward departure. The Court has already considered Uniroyal's relatively minor degree of involvement in looking at volumetrics. The Court is also not persuaded that Uniroyal is completely uninvolved, as it would have the Court find. It arranged for production of hazardous materials through a tolling arrangement, and it was aware of the production of hazardous wastes that would be produced as a result of the product. It benefitted from the production of hazardous materials at the Site.

It is, therefore, not inequitable to place a larger percentage of costs on Uniroyal than just what the difference in volume would support. In Browning-Ferris Industries of Illinois, Inc. v. Ter Maat, 195 F.3d 953 (7th Cir. 1999), the Court found that allocating a larger share of responsibility to one responsible party who had operated the landfill for fewer years and dumped less waste in it than other parties was equitable. The Court found that the polluter's conduct was a sufficient though not necessary condition of the clean up. Similarly, here, the production of 2,4,5-T for Uniroyal which resulted in the production of hazardous wastes was a sufficient condition for the clean up. The Court previously found that some of the drums and tanks contained dioxin contaminated waste from the production of Uniroyal's 2,4,5-T. That is, but for the production of 2,4,5-T for Uniroyal, there would not be a certain amount of wastes left and ultimately stored in the drums that had to be incinerated.

The Court finds that an "upward departure" is warranted in this instance. The percentage will be small given Uniroyal's limited involvement with the Site, but takes into account Uniroyal's role in the generation of hazardous material.

The Court has also given consideration to the parties' cooperation with government officials. Hercules responded to EPA's Orders under Section 106 of CERCLA and undertook extensive remediation. Hercules' efforts arguably had some effect on reducing the costs of remediation, and therefore Uniroyal's liability. Uniroyal did not respond, taking the position that it had cause to disregard Section 106 Orders because the Court did not find it liable until 1997. The Court notes, however, that the case on which it relied for finding Uniroyal liable as an arranger, United States v. Aceto Agricultural Chemicals Corp., 872 F.2d 1373 (8th Cir. 1989), had been decided several years before the first 106 Order. Thus, the Court finds that the sixth Gore factor also justifies finding Uniroyal to be responsible for more than the 1.76 percent and that Uniroyal and Hercules should share, pro rata, the orphan shares of Reasor-Hill and Vertac.

Hercules points to a number of other factors that the Court should consider in allocating the costs to reduce its costs. For example, Hercules introduced evidence that Vertac was not as concerned about safety and cleanliness as Hercules and that the plant went downhill under Vertac.

There is no doubt that Hercules' safety and environmental programs are to be commended. However, the degree of care used in Hercules in handling the waste does not have any weight in allocating the costs between Uniroyal and Hercules. Hercules owned and operated the plant, and therefore was in a position to oversee the care used at plant site. As discussed above, Hercules' safety and maintenance programs are laudatory; however, that being so does not mean that Uniroyal should assume more of the costs. Uniroyal was in no position to manage the disposal of any hazardous materials.

Hercules also introduced evidence regarding the knowledge the scientific community had of the problems with dioxin at the time Hercules manufactured the herbicides and pesticides. Although Hercules learned of the presence of dioxin by the mid-1960s, the technology did not exist at that time to adequately analyze the presence of dioxin in the soil or water during the years that Hercules operated the plant. Furthermore, the possibility of a link of dioxin to cancer did not surface until the mid to late 1970s.

The evidence regarding the state of knowledge of dioxin is interesting but irrelevant to this proceeding. It does not negate that the Court has found hazardous materials at the Site. . . .

In sum, after consideration of all the evidence, the Court finds that Uniroyal should be responsible for 2.6 percent of the costs for which it is jointly and severally liable. This includes the orphan shares. Thus, the parties are entitled to contribution from one another consistent with the allocation findings expressed herein.

The parties are directed to consult with each other, and the EPA regarding the offsets from other PRPs, the interest calculations, and the allocations as set forth in this Order. If the parties can agree on the amount, they should submit a proposed precedent for judgment within twenty days of the date of this Order. If not, each party should submit a proposed precedent setting forth its position.

NOTES AND QUESTIONS

1. **On Remand.** The Eighth Circuit did not disturb the district court's allocation, but did remand for an evidentiary hearing on claims of divisibility advanced by Hercules. The district court then found against Hercules on all of its divisibility claims, except for one dealing with a discrete part of the site that accounted for a small share of the over $100 million in cleanup costs incurred so far. The district court reaffirmed its original allocation of liability after making this minor adjustment in total costs. U.S. v. Vertac Chemical Corp. 364 F. Supp. 2d 94 (E.D. Ark. 2005).

2. **Who Can Blame Them?** PRPs raise diverse considerations in a contribution action, limited only by their anticipation of what might be a plausible appeal to the equitable discretion of the trial judge. In a case such as *Vertac*, where each percentage point of liability is worth nearly $1 million, PRPs are perhaps not be criticized for the diversity of considerations that they bring to the court's attention.

3. **The Gore Factors.** Do the Gore factors make more sense when the court is trying to allocate liability among generators of wastes than they do when trying to allocate liability between a group of generators and an owner? Consider a group of generators representing 70 percent of the total wastes shipped to the site, none of whom played any active role in disposing or monitoring the waste once it reached the site. The previous site owner generated no waste, but failed to dispose of other parties' waste properly. Once the current owner found out about the waste, she took immediate measures to contain the contamination and cooperated fully with government authorities. How do the Gore factors apply?

4. **Equitable Factors.** Courts have refused to limit the equitable factors that they are able to consider, treating this as a matter of case-by-case judgment. They can consider several factors or only one (e.g., volumetric allocation with equal weighting of all wastes; duration of ownership when allocating among owners). One court recently identified a list of (sometimes overlapping) factors relevant to other courts' holdings: "(1) the parties' relative fault or culpability, (2) the ability of the parties to demonstrate that their contribution to a discharge, release or disposal of a hazardous waste can be distinguished, (3) the amount of hazardous waste involved, (4) the degree of toxicity, (5) the degree of involvement of the parties in the generation, transportation, treatment, storage or disposal of the hazardous waste, (6) the degree of care exercised by the parties with respect to the hazardous waste, (7) the degree of cooperation by the parties with government agencies to prevent harm to the public health or the environment, (8) financial resources or economic status, (9) economic benefits received by the parties from contaminating activities or remediation, (10) knowledge and/or acquiescence of the parties in the contaminating activities, and (11) contracts between the parties." Waste Management of Alameda Cty. v. East Bay Regional Park Dist., 135 F. Supp. 2d 1071 (N.D. Cal. 2001).

5. **Zero Allocation for De Minimis Contributors.** The amount of cleanup attributable to Uniroyal's arranging was calculated by it to be 1.58 percent by volume. Is there a level of contribution so minor that a PRP ought to bear none of the costs of cleanup? In Acushnet Co. v. Mohasco Corp., 191 F.3d 69,

77 (1st Cir. 1999), cited by the *Vertac* district court, the First Circuit upheld grants of summary judgment and judgments according to law to three small contributors to a site prior to a full allocation trial. One PRP had offered uncontradicted testimony that the creosote-soaked telephone poles that it had disposed of at the site could not leach polycyclic aromatic hydrocarbons (PAHs) into the groundwater at concentrations greater than the background level. Three others had deposited wastes that were minuscule in quantity compared to the entire site—in one case the court speculated that the PRP's contribution would equate to a 1 in 500,000th share. Acushnet v. Coaters, 948 F. Supp. 128 (D. Mass. 1996). The district court acknowledged the fact that the linchpin of a contribution action is a holistic consideration of all the relevant equitable factors, so that it was impossible to identify any single bright-line criterion for granting summary dismissal to de minimis PRPs. Nonetheless, the court concluded that in a contribution action, the plaintiff bore a burden of proving a "minimum standard of significance of [a] defendant's responsibility as a source of one or more hazardous substances at the site." One determinant of that threshold-of-significance was a showing of "reasons for court intervention that outweigh the public interest against recognizing causes of action the enforcement of which exceed the added resources that would be tapped for waste-site remediation." Id. at 136. The court seems to say, in other words, plaintiffs needed to show that they are reasonably likely to recover more from a PRP than the public and private resources required to adjudicate that liability.

The First Circuit affirmed the district court decision, although it concluded that insofar as any element of the district court's decision turned on a conclusion that a PRP's contribution to the site had not caused the plaintiff to incur any response costs was inappropriate and out of place in a section 113(f) contribution action. 191 F.3d at 72. There is no "minimum quantity of hazardous waste before liability may be imposed [under CERCLA] . . . [A]ny reasonable danger of release, however insignificant, would seem to give rise to liability." Id. at 76. However, while de minimis PRPs are to be held joint and severally liable at the liability stage of the trial, unless they can show divisibility, "[t]his does not mean . . . that the de minimis polluter must necessarily be held liable for all response costs. . . . [A] defendant may avoid . . . liability for response costs in a contribution action under §113(f) if it demonstrates that its share of hazardous waste deposited at the site constitutes no more than background amounts of such substances in the environment and cannot concentrate with other wastes to produce higher amounts. This rule is not based on CERCLA's causation requirement, but it is logically derived from §113(f)'s express authorization that a court take equity into account when fixing each defendant's fair share of response costs. We caution, however, that not every de minimis polluter will elude liability in this way. As always, an equitable determination must be justified by the record. . . . On the whole, the costs and inherent unfairness in saddling a party who has contributed only trace amounts of hazardous waste with joint and several liability for all costs incurred outweigh the public interest in requiring full contribution from de minimis polluters." Id. at 77-79.

6. **Allocating Orphan Shares.** PRPs who have gone out of business, been declared insolvent, or cannot be located leave behind "orphan shares" of liability. Superfund liability is joint and several, so that any or all of the remaining PRPs can be held liable for 100 percent of response costs, including the orphan shares. How should those orphan shares be dealt with in a contribution action, where the ruling concept is equitable allocation? Consider a site in which the site

owner (O) has paid 100 percent of the cleanup expenses, totaling $1 million. O then brings a contribution action against another PRP, G. The contribution court allocates responsibility 20 percent to O, 20 percent to G, and 60 percent to D, a defunct corporation with no remaining assets. O can argue that it ought to bear only its 20 percent share of responsibility, in which case G is assigned the remaining 80 percent. G can make the identical argument, which would leave O with the remaining 80 percent. Both of these inequitable results are avoided if the contribution court divides up all the liability among the solvent plaintiff and defendant only. In that case, each end up bearing 50 percent of the cleanup costs, including the orphan shares. The burden of the orphan shares is shared among them in proportion to their comparative degrees of responsibility. This result is consistent with the Restatement of Torts §886A(2), and followed in a number of CERCLA decisions. E.g., Final Creek Group v. Newmont Mining Corp., 118 F.3d 1298, 1301-1306 (9th Cir. 1997).

7. Settlements. Does this same principle work in cases where the plaintiff has settled with some of the PRPs, or simply has not sued all of them for contribution? Suppose that D was not solvent, but had settled with O for $100,000. How should the court allocate liability? Should the court continue to limit its allocation just to the parties before the court according to their comparative degrees of responsibility? Is G liable to O for 50 percent of total cleanup costs ($500,000) or only 50 percent of the remaining costs ($450,000)? If the amount of G's settlement is to be subtracted prior to allocation, should O bear responsibility for allowing D to make a "sweetheart" settlement? After all, if O had settled with D for the whole amount of D's liability, G would only pay $200,000. Would it matter if comparative responsibility had been completely unclear at the time of the settlement? The following decision bears on these questions.

|| ***AKZO Nobel Coatings, Inc. v. Aigner Corp.*** ||
|| **197 F.3d 302 (7th Cir. 1999)** ||

EASTERBROOK, Circuit Judge.

[This is an appeal from a contribution action brought by Akzo against a consortium of other PRPs, including Aigner and about 50 others, all generators of hazardous wastes. After hearing arguments on other equitable allocation formulas, the district court settled on dividing liability among the plaintiff and defendants on the basis of the volume of hazardous waste disposed at the site, named Fisher-Calo, with all wastes being weighted equally.]

Having decided that all gallons of solvents shipped to Fisher-Calo count equally, the court then ordered Akzo to pay approximately one third more than equal-weighting implies. Akzo generated approximately 9% by volume of all solvents that Fisher-Calo processed, but the court ordered Akzo to reimburse Aigner for approximately 13% of the costs that Aigner has incurred or will expend in completing the cleanup. Aigner and the other firms in its consortium sent about 71% of the total volume of solvents to the Fisher-Calo site, so Akzo's shipments are approximately 13% of the Akzo + Aigner total; other shipments and shippers were ignored because they are not parties to this suit.

According to the district court, this outcome is required by the Uniform Comparative Fault Act. The district court read §2 and §6 of the UCFA to provide that the responsibility of non-parties must be disregarded, even if they are financially able to pay (indeed, even if they already *have paid*) their share of the cleanup. To take a simple example, suppose Firm A is responsible for 40% of the pollutants, Firm B for 10%, and Firm C for 50%. Firm A agrees with the EPA to perform the cleanup and sues B for contribution. On the district court's reading of the UCFA, B must pay 20% of the total cleanup costs, because B sent 20% of the pollutants that A and B generated jointly. That C is able to pay its 50% share—indeed, that C has *already* paid 50%, and that the outcome of the suit between A and B will leave A bearing only 30% of the total costs—is irrelevant on the district court's (and Aigner's) understanding of the UCFA. A polluter that agreed to clean up a Superfund site could turn a tidy profit if this were so. Suppose that ten firms, A through J, sent 10% each, and that A, having agreed to do the cleanup work, sues B for contribution. Firms A and B are responsible for equal volumes of wastes, so the court would order B to pay 50% of the total cleanup costs. Next A sues C and recovers another 50%. If all of Firms B through J were good for the judgments, then A would recover 450% of its total outlay for pollution control. Even if the court set a cap of 100%, to prevent A from making a profit, the upshot would be that of ten equally responsible polluters, B and C would pay 50% each, and the other eight would pay nothing. That is not a sensible outcome of a process that is supposed to yield an "equitable" allocation of expenses.

Akzo contends that the UCFA requires the district court to undertake a global assessment of responsibility, so that Akzo cannot be required to pay anything until every shipper's share has been determined. That might take years of trial time. Akzo would be happy to skip the trial and chip in 9%, but that would leave Aigner holding the bag if the other shippers were unable to pay their shares. Aigner, for its part, contends that the UCFA requires courts to ignore non-parties just as the district court concluded. None of these approaches is sound. Akzo's would either complicate an already difficult allocation process or saddle firms such as Aigner with excess costs. The Supreme Court has cautioned against the adoption of any contribution rule that would complicate litigation. . . . Aigner's approach would lead to disproportionate liability, with contribution shares turning not on actual responsibility (or on the actual collections of the party performing the cleanup) but on litigation strategy. It is of course possible that both sides are wrong, and that the UCFA requires the inclusion of either pollution shares of, or the actual recoveries from, the additional parties with which Aigner has reached settlements. But we resist all temptation to give the UCFA a close reading—and this despite the fact that Akzo and Aigner agreed in the district court that it supplies the rule of decision. Section 113(f)(1) provides otherwise: "Such claims [for contribution] shall be brought in accordance with this section and the Federal Rules of Civil Procedure, and shall be governed by Federal law." The UCFA is not a federal law, and we are not bound by the parties' agreement to an inapplicable body of legal rules. . . .

Although federal law governs, it is possible and often desirable to borrow a rule from state law, when the alternative is judicial invention. . . . The reference to "Federal law" in §113(f)(1) implies that the law should be nationally uniform, rather than varying according to each state's idea of appropriate contribution. Yet the UCFA would not be an attractive national rule. Unlike the Uniform Commercial Code [upon which the Supreme Court has looked for guidance in other contexts], the UCFA has not been adopted throughout the United States. Only two states (Iowa and Washington) have enacted the UCFA; eleven have adopted the Uniform Contribution Among Tortfeasors Act, which supplies a different approach to contribution; the rest resolve contribution issues through the common law or non-uniform statutes. When one of the litigants has settled with a third party, the UCFA reduces other shares by the percentage of total fault of the person released in the settlement (UCFA §2); this is the source of Akzo's contention that the district court must hold a comprehensive trial to determine every shipper's share of liability. The UCATA, by contrast, reduces liability only by the dollar amount of third-party settlements (UCATA §4). These competing approaches can produce substantial differences in incentives to settle and in the complexity of litigation. . . . To the extent language in §113 speaks to the issue, it prefers the approach of the UCATA: A settlement with the United States or a state "does not discharge any of the other potentially liable persons unless its terms so provide, but it reduces the potential liability of the others by the amount of the settlement." Section 113(f)(2), 42 U.S.C. §9613(f)(2). Adopting the UCFA as a federal rule would undermine that decision.

As a proposition of federal law, the district court's approach has nothing to recommend it, for it produces disparities in liability when third parties have settled. We assume, with the district court, that the proportionate share of the parties is a good starting point. Suppose that Akzo and Aigner were the only two financially sound parties responsible for the pollution. Then the final contribution shares properly would reflect only their relative responsibility, and the 13% share for Akzo would stand. But they are not. Aigner has settled with some other firms that sent solvents to Fisher-Calo and with some past owner-operators of portions of the site. It has claims pending against still more potentially responsible parties. It is very unlikely that 13% is an accurate estimate of Akzo's share among the financially sound firms that will eventually chip in.

[McDermott v. AmClyde, 511 U.S. 202 (1994)] considered at length the proper treatment of settling parties under a body of federal law that includes contribution—the law of admiralty. The Court deemed two approaches "closely matched" (511 U.S. at 217): claim reduction (also known as "proportionate share"), see Restatement (2d) of Torts §886A Comment m(3), and reduction *pro tanto* by the actual amounts recovered in settlements, see *Restatement* §886A Comment m(2). The claim-reduction approach requires the court to determine the responsibility of all firms that have settled, as well as those still involved in the litigation, and to ignore any firms that have not settled. To return to the ten-firm hypothetical above, if Firm A had settled with C and D, then their shares of responsibility (and the corresponding cleanup costs) would be excluded from the calculation. In a contribution suit between A and B, Firm B would be ordered to pay 50% of the costs after excluding C and D, or 40% of the total costs of restoring the site. It would not matter how much A actually had recovered from C and D. By contrast, under the *pro tanto* approach, anything A recovered from C and D in settlement would be deducted from the total cleanup costs, and the court would order A and B to bear the remaining costs equally. In *McDermott* the Court adopted claim reduction, deeming it most compatible with the way related issues in admiralty have been handled.

If as *McDermott* explained the choice between the *pro tanto* approach and claim reduction is a tossup, 511 U.S. at 217, then it is best to match the handling of settlements with the way intersecting principles of law work. For admiralty that meant claim reduction. For CERCLA the most closely related rule of law is §113(f)(2), which reduces third-party claims by the actual cash value of settlements reached with governmental bodies. Extending the *pro tanto* approach of §113(f)(2) to claims under §113(f)(1) enables the district court to avoid what could be a complex and unproductive inquiry into the responsibility of missing parties. The extended litigation between Akzo and Aigner well illustrates the difficulties of fixing responsibility for wastes sent years (if not decades) ago to a firm that did not keep good records and contaminated a wide area. Excluding only actual collections from third parties enables the court to conserve its resources.

On remand, the district court should determine how much Aigner has collected from third parties in settlement, then require Akzo to pay 12.56% of the costs net of those recoveries, rather than of Aigner's total outlay. The total must be reduced not only by collections Aigner has realized to date, but also by future third-party payments. Phrasing Akzo's liability as "12.56% of the cleanup cost net of third-party collections" or some similar formula will avoid any need to reopen the judgment under Fed. R. Civ. P. 60(b)(5) to account for the outcome of litigation now pending or to be filed in the future.

If some of Aigner's settlements provide for percentage-of-cost payments rather than cash payments, then the district court should exclude that percentage from the pool. (To this extent the *pro tanto* approach works like claim reduction, but without the need for the court to determine the responsibility of the settling parties.) Even if, as Akzo believes, Aigner settled for too little with any of these third parties, it is not free to bring its own contribution actions against them. *McDermott* labeled "clearly inferior" the possibility of collecting more from parties who reached private settlements in good faith. 511 U.S. at 211. A potentially responsible party (PRP in CERCLA jargon) that wants to guard against inadequate collections from third parties must either intervene in the suits against them or challenge the bona fides of the settlements immediately after they are reached. Id. at 212-14. . . .

The judgment is vacated to the extent it quantifies Akzo's contribution liability, and the case is remanded for further proceedings consistent with this opinion.

PROBLEM EXERCISE: CERCLA COST ALLOCATION, SETTLEMENTS, AND CONTRIBUTION

Suppose that Scientific Disposal Services owns and operates a dumpsite that has been listed on the National Priorities List for cleanup under the Superfund program. Scientific ceases operations and EPA excavates and removes some drums buried at the site. After performing a remedial investigation/feasibility study (RI/FS), EPA issues a record of decision (ROD) calling for removal of hot spots of soil contaminated with metals, a pump-and-treat system to remediate groundwater contaminated with metals and organic wastes, construction of a slurry wall to prevent further off-site migration of contaminants, and installation of a clay cap over the entire site, including the municipal landfill. EPA estimates that the total cost of remedial action will be $60 million.

Question One. If the PRPs believe that EPA has selected a remedy that is too expensive, what legal action can they take to challenge it? See CERCLA §121.

Question Two. Assume that you are the attorney for Toxicology Lab, which shipped only a small quantity of arsenic in a metal drum to the site. What would you advise your client concerning potential liability? What should Toxicology do to try to minimize its liability?

Question Three. Amalgamated Pesticide has disposed liquid wastes containing dioxin, among other hazardous substances. True Value shipped metallic waste to Scientific with the understanding that they will be recycled, which Scientific did not do. And Toxicology shipped one metal drum. Prior to Scientific, an industrial firm owned the site and disposed of small amounts of their own waste at the site. The PRPs would like to reach agreement among themselves concerning how to allocate the costs of the remedial action. What arguments would each of the PRPs make in an effort to minimize their share of the costs? How should they proceed in an effort to reach agreement on cost allocation? If they fail to agree, what legal options are open to EPA and the PRPs to resolve the cost allocation issues?

Question Four. Suppose that a wealthy developer expresses interest in purchasing the site in order to build a baseball stadium on the property after its environmental problems have been remediated. The developer is willing to contribute $2 million toward the cost of remedial action, in return for ironclad assurances that she will incur no further liability. What options are available to the developer?

6. *Has Superfund Worked?*

Now that CERCLA is more than a quarter-century old, every aspect of the CERCLA program has been extensively analyzed and criticized, often from several angles at once. The major complaints can be summarized as follows:

1. Joint and several liability results in unfair allocations of financial responsibility.
2. A litigation-driven system funnels too much CERCLA money into transactions costs and too little into site cleanup.
3. The cleanup process is too slow and often ineffective.
4. Cleanup standards are too stringent; one-size-fits-all health-based standards are inappropriate and impair productive uses of land.
5. Where EPA does have discretion, remedies are uneven from site to site, often driven by the effectiveness of community lobbying.

Over the years, EPA and the Congress have taken some steps to address each of these concerns. Joint and several liability has been modified by innocent purchaser and bona fide purchaser exemptions, by clearer rules regarding lender liability, by exemptions for residential homeowners, and by modifications in agency settlement policies. Litigation costs have diminished as a proportion of total CERCLA-related expenditures because a larger number of cleanups occur without costly front-end litigation, although contribution lawsuits can still be complex and costly. The Superfund program has been successful in leveraging private resources, and has generated $8 in private response costs for every $1 spent on enforcement. Overall, private parties had put $22.8 billion into site cleanup during the life of the program, through FY 2004. EPA, FY 2004 Superfund Annual Report at 15. These cleanup efforts have reduced human exposures. EPA now identifies 1,242 of the 1,493 NPL sites with human health exposures as being "under control," "meaning that protective controls were in place to prevent any unacceptable human exposures under current land and ground water use." Id. at 17.

Cleanup standards are criticized both by PRPs, who generally complain they are too stringent, and by communities near the sites, who have the opposite concern. Hurricane Katrina has vividly illustrated the importance of proper cleanup. There are three Superfund sites in New Orleans, and all of them were flooded by Katrina and the failure of the levees. Each had employed cleanup standards that left part of the hazardous substances at the site, and as a result the flooding has spread those substances throughout the region. At the Agriculture Street Site, sometimes known as the "black Love Canal" because the community surrounding it is 60 to 80 percent minority,

> EPA's choice of a remedy for the site has significantly exacerbated [the] damage. Instead of excavating the site, treating contaminated soil in situ, or even installing a liner that would prevent the landfill's contents from washing away, EPA decided that its final remedy would be limited excavation of less than two-thirds of the site and the placement of two feet of clean fill on top of the buried waste. An Unnatural Disaster: The Aftermath of Hurricane Katrina by Member Scholars of the Center for Progressive Reform at 20 (2005). Available at *http://www.progressivereform.org/Unnatural_Disaster_512.pdf.*

EPA has been attempting to quantify the benefits of the Superfund program, but to date its efforts have not been successful. Recently, EPA presented a partial draft document to its Science Advisory Board describing how it proposed to quantify three measures of benefits—health benefits, reductions in injuries to ecosystems, and protection of groundwater. The most well-developed of EPA's valuation techniques involved calculation of increased property values around Superfund sites. (How are such studies relevant to the three benefits that EPA is trying to measure?) The SAB, however, concluded that while such studies provided some information on the benefit of living farther away from a Superfund site, they did not provide a "credible estimate of the monetary value of the retrospective benefits of the Superfund program." Superfund Benefits Analysis Advisory Panel, Draft Advisory on Superfund Benefits Analysis, April 25, 2005, at 5. The SAB found numerous deficiencies in other aspects of the benefits study and concluded that EPA was quite far away from being able to measure such benefits.

The PRP community continues to search for ways to off-load responsibility for pre-CERCLA sites, relying in substantial part on the argument that CERCLA so dramatically changed the rules of the game that imposing retroactive joint and several liability for CERCLA-standard cleanups is unfair. As a constitutional matter, this argument was found wanting in *Olin Corp.,* page 371, but that case's result does not dispose of the issue as a political argument. The alternative to PRP liability for old sites would be some form of public works program, funded through general revenue and Superfund taxes.

As the CERCLA program matures, experience under the program itself becomes a factor weighing against substantial modifications in the liability standards for a subset of sites. A study by Resources for the Future (RFF) examined the impact of five different options for CERCLA liability, including several that would relieve PRPs of liability for certain categories of sites. Among its overall conclusions was the observation that "[a]ny alternative that eliminates Superfund liability for a subset of sites could diminish—if not eliminate—the current incentives PRPs face both to clean up sites not on the NPL, and also to carefully handle hazardous substances not regulated under other statutes." Moreover, it concludes that any liability modification at this stage will create some new inequities:

> Those PRPs who have already stepped forward and begun to pay for cleanups at sites like those to be released from liability under [one of the

options reviewed in the study] would be unfairly treated if, as we suspect is likely, they are not reimbursed for the costs they have incurred. This potential inequity would carry with it a very important incentive effect: the message that it may not be wise to comply immediately with environmental laws because, if one hangs back and waits, the law may be changed. [K. Probst & P. Portney, Assigning Liability for Superfund Cleanups: An Analysis of the Policy Options 46 (1992).]

Another study confirmed that fairness among PRP classes is the fundamental issue in the allocation debate: There is less than a 4 percent difference between the total costs of cleanups under the most and least expensive financing and liability schemes examined by the study. Probst et al., Footing the Bill for Superfund Cleanups: Who Pays and How? (1995).

To date, the Justice Department has consistently opposed any option that would eliminate strict, joint and several, and retroactive liability, claiming that such liability is essential to vindicating the polluter pays principle that is at the heart of CERCLA. Schiffer, Keep Superfund Liability Intact, Envtl. Forum, Sept./Oct. 1995, at 25. The attribute of CERCLA that remains the hardest to quantify is the degree of care handlers of hazardous substances exercise now in light of the prospect of Superfund liability if they fail to take care. As the program matures and the old sites are addressed, this going-forward aspect of CERCLA, which was a strong motivator for the law in the first place, will become increasingly prominent—but no less easy to quantify.

The Hamilton and Viscusi analysis of Superfund risk assessments and remediation efforts emphasized that the program's emphasis on maximum individual risk exposure and its neglect of population risk exposure have resulted in Superfund remediation not being done in a way that meets cost-effectiveness tests. They found that "95 percent of the cleanup dollars are spent to clean up 0.5 percent of the expected cancer risks." Hamilton & Viscusi, Calculating Risks 212 (1999). They also found that remediation expenditures covary with the degree of political organization of the surrounding communities in a way they describe as "perverse." "Residents influence cleanups most when site risks are low and the costs per cancer case avoided are high." Id. at 213. In part, they attribute this phenomenon to the fact that "remediations have benefits concentrated in the immediate area of the site and costs dispersed nationwide across taxpayers and consumers." Id. at 212-213. Thus, in the struggle between risk avoidance and cost-effectiveness, EPA receives citizen-based pressure on only one side.

Revisions of Superfund emerged from a significant private party effort in 1995. The National Commission on Superfund was made up of a representative group of CERCLA stakeholders, and it was able to issue a consensus proposal on Superfund reforms that the Clinton administration eventually endorsed. The consensus proposal contained major modifications with respect to cleanup standards that retained a national health-based focus but incorporated adjustments in response to site-specific considerations, including future land use, as well as recognizing technological infeasibility in the remediation selection process. With respect to liability, the consensus proposal would have retained strict, joint, and several liability as the standard courts could impose. In addition, building on EPA experiments with nonbinding allocations of responsibility, it would have provided an attractive prelitigation settlement option to PRPs that would have assigned individual shares on the basis of equitable standards identified in the legislation, in effect offering each PRP a way to resolve its own "several" liability at the outset. Steinzor, The Reauthorization of Superfund: Can the Deal of the Century Be Saved? 25 Envtl. L. Rep. 10016 (1995).

The reform proposal died in last-minute wrangling in Congress, and no comprehensive reform package has garnered much support since.

NOTES AND QUESTIONS

1. How important do you think it is for remedial actions to achieve levels of cleanup that are consistent from site to site? How should EPA deal with the tension between CERCLA's preferences for permanent remedies and for treatment and its cost-effectiveness requirement?

2. Some observers have attributed the controversy over EPA's implementation of Superfund to a lack of consensus over the proper goals of CERCLA and inherent tension between CERCLA's goal of promptly and effectively cleaning up hazardous substance releases and its goal of shifting cleanup costs to responsible parties. According to consultants for an industry coalition on Superfund:

> [B]ecause the general goal of cleanup may be simply unachievable either from a technological or a cost standpoint, it is difficult to articulate national and workable cleanup objectives. Even after Section 121 of SARA addressed the "how clean is clean" issue, the exact level of required cleanup has not been specified by Congress, the EPA or the courts. Also, this country has now had wide experience with the articulation of unachievable goals in environmental legislation, a form of environmental brinksmanship. There is an emerging consensus among policy analysts that the concept has outlived its early utility as a means of building public support for environmental programs and for effectively achieving the basic objectives of any program of pollution reduction, but the idea retains considerable currency in some quarters. Section 121 of SARA adopts technology-forcing cleanup standards, but does not define a level of expected technology development and discharge reduction goals comparable to definitions in the Clean Air and Water Acts. To complicate matters further, Section 121 embodies the same uncertainty about the relevance of economic analysis in setting and achieving standards of other environmental programs. [Coalition on Superfund, Coalition on Superfund Research Report 3-23-24 (1989).]

Do you agree that Superfund's goals are too ambitious? How, if at all should they be modified? Does EPA's difficulty in finding a satisfactory answer to the "how clean is clean" problem stem from an inherent tension between CERCLA's preference for remedies that are both permanent and cost-effective?

3. Hamilton and Viscusi find that the political organization of local residents makes a difference in how much money EPA spends on cleanup, often at sites where their study finds little risk. Although it is true that local residents have a strong bias in favor of expensive cleanups, and that there are no citizen organizations arguing against expensive measures at any specific site, the PRP community at each location does have great incentive to push EPA to lower costs, and these PRP communities often include corporations of significant size. Why do you suppose they appear continually to lose the battle for more cost-effective cleanup standards?

4. Hamilton and Viscusi also analyzed the effect of reforming CERCLA so that it employed risk assessment and cost-benefit analysis in its site selection and remediation decisions. Because so much money is spent on sites that pose relatively little population risk, they found that substantial program savings could

be gained. EPA spent $2.2 billion at the 145 sites they analyzed; $1.4 billion of this was spent at large sites "to reduce cancers at a cost above $100 million per cancer case averted." Hamilton & Viscusi, Calculating Risks 229 (1999).

In their view, employing risk assessment and cost-benefit analysis could have a positive effect on environmental equity concerns. Minority populations were more concentrated around sites that would pass a benefit-cost test for cleanup than they were on average around the entire sample. Id. at 235. Placing a site on the NPL in the first place was another part of the process that Hamilton and Viscusi found was affected by community pressure, which they believe operates adversely to minority interests. "In sum, risk assessment and benefit-cost analysis may reduce environmental inequities by reducing the role for constituent pressure in remediations and by focusing attention on high health risks, which often occur in minority communities. Basing cleanup decisions on the merits as reflected by assessments of costs and benefits is the risk policy analogue of equal opportunity policies in the labor market. Equal risk protection may thus ameliorate the environmental inequities that result from the powerful influence of political forces." Id. at 236. Bearing in mind that their analysis was of sites where RODs had been compiled in 1991-1992, do you think their analysis would be borne out if a similar study were conducted today? If cost-benefit analysis favors minority communities, is that a reason to adopt it? If minority communities are now faring better under a system subject to political influence, is that a reason to retain the current system?

E.   DUMPSITE REGULATION, THE DORMANT COMMERCE CLAUSE, AND ENVIRONMENTAL JUSTICE CONCERNS

As federal policy has regulated land disposal with increasing stringency, this option has become much more costly. RCRA's minimum technology standards for subtitle C facilities and the new subtitle D standards for municipal dumps have reduced the supply, and increased the cost, of land disposal facilities. The RCRA land ban has created explicit technology-based standards for treatment of hazardous wastes. By restricting the use of land disposal facilities, the land ban and regulations that raise the costs of land disposal, along with the fear of CERCLA liability, have substantially increased incentives for waste reduction, and recycling. While significant progress is being made in waste reduction, controversies over whose waste is being disposed of where continue to create tensions among states.

As awareness of the environmental hazards of waste disposal has increased, the siting of new waste disposal capacity has become a particularly controversial issue. Low-income and minority communities that often hosted such facilities are now resisting them on environmental justice grounds. States that have become dumping grounds for waste generated in other states have tried a variety of measures to restrict waste imports. These measures frequently have been struck down on constitutional grounds. The sections that follow examine controversies spawned by the search for disposal alternatives and the controversies they have spawned, including Commerce Clause restrictions. These include the impact of environmental justice concerns on facility siting.

1. Commerce Clause Limitations

The production of growing quantities of solid waste, the increasingly stringent regulation of sanitary and hazardous landfills, and the enormous unpopularity of such facilities to the local communities in which they are located have combined to make new land-based waste disposal capacity a scarce commodity. When a particular state receives more out-of-state waste bound for disposal inside the state than it exports, placing limits on the importation of waste presents one possible strategy for that state to mitigate the problems associated with dwindling capacity.

Consider the situation Alabama faced with the hazardous waste facility owned and operated by Chemical Waste Management in Sumter County, near Emelle, Alabama. With a population approximately 70 percent black, more than one-third of Sumter's residents live below the poverty line, making it one of Alabama's poorest counties. Emelle itself is a small community of fewer than 1,000 residents, 90 percent of whom are black. Robert D. Bullard, Dumping in Dixie 59-60 (2d ed. 1994). In 1989, 17 percent of the landfilled hazardous waste in the country was shipped to Emelle, totalling some 488,000 tons, up from 341,000 tons in 1985. These amounts are vastly in excess of the amount of hazardous waste shipped out of the state by Alabama generators.

When Alabama sought to reduce the volume of wastes being received at Chem Waste's site, it thought first of reducing the flow of out-of-state wastes, thus preserving the facility's capacity to deal with waste generated in Alabama. One of the chief obstacles such a strategy faces is the Commerce Clause, which vests in the Congress the power "to regulate commerce . . . among the several states." In 1978, the Supreme Court decided the following case, dealing with an early New Jersey attempt to limit the importation of municipal solid waste ("garbage") to its landfills.

|| **Philadelphia v. New Jersey** ||
|| **437 U.S. 617 (1978)** ||

MR. JUSTICE STEWART delivered the opinion of the Court.

A New Jersey law prohibits the importation of most "solid or liquid waste which originated or was collected outside the territorial limits of the State. . . ." In this case we are required to decide whether this statutory prohibition violates the Commerce Clause of the United States Constitution.

The statutory provision in question is ch. 363 of 1973 N.J. Laws, which took effect in early 1974. In pertinent part it provides:

> No person shall bring into this State any solid or liquid waste which originated or was collected outside the territorial limits of the State, except garbage to be fed to swine in the State of New Jersey, until the commissioner [of the State Department of Environmental Protection] shall determine that such action can be permitted without endangering the public health, safety, and welfare and has promulgated regulations permitting and regulating the treatment and disposal of such waste in this State.

N.J. Stat. Ann. §13:11-10 (West Supp. 1978).

[Private landfill owners in New Jersey, as well as several out-of-state cities, including Philadelphia, all of whom had disposal contracts with New Jersey landfills, sued in state court. The New Jersey Supreme Court upheld the statute as a legitimate health and safely statute that did not economically discriminate against interstate commerce and only slightly burdened it. The United States Supreme Court first remanded the case to the New Jersey court, instructing it to consider whether the New Jersey statute had been preempted by the newly enacted Resources Conservation and Recovery Act of 1976. The New Jersey court found no preemption. The plaintiffs appealed once again. After agreeing that no preemption had occurred, the Supreme Court proceeded to the Commerce Clause issues.]

II

[First, the Court held that out-of-state wastes are "commerce" within the meaning of the Commerce Clause. Cases upholding quarantine laws that prohibited the importation of, for example, disease-carrying animal carcasses, sometimes state that these items were "not legitimate subjects of trade and commerce." The Court explained that in so stating, such cases were "stating [a] conclusion, not the starting point of [their] reasoning."]

III

A

Although the Constitution gives Congress the power to regulate commerce among the States, many subjects of potential federal regulation under that power inevitably escape congressional attention "because of their local character and their number and diversity." South Carolina State Highway Dept. v. Barnwell Bros., Inc., 303 U.S. 177, 185. In the absence of federal legislation, these subjects are open to control by the States so long as they act within the restraints imposed by the Commerce Clause itself. The bounds of these restraints appear nowhere in the words of the Commerce Clause, but have emerged gradually in the decisions of this Court giving effect to its basic purpose. That broad purpose was well expressed by Mr. Justice Jackson in his opinion for the Court in H. P. Hood & Sons, Inc. v. Du Mond, 336 U.S. 525, 537-538:

> This principle that our economic unit is the Nation, which alone has the gamut of powers necessary to control the economy, including the vital power of erecting customs barriers against foreign competition, has as its corollary that the states are not separable economic units. As the Court said in Baldwin v. Seelig, 294 U.S. [511], 527, "what is ultimate is the principle that one state in its dealings with another may not place itself in a position of economic isolation."

The opinions of the Court through the years have reflected an alertness to the evils of "economic isolation" and protectionism, while at the same time recognizing that incidental burdens on interstate commerce may be unavoidable when a State legislates to safeguard the health and safety of its people. Thus, where simple economic protectionism is effected by state legislation, a virtually per se rule of invalidity has been erected. The clearest example of such legislation is a law that overtly blocks the flow of interstate commerce at a State's borders. Cf. Welton v. Missouri, 91 U.S. 275. But where other legislative objectives are credibly advanced and there is no patent discrimination against interstate trade, the Court has adopted a much more flexible approach, the general contours of which were outlined in Pike v. Bruce Church, Inc., 397 U.S. 137, 142:

> Where the statute regulates evenhandedly to effectuate a legitimate local public interest, and its effects on interstate commerce are only incidental, it will be upheld unless the burden imposed on such commerce is clearly excessive in relation to the putative local benefits. . . . If a legitimate local purpose is found, then the question becomes one of degree. And the extent of the burden that will be tolerated will of course depend on the nature of the local interest involved, and on whether it could be promoted as well with a lesser impact on interstate activities.

The crucial inquiry, therefore, must be directed to determining whether ch. 363 is basically a protectionist measure, or whether it can fairly be viewed as a law directed to legitimate local concerns, with effects upon interstate commerce that are only incidental.

B

The purpose of ch. 363 is set out in the statute itself as follows:

> The Legislature finds and determines that . . . the volume of solid and liquid waste continues to rapidly increase, that the treatment and disposal of these wastes continues to pose an even greater threat to the quality of the environment of New Jersey, that the available and appropriate landfill sites within the State are being diminished, that the environment continues to be threatened by the treatment and disposal of waste which originated or was collected outside the State, and that the public health, safety, and welfare require that the treatment and disposal within this State of all wastes generated outside of the State be prohibited.

The New Jersey Supreme Court accepted this statement of the state legislature's purpose. The state court additionally found that New Jersey's existing landfill sites will be exhausted within a few years; that to go on using these sites or to develop new ones will take a heavy environmental toll, both from pollution and from loss of scarce open lands; that new techniques to divert waste from landfills to other methods of disposal and resource recovery processes are under development, but that these changes will require time; and finally, that "the extension of the lifespan of existing landfills, resulting from the exclusion of out-of-state waste, may be of crucial importance in preventing further virgin wetlands or other undeveloped lands from being devoted to landfill purposes." Based on these findings, the court concluded that ch. 363 was designed to protect, not the State's economy, but its environment, and that its substantial benefits outweigh its "slight" burden on interstate commerce.

The appellants strenuously contend that ch. 363, "while outwardly cloaked 'in the currently fashionable garb of environmental protection,' . . . is actually no more than a legislative effort to suppress competition and stabilize the cost of solid waste disposal for New Jersey residents. . . ." They cite passages of legislative history suggesting that the problem addressed by ch. 363 is primarily financial: Stemming the flow of out-of-state waste into certain landfill sites will extend their lives, thus delaying the day when New Jersey cities must transport their waste to more distant and expensive sites.

The appellees, on the other hand, deny that ch. 363 was motivated by financial concerns or economic protectionism. In the words of their brief, "[no] New Jersey commercial interests stand to gain advantage over competitors from outside the state as a result of the ban on dumping out-of-state waste." Noting that New Jersey landfill operators are among the plaintiffs, the appellee's brief argues that "[the] complaint is not that New Jersey has forged an economic preference for its own commercial interests, but rather that it has denied a small group of its entrepreneurs an economic opportunity to traffic in waste in order to protect the health, safety, and welfare of the citizenry at large."

This dispute about ultimate legislative purpose need not be resolved, because its resolution would not be relevant to the constitutional issue to be decided in this case. Contrary to the evident assumption of the state court and the parties, the evil of protectionism can reside in legislative means as well as legislative ends. Thus, it does not matter whether the ultimate aim of ch. 363 is to reduce the waste disposal costs of New Jersey residents or to save remaining open lands from pollution, for we assume New Jersey has every right to protect its residents' pocketbooks as well as their environment. And it may be assumed as well that New Jersey may pursue those ends by slowing the flow of all waste into the State's remaining landfills, even though interstate commerce may incidentally be affected. But whatever New Jersey's ultimate purpose, it may not be accomplished by discriminating against articles of commerce coming from outside the State unless there is some reason, apart from their origin, to treat them differently. Both on its face and in its plain effect, ch. 363 violates this principle of nondiscrimination.

The Court has consistently found parochial legislation of this kind to be constitutionally invalid, whether the ultimate aim of the legislation was to assure a steady supply of milk by erecting barriers to allegedly ruinous outside competition, Baldwin v. G. A. F. Seelig, Inc., 294 U.S., at 522-524; to create jobs by keeping industry within the State, Foster-Fountain Packing Co. v. Haydel, 278 U.S. 1, 10; or to preserve the State's financial resources from depletion by fencing out indigent immigrants, Edwards v. California, 314 U.S. 160, 173-174. In each of these cases, a presumably legitimate goal was sought to be achieved by the illegitimate means of isolating the State from the national economy.

Also relevant here are the Court's decisions holding that a State may not accord its own inhabitants a preferred right of access over consumers in other States to natural resources located within its borders. West v. Kansas Natural Gas Co., 221 U.S. 229; Pennsylvania v. West Virginia, 262 U.S. 553. These cases stand for the basic principle that a "State is without power to prevent privately owned articles of trade from being shipped and sold in interstate commerce on the ground that they are required to satisfy local demands or because they are needed by the people of the State." Foster-Fountain Packing Co. v. Haydel, supra, at 10.

The New Jersey law at issue in this case falls squarely within the area that the Commerce Clause puts off limits to state regulation. On its face, it imposes on out-of-state commercial interests the full burden of conserving the State's remaining landfill space. It is true that in our previous cases the scarce natural resource was itself the article of commerce, whereas here the scarce resource and the article of commerce are distinct. But that difference is without consequence. In both instances, the State has overtly moved to slow or freeze the flow of commerce for protectionist reasons. It does not matter that the State has shut the article of commerce inside the State in one case and outside the State in the other. What is crucial is the attempt by one State to isolate itself from a problem common to many by erecting a barrier against the movement of interstate trade. The appellees argue that not all laws which facially discriminate against out-of-state commerce are forbidden protectionist regulations. In particular, they point to quarantine laws, which this Court has repeatedly upheld even though they appear to single out interstate commerce for special treatment. In the appellees' view, ch. 363 is analogous to such health-protective measures, since it reduces the exposure of New Jersey residents to the allegedly harmful effects of landfill sites.

It is true that certain quarantine laws have not been considered forbidden protectionist measures, even though they were directed against out-of-state commerce. But those quarantine laws banned the importation of articles such as diseased livestock that required destruction as soon as possible because their very movement risked contagion and other evils. Those laws thus did not discriminate against interstate commerce as such, but simply prevented traffic in noxious articles, whatever their origin.

The New Jersey statute is not such a quarantine law. There has been no claim here that the very movement of waste into or through New Jersey endangers health, or that waste must be disposed of as soon and as close to its point of generation as possible. The harms caused by waste are said to arise after its disposal in landfill sites, and at that point, as New Jersey concedes, there is no basis to distinguish out-of-state waste from domestic waste. If one is inherently harmful, so is the other. Yet New Jersey has banned the former while leaving its landfill sites open to the latter. The New Jersey law blocks the importation of waste in an obvious effort to saddle those outside the State with the entire burden of slowing the flow of refuse into New Jersey's remaining landfill sites. That legislative effort is clearly impermissible under the Commerce Clause of the Constitution.

Today, cities in Pennsylvania and New York find it expedient or necessary to send their waste into New Jersey for disposal, and New Jersey claims the right to close its borders to such traffic. Tomorrow, cities in New Jersey may find it expedient or necessary to send their waste into Pennsylvania or New York for disposal, and those States might then claim the right to close their borders. The Commerce Clause will protect New Jersey in the future, just as it protects her neighbors now, from efforts by one State to isolate itself in the stream of interstate commerce from a problem shared by all. The judgment is Reversed.

MR. JUSTICE REHNQUIST, with whom THE CHIEF JUSTICE joins, dissenting.

The question presented in this case is whether New Jersey must . . . . continue to receive and dispose of solid waste from neighboring States, even though these will inexorably increase the health problems discussed above. The Court answers this question in the affirmative. New Jersey must either prohibit *all* landfill operations, leaving itself to cast about for a presently nonexistent solution to the serious problem of disposing of the waste generated within its own borders, or it must accept waste from every portion of the United States, thereby multiplying the health and safety problems which would result if it dealt only with such wastes generated within the State. Because past precedents establish that the Commerce Clause does not present appellees with such a Hobson's choice, I dissent.

The Court recognizes that States can prohibit the importation of items "which, on account of their existing condition, would bring in and spread disease, pestilence, and death, such as rags or other substances infected with the germs of yellow fever or the virus of small-pox, or cattle or meat or other provisions that are diseased or decayed, or otherwise, from their condition and quality, unfit for human use or consumption." Bowman v. Chicago & Northwestern R. Co., 125 U.S. 465, 489 (1888). As the Court points out, such "quarantine laws have not been considered forbidden protectionist measures, *even though they were directed against out-of-state commerce.*"

In my opinion, these cases are dispositive of the present one. Under them, New Jersey may require germ-infected rags or diseased meat to be disposed of as best as possible within the State, but at the same time prohibit the *importation* of such items for disposal at the facilities that are set up within New Jersey for disposal of such material generated within the State. The physical fact of life that New Jersey must somehow dispose of its own noxious items does not mean that it must serve as a depository for those of every other State. Similarly, New Jersey should be free under our past precedents to prohibit the importation of solid waste because of the health and safety problems that such waste poses to its citizens. The fact that New Jersey continues to, and indeed must continue to, dispose of its own solid waste does not mean that New Jersey may not prohibit the importation of even more solid waste into the State. I simply see no way to distinguish solid waste, on the record of this case, from germ-infected rags, diseased meat, and other noxious items.

The Court's effort to distinguish these prior cases is unconvincing. It first asserts that the quarantine laws which have previously been upheld "banned the importation of articles such as diseased livestock that required destruction as soon as possible because their very movement risked contagion and other evils." According to the Court, the New Jersey law is distinguishable from these other laws, and invalid, because the concern of New Jersey is not with the *movement* of solid waste but with the present inability to safely *dispose* of it once it reaches its destination. But I think it far from clear that the State's law has as limited a focus as the Court imputes to it: Solid waste which is a health hazard when it reaches its destination may in all likelihood be an equally great health hazard in transit.

Even if the Court is correct in its characterization of New Jersey's concerns, I do not see why a State may ban the importation of items whose movement risks contagion, but cannot ban the importation of items which, although they may be transported into the State without undue hazard, will then simply pile up in an ever increasing danger to the public's health and safety. The Commerce Clause was not drawn with a view to having the validity of state laws turn on such pointless distinctions.

Second, the Court implies that the challenged laws must be invalidated because New Jersey has left its landfills open to domestic waste. But, as the Court notes, this Court has repeatedly upheld quarantine laws "even though they appear to single out interstate commerce for special treatment." The fact that New Jersey has left its landfill sites open for domestic waste does not, of course, mean that solid waste is not innately harmful. Nor does it mean that New Jersey prohibits importation of solid waste for reasons other than the health and safety of its population. New Jersey must out of sheer necessity treat and dispose of its solid waste in some fashion, just as it must treat New Jersey cattle suffering from hoof-and-mouth disease. It does not follow that New Jersey must, under the

Commerce Clause, accept solid waste or diseased cattle from outside its borders and thereby exacerbate its problems.

NOTES AND QUESTIONS

1. **Some Commerce Clause Background.** Efforts to preserve local access to natural resources have faced constitutional obstacles in the past. In Pennsylvania v. West Virginia, 262 U.S. 553 (1923), the Supreme Court struck down a West Virginia statute requiring producers of natural gas to give West Virginia residents preference over nonresident consumers in the purchase of natural gas. The West Virginia legislature had wanted to insulate state residents in the case of gas shortages and believed this was permissible because the gas originated in West Virginia. However, the Court stated that "[n]atural gas is a lawful article of commerce, and its transmission from one state to another for sale and consumption in the latter is interstate commerce." Id. at 596. West Virginia's stated interest in conserving natural resources could not justify the measure because "the purpose of its conservation is in a sense commercial—the business welfare of the State, as coal might be, or timber. . . . If the States have such power a singular situation might result. Pennsylvania might keep its coal, the Northwest its timber, the mining states their minerals. . . . Commerce will be halted at state lines." Id. at 599. In *West Virginia* and similar cases, the states' ostensible purpose was the conservation of a scarce resource. Should landfill capacity be viewed as a resource analogous to natural gas reserves?

In a case that some have thought hard to square with the recent Commerce Clause decisions, the Supreme Court has held that Montana could charge an out-of-state license fee for hunting Montana elk that was 25 times larger than the fee charged in-staters. Baldwin v. Fish & Game Comm'n, 436 U.S. 371 (1978). *Baldwin* was decided under the Privileges and Immunities Clause, not the Commerce Clause. The Court recognized that states were not "obliged to share those things they held in trust for their own people." Id. at 384. Moreover, such policies "manifest the State's special interest in regulating and preserving wildlife for the benefit of its citizens." Id. at 392. However, in a concurring opinion, Chief Justice Burger limited the majority holding by stating that if the wildlife became involved in interstate commerce, then access cannot be restricted in a manner that violates the Commerce Clause. Professor Tribe has the following to say about *Baldwin:*

> There . . . appear to be some goods and services that a state's citizens, having created or preserved for themselves, are entitled to keep for themselves. Thus Montana's carefully-tended elk herds are akin to public libraries, public schools, state universities, state-supported hospitals, and public welfare programs—things that the Court has suggested that a state may reserve for the use or enjoyment of its citizens. The Court implied in *Baldwin* that it would approve even a total exclusion of nonresident hunters upon a showing by the state that any additional hunting opportunities beyond those Montana chose to reserve to its citizens would endanger the elk population to the point of extinction. [L. Tribe, American Constitutional Law 539 (2d ed. 1988).]

A year after *Baldwin,* the Court decided Hughes v. Oklahoma, 441 U.S. 322 (1979). At issue was an Oklahoma statute banning the export of minnows caught in state waters. The state defended the ban as a conservation measure. The Court struck down the statute in a 7-2 decision. Once wild animals or other natural resources became objects in interstate commerce, said the Court, state laws concerning them had to be judged by the same Commerce Clause standards that are applicable to other items of commerce. While recognizing that conservation was a legitimate state interest, the majority held that the state had not shown its ban to be the least discriminatory means of furthering that interest. "Far from choosing the least discriminatory alternative, Oklahoma has chosen to 'conserve' its minnows in the way that most overtly discriminates against interstate commerce." 441 U.S. at 337-338.

In another line of decisions, the Supreme Court has taken a considerably more permissive view of efforts by states to ensure that state-created resources be reserved for use by their citizens. For example, in Reeves v. Stake, 447 U.S. 429 (1980), the Supreme Court upheld a South Dakota statute reserving all cement produced by a state-owned cement plant for use by state residents, in the event orders exceeded supply. According to the Court, "[c]ement is not a natural resource, like coal, timber, wild game, or minerals. . . . It is the end product of a complex process whereby a costly physical plant and human labor act on raw materials. South Dakota has not sought to limit access to the State's limestone or other materials used to make cement." Id. at 443-444. The Court acknowledged that South Dakota's policies "reflect the essential and patently unobjectionable purpose of state government—to serve the citizens of the State." Id. at 442.

2. **Back to Alabama.** In 1989, Alabama enacted a ban on the importation of hazardous wastes from any state that did not itself have a commercial hazardous waste facility. It attempted to distinguish its hazardous waste ban from New Jersey's garbage ban on the ground that hazardous waste posed greater health hazards. The Eleventh Circuit found this no basis for permitting a facially discriminatory state statute, and it declared Alabama's ban unconstitutional. National Solid Waste Management Association v. Alabama, 910 F.2d 713 (11th Cir. 1990).

In April 1990, the Alabama legislature adopted a different strategy. It enacted a law that (a) imposed a "base fee" of $25.60 per ton on all hazardous wastes disposed of in the state, (b) imposed an "additional fee" of $72.00 per ton on all out-of-state hazardous waste disposed of in the state, and (c) placed a cap on the amount of hazardous waste that could be disposed of in any Alabama facility during any one-year period.

ChemWaste challenged this new statute, which was struck down by the Supreme Court. Chemical Waste Management, Inc. v. Hunt, 504 U.S. 334 (1992). Holding that a facially discriminatory statute faces "the strictest scrutiny of any purported legitimate local purpose and of the absence of discriminatory alternatives," the Court found that "ultimately, the State's concern focuses on the volume of the waste entering the Emelle facility," and that there were other, less discriminatory means of reducing that volume. 504 U.S. at 344-345. As he did in Philadelphia v. New Jersey, Chief Justice Rehnquist dissented. Emphasizing the strength of Alabama's legitimate interest in a "safe and attractive environment," the Chief Justice saw the case as one in which the state was using its taxing authority to prevent the export of a valuable commodity—the "safe environment that attends appropriate disposal of hazardous wastes"—out of state. Especially when this commodity is a "public good that the state has helped to produce," the Chief Justice concluded that the Alabama statute was constitutionally permissible. 504 U.S. at 349.

3. **Oregon.** The *Chemical Waste* majority suggested that a differential fee or tax structure might be permissible under the Commerce Clause if the state had a basis for concluding that out-of-state waste imposed differential burdens on the state receiving the waste. The Court suggested "a generally applicable per-ton additional fee on all hazardous waste disposed of within Alabama, or a per-mile tax on all vehicles transporting hazardous waste across Alabama roads, or an evenhanded cap on the total tonnage landfilled at Emelle, which would curtail volume from all sources." 504 U.S. at 345.

Even as the *Chemical Waste* litigation was proceeding, Oregon was pursuing this avenue. In 1989, it enacted legislation instructing its Environmental Quality Commission to set a surcharge "based on the costs to the State of Oregon and its political subdivisions of disposing of solid waste generated out-of-state which are not otherwise paid for" under specified statutes. After rulemaking the Commission set this figure at $2.25 per ton, compared to the $0.85 per ton fee the legislation charged to in-state waste haulers. Out-of-state haulers challenged this arrangement on Commerce Clause grounds. The Supreme Court analyzed the case using the "virtually per se rule of invalidity" of Philadelphia v. New Jersey, because the statute by its express terms treated in- and out-of-state waste differently.

Oregon did not claim that its costs of disposal differed between the two kinds of waste, nor that there were any health concerns unique to out-of-state waste. They justified the surcharge as means of recouping from out-of-state haulers an amount approximately equal to the costs of disposal that Oregon and its citizens pay, through income taxes and other means, that are not reflected in the $0.85 per ton fee. The Court, per Justice Thomas, held that such a "compensating tax" could only be justified if Oregon could point to other charges assessed against in-state haulers for which the surcharge was compensating, which it could not. It rejected the notion that Oregon could recoup the subsidies it was in effect providing to waste disposal, because income taxes and the disposal surcharge were taxing events that were not equivalent, and the Court refused to enter the "morass" of weighing comparative tax burdens. Chief Justice Rehnquist, joined by Justice Blackmun, dissented. He argued that because Oregon was imposing restrictions on its own citizens' generation of solid waste (through various state and local programs), thereby trying to preserve a scarce state recourse—landfill capacity—"it is not discriminating against interstate commerce by preventing the uncontrolled transfer of out-of-state solid waste into the State." Oregon Waste Systems, Inc. v. Department of Envtl. Quality, 511 U.S. 93 (1994).

4. **Michigan.** Michigan adopted a state law requiring each county to formulate a waste management plan that demonstrated that it had adequately arranged for disposal of solid wastes generated in the county over the next 20 years. The law also authorized a county to refuse to dispose of wastes from outside the county, ostensibly as a means for the county to preserve its own capacity to demonstrate adequate arrangements for its own wastes. The Supreme Court held that the fact that such a county ban would discriminate against wastes from elsewhere in Michigan as well as from outside the state did not save the law from invalidity under the Commerce Clause. Chief Justice Rehnquist dissented, this time joined by Justice Blackmun. Fort Gratiot Sanitary Landfill, Inc. v. Michigan Department of Natural Resources, 504 U.S. 353 (1992).

5. **Are There Other State Options?** In light of *Fort Gratiot, Chemical Waste Management,* and *Oregon Waste Systems,* what, if anything, can a state do to discourage importation of hazardous or solid waste that will not violate the

dormant Commerce Clause? See, e.g., Government Suppliers Consolidating Servs. v. Bayh, 753 F. Supp. 769 (D. Ind. 1990) (striking down a two-tier fee system, on a rationale similar to *Chemical Waste Management*'s); BFI Medical Waste Sys. v. Whatcom County, 983 F.2d 911 (9th Cir. 1993) (citing *Fort Gratiot* in striking down a law authorizing a county option system similar to that at issue in *Fort Gratiot*). See also In re Southeast Arkansas Landfill, Inc. v. Arkansas, 981 F.2d 372 (8th Cir. 1992) (an Arkansas law limiting the amount of solid waste generated outside regional planning districts that landfills within the district could accept violates the Commerce Clause); Chemical Waste Management v. Templet, 967 F.2d 1058 (5th Cir. 1992) (prohibition of import or disposal of hazardous waste originating in foreign nations violates dormant Commerce Clause). But see Medical Waste Assocs. Ltd. v. Mayor and City Council of Baltimore, 966 F.2d 148 (4th Cir. 1992) (city ordinance requiring medical waste incinerator to burn only wastes generated within city does not violate Commerce Clause).

6. **Recycling Programs.** Wisconsin sought to promote recycling by enacting a statute prohibiting the land disposal of eleven specific materials that the state deemed to be recyclable. The only such waste excepted from the law's prohibition was waste generated in communities with "an effective recycling program" as defined by the statute. While a federal district court upheld the law as facially nondiscriminatory, the Seventh Circuit reversed. The court concluded that the law discriminated against interstate commerce by attempting to "control[] the conduct of those engaged in commerce occurring wholly outside the State of Wisconsin. . . ." National Solid Wastes Mgmt. Ass'n v. Meyer, 63 F.3d 652, 658 (7th Cir. 1995). The court explained that the law's basic infirmity was that it required all persons in out-of-state communities to adhere to "effective recycling programs" whether or not they shipped their waste to Wisconsin in order for any members of their community to have access to Wisconsin landfills. The court indicated that Wisconsin could have pursued less discriminatory alternatives by applying the law only to persons who dispose of waste in Wisconsin or by requiring that all waste disposed in the state be processed first in a materials recovery facility that separates the eleven listed materials. 63 F.3d at 662.

7. **Nondiscriminatory Measures.** Could a state avoid the problem of facially discriminatory legislation by simply banning all waste disposal within the boundaries of the state regardless of where the waste was generated? How would such a measure differ from the legislation struck down in Fort Gratiot Sanitary Landfill, Inc. v. Michigan Department of Natural Resources, 504 U.S. 353 (1992), discussed in Note 4 above? Such a law effectively would require that all waste generated in the state be exported. Could it survive constitutional scrutiny under the Commerce Clause?

8. **Other Nondiscriminatory Measures.** Measures that the Court determines regulate "even-handedly" are still subject to review, but under the more lenient *Pike Church* test, page 441, above. Avoiding the "virtually per se rule of invalidity" requires more than a statute that is nondiscriminatory on its face. For example, the Fort Gratiot statute did not expressly single out out-of-state waste and still was held to be discriminatory and subject to the tougher standard. As states continue to pursue ways of addressing their dwindling landfill problems, they can enact statutes that require intensive factual review to determine which test applies and whether the provisions are constitutional.

9. **Discriminatory Purpose.** Even facially nondiscriminatory measures regulating waste disposal may be constitutionally suspect under the dormant Commerce Clause if there is evidence that they were enacted expressly to

disadvantage waste originating out of state. In March and April 1999, the Virginia General Assembly enacted legislation to cap the amount of municipal solid waste (MSW) that Virginia landfills can accept and to restrict the use of barges and trucks to transport such waste. The legislation was adopted after then-Governor James Gilmore declared that "the home state of Washington, Jefferson, and Madison has no intention o[f] becoming New York's dumping ground." In Waste Management Holdings, Inc. v. Gilmore, 252 F.3d 316 (4th Cir. 2001), the Fourth Circuit found unmistakable evidence that the purpose of the legislation was "to reduce the flow of MSW generated outside Virginia into Virginia for disposal." While the court found that "MSW generated outside Virginia poses health and safety risks not posed by MSW generated inside Virginia," it concluded that most of the Virginia regulations could not be justified as the least discriminatory means for achieving the state's health and safety goals.

10. **Flow Control Laws.** Some states have sought to address the dwindling supply of landfill capacity, as well as the environmental degradation caused by such landfills, through strategies that seek to minimize the amount of waste that needs to be landfilled. Recyclable materials can be separated from the waste stream through curbside recycling, separation at a centralized facility, or a combination of these approaches. Much waste can also be incinerated. Incineration brings its own environmental concerns, but some localities have used it as a least-worst approach to waste disposal. Central waste sorting facilities and waste-to-energy facilities represent costly capital investments. To ensure their viability local governments have sought ways to ensure that the facilities will receive a reliable flow of waste material once they have been constructed. This has led to the development of a number of "flow control" laws and regulations throughout the United States.

New Jersey, for example, has been one of the leaders in flow control waste management systems. In something of a reversal from its efforts initially to restrict the importation of out-of-state waste, which led to the decision in Philadelphia v. New Jersey, in the 1990s New Jersey built a statewide system of waste-to-energy incinerators, associated landfills, and recycling centers that it underwrote with some $1.7 billion in government bonds. It also enacted a set of rules to assure the operators of these facilities that they would have minimum flows of waste material—in effect, adopting a strategy of keeping much of its waste in the state. Nationwide, it has been estimated that there is some $20 billion in bond debt for similar waste facilities, as well as a number of accompanying flow control ordinances or laws to provide raw materials to those facilities.

The constitutionality of these strategies was addressed by the Supreme Court in the following decision.

C & A Carbone, Inc. v. Town of Clarkstown
511 U.S. 383 (1994)

JUSTICE KENNEDY delivered the opinion of the Court.

. . . The town of Clarkstown, New York, lies in the lower Hudson River valley, just upstream from the Tappan Zee Bridge and by highway minutes from New Jersey. Within the town limits are the village of Nyack and the hamlet of West Nyack. In August 1989, Clarkstown entered into a consent decree with the New York State Department of Environmental Conservation. The town agreed to close its landfill located on Route 303 in West Nyack and build a new solid waste transfer station on the same site. The station would receive bulk solid waste and separate recyclable from nonrecyclable items. Recyclable waste would be baled for shipment to a recycling facility; nonrecyclable waste, to a suitable landfill or incinerator.

The cost of building the transfer station was estimated at $1.4 million. A local private contractor agreed to construct the facility and operate it for five years, after which the town would buy it for one dollar. During those five years, the town guaranteed a minimum waste flow of 120,000 tons per year, for which the contractor could charge the hauler a so-called tipping fee of $81 per ton. If the station received less than 120,000 tons in a year, the town promised to make up the tipping fee deficit. The object of this arrangement was to amortize the cost of the transfer station: The town would finance its new facility with the income generated by the tipping fees.

The problem, of course, was how to meet the yearly guarantee. This difficulty was compounded by the fact that the tipping fee of $81 per ton exceeded the disposal cost of unsorted solid waste on the private market. The solution the town adopted was the flow control ordinance here in question, Local Laws 1990, No. 9 of the Town of Clarkstown. The ordinance requires all nonhazardous solid waste within the town to be deposited at the Route 303 transfer station. Id. §3.C (waste generated within the town), §5.A (waste generated outside and brought in). Noncompliance is punishable by as much as a $1,000 fine and up to 15 days in jail. §7.

The petitioners in this case are C & A Carbone, Inc., a company engaged in the processing of solid waste, and various related companies or persons, all of whom we designate Carbone. Carbone operates a recycling center in Clarkstown, where it receives bulk solid waste, sorts and bales it, and then ships it to other processing facilities—much as occurs at the town's new transfer station. While the flow control ordinance permits recyclers like Carbone to continue receiving solid waste. §3.C, it requires them to bring the nonrecyclable residue from that waste to the Route 303 station. It thus forbids Carbone to ship the nonrecyclable waste itself, and it requires Carbone to pay a tipping fee on trash that Carbone has already sorted. . . .

At the outset we confirm that the flow control ordinance does regulate interstate commerce, despite the town's position to the contrary. The town says that its ordinance reaches only waste within its jurisdiction and is in practical effect a quarantine: It prevents garbage from entering the stream of interstate commerce until it is made safe. This reasoning is premised, however, on an outdated and mistaken concept of what constitutes interstate commerce.

While the immediate effect of the ordinance is to direct local transport of solid waste to a designated site within the local jurisdiction, its economic effects are interstate in reach. The Carbone facility in Clarkstown receives and processes waste from places other than Clarkstown, including from out of State. By requiring Carbone to send the nonrecyclable portion of this waste to the Route 303 transfer station at an additional cost, the flow control ordinance drives up the cost for out-of-state interests to dispose of their solid waste. Furthermore, even as to waste originating in Clarkstown, the ordinance prevents everyone except the favored local operator from performing the initial processing step. The ordinance thus deprives out-of-state businesses of access to a local market. These economic effects are more than enough to bring the Clarkstown ordinance within the purview of the Commerce Clause. It is well settled that actions are within the domain of the Commerce Clause if they burden interstate commerce or impede its free flow.

The real question is whether the flow control ordinance is valid despite its undoubted effect on interstate commerce. For this inquiry, our case law yields two lines of analysis: first, whether the ordinance discriminates against interstate commerce, *Philadelphia,* 437 U.S. at 624; and second, whether the ordinance imposes a burden on interstate commerce that is "clearly excessive in relation to the putative local benefits," Pike v. Bruce Church, Inc., 397 U.S. 137, 142 (1970). As we find that the ordinance discriminates against interstate commerce, we need not resort to the *Pike* test. . . .

The central rationale for the rule against discrimination is to prohibit state or municipal laws whose object is local economic protectionism, laws that would excite those jealousies and retaliatory measures the Constitution was designed to prevent. We have interpreted the Commerce Clause to invalidate local laws that impose commercial barriers or discriminate against an article of commerce by reason of its origin or destination out of State. See, e.g., *Philadelphia,* supra (striking down New Jersey statute that prohibited the import of solid waste); Hughes v. Oklahoma, 441 U.S. 322 (1979) (striking down Oklahoma law that prohibited the export of natural minnows).

Clarkstown protests that its ordinance does not discriminate because it does not differentiate solid waste on the basis of its geographic origin. All solid waste, regardless of origin, must be processed at the designated transfer station before it leaves the town. Unlike the statute in *Philadelphia,* says the town, the ordinance erects no barrier to the import or export of any solid waste but requires only that the waste be channeled through the designated facility.

Our initial discussion of the effects of the ordinance on interstate commerce goes far toward refuting the town's contention that there is no discrimination in its regulatory scheme. The town's own arguments go the rest of the way. As the town itself points out, what makes garbage a profitable business is not its own worth but the fact that its possessor must pay to get rid of it. In other words, the article of commerce is not so much the solid waste itself, but rather the service of processing and disposing of it.

With respect to this stream of commerce, the flow control ordinance discriminates, for it allows only the favored operator to process waste that is within the limits of the town. The ordinance is no less discriminatory because in-state or in-town processors are also covered by the prohibition. In Dean Milk Co. v. Madison, 340 U.S. 349 (1951), we struck down a city ordinance that required all milk sold in the city to be pasteurized within five miles of the city lines. We found it "immaterial that Wisconsin milk from outside the Madison area is subjected to the same proscription as that moving in interstate commerce." Id., at 354, n. 4. . . .

In this light, the flow control ordinance is just one more instance of local processing requirements that we long have held invalid. . . . The essential vice in laws of this sort is that they bar the import of the processing service. Out-of-state meat inspectors, or shrimp hullers, or milk pasteurizers, are deprived of access to local demand for their services. Put another way, the offending local laws hoard a local resource—be it meat, shrimp, or milk—for the benefit of local businesses that treat it.

The flow control ordinance has the same design and effect. It hoards solid waste, and the demand to get rid of it, for the benefit of the preferred processing facility. The only conceivable distinction from the cases cited above is that the flow control ordinance favors a single local proprietor. But this difference just makes the protectionist effect of the ordinance more acute. In *Dean Milk*, the local processing requirement at least permitted pasteurizers within five miles of the city to compete. An out-of-state pasteurizer who wanted access to that market might have built a pasteurizing facility within the radius. The flow control ordinance at issue here squelches competition in the waste-processing service altogether, leaving no room for investment from outside.

Discrimination against interstate commerce in favor of local business or investment is *per se* invalid, save in a narrow class of cases in which the municipality can demonstrate, under rigorous scrutiny, that it has no other means to advance a legitimate local interest. Maine v. Taylor, 477 U.S. 131 (1986) (upholding Maine's ban on the import of baitfish because Maine had no other way to prevent the spread of parasites and the adulteration of its native fish species). A number of *amici* contend that the flow control ordinance fits into this narrow class. They suggest that as landfill space diminishes and environmental cleanup costs escalate, measures like flow control become necessary to ensure the safe handling and proper treatment of solid waste.

The teaching of our cases is that these arguments must be rejected absent the clearest showing that the unobstructed flow of interstate commerce itself is unable to solve the local problem. The Commerce Clause presumes a national market free from local legislation that discriminates in favor of local interests. Here Clarkstown has any number of nondiscriminatory alternatives for addressing the health and environmental problems alleged to justify the ordinance in question. The most obvious would be uniform safety regulations enacted without the object to discriminate. These regulations would ensure that competitors like Carbone do not underprice the market by cutting corners on environmental safety.

Nor may Clarkstown justify the flow control ordinance as a way to steer solid waste away from out-of-town disposal sites that it might deem harmful to the environment. To do so would extend the town's police power beyond its jurisdictional bounds. States and localities may not attach restrictions to exports or imports in order to control commerce in other states. Baldwin v. G.A.F. Seelig, Inc., 294 U.S. 511 (1935) (striking down New York law that prohibited the sale of milk unless the price paid to the original milk producer equalled the minimum required by New York).

The flow control ordinance does serve a central purpose that a nonprotectionist regulation would not: It ensures that the town-sponsored facility will be profitable, so that the local contractor can build it and Clarkstown can buy it back at nominal cost in five years. In other words, as the most candid of *amici* and even Clarkstown admit, the flow control ordinance is a financing measure. By itself, of course, revenue generation is not a local interest that can justify discrimination against interstate commerce. Otherwise States could impose discriminatory taxes against solid waste originating outside the State. . . .

Clarkstown maintains that special financing is necessary to ensure the long-term survival of the designated facility. If so, the town may subsidize the facility through general taxes or municipal bonds. But having elected to use the open market to earn revenues for its project, the town may not employ discriminatory regulation to give that project an advantage over rival businesses from out of State. . . .

State and local governments may not use their regulatory power to favor local enterprise by prohibiting patronage of out-of-state competitors or their facilities. We reverse the judgment and remand the case for proceedings not inconsistent with this decision.

It is so ordered.

[In an opinion concurring in the judgment, JUSTICE O'CONNOR expressed the view that the town's ordinance was "unconstitutional not because of facial or effective discrimination against interstate commerce, but rather because it imposes an excessive burden on interstate commerce."]

JUSTICE SOUTER, with whom THE CHIEF JUSTICE and JUSTICE BLACKMUN join, dissenting.

The majority may invoke "well-settled principles of our Commerce Clause jurisprudence," but it does so to strike down an ordinance unlike anything this Court has ever invalidated. Previous cases have held that the "negative" or "dormant" aspect of the Commerce Clause renders state or local legislation unconstitutional when it discriminates against out-of-state or out-of-town businesses such as those that pasteurize milk, hull shrimp, or mill lumber, and the majority relies on these cases because of what they have in common with this one: out-of-state processors are excluded from the local market (here, from the market for trash processing services). What the majority ignores, however, are the differences between our local processing cases and this one: the exclusion worked by Clarkstown's Local Law 9 bestows no benefit on a class of local private actors, but instead directly aids the government in satisfying a traditional governmental responsibility. The law does not differentiate between all local and all out-of-town providers of a service, but instead between the one entity responsible for ensuring that the job gets done and all other enterprises, regardless of their location. The ordinance thus falls outside that class of tariff or protectionist measures that the Commerce Clause has traditionally been thought to bar States from enacting against each other, and when the majority subsumes the ordinance within the class of laws this Court has struck down as facially discriminatory (and so avails itself of our "virtually *per se* rule" against such statutes, see Philadelphia v. New Jersey, 437 U.S. 617, 624 (1978)), the majority is in fact greatly extending the Clause's dormant reach.

There are, however, good and sufficient reasons against expanding the Commerce Clause's inherent capacity to trump exercises of state authority such as the ordinance at issue here. There is no indication in the record that any out-of-state trash processor has been harmed, or that the interstate movement or disposition of trash will be affected one whit. To the degree Local Law 9 affects the market for trash processing services, it does so only by subjecting Clarkstown residents and businesses to burdens far different from the burdens of local favoritism that dormant Commerce Clause jurisprudence seeks to root out. The town has found a way to finance a public improvement, not by transferring its cost to out-of-state economic interests, but by spreading it among the local generators of trash, an equitable result with tendencies that should not disturb the Commerce Clause and should not be disturbed by us.

[The concurring opinion of Justice O'Connor is omitted.]

NOTES AND QUESTIONS

1. Unlike the surcharges in *Chemical Waste Management* and *Oregon Waste Systems,* the Clarkstown ordinance applied to all solid waste brought within the

town's jurisdiction without regard to its point of origin. Why did the Court majority find that the Clarkstown ordinance discriminated against interstate commerce?

2. A private contractor had agreed to build Clarkstown's $1.4 million transfer station and to sell it to the town for $1 after operating it for five years. Would it have made any difference to the outcome of the case if the city owned the facility instead, having built it with municipal funds? See Atlantic Coast Demolition & Recycling v. Board of Chosen Freeholders of Atlantic County, 112 F.3d 652 (3d Cir. 1997) (striking down New Jersey's statewide flow control scheme, which included many municipally owned and financed facilities).

3. In light of *Carbone*, would it violate the dormant Commerce Clause for a municipality to hire a single private company to collect all garbage generated in the town and to arrange to have the garbage incinerated in a single private incinerator? In USA Recycling, Inc. v. Town of Babylon, 66 F.3d 1272 (2d Cir. 1995), the Second Circuit reversed a district court's decision to grant an injunction against such an arrangement. The court concluded that *Carbone* did not strip local governments of their long-standing authority to collect and dispose of garbage. The court conceded that the town of Babylon had effectively "created monopolies in the waste collection and disposal markets by taking over both markets and then hiring independent contractors to provide services on the Town's behalf." Id. at 1275-1276. However, the court found that this arrangement "neither discriminates against, nor imposes any incidental burdens on, interstate commerce." Id. at 1276. Prior to the decision in *Carbone*, Babylon had employed a flow control ordinance to help finance construction and operation of a municipal incinerator. The ordinance had required all solid waste collected in the town to be disposed of at the incinerator and it imposed tipping fees on garbage haulers who delivered waste there. After the *Carbone* decision, the town responded by assuming full responsibility for waste disposal, financed through assessments on commercial property, and it contracted to send all the town's waste to the incinerator. The Second Circuit concluded that this arrangement was dramatically different from the flow control ordinance invalidated in *Carbone* because it did not require local businesses to buy services from anyone. "Instead, the Town unilaterally provides garbage services to everyone" within its jurisdiction. Id. at 1283. See also SSC Corp. v. Town of Smithtown, 66 F.3d 502 (2d Cir. 1995); Bennett Electric Co. v. Village of Miami Shores, 11 F. Supp. 2d 1348 (S.D. Fla. 1998), reaching similar results. These cases hold that a municipality may, if it chooses, "eliminate[] the [garbage collection services] market entirely," by taking over the provision of a "traditional municipal service" itself. *USA Recycling*, 66 F.3d at 1283.

4. In the early aftermath of *Carbone*, it appeared that federal legislation authorizing flow control restrictions might be forthcoming, as municipalities with bonded indebtedness for facility construction pressed their case on the Congress, and as about 10 percent of those bonds were downgraded in quality ratings or placed on a credit watch because of facilities' need to reduce tipping fees in the face of increased competition. BNA State Environment Daily, Mar. 20, 1997. In order to reduce industry opposition, flow control proponents agreed to seek such authority only for those governments that had enacted flow control measures before *Carbone* was decided, and only until their bond financing was retired.

Flow control relief, however, became joined with the interstate waste transport issue, which pits net importing states, who favor Congress authorizing states to restrict importation of waste, against net exporting states, who oppose it. That opposition is joined by others who espouse free market principles, as well as by some environmental groups. Thus far, the impasse has deadlocked action on both flow control and interstate transport.

5. Some environmentalists oppose federal legislation that would authorize states to ban waste imports on the ground that such laws discourage the development of better technologies for waste disposal. See, e.g., Congress Should Not Allow States to Ban Interstate Transport of Waste, Industry Says, 22 Envtl. Rep. 107 (1991). Do you agree? Grassroots environmental organizations look more favorably on proposals to authorize waste import bans. Environmentalists Release RCRA Wish List: Interstate Transport, Medical Waste Left Out, 22 Envtl. Rep. 334 (1991). Why do you think the views of the national groups diverge from those of the local groups on this subject?

6. Spurred in part by the NIMBY syndrome, local governments may be inclined to use their land use authorities to ban *all* land disposal of certain kinds of wastes, especially hazardous wastes, regardless of point of origin. These efforts face no Commerce Clause obstacles. Interestingly, however, federal legislation—which some states are hoping will *authorize* certain waste disposal bans (bans on out-of-state wastes)—may now operate to *prohibit* other kinds of waste disposal bans. See Rollins Environmental Services, Inc. v. Parish of St. James, 775 F.2d 627 (5th Cir. 1985) (effort to prohibit siting of PCB transfer facility preempted by section 18(a)(2) of the Toxic Substances Control Act).

2. Siting Controversies and the Environmental Justice Movement

One of the major focal points of the environmental justice movement has been on the siting of locally undesirable land uses (LULUs), such as hazardous waste treatment and disposal facilities, sanitary landfills, and nuclear reactors. See the discussion in Chapter 1, pages 15-24. As noted in Chapter 1, some controversy attends the question of whether the pattern of LULUs presently located in largely poor, minority communities—such as the ChemWaste facility in Emelle, Alabama, discussed earlier in this chapter—is more attributable to decisions made to site in such locations or to the subsequent movement of populations to communities neighboring such facilities, which often offer low-cost housing because of the property value–depressing effects of the LULU. However that historical question is resolved, there can be little doubt that the concerns raised by the environmental justice movement have produced much more sensitivity to the distributional justice issues posed by such siting decisions now and in the future.

The Nuclear Regulatory Commission responded to President Clinton's Executive Order 12,898 by adjusting its procedures for evaluating licensing applications. The following excerpts are from an opinion of its Atomic Safety and Licensing Board, which found insufficient attention had been paid to compliance with 12,898 in the NRC staff evaluation of a uranium enrichment plant proposed to be sited near predominantly minority communities in Louisiana.

	In the Matter of Louisiana Energy	
	Services, L.P.	
	Decision of the Nuclear Regulatory Commission	
	Atomic Safety and Licensing Board, May 1, 1997	

Before Administrative Judges MOORE, COLE and SHON.

This Final Initial Decision addresses the remaining contention—environmental justice contention J.9—filed by the Intervenor, Citizens Against Nuclear Trash ("CANT"), in this combined construction permit-operating license proceeding. The Applicant, Louisiana Energy Services, L.P. ("LES"), seeks a 30-year materials license to possess and use byproduct, source, and special nuclear material in order to enrich uranium using a gas centrifuge process at the Claiborne Enrichment Center ("CEC"). The Applicant plans to build the CEC on a 442-acre site in Claiborne Parish, Louisiana, that is immediately adjacent to and between the unincorporated African-American communities of Center Springs and Forest Grove, some five miles from the town of Homer, Louisiana. . . .

The community of Forest Grove was founded by freed slaves at the close of the Civil War and has a population of about 150. Center Springs was founded around the turn of the century and has a population of about 100. The populations of Forest Grove and Center Springs are about 97 percent African American. Many of the residents are descendants of the original settlers and a large portion of the landholdings remain with the same families that founded the communities. Aside from Parish Road 39 and State Road 9, the roads in Center Springs or Forest Grove are either unpaved or poorly maintained. There are no stores, schools, medical clinics, or businesses in Center Springs or Forest Grove. The Intervenor's evidence was undisputed that from kindergarten through high school the children of Center Springs and Forest Grove attend schools that are largely racially segregated. Many of the residents of the communities are not connected to the public water supply. Some of these residents rely on groundwater wells while others must actually carry their water because they have no potable water supply.

Although none of the parties put in any specific statistical evidence on the income and educational level of the residents of Forest Grove and Center Springs, the 1990 United States Bureau of the Census statistics in the record show they are part of a population that is among the poorest and most disadvantaged in the United States. Claiborne Parish is one of the poorest regions of the United States with a total population in 1990 of 17,405 and a racial makeup of 53.43 percent white and 46.09 percent African American. Over 30 percent of the parish population lives below the poverty level with over 58 percent of the black population and 11 percent of the white population living below the poverty line. Per capita income of the black population of Claiborne Parish is only 36 percent of that of the white population, compared to a national average of 55 percent. Over 69 percent of the black population of Claiborne Parish earns less than $15,000 annually, 50 percent earns less than $10,000, and 30 percent earns less than $5,000. In contrast, among whites in the parish, 33 percent earn less than $15,000 annually, 21.5 percent earn less than $10,000, and 6.5 percent earn less than $5,000. In Claiborne Parish, over 31 percent of blacks live in households in which there are no motor vehicles and over 10 percent live in households that lack complete plumbing. Over 50 percent of the African-American households in the parish have only one parent, 58 percent of the black population has less than a high school education, including almost 33 percent of the parish black population over 24 years old that has not attained a ninth grade education. . . .

The CEC site selection process began with a coarse screening of the 48 contiguous states to identify a region of the United States for the facility. This Coarse Screening Phase applied various selection criteria involving the service area of sponsoring electric utilities, transportation distances, and seismic and severe storm factors. In October 1987, the siting consultants recommended northern Louisiana to the Steering Committee as the regional location for the facility and the Steering Committee adopted this recommendation.

Because of a hold on the project, it was not until the spring of 1988 that the site selection consultants conducted what the ER labels a two-phase intermediate screening process to select the most suitable host community. In Intermediate Phase I, communities across northern Louisiana within 45 miles of Interstate 40 were solicited with the assistance of the Louisiana Department of Economic Development. The candidate communities were asked to nominate potential sites based on a set of criteria that, inter alia, indicated the proposed facility was a chemical plant. In answer to the solicitation, 21 communities in 19 parishes with over 100 sites responded and expressed an interest in hosting the project.

According to the ER, during Intermediate Phase I, the site selection personnel then visited each of the communities and, applying a second set of criteria, reduced to nine the number of candidate communities. . . .

The purpose of the second phase of intermediate screening was to select a host community from the nine communities still under consideration. . . .

During this phase, Mr. Engwall scored the remaining nine candidate communities against another set of criteria that had been refined and expanded from those used in the first intermediate phase. . . .

Mr. Engwall visited a number of the communities previously visited by his predecessor to learn more about Mr. Schaperkotter's evaluative process. His visits included several communities that had been eliminated in Intermediate Phase I because they had expressed a renewed interest or proposed additional sites. Mr. Engwall also visited each of the nine remaining candidate communities, including Homer, which he visited for the first time on May 22, 1989. . . . Based on Mr. Engwall's scoring, Homer was the highest rated community, with Winnsboro the runner up. The Steering Committee then selected Homer as the host community. On June 9, 1989, the then Senator of Louisiana, Bennett Johnson, came to Homer and announced that it had been selected as the CEC host community.

After selecting Homer as the host community, the ER states that a fine screening process, in two phases, was employed to obtain the three most preferred sites from the six sites nominated by Homer community leaders. In what the ER describes as Fine Screening Phase I, Mr. Engwall scored each of the six sites using the K-T decisional analysis against another set of criteria developed in conjunction with the Steering Committee. Although 11 sites in Claiborne Parish were initially nominated by community leaders, five sites were immediately dropped by Mr. Engwall for failing to meet the selection criteria and only six sites were seriously considered and scored. On the basis of the K-T analysis, the LeSage site was top rated and recommended for selection, pending confirmatory on-site studies. . . .

Intervenor witness Dr. Bullard in his prefiled direct testimony stated that, in his opinion, the process for selecting the CEC site was, among other things, biased and that racial considerations were a factor in the site selection process. Dr. Bullard based his conclusion that the CEC siting process was racially discriminatory on four major points. According to Dr. Bullard, the first factor and the most significant indication that institutionalized racism played a part in the site selection, was the fact that, at each progressively narrower stage of the site selection process, the level of poverty and African Americans in the local population rose dramatically, until it culminated in the selection of a site with a local population that is extremely poor and 97 percent African American. Specifically, Dr. Bullard stated:

> . . . [T]he aggregate average percentage of black population for a one mile radius around all of the 78 sites [that LES claims it seriously considered as candidate sites] (in 16 parishes) is 28.35 percent. When LES completed its initial site cuts, and reduced the list to 37 sites within nine communities (parishes), including Homer, the aggregate percentage of black population rose to 36.78 percent. When LES then further limited its focus to six sites in Claiborne Parish, the aggregate average percent black population rose again, to 64.74 percent. The final site selected, the "LeSage" site, has a 97.1 percent black population within a one-mile radius. . . .

Next, Dr. Bullard asserted, Mr. Engwall compounded the problem by using invalid and biased considerations in comparing the population level of the LeSage site to that of the Emerson site. The Emerson site, which was the overall second highest rated site in Fine Screening Phase I, was given a "low population" score of 7, yielding a significantly lower weighted score of 56. . . . [W]hen asked what he saw that caused him to score the site a seven, Mr. Engwall answered "[p]robably the proximity to the lake." Mr. Engwall went on to explain that "[w]e just felt opinionwise people would probably not want this plant to be close to their pride and joy of their lake where they go fishing." The significance of the lake, Dr. Bullard asserted, also was emphasized a few pages earlier in his deposition when Mr. Engwall testified that the Emerson site was rated neutral to slightly negative because

> [i]t was right on the edge of this lake. This lake is a very nice lake. This lake is the pride and joy of this part of Louisiana, nice boating, nice homes along the lake. It was felt that an industrial facility real close to that lake would not be in keeping with the existing usage, which was nice homes, vacation and fishing, hunting.

Based on Mr. Engwall's deposition testimony, Dr. Bullard concluded it was clear that quality of life considerations improperly affected Mr. Engwall's scoring of the low population criterion for the Emerson site given that, at this stage of the evaluation process, there were no site specific criterion related to quality of life. He further maintained that Mr. Engwall's biased judgment on the quality of life concern regarding the desirability of avoiding the lakeside site where white, middle class people lived was directly related to the relative scoring of the low population criterion. Dr. Bullard asserted that the total effect of Mr. Engwall's actions was to discriminate against the Forest Grove and Center Springs communities because their residents' lifestyle and socioeconomic status were on a much lower plane.

The third factor Dr. Bullard testified about was racial discrimination inherent in the Fine Screening Phase I criterion of not siting the facility within at least 5 miles of institutions such as schools, hospitals, and nursing homes. He asserted that by its own terms, this criteria is inherently biased toward the selection of sites in minority and poor areas because these areas generally lack institutions such as schools, hospitals, and nursing homes that are the focus of this criteria. Dr. Bullard stated that even though Forest Grove and Center Springs are five miles from the nearest town, there are no schools, hospitals, or medical facilities of any kind or, for that matter, any other service institution in either community. He stated that, while it is not necessarily inappropriate to attempt to site a hazardous facility in an area that is far from these institutions, this criterion cannot be applied equitably unless the process is enlightened by consideration of the demographics of the affected population. Otherwise, he stated, disadvantaged populations will invariably be favored as hosts for more hazardous facilities as is evidenced by the fact that minority communities already host a disproportionate share of prisons, half-way houses, and mental institutions.

The fourth and final point, according to Dr. Bullard, was the use of various community support criteria in the selection process that had the effect of discriminating against the people of Forest Grove and Center Springs. He testified that during the siting process LES relied upon the opinions of Homer, a community five miles from the actual host community. This was inappropriate, he concluded, because Homer stood to minimize the risks and maximize the benefit to itself by placing the facility a good distance from its own residents. In contrast, the actual host communities of Forest Grove and Center Springs were never informed of the siting decision until it was too late for the residents to affect the selection process.

This was particularly significant, Dr. Bullard testified, because the principal criteria for site selection were support from the community and opinion leaders in the community. Indeed, LES considered it of primary importance that the facility should be located in a locale where it would be considered a community asset. . . . According to Dr. Bullard, the groups of community leaders with whom LES met and with whom it consulted to form its opinion of "community support," "active and cohesive community leadership," and "community leader preferences," were dominated by the Claiborne Parish Industrial Development Foundation—on which Forest Grove and Center Springs have no representatives—and elected officials from the towns of Homer and Haynesville, rather than Forest Grove and Center Springs. Thus, Dr. Bullard concluded that a racially neutral site selection process was perverted to give certain communities the discretion to decide who should accept the adverse impacts of the proposed facility. . . .

C. LICENSING BOARD DETERMINATION

The nondiscrimination component of Executive Order 12,898 requires that the NRC conduct its licensing activities in a manner that "ensures" those activities do not have the effect of subjecting any persons or populations to discrimination because of their race or color. 3 C.F.R. at 861. In the FEIS and in its prefiled direct testimony, the Staff stated that it sought to determine whether race played a role in the CEC site selection process by reviewing the information in the Applicant's ER. In taking this action, the Staff necessarily recognized the agency's obligation under the nondiscrimination component of the President's environmental justice directive to make sure the site selection process conducted by the original venturers in what subsequently became the LES project was free from racial discrimination.

In the circumstances presented in this licensing action, however, by limiting its consideration to a facial review of the information in the Applicant's ER, the Staff has failed to comply with the President's directive. As we discuss more fully below, a thorough and in-depth investigation of the Applicant's siting process by the Staff is essential to insure compliance with the President's nondiscrimination directive if that directive is to have any real meaning. Moreover, such a thorough Staff investigation is needed not only to comply with Executive Order 12,898, but to avoid the constitutional ramifications of the agency becoming a participant in any discriminatory conduct through its grant of a license.

Racial discrimination in the facility site selection process cannot be uncovered with only a cursory review of the description of that process appearing in an applicant's environmental report. If it were so easily detected, racial discrimination would not be such a persistent and enduring problem in American society. Racial discrimination is rarely, if ever, admitted. Instead, it is often rationalized under some other seemingly racially neutral guise, making it difficult to ferret out. Moreover, direct evidence of racial discrimination is seldom found. Therefore, under the circumstances presented by this licensing action, if the President's nondiscrimination directive is to have any meaning a much more thorough investigation must be conducted by the Staff to determine whether racial discrimination played a role in the CEC site selection process. . . .

Because this agency's primary responsibilities historically have dealt with technical concerns, investigating whether racial discrimination played a part in a facility siting decision is far afield from the Staff's past activities. Indeed, because racial discrimination questions have not previously been involved in agency licensing activities, this is an area in which the Staff has little experience or expertise. Nevertheless, if the President's directive is to have any meaning in this particular licensing action, the Staff must conduct an objective, thorough, and professional investigation that looks beneath the surface of the description of the site selection process in the ER. In other words, the Staff must lift some rocks and look under them.

Substantial evidence presented by the Intervenor in this proceeding demonstrates why it is imperative that the Staff conduct such a thorough investigation. As we have noted, direct evidence of racial discrimination is rare. Nonetheless, the Intervenor's evidence, the most significant portions of which are largely unrebutted or ineffectively rebutted, is more than sufficient to raise a reasonable inference that racial considerations played some part in the site selection process such that additional inquiry is warranted. In so stating, we do not make specific findings on the current record that racial discrimination did or did not influence the site selection process. When stripped of its abundant irrelevant chaff, the record is simply inadequate, objectively viewed, to reach any conclusion with the requisite degree of confidence. A finding that the selection process was tainted by racial bias is far too serious a determination, with potentially long-lasting consequences, to render without the benefit of a thorough and professional Staff investigation aided by whatever outside experts as may be necessary. Additionally, the Applicant, because of the allocation of the burden of proof in the adjudicatory process and the nature of this particular subject matter, is, to some extent, in the position of proving a negative. Thus, in this instance any finding that racial considerations either did or did not play a part in the site selection process should be made only after the Staff has undertaken a complete and systematic examination of the entire process. . . .

Looking to the record of this proceeding, the Intervenor's statistical evidence . . . shows that as the site selection process progressed and the focus of the search narrowed, the level of minority representation in the population rose dramatically. The Intervenor's analysis did not include one of the 79 seriously considered proposed CEC sites because it was not clearly identified on the large map on which the siting consultants had marked the proposed sites. Of the remaining 78 proposed sites, however, the Intervenor's analysis reveals that the aggregate average percentage of black population within a one-mile radius of each of the sites across 16 parishes is 28.35 percent. After the initial site cuts reduced the list to 37 sites in nine parishes, including the sites in Claiborne Parish, the aggregate percentage of black population rose to 36.78 percent. Then, when the search narrowed to the six sites in Claiborne Parish, the aggregate average percent of black population increased to 64.74 percent. Ultimately, the process culminated in a chosen site with a black population of 97.1 percent within a one-mile radius of the LeSage site, which is the site with the highest percent black population of all 78 examined sites. This statistical evidence very strongly suggests that racial considerations played a part in the site selection process. It does not, of course, rule out all possibility that race played no part in the selection process. Nonetheless, the Intervenor's statistical evidence clearly indicates that the probability of this being the case is unlikely. Certainly, the possibility that racial considerations played a part in the site selection cannot be passed off as mere coincidence. . . .

To summarize, the Intervenor's statistical evidence and its evidence concerning the application of the low population criterion stand as significant probative evidence in the current record that racial considerations played a part in the site selection process. This evidence demonstrates that a thorough Staff investigation of the site selection process is needed in order to comply with the President's nondiscrimination directive in Executive Order 12,898. The Intervenor did provide other evidence concerning the inherent racial bias in the fine screening criterion of siting the facility five miles from institutions such as schools, hospitals, and nursing homes and evidence on the manner in which various community opinion and support criteria in the selection process discriminated against the minority communities of Forest Grove and Center Springs. This evidence is, at most, only indirectly indicative that racial considerations played a part in the site selection process. Nevertheless, when coupled with the Intervenor's statistical evidence and its evidence concerning the application of the low population criterion, this further Intervenor evidence raises concerns that deserve attention and should be further carefully analyzed as part of the Staff investigation. . . .

NOTES AND QUESTIONS

1. There can be difficult methodological problems in assessing whether siting decisions have disproportionate impacts on minorities and the poor. As noted in Chapter 1 different conclusions can be reached depending upon whether siting decisions are analyzed by census block, postal zip code, or county. What methodology was used in the Louisiana siting controversy?

2. Does the Licensing Board's decision mean that whenever a site is selected near communities that have the highest minority population of all candidate sites, a license must be denied to comply with Executive Order 12,898? What other factors were present in this case that convinced the Board to deny the license?

3. What should the NRC staff do in response to the Board's decision? Is there any way in which they could continue to support licensing at the site selected by Louisiana Energy Services and still comply with Executive Order 12,898?

4. Examining environmental justice claims continues to be a part of NRC's environmental impact assessment process under NEPA. In making these assessments, the NRC says its approach to "environmental justice [is] to look at disparate environmental harms, not disparate economic benefits." NRC, In the Matter of Private Fuel Storage LLC (Independent Spent Fuel Storage Installation), CLI 04-04 (Feb. 4, 2004). In the Matter of Private Fuel Storage licensing proceeding, it found that the members of a particular band of the Goshute Indians in Utah would receive economic benefits greater than the environmental harms to which they would be exposed, and thus that environmental justice concerns had been adequately addressed. Id. Is this approach to environmental justice consistent with the Executive Order?

5. Arguing "that environmental justice is not cost-free," a report published by Resources for the Future observes:

> At least in theory, to the extent that priority is given to addressing the environmental needs of minorities and the poor, it may not be given to actions that may protect a larger number of people. The overarching strategy of environmental protection in this country has been based not on a standard of justice that assumes government regulation should be directed to improving the conditions of some particular members of society but on utilitarian principles—the greatest good for the greatest number of people. These utilitarian principles are incorporated into environmental policies through such tools as benefit-cost analysis and, more recently, comparative risk. The potential conflict between environmental justice and utilitarianism will not be easy to reconcile.

J. Clarence Davies & Jan Mazurek, Regulating Pollution: Does the U.S. System Work? 37 (1997). Do you agree? How would you respond in the context of the siting dispute addressed by the Licensing Board?

6. Efforts to challenge siting decisions on equal protection grounds generally have been unsuccessful because it is extremely difficult to prove intentional discrimination, as required to establish that state action violates the Fourteenth Amendment. In Bean v. Southwestern Waste Management Corp., 482 F. Supp. 673 (S.D. Tex. 1979), aff'd without opinion, 782 F.2d 1038 (5th Cir. 1986), a court held that statistical evidence of disparate impact was insufficient to establish intentional discrimination in the selection of a solid waste disposal site despite the fact that the community originally was told that a shopping mall or steel mill was being constructed. In R.I.S.E., Inc. v. Kay, 768 F. Supp. 1144 (E.D. Va. 1991), a court rejected a claim that a county's decision to site a landfill in a predominantly black community violated the Equal Protection Clause despite statistical evidence of racially disproportionate impact. The court concluded that "the Equal Protection Clause does not impose an affirmative duty to equalize the impact of official decisions on different racial groups." Id. at 1150.

3.   Factors Affecting Siting Decisions: The Yucca Mountain Case Study

Apart from the legal difficulties that surround the search for land-based disposal locations, weighing the pros and cons of locating large deposits of potentially harmful waste materials introduces complex problems and uncertainties. No single siting decision highlights these complexities and uncertainties better than the federal government's decades-long search to create a disposal facility for spent nuclear fuel and high-level radioactive waste. In recent years, that effort has focused on Yucca Mountain, Nevada, a site 90 miles northwest of Las Vegas. On February 14, 2002, U.S. Secretary of Energy Spencer Abraham, acting under Section 114(a) of the Nuclear Waste Policy Act, 42 U.S.C. §10101ff, formally recommended that President Bush approve Yucca Mountain as the site for the geologic repository for nuclear waste. President Bush approved the siting recommendation and forwarded it to Congress, which endorsed the project in July 2002. This action permitted the Department of Energy to take the next step in the project, which is to make application to the Nuclear Regulatory Commission for an operating permit for the site, which DOE is currently preparing. While campaigning in Nevada during the 2000 presidential campaign, Bush had criticized the Clinton-Gore administration for proceeding with the Yucca Mountain project. Citing the risks of groundwater contamination from waste that will remain radioactive for tens of thousands of years and the risks of transporting 70,000 tons of such waste from all over the country, opponents of the project are pursuing every legal avenue they can to oppose the siting decision.

PROBLEM EXERCISE: SHOULD THE NATION'S HIGH-LEVEL RADIOACTIVE WASTE BE DEPOSITED IN YUCCA MOUNTAIN?

For many years civilian and defense-related activities have produced spent nuclear fuel and high-level radioactive waste. These materials have accumulated—and continue to accumulate—at 72 commercial and 5 Department of Energy (DOE) sites across the United States. Disposal of this waste poses an unprecedented challenge because it will remain highly radioactive for thousands of years. DOE is building a repository for the waste inside Yucca Mountain in Nevada. The repository will be located at least 200 meters (660 feet) below the surface and at least 160 meters (530 feet) above the present-day water table. Further background information concerning Yucca Mountain is available on the website of DOE's Office of Civilian Radioactive Waste Management at *http://www.ocrwm.doe.gov/*.

Arguments in Favor of the Yucca Mountain Repository

Proponents of building the repository at Yucca Mountain argue that it is critical to national security, nuclear nonproliferation, and the ongoing environmental cleanup at former nuclear weapons production sites. More than 161 million Americans live within 75 miles of temporary nuclear waste storage sites. These sites were not designed to contain the waste for extended periods of time or to withstand terrorist attacks. Nuclear materials would be far better secured in a deep underground repository at Yucca Mountain. While Nevada has not generated any waste from nuclear powerplants, the state will be adequately compensated for accepting the nation's radioactive waste.

DOE argues that experts throughout the world support its view that the safest and most feasible method for disposing of highly radioactive material is to store it deep underground. The physical characteristics that render Yucca Mountain a suitable site for waste disposal include: (1) its remote location and long distance from a large population center—100 miles from Las Vegas, Nevada; (2) its very dry climate—less than 6 inches of rainfall a year (water is the primary means by which radio-nuclides disposed of at Yucca Mountain could reach the accessible environment); and (3) its extremely deep water table—800 to 1,000 feet below the level of the potential repository.

Arguments in Opposition to the Yucca Mountain Repository

Opponents of the Yucca Mountain repository argue that it is riskier to ship highly radioactive material from all over the country to Yucca Mountain than it would be to leave it dispersed at current sites. They note the risks of accidents during transport and that highly radioactive waste could be an attractive target for terrorist attacks, particularly when shipments pass through populated areas. Las Vegas Sun, Nevada to Emphasize Terrorist Threats to Shipping Nuclear Waste, Jan. 10, 2002. (Republican Governor Kenny Guinn and Republican Senator John Ensign of Nevada argued that radioactive waste shipments are a potential target to terrorist attacks since the waste will be carried on the nation's interstates via trucks or on our nation's railways.) Supporters of the dump say the waste will be transported in special canisters strong enough to withstand any crash or attack.

Opponents of the project argue that the Yucca Mountain site should be disqualified because subsurface fracturing would allow contaminated ground-water to reach the environment in less than the 1,000 years required by DOE's original 1984 site suitability guidelines (10 C.F.R. Part 960). DOE responds that these guidelines have been superseded by Yucca Mountain-specific guidelines it promulgated in 2001. (10 C.F.R. Part 963). Project opponents also argue that earthquakes and volcanoes will cause releases of radioactive waste. The DOE maintains that its EIS has adequately taken these concerns into account.

Question One.   Should the nation's high-level radioactive waste be deposited in a repository at Yucca Mountain, Nevada? What should be the principal considerations on which this decision should be based?

Question Two.   If the waste is not deposited in a repository at Yucca Mountain, what should be done with it to protect human health and the environment against the risks it poses for the next several thousand years? Can any present-day policy protect adequately against risks extending so far into the future?

Question Three.   Nevada residents and officials strongly oppose siting a high-level nuclear waste repository in their state. They maintain that it is grossly unfair to their state since it has no nuclear powerplants that generated the waste and that state residents already have suffered unfairly by being exposed to nuclear fallout from the federal government's Nevada nuclear test range. Is it fair to make Nevada accept this facility despite its vigorous opposition?

Question Four.   The 2002 congressional action constituted the final legislative hurdle the Yucca Mountain project faces, but there are a number of regulatory obstacles remaining. One of these involves standards for radioactive releases. Section 801 of the Energy Policy Act of 1992 provides that the EPA "shall, based upon and consistent with the findings and recommendations of the National Academy of Sciences, promulgate, by rule, public health and safety standards for protection of the public from releases from radioactive materials stored or disposed of in the repository at the "Mountain site." Pursuant to this provision, EPA promulgated standards requiring the DOE to "demonstrate, using performance assessment, that there is a reasonable expectation that, for 10,000 years following disposal, the reasonably maximally exposed individual receives no more than an annual committed effective dose equivalent of 150 microsieverts (15 millirems) from releases from the undisturbed Yucca Mountain disposal system." The National Academy of Sciences, however, had issued a report indicating that there was no scientific basis for limiting a performance standard for Yucca to 10,000 years and that peak radiation exposures could occur tens of thousands and even hundreds of thousands of years in the future. Comm. on Technical Bases for Yucca Mountain Standards, Nat'l Research Council, Technical Bases for Yucca Mountain Standards (1995). The inconsistency between EPA's regulation and the NAS study led a U.S. Court of Appeals to overturn the EPA regulation because it violated section 801 of the Energy Policy Act. Nuclear Energy Institute, Inc. v. Environmental Protection Agency, 373 F.3d 1251, 1262 (D.C. Cir. 2004). EPA is in the process of reformulating its radioactivity standard. How realistic is it to expect that any standards promulgated today can ensure the control of risks tens of thousands of years in the future?

Question Five.   Also damaging to the effort to license Yucca Mountain may be the revelations that federal employees falsified data on water leakage into the facility. Falsified Yucca Data Could Complicate New EPA Radiation Standard, Inside EPA, April 1, 2005. This could "support the project opponents' claim that the site is unsuitable because water moves through the mountain much quicker than earlier anticipated, greatly increasing the likelihood of a radiation release from interred nuclear waste." Id. Has the dearth of salient alternatives to Yucca Mountain created a temptation to cut corners in performing objective analyses of the project? Do the difficulties experienced in developing a safe repository for disposal of high-level radioactive waste indicate that society should be more careful in the future to resolve uncertainties before launching technologies known to create severe risks that will persist for tens of thousands of years?

=5=

Air Pollution Control

There has always been a big gap between industrial leaders who say they cannot do something and their engineers, who usually figure out a way to do it. Before Congress passed the 1970 Clean Air Act, Detroit argued that significant pollution reductions would be utterly impractical or prohibitively expensive. Then along came the catalytic converter that, at modest cost, eventually cut harmful tailpipe emissions by 95 percent. Likewise, the oil companies predicted economic doom when Congress mandated cleaner fuels in 1990. Their chemists, however, have since managed to produce such fuels without disturbing profits.

—*New York Times editorial**

In 2003, ozone levels nationwide were the lowest they have been since 1980. Yet ozone continues to be a pervasive air pollution problem, affecting many areas across the country and, at times, harming millions of people, sensitive vegetation, and ecosystems.

—*The U.S. Environmental Protection Agency***

A. THE AIR POLLUTION PROBLEM

Air pollution has been a persistent problem of the Industrial Age, much of it traceable to the combustion of fossil fuels for energy in electrical generating units, in automobiles, and in industry. Even when they are not combusted for fuels, hydrocarbons contribute to air pollution through the release of vapors from chemical solvents, paints, and at gasoline filling stations, as well as by virtue of being the feedstock for the petrochemical industry, which has given us some of our most serious toxic substances problem, some of them airborne. Sources of air pollution are diverse, including most major industries, automobiles, trucks, buses, trains, planes and motorboats, hazardous waste sites and sanitary landfills, dry cleaners, construction sites, gas stations, lawnmowers, fireplaces, and wood-stoves. The diversity of sources and of the discrete pollutants each source typically emits have strongly influenced the regulatory strategies employed to improve air quality.

Certain conventional air pollutants have become nearly ubiquitous, originating from many diverse sources and posing risks to human health and

---

*Detroit Turns a Corner, Jan. 11, 1998, at 18.
**The Ozone Report (April 2004)

467

welfare. These include: carbon monoxide, sulfur dioxide, oxides of nitrogen, volatile organic compounds, particulates, and lead. For these pollutants, the Clean Air Act establishes a regulatory regime in which EPA sets national ambient air quality standards for each of them, after first establishing criteria that relate exposure to these air pollutants to adverse effects on human health and welfare. Each of the pollutants just named is regulated in this way, either as a so-called criteria pollutant or as a precursor to such pollutants.

These ubiquitous pollutants can cause serious health problems or exacerbate existing problems. Figure 5.1 presents a recent EPA description of the health problems associated with ozone. Ozone has proven the most difficult air pollution problem to resolve if measured by the number of Americans who continue to live in areas of the country that exceed the national air quality standards. As of 2003, more than 100 million Americans lived in air basins with poor ozone air quality. EPA, The Ozone Report: Measuring Progress Through 2003 (EPA 454/K-04-001, April 2004), at 1. Other air pollutants can cause even more serious adverse effects, including birth defects, heart attacks, cancer, cognitive impairment, and other forms of morbidity and mortality. (For descriptions of adverse health effects of other pollutants, refer to the website identified in Figure 5.1.)

Occasionally, acute episodes of severe exposures have generated a great deal of public attention. For example, on October 26, 1948, residents of Donora, Pennsylvania, awoke to find that a blanket of warm air above a cool air mass had trapped the pollutants emitted from the town's factories. The deadly inversion lasted for four days. Within two days, visibility had been sharply reduced and the town's doctors were flooded with people with breathing difficulties. Twenty people and numerous animals died; more than half of the town's 12,000 residents became ill. Devra Davis, When Smoke Ran Like Water 5-30 (2002). Such acute episodes no longer occur in the United States, except occasionally in the immediate vicinity of a chemical fire before people can be evacuated, but acute exposures are still a serious problem in a growing number of developing countries. More than two-thirds of the global urban population, mostly in developing countries, breathes air that has unhealthy levels of particulate matter at least part of the year, and major cities outside the United States experience very high average concentrations, with peak levels higher still. Addressing the health effects that are associated with chronic exposures presents problems for regulators attempting to achieve air pollution levels that will protect the public health. Populations move, air pollutants interact, and levels of pollution are not constant. Factors other than chronic exposure to air pollution also are associated with many of the health effects, especially the respiratory diseases. Lifestyle factors, particularly smoking, are strong contributors. In such circumstances it is difficult to determine how to establish air pollution controls sufficient to protect the public health.

Four of the conventional pollutants—carbon monoxide, volatile organic compounds, oxides of nitrogen, and lead—are produced by the internal combustion engines that drive cars and trucks. Such engines are the primary sources of carbon monoxide, although all fossil fuel combustion processes, including utility and other industrial boilers, produce it to some extent as carbon from the fuel bonds with single oxygen atoms. Oxides of nitrogen are produced by combustion because nitrogen in the air is oxidized by the heat produced during combustion. Unburned, as well as partially unburned, hydrocarbons or volatile

---

FIGURE 5.1
Adverse Health Effects Associated with Ozone

Ozone is the prime ingredient of smog in our cities and other areas of the country. . . . When inhaled, even at very low levels, ozone can: cause acute respiratory problems; aggravate asthma; cause significant temporary decreases in lung capacity of 15 to over 20 percent in some healthy adults; cause inflammation of lung tissue; lead to hospital admissions and emergency room visits [10 to 20 percent of all summertime respiratory-related hospital visits in the northeastern U.S. are associated with ozone pollution]; and impair the body's immune system defenses, making people more susceptible to respiratory illnesses, including bronchitis and pneumonia.

Children are most at risk from exposure to ozone. The average adult breathes 13,000 liters of air per day. Children breathe even more air per pound of body weight than adults. Because children's respiratory systems are still developing, they are more susceptible than adults to environmental threats. Ground-level ozone is a summertime problem. Children are outside playing and exercising during the summer months at summer camps, playgrounds, neighborhood parks and in backyards.

Asthma is a growing threat to children and adults. Children make up 25 percent of the population and comprise 40 percent of the asthma cases. Fourteen Americans die every day from asthma, a rate three times greater than just 20 years ago. African-Americans die at a rate six times that of Caucasians. For asthmatics having an attack, the pathways of the lungs become so narrow that breathing becomes akin to sucking a thick milk shake through a straw. Ozone can aggravate asthma, causing more asthma attacks, increased use of medication, more medical treatment and more visits to hospital emergency clinics.

Even moderately exercising healthy adults can experience 15 to over 20 percent reductions in lung function from exposure to low levels of ozone over several hours. Damage to lung tissue may be caused by repeated exposures to ozone—something like repeated sunburns of the lungs—and this could result in a reduced quality of life as people age. Results of animal studies indicate that repeated exposure to high levels of ozone for several months or more can produce permanent structural damage in the lungs. Among those most at risk to ozone are people who are outdoors and moderately exercising during the summer months. This includes construction workers and other outdoor workers.

Source: http://www.epa.gov/ttn/oarpg/naaqsfin/o3health.html

---

organic compounds (VOCs) escape from internal combustion engines and from oil refineries and chemical plants, as well as from evaporation in gasoline stations and fuel storage areas, dry cleaners, oil-based paint applications, and gas tanks.

The major sources of sulfur oxides are coal combustion and to a lesser extent oil combustion. The major locations for such combustion are utility power plants, although industrial boilers and residential heating also contribute to emissions. Particulates also originate from these sources, but in certain locations agricultural operations can discharge more significant quantities of particulates, as can forest fires. Fugitive dust from mining sites, construction sites, and the like also can be a significant localized source of particulate matter.

B.   THE CLEAN AIR ACT: BASIC PRINCIPLES

The principal statutory authorities for controlling air pollution are contained in the Clean Air Act. While other federal environmental laws can be used to address some aspects of air pollution (e.g., air emissions from hazardous waste disposal facilities are regulated under RCRA, air contaminants in the workplace are regulated under the OSH Act, and the Emergency Planning and Community Right to Know Act requires reporting of toxic air emissions), the Clean Air Act establishes comprehensive sets of measures to control outdoor air pollution throughout the nation.

The Clean Air Act Amendments of 1970 were the first in a series of comprehensive, medium-based federal regulatory statutes enacted in the 1970s to protect the environment. Because most of these laws emerged from the same congressional committees, the concepts and language adopted in the Clean Air Act provided important precedents for much of the environmental legislation that followed. These modern statutory authorities were preceded by a history of litigation sounding in private and public nuisance, which was reviewed in Chapter 2. The Georgia v. Tennessee Copper Co. litigation discussed there illustrates how virtually uncontrolled emissions from industrial facilities caused such substantial environmental damage that equitable remedies were imposed. Municipal smoke abatement ordinances were among the first environmental regulations adopted in the United States, with ordinances in Chicago, Cincinnati, New York, and Pittsburgh, among others, dating back to the 1880s and 1890s.

Some air pollution problems can be adequately addressed through litigation or municipal ordinances. Many facets of the air pollution problem, however, transcend municipal boundaries, and problems originating in numerous sources create insurmountable difficulties in proving causation and fashioning complete relief. The growth of nonlocalized and widespread air pollution problems associated with the automobile and with rapid industrialization outstripped the ability of these earlier regulatory approaches. The first state air regulation agency was created in Oregon in 1952. California's love affair with the automobile produced sufficient smog so that in 1959 that state became the first jurisdiction in the nation to enact laws that established air quality standards and began to determine what level of controls on vehicle emissions would be necessary to meet them.

Federal air pollution law began with the Clean Air Act of 1963, 42 U.S.C. §§1857-1857c-9 (1964), but the 1970 Amendments marked a significant departure from prior approaches and stamped federal regulatory policy with major features that it retains today. The 1970 Amendments were followed by significant modifications in 1977 and then again in 1990.

The diversity of air pollution problems, sources of air pollution, available regulatory strategies, and governments empowered to regulate different aspects of those problems have produced a very complex national regulatory strategy. Here is a highly simplified overview.

The centerpiece of federal law involves controlling the six criteria pollutants. Through the EPA, the federal government establishes *national ambient air quality standards* (NAAQSs) for these pollutants (§§108, 109). State governments then decide how the numerous *existing sources* within their jurisdictions whose emissions contribute to the ambient levels of these pollutants ought to be controlled in order to meet those NAAQSs for their jurisdictions. Each state's set of regulations to meet the NAAQSs is called its *state implementation plan* (SIP) (§110). Among other requirements, each SIP must avoid interfering with the efforts of other states to achieve compliance with the NAAQSs (§§110(a)(2)(D), 126). If a state does not prepare a SIP that meets the requirements of the Act, EPA must prepare a federal implementation plan (FIP) that ensures the NAAQSs will be met. See page 503.

As a further elaboration on the basic NAAQS/SIP structure, federal law now classifies parts of the country that continue to exceed the NAAQSs as *non-attainment* areas (NAs). It also classifies areas that have air quality better than the NAAQSs are classified as attainment areas regulated by a *prevention of significant deterioration* (PSD) program designed to maintain healthy air. The law also contains visibility protections for national parks and other areas where visibility is found to have special value (§169A), and these must be taken into account before new pollution sources can be approved. See section D2, below, for discussion of the NA and PSD programs.

All *new source performance standards* for stationary sources of air pollution are established by the EPA (§111). The Act mandates a permitting program for new sources, through which the various new source standards are implemented and enforced (Title V).

The transportation sector currently contributes 76.6, 49.1, and 39.8 percent of the total national emissions of CO, NOx, and VOCs, respectively. To address transportation emissions, EPA regulates both the *content* of fuels burned by *mobile sources* of air pollution—cars, trucks, and buses—and the *emissions standards* for new vehicles (§§202-234) (in some instances, Congress has enacted the exact numerical limitations for mobile source emissions and fuel content). All state authority to regulate auto emissions is preempted by the federal statute (§209), except California's. In contrast, states have plenary authority to affect the use of motor vehicles within their jurisdiction through *transportation control plans* (TCPs), by increasing the use of mass transit, and in other ways. See section F, below, for discussion of federal regulation of mobile sources and fuel content. Occasionally, the federal government has developed TCPs itself or has enacted laws requiring specific transportation control measures, such as the employee trip reduction program included in the 1990 Amendments, but attempts to federalize TCPs have failed. What do you believe explains the different elements of the allocation of authority over the motor vehicle segment of the air pollution problem?

In addition to the responsibilities already noted, EPA establishes national emissions standards for existing sources of hazardous air pollutants, pollutants thought to pose a particularly acute danger to public health (§112). Hazardous air pollutant controls are discussed in Chapter 3, on pages 271-278. EPA also administers a national program for the reduction of acid rain (Title IV), see section E, below, as well as for the elimination of pollutants that destroy the ozone layer, such as chlorofluorocarbons (Title VI).

This overview of the Clean Air Act shows that it assigns responsibilities for addressing different aspects of our country's air pollution problems to federal and state governments. Figure 5.2 summarizes the major responsibilities. In addition, the Act establishes some regional entities to deal with problems that are inevitably multistate in nature, notably the Ozone Transport Commission, composed of the District of Columbia and the 12 states in the Northeast from Maryland to Maine, to assist in developing coordinated measures to respond to the interstate ozone problems in that region (§184).

FIGURE 5.2
Clean Air Act—Major Programs

Regulatory Targets	Federal			States
	General	NA	PSD	
EXISTING SOURCES		✓		✓
EXISTING HAP SOURCES	✓			
NEW SOURCES	✓	✓	✓	
ACID RAIN SOURCES	✓			
OZONE DEPLETING SOURCES	✓			
SMALL SOURCES				✓
VEHICLE EXHAUST	✓			
FUEL CONTENT	✓	✓	✓	
I/M PROGRAMS	✓			
USE (TCPs)				✓

Check mark (✓) for federal gov't indicates it sets the standards, even if state administers them in its SIP. NA refers to programs that apply only in nonattainment areas. PSD refers to programs that apply only in clean air areas subject to nondeterioration rules.

Certainly the Clean Air Act has had considerable success. Overall, aggregate emissions of the criteria pollutants have fallen by about 25 percent, at the same time as Gross Domestic Product increased by 161 percent, energy consumption increased 42 percent, and vehicle miles traveled increased 149 percent. The reduction of lead emissions is perhaps the singular success story in air pollution control. EPA has drastically reduced airborne lead in the United States by banning the use of lead additives in gasoline. For details on lead emissions and their control, see Chapter 1, page 34, and Chapter 3, page 181. Figure 5.3 shows EPA data showing trends for the major air pollutants since 1970. At the same time, the Clean Air Act has become a prime target of critics and reformers who argue that the usefulness of existing regulatory approaches has been exhausted and that new strategies must be adopted to make further progress with respect to our remaining air quality issues. In some respects, the existing Air Act has already partially responded to calls for reform. The 1990 Amendments include an expanded deployment of incentive-based regulatory instruments, most notably the acid rain reduction program. See section E. These Amendments also recognize that end-of-the-pipe controls, whether they be at the end of an automobile tailpipe or at the end of a factory's smokestack, are going to be inadequate to achieve the NAAQSs in some major population centers. Thus, the 1990 Amendments require some nonattainment areas to participate in a clean fuels program, use market incentives to

FIGURE 5.3
National Air Pollutant Emissions Estimates
(fires and dust excluded) for Major Pollutants

	Millions of Tons Per Year							
	1970	1975	1980	1985[1]	1990	1995	2000[1]	2005[2]
Carbon Monoxide (CO)	197.3	184.0	177.8	169.6	143.6	120.0	102.4	89
Nitrogen Oxides (NOx)[3]	26.9	26.4	27.1	25.8	25.2	24.7	22.3	19
Particulate Matter (PM)[4]								
PM10	12.2[1]	7.0	6.2	3.6	3.2	3.1	2.3	2
PM2.5[5]	NA	NA	NA	NA	2.3	2.2	1.8	2
Sulfur Dioxide (SO$_2$)	31.2	28.0	25.9	23.3	23.1	18.6	16.3	15
Volatile Organic Compounds (VOC)	33.7	30.2	30.1	26.9	23.1	21.6	16.9	16
Lead[6]	0.221	0.16	0.074	0.022	0.005	0.004	0.003	0.003
Totals[7]	301.5	275.8	267.2	249.2	218.2	188.0	160.2	138.7

1. In 1985 and 1996 EPA refined its methods for estimating emissions. Between 1970 and 1975, EPA revised its methods for estimating particulate matter emissions.
2. The estimates for 2005 are preliminary.
3. NOx estimates prior to 1990 include emissions from fires. Fires would represent a small percentage of the NOx emissions.
4. PM estimates do not include condensable PM, or the majority of PM2.5 that is formed in the atmosphere from 'precursor' gases such as SO$_2$ and NOx.
5. EPA has not estimated PM2.5 emissions prior to 1990.
6. The 1999 estimate for lead is used to represent 2000 and 2003 because lead estimates do not exist for these years.
7. PM2.5 emissions are not added when calculating the total because they are included in the PM10 estimate.

Source: EPA Air Trends—Continued Progress Through 2004. http://www.epa.gov/air-trends/2006/econ-emissions.html

encourage utilities to switch to low-polluting fuels, and institute programs to promote the development of low-emissions vehicles.

As you study the Clean Air Act, reflect on whether or not the country's air pollution strategy needs another major overhaul, either with respect to its goals, its methods for achieving those goals, or both.

AIR POLLUTION CONTROL: A PATHFINDER

The federal Clean Air Act is the principal source of statutory authority for controlling air pollution. Originally enacted in 1963 and amended in 1967, the Act did not provide for comprehensive national regulation until the Clean Air Act Amendments of 1970 were adopted. The 1970 Amendments established the basic program for controlling air pollution that remains in effect today. The Clean

Air Act was amended in comprehensive fashion in 1977, and, after a long legislative struggle, again in 1990. Although they are the product of more than a decade of legislative debate, the massive Clean Air Act Amendments of 1990 generated remarkably little formal legislative history. Because the conference committee did not complete its work until just before adjournment, Congress simply ran out of time to prepare an elaborate conference report. While the Amendments occupy nearly 100 pages of tiny print in the October 26, 1990, Congressional Record (pp. H13101-13197), the Joint Explanatory Statement of the Committee of Conference occupies less than 7 pages (H13197-13203). A more detailed explanation of the legislation was inserted into the October 27, 1990, Congressional Record by Senator Baucus, the floor manager of the legislation (S16969-16983).

A useful guide to the 1990 Amendments is J. Quarles and W.H. Lewis, Jr., The NEW Clean Air Act: A Guide to the Clean Air Program as Amended in 1990 (1990). A more detailed guide to the structure of the current Clean Air Act is a three-part series of articles that appeared in the Environmental Law Reporter from April through June 1992. Garrett & Winner, A Clean Air Act Primer: Part I, 22 Envtl. L. Rep. 10159 (1992) (history and structure of the Act, NAAQSs, SIPs, and non-attainment); Part II, 22 Envtl. L. Rep. 10235 (PSD, new and modified sources, acid deposition control, NESHAPs, mobile sources); Part III, 22 Envtl. L. Rep. 10301 (new permit program, enforcement, judicial review, protection of the stratospheric ozone layer, legislative history).

EPA regulations implementing the Clean Air Act are found at 40 G.F.R. parts 50-97. EPA's Office of Air and Radiation maintains a website at *www.epa.gov/oar/*. Current data are available on its AIRlinks website, *www.epa.gov/airlinks/*. It also has a site devoted to the growing number of market-based systems of pollution control, *www.epa.gov/airmarkets/*.

To understand why the Clean Air Act has become such a complex beast, it is important to appreciate its historical background. A useful survey of how the federal role in air pollution control evolved is contained in J. Krier & E. Ursin, Pollution and Policy (1977). An early history of the Act that emphasizes the many institutional actors that influenced its implementation is R. Shep Melnick, Regulation and the Courts: The Case of the Clean Air Act (1983). William Pederson's classic article, Why the Clean Air Act Works Badly, 199 U. Pa. L. Rev. 1059 (1981), spurred interest in the development of the kind of permit program now incorporated in the 1990 Amendments. Craig Oren has provided the most detailed guide to the impenetrable PSD provisions of the Act. Oren, Prevention of Significant Deterioration: Control-Compelling Versus Site-Shifting, 74 Iowa L. Rev. 1 (1988); Oren, Detail and Delegation: A Study in Statutory Specificity, 15 Colum. J. Envtl. L. 143 (1990). The American Bar Association publishes an excellent handbook. Robert J. Martineau, Jr. & Daniel P. Novello eds., The Clean Air Handbook (2d ed. 2004).

MAJOR PROVISIONS OF THE CLEAN AIR ACT

TITLE I Section 108: requires EPA to identify "air pollutants" anticipated to endanger public health or welfare and to publish air quality criteria.

Section 109: requires EPA to adopt nationally uniform ambient air quality standards (NAAQSs) for criteria air pollutants.

Section 110: requires states to develop and submit to EPA for approval state implementation plans (SIPs) specifying measures to assure that air quality within each state meets the NAAQSs.

Section 111: requires EPA to establish nationally uniform, technology-based standards for major new stationary sources of air pollution—New Source Performance Standards (NSPSs).

Section 112: mandates technology-based standards to reduce listed hazardous air emissions from major sources in designated industrial categories, with additional regulation possible if necessary to protect public health with an "ample margin of safety."

Part C (Sections 160-169A): specifies requirements to prevent significant deterioration of air quality (PSD) for areas with air quality that exceeds the NAAQSs.

Part D (Sections 171-178): specifies requirements for areas that fail to meet the NAAQSs (nonattainment areas).

TITLE II (Sections 202-216): requires EPA to establish nationally uniform emissions standards for automobiles and light trucks that manufacturers must meet by strict deadlines.

TITLE III Section 304: authorizes citizen suits against violators of emissions standards and against the EPA administrator for failure to perform nondiscretionary duties.

Section 307: authorizes judicial review of nationally applicable EPA actions exclusively in the U.S. Court of Appeals for the District of Columbia Circuit.

TITLE IV (Sections 401-416): creates a system of marketable allowances for sulfur dioxide emissions from power plants and major industrial sources to reduce acid precipitation.

TITLE V (Sections 501-507): requires permits for all major industrial sources with state administration and federal oversight.

TITLE VI (Sections 601-617): establishes a program for controlling substances that contribute to depletion of stratospheric ozone.

C. NATIONAL AMBIENT AIR QUALITY STANDARDS

From the beginning, the goal of achieving air quality levels throughout the country that protect the public health and welfare has constituted the heart of the Clean Air Act. In this section we examine how the Act establishes national ambient air quality standards for the most common pollutants. The subsequent section then explores some problems in implementing practical programs that will achieve those standards, as well as how those programs have evolved over time as we have attempted to solve those problems.

The basic idea behind the Clean Air Act is deceptively simple: For the most common pollutants, the federal government will determine national ambient air quality standards (NAAQSs) and then the states will decide how to control local pollution sources so as to meet those standards. As you study the following materials, try to appreciate how complicated each step in this process actually is. Should Congress have anticipated the difficulties and written legislation that would have coped with them better? Do the difficulties suggest that these simple ideas are conceptually flawed and should be abandoned? If so, what principles should guide the nation's air pollution policies? Keep your eye on these questions as you are introduced to the intricacies of the Clean Air Act.

1.   Establishing NAAQSs

Section 109 of the Clean Air Act requires the EPA administrator to set primary NAAQSs at the level "which in the judgment of the Administrator, based on [the ambient air quality] criteria and allowing an adequate margin of safety, are requisite to protect the public health." The air quality criteria are supposed to "accurately reflect the latest scientific knowledge useful in indicating the kind and extent of all identifiable effects on public health or welfare which may be expected from the presence of such pollutant in the ambient air," CAA §108(a)(2).

Each step in this process is difficult and controversial. Scientific data are often lacking or inconsistent. EPA often has to interpret very limited evidence of adverse health effects based on data drawn from a tiny portion of the population exposed to certain pollutants. These health effects may vary depending on both the magnitude and the duration of exposures. The very idea of a health effect is also not fixed. Is a "health effect" any detectable change in blood chemistry, or only changes proved to have an adverse effect on bodily functions? What populations should be used as the measure of effects, given that small children and the elderly may be more susceptible to effects of air pollution? Should it matter that most human exposure to a particular air pollutant is from nonair sources? What constitutes a margin of safety if there is no known threshold for a particular pollutant?

The answer to each of these questions is crucial, because the ambient air quality standards serve as the basis for both short-term and longer-term exposure limits applicable to the entire nation, with potentially billions of dollars in industry control costs dependent on the outcome.

The regulatory burden involved in establishing a NAAQS is so demanding that EPA has strong incentives to avoid making frequent changes in such standards, much less to promulgate new ones. Whenever EPA promulgates or revises an ambient standard, every SIP must be amended and reviewed. At the time of enactment of the Act in 1970, air quality criteria already had been promulgated for five major pollutants: sulfur oxides, particulates, carbon monoxide, hydrocarbons, and photochemical oxidants. A sixth, nitrogen oxides, was added by EPA in 1971. Only one other pollutant, lead, has been added since then, as a result of a citizen suit. NRDC v. Train, 545 F.2d 320 (2d Cir. 1976). Lead was a unique case because EPA had formally recognized the health risk of airborne

FIGURE 5.4
National Ambient Air Quality Standards
Primary (health related)

Pollutant	Averaging Time	Concentration
PM_{10}	Annual arithmetic mean	$50\ \mu g/m^3$
	24-hour	$150\ \mu/m^3$
$PM_{2.5}$	Annual arithmetic mean	$15\ \mu g/m^3$
	24-hour	$65\ \mu g/m^3$
SO_2	Annual arithmetic mean	(0.03 ppm)
		$80\ \mu g/m^3$
	24-hour	(0.14 ppm)
		$365\ \mu g/m^3$
CO	8-hour	9 ppm
		$(10\ \mu g/m^3)$
	1-hour	35 ppm
		$(40\ \mu g/m^3)$
NOx	Annual arithmetic mean	0.053 ppm
		$(100\ \mu g/m^3)$
Ozone	8-hour	0.08 ppm
Lead	Maximum quarterly average	$1.5\ \mu g/m^3$

Secondary (welfare-related) standards are the same as primary for PM, NOx, ozone, and lead. The SO_2 secondary standard is $1300\ \mu g/m^3$ over a 3-hour average. CO has no secondary standard.

lead when it promulgated regulations under section 211 to limit lead in gasoline. In this situation, the court concluded that EPA had a nondiscretionary duty to set national ambient standards. More recent litigation suggests some uncertainty as to the specific actions necessary to trigger nondiscretionary duties. See, e.g., Thomas v. New York, 802 F.2d 1443 (D.C. Cir. 1986).

The current NAAQSs are listed in Figure 5.4. Notice that the concentrations of pollutants specified by the standards are expressed in terms of averages over different periods of time. Why would the standards be based on averages over different periods of time? Primary standards are to protect the public health "allowing an adequate margin of safety," while secondary standards are "to protect the public welfare from any known or anticipated adverse effects" of air pollution.

For two decades, the leading case interpreting sections 108 and 109 has been an appellate court decision involving the national ambient air quality standard for lead. A trade association representing lead producers and users, the Lead Industries Association (LIA), and a lead producer, the St. Joe Minerals Corporation, sought to have the standard invalidated on a variety of grounds. The decision that follows established several important principles concerning EPA's authority to set NAAQSs. One of those principles is that the Clean Air Act requires NAAQS to be set based on public health considerations alone, without balancing those considerations against the costs of meeting them. Costs play a more substantial role in other steps of multi-step statutory processes for achieving air quality, but they play no role in setting the NAAQS. Over the years, this principle was reiterated in Court of Appeals decisions, but the Supreme Court had never taken up the issue until its 2001 decision in Whitman v. American

Trucking Ass'ns, pages 486-492. Because *American Trucking* has replaced *Lead Industries* as the leading authority on this principle, the portions of *Lead Industries* relevant to it are no longer included in the casebook.

The following excerpt from *Lead Industries* addresses the findings that EPA must make in order to justify setting a NAAQS on the basis of adverse health effects. In setting the standard for airborne lead, the administrator was concerned about lowering the levels of lead in the blood of the sensitive population, namely children in urban areas. EPA made the decision that "the maximum safe individual blood lead level should be no higher than the blood lead level used by the Centers for Disease Control in screening children for lead poisoning," 647 F.2d at 1144, which at the time was 30 μg/dl. In order to achieve its goal of lowering 99.5 percent of the target population to blood lead levels below 30 μg/dl, EPA calculated that the average total blood lead level in that population would have to be 15 μg/dl. This was based on an assumption that the ratio of airborne lead to blood lead levels was 1:2. While this was consistent with some existing studies, the EPA conceded that the relationship between airborne lead and blood lead was only imperfectly understood. EPA also employed a combination of partial studies and some assumptions to conclude that nonair sources of lead (e.g., lead-based paint, lead from canned foods and pipes) contributed 12 μg/dl to blood lead levels of children, on average. In accordance with these conclusions, the EPA set the primary air standard at 1.5 μg/dl.

|| *Lead Industries Association v. EPA* ||
647 F.2d 1130 (D.C. Cir. 1980)

J. SKELLY WRIGHT, Chief Judge:

[Petitioner Lead Industries Assn. (LIA) asserted that EPA lacked sufficient evidence to justify setting the lead NAAQS as low as it had.]

LIA argues that the legislative history of the Act indicates that Congress only intended to protect the public against effects which are known to be *clearly harmful* to health, maintaining that this limitation on the Administrator's statutory authority is necessary to ensure that the standards are not set at a level which is more stringent than Congress contemplated. The Administrator, on the other hand, agrees that primary air quality standards must be based on protecting the public from "adverse health effects," but argues that the meaning LIA assigns to that phrase is too limited. In particular, the Administrator contends that LIA's interpretation is inconsistent with the precautionary nature of the statute, and will frustrate Congress' intent in requiring promulgation of air quality standards. . . .

We agree that LIA's interpretation of the statute is at odds with Congress' directive to the Administrator. . . . The Senate Report explains that the Administrator is to set standards which ensure that there is "an absence of adverse effects." But LIA would require a further showing—that the effects on which the standards were based are *clearly* harmful or *clearly* adverse. We cannot, however, find the source of this further restriction that LIA would impose on the Administrator's authority. It may be that it reflects LIA's view that the Administrator must show that there is a "medical consensus that [the effects on which the standards were based] are harmful. . . ." If so, LIA is seriously mistaken. This court has previously noted that some uncertainty about the health effects of air pollution is inevitable. And we pointed out that "[a]waiting certainty will often allow for only reactive, not preventive regulat[ory action]." Ethyl Corp. v. EPA, 541 F.2d 1, 25 (D.C. Cir 1976) (*en banc*). Congress apparently shares this view; it specifically directed the Administrator to allow an adequate margin of safety to protect against effects which have not yet been uncovered by research and effects whose medical significance is a matter of disagreement. . . . Moreover, it is significant that Congress has recently acknowledged that more often than not the "margins of safety" that are incorporated into air quality standards turn out to be very modest or nonexistent, as new information reveals adverse health effects at pollution levels once thought to be harmless. See H.R. Rep. No. 95-294, at 103-117. Congress' directive to the Administrator to allow an "adequate margin of safety" alone plainly refutes any suggestion that the Administrator is only authorized to set primary air quality standards which are designed to protect against health effects that are known to be clearly harmful.

NOTES AND QUESTIONS

1. Subsequent to this decision, CDC lowered the screening level to 25 μg/dl, and in 1991 it lowered the level again, to 10 μg/dl. What impact, if any, should this have on the level of the NAAQS? What if it were impossible to get 99.5 percent of the children's blood lead levels below the CDC level, due to their exposure to other sources of lead?

2. In Chapter 2, we introduced the trade-off between regulatory strategies that are inflexible but relatively easy to administer and more complex but more flexible strategies. There, the contrast was between nationally uniform technology-based standards and cost-benefit balancing standards. See pages 137-142. Proponents of greater flexibility have criticized the nationally uniform ambient standards of the Clean Air Act as well. In an early article, Professor Krier argued that uniform standards are a "fundamentally mistaken end":

> To justify uniform standards as efficient in cost-minimization terms one would have to assume that the costs of a given level of pollution and a given level of control are the same across the nation. This assumption, however, is manifestly not valid. For example, aesthetic costs and materials losses will be functions of the varying resource endowments, degree of development, and human attitudes that exist in different regions. Even health costs—which were of the greatest concern to Congress in passing the 1970 legislation—vary from place to place. Since such costs represent the aggregate of individual health effects, and since population varies significantly by region, so too will total health costs. If one believes that per capita and not aggregate health costs should be the relevant factor, efficiency considerations would still suggest some variation in air quality levels. This is because the costs of pollution control will also vary, depending upon population, density and nature of development, and meteorological and topographical conditions in any particular region. In short, since the costs of pollution and the costs of control vary across the country, it is difficult to see how a uniform standard can begin to take the varying costs into account. The standard that minimizes total costs for a region in Iowa is hardly likely to do so for all the regions of California or New York or Colorado as well. To require adherence to the same stringent standard everywhere will in many areas result in the imposition of control costs which are much larger than the pollution costs avoided. [Krier, The Irrational National Air Quality Standards: Macro- and Micro-Mistakes, 22 UCLA L. Rev. 323, 336-337 (1974).]

Krier contends that the only defensible rationale for nationally uniform standards is that it is simply too costly to set regional standards. In light of his criticisms, why do you suppose that Congress chose the nationally uniform approach?

The *Lead Industries* opinion describes the 1970 Clean Air Act Amendments as Congress's effort at " 'taking a stick to the States.' . . . Congress was well aware that, together with Section 108 and 110, Section 109 imposes requirements of a 'technology-forcing' character." 647 F.2d at 1145. Does this characterization affect your answer?

Greater flexibility in standard setting, and especially the ability to balance costs of compliance against benefits on a localized level, is one of the center-pieces of reform proposed by most of the reinventing environmental regulation reports referenced in the opening chapter of this casebook. For more on the arguments in favor of cost-benefit analysis in setting the NAAQS, see the notes after *American Trucking*, below.

3. At the time Professor Krier wrote the quoted article, states had just barely begun to implement their SIPs. Subsequently, it has become apparent that the SIP-writing process provides an occasion for states to take into account variations in pollution abatement costs in allocating emission controls among industries. For instance, a study of the paper industry has found that the stringency of pollution controls in SIPs tends to vary with differences in costs and benefits. R. Luken, Efficiency in Environmental Regulation: A Benefit-Cost Analysis of Alternative Approaches (1990).

As we will see below, states also have varied considerably in their progress toward attainment of the standards. Indeed, Krier now argues that national uniformity has been a chimerical goal of the Clean Air Act in light of the variable compliance history of different parts of the country. J. Krier, On the Topology of Uniform Environmental Standards in a Federal System—And Why It Matters, 54 Md. L. Rev. 1226 (1995). He maintains that it would be wiser and more efficient to abandon the fiction of uniformity in light of the "enormous costs, laughable delays, and extraordinary burdens" being incurred "for the sake of someday achieving standards that are, in the extreme cases, probably impossible and in many instances not worthwhile." Id. at 1241.

4. Section 108(a) requires EPA to publish air quality criteria for any pol-lutant that contributes to air pollution that may endanger public health or welfare if its presence "in the ambient air results from numerous or diverse mobile or stationary sources." Lead is the only new criteria air pollutant that has been added to EPA's initial list and, as explained above, this occurred only because of a successful citizen suit. NRDC v. Train, 545 F.2d 320 (2d Cir. 1976). Similar litigation has been initiated by the states of Connecticut, Maine, and Massachusetts to compel EPA to establish a NAAQS for carbon dioxide, due to its contribution to global warming and climate change. During the Clinton administration the general counsel of EPA had issued a legal opinion conclud-ing that CO_2 was covered by sections 108 and 109, but EPA did not begin proceedings to establish a NAAQS. The change of administrations in 2001 brought a new legal opinion from EPA's new general counsel, which repudiated the earlier conclusion. President Bush also repudiated a campaign pledge to regulate CO_2 and announced that the United States was withdrawing from the Kyoto Protocol that established worldwide controls on greenhouse gases that contribute to global warming and climate change. (See pages 1063-1071 for discussion of Kyoto.) The lawsuit by the state attorneys general followed.

PROBLEM EXERCISE: A NAAQS FOR CO$_2$?

Should a national ambient air quality standard (NAAQS) be established for carbon dioxide (CO$_2$) in light of evidence that it is the most significant greenhouse gas that contributes to global warming?

Question One. Should CO$_2$ be considered a criteria pollutant under section 108 of the CAA? This section applies to pollutants emitted from numerous or diverse sources whose emissions "cause or contribute to air pollution which may reasonably be anticipated to endanger public health or welfare." The states argue that: (1) CO$_2$ is emitted by numerous and diverse sources, (2) it contributes to the buildup of atmospheric concentrations of greenhouse gases, (3) these gases already are adversely affecting the earth's climate, and (4) changes in climate are known or may reasonably be anticipated to be causing a wide range of adverse effects on human health or welfare including heat stress, extreme storms, increased formation of ground-level ozone, and changes in the distribution and severity of diseases.

Question Two. Is CO$_2$ an "air pollutant"? Section 302(g) of the CAA broadly defines "air pollutant" to include "any physical, chemical, biological, radioactive . . . substance or matter which is emitted into or otherwise enters the ambient air." On April 10, 1998, EPA General Counsel Jonathan Z. Cannon issued an opinion concluding that CO$_2$ meets this definition. Opponents of CO$_2$ regulation argue that it is not a pollutant, but rather "a colorless, odorless gas that cannot be seen nor smelled," that "does not contaminate or defile things," but rather "enhances and actually makes possible the very existence of life on earth." *www.co2science.org*. Proponents of regulation argue that CO$_2$ should be considered a pollutant because it, like many other naturally occurring chemicals, becomes harmful when emitted in excessive amounts.

Question Three. In August 2003 EPA General Counsel Robert Fabricant issued a new opinion reversing the earlier position that CO$_2$ is an air pollutant covered by the CAA. Fabricant relied in part on a Supreme Court decision, FDA v. Brown and Williamson Tobacco Corp., 529 U.S. 120 (2000). In that case, FDA had asserted jurisdiction over tobacco under its authority to regulate drugs and medical devices. While tobacco did seem to fall well within the plain meaning of the FFDCA, the Court, in a 5-4 ruling, held that FDA lacked jurisdiction to regulate it. Subsequent to the enactment of the FFDCA, Congress had enacted a number of statutes that expressly contemplated the continued marketing of tobacco, and that aimed at regulating tobacco advertising. Under one reading of the FFDCA, however, if the FDA took jurisdiction over tobacco it would end up having to ban it, since the statute permits the FDA to approve marketing of drugs only if it can be done in a manner that is safe and effective. Despite FDA's protestations that it had no intention to ban tobacco products, the Court expressed the view that it might be required to do so if the agency had jurisdiction to regulate tobacco products. Additionally, prior to the agency's conclusion that tobacco products were being used as nicotine delivery devices, FDA Commissioners and high officials in HHS had repeatedly testified in Congress that the FDA lacked jurisdiction to regulate tobacco. The Court felt that the subsequent legislation Congress had enacted had "effectively ratified that position." 529 U.S. at 157. The Court concluded that on the basis of this record, Congress could not be presumed to have given the FDA jurisdiction of such "extraordinary" significance, over a large industry entirely different from any it had exercised jurisdiction over previously, without a better indication than the general wording of a jurisdictional provision of the FDA's statute.

How applicable is the *Brown and Williamson* decision to EPA's jurisdiction over emissions of greenhouse gases such as carbon dioxide? See Judge Tatel's dissenting opinion in Massachusetts v. EPA, 415 F.3d 50, 61 (D.C. Cir. 2005), a case in which a sharply divided court rejected a claim by environmental groups that EPA must regulate emissions of CO_2 from automobiles under section 202(a)(1) of the Clean Air Act because they are air pollutants that may endanger public welfare. The Supreme Court has agreed to review this decision.

Question Four. To justify its rejection of a petition to regulate emissions of greenhouse gases from automobiles, EPA concluded that it should not commence rulemaking "[u]ntil more is understood about the causes, extent and significance of climate change and the potential options for addressing it." 68 Fed. Reg. 52,822, 52,931 (Sept. 8, 2003). Is this consistent with Ethyl Corp. v. EPA, , 541 F.2d 1 (D.C. Cir. 1976) (en banc), discussed in Chapter 3 on pages 176-177? Petitioners in Massachusetts v. EPA thought not, but Judge Randolph argued that "*Ethyl* supports EPA, not petitioners" because it "gives the Administrator considerable discretion" to act not solely on the basis of scientific assessments, but also to make "policy judgments" concerning whether regulation was appropriate. 415 F.3d at 57-58. Do you agree with Judge Randolph's interpretation of *Ethyl*?

Question Five. Could EPA regulate emissions of greenhouse gases from new motor vehicles under section 202 of the Clean Air Act? Section 202 requires EPA to issue standards to control emissions from such sources that cause or contribute to air pollution that may reasonably be anticipated to endanger public health or welfare. In July 2002 California enacted legislation requiring "the maximum feasible reduction" in emissions of greenhouse gases from mobile sources in the state by the end of the decade. Can California legally do so? See CAA §209, 42 U.S.C. §7543, and page 577, below.

2. Revising NAAQSs

EPA is required to review and revise its air quality criteria and the NAAQSs at five-year intervals. Section 109(d) of the Clean Air Act directs EPA to "complete a thorough review" of the criteria and the NAAQSs and to make such revisions to them "as may be appropriate." To assist the agency in performing these tasks, EPA is required to appoint an independent scientific review committee, the Clean Air Scientific Advisory Committee (CASAC), which reviews the scientific data relied upon by the agency and recommends revisions in the criteria and the NAAQSs. While CASAC helps EPA to improve the quality of its analysis, its composition sometimes is controversial because it can include experts who work for industries EPA regulates. See S. Jasanoff, The Fifth Branch: Science Advisors as Policymakers 101-122 (1990).

Pursuant to these requirements, EPA in 1982 published new air quality criteria for particulate matter and sulfur oxide. The new criteria discussed in some detail how emissions of sulfur oxides contributed to the acid deposition problem. Despite issuing a three-volume "Critical Assessment" of the effects of sulfur oxides on acid deposition in 1984, EPA took no action with respect to revisions of the NAAQS.

In Environmental Defense Fund v. Thomas, 870 F.2d 892 (2d Cir. 1989), several environmental groups and six states sued EPA for failing to revise the

NAAQS for sulfur oxides. The plaintiffs argued that EPA was required to revise the NAAQS to prevent acid deposition because the agency had published new criteria documents finding that sulfur oxide contributed to the acid deposition problem. EPA argued that the "as may be appropriate" language of section 109(d) made any decision concerning revision of the NAAQS wholly discretionary. The Second Circuit rejected the arguments made by both EPA and the plaintiffs. The court concluded that although it could not dictate to EPA whether or how the NAAQS should be revised, "the Administrator must make *some* decision regarding the revision of the NAAQS" that itself would be subject to judicial review. 870 F.2d at 896. By publishing revised criteria documents, EPA "triggered a duty" on its part "to address and decide whether and what kind of revision is necessary." Id. at 900.

As noted above, EPA has been reluctant to revise its NAAQSs in part because of the enormous administrative burden such revisions would generate. Whenever EPA changes a NAAQS, each state must prepare a revised state implementation plan (SIP) that must then undergo a cumbersome process of EPA review and approval. Lengthy delays have occurred in the revision of air quality criteria as members of CASAC struggle to reach consensus on the significance of new data.

Scientific uncertainty has been the principal rationale used by EPA when it has declined to revise NAAQSs, despite new evidence indicating that certain pollutants contribute to health or environmental damages at lower levels of exposure than previously thought. EPA cited scientific uncertainty when it announced in August 1994 that it would not revise the NAAQS for carbon monoxide. 59 Fed. Reg. 38,906 (1994). While expressing concern about the growing body of scientific evidence associating nitrogen deposition with ecological damage, EPA proposed in October 1995 not to revise the NAAQS for nitrogen oxides. Standard for Nitrogen Dioxide Adequate to Protect Health, Environment, EPA Says, 23 Envtl. Rep. 1035 (1995).

The question of how much protection the NAAQSs should afford sensitive populations has assumed increasing importance. In the *Lead Industries Association* decision, the D.C. Circuit stated that "air quality standards must also protect individuals who are particularly sensitive to the effects of pollution." 647 F.2d at 1153. The court noted that the Senate Report on the 1970 Clean Air Amendments was "particularly careful to note that especially sensitive persons such as asthmatics and emphysematics are included within the group that must be protected." Id. at 1152. Concern about the effect of air pollution on asthmatics has increased as the health problems of asthmatics have become more apparent. The hospitalization rate for asthmatics has nearly tripled in the United States since 1970 and it rose by 43 percent between 1979 and 1987 for children under 15, an increase that cannot be accounted for solely by better diagnoses. Link Between Asthma and "Safe" Ozone Levels Is Studied, N.Y. Times, Aug. 8, 1991, at C3. As EPA's description of ozone's adverse health effects suggests, the link between ozone and asthma is now firmly established. See Figure 5.1, above.

SO_2 has also been associated with asthma. Notwithstanding this, in 1988, EPA proposed not to revise its primary and secondary NAAQSs for SO_2. It did express concern over the effects of short-term SO_2 peaks on asthmatics, and solicited public comment on the possibility of adding a new one-hour primary standard for SO_2 of 0.4 ppm. 53 Fed. Reg. 14,926 (1988). The agency subsequently estimated that 68,000 to 166,000 asthmatics could be exposed to at least one peak SO_2 concentration while exercising outdoors and that total exposure events could range from 180,000 to 395,000. 59 Fed. Reg. 58,967 (1994). One reason EPA was reluctant to revise the NAAQS was that short-term peaks of SO_2 are concentrated in the vicinity of several hundred large emissions sources, including power plants and petroleum refineries, and hence national standards may be inappropriate.

In November 1994, EPA proposed three alternatives for protecting asthmatics from short-term exposures: (1) a five-minute SO_2 NAAQS of 0.60 ppm; (2) a new program requiring the use of section 303's emergency response authorities against sources whenever SO_2 levels exceed a 0.60 ppm "trigger" over a five-minute period; and (3) targeting particular sources of SO_2 peaks for more vigorous enforcement of existing standards through a program of enhanced monitoring and inspections. 50 Fed. Reg. 58,958 (1994). In 1995, EPA issued a proposed rule elaborating on these options. 60 Fed. Reg. 12,492 (1995).

The main beneficiaries of a short-term standard would be asthmatics who suffer temporary and reversible bronchoconstriction while exercising. What significance should be attached to the temporary nature of these effects and the fact that they also can be induced by other stimuli? In *Lead Industries Association*, the D.C. Circuit rejected the notion that a primary NAAQS can only be used to protect against health effects known to be "clearly harmful." 647 F.2d at 1148. Can it be used to protect against bronchoconstriction experienced by asthmatics? One type of asthma medication can be effective in preventing bronchoconstriction if taken shortly before exposure to SO_2. But SO_2 exposures are unpredictable and the medication is not widely used. Should the fact that asthmatics can avoid adverse reactions to SO_2 by taking medication prior to exercising influence EPA's decision in any way? More generally, when EPA establishes NAAQSs, can it discount the adverse health effects of air pollutants that can be avoided by staying indoors or by not exercising?

While noting that its cost estimates may be overstated, EPA estimated that compliance with a five-minute SO_2 NAAQS would cost $1.75 billion annually in the year 2005. Most of these costs would be borne by the utility sector. If the standards were modified to permit five exceedances instead of one before a violation occurs, its cost would be reduced to $560 million annually. 60 Fed. Reg. 12,512 (1995). EPA was unable to quantify the benefits of a five-minute NAAQS. What relevance, if any, does this information have for EPA's decision concerning the NAAQS? Does it suggest that it would be "too expensive" for EPA to adopt a five-minute NAAQS? Can EPA legally consider costs when establishing a NAAQS?

In May 1996, EPA announced its decision not to adopt a new short-term exposure NAAQS for SO_2. 61 Fed. Reg. 25,566 (1996). EPA conceded that exposure to short-term peak SO_2 concentrations causes bronchoconstrictive responses in exercising asthmatics, but it noted a divergence of opinion in the medical community concerning the significance of these effects. Although it acknowledged that "repeated occurrences of such effects should be regarded as significant from a public health standpoint," it concluded that this problem was more appropriately addressed at the state level.

Public health and environmental organizations sued EPA for its failure to adopt a short-term standard. In 1998, the D.C. Circuit Court of Appeals remanded the decision to EPA for further explanation, saying that EPA had failed to explain why exposure to peak SO_2 concentrations does not amount to a "public health" problem within the meaning of the Act. American Lung Association v. EPA, 134 F.3d 388 (D.C. Cir. 1998). "The link," the court wrote, "between this conclusion and the factual record as interpreted by EPA—that 'repeated' exposure is 'significant' and that thousands of asthmatics are exposed more than once a year—is missing. Why is the fact that thousands of asthmatics can be expected to suffer atypical physical effects from repeated five-minute bursts of high-level sulfur dioxide not a public health problem? Why are from 180,000 to 395,000 annual 'exposure events' . . . so 'infrequent' as to warrant no regulatory action? Why are disruptions of ongoing activities, use of medication, and hospitalization not 'adverse health effects' for asthmatics? . . . Without answers to these questions, the Administrator cannot fulfill her responsibility under the Clean Air Act to establish NAAQS's 'requisite to protect the public health.' . . . Given the gaps in the Final Decision's reasoning, we must remand this case to permit the Administrator to explain her conclusions more fully."

As of February 2006, EPA still has not completed its revised rulemaking in response to the *American Lung Ass'n* decision.

Notwithstanding the SO$_2$ example, EPA does sometimes revise NAAQS. Spurred by a court challenge and mounting evidence of health effects not accounted for the last time EPA examined the particulate (PM) and ozone standards, EPA undertook review of those NAAQS and concluded that each should be revised. In 1997 EPA lowered the ozone standard from 0.12 ppm over a one-hour average to 0.08 ppm over an eight-hour average. While keeping the existing PM standard in place, it added a standard for fine particles of 2.5 microns or less, setting it at 15 µg per cubic meter on average annually, and at 65 µg per cubic meter over a 24-hour average. 62 Fed. Reg. 38,652 (1997), 62 Fed. Reg. 38,762 (1997).

Data available to EPA in early 2002 indicate that 638 counties are likely to violate the new ozone standards, while 330 counties are likely to violate the new fine particles standard, compared with 106 and 41, respectively, under the old standards. Exceedances for ozone are concentrated in the Northeast corridor and along the southern California coast. Stakeholders Prepare for Air Quality Rule Implementation Battle, Inside EPA (March 29, 2002).

Using models that projected costs to the year 2010, EPA estimates the new ozone standards would impose costs of $1.1 billion annually. While unable to quantify all health benefits, EPA estimates quantifiable benefits in a range from $0.4 billion to $2.1 billion per year. For PM, the comparable figures are $8.6 billion in costs, and a range of $19 to $104 billion in benefits. EPA Regulatory Impact Analysis for the Particulate Matter and Ozone Rule, Tables ES-3 and ES-4 (July 17, 1997). The PM benefits are largely attributed to new research linking specific components of concern such as acid aerosols, sulfates, nitrates, some metals, and diesel particulates, all of which are found predominantly on the fine particles, to adverse health effects. The existing PM standard had permitted compliance through the use of technologies not designed to reduce the fine particles. Among the studies supporting the PM standard was a comprehensive epidemiological study of the medical records of more than 550,000 people in 151 cities, which found death rates 15 to 17 percent greater in cities with high levels of particulates, after controlling for other factors. Health et al., Particulates Air Pollution as a Predictor of Mortality in a Prospective Study of U.S. Adults, 151 Am. J. of Respiratory & Critical Care 669 (1995). Even in cities that were in compliance with the NAAQS for particulates, death rates were 3 to 8 percent higher than in complying cities with lower levels of exposure.

The new NAAQSs were immediately challenged by many parties. In 1999, a three-judge panel of the D.C. Circuit voted 2-1 to invalidate both the ozone and the PM NAAQS. American Trucking Ass'n v. EPA, 175 F.3d 1027 (D.C. Cir. 1999). Industry groups had argued in their petitions that *Lead Industries* was not controlling, and that EPA had erred in failing to consider the costs of compliance in setting the standards. One industry petition also briefly argued that if the Clean Air Act really did compel the administrator of EPA to set NAAQS without taking costs into account, then the delegation of authority was in effect standardless, because it did not identify how any point above zero could be chosen as a NAAQS, at least when EPA was considering a pollutant where there was no clear evidence of a level above zero where the pollutant had no adverse effects. Industry petitions also raised a number of other challenges to the evidence and to details in EPA's interpretation of the 1990 Amendments.

When the panel decision was announced, it rested on a much more breathtaking legal theory than anyone had anticipated. The panel acknowledged that EPA had provided information on criteria that it took into account in setting the NAAQS, such as the severity of adverse health effects at different levels of exposure, the number of people affected, the quality of the scientific evidence, and so on. Nonetheless, it concluded that EPA had violated the constitutional doctrine against delegating legislative authority to the executive branch because the agency had failed to identify how these criteria would all be combined to reach a judgment as to why a specific level would be chosen. Without identifying such a "determinate standard," the panel wrote, "it is as though Congress commanded EPA to select 'big guys,' and EPA announced that it would evaluate candidates based on height and weight, but revealed no cut-off point. The announcement, though sensible in what it does say, is fatally incomplete. The reasonable person responds, 'How tall? How heavy?' " Id. at 1034.

The panel's decision was both novel and potentially far-reaching. Previously, the non-delegation doctrine had only been invoked by the Supreme Court as a check on Congress's authority. Here, however, the panel did not find the Clean Air Act to be irretrievably flawed on non-delegation grounds. Instead, it held that EPA had failed to cure any non-delegation problem by not announcing a determinate standard or formula for combining all the relevant criteria. The theory was potentially far-reaching because its logic could be applied to many other areas of administrative rulemaking, both at EPA and in other agencies. Few were surprised when the Supreme Court accepted the case for review, thereby providing the Court with its first opportunity to review the proper interpretation of the standard-setting provisions of the Clean Air Act for NAAQSs.

|| *Whitman v. American Trucking Ass'ns* ||
531 U.S. 457 (2001)

JUSTICE SCALIA delivered the opinion of the Court.

These cases present the following questions: (1) Whether §109(b)(1) of the Clean Air Act (CAA) delegates legislative power to the Administrator of the Environmental Protection Agency (EPA). (2) Whether the Administrator may consider the costs of implementation in setting national ambient air quality standards (NAAQS) under §109(b)(1). (3) Whether the Court of Appeals had jurisdiction to review the EPA's interpretation of Part D of Title I of the CAA, 42 U.S.C. §7501-7515, with respect to implementing the revised ozone NAAQS. (4) If so, whether the EPA's interpretation of that part was permissible. . . .

II

In *Lead Industries Assn., Inc. v. EPA,* [pages 478-479], the District of Columbia Circuit held that "economic considerations [may] play no part in the promulgation of ambient air quality standards under Section 109" of the CAA. In the present cases, the court adhered to that holding, 175 F.3d, at 1040-1041, as it had done on many other occasions. Respondents argue that these decisions are incorrect. We disagree; and since the first step in assessing whether a statute delegates legislative power is to determine what authority the statute confers, we address that issue of interpretation first and reach respondents' constitutional arguments in Part III, *infra.*

Section 109(b)(1) instructs the EPA to set primary ambient air quality standards "the attainment and maintenance of which . . . are requisite to protect the public health" with "an adequate margin of safety." Were it not for the hundreds of pages of briefing respondents have submitted on the issue, one would have thought it fairly clear that this text does not permit the EPA to consider costs in setting the standards. The language, as one scholar has noted, "is absolute." D. Currie, Air Pollution: Federal Law and Analysis 4-15 (1981). The EPA, "based on" the information about health effects contained in the technical "criteria" documents compiled under §108(a)(2), is to identify the maximum airborne concentration of a pollutant that the public health can tolerate, decrease the concentration to provide an "adequate" margin of safety, and set the standard at that level. Nowhere are the costs of achieving such a standard made part of that initial calculation.

Against this most natural of readings, respondents make a lengthy, spirited, but ultimately unsuccessful attack. They begin with the object of §109(b)(1)'s focus, the "public health." When the term first appeared in federal clean air legislation—in the Act of July 14, 1955 (1955 Act), 69 Stat. 322, which expressed "recognition of the dangers to the public health" from air pollution—its ordinary meaning was "[t]he health of the community." Webster's New International Dictionary 2005 (2d ed. 1950). Respondents argue, however, that §109(b)(1), as added by the Clean Air Amendments of 1970 (1970 Act), 84 Stat. 1676, meant to use the term's secondary meaning: "[t]he ways and means of conserving the health of the members of a community, as by preventive medicine, organized care of the sick, etc." Ibid. Words that can have more than one meaning are given content, however, by their surroundings, *FDA v. Brown & Williamson Tobacco Corp.,* 529 U.S. 120, 132-133 (2000); *Jones v. United States,* 527 U.S. 373, 389 (1999), and in the context of §109(b)(1) this second definition makes no sense. Congress could not have meant to instruct the Administrator to set NAAQS at a level "requisite to protect" "the art and science dealing with the protection and improvement of community health." Webster's Third New International Dictionary 1836 (1981). We therefore revert to the primary definition of the term: the health of the public.

Even so, respondents argue, many more factors than air pollution affect public health. In particular, the economic cost of implementing a very stringent standard might produce health losses sufficient to offset the health gains achieved in cleaning the air—for example, by closing down whole industries and thereby impoverishing the workers and consumers dependent upon those industries. That is unquestionably true, and Congress was unquestionably aware of it. Thus, Congress had commissioned in the Air Quality Act of 1967 (1967 Act) "a detailed estimate of the cost of carrying out the provisions of this Act; a comprehensive study of the cost of program implementation by affected units of government; and a comprehensive study of the economic impact of air quality standards on the Nation's industries, communities, and other contributing sources of pollution." §2, 81 Stat. 505. The 1970 Congress, armed with the results of this study, see The Cost of Clean Air, S. Doc. No. 91-40 (1969) (publishing the results of the study), not only anticipated that compliance costs could injure the public health, but provided for that precise exigency. Section 110(f)(1) of the CAA permitted the Administrator to waive the compliance deadline for stationary sources if, inter alia, sufficient control measures were simply unavailable and "the continued operation of such sources is *essential . . . to the public health* or welfare." 84 Stat. 1683 (emphasis added). Other provisions explicitly permitted or required economic costs to be taken into account in implementing the air quality standards. Section 111(b)(1)(B), for example, commanded the Administrator to set "standards of performance" for certain new sources of emissions that as specified in §111(a)(1) were to "reflec[t]the degree of emission limitation achievable through the application of the best system of emission reduction which (taking into account the cost of achieving such reduction) the Administrator determines has been adequately demonstrated." Section 202(a)(2) prescribed that emissions standards for automobiles could take effect only "after such period as the Administrator finds necessary to permit the development and application of the requisite technology, giving appropriate consideration to the cost of compliance within such period." 84 Stat. 1690. See also §202(b)(5)(C) (similar limitation for interim standards); §211(c)(2) (similar limitation for fuel additives); §231(b) (similar limitation for implementation of aircraft emission standards). Subsequent amendments to the CAA have added many more provisions directing, in explicit language, that the Administrator consider costs in performing various duties. See, e.g., 42 U.S.C. §7545(k)(1) (reformulate gasoline to "require the greatest reduction in emissions . . . taking into consideration the cost of achieving such emissions reductions"); §7547(a)(3) (emission reduction for nonroad vehicles to be set "giving appropriate consideration to the cost" of the standards). We have therefore refused to find implicit in ambiguous sections of the CAA an authorization to consider costs that has elsewhere, and so often, been expressly granted.

Accordingly, to prevail in their present challenge, respondents must show a textual commitment of authority to the EPA to consider costs in setting NAAQS under §109(b)(1). And because §109(b)(1) and the NAAQS for which it provides are the engine that drives nearly all of Title I of the CAA, 42 U.S.C. §7401-7515, that textual commitment must be a clear one. Congress, we have held, does not alter the fundamental details of a regulatory scheme in vague terms or ancillary provisions—it does not, one might say, hide elephants in mouseholes. Respondents' textual arguments ultimately founder upon this principle.

Their first claim is that §109(b)(1)'s terms "adequate margin" and "requisite" leave room to pad health effects with cost concerns. Just as we found it "highly unlikely that Congress would leave the determination of whether an industry will be entirely, or even substantially, rate-regulated to agency discretion—and even more unlikely that it would achieve that through such a subtle device as permission to 'modify' rate-filing requirements," MCI Telecommunications Corp. v. American Telephone & Telegraph Co., so also we find it implausible that Congress would give to the EPA through these modest words the power to determine whether implementation costs should moderate national air quality standards. Accord Christensen v. Harris County, 529 U.S. 576, 590n. (2000) (Scalia, J., concurring in part and concurring in judgment)

("The implausibility of Congress's leaving a highly significant issue unaddressed (and thus 'delegating' its resolution to the administering agency) is assuredly one of the factors to be considered in determining whether there is ambiguity" (emphasis deleted)).

The same defect inheres in respondents' next two arguments: that while the Administrator's judgment about what is requisite to protect the public health must be "based on [the] criteria" documents developed under §108(a)(2), see §109(b)(1), it need not be based solely on those criteria; and that those criteria themselves, while they must include "effects on public health or welfare which may be expected from the presence of such pollutant in the ambient air," are not necessarily limited to those effects. Even if we were to concede those premises, we still would not conclude that one of the unenumerated factors that the agency can consider in developing and applying the criteria is cost of implementation. That factor is both so indirectly related to public health and so full of potential for canceling the conclusions drawn from direct health effects that it would surely have been expressly mentioned in §§108 and 109 had Congress meant it to be considered. Yet while those provisions describe in detail how the health effects of pollutants in the ambient air are to be calculated and given effect, see §108(a)(2), they say not a word about costs.

Respondents point, finally, to a number of provisions in the CAA that *do* require attainment cost data to be generated. Section 108(b)(1), for example, instructs the Administrator to "issue to the States," simultaneously with the criteria documents, "information on air pollution control techniques, which information shall include data relating to the cost of installation and operation." And §109(d)(2)(C)(iv) requires the Clean Air Scientific Advisory Committee to "advise the Administrator of any adverse public health, welfare, social, economic, or energy effects which may result from various strategies for attainment and maintenance" of NAAQS. Respondents argue that these provisions make no sense unless costs are to be considered in setting the NAAQS. That is not so. These provisions enable the Administrator to assist the States in carrying out their statutory role as primary *implementers* of the NAAQS. It is to the States that the Act assigns initial and primary responsibility for deciding what emissions reductions will be required from which sources. It would be impossible to perform that task intelligently without considering which abatement technologies are most efficient, and most economically feasible—which is why we have said that "the most important forum for consideration of claims of economic and technological infeasibility is before the state agency formulating the implementation plan," *Union Elec. Co. v. EPA,* [page 497]. Thus, federal clean air legislation has, from the very beginning, directed federal agencies to develop and transmit implementation data, including cost data, to the States. See 1955 Act, §2(b), 69 Stat. 322; Clean Air Act of 1963, amending §§3(a), (b) of the CAA, 77 Stat. 394; 1967 Act, §§103(a)-(d), 104, 107(c), 81 Stat. 486-488. That Congress chose to carry forward this research program to assist States in choosing the means through which they would implement the standards is perfectly sensible, and has no bearing upon whether cost considerations are to be taken into account in formulating the standards.

It should be clear from what we have said that the canon requiring texts to be so construed as to avoid serious constitutional problems has no application here. No matter how severe the constitutional doubt, courts may choose only between reasonably available interpretations of a text. The text of §109(b), interpreted in its statutory and historical context and with appreciation for its importance to the CAA as a whole, unambiguously bars cost considerations from the NAAQS-setting process, and thus ends the matter for us as well as the EPA.[4] We therefore affirm the judgment of the Court of Appeals on this point.

III

Section 109(b)(1) of the CAA instructs the EPA to set "ambient air quality standards the attainment and maintenance of which in the judgment of the Administrator, based on [the] criteria [documents of §108] and allowing an adequate margin of safety, are requisite to protect the public health." The Court of Appeals held that this section as interpreted by the Administrator did not provide an "intelligible principle" to guide the EPA's exercise of authority in setting NAAQS. "[The] EPA," it said, "lack[ed] any determinate criteria for drawing lines. It has failed to state intelligibly how much is too much." 175 F.3d, at 1034. The court hence found that the EPA's interpretation (but not the statute itself) violated the nondelegation doctrine. *Id.*, at 1038. We disagree.

In a delegation challenge, the constitutional question is whether the statute has delegated legislative power to the agency. Article I, §1, of the Constitution vests "[a]ll legislative Powers herein granted . . . in a Congress of the United States." This text permits no delegation of those powers, *Loving v. United States,* 517 U.S. 748, 771 (1996), and so we repeatedly have said that when Congress confers decision making authority upon agencies *Congress* must "lay down by legislative act an intelligible principle to which the person or body authorized to [act] is directed to conform." We have never suggested that an agency can cure an unlawful delegation of legislative power by adopting in its discretion a limiting construction of the statute. Both *Fahey* v. *Mallonee,* 332 U.S. 245, 252-253 (1947), and *Lichter v. United States,* 334 U.S. 742, 783 (1948), mention agency regulations in the course of their nondelegation discussions, but *Lichter* did so because a subsequent Congress had incorporated the regulations into a revised version of the statute, *ibid.,* and *Fahey* because the customary practices in the area, implicitly incorporated into the statute, were reflected in the regulations. 332 U.S., at 250. The idea that an agency can cure an unconstitutionally standardless delegation of power by declining to exercise some of that power seems to us internally contradictory. The very choice of which portion of the power to exercise—that is to say, the prescription of the standard that Congress had omitted—would *itself* be an exercise of the forbidden legislative authority. Whether the statute delegates legislative power is a question for the courts, and an agency's voluntary self-denial has no bearing upon the answer.

We agree with the Solicitor General that the text of §109(b)(1) of the CAA at a minimum requires that "[f]or a discrete set of pollutants and based on published air quality criteria that reflect the latest scientific knowledge, [the] EPA must establish uniform national standards at a level that is requisite to protect public health from the adverse effects of the pollutant in the ambient air." Tr. of Oral Arg. in No. 99-1257, p. 5. Requisite, in turn, "mean[s] sufficient, but not more than necessary." *Id.*, at 7. These limits on the EPA's discretion are

---

4. Respondents' speculation that the EPA is secretly considering the costs of attainment without telling anyone is irrelevant to our interpretive inquiry. If such an allegation could be proved, it would be grounds for vacating the NAAQS, because the Administrator had not followed the law. It would not, however, be grounds for this Court's changing the law.

strikingly similar to the ones we approved in *Touby v. United States,* 500 U.S. 160 (1991), which permitted the Attorney General to designate a drug as a controlled substance for purposes of criminal drug enforcement if doing so was " 'necessary to avoid an imminent hazard to the public safety.' " *Id.,* at 163. They also resemble the Occupational Safety and Health Act provision requiring the agency to " 'set the standard which most adequately assures, to the extent feasible, on the basis of the best available evidence, that no employee will suffer any impairment of health' "—which the Court upheld in *Industrial Union Dept., AFL-CIO v. American Petroleum Institute,* [pages 183-193], and which even then-Justice Rehnquist, who alone in that case thought the statute violated the nondelegation doctrine, see *id.,* at 671 (opinion concurring in judgment), would have upheld if, like the statute here, it did not permit economic costs to be considered. See *American Textile Mfrs. Institute, Inc.* v. *Donovan,* 452 U.S. 490, 545 (1981) (Rehnquist J., dissenting).

The scope of discretion §109(b)(1) allows is in fact well within the outer limits of our nondelegation precedents. In the history of the Court we have found the requisite "intelligible principle" lacking in only two statutes, one of which provided literally no guidance for the exercise of discretion, and the other of which conferred authority to regulate the entire economy on the basis of no more precise a standard than stimulating the economy by assuring "fair competition." See *Panama Refining Go. v. Ryan,* 293 U.S. 388 (1935); *A. L. A. Schechter Poultry Corp.* v. *United States,* 295 U.S. 495 (1935). We have, on the other hand, upheld the validity of §11(b)(2) of the Public Utility Holding Company Act of 1935, 49 Stat. 821, which gave the Securities and Exchange Commission authority to modify the structure of holding company systems so as to ensure that they are not "unduly or unnecessarily complicate[d]" and do not "unfairly or inequitably distribute voting power among security holders." *American Power & Light Co. v. SEC,* 329 U.S. 90, 104 (1946). We have approved the wartime conferral of agency power to fix the prices of commodities at a level that " 'will be generally fair and equitable and will effectuate the [in some respects conflicting] purposes of th[e] Act.' " *Yakus v. United States,* 321 U.S. 414, 420, 423-426 (1944). And we have found an "intelligible principle" in various statutes authorizing regulation in the "public interest." See, *e.g., National Broadcasting Co.* v. *United States,* 319 U.S. 190, 225-226 (1943) (FCC's power to regulate airwaves); *New York Central Securities Corp.* v. *United States,* 287 U.S. 12, 24-25 (1932)(ICC's power to approve railroad consolidations). In short, we have "almost never felt qualified to second-guess Congress regarding the permissible degree of policy judgment that can be left to those executing or applying the law." *Mistretta v. United States,* 488 U.S. 361, 416 (1989) (Scalia J., dissenting); see *id.,* at 373 (majority opinion).

It is true enough that the degree of agency discretion that is acceptable varies according to the scope of the power congressionally conferred. While Congress need not provide any direction to the EPA regarding the manner in which it is to define "country elevators," which are to be exempt from new-stationary-source regulations governing grain elevators, see §7411(i), it must provide substantial guidance on setting air standards that affect the entire national economy. But even in sweeping regulatory schemes we have never demanded, as the Court of Appeals did here, that statutes provide a "determinate criterion" for saying "how much [of the regulated harm] is too much." 175 F.3d, at 1034. In *Touby,* for example, we did not require the statute to decree how "imminent" was too imminent, or how "necessary" was necessary enough, or even—most relevant here—how "hazardous" was too hazardous. 500 U.S., at 165-167. Similarly, the statute at issue in *Lichter* authorized agencies to recoup "excess profits" paid under wartime Government contracts, yet we did not insist that Congress specify how much profit was too much. 334 U.S., at 783-786. It is therefore not conclusive for delegation purposes that, as respondents argue, ozone and particulate matter are "nonthreshold" pollutants that inflict a continuum of adverse health effects at any airborne concentration greater than zero, and hence require the EPA to make judgments of degree. "[A] certain degree of discretion, and thus of lawmaking, inheres in most executive or judicial action." *Mistretta v. United States, supra,* at 417 (Scalia J., dissenting) (emphasis deleted); see 488 U.S., at 378-379 (majority opinion). Section 109(b)(1) of the CAA, which to repeat we interpret as requiring the EPA to set air quality standards at the level that is "requisite"—that is, not lower or higher than is necessary—to protect the public health with an adequate margin of safety, fits comfortably within the scope of discretion permitted by our precedent.

We therefore reverse the judgment of the Court of Appeals remanding for reinterpretation that would avoid a supposed delegation of legislative power. It will remain for the Court of Appeals—on the remand that we direct for other reasons—to dispose of any other preserved challenge to the NAAQS under the judicial-review provisions contained in 42 U.S.C. §7607(d)(9).

IV

[The Court went on to find that EPA had misinterpreted the impact of provisions added to the Act in the 1990 Amendments (Subpart 2 of Part D of Title I) specifying implementation schedules for ozone nonattainment areas. The Court rejected EPA's claim that this issue was not properly before it because it found that EPA's "interim implementation policy" was sufficiently final and ripe for judicial review. Recognizing that some parts of Subpart 2 may be "ill-fitted" for implementation of a revised ozone standard, the Court expressed doubt "that Congress clearly intended Subpart 2 to be the exclusive, permanent means of enforcing a revised ozone standard in nonattainment areas." In this respect the Court departed from the D.C. Circuit's interpretation of the impact of Subpart 2. However, while acknowledging the statute's ambiguity on this issue, the Court refused to defer to EPA's interpretation that Subpart 2 was entirely inapplicable to a revised ozone NAAQS because it deemed it unreasonable to think that Congress would let EPA render Subpart 2 nugatory simply by revising the ozone NAAQS. Thus the Court remanded this aspect of the case back to EPA "to develop a reasonable interpretation of the nonattainment implementation provisions" as applied to a revised ozone NAAQS.]

NOTES AND QUESTIONS

1. The Court unanimously rejects the D.C. Circuit's holding that an agency could cure an unconstitutional delegation of legislative power by developing an "intelligible principle" to confine its exercise of its discretion. In his opinion for the Court, Justice Scalia argues that "the prescription of the standard that Congress had omitted would itself be an exercise of the forbidden legislative authority." Noting that the Court has only twice struck down statutes

on non-delegation grounds, Justice Scalia found that the scope of discretion afforded EPA by section 109(b)(1) is "well within the outer limits of [the Court's] nondelegation precedents." He did so even though he concludes that to avoid non-delegation problems Congress must provide more substantial guidance when it authorizes regulations that can affect the entire nation's economy. Where did the Court find adequate guidance in section 109(b)(1)? In light of this decision, what must EPA do in the future when deciding at what level to set the NAAQSs?

2. How does the Court compare the non-delegation issue in this case with the non-delegation challenge raised against OSHA's Benzene standard in Industrial Union Dept., AFL-CIO v. American Petroleum Institute, page 183.

3. While the Court was unanimous in rejecting the notion that the Clean Air Act violated the non-delegation doctrine, some Justices had different views of how the doctrine should be interpreted. In a concurring opinion, Justice Stevens, joined by Justice Souter, argued that the Court should simply acknowledge that the power delegated to EPA is "legislative," but uphold the delegation as constitutional because it is adequately limited by the terms of the authorizing statute. Stevens and Souter maintained that neither Article I, §1, which vests "All legislative Powers" in the Congress, nor Article II, §1, which vests the "executive Power" in the President, purports to limit the authority of either to delegate authority to others. Thus, in their view, executive agency rulemaking "pursuant to a valid delegation from Congress is 'legislative,' but constitutional so long as the delegation provides a sufficiently intelligible principle" for exercising that authority. By contrast, Justice Thomas argued in another concurrence that even delegations accompanied by intelligible principles may be struck down as unconstitutional if the significance of the decision is simply too great to enable it to be delegated constitutionally.

4. The Court apparently did not think that the question of whether costs may be considered in setting NAAQSs was even a close one. As Justice Scalia wryly noted, "Were it not for the hundreds of pages of briefing respondents have submitted on the issue, one would have thought it fairly clear that this text does not permit the EPA to consider costs in setting the standards." In a concurring opinion not joined by any other Justice, Justice Breyer stressed that the Act does not require the elimination of all risk simply because it mandates a cost-blind standard-setting process. Citing the observation in Justice Stevens' plurality opinion in *Benzene* (page 183) that "the word 'safe' is not the equivalent of 'risk-free,'" Justice Breyer argues that what is "requisite" to protect public health will "vary with background circumstances, such as the public's ordinary tolerance of the particular health risk in the particular context at issue." He maintains that the EPA Administrator has considerable discretion in standard-setting under the statute because she can consider estimates of comparative health risks, the severity of adverse effects, the number and distribution of people affected by a pollutant, and the uncertainties surrounding each estimate. Additional background information on the *American Trucking* litigation may be found in Schroeder, The Story of American Trucking: The Blockbuster that Misfired, in Environmental Law Stories 321 (R.J. Lazarus & O.A. Houck eds., 2005).

5. The *American Trucking* case was argued in the Supreme Court on November 7, 2000. While awaiting the Court's decision, EPA received significant support for its view of the health risks through a study linking particulate levels to substantial increases in mortality rates. Laura Johannes, Study Shows Need for

Tougher Air Rules, Wall St. J., Dec. 14, 2000, at B10. The study by researchers at Johns Hopkins and Yale Universities examined mortality rates in 20 U.S. cities following spikes in particulate pollution during the period from 1987 to 1994. It found that mortality rates increased immediately during the 24 hours following increases in particulate pollution. Unlike previous research, the study was able to isolate the effects of changes in participate pollution from the effects of other pollutants. Subsequent work by Dr. Samet and colleagues strengthened these findings in a study examining the relationship between ozone and death rates in 95 large urban areas between 1987 and 2000. It is the first conclusive evidence that higher smog levels—in addition to fine particulate matter—contribute to death, and that a reduction of 10 ppm in ozone levels could save 4,000 lives a year. Michelle L. Bell et al., Ozone and Short-term Mortality in 95 U.S. Urban Communities, 1987-2000, 2004 JAMA 372-378 (2004). Had mortality been recognized as an adverse health effect in 1997, EPA's calculation of monetized benefits from the revised ozone standard would have increased dramatically. EPA is now considering the possibility of proposing even stricter ozone standards in 2007. Inside EPA, New Ozone Research Could Boost EPA Benefits Estimates in Air Rules (July 8, 2005).

6. The holding in Part IV, finding the relationship of the provisions governing implementation of revised standards and the provisions governing statutorily established compliance timetables to be ambiguous, is one of the few times Justice Scalia has ruled that a significant question of statutory interpretation was not clear, and hence could be decided at the first step of a *Chevron* analysis. The consequence of Part IV was a remand to the agency to reconsider that relationship and promulgate a new approach to implementing the revised NAAQS. On April 30, 2004, EPA issued a revised implementation schedule for the 8-hour ozone standard. 69 Fed. Reg. 23,951, and also issued area quality designations for the new standard, declaring 474 counties throughout the country to be out of attainment for the 8-hour standard, and hence subject to the revised nonattainment rules set forth in the EPA plan. 69 Fed. Reg. 21,715. On nonattainment generally, see Section D2A.

7. Opponents of the revised NAAQS vigorously lobbied the incoming Bush Administration to reconsider the standards themselves, in addition to their implementation. In what one paper called "arguably the biggest victory for environmentalists since President Bush took office," the administration retained the standards in their current form. Traci Watson, Bush to Keep Tough Air Rules, USA Today 1A (May 18, 2001). In March 2002, the *American Trucking* panel of the D.C. Circuit, on remand of the case from the Supreme Court, upheld the standards against industry challenges that they were arbitrary and capricious. American Trucking Ass'ns v. EPA, 283 F.3d 355 (D.C. Cir. 2002).

8. The *American Trucking* decision indicates that the Court is loathe to extend its revival of dormant constitutional limits on regulatory authority to dismantle basic elements of the federal regulatory infrastructure. As the oldest, most established and arguably most successful federal environmental statute, the Clean Air Act was a particularly ill-chosen target for a non-delegation claim. The Court also was unimpressed with the tired old tactic of pitting the environment against the economy. Opponents of the Act argued that massive overregulation is inevitable if benefit-cost analysis is not used. However, when industry counsel told the Court at oral argument that "we can't live with" such a law, Chief Justice Rehnquist replied that we seem to have done pretty well with it for decades. The Court seems to have appreciated the notion that Congress

intended for Clean Air standards to help stimulate the development of new pollution control technology when needed to protect public health.

9. Notwithstanding the legal decision in *American Trucking,* the policy wisdom of the health-based orientation of the NAAQSs remains a source of criticism, as it has from the very beginning. See page 479, above. Critics have focused especially on the case of no-threshold pollutants, such as ozone and PM, where any level of exposure above zero guarantees some risk of adverse health effects. In at least these cases, critics say, EPA must be able to consider compliance costs. Do you agree?

According to some, a major problem with the NAAQS approach is the obstacle it creates to candid public debate about air quality goals because the EPA cannot explicitly discuss its considerations of costs, even though it must of necessity think about costs. See, e.g., M. Landy, M. Roberts & S. Thomas, The Environmental Protection Agency: Asking the Wrong Questions, ch. 3 (1990); Eads, The Confusion of Goals and Instruments: The Explicit Consideration of Costs in Setting National Ambient Air Quality Standards, in To Breathe Fresh Air (M. Gibson ed., 1985).

10. In a ruling not challenged by EPA in the Supreme Court, the Court of Appeals held that EPA erred in setting the ozone standard without taking into account the "health benefits of tropospheric ozone as a shield from the harmful effects of the sun's ultraviolet rays." Relying upon the language in section 108(a)(2) requiring EPA to issue criteria "indicating the kind and extent of all identifiable effects [of the criteria pollutant] on health," and the language of section 109 requiring the NAAQS to be "based" on the criteria, the court found that EPA had to consider both the negative and the positive health effects of reducing ambient levels. 175 F.3d at 1051-1054.

Debate over the opinion thus becomes another battleground on the issue raised in Chapter 3 as to whether risk-risk trade-offs ought to be considered whenever the government regulates exposure to a potentially harmful substance. Compare the result here with NRDC v. EPA, 902 F.2d 962 (D.C. Cir. 1990), where, in the course of upholding EPA's previous PM standard, the court rejected as "entirely without merit" the claim that EPA had erred in not considering the "health consequences of unemployment" potentially caused by the standard. 902 F.2d at 973. Are these two consistent?

D. ATTAINING AND MAINTAINING THE NAAQSs

1. *Implementation and Compliance—The Basic Structure*

Writing national ambient air quality standards is just the beginning of the Clean Air Act program. Those standards have no effect on reducing environmental damage and adverse health effects until they have been implemented—until actual sources of pollution have reduced emissions. Implementation entails numerous decisions regarding which sources of each criteria pollutant should abate their present emissions so that the net effect of emissions from all sources does not exceed the standards. (In 1977, the program became even more complex when Congress enacted programs to maintain air quality in regions of the country where the pollution levels are currently less than the ambient standards. See pages 510-519. In this section's discussion of the basic implementation process, we generally refer simply to attaining the standards, though the CAA's goal is actually the attaining and maintaining of air quality.) Subsequently, it entails compliance checking and enforcement to see that the individualized limitations are being met.

The NAAQSs define the minimum acceptable levels of air quality to be achieved throughout the nation for the criteria air pollutants. While EPA promulgates the NAAQSs, the task of deciding precisely how to achieve them is left largely to the states, subject to EPA review and approval. Section 110 of the Act gives each state the responsibility for developing a state implementation plan (SIP) that details how compliance with the NAAQSs will be achieved in each air quality control region (AQCR). SIPs are at the heart of what has been described as the Clean Air Act's "bold experiment in cooperative federalism." Bethlehem Steel Corp. v. Gorsuch, 742 F.2d 1028, 1036 (7th Cir. 1984).

To develop an acceptable SIP, each state first has to determine existing and projected levels of the criteria air pollutant in each AQCR within the state's boundaries. These data are used to determine what emissions reductions are necessary to comply with the NAAQS for the pollutant. The state has to inventory sources of emissions and project their expected future growth. It then must confront the politically sensitive task of deciding what control strategies to employ and how to allocate the burden of emission reductions among sources. Finally, the state must demonstrate to EPA that the measures adopted in its SIP are adequate to attain and maintain compliance with the NAAQS.

Section 110 specifies in detail the types of provisions states must include in their SIPs to obtain EPA approval. EPA's more than 1,700 pages of regulations are even more particular. 40 C.F.R. pts. 51-52 (1999). SIPs must provide for quantified emission limits, compliance timetables, monitoring and enforcement programs, limits on interstate pollution, measures that ensure compliance with nonattainment and PSD requirements, and assurances that the state has adequate resources and the legal authority to implement its plan. §110(a)(2). States have the most discretion in deciding how to regulate existing stationary sources, as other parts of the Clean Air Act impose emissions controls on mobile sources (Title II, discussed below in section F) and new sources (section 111's new source performance standards). Most states have adopted some form of categorical emissions limits for existing stationary sources, usually based on judgments about what was technologically achievable and economically affordable. Among the emissions control strategies that the Clean Air Act now specifically endorses, but does not require states to adopt, are "economic incentives such as fees, marketable permits, and auctions of emissions rights." §110(a)(2).

The 1970 Clean Air Amendments directed each state to develop SIPs that would achieve compliance with the primary NAAQSs "as expeditiously as practicable," but no later than three years from the date the SIP is approved. Secondary standards were to be achieved within "a reasonable time." Section 116 of the Act expressly preserves the authority of states to adopt emissions standards that are stricter than the national standards.

The 1970 Act required states to submit their initial SIPs to EPA for review within nine months after a NAAQS was promulgated. (The 1990 Amendments now give states three years to submit a SIP after a NAAQS is promulgated or revised unless EPA specifies a shorter time period. §110(a)(1).) The 1990 Amendments give EPA 12 months to approve or disapprove each state's submission.

§110(k)(2). (The 1970 Act gave EPA four months to act.) Upon EPA approval, the SIP becomes federally enforceable. A state that fails to submit a SIP or that submits an inadequate one whose deficiencies are not cured within a specified time period becomes subject to certain sanctions under section 179, including a loss of federal highway funds. If such a state fails to win EPA approval for a new SIP within two years after its SIP submission is disapproved, section 110(c) requires EPA to promulgate a federal implementation plan (FIP) for the state.

The Supreme Court helped flesh out the contours of the federal-state partnership embodied in the Clean Air Act in two decisions involving the initial generation of SIPs submitted in response to the 1970 Amendments. In *Train v. Natural Resources Defense Council*, 421 U.S. 60 (1975), the Court upheld EPA's decision to approve a SIP that included a variance procedure for sources that found it difficult to comply with the state's immediately effective categorical emissions limits. So long as the SIP provided for timely attainment and maintenance of the NAAQS and met the Act's other requirements, the Court held that EPA must approve it. The Court explained that:

> The Act gives the Agency no authority to question the wisdom of a State's choices of emissions limitations if they are part of a plan which satisfies the standards of §110(a)(2), and the Agency may devise and promulgate a specific plan of its own only if a State fails to submit an implementation plan which satisfies those standards. §110(c). Thus, so long as the ultimate effect of a State's choice of emission limitations is compliance with the national standards for ambient air, the State is at liberty to adopt whatever mix of emission limitations it deems best suited to its particular situation. [421 U.S. at 179.]

This decision indicated that states had considerable freedom to choose what regulatory strategies to employ to meet the NAAQSs. During its very next term, the Court was asked to decide whether a state had gone too far in exercising that freedom.

In the case below, Missouri had adopted a SIP that required substantial reductions in emissions of SO_2 in the St. Louis metropolitan area, where SO_2 levels exceeded the NAAQS. Union Electric Company, the electric utility servicing St. Louis, challenged EPA's approval of Missouri's SIP. The utility argued that EPA should not have approved the SIP because it required the utility to do what was economically and technologically impossible.

Union Electric Company v. EPA
427 U.S. 246 (1976)

JUSTICE MARSHALL delivered the opinion of the Court.

... The Administrator's position is that he has no power whatsoever to reject a state implementation plan on the ground that it is economically and technologically infeasible. ... After surveying the relevant provisions of the Clean Air Amendments of 1970 and their legislative history, we agree that Congress intended claims of economic and technological infeasibility to be wholly foreign to the Administrator's consideration of a state implementation plan.

... [T]he 1970 Amendments to the Clean Air Act were a drastic remedy to what was perceived as a serious and otherwise unchecked problem of air pollution. The Amendments place the primary responsibility for formulating pollution control strategies on the States, but nonetheless subject the States to strict minimum compliance requirements. These requirements are of a "technology-forcing character," Train v. NRDC, and are expressly designed to force regulated sources to develop pollution control devices that might at the time appear to be economically or technologically infeasible.

This approach is apparent on the face of §110(a)(2). The provision sets out eight criteria that an implementation plan must satisfy, and provides that if these criteria are met and if the plan was adopted after reasonable notice and hearing, the Administrator "shall approve" the proposed state plan. The mandatory "shall" makes it quite clear that the Administrator is not to be concerned with factors other than those specified, and none of the eight factors appears to permit consideration of technological or economic infeasibility. . . .

Amici Appalachian Power Co. et al. . . . claim that the States are precluded from submitting implementation plans more stringent than federal law demands by §110(a)(2)'s second criterion—that the plan contain such control devices "as may be necessary" to achieve the primary and secondary air quality standards. §110(a)(2)(B). The contention is that an overly restrictive plan is not "necessary" for attainment of the national standards and so must be rejected by the Administrator. . . .

We read the "as may be necessary" requirement of §110(a)(2)(B) to demand only that the implementation plan submitted by the State meet the "minimum conditions" of the Amendments. Beyond that, if a State makes the legislative determination that it desires a particular air quality by a certain date and that it is willing to force technology to attain it—or lose a certain industry if attainment is not possible—such a determination is fully consistent with the structure and purpose of the Amendments, and §110(a)(2)(B) provides no basis for the EPA Administrator to object to the determination on the grounds of infeasibility. . . .

Our conclusion is bolstered by the recognition that the Amendments do allow claims of technological and economic infeasibility to be raised in situations where consideration of such claims will not substantially interfere with the primary congressional purpose of prompt attainment of the national air quality standards. Thus, we do not hold that claims of infeasibility are never of relevance in the formulation of an implementation plan or that sources unable to comply with emissions limitations must inevitably be shut down.

Perhaps the most important forum for consideration of claims of economic and technological infeasibility is before the state agency formulating the implementation plan. So long as the national standards are met, the State may select whatever mix of control devices it desires, and industries with particular economic or technological problems may seek special treatment in the plan itself. Moreover, if the industry is not exempted from, or accommodated by, the original plan, it may obtain a variance, as petitioner did in this case; and the variance, if granted after notice and a hearing, may be submitted to the EPA as a revision of the plan. Lastly, an industry denied an exemption from the implementation plan, or denied a subsequent variance, may be able to take its claims of economic or technological infeasibility to the state courts. . . .

. . . [T]he State has virtually absolute power in allocating emissions limitations so long as the national standards are met. . . . Congress plainly left with the States, so long as the national standards were met, the power to determine which sources would be burdened by regulation and to what extent. Technology forcing is a concept somewhat new to our national experience and it necessarily entails certain risks. But Congress considered those risks in passing the 1970 Amendments and decided that the dangers posed by uncontrolled air pollution made them worth taking. Petitioner's theory would render that considered legislative judgment a nullity, and that is a result we refuse to reach.

NOTES AND QUESTIONS

1. The Court's decision confirmed the important role states were to play in deciding how to achieve compliance with the NAAQSs. While it established that states were free to "force" technology, few chose to do so in practice. Indeed, Missouri's SIP provided for temporary variances to sources that could not comply immediately. Pursuant to these provisions, Union Electric subsequently obtained a variance from the state and did not have to shut down.

2. In a concurring opinion joined by Chief Justice Burger, Justice Powell decried the "Draconian possibility" that the Clean Air Act could precipitate "the shutdown of an urban area's electrical service" that would "sacrifice the well-being of a large metropolitan area" to "technologically impossible" demands. 427 U.S. at 272 (Powell, J., concurring). The papers of the late Justice Thurgood Marshall reveal that during the Court's deliberations on the case Justice Rehnquist also expressed the view that the Act is a "harsh and draconian statute." Chief Justice Burger expressed the view that "the problems in this case are a consequence of letting a lot of little boys on Congressional staffs write legislation in noble prose that often takes little account of realities." Percival, Environmental Law in the Supreme Court: Highlights From the Marshall Papers, 23 Envtl. L. Rep. 10,606, 10,617 (1993). Do you agree that the Clean Air Act is so draconian that Congress did not appreciate the "realities" to which Chief Justice Burger refers? Is there anything in section 110(a)(2) that precludes states from taking such considerations into account when developing their SIPs? In a footnote not reproduced above, the Court noted that other portions of the Act expressly permit consideration of compliance costs and the state of existing technology, such as section 111's new source performance standards (NSPSs). Why would Congress require that such factors be taken into consideration for NSPSs, but not for achieving compliance with the NAAQSs?

3. Many states developed SIPs that sought to minimize the burden on local industry while appearing on paper to promise attainment of the NAAQSs. EPA's crucial role in reviewing SIPs is to ensure that they include measures that will in fact result in attainment and maintenance of the NAAQSs. Yet this requires EPA to have a crystal ball whose accuracy is heavily dependent on air quality modeling, which some view as "more sorcery than science." Reed, State Implementation Plans, in Law of Environmental Protection 11-28 (S. Novick ed., 1988). Does the Court's decision imply that EPA cannot disapprove a SIP that relies primarily on measures so draconian that there is no reasonable prospect that they would be implemented in practice?

4. Air quality dispersion models are subject to tremendous uncertainties, particularly as the number of sources increases and as pollutants travel longer distances. Courts generally have supported EPA's use of computer models, recognizing that they inevitably are subject to considerable uncertainty. See, e.g., Cleveland Elec. Illuminating Co. v. EPA, 572 F.2d 1150 (6th Cir. 1978). But there have been exceptions. In Ohio v. EPA, 784 F.2d 226 (6th Cir. 1986), the Sixth Circuit rejected EPA's use of a model, citing the absence of empirical validation

of the model's results and studies at other sites that had produced "unimpressive" results. Cf. Connecticut v. EPA, 696 F.2d 147 (2d Cir. 1982) (burden on petitioners to demonstrate availability of better model).

5. While states have considerable freedom in choosing how to comply with the NAAQSs, the Clean Air Act does impose some limitations on the kind of controls states can employ. Section 123 bars states from relying on intermittent controls that try to vary the timing of emissions to coincide with times of favorable atmospheric conditions. As long as the end result complies with the NAAQS, why should states be prohibited from demonstrating compliance by "cutting emissions only when meteorological conditions likely will . . . concentrate [pollution] under a temperature inversion"? Section 123 also bars states from relying on tall stacks to disperse air pollutants, the strategy initially used by the copper smelters in Georgia v. Tennessee Copper Company, discussed in Chapter 2. Why should the use of tall stacks be barred as a SIP compliance strategy?

6. States seeking approval for SIP revisions have sometimes encountered lengthy delays. In General Motors v. United States, 496 U.S. 530 (1990), the Supreme Court held that EPA's failure to act for more than 32 months on a proposed SIP revision did not bar enforcement against a source whose violation of an existing SIP would be cured by the proposed SIP revision. The Court held that EPA can enforce the existing SIP even if the agency had delayed unreasonably action on the proposed SIP revision. Is this result fair? The 1990 Amendments now mandate that EPA take action on proposed SIP revisions within 12 months of their submission, §110(k).

7. The CAA contemplates an evolving program of air quality controls, in which Congress or EPA will from time to time revise or add to air quality requirements, thereby triggering downstream adjustments by the implementing agencies and ultimately compliance and enforcement officials. Congress, for example, revised the Act in 1977 to add requirements related to the prevention of significant deterioration and nonattainment issues, as well as visibility-related requirements. In 1990, it adopted a program to address the process of acid deposition. The EPA not only issues original NAAQSs; it is also under a statutory obligation to revisit them every five years in light of new scientific information. EPA can also discover after a SIP has been approved that in fact it will be inadequate to meet the requirements of the Act. When one of these developments occurs, section 110(k)(5) gives EPA express authority to "call[] for plan revisions."

8. As it is preparing to issue a SIP call, EPA frequently has an opinion as to the best way to respond to the deficiency that it has discovered in existing SIPs (either because the requirements for them have been revised by the agency or the Congress or because one or more have been found to be inadequate to meet the requirements of the Act). In recent years, for instance, EPA has had a strong preference for emissions trading systems for addressing a variety of ambient problems. See pages 550-556 for discussion of such systems. The general design of the statute, however, pursuant to its system of cooperative federalism, leaves the selection of the best way to respond to the national requirements up to the States in the first instance. Can EPA decide that a SIP is "inadequate" unless it adopts the preferred approach of EPA? The following decision confronts an instance in which this question arose.

9. As background to the following decision, the 1990 Amendments enacted a variety of new provisions to address the ozone problem, especially the interstate and regional nature of the problem. (For further discussion, see pages 534-543.) One of these created the Northeast Ozone Transport Commission (OTC),

composed of representatives of 12 northeastern states plus the District of Columbia. §184. The Act authorized the Commission to recommend control measures for the region "necessary to bring any area in such region into attainment" with the ozone NAAQS. §184(c)(1). Pursuant to that authorization, the Commission petitioned EPA to recognize that adoption of the California Low Emission Vehicle (LEV) program—which imposes stricter ozone controls than the federal auto emissions standards—was such a "necessary" control measure. (California is the one state in the nation permitted to write emissions standards for automobiles that differ from the national standards. Other states are also permitted to adopt California's standards instead of the national ones.) Uncertain as to the constitutional soundness of the OTC provisions, EPA ultimately responded to the OTC petition by issuing an order both under the Ozone Transport Commission provisions of the Act and under its section 110(k)(5) SIP call authority. EPA found the California LEV program to be necessary for the 13 member jurisdictions; it also found that the SIPs of these jurisdictions were "substantially inadequate" unless they either adopted the California LEV program or else instituted alternative measures that were highly infeasible and more draconian than adopting the LEV program.

EPA's action was challenged. The portion of the Court of Appeals decision addressing EPA's SIP call authority is reproduced below.

Virginia v. EPA
108 F.3d 1397 (D.C. Cir. 1997)

RANDOLPH, Circuit Judge.

[The court determined that EPA's SIP call effectively ordered the adoption of the California standards, because the measures required of a state choosing not to adopt it were so "unreasonable and impracticable" as to amount to no "real alternative" at all.]

Does section 110 give EPA the authority to condition approval of a state's plan on the state's adoption of control measures EPA has chosen? . . . [W]e are aware of no case (EPA has cited none) supporting the proposition EPA now urges upon us, namely, that under section 110 EPA may condition approval of a state's implementation plan on the state's adopting a particular control measure, here the California Low Emission Vehicle program. . . .

Section 110 governs the interplay between the states and EPA with respect to the formulation and approval of such State Plans. The basic procedure is that "each state determines an emission reduction program for its nonattainment areas, subject to EPA approval, within deadlines imposed by Congress." Natural Resources Defense Council v. Browner, 57 F.3d 1122, 1123 (D.C. Cir. 1995).

Should a state fail to submit an implementation plan, or should its plan fail to provide the required reductions in air pollution, certain penalties—some mandatory, others at EPA's discretion—may follow. . . . The noncomplying state may, for instance, be prevented from spending federal highway money in nonattainment areas. . . . This sanction becomes mandatory if the state fails to implement an adequate State Plan within 24 months of EPA's finding that the state's proposed plan is deficient. . . . At that same point, EPA must impose a "federal implementation plan" ("Federal Plan") on those areas of the state in nonattainment. . . . The Federal Plan "provides an additional incentive for state compliance because it rescinds state authority to make the many sensitive technical and political choices that a pollution control regime demands." Natural Resources Defense Council, 57 F.3d at 1124.

In 1975, the Supreme Court analyzed section 110's "division of responsibilities" between the states and the federal government. Train v. Natural Resources Defense Council. . . .

[A]"broader issue," the Court thought, was at stake in the case—namely, "whether Congress intended the States to retain any significant degree of control over the manner in which they attain and maintain national standards." . . . The Act expressly gave the states initial responsibility for determining the manner in which air quality standards were to be achieved. . . . Section 107(a) of the Act read then, as it does now: "Each State shall have the primary responsibility for assuring air quality within the entire geographic area comprising such State by submitting an implementation plan which will specify *the manner* in which national primary and secondary ambient air quality standards will be achieved and maintained within each air quality control region in such State" (emphasis added). In light of section 107(a), the Court construed section 110: . . .

> [So] long as the ultimate effect of a State's choice of emission limitations is compliance with the national standards for ambient air, the State is at liberty to adopt whatever mix of emission limitations it deems best suited to its particular situation. . . .

The Supreme Court repeated this interpretation in Union Electric Co. v. EPA: section 110 left to the states "the power to determine which sources would be burdened by regulations and to what extent."

[Bethlehem Steel Corp. v. Gorsuch, 742 F.2d 1028 (7th Cir. 1984) similarly stated:]

> [T]he Clean Air Act creates a partnership between the states and the federal government. The state proposes, the EPA disposes. The federal government through the EPA determines the ends—the standards of air quality—but Congress has given the states the initiative and a broad responsibility regarding the means to achieve those ends through state implementation plans and timetables of compliance. . . . The Clean Air Act is an experiment in federalism, and the EPA may not run roughshod over the procedural prerogatives that the Act has reserved to the states, . . . especially when, as in this case, the agency is overriding state policy. . . .

[T]he 1990 amendments did not alter the division of responsibilities between EPA and the states in the section 110 process. It was with this understanding that we recently summarized the statutory system: "The states are responsible in the first instance for meeting the" national ambient standards "through state-designed plans that provide for attainment, maintenance, and enforcement of the" national standards "in each air quality control region. Thus, each state determines an emission reduction program for its nonattainment areas, subject to EPA approval, within deadlines imposed by Congress." . . .

Because section 110 does not enable EPA to force particular control measures on the states, EPA's authority to promulgate the rule under review must be derived from section 184 alone. [The court then held that section 184 provides EPA general authority to order adoption of specific control measures recommended by OTC, but that other provisions of the Act—section 177 read together with section 202—specifically prohibit EPA from compelling any state to adopt auto emissions standards different from the national standards. The court concluded that this specific prohibition prevailed over the general grant of authority.]

In sum, we hold that EPA may not, under section 110, condition approval of a state's implementation plan on the state's adoption of a particular control measure. We also hold that EPA may not, under section 184, circumvent section 177, as we interpret it in light of section 202. For the reasons given, we hold that the SIP call EPA issued with respect to each state and the District of Columbia cannot stand.

The petitions for review are granted and the rule is vacated in its entirety.

So ordered.

NOTES AND QUESTIONS

1. Why did EPA choose to include in its SIP call the instruction that states adopt a specific control measure, namely, the California LEV standards? Why did EPA think it would not be sufficient to base its SIP call simply upon a determination that the current ozone controls contained in the SIPs of the 13 jurisdictions within the OTC were substantially inadequate and interfered with the ability of neighboring states to meet the NAAQS?

2. Should a state choose not to submit a SIP that the EPA can determine to be adequate, the Act does provide a mechanism for the federal government to step in and make all the choices that would normally be reserved to the states. As indicated in Virginia v. EPA, above, EPA must promulgate a federal implementation plan (FIP) 24 months after finding deficient a state implementation plan. EPA has been very reluctant to exercise this authority, however.

Sometimes EPA has been able to avoid writing FIPS by exercising its "conditional approval" authority for SIPs. Section 110(k)(4), added in 1990, authorizes EPA to condition its approval of a SIP on the state promulgating revisions that will bring the SIP into complete compliance so long as the SIP's deficiencies are minor and corrected within one year. EPA attempted to use section 110(k)(4) to approve conditionally SIPs that promised to adopt adequate measures within a year. In Natural Resources Defense Council v. EPA, 22 F.3d 1125, 1134-1136 (D.C. Cir. 1994), the D C Circuit held that this was illegal because "the conditional approval mechanism was intended to provide the EPA with an alternative to disapproving substantive, but not entirely satisfactory, SIPs submitted by the statutory deadlines and not, as EPA has used it, as a means of circumventing those deadlines." (Section 110(k)(4) superseded a more loosely phrased provision, under which EPA had adopted "partial" and "conditional" approvals of plans in situations where it otherwise might have had to impose bans on new construction in order to ensure NAAQS compliance. See City of Seabrook v. EPA, 659 F.2d 1349 (5th Cir. 1981) (upholding EPA's practice); but see Connecticut Fund for the Environment v. EPA, 696 F.2d 147 (2d Cir. 1982) (allowing conditional approvals but finding them insufficient to allow the state to avoid a construction ban).)

As an even more drastic way to avoid the FIP requirement, sometimes it has appeared the EPA has approved SIPs that had no realistic chance of attaining the NAAQSs. Occasionally, environmental organizations sued EPA to force it to write a FIP. After Abramowitz v. EPA, 832 F.2d 1071 (9th Cir. 1987), held in the case of the South Coast Air Basin that EPA's duty to do so was clear and mandatory, EPA was faced with developing a FIP that would cause massive economic and social dislocation or a FIP that would authorize decades of noncompliance. It opted not to pursue the option of adopting "a plan that provides for attainment in the South Coast immediately or even within five years," because such a plan "would have to prohibit most traffic, shut down major business activity, curtail the use of important consumer goods, and ... destroy the economy of the South Coast, so that most of the population would be forced to resettle elsewhere." 53 Fed. Reg. 49,494, 49,495 (1988).

The Act also provides a series of sanctions EPA can apply against states that fail to submit satisfactory SIPs, including suspension of federal highway funds and increasing the ratio of pollution offsets required before new pollution sources can be located within nonattainment areas. In the past, EPA sometimes withheld sanctioning noncompliant states, but in 1990 Congress added section 179, which requires EPA to impose sanctions on states that fail to rectify deficiencies in the SIP submissions within 18 months.

3. Conflicts over the division of authority between state and federal governments can arise at other places in the implementation process as well. For example, section 113 gives EPA the authority to order SIP compliance by a pollution source if EPA determines it is not complying. That section also permits EPA to become the primary enforcer of SIPs if EPA detects "widespread" failure of the state to enforce its own regulations.

4. The following decision involves a dispute over the respective roles of state and federal government in administering the Prevention of Significant Deterioration Program (PSD), see pages 510-514, which the Congress added to the statute in 1977.

In the following case, Alaska had the initial authority for administering the PSD program. When the state agency and EPA disagreed over whether the PSD requirements had been met, EPA issued an order to prevent any construction at the proposed site. Alaska sued, claiming that the state agency's determination was conclusive and that EPA had no authority to overrule it administratively. EPA's only recourse, in Alaska's view, was to sue the state agency in state court. In a 5-4 opinion, the Court sided with EPA. The dissent, which seems influenced by the Court's recently heightened interest in protecting state autonomy, thought that EPA's interpretation failed to grant the appropriate amount of finality to the state of Alaska's determination and concluded that the state permit decision could not be overruled by "administrative fiat."

Alaska Department of Environmental Conservation v. Environmental Protection Agency
540 U.S. 461 (2004)

JUSTICE GINSBURG delivered the opinion of the Court in which JUSTICES STEVENS, O'CONNOR, SOUTER and BREYER joined.

[Introductory Note: When the Red Dog Mine, owned by Cominco, Inc., decided to expand its production of zinc concentrate, it needed to increase its on-site electrical generating capacity. The airshed around the Mine, located some 100 miles north of the Arctic Circle, was subject to the requirements of the PSD provisions of the Clean Air Act. Because the expansion would add more than 40 tons of nitrogen oxide per year to the air emissions at the site, the expansion plans triggered a PSD requirement that the new generating capacity come equipped with Best Available Control Technology (BACT). BACT is defined as "an emission limitation based on the maximum degree of [pollution] reduction . . . which the permitting authority, on a case-by-case basis, taking into account energy, environmental, and economic impacts and other costs, determines is achievable for [the] facility." An acceptable PSD program, including preconstruction review to ensure compliance with BACT limitations, is an element of the state implementation plan (SIP), and in the case of a state with an approved SIP for the area, the permitting agency is the state air quality agency, in this case the Alaska Department of Environmental Conservation (ADEC).

Red Dog first proposed to supply its additional electrical needs by increasing operation of a standby generator already at the facility. ADEC determined that BACT for the standby generator was a process known as selective catalytic reduction (SCR), which reduces NOx emissions by 90 percent. Red Dog then modified its expansion plans, proposing to install an entirely new generator, designated MG-17, for which it suggested that an alternative technology, Low NOx, be adopted by ADEC as BACT. Low NOx removes 30 percent of nitrogen emissions. ADEC issued a draft PSD permit that determined Low NOx to be BACT for both generators. ADEC's staff analysis had determined that SCR was technologically, environmentally, and economically feasible for the Red Dog generators. Nonetheless, ADEC accepted Red Dog's plan to fit all its generators with Low NOx, which would enable the plant as a whole to meet emissions reductions commensurate with applying SCR to the two generators. In fact, under some operating assumptions, Red Dog asserted, its alternative would achieve nearly 400 tons per year lower emissions than applying SCR to just the two generators. Accordingly, ADEC concluded that the proposal "achieve[d] a similar maximum NOx reduction as the most stringent controls; [could] potentially result in a greater NOx reduction; and is logistically and economically less onerous to [Red Dog]."

EPA and other federal agencies objected, stating that the PSD provisions required BACT, and could not be satisfied by imposing new controls on other emissions units. Rather than challenge this, ADEC issued a second draft permit that dropped the offsetting emissions justification, and simply concluded that Low NOx was BACT for the two generators. ADEC acknowledged that it had received no information from Red Dog enabling it to draw any conclusion as to the impact of the costs of SCR on Red Dog's profitability, but it nonetheless concluded that SCR imposed a disproportionate cost on the mine. ADEC employed a comparison with the cost impacts on a rural Alaska utility to conclude that SCR implied a 20 percent price increase, but provided no economic basis for the comparison in its technical analysis.

EPA objected to the second draft. Red Dog, EPA claimed, "has not adequately demonstrated any site-specific factors to support [the mine's] claim that the installation of SCR is economically infeasible at the Red Dog Mine. Therefore, elimination of SCR as BACT based on cost-effectiveness grounds is not supported by the record and is clearly erroneous." Nonetheless, ADEC issued the final permit without supplementing its analysis. EPA then issued an order preventing Red Dog from proceeding with construction. EPA was exercising its authority under section 113(a)(5) to "issue an order prohibiting construction" "whenever . . . EPA finds that a State is not acting in compliance with any requirement . . . relating to the construction of new sources," as well as its authority under section 167 to "take such measures, including issuance of an order . . . to prevent the construction . . . of a major emitting facility which does not conform to the [PSD] requirements."]

III

A

Centrally at issue in this case is the question whether EPA's oversight role, described by Congress in CAA §§113(a)(5) and 167, extends to ensuring that a state permitting authority's BACT determination is reasonable in light of the statutory guides. Sections 113(a)(5) and 167 lodge in the Agency encompassing supervisory responsibility over the construction and modification of pollutant emitting facilities in areas covered by the PSD program. In notably capacious terms, Congress armed EPA with authority to issue orders stopping construction when "a State is not acting in compliance with any [CAA] requirement or prohibition . . . relating to the construction of new sources or the modification of existing sources," §7413(a)(5), or when "construction or modification of a major emitting facility . . . does not conform to the requirements of [the PSD program]," §7477. . . .

All parties agree that one of the "many requirements in the PSD provisions that the EPA may enforce" is "that a [PSD] permit contain a BACT limitation." It is therefore undisputed that the Agency may issue an order to stop a facility's construction if a PSD permit contains no BACT designation.

EPA reads the Act's definition of BACT, together with CAA's explicit listing of BACT as a "[p]reconstruction requiremen[t]," to mandate not simply a BACT designation, but a determination of BACT faithful to the statute's definition. In keeping with the broad oversight role §§113(a)(5) and 167 vest in EPA, the Agency maintains, it may review permits to ensure that a State's BACT determination is reasonably moored to the Act's provisions. We hold, as elaborated below, that the Agency has rationally construed the Act's text and that EPA's construction warrants our respect and approbation.

BACT's statutory definition requires selection of an emission control technology that results in the "maximum" reduction of a pollutant "achievable for [a] facility" in view of "energy, environmental, and economic impacts, and other costs." This instruction, EPA submits, cabins state permitting authorities' discretion by granting only "authority to make reasonable BACT determinations," i.e., decisions made with fidelity to the Act's purpose "to insure that economic growth will occur in a manner consistent with the preservation of existing clean air resources." . . .

EPA stresses Congress' reason for enacting the PSD program—to prevent significant deterioration of air quality in clean-air areas within a State and in neighboring States. That aim, EPA urges, is unlikely to be realized absent an EPA surveillance role that extends to BACT determinations. The Agency notes in this regard a House Report observation:

> "Without national guidelines for the prevention of significant deterioration a State deciding to protect its clean air resources will face a double threat. The prospect is very real that such a State would lose existing industrial plants to more permissive States. But additionally the State will likely become the target

of" economic-environmental blackmail "from new industrial plants that will play one State off against another with threats to locate in whichever State adopts the most permissive pollution controls." H.R. Rep. No. 95-294, p. 134 (1977), U.S. Code Cong. & Admin. News 1977, 1077, 1213.

The House Report further observed that "a community that sets and enforces strict standards may still find its air polluted from sources in another community or another State." Federal agency surveillance of a State's BACT designation is needed, EPA asserts, to restrain the interjurisdictional pressures to which Congress was alert.

The CAA construction EPA advances in this litigation is reflected in inter-pretive guides the Agency has several times published. . . . We "normally accord particular deference to an agency interpretation of 'longstanding' duration," . . .

We have previously accorded dispositive effect to EPA's interpretation of an ambiguous CAA provision. See *Chevron U.S.A. Inc. v. Natural Resources Defense Council, Inc.; Union Elec.* The Agency's interpretation in this case, presented in internal guidance memoranda, however, does not qualify for the dispositive force described in *Chevron.* See Christensen v. Harris County, 529 U.S. 576, 587 (2000) ("Interpretations such as those in . . . policy statements, agency manuals, and enforcement guidelines, all of which lack the force of law—do not warrant Chevron-style deference."). Cogent "administrative interpretations . . . not [the] products of formal rulemaking . . . nevertheless warrant respect." We accord EPA's reading of the relevant statutory provisions that measure of respect.

B

. . . ADEC argues that the statutory definition of BACT unambiguously assigns to "the permitting authority" alone determination of the control technol-ogy qualifying as "best available." . . . EPA's enforcement role, ADEC maintains, is restricted to the requirement "that the permit contain a BACT limitation."

Understandably, Congress entrusted state permitting authorities with initial responsibility to make BACT determinations "case-by-case." A state agency, no doubt, is best positioned to adjust for local differences in raw materials or plant configurations, differences that might make a technology "unavailable" in a particular area. But the fact that the relevant statutory guides—"maximum" pollution reduction, considerations of energy, environmental, and economic impacts—may not yield a "single, objectively 'correct' BACT determination" surely does not signify that there can be no unreasonable determinations. Nor does Congress' sensitivity to site-specific factors necessarily imply a design to preclude in this context meaningful EPA oversight under §§113(a)(5) and 167. EPA claims no prerogative to designate the correct BACT; the Agency asserts only the authority to guard against unreasonable designations.

Under ADEC's interpretation, EPA properly inquires whether a BACT determination appears in a PSD permit but not whether that BACT determina-tion "was made on reasonable grounds properly supported on the record." Congress, however, vested EPA with explicit and sweeping authority to enforce CAA "requirements" relating to the construction and modification of sources under the PSD program, including BACT. We fail to see why Congress, having expressly endorsed an expansive surveillance role for EPA in two independent CAA provisions, would then implicitly preclude the Agency from verifying sub-stantive compliance with the BACT provisions and, instead, limit EPA's superintendence to the insubstantial question whether the state permitting authority had uttered the key words "BACT."

We emphasize, however, that EPA's rendition of the Act's less than crystalline text leaves the "permitting authority" considerable leeway. The Agency acknowledges "the need to accord appropriate deference" to States' BACT designations and disclaims any intention to " 'second guess' state decisions," 63 Fed. Reg., at 13,797. Only when a state agency's BACT determination is "not based on a reasoned analysis," may EPA step in to ensure that the statutory requirements are honored. . . .

Even if the Act imposes a requirement of reasoned justification for a BACT determination, ADEC ultimately argues, such a requirement may be enforced only through state administrative and judicial processes. State review of BACT decisions, according to ADEC, allows development of an adequate factual record, properly imposes the burden of persuasion on EPA when it challenges a State's BACT determination, and promotes certainty. Unless EPA review of BACT determinations is channeled into state administrative and judicial forums, ADEC suggests, "there is nothing to prevent the EPA from invalidating a BACT determination at any time—months, even years, after a permit has been issued."

It would be unusual, to say the least, for Congress to remit a federal agency enforcing federal law solely to state court. We decline to read such an uncommon regime into the Act's silence. EPA, the expert federal agency charged with enforcing the Act, has interpreted the BACT provisions and its own §§113(a)(5) and 167 enforcement powers not to require recourse to state processes before stopping a facility's construction. That rational interpretation, we agree, is surely permissible . . .

The Ninth Circuit's review of EPA's order is in keeping with our holding that EPA may not reduce the burden it must carry by electing to invoke its stop-construction-order authority. Specifically, the Court of Appeals rested its judgment on what EPA showed from ADEC's own report: "(1) Cominco failed to meet its burden of demonstrating [to ADEC] that SCR was economically infeasible; and (2) ADEC failed to provide a reasoned justification for its elimination of SCR as a control option." 298 F.3d, at 823. EPA's conclusions, and the basis for them, support the Court of Appeals' determination that the federal Agency's grounds for issuing the orders under review were not "arbitrar[y] and capriciou[s]." Ibid. Our own analysis, similarly hinges on the question whether ADEC's BACT determination was a reasonable one. Our analysis would have taken the same path had EPA initiated a civil action pursuant to §113(a)(5)(C), or if the suit under consideration had been filed initially in state court. . . .

In sum, EPA interprets the Act to allow substantive federal Agency surveillance of state permitting authorities' BACT determinations subject to federal court review. We credit EPA's longstanding construction of the Act and confirm EPA's authority, pursuant to §§113(a)(5) and 167, to rule on the reasonableness of BACT decisions by state permitting authorities.

IV

A

We turn finally, and more particularly, to the reasons why we conclude that EPA properly exercised its statutory authority in this case. ADEC urges that, even if the Act allows the Agency to issue stop-construction orders when a state permitting authority unreasonably determines BACT, EPA acted impermissibly in this instance. . . .

Because the Act itself does not specify a standard for judicial review in this instance, we apply the familiar default standard of the Administrative Procedure Act, 5 U.S.C. §706(2)(A), and ask whether the Agency's action was "arbitrary, capricious, an abuse of discretion, or otherwise not in accordance with law." Even when an agency explains its decision with "less than ideal clarity," a reviewing court will not upset the decision on that account "if the agency's path may reasonably be discerned." EPA's three skeletal orders to ADEC and Cominco surely are not composed with ideal clarity. These orders, however, are properly read together with accompanying explanatory correspondence from EPA; so read, the Agency's comments and orders adequately ground the determination that ADEC's acceptance of Low NOx for MG-17 was unreasonable given the facts ADEC found.

Employing [EPA's recommended top-down method for determining BACT] in the May 1999 draft permit, ADEC first concluded that SCR was the most stringent emission-control technology that was both "technically and economically feasible." That technology should have been designated BACT absent "technical considerations, or energy, environmental, or economic impacts justif[ying] a conclusion that [SCR was] not 'achievable' in [this] case." New Source Review Manual, p. B2. ADEC nevertheless selected Low NOx as BACT; ADEC did so in May 1999 based on Cominco's suggestion that fitting all Red Dog Mine generators with Low NOx would reduce aggregate emissions.

In September and December 1999, ADEC again rejected SCR as BACT but no longer relied on Cominco's suggestion that it could reduce aggregate emissions by equipping all generators with Low NOx. ADEC candidly stated that it aimed "[t]o support Cominco's Red Dog Mine Production Rate Increase Project, and its contributions to the region." In these second and third rounds, ADEC rested its selection of Low NOx squarely and solely on SCR's "disproportionate cost."

EPA concluded that ADEC's switch from finding SCR economically feasible in May 1999 to finding SCR economically infeasible in September 1999 had no factual basis in the record. . . .

We do not see how ADEC, having acknowledged that no determination "[could] be made as to the impact of [SCR's] cost on the operation . . . and competitiveness of the [mine]," could simultaneously proffer threats to the mine's operation or competitiveness as reasons for declaring SCR economically infeasible. ADEC, indeed, forthrightly explained why it was disarmed from reaching any judgment on whether, or to what extent, implementation of SCR would adversely affect the mine's operation or profitability: Cominco had declined to provide the relevant financial data, disputing the need for such information and citing "confidentiality concerns." . . . No record evidence suggests that the mine, were it to use SCR for its new generator, would be obliged to cut personnel, or raise zinc prices. Absent evidence of that order, ADEC lacked cause for selecting Low NOx as BACT based on the more stringent control's impact on the mine's operation or competitiveness. . . .

In short, as the Ninth Circuit determined, EPA validly issued stop orders because ADEC's BACT designation simply did not qualify as reasonable in light of the statutory guides.

In its briefs to this Court, ADEC nonetheless justifies its selection of Low NOx as BACT for MG-17 on the ground that lower aggregate emissions would

result from Cominco's "agree[ment] to install Low NOx on all its generators.". . . . We need not dwell on ADEC's attempt to resurrect Cominco's emissions-offsetting suggestion, adopted in the initial May 1999 draft permit, but
thereafter dropped. As ADEC acknowledges, the final PSD permit did not offset
MG-17's emissions against those of the mine's six existing generators, installations that were not subject to BACT. ADEC recognized in September and
December 1999 that a State may treat emissions from several pollutant sources
as falling under one "bubble" for PSD permit purposes only if every pollutant
source so aggregated is "part of the permit action." Offsetting new emissions
against those from any of the mine's other generators, ADEC agreed, "[was] not
a consideration of the BACT review provided for by the applicable law or guidelines," for those generators remained outside the permit's compass. ADEC
plainly did not, and could not, base its December 10, 1999 permit and technical
analysis on an emissions-offsetting rationale drawing in generators not subject to
BACT. Id., at 111-112. By that time, only MG-17 was "part of the permit
action." . . .

The judgment of the Court of Appeals is accordingly Affirmed.

The dissenting opinion of JUSTICE KENNEDY, in which THE CHIEF JUSTICE,
JUSTICE SCALIA, and JUSTICE THOMAS join, is omitted.

2.   The Evolution of the Programs to Achieve and Maintain the NAAQS

A.   Nonattainment and Prevention of Significant Deterioration

As we have gained experience with the difficulties inherent in achieving and
maintaining the NAAQS and with the various regulatory options available, the
basic implementation structure reviewed in the previous section has evolved
considerably. The first substantial evolutionary steps for the Clean Air Act's
ambient air quality program were taken by the EPA even prior to any formal
amendments to the Act. A 1972 district court decision had ruled that the statutory purpose to "protect and enhance" air quality imposed on EPA an obligation
to write rules that would prevent the deterioration of air quality that was presently
better than required by the NAAQS. In an unusual trajectory of judicial review,
this decision by Judge Pratt became law of the land when it was first sustained in
an unpublished per curiam decision in the D.C. Circuit and then again by an
equally divided Supreme Court. Sierra Club v. Ruckelshaus, 344 F.S. 253 (D.D.C.
1972), aff'd per curiam, 2 Envtl. L. Rep. 20656 (D.C. Cir. 1972), aff'd by an
equally divided court mem. sub nom. Fri v. Sierra Club, 412 U.S. 541 (1973).
The equal division of the Supreme Court came about because the Hunton and
Williams law firm represented parties in the litigation and Justice Lewis Powell
followed his then-policy of recusing himself from litigation in which his former
firm was involved. (In the years after *Fri*, Justice Powell abandoned this policy.) In
response to this decision, EPA created a requirement that states include in their
SIPs a program for the preconstruction review of stationary sources, designed to
prevent significant deterioration of so-called "clean air" areas.

Later, in 1976, EPA turned its attention to the unavoidable evidence that
SIPs were not going to bring many parts of the country that were currently
exceeding the NAAQS into compliance in time to meet the statutory deadlines.

Notwithstanding *Union Electric*'s endorsement of the idea that the CAA was meant to apply strong medicine to the air quality problem, solving the air quality problems of dirty air areas was viewed as nearly intractable. The states saw that only draconian measures such as severe restrictions on automobile movement, expensive and perhaps unachievable controls on existing sources and moratoria on new stationary source construction would be adequate if the deadlines were to be met—and they declined to submit SIPs that contained such unpopular measures. The CAA provides EPA with back up authority to issue federal implementation plans (FIPs) if state plans prove inadequate, but the EPA was equally reluctant to exercise that authority. EPA had some disastrous early experiences with FIPs, including several instances in which it wrote FIPs that included significant land use and transportation controls, such as vehicle inspection and maintenance programs, bus and carpool lanes, parking fees, and, in the case of a FIP covering the South Coast Air Basin in California (which includes Los Angeles), severe gas rationing. State and public reaction to these plans was intensely hostile, and in 1974 Congress stripped EPA of any authority to include land use and transportation controls in a FIP. To avoid its own statutory obligation to write FIPs, EPA gave generous interpretations to the adequacy of state submissions and approved some SIPs that subsequently proved to be inadequate.

Eventually, the inadequacy of the SIPs could no longer be ignored. Faced with the prospect of having the CAA be the cause of prohibiting new construction in any area of the country that was not attaining the NAAQS, the EPA crafted an "offset policy." The policy aimed at permitting continued economic expansion in the nonattainment areas, provided that plants complied with requirements that included applying more stringent control technologies than the NSPS, certifying that any other facilities owned by the owner of the new construction were complying with their SIP obligations, and finding ways to "offset" the additional pollutants from the new sources through reductions of similar pollutants coming from existing sources. These offsets had to be greater than 1 to 1, so that in principle the placement of a new facility would result in net improvement in air quality in the area. The idea behind the offset program was to put nonattainment regions on a glide path to eventual compliance with the NAAQS.

Whether the offset program would have survived judicial challenge will never be known, because Congress revisited the CAA for its first major revisions in 1976, and the next year enacted the 1977 Clean Air Act Amendments. These Amendments superseded the agency-created programs for the prevention of significant deterioration (PSD) and nonattainment (NA), by creating statutory programs that built on these early agency efforts. See Title I, Part C, 42 U.S.C. §§7470-7492 (PSD program); Part D, 42 U.S.C. §§7501-7515 (NA program). The basic NA and PSD statutory structures were subsequently refined once again in 1990. These provisions supply the statutory backdrop for the ongoing efforts of the states and the EPA to bring NA areas of the country into compliance and for maintaining air quality in clean air areas. (For good histories of the PSD program over the 1977-1990 time period, see Oren, Prevention of Significant Deterioration: Control-Compelling Versus Site-Shifting, 74 Iowa L. Rev. 1 (1988); Oren, Detail and Delegation: A Study in Statutory Specificity, 15 Colum. J. Envtl. L. 143 (1990). On both PSD and NA, see Theodore L. Garrett & Sonya D. Winner, "A Clean Air Act Primer," Clean Air Deskbook, Environmental Law Institute (1992).)

When Congress revised these programs in 1990, they still faced the reality that the existing regulatory structure, even as modified in 1977, was not moving

FIGURE 5.5
Attainment and Nonattainment Areas in the U.S. 8-hour Ozone Standard

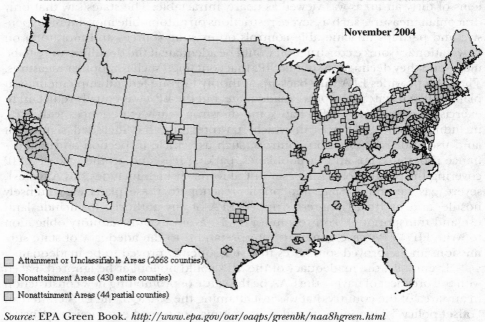

November 2004

☐ Attainment or Unclassifiable Areas (2668 counties)
▨ Nonattainment Areas (430 entire counties)
▨ Nonattainment Areas (44 partial counties)

Source: EPA Green Book. *http://www.epa.gov/oar/oaqps/greenbk/naa8hgreen.html*

the country toward compliance, and that large numbers of Americans continued to live in areas that were nonattainment for one or more of the criteria pollutants. Urban areas were the most difficult of the problems that needed solving, with ozone nonattainment being the hardest one to solve, due to the fact that automobiles are major contributors to the problem, as are emissions from remote sources that are transported by wind circulation to urban and other areas. EPA has designated 126 such areas, based on air quality data from 2001-2003. In EPA's words, "the vast majority of these are in the East (404 counties or partial counties), and are home to more than one-third of all Americans." EPA, Evaluating Ozone Control Programs in the Eastern United States: Focus on the NOx Budget Trading Program, pp. 1-2. EPA-454-K-05-001 (2005). Figure 5.5 shows the ozone nonattainment areas as of November 2004, based on the 8-hour ozone standard that was eventually sustained in the *American Trucking* litigation, pages 486-492. For maps of nonattainment areas for other pollutants, see the web page for this casebook, or go to *http://www.epa.gov/air/oaqps/greenbk/*.

Besides making other refinements in the NA program, the 1990 Amendments created an elaborate regulatory system to address the ozone problem, 42 U.S.C. §§7511ff, and less elaborate ones for carbon monoxide and PM, §§7512, 7513. The ozone program creates different gradations of nonattainment, varying from moderate to extreme, and then imposes increasingly stringent regulatory requirements on them.

States must require reasonably available control technology (RACT) on existing stationary sources, while major new stationary sources in NA areas must install emissions control technology that will meet a "lowest achievable emissions reduction" (LAER) standard for that source. The definition of major source varies by nonattainment region; the worse the air quality problem, the

FIGURE 5.6
Ozone Non Attainment SIP Requirements

Marginal Areas:

- Must inventory emissions sources
- Apply RACT to existing sources
- Improve Auto Inspection & Maintenance Program
- Apply LAER to new & modified major sources
- Major source thresholds = 100 tons per year (tpy)
- Emissions offsets must be 1.1 to 1

Moderate Areas—all Marginal requirements plus:

- 15% progress required in 5 years
- Emissions offsets must be 1.15 to 1

Serious Areas—all Moderate requirements plus:

- Enhanced air quality monitoring
- Enhanced I/M program
- Clean fuel vehicle program
- Transportation control measures
- Major source threshold for VOCs = 50 tpy
- Emissions offsets must be 1.2 to 1

Severe Areas (I and II)—all Serious requirements plus

- Major source threshold for VOCs = 25 tpy
- Stricter transportation control measures
- Emissions offsets of 1.3 to 1
- Use of reformulated gasoline

Extreme Areas—all Severe requirements plus

- Major source threshold for VOCs = 10 tpy
- Emissions offsets of 1.5 to 1

lower the threshold for being considered a major source. Major sources must also meet offset requirements similar to those first instituted through EPA regulations in 1976, but once again these now vary according to the severity of the air quality problem at their location. Offset requirements range from 1.5 to 1 in the most extreme ozone nonattainment area down to 1.1 to 1 for marginal areas. (No areas are currently classified as extreme for ozone).

With respect to the PSD program, "increments" by which an area can increase air pollution over an historical baseline form the regulatory bedrock of the program. Clean areas are assigned to one of three Classes, each with different increments. The most stringent controls are of Class I areas, which are national parks, forests, wilderness areas and other areas of special air quality concern. Separate visibility protections also apply to these areas. Class II and Class III areas permit successively more incremental air pollution, but in no case can the NAAQS be exceeded.

If the classification and increment framework provide the bases for the PSD regulatory program, then the preconstruction review of new stationary sources of air pollutants is its operational center, as well as the source of most of the controversies over the program. The PSD program, like the NA program, requires preconstruction review of all major new stationary sources, including major modifications of existing sources, that are located in areas currently in attainment or unclassified for one or more criteria pollutant and that will emit or have the potential to emit "significant" amounts of at least one of the criteria pollutants. 42 U.S.C. §7475. (The definitions of "major" and "significant" vary, however, between the two programs and also according to the pollutants that are involved.) The review entails a multi-step process first to determine whether the new source is one that requires full preconstruction review, next to calculate the relevant baseline for assessing how much of the area's increment remains available, and to perform air quality modeling that attempts to assess the impact of the new source on the available increment, and finally to perform an analysis of the "best available control technology" (BACT) for that category of new source. These steps are largely similar to those required by preconstruction review in NA areas, except that the threshold levels for major sources vary between the programs, the NA program does not require an area-wide baseline determination, since no increment depletion analysis is required, and the two programs stipulate different—although both stringent—technology-based standards at the end of the process.

Over the years, EPA has worked to provide unified guidance on the processes that new or modified sources must go through to comply with the statute's various air quality requirements, while at the same time developing unique guidance for the steps that are unique to the different preconstruction review requirements. In 1990, Congress amended the CAA to specify some of the preconstruction review requirements, adding a national permitting system in Title V, sections 502-507 of the 1990 Amendments. Title V applies to CAA programs aimed at existing sources, such as the acid rain program, as well as the new and modified source requirements. (On acid rain, see section D2E.) Its rules for preconstruction reviews, together with the agency regulations implementing those reviews, have become known as the New Source Review program, or NSR.

B.   NEW SOURCE REVIEW FOR PSD AND NA

New Source Review is a critical component of efforts to maintain air quality in PSD areas and of efforts to improve air quality in NA areas. It has also been a source of friction between facility owners, EPA, and state air quality agencies, as the *ADEC* decision, pages 510-514, illustrates. Facility owners find the process time-consuming and expensive, and as a result are continually probing the limits of the various ways in which NSR can be avoided. In order to be subject to NSR, a new source must increase air emissions for a covered pollutant above the statutory threshold amounts. One way to avoid NSR, then, is to take advantage of EPA's recognizing an entire facility as a single source, rather than treating each individual emissions location at a larger facility as a source. This provides an existing facility, with existing emissions, the possibility of reducing emissions somewhere in its operation in sufficient amount to stay below the threshold ceilings that trigger NSR, even after the new emissions have been added. (The legality of EPA's interpretation of the Clean Air Act to permit treating each facility as operating under a "bubble" in this way was upheld in the seminal *Chevron* decision. See pages 160-162.)

For example, a coal-fired power plant currently emitting SO_2, and consisting of three separate generating units might propose to build a fourth generating unit at the facility. It might decide to install state of the art emissions control devices on one or more of the existing units in order to reduce these emissions sufficiently so that the net emissions of the new unit plus the existing units is kept below the major source threshold. In this way, the net emissions of the facility—new pollution minus contemporaneous reductions in existing emissions—would not trigger review.

This technique, called "netting out," is one way to avoid NSR. (Sources can also net out by agreeing to enforceable restrictions on emissions within their plant, for instance by agreeing to limitations on hours of operations). Netting out is not always available or attractive to the source. The Red Dog Mine had considered netting out as a way to avoid having to install BACT, but it dropped the idea. See the last full paragraph of the *ADEC* decision, page 514. Why do you suppose it chose not to net out? Besides netting, sources are looking for other ways to avoid NSR. One group of facilities that have apparently been very creative in finding other ways to avoid review are coal-fired power plants already in existence in 1977, when the Amendments establishing PSD and NA preconstruction review were enacted. These plants still constitute a considerable portion of U.S. coal-fired generating capacity. For instance, Duke Energy's entire coal-fired generating capacity consists of eight plants in North and South Carolina, with a total of 30 separate generating units, all of which were constructed between 1940 and 1975.

Because the CAA deals with existing sources and new sources differently, facilities such as those operated by Duke Energy did not become subject to new source performance standards or to NSR under either the PSD or the NA programs when those programs were enacted. They should become subject to the applicable NSR requirements, however, if and when they are modified in ways that would produce additional net emissions sufficient to exceed threshold levels for major sources. This is because whenever the CAA has a requirement that applies to new sources, that requirement also applies to "modifications" of existing facilities. E.g., 42 U.S.C. §7411(a)(4) (NSPS applies to modified sources). The statute, furthermore, gives "modified" a very expansive meaning: A stationary source is "modified" whenever it undergoes "any physical change in, or change in the method of operation of, a stationary source which increases the amount of any air pollutant emitted by such source or which results in the emission of any air pollutant not previously emitted." Id. See also sections 7475(a), 7479(2)(C) (PSD program applies to any "major emitting facility on which construction is commenced" after the effective date of the program; "construction" defined as "includ[ing] the modification (as defined in section 7411(a)(4) of this title) of any source or facility"); sections 7501(4), 7502(5), 7503(a)(2) (NA program applies to any "new or modified major stationary source" and " 'modified' means the same as the term 'modification' as used in section 7411(a)(4) . . .").

The legislative history of the CAA supports the conclusion that in covering "modified" sources with the language quoted above the Congress was providing a limited grace period for existing sources, permitting them to operate for the remainder of their economically useful lives, then putting their owners to the choice of closing the plants down or upgrading them to last longer while at the same time abiding by any applicable NSR requirements.

Longstanding EPA regulations provide that certain kinds of changes in a facility will not constitute a physical or operational change that triggers NSR. One of these categories exempts "maintenance, repair, and replacement which the Administrator determines to be routine for a source category. . . ." 40 C.F.R. §52.21(b)(2)—the RMRR exemption. This exemption would be consistent with the legislative history of the CAA so long as the maintenance, repair, and replacement were not of a kind that prolonged the otherwise calculated economically useful life of a facility. If it did serve to prolong that life, however, that would seem inconsistent with the limited grace period that Congress believed it was providing existing sources.

The first lawsuit addressing the application of the RMRR exemption arose when Wisconsin Power (WEPCO) contested an EPA determination that the renovations it planned for some of its coal-fired generating units could not qualify for an RMRR exception. "WEPCO proposes to replace rear steam drums on units 2, 3, 4 and 5; each of these steam drums measures 60 feet in length, 50.5 inches in diameter and 5.25 inches in thickness. In addition, WEPCO plans to replace another major component, the air heaters, in units 1-4. To implement this four-year program, WEPCO will need to make the replacements by taking the units successively out of service for nine-month periods." Wisconsin Elec. Power Co. v. Reilly, 893 F.2d 901, 907-908 (7th Cir. 1990). Employing an analysis that it termed "case-by-case," and that weighed "the nature, extent, purpose, frequency, and cost of the work, as well as other relevant factors, to arrive at a common-sense finding," id. at 911, EPA found these changes to be non-routine and the court upheld the determination. (Perhaps internal company memoranda referring to these renovations as "life-extension projects" had something to do with the result.)

For the next decade after *WEPCO*, states did not receive many NSR inquiries or permit submissions from existing sources and yet existing power plants seemed to be continuing to operate even though they were getting very old. In a 2002 analysis, GAO found that coal-fired power plants put into operation prior to 1972 still comprise 57 percent of the active fossil-fired plants in the country today. Government Accounting Office, Air Pollution: Emissions from Older Electricity Generating Units at 2 (June 2002). GAO estimated that on average the older units emit twice the amount of SO_2 per megawatt-hour generated than new units and 25 percent more NOx than new units. Id. at 7. Curious as to why it was not seeing more NSR inquiries or submissions, EPA undertook an industry-wide investigation. After some prodding by states led by New York, EPA announced an NSR enforcement campaign, aimed at bringing actions against utilities, such as Duke Energy, whom EPA believed had made nonroutine physical changes in one or more of their generating units without complying with NSR. In November 1999, EPA filed lawsuits against seven electric utilities and a total of 51 power plants. John Fiakla, EPA Sues 7 Utilities, Tells TVA to Stop Practices, Wall St. J., Nov. 4, 1999, at A1. The lawsuits alleged that the utility companies had in fact invested in major life-extending capital improvements at the power plants without going through new source review. The utilities countered that their activities constituted "routine maintenance" necessary to ensure the reliability of electrical supply. Wald, Old Plants with New Parts Present a Problem to EPA, N.Y. Times, Dec. 26, 1999, at A17. All told, in 1999 and 2000, EPA commenced litigation against ten utility companies. Jeanhee Hong, A New Deal for New Source Review, Trends, Vol. 37, no. 3, at 1 (Jan./Feb. 2006).

The utilities strenuously contested EPA's interpretation of plant alterations that trigger NSR, claiming that EPA was contradicting long-standing understandings by advancing "regulatory interpretations . . . best described as 'lawmaking by litigation.'" Peter E. Seley, Lawmaking Through Litigation: EPA's Gamble on New Source Review, 15 Nat. Resources & Env. 260, 260 (2001). Notwithstanding industry outcry, EPA had a number of successes in the closing months of the Clinton administration, when several utility defendants reached agreements on the principles of settlements with EPA. Virginia Electric Power Company (VEPCO) agreed to reduce significantly emissions of NOx and sulfur dioxide at a capital cost of $1.2 billion in addition to paying fines and underwriting supplemental environmental projects. Air Pollution: Virginia Utility Agrees to Major Reductions in NOx and Sulfur Dioxide at Eight Plants to Cut Transport, BNA Daily Envtl. Rep. (Nov. 17, 2000). Under a phased-in, ten-year schedule, VEPCO said it would reduce its NOx emissions from 105,000 tons per year (tpy) to 30,000 tpy. Installation of modern scrubbers will also reduce sulfur dioxide emissions from a current level of 263,000 tpy to 82,000 tpy. Cinergy Corporation, a Cincinnati-based utility, subsequently reached a similar settlement agreement. In addition to paying fines and underwriting supplemental environmental agreements, Cinergy said it would spend $1.4 billion installing up-to-date pollution reduction equipment. BNA Daily Envtl. Rep. (Dec. 27, 2000).

Some utilities chose to litigate rather than settle, however. As the litigation unfolded, the cases focused on three claims by the utilities. First, they claimed their renovations were RMRR under prior guidance issued by EPA, and that the interpretation of RMRR that EPA was putting forth in the lawsuits was in effect a new interpretation for which they lacked fair notice and therefore it should not have applied to them. Second, EPA based part of its determination of RMRR on whether the capital improvements were routine for the specific unit being evaluated. Industry claimed this was the wrong standard, and that their improvements were routine because they were routine for the industry. Separate from their specific criticisms of RMRR, the utilities also objected to how EPA was determining whether or not their actions had increased emissions. EPA took the position that the question of an emissions increase was to be answered by whether or not the facility's projected emissions over an annual time period after the improvements exceeded its actual emissions over an annual time period prior to the improvements. The utilities claimed that the proper calculation was whether or not the unit's hourly emissions rate was made greater by the capital improvements. One situation in which these different methods would have great consequences is the case of an improvement that makes operating the unit more efficient or economical, such that the company might choose to run it for more hours during the year after the improvements. In that case, its annual emissions would go up even though its hourly emissions rate might not (indeed, the hourly emissions rate might even fall), simply because it was run longer. Because most of the changes the utilities had made did not increase the unit's hourly emissions rate, winning on this point alone would secure them a meaningful victory regardless of the outcome of the other two arguments.

As of February 2006, four decisions in EPA enforcement actions against utilities had been issued in four different district court actions. Only one of these has produced an appealable ruling, however. In United States v. Duke Energy Corp., 278 F. Supp. 2d 619 (M.D.N.C. 2003), the court ruled on cross summary judgment motions, finding for the utility on both the routine in the industry versus routine at the unit issue and the total emissions versus emissions rate question. An appeal to the Fourth Circuit produced the following result.

United States v. Duke Energy Corp.
411 F.3d 539 (4th Cir. 2005), cert. granted, May 15, 2006

DIANA GRIBBON MOTZ, Circuit Judge.

The United States brought this enforcement action against Duke Energy Corporation, which provides North Carolina and South Carolina with electricity generated from eight plants located throughout the two states. The United States maintains that Duke Energy on numerous occasions modified these plants without first obtaining appropriate permits in violation of the Clean Air Act. The district court granted summary judgment to Duke Energy. We affirm, albeit for somewhat different reasons than those relied on by the district court.

I

The Clean Air Act is a complex statute supported by an elaborate regulatory scheme; both have a complicated history. This case involves two different, but complementary provisions of the Act: the New Source Performance Standards ("NSPS") provisions, and the Prevention of Significant Deterioration ("PSD") provisions.

To help attain and thereafter maintain [the NAAQS], the 1970 amendments enacted the NSPS provisions, which required the EPA to promulgate standards regulating emissions from both newly constructed and modified sources of pollution at power plants. Congress defined "modification" in the NSPS provisions as "any physical change in, or change in the method of operation of, a stationary source which increases the amount of any air pollutant emitted by such source or which results in the emission of any air pollutant not previously emitted."

Since 1971, the EPA has promulgated NSPS regulations that define "modification" in virtually the same words as the statute. *See, e.g.,* 36 Fed. Reg. 24,876, 24,877 (Dec. 23, 1971); 40 C.F.R. §60.2 (1976); 40 C.F.R. §60.2 (2004). In 1975, the EPA added a regulation elaborating on this definition and further defining "modification" by reference to an increase in the hourly emission rate: a modification includes "any physical or operational change to an existing facility which results in an increase in the emission rate to the atmosphere of any [regulated] pollutant," measured not in tons per year, but in kilograms per hour. 40 Fed. Reg. 58,416, 58,419 (Dec. 16, 1975) (codified at 40 C.F.R. §60.14(a) & (b)).

Congress thereafter enacted a PSD program in the Clean Air Act Amendments of 1977.

The PSD program imposes, *inter alia,* preconstruction review and permit requirements on new or modified sources in areas that have attained or exceeded their air quality standards. Unlike the NSPS program, the PSD program does not focus primarily on technology-based controls, but on the "net emissions from an entire plant resulting from construction or modification of one or more emitting sources within the plant." And so, while NSPS centers on technological controls at an individual pollution-emitting apparatus, PSD fixes on the actual emissions from a site.

The EPA promulgated regulations under the PSD provisions of the statute in 1978. Under the 1980 PSD regulations, a plant cannot engage in a "major modification" of equipment without first undergoing the EPA's permit process and acquiring a permit. The EPA's PSD regulations define a "major modification" as "any physical change in or change in the method of operation of a major stationary source that would result in a significant net emissions increase of any pollutant subject to regulation under the Act." A "net emissions increase" is "[a]ny increase in actual emissions from a particular physical change or change in the method of operation" of a unit. The PSD regulations measure emissions increases relative to a baseline calculation of "actual emissions," i.e., "the average rate, in tons per year, at which the unit actually emitted" the regulated pollutant for, usually, the two years prior to date of measurement, "using the unit's actual operating hours, production rates, and types of materials processed, stored, or combusted" during the selected time period.

II

A

Duke Energy's eight plants in the Carolinas include thirty coal-fired generating units that were placed in service between 1940 and 1975. Each unit contains, as one of its three major components, a boiler, which is a large structure from six to twenty stories tall containing thousands of steel tubes. The tubes are arranged into sets of tube assemblies, including economizer tubes, in which water is initially heated; furnace waterwall tubes, in which water evaporates to steam; superheater tubes, in which the temperature of the steam is raised before being released into a turbine; and reheater tubes, in which steam released from the turbine is reheated and returned to the turbine.

Between 1988 and 2000, as part of a plant modernization program, Duke Energy engaged in twenty-nine projects on the coal-fired generating units, most of which consisted of replacing and/or redesigning one or more of the boiler tube assemblies. These projects would both extend the life of the generating units and allow the units to increase their daily hours of operation. Duke Energy did not apply for or acquire new permits from the EPA for these projects, some of which, according to the Government, cost "more than seven times the original cost of the unit."

The EPA and the Intervenors maintain that these life-extension projects constitute "major modifications" of Duke Energy's furnaces as defined in the PSD statutory and regulatory provisions—that is, physical changes leading to a significant net emissions increase—and thus Duke Energy was required to obtain permits for them. The EPA does not contend that the post-project hourly rate of emissions increased. Rather, it argues that the PSD requires measurement of the net emissions increase by using an "actual-to-projected-actual" test, comparing the actual pre-project emissions from a unit to the projected post-project emissions, which takes into account a unit's ability to operate for more hours. Because the Duke Energy projects enable the units to operate for more hours each day, they will lead to an increase in actual yearly emissions.

Duke Energy counters that its projects do not constitute modifications subject to PSD because they did not increase the units' levels of emissions. The company maintains that, under the PSD program, a net emissions increase will result only if there is an increase in the hourly rate of emissions. Because none of its projects increased a unit's hourly capacity to emit pollution (but increased only the number of hours the unit could operate), the projects did not increase emissions from pre-project levels, and so, according to Duke Energy, it did not have to obtain permits.

B

The district court agreed with Duke Energy. It held that a modification subject to PSD exists only if there is a post-project increase in the hourly rate of emissions.[2]

After resolution of this legal issue, the parties stipulated that the Duke Energy projects would not result in an increase in the hourly rate of emissions. The court then entered summary judgment for Duke Energy.

III

In cases in which an agency's interpretation of its regulations are at issue, a court engages in a modified *Chevron* analysis. *See Chevron U.S.A., Inc. v. Natural Res. Def. Council* [pages 160-162]. First, as in the usual *Chevron* analysis, a court must determine "whether Congress has directly spoken to the precise question at issue." "The judiciary is the final authority on issues of statutory construction" and "[i]f a court, employing traditional tools of statutory construction, ascertains that Congress had an intention on the precise question at issue, that intention is the law and must be given effect." Only if the statute is silent or ambiguous on the point is Congress deemed to have delegated authority to the agency to clarify the point in its regulations. Thus, only in such cases does a court examine the regulation itself, determining its legitimate meaning, asking whether the regulation is based on a permissible construction of the statute, and, if so, deferring to it.

The EPA and the Intervenors expressly acknowledge that these principles govern our review in the case at hand. They fail to understand, however, that straightforward application of these principles can lead to only one conclusion: affirmance of the judgment of the district court.

This is so because Congress has indeed "directly spoken to the precise question at issue." As the EPA itself concedes, the critical first "question at issue" here is whether the EPA "can interpret the statutory term 'modification'

---

2. Duke Energy asserted in the alternative that its projects constitute maintenance, repair and replacement that is routine in the utility industry and, for this reason, were exempt from the permit requirements. The EPA and the Intervenors disagreed, contending that this regulatory exemption only applies to repairs and replacements routine within the life of a generating unit and, therefore, Duke Energy's life-enhancing projects did not qualify for this exemption. The district court again agreed with Duke Energy's interpretation, but held that there was insufficient evidence to grant summary judgment to Duke Energy on this claim. Given our resolution of this case, we need not reach this question.

under PSD differently from how EPA interpreted that term" in the NSPS. As the EPA also concedes, Congress expressly defined "modification" in the NSPS provisions of the Clean Air Act, 42 U.S.C. §7411(a), and then expressly directed that the PSD provisions of the Act employ this same definition. *See* 42 U.S.C. 7479(2)(c) (providing that "construction" in the PSD includes "modification . . . as defined in section 7411(a)"). When Congress mandates that two provisions of a single statutory scheme define a term identically, the agency charged with administering the statutory scheme cannot interpret these identical definitions differently. Thus, because Congress mandated that the PSD definition of "modification" be identical to the NSPS definition of "modification," the EPA cannot interpret "modification" under the PSD inconsistently with the way it interprets that term under the NSPS.

Common sense would seem to dictate this result. Supreme Court precedent certainly does. *See Rowan Cos. v. United States,* 452 U.S. 247, 101 S. Ct. 2288, 68 L. Ed. 2d 814 (1981). In *Rowan,* the Court faced a situation strikingly similar to the one at hand, and held that when Congress itself provided "substantially identical" statutory definitions of a term in different statutes, the agency charged with enforcing the statutes could not interpret the statutory definitions "differently."

The question presented in *Rowan* was whether the Commissioner of the Internal Revenue Service could interpret the statutory term "wages" differently for, on the one hand, the Federal Insurance Contributions Act ("FICA") and the Federal Unemployment Tax Act ("FUTA"), and, on the other, the statute governing income-tax withholding. Congress had defined the term "wages" in these statutes in substantially the same language: for both FICA and FUTA, "wages" were defined as "all remuneration for employment, including the cash value of all remuneration paid in any medium other than cash"; for income tax withholding, "wages" were defined as "all remuneration (other than fees paid to a public official) for services performed by an employee for his employer, including the cash value of all remuneration paid in any medium other than cash." The Commissioner, however, issued regulations interpreting "wages" under FICA and FUTA to include the value of meals and lodging provided to employees for the convenience of the employer, and "wages" under the income-tax withholding statute to exclude this value.

In holding the Commissioner's interpretation impermissible, the Court relied on the plain language of the statutes and their legislative history. First, the Court noted that when Congress enacted the precursors to FICA and FUTA as part of the Social Security Act of 1935, it chose "wages" as the basis for employer taxation and then statutorily defined the term. Similarly, seven years later, when Congress enacted the original income-tax withholding statute, it chose "wages" as the basis for taxation and statutorily defined the term "in substantially the same language that it used in FICA and FUTA." The *Rowan* Court held that, "[i]n view of this sequence of consistency, the plain language of the statute is strong evidence that Congress intended 'wages' to mean the same thing under FICA, FUTA, and income-tax withholding." The Court then examined the statutes' history, finding indications that Congress intended to "coordinate the income-tax withholding system with FICA and FUTA . . . to promote simplicity and ease of administration," and concluding that "[c]ontradictory interpretations of substantially identical definitions do not serve that interest."

The plain language of the Clean Air Act provides even stronger evidence that Congress intended the statutory definitions of "modification" in the PSD and NSPS provisions to be interpreted identically. While Congress used only "substantially the same language" in the statutory definitions at issue in *Rowan,* here Congress mandated that the definition of "modification" in the PSD provisions precisely mirror the definition of "modification" in the NSPS provision. Congress did this by directly incorporating the NSPS definition, which it had enacted in 1970, into the PSD provisions, which it enacted seven years later. *See* Pub. L. No. 95-190, 91 Stat. 1393, 1402 (1977) ("The term 'construction' when used in connection with any source or facility, includes the modification (as defined in [section 7411(a)]) of any source or facility."); 42 U.S.C. §7479(2)(C).

Moreover, as in *Rowan,* the legislative history of the statutes at issue here does not in any way suggest that Congress intended these identical statutory definitions to receive different interpretations.

The EPA and Intervenors . . . emphasize the "vital differences" between PSD and NSPS. We do not ignore or minimize those differences. Although both statutes are part of the Clean Air Act and designed to serve its purpose "to protect and enhance the quality of the Nation's air resources so as to promote the public health and welfare and the productive capacity of its population," 42 U.S.C. §7401(b)(1), they address somewhat different problems. PSD exists primarily to prevent significant deterioration of ambient air quality in areas meeting clean air standards, while NSPS requires new sources to implement particular technologies to limit their own emissions. These differences have led us and other courts to approve different regulatory definitions for an identical statutory term in the two statutes. In *PEPCo,* for example, we held that "significant difference[s] between the PSD and NSPS programs" justified a different interpretation of the statutory term "stationary source." 650 F.2d at 518. But in *PEPCo,* although Congress had defined the term "stationary source" in the NSPS provisions it had *not* defined that term in the PSD provisions. Thus, while in *PEPCo* both statutes contained the same *term,* the statutes did not *define* that term in the same manner; nor was the use of the term in the PSD provisions linked to the statutory definition of the term in the NSPS provisions. Similarly, in *Northern Plains Resource Council,* the Ninth Circuit allowed the EPA to interpret the statutory term "commenced" differently in the NSPS and PSD regulations. 645 F.2d at 1357. But again, although one statute—there the PSD provisions—defined the term, the other—the NSPS provisions—did *not.* And, Congress had not linked the PSD definition of the term to its use in the NSPS provisions of the statute.

PEPCo . . . illustrate[s] the principle that the same word or phrase will generally be presumed to have the same meaning when used in different parts of the statute, but this "presumption of the uniform usage . . . relents" when there is "a variation in the connection in which the words are used as reasonably to warrant the conclusion that they were employed in different parts of the act with different intent." *Gen. Dynamics Land Sys., Inc. v. Cline,* 540 U.S. 581, 124 S. Ct. 1236, 1245, 157 L. Ed. 2d 1094 (2004) (internal quotation marks and citation omitted). Thus, in *PEPCo . . . ,* the difference in purpose between the NSPS and PSD programs justified the conclusion that the same words had different meanings in the two sections of the statute.

In the case before us, however, the presumption of uniform usage has become effectively irrebutable because Congress' decision to create identical statutory definitions of the term "modification" has affirmatively mandated that this term be interpreted identically in the two programs. The different purposes of the NSPS and PSD programs cannot override that mandate. Neither the United States nor the Intervenors have cited a single case in which any court has held that identical statutory *definitions* can be interpreted differently by the agency charged with enforcement of the statute. Moreover, in *Rowan* the Supreme Court expressly rejected the argument, which was successful in the Fifth Circuit, that the different purposes of FICA/FUTA and income-tax withholding justified the different regulatory interpretations of the same statutory definition. The *Rowan* Court concluded that to permit the Commissioner to interpret the same statutory terms differently would "fail to implement the congressional mandate in a consistent and reasonable manner."

So it is here. Congress mandated that the PSD statute incorporate the NSPS statutory definition of "modification." No one disputes that prior to enactment of the PSD statute, the EPA promulgated NSPS regulations that define the term "modification" so that only a project that increases a plant's *hourly* rate of emissions constitutes a "modification." The EPA must, therefore, interpret its PSD regulations defining "modification" congruently. Of course, this does not mean that this regulatory interpretation must be retained indefinitely. The EPA retains its authority to amend and revise this and other regulations "through exercise of appropriate rulemaking powers." Indeed, the parties point out that the EPA has already amended some of the regulations at issue here. As long as Congress mandates that "modification" be defined identically in the NSPS and PSD statutes, however, EPA must interpret that term in a consistent manner in the NSPS and PSD regulations.

IV

For the foregoing reasons, the judgment of the district court is *AFFIRMED.*

NOTES AND QUESTIONS

1. Is the interpretation given by the court to what constitutes an increase in emissions consistent with the idea of a limited grace period for existing sources? Notice that the court refers to Duke Energy's capital investments as ones that would extend the life of the generating units.

2. What was EPA's argument that the NSPS and PSD programs served different purposes? How do those different purposes support different interpretations of what constitutes an emissions increase?

3. Suppose that the Congress had written out the same definition of modification in the PSD section of the CAA as found in the NSPS section, instead of referencing the NSPS definition. Under the Court's analysis, would EPA then have had a stronger argument that the different purposes served by the NSPS and the PSD programs justified giving different meanings to the idea of an emissions increase in the two programs? Consider that the concept of what constitutes an increase in emissions would be ambiguous in both sections of the statute. Under those circumstances, *Chevron* instructs the courts to defer to reasonable constructions of the statute. Can it be reasonable for EPA to interpret an increase in emissions one way in one portion of the statute, and then a different way in a second portion? Would you infer from Congress's use of the same concept in two sections of the statute that Congress meant EPA to resolve ambiguities in the same way in each section, or that it meant EPA to exercise its expertise in

resolving those ambiguities, with it being possible that EPA might reasonably conclude the ambiguity ought to be resolved differently in the two cases?

4. Recall that deciding whether a facility needs to go through the NSR approval process entails a two-step inquiry: (1) has there been a physical or operational change that (2) results in an increase in emissions? EPA and the utility companies disagreed over EPA's interpretation of the requirements of each. *Duke Energy,* however, addressed only the second step. See note 2 of the opinion. The principal issues in dispute regarding the first step, as already indicated, concern whether EPA's pattern of varying interpretations of the RMRR exemption meant that utility companies lacked fair notice of the interpretation upon which EPA was basing its enforcement actions. In U.S. v. Southern Indiana Gas and Electric Co., 245 F. Supp. 2d 994 (S.D. Ind. 2003) (*SIGECO*), the district court rejected the fair notice argument, concluding that since *WEPCO,* EPA had been sufficiently consistent in reiterating the "case-by-case, fact intensive" nature of the RMRR review, as well as the major considerations that go into that review. Beyond arguing lack of fair notice, defendant utilities have also argued that what is "routine" must be decided by reference to the industry as a whole, not by reference to the repair and maintenance history of the specific unit being reviewed. On this issue, the district courts have split. Both *SIGECO* and U.S. v. Ohio Edison, 276 F. Supp. 2d 829 (S.D. Ohio, Aug. 7, 2003) found in favor of EPA on this issue, while the lower court in *Duke Energy,* U.S. v. Duke Energy, 278 F. Supp. 2d 619 (M.D.N.C. 2003), and U.S. v. Alabama Power Co. 372 F. Supp. 2d 1283 (N.D. Ala. 2005) have ruled for the utility defendants.

5. The Department of Justice petitioned for a rehearing en banc in *Duke Energy,* but when that was denied it declined to petition for certiorari. Several environmental intervenors did petition for Supreme Court review, however, and the Court announced in May 2006 that it would hear the case during its October 2006 Term. Environmental Defense v. Duke Energy Corp., No. 05-848. This is only the third time that the Supreme Court has ever agreed to review a case solely at the behest of an environmental organization over the opposition of the government and the regulated community. One issue that will be raised before the Supreme Court is the question whether the Fourth Circuit transgressed the judicial review provisions of section 307(b) of the Clean Air Act, which provide for exclusive venue in the D.C. Circuit for challenges to nationally applicable regulatory decisions.

6. One reason that some utilities chose to litigate rather than settle EPA's enforcement actions is that they were hoping that a new President and administration might result in a change in EPA's approach to enforcement. When President Bush assumed office in January 2001, one of his first actions was to ask Vice President Cheney to head an energy policy task force to make recommendations on a comprehensive national energy policy. One of the task force's recommendations was to revise the New Source Review program to respond to industry complaints that its requirements were stifling capital investments that could improve energy efficiency and reduce dependence on foreign energy sources. On December 31, 2002, EPA issued a set of regulatory changes designed to "reduce burden, maximize operating flexibility, improve environmental quality, provide additional certainty, and promote administrative efficiency" in the NSR program for PSD and NA. 67 Fed. Reg. 80,166, 80,189 (Dec. 31, 2002).

7. The new NSR regulations revised some of the methodology to be used in calculating whether a physical or operational change increased emissions, spelled out several situations in which a facility would be exempt from making

such a calculation, and revised some other aspects of the NSR procedures as well. As for determining whether a change increased emissions, EPA first altered the way a facility should establish its existing emissions baseline against which to compare its post-change emissions. Previously, EPA's NSR regulations as applied to the PSD and NA programs had provided that "[m]ajor modification means any physical change in or change in the method of operation of a major stationary source that would result in a significant net emissions increase of any pollutant subject to regulation under the Act." 45 Fed. Reg. 52,676, 52,735 (Aug. 7, 1980). "Net emissions increase" was defined as "any increase in actual emissions from a particular physical change or change in method of operation" after the source had taken into account, through the "netting" process, any other contemporaneous changes in emissions at the facility. Id. at 52,736. Then EPA defined "actual emissions":

> (ii) In general, actual emissions as of a particular date shall equal the average rate, in tons per year, at which the unit actually emitted the pollutant during a two-year period which proceeds the particular date and which is representative of normal source operation. The Administrator shall allow the use of a different time period upon a determination that it is more representative of normal source operation. Actual emissions shall be calculated using the unit's actual operating hours, production rates, and types of materials processed, stored, or combusted during the selected time period.
> (iii) The Administrator may presume that source-specific allowable emissions for the unit are equivalent to the actual emissions of the unit.
> (iv) For any emissions unit which has not begun normal operations on the particular date, actual emissions shall equal the potential to emit of the unit on that date. Id. at 52,737.

In its 2002 regulations, EPA changed the procedure for calculating actual emissions to permit the facility to choose any 24-month period during the previous 10 years of operation. The change was designed to allow facilities to choose the highest emissions period during this 10-year period.

8. Once actual emissions are determined, EPA's 2002 regulations provided that these are to be compared to the annual emissions that the facility projects will be actually emitted from the facility after the change. This "actual-to-projected-actual" calculation is the same one described (and rejected) by the *Duke Energy* court. It requires that increased emissions resulting from increases in hours of operation be counted in the projection of actual future emissions. However, in another NSR revision, EPA provided that the facility need not count in its projected actual emissions any increases that "an existing unit could have accommodated during the consecutive 24-month period used to establish the baseline actual emissions . . . and that are also unrelated to the particular project, including any increased utilization due to product demand growth." 67 Fed. Reg. at 80,277. This "demand growth exclusion" had already been available to utilities under the prior rule; the 2002 changes made it available to all stationary sources.

9. States and environmental organizations challenged a number of features of the 2002 regulations as being too lax and contrary to the CAA. Industry groups challenged several features as being too stringent, contrary to prior judicial decisions and inconsistent with the CAA. Other state intervenors defended EPA's rule. In June 2005, just nine days after the decision of the Fourth Circuit in *Duke Energy*, the D.C. Circuit rendered its decision on these challenges.

New York v. EPA
413 F.3d 3 (D.C. Cir. 2005)

Before: ROGERS and TATEL, Circuit Judges, and WILLIAMS, Senior Circuit Judge.

PER CURIAM.

In 1977, Congress amended the Clean Air Act ("CAA" or "the Act") to strengthen the safeguards that protect the nation's air quality. Among other things, these amendments directed that major stationary sources undertaking modifications must obtain preconstruction permits, as must major new sources, through a process known as "New Source Review" ("NSR"). According to a preexisting definition referenced in the 1977 amendments, a source undertakes a modification when "any physical change . . . or change in the method of operation . . . which increases the amount of any air pollutant emitted by such source" occurs. The Environmental Protection Agency ("EPA") has interpreted this rather terse definition in numerous rules, including ones issued in 1980, 1992, and most recently in 2002.

Industry, government, and environmental petitioners now challenge this 2002 rule, which departs sharply from prior rules in several significant respects. Roughly speaking, industry petitioners argue that the 2002 rule interprets "modification" too broadly, while government and environmental petitioners argue that the rule's interpretation is too narrow. Industry petitioners have also revived previously stayed challenges to EPA's earlier rule.

Today, we reject challenges to substantial portions of the 2002 rule. . . .

I. BACKGROUND

EPA's 1975 NSPS regulation, like its earlier 1971 regulation, elaborated upon [the] statutory definition of a "modified source," doing so in provisions whose meaning the parties debate today. One part of the 1975 regulation provided that " '[m]odification' means any physical change in, or change in the method of operation of, an existing facility which increases the amount of any air pollutant (to which a standard applies) emitted into the atmosphere by that facility." 40 Fed. Reg. 58,416, 58,418 (Dec. 16, 1975). Using somewhat different terms, another part of the 1975 regulation stated that "any physical or operational change to an existing facility which results in an increase in the emission rate to the atmosphere of any pollutant to which a standard applies shall be considered a modification within the meaning . . . of the Act," with "[e]mission rate . . . expressed as kg/hr of any pollutant discharged into the atmosphere." 40 Fed. Reg. at 58,419. Yet neither the 1975 regulation nor its preamble explained why EPA found it necessary to offer these two separate glosses on "modification."

Adding to the confusion, EPA put forth yet another definition of "modification" in a 1974 regulation implementing what became known as the regulatory "Prevention of Significant Deterioration" ("PSD") program. Seeking to prevent backsliding in regions whose air quality met NAAQS, this program required new sources and sources undertaking modifications to obtain preconstruction permits. The regulation defined "modification" in a manner that closely tracked—but didn't precisely mirror—the NSPS regulatory definition, stating that "[t]he phrases 'modification' or 'modified source' mean any physical change in, or change in the method of operation of, a stationary source which increases the emission rate of any pollutant for which a national standard has been promulgated." 39 Fed. Reg. 42,510, 42,514 (Dec. 5, 1974). The regulation's preamble further provided that the term "modified source" was meant "to be consistent with the definition used in [NSPS]." Id. at 42,513.

Both the NSPS and PSD regulations listed certain exceptions to what constitutes a "modification," though once again the precise content of the regulations varied. The 1974 PSD and the 1971 NSPS regulations provided that:

> (1) Routine maintenance, repair, and replacement shall not be considered a physical change, and (2) The following shall not be considered a change in the method of operation: (i) An increase in the production rate, if such increase does not exceed the operating design capacity of the source; (ii) An increase in the hours of operation; (iii) Use of an alternative fuel or raw material [under certain conditions].

The 1975 NSPS regulation not only phrased its exceptions differently, but also added a few additional ones:

> The following shall not, by themselves, be considered modifications under this part: (1) Maintenance, repair, and replacement which the Administrator determines to be routine . . .; (2) An increase in production rate of an existing facility, if that increase can be accomplished without a capital expenditure on the stationary source containing that facility; (3) an increase in the hours of operation; (4) Use of an alternative fuel or raw material [under certain conditions] . . .; (5) The addition or use of any system whose primary function is the reduction of air pollutants . . .; (6) The relocation or change in ownership of an existing facility.

In its various permutations, this regulatory framework had not been long in place when, in 1977, Congress amended the CAA yet again. These amendments drew upon, expanded, and superseded the regulatory PSD program. In particular, the amendments strengthened the Act by (1) expressly creating a preconstruction review process for new or modified major sources located in "nonattainment" areas (i.e., areas which failed to meet NAAQS), see generally 42 U.S.C. §§7501-7515; and (2) expressly providing a parallel preconstruction review process in PSD areas (i.e., areas which met NAAQS or where there was insufficient information to evaluate whether NAAQS were met), see generally id. §§7470-7492. The parties refer to the first as "Nonattainment New Source Review" ("NNSR"), to the second as "Prevention of Significant Deterioration" ("PSD"), and to both collectively as "New Source Review" ("NSR"). We shall do the same. . . .

In sum, the 1977 amendments carved out a significant difference between existing sources on the one hand and new or modified sources on the other. The former faced no NSR obligations—in the common phrase, they were "grandfathered"—while the latter were subject to strict standards. Limiting NSR to new or modified sources was one method of accomplishing the amendments' goal of "a proper balance between environmental controls and economic growth," id. at 27,076 (Aug. 4, 1977) (statement of Rep. Waxman).

EPA promulgated an NSR regulation in 1978. . . . The 1978 regulation defined a major "modification" as a "physical change, change in the method of operation of, or addition to a stationary source which increases the potential emission rate of any air pollutant regulated under the act." The phrase "potential emission rate," though new to EPA regulations relating to "modification," went unchallenged during ensuing litigation over other aspects of the 1978 regulation. That litigation culminated in this circuit's Alabama Power Co. v. Castle decision, issued initially as a brief opinion, 606 F.2d 1068 (D.C. Cir. 1979), that was superseded six months later by a much longer one, 636 F.2d 323.

In the period between the two *Alabama Power* opinions, EPA proposed a new NSR regulation. The proposed definition of modification continued focusing on potential emissions rates rather than actual emissions. 44 Fed. Reg. 51,924, 51,952 (Sept. 5, 1979). After the issuance of the revised *Alabama Power* opinion, however, EPA changed its definition of modification. The final 1980 rule defined the term [as set forth in the note 7, page 525]. In contrast to the proposed regulation's approach, this regulation emphasized "actual emissions." Justifying the shift, EPA explained in the regulation's preamble that while the initial *Alabama Power* decision had used the phrase "potential to emit," the later opinion used language that, "like the [statutory] definition, suggest[ed] changes in actual emissions," and that EPA had followed suit. Finally, the 1980 regulation provided that "[a] physical change or change in the method of operation shall not include . . . an increase in the hours of operation or in the production rate."

Several parties petitioned this court for review of the 1980 rule, but we stayed that challenge because of ongoing settlement discussions with EPA. Ultimately, EPA and the parties entered into an agreement providing that the agency would undertake a new rulemaking and that if the new rule failed to meet certain conditions, the parties could revive their stayed petitions.

In the proceedings before us today, industry petitioners and EPA dispute what the 1980 rule meant. Both agree that for a source to undertake a modification, it must first make a physical or operational change other than an increase in the hours of operation. They disagree over how to measure an "increase" in emitted pollutants once a change has occurred. According to industry petitioners, the 1980 regulation provided that an emissions "increase" occurs only if the maximum hourly emissions rate goes up as a result of the physical or operational change. According to EPA, however, an increase occurs under the 1980 regulations if, after netting, a source's past annual emissions (typically measured by averaging out the two "baseline" years prior to the change) are less than future annual emissions (measured by calculating the source's potential to emit after the change). EPA proffered this interpretation, which quickly became known as the "actual-to-potential" test, in proceedings leading up to Puerto Rican Cement Co. v. EPA, 889 F.2d 292 (1st Cir. 1989), and Wisconsin Electric Power Co. v. Reilly, 893 F.2d 901 (7th Cir. 1990) ("*WEPCo*"). EPA also referred to this interpretation in its preambles to later rules, see 57 Fed. Reg. 32,314, 32,328 (July 21, 1992); 67 Fed. Reg. 80,186, 80,199 (Dec. 31, 2002).

Puerto Rican Cement's facts illustrate the practical difference between industry's and EPA's interpretations. In that case, a factory sought to make a physical change: it would replace old cement kilns that operated 60% of the time with a new kiln that would emit fewer pollutants per hour. "If operated to achieve about the same level of production [as the old ones], the new kiln will pollute far less than the older kilns; but, if the Company operates the new kiln at significantly higher production levels, it will emit more pollutants than did the older kilns." Under the actual-to-potential test, the company "increased" its emissions after the change, making it subject to NSR: operated at full potential, the new kiln would emit more pollutants than the old kilns had emitted when actually in operation. Under the interpretation urged by industry petitioners, however, the company had not undergone an "increase" in emissions—and thus would not trigger NSR—since the new kiln would have a lower hourly emissions rate than the old ones. Siding with EPA, the First Circuit agreed that the company had to obtain an NSR permit to make the intended change.

EPA issued a proposed rule in 1996, followed by a 1998 Notice of Availability ("NOA") requesting additional comment on several issues, followed in turn by a four-year hiatus. In the meantime, EPA began investigating numerous sources for noncompliance with the existing NSR program. It ended up bringing complaints against thirty-two utilities in ten states.

In 2002, EPA issued a new final rule to "reduce burden, maximize operating flexibility, improve environmental quality, provide additional certainty, and promote administrative efficiency." This rule departed from the prior rules in several significant respects relevant to this litigation. It adopted the actual-to-projected-actual test for all existing sources, though leaving sources the option to continue using the actual-to-potential test if they preferred.

Numerous petitioners now challenge the 2002 rule. . . .

In considering these challenges, we apply a highly deferential standard of review. We may set aside a regulation only if it exceeds EPA's "statutory jurisdiction, authority, or limitations" or is "arbitrary, capricious, an abuse of discretion, or otherwise not in accordance with law." 42 U.S.C. §7607(d)(9).

As to EPA's interpretation of the CAA, we proceed under *Chevron*'s familiar two-step process. In the first step ("Chevron Step 1"), we determine whether, based on the Act's language, legislative history, structure, and purpose, "Congress has directly spoken to the precise question at issue." If so, EPA must obey. But if Congress's intent is ambiguous, we proceed to the second step ("Chevron Step 2") and consider "whether the agency's [interpretation] is based on a permissible construction of the statute." If so, we will give that interpretation "controlling weight unless [it is] arbitrary, capricious, or manifestly contrary to the statute."

Aside from statutory interpretation, we evaluate EPA's actions based on traditional administrative law principles. "Where, as here, the issue before us requires a high level of technical expertise, we must defer to the informed discretion of the responsible federal agencies." After a "searching and careful inquiry" into the facts, we will find EPA's actions arbitrary and capricious if the agency has failed to "examine the relevant data and articulate a satisfactory explanation for its action, including a rational connection between the facts found and the choice made," *Motor Vehicle Mfrs. Ass'n v. State Farm Mut. Auto. Ins. Co.*, or has reached a conclusion unsupported by substantial evidence. The standard of review "does not," however, "permit us to substitute our policy judgment for that of the Agency."

II. INDUSTRY CHALLENGES

Various firms and industry associations . . . attack the 2002 rule's definition of "modification" for NSR purposes on the ground that it unlawfully differs from its definition for NSPS purposes. While the NSPS regulatory definition of modification allegedly focuses on the hourly rate of emissions, the NSR definition focuses on net emissions increases measured in tons per year. Compare 40 C.F.R. §60.14 (NSPS), with id. §52.21(b)(2)(ii) (NSR). Industry claims that this divergence is unlawful because Congress intended to adopt for NSR purposes the NSPS regulatory definition in existence at the time of the 1977 amendments. (Industry petitioners also challenge the 1980 rule's definition of modification in the NSR context to the extent that it differs from the NSPS definition.) We are not convinced. . . .

A

Modification. Industry rests its claim that modification must have the same regulatory meaning for NSR as prevailed for NSPS in 1977 on the fact that Congress, by a cross-reference, used the same language in both statutory contexts. Thus, the NNSR portion of the Act provided:

> The terms "modifications" and "modified" mean the same as the term "modification" as used in section 7411(a)(4) of this title. 42 U.S.C. §7501(4).

Similarly, the PSD portion of the statute provides that "construction" includes "the modification (as defined in section 7411(a) of this title) of any source or facility." Id. §7479(2)(C). So far as appears, then, these incorporations by reference are the equivalent of Congress's having simply repeated in the NSR context the definitional language used before in the NSPS context.

We have (naturally) required indications in the statutory language or history to infer that Congress intended to incorporate into a statute a preexisting regulatory definition. Industry suggests there is "abundant indication" of such intent, pointing to Congress's having said that modification (in the NNSR portion of the statute) has the meaning of the same word "as used in" the NSPS portion of the statute. It also cites a conference committee report that explains agreement to cover modification as well as construction in Part C of the Act (PSD) (a point apparently originally excluded unintentionally) by saying that construction is being defined "to conform to usage in other parts of the Act." See 123 Cong. Rec. 32,253 (Nov. 1, 1977). But the phrases "usage" and "used in" refer not to regulatory usage, but only to usage in the statute itself. They tell us no more than if Congress had used a little more ink and repeated the NSPS definitions verbatim. Elsewhere in the Act, moreover, Congress did incorporate regulatory provisions expressly by reference. See, e.g., Pub. L. No. 95-95, §129(a)(1), 91 Stat. 685, 745 (1977) ("the interpretative regulation of the Administrator of the Environmental Protection Agency published in 41 Federal Register 55524 . . . shall apply. . . . ") (incorporating EPA's offset ruling); 42 U.S.C. §7502 note. Congress's failure to use such an express incorporation of prior regulations for "modification" cuts against the proposed inference.

Industry petitioners also invoke *Bragdon v. Abbott*, 524 U.S. 624, 632, 118 S. Ct. 2196, 141 L. Ed. 2d 540 (1998), for the proposition that when Congress repeats a well-established term, it implies that Congress intended the term to be construed in accordance with preexisting regulatory interpretations. But that proposition does industry little good here, as the regulatory definitions in the NSPS and PSD programs already differed at the time of the 1977 amendments.

In fact, the NSPS regulations adopted in 1975 and in force at the time of the 1977 CAA amendments themselves used two different (and possibly inconsistent) definitions of modification. Section 60.2(h) defined modification to include "any physical change in, or change in the method of operation of, an existing facility which increases the amount of any air pollutant (to which a standard applies) emitted into the atmosphere by that facility." 40 Fed. Reg. at 58,418 (previously codified at 40 C.F.R. §60.2(h) (1976)). But 40 C.F.R. §60.14(a) provided that "any physical or operational change to an existing facility which results in an increase in the emissions rate to the atmosphere of any pollutant to which a standard applies shall be considered a modification," and §60.14(b) specified that the emissions rate should be expressed in "kg/hr of any pollutant discharged into the atmosphere." Industry's briefs, curiously, mention only §60.14, never §60.2(h). Given the two quite differently worded regulatory definitions of "modification" within the NSPS program at the time of the 1977 amendments, it would take a rather pointed indication from Congress to support the idea that it expressly adopted one of them for NSR. No such indication exists. We express no opinion as to whether Congress intended to require that EPA use identical regulatory definitions of modification across the NSPS and NSR programs. Cf. *Duke Energy* [pages 518-523]. That argument was not made by industry petitioners in their opening brief and is therefore waived. See Verizon Tel. Cos. v. FCC, 292 F.3d 903, 911-912 (D.C. Cir. 2002). As industry makes no attack at all on the reasonableness of EPA's definition of modification for NSR (apart from its divergence from one of the 1975 NSPS definitions), we reject this portion of industry's challenge to the 1980 and the 2002 rules.

EPA acknowledges that fewer changes will trigger NSR under the 2002 rule than under the 1980 rule. However, based on its experience and its Environmental Impact Analysis . . . EPA "believe[s] that the environment will not be adversely affected" . . . because NSR is not the primary mechanism for reducing emissions from existing sources. EPA explains in its Report to the President:

> The NSR program is by no means the primary regulatory tool to address air pollution from existing sources. The Clean Air Act provides for several other public health-driven and visibility-related control efforts: for example, the National Ambient Air Quality Standards Program implemented through enforceable State Implementation Plans, the NOx SIP Call, the Acid Rain Program, the Regional Haze Program, etc. Thus, while NSR was designed by Congress to focus particularly on sources that are newly constructed or that make major modifications, Congress provided numerous other tools for assuring that emissions from existing sources are adequately controlled.

EPA, New Source Review: Report to the President 3-4 (2002).

IX. CONCLUSION

Accordingly, we deny the petitions of government, environmental, and industry petitioners [except as to minor provisions not included in this excerpt—see note 5, below].

NOTES AND QUESTIONS

1. Well after oral argument in this case, and just nine days prior to the panel issuing its decision, the *Duke Energy* decision concluded that the CAA required the regulatory definitions of modification to be the same for the NSPS and the PSD programs. Industry petitioners quickly brought the result in that case to the attention of the D.C. Circuit panel through the submission of a post-argument

supplemental filing of letters. How did the D.C. Circuit address the relevance of the *Duke Energy* ruling? Notice that while the Supreme Court's *Rowan* decision played a prominent role in the Fourth Circuit's ruling, it was not mentioned in the D.C. Circuit's opinion. In fact, *Rowan* had not been raised by any party in the Fourth Circuit either; it entered the case after the Fourth Circuit panel on its own motion asked for supplemental briefing on the relevance of the case for the issues before it. Is there any malpractice liability lurking in the D.C. Circuit case for the parties who did not brief the *Rowan* argument in their opening briefs? If the D.C. Circuit panel had reached the *Duke Energy* rating, would it have agreed or disagreed with it?

2. EPA's changes to its NSR regulations are designed to make it easier for facilities to avoid new source review. Does this reflect a basic problem with a strategy of regulating new sources of pollution more stringently than existing sources—that it encourages prolonging the life of old sources to take advantage of more relaxed emissions standards? Compare this approach with that of the Oil Pollution Act, see pages 121-126, which phased in its double-hull requirement for oil tankers on a schedule based on the age of existing tankers. Which one is a better approach?

3. When the EPA announced its 2002 rule changes, EPA Administrator Whitman had said that the revisions would not affect the government's litigation strategy with respect to claimed violations of the old rules from actions taken by facilities prior to the rule changes. After Administrator Whitman left the Agency, however, Inside EPA reported that "in a controversial move, EPA enforcement chief J.P. Suarez told enforcement staff . . . to set aside cases not yet filed that do not meet the requirements of the new rules, which would primarily affect utility cases." Inside EPA, "EPA Retreat on NSR Enforcement Could Buoy State Legal Strategies" (Nov. 14, 2003). Is this a justifiable enforcement policy? How significant is it in light of the *Duke Energy* decision, pages 518-523?

4. Much of the controversy surrounding NSR has been over the ambiguities in the case-by-case nature of the determination that a capital improvement project comes within the routine maintenance, replacement, and repair exemption. Interestingly, neither of the two circuit court opinions to date has reached the objections the utility companies have been raising to EPA's interpretation of that exemption. There has been RMRR-related activity on the regulatory front, however. In 2003, EPA promulgated a revision of RMRR that adopted a bright line test for determining whether or not a capital project qualified for the exemption. Under the new Equipment Replacement Rule (ERP), a capital project at an existing facility is exempt from NSR if: (1) the project replaces existing equipment with identical ones, or ones that serve the same purpose; (2) project costs do not exceed 20 percent of the current replacement value of the entire unit; (3) the project does not alter the basic design of the unit or cause it to exceed any applicable emissions limitations that applies to the unit. 68 Fed. Reg. 61,248, 62,252. In December 2003, a panel of the D.C. Circuit stayed implementation of the ERP based on its belief that challengers had shown a reasonable likelihood of success on the merits. New York v. EPA, 03-1380, Dec. 24, 2003. As of this writing, the court has not issued a final decision.

5. The rule under review in New York v. EPA contained a number of other changes in the complex NSR rules. The court upheld the great majority of them. It upheld the EPA's extension of the demand growth exclusion (see note 8, page 525) to non-utility sources on the ground that EPA was correct in interpreting the statute "as requiring 'a causal link' between the proposed change and any

post-change increase in emissions," and that the 2002 regulations were a reasonable way to implement that requirement. It also upheld EPA's decision to let a source select any 24-month period from the 10 years to use as a baseline against which to determine whether an emissions increase will occur. However, the court struck down the regulation's provision that no recordkeeping of actual post-change emissions was required of a source that determined there was no "reasonable possibility" that a physical operational change might result in increased emissions. "Of course," the panel wrote, "one might wonder why sources with no 'reasonable possibility' of significantly increased emissions should keep records at all. If EPA actually knew which sources had no 'reasonable possibility' of triggering NSR, these sources would obviously have no need to keep records. The problem is that EPA has failed to explain how, absent recordkeeping, it will be able to determine whether sources have accurately concluded that they have no 'reasonable possibility' of significantly increased emissions. We recognize that less burdensome requirements may well be appropriate for sources with little likelihood of triggering NSR, but EPA needs to explain how its recordkeeping and reporting requirements allow it to identify such sources. . . . At oral argument, EPA counsel asserted that under the reasonable possibility standard, enforcement authorities could conduct inspections and request information. Although conceding that nothing in the record addressed how authorities could access data through these mechanisms once a source had failed to keep records, counsel maintained that the methodology is enforceable simply because such actions are 'inherent' in EPA's enforcement authority. EPA certainly has such inherent enforcement authority, but even inherent authority depends on evidence. . . . Because EPA has failed to explain how it can ensure NSR compliance without the relevant data, the court remanded for it either to provide an acceptable explanation for its 'reasonable possibility' standard or to devise an appropriately supported alternative."

The court upheld the use of Plantwide Applicability Limitations (PALs), which it described as a way to give "sources the flexibility to respond rapidly to market changes and to eliminate the administrative burdens of 'netting out' of NSR under the 1980 rule . . . Under [the PAL method], a change does not 'increase' net emissions and thus does not trigger NSR as long as source-wide emissions remain below the [amounts]specified in the source's PAL permit. The PAL is calculated by adding a 'significant' margin to the baseline actual emissions from any two-year period within the ten-year period immediately preceding the permit application. The PAL permit is effective for ten years, and may be renewed prior to the expiration of the initial ten-year term. With the PAL option comes various monitoring and recordkeeping requirements. The source must employ a 'monitoring system that accurately determines plantwide emissions of the PAL pollutant.' The monitoring system must be approved by EPA. The source must keep 'all records necessary to determine compliance' with the PAL permit 'including a determination of each emission unit's 12-month rolling total emissions.' " The court concluded that because the "CAA is silent on how to calculate emissions increases . . . the court must defer to EPA's assessment of the environmental benefits of PALs, which is based on the agency's expert evaluation of technical data from the pilot projects."

The court, however, struck down both the Clean Units and the Pollution Control Projects (PCPs) regulations. Each of these regulations permitted a facility to avoid NSR so long as they maintained their status—for Clean Units, by installing and maintaining state-of-the-art pollution technology, for PCPs by undertaking "environmentally beneficial" measures—even if some emissions at the facility increased over the threshold amounts otherwise applicable. The court ruled that this violated the CAA. When Congress defined a modified source as one that increased emissions "of any air pollutant emitted from the source," it meant to focus on the actual emissions of pollutants. Accordingly, EPA lacked discretion to ignore significant emissions increases from Clean Units or PCPs.

6. Following the decisions in New York v. EPA and *Duke Energy*, EPA proposed to revise the test for determining whether an electrical generating unit's capital improvements increased emissions under NSR review, to make it the same as that used under NSPS review, namely a comparison of hourly emissions rates before and after the improvement. 70 Fed. Reg. 61,081 (Oct. 20, 2005). This action is consistent with *Duke Energy*, but is it consistent with the holding in New York v. EPA? At about the same time, EPA issued guidance to its regional offices that although it would continue to pursue the pending enforcement actions, the agency would only initiate future actions against improvements that violated current NSR standards, even if the improvements had occurred years ago while the old standards were in effect. Jeanhee Hong, A New Deal for New Source Review, Trends, Vol. 37, no. 3, at 12 (Jan./Feb. 2006).

7. When EPA responded to challengers' complaints in the principal case, above, that the changes in NSR procedures would have deleterious effects on the environment, one of the Agency's responses was that NSR was only one of several federal air quality programs that served to reduce pollution from stationary sources. As air quality programs under the CAA now are well into their fourth decade, it is indeed true that the country's most persistent air quality problems are being addressed by an overlapping complex of approaches, each based on different regulatory authorities contained in the statute. One very noticeable evolution in air quality programming has been federal actions aimed at addressing persistent air quality problems that involve multi-state regions. Another has been in the use of programs permitting affected sources to trade allowable emissions among themselves in order to seek the most cost-effective combination of controls as possible. These two developments are frequently combined. After identifying a multi-state problem that involves numerous stationary sources, EPA will promulgate a system for trading emissions allowances among affected sources as a means of achieving desired results. The next two sections address each of these developments.

C. MULTI-STATE AIR QUALITY PROBLEMS

Air pollution does not respect state boundaries. The interstate nature of many air quality problems has simultaneously been one of the persistent justifications for a federal air quality statute and one of the most difficult problems for programs under the CAA to address. From the beginning, state implementation plans were supposed to be responsive to complaints that emissions from within its boundaries were interfering with air quality in a downwind state. The current version of this requirement provides that states must include in their SIPs provisions prohibiting emissions activity that will "contribute significantly to non-attainment, or interfere with maintenance by, any other state with respect to any [NAAQS]," and a similar provision preventing significant interference with PSD or visibility protection efforts by other states was added in 1977.

§110(a)(2)(D)(i). Likewise, the CAA has for decades contained a provision permitting a downwind state to petition the EPA for a finding that a major stationary source or group of sources was interfering with the downwind state's air quality efforts in violation of their section 110(a)(2)(D)(i) obligations. §126. (Section 126 as currently drafted refers to a state's section (a)(2)(D)(ii) obligations, but EPA determined that this reference was a scrivener's error which arose when the provisions of section 110 were renumbered after elimination of one of its subparts, and the D.C. Circuit has agreed. Appalachian Power Co. v. EPA, 249 F.3d 1032 (D.C. Cir. 2001).) Until recently, however, neither of these provisions has been successful in producing concrete measures designed to help downwind states address air quality problems that have a significant interstate component.

Perhaps the most obvious of the interstate NAAQS problems has been the ozone problem in the Northeast and along the eastern seaboard of the United States. See Figure 5.5. Ozone is the product of chemical interaction of volatile organic compounds and oxides of nitrogen in the presence of sunlight. Major sources of these precursor pollutants include vehicles, electric utilities, industrial facilities, gasoline vapors (at filling stations and petroleum plants, for example), chemical solvents, as well as natural sources. Because sunlight accelerates the chemical reactions that produce ozone, the problem is worse in the summer months; May through September is considered "ozone season." The problem is worse in urban areas, due to the concentration of local sources of the precursors, but as EPA explains, "even rural areas with relatively low amounts of local emissions may experience high ozone levels because the wind transports ozone and the pollutants that form it hundreds of miles away from their original sources." EPA, The Ozone Report: Measuring Progress through 2003 (EPA 454/K-04-001, April 2004), p. 1.

In 1990, the Congress added section 184 to the CAA as one method for addressing the northeastern regional ozone problem. That section created the Ozone Transport Commission (OTC), composed of representatives of the twelve eastern seaboard states from Virginia to Maine, plus the District of Columbia. The EPA and the OTC are charged with jointly studying the ozone problem. By majority vote, the OTC can develop recommendations for additional control measures that it determines are "necessary to bring [any region within the OTC] into attainment. . . ." §184((c). Section 176 also authorizes the creation of additional interstate ozone commissions. The dispute over EPA's authority to order specific compliance measures that culminated in Virginia v. EPA, pages 501-503, began as a recommendation from the OTC under this section.

Besides section 184, section 110 of the CAA gives the EPA authority to call for a revision of any SIP whenever EPA determines that the current plan is "substantially inadequate to attain or maintain the relevant NAAQS, to mitigate adequately the interstate pollutant transport described in §176A or §184, or to otherwise comply with any requirement of this Act. . . ." §110(k)(5). Among the requirements covered by the last phrase of section 110(k)(5) are those relating to the prohibition on sources significantly contributing to NA, PSD, or visibility problems of other states.

In 1998, EPA invoked this section 110(k)(5) authority to address the regional transport of NOx on the basis of the contribution of states to the ozone problems of other states in a region consisting of 22 states and the District of Columbia. Much of the factual basis for this "NOx SIP Call" was gathered as a result of the work of EPA, the OTC, and other states trying better to understand the nature of the regional transport problem. The rule and the litigation following it were complicated by the fact that EPA's 1997 revision of the ozone NAAQS was being challenged in litigation that was finally resolved by the Supreme Court in the *American Trucking* decision, pages 486-492. Prior to the Supreme Court's ruling, the D.C. Circuit had stayed implementation of the new 8-hour ozone standard. Eventually, however, challenges by Midwestern states, electric utilities, and industry groups were resolved in the following decision.

Michigan v. EPA
213 F.3d 663 (D.C. Cir. 2000)

Before: WILLIAMS, SENTELLE and ROGERS, Circuit Judges.
Opinion PER CURIAM.

INTRODUCTION

In October 1998 EPA issued a final rule mandating that 22 states and the District of Columbia revise their SIPs to mitigate the interstate transport of ozone. EPA uniformly required that each state reduce nitrogen oxides (NOx—an ozone precursor) by the amount accomplishable by what EPA dubbed "highly cost-effective controls," namely, those controls EPA found capable of removing NOx at a cost of $2000 or less per ton. Numerous petitions for review challenge various aspects of EPA's decision.

I.   GENERAL CLAIMS...

C.   Determining "Significant" Contribution

Section 110(a)(2)(D)(i)(I) requires states to prohibit any source within the state from "emitting any air pollutant in amounts which will . . . contribute significantly to nonattainment in, or interfere with maintenance by, any other state with respect to any [NAAQS]." It applies only to states that "contribute significantly" to nonattainment in a downwind state. Petitioners make essentially four arguments challenging EPA's determination of "significance": (1) EPA acted contrary to precedent; (2) EPA considered forbidden factors, namely, costs of reduction; (3) EPA irrationally imposed uniform NOx controls on the states; (4) EPA's determination was so devoid of intelligible principles as to violate the nondelegation doctrine.

1.   Past Precedent

Before the 1990 amendments to the Clean Air Act, §110(a)(2)(E)(I) directed the EPA to insist on SIP provisions adequate to prevent sources within a state from emitting air pollution that would "prevent attainment or maintenance [of primary or secondary standards] by any other State." In a number of decisions EPA found, with approval of the courts, that various emissions of a particular state, having a proportionate impact on some downwind state greater than the impacts involved here, did not meet that standard. According to the states, these decisions, and what they claim to be Congress's implicit endorsement in the 1990 amendments, bar EPA from regarding the ozone emissions here as "significant" within the meaning of §110(a)(2)(D)(i)(I). Thus the states would equate the old standard—"prevent attainment"—with the new standard: "contribute significantly to nonattainment."

Nothing in the text of the new section or any other provision of the statute spells out a criterion for classifying "emissions activity" as "significant." Nor did EPA, under the then-existing provision, bind itself to any criterion. Further, given EPA's finding as to the cumulative effects of the pollutants that generate ozone, EPA might well be able to distinguish this case from the sulfur dioxide cases that the states have cited. See 63 Fed. Reg. at 57,359. ("The chemical reactions that create ozone take place while the pollutants are being blown through the air by the wind, which means that ozone can be more severe many miles away from the source of emissions than it is at the source.") But the states point to nothing suggesting any prior adoption by EPA of any binding concept of how much was too much, so the claim falls short at the threshold.

2.   Consideration of Costs

Petitioners claim §110(a)(2)(D)(i)(I) does not permit EPA to take into consideration the cost of reducing ozone. The full section provides that SIPs must contain provisions adequately prohibiting

> any source or other type of emissions activity within the State from emitting any air pollutant in amounts which will . . . contribute significantly to nonattainment in, or interfere with maintenance by, any other State with respect to any such national primary or secondary ambient air quality standard.

Before reviewing the petitioners' attacks we must first describe how EPA went about the business at hand. It first determined that 23 jurisdictions are "significant" contributors to downwind nonattainment. In making this listing EPA drew lines based on the magnitude, frequency, and relative amount of each state's ozone contribution to a nonattainment area. For example, in one calculation it looked at the number of NOx parts per billion ("ppb") that a candidate state's emissions made to exceedances in specific downwind locations (examined as a proportion of those exceedances). Indiana was found to contribute at least 2 ppb to 4% of the 1-hour ozone exceedances in New York City, and was deemed a "significant contributor" to nonattainment there. On the other hand, Alabama, Georgia, Massachusetts, Missouri, South Carolina, Tennessee, and Wisconsin were not deemed "significant contributors" to New York City nonattainment because none of these states ever contributed more than 2 ppb to a 1-hour exceedance in that area. Although EPA looked at other measures, e.g., the percentage contribution of a state's emissions to total concentrations in a specified area, no one quarrels either with its use of multiple measures, or with the way it drew the line at this stage.

Although the dividing line was a very low threshold of contribution, in the end EPA's rule called for termination of only a subset of each state's contribution. EPA decided that the 23 "significant contributors" need only reduce their ozone by the amount achievable with "highly cost-effective controls." Thus, once a state had been nominally marked a "significant contributor," it could satisfy the statute, i.e., reduce its contribution to a point where it would not be "significant" within the meaning of §110(a)(2)(D)(i)(I), by cutting back the amount that could be eliminated with "highly cost-effective controls." EPA's design was to have a lot of states make what it considered modest NOx reductions, uniformly limited to ones that could be achieved (in EPA's estimate) for less than $2000 a ton. As a result, naturally, the ultimate line of "significance," whether measured in volume of NOx emitted or arriving in nonattainment areas, would vary from state to state depending on variations in cutback costs.

State and Industry/Labor petitioners argue that this approach runs afoul of §110(a)(2)(D), which they read as prohibiting any consideration of costs or cost-effectiveness in determining what contributions are "significant." . . .

By its terms the statute is focused on "amounts" of "emissions activity" that "contribute significantly to nonattainment." The fundamental dispute is over the clarity of the phrase "contribute significantly." Must EPA simply pick some flat "amount" of contribution, based exclusively on health concerns, such that any excess would put a state in the forbidden zone of "significance"? Or was it permissible for EPA to consider differences in cutback costs, so that, after reduction of all that could be cost-effectively eliminated, any remaining "contribution" would not be considered "significant"? In deciding on the permissible ceiling, EPA used "significant" in the second way.

The term "significant" does not in itself convey a thought that significance should be measured in only one dimension—here, in the petitioners' view, health alone. Indeed, "significant" is a very odd choice to express unidimensionality; consider the phrase "significant other." In some contexts, "significant" begs a consideration of costs. In finding a threshold requirement of "significant risk" in §3(8) of the Occupational Health and Safety Act, a plurality of the Supreme Court understood a "significant" risk as something more than a "mathematical straitjacket," and held that "[s]ome risks are plainly acceptable and others are plainly unacceptable." [*Benzene*, pages 182-193]. The plurality withheld judgment on whether the Act required a "reasonable correlation between costs and benefits," but the upshot of inserting the adjective "significant" was a consideration of which risks are worth the cost of elimination. OSHA has since interpreted §3(8) and regulation of "significant risk" to require "cost-effective protective measures" and set standards with an eye toward "the costs of safety standards [being] reasonably related to their benefits." See International Union v. OSHA (Lockout/Tagout II), 37 F.3d 665, 668-69 (D.C. Cir. 1994) (quoting OSHA's final rule). OSHA's reaction to the term "significant" seems to confirm what some commentators have asked rhetorically: "[C]an an agency sensibly decide whether a risk is 'significant' without also examining the cost of eliminating it?" Stephen G. Breyer, Richard B. Stewart, Cass R. Sunstein & Matthew L. Spitzer, Administrative Law and Regulatory Policy 5 (4th ed. 1999).

Petitioners conspicuously fail to describe the intellectual process by which EPA would determine "significance" if it may consider only health. EPA has determined that ozone has some adverse health effects—however slight—at every level. Without consideration of cost it is hard to see why any ozone-creating emissions should not be regarded as fatally "significant" under §110(a)(2)(D)(i)(I). Perhaps EPA might (under such a rule) let the upwind states off at the stringency level of the programs imposed on non-attainment areas, but petitioners do not explain how "significance" can exclude cost but admit equity.

Although the ambiguity of the word "significant" and the implications of a health-only reading are potentially fatal flaws in petitioners' theory (aside from their own inability to discern the "plain language" consistently), the most formidable obstacle is the settled law of this circuit. It is only where there is "clear congressional intent to preclude consideration of cost" that we find agencies barred from considering costs. NRDC, 824 F.2d at 1163; see also George E. Warren Corp. v. EPA, 159 F.3d 616, 622-24 (D.C. Cir. 1998), reh'g granted, 164 F.3d 676 (D.C. Cir. 1999); Grand Canyon Air Tour Coalition v. FAA, 154 F.3d 455, 475 (D.C. Cir. 1998), cert. denied, 526 U.S. 1158, 119 S. Ct. 2046, 144 L. Ed. 2d 214 (1999); NRDC v. EPA, 937 F.2d 641, 643-646 (D.C. Cir. 1991); cf. International Bhd. of Teamsters v. United States, 735 F.2d 1525, 1528-1529 (D.C. Cir. 1984) (construing mandate to adopt "reasonable requirements" for safety as allowing consideration of cost).

In *NRDC* we considered §112 of the Clean Air Act, requiring EPA to set an air quality standard for hazardous pollutants with an "ample margin of safety" to protect the public health. We held that this phrase did not preclude a consideration of costs. In *George E. Warren Corp.* we acknowledged that the statutory scheme for the reformulated gasoline program had the "overall goal" of improving air quality and "reducing air pollution." But because there was nothing "in the text or structure of the statute to indicate that the Congress intended to preclude the EPA from considering the effects a proposed rule might have upon the price and supply of gasoline," we found no such preclusion even though the provision at issue contained no allusion whatever to such effects. Similarly, in *Grand Canyon Air Tour* the statute required the FAA to devise a plan for "substantial restoration of the natural quiet" in the Grand Canyon area, but we found nothing impermissible in the FAA's consideration of costs to the air tourism industry in deciding how "substantial" that restoration must be. In *NRDC v. EPA* we considered whether EPA permissibly used cost-benefit analysis in refusing to classify a particular polluting source as "major." The petitioners argued that cost considerations were precluded, and we stated: "[W]hile the statutory language and legislative history do not bar petitioners' construction, they provide little support and no necessity for it." We affirmed EPA's use of cost-benefit analysis. . . . So too here. . . .

III. FEDERALISM . . .

A. NOx Budgets

. . . EPA ordered the challenged SIP call under the authority of section 110(k)(5) in order to address significant contribution to 1-hour ozone nonattainment as described under section 110(a)(2)(D). In fashioning the SIP call, EPA focused on [the] determination that "[r]egional NOx emissions reductions are effective in producing ozone benefits." EPA also [considered] that while NOx controls are effective in addressing regional ozone problems, VOC controls are most effective locally and are most advantageous to urban nonattainment areas. Because . . . NOx reductions provide the key to addressing regional ozone problems, EPA's SIP call addresses regional ozone nonattainment through NOx emissions "budgets" established by the agency for each covered state. The budgets represent the amount of allowable NOx emissions remaining after a covered state prohibits the NOx amount contributing significantly to downwind nonattainment. While EPA calculated the budgets using highly cost-effective emission controls, the agency allows the states to choose the control measures necessary to bring their emissions within the budget requirements. Under EPA's budget plan, a state "may choose from a broader menu of cost-effective, reasonable alternatives" including alternatives that "may even be more advantageous in light of local concerns." In fact, EPA has stated that the states have "full discretion in selecting the controls, so that [the states]may choose any set of controls that would assure achievement of the budget." In addition, each state has the option of adopting an interstate trading program that allows it to purchase NOx "allowances" from sources that have elected to over-control. The SIP call also gives the states the option in some circumstances to use "banked" allowances (i.e., allowances from prior years) to comply with emissions limits.

Petitioners assert that EPA's NOx budget program impermissibly intrudes on the statutory right of the states to fashion their SIP submissions in the first instance. In support of this position, the petitioners primarily rely on our decision in [*Virginia v. EPA*, pages 501-503] where we held that EPA may not use a section 110(k)(5) SIP call to order states to adopt a particular approach to achieving the SIP requirements listed in section 110. Under the rule at issue in *Virginia*, EPA required states to adopt California's vehicle emission program and in effect set the numerical emissions limitations and mandated the means for the states to achieve the necessary emissions reductions. That case involved an EPA rule that required several states to reduce ozone precursors by a particular program and only allowed states to implement a more stringent program as an alternative or substitute. We held that EPA's approach exceeded its authority under section 110 because each state retains the authority to determine in the first instance the necessary and appropriate control measures needed to satisfy section 110's standards.

Our holding in *Virginia* was mandated by the Supreme Court's decision in Train v. NRDC, 421 U.S. 60 (1975). *Train* involved a challenge to Georgia's procedures for revising source-specific emission limits adopted in a SIP. The *Train* Court held that states have the authority under the CAA to initially propose specific emission limitations. The Court defined "emission limitations" as "*regulations of the composition of substances* emitted into the ambient air from such sources as power plants, service stations, and the like. They are the *specific rules to which operators of pollution sources are subject,* and which if enforced should result in ambient air which meets the national standards (emphasis added). The Court further held that EPA has only "a secondary role in the process of determining and enforcing the *specific, source-by-source* emission limitations." (Emphasis added.) The *Train* decision and subsequent precedent make clear that section 110 left to the states "the power to [initially] determine *which sources* would be burdened by regulation and to *what extent.*" [*Union Electric*, pages 497-499]; cf. *Virginia* (involving a source-specific program). As we elaborated in *Virginia*, "the Supreme Court decided . . . that [section 110] did not confer upon EPA the authority to condition approval of [a state's] implementation plan . . . on the state's adoption of a specific control measure." For the reasons set forth below, we conclude that the NOx budgets do not fall within the realm of impermissible SIP call regulation as defined in *Virginia* and *Train*.

Given the *Train* and *Virginia* precedent, the validity of the NOx budget program underlying the SIP call depends in part on whether the program in effect constitutes an EPA-imposed control measure or emission limitation triggering the *Train-Virginia* federalism bar: in other words, on whether the program constitutes an impermissible source-specific means rather than a permissible end goal. However, the program's validity also depends on whether EPA's budgets allow the covered states real choice with regard to the control measure options available to them to meet the budget requirements.

Section 110(a)(2)(D) requires SIPs to contain adequate provisions prohibiting emissions from "any source or other type of emissions activity within the State" that "contribute significantly" to NAAQS nonattainment in another state. Here, EPA mandates that 22 states and the District of Columbia implement section 110(a)(2)(D) using its NOx budget system. In essence, the NOx budget in question is an EPA mandate prohibiting NOx emissions in the 23 jurisdictions from exceeding a tonnage specific to that jurisdiction. Of concern to petitioners, the budget rule prohibits states from seeking compliance, in whole or part, by controlling VOC emissions even though VOCs as well as NOx emissions contribute to ozone problems.

Yet, the budget plan's defining aspects do not necessarily cause the program to conflict with the limiting principles contained in *Train* and *Virginia.* Analyzing the budget rule together with the relevant precedent, we hold that based on section 110's silence, EPA reasonably interpreted section 110 as providing it with the authority to determine a state's NOx significant contribution level and agree with EPA that the EPA budget plan does no more than project whether states have reduced emissions sufficiently to mitigate interstate transport.

Under section 110, EPA must "approve a [SIP] submittal as a whole if it meets all of the applicable requirements of [the Act]." While the states have considerable latitude in fashioning SIPs, the CAA "nonetheless subject[s] the States to strict minimum compliance requirements" and gives EPA the authority to determine a state's compliance with the requirements. *Union Electric.* Given EPA's authority to ensure that submitted SIPs adequately prohibit significantly contributing emissions, EPA permissibly relied on its general rulemaking authority to prospectively inform the states of EPA's significance determinations.

Moreover, EPA does not tell the states how to achieve SIP compliance. Rather, EPA looks to section 110(a)(2)(D) and merely provides the levels to be achieved by state-determined compliance mechanisms. Specifically, EPA set NOx reduction levels based, in part, on assumptions about reductions obtainable through highly cost-effective controls. However, EPA made clear that states do not have to adopt the control scheme that EPA assumed for budget-setting purposes. States can choose from a myriad of reasonably cost-effective options to achieve the assigned reduction levels. While EPA bases the budgets here on "highly cost-effective" control measures, the states remain free to implement other "cost-effective" or "reasonably cost-effective" measures in place of the ones identified by EPA. More importantly, EPA went so far as to give the states "full discretion in selecting . . . controls," thereby allowing states to attain their budgets by imposing even quite unreasonable, very cost-ineffective controls. In *Virginia,* we did not bar EPA from permitting more costly alternatives but rather alternatives states would consider "unreasonable or impracticable." Here, EPA accommodates *Virginia*'s mandate by allowing reasonable control alternatives and allowing states to focus reduction efforts based on local needs or preferences. Thus, real choice exists for the covered states.

In sum, we conclude that EPA's NOx budget program reasonably establishes reduction levels and leaves the control measure selection decision to the states. In addition, unlike the rule invalidated in *Virginia,* states implementing alternative control measures will not be penalized with more stringent emissions targets. Since the challenged budget program does not mandate a "specific, source-by-source emission limitation[ ]," the NOx budget plan does not run afoul of *Train* or *Virginia.* . . .

We vacate EPA's final rule with respect to [the inclusion of parts of] Wisconsin and Missouri, and Georgia [in the SIP call]. These cases are remanded for further consideration in light of this opinion. We hold that EPA failed to provide adequate notice of a change in the definition of an electric generating unit, and that EPA did not provide adequate notice of a change in the control level assumed for large stationary internal combustion engines. These cases are also remanded.

In all other respects, the petitions for review are denied.

So ordered.

NOTES AND QUESTIONS

1. In its NOx SIP call, EPA provided "each state [with]the option of adopting an interstate trading program that allows it to purchase NOx 'allowances' from sources that have elected to over-control." While EPA could not compel the states to participate in such a trading program, in recent years this sort of program has become EPA's preferred approach to addressing many air quality problems involving multiple sources. This approach is frequently called a cap-and-trade program, because it first establishes a ceiling on the amount of allowable emissions (in this case, EPA refers to this state-by-state cap as the NOx Budget), and then permits the affected parties to trade "allowances." Thus any state can meet the NOx Budget by assigning an initial allowance amount to contributing sources and then letting them trade allowances. Presumably sources facing high abatement costs will try to purchase allowances from sources with low compliance costs, right? The original cap-and-trade program under the Clean Air Act was established by the Congress in the 1990 Amendments to address the problem of acid deposition. The workings of that cap-and-trade program, which are broadly representative of how cap-and-trade programs generally function, are described in greater detail at pages 550-553.

2. Do you agree that the idea of a "significant" contribution to a pollution problem cannot be determined sensibly without considering the costs of reducing the contribution? Recall the distinction developed in Chapter 3 between risk assessment and risk management. Could the significance decision be a matter of risk assessment that is made without consideration of costs, with the risk management decision then taking into account costs as one of a number of factors relevant to deciding what to do about the risk?

3. Petitioners challenged EPA's using $2,000/ton cost-of-removal as the basis for the NOx budget on the ground that EPA had arbitrarily chosen that dollar amount, with nothing in the statute to guide its decision of that number, instead of $1,000 or $4,000, for example. After the Supreme Court's decision in *American Trucking*, pages 482-492, this objection would no longer be phrased in non-delegation language, but is it an otherwise valid objection?

4. Why does the NOx SIP call not run afoul of what the court termed the *Train-Virginia* federalism bar?

5. Phase I of the EPA NOx budget program went into effect in 2003. All states that were covered by the final rule decided to participate in the cap-and-trade program, and nearly all their revised SIPs have now been approved. For 2004 EPA reports nearly 100 percent compliance from the approximately 2,500 units covered by the cap-and-trade program. Eighty-five percent of covered units are fossil-fuel-fired electrical generating facilities. EPA, Evaluating Ozone

Control Programs in the Eastern United States: Focus on the NOx Budget Trading Program, page 6, Figure 4, EPA-454-K-05-001 (2005). EPA reports that electrical power industry NOx emissions during ozone season were "about 30 percent lower than in 2003, when a limited number of states were subject to NOx SIP Call requirements; 50 percent lower than in 2000, before the NOx SIP Call was implemented; and 70 percent lower than in 1990, before implementation of the Clean Air Act Amendments." Id., Executive Summary, p. 2. As for overall ozone air quality, EPA reports that "in most of the eastern United States, reductions in ozone concentrations (adjusted for weather) more than doubled after the NOx SIP Call was implemented. Ozone concentrations declined where EPA expected they would. Areas with the greatest decline in ozone concentrations are near, and downwind of, areas with greatest reductions in NOx emissions." Id.

6. A number of the northeastern-most states in the OTC were not content to wait upon EPA's SIP call approach. They filed section 126 petitions, claiming that stationary sources upwind of them, including in some states outside the OTC, were interfering with their ability to comply with the ozone NAAQS. On April 30, 1999, EPA found these petitions to be largely meritorious. 64 Fed. Reg. 28,250 (1999). See also 64 Fed. Reg. 33,956 (1999) (staying effective date of April 30 final rule until Nov. 30, 1999). EPA did not immediately trigger the requirements that upwind sources cease their interference with downwind state compliance, however, because it preferred to address the problem through its SIP call approach. What are the differences between the implementation options available to EPA under section 126 as compared with section 110(k)(5)? Why might EPA have preferred to rely upon its SIP call authority?

In December 1999, EPA did grant section 126 petitions filed by New York, Connecticut, Massachusetts, and Pennsylvania. Wald, EPA Is Ordering 392 Plants to Cut Pollution in Half, N.Y. Times, Dec. 18, 1999, at A1. It then issued a rule mandating a cap-and-trade program for affected sources that was premised on the same analysis that EPA had used as the basis for the NOx SIP call, assigning NOx allowances to major sources, based upon application of the same "highly effective controls" which EPA had included in the SIP call. The order affects nearly 400 plants, mostly utility power plants, in 12 states as far south as North Carolina and as far west as Indiana. EPA estimates compliance costs at $950 million per year. In the decision below, D.C. Circuit upheld the vast bulk of EPA's 126 rule.

Appalachian Power Co. v. EPA
249 F.3d 1032 (D.C. Cir. 2001)

Before: WILLIAMS, GINSBURG and SENTELLE, Circuit Judges.
Opinion for the Court filed PER CURIAM.

In response to petitions from several northeastern states that alleged that nitrogen oxide emitted in neighboring states was harming their local air quality, the Environmental Protection Agency promulgated a rule that requires many NOx emitting facilities in several midwestern and southeastern states to conform to emission limits set by the EPA and to participate in an emissions trading program. Numerous petitioners challenge the rule as inconsistent with the Clean Air Act, arbitrary and capricious, and technically deficient. We uphold most aspects of the rule but remand several particulars to the Agency for reconsideration.

I. BACKGROUND

On January 18, 2000, the Environmental Protection Agency ("EPA") issued its final rule to control emissions of nitrogen oxide ("NOx") under section 126 of the Clean Air Act ("CAA"). In the January rule, the EPA made final its findings that stationary sources of NOx emissions in twelve upwind states and the District of Columbia contribute significantly to ozone nonattainment in northeastern states. This finding triggers direct federal regulation of stationary sources of NOx in the upwind states. The rule further established a "cap and trade" system for NOx emissions within each upwind jurisdiction. Covered sources must obtain NOx emission allowances to cover their emissions, adopt additional emission controls, or cease operations. Numerous petitions for review challenge various aspects of the rule.

A. Statutory Framework

. . . Much air pollution is a local or regional problem. Some pollution, however, is caused or augmented by emissions from other states. Emissions from "upwind" regions may pollute "downwind" regions. Several provisions of the CAA are designed to address such transboundary air pollution. In particular, section 110(a)(2)(D)(i)(I) of the Act requires states to prohibit emissions within the state in amounts that will "contribute significantly to nonattainment in, or interfere with maintenance by, any other State" of the NAAQS.

CAA section 126 provides a mechanism whereby downwind states may petition the EPA to directly regulate upwind sources of pollution. Under section 126(b), 42 U.S.C. §7426(b), a downwind state "may petition the Administrator for a finding that any major source or group of stationary sources emits or would emit any air pollutant in violation" of CAA section 110(a)(2)(D). Once the EPA makes a section 126(b) finding, section 126(c) provides that:

> it shall be a violation of this section and the applicable implementation plan in such State—
> (1) for any major proposed new (or modified) source with respect to which a finding has been made under subsection (b) of this section to be constructed or to operate in violation [of this section or section 110], or
> (2) for any major existing source to operate more than three months after such finding has been made with respect to it.
> The Administrator may allow the continued operation of existing sources beyond three months provided such sources comply with emission limitations and compliance schedules provided by the Administrator which "bring about compliance . . . as expeditiously as practicable, but in no case later than three years after the date of such finding." Id. . . .

Because the section 126 petitions raised many of the same issues as the NOx SIP call, and would require comparable emission reductions, the EPA coordinated its response to the section 126 petitions with the NOx SIP call rulemaking.

In a final rule published on May 25, 1999, the EPA determined that NOx emissions in twelve states and the District of Columbia contribute significantly to nonattainment of the one-hour ozone NAAQS in Connecticut, Massachusetts,

New York, and Pennsylvania. The twelve states are Delaware, Indiana, Kentucky, Maryland, Michigan, New Jersey, New York, North Carolina, Ohio, Pennsylvania, Virginia, and West Virginia.

Rather than make section 126 findings at that time, however, the EPA determined that it was appropriate to postpone such findings pending the resolution of the NOx SIP call process. Accordingly, the EPA issued a rule providing that the findings would automatically be deemed made with regard to sources from a given state should that state fail to comply with a NOx SIP call deadline. The EPA based this decision on the judgment that full compliance with the NOx SIP call would obviate the need for section 126 findings. Once made, the section 126 findings would require covered sources to come into compliance no later than May 1, 2003. Sources that failed to comply by that date would be required to cease operations.

[Orders issued by the D.C. Circuit in the *American Trucking* and Michigan v. EPA cases, pages 486-492 and 536-542, caused EPA to rethink its deferral approach to the 126 petitions, and it moved ahead with them independently.]

In response to these orders, the EPA revised the section 126 rule. In particular, the EPA made the requested findings of significant contributions, granting the relevant portions of the section 126 petitions and delinking the section 126 findings from compliance with the NOx SIP call. The EPA explained that it was "implementing the requirements of section 126 of the CAA in the absence of any currently effective requirement for upwind States to address the interstate pollution transport problems themselves." Instead, the EPA's new rule contained a provision to withdraw the relevant findings upon approval of a NOx SIP in accordance with the October 1998 NOx SIP call.

As with the NOx SIP call, the EPA considered both NOx emissions and the cost of control in determining which sources contribute significantly to downwind ozone nonattainment. Based upon its analysis of the cost of emissions controls, the EPA concluded that measures which can reduce NOx emissions for $2,000 or less per ton are highly cost-effective. The EPA then divided NOx emission sources into various categories and determined the level of emission reduction that would be highly cost-effective for each category.

The section 126 rule also established an emission allowance "cap and trade" program, known as the Federal NOx Budget Trading Program. Under this program, originally outlined in the May 1999 rule, regulated sources are allocated tradeable NOx emission allowances and are prohibited from emitting more NOx than the amount of allowances held. If a facility emits more than its initial allowance allocation, it must purchase additional allowances from another facility, reduce its emissions, or cease operations.

To determine the initial allocations, the EPA established a NOx emission cap for each upwind state. Each state's cap is based upon expected emission reductions from highly cost-effective controls in that state as of 2007. Ninety-five percent of each state's cap is allocated proportionally among existing sources based upon each facility's heat input. Five percent of the cap is set aside for future, as-yet-unproposed sources. These initial allocations will apply for the 2003-07 time period. The EPA will issue revised allocations for the 2008-12 time period, and every five years thereafter.

Since the issuance of the final section 126 rule, this Court has ruled on various challenges to the EPA's NOx SIP call. In *Michigan v. EPA* [pages 536-542], we upheld the SIP call in most respects, remanding portions of the rule to the EPA. Of greatest relevance to these proceedings, we upheld the

EPA's analyses of interstate transport of NOx emissions and its use of cost-effectiveness criteria in determining which upwind sources "contribute significantly" to nonattainment in downwind states. Subsequently, we entered an order amending the deadline for full implementation of NOx SIP revisions from May 1, 2003 to May 31, 2004.

After the EPA published the final section 126 rule in January 2000, numerous groups petitioned this Court for review. Among the petitioners are a group of upwind states from the midwestern and southeastern United States ("MW & SE State Petitioners"); utilities and other operators of electric generating facilities ("Non-State Petitioners"); companies that operate non-electric generating/industrial facilities ("Non-EGU Petitioners"); and several individual companies that have facility-specific concerns ("Facility-Specific Petitioners"). A group of northeastern states ("NE State Petitioners") also petitioned for review alleging that the EPA's rule did not go far enough in controlling upwind NOx emissions. The northeastern states otherwise intervened in support of the EPA, as did a group of environmental organizations. The various petitions for review were consolidated into this case.

II. COMMON AND GENERAL ISSUES

The EPA maintains that its approach is necessitated by the "language and purposes of section 126" and that it is consistent with "the language of section 110, the cooperative federalism structure of title I of the CAA, [and this] court's decision to stay the deadlines for States to submit SIP revisions under the NOx SIP call." . . . Petitioners disagree. They argue that §§110 and 126 require the agency to refrain from making any §126 findings while the NOx SIP call is ongoing, and that a similar constraint is imposed by the doctrine of "cooperative federalism" that this court has recognized as being embodied in the Act.

The petitioners' primary argument . . . is that Title I of the Clean Air Act is animated by a commitment to "cooperative federalism" under which the EPA is to determine what level of air quality is required but must defer in the first instance to the judgments of the states regarding how to achieve that level. This principle, according to the petitioners, requires that a SIP call inviting states to respond to the problem of interstate transport be the preferred remedy, while direct federal regulation of sources, as authorized by §126, must be a last resort reserved for cases in which states cannot or do not meet their SIP obligation.

In *Michigan* this court assessed the legality of the emissions budgets that the EPA assigned to each state as part of the NOx SIP call with respect to what we called the "*Train-Virginia* federalism bar." We referred there to our holding in Virginia v. EPA, that under §110 each state retains the power, in its SIP, to determine how it will achieve the NAAQS, and that the EPA may not dictate to a state a particular "source-specific means" to that end, a proposition for which we relied upon *Train*. This principle, of course, cannot be absolute in the face of §126, which contemplates that in at least some circumstances the EPA will directly regulate sources within a state. Neither *Train* and *Virginia* nor *Michigan* considered the interaction of their holdings with §126, but in its 1999 rule the EPA noticed the tension between §126 and the *Train-Virginia* line of cases, and properly sought to accommodate the two:

Section 126 is somewhat unusual in Title I [of the CAA] in that it authorizes EPA to control sources directly, rather than providing a means for EPA to encourage states to control those sources. In that sense, it is similar to the provisions for federal implementation plans in §110(c). With both of these provisions, Congress provided tools for direct federal action to address serious failures of state action. Nevertheless, Congress' clear preference throughout Title I is that states are to decide and plan how they will control their sources of air pollution.

The petitioners contend that the delay in the NOx SIP call deadline, because it did not affect the "Congress' clear preference" for state implementation decisions, should not have altered the EPA's determination that the SIP call takes precedence over §126. The EPA, however, is obligated not only to give to §110 a meaning that is consistent with *Train* and *Virginia*, but also reasonably to construe §126. The EPA, which considers the two provisions to be "independent statutory tools to address the problem of interstate pollution transport" that the EPA may deploy either singly or in tandem, reasonably construes both provisions. . . .

[T]hree critical provisions of §126 would lose their force if, as the petitioners suggest, the lengthened timetable of the NOx SIP call were to suspend the §126 process. First, §126 emphatically requires that any source found to contribute to downwind nonattainment may in no event be permitted to operate for more than three years after such finding. Second, under §126 "[r]elief does not depend upon any action by the upwind states, as is necessary for a SIP revision." Third, relief under §126 is independent also of the discretionary policy preferences of the EPA; the agency must act upon a request for a §126 finding within 60 days. Under the EPA's approach, of course, §126 retains each of these features. See, e.g., Jan. 2000 Rule, 65 Fed. Reg. at 2681/1 ("Congress provided section 126 to downwind states as a critical remedy to address pollution problems . . . otherwise beyond their control, and EPA has no authority to refuse to act under this section.").

The petitioners argue, however, that the EPA's construction deprives §110 of its force because it constrains the development of the SIP: sources subject to a §126 finding will be bound by emissions limitations set by the agency, and by the emissions trading program, . . . even if the state in which they are located prefers to regulate different sources or to use different methods to mitigate downwind nonattainment. The petitioners argue that such constraints violate §110 as interpreted in *Virginia*, but they plainly do not. In *Virginia*, this court disapproved the EPA's plan to reject SIPs that did not incorporate particular limits upon emissions from new cars; we held that the EPA may not, as part of the "section 110 process," intervene in a state's choice of how to reach the NAAQS. We did not suggest that under §110 states may develop their plans free of extrinsic legal constraints. Indeed, SIP development, like any environmental planning process, commonly involves decision-making subject to various legal constraints. That §126 imposes one such limitation—and it is surely not the only independent provision of federal law to do so—does not affect a state's discretion under §110.

VI. CONCLUSION

In summary, we remand the rules to the EPA to allow the agency to (1) properly justify either the current or a new set of [utility power plant] utilization growth factors to be used in estimating utilization in 2007, and (2) either alter or properly justify its categorization of cogenerators that sell electricity to the electric grid as EGUs. With respect to all other issues, including those not discussed expressly herein, the petitions are denied.

NOTES AND QUESTIONS

1. While upholding the vast majority of EPA's rule, the court did find that certain projections EPA had made for growth in electric power generation were unsupported by the record, and that EPA had failed to justify adequately why it has chosen to classify facilities that co-generated both energy used in some industrial activity and electricity for sale to the grid as electrical generating units instead of nonelectrical generating units.

2. If EPA is under a mandatory duty to act when presented with a meritorious section 126 petition, was its original decision to defer action on the petitions pending implementation of the NOx SIP call justifiable?

3. The obligations imposed on facilities via the section 126 petition essentially duplicate those resulting from the NOx SIP call, because all the state affected by the call have elected to adopt the EPA's NOx trading program. The section 126 obligations affect pollution sources in only 12 states plus the District of Columbia, while the NOx SIP call affects 22 states. Why the difference in coverage? Does the difference in coverage suggest one reason EPA might prefer to regulate pursuant to a SIP call rather than by responding to section 126 petitions? What other reasons might EPA have to prefer one approach over the other?

4. For the first several decades of CAA implementation, EPA's approach to exercising authority over multi-state pollution problems had been very cautious, and it was often accused of failing to implement the statutory provisions that called on upwind states to be "good neighbors." In recent years, however, interstate rules such as the NOx SIP call and the section 126 petitions have been given high priority at the Agency and once implemented will deserve credit for improving regional air quality. What explains this apparent change in approach to multi-state regional air quality problems?

5. EPA continues to explore multi-state initiatives to reduce levels of the critiera pollutants, and it continues to employ trading programs as an integral component of them. On May 12, 2005, it finalized its Clean Air Interstate Rule (CAIR) aimed at reducing levels of sulfur dioxide and nitrogen oxides in order to help achieve the lowered NAAQS for ozone and PM2.5. 70 Fed. Reg. 25,162 (May 12, 2005). (Sulfur dioxide and NOx are precursors of fine particles, many of which are formed through chemical reactions in the atmosphere. Nitrogen oxides, as already discussed, are ozone precursors.) The CAIR is a SIP call directed at 28 states in the Eastern and Midwestern parts of the country and is based on air quality analyses similar to those that have formed the basis for EPA's NOx SIP call and its response to the section 126 petitions. The CAIR gives these states the option of participating in a cap-and-trade program for fossil-fuel-fired electrical generating units or else selecting other options for achieving the required SO_2 and NOx reductions.

Both the CAIR and the NOx SIP call impose NOx budgets on states and facilities, with the budget assignments being slightly more stringent under the CAIR, where they overlap. Describing the relationship between the CAIR and the NOx SIP call, however, is complicated. Six states covered by CAIR are not in the NOx SIP call. One state, Rhode Island, is subject to the NOx SIP call, but not to the CAIR. It is also complicated by the fact that the CAIR's concern over NOx is based on both PM and ozone concerns and addresses both PM2.5 precursors and ozone precursors, whereas the NOx SIP call is aimed exclusively at ozone. The seasonal variations for ozone mean that particular attention must be given to emissions during the ozone season, May through September, whereas the PM2.5 concerns are constant year-round. For the states subject to both CAIR and the NOx SIP call, EPA says:

> "States subject to the CAIR for PM2.5 [will] be subject to an annual limitation and . . . States subject to the CAIR for ozone [will] be subject to an ozone season limitation. This means that States subject to the CAIR for both PM2.5 and ozone are subject to both an annual and an ozone season NOX limitation. . . . States subject to the CAIR for ozone only are only subject to an ozone season NOX limitation. To implement these NOX limitations, EPA will establish and operate two NOX trading programs, i.e., a CAIR annual NOX trading program and a CAIR ozone season NOX trading program. The CAIR ozone season NOX trading program will replace the current NOX SIP Call as discussed in more detail later in this section." 70 Fed. Reg. at 25,289-25,290.

6. The CAIR seeks to accomplish some of the programming President Bush had put forth in his Clear Skies proposal, which would have introduced an expanded cap-and-trade program for NOx, replacing the SIP call program in 2008. However, Clear Skies stalled in the Congress and the EPA decided to go forward with CAIR.

7. In an unusual move, along with promulgating the CAIR, the EPA announced that it was going to develop a Federal Implementation Plan to be ready to go in case any state submitted unsatisfactory SIP revisions, but in advance of any state's SIP having been found to be inadequate. The FIP, quite naturally, would implement the cap-and-trade program provisions that are set forth in the CAIR as a state option. As already discussed, EPA has historically been extremely reluctant to promulgate a FIP. What explains its change in approach?

8. Separately from the section 126 petitions filed by the northeastern states, in 2004 North Carolina filed a section 126 petition charging that 11 power plants owned and operated by the Tennessee Valley Authority were interfering with North Carolina's efforts to meet particulate matter and ozone standards. Similarly to how it had coordinated its earlier section 126 response to the NOx SIP call, EPA relied upon its CAIR rule in responding to North Carolina. In this case, however, it chose to deny the petition and to rely exclusively upon the CAIR and the issuance of a standby FIP for the affected areas instead. 40 Fed. Reg. 49,708 (Aug. 24, 2005). North Carolina has now filed a common law public nuisance action against the TVA, based upon the adverse health effects it alleges are being caused by the utility's emissions, thereby returning air quality regulation to its common law roots. Wade Rawlins, N.C. Sues TVA for Cleaner Air, Raleigh News & Observer at A1 (Jan. 31, 2006). For the antecedents to North Carolina's action, see Georgia v. Tennessee Copper Co., Chapter 2, pages 82-84.

9. In addition to its good neighbor provisions aimed at multi-state pollution problems, the CAA has an international good neighbor provision. Now, Canadian environmentalists are considering filing a suit under section 115 against EPA, based on the claim that the CAIR is inadequate to stop emissions from seven Midwestern states—Ohio, Illinois, West Virginia, Indiana, Kentucky,

Michigan, and Pennsylvania—from interfering with air quality in eastern
Canada. Inside EPA, "Canadian Environmentalists Threaten Suit Over EPA's
Interstate Air Rule," July 8, 2005. Read section 115. Does it grant EPA the same
authority with respect to multi-national pollution problems as section
110(a)(2)(D)(i) does with respect to multi-state problems? How would you
expect EPA to respond to such a petition?

D. CAP-AND-TRADE AND OTHER ECONOMIC INCENTIVE PROGRAMS

The NOx SIP call, the section 126 response, and the CAIR all reflect EPA's
preference for addressing multi-source, regional air pollution problems by use
of cap-and-trade programs. Cap-and-trade is the most well known of a variety of
programs described by EPA as economic incentive programs, or EIPs. Other
examples of EIPs include the netting or bubbling options that can avoid the
need for modifications of new sources from having to comply with NSR. See
page 515. EIPs all share a common characteristic: They provide facility owners
an option of complying with some specific emissions requirement or searching
for alternative emissions reductions that then permits the facility to avoid complying with those specific requirements. When netting is involved, this option
provides an incentive for the facility to look for lower cost alternatives within the
facility. When cap-and-trade markets are involved, it creates an incentive for the
facility to look for a trading partner who will contract with the facility. In each
case, facilities are presumed to look for the lower-cost alternative—complying
with the emissions limits where that is less costly, or netting or trading when that
is less costly.

Numerous cap-and-trade programs are now in existence or being proposed, in dealing with air quality, water quality, and a variety of other environmental issues. The flagship program remains the one that Congress created in
1990 to address the problem of acid deposition, both because it has been until
recently the largest and most comprehensive program and because its notable
success has made it the poster-child for those who support using cap-and-trade
in the widest possible variety of circumstances. The following section focuses on
the acid deposition program.

In 1994, EPA issued policy guidance for states interested in implementing
cap-and-trade programs as compliance mechanisms for various elements of the
Clean Air Act. EPA, Economic Incentive Program Rules, 59 Fed. Reg. 16,609
(1994). In developing these rules, EPA drew on the experience of the South
Coast Air Quality Management District (SCAQMD) in California, whose jurisdiction includes the Los Angeles Air Basin, which has the most significant air
quality problems in the United States. Since the early 1990s, SCAQMD has been
developing and implementing a number of trading mechanisms to assist in the
reduction of emissions. See Drury et al., Pollution Trading and Environmental
Injustice: Los Angeles' Failed Experiment in Air Quality Policy, 9 Duke Envtl.
Law & Pol'y F. 231 (1999). Instead of writing specific regulations for existing
sources, SCAQMD is relying largely upon a declining cap-and-trade approach to
emissions reduction.

One component of SCAQMD's efforts is its Rule 1610 program, pursuant
to which "licensed car scrappers" can acquire and then destroy old cars (which
disproportionately contribute to car-related pollution), thereby obtaining from

Figure 5.7
How a Cap and Trade Program Works

1. The regulating authority sets a cap on total mass emissions for a group of sources for a fixed compliance period (e.g., one year).
2. The regulating authority divides the cap into allowances, each representing an authorization to emit a specific quantity of pollutant (e.g., 1 ton of SO_2).
3. The regulating authority distributes allowances.
4. For the compliance period, each source measures and reports all of its emissions.
5. At the end of the period, each source must surrender allowances to cover the quantity of the pollutant it emitted.
6. If a source does not hold sufficient allowances to cover its emissions, the regulating authority imposes penalties.

SCAQMD emissions credits representing the emissions eliminated by removing the car from service. A second central component is the Regional Clean Air Incentives Market (RECLAIM), which allocates an annually declining number of emissions credits to each covered source. Sources cannot emit more pollution than the credits that they own, so their choices are (1) to match their emissions to their assigned credits; (2) to emit less than their assigned credits and sell excess credits; or (3) to emit more than their assigned credits after they have purchased additional credits. Credits can be purchased from other stationary sources or from licensed car scrappers. RECLAIM currently applies to SO_2 and NOx emissions. Efforts to add VOCs to RECLAIM have been stalled due to concerns over the inability to monitor those emissions, as well as concerns about exacerbating hot spots of toxic VOC emissions.

The following problem exercise explores some of the issues raised by programs such as those being implemented by SCAQMD.

PROBLEM EXERCISE: ECONOMIC INCENTIVE PROGRAMS

Rule 1610 permits scrapped cars to come from anywhere within the four-county South Coast Air Basin. To date, most of the emissions credits produced from the Rule 1610 program have been purchased by four oil refineries and marine terminals, three of which are located close together in the communities of Wilmington and San Pedro.

Question One. What concerns might arise from a program that permits widely dispersed automobile-related emissions reductions to substitute for pollution control at three concentrated pollution facilities? How might those concerns be mitigated?

Question Two. The populations living near the three marine terminals are approximately 80 percent minority (largely Latino), compared with a South Coast Air Basin minority population of 36 percent. Does this raise an environmental justice issue? If so, can EPA permit the California implementation plan to include the Rule 1610 trading program, consistent with the President's Executive Order on environmental justice and EPA's own policies, discussed at pages 19-20, above?

Question Three. SCAQMD's Rule 1610 emissions credits are based on the assumption that scrapped automobiles would have been driven an average of

5,000 miles per year for an additional three years. Recent estimates suggest that between 100,000 and 200,000 automobiles would be scrapped or abandoned annually within the South Coast Air Basin without the intervention of the Rule 1610 program. Approximately 25,000 cars have been scrapped under that program. What issues do these facts raise about the legitimacy of permitting credits under the 1610 program to offset pollution from the marine terminals?

Question Four.   A source must own emissions credits equal to its emissions. SCAQMD permits sources to calculate emissions based on formulas— emissions factors—developed by EPA. These are necessarily averages, meaning that within any source category half of the sources will have higher actual emissions, even if the emissions factors are accurate, which they sometimes are not. See EPA, Compilation of Air Pollutant Emissions Factors, AP-42, Fifth Edition, Vol. I, pages 3-4 (available on the Internet; see this casebook's website). In fact, documents obtained through the Freedom of Information Act indicate that the marine terminals measured their actual emissions, and that those emissions ranged from 10 to 1,000 times higher than the amounts calculated using emissions factors. How does this discrepancy affect the RECLAIM program?

The Title IV acid rain program requires power plants to install continuous emissions monitors (CEMs) to provide accurate dates on actual emissions. §§402, 412. Should SCAQMD require CEMs?

Question Five.   The baseline of SCAQMD's declining cap-and-trade program—the amount of credits initially allocated to each source—was set based on the highest annual level of source emissions for the five years prior to the program's initiation. Industry resisted basing credits on the immediate past year because the South Coast Air Basin was in recession. In the first three years of RECLAIM, actual industrial emissions of NOx declined by approximately 3 percent, while the amount of the RECLAIM cap declined 30 percent. In 2001, an EPA official observed that "for seven years, the program did absolutely nothing." Should SCAQMD have chosen a different baseline?

SCAQMD's record with RECLAIM provides a number of cautionary lessons concerning possible pitfalls that need to be taken into account in deciding whether cap-and-trade is a desirable regulatory instrument in particular circumstances. The problems with Rule 1610 and with an inflated baseline are illustrative. The inflated baseline concern was brought home vividly when California experienced electrical shortages in 2000. Supply shortages prompted Los Angeles area utilities to run gas turbine facilities (normally used only at times of peak consumption) much more often than usual. As a result, RECLAIM faced a sudden demand for NOx credits to cover the emissions from the turbines. Prices fluctuated wildly, sometimes topping $50,000 a ton, because there was an inadequate supply of credits. The tight market revealed that many facilities were still relying on purchasing readily-available RECLAIM credits rather than installing pollution controls. In subsequent investigative reporting, the Los Angeles Times reported that "local air quality officials acknowledge that, from its inception, [RECLAIM] was embedded with powerful disincentives to cut smog. This is because they seeded it with too many credits, about 40% more than real-world emissions. Credits were so plentiful and cheap for so long that companies grew addicted to buying them instead of spending more for pollution controls." Gary Polakovic, Innovative Smog Plan Makes Little Progress, L.A. Times, April 17, 2001, at B1. The SCAQMD estimated that the air emission targets it had set for that year would be exceeded by 14 percent. Id.

Some analysts believe that another reason RECLAIM stumbled in 2001 was because the program did not permit the "banking" of emissions credits. Banking, or saving allowances by "overcomplying" today so that the unused credits can be used in future years, is a feature of cap-and-trade programs under EPA's EIP guidance. "RECLAIM is the exception that proves the rule with respect to allowance banking. One way to help avoid the spike in prices would have been to allow allowance banking (in a simple form) all along. Had banking been allowed, sources with low-cost abatement options would have had an incentive to adopt them early and retain the allowances for future periods, even in the case where allocations were higher than the current demand for emissions. . . ." Burtraw et al., Economics of Pollution Trading for SO₂ and NOx, Resources for the Future Discussion Paper 05-05 (March 2005), at 37.

The SCAQMD relieved the market pressure in May 2001 by removing electric generating facilities from NOx market, and adopting for them a technology-based compliance plan, requiring existing facilities to install Best Available Retrofit Control Technology. This and other changes returned the RECLAIM market prices to more customary trading levels. By 2005, SCAQMD could report that "in Calendar Year 2004, the price trend for NOx [credits] valid for the same period returned to the pattern seen prior to the energy crisis in 2000, in that prices for [credits] started out high at the beginning of the compliance year and gradually declined over the course of the year. NOx [credits] that expired in December 2003 and June 2004 were traded at prices less than \$1 per pound in the 60-day period following their expiration date during which facilities are allowed to trade to reconcile their emissions." SCAQMD, Annual RECLAIM Audit Report for the 2003 Compliance Year, pages 2-12 (March 2005).

For more on the possible hazards of employing emissions trading programs to resolve environmental issues, see the Center for Progressive Reform's Perspective on Emissions Trading: *http://www.progressivereform.org/perspectives/emissions.cfm.*

E. ACID DEPOSITION

In 1990, Congress amended the CAA to add Title IV, addressing the problem of acid deposition. Acid deposition results from sulfur dioxides and nitrogen oxides forming acids in the atmosphere and then being deposited on land, either in dry form or in the form of acid rain. Contributors to the problem include local emissions sources, trucks, and autos. They also include distant sources that send their emissions high enough into the atmosphere to be carried long distances before they are acidified and deposited. Many of these long-range sources exist because the federal program failed sufficiently to understand and address multi-state pollution problems soon enough. In the 1970s, utility companies had responded to increasingly stringent control of local air pollution by building tall stacks that could project pollution plumes into the upper atmosphere, sending the pollution long distances. More than 175 stacks higher than 500 feet were constructed after enactment of the 1970 Act. This practice was terminated by section 123 of the 1977 Amendments, but not before utility companies had constructed the 111 "big dirties" that are the primary sources of acid rain in the eastern United States. In the 1990 Amendments, Congress finally created an extensive program to control interstate pollution in response to the acid rain problem.

The issue of acid deposition is intensely regional: Midwestern power plants contribute a major share of the pollution that causes acid deposition in the eastern part of the country. EPA dodged the divisive issue for years, abetted for a portion of that time by uncertainty over the causes and effects of the problem. Environmental organizations and eastern states pursued litigation strategies under existing Air Act provisions, but the courts, taking notice of Congress's and EPA's silence on the issue, refused to order EPA to act. See, e.g., New York v. EPA, 852 F.2d 574 (D.C. Cir. 1988).

In its 1981 Report, To Breathe Clean Air, the National Commission on Air Quality (created by the 1977 Amendments), recommended significant reductions in sulfur oxide emissions affecting the eastern states, despite the uncertainties and the potential of multiple factors contributing to forest dieback. Action on that report came nine years later, with the 1990 Amendments.

When Congress enacted Title IV in 1990 it relied exclusively on a cap-and-trade program.

The acid rain program begins with a nationwide cap on emissions. By the year 2000, sulfur dioxide emissions from fossil fuel–fired electric power plants had to be reduced by 10 million tons per year from 1980 levels. Nitrogen oxide emissions also had to be reduced, by approximately 2 million tons per year below 1980 levels.

Reductions are to be achieved in two phases. "Phase I applied primarily to the largest coal-fired electric generation sources from 1995 through 1999 for SO_2 and from 1996 through 1999 for NOx. Phase II for both pollutants began in 2000. For SO_2, it applies to thousands of combustion units generating electricity nationwide; for NOx it generally applies to affected units that burned coal during 1990-1995." EPA, Acid Rain Program 2003 Progress Report 3 (2004). More specifically, Phase I applied to the 111 big dirties; the second phase applies to all power plants within the 48 contiguous states and the District of Columbia, plus additional sources. Compliance with the program is enhanced by continuous monitoring requirements and stiff penalties for violations.

The potential for trading is created by allocating pollution allowances to sources based on their past emissions and fuel consumption. In making these initial allocations to power plants, the government had good historical data, and Congress incorporated numerical allocations for the Phase I power plants directly into the text of the Act. §404(e), Table A. An allowance permits the holder to emit one ton of sulfur dioxide during or after the calendar year of issuance. Allowances may be reallocated within a company to cover multiple units, transferred to another owner, or even transferred to a later year.

In order to satisfy additional political objectives and operational concerns, the statute includes a number of provisions for "bonus" allowances. For instance, bonus allowances could have been obtained in Phase I by:

- units that install scrubbers and need an additional two years' delay;
- units that emit less than a specified amount of sulfur dioxide per unit of energy prior to 1995 receive two-for-one allowances, not to exceed 3.5 million allocated on a first-come, first-served basis;
- units that reduce emissions through the use of conservation or renewable energy and meet other related conditions can obtain bonuses from a pool of 300,000 allowances; and
- a pool of 200,000 allowances for each year of Phase I was available to utilities in Indiana, Ohio, and Illinois.

A different set of extensions and bonus opportunities is provided in Phase II to reward utilities that invest in "clean coal" technology, conservation, and renewable energy, to ease the transition for utilities in ten midwestern states, and to compensate utilities in "clean states"—states that had achieved low emission levels by 1985. To further complicate matters, industrial units can be brought into the Phase I and II programs. This can occur by voluntary "opt in" (why would an industry want to do this?) or by regulation, should EPA determine that industrial emissions are expected to exceed 5.6 million tons per year on the basis of a 20-year forecast. Finally, in order to promote the creation of a market and the availability of allowances, EPA withholds 2.8 percent of each unit's allowance allocation for auction each year. By 2003, sources subject to the acid rain program had reduced SO_2 emisisons by 32 percent compared to 1990 figures. Acid Rain Program 2003 Progress Report at 3.

The structure of the Title IV program and the nature of the environmental problem it addresses provide it with some advantages compared with more localized trading programs, such as RECLAIM. One difficulty with allowing trading for most conventional air pollutants is that the location and timing of emissions determines the severity of pollution; trading must be confined to identical pollutants within a single airshed or additional adjustments must be made to account for concentration and other measures of impact. T. Tietenberg, Emissions Trading: An Exercise in Reforming Pollution Policy (1985); Levin & Elman, The Case for Environmental Incentives, Envtl. Forum 7-11 (Jan.-Feb. 1990). In contrast, acid rain offers a problem well suited to a trading approach, since emissions reductions are of relatively constant value over time and space. Dudek & Palmisano, Emissions Trading: Why Is This Thoroughbred Hobbled?, 13 Colum. J. Envtl. L. 217 (1988).

A closely related problem is the need for sufficient trades to assure permits are available on competitive terms. This may not occur if the relevant market is small; for example, a pollutant emitted by only a few sources in an airshed. The large size of the national market for SO_2 trades lessens these concerns, and several provisions were included in the program specifically to promote the evolution of a competitive market, such as the restoration of some allowances for annual auction.

The Title IV program has been successful by many measures. Trading in allowances has been active. One of the surprises has been the price at which allowances trade—much lower than was initially projected. At the time of enactment of the 1990 Amendments, projections had the allowances selling at between $1,000 and $1,500 each, based on the assumption that most utilities would need to install scrubbers to achieve the required emission reductions. Prices, however, have fluctuated between $50 and somewhat more than $200, reflecting the fact that companies have employed less expensive compliance techniques, even though the cost of scrubbers has also fallen significantly since 1990. Most utilities instead switched to low-sulfur coal or to blended fuel, which became a much more economical alternative due to plunging transportation costs following railroad deregulation. Ellerman, Schmalenese, Joskow, Montero & Bailey, Emissions Trading Under the U.S. Acid Rain Program: Evaluation of Compliance Costs and Allowance Market Performance 66 (1997).

Utility companies also "overcomplied" in the early years of the program, often with the purpose of banking allowances for use in Phase II, when their initial allocation were further reduced. The amount of allowances banked by Phase I units grew steadily until Phase II began. Now firms are apparently drawing down from banked allowances to help meet the more stringent requirements of Phase II, as banked allowance accounts shrunk by a total of 1.1 million in 2003. In 2003, current allowances under the Tide IV program amounted to 9.54 million. Another 8.6 million had been banked, meaning that 18.2 million allowances were available for use that year. However, sources emitted only 10.6 million tons in 2003, 1.1 million over the allowances granted in 2003, but still a 32 percent reduction from 1990 levels. Acid Rain Program 2003 Progress Report at 4.

Title IV also allows companies that were not initially covered by the Phase I program to opt in to it. A number of companies have elected to do so, in order to build up emissions allowances for sale later on. (Opt-in firms are able to wait until the first week in December to see if they have had a good emission year, compared with their historical average. If their actual emissions are low, they can opt in and collect last-minute excess allowances for the year.) The same study that documented more fuel switching than expected also reported that the program's opt-in provisions may actually have resulted in a net increase in emissions due to overly generous allowance allocations to facilities that would have opted in anyway. Ellerman et al.

An EPA study released in November 1995 estimated that the reductions in SO_2 emissions required by Title IV will produce annual health benefits in the eastern United States with a monetary value ranging from $12 to $78 billion by the year 2010. These reductions also were estimated to produce between $290 million and $1.87 billion in annual health benefits in Canada. EPA, Human Health Benefits from Sulfate Reduction Under Title IV of the 1990 Clean Air Act Amendments 8 (1995). Most of these benefits are calculated to result from reductions in premature deaths (more than 9,600 per year) and reduced cases of chronic bronchitis (more than 14,500 per year). These estimates do not even include the environmental benefits of reduced damage to forests, lakes, streams, and buildings, or of improved visibility—benefits that played a central role in the debate over enactment. Because the costs of complying with Title IV were then expected to be only $2 to $3 billion per year, the program looked like a terrific bargain. Mathews, Clean Sweeps: Two Success Stories for the Environment, Wash. Post, Dec. 18, 1995, at A23. Title IV looks like an even better bargain now because projected compliance costs have continued to fall. A recent cost estimate is $1.1 billion/year in the year 2010. Carlson, Burtraw, Cropper & Palmer, SO_2 Control by Electric Utilities: What are the Gains from Trade?, 108 J. Pol. Econ. 1292-1326 (2000). OMB has estimated that the acid rain program has a benefits-to-cost ratio of 40:1, and the largest quantified human health benefits of any program instituted in the past 10 years. OMB, Office of Information and Regulatory Affairs, Informing Regulatory Decisions: 2003 Report to Congress on the Costs and Benefits of Federal Regulations and Unfunded Mandates on State, Local, and Tribal Entities (2003), *www.whitehouse.gov/omb/inforeg/2003_cost-ben_final_rpt.pdf.*

NOTES AND QUESTIONS

1. How was the objective of reducing sulfur dioxide emissions by 10 million tons per year chosen? One factor may have been a study of the costs per ton of emissions reduction by the Congressional Budget Office (CBO). The CBO estimated that costs would be $270 per ton for an 8-million-ton-per-year program, $360 per ton in a 10-million-ton-per-year program, and $720 per

ton in a 12-million-ton-per-year program. CBO, Curbing Acid Rain: Cost, Budget, and Coal-Market Effects xix (1986).

2. What is the legal status of allowances? The Act states they are not "property" rights but rather "limited authorizations." EPA can, for example, reduce their value by ratcheting down Phase II allowances pro rata if necessary to stay within the 8.95-million ton annual cap.

3. What is the relationship between the allowances and other regulatory requirements, including the ambient air quality standards for sulfur dioxide and the new source standards for power plants? If trading stimulates technological innovation (as economists predict), will this trigger more stringent technology-based requirements for new sources, and if so, will this undermine the value of allowances?

4. Since utility investments are subject to state regulation, utilities may have incentives quite different from those of other businesses. For example, because they have long planning horizons they may prefer to hold on to allowances in order to ensure an adequate supply in the future, unless an effective options market develops. They may also question the value of selling allowances if state regulators demand that most of the earnings obtained be passed on to the customers who paid for the pollution control measures earlier through higher rates. Utilities that share power regionally through power pools also will have to establish rules governing whether allowances can be pooled.

5. Why should existing sources be given allowances? Doesn't this policy discriminate against new sources and reward utilities for their past pollution? Consider other ways in which emission rights might have been distributed. What explains the distribution chosen by Congress?

6. If trading offers such large opportunities for cost reductions, where does resistance to it originate? One study suggests that the only constituency for efficiency has been economists. See S. Kelman, What Price Incentives? Economists and the Environment (1981). Others suggest a variety of factors. Some environmentalists express moral outrage at the notion of "rights to pollute"; they also may resent industry profits from trades. Many fear that trading systems will be difficult to police effectively, resulting in higher levels of emissions than otherwise would be the case. See the discussion of economic incentive programs, pages 550-553. If this last reason is valid, then the use of cap-and-trade may snowball as its use increases and people become more familiar with it. Regulators and industry may prefer the system they know, and the latter also may be concerned by the prospects of additional costs for the acquisition of permits. See generally Hahn & Stavins, above; Hanley, Hallet & Moffatt, Why Is More Notice Not Taken of Economists' Prescriptions for the Control of Pollution?, 22 Env. & Planning 1241 (1990).

7. Can trading schemes, even if they are policed rigorously, result in increased pollution? One result of the use of trading mechanisms may be that companies whose emissions otherwise would be below legal limits will acquire pollution rights to sell to other companies. By ensuring that companies in the aggregate discharge the maximum levels of pollution permitted by law, allowance trading may increase emissions. Of course, the overall levels of allowable pollution permitted could be ratcheted downward to counteract this tendency.

8. Recall the offset provisions of the Clean Air Act that govern new sources in nonattainment areas. The Minnesota Mining and Manufacturing Company (3M), a pioneer in source reduction, has a corporate policy that it will neither

use nor sell offset allowances it acquires by voluntarily reducing emissions of chemicals. "Top management felt if we sold credits all we would have done is transfer emissions, not reduce them," explains a company spokesperson. 3M has returned credits (reportedly worth more than $1 million) that otherwise would have allowed emissions of more than 1,000 pounds of organic solvents per day in the Los Angeles area. Holusha, Hutchinson No Longer Holds Its Nose, N.Y. Times, Feb. 3, 1991, at C1. Is such a decision economically rational? (The company does take a tax deduction for the value of the credits.) Should such voluntary emissions reductions be taken into account in determining the amount by which other sources must reduce emissions? According to a company spokesperson, 3M later made an exception to its policy to sell some emissions credits to a Procter & Gamble facility in Camarillo, California in order to prevent job losses. 3M donated the proceeds of the sale to an environmental group.

9. In January 1993, the Long Island Lighting Company (LILCO) announced plans to sell emissions allowances to an undisclosed company believed to be located in the Midwest. Some environmentalists expressed concern that such a transaction would increase emissions from sources in the Midwest that contribute to acid deposition in New York, while reducing emissions from LILCO's stacks, which usually drift over the Atlantic Ocean. Should utilities be required to disclose the details of allowance sales and purchases including the location of the parties involved in the transactions? Are there circumstances in which it might make sense to impose geographical restrictions on sales of allowances? EPA maintains that even if individual trades arguably aggravate the distribution of pollution, the overall emissions reductions mandated by Title IV will require midwestern utilities to reduce emissions substantially. Dao, A New, Unregulated Market: Selling the Right to Pollute, N.Y. Times, Feb. 6, 1993, at A1. Should allowance trades be subject to environmental impact statement requirements? Overall, NOx reductions seem to be occurring where they should. The states with the highest emissions prior to 1990 are also the states where the largest reductions have occurred, with the midwestern states of Ohio, Indiana, Illinois, and Missouri leading the way.

10. A trade between utilities at opposite ends of the country that did not raise environmental concerns was announced in November 1994. An Arizona utility, Arizona Public Service, traded 25,000 allowances to the Niagara Mohawk Power Corporation in upstate New York. Niagara Mohawk agreed to donate the allowances to an environmental group that would retire them unused, enabling the utility to take a $3.75 million tax deduction. Niagara Mohawk promised to use the money saved from the tax deduction to reduce greenhouse gas emissions by 1.75 million tons. The credit for the reductions in greenhouse gases was then transferred to Arizona Public Service to help it satisfy its voluntary commitment to reduce greenhouse emissions as part of the Climate Change Accord, which several utilities signed in April 1994. Passell, For Utilities, New Clean-Air Plan, N.Y. Times, Nov. 18, 1994, at D1.

11. Some environmental and public health groups are acquiring allowances and then letting them expire unused in order to *reduce* permissible levels of pollution. In March 1994, the Maryland Environmental Law Society (MELS) became the first law student group to purchase allowances. Five other law schools followed suit in 1995. Students Buy and Hold Pollution Rights, N.Y. Times, March 31, 1995, at A28. A nonprofit group formed expressly for the purpose of retiring allowances, the National Healthy Air License Exchange (INHALE), purchased 150 allowances in 1995 and more than 300 at the CBOT's 1996 auction.

12. By encouraging utilities to switch to low-sulfur coal, Title IV has had a profound impact on the domestic coal industry. Demand for low-sulfur coal has soared, while many mines with high-sulfur lodes have been forced to close. This has caused significant dislocations in many communities. Some states have attempted to require their local utilities to continue using high-sulfur local coal. Such a law was challenged in the case below by an alliance of western coal companies.

Alliance for Clean Coal v. Bayh
72 F.3d 556 (7th Cir. 1995)

CUMMINGS, Circuit Judge:

Because of the sulfur contained in the coal they burn, coal-fired generating plants are a principal source of atmospheric sulfur dioxide emissions. The sulfur content of coal burned by utilities depends upon the geological origin of the coal: whereas coal mined in the western United States has the lowest sulfur content, almost all of the coal mined in the "Illinois Basin," including most of Illinois and parts of Indiana and western Kentucky, has a relatively high sulfur content.

Congressional enactment of the Clean Air Act Amendments of 1970 required newly constructed generating units to use systems of emissions control approved by the Environmental Protection Agency ("EPA"). The EPA initially provided two methods for controlling sulfur dioxide emissions: (1) the use of low-sulfur coal; and (2) the installation of a device to scrub high-sulfur coal emissions before they reach the atmosphere. Because scrubbing was costlier than using low-sulfur western coal, states producing high-sulfur coal suffered competitively. In 1990 the Clean Air Act was amended again to require drastic reductions in industrial sulfur dioxide emissions by the year 2000. 42 U.S.C. §§7401-7671q. The 1990 Act implemented an innovative market-driven approach to emissions regulation, allowing for the free transfer of emissions "allowances." The Act is aimed at reducing emissions efficiently and allows utilities to meet the standards in the cheapest manner possible. To comply with the new emissions limitations, utilities now have a choice of the following strategies: (1) installing pollution control devices; (2) using low-sulfur coal; (3) purchasing allowances to emit sulfur dioxide; (4) switching to another fuel; (5) closing down certain units; (6) offsetting emissions at one plant by over-complying at another; or (7) adopting some combination. According to [appellant] Alliance [for Clean Coal], because of the high costs associated with installing pollution devices, the 1990 amendments should result in a decline in demand for the Illinois Basin's high-sulfur coal.

High-sulfur coal-mining states like Indiana considered legislation responsive to the foregoing federal acts. Thus in 1991 Indiana adopted its [Environmental Compliance Plans Act] ECPA. This statute permits electric utilities to avail themselves of early prudency review by submitting plans for complying with the federal legislation to the Commission. In order to approve a utility's plan, the Commission must find that the plan (A) meets the Clean Air Act Amendments of 1990; (B) constitutes a reasonable and least cost strategy over the life of the investment consistent with providing reliable, efficient, and economical electrical service; (C) is in the public interest; and (D) either:

> (i) provides for continued or increased use of Indiana coal in the coal-consuming electric generating units owned or operated by the public utility and affected by the Clean Air Act Amendments of 1990; or

(ii) if the plan does not provide for continued or increased use of Indiana coal, such nonprovision is justified by economic considerations including the effects in the regions of Indiana in which the mining of coal provides employment and in the service territory of the public utility. 1C §8-1-27-8(1).

A plan that has a negative impact on Indiana coal is subject to continuing annual surveillance. . . .

In the court below Alliance moved for summary judgment on the ground that the ECPA unjustifiably discriminated against interstate commerce. The district court concluded that the ECPA was intended to promote high-sulfur coal at the expense of western coal and unconstitutionally burdens interstate commerce. . . .

The threshold inquiry we must make in deciding whether the ECPA violates the Commerce Clause is whether it "is basically a protectionist measure, or if it can fairly be viewed as a law directed to legitimate local concerns with effects upon interstate commerce that are only incidental." *Oregon Waste Systems, Inc. v. Dept. of Environmental Quality*, 114 S. Ct. 1345, 1350 (1994).

As the district judge recognized, the outcome of this case is controlled by *Alliance for Clean Coal v. Miller*, 44 F.3d 591 (7th Cir. 1995). There we invalidated the Illinois Coal Act, also enacted on the heels of the Clean Air Act Amendments of 1990, on the ground that it was repugnant to the Commerce Clause of the United States Constitution. The Illinois Coal Act provided that in preparing and approving compliance plans, the Illinois Commerce Commission and utilities were required to "take into account . . . the need to maintain and preserve as a valuable State resource the mining of coal in Illinois." Id. at 593-594. The Act also encouraged implementing scrubbers to allow the continued use of high-sulfur coal by guaranteeing utilities the ability to recover the installation costs of scrubbers by including such costs in their rate base. Id. We stated "the Illinois Coal Act is a none-too-subtle attempt to prevent Illinois electric utilities from switching to low-sulphur western coal as a Clean Air Act compliance option." Id. at 595. Therefore, we concluded that the Act was "repugnant to the Commerce Clause and the principle of a unitary national economy which that clause was intended to establish." Id.

The ECPA contains provisions that are virtually identical to the sections of the Illinois Coal Act discussed above. First, in determining whether to approve a plan that includes a compliance option calling for a decrease in the use of Indiana coal, the ECPA requires the Commission to take into account "the effects in the regions of Indiana in which the mining of coal provides employment and in the service territory of the public utility." The ECPA also provides incentives for utilities to install scrubbers to continue to use high-sulfur fuel by guaranteeing a recoupment of the implementation costs.

We agree with the district court that, just as in *Miller*, the ECPA discriminates against interstate commerce based solely upon geographic origin, and thus violates the Commerce Clause. The clear intent of the statute is to benefit Indiana coal at the expense of western coal. The fact that the ECPA does not explicitly forbid the use of out-of-state coal or require the use of Indiana coal, but "merely encourages" utilities to use high-sulfur coal by providing economic incentives does not make the ECPA any less discriminatory. . . .

Because the ECPA discriminates against interstate commerce, the burden lies with the defendants to prove that this discrimination is justified by a legitimate and compelling governmental interest. [Wyoming v. Oklahoma, 502 U.S.

437, 456 (1992).] Defendants provide the following justification. They argue that a viable competitive Midwest high-sulfur coal market is a major component of low-cost electrical service by Indiana utilities and that the ECPA seeks only to ensure that market. . . . However, ensuring such a regional market is not a proper justification for discriminating against interstate commerce. . . .

While we do not doubt that a healthy Indiana mining industry and a fully employed workforce may aid Indiana in achieving a low cost electrical service, that is not a legitimate justification for discrimination against interstate commerce. Protection of local, or even regional, industry is simply not a legislative action that is consistent with the Commerce Clause.

NOTES AND QUESTIONS

1. PSI Energy, Inc. intervened on the side of the plaintiff in this case, while the United Mine Workers intervened on the side of the state. Shortly after the 1990 Amendments were signed into law, James E. Rogers Jr., the chairman of PSI, had stated in an interview that switching to low-sulfur coal was an option that he had ruled out. He noted that half of the coal burned by the utility came from Indiana mines and that "[s]ome of the coal companies are our largest customers. . . ." He continued, "Because of the politics of the state, because of who we serve, we have to comply with clean air [regulations] and continue to use high-sulfur coal." Lippman, Clean Air Law Forces Choices, Wash. Post, Nov. 27, 1990, at D1, D4. In light of its prior support for continued use of local, high-sulfur coal, why would PSI now support a legal challenge to the Indiana law?

2. Coal mines in the West and in eastern Kentucky and southern West Virginia where low-sulfur coal is found are thriving due to the shift in demand toward low-sulfur coal. However, in other places in the East that are heavily dependent on the mining of high-sulfur coal, the economic impact of this shift in demand has been severe, as many high-sulfur coal mines have closed and many miners have lost their jobs. Kilborn, East's Coal Towns Wither in the Name of Cleaner Air, N.Y. Times, Feb. 15, 1996, at A1. Between 1990 and 1995, coal production in the eastern United States fell 14 percent, while in the West it has increased by 26 percent. Id. at A16. Altogether nearly 1,000 coal mines in the United States have closed since 1990, leaving 2,500; yet coal production nationwide is at a record 1.05 billion tons annually. Should the environmental justice movement be concerned about the impact of regulation on miners' jobs?

3. Should the environmental laws attempt to compensate those who are adversely affected when regulation alters demand for particular products? One of the most hotly debated provisions in the 1990 Amendments was the creation of a program to provide financial assistance to displaced miners. The program pays for miners who lose their jobs due to the shift away from high-sulfur coal to go to school for two years to learn new skills and it generally keeps unemployment benefits, that normally would expire after six months, running for the duration. Id.

4. Instead of requiring utilities to purchase local coal, could a state choose to subsidize the coal industry directly? For example, in 1996 the Virginia General Assembly adopted legislation to subsidize the price of local coal by two dollars per ton through a complicated tax-credit formula for coal mining companies in the state. Relief for Coal Industry, Wash. Post, Mar. 2, 1996, at B3. Would this $188 million subsidy program violate the dormant Commerce Clause? Recall

Justice Kennedy's majority opinion in the *Carbone* decision in Chapter 3. Could a state purchase local coal and provide it to utilities at a reduced price without violating the dormant Commerce Clause?

E.   MOBILE SOURCE CONTROLS: A TECHNOLOGY-FORCING VENTURE

Emissions from automobiles and other mobile sources were the first forms of air pollution subjected to national regulation, and emissions from mobile source exhaust were subjected to regulation by California in 1965. As we will discuss in a moment, emissions regulations have been successful in achieving a dramatic reduction in the amount of pollution mobile sources produce per vehicle mile traveled. Nonetheless, emissions from automobiles and other mobile sources have also become an increasing fraction of the national air pollution load for carbon monoxide and oxides of nitrogen, which are produced when the internal combustion engine burns gasoline or diesel fuel. The reason: other sources are being better controlled, while the effects of lower emissions per vehicle mile traveled is being offset by a dramatic increase in the number of automobiles, trucks, and buses on the road today and in the number of vehicle miles traveled. Figure 5.8 illustrates the problem by charting the relationship between VOCs emitted per vehicle mile traveled compared with total vehicle miles traveled. How can we reduce ambient levels of the pollutants associated with mobile sources once end-of-the-pipe emissions control technology for such sources has taken us as far as it can?

FIGURE 5.8
Ozone Emissions Reductions Offset by Increased Vehicle Use

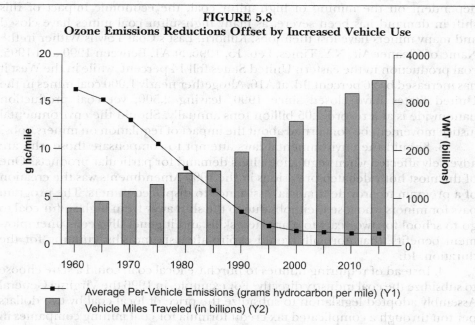

Average Per-Vehicle Emissions (grams hydrocarbon per mile) (Y1)

Vehicle Miles Traveled (in billions) (Y2)

Source: U.S. EPA (last modified July 20, 1998). *http://www.epa.gov/oms/04-ozone.htm*

One answer, of course, is to transition from fossil-fuel-driven forms of transportation to other kinds. The options range from the hydrogen fuel cell vehicles to battery powered. The CAA has little directly to say about that transition, although California's ZEV auto emissions program, see pages 569-571, has stimulated the development of alternative fuel vehicles, and that program could not have been promulgated if Congress had failed to exempt California from the statutory preemption that prevents other states from adopting emissions standards different from the federal standards. Transition to cleaner fossil fuels, such as natural gas or synthetic fuels from clean coal technologies would achieve partial benefits in the interim. The 1990 Amendments did direct EPA to develop standards for "clean alternative fuel," sections 241 et seq., exempting them from certain transportation control measures and requiring serious, severe, and extreme NA areas for ozone to adopt clean fuel programs for vehicle fleets. Otherwise, reducing the air pollution impacts of the fossil-fuel-powered internal combustion vehicle comes from one of three strategies. One is to install equipment on each vehicle to capture pollutants before they become ambient. Historically, this was the first strategy employed, and such improvement as we have achieved in the mobile source sector are primarily attributable to this technique. Second, adjustments can be made in the composition of the fuel burned by mobile sources, including the complete elimination of hazardous additives. The amazing success we have had in reducing the adverse health effects of lead on children has come directly from the phasedown and then the phaseout of lead additives in gasoline. See pages 180-182. The 1990 Amendments

FIGURE 5.9

emphasized fuel content strategies more than any previous version of the CAA. It established detailed statutory requirements for the content of reformulated gasoline to reduce emissions of volatile chemicals and toxic air pollutants. (Section 211(k), which contains the new requirements, has more words than the entire fuels-related provisions of the CAA had contained up until then.) Third, we can reduce the rate at which we use mobile sources. This section reviews the contributions of each of these approaches to solving the problem of mobile source pollution.

1. Emissions Standards

The initial federal entry into the problem of mobile source emissions was the Schenck Act, which directed the Surgeon General to study the impact of motor vehicle emissions on human health. At the time, little was known either about the composition of auto emissions or about their environmental consequences. The automobile manufacturers, as chronicled in Ralph Nader's Unsafe at Any Speed (1965), downplayed the issue and resisted calls for research.

California was out in front of the federal effort. In 1960, the state established an emissions control board to oversee the development of emissions control equipment, establishing deadlines for the installation of emissions controls starting from the date the board certified that two satisfactory devices had been developed. Installation was required on new and used cars, and the law was enforced by refusals to register vehicles that lacked control devices. The California board certified seven devices by November 1962, and the registration requirements went into effect in 1965, over the vigorous opposition of the automobile manufacturers.

Congress took modest steps in 1965 and 1967, authorizing the secretary of HEW to establish auto emissions standards after considering costs and "technological feasibility," but the start of significant federal efforts can be traced to President Nixon's 1970 special message to Congress on the environment. In it, he endorsed even tighter controls on vehicle emissions based on estimates of the lowest emissions levels attainable with developing technology. Yet he recognized that even such stringent controls eventually would be insufficient because growth of the vehicle fleet could cancel out progress from emissions controls. Thus, he proposed the development of clean alternatives to the internal combustion engine:

> Our responsibility now is also to look beyond the Seventies, and the prospects then are uncertain. Based on present trends, it is quite possible that by 1980 the increase in the sheer number of cars in densely populated areas will begin outrunning the technological limits of our capacity to reduce pollution from the internal combustion engine. . . . [U]nless vehicles with an alternative, low-pollution power source are available, vehicle-caused pollution will once again begin an inexorable increase. Therefore, prudence dictates that we move now to ensure that such a vehicle will be available if needed. [R. Nixon, Public Papers of the President 101 (1970).]

President Nixon ordered federal agencies to begin research and development for unconventional vehicles. As an incentive to the private sector to develop such vehicles, he pledged that federal agencies would purchase them even if they cost more than conventional vehicles.

In the 1970 Clean Air Act, Congress imposed "strong medicine" on automobile manufacturers to force the development of greatly improved emissions control technology. In what one senator described as perhaps the "biggest industrial judgment that has been made in the U.S. in this century," 116 Cong. Rec. 33085 (1970) (remarks of Sen. Baker), Congress directed automotive manufacturers to curtail emissions of hydrocarbons and carbon monoxide from new vehicles by 90 percent within five years, and a similar reduction in NOx by one year later. Congress decided on a 90 percent reduction by relying on the simple notion that since air pollution levels in major cities were approximately five times the expected levels of the NAAQSs, emissions would need to be reduced by at least 80 percent, with an additional 10 percent necessary to provide for growing vehicle use. S. Rep. No. 91-1196, 91st Cong., 2d Sess. at 25 (1970). A committee staff member involved in the legislative drafting process described the 90 percent rollback requirements as "a back of the envelope calculation. . . . We didn't have any particular methodology. We just picked what sounded like a good goal." Easterbrook, Cleaning Up, Newsweek, July 24, 1989, at 29. An earlier report from HEW's National Air Pollution Control Administration (which was absorbed into EPA when that agency was created) had estimated that reductions of 92.7 percent for CO, 99 percent for hydrocarbons, and 93.6 for NOx would be required to achieve healthy air levels, so there was some support for the general range of reductions being demanded. NACPA, Federal Motor Vehicle Emissions Goals for Carbon Monoxide, Hydrocarbons, and Nitrogen Oxides, Based on Desired Air Quality Levels, J. Air Pollution Control Ass'n, Aug. 1970, 20(8): 519-524. President Nixon had proposed a 1980 deadline for these standards to be met, but after Senator Nelson proposed banning the internal combustion engine by 1975, Senator Muskie fashioned a "compromise" appending the earlier deadline to the administration's bill.

The mobile source regulations present a classic example of the technology-forcing concept introduced in Chapter 2. Congress adopted the rollback requirements with full knowledge that the technology to meet them did not yet exist, might not be available by the deadline, and had an unknown cost. The legislation gave EPA the power, at least in theory, to shut down the entire automobile industry if it failed to comply. The "statute was, indeed, deliberately designed as 'shock treatment' to the industry." International Harvester v. Ruckelshaus, 478 F.2d 615, 648 (D.C. Cir. 1973). The auto companies began a battle in the courts, the Congress, and the media that continues to this day.

Concerned that auto manufacturers might not be able to meet the deadline, Congress had provided the EPA administrator with limited discretion to grant the automobile companies a one-year extension, if the administrator determined that (i) such an extension was essential to the public interest or the public health and welfare, (ii) the auto companies had made all good-faith efforts to comply, (iii) the company petitioning for the extension had established that effective control technology was not available to meet the standards, and (iv) a study conducted by the National Academy of Sciences was consistent with the company's claim. §205(b)(5)(D).

Faced with such a petition, Administrator Ruckelshaus denied an extension on the ground that the companies had not met their burden with respect to requirement (iii). The administrator's conclusions depended heavily on EPA's own extrapolations from limited laboratory experiments with one design of the catalytic converter. The Agency reasoned that, although the technology had not yet been demonstrated (in 1972, when the petition was filed) to be able to meet

the standards over a 50,000-mile vehicle life as required under the Act, anticipated continued development of the technology would result in 1975 model
year cars being able to meet the standards. Hence, in EPA's judgment, the
technology was "available."

In International Harvester v. Ruckelshaus, 478 F.2d 615 (D.C. Cir. 1973),
the D.C. Circuit overturned EPA's decision not to extend the deadline.
Reasoning that the risks associated with an erroneous denial of the extension
were much greater than those associated with an erroneous grant, the court
placed the burden of rebutting the companies' initial showing of nonavailability
on EPA and found that the Agency had not met that burden.

This was not the last extension the auto industry received. EPA also granted
a one-year extension of the 1976 deadline for nitrogen oxide controls. Congress
amended the Clean Air Act in 1977 to grant the auto industry further extensions.
As a result of these extensions, the original hydrocarbon and carbon monoxide
standards did not take effect until 1980 and 1981 respectively, the very dates the
industry originally had forecast that it could meet. The final nitrogen oxide
standard was relaxed and the deadline extended to 1981.

In the 1990 Amendments, Congress lowered some of the exhaust standards
once again, to 3.4 grams per mile for carbon monoxide, 0.4 for NOx, and 0.41
for hydrocarbons. It also instructed EPA to study whether further reductions
were necessary and feasible. After issuing a "Tier II" report to Congress in 1998,
EPA proposed stricter new Tier II standards in May 1999. 64 Fed. Reg. 26,004
(1999).

In December 1999 EPA adopted far-reaching exhaust and fuel content regulations. The standards require a 77 percent reduction in emissions from automobiles beginning in the 2004 model year; for the first time they extend the same
strict automobile standards to sport utility vehicles (SUVs), pick-up trucks, and
minivans beginning in the 2007 model year; and they require a 90 percent reduction in the sulfur content of gasoline by 2004 (lowering the standard to 30 ppm
from a current average of 300 ppm). The standards are estimated to cost oil
refiners and automobile manufacturers $5.3 billion in increased compliance
costs, raising the price of new vehicles by $100 to $200 and adding a cent or
two to the price of gasoline. However, the emissions reductions projected
under the rules are designed to prevent 4,300 premature deaths annually and
173,000 cases of asthma and other respiratory illnesses among children, generating health-related benefits with an estimated value of $25.2 billion. K. Bradsher,
Clinton Allays Criticism on New Pollution Rules, N.Y. Times, Dec. 22, 1999, at A20.

Assessments of the mobile source experience are mixed. Some believe it
confirms the notion that "there is a certain comfort in being asked for the
impossible: you know you will not actually have to do it." Margolis, The Politics
of Auto Emissions, 49 Pub. Interest 3, 13 (1977). Others liken it to the fairy tale
Rumpelstiltskin, wherein a maiden is ordered to weave straw into gold, a seemingly
impossible task that she miraculously accomplishes. D. Currie, Air Pollution:
Federal Law and Analysis (1981). It seems clear that emissions control technology would not have developed as quickly as it did without the regulations. Only a
few months after the International Harvester remand, General Motors announced
that it would install catalytic converters in all its 1975 model year cars that would
last the life of the car while permitting improved fuel economy. See Ditlow,
Federal Regulation of Motor Vehicle Emissions Under the Clean Air Amendments of 1970, 4 Ecology L.Q. 495, 514-516 (1975). Most vehicles failed to comply
with even the revised standards, however, due to differences between test results

for prototypes and actual performance on the road. Nevertheless, emissions controls ultimately produced dramatic reductions in vehicle emissions. As Currie notes, even though the industry knew EPA would not shut it down, perhaps "the cosmetic efforts industry felt compelled to make in order to establish its good faith could not, given the resourcefulness of its engineers, but have produced some improvement." D. Currie, above, at 2-114. Others argue that emissions controls were not a good investment, particularly since they encouraged consumers to keep older cars longer. R. Crandall, H. Gruenspecht, T. Keeler & L. Lave, Regulating the Automobile 115-116 (1986).

Technology forcing and technology forecasting may be to some extent inherently at odds. If the nature of the solution were evident, "forcing" would not be necessary. NRDC attorney David Doniger argued that "before a regulation exists, industry has little incentive to invent effective controls. Invariably industry later finds better and cheaper ways to cut emissions, so actual costs are nowhere near the dire predictions." Easterbrook, above, at 32.

NOTES AND QUESTIONS

1. Who should be responsible for developing improved emissions control technology—the auto manufacturers, the government, or independent entrepreneurs? California's ZEV program (see next section) was premised on the notion that technology-forcing regulation would encourage entrepreneurs to develop technology, although auto manufacturers were reluctant to use devices developed by others. In 1969 the federal government sued the four largest auto manufacturers, alleging that they had conspired to delay the development of emissions control devices. The suit was settled by consent decree. United States v. Automobile Manufacturers Association, 307 F. Supp. 617 (C.D. Calif. 1969), aff'd sub nom. City of New York v. United States, 397 U.S. 248 (1970). Why would California's initial program premise the deadline for installing emissions control devices on certification that at least *two* such devices existed?

2. Professor Currie notes that it was never likely that EPA would seek to shut down the automobile industry. Why, then, was the law effective at all? Why didn't the manufacturers simply ignore the law and call EPA's bluff? See sections 203(a)(1) and 205. Do these sections provide an adequate answer?

3. A major challenge faced by technology-forcing regulation is the question of what combination of carrots and sticks to use to provide an incentive for the development of new technology. The Clean Air Act's imposition of a deadline, coupled with the escape hatch of an extension, provided the auto industry with considerable incentives to maintain that the deadline could not be met and to lobby for extensions. In effect, the auto industry and EPA were engaged in a high-stakes game of chicken. Can you think of any alternative approaches to technology forcing that would avoid the all-or-nothing character of an absolute deadline while providing incentives for companies to develop control technology? Could a scheme of escalating taxes imposed on manufacturers of nonconforming vehicles guarantee the attainment of emissions control goals? Could tradeable emissions rights work for auto manufacturers?

4. Crandall notes the problem created by giving people an incentive to retain older cars longer and thereby avoid the expense of emissions controls and energy efficiency standards. In 1969, 12 percent of cars in the United States were 10 years old or older. By 1987 the figure had increased to 29 percent. States

could regulate pre-Clean Air Act vehicles if they chose to do so. See T. Jorling, The Federal Law of Air Pollution Control, in Federal Environmental Law 1128-1130 (E. Dolgin & T. Guilbert eds., 1974).

Understanding that the emissions control approach to the mobile source problem would in the future be less and less able to achieve significant gains, governments have been exploring other approaches to the problem as well.

2. Fuel Content

The Act authorizes the EPA to restrict or prohibit the use of any fuel additive that "causes, or contributes, to air pollution which may reasonably be anticipated to endanger the public health or welfare." §211(c). The Administrator used this authority to restrict the lead content of gasoline, see Ethyl Corp. v. EPA, page 176, to dramatic effect, as the correlation between lead content in children's blood to controls on lead in gasoline demonstrates. Unfortunately, the approach taken with lead has little direct applicability to the contributions that fuel content makes to the other criteria pollutants, because carbon monoxide, volatile organic compounds, and oxides of nitrogen are inevitable products of the combustion process. Still, some gains with respect to these emissions can be obtained by adjusting fuel content because gasoline is a complex mixture of a variety of hydrocarbons and other chemicals whose content can be varied at the refinery. In 1990, Congress added some clean fuel provisions establishing two different clean fuels programs. One requires the use of reformulated gasoline, which results in lower hydrocarbon emissions, in regions of the country that are nonattainment for ozone. The second requires the use of oxygenated gasoline, which reduces carbon monoxide emissions, in regions of the country that are nonattainment for carbon monoxide.

The oxygenated gasoline program requires gasoline to contain a minimum oxygen content to ensure more complete combustion and hence lower carbon monoxide emissions. Additives, such as ethanol and MTBE, are used to achieve the required oxygen content. After the 1990 Amendments, MTBE was the preferred option of many refineries in achieving the statutory requirement. It has since proven to be an outstanding example of unintended adverse environmental consequences, perhaps rivaling in scope the ill-advised authorization of tall chimney stacks to comply with early local air pollution demands. Tall stacks greatly exacerbated the acid rain problem, page 553. As for MTBE, it has been leaking from underground gasoline storage tanks and contaminating groundwater systems. Because MTBE is soluble in water it travels much greater distances than other gasoline components once it has leaked into the groundwater. We now know it is a likely human carcinogen, as well. MTBE use was initially stimulated by EPA decisions prior to the 1990 Amendments, namely the decisions to remove lead additives from gasoline. MTBE is one of the substitutes used to enhance octane levels. Subsequently, the fuel content provisions of the 1990 Amendments greatly stimulated its use. See McGarity, MTBE: A Precautionary Tale, 28 Harv. Envtl. L. Rev. 281 (2004).

Even prior to Congress's enactment of CAA reformulated gasoline standards, a version of reformulated gasoline had been developed by ARCO in the 1960s as a substitute for leaded gasoline. Congress thus built on existing industry expertise in writing the clean fuels provisions, although not without some interesting twists. The original legislative proposal of President George H.W.

Bush contained provisions that would have led to the introduction of alternative (nonpetroleum) fuels. The oil companies and oxygenate additive manufacturers opposed these measures and were eventually successful in substituting the current clean fuels provisions for them, although they argued that the clean fuels standards actually adopted were too tough for them to meet. William Rosenberg, then EPA Assistant Administrator for Air, described what happened when Congress called their bluff: "Three days before the conference committee finished its work, representatives of the oil industry said they couldn't make reformulated gasoline to meet the standard. Three days after they finished, Amoco started selling it on Pennsylvania Avenue." Bush Signs Clean Air Act Amendment, Predicts Benefits for All U.S. Citizens, 21 Envtl. Rep. 1387 (1990).

The reformulated gasoline program currently applies to ten metropolitan regions with severe ozone problems—Los Angeles, San Diego, Hartford, New York, Philadelphia, Chicago, Baltimore, Houston, Milwaukee, and Sacramento—although other areas can and have opted in to the program if they wish to employ reformulated gasoline as a means for improving air quality. This program has had beneficial effects, because reformulated gasoline reduces hydrocarbon emissions by 15 percent and, as an added bonus, reduces toxic emissions by roughly the same amount. Mobil Oil, which had opposed the program as too costly, now declares: "In retrospect, we were wrong. Air quality is improving, at a cost acceptable to the motoring public." Mobil Corporation advertisement, Oct. 27, 1994.

Reformulating gasoline is a strategy limited by the demands of the engine and the original content of crude oil. EPA continues to study alternative fuels and has been involved in a number of pilot or study projects involving propane, methanol, ethanol, and other alternatives. Each fuel has its advantages and disadvantages. Compressed natural gas (CNG), for example, results in substantially less carbon monoxide but slightly more nitrogen oxide. Concern about global warming may favor certain fuels more than others: reformulated gasoline results in a slight increase in emissions of carbon dioxide, a greenhouse gas, while CNG and ethanol can reduce carbon dioxide. Figure 5.10 summarizes the significant characteristics of the major alternative fuels currently being studied.

3.   Alternative Vehicles

Shortly before the 1990 Amendments were enacted, California exercised its unique ability to promulgate its own emissions standards to institute a program that took technology forcing a step beyond anything the federal government had attempted. California's initial Zero Emissions Vehicle (ZEV) standards required each manufacturer's vehicle fleet sold in California to meet an overall fleet average for emissions, which declined each year to the year 2003, with a certain percentage of the fleet required to be zero emissions vehicles, an objective that could be met only by non-fossil-fuel-driven vehicles (e.g., battery-electric card or hydrogen fuel cell vehicles). Part of the ZEV mandate could be met by sale of autos that were close to zero emissions; the standards established various categories of automobiles that come close to being ZEV, such as low emission vehicles, ultra low emission vehicles, and partial zero emission vehicles (LEV, ULEV and PZEV, respectively).

Manufacturers never succeeded in producing marketable ZEVs, and as the deadline for doing so approached, California's Air Resources Board (CARB)

FIGURE 5.10
Comparison of Alternative Fuels

Fuel	Advantages	Disadvantages
Electricity	–Potential for zero vehicle emissions –Power plant emissions easier to control –Can recharge at night when power demand is low	–Current technology is limited –Higher vehicle cost; lower vehicle range, performance –Less convenient refueling
Ethanol	–Excellent automotive fuel –Very low emissions of ozone-forming hydrocarbons and toxics –Made from renewable sources –Can be domestically produced	–High fuel cost –Somewhat lower vehicle range
Methanol	–Excellent automotive fuel –Very low emissions of ozone-forming hydrocarbons and toxics –Can be made from a variety of feedstocks, including renewables	–Fuel could initially be imported –Somewhat lower vehicle range
Natural gas (methane)	–Very low emissions of ozone-forming hydrocarbons, toxics, and carbon monoxide –Can be made from a variety of feedstocks, including renewables –Excellent fuel, especially for fleet vehicles	–Higher vehicle cost –Lower vehicle range –Less convenient refueling
Propane	–Cheaper than gasoline today –Most widely available clean fuel today –Somewhat lower emissions of ozone-forming hydrocarbons and toxics –Excellent fuel, especially for fleet vehicles	–Cost will rise with demand –Limited supply –No energy security or trade balance benefits
Reformulated gasoline	–Can be used in all cars without changing vehicles or fuel distribution system –Somewhat lower emissions of ozone-forming hydrocarbons, nitrogen oxides, and toxics	–Somewhat higher fuel cost –Few energy security or trade balance benefits

Source: U.S. EPA (last modified July 20, 1998). *http://www.epa.gov/otag/consumer/06-clean.pdf*

extended the deadlines several times. The current version of the program was introduced in 2003, partially as the result of litigation filed by the auto manufacturers. They argued that because the only way to comply with California's standards for near ZEV vehicles was to market cars with very high fuel efficiency, these emissions standards amounted to fuel efficiency standards and as such were preempted by The Energy Policy and Conservation Act of 1975, which authorizes the National Highway Traffic Safety Administration to set fuel efficiency standards, and preempts state standards. The manufacturers prevailed in district court, and before the Ninth Circuit could decide the case, the CARB and the manufacturers reached a settlement that produced the 2003 regulations. The 2003 regulations once again set ZEV goals, but also establish an "alternative compliance path" that manufacturers can meet by selling hybrid electric vehicles (HEVs) if they meet certain technological requirements.

While they have not yet succeeded in stimulating a commercially viable ZEV, the California standards have been technology forcing. CARB claims that the ZEV regulation "spurred advances in natural gas and other alternative fueled vehicles, super-clean gasoline vehicles, fuel efficient hybrids that are powered by a combination of electric motors and internal combustion engines, and fuel cell vehicles powered by electricity created from pollution-free hydrogen. We are seeing large numbers of PZEVs on the road and expect many more PZEVs and AT PZEVs [HEVs that satisfy certain advanced technology standards] in the years to come." CARB, 2003 Zero Emission Vehicle Program Changes Fact Sheet (March 18, 2004), available at *http://www.arb.ca. gov/msprog/zevprog/factsheets/2003zevchanges.pdf.*

California's program has had repercussions well beyond the state's borders. As the remaining options available to other states to meet the ozone NAAQS have been dwindling, the OTC states, which have significant ozone problems, began to adopt California's standards, exercising a choice that the CAA gave them, even as it was preempting their ability to enact their own unique standards. That election withstood judicial standards by manufacturers, but only if the standards adopted by other states were identical to current California standards. This meant that each time California revises its standards, other states have only two choices—revise their standards to match California's, or revert to the federal standards. Association of International Automobile Mfrs. v. Massachusetts Dept. of Envtl. Protection, 208 F.3d 1 (1st Cir. 2000).

Concerned particularly about the ZEV sales quota in the California program, auto manufacturers worked with EPA to construct a voluntary national LEV (NLEV) program that would lower emissions levels from the federal baseline. In 1997, EPA announced the framework for the NLEV program that would permit states to elect to participate in that program voluntarily, although under terms that were legally enforceable once states opted in. 62 Fed. Reg. 31,192 (1997).

NOTES AND QUESTIONS

1. Cars designed to meet California's LEV standard are somewhat more expensive to purchase, though cost estimates vary substantially, ranging from $100 to $1,200 per car. In light of the increased cost of vehicles under the LEV standard, why would the OTC states want to adopt it? Had the OTC states not acted in concert, how likely is it that any individual state would have opted for the California standards? Given their opposition to tighter emissions controls, why would the automobile manufacturers offer to produce a 49-state car that provides emissions reductions equivalent to the LEV standard?

2. Why mandate a sales quota for *zero* emission vehicles, as opposed to simply mandating more rapid adoption of very low emission levels? Why might different interest groups support or oppose ZEV requirements? Consider environmentalists, federal regulators, the oil industry, and electric utilities. Is California's interest in electric vehicles likely to be unique? Should it make any difference to policy makers that there may be a promising export market for electric vehicles? See C. Moore & A. Miller, Green Gold (1994). How would this benefit be addressed within the regulatory framework for clean air?

3. In response to the first technology-forcing directive, the 1970 Clean Air Act's call for a 90 percent reduction in emissions per vehicle, auto executives publicly warned that it "could prevent continued production of automobiles" and "do irreparable damage to the American economy." Weisskopf, Auto Pollution Debate Has Ring of the Past, Wash. Post, March 26, 1990, at A1. The industry reacted similarly to the 1975 legislation mandating Corporate Average Fuel Economy standards. Both standards were successfully met, although not without added costs to consumers. Miller, Cleaning the Air While Filling Corporate Coffers, 1990 Annual Survey of American Law 69 (1990). Given the

examples of successful innovation in response to regulation, why isn't this approach used more often? Will agencies have more difficulty defending standards based on technology not already widely used? See Stewart, Regulation, Innovation, and Administrative Law: A Conceptual Framework, 69 Cal. L. Rev. 1259, 1300 (1981). Would more precise legislative language help? See NRDC v. Herrington, 768 F.2d 1355, 1391-1400 (1985) (standards based on "maximum technologically feasible" levels).

4. Does technology forcing make economic sense? Isn't it possible that technology may be developed that isn't worth the cost? See Harrington, Walls & McConnell, Using Economic Incentives to Reduce Auto Pollution, Issues in Science and Technology, Winter 1994-1995, pp. 26-32; R. Crandall et al., Regulating the Automobile (1986) (arguing that the marginal costs of meeting air quality goals greatly exceed the marginal benefits). Liability for automakers who fail to meet the ZEV standard is limited to $5,000 times 2 percent of vehicles sold in California and "credits" may be obtained from other companies. If making a consumer-desirable electric car is as impossible as the auto industry claims, why are they investing millions in attempting to meet the regulations? Wouldn't it make more sense to pay the fines and anticipate repeal of the standards in response to evidence that consumers won't buy electric cars? A variation of this strategy anticipated by some observers is that car companies will subsidize small firms to outfit standard car bodies as electric cars, probably using their smallest and lowest cost models. D. Wallace, Environmental Policy and Industrial Innovation (1995). What risks might be associated with such strategies?

5. According to some accounts, California's ZEV standard surprisingly can be attributed to the dream of Roger Smith, then CEO of General Motors (GM). Smith had taken a personal interest in GM's development of a solar-powered racer in the 1980s and saw its potential as the basis for development of electric cars. GM had some advantage in making components for electric vehicles since its subsidiaries included Hughes, Delco-Remy, and Rockwell. The initial product of this effort was the Impact, an electric car prototype exhibited at the Los Angeles Motor Show with great fanfare early in 1990. The Impact went from 0 to 60 miles per hour faster than a Nissan 300ZX and was described by Popular Science as "possibly the best-handling and performing small car that GM has ever turned out." Sperling, Gearing Up for Electric Cars, Issues in Science and Technology 33, Winter 1994-1995, at 35. After this enthusiastic reception, GM announced in April 1990 that it would make a major additional investment in the Impact. This development bolstered the decision by the California legislature to approve the ZEV regulation in September 1990. However, in the two years that followed, Smith retired, GM announced record losses (over $12 billion in 1991 and 1992), and investment in the Impact program was substantially reduced. Wallace, at 162. In January 1996, the General Motors Corporation announced that it would begin selling an electric car, called the EV1, in selected areas of the West in fall 1996. GM stated that the EV1, a product of the Impact program, would have a range of 70-90 miles between charges and would sell in the mid-$30,000 price range. Fisher, G.M., in a First, Will Market a Car Designed for Electric Power, N.Y. Times, Jan. 5, 1996, at A6. In recent years, GM and other manufacturers have shifted their research interests away from electric battery vehicles and toward hybrids and hydrogen-powered vehicles.

6. President G.W. Bush has advocated the development of new car technologies, including hydrogen vehicles. In his 2003 State of the Union Address,

the President extolled the virtues of hydrogen-powered vehicles, and proposed a $1.2 billion multi-year program to develop them. At that time he said, "A simple chemical reaction between hydrogen and oxygen generates energy, which can be used to power a car—producing only water, not exhaust fumes. With a new national commitment, our scientists and engineers will overcome obstacles to taking these cars from laboratory to showroom—so that the first car driven by a child born today could be powered by hydrogen, and pollution-free. Join me in this important innovation—to make our air significantly cleaner, and our country much less dependent on foreign sources of energy." In 2005, the Congress passed energy legislation that will provide up to $3,400 per vehicle in tax credits to consumers for purchase of fuel efficient, low emissions cars, based on their fuel savings potential.

7. The ZEV program is not the only air quality innovation to come from California. Another way to stimulate the introduction of alternative fuel vehicles into the market is to impose purchasing requirements on different entities who purchase quantities of vehicles, such as school districts, police departments, or private companies. In an effort to improve the air quality situation there, the regional air quality agency responsible for the Los Angeles air basin instituted a set of requirements for the owners of vehicle fleets to purchase "clean fuel" vehicles, meaning vehicles that ran on fuels other than gasoline or diesel (the rules were aimed primarily at reducing the number of diesel-powered vehicles in the air basin, as diesel exhausts contribute significant amounts of toxic as well as criteria pollution), such as natural gas or electricity. The agency, however, did not seek to utilize California's exemption from the CAA provision preempting state emissions standards, because it claimed that the fleet rules were purchasing requirements and not emissions standards. Thus, California did not apply for a waiver for the Los Angeles rules, as the statute requires if California seeks to adopt a standard different from the federal. Auto and engine manufacturers challenged the fleet rules claiming that they were preempted by the Clean Air Act. The challenge reached the Supreme Court, which rendered the following decision.

	Engine Manufacturers Association v.	
	South Coast Air Quality Management District	
	541 U.S. 246 (2004)	

JUSTICE SCALIA delivered the opinion of the Court. . . .

I

The [South Coast Air Quality Management District, or District] is responsible under state law for developing and implementing a "comprehensive basin wide air quality management plan" to reduce emission levels and thereby achieve and maintain "state and federal ambient air quality standards." Between June and October 2000, the District adopted six Fleet Rules. The Rules govern operators of fleets of street sweepers (Rule 1186.1), of passenger cars, light-duty trucks, and medium-duty vehicles (Rule 1191), of public transit vehicles and urban buses (Rule 1192), of solid waste collection vehicles (Rule 1193), of airport passenger transportation vehicles, including shuttles and taxicabs picking up airline passengers (Rule 1194), and of heavy-duty on-road vehicles (Rule 1196). All six Rules apply to public operators; three apply to private operators as well (Rules 1186.1, 1193, and 1194).

The Fleet Rules contain detailed prescriptions regarding the types of vehicles that fleet operators must purchase or lease when adding or replacing fleet vehicles. Four of the Rules (1186.1, 1192, 1193, and 1196) require the purchase or lease of "alternative-fuel vehicles," and the other two (1191 and 1194) require the purchase or lease of either "alternative-fueled vehicles" or vehicles that meet certain emission specifications established by the California Air Resources Board (CARB).

In August 2000, petitioner Engine Manufacturers Association sued the District and its officials, also respondents, claiming that the Fleet Rules are preempted by §209 of the CAA, which prohibits the adoption or attempted enforcement of any state or local "standard relating to the control of emissions from new motor vehicles or new motor vehicle engines." 42 U.S.C. §7543(a). [The District Court upheld the fleet rules, reasoning that] "where a state regulation does not compel manufacturers to meet a new emissions limit, but rather affects the purchase of vehicles, as the Fleet Rules do, that regulation is not a standard." The Ninth Circuit affirmed on the reasoning of the District Court.

II

Section 209(a) of the CAA states:

"No State or any political subdivision thereof shall adopt or attempt to enforce any standard relating to the control of emissions from new motor vehicles or new motor vehicle engines subject to this part. No State shall require certification, inspection, or any other approval relating to the control of emissions . . . as condition precedent to the initial retail sale, titling (if any), or registration of such motor vehicle, motor vehicle engine, or equipment." 42 U.S.C. §7543(a).

The District Court's determination that this express preemption provision did not invalidate the Fleet Rules hinged on its interpretation of the word "standard" to include only regulations that compel manufacturers to meet specified emission limits. This interpretation of "standard" in turn caused the court to draw a distinction between purchase restrictions (not pre-empted) and sale restrictions (pre-empted). Neither the manufacturer-specific interpretation of "standard" nor the resulting distinction between purchase and sale restrictions finds support in the text of §209(a) or the structure of the CAA.

"Statutory construction must begin with the language employed by Congress and the assumption that the ordinary meaning of that language accurately expresses the legislative purpose." *Park 'N Fly, Inc. v. Dollar Park & Fly, Inc.,* 469 U.S. 189, 194 (1985). Today, as in 1967 when §209(a) became law, "standard" is defined as that which "is established by authority, custom, or general consent, as a model or example; criterion; test." Webster's Second New International Dictionary 2455 (1945). The criteria referred to in §209(a) relate to the emission characteristics of a vehicle or engine. To meet them the vehicle or engine must not emit more than a certain amount of a given pollutant, must be equipped with a certain type of pollution-control device, or must have some other design feature related to the control of emissions. This interpretation is consistent with the use of "standard" throughout Title II of the CAA (which governs emissions from moving sources) to denote requirements such as numerical emission levels with which vehicles or engines must comply, *e.g.,* 42 U.S.C. §7521(a)(1)(B)(ii), or emission-control technology with which they must be equipped, *e.g.,* §7521(a)(6).

Respondents, like the courts below, engraft onto this meaning of "standard" a limiting component, defining it as only "[a] *production* mandat[e] that require[s] *manufacturers* to ensure that the vehicles they produce have particular emissions characteristics, whether individually or in the aggregate." This confuses standards with the means of enforcing standards. Manufacturers (or purchasers) can be made responsible for ensuring that vehicles *comply* with emission standards, but the standards themselves are separate from those enforcement techniques. While standards target vehicles or engines, standard-enforcement efforts that are proscribed by §209 can be directed to manufacturers or purchasers.

The distinction between "standards," on the one hand, and methods of standard enforcement, on the other, is borne out in the provisions immediately following §202. These separate provisions enforce the emission criteria—*i.e.*, the §202 standards. Section 203 prohibits manufacturers from selling any new motor vehicle that is not covered by a "certificate of conformity." Section 206 enables manufacturers to obtain such a certificate by demonstrating to the EPA that their vehicles or engines conform to the §202 standards. Sections 204 and 205 subject manufacturers, dealers, and others who violate the CAA to fines imposed in civil or administrative enforcement actions. By defining "standard" as a "production mandate directed toward manufacturers," respondents lump together §202 and these other distinct statutory provisions, acknowledging a standard to be such only when it is combined with a mandate that prevents manufacturers from selling non-complying vehicles. . . .

Respondents contend that their qualified meaning of "standard" is necessary to prevent §209(a) from preempting "far too much" by "encompass[ing] a broad range of state-level clean-air initiatives" such as voluntary incentive programs. But it is hard to see why limitation to mandates on manufacturers is necessary for this purpose; limitation to mandates on manufacturers and purchasers, or to mandates on *anyone,* would have the same salvific effect. We need not resolve application of §209(a) to voluntary incentive programs in this case, since all the Fleet Rules are mandates.

In addition to having no basis in the text of the statute, treating sales restrictions and purchase restrictions differently for preemption purposes would make no sense. The manufacturer's right to sell federally approved vehicles is meaningless in the absence of a purchaser's right to buy them. It is true that the Fleet Rules at issue here cover only certain purchasers and certain federally certified vehicles, and thus do not eliminate all demand for covered vehicles. But if one State or political subdivision may enact such rules, then so may any other; and the end result would undo Congress's carefully calibrated regulatory scheme.

A command, accompanied by sanctions, that certain purchasers may buy only vehicles with particular emission characteristics is as much an "attempt to enforce" a "standard" as a command, accompanied by sanctions, that a certain percentage of a manufacturer's sales volume must consist of such vehicles. We decline to read into §209(a) a purchase/sale distinction that is not to be found in the text of §209(a) or the structure of the CAA. . . .

IV

The courts below held all six of the Fleet Rules to be entirely outside the preemptive reach of §209(a) based on reasoning that does not withstand scrutiny. In light of the principles articulated above, it appears likely that at least certain aspects of the Fleet Rules are pre-empted. For example, the District may have attempted to enforce CARB's ULEV, SULEV, and ZEV standards when, in Rule 1194, it required 50% of new passenger-car and medium-duty-vehicle purchases by private airport-shuttle van operators to "meet ULEV, SULEV, or ZEV emission standards" after July 1, 2001, and 100% to meet those standards after July 1, 2002.

It does not necessarily follow, however, that the Fleet Rules are preempted *in toto.* We have not addressed a number of issues that may affect the ultimate disposition of petitioners' suit, including the scope of petitioners' challenge, whether some of the Fleet Rules (or some applications of them) can be characterized as internal state purchase decisions (and, if so, whether a different standard for preemption applies), and whether §209(a) preempts the Fleet Rules even as applied beyond the purchase of new vehicles (*e.g.,* to lease arrangements or to the purchase of used vehicles). These questions were neither passed on below nor presented in the petition for certiorari. They are best addressed in the first instance by the lower courts in light of the principles articulated above.

The judgment is vacated, and the case is remanded for further proceedings consistent with this opinion.

It is so ordered.

[The dissenting opinion of Justice Souter is omitted.]

NOTES AND QUESTIONS

1. The motivating force behind the federal preemption of all emissions standards except California's was to ensure that there would be no "third vehicle" that manufacturers would have to produce if they wanted to sell cars in any American market. This was the rationale behind the decisions in which state adoption of California's standards has been litigated: If states adopted California's ZEV standards precisely, they were not thereby creating a regulatory third vehicle, but if the standards differed they were. See, e.g. Ass'n of International Automobile Mfrs. v. Mass. Dept. of Envtl. Protection, 208 F.3d 1 (1st Cir. 2000). Do SCAQMD's fleet rules create a regulatory "third vehicle"? If not, why should they be preempted?

2. On remand, the district court decided one of the questions left open by the Supreme Court in favor of SCAQMD. As directed at governmental fleet owners, the fleet rules constituted propriety actions, or decisions by the state regarding how public monies would be spent. As such, they fell within the market participation doctrine with respect to preemption, which requires Congress's intent to preempt such propriety actions to be "clear and manifest" from the statute. Reasoning that the fleet rules as applied to such fleets did not amount to a direction to auto manufacturers to market a third vehicle, that such rules had no discernible effect on private markets, and that enforcing such rules was consistent with the CAA's general approach of encouraging states to take the lead in solving air quality problems, the court ruled that the CAA lacked such clear and manifest expression of congressional desire to preempt such rules. The court declined to resolve the enforceability of the fleet rules as applied to fleets leased by public entities. Engine Mfrs. Ass'n v. So. Coast Air Quality Management Dist., U.S.D.C., E.D. of California, No. CV00-00-54FMC

(BQRX), 2005 WL 1163437 (May 5, 2005). However, in the wake of the court's decision, SCAQMD announced that it was resuming enforcement of its rules as applied to "privately owned fleets under contract to or operated under an exclusive license with public agencies. The affected fleets include school bus, transit bus, street sweeping, airport ground-access and refuse collection fleets owned and operated by private entities under contract or license to public agencies." SCAQMD Advisory, July 25, 2005. See *http://www.aqmd.gov/news1/ 2005/FleetRuleAdvisoryPR.html.*

3. The California Air Resources Board has adopted regulations to control emissions of carbon dioxide and other greenhouse gases from new cars and light trucks beginning with the 2009 model year. These standards are particularly significant because they represent the first effort by a state to regulate emissions of greenhouse gases from motor vehicles, which are a substantial source of such emissions. California is the largest automobile market in the United States and other states may decide to adopt these standards if they survive legal challenges. In December 2004 automobile manufacturers challenged California's regulations in a lawsuit filed in federal court for the Central District of California. Central Valley Chrysler-Jeep, Inc. v. Witherspoon, CIV-F-04-6663-REC-LJO. The plaintiff auto manufacturers argue that the regulations are preempted by federal law because the only practicable way to comply with them is to improve fuel economy which already is regulated by federal standards established by the National Highway Transportation Safety Administration (NHTSA).

4. Transportation Control Plans and Other Measures Directly Affecting Drivers

The final set of strategies for reducing auto-related pollution targets the behavior of Americans. A study conducted by the South Coast Air Quality Management District in the late 1980s showed a rush hour vehicle occupancy rate of 1.13 persons. Oren, How a Mandate Came from Hell: The Makings of the Federal Employee Trip Reduction Program, 28 Envtl. Law 267, 296 (1998). Although this figure may vary somewhat from city to city, it is representative of the fact that a high percentage of automobile use consists of moving a single individual from his or her home to work each day. Increasing the occupancy rate or shifting users to mass transit or van pooling can have appreciable effects on air pollution by reducing vehicle miles traveled.

Authorities who wish to develop transportation control measures theoretically have a number of techniques at their disposal. Among other measures, they can raise the price of gasoline or the price of parking in downtown areas, create high occupancy vehicle lanes, or subsidize mass transit. After being sued for its failure to perform a mandatory duty of writing a FIP for the Los Angeles air basin that would achieve NAAQS compliance by 1975, EPA once announced a FIP that included gasoline rationing among other measures sufficient to reduce automobile use by 80 percent. As Craig Oren reports it, "[that] announcement triggered an adverse public reaction from which, as then-Administrator Lee Thomas said in 1977, '[t]he foundations of EPA are still trembling,'" Id. at 278. In general, measures that impose costs on drivers in an effort to affect automobile use for environmental purposes have met with resistance and opposition. Programs that make other options voluntarily available to drivers, such as high occupancy vehicle lanes, meet with less opposition but have not made significant inroads into the air pollution problem.

The federal government's latest experience with transportation control measures involved provisions in the 1990 Amendments creating an employee trip reduction program, through which major employers were to be responsible for increasing vehicle occupancy or else shifting employees from their private automobiles to van pools and other forms of more environmentally benign transport. §182(d)(1)(B). Before EPA could fully implement the program, it became mired in disputes and controversies. In 1995 Congress rescinded the provisions. House, Senate Approve "Corrections Day" Bill to Make Air Act Employee Commute Plan Optional, 26 Envtl. Rep. 1551 (1995). Accounts of the entire state and federal history with various transportation control measures can be found in Oren, cited above, as well as in McGarity, Regulating Commuters to Clear the Air: Some Difficulties in Implementing a National Program at a Local Level, 27 Pac. L.J. 1521 (1996).

Inspection and maintenance (I/M) programs are not transportation control measures in the sense used here. We discuss them in this section, however, because they share a crucial and politically significant feature with such measures: By requiring car owners to have their vehicles regularly inspected and then requiring them to repair any emission control deficiencies, they directly regulate the behavior of car owners.

The 1990 Amendments require more aggressive I/M programs for areas that are nonattainment for ozone or carbon monoxide. An effective I/M program promises to ensure that cars complying with emissions limits when new will continue to do so over their lifetime, but the real targets of I/M programs are the 10 percent of operating vehicles that account for 50 percent of the pollution from mobile sources. Twenty-two states and the District of Columbia have I/M programs in place, but the 1990 Amendments provide more rigorous requirements than any state currently has in place. Pivotal to these requirements is the use of expensive dynamometer testing of cars (approximately $140,000 per machine) to gain more accurate readings of emissions during acceleration, deceleration, and cruising than can be achieved by the stationary tailpipe sensor systems currently used by those states that have I/M programs in place. Because EPA worried about fraudulent practices associated with state programs in which testing stations also did repairs, its implementing regulations contained a presumption that centralized testing facilities would be employed—meaning that many states would have to construct new testing facilities, and that motorists would be faced with a procedure much less convenient than stopping in at a local gas station or dealership service shop. These provisions were upheld in NRDC v. EPA, 22 F.3d 1125 (D.C. Cir. 1994).

Criticism of the I/M program began almost as soon as the 1990 Amendments were passed, and increased as EPA was tardy in promulgating implementing regulations. In several states that implemented programs using EPA's preferred dynamometer machinery, motorists encountered long lines at testing stations and erroneous readings. Because testing stations cannot repair vehicles, and repair shops cannot provide official certifications, noncomplying vehicles have been "ping-ponged" back and forth from testing station to repair shop. Hostility to the I/M program grew so strong in Maine that the state has discontinued it, with the governor proposing alternative programs of reformulated gasoline use, vapor recovery at gas pumps, and other pollution controls to achieve the gains that the I/M program was supposed to achieve. Other states have either refrained from implementing the I/M program altogether, or have crafted programs that do not completely comply with EPA's regulations. EPA is seeking ways to make its requirements more flexible in an effort to meet state concerns.

NOTES AND QUESTIONS

1. The rationale behind the more stringent I/M requirements in the 1990 Clean Air Act was the recognition that, with increasingly stringent controls on new cars, an increasing proportion of auto emissions would come from older cars. Moreover, any requirements that increase the cost of new cars will encourage longer retention of old ones. The result is that roughly half of all CO emissions are estimated to come from only 8 percent of vehicles. Identifying and removing these "gross polluters" has economic and equity justifications as well as environmental benefits, since removing them may be much less expensive per unit of emission reduction and allowing drivers of those cars to continue their high level of emissions is also unfair. With these seemingly compelling purposes, why have the I/M requirements been so strongly opposed by states? Is it because the requirements apply to every car owner in large urban areas, imposing environmental duties on individuals rather than on corporations? One critic compares the program to "requiring every resident of a crime ridden neighborhood to spend 15 minutes in jail." Henderson, Dirty Driving, Policy Rev. 56, 60 (Spring 1992). If so, what does this mean in terms of future support for achieving air quality goals? Note that with the increasing effectiveness of controls on major stationary sources, an increasing percentage of pollution is from smaller sources.

2. As discussed above, one reason for states' opposition has been EPA's initial insistence on centralized testing facilities to separate testing from repair. To what extent was EPA responding to a congressional directive versus its own judgment of what is necessary for an effective program? See §182(c)(3)(C)(vi) and H.R. Rep. No. 490 at 239. Can you imagine more creative strategies EPA might use to balance the state interest in providing convenience with EPA's need to assure a credible testing system?

3. Economists argue that to be cost-effective, policies for controlling motor vehicle emissions should try to (1) reduce total emissions at the places and times when pollution is most serious; (2) give motorists incentives to reduce pollution; and (3) evaluate progress on the basis of actual emissions rather than modeling estimates. Harrington & Walls, Shifting Gears: New Directions for Cars and Clean Air, Resources, Spring 1994, at 5. How would you evaluate the following options using these criteria: (a) gasoline reformulated to burn more cleanly, (b) improved vehicle I/M programs, (c) mandates to sell alternative-fuel vehicles that use methanol or compressed natural gas, (d) mandates to sell electric cars, (e) programs providing bounties to encourage consumers to scrap old cars, (f) tighter emissions controls on vehicles, (g) an increase in the gasoline tax to discourage driving, and (h) car registration fees that vary, depending upon the vehicle's expected emissions?

=6=

|| *Water Pollution Control* ||

The federal Clean Water Act (CWA) could lay claim to being the most successful environmental program in America. Since its enactment in 1972, industrial discharges to the nation's waters are precipitously down, rates of wetlands loss have slowed and in some regions even reversed, and municipal loadings . . . have dropped by nearly 50 percent while their populations served have doubled. . . .

Yet, we do not have clean water. . . . What has gone wrong, of course, is that unregulated sources have blossomed like algae to consume the gains. . . . Individually small, it is their cumulative impacts that are the problem. . . . Most importantly, they are by nature diffuse, not outfalls from pipes, and therefore long considered to be beyond those regulatory requirements of the Clean Water Act that have led to its success.

Which would end the story, but for the remarkable resurrection of a long-dormant provision of the Clean Water Act, Sec. 303(d), now taking the field and forcing a showdown on the last water quality frontier, nonpoint source pollution.

—Oliver A. Houck*

Water is nature's most precious resource. Most of the water on Earth today was on this planet shortly after its formation several billion years ago, "and it may be about all the planet will ever have." William K. Stevens, Water: Pushing the Limits of an Irreplaceable Resource, 14 Nat. Res. & Envt. 3 (Summer 1999). The vast majority of this water—97.5 percent—is salt water found in the oceans. The 2.5 percent that constitutes the world's freshwater supply is primarily locked in glaciers. Only eight-thousandths of the water on earth is part of the renewable freshwater supply found on land, and it is this resource that, except for oxygen, "is the most vital substance on the planet" for human existence. Id.

Water has been a source of enormous conflict throughout history as humans have competed to trap it, "tap it, rechannel it, transfer it, pollute it, consume it, feed it to livestock, ladle it onto farm fields (by far the biggest single use) and flush it through factories, power plants and toilets." Id. This human activity has significantly altered the planet's water cycle, disrupting freshwater ecosystems. After discussing the changing nature and scope of water pollution problems, this chapter reviews legal authorities for protecting water resources. It then examines controls on discharges from point sources, water-quality-based controls, and wetland protection programs. The chapter concludes by exploring efforts to redirect policy toward a watershed protection approach that seeks to address serious problems caused by pollution from nonpoint sources.

---

*TMDLs IV: The Final Frontier, 29 Envtl. L. Rep. 10469 (Aug. 1999).

A.   WATER POLLUTION PROBLEMS

Although our understanding of water pollution problems is improving significantly, it is surprising how much we don't know. Despite decades of research and regulation, it is still not possible to make a comprehensive assessment of the quality of the nation's waters. When EPA attempted to summarize for Congress the state of the nation's waters in 2000, it found that water quality data were available for only about 19 percent of the nation's river and stream miles, 43 percent of its acres of lakes and ponds, and 36 percent of its estuarine square miles. The agency found that nearly 40 percent of assessed river and stream miles, 46 percent of assessed lake acres, and more than 50 percent of assessed estuarine areas did not meet applicable water quality standards. EPA, 2000 National Water Quality Inventory (2001). It has long been recognized that these data were inadequate to permit an objective, overall assessment of whether the quality of the nation's waters is getting better or worse. While efforts are being made to improve water quality monitoring, some conclusions are possible. Clearly there have been some dramatic improvements in water quality in certain rivers and lakes, though coastal and estuarine waters have been under severe stress. The conclusions of the following summary of the successes and challenges facing efforts to protect water quality in the United States remain valid today.

Browner & Glickman, Clean Water Action Plan: Restoring and Protecting America's Waters
1 (1998)

For the past 25 years, federal, state, territorial, tribal, and local governments have worked with the public and businesses to implement a variety of programs to improve the quality of the nation's water resources, including programs established by the Clean Water Act, the Coastal Zone Management Act, the 1990 and 1996 Farm Bills, and other laws. These efforts have resulted in a dramatic reduction in water pollution and, in many cases, a rebirth of the diverse environmental, recreational, and economic values of many of the nation's most treasured waters. At the same time, serious water pollution problems persist throughout the country. Water pollution today degrades the quality of rivers, lakes, and coastal waters, but also affects quality of life by reducing recreational opportunities, undermining local economic prosperity, and threatening drinking water supplies and public health.

Clean Water Successes

All Americans can be proud of the progress the nation has made toward clean water over the past 25 years:

- In 1972, most estimates were that only 30 to 40 percent of assessed waters met water quality goals such as being safe for fishing and swimming. Today, state monitoring data indicate that between 60 to 70 percent of assessed waters meet state water quality goals.

- Twenty-five years ago, wetland losses were estimated at 460,000 acres each year. Today, wetland losses are estimated to be about one-fourth of that rate.
- Since 1982, soil erosion from cropland has been reduced by more than one-third, saving over a billion tons of soil each year and substantially reducing sediments, nutrients, and other pollutants that reach streams, lakes, and rivers.
- Twenty-five years ago, sewage treatment plants served only 85 million people. Today, the number of people who have access to adequate wastewater treatment facilities has more than doubled, to 173 million people.
- Compliance with national standards for discharges from industrial facilities results in the removal of billions of pounds of pollutants from wastewater each year.

Describing water quality accomplishments purely in terms of statistics, however, does not do them justice and leaves much unsaid. Many Americans can still remember the disastrous condition of many of the nation's waters before the Clean Water Act. A stench rose from Lake Erie. People said the Androscoggin River in Maine was "too thick to paddle and too thin to plow." The Connecticut River was thought of as "the best-landscaped sewer in the country." Oregon's Willamette River was off limits to recreation and the mighty salmon perished. Boston Harbor was called "America's dirtiest harbor." And the Cuyahoga River burned. Today, these waters are well on the way to recovery and form an individual piece of the larger success story of the Clean Water Act. . . .

Foundations of Success

The progress to date in reducing water pollution is largely the result of the aggressive implementation of a wide array of programs created by the 1972 Clean Water Act and other laws. Although some of the most dramatic successes have come from control of discharges from sewage treatment and industrial facilities, all levels of government, the private sector, and concerned citizens have played essential roles in reducing water pollution.

Improving Sewage Treatment

Perhaps the single biggest reason for the dramatic progress in reducing water pollution is the remarkable improvement in the treatment of municipal wastewater. When left untreated, raw sewage, wastewater, and street debris can spill into waterways, degrading water quality, imposing a danger to public health, impairing recreational activities, and limiting commercial fishing and shellfishing.

Federal, state, tribal, and local governments made this success possible by investing close to $100 billion since 1972. But perhaps more important than providing funds, the Clean Water Act provided uniform national treatment standards (i.e., secondary treatment) for all sewage treatment systems across the country. This national commitment to a single sewage treatment goal helped overcome extended debates over treatment levels and forged a partnership among engineering professionals, construction contractors, and government that became the foundation for the successful construction of almost 14,000 municipal sewage treatment facilities.

Controlling Industrial Waste

Progress in improving water quality does not result from sewage treatment alone. Controls over thousands of industrial discharges were imposed at the same time that municipalities were improving sewage treatment facilities nationwide. Today, more than 50 major categories of industry comply with national, minimum standards for the discharge of conventional and toxic pollutants. Compliance with these national standards results in the removal of billions of pounds of conventional pollutants and more than one billion pounds of toxic water pollutants from industrial discharges each year. . . .

Today's Water Quality Challenges

Despite significant progress in reducing water pollution, serious water quality problems persist throughout the country. The bottom line of the assessments described below is that about 1,000 of the over 2,000 watersheds nationally are in need of restoration and protection efforts in order to meet clean water goals.

Too Many Waters Are Impaired

Every two years, states report on the condition of their waters and the EPA provides a summary report of this information to Congress. In 1996, the states found that:

- Of the *rivers and streams* surveyed (19 percent of all stream miles), 36 percent were partially or fully impaired and water quality threatened in an additional 8 percent.
- Of the surveyed *lakes* (40 percent of all lake acres), 39 percent were partially or fully impaired, with water quality threatened in an additional 10 percent.
- Of the *estuaries* surveyed by coastal states (72 percent of all estuarine waters), 38 percent are reported to be partially or fully impaired, with water quality threatened in an additional 4 percent.
- Of the *Great Lakes* shore miles surveyed (94 percent of all shore miles), 97 percent were reported to be partially or fully impaired, with water quality threatened in an additional 1 percent.

Based on water quality monitoring, states and tribes identify water bodies that do not meet or are not expected to meet water quality standards even after implementation of national minimum controls over sewage and industrial discharges. In 1996, states and tribes identified about 15,000 water bodies not meeting water quality goals. . . .

Index of Watershed Indicators—A Watershed View

. . . The *Index of Watershed Indicators* organizes information on 15 indicators of watershed health and uses them to assess the condition and vulnerability to future degradation of the aquatic system in each of the more than 2,000 watersheds in the country. . . . The *Index* suggests that:

- Sixteen percent of the watersheds in the continental United States have good water quality;
- Thirty-six percent have moderate water quality problems;

- Twenty-one percent have serious water quality problems; and
- Twenty-seven percent of the watersheds lack sufficient information to make an overall assessment. In addition, the *Index of Watershed Indicators* reveals that one in 14 of the nation's watersheds are vulnerable to future problems.

Other Perspectives on Water Quality

There are several other important perspectives on the condition of the nation's waters: . . .

- . . . [H]abitat loss, pollution, and over-fishing have reduced populations of coastal fish and other species to historically low levels of abundance and diversity. Rapid population growth and increasing demand for recreation and economic development in many coastal areas have degraded natural resources and have led to declines in both environmental integrity and general productivity.
- Contamination of the nation's waters from atmospheric sources is a pervasive and complex problem. Not only are the sources of toxic contaminants in the air diverse—including fossil fuel combustion, incinerators, mobile sources, and industrial and agricultural activity—but wind currents often carry these substances for long distances before they are deposited. As much as 90 percent of certain toxic pollutants in the Great Lakes has been attributed to airborne deposition. . . .

Polluted Runoff Is the Most Important Source of Water Pollution

Leading causes of water quality impairments reported by states include siltation, nutrients, bacteria, oxygen-depleting substances, metals, habitat alteration, pesticides, and organic toxic chemicals. The majority of this pollution results from polluted runoff. Nationally, agriculture is the most extensive source of water pollution, affecting 70 percent of impaired rivers and streams and 49 percent of impaired lake acres. Other national or regional sources include municipal point sources, hydrologic and habitat modification, urban runoff and storm water, resource extraction, removal of streamside vegetation, and forestry.

Consequences of Water Pollution

Water pollution clearly degrades environmental quality, but it also diminishes recreational and economic opportunities and poses clear threats to public health. There is growing evidence that degradation of rivers, lakes, and coastal waters takes a toll on recreation and the economy.

- In the Gulf of Mexico, a hypoxic zone (an area with low levels of oxygen) threatens the livelihood of fishermen. The area is affected by excess amounts of nutrients from the Mississippi River watershed, which ultimately drains into the Gulf of Mexico.
- Of the nation's 382 million acres of croplands, over 70 million acres suffer erosion rates that threaten long-term productivity. Poor land management and agricultural practices directly affect hundreds of thousands of the nation's surface waters.
- Polluted runoff from urban and agricultural areas adds sediment into waters that carry it downstream and deposit it into harbors or reservoirs.

Federal and non-federal dredging in coastal areas and the disposal of dredged materials costs about $1 billion per year.

Perhaps most important, there is growing recognition that water pollution poses serious threats to public health.

- In certain Maryland and Virginia tributaries to the Chesapeake Bay and in the Neuse River in North Carolina, the microorganism *Pfiesteria* has killed fish and may pose a risk to people. Other harmful algal blooms and biotoxins have also affected the health and taken the lives of people, in addition to harming fish, shellfish, and other wildlife. *Pfiesteria* and harmful algal blooms have been associated with excessive nutrients in water.
- People have become sickened and as many as 100 have died in Milwaukee from ingesting *Cryptosporidium,* a disease-causing microorganism in drinking water.
- In 1996, 2,193 fish consumption advisories were issued in 48 states. Mercury, PCBs, chlordane, dioxin, and DDT were responsible for almost all fish consumption advisories in 1996.
- Coastal states report unhealthy levels of pollution-related bacteria at swimming beaches; there were more than 2,500 beach closings and advisories in 1996. Illnesses caused by these bacteria are of special concern to families with children.
- Polluted runoff and discharges from thousands of abandoned mines cause water quality degradation, diminish recreational uses, threaten drinking water sources, and harm fish and wildlife habitats.

NOTES AND QUESTIONS

1. In what respects do water pollution problems differ from air pollution problems? Which should be easier to control—water pollution or air pollution? Which is more naturally variable in quality—water or air? How should regulatory policy take these differences into account?

2. Figure 6.1 lists some of the principal point and nonpoint sources of water pollution and the types of pollutants they generate. Biochemical oxygen demand (BOD) measures the oxygen-depleting capacity of substances such as organic wastes and chemicals that consume oxygen as they decompose. Human and animal wastes contribute bacteria to water, such as fecal coliform and fecal streptococcus. Nitrogen and phosphorus discharges cause nutrient overenrichment and algae blooms. Siltation and soil erosion block sunlight necessary for the growth of submerged aquatic vegetation. Figure 6.1 is not a comprehensive list of the sources of water quality problems. As noted earlier, atmospheric deposition of pollutants can be a major factor degrading water quality; altered stream flows also affect the health of aquatic ecosystems.

3. A general idea of the leading causes and sources of water pollution is provided by Figures 6.2 and 6.3. Figure 6.2 provides a rough index of the relative contributions of different pollutants to overall water quality problems in rivers and streams. Figure 6.3 shows the different industries and activities responsible for such pollution. As the figures indicate, nonpoint sources now are generating the most serious problems affecting nearly every major watershed, although the

FIGURE 6.1
Pollutants and Their Sources

	BOD	Bacteria	Nutrients	Ammonia	Turbidity	TDS	Acids	Toxics
Point Sources								
Municipal Sewage Treatment Plants	•	•	•	•				•
Industrial Facilities		•						•
Combined Sewer Overflows	•	•	•	•	•	•		•
Nonpoint Sources								
Agricultural Runoff	•	•	•		•	•		•
Urban Runoff	•	•	•		•			•
Construction Runoff			•		•			•
Mining Runoff					•		•	•
Septic Systems	•	•	•					•
Landfills/Spills	•							•
Silviculture Runoff	•		•		•			•

Source: Modified from 1986 305(b) National Report.
Abbreviations: Biological Oxygen Demand, BOD; Total Dissolved Solids, TDS.

precise sources vary from state to state. Nutrient runoff from commercial fertilizers is widely credited with causing a huge "dead zone" in the Gulf of Mexico. "The waters of northern Wisconsin are polluted by dairy farms, in North Carolina by hogs, in Maryland by chickens, in south Florida by sugar, in Wyoming by beef cattle, in Oregon by clearcuts, in Maine by logging roads." Houck, TMDLs IV: The Final Frontier, 29 Envtl. L. Rep. 10469, 10470 (1999).

4. Despite improvements in sewage treatment technology, more than 1,000 cities still use combined sewer overflow (CSO) systems that channel storm water through sewers. Council on Environmental Quality, Environmental Quality: Along the American River 153 (1997). In major storms these systems discharge untreated sewage directly into surface waters. In a report to Congress in 2002, EPA estimated that CSOs result in the untreated discharge of 850 billion gallons of untreated waste annually and that the cost of fully controlling these discharges over the next 20 years would be $140 billion. EPA, Report to Congress on Impacts and Control of Combined Sewer Overflows and Sanitary Sewer Overflows (2002).

5. For an assessment of the effect of the Clean Water Act on water quality see William L. Andreen, Water Quality Today—Has the Clean Water Act Been a Success? 55 Ala. L. Rev. 537 (2004). Professor Andreen writes that the Act "has been remarkably successful in doing what it was designed to do." He notes that the "implementation of technology-based limitations has produced substantial reductions in industrial pollution, and the sums expended on the construction grants program have produced real dividends in terms of water quality." Id.

FIGURE 6.2
Leading Causes of Pollution in U.S. Rivers and Streams*

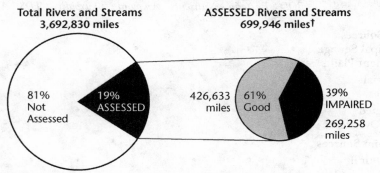

Total Rivers and Streams
3,692,830 miles

ASSESSED Rivers and Streams
699,946 miles†

81% Not Assessed   19% ASSESSED

426,633 miles   61% Good   39% IMPAIRED   269,258 miles

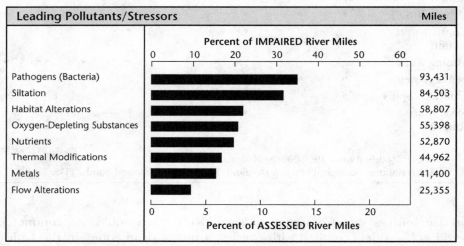

Leading Pollutants/Stressors	Miles

Percent of IMPAIRED River Miles

	Miles
Pathogens (Bacteria)	93,431
Siltation	84,503
Habitat Alterations	58,807
Oxygen-Depleting Substances	55,398
Nutrients	52,870
Thermal Modifications	44,962
Metals	41,400
Flow Alterations	25,355

Percent of ASSESSED River Miles

States assessed 19% of the total miles of rivers and streams for the 2000 report. The larger pie chart on the left illustrates this proportion. The smaller pie chart on the right shows that, for the subset of assessed waters, 61% are rated as good and 39% as impaired. When states identify waters that are impaired, they also describe the sources of pollutants associated with the impairment. The bar chart presents the leading sources and the number of river and stream miles they impact. The percent scales on the upper and lower x-axes of the bar chart provide different perspectives on the magnitude of the impact of these sources. The lower axis compares the miles impacted by the source to the total ASSESSED miles. The upper axis compares the miles impacted by the source to the total IMPAIRED miles.

Based on data contained in Appendix A, Table A-5.

*Excluding unknown and natural sources.

†Includes miles assessed as not attainable.

Note: Percentages do not add up to 100% because more than one pollutant or source may impair a river segment.

Source: U.S. Environmental Protection Agency, Office of Water, *National Water Quality Inventory: 2000 Report to Congress (http://www.epa.gov/305b/2000report/chp2.pdf)*

FIGURE 6.3

Leading Sources of Pollution in U.S. Rivers and Streams

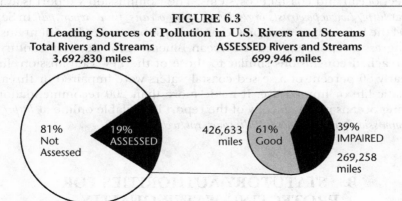

Total Rivers and Streams	ASSESSED Rivers and Streams
3,692,830 miles	699,946 miles

81% Not Assessed   19% ASSESSED

426,633 miles 61% Good   39% IMPAIRED 269,258 miles

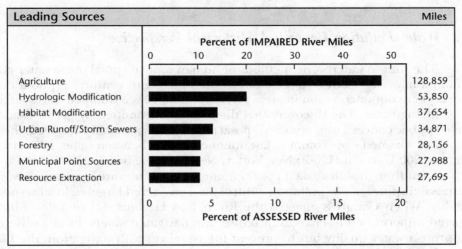

Leading Sources   **Miles**

Percent of IMPAIRED River Miles

Leading Sources	Miles
Agriculture	128,859
Hydrologic Modification	53,850
Habitat Modification	37,654
Urban Runoff/Storm Sewers	34,871
Forestry	28,156
Municipal Point Sources	27,988
Resource Extraction	27,695

Percent of ASSESSED River Miles

Source: U.S. Environmental Protection Agency, Office of Water, *National Water Quality Inventory: 2000 Report to Congress* (http://www.epa.gov/305b/2000report/chp2.pdf)

at 542. Yet significant problems remain. In addition to the problems of pollution from nonpoint sources and the destruction and degradation of wetlands, Andreen notes: "Permit compliance is too inconsistent; too many industrial facilities that discharge toxics to municipal sewer systems fail to meet pretreatment standards; too many municipal systems experience sewer overflows when it rains; too many rivers suffer from altered flows; and most municipal systems are aging and will soon need major renovation."

6. Two major commission reports have focused attention on environmental problems in coastal and ocean waters. In June 2003, the Pew Oceans Commission issued a report, America's Living Oceans: Charting a Course for Sea Change, which concluded that "America's oceans are in crisis and the stakes could not be higher." Among the problems highlighted by the report are coastal development and sprawl destroying wetlands and estuaries, overfishing, nutrient runoff in coastal rivers and bays, and the introduction of invasive species. The Commission, which included a diverse group of American leaders with backgrounds in science, fishing, conservation, government, education, business, and philanthropy, recommended significant legal and policy reforms

to protect ocean and coastal ecosystems. The Commission's report is available online at *http://www.pewtrusts.org/pdf/env_pew_oceans_final_report.pdf*. In September 2004 the U.S. Commission on Ocean Policy submitted to President Bush and the Congress a report entitled An Ocean Blueprint for the 21st Century. The report reached conclusions similar to those of the Pew Commission, finding that nearly 80 percent of assessed coastal waters were impaired or threatened for aquatic life or human use. It made more than 200 recommendations for improving oceans policy. A copy of the report is available online at *http://www. oceancommission.gov/documents/full_color_rpt/welcome.html*.

B.   STATUTORY AUTHORITIES FOR PROTECTING WATER QUALITY

1.   *Water Pollution Control: A Historical Perspective*

The shift to waterborne methods of human waste disposal made water pollution a major concern of large cities in the nineteenth century. Typhoid outbreaks were not uncommon in areas where raw sewage was dumped into sources of drinking water. The discovery that disease was transmitted by germs exacerbated public concern over sewage disposal practices. As noted in Chapter 2, these practices spawned early common law nuisance actions between states. Missouri v. Illinois, 200 U.S. 496 (1906); New York v. New Jersey, 256 U.S. 296 (1921).

Even though states asked the Supreme Court to umpire interstate sewage disposal disputes, water pollution control was considered largely a local responsibility. When Congress enacted the Rivers and Harbors Act of 1899, which barred unpermitted discharges of refuse into navigable waters, its aim was not to protect water quality but to prevent interferences with navigation, the lifeblood of American commerce then. After major U.S. cities began chlorinating their drinking water, typhoid outbreaks were virtually eliminated by 1930. V. Tschinkel, The Rise and Fall of Environmental Expertise, in Technology and the Environment 160 (J. Ausabel & H. Sladovich eds., 1989). Public concern over water pollution shifted to its impact on recreation and aquatic life. See, e.g., New Jersey v. City of New York, 284 U.S. 585 (1931).

After World War II water pollution problems intensified as industrial activity accelerated. Congress initially responded by funding research and by providing federal grants for state water pollution control programs in the Water Quality Act of 1948. Federal funding was expanded in the Federal Water Pollution Control Act of 1956, enacted despite President Eisenhower's opposition to direct federal aid for the construction of municipal sewage treatment facilities.

Like the legislation that preceded enactment of the 1970 Clean Air Act, the Federal Water Pollution Control Act in theory authorized the federal government to act against interstate pollution through a cumbersome procedure of abatement conferences. In the Water Quality Act of 1965, Congress strengthened these provisions by requiring states to adopt water quality standards for interstate waters subject to the approval of a new agency, the Federal Water Pollution Control Administration. If a state did not adopt water quality standards within two years the federal government in theory could intervene and adopt its own standards, after a lengthy and difficult process. States also were required to promulgate state implementation plans, though federal officials could not impose an implementation plan if a state failed to act. As a result, even when water quality standards were adopted, there was no effective mechanism to translate them into workable requirements on individual dischargers, and the federal government had no meaningful enforcement authority. Barry, The Evolution of the Enforcement Provisions of the Federal Water Pollution Control Act: A Study of the Difficulty in Developing Effective Legislation, 86 Mich. L. Rev. 1103 (1970). Thus, it is not surprising that the 1965 Act produced only slow progress. By 1972 only about one-half of the states had water quality standards, and the Senate Committee on Public Works (chaired by Senator Muskie) issued a report concluding that "the Federal water pollution program . . . has been inadequate in every vital aspect."

Despite amendments gradually expanding and strengthening federal authorities, the modern era of comprehensive federal regulation of water pollution was not born until enactment of the Federal Water Pollution Control Act of 1972. An unlikely catalyst for this legislation was the revival of the long-dormant Rivers and Harbors Act of 1899, or, as it came to be known, the Refuse Act. To protect navigation, section 13 of the Act prohibited discharges into navigable waters of the United States of "any refuse matter of any kind or description whatever other than that flowing from streets and sewers and passing therefrom in a liquid state." Exceptions were to be made only with the permission of the Secretary of the Army. The Act had not been considered a pollution control law until two Supreme Court decisions in the 1960s construed the Act to encompass discharges of industrial wastes, whether or not they threatened navigation. United States v. Republic Steel Corp., 362 U.S. 482 (1960); United States v. Standard Oil Co., 384 U.S. 224 (1966).

The discharges at issue in those cases could have been found in virtually any waterway around the country. In 1970 Congressman Henry Reuss of Wisconsin, chairman of the House Subcommittee on Conservation and Natural Resources, saw the Refuse Act's promise as a tool for dramatic action against the growing water pollution problem. His subcommittee issued a report publicizing the Act's *qui tam* provisions, a common law remedy allowing citizens to prosecute crimes and keep half of the fines paid. Reuss cleverly decided to test these provisions by compiling a list of 270 Wisconsin companies discharging wastes without a permit. Suits were brought against four companies, and the Congressman sent his share of the resulting fines back to the state Department of Natural Resources to help fund construction of sewage treatment plants. See Comment, Discharging New Wine into Old Wineskins: The Metamorphosis of the Rivers and Harbors Act of 1899, 33 U. Pitt. L. Rev. 483 (1972). Several hundred suits ultimately were filed under the Refuse Act, though the average fine collected was only about $2,000. R. Zener, The Federal Law of Water Pollution Control, in Federal Environmental Law 785-786 (E. Dolgin & T. Guilbert eds., 1974).

The Refuse Act experience illustrates the capacity of different institutional actors to influence the evolution of environmental policy as issues move between the courts, the executive branch, and the Congress. Congressman Reuss's role illustrates one of the unique features of American environmental law—the fact that one person can make an enormous difference by looking for laws applicable to new problems and by using the courts to demand that they be enforced. His actions helped change the political dynamic by creating an immediate demand among dischargers for some form of permit program to protect them from lawsuits. In December 1970, while legislation was being debated in Congress,

President Nixon by executive order created a permit program to be adminis-tered by the Army Corps of Engineers and EPA. After the administration announced that it would not take enforcement action against any discharger that had applied for a permit, more than 23,000 permit applications were filed. Ironically, the permit program faltered when a court enjoined its operation for failure to comply with the environmental impact statement requirement of the new National Environmental Policy Act (NEPA). Kalur v. Resor, 335 F. Supp. 1 (D.D.C. 1971). Before that decision could be appealed, Congress acted.

2. Statutory Authorities

Spurred by the Refuse Act experience and growing concern over the demon-strated inadequacies of state water pollution controls, Congress in October 1972 adopted the Federal Water Pollution Control Act Amendments (FWPCA), or, as now called, the Clean Water Act. Pub. L. 92-500, 33 U.S.C. §§1251 et seq. The FWPCA was enacted when Congress overrode a veto by President Nixon, who opposed its massive increase in federal funds for sewage treatment. (Nixon's subsequent effort to impound half of the funds authorized resulted in the enact-ment of the Congressional Budget and Impoundment Act of 1974.)

In order "to restore and maintain the chemical, physical, and biological integrity of the Nation's waters," the FWPCA broke new ground in three impor-tant areas. First, it mandated the imposition of technology-based discharge limits that "facilitate enforcement by making it unnecessary to work backward from an overpolluted body of water to determine which point sources are responsible and which must be abated." EPA v. California ex rel. State Water Resources Control Board, 426 U.S. 200, 204 (1976). Second, as a result of experi-ence with the Refuse Act, Congress imposed a nationwide permit system on point source dischargers while retaining the previously required water quality standards. This served "to transform generally applicable effluent limitations and other standards—including those based on water quality—into the obliga-tions (including a timetable for compliance) of the individual discharger." 426 U.S. at 204-205. Finally, Congress substantially expanded the federal role in financing construction of municipal treatment facilities.

The FWPCA, which was renamed the Clean Water Act when amended in 1977, remains the principal federal statute regulating water pollution. As indi-cated in the following text, the Clean Water Act is not the only federal statute that seeks to protect water quality. In 1972 Congress also enacted the Marine Protection, Research, and Sanctuaries Act, known as the Ocean Dumping Act, and the Coastal Zone Management Act.

The Ocean Dumping Act prohibits all dumping of wastes in the ocean except where permits are issued by EPA (for nondredged materials) or by the U.S. Army Corps of Engineers (for dredged materials). Permits are conditioned on a showing that the dumping will not "unreasonably degrade" the environ-ment. A major motivation for the Act was to prevent dischargers from evading the Clean Water Act's permit requirements by simply dumping wastes into the ocean. While EPA's stated policy since 1973 has been to phase out all ocean dumping, Congress eventually had to amend the Ocean Dumping Act to estab-lish deadlines for phasing out dumping of industrial waste and municipal sew-age sludge. After New York City won an extension of the deadline for ending ocean dumping of sewage sludge in City of New York v. EPA, 543 F. Supp. 1084

(S.D.N.Y. 1981), the Act was amended in 1988 to impose escalating disposal fees (increasing over time from $100 to $200 per ton), culminating in a ban on such dumping in 1992.

The Coastal Zone Management Act provides financial assistance to encourage states to adopt federally approved coastal management plans. The Act requires certification that activities affecting land or water use in a coastal zone conform to such plans before federal permits can be issued. Legislation to require *all* states to develop land use control plans had passed the Senate in 1972 but ultimately failed to win adoption despite President Nixon's support for establishing a national land use policy. In 1990, Congress adopted the Oil Pollution Act, see page 124, and strengthened the Coastal Zone Management Act to require states with approved plans to adopt measures to control nonpoint source pollution. By 1991, coastal management programs had been developed for 29 states and territories, covering nearly 95 percent of the U.S. coastline and the shores of the Great Lakes. GEQ, Environmental Quality—22nd Annual Report 38 (1992).

In addition to the statutes, discussed above, the Safe Drinking Water Act regulates the quality of drinking water supplied by public water systems. RCRA and CERCLA have considerable relevance for groundwater protection and remediation, as discussed in Chapter 4. Many states also have adopted their own groundwater protection legislation. This chapter focuses primarily on the regulatory programs established under the federal Clean Water Act to control pollution of surface waters and to encourage states to develop programs to address nonpoint sources.

PRINCIPAL FEDERAL LAWS ADDRESSING WATER POLLUTION

The Clean Water Act prohibits all unpermitted discharges into the waters of the United States (including the territorial sea) of pollutants from point sources, imposes effluent limitations on dischargers, and requires statewide planning for control of pollution from nonpoint sources.

The Ocean Dumping Act prohibits in the area seaward of the inner boundary of the U.S. territorial sea the transportation of wastes for dumping and the dumping of wastes unless a permit has been obtained. EPA is responsible for issuing permits for all materials except for dredged materials, for which permits must be obtained from the U.S. Army Corps of Engineers.

The Oil Pollution Act makes owners of vessels discharging oil liable for costs of cleanup; establishes an Oil Spill Liability Trust Fund to pay response costs; and imposes minimum design standards to prevent spills by vessels operating in U.S. waters.

The Coastal Zone Management Act offers federal financial assistance to states that adopt federally approved coastal management plans and requires federal actions in coastal areas to be consistent with state programs. Amended in 1990 to require states to adopt programs to control nonpoint sources of coastal water pollution.

The Safe Drinking Water Act regulates contaminants in drinking water supplied by public water systems, establishes a permit program regulating the underground injection of hazardous waste, and restricts activities that threaten sole-source aquifers.

---

3.   *The Structure of the Clean Water Act*

The Clean Water Act is the most comprehensive source of federal regulatory authority to control water pollution. To assist you in developing an understanding of the structure of the Clean Water Act, the major provisions of the Act are outlined below. Following a brief description of these provisions, their operation and implementation are discussed in more detail in the sections that follow.

MAJOR PROVISIONS OF THE
CLEAN WATER ACT

§101 Goals. Declares national goals of fishable/swimmable waters by 1983 and the elimination of pollutant discharges into navigable waters by 1985.

§301 Effluent Limitations. Prohibits "the discharge of any pollutant" (defined in §502(12) as the addition of any pollutant to navigable waters from any point source or to the waters of the ocean or contiguous zone from any point source other than a vessel) except those made in compliance with the terms of the Act, including the permit requirements of section 402. Imposes multi-tiered effluent limitations on existing sources whose stringency and timing depends on the nature of the pollutant discharged and whether the outfall is directed to a water body or a publicly owned treatment works (POTW).

§302 Water Quality Related Effluent Limitations. Authorizes the imposition of more stringent effluent limitations when necessary to prevent interference with the attainment or maintenance of desired water quality.

§303 Water Quality Standards & TMDLs. Requires states and tribes to adopt and to review triennially water quality criteria and standards subject to EPA approval, to identify waters where effluent limits are insufficient to achieve such standards, and to establish total maximum daily loads (TMDLs) of pollutants for such waters.

§304 Federal Water Quality Criteria and Guidelines. Requires EPA to adopt water quality criteria and guidelines for effluent limitations, pretreatment programs, and administration of the NPDES permit program.

§306 New Source Performance Standards. Requires EPA to promulgate new source performance standards reflecting best demonstrated control technology.

§307 Toxic and Pretreatment Effluent Standards. Requires dischargers of toxic pollutants to meet effluent limits reflecting the best available technology economically achievable. Requires EPA to

establish pretreatment standards to prevent discharges from interfering with POTWs.

§309 Enforcement Authorities. Authorizes compliance orders and administrative, civil, and criminal penalties for violations of the Act.

§319 Nonpoint Source Management Programs. Requires states and tribes to identify waters that cannot meet water quality standards due to nonpoint sources, identify the activities responsible for the problem, and prepare management plans identifying controls and programs for specific sources.

§401 State Water Quality Certification. Requires applicants for federal licenses or permits that may result in a discharge into navigable water to obtain a certification from the state in which the discharge will occur that it will comply with various provisions of the Act.

§402 NPDES Permit Program. Establishes a national permit program, the national pollution discharge elimination system (NPDES), that may be administered by EPA or by states or Indian tribes under delegated authority from EPA.

§404 Dredge and Fill Operations. Requires a permit from the Army Corps of Engineers for the disposal of dredged or fill material into navigable waters with the concurrence of EPA unless associated with "normal" farming.

§505 Citizen Suits. Authorizes citizen suits against any person who violates an effluent standard or order, or against EPA for failure to perform a nondiscretionary duty.

§509 Judicial Review. Authorizes judicial review of certain EPA rulemaking actions in the U.S. Courts of Appeals.

§518 Indian Tribes. Authorizes EPA to treat Indian tribes as states for purposes of the Act for tribes that have governing bodies carrying out substantial governmental duties and powers.

The Clean Water Act adopts breathtakingly ambitious goals in section 101(a) ("that the discharge of pollutants into the navigable waters be eliminated by 1985," section 101(a)(1), and that fishable/swimmable waters be achieved "wherever attainable" by July 1, 1983, section 101(a)(2)) that suggest a virtually cost-blind determination to control water pollution. While the Act concentrates its regulatory firepower on pollution from point sources, in 1987 Congress added section 101(a)(7), which articulates a new goal of developing and implementing "programs for the control of nonpoint sources of pollution," §101(a)(7).

The construction grants program of the Act, which provided $54 billion in federal funds to build sewage treatment plants between 1972 and 1990, played an important role in federal-state interactions until it was replaced by a revolving loan fund. The program often had produced a tug-of-war between federal and local officials, with the latter seeking to use federal funds to encourage development by extending their sewer systems and the former bent on ensuring that treatment works were constructed at the end of the sewer line.

The heart of the Clean Water Act is section 301's requirement for nationally uniform, technology-based limits on point source discharges administered through a national permit program required by section 402. CEQ explained the rationale for this approach as follows:

> Perhaps the predominant influence on the law was the universal recognition that basing compliance and enforcement efforts on a case-by-case judgment of a particular facility's impacts on ambient water quality is both scientifically and administratively difficult. To minimize the difficulties in relating discharges to ambient water quality, the law requires minimum effluent limitations for each category of discharger, based on technological and economic feasibility, regardless of receiving water requirements. [CEQ, Environmental Quality—1973, at 171 (1973).]

Congress mandated that standards be uniform by industrial category, recognizing that industries varied in their capabilities for reducing pollution. Existing dischargers were to employ "best practicable" control technology (BPT) by 1977 and "best available" technology (BAT) by 1983. New dischargers were required by section 306 to meet BAT-based requirements.

Implementation of these requirements, like implementation of the Clean Air Act, has featured missed deadlines, lawsuits, court orders, and, ultimately, statutory extensions. Congress in 1977 adopted major amendments to the Clean Water Act that extended the deadlines for compliance with the technology-based effluent limitations and that adjusted the requirements for certain dischargers. The BAT deadline was extended to July 1, 1984, for dischargers of toxic pollutants. For dischargers of "conventional pollutants"—BOD, fecal coliform, suspended solids, and pH—BAT requirements were relaxed. Instead of BAT, they were required to achieve "best conventional" technology (BCT) by July 1, 1984, if the incremental benefit of such upgrading exceeded the costs. §304(b)(4). In 1987 these deadlines again were extended because it had taken EPA far longer to establish effluent limitations than anticipated.

The 1972 Act required POTWs to provide secondary treatment by 1977 and advanced treatment by 1983. Congress later extended the secondary treatment deadline to July 1988 and eliminated the advanced treatment requirement. POTWs also were required to obtain permits for sludge disposal. Industrial dischargers into POTWs were required by section 307(b) to obtain pretreatment permits to assure that their waste discharges do not interfere with the treatment process. In 1987 Congress allowed POTWs discharging into "marine waters" to receive a waiver from secondary treatment requirements if there was no interference with water quality standards. §301(h). Effluent limits on point source discharges are discussed in section C, below. A summary of how they have changed over time is presented in Figure 6.4.

The system of ambient water quality standards that Congress had initiated in the 1965 Act was retained primarily to be used as a backup when effluent limitations proved insufficient to protect water quality. States must designate uses for which the water bodies within their jurisdiction are to be protected subject to EPA review of their adequacy to "protect the public health or welfare, enhance the quality of water, and serve the purposes of this Act." §303(c)(2). Permits for point sources must incorporate any more stringent conditions necessary to meet water quality standards, which may be modified for conventional pollutants only if EPA finds the added costs bear no reasonable relationship to the benefits. §302(a). Section 303(d) requires states and tribes to identify waters that do not meet water quality standards and to establish total maximum daily loads (TMDLs) for pollutants that cause violations of such standards. In 1987,

FIGURE 6.4
Technology-Based Effluent Limits and Deadlines for Compliance

Source	1972 Act	1977 Amendments	1987 Amendments
INDUSTRIAL FACILITIES	BPT by 1977 BAT by 1983	For toxics BAT by 1984 or within 3 years For conventional pollutants BCT by 1984	For toxics BAT and for conventional pollutants BCT as soon as possible or within 3 years and no later than 3/31/89
		1981 Amendments	
POTWs	Secondary treatment by 1977 Advanced treatment by 1983	Secondary treatment by 1988 Advanced treatment requirement eliminated	

Congress in section 304(*l*) required states to identify waters impaired by toxic pollutants and to establish individual control strategies for sources of such pollutants. Water quality-based controls are discussed in section D, below.

Nonpoint sources of water pollution are not subject to permit requirements. While section 208 of the Act has long required states to engage in area-wide planning that can encompass measures to control nonpoint source pollution, this program has been ineffective. In 1987 Congress added section 319, which requires states to identify waters impaired by nonpoint source pollution and the sources of such pollution and to prepare management plans for controlling it, subject to EPA approval. See section F, below.

Section 404 establishes a permit requirement for disposal of dredged and fill material into navigable waters. As discussed in section E, this permit program, which is administered jointly by the Army Corps of Engineers and EPA, plays an important role in efforts to protect wetlands.

The National Pollutant Discharge Elimination System (NPDES), created in section 402, is the administrative system for issuance of permits to the thousands of individual point source dischargers. States meeting minimum federal requirements may assume primary responsibility for issuance of permits. In states that decline to do so, EPA is required to administer the permit program. EPA retains oversight authority over state permit decisions as well as independent enforcement authority. The Act provides several enforcement options, including administrative compliance orders, administrative penalties, and civil and criminal fines in government actions taken under section 309. Citizen enforcement suits are authorized by section 505(a). Enforcement problems are discussed in Chapter 10, which compares the Clean Water Act's enforcement authorities with those contained in other federal environmental laws.

NOTES AND QUESTIONS

1. The "zero discharge" and "fishable/swimmable" goals contained in section 101(a) have been widely condemned by economists, who question the logic of even articulating an aspirational standard that appears so expensive and

infeasible. Why would Congress adopt such a seemingly unrealistic goal? One clue may be found in Senator Muskie's statement during the debates prior to enactment that "[w]hat we need to produce the technology required by the bill is a national commitment to what we want to achieve—come up with modern technology, new and changed. . . ."

2. Consider the principal types of pollution control regulations mandated by the Clean Water Act: (1) a general prohibition on point source discharges except as authorized by permits requiring (a) compliance with technology-based effluent limitations or (b) more stringent effluent limitations when necessary to protect the quality of receiving waters, (2) pretreatment requirements for dischargers to POTWs, and (3) permit requirements for dredge and fill operations. Is the range of controls available under the Clean Water Act more extensive or less extensive than that available under the Clean Air Act? Which Act is most likely to force the development of new technology?

3. Economists have been extremely critical of the Clean Water Act's use of nationally uniform effluent standards for classes and categories of industries. They note that a discharge may be insignificant in one water body (e.g., the Mississippi) but catastrophic in another (a small trout stream or a lake that supplies a town's water supply). Consequently, the benefits of control will vary geographically. Moreover, a focus on the technology available to each industry may result in inefficient allocation of costs *among* industries that may have different costs for controlling the same pollution. Pedersen, Turning the Tide on Water Quality, 15 Ecology L.Q. 69, 83 (1988).

You may recall similar concerns in the context of the Clean Air Act. Is the case of uniformity any different in the context of water quality? Cf. Currie, Congress, the Court, and Water Pollution, 1977 Sup. Ct. Rev. 39 (uniformity can lead to overexpenditure but use-based regulation assumes greater knowledge than is practical, is inadequate to allow for growth, does not deal with high concentrations in mixing zones, and does not address aesthetic concerns).

4. A. Myrick Freeman III has estimated that the costs of federal water pollution control policy in 1985 ranged from $25 to $30 billion, while the range of estimated benefits was only $6 to $28 billion. Freeman, Water Pollution Policy, in Public Policies for Environmental Protection 125-126 (P. Portney ed., 1990). While Freeman notes that these estimates probably understate benefits (by excluding the benefits of controls on toxic effluents) and overestimate costs (because engineering estimates fail to reflect cost-reducing technological innovation), he deems it likely that costs outweigh benefits in the aggregate. Freeman argues that the Clean Water Act's current approach should be replaced with "the principle that pollution control policies should be designed to maximize the net benefits from pollution control activities." Id. at 127. Do you agree? Freeman would set water quality standards for each segment of a water body at the point where the "marginal benefits of raising water quality to that point would just equal the marginal cost of doing so," and effluent reduction requirements would vary across dischargers even within the same industrial category. Why do you think Congress eschewed Freeman's approach to pollution control?

5. The distinction between water quality standards and effluent limitations is critical. Water quality standards describe tolerable limits for particular uses (e.g., water suitable for swimming may be limited to no more than 200 fecal coliform bacteria per 100 milliliters). Effluent standards describe an amount of pollution discharged in a time period (e.g., 1 pound of *x* pollutant per day) or more typically a maximum amount per unit of production (e.g., 1 pound of

x per ton of steel). Which type of system is more responsive to considerations of economic efficiency? Which is more responsive to equity concerns?

Water quality standards are roughly comparable to ambient air quality standards. Why was Congress willing to adopt a regulatory scheme for air quality based on ambient standards at almost the same time it was coming to the conclusion that such a system had been a failure in the context of water pollution? Some authorities advocate reconsideration of the water quality standards approach; e.g., Pedersen, above. Based on the Clean Air Act experience, how could such a system be employed effectively?

4.   The Scope of Federal Authority to Regulate Water Pollution

The Clean Water Act prohibits unpermitted discharges of pollutants to "navigable waters." The term "navigable waters" is defined in section 502(7) to mean "the waters of the United States, including the territorial seas." Questions concerning how broadly to interpret "waters of the United States" and the extent of Congress's constitutional authority to regulate certain waters have generated considerable litigation.

One issue concerns whether discharges to groundwater or deep well injection of wastes could be regulated under the Clean Water Act. A few early decisions suggested that the Act could be used to regulate such discharges in order to protect surface waters. For example, in United States v. GAF Corp., 389 F. Supp. 1379, 1383 (S.D. Tex. 1975), a district court suggested that the Clean Water Act could be used to regulate deep well injection if the discharges "flow into or otherwise affect surface waters." See also United States Steel Corp. v. Train, 556 F.2d 822 (7th Cir. 1977). However, Exxon Corp. v. Train, 554 F.2d 1310 (5th Cir. 1977), held that the Clean Water Act did not give EPA authority over deep well injection where the wells are not connected to surface waters. Following this decision, EPA has declined to assert such jurisdiction. See also Village of Oconomowoc Lake v. Dayton Hudson Corp., 24 F.3d 962 (7th Cir. 1994).

Courts remain split. For example, in Quivira Mining Co. v. United States, 765 F.2d 126 (10th Cir. 1985), the Tenth Circuit held that EPA has the power to require NPDES permits for discharges into a remote arroyo because they could reach surface waters through underground aquifers. But in Umatilla Water Quality Protective Ass'n v. Smith Frozen Foods, 962 F. Supp. 1312 (D. Or. 1997), a district court declined to apply the Clean Water Act to discharges to groundwater hydrologically connected to surface waters, noting that EPA had not asserted such authority and Oregon already had a separate permit program for groundwater discharges.

The question of what constitutes the "waters of the United States" for purposes of defining the jurisdictional limits of federal authority under the Clean Water Act is enormously important even apart from the issue of controlling discharges to groundwater. It is estimated that approximately 98 to 99 percent of the nation's water bodies are not waters that would be considered traditionally navigable. The quality of navigable waters is significantly affected by the quality of both their nonnavigable tributaries and of wetlands adjacent to both navigable waters and their nonnavigable tributaries. In the case that follows the U.S. Supreme Court considered whether wetlands adjacent, but not physically connected to, navigable waters were part of the "waters of the

United States," covered by the Clean Water Act's section 404 permit program. Both section 404 and section 402 of the Clean Water Act use "navigable waters" as their touchstone for federal jurisdiction.

United States v. Riverside Bayview Homes, Inc.
474 U.S. 121 (1985)

WHITE, J., delivered the opinion for a unanimous Court.

This case presents the question whether the Clean Water Act, together with certain regulations promulgated under its authority by the Army Corps of Engineers, authorizes the Corps to require landowners to obtain permits from the Corps before discharging fill material into wetlands adjacent to navigable bodies of water and their tributaries.

The relevant provisions of the Clean Water Act originated in the Federal Water Pollution Control Act Amendments of 1972 and have remained essentially unchanged since that time. Under §§301 and 502 of the Act, any discharge of dredged or fill materials into "navigable waters"—defined as the "waters of the United States"—is forbidden unless authorized by a permit issued by the Corps of Engineers pursuant to §404. After initially construing the Act to cover only waters navigable in fact, in 1975 the Corps issued interim final regulations redefining "the waters of the United States" to include not only actually navigable waters but also tributaries of such waters, interstate waters and their tributaries, and nonnavigable intrastate waters whose use or misuse could affect interstate commerce. 40 Fed. Reg. 31320 (1975). More importantly for present purposes, the Corps construed the Act to cover all "freshwater wetlands" that were adjacent to other covered waters. A "freshwater wetland" was defined as an area that is "periodically inundated" and is "normally characterized by the prevalence of vegetation that requires saturated soil conditions for growth and reproduction." 33 C.F.R. §209.120(d)(2)(h) (1976). In 1977 the Corps refined its definition of wetlands by eliminating the reference to periodic inundation and making other minor changes. The 1977 definition reads as follows:

> The term "wetlands" means those areas that are inundated or saturated by surface or ground water at a frequency and duration sufficient to support, and that under normal circumstances do support, a prevalence of vegetation typically adapted for life in saturated soil conditions. Wetlands generally include swamps, marshes, bogs and similar areas. 33 CFR §323.2(c) (1978).

In 1982, the 1977 regulations were replaced by substantively identical regulations that remain in force today. See 33 C.F.R. §323.2 (1985).

Respondent Riverside Bayview Homes, Inc. (hereafter respondent), owns 80 acres of low-lying, marshy land near the shores of Lake St. Clair in Macomb County, Michigan. In 1976, respondent began to place fill materials on its property as part of its preparations for construction of a housing development. The Corps of Engineers, believing that the property was an "adjacent Wetland" under the 1975 regulation defining "waters of the United States," filed suit in the United States District Court for the Eastern District of Michigan, seeking to enjoin respondent from filling the property without the permission of the Corps.

The District Court held that the portion of respondent's property lying below 575.5 feet above sea level was a covered wetland and enjoined respondent from filling it without a permit. Respondent appealed, and the Court of Appeals remanded for consideration of the effect of the intervening 1977 amendments to the regulation. On remand, the District Court again held the property to be a wetland subject to the Corps' permit authority.

Respondent again appealed, and the Sixth Circuit reversed. 729 F.2d 391 (1984). The court construed the Corps' regulations to exclude from the category of adjacent wetlands—and hence from that of "waters of the United States"—wetlands that were not subject to flooding by adjacent navigable waters at a frequency sufficient to support the growth of aquatic vegetation. . . . Under the court's reading of the regulations, respondent's property was not within the Corps' jurisdiction, because its semi-aquatic characteristics were not the result of frequent flooding by the nearby navigable waters. Respondent was therefore free to fill the property without obtaining a permit.

We granted certiorari to consider the proper interpretation of the Corps' regulations defining "waters of the United States" and the scope of the Corps' jurisdiction under the Clean Water Act, both of which were called into question by the Sixth Circuit's ruling. We now reverse.

[The Court rejected the Sixth Circuit's interpretation of the Corps' regulations and held that they do not require frequent flooding by navigable waters. Rather, "saturation by either surface or ground water is sufficient to bring an area within the category of wetlands, provided that the saturation is sufficient to and does support wetland vegetation." This interpretation "plainly bring[s respondent's] property within the category of wetlands as defined by the current regulations."] Hence, it is part of the "waters of the United States" as defined by 33 C.F.R. §323.2 (1985), and if the regulation itself is valid as a construction of the term "waters of the United States" as used in the Clean Water Act, a question which we now address, the property falls within the scope of the Corps' jurisdiction over "navigable waters" under §404 of the Act.

An agency's construction of a statute it is charged with enforcing is entitled to deference if it is reasonable and not in conflict with the expressed intent of Congress. Accordingly, our review is limited to the question whether it is reasonable, in light of the language, policies, and legislative history of the Act for the Corps to exercise jurisdiction over wetlands adjacent to but not regularly flooded by rivers, streams, and other hydrographic features more conventionally identifiable as "waters."

On a purely linguistic level, it may appear unreasonable to classify "lands," wet or otherwise, as "waters." Such a simplistic response, however, does justice neither to the problem faced by the Corps in defining the scope of its authority under §404(a) nor to the realities of the problem of water pollution that the Clean Water Act was intended to combat. In determining the limits of its power to regulate discharges under the Act, the Corps must necessarily choose some point at which water ends and land begins. Our common experience tells us that this is often no easy task: the transition from water to solid ground is not necessarily or even typically an abrupt one. Rather, between open waters and dry land may lie shallows, marshes, mudflats, swamps, bogs—in short, a huge array of areas that are not wholly aquatic but nevertheless fall far short of being dry land. Where on this continuum to find the limit of "waters" is far from obvious.

Faced with such a problem of defining the bounds of its regulatory authority, an agency may appropriately look to the legislative history and underlying policies of its statutory grants of authority. Neither of these sources provides unambiguous guidance for the Corps in this case, but together they do support the reasonableness of the Corps' approach of defining adjacent wetlands as "waters" within the meaning of §404(a). Section 404 originated as part of the Federal Water Pollution Control Act Amendments of 1972, which constituted a comprehensive legislative attempt "to restore and maintain the chemical, physical, and biological integrity of the Nation's waters." CWA §101. This objective incorporated a broad, systemic view of the goal of maintaining and improving water quality: as the House Report on the legislation put it, "the word 'integrity' . . . refers to a condition in which the natural structure and function of ecosystems is [*sic*] maintained." H.R. Rep. No. 92-911, p. 76 (1972). Protection of aquatic ecosystems, Congress recognized, demanded broad federal authority to control pollution, for "[w]ater moves in hydrologic cycles and it is essential that discharge of pollutants be controlled at the source." S. Rep. No. 92-414, p. 77 (1972).

In keeping with these views, Congress chose to define the waters covered by the Act broadly. Although the Act prohibits discharges into "navigable waters," the Act's definition of "navigable waters" as "the waters of the United States" makes it clear that the term "navigable" as used in the Act is of limited import. In adopting this definition of "navigable waters," Congress evidently intended to repudiate limits that had been placed on federal regulation by earlier water pollution control statutes and to exercise its powers under the Commerce Clause to regulate at least some waters that would not be deemed "navigable" under the classical understanding of that term.

Of course, it is one thing to recognize that Congress intended to allow regulation of waters that might not satisfy traditional tests of navigability; it is another to assert that Congress intended to abandon traditional notions of "waters" and include in that term "wetlands" as well. Nonetheless, the evident breadth of congressional concern for protection of water quality and aquatic ecosystems suggests that it is reasonable for the Corps to interpret the term "waters" to encompass wetlands adjacent to waters as more conventionally defined. Following the lead of the Environmental Protection Agency, the Corps has determined that wetlands adjacent to navigable waters do as a general matter play a key role in protecting and enhancing water quality:

> The regulation of activities that cause water pollution cannot rely on . . . artificial lines . . . but must focus on all waters that together form the entire aquatic system. Water moves in hydrologic cycles, and the pollution of this part of the aquatic system, regardless of whether it is above or below an ordinary high water mark, or mean high tide line, will affect the water quality of the other waters within that aquatic system.
>
> For this reason, the landward limit of Federal jurisdiction under Section 404 must include any adjacent wetlands that form the border of or are in reasonable proximity to other waters of the United States, as these wetlands are part of this aquatic system. 42 Fed. Reg. 37128 (1977).

We cannot say that the Corps' conclusion that adjacent wetlands are inseparably bound up with the "waters" of the United States—based as it is on the Corps' and EPA's technical expertise—is unreasonable. In view of the breadth of federal regulatory authority contemplated by the Act itself and the inherent difficulties of defining precise bounds to regulable waters, the Corps' ecological judgment about the relationship between waters and their adjacent wetlands provides an adequate basis for a legal judgment that adjacent wetlands may be defined as waters under the Act.

This holds true even for wetlands that are not the result of flooding or permeation by water having its source in adjacent bodies of open water. The Corps has concluded that wetlands may affect the water quality of adjacent lakes, rivers, and streams even when the waters of those bodies do not actually inundate the wetlands. . . . Again, we cannot say that the Corps' judgment in these matters is unreasonable, and we therefore conclude that a definition of "waters of the United States" encompassing all wetlands adjacent to other bodies of water over which the Corps has jurisdiction is a permissible interpretation of the Act. Because respondent's property is part of a wetland that actually abuts on a navigable waterway, respondent was required to have a permit in this case. . . .

NOTES AND QUESTIONS

1. Acknowledging the difficulty of defining jurisdictional boundaries with precision, the Court in *Riverside Bayview* appeared to endorse a functional approach that interprets the jurisdictional reach of section 404 expansively to promote the goals of the Act. The decision reflects concern that a more restrictive interpretation of regulatory authority could undermine the congressional goal of providing comprehensive protection to water quality.

2. While the federal government has not sought to extend its jurisdiction to groundwater, EPA and the Corps broadly defined "waters of the United States" to include not only waters used in, or susceptible to use in interstate commerce, but also:

(3) All other waters such as intrastate lakes, rivers, streams (including intermittent streams), mudflats, sandflats, wetlands, sloughs, prairie potholes, wet meadows, playa lakes, or natural ponds, the use, degradation or destruction of which could affect interstate or foreign commerce including any such waters:

> (i) Which are or could be used by interstate or foreign travelers for recreational or other purposes; or
> (ii) From which fish or shellfish are or could be taken and sold in interstate or foreign commerce; or
> (iii) Which are or could be used for industrial purposes by industries in interstate commerce. 33 C.F.R. §328.3(a) (Corps), 40 C.F.R. §230.3(s)(3) (EPA).

3. In a preamble to its regulations, the Corps also suggested that "waters of the United States" include waters that could be used as habitat by migratory birds or endangered species or to irrigate crops sold in interstate commerce. In Hoffman Homes, Inc. v. Administrator, EPA, 999 F.2d 256 (7th Cir. 1993), the Seventh Circuit considered whether section 404's reach extended to an isolated, one-acre wetland. Unlike the wetland area in *Riverside Bayview,* the wetland in *Hoffman Homes* was not adjacent to another body of water, but rather was separated from a small creek by 750 feet. EPA argued that Clean Water Act jurisdiction could be premised on the notion that the wetland was a suitable or potential habitat for migratory birds. The Seventh Circuit agreed with EPA that federal jurisdiction could be premised on a potential effect on interstate commerce, but it found that the agency had failed to provide sufficient evidence to support the conclusion that the wetland was a suitable habitat for migratory birds. The court noted that there was no evidence that migratory birds actually used the wetland

and that the area was not shown to have "characteristics whose use by and value to migratory birds is well established . . ." 999 F.2d at 261. Thus, it found that the wetland was not subject to section 404.

4. The Supreme Court's decision in United States v. Lopez, 514 U.S. 549 (1995), raised new questions concerning the jurisdictional reach of the Clean Water Act. In *Lopez*, the Court held that the Commerce Clause did not give Congress the authority to prohibit the possession of firearms in the vicinity of schools because the statute at issue regulated an activity that did not "substantially affect" interstate commerce. Unlike the statute in *Lopez*, which contained "no jurisdictional element which would ensure, through case-by-case inquiry, that the firearm possession in question affects interstate commerce," 514 U.S. at 561, the Clean Water Act extends only to "waters of the United States," 33 U.S.C. §1362(7). However, because *Lopez* now requires that regulated activities *substantially* affect interstate commerce, some activities previously deemed regulable because they had some potential effect on interstate commerce could escape federal jurisdiction if their impact is not considered substantial enough. In Solid Waste Agency of Northern Cook County v. U.S. Army Corps of Engineers (SWANCC) the Court was asked to consider whether Congress has the constitutional authority to regulate isolated wetlands used by migratory birds. The provision of the Army Corps of Engineers' definition of "waters of the United States" that extends section 404 jurisdiction on the basis of the use of waters by migratory birds was challenged in this case. Relying on *Lopez*, the petitioner in *SWANCC* argued that Congress could not require it to obtain a federal permit under section 404(a) of the Clean Water Act before it filled an abandoned sand and gravel pit to create a landfill. The Seventh Circuit had upheld application of section 404(a) to the isolated wetland, finding that because it served as habitat for migratory birds, substantial effects on interstate commerce could be inferred from the millions of hunters and bird watchers who travel interstate in pursuit of birds.

SWANCC involved land that had been used as a sand and gravel pit mine prior to 1960. Subsequently, the excavation trenches became permanent and seasonal ponds, and the entire area was overgrown. The county solid waste agency proposed to convert the site into a landfill. The Corps initially declined to assert section 404 jurisdiction over the site because it believed that the site contained no jurisdictional wetlands. Later, it reversed its position upon learning that the site was visited by over 100 species of migratory birds. After the Seventh Circuit found for the Corps in a challenge to the Corps' jurisdiction, the solid waste agency sought and was granted certiorari in the Supreme Court. In the following 5-4 decision, the Supreme Court reversed.

Solid Waste Agency of Northern Cook County v. U.S. Army Corps of Engineers
531 U.S. 159 (2001)

CHIEF JUSTICE REHNQUIST delivered the opinion of the Court.

. . . Section 404(a) grants the Corps authority to issue permits "for the discharge of dredged or fill material into the navigable waters at specified disposal sites." The term "navigable waters" is defined under the Act as "the waters of the United States, including the territorial seas." §1362(7). The Corps has issued regulations defining the term "waters of the United States" to include "waters such as intrastate lakes, rivers, streams (including intermittent streams), mudflats, sandflats, wetlands, sloughs, prairie potholes, wet meadows, playa lakes, or natural ponds, the use, degradation or destruction of which could affect interstate or foreign commerce. . . ." 33 CFR §328.3(a)(3)(1999).

In 1986, in an attempt to "clarify" the reach of its jurisdiction, the Corps stated that §404(a) extends to intrastate waters:

> a. Which are or would be used as habitat by birds protected by Migratory Bird Treaties; or
> b. Which are or would be used as habitat by other migratory birds which cross state lines; or
> c. Which are or would be used as habitat for endangered species; or
> d. Used to irrigate crops sold in interstate commerce.

51 Fed.Reg. 41217. This last promulgation has been dubbed the "Migratory Bird Rule." . . .

This is not the first time we have been called upon to evaluate the meaning of §404(a). In United States v. Riverside Bayview Homes, Inc., 474 U.S. 121 (1985), we held that the Corps had §404(a) jurisdiction over wetlands that actually abutted on a navigable waterway. In so doing, we noted that the term "navigable" is of "limited import" and that Congress evidenced its intent to "regulate at least some waters that would not be deemed 'navigable' under the classical understanding of that term." But our holding was based in large measure upon Congress' unequivocal acquiescence to, and approval of, the Corps' regulations interpreting the CWA to cover wetlands adjacent to navigable waters. See id. at 135-139. We found that Congress' concern for the protection of water quality and aquatic ecosystems indicated its intent to regulate wetlands "inseparably bound up with the 'waters' of the United States."

It was the significant nexus between the wetlands and "navigable waters" that informed our reading of the CWA in *Riverside Bayview Homes*. Indeed, we did not "express any opinion" on the "question of the authority of the Corps to regulate discharges of fill material into wetlands that are not adjacent to bodies of open water. . . ." In order to rule for respondents here we would have to hold that the jurisdiction of the Corps extends to ponds that are *not* adjacent to open water. But we conclude that the text of the statute will not allow this. . . .

Respondents next contend that whatever its original aim in 1972, Congress charted a new course five years later when it approved the more expansive definition of "navigable waters" found in the Corps' 1977 regulations. In July 1977, the Corps formally adopted 33 CFR §323.2(a)(5)(1978), which defined "waters of the United States" to include "isolated wetlands and lakes, intermittent streams, prairie potholes, and other waters that are not part of a tributary system to interstate waters or to navigable waters of the United States, the degradation or destruction of which could affect interstate commerce." Respondents argue that Congress was aware of this more expansive interpretation during its 1977 amendments to the CWA. Specifically, respondents point to a failed House bill, H.R. 3199, that would have defined "navigable waters" as "all waters which are presently used, or are susceptible to use in their natural condition or by reasonable improvement as a means to transport interstate or foreign commerce." The failure to pass legislation that would have overturned the Corps' 1977 regulations and the extension of jurisdiction in §404(g) to waters "other than" traditional "navigable waters," respondents submit, indicate that Congress recognized and accepted a broad definition of "navigable waters" that includes nonnavigable, isolated, intrastate waters.

Although we have recognized congressional acquiescence to administrative interpretations of a statute in some situations, we have done so with extreme care. . . . A bill can be proposed for any number of reasons, and it can be rejected for just as many others. The relationship between the actions and inactions of the 95th Congress and the intent of the 92d Congress in passing §404(a) is also considerably attenuated. Because "subsequent history is less illuminating than the contemporaneous evidence," *Hagen v. Utah*, 510 U.S. 399, 420 (1994), respondents face a difficult task in overcoming the plain text and import of §404(a).

We conclude that respondents have failed to make the necessary showing that the failure of the 1977 House bill demonstrates Congress' acquiescence to the Corps' regulations or the "Migratory Bird Rule," which, of course, did not first appear until 1986. Although respondents cite some legislative history showing Congress' recognition of the Corps' assertion of jurisdiction over "isolated waters," as we explained in *Riverside Bayview Homes*, "[i]n both Chambers, debate on the proposals to narrow the definition of navigable waters centered largely on the issue of wetlands preservation." Beyond Congress' desire to regulate wetlands adjacent to "navigable waters," respondents point us to no persuasive evidence that the House bill was proposed in response to the Corps' claim of jurisdiction over non-navigable, isolated, intrastate waters or that its failure indicated congressional acquiescence to such jurisdiction. . . .

We thus decline respondents' invitation to take what they see as the next ineluctable step after *Riverside Bayview Homes*, holding that isolated ponds, some only seasonal, wholly located within two Illinois counties, fall under §404(a)'s definition of "navigable waters" because they serve as habitat for migratory birds. As counsel for respondents conceded at oral argument, such a ruling would assume that "the use of the word navigable in the statute . . . does not have any independent significance." We cannot agree that Congress' separate definitional use of the phrase "waters of the United States" constitutes a basis for reading the term "navigable waters" out of the statute. We said in *Riverside Bayview Homes* that the word "navigable" in the statute was of "limited effect" and went on to hold that §404(a) extended to nonnavigable wetlands adjacent to open waters. But it is one thing to give a word limited effect and quite another to give it no effect whatever. The term "navigable" has at least the import of showing us what Congress had in mind as its authority for enacting the CWA: its traditional jurisdiction over waters that were or had been navigable in fact or which could reasonably be so made.

Respondents—relying upon all of the arguments addressed above—contend that, at the very least, it must be said that Congress did not address the precise question of §404(a)'s scope with regard to nonnavigable, isolated, intrastate waters, and that, therefore, we should give deference to the "Migratory Bird Rule." See, e.g., Chevron U.S.A. Inc. v. Natural Resources Defense Council, Inc., 467 U.S. 837 (1984). We find §404(a) to be clear, but even were we to agree with respondents, we would not extend *Chevron* deference here.

Where an administrative interpretation of a statute invokes the outer limits of Congress' power, we expect a clear indication that Congress intended that result. . . .

Twice in the past six years we have reaffirmed the proposition that the grant of authority to Congress under the Commerce Clause, though broad, is not unlimited. See United States v. Morrison, 529 U.S. 598 (2000); United States v. Lopez, 514 U.S. 549 (1995). . . .

These are significant constitutional questions raised by respondents' application of their regulations, and yet we find nothing approaching a clear statement from Congress that it intended §404(a) to reach an abandoned sand and gravel pit such as we have here. Permitting respondents to claim federal jurisdiction over ponds and mudflats falling within the "Migratory Bird Rule" would result in a significant impingement of the States' traditional and primary power over land and water use. Rather than expressing a desire to readjust the federal-state balance in this manner, Congress chose to "recognize, preserve, and protect the primary responsibilities and rights of States . . . to plan the development and use . . . of land and water resources . . ." 33 U.S.C. §1251(b). We thus read the statute as written to avoid the significant constitutional and federalism questions raised by respondents' interpretation, and therefore reject the request for administrative deference.

We hold that 33 CFR §328.3(a)(3)(1999), as clarified and applied to petitioner's balefill site pursuant to the "Migratory Bird Rule," 51 Fed.Reg. 41217 (1986), exceeds the authority granted to respondents under §404(a) of the CWA. The judgment of the Court of Appeals for the Seventh Circuit is therefore
Reversed.

NOTES AND QUESTIONS

1. In a sharp dissent, Justice Stevens, joined by Justices Souter, Ginsburg, and Breyer, argued that the Court had misapprehended the meaning of both the 1972 Act and Congress's 1977 acquiescence in the Corps' more expansive regulations.

2. How did the Court distinguish *Riverside Bayview Homes?* Compare the approach to statutory construction used in *Riverside Bayview* with the approach used in *SWANCC.* Why does the Court find that wetlands adjacent to navigable waters are covered by §404 in *Riverside Bayview,* but that the isolated wetlands in *SWANCC* are not? Does the statutory language make any distinction between these two? The U.S. Army Corps of Engineers argued in its brief that the term "isolated wetlands" is misleading because waters that are remote from and lack a direct connection to navigable waters may have other hydrologic connections to, and affect the quality of, traditional navigable waters, e.g., through groundwater connections and flood and erosion control.

3. Why did the Court reject the Corps' argument for *Chevron* deference to its interpretation of the scope of its authority? Is the Court's use of *Chevron* in *SWANCC* consistent with its treatment in *Riverside Bayview?* See Michael P. Healy, Textualism's Limits on the Administrative State: Of Isolated Waters, Barking Dogs, and *Chevron,* 31 Envtl. L. Rep. 10928 (2001).

4. *SWANCC* was decided by the same 5-4 lineup of Justices that prevailed in *Lopez.* While the Court declined to reach the *Lopez* question by refusing to decide whether Congress had the constitutional authority to regulate isolated wetlands, how did the constitutional question affect the Court's ultimate holding in *SWANCC?*

5. In January 2003 EPA and the Army Corps of Engineers solicited comment on how they should redefine "waters of the United States" in response to *SWANCC.* 68 Fed. Reg. 1991 (2003). The two agencies issued a joint memorandum stating that *SWANCC* "squarely eliminates CWA jurisdiction over isolated waters that are intrastate and non-navigable, where the sole basis for asserting

federal jurisdiction is the actual or potential use of the waters as habitat for migratory birds that cross state lines in their migrations." Despite concern that EPA and the Corps would issue a more restrictive definition of "waters of the United States," the agencies abandoned this effort in December 2003 following a White House meeting where a group of Republican sportsmen persuaded President Bush not to weaken wetlands protections.

6. Most lower courts interpreted *SWANCC* as restricting federal authority only where it turned solely on the potential presence of migratory birds. See United States v. Deaton, 332 F.3d 698 (4th Cir. 2003); United States v. Rapanos, 339 F.3d 447 (6th Cir. 2003); United States v. Gerke, 412 F.3d 804 (7th Cir. 2005); Headwaters, Inc. v. Talent Irrigation Dist., 243 F.3d 526 (9th Cir. 2001); Parker v. Scrap Metal Processors, Inc., 386 F.3d 993 (11th Cir. 2004). But the Fifth Circuit in Rice v. Harken Exploration Co., 250 F.3d 264 (5th Cir. 2001) and In re Needham, 354 F.3d 340 (5th Cir. 2003), concluded that federal jurisdiction extended only to waters that are actually navigable or adjacent to an open body of navigable water. The U.S. Supreme Court agreed to review two Sixth Circuit decisions that upheld federal jurisdiction over wetlands adjacent to non-navigable tributaries of navigable waters. The *Rapanos* case involved review of a civil enforcement judgment, United States v. Rapanos, 376 F.3d 629 (6th Cir. 2004), against a man who had been convicted of criminal violations of §404 for filling wetlands in open defiance of both a state cease-and-desist order and an EPA administrative compliance order. The *Rapanos* case was consolidated with review of Carabell v. U.S. Army Corps of Engineers, 391 F.3d 704 (6th Cir. 2004), which had upheld §404 jurisdiction over wetlands separated by an earthen berm from a non-navigable tributary of navigable waters. On June 19, 2006, a sharply divided Court issued the following decision.

Rapanos v. United States
126 S.Ct. 2208 (2006)

JUSTICE SCALIA announced the judgment of the Court, and delivered an opinion, in which THE CHIEF JUSTICE, JUSTICE THOMAS, and JUSTICE ALITO join.

. . . We first addressed the proper interpretation of 33 U.S.C. §1362(7)'s phrase "the waters of the United States" in United States v. Riverside Bayview Homes, Inc., 474 U.S. 121 (1985). That case concerned a wetland that "was adjacent to a body of navigable water," because "the area characterized by saturated soil conditions and wetland vegetation extended beyond the boundary of respondent's property to . . . a navigable waterway." *Id.* at 131; see also 33 CFR §328.3(b) (2004). Noting that "the transition from water to solid ground is not necessarily or even typically an abrupt one," and that "the Corps must necessarily choose some point at which water ends and land begins," 474 U.S., at 132, we upheld the Corps' interpretation of "the waters of the United States" to include wetlands that "actually abut[ted] on" traditional navigable waters. *Id.* at 135. . . .

In *SWANCC,* we considered the application of the Corps' "Migratory Bird Rule" to "an abandoned sand and gravel pit in northern Illinois." 531 U.S., at 162. Observing that "[i]t was the *significant nexus* between the wetlands and 'navigable waters' that informed our reading of the CWA in *Riverside Bayview*," *id.* at 167 (emphasis added), we held that *Riverside Bayview* did not establish "that the jurisdiction of the Corps extends to ponds that are not adjacent to open water." 531 U.S., at 168 (emphasis deleted). On the contrary, we held that "nonnavigable, isolated, intrastate waters," *id.* at 171—which, unlike the wetlands at issue in *Riverside Bayview,* did not "actually abu[t] on a navigable waterway," 531 U.S. at 167—were not included as "waters of the United States." . . .

The *Rapanos* petitioners contend that the terms "navigable waters" and "waters of the United States" in the Act must be limited to the traditional definition of *The Daniel Ball,* which required that the "waters" be navigable in fact, or susceptible of being rendered so. See 10 Wall., at 563. But this definition cannot be applied wholesale to the CWA. The Act uses the phrase "navigable waters" as a *defined* term, and the definition is simply "the waters of the United States." 33 U.S.C. §1362(7). Moreover, the Act provides, in certain circumstances, for the substitution of state for federal jurisdiction over "navigable waters . . . *other than* those waters which are presently used, or are susceptible to use in their natural condition or by reasonable improvement as a means to transport interstate or foreign commerce . . . including wetlands adjacent thereto." §1344(g)(1) (emphasis added). This provision shows that the Act's term "navigable waters" includes something more than traditional navigable waters. We have twice stated that the meaning of "navigable waters" in the Act is broader than the traditional understanding of that term, *SWANCC,* 531 U.S., at 167; *Riverside Bayview,* 474 U.S., at 133. We have also emphasized, however, that the qualifier "navigable" is not devoid of significance.

We need not decide the precise extent to which the qualifiers "navigable" and "of the United States" restrict the coverage of the Act. Whatever the scope of these qualifiers, the CWA authorizes federal jurisdiction only over "waters." 33 U.S.C. §1362(7). The only natural definition of the term "waters," our prior and subsequent judicial constructions of it, clear evidence from other provisions of the statute, and this Court's canons of construction all confirm that "the waters of the United States" in §1362(7) cannot bear the expansive meaning that the Corps would give it.

The Corps' expansive approach might be arguable if the CWA defined "navigable waters" as "water of the United States." But "the waters of the United States" is something else. The use of the definite article ("the") and the plural number ("waters") show plainly that §1362(7) does not refer to water in general. In this form, "the waters" refers more narrowly to water "[a]s found in streams and bodies forming geographical features such as oceans, rivers, [and] lakes," or "the flowing or moving masses, as of waves or floods, making up such streams or bodies." Webster's New International Dictionary 2882 (2d ed. 1954) (hereinafter Webster's Second). On this definition, "the waters of the United States" include only relatively permanent, standing or flowing bodies of water. The definition refers to water as found in "streams," "oceans," "rivers," "lakes," and "bodies" of water "forming geographical features." *Ibid.* All of these terms connote continuously present, fixed bodies of water, as opposed to ordinarily dry channels through which water occasionally or intermittently flows. Even the least substantial of the definition's terms, namely "streams," connotes a continuous flow of water in a permanent channel—especially when used in company with other terms such as "rivers," "lakes," and "oceans." None of these terms encompasses transitory puddles or ephemeral flows of water.

The restriction of "the waters of the United States" to exclude channels containing merely intermittent or ephemeral flow also accords with the commonsense understanding of the term. In applying the definition to "ephemeral streams," "wet meadows," storm sewers and culverts, "directional sheet flow during storm events," drain tiles, man-made drainage ditches, and dry arroyos in the middle of the desert, the Corps has stretched the term "waters of the United States" beyond parody. The plain language of the statute simply does not authorize this "Land Is Waters" approach to federal jurisdiction.

In addition, the Act's use of the traditional phrase "navigable waters" (the defined term) further confirms that it confers jurisdiction only over relatively *permanent* bodies of water. The Act adopted that traditional term from its pre-decessor statutes. On the traditional understanding, "navigable waters" included only discrete *bodies* of water. For example, in *The Daniel Ball,* we used the terms "waters" and "rivers" interchangeably. 10 Wall., at 563. And in *Appalachian Electric,* we consistently referred to the "navigable waters" as "waterways." Plainly, because such "waters" had to be navigable in fact or sus-ceptible of being rendered so, the term did not include ephemeral flows. As we noted in *SWANCC,* the traditional term "navigable waters"—even though defined as "the waters of the United States"—carries *some* of its original sub-stance: "[I]t is one thing to give a word limited effect and quite another to give it no effect whatever." That limited effect includes, at bare minimum, the ordinary presence of water.

Our subsequent interpretation of the phrase "the waters of the United States" in the CWA likewise confirms this limitation of its scope. In *Riverside Bayview,* we stated that the phrase in the Act referred primarily to "rivers, streams, and other *hydrographic features more conventionally identifiable as 'waters'*" than the wetlands adjacent to such features. 474 U.S., at 131 (emphasis added). We thus echoed the dictionary definition of "waters" as referring to "streams and bodies *forming geographical features* such as oceans, rivers, [and] lakes." Web-ster's Second 2882 (emphasis added). Though we upheld in that case the inclu-sion of wetlands abutting such a "hydrographic featur[e]"—principally due to the difficulty of drawing any clear boundary between the two—nowhere did we suggest that "the waters of the United States" should be expanded to include, in their own right, entities other than "hydrographic features more conventionally identifiable as 'waters.'" Likewise, in both *Riverside Bayview* and *SWANCC,* we repeatedly described the "navigable waters" covered by the Act as "open water" and "open waters." Under no rational interpretation are typically dry channels described as "*open* waters."

Most significant of all, the CWA itself categorizes the channels and con-duits that typically carry intermittent flows of water separately from "navigable waters," by including them in the definition of "'point source.'" The Act defines "'point source'" as "any discernible, confined and discrete conveyance, including but not limited to any pipe, ditch, channel, tunnel, conduit, well, discrete fissure, container, rolling stock, concentrated animal feeding opera-tion, or vessel or other floating craft, from which pollutants are or may be dis-charged." 33 U.S.C. §1362(14). It also defines "'discharge of a pollutant'" as "any addition of any pollutant *to* navigable waters *from* any point source." §1362(12)(A) (emphases added). The definitions thus conceive of "point sources" and "navigable waters" as separate and distinct categories. The defini-tion of "discharge" would make little sense if the two categories were signifi-cantly overlapping. The separate classification of "ditch[es], channel[s], and conduit[s]"—which are terms ordinarily used to describe the watercourses through which *intermittent* waters typically flow—shows that these are, by and large, *not* "waters of the United States."

Moreover, only the foregoing definition of "waters" is consistent with the CWA's stated "policy of Congress to recognize, preserve, and protect the primary responsibilities and rights of the States to prevent, reduce, and eliminate pollution, [and] to plan the development and use (including restoration, preservation, and enhancement) of land and water resources . . . ." §1251(b). . . .

Even if the phrase "the waters of the United States" were ambiguous as applied to intermittent flows, our own canons of construction would establish that the Corps' interpretation of the statute is impermissible. As we noted in *SWANCC*, the Government's expansive interpretation would "result in a significant impingement of the States' traditional and primary power over land and water use." . . .

Likewise, just as we noted in *SWANCC*, the Corps' interpretation stretches the outer limits of Congress's commerce power and raises difficult questions about the ultimate scope of that power. (In developing the current regulations, the Corps consciously sought to extend its authority to the farthest reaches of the commerce power. See 42 Fed.Reg. 37127 (1977).) Even if the term "the waters of the United States" were ambiguous as applied to channels that sometimes host ephemeral flows of water (which it is not), we would expect a clearer statement from Congress to authorize an agency theory of jurisdiction that presses the envelope of constitutional validity.

In sum, on its only plausible interpretation, the phrase "the waters of the United States" includes only those relatively permanent, standing or continuously flowing bodies of water "forming geographic features" that are described in ordinary parlance as "streams[,] . . . oceans, rivers, [and] lakes." See Webster's Second 2882. The phrase does not include channels through which water flows intermittently or ephemerally, or channels that periodically provide drainage for rainfall. The Corps' expansive interpretation of the "the waters of the United States" is thus not "based on a permissible construction of the statute." *Chevron*, 467 U.S., at 843. . . .

When we characterized the holding of *Riverside Bayview* in *SWANCC*, we referred to the close connection between waters and the wetlands that they gradually blend into: "It was the *significant nexus* between the wetlands and 'navigable waters' that informed our reading of the CWA in *Riverside Bayview Homes*." 531 U.S. at 167 (emphasis added). In particular, *SWANCC* rejected the notion that the ecological considerations upon which the Corps relied in *Riverside Bayview*—and upon which the dissent repeatedly relies today—provided an *independent* basis for including entities like "wetlands" (or "ephemeral streams") within the phrase "the waters of the United States." *SWANCC* found such ecological considerations irrelevant to the question whether physically isolated waters come within the Corps' jurisdiction. It thus confirmed that *Riverside Bayview* rested upon the inherent ambiguity in defining where water ends and abutting ("adjacent") wetlands begin, permitting the Corps' reliance on ecological considerations *only to resolve that ambiguity* in favor of treating all abutting wetlands as waters. Isolated ponds were not "waters of the United States" in their own right and presented no boundary-drawing problem that would have justified the invocation of ecological factors to treat them as such.

Therefore, *only* those wetlands with a continuous surface connection to bodies that are "waters of the United States" in their own right, so that there is no clear demarcation between "waters" and wetlands, are "adjacent to" such waters and covered by the Act. Wetlands with only an intermittent, physically remote hydrologic connection to "waters of the United States" do not implicate the boundary-drawing problem of *Riverside Bayview,* and thus lack the necessary connection to covered waters that we described as a "significant nexus" in *SWANCC.* Thus, establishing that wetlands such as those at the Rapanos and Carabell sites are covered by the Act requires two findings: First, that the adjacent channel contains a "wate[r] of the United States," (*i.e.,* a relatively permanent body of water connected to traditional interstate navigable waters); and second, that the wetland has a continuous surface connection with that water, making it difficult to determine where the "water" ends and the "wetland" begins. . . .

Because the Sixth Circuit applied the wrong standard to determine if these wetlands are covered "waters of the United States," and because of the paucity of the record in both of these cases, the lower courts should determine, in the first instance, whether the ditches or drains near each wetland are "waters" in the ordinary sense of containing a relatively permanent flow; and (if they are) whether the wetlands in question are "adjacent" to these "waters" in the sense of possessing a continuous surface connection that creates the boundary-drawing problem we addressed in *Riverside Bayview.*

JUSTICE KENNEDY, concurring in the judgment.

These consolidated cases require the Court to decide whether the term "navigable waters" in the Clean Water Act extends to wetlands that do not contain and are not adjacent to waters that are navigable in fact. In *SWANCC,* the Court held, under the circumstances presented there, that to constitute " 'navigable waters' " under the Act, a water or wetland must possess a "significant nexus" to waters that are or were navigable in fact or that could reasonably be so made. In the instant cases neither the plurality opinion nor the dissent by Justice Stevens chooses to apply this test; and though the Court of Appeals recognized the test's applicability, it did not consider all the factors necessary to determine whether the lands in question had, or did not have, the requisite nexus. In my view the cases ought to be remanded to the Court of Appeals for proper consideration of the nexus requirement . . . .

Riverside Bayview and *SWANCC* establish the framework for the inquiry in the cases now before the Court: Do the Corps' regulations, as applied to the wetlands in *Carabell* and the three wetlands parcels in *Rapanos,* constitute a reasonable interpretation of "navigable waters" as in *Riverside Bayview* or an invalid construction as in *SWANCC?* Taken together these cases establish that in some instances, as exemplified by *Riverside Bayview,* the connection between a nonnavigable water or wetland and a navigable water may be so close, or potentially so close, that the Corps may deem the water or wetland a "navigable water" under the Act. In other instances, as exemplified by *SWANCC,* there may be little or no connection. Absent a significant nexus, jurisdiction under the Act is lacking. Because neither the plurality nor the dissent addresses the nexus requirement, this separate opinion, in my respectful view, is necessary . . . .

[Justice Kennedy then rejects the plurality's interpretation that only waters with a continuous surface connection to standing or continuously flowing waters are covered by §404. He argues that this is contrary to the statutory text and congressional purpose.]

In sum the plurality's opinion is inconsistent with the Act's text, structure, and purpose. As a fallback the plurality suggests that avoidance canons would compel its reading even if the text were unclear. In *SWANCC,* as one reason for rejecting the Corps' assertion of jurisdiction over the isolated ponds at issue there, the Court observed that this "application of [the Corps'] regulations" would raise significant questions of Commerce Clause authority and encroach on traditional state land-use regulation. . . .

The concerns addressed in *SWANCC* do not support the plurality's interpretation of the Act. In *SWANCC,* by interpreting the Act to require a significant nexus with navigable waters, the Court avoided applications—those involving waters without a significant nexus—that appeared likely, as a category, to raise constitutional difficulties and federalism concerns. Here, in contrast, the plurality's interpretation does not fit the avoidance concerns it raises. On the one hand, when a surface-water connection is lacking, the plurality forecloses jurisdiction over wetlands that abut navigable-in-fact waters—even though such navigable waters were traditionally subject to federal authority. On the other hand, by saying the Act covers wetlands (however remote) possessing a surface-water connection with a continuously flowing stream (however small), the plurality's reading would permit applications of the statute as far from traditional federal authority as are the waters it deems beyond the statute's reach. Even assuming, then, that federal regulation of remote wetlands and nonnavigable waterways would raise a difficult Commerce Clause issue notwithstanding those waters' aggregate effects on national water quality, but cf. Wickard v. Filburn, 317 U.S. 111 (1942), the plurality's reading is not responsive to this concern. As for States' "responsibilities and rights," §1251(b), it is noteworthy that 33 States plus the District of Columbia have filed an *amici* brief in this litigation asserting that the Clean Water Act is important to their own water policies. These *amici* note, among other things, that the Act protects downstream States from out-of-state pollution that they cannot themselves regulate . . .

Consistent with *SWANCC* and *Riverside Bayview* and with the need to give the term "navigable" some meaning, the Corps' jurisdiction over wetlands depends upon the existence of a significant nexus between the wetlands in question and navigable waters in the traditional sense. The required nexus must be assessed in terms of the statute's goals and purposes. Congress enacted the law to "restore and maintain the chemical, physical, and biological integrity of the Nation's waters," 33 U.S.C. §1251(a), and it pursued that objective by restricting dumping and filling in "navigable waters," §§1311(a), 1362(12). With respect to wetlands, the rationale for Clean Water Act regulation is, as the Corps has recognized, that wetlands can perform critical functions related to the integrity of other waters—functions such as pollutant trapping, flood control, and runoff storage. 33 CFR §320.4(b)(2). Accordingly, wetlands possess the requisite nexus, and thus come within the statutory phrase "navigable waters," if the wetlands, either alone or in combination with similarly situated lands in the region, significantly affect the chemical, physical, and biological integrity of other covered waters more readily understood as "navigable." When, in contrast, wetlands' effects on water quality are speculative or insubstantial, they fall outside the zone fairly encompassed by the statutory term "navigable waters."

Although the dissent acknowledges that wetlands' ecological functions vis-à-vis other covered waters are the basis for the Corps' regulation of them, it concludes that the ambiguity in the phrase "navigable waters" allows the Corps to construe the statute as reaching all "non-isolated wetlands," just as it construed the Act to reach the wetlands adjacent to navigable-in-fact waters in *Riverside Bayview.* This, though, seems incorrect. The Corps' theory of jurisdiction in these consolidated cases—adjacency to tributaries, however remote and insubstantial—raises concerns that go beyond the holding of *Riverside Bayview,* and so the Corps' assertion of jurisdiction cannot rest on that case.

As applied to wetlands adjacent to navigable-in-fact waters, the Corps' conclusive standard for jurisdiction rests upon a reasonable inference of ecologic interconnection, and the assertion of jurisdiction for those wetlands is sustainable under the Act by showing adjacency alone. That is the holding of *Riverside Bayview*. Furthermore, although the *Riverside Bayview* Court reserved the question of the Corps' authority over "wetlands that are not adjacent to bodies of open water," and in any event addressed no factual situation other than wetlands adjacent to navigable-in-fact waters, it may well be the case that *Riverside Bayview*'s reasoning—supporting jurisdiction without any inquiry beyond adjacency—could apply equally to wetlands adjacent to certain major tributaries. Through regulations or adjudication, the Corps may choose to identify categories of tributaries that, due to their volume of flow (either annually or on average), their proximity to navigable waters, or other relevant considerations, are significant enough that wetlands adjacent to them are likely, in the majority of cases, to perform important functions for an aquatic system incorporating navigable waters.

The Corps' existing standard for tributaries, however, provides no such assurance. As noted earlier, the Corps deems a water a tributary if it feeds into a traditional navigable water (or a tributary thereof) and possesses an ordinary high-water mark, defined as a "line on the shore established by the fluctuations of water and indicated by [certain] physical characteristics," §328.3(e). This standard presumably provides a rough measure of the volume and regularity of flow. Assuming it is subject to reasonably consistent application, it may well provide a reasonable measure of whether specific minor tributaries bear a sufficient nexus with other regulated waters to constitute "navigable waters" under the Act. Yet the breadth of this standard—which seems to leave wide room for regulation of drains, ditches, and streams remote from any navigable-in-fact water and carrying only minor water-volumes towards it—precludes its adoption as the determinative measure of whether adjacent wetlands are likely to play an important role in the integrity of an aquatic system comprising navigable waters as traditionally understood. Indeed, in many cases wetlands adjacent to tributaries covered by this standard might appear little more related to navigable-in-fact waters than were the isolated ponds held to fall beyond the Act's scope in *SWANCC*.

When the Corps seeks to regulate wetlands adjacent to navigable-in-fact waters, it may rely on adjacency to establish its jurisdiction. Absent more specific regulations, however, the Corps must establish a significant nexus on a case-by-case basis when it seeks to regulate wetlands based on adjacency to nonnavigable tributaries. Given the potential overbreadth of the Corps' regulations, this showing is necessary to avoid unreasonable applications of the statute. Where an adequate nexus is established for a particular wetland, it may be permissible, as a matter of administrative convenience or necessity, to presume covered status for other comparable wetlands in the region. That issue, however, is neither raised by these facts nor addressed by any agency regulation that accommodates the nexus requirement outlined here.

This interpretation of the Act does not raise federalism or Commerce Clause concerns sufficient to support a presumption against its adoption. To be sure, the significant nexus requirement may not align perfectly with the traditional extent of federal authority. Yet in most cases regulation of wetlands that are adjacent to tributaries and possess a significant nexus with navigable waters will raise no serious constitutional or federalism difficulty. As explained earlier, moreover, and as exemplified by *SWANCC*, the significant-nexus test itself prevents problematic applications of the statute. The possibility of legitimate Commerce Clause and federalism concerns in some circumstances does not require the adoption of an interpretation that departs in all cases from the Act's text and structure. See Gonzalez v. Raich, 545 U.S. 1 (2005).

In both the consolidated cases before the Court the record contains evidence suggesting the possible existence of a significant nexus according to the principles outlined above. Thus the end result in these cases and many others to be considered by the Corps may be the same as that suggested by the dissent, namely, that the Corps' assertion of jurisdiction is valid. Given, however, that neither the agency nor the reviewing courts properly considered the issue, a remand is appropriate, in my view, for application of the controlling legal standard.

JUSTICE STEVENS, with whom JUSTICE SOUTER, JUSTICE GINSBURG, and JUSTICE BREYER join, dissenting.

. . . The narrow question presented in No. 04-1034 is whether wetlands adjacent to tributaries of traditionally navigable waters are "waters of the United States" subject to the jurisdiction of the Army Corps; the question in No. 04-1384 is whether a manmade berm separating a wetland from the adjacent tributary makes a difference. The broader question is whether regulations that have protected the quality of our waters for decades, that were implicitly approved by Congress, and that have been repeatedly enforced in case after case, must now be revised in light of the creative criticisms voiced by the plurality and Justice Kennedy today. Rejecting more than 30 years of practice by the Army Corps, the plurality disregards the nature of the congressional delegation to the agency and the technical and complex character of the issues at stake. Justice Kennedy similarly fails to defer sufficiently to the Corps, though his approach is far more faithful to our precedents and to principles of statutory interpretation than is the plurality's.

In my view, the proper analysis is straightforward. The Army Corps has determined that wetlands adjacent to tributaries of traditionally navigable waters preserve the quality of our Nation's waters by, among other things, providing habitat for aquatic animals, keeping excessive sediment and toxic pollutants out of adjacent waters, and reducing downstream flooding by absorbing water at times of high flow. The Corps' resulting decision to treat these wetlands as encompassed within the term "waters of the United States" is a quintessential example of the Executive's reasonable interpretation of a statutory provision. See *Chevron*, 467 U.S., at 842-845.

Our unanimous decision in *Riverside Bayview* was faithful to our duty to respect the work product of the Legislative and Executive Branches of our Government. Today's judicial amendment of the Clean Water Act is not.

NOTES AND QUESTIONS

1. Given the 4-1-4 split of the Justices, what is the Court's holding?

2. On remand, what must the government show to satisfy Justice Kennedy's "substantial nexus" test? Can the Corps still rely on the proximity of wetlands it seeks to regulate to tributaries of navigable waters?

3. How do the plurality, Justice Kennedy, and the dissenters each differ in their interpretation of what was decided by the Court in *Riverside Bayview* and *SWANCC*?

4. In a concurring opinion, Chief Justice Roberts expressed regret that because "no opinion commands a majority of the Court . . . [l]ower courts and regulated entities will now have to feel their way on a case-by-case basis." He suggested that this problem "could have been avoided" if the Corps had issued new regulations clarifying §404's reach because such regulations would qualify for *Chevron* deference. Is the Chief Justice suggesting that *Chevron* deference would leave the Corps free to adopt a broader definition of "waters of the United States" than that articulated by Justice Scalia?

5. In other portions of his opinion, Justice Scalia claimed that §404 imposes high costs on landowners and he dismissed ecological concerns about filling wetlands. Justice Kennedy called Scalia's opinion "unduly dismissive" of the "[i]mportant public interests . . . served by the Clean Water Act in general and by the protection of wetlands in particular." Justice Stevens decried the plurality's "antagonism to environmentalism." Responding to Scalia's claim that his dissent is "policy-laden" Stevens observed that "[t]he policy considerations that have influenced my thinking are Congress' rather than my own."

6. Could the plurality's interpretation of "waters of the U.S." affect federal jurisdiction to require NPDES permits under §402? While both §404 and §402 use the same jurisdictional terms, Justice Scalia emphatically rejected the government's argument that it could. He notes that "[t]he Act does not forbid the 'addition of any pollutant *directly* to navigable waters from any point source,' but rather the 'addition of any pollutant *to* navigable waters.'" §1362(12)(A) (emphasis added); §1311(a). Thus, he maintains that "the discharge into intermittent channels of any pollutant *that naturally washes downstream* likely violates §1311(a), even if the pollutants discharged from a point source do not emit 'directly into' covered waters, but pass 'through conveyances' in between."

C.   REGULATION OF DISCHARGES FROM POINT SOURCES

Building on the Refuse Act's simple strategy of requiring a permit for all discharges to navigable waters, section 301(a) of the Clean Water Act flatly declares that "the discharge of any pollutant by any person shall be unlawful," except in compliance with certain sections of the Act, including the permit requirements of section 402 (discharge of pollutants) and section 404 (discharge of dredged or fill material). Permits to discharge pollutants are governed by section 402's national pollution discharge elimination system (NPDES) program and must incorporate effluent limitations—restrictions on the quantities of pollutants that may be discharged—mandated by section 301. Section 404 establishes a separate permit program that allows discharges of dredged or fill material into wetlands at sites designated in the permit. Thus, on its face the Act appears to be both remarkably simple and comprehensive: It prohibits all discharges of water pollutants unless the discharger has a permit that incorporates effluent limitations and it requires separate permits for discharges of dredged or fill material in regulated wetlands.

As with so many other areas of environmental regulation, the definition of "regulatory targets" under the Clean Water Act becomes more complicated the closer one looks. Section 502(12) of the Act defines "discharge of a pollutant" to include "any addition of any pollutant to navigable waters from any point source" or "to the waters of the contiguous zone or the ocean from any point source other than a vessel or other floating craft." This language indicates that the Act's permit requirements do not cover *all* pollutant discharges, but rather only discharges from point sources that involve the addition of a pollutant. Thus what is meant by the "addition of any pollutant . . . from any point source" will have important jurisdictional consequences.

1. Defining the "Addition of Any Pollutant"

As noted above, for a pollutant discharge to be regulated under either section 402 or 404, it must meet the statutory definition of "discharge" which requires that it involve the "addition of any pollutant." Just as some of the most important cases defining "navigable waters" arose in the context of section 404's permit program, so too have many of the cases defining what constitutes a "discharge" for purposes of the Act. Since the late 1970s, the U.S. Army Corps of Engineers had maintained that de minimis discharges associated with normal dredging activities were not covered by section 404. However, in 1993 the Corps adopted a final rule (known as the "Tulloch Rule" after the lawsuit that inspired it) to clarify that excavation activities producing any incidental redeposit of dredged materials, "however temporary or small," require section 404 permits when they would degrade or destroy wetlands. 58 Fed. Reg. 45,008 (1993). In the case that follows the Tulloch Rule was challenged by a trade association that argued that incidental redeposits of dredged materials could not be regulated as "discharges" because they did not result in the net addition of any pollutants to receiving waters.

	National Mining Association v.	
	Army Corps of Engineers	
	145 F.3d 1399 (D.C. Cir. 1998)	

WILLIAMS, Circuit Judge:

Section 404 of the Clean Water Act (the "Act") authorizes the United States Army Corps of Engineers (the "Corps") to issue permits "for the discharge of dredged or fill material into the navigable waters at specified disposal sites." 33 U.S.C. §1344. Section 301(a) of the Act provides that the "discharge of any pollutant by any person" is unlawful unless in compliance with Act's permit requirements, including those of §404. Id. §1311(a). "Discharge," in turn, is defined as "any addition of any pollutant to navigable waters from any point source." Id. §1362(12).

In 1986 the Corps issued a regulation defining the term "discharge of dredged material," as used in §404, to mean "any addition of dredged material into the waters of the United States," but expressly excluding "de minimis, incidental soil movement occurring during normal dredging operations." 51 Fed. Reg. 41,206, 41,232 (Nov. 13, 1986). In 1993, responding to litigation, the Corps issued a new rule removing the de minimis exception and expanding the definition of discharge to cover "any addition of dredged material into, *including any redeposit of dredged material within,* the waters of the United States." 33 CFR

§323.2(d)(1) (emphasis added). Redeposit occurs when material removed from the water is returned to it; when redeposit takes place in substantially the same spot as the initial removal, the parties refer to it as "fallback." In effect the new rule subjects to federal regulation virtually all excavation and dredging performed in wetlands.

The plaintiffs, various trade associations whose members engage in dredging and excavation, mounted a facial challenge to the 1993 regulation, claiming that it exceeded the scope of the Corps' regulatory authority under the Act by regulating fallback. . . .

The 1993 rulemaking under challenge here was prompted by a lawsuit, North Carolina Wildlife Federation v. Tulloch, Civ. No. C90-713-CIV-5-BO (E.D.N.C. 1992), concerning a developer who sought to drain and clear 700 acres of wetlands in North Carolina. See 58 Fed. Reg. at 45,016. Because the developer's efforts involved only minimal incidental releases of soil and other dredged material, the Corps' field office personnel determined that, under the terms of the 1986 regulation, §404's permit requirements did not apply. Environmental groups, concerned by what they viewed as the adverse effects of the developer's activities on the wetland, filed an action seeking enforcement of the §404 permit requirement. As part of the settlement of the Tulloch case (a settlement to which the developer was not a party), the two administering agencies agreed to propose stiffer rules governing the permit requirements for land-clearing and excavation activities. The result—the regulation at issue here—has come to be called the "Tulloch Rule."

As mentioned above, the Tulloch Rule alters the preexisting regulatory framework primarily by removing the de minimis exception and by adding coverage of incidental fallback. Specifically, the rule defines "discharge of dredged material" to include "any addition, *including any redeposit,* of dredged material, including excavated material, into waters of the United States which is incidental to any activity, including mechanized landclearing, ditching, channelization, or other excavation." 33 CFR §323.2(d)(1)(iii) (emphasis added).

The Tulloch Rule does have its own de minimis exception, but it is framed in terms of the Act's overall goals. A permit is not required for "any incidental addition, including redeposit, of dredged material associated with any activity that does not have or would not have the effect of destroying or degrading an area of waters of the United States." 33 CFR §323.2(d)(3)(i). Persons engaging in "mechanized landclearing, ditching, channelization and other excavation activity," however, bear the burden of proving to the Corps that their activities would not have destructive or degrading effects. Id. Degradation is defined as any effect on the waters of the United States that is more than de minimis or inconsequential. Id. §323.2(d)(5). Thus, whereas the 1986 rule exempted de minimis soil movement, the Tulloch Rule covers all discharges, however minuscule, unless the Corps is convinced that the *activities with which they are associated* have only minimal adverse effects. In promulgating the new rule the Corps "emphasized that the threshold of adverse effects for the de minimis exception is a very low one." 56 Fed. Reg. at 45,020.

It is undisputed that by requiring a permit for "*any* redeposit," 33 CFR §323.2(d)(1)(iii) (emphasis added), the Tulloch Rule covers incidental fallback. According to the agencies, incidental fallback occurs, for example, during dredging, "when a bucket used to excavate material from the bottom of a river, stream, or wetland is raised and soils or sediments fall from the bucket back into the water." Agencies' Br. at 13. (There is no indication that the rule would not also reach soils or sediments falling out of the bucket even before it emerged from the water.) Fallback and other redeposits also occur during mechanized landclearing, when bulldozers and loaders scrape or displace wetland soil, see 58 Fed. Reg. 45,017-18, as well as during ditching and channelization, when draglines or backhoes are dragged through soils and sediments. See id. at 45,018. Indeed, fallback is a practically inescapable by-product of all these activities. In the preamble to the Tulloch Rule the Corps noted that "it is virtually impossible to conduct mechanized landclearing, ditching, channelization or excavation in waters of the United States without causing incidental redeposition of dredged material (however small or temporary) in the process." Id. at 45,017. As a result, the Tulloch Rule effectively requires a permit for all those activities, subject to a limited exception for ones that the Corps in its discretion deems to produce no adverse effects on waters of the United States. . . .

The plaintiffs claim that the Tulloch Rule exceeds the Corps' statutory jurisdiction under §404, which, as we have noted, extends only to "discharge," defined as the "addition of any pollutant to navigable waters." 33 U.S.C. §§1344, 1362(12). It argues that fallback, which returns dredged material virtually to the spot from which it came, cannot be said to constitute an addition of anything. Therefore, the plaintiffs contend, the Tulloch Rule conflicts with the statute's unambiguous terms and cannot survive even the deferential scrutiny called for by Chevron U.S.A., Inc. v. NRDC, 467 U.S. 837, 81 L. Ed. 2d 694, 104 S. Ct. 2778 (1984). The "jurisdictional" character of the issue has no effect on the level of deference, Oklahoma Natural Gas Co. v. FERC, 307 U.S. App. D.C. 414, 28 F.3d 1281, 1283-84 (D.C. Cir. 1994), as the plaintiffs seem to acknowledge by their silence on the subject.

The agencies argue that the terms of the Act in fact demonstrate that fallback may be classified as a discharge. The Act defines a discharge as the addition of any pollutant to navigable waters, 33 U.S.C. §1362(12), and defines "pollutant" to include "dredged spoil," as well as "rock," "sand," and "cellar dirt." Id. §1362(6). The Corps in turn defines "dredged material" as "material that is excavated or dredged from waters of the United States," 33 CFR §323.2(c), a definition that is not challenged here. Thus, according to the agencies, wetland soil, sediment, debris, or other material in the waters of the United States undergoes a legal metamorphosis during the dredging process, becoming a "pollutant" for purposes of the Act. If a portion of the material being dredged then falls back into the water, there has been an addition of a pollutant to the waters of the United States. Indeed, according to appellants National Wildlife Federation et al. ("NWF"), who intervened as defendants below, this reasoning demonstrates that regulation of redeposit is actually *required* by the Act.

We agree with the plaintiffs, and with the district court, that the straight-forward statutory term "addition" cannot reasonably be said to encompass the situation in which material is removed from the waters of the United States and a small portion of it happens to fall back. Because incidental fallback represents a net withdrawal, not an addition, of material, it cannot be a discharge. As we concluded recently in a related context, "the nearest evidence we have of definitional intent by Congress reflects, as might be expected, that the word 'discharge' contemplates the addition, not the withdrawal, of a substance or substances." North Carolina v. FERC, 324 U.S. App. D.C. 209, 112 F.3d 1175, 1187 (D.C. Cir. 1997). The agencies' primary counterargument—that fallback constitutes an "addition of any pollutant" because material becomes a pollutant only upon being dredged—is ingenious but unconvincing. Regardless of any legal metamorphosis that may occur at the moment of dredging, we fail to see how there can be an addition of *dredged material* when there is no addition of *material*. Although the Act includes "dredged spoil" in its list of pollutants, 33 U.S.C. §1362(6), Congress could not have contemplated that the attempted removal of 100 tons of that substance could constitute an addition simply because only 99 tons of it were actually taken away.[1] In fact the removal of material from the waters of the United States, as opposed to the discharge of material into those waters, is governed by a completely independent statutory scheme. Section 10 of the Rivers and Harbors Act of 1899, 33 U.S.C. §403, makes it illegal "to excavate or fill" in the navigable waters of the United States without the Corps' approval. As the general counsel of the Army noted in a law review article published a few years after the passage of the Clean Water Act, Congress enacted "two separate statutory frameworks. Section 10 of the 1899 Act covers the act of dredging, while Section 404 [of the Clean Water Act] covers the disposal of the dredged material." Charles D. Ablard and Brian B. O'Neill, Wetland Protection and Section 404 of the Federal Water Pollution Control Act Amendments of 1972: A Corps of Engineers Renaissance, 1 Vt. L. Rev. 51, 93 (1976).

The agencies, though acknowledging that the Tulloch Rule effectively requires a permit for all mechanized landclearing, ditching, channelization or excavation in waters of the United States, see 58 Fed. Reg. at 45,017, locate their permitting requirement under §404, not under the Rivers and Harbors Act's explicit coverage of "excavat[ion]." The explanation for this choice is apparently that the scope of the Corps' geographic jurisdiction is narrower under the Rivers and Harbors Act than under the Clean Water Act, extending only to waters subject to the ebb and flow of the tide, or waters that are used, have been used, or may be susceptible for use to transport interstate or foreign commerce. 33 CFR §329.4; see also id. §328.1 (noting difference between geographic jurisdiction under the two statutes).

There may be an incongruity in Congress' assignment of extraction activities to a statute (the Rivers and Harbors Act) with a narrower jurisdictional sweep than that of the statute covering discharges (the Clean Water Act). This incongruity, of course, could be cured either by narrowing the jurisdictional reach of the Clean Water Act or broadening that of the Rivers and Harbors Act. But we do not think the agencies can do it simply by declaring that incomplete removal constitutes addition.

The agencies also point to some specific exemptions set forth in §404(f) of the Act in support of their view that fallback can reasonably be said to constitute discharge. Congress added the subsection in 1977, apparently in response to the broad construction of "discharge" in the 1977 regulations. It provides that "the discharge of dredged or fill material . . . is not prohibited . . . or otherwise

---

1. The unreasonableness of the agencies' statutory interpretation was illustrated by some of the hypotheticals posed at oral argument. For instance, counsel for the agencies admitted that under their interpretation of the term "discharge" in §301(a), it "might very well" be permissible to require any landowner in the United States wishing to cut down a tree in a wetland to obtain a §402 permit, since 33 U.S.C. §1362(6) defines "pollutant" to include "biological material." Oral Arg. Tr. at 22. Similarly, counsel agreed that the Corps could require a permit to ride a bicycle across a wetland under its interpretation of §404, although bicycle-riding seems—for now—to be exempted under the Tulloch Rule as an activity that does not generally destroy or degrade waters of the United States. Oral Arg. Tr. at 25; see 58 Fed. Reg. at 45,023 (indicating that "walking, grazing, vehicular traffic, and boating" would not generally be regulated).

subject to regulation" under the Act's permitting requirements when the discharge results from any of a number of specifically exempted activities, including "normal farming, silviculture, and ranching activities such as plowing, seeding, cultivating, [or] minor drainage," 33 U.S.C. §1344(f)(1)(A), and "maintenance of drainage ditches," id. §1344(f)(1)(C). After listing these exemptions, §404(f) provides that a permit shall nonetheless be required for any activity "having as its purpose bringing an area of the navigable waters into a use to which it was not previously subject, where the flow or circulation of navigable waters may be impaired or the reach of such waters be reduced." Id. §1344(f)(2).

The agencies claim these exemptions show that as a general matter Congress considered fallback to be covered by §404. They especially note that §404(f)(1) uses the term "*discharge* of dredged or fill material" to describe the consequences of the protected activities, supposedly reflecting a congressional belief that fallback is a form of discharge.

We find the exemptions far less telling. Some of the named activities—plowing, ditch maintenance, and the like—may produce fallback, but they may also produce actual discharges, i.e., additions of pollutants, so that §404(f) accomplishes a useful purpose simply by exempting them insofar as they produce the latter. Some others, such as seeding, seem to us just as unlikely to produce fallback as actual discharge, so we are reluctant to draw any inference other than that Congress emphatically did not want the law to impede these bucolic pursuits.

NWF complains that our understanding of "addition" reads the regulation of dredged material out of the statute. They correctly note that since dredged material comes from the waters of the United States, 33 CFR §323.2(c), any discharge of such material into those waters could technically be described as a "redeposit," at least on a broad construction of that term. The Fifth Circuit made a similar observation fifteen years ago: "'[D]redged' material is by definition material that comes from the water itself. A requirement that all pollutants must come from outside sources would effectively remove the dredge-and-fill provision from the statute." Avoyelles Sportsmen's League v. Marsh, 715 F.2d 897, 924 n.43 (5th Cir. 1983). But we do not hold that the Corps may not legally regulate some forms of redeposit under its §404 permitting authority.[2] We hold only that by asserting jurisdiction over "*any* redeposit," including incidental fallback, the Tulloch Rule outruns the Corps' statutory authority. Since the Act sets out no bright line between incidental fallback on the one hand and regulable redeposits on the other, a reasoned attempt by the agencies to draw such a line would merit considerable deference. Cf. Dubois v. U.S. Dep't of Agriculture, 102 F.3d 1273, 1296-99 (1st Cir. 1996) (although movement of pollutants within the same body of water might not constitute an "addition" for purposes of NPDES permit requirement, movement from one body of water to a separate one with different water quality is an addition). But the Tulloch Rule makes no effort to draw such a line, and indeed its overriding purpose appears to be to expand the Corps' permitting authority to encompass incidental fallback and, as a result, a wide range of activities that cannot remotely be said to "add" anything to the waters of the United States . . .

---

2. Even the plaintiffs concede that under a broad reading of the term "redeposit," "a redeposit could be an addition to [a] new location and thus a discharge." Plaintiffs' Br. at 17.

In a press release accompanying the adoption of the Tulloch Rule, the White House announced: "Congress should amend the Clean Water Act to make it consistent with the agencies' rulemaking." White House Office on Environmental Policy, Protecting America's Wetlands: A Fair, Flexible, and Effective Approach 23 (Aug. 24, 1993). While remarkable in its candor, the announcement contained a kernel of truth. If the agencies and NWF believe that the Clean Water Act inadequately protects wetlands and other natural resources by insisting upon the presence of an "addition" to trigger permit requirements, the appropriate body to turn to is Congress. Without such an amendment, the Act simply will not accommodate the Tulloch Rule. The judgment of the district court is Affirmed.

SILBERMAN, Circuit Judge, concurring:

I join the opinion of the court and write separately only to make explicit what I think implicit in our opinion. We hold that the Corps' interpretation of the phrase "*addition* of any pollutant to navigable waters" to cover incidental fallback is "unreasonable," which is the formulation we use when we have first determined under *Chevron* that neither the statutory language nor legislative history reveals a precise intent with respect to the issue presented—in other words, we are at the second step of the now-familiar *Chevron* Step I and Step II analysis. See, e.g., Whitecliff, Inc. v. Shalala, 20 F.3d 488 (D.C. Cir. 1994); Fedway Associates, Inc. v. United States Treasury, 976 F.2d 1416 (D.C. Cir. 1992); Abbott Labs. v. Young, 920 F.2d 984 (D.C. Cir. 1990); Associated Gas Distribs. v. FERC, 899 F.2d 1250 (D.C. Cir. 1990). As our opinion's discussion of prior cases indicates, the word addition carries both a temporal and geographic ambiguity. If the material that would otherwise fall back were moved some distance away and then dropped, it very well might constitute an "addition." Or if it were held for some time and then dropped back in the same spot, it might also constitute an "addition." But the structure of the relevant statutes indicates that it is unreasonable to call incidental fallback an addition. To do so perforce converts *all* dredging—which is regulated under the Rivers and Harbors Act—into discharge of dredged material which is regulated under the Clean Water Act.

Moreover, that Congress had in mind either a temporal or geographic separation between excavation and disposal is suggested by its requirement that dredged material be discharged at "specified disposal sites," U.S.C. §1344 (1994), a term which simply does not fit incidental fallback.

The Corps attempts to avoid these difficulties by asserting that rock and sand are magically transformed into pollutants once dredged, so *all* dredging necessarily results in an addition of pollutants to navigable waters. But rock and sand only become pollutants, according to the statute, once they are "discharged into water." 33 U.S.C. §1362(6) (1994). The Corps' approach thus just leads right back to the definition of discharge.

NOTES AND QUESTIONS

1. The Tulloch Rule was designed to prevent developers from simply draining wetlands as an end run around the section 404 permit process. As the court notes, those who can convince the Corps that their dredging activities would not destroy or degrade wetlands are exempt from the permit requirement. Why not permit the Corps to define the scope of activities covered by section 404's permit

requirement by reference to the prospective environmental impact of the activity? What, in the court's view, was the critical defect in the Tulloch Rule?

2. The court notes that section 10 of the Rivers and Harbors Act explicitly regulates dredging activities by making it illegal "to excavate or fill" in navigable waters without the approval of the Corps. In light of this requirement, why does the Corps need to rely on section 404 to block the draining of wetlands?

3. As a result of the court's decision, what activities are now considered to involve the discharge of a pollutant and what activities are not? The National Wildlife Federation argued that invalidation of the Tulloch Rule could exempt all redeposits of dredged material from section 404 even when the material is redeposited in wetlands areas. Why does the court disagree? What redeposits would be regulable under section 404 in light of the court's decision? Where would Judge Silberman draw the line? In United States v. Deaton, 209 F.3d 331 (4th Cir. 2000), the Fourth Circuit rejected the argument that sidecasting of dredged material cannot be regulated under section 404 because it results in no net increase in the amount of material present in the wetland. The court concluded that "Congress determined that plain dirt, once excavated from the waters of the United States, could not be redeposited into those waters without causing harm to the environment." 209 F.3d at 336.

4. In the immediate aftermath of the *National Mining* decision, it was estimated that at least 20,000 acres of wetlands were degraded or destroyed and 150 miles of streams channelized without environmental review or mitigation. To close this loophole, EPA and the Corps issued new regulations in January 2001 that clarified the types of activities likely to result in a discharge of dredged material requiring a permit under section 404. 66 Fed. Reg. 4549. The regulations modify the definition of "discharge of dredged materials" to create a rebuttable presumption that the use of mechanized earth-moving equipment to conduct land clearing, ditching, channelization, in-stream mining, or other earth-moving activity in waters of the United States results in a discharge of dredged material, unless project-specific evidence shows that the activity causes only "incidental fallback." The regulations also provide a definition of what constitutes nonregulable incidental fallback that is consistent with the court's decision.

5. After initially delaying for 60 days the effective date of the new regulations redefining "discharge of dredged materials," the incoming Bush administration allowed the rules to take effect in April 2001. EPA Administrator Christine Todd Whitman strongly endorsed the regulations as an important step toward protecting the nation's wetlands. She noted that no regulatory action could fully close the loophole in the Clean Water Act created by the *National Mining* decision, which only Congress can correct.

"*Discharge of a Pollutant*": *the* **Borden Ranch** *and* **Miccosukee** *Cases*

The U.S. Supreme Court has considered the question of what constitutes the "discharge of a pollutant" under the Clean Water Act in cases it reviewed in 2002 and 2004. In December 2002 the Court reviewed a decision by the Ninth Circuit in Borden Ranch Partnership v. U.S. Army Corps of Engineers, 261 F.3d 810 (9th Cir. 2001), affirmed by an equally divided Court, 537 U.S. 99 (2002). By a 2-1 vote a panel of the Ninth Circuit upheld a judgment that a real estate developer, Angelo Tsakopoulos, had violated section 404 by using "deep ripping" equipment to punch holes in a dense layer of soil (a clay pan) beneath a wetland to allow surface waters to penetrate and drain the wetlands. Citing United States v. Deaton, see note 3 above on this page, the court majority

held that "activities that destroy the ecology of a wetland are not immune from
the Clean Water Act merely because they do not involve the introduction of
material brought in from somewhere else." 261 F.3d at 814-815. It concluded
that deep ripping can constitute a discharge of a pollutant regulated under the
Clean Water Act because it causes soil to be "wrenched up, moved around, and
redeposited somewhere else." Id. at 815. In a footnote the majority distinguished *National Mining Association* as a case involving only "incidental fallback."
The court observed that the deep ripping does not involve mere incidental
fallback, but constitutes environmental damage sufficient to constitute a regulable redeposit. A dissenting judge argued that *National Mining Association*
should be extended to exempt deep ripping, because it involves the plowing
of land and not the addition of dredged materials.

In the U.S. Supreme Court lawyers for Tsakopoulos challenged this Ninth
Circuit's conclusion that deep ripping constitutes the discharge of a pollutant.
Shortly after hearing oral argument, the Court announced that it had split 4-4,
affirming the Ninth Circuit's decision by an equally divided Court. The split was
the result of Justice Anthony Kennedy recusing himself from the case because he
is an acquaintance of Tsakopoulos.

A year later the Court reviewed a decision by the Eleventh Circuit that
had held that a section 402 NPDES permit was required for pumps that
moved water polluted by stormwater runoff from a canal to a reservoir as part
of the South Florida Flood Control Project because the pumping of the polluted
water constituted the discharge of a pollutant. The Court reached the following
decision.

|| *South Florida Water Management*
District v. Miccosukee Tribe of Indians
541 U.S. 95 (2004) ||

Justice O'Connor delivered the opinion of the Court.

Petitioner South Florida Water Management District operates a pumping
facility [S-9] that transfers water from a canal [C-11] into a reservoir [WCA-3] a
short distance away. Respondents Miccosukee Tribe of Indians and the Friends
of the Everglades brought a citizen suit under the Clean Water Act contending
that the pumping facility is required to obtain a discharge permit under the
National Pollutant Discharge Elimination System. The District Court agreed and
granted summary judgment to respondents. A panel of the United States Court
of Appeals for the Eleventh Circuit affirmed. . . .

Congress enacted the Clean Water Act (Act) in 1972. Its stated objective
was "to restore and maintain the chemical, physical, and biological integrity of
the Nation's waters." 33 U.S.C. §1251. To serve those ends, the Act prohibits
"the discharge of any pollutant by any person" unless done in compliance with
some provision of the Act. §1311(a). The provision relevant to this case, §1342,
establishes the National Pollutant Discharge Elimination System, or "NPDES."
Generally speaking, the NPDES requires dischargers to obtain permits that
place limits on the type and quantity of pollutants that can be released into
the Nation's waters. The Act defines the phrase "'discharge of a pollutant'"
to mean "any addition of any pollutant to navigable waters from any point
source." §1362(12). A "'point source,'" in turn, is defined as "any discernible,

confined and discrete conveyance," such as a pipe, ditch, channel, or tunnel, "from which pollutants are or may be discharged." §1362(14).

According to the Tribe, the District cannot operate S-9 without an NPDES permit because the pump station moves phosphorous-laden water from C-11 into WCA-3. The District does not dispute that phosphorous is a pollutant, or that C-11 and WCA-3 are "navigable waters" within the meaning of the Act. The question, it contends, is whether the operation of the S-9 pump constitutes the "discharge of [a] pollutant" within the meaning of the Act.

[The Court first rejected the water district's claim that the pump could not be considered a point source because it did not generate the pollutants in the waters it pumped—see discussion on page 624.]

. . . For purposes of determining whether there has been "any addition of any pollutant to navigable waters from any point source," ibid., the Government contends that all the water bodies that fall within the Act's definition of "'navigable waters'" (that is, all "the waters of the United States, including the territorial seas," §1362(7)) should be viewed unitarily for purposes of NPDES permitting requirements. Because the Act requires NPDES permits only when there is an addition of a pollutant "to navigable waters," the Government's approach would lead to the conclusion that such permits are not required when water from one navigable water body is discharged, unaltered, into another navigable water body. That would be true even if one water body were polluted and the other pristine, and the two would not otherwise mix. Under this "unitary waters" approach, the S-9 pump station would not need an NPDES permit.

The "unitary waters" argument focuses on the Act's definition of a pollutant discharge as "any addition of any pollutant to navigable waters from any point source." §1362(12). The Government contends that the absence of the word "any" prior to the phrase "navigable waters" in §1362(12) signals Congress' understanding that NPDES permits would not be required for pollution caused by the engineered transfer of one "navigable water" into another. It argues that Congress intended that such pollution instead would be addressed through local nonpoint source pollution programs. Section 1314(f)(2)(F), which concerns nonpoint sources, directs the Environmental Protection Agency (EPA) to give States information on the evaluation and control of "pollution resulting from . . . changes in the movement, flow, or circulation of any navigable waters or ground waters, including changes caused by the construction of dams, levees, channels, causeways, or flow diversion facilities."

We note, however, that §1314(f)(2)(F) does not explicitly exempt nonpoint pollution sources from the NPDES program if they also fall within the "point source" definition. And several NPDES provisions might be read to suggest a view contrary to the unitary waters approach. For example, under the Act, a State may set individualized ambient water quality standards by taking into consideration "the designated uses of the navigable waters involved." 33 U.S.C. §1313(c)(2)(A). Those water quality standards, in turn, directly affect local NPDES permits; if standard permit conditions fail to achieve the water quality goals for a given water body, the State must determine the total pollutant load that the water body can sustain and then allocate that load among the permitholders who discharge to the water body. §1313(d). This approach suggests that the Act protects individual water bodies as well as the "waters of the United States" as a whole.

The Government also suggests that we adopt the "unitary waters" approach out of deference to a longstanding EPA view that the process of "transporting, impounding, and releasing navigable waters" cannot constitute an "'addition'" of pollutants to "'the waters of the United States.'" Brief for United States as Amicus Curiae 16. But the Government does not identify any administrative documents in which EPA has espoused that position. Indeed, an amicus brief filed by several former EPA officials argues that the agency once reached the opposite conclusion. See Brief for Former Administrator Carol M. Browner et al. as Amici Curiae 17 (citing In re Riverside Irrigation Dist., 1975 WL 23864 (Off. Gen. Couns., June 27, 1975) (irrigation ditches that discharge to navigable waters require NPDES permits even if they themselves qualify as navigable waters)). The "unitary waters" approach could also conflict with current NPDES regulations. For example, 40 CFR §122.45(g)(4) (2003) allows an industrial water user to obtain "intake credit" for pollutants present in water that it withdraws from navigable waters. When the permit holder discharges the water after use, it does not have to remove pollutants that were in the water before it was withdrawn. There is a caveat, however: EPA extends such credit "only if the discharger demonstrates that the intake water is drawn from the same body of water into which the discharge is made." The NPDES program thus appears to address the movement of pollutants among water bodies, at least at times.

Finally, the Government and numerous amici warn that affirming the Court of Appeals in this case would have significant practical consequences. If we read the Clean Water Act to require an NPDES permit for every engineered diversion of one navigable water into another, thousands of new permits might have to be issued, particularly by western States, whose water supply networks often rely on engineered transfers among various natural water bodies. Many of those diversions might also require expensive treatment to meet water quality criteria. It may be that construing the NPDES program to cover such transfers would therefore raise the costs of water distribution prohibitively, and violate Congress' specific instruction that "the authority of each State to allocate quantities of water within its jurisdiction shall not be superseded, abrogated or otherwise impaired" by the Act. §1251(g). On the other hand, it may be that such permitting authority is necessary to protect water quality, and that the States or EPA could control regulatory costs by issuing general permits to point sources associated with water distribution programs. See 40 CFR §§122.28, 123.25 (2003). Indeed, that is the position of the one State that has interpreted the Act to cover interbasin water transfers. See Brief for Pennsylvania Department of Environmental Protection as Amicus Curiae 11-18.

Because WCA-3 and C-11 are both "navigable waters," adopting the "unitary waters" approach would lead to the conclusion that the District may operate S-9 without an NPDES permit. But despite its relevance here, neither the District nor the Government raised the unitary waters approach before the Court of Appeals or in their briefs respecting the petition for certiorari. (The District adopted the position as its own in its reply brief on the merits.) Indeed, we are not aware of any reported case that examines the unitary waters argument in precisely the form that the Government now presents it. As a result, we decline to resolve it here. Because we find it necessary to vacate the judgment of the Court of Appeals with respect to a third argument presented by the District, the unitary waters argument will be open to the parties on remand.

In the courts below, as here, the District contended that the C-11 canal and WCA-3 impoundment area are not distinct water bodies at all, but instead are two hydrologically indistinguishable parts of a single water body. The Government agrees with the District on this point, claiming that because the C-11 canal and WCA-3 "share a unique, intimately related, hydrological association," they "can appropriately be viewed, for purposes of Section 402 of the Clean Water Act, as parts of a single body of water." Brief for United States in Opposition 13. The Tribe does not dispute that if C-11 and WCA-3 are simply two parts of the same water body, pumping water from one into the other cannot constitute an "addition" of pollutants. As the Second Circuit put it in *Trout Unlimited*, "[i]f one takes a ladle of soup from a pot, lifts it above the pot, and pours it back into the pot, one has not 'added' soup or anything else to the pot." 273 F. 3d, at 492. What the Tribe disputes is the accuracy of the District's factual premise; according to the Tribe, C-11 and WCA-3 are two pots of soup, not one.

The record does contain information supporting the District's view of the facts. Although C-11 and WCA-3 are divided from one another by the L-33 and L-37 levees, that line appears to be an uncertain one. Because Everglades soil is extremely porous, water flows easily between ground and surface waters, so much so that "[g]round and surface waters are essentially the same thing." App. 111, 117. C-11 and WCA-3, of course, share a common underlying aquifer. Moreover, the L-33 and L-37 levees continually leak, allowing water to escape from WCA-3. This means not only that any boundary between C-11 and WCA-3 is indistinct, but also that there is some significant mingling of the two waters; the record reveals that even without use of the S-9 pump station, water travels as both seepage and groundwater flow between the water conservation area and the C-11 basin. App. 172, see also id., at 37 (describing flow between C-11 and WCA-3 as "cyclical").

The parties also disagree about how the relationship between S-9 and WCA-3 should be assessed. At oral argument, counsel for the Tribe focused on the differing "biological or ecosystem characteristics" of the respective waters, while counsel for the District emphasizes the close hydrological connections between the two. Despite these disputes, the District Court granted summary judgment to the Tribe. It applied a test that neither party defends; it determined that C-11 and WCA-3 are distinct "because the transfer of water or its contents from C-11 into the Everglades would not occur naturally." The Court of Appeals for the Eleventh Circuit endorsed this test. 280 F. 3d, at 1368.

We do not decide here whether the District Court's test is adequate for determining whether C-11 and WCA-3 are distinct. Instead, we hold only that the District Court applied its test prematurely. Summary judgment is appropriate only where there is no genuine issue of material fact. The record before us leads us to believe that some factual issues remain unresolved. The District Court certainly was correct to characterize the flow through the S-9 pump station as a non-natural one, propelled as it is by diesel-fired motors against the pull of gravity. And it also appears true that if S-9 were shut down, the water in the C-11 canal might for a brief time flow east, rather than west, as it now does. But the effects of shutting down the pump might extend beyond that. The limited record before us suggests that if S-9 were shut down, the area drained by C-11 would flood quite quickly. See 280 F. 3d, at 1366 ("Without the operation of the S-9 pump station, the populated western portion of Broward County would flood within days"). That flooding might mean that C-11 would no longer be a "distinct body of navigable water," id., at 1368, but part of a larger water body extending over WCA-3 and the C-11 basin. It also might call into question the Eleventh Circuit's conclusion that S-9 is the cause in fact of phosphorous addition to WCA-3. Nothing in the record suggests that the District Court considered these issues when it granted summary judgment. Indeed, in ordering later emergency relief from its own injunction against the operation of the S-9 pump station, the court admitted that it had not previously understood that shutting down S-9 would "literally ope[n] the flood gates." Id., at 1371.

We find that further development of the record is necessary to resolve the dispute over the validity of the distinction between C-11 and WCA-3. After reviewing the full record, it is possible that the District Court will conclude that C-11 and WCA-3 are not meaningfully distinct water bodies. If it does so, then the S-9 pump station will not need an NPDES permit. In addition, the Government's broader "unitary waters" argument is open to the District on remand. Accordingly, the judgment of the United States Court of Appeals for the Eleventh Circuit is vacated, and the case is remanded for further proceedings consistent with this opinion.

NOTES AND QUESTIONS

1. While agreeing with the majority's conclusion that the pump was a "point source," Justice Scalia dissented from the Court's decision to vacate and remand for consideration of the federal government's "unitary waters" theory. He maintained that the government's theory was not properly before the Court because it was not among the questions the Court had agreed to review.

2. The Court's decision indicates that NPDES permits may be required for pumps that convey polluted water from one water body to another even if the pollutants are the product of stormwater runoff. However, in light of the Court's remand to consider the "unitary waters" theory, a permit may not be required unless the canal and wetland area are considered distinct water bodies. How should the court below respond to the Court's remand? What test, if any, can be used to determine if the canal and wetland areas are "meaningfully distinct water bodies"?

3. What are the implications of the Justice Department's "unitary waters" theory? If all navigable waters are "viewed unitarily for purpose of NPDES permitting requirements," would that preclude a finding that the conveyance of polluted water from one water body to another is a "discharge of a pollutant" subject to regulation under the Clean Water Act regardless of its environmental consequences for the receiving waters?

4. Section 401 of the Clean Water Act, discussed in Part D2 of this chapter, requires applicants for federal approval of any activity "which may result in any discharge into the [Nation's] navigable waters" to seek state approval. In S.D. Warren v. Maine Board of Environmental Protection, 126 S. Ct. 1843 (2006), the U.S. Supreme Court rejected the claim that because a dam did not "add" any pollutants to water flowing through it, relicensing of a hydroelectric project was not an activity subject to section 401. The Court distinguished Miccosukee by noting that it involved construction of section 402 of the Act, not section 401, and that the two sections serve different purposes and use different language to reach them. It explained:

> The question in Miccosukee was whether a pump between a canal and an impoundment produced a "discharge of a pollutant" within the meaning of §402, see 541 U.S., at 102-103, and the Court accepted the shared view of the parties that if two identified volumes of water are "simply two parts of the same water body, pumping water from one into the other cannot constitute an 'addition' of pollutants," id., at 109. Miccosukee was thus concerned only with whether

an "addition" had been made (phosphorous being the substance in issue) as required by the definition of the phrase "discharge of a pollutant"; it did not matter under §402 whether pumping the water produced a discharge without any addition. In sum, the understanding that something must be added in order to implicate §402 does not explain what suffices for a discharge under §401.

26 S. Ct., at 1850.

The Court also noted that when applied to water, the term "discharge" commonly means "flowing or issuing out" and that the relicensing of hydroelectric projects had long been viewed as requiring section 401 certification. It observed that the section 401 certification process is an essential means for preserving state authority to address water quality problems because dams may affect water quality by changing a river's flow, movement, and circulation.

5. In a footnote to its decision in *S.D. Warren*, the Supreme Court described its *Miccosukee* decision as "at odds" with the argument that the transfer of polluted water from a canal to a connected impoundment constituted an "addition" of a pollutant, triggering section 402's permit requirement. The Court observed that:

> The fact that the parties in *Miccosukee* conceded that the water being pumped was polluted does not transform the Court's analysis from one centered on the word "addition" to one centered on the word "discharge." Before *Miccosukee*, one could have argued that transferring polluted water from a canal to a connected impoundment constituted an "addition." *Miccosukee* is at odds with that construction of the statute, but it says nothing about whether the transfer of polluted water from the canal to the impoundment constitutes a "discharge."

Id. at n. 6.

6. After *Miccosukee* was decided, EPA General Counsel Ann Klee issued a memorandum to regional administrators concluding that water transfers— "activities that convey or connect navigable waters without subjecting the water to intervening industrial, municipal, or commercial use"—are not subject to regulation under section 402's permit program. Memorandum from Ann R. Klee to Regional Administrators, regarding "Agency Interpretation on Applicability of Section 402 of the Clean Water Act to Water Transfers" (Aug. 5, 2005). The memorandum announced that EPA would initiate a rulemaking process to address how water transfers should be regulated.

7. While the Court in *Miccosukee* had no trouble finding that a pump constituted a point source even though it did not generate the pollutants it conveyed, the question of what constitutes a point source remains alive in other circumstances. At oral argument in the Supreme Court in the *Borden Ranch* case, there was considerable discussion of the meaning of "point source" and whether a deep ripper could qualify as one. Justice Scalia was skeptical of the notion that anything that moved dirt could be considered a conveyance that would make it a point source, arguing that under this view anyone who used a rake on a beach could be considered a point source. The government noted that a deep ripper is an enormous piece of specialized machinery that weighs over 100,000 pounds and whose very purpose is to move dirt. We now turn to the question of what constitutes a point source under the Clean Water Act.

2.   *Defining "Point Sources" Subject to Permit Requirements*

Why would Congress have chosen to focus federal water pollution control efforts almost exclusively on point source discharges? Congress was aware that nonpoint sources made a considerable contribution to water pollution, though it may not have fully appreciated their importance. But it recognized that point sources are easier to control, both politically and administratively, particularly when pollution control technology emphasized end-of-the-pipe solutions. Control of nonpoint source pollution requires some form of land use control, which has been politically unpopular, even at the state level, as we will see in Chapter 7. Thus, it was not until the Clean Water Act was amended in 1987 that Congress explicitly identified control of nonpoint source pollution as a goal of the Act.

Even limited to point source dischargers, implementation of a national permit program posed major administrative challenges for EPA. Recognizing the enormous task it faced, EPA announced that it would focus first on processing permit applications from major dischargers in areas where water pollution was the worst. Fearing that it would have to process millions of permit applications, the Agency also issued regulations exempting certain categories of point sources from the Act's permit requirements on the ground of administrative infeasibility. An environmental group challenged EPA's decision in the case that follows.

NRDC v. Costle
568 F.2d 1369 (D.C. Cir. 1977)

LEVENTHAL, Circuit Judge:

In 1973 the EPA Administrator issued regulations that exempted certain categories of "point sources" of pollution from the permit requirements of §402. The Administrator's purported authority to make such exemptions turns on the proper interpretation of §402.

A "point source" is defined in §502(14) as "any discernible, confined and discrete conveyance, including but not limited to any pipe, ditch, channel, tunnel, conduit, well, discrete fissure, container, rolling stock, concentrated animal feeding operation, or vessel or other floating craft, from which pollutants are or may be discharged."

The 1973 regulations exempted discharges from a number of classes of point sources from the permit requirements of §402, including all silvicultural point sources; all confined animal feeding operations below a certain size; all irrigation return flows from areas of less than 3,000 contiguous acres or 3,000 noncontiguous acres that use the same drainage system; all nonfeedlot, nonirrigation agricultural point sources; and separate storm sewers containing only storm runoff uncontaminated by any industrial or commercial activity. The EPA's rationale for these exemptions is that in order to conserve the Agency's enforcement resources for more significant point sources of pollution, it is necessary to exclude these smaller sources of pollutant discharges from the permit program.

The National Resources Defense Council, Inc. (NRDC) sought a declaratory judgment that the regulations are unlawful under the FWPCA. Specifically, NRDC contended that the Administrator does not have authority to exempt any class of point source from the permit requirements of §402. It argued that Congress in enacting §§301, 402 of the FWPCA intended to prohibit the discharge of pollutants from *all* point sources unless a permit had been issued to the discharger under §402 or unless the point source was explicitly exempted from the permit requirements by statute. The District Court granted NRDC's motion for summary judgment. It held that the FWPCA does not authorize the Administrator to exclude any class of point sources from the permit program. NRDC v. Train, 396 F. Supp. 1393 (D.D.C. 1975). The EPA has appealed to this court. . . .

I. Legislative History

The NPDES permit program established by §402 is central to the enforcement of the FWPCA. It translates general effluent limitations into the specific obligations of a discharger. . . .

The appellants argue that §402 not only gives the Administrator the discretion to grant or refuse a permit, but also gives him the authority to exempt classes of point sources from the permit requirements entirely. They argue that this interpretation is supported by the legislative history of §402 and the fact that the unavailability of this exemption power would place an unmanageable administrative burden on EPA. . . .

Under the EPA's interpretation the Administrator would have broad discretion to exempt large classes of point sources from any or all requirements of the FWPCA. This is a result that the legislators did not intend. Rather they stressed that the FWPCA was a tough law that relied on explicit mandates to a degree uncommon in legislation of this type. . . .

There are innumerable references in the legislative history to the effect that the Act is founded on the "basic premise that a discharge of pollutants without a permit is unlawful and that discharges not in compliance with the limitations and conditions for a permit are unlawful." Even when infeasibility arguments were squarely raised, the legislature declined to abandon the permit requirement. . . .

The wording of the statute, legislative history, and precedents are clear: the EPA Administrator does not have the authority to exempt categories of point sources from the permit requirements of §402. . . .

II. Administrative Infeasibility

The appellants have stressed in briefs and at oral argument the extraordinary burden on the EPA that will be imposed by the above interpretation of the scope of the NPDES program. The spectre of millions of applications for permits is evoked both as part of appellants' legislative history argument—that Congress could not have intended to impose such burdens on the EPA—and as an invitation to this court to uphold the regulations as deviations from the literal terms of the FWPCA necessary to permit the agency to realize the general objectives of that act. . . .

A. Uniform National Effluent Limitations

EPA argues that the regulatory scheme intended under Titles III and IV of the FWPCA requires, first, that the Administrator establish national effluent limitations and, second, that these limitations be incorporated in the individual permits of dischargers. EPA argues that the establishment of such limitations is simply not possible with the type of point sources involved in the 1973 regulations, which essentially involve the discharge of runoff—i.e., wastewaters generated by rainfall that drain over terrain into navigable waters, picking up pollutants along the way. . . .

EPA contends that certain characteristics of runoff pollution make it difficult to promulgate effluent limitations for most of the point sources exempted by the 1973 regulations:

> The major characteristic of the pollution problem which is generated by runoff . . . is that the owner of the discharge point . . . has no control over the quantity of the flow or the nature and amounts of the pollutants picked up by the runoff. The amount of flow obviously is unpredictable because it results from the duration and intensity of the rainfall event, the topography, the type of ground cover and the saturation point of the land due to any previous rainfall. Similar factors affect the types of pollutants which will be picked up by that runoff, including the type of farming practices employed, the rate and type of pesticide and fertilizer application, and the conservation practices employed. . . .
>
> An effluent limitation must be a precise number in order for it to be an effective regulatory tool; both the discharger and the regulatory agency need to have an identifiable standard upon which to determine whether the facility is in compliance. That was the principle of the passage of the 1972 Amendments.

Implicit in EPA's contentions is the premise that there must be a uniform effluent limitation prior to issuing a permit. That is not our understanding of the law. . . .

As noted in NRDC v. Train [510 F.2d 692 (D.C. Cir. 1975)], the primary purpose of the effluent limitations and guidelines was to provide uniformity among the federal and state jurisdictions enforcing the NPDES program and prevent the "Tragedy of the Commons" that might result if jurisdictions can compete for industry and development by providing more liberal limitations than their neighboring states. 510 F.2d at 709. The effluent limitations were intended to create floors that had to be respected by state permit programs.

But in NRDC v. Train it was also recognized that permits could be issued before national effluent limitations were promulgated and that permits issued subsequent to promulgation of uniform effluent limitations could be modified to take account of special characteristics of subcategories of point sources. . . .

In [*Train*] this court fully appreciated that technological and administrative constraints might prevent the Administrator from developing guidelines and corresponding uniform numeric effluent limitations for certain point sources anytime in the near future. The Administrator was deemed to have the burden of demonstrating that the failure to develop the guidelines on schedule was due to administrative or technological infeasibility. 510 F.2d at 713. Yet the underlying teaching was that technological or administrative infeasibility was a reason for adjusting court mandates to the minimum extent necessary to realize the general objectives of the Act. It is a number of steps again to suggest that these problems afford the Administrator the authority to exempt categories of point sources from the NPDES program entirely.

With time, experience, and technological development, more point sources in the categories that EPA has now classed as exempt may be amenable to national effluent limitations achieved through end-of-pipe technology or other means of pollution control. . . .

In sum, we conclude that the existence of uniform national effluent limitations is not a necessary precondition for incorporating into the NPDES program pollution from agricultural, silvicultural, and storm water runoff point sources. The technological or administrative infeasibility of such limitations may result in adjustments in the permit programs, as will be seen, but it does not authorize the Administrator to exclude the relevant point source from the NPDES program.

B.   Alternative Permit Conditions Under §402(a)

EPA contends that even if it is possible to issue permits without national effluent limitations, the special characteristics of point sources of runoff pollution make it infeasible to develop restrictions on a case-by-case basis. EPA's implicit premise is that whether limitations are promulgated on a class or individual source basis, it is still necessary to articulate any limitation in terms of a numerical effluent standard. That is not our understanding.

Section 402 provides that a permit may be issued upon condition "that such discharge will meet either all applicable requirements under sections 301, 302, 306, 307, 308 and 403 of this Act, *or prior to taking of necessary implementing actions relating to all such requirements, such conditions as the Administrator determines are necessary to carry out the provisions of this Act.*" 33 U.S.C. §1342(a) (Supp. V 1975) (emphasis added). This provision gives EPA considerable flexibility in framing the permit to achieve a desired reduction in pollutant discharges. The permit may proscribe industry practices that aggravate the problem of point source pollution. . . .

[W]hen numerical effluent limitations are infeasible, EPA may issue permits with conditions designed to reduce the level of effluent discharges to acceptable levels. This may well mean opting for a gross reduction in pollutant discharge rather than the fine-tuning suggested by numerical limitations. But this ambitious statute is not hospitable to the concept that the appropriate response to a difficult pollution problem is not to try at all.

It may be appropriate in certain circumstances for the EPA to require a permittee simply to monitor and report effluent levels; EPA manifestly has this authority. Such permit conditions might be desirable where the full extent of the pollution problem is not known.

C.   General Permits

Finally, EPA argues that the number of permits involved in the absence of an exemption authority will simply overwhelm the Agency. Affidavits filed with the District Court indicate, for example, that the number of silviculture point sources may be over 300,000 and that there are approximately 100,000 separate storm sewer point sources. We are and must be sensitive to EPA's concerns of an intolerable permit load. But the District Court and the various parties have suggested devices to mitigate the burden—to accommodate within a practical regulatory scheme Congress' clear mandate that all point sources have permits. All that is required is that EPA make full use of its interpretational authority. The existence of a variety of options belies EPA's infeasibility arguments.

Section 402 does not explicitly describe the necessary scope of a NPDES permit. The most significant requirement is that the permit be in compliance with limitation sections of the Act described above. As a result NRDC and the District Court have suggested the use of area or general permits. The Act allows such techniques. Area-wide regulation is one well-established means of coping with administrative exigency. An instance is area pricing for natural gas producers, which the Supreme Court upheld in Permian Basin Area Rate Cases, 390 U.S. 747 (1968). A more dramatic example is the administrative search warrant which may be issued on an area basis despite the normal Fourth Amendment requirement of probable cause for searching specific premises. Camara v. Municipal Court, 387 U.S. 523 (1967).

In response to the District Court's order, EPA promulgated regulations that make use of the general permit device. 42 Fed. Reg. 6846-53 (Feb. 4, 1977). The general permit is addressed to a class of point source dischargers, subject to notice and opportunity for public hearing in the geographical area covered by the permit. Although we do not pass on the validity of the February 1977 regulations, they serve to dilute an objection of wholesale infeasibility.

Our approach is not fairly subject to the criticism that it elevates form over substance [such] that the end result will look very much like EPA's categorical exemption. It is the function of the courts to require agencies to comply with legislative intent when that intent is clear, and to leave it to the legislature to make adjustments when the result is counterproductive. At the same time, where intent on an issue is unclear, we are instructed to afford the administering agency the flexibility necessary to achieve the general objectives of the Act. . . . These lines of authority conjoin in our approach. We insist, as the Act insists, that a permit is necessary; the Administrator has no authority to exempt point sources from the NPDES program. But we concede necessary flexibility in the shaping of the permits that is not inconsistent with the clear terms of the Act.

There is also a very practical difference between a general permit and an exemption. An exemption tends to become indefinite: the problem drops out of sight, into a pool of inertia, unlikely to be recalled in the absence of crisis or a strong political protagonist. In contrast, the general or area permit approach forces the Agency to focus on the problems of specific regions and requires that the problems of the region be reconsidered at least every five years, the maximum duration of a permit. . . .

NOTES AND QUESTIONS

1. In general, the more comprehensive a regulatory program is, the greater is the administrative burden on the agency that must implement it. At some point the universe of regulatory targets becomes so large that it simply is not feasible to apply the same standards to all. Rather than requiring that *all* point sources be regulated, would it make more sense to give EPA the authority to require permits for whatever sources (point or nonpoint) that it determines pose the greatest problems? If EPA had the authority to issue permits authorizing discharges, why did it not have the authority to exempt point sources from permit requirements?

2. The court offers several suggestions for easing the administrative burden of permitting the sources EPA sought to exempt, including the use of general permits and other alternatives to numerical effluent limitations. Is there any "very practical difference" between a general or area-wide permit and an exemption, and if so, how could a general permit contribute to achieving the objectives of the Act?

3. Under what circumstances should pollutant discharges that occur due to weather conditions be considered discharges from point sources? The American Iron and Steel Institute had argued that only "volitional flows" that add pollutants to navigable waters should be considered point source discharges. Would this interpretation be more sensible because it would exempt from permit requirements natural runoff that happens to flow through a discrete conveyance? Or should it depend on whether or not the conveyance usually collects pollution? Why not simply abandon the point-nonpoint source distinction in favor of one that turns on whether the discharge is caused by human activities or naturally occurring ones? Would this be an easy distinction to make? Should the determination of point source status depend instead on how amenable the discharge is to control?

4. Examine the current statutory definition of "point source," which is contained in section 502(14). Note that the definition is the same as that quoted in NRDC v. Costle, except that Congress has added a sentence exempting "agricultural stormwater discharges and return flows from irrigated agriculture." Return flows from irrigated agriculture were exempted in the 1977 Amendments in response to NRDC v. Costle. This exemption has generated considerable criticism because agricultural irrigation has created severe pollution problems in some areas. For example, at California's Kesterson National Wildlife Refuge, return flows produced a buildup of naturally occurring selenium in concentrations toxic to wildlife.

5. In the 1987 Amendments, Congress required NPDES permits for storm water discharges associated with industrial activity and those from municipal separate storm sewer systems (MS4s) serving a population of 100,000 or more. §402(p). Congress confirmed that permits for industrial storm water discharges must meet all applicable provisions of section 301 and section 402 including BAT/BCT, section 402(p)(3)(A), and it required that municipal permits prohibit non-storm water discharges into storm sewers while requiring controls to reduce pollutant discharges "to the maximum extent practicable." §402(p)(3)(B). Faced with permit requirements applicable to 114,000 industrial facilities and 220 cities, 55 Fed. Reg. 47,990 (1990), EPA belatedly issued permit application regulations under court order in October 1990. In April 1992, EPA adopted a four-tiered approach to industrial storm water permitting that relies on general permits for most dischargers. 57 Fed. Reg. 11,394 (1992). If storm water discharges in particular watersheds, or from certain industries or specific facilities, are found to contribute to water quality problems, watershed-, industry-, or facility-specific permits may be required. In 1999 EPA issued Phase II of its storm water regulations, which broadened their reach to include smaller municipalities and construction sites that disturb between one and five acres of land. In Environmental Defense Center v. EPA, 344 F.3d 832 (9th Cir. 2003), the Ninth Circuit upheld EPA's authority to issue the Phase II rules and it rejected claims that they violated the Tenth Amendment. However, the court held that EPA must provide for public review of notices of intent to obtain coverage under the Phase II general permit because these notices indicate how dischargers plan to comply with the requirement to reduce discharges "to the maximum extent practicable."

6. Figure 6.5 shows the relative contributions of different types of point sources to pollutant discharges. As the figure indicates, combined sewer overflows (CSOs) are now the largest source of point source discharges, followed by conventional industrial discharges and discharges from sewage treatment

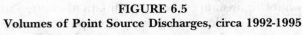

FIGURE 6.5
Volumes of Point Source Discharges, circa 1992-1995

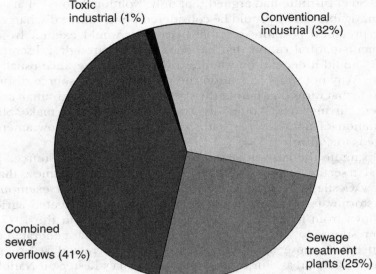

Based on U.S. Environmental Protection Agency, Permit Compliance System, unpublished.
NOTE: Totals include: sewage treatment plants, 3,318 million pounds in 1992; combined
sewer overflows, 5,340 million pounds in 1992; toxic industrial, 146 million pounds in 1995;
and conventional industrial, 4,170 million pounds in 1995.
Source: Council on Environmental Quality.

plants. In 1999 EPA estimated that nearly 350,000 NPDES permits had been issued, a number that may rise to 500,000 as an expanded storm water permit program is implemented. EPA, Interim Framework to Ensure Issuance of Timely and High Quality NPDES Permits (1999). As the universe of facilities requiring an NPDES permit has expanded, a backlog of expired permits has developed. EPA estimates that 28 percent of major individual permits have expired and that the percentage of minor permits that have expired is even larger.

7. Is it clear that all of the sources EPA sought to exempt from permit requirements in NRDC v. Costle were indeed point sources? Industry intervenors argued that some of them were not. Does the court ever specify what a point source is? In the case below, the U.S. Court of Appeals for the Second Circuit addressed the question whether a person can be a point source for purposes of the Clean Water Act.

United States v. Plaza Health Laboratories, Inc.
3 F.3d 643 (2d Cir. 1993)

Before: OAKES, REARSE, and PRATT, Circuit Judges. GEORGE C. PRATT, Circuit Judge:

Defendant Geronimo Villegas appeals from a judgment entered in the United States District Court for the Eastern District of New York, Edward R.

Korman, Judge, convicting him of two counts of knowingly discharging pollutants into the Hudson River in violation of the Clean Water Act ("CWA"). See 33 U.S.C. §§1311 and 1319(c)(2). . . .

FACTS AND BACKGROUND

Villegas was co-owner and vice president of Plaza Health Laboratories, Inc., a blood-testing laboratory in Brooklyn, New York. On at least two occasions between April and September 1988, Villegas loaded containers of numerous vials of human blood generated from his business into his personal car, and drove to his residence at the Admirals Walk Condominium in Edgewater, New Jersey. Once at his condominium complex, Villegas removed the containers from his car and carried them to the edge of the Hudson River. On one occasion he carried two containers of the vials to the bulkhead that separates his condominium complex from the river, and placed them at low tide within a crevice in the bulkhead that was below the high-water line.

On May 26, 1988, a group of eighth graders on a field trip at the Alice Austin House in Staten Island, New York, discovered numerous glass vials containing human blood along the shore. Some of the vials had washed up on the shore; many were still in the water. Some were cracked, although most remained sealed with stoppers in solid-plastic containers or ziplock bags. Fortunately, no one was injured. That afternoon, New York City workers recovered approximately 70 vials from the area.

On September 25, 1988, a maintenance worker employed by the Admirals Walk Condominium discovered a plastic container holding blood vials wedged between rocks in the bulkhead. New Jersey authorities retrieved numerous blood vials from the bulkhead later that day.

Ten of the retrieved vials contained blood infected with the hepatitis-B virus. All of the vials recovered were eventually traced to Plaza Health Laboratories. . . .

Villegas contends that one element of the CWA crime, knowingly discharging pollutants from a "point source," was not established in his case. He argues that the definition of "point source," 33 U.S.C. §1362(14), does not include discharges that result from the individual acts of human beings. Raising primarily questions of legislative intent and statutory construction, Villegas argues that at best, the term "point source" is ambiguous as applied to him, and that the rule of lenity should result in reversal of his convictions. . . .

1. Language and Structure of Act

Human beings are not among the enumerated items that may be a "point source." Although by its terms the definition of "point source" is nonexclusive, the words used to define the term and the examples given ("pipe, ditch, channel, tunnel, conduit, well, discrete fissure," etc.) evoke images of physical structures and instrumentalities that systematically act as a means of conveying pollutants from an industrial source to navigable waterways.

In addition, if every discharge involving humans were to be considered a "discharge from a point source," the statute's lengthy definition of "point source" would have been unnecessary. It is elemental that Congress does not add unnecessary words to statutes. Had Congress intended to punish any human being who polluted navigational waters, it could readily have said: "any person who places pollutants in navigable waters without a permit is guilty of a crime."

The Clean Water Act generally targets industrial and municipal sources of pollutants, as is evident from a perusal of its many sections. Consistent with this focus, the term "point source" is used throughout the statute, but invariably in sentences referencing industrial or municipal discharges. See, e.g., 33 U.S.C. §1311 (referring to "owner or operator" of point source); §1311(e) (requiring that effluent limitations established under the Act "be applied to all point sources of discharge"); . . .

Finally on this point, we assume that Congress did not intend the awkward meaning that would result if we were to read "human being" into the definition of "point source." Section 1362(12)(A) defines "discharge of a pollutant" as "any addition of any pollutant to navigable waters from any point source." Enhanced by this definition, §1311(a) reads in effect "the addition of any pollutant to navigable waters *from any point source by any person* shall be unlawful" (emphasis added). But were a human being to be included within the definition of "point source," the prohibition would then read: "the addition of any pollutant to navigable waters *from any person by any person* shall be unlawful," and this simply makes no sense. As the statute stands today, the term "point source" is comprehensible only if it is held to the context of industrial and municipal discharges.

2.   Legislative History and Context

. . . The legislative history of the CWA, while providing little insight into the meaning of "point source," confirms the act's focus on industrial polluters. Congress required NPDES permits of those who discharge from a "point source." The term "point source," introduced to the act in 1972, was intended to function as a means of identifying industrial polluters—generally a difficult task because pollutants quickly disperse throughout the subject waters. The Senate report for the 1972 amendments explains:

> In order to further clarify the scope of the regulatory procedures in the Act the Committee had added a definition of point source to distinguish between control requirements where there are *specific confined conveyances, such as pipes*, and control requirements which are imposed to control runoff. The control of pollutants from runoff is applied pursuant to section 209 and the authority resides in the State or other local agency.

S. Rep. No. 92-414, reprinted in 1972 U.S.C.C.A.N. 3668, 3744. . . .

We find no suggestion either in the act itself or in the history of its passage that Congress intended the CWA to impose criminal liability on an individual for the myriad, random acts of human waste disposal, for example, a passerby who flings a candy wrapper into the Hudson River, or a urinating swimmer. Discussions during the passage of the 1972 amendments indicate that Congress had bigger fish to fry. . . .

In sum, although Congress had the ability to so provide, §1362(14) of the CWA does not expressly recognize a human being as a "point source"; nor does the act make structural sense when one incorporates a human being into that definition. The legislative history of the act adds no light to the muddy depths of this issue, and cases urging a broad interpretation of the definition in the civil-penalty context do not persuade us to do so here, where Congress has imposed heavy criminal sanctions. Adopting the government's suggested flexibility for the definition would effectively read the "point source" element of the crime out of the statute, and not even the EPA has extended the term "point source" as far as is urged here.

We accordingly conclude that the term "point source" as applied to a human being is at best ambiguous.

B. Rule of Lenity

In criminal prosecutions the rule of lenity requires that ambiguities in the statute be resolved in the defendant's favor. . . .

Since the government's reading of the statute in this case founders on our inability to discern the "obvious intention of the legislature," Huddleston, 415 U.S. at 831, to include a human being as a "point source," we conclude that the criminal provisions of the CWA did not clearly proscribe Villegas' conduct and did not accord him fair warning of the sanctions the law placed on that conduct. Under the rule of lenity, therefore, the prosecutions against him must be dismissed. . . .

OAKES, Circuit Judge, dissenting:

. . . [B]ecause I do not agree that a person can never be a point source, and because I believe that Mr. Villegas' actions, as the jury found them, fell well within the bounds of activity proscribed by the Clean Water Act's bar on discharge of pollutants into navigable waters, I am required to dissent. . . .

I begin with the obvious, in hopes that it will illuminate the less obvious: the classic point source is something like a pipe. This is, at least in part, because pipes and similar conduits are needed to carry large quantities of wastewater, which represents a large proportion of the point source pollution problem. Thus, devices designed to convey large quantities of wastewater from a factory or municipal sewage treatment facility are readily classified as point sources. Because not all pollutants are liquids, however, the statute and the cases make clear that means of conveying solid wastes to be dumped in navigable waters are also point sources. See, e.g., 33 U.S.C. §1362(14) ("rolling stock," or railroad cars, listed as an example of a point source); Avoyelles Sportsmen's League, Inc. v. Marsh, 715 F.2d 897, 922 (5th Cir. 1983) (backhoes and bulldozers used to gather fill and deposit it on wetlands are point sources).

What I take from this look at classic point sources is that, at the least, an organized means of channeling and conveying industrial waste in quantity to navigable waters is a "discernible, confined and discrete conveyance." The caselaw is in accord: courts have deemed a broad range of means of depositing pollutants in the country's navigable waters to be point sources. See, e.g., Rybachek v. EPA, 904 F.2d 1276 (9th Cir. 1990) (placer mining; sluice box from which discharge water is redeposited in stream is point source, despite provisions protecting some mining activities); United States v. M.C.C. of Fla., Inc., 772 F.2d 1501, 1505-1506 (11th Cir. 1985) (tugs redepositing dirt from bottom of water body onto beds of water grass are point sources discharging the dirt), vacated on other grounds, 481 U.S. 1034 (1987) (defendants' right to jury trial); Sierra Club v. Abston Constr. Co., 620 F.2d 41, 45 (5th Cir. 1980) (spill

of contaminated runoff from strip mine, if collected or channeled by the operator, is point source discharge); United States v. Earth Sciences, Inc., 599 F.2d
368, 374 (10th Cir. 1979) (same); Appalachian Power Co. v. Train, 545 F.2d
1351, 1372 (4th Cir. 1976) (same); O'Leary v. Moyer's Landfill, Inc., 523 F.
Supp. 642, 655 (E.D. Pa. 1981) (same). Nor have courts been inclined to exclude
mining or agricultural point sources, despite the fact that portions of the Clean
Water Act protect these industries to some extent. . . .

Further, the legislative history indicates that the Act was meant to control
periodic, as well as continuous, discharges. S. Rep. No. 92-414, 92d Cong. 1st
Sess. (1971), reprinted at 1972 U.S.C.C.A.N. 3668, 3705.

In short, the term "point source" has been broadly construed to apply to a
wide range of polluting techniques, so long as the pollutants involved are not
just humanmade, but reach the navigable waters by human effort or by leaking
from a clear point at which wastewater was collected by human effort. From
these cases, the writers of one respected treatise have concluded that such a
"man-induced gathering mechanism plainly is the essential characteristic of a
point source" and that a point source, "put simply, . . . is an identifiable conveyance of pollutants." 5 Robert E. Beck, Waters & Water Rights §53.01(b)(3) at
216-17 (1991). . . .

. . . [T]o further refine the definition of "point source," I consider what it
is that the Act does not cover: nonpoint source discharges.

Nonpoint source pollution is, generally, runoff: salt from roads, agricultural chemicals from farmlands, oil from parking lots, and other substances
washed by rain, in diffuse patterns, over the land and into navigable waters. The
sources are many, difficult to identify and difficult to control. Indeed, an effort
to greatly reduce nonpoint source pollution could require radical changes in
land use patterns which Congress evidently was unwilling to mandate without
further study. The structure of the statute—which regulates point source pollution closely, while leaving nonpoint source regulation to the states under the
Section 208 program—indicates that the term "point source" was included in
the definition of discharge so as to ensure that nonpoint source pollution
would not be covered. Instead, Congress chose to regulate first that which
could easily be regulated: direct discharges by identifiable parties, or point
sources.

This rationale for regulating point and nonpoint sources differently—
that point sources may readily be controlled and are easily attributable to a
particular source, while nonpoint sources are more difficult to control without
radical change, and less easily attributable, once they reach water, to any particular responsible party—helps define what fits within each category. Thus,
Professor Rodgers has suggested, "the statutory 'discernible, confined and
discrete conveyance' . . . can be understood as singling out those candidates
suitable for control-at-the-source." 2 William H. Rodgers, Jr., Environmental
Law: Air and Water §4.10 at 150 (1986). And, as Professor Rodgers notes, "case
law confirms the controllability theory, adding to it a responsibility component,
so that 'point sources' are understood both as sources that can be cleaned
up and as sources where fairness suggests the named parties should do the
cleaning." Id. . . .

While Villegas' activities were not prototypical point source discharges—in
part because he was disposing of waste that could have been disposed of on land,
and so did not need a permit or a pipe—they much more closely resembled a
point source discharge than a nonpoint source discharge. First, Villegas and his

lab were perfectly capable of avoiding discharging their waste into water: they were, in Professor Rodgers' terms, a "controllable" source.

Furthermore, the discharge was directly into water, and came from an identifiable point, Villegas. Villegas did not dispose of the materials on land, where they could be washed into water as nonpoint source pollution. Rather, he carried them, from his firm's laboratory, in his car, to his apartment complex, where he placed them in a bulkhead below the high tide line. I do not think it is necessary to determine whether it was Mr. Villegas himself who was the point source, or whether it was his car, the vials, or the bulkhead: in a sense, the entire stream of Mr. Villegas' activity functioned as a "discrete conveyance" or point source. The point is that the source of the pollution was clear, and would have been easy to control. Indeed, Villegas was well aware that there were methods of controlling the discharge (and that the materials were too dangerous for casual disposal): his laboratory had hired a professional medical waste handler. He simply chose not to use an appropriate waste disposal mechanism.

Villegas' method may have been an unusual one for a corporate officer, but it would undermine the statute—which, after all, sets as its goal the elimination of discharges, 33 U.S.C. §1311(a)—to regard as "ambiguous" a Congressional failure to list an unusual method of disposing of waste. I doubt that Congress would have regarded an army of men and women throwing industrial waste from trucks into a stream as exempt from the statute. Since the Act contains no exemption for de minimus violations—since, indeed, many Clean Water Act prosecutions are for a series of small discharges, each of which is treated as a single violation—I cannot see that one man throwing one day's worth of medical waste into the ocean differs (and indeed, with this type of pollution, it might be that only a few days' violations could be proven even if the laboratory regularly relied on Villegas to dispose of its waste by throwing it into the ocean). A different reading would encourage corporations perfectly capable of abiding by the Clean Water Act's requirements to ask their employees to stand between the company trucks and the sea, thereby transforming point source pollution (dumping from trucks) into nonpoint source pollution (dumping by hand). Such a method is controllable, easily identifiable, and inexcusable. To call it nonpoint source pollution is to read a technical exception into a statute which attempts to define in broad terms an activity which may be conducted in many different ways. . . .

I do not think technical arguments about whether the toxic substances were in discrete containers are fruitful when the activity is discrete, conveys pollutants, and is confined to a clear, traceable single source. When a company chooses to use the nation's waters as a dumpsite for waste it has created and gathered in a manageable place,[7] it should ask for a permit or face prosecution.

I am of course given pause, however, by the nature of the criminal sanctions attached to point source discharges under §1319. Given the broad statutory definitions of pollutant and point source, it would appear that a knowing violation would include intentionally throwing a candy wrapper into the ocean—and that this is an activity which could subject the thrower to a $25,000 fine and three years in jail. It seems improbable to me that this could have been Congress' intent. Consequently, I would with the majority read the statute as ambiguous as it pertains to individual litterers, as opposed to disposers

---

7. I mean to distinguish a company whose agricultural or other activity leaves pollutants dispersed on the land, which may then find their way into the nation's waters.

of industrial and municipal waste.[8] The latter were the principal targets of the authors of the CWA, and, as professional creators of waste, charged with knowledge that disposal of waste into navigable waters is a crime.

NOTES AND QUESTIONS

1. The court majority says that the Clean Water Act was never designed to address the random, individual polluter. Why not? Is the court majority correct when they argue that interpreting "point source" to embrace humans could subject to criminal penalties a urinating swimmer or a passerby who flings a candy wrapper into surface waters?

2. In a portion of the majority opinion not reproduced above, the court noted that the Rivers and Harbors Act makes it a misdemeanor "to throw, discharge, or deposit . . . any refuse matter" into surface waters. Why do you think the government chose not to prosecute Mr. Villegas under this statute, which would not have presented the "point source" problem?

3. The court invokes the rule of lenity to resolve statutory ambiguities in favor of a defendant in a criminal case. The purpose of this rule is to ensure that individuals will have fair warning concerning what behavior is criminal. Do you think that most people would consider the dumping of contaminated vials of blood into water where they could wash onto beaches on which children play to be a criminal act?

4. On what does Judges Oakes premise his dissenting view that persons are point sources? Is he right that under the majority's interpretation a company could avoid compliance with the Clean Water Act simply by having its employees hurl waste into water? How would Judge Oakes deal with the problem of criminalizing the urinating swimmer or the candy wrapper tosser? Concerned that this decision could undermine the Clean Water Act, the government appealed to the Supreme Court, but the Court declined to review the case. United States v. Villegas, cert. denied, 512 U.S. 1245 (1994).

5. In a subsequent case, Judge Oakes, writing for a unanimous court, reversed a district court holding that a liquid manure spreading operation was not a point source for purposes of the Clean Water Act. In Concerned Area Residents for the Environment v. Southview Farm, 34 F.3d 114 (2d Cir. 1994), the Second Circuit held that because the liquid manure was collected by human effort and channelled through ditches that led to a stream, the operation was a point source. The court also held that manure spreading vehicles used by the operation were point sources because they collected liquid manure and discharged it on fields from which the manure directly flowed into navigable waters. It rejected arguments that the operation involved "agricultural stormwater discharges" exempted from the definition of "point source" in

---

8. An alternative—that the Act applies only to major discharges—seems to me both administratively unworkable (where does one draw the line?) and inconsistent with the statute and case law. The statutory definition of "discharge" refers to "any" addition of "any" pollutant from "any" point source, indicating a congressional intent to bar all, even minor, violations. Further, the D.C. Circuit has held that EPA has no discretion to limit regulation of point sources to those it deems most significant. National Resources Defense Council, Inc. v. Costle, 568 F.2d 1369, 1374 (D.C. Cir. 1977). This, too, indicates that small as well as large point sources are governed by the Act.

section 502(14), finding that it instead involved the kind of "concentrated animal feeding operation" (CAFO) specifically listed in the point source definition.

6. Improperly managed animal feeding operations (AFOs) now are widely recognized as an important source of water pollution. EPA estimates that out of 1.3 million farms with livestock, approximately 238,000 maintain confined animal feeding operations (CAFOs). These CAFOs produce more than 500 million tons of animal manure each year, more than three times the amount of waste excreted by humans. In March 1999 EPA and USDA issued their "Unified National Strategy for Animal Feeding Operations." The strategy sought to accelerate the issuance of NPDES permits for large CAFOs (i.e., operations with greater than 1,000 animal units) and to require that comprehensive nutrient management plans be incorporated in these permits. In December 2002, EPA issued final CAFO regulations that require approximately 15,500 large CAFOs to apply for NDPES permits by 2006. The regulations require these entities to apply for a permit, submit an annual report, and develop and follow a plan for handling manure and wastewater. Large CAFOs are defined in the rule as operations raising more than 1,000 cattle, 700 dairy cows, 2,500 swine, 10,000 sheep, 125,000 chickens, 82,000 laying hens, or 55,000 turkeys in confinement. As revised in 2003, EPA's regulations require all CAFOs to apply for NPDES permits and to develop and implement nutrient management plans. 68 Fed. Reg. 7176 (2003).

7. Consider whether or not the following activities involve discharges from point sources that require an NPDES permit. Is a dam that discharges water whose oxygen content has been reduced due to the dam's presence a point source? See National Wildlife Fed. v. Gorsuch, 693 F.2d 156 (D.C. Cir. 1982) (EPA properly determined that Congress did not intend to require dams to obtain NPDES permits). Does the discharge of dead fish from a hydroelectric plant's penstocks require an NPDES permit? See National Wildlife Fed. v. Consumers Power Co., 862 F.2d 580 (6th Cir. 1988) (no permit required following holding in *Gorsuch*). Is a permit required if toxic materials are discharged into a stream when a settling pond used to process gold ore overflows during an unusually sudden snowmelt? See United States v. Earth Sciences, Inc., 599 F.2d 368 (10th Cir. 1979) (permit required because Congress defined "point source" to embrace "the broadest possible definition of any identifiable conveyance from which pollutants might enter the waters of the United States"); see also Sierra Club v. Abston Constr. Co., 620 F.2d 41 (5th Cir. 1980) (surface runoff from strip mine is a point source when spoil piles are designed so that it is reasonably likely pollutants will be discharged through ditches or other discrete conveyances); compare section 402(1) (1987 amendment exempting from permit requirements discharges of storm water runoff from oil, gas, and mining operations that do not come into contact with products or waste material). Are a series of surface impoundments designed to capture, contain, and evaporate toxic runoff from an abandoned mine a point source when their contents occasionally spill into a nearby river? See Committee to Save Mokelumne River v. East Bay Mun. Util. Dist., 13 F.3d 305 (9th Cir. 1993) (impoundments held to be a point source, although a concurring judge noted that because the facility was like a dam and had been constructed to help reduce pollution, he would have been willing to defer to EPA if it had determined that the facility was not a point source). Is the application of aquatic herbicides to irrigation canals a discharge from a point source that must be authorized by an NPDES permit? (In Headwaters Inc. v. Talent Irrigation District, 243 F.3d 526 (9th Cir. 2001), the court said that it was.)

8. As noted above, the U.S. Supreme Court addressed the question whether a pump moving polluted water from a canal to a reservoir is a point source in *South Florida Water Management District v. Miccosukee Tribe of Indians*, 541 U.S. 95 (2004). The water district had argued that section 402's permit requirement only applies when pollutants originate from a point source and not when they merely pass through them. The Court unanimously rejected this argument. The Court wrote:

> A point source is, by definition, a "discernible, confined, and discrete *conveyance*." §1362(14) (emphasis added). That definition makes plain that a point source need not be the original source of the pollutant; it need only convey the pollutant to "navigable waters," which are, in turn, defined as "the waters of the United States." §1362(7). Tellingly, the examples of "point sources" listed by the Act include pipes, ditches, tunnels, and conduits, objects that do not themselves generate pollutants but merely transport them. §1362(14). In addition, one of the Act's primary goals was to impose NPDES permitting requirements on municipal wastewater treatment plants. See, e.g., §1311(b)(1)(B) (establishing a compliance schedule for publicly owned treatment works). But under the District's interpretation of the Act, the NPDES program would not cover such plants, because they treat and discharge pollutants added to water by others. We therefore reject the District's proposed reading of the definition of " 'discharge of a pollutant' " contained in §1362(12). That definition includes within its reach point sources that do not themselves generate pollutants. 541 U.S., at 105.

3. Technology-Based Effluent Limitations

At the heart of the Clean Water Act are technology-based effluent limitations applicable to all point source dischargers and implemented through enforceable permits. Congress intended that the effluent limits be uniform throughout the nation for "similar point sources with similar characteristics," in part to prevent geographic competition for industry from undermining water pollution control standards. As noted above, this approach is criticized by economists who favor standards that would base controls on individualized assessments of costs and benefits. Consider whether more flexible standards realistically could be implemented by EPA as you learn about the Agency's difficulties in implementing the existing technology-based approach.

A. APPLICATION TO INDUSTRIAL DISCHARGES

i. The Development of Effluent Limitations

The 1972 Act sought to force existing dischargers to employ progressively more stringent pollution control technology in two phases. Section 301(b)(1) originally required existing sources to employ the "best practicable control technology currently available" (BPT) by July 1, 1977, followed by the "best available technology economically achievable for each category or class" (BAT) by July 1, 1983. New sources were required by section 306 to meet a more stringent standard that would reduce their effluents to the greatest degree "achievable through application of the best available demonstrated control technology" (BADT), which could include process changes and a zero-discharge standard.

EPA faced a formidable task in determining how to translate technology-based standards into enforceable limits on industrial source categories. Section 304(b) of the FWPCA gave EPA one year to publish guidelines identifying the degree of effluent reduction attainable through the application of the levels of technology required by the Act. Swift action was crucial because Congress had given EPA and the states only two years to implement the new NPDES permit program. The Act specified that a discharger would not be considered in violation of the Act for the first two years after enactment if it had applied for a permit within six months of enactment. Congress had contemplated that the states would shoulder most of the actual burden of issuing permits (permits may be issued either by EPA or by states with programs approved by EPA), and it had required EPA to issue procedural guidelines to govern state operation of the NPDES permit program within two months after enactment of the Act.

Six months after enactment of the Clean Water Act, EPA had received nearly 33,000 applications for NPDES permits. By mid-1974 EPA had received 65,000 applications, but only 15 states had taken over responsibility for permit issuance. It soon became apparent that EPA would have to write more than 50,000 permits and define the range of technologically possible effluent limits for dozens of different industries, an enormous technical and administrative burden. The process of writing permits had already begun due to the Refuse Act experience, but without the detailed, industry-based assessment of technology dictated by section 304. Moreover, the section 304 process was supposed to be completed in only 12 months. Recall, too, that EPA was then a new agency with equally substantial tasks under the Clean Air Act.

EPA recognized that it would be unable to meet the one-year deadline in section 304(b)(1)(A) for promulgating effluent guidelines for classes and categories of point sources. The Agency announced that instead it would publish the guidelines in three groups over a two-year period, concentrating first on the 27 industry categories identified by section 306(b)(1)(A) as targets for new source performance standards. NRDC then sued EPA for failure to meet the deadline for issuing the guidelines, and EPA was placed on a court-ordered schedule requiring issuance of guidelines for all point source effluent discharges by December 31, 1974. NRDC v. Train, 510 F.2d 692 (D.C. Cir. 1975).

To further complicate matters, it soon became apparent that the Act was ambiguous concerning a crucial point: Were effluent limits intended to be uniform by industry, or individually determined with reference to the industry effluent guidelines required by section 304? Section 304(b) required EPA to "publish regulations providing guidelines for effluent limitations," but EPA had not issued such guidelines when it adopted effluent limits for existing sources under section 301(b) and for new sources under section 306. EPA needed to issue regulations rapidly to give industries subject to them time to meet the 1977 deadline for installing certain levels of pollution control technology.

EPA determined that it would issue industry-wide effluent limitations under section 301 without waiting to promulgate guidelines under section 304(b). It proceeded to set numerical limits for various pollutants that were to be applied to different industries based on analyses of the capabilities of alternative pollution control technologies. Dischargers argued that effluent limits should be determined in individual permit proceedings and that issuance of the guidelines was a prerequisite to issuance of individual permits. Had this argument prevailed, final permit issuance would have been delayed for years, and industry would have been afforded many more opportunities to seek plant-specific adjustments in effluent limits during permit proceedings.

After six different United States Courts of Appeals reached varying opinions on this question, the Supreme Court finally resolved the issue in Du Pont v. Train, 430 U.S. 112 (1977). The Court agreed with EPA that section 301 limitations "are to be adopted by the Administrator, . . . they are to be based primarily on classes and categories, and . . . they are to take the form of regulations." 430 U.S. at 129. The Court noted that the Act's BAT requirement provided expressly for regulation by "categories and classes" of dischargers, language difficult to reconcile with case-by-case permits. 430 U.S. at 126. While the Act's BPT requirement did not contain similar language, the Court held that industry-wide BPT regulation was permissible "so long as some allowance is made for variations in individual plants as EPA has done by including a variance clause in its 1977 limitations." 430 U.S. at 128. The Court noted the "impossible burden" that would be imposed on EPA were it to be required to determine BPT in tens of thousands of individual permits proceedings sufficiently in advance of the 1977 compliance deadline. Id. at 132-133.

The *Du Pont* decision established the validity of EPA's basic approach. What remained was the task of defining, implementing, and defending effluent limitations for every industrial category. Because the BPT effluent limitations had not been issued at the time most of the first round of discharge permits were issued, most permits did not contain categorical limits on discharges but rather incorporated individually negotiated limits based on the permit writer's "best professional judgment." Thus, the imposition of nationally uniform, categorical effluent limits was deferred long beyond the initial deadlines.

The task of implementing sections 301 and 304 required an enormous administrative effort. EPA discovered that it was even more complicated than expected. While only 27 industrial categories were identified in the Act, EPA identified 180 industrial subcategories and 45 other classifications for which it believed distinct effluent standards were needed. CEQ Environmental Quality—1974, at 141 (1974). Relying heavily on outside contractors for analysis of treatment technologies and industrial processes, EPA promulgated effluent guidelines for 30 industries by July 1974. The BPT guidelines, reflecting the performance of technology to be employed by 1977, relied largely on end-of-the-pipe treatment technologies for common pollutants and their parameters (e.g., biochemical oxygen demand, metals, pH, total suspended solids). The BAT guidelines, to be achieved by 1983, emphasized not only control technology but also process changes that for a few industries could result in attainment of the "no discharge" goal. Id. at 142.

EPA's effluent standards were invariably challenged in court. By 1977, more than 200 lawsuits had been filed. While this litigation delayed implementation of the effluent limits, judicial decisions helped clarify the requirements of the Act. Claims that the condition of receiving waters should be taken into account in establishing effluent limitations were rejected in Weyerhaeuser Co. v. Costle, 590 F.2d 101 (D.C. Cir. 1978). In EPA v. National Crushed Stone Association, 449 U.S. 64 (1980), the Supreme Court held that firms could be required to comply with technology-based effluent limits that would force some firms in an industry subcategory to go out of business. In many other cases courts reviewed industry claims that the technology was not available to comply with EPA's standards. By 1989, United States Courts of Appeals had decided at least 27 cases challenging the validity of effluent guidelines.

See Chemical Manufacturers Association v. EPA, 870 F.2d 177, 198 n.39 (5th Cir. 1989).

Section 308 of the Clean Water Act gives EPA data collection authority to assist in the development of effluent guidelines. This authority includes the right to impose record-keeping, sampling, and reporting requirements on point sources and a right of entry to inspect and gather data on the premises of such sources. A study of the guidelines development process found that this authority had not been of much help to EPA in developing BPT standards because legal challenges by industry delayed data gathering and "forced data collection through Section 308 authority created or worsened an adversarial relationship between EPA and an industry." W. Magat, A. Krupnick & W. Harrington, Rules in the Making 36 (1986). As a result, "[i]ndustry was capable of manipulating the rulemaking process by withholding data on costly, but effective, abatement technologies and by supplying excessive and confusing data." Id.

The process used by EPA to develop effluent standards for industrial dischargers is illustrated in Figure 6.6. As EPA acquired more experience in promulgating effluent standards, the process improved somewhat, though it remains extraordinarily cumbersome and data-intensive. EPA staff may take as many as 20 samples of wastewater at a plant and analyze each for 100 different pollutants in order to contribute to development of a data base to support effluent guidelines. Settlement with NRDC Puts EPA on Schedule to Issue Effluent Guidelines for 20 Industries, 22 Envtl. Rep. 2323, 2324 (1992).

William Pedersen views the process of establishing effluent guidelines to be a wasteful exercise that leads to standards that quickly become out of date:

> Each guideline has required a major and expensive rulemaking. Most of the effort was spent on exploring, for EPA's education, details of the costs and achievable reductions for various technologies in the industry under consideration at the time the guideline was being developed. That knowledge had only short-term value; it quickly became outdated with economic changes and the advance of technology. Moreover, the process demanded that EPA develop expertise in an impossibly wide variety of fields, duplicating knowledge already acquired by the industries involved. [Pedersen, Turning the Tide on Water Quality, 15 Ecology L.Q. 69, 85 (1988).]

Pedersen maintains that the fundamental flaw in the effluent standards is their technology-based approach, which "makes environmental performance irrelevant" while bringing costs to center stage. The result "has been a slight and variable willingness to cut back unduly strict requirements, coupled with a complete inability to strengthen unduly lenient standards." Id. at 87.

ii. Effluent Standards for Toxic Water Pollutants

Ironically, Congress turned to technology-based effluent standards because of wide agreement that water quality-based approaches were far more difficult to implement. In the one area where Congress initially sought to retain a water quality-based approach—control of toxic pollutants—EPA soon agreed to substitute a technology-based approach as well. Deficiencies in this approach resulted in yet another shift in regulatory emphasis when the 1987 Amendments placed renewed emphasis on a water quality-based approach for controlling toxics, as we will see in section D.

FIGURE 6.6
The Industrial Water Pollution Standard-Setting Process

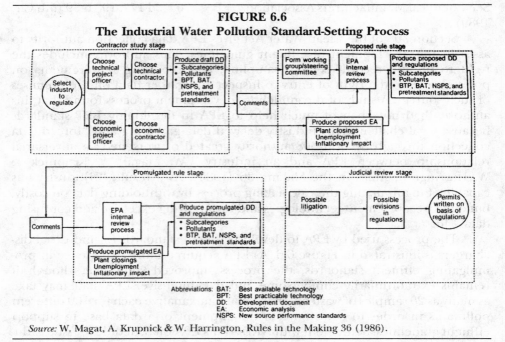

Source: W. Magat, A. Krupnick & W. Harrington, Rules in the Making 36 (1986).

The 1972 Act reflected congressional concern that discharges of toxic pollutants posed potentially serious health risks. Thus, Congress created a regulatory scheme for toxics very different from the technology-based program otherwise applicable to point sources. To implement section 101(a)(3)'s ambitious goal that there be no discharge of "toxic pollutants in toxic amounts," section 307(a) of the 1972 Act required EPA to establish a list of toxic water pollutants and to set health-based standards for controlling them within 90 days. Unlike the technology-based standards, in which cost considerations could play a limited role, these regulations were to be strictly health-based and were to be established without regard to cost, technological feasibility, or economic impact.

EPA found the task Congress had given it to be hopelessly difficult. After proposing standards for nine toxic water pollutants, the agency determined that defensible standards could not be promulgated given the dearth of available data on aquatic toxicology and the fate and transport of pollutants. Environmental groups brought several lawsuits against EPA after it missed the deadline for promulgating standards under section 307(a).

After lengthy negotiations between EPA and the environmental groups and several meetings with industry intervenors, a comprehensive settlement agreement was reached. Incorporated into a consent decree, called the "Flannery Decree" after the judge who approved it, the settlement committed EPA to a schedule for promulgating effluent guidelines, pretreatment standards, and new source performance standards for 65 toxic pollutants and 21 industries. The agreement shifted EPA's focus from health-based regulation to technology-based standards with tight deadlines for issuance.

The Flannery Decree was subsequently ratified, amended in some details, and incorporated in section 301 of the Act by the 1977 Amendments.

A statement by the House conferees noted that the approach in section 307(a) had failed primarily due to "the formal, cumbersome rulemaking process."

Although the Flannery Decree originally required EPA to establish technology-based standards for 65 toxic pollutants discharged by 21 primary industries, it was subsequently broadened to cover 126 pollutants from 34 industrial categories. These 126 pollutants, which by no means include all significant toxic pollutants of concern today, became known as "priority pollutants."

iii. Variances

The trade-off between flexibility and complexity is well illustrated by efforts to fine-tune national effluent standards. Standards established for industrial categories containing as many as 100 or more dischargers may be inappropriate for individual plants with special circumstances not easily taken into account in a national standard. For example, a plant may have a shortage of land on which to build additional waste treatment capacity, or air quality controls may prevent the use of certain treatment processes. How should EPA take such factors into account without either defeating the goal of nationally uniform standards or hopelessly complicating the standard-setting process?

The 1972 Act did not explicitly address this issue other than to allow EPA flexibility to define additional industry subcategories. In its early regulations, EPA devised an alternative approach allowing individual permit applicants an opportunity to request a variance for factors "fundamentally different" from those considered by EPA. As noted above, in the *Du Pont* decision the Supreme Court strongly endorsed this "FDF variance" for BPT, although it later held in EPA v. National Crushed Stone Association, 449 U.S. 64 (1980), that EPA need not consider an individual firm's ability to afford BPT requirements.

While Congress authorized some modifications of effluent standards in sections 301(c) and 301(g), the 1977 Amendments added section 301(*l*), which prohibited modification of any requirements applicable to toxic pollutants. In Chemical Manufacturers Association v. NRDC, 470 U.S. 116 (1985), the Supreme Court reviewed a Third Circuit decision holding that FDF variances could not be granted for discharges of toxics into sewage treatment systems, which are known as "indirect" discharges and governed by the pretreatment program. The Court had to decide whether an FDF variance was a "modification" in the sense used by section 301(*l*).

‖ ***Chemical Manufacturers*** ‖
‖ ***Association v. NRDC*** ‖
‖ **470 U.S. 116 (1985)** ‖

JUSTICE WHITE delivered the opinion of the Court.

Section 301(*l*) states that EPA may not "modify" any requirement of §301 insofar as toxic materials are concerned. EPA insists that §301(*l*) prohibits only those modifications expressly permitted by other provisions of §301, namely, those that §301(c) and §301(g) would allow on economic or water-quality grounds. Section 301(*l*), it is urged, does not address the very different issue of FDF variances. . . .

A

NRDC insists that the language of §301(*l*) is itself enough to require affirmance of the Court of Appeals, since on its face it forbids any modifications of the effluent limitations that EPA must promulgate for toxic pollutants. If the word "modify" in §301(*l*)is read in its broadest sense, that is, to encompass any change or alteration in the standards, NRDC is correct. But it makes little sense to construe the section to forbid EPA to amend its own standards, even to correct an error or to impose stricter requirements. . . . As NRDC does and must concede, §301(*l*) cannot be read to forbid every change in the toxic waste standards. The word "modify" thus has no plain meaning as used in §301(*l*), and is the proper subject of construction by EPA and the courts. . . . We should defer to [EPA's] view unless the legislative history or the purpose and structure of the statute clearly reveal a contrary intent on the part of Congress. NRDC submits that the legislative materials evince such a contrary intent. We disagree. . . .

[Based on an examination of the legislative history of section 301(*l*), the Court concludes that Congress intended for it to bar only waivers based on the economic capability of dischargers under section 301(c) or on water quality considerations under section 301(g).]

After examining the wording and legislative history of the statute, we agree with EPA and CMA that the legislative history itself does not evince an unambiguous congressional intention to forbid all FDF waivers with respect to toxic materials.

C

Neither are we convinced that FDF variances threaten to frustrate the goals and operation of the statutory scheme set up by Congress. The nature of FDF variances has been spelled out both by this Court and by the Agency itself. The regulation explains that its purpose is to remedy categories which were not accurately drawn because information was either not available to or not considered by the Administrator in setting the original categories and limitations. An FDF variance does not excuse compliance with a correct requirement, but instead represents an acknowledgement that not all relevant factors were taken sufficiently into account in framing that requirement originally, and that those relevant factors, properly considered, would have justified—indeed, required—the creation of a subcategory for the discharger in question. As we have recognized, the FDF variance is a laudable corrective mechanism, "an acknowledgment that the uniform . . . limitation was set without reference to the full range of current practices, to which the Administrator was to refer." EPA v. National Crushed Stone Assn., 449 U.S. 64, 77-78 (1980). It is, essentially, not an exception to the standard-setting process, but rather a more fine-tuned application of it.

We are not persuaded by NRDC's argument that granting FDF variances is inconsistent with the goal of uniform effluent limitations under the Act. . . .

NRDC concedes that EPA could promulgate rules under §307 of the Act creating a subcategory for each source which is fundamentally different from the rest of the class under the factors the EPA must consider in drawing categories. The same result is produced by the issuance of an FDF variance for the same failure properly to subdivide a broad category. Since the dispute is therefore reduced to an argument over the means used by EPA to define subcategories of indirect dischargers in order to achieve the goals of the Act, these are particularly persuasive cases for deference to the Agency's interpretation.

NRDC argues, echoing the concern of the Court of Appeals below, that allowing FDF variances will render meaningless the §301(*l*) prohibition against modifications on the basis of economic and water quality factors. That argument ignores the clear difference between the purpose of FDF waivers and that of §301(c) and (g) modifications, a difference we explained in *National Crushed Stone*. A discharger that satisfies the requirements of §301(c) qualifies for a variance "simply because [it] could not afford a compliance cost that is not fundamentally different from those the Administrator has already considered" in creating a category and setting an effluent limitation. 449 U.S., at 78. A §301(c) modification forces "a displacement of calculations already performed, not because those calculations were incomplete or had unexpected effects, but only because the costs happened to fall on one particular operator, rather than on another who might be economically better off." Ibid. FDF variances are specifically unavailable for the grounds that would justify the statutory modifications. Both a source's inability to pay the foreseen costs, grounds for a §301(c) modification, and the lack of a significant impact on water quality, grounds for a §301(g) modification, are irrelevant under FDF variance procedures.

EPA and CMA point out that the availability of FDF variances makes bearable the enormous burden faced by EPA in promulgating categories of sources and setting effluent limitations. Acting under stringent timetables, EPA must collect and analyze large amounts of technical information concerning complex industrial categories. Understandably, EPA may not be apprised of and will fail to consider unique factors applicable to atypical plants during the categorical rulemaking process, and it is thus important that EPA's nationally binding categorical pretreatment standards for indirect dischargers be tempered with the flexibility that the FDF variance mechanism offers, a mechanism repugnant to neither the goals nor the operation of the Act.

III

Viewed in its entirety, neither the language nor the legislative history of the Act demonstrates a clear congressional intent to forbid EPA's sensible variance mechanism for tailoring the categories it promulgates. In the absence of a congressional directive to the contrary, we accept EPA's conclusion that §301(*l*) does not prohibit FDF variances.

JUSTICE MARSHALL, . . . dissenting.

. . . EPA's argument that §301(*l*) proscribes only those modifications otherwise authorized by §§301(c) and (g) . . . is clearly inconsistent with congressional intent; the plain meaning of the statute and its legislative history show a clear congressional intent to ban all "modifications." . . .

If these two modifications are the only ones now prohibited, the result is wholly counterintuitive. EPA is in effect contending that economic and water-quality factors present the most compelling case for modification of the standard in the nontoxic context—as they are explicitly authorized by statute—but the least compelling case for modification in the toxic context—as they are the only modifications prohibited by §301(*l*). As might be expected, EPA does not present any theory, much less a logical argument, for evidence in the legislative history, to support this extremely inconsistent result. . . .

EPA's second construction of the statutory scheme is, on the surface, a more plausible one. EPA argues that FDF variances do not excuse compliance with the correct standards, but instead provide a means for setting more appropriate standards. It is clear that, pursuant to §307(b)(2), EPA can "revise" the pretreatment standards, as long as it does so "following the procedure established . . . for the promulgation of such standards." The statute contemplates that the standards will be set and revised through notice-and-comment rulemaking and will be applicable to categories of sources. EPA argues that such a "revision," which is clearly not proscribed by §301(*l*), would be substantively indistinguishable from an FDF variance. . . .

To support its argument, EPA points out that the factors that may justify an FDF variance are the same factors that may be taken into account in setting and revising the national pretreatment standards. . . . EPA acknowledges that the statute requires that the national pretreatment standards be established—and therefore revised—for "categories" of dischargers and not on a case-by-case basis. It argues, however, that nothing in the Clean Water Act precludes EPA from defining a subcategory that has only one discharger.

The logic of EPA's position is superficially powerful. If EPA can, through rulemaking, define a subcategory that includes only one discharger, why should it not be able to do so through a variance procedure? In fact, if rulemaking and the variance procedure were alternative means to the same end, I might have no quarrel with EPA's position, which the Court has accepted. . . .

However, the Agency's position does not withstand more than superficial analysis. An examination of the legislative history of the 1972 amendments to the Clean Water Act—the relevance of which both the Court and EPA ignore— reveals that Congress attached great *substantive* significance to the method used for establishing pollution control requirements.

The Conference Committee Report directed EPA to "make the determination of the economic impact of an effluent limitation on the basis of classes and categories of point sources, *as distinguished from a plant by plant determination.*" 1972 Leg. Hist. 304 (emphasis added). . . .

The legislative history also makes clear why Congress found it so important that the standards be set for "categories" of dischargers, and not for individual dischargers. Congress intended to use the standards as a means to "force" the introduction of more effective pollution control technology. . . . By requiring that the standards be set by reference to either the "average of the best" or very "best" technology, the Act seeks to foster technological innovation. . . .

Unlike the statutory revision mechanism of §307(b), FDF variances are set not by reference to a category of dischargers, but instead by reference to a single discharger. In evaluating an application for a variance, EPA does not look at the group of dischargers in the same position as the applicant, but instead focuses solely on the characteristics of the applicant itself. Under the FDF program, there is no mechanism for EPA to ascertain whether there are any other dischargers in that position. Moreover, there is no mechanism for EPA to group together similarly situated dischargers. Quite to the contrary, a scheme in which the initial screening may be done by the individual States, at times determined by when the variance application is filed, is unlikely to lead to the identification of new subcategories. . . .

In the aggregate, if EPA defines a new pretreatment subcategory through rulemaking, the BAT-level pollution control requirement of each discharger would be determined by reference to the capability of the "best" performer. In contrast, if EPA provides individual variances to each plant in this group, only one discharger would have a requirement based on the capability of the best performer—the best performer itself. The others would necessarily be subject to less stringent standards. . . .

It is true, of course, that even the statutory revision procedure might identify a subcategory with only one discharger. That procedure, however, will have established that this discharger is uniquely situated. In contrast, an FDF variance sets an individual requirement even where there may be similarly situated dischargers.

NOTES AND QUESTIONS

1. How do the majority and the dissent differ in their characterizations of the purpose of FDF variances? To what extent do these differences reflect different conceptions of the role of the effluent standards in forcing the development of improved pollution control technology?

2. The Court split 5-4 in this case, with three other Justices joining Justice Marshall's dissent. Justice Marshall's papers reveal that the outcome was even closer than the vote suggests. When the Justices met to vote on the merits, following oral argument, they split 4-4, with Justice White finding the case too close to call. A week later, Justice White voted in favor of EPA, while still expressing some doubt about the outcome. He then was assigned to write the majority opinion, and expressed some ambivalence about the result after seeing Justice Marshall's "very good dissent." Percival, Environmental Law in the Supreme Court: Highlights from the Marshall Papers, 23 Envtl. L. Rep. 10606, 10613 (1993).

3. At the time the Court decided this case, EPA headquarters had received 58 applications for FDF variances and granted only four. Pedersen, Turning the Tide on Water Quality, 15 Ecology L.Q. 69, 86 n.81 (1988). By September 1995, EPA had granted only eight FDF variances, while denying nearly 200. Given the small number of favorable applications for variances, why do you think there has been so much litigation concerning them? What impact is the availability of FDF variances likely to have on the administrative costs of implementing effluent limitations?

4. BAT regulations are now coming into effect for many industries, spurring more applications for FDF variances. Because these applications generally require EPA to assess plant-specific technical data on production processes and control technologies, EPA has been slow to rule on such applications, taking an average of three years to process them. To expedite the FDF process, the 1987 Amendments required EPA to rule on FDF variance applications within 180 days of submission, a deadline that EPA has found to be difficult to meet. EPA's failure to meet this deadline has been held not to stay a discharger's obligation to comply with the effluent limits that are the subject of the application. See Chemical Manufacturers Association v. EPA, 870 F.2d 177 (5th Cir. 1989) (citing §505(a)(2)).

5. The 1987 CWA Amendments specifically addressed the FDF variance for the first time. A new section 301(n) sets out permissible grounds for FDF variances for toxic pollutants. Could the FDF variance provision ever be used to justify more *stringent* conditions on a discharger? What circumstances might justify such action, and how might it come about? EPA's regulations allow for the possibility. Does section 301(n)?

iv.   Effluent Limitations: The State of the Art

The process of implementing the Clean Water Act's technology-based approach to water pollution control has been laborious, technically complex, and marked by repeated delays and missed deadlines. Having "shifted our faith from science to engineering," Houck, The Regulation of Toxic Pollutants Under the Clean Water Act, 21 Envtl. L. Rep. 10528, 10536 (1991), the Act and the Flannery Decree forced EPA to make engineering judgments based on detailed studies of production processes and pollution control technologies on an industry subcategory-by-subcategory basis. Many effluent guidelines have taken five or more years to develop. 55 Fed. Reg. 80, 81 (1990). When ultimately implemented, "BAT had lost its bite," though it "has probably been the most effective pollution control program in the world in terms of producing identifiable abatement—short of outright bans—if only because alternative programs have proven equally burdensome and so much less effective." Houck, above, at 10538, 10541.

The Flannery Decree ultimately produced numerous effluent guidelines, but it did not ensure comprehensive coverage of industrial dischargers. By 1990, EPA had promulgated effluent guidelines and standards covering 51 categories of dischargers and had completed all but one of the rulemakings required under the Flannery Decree. Despite this progress, EPA's effluent guidelines remained far from comprehensive. Nearly 80 percent of existing industrial dischargers of toxics (59,338 of 74,525) still were not covered by BAT standards. Natural Resources Defense Council v. Reilly, 32 ERC (BNA) 1969, 1972 n.25 (D.D.C. 1991). Moreover, the guidelines that had been issued by EPA often failed to cover significant substances or were based on data that were woefully outdated. As a result, even though all dischargers must have a permit, large quantities of toxics were being discharged because they were uncontrolled or poorly controlled in existing permits.

When it amended the Clean Water Act in 1987, Congress expressly required EPA to strengthen, expand, and revise existing technology-based controls to ensure that significant sources of discharges did not escape regulation. Congress added section 304(m), which required EPA to review and revise existing effluent guidelines by set deadlines, and to establish new effluent guidelines and new source performance standards for dischargers of toxics and unconventional pollutants not previously covered by such standards.

While the Clean Water Act's technology-based effluent limits have generated significant reductions in pollution from industrial sources, they have received considerable criticism from many quarters. Industry groups argue that the standards are inflexible and inefficient because they do not take into account the condition of receiving waters or differences among firms in the marginal costs of controlling pollution. Environmentalists decry the length of time it takes EPA to issue technology-based standards and the weakness of the ultimate standards EPA has set. Technology-based standards also provide little incentive for industries to develop better pollution control technology and they do not guarantee that health-based goals will be achieved.

Consider, for example, EPA's effluent guidelines for the organic chemical, plastics, and synthetic fiber (OCPSF) industries. When EPA issued the standards after 11 years of study and rulemaking proceedings, the agency had produced an administrative record more than 600,000 pages long. The standards then were challenged in court by a variety of industry groups and NRDC. Legal briefs in the litigation consumed more than 3,000 pages with a

9,000 page appendix. The court ultimately remanded standards for 20 pollutants to EPA on the ground that the agency had failed "to demonstrate a reasonable basis for its conclusion that in-plant treatment can eliminate pollutants as effectively as end-of-the-pipe systems" on which biological treatment is used. Chemical Mfrs. Ass'n v. EPA, 870 F.2d 177 (5th Cir. 1989). The court also agreed with NRDC that EPA had erred by failing to consider recycling technologies when establishing a new source performance standard (NSPS). The court concluded that when 36 plants—more than one-quarter of the industry—already had achieved zero discharges through recycling, it was arbitrary and capricious for EPA not to consider recycling technology when setting the NSPS. Six years after the court's decision, EPA still had not completed action on all of the issues remanded to it by the court.

Frustration with technology-based standards is inspiring proposals for more flexible and more efficient approaches for controlling water pollution. In March 1995, the Clinton administration supported proposals to allow companies that agree to adopt innovative treatment approaches to prevent pollution to take more time to comply with effluent standards. B. Clinton & A. Gore, Reinventing Environmental Regulations 43 (1995). It also endorsed effluent trading, which would allow sources that reduce pollution below the required minimum to acquire pollution allowances that could be sold to other firms. The administration estimated that trades between industrial point sources could save between $8.4 million and $1.9 billion in compliance costs for industry. Id. at 19. To provide an incentive for pollutant reductions that exceed technology-based standards, others have proposed to impose effluent charges or to negotiate a "public contract" between regulators and industries that will require pollution to be phased out over a fixed period of time.

NOTES AND QUESTIONS

1. Should effluent trading be permitted between industrial point sources? What advantages would it have? What disadvantages? Would it be possible to implement such a system without changing existing law?

2. Oliver Houck concludes that the stringency of EPA's technology-based standards often depends primarily on the industry's political clout:

> It is an astonishing but commonplace fact that when a BAT-limited industry is required to reduce x further—due to water quality, health, public relations, or other considerations—it finds the ability to do so. In this regard, BAT appears to be more a problem of lead time and amortization of costs than a problem of engineering. BAT remains as driven by the most an industry will accept as by the most it can do.
>
> This conclusion is reinforced by the equally disturbing fact that discharge standards have emerged unevenly, with a heavy "zero discharge" hand on such unfortunates as seafood canners and placer mine operators, and a remarkably blind eye to available closed-cycle systems for some of the nation's highest-volume dischargers of broad-spectrum toxins. The disparities in these standards reflect nothing more starkly than a disparity in clout. These disparities are amplified by the fact that, for the decade of the 1980s, EPA only worked with any intensity on that limited group of industries and that limited set of toxic compounds mandated by the 1976 decree. [Houck, The Regulation of Toxic Pollutants Under the Clean Water Act, 21 Envtl. L. Rep. 10528, 10539 (Sept. 1991).]

Does this experience suggest that a technology-*forcing* approach to regulation should be employed more extensively? Would industries with little political clout be any better off under alternative approaches to regulation?

B.   POTWs AND THE PRETREATMENT PROGRAM

Sewage disposal became a water pollution problem in the late nineteenth century when urban areas turned to sewer systems for disposing of human waste. The percentage of the U.S. population served by sewer systems rose from 3 percent in 1860 to 33 percent in 1900 and 50 percent in 1930. Council on Environmental Quality, Environmental Quality—1974, at 144 (1974). Sewer systems improved sanitary conditions in cities by collecting waste and transporting it downstream. While it was widely assumed that rivers and streams could easily assimilate wastes, growing volumes of raw sewage eventually created problems so severe that water pollution became a national concern. By 1910, 38 percent of the nation's population was served by sewer systems, but only 4 percent was served by sewage treatment plants. Id.

Municipalities were reluctant to invest in expensive treatment facilities that would primarily benefit downstream populations. Beginning in 1956, the federal government sought to overcome this resistance by providing federal funds for the construction of sewage treatment plants. Nearly $100 billion in federal, state, tribal, and local funds has been invested in the construction of thousands of sewage treatment plants, which now serve 173 million people with at least secondary treatment systems. However, the continued expansion of sewer systems has outpaced the expansion of treatment capacity in some areas, such as New York City. Gold, Despite Decades of Spending, Sewage Plants Are Full Up, N.Y. Times, Aug. 18, 1991, at E16.

Publicly owned wastewater treatment works (POTWs) are regulated separately from industrial point source dischargers under the Clean Water Act, which applies a separate set of effluent limits to them under section 301(b)(1)(B) of the Act. In 1972, Congress required POTWs to achieve at least secondary treatment levels by 1977 and an even more advanced level of treatment by 1983. The latter requirement was eliminated in 1981, though limits more stringent than secondary treatment limits may still be imposed if necessary to meet applicable water quality standards. §301(b)(1)(C). Congress also relaxed treatment requirements in 1977 when it added section 301(h), which authorizes POTWs discharging directly into marine waters to waive secondary treatment requirements in certain circumstances.

POTWs are substantial point source dischargers (see Figure 6.5 on page 636) whose effluent contains by-products of municipal sewage and industrial discharges subject to the pretreatment program (see Figure 6.1 on page 587). Sludge is the potentially hazardous by-product of the treatment process, which POTWs must manage in large quantities. Most sludge is disposed on land; it no longer may legally be dumped into the ocean as New York City and some of its neighbors in New Jersey had done for years. The 1987 Amendments added section 405 to the Clean Water Act, which required EPA to develop standards for disposal of sewage sludge to be implemented through the NPDES permits issued to POTWs.

In 1993, EPA issued regulations governing the use and disposal of sewage sludge pursuant to section 405(d) of the Clean Water Act. 58 Fed. Reg. 9,248 (1993). The regulations impose numeric limits on concentrations of various heavy metals and pathogens in sewage sludge that apply except when sludge is taken to a municipal landfill. EPA's decision to exempt from the numeric limits sludge taken to municipal landfills was upheld in Sierra Club v. EPA, 992 F.2d 337 (D.C. Cir. 1993). The court found that EPA had insufficient information to establish scientifically defensible numeric limits on sludge taken to such landfills. In Leather Industries of America v. EPA, 40 F.3d 392 (D.C. Cir. 1994), EPA's numeric limits on selenium and chromium in sludge were struck down as insufficiently supported in the administrative record. However, the court upheld EPA's refusal to provide for site-specific variances and it confirmed that the agency has the authority to regulate sludge to protect against phytotoxicity, the reduction in crop yields that occurs when plants absorb toxic metals.

Section 405(e) of the Clean Water Act specifies that "the manner of disposal or use of sludge is a local determination" so long as federal regulations are not violated. In Welch v. Board of Supervisors of Rappahannock County, 860 F. Supp. 328 (W.D. Va. 1994), a county ordinance banning the application of sewage sludge to farmland was held not to be preempted by federal law because state and local governments may adopt more stringent limits on sludge disposal, so long as they at least meet federal minimum standards.

As controls on toxic discharges into surface waters have been strengthened, more pressure has been placed on a particularly weak link in the Clean Water Act's system of controls: the pretreatment program. Many industrial sources have chosen to avoid the NPDES permit process and to escape RCRA standards by discharging toxics and hazardous waste into sewers. These indirect dischargers are exempt from NPDES permit requirements. (Remember that the NPDES requirements apply only to point sources that discharge into surface waters and that domestic sewage is exempt from regulation as a hazardous waste under RCRA.) The Office of Technology Assessment reported in 1987 that more than 160,000 industrial facilities discharged more than one trillion gallons of wastewater containing RCRA hazardous wastes into municipal sewers each year. If not treated at industrial facilities, these "indirect" waste discharges would contain 160,000 metric tons of hazardous components, including 62,000 metric tons of metals that are priority pollutants, 40,000 tons of organic chemicals that are priority pollutants, and 64,000 tons of other hazardous organic chemicals. OTA, Wastes in Marine Environments 212 (1987).

The rationale for exempting indirect dischargers from the NPDES program was that it would be redundant to require controls on discharges that already would be subject to treatment in POTWs. To prevent indirect discharges from interfering with the operation of POTWs, section 307 of the Clean Water Act requires pretreatment of such discharges to control pollutants that are not susceptible to treatment by POTWs. EPA has promulgated general pretreatment regulations that prohibit the discharge of pollutants that might interfere with or pass through POTWs and that require the development of local pretreatment programs. In Arkansas Poultry Federation v. EPA, 852 F.2d 324 (8th Cir. 1988), the Eighth Circuit upheld EPA's definitions of "interference" and "pass through," which provide that indirect dischargers may only be penalized for discharges that actually cause permit violations at POTWs. EPA is promulgating technologically based pretreatment requirements on an industry-wide basis ("categorical pre-treatment requirements"). Individual POTWs also are authorized to impose local limits.

Plagued with problems of nonimplementation and lax enforcement, the pretreatment program had long been considered by many to be a failure, though belated efforts to beef up enforcement appear to be producing some results. Problems with the program are described in Houck, Ending the War: A Strategy to Save America's Coastal Zone, 47 Md. L. Rev. 358, 384-388 (1988). Professor Houck questions the basic premise of assigning responsibility for implementing a national program to local governments. He notes that "even if the purpose of a *national* discharge program were to offset the political pressures placed on states to relax their programs, those same pressures are even more formidable at the local level, producing a wide variety of standards and levels of compliance among the local municipal systems." Houck also questions the basic concept on which the nation's sewage disposal policy is founded: using waterways for sewage disposal, which he terms "a little barbaric." He notes that alternative technology exists that could avoid "the illogic of first putting human wastes into our water and then building ever more expensive plants to take them out." Id. at 381-383. But given the enormous investment society has made in waterborne sewage disposal systems, he recognizes the futility of his complaint.

NOTES AND QUESTIONS

1. Is the delegation of program authority to hundreds of local entities subject to intense local political pressure from dischargers a basic flaw in the pretreatment program? Why doesn't support for a clean environment effectively counterbalance local political pressures? Many federal environmental programs delegated to the states are subject to EPA supervision. EPA must approve POTWs' pretreatment programs. Could the system of program delegation be improved, or is the concept fundamentally flawed? Is the basic problem that indirect dischargers are too numerous and mobile to be subject to effective enforcement action?

2. One reason why so many toxic materials are discharged into sewers is the domestic sewage exclusion to RCRA. RCRA's definition of "solid waste" expressly exempts "solid or dissolved materials in domestic sewage . . . or industrial discharges which are point sources subject to permits under section [402 of the Clean Water Act]." RCRA §1004(27). Thus, facilities can escape RCRA regulation by discharging hazardous waste into surface waters subject to NPDES permits, and they can escape the NPDES permit process by discharging such waste into sewers. Should the domestic sewage exclusion apply to hazardous waste mixed with sewage from an industrial plant rather than from residences? In Comite Pro Rescate de la Salud v. Puerto Rico Aqueduct and Sewer Authority, 888 F.2d 180 (1st Cir. 1989), the First Circuit said no.

3. The pretreatment program was supposed to prevent the domestic sewage exclusion from causing harm. When Congress amended RCRA in 1984, it required EPA to undertake a comprehensive study of the impact of the domestic sewage exclusion. RCRA §3018. EPA completed the Domestic Sewage Study in February 1986. The study found that many significant hazardous waste discharges are not covered by existing pretreatment regulations because they involve chemicals that, while hazardous, are not among the 126 priority pollutants covered by the Flannery Decree. The study noted that pretreatment standards for certain industries "do not specifically regulate nonpriority organics, despite the fact that many of these pollutants are discharged in significant concentrations and/or loadings." More than 38.3 million pounds of toxic pollutants discharged annually were not covered by effluent limits under the Flannery

Decree, and more than 7.2 million pounds of hazardous metals and between 81 and 132 million pounds of priority hazardous organic constituents were discharged to POTWs even after implementation of categorical pretreatment standards. EPA, Report to Congress on the Discharge of Hazardous Wastes to Publicly Owned Treatment Works 7-9 (Feb. 1986).

4. In response to its Domestic Sewage Study, EPA in 1990 revised its pretreatment regulations. 55 Fed. Reg. 30,082 (1990). While the new regulations place numerical limits on discharges of ignitable waste, restrictions on discharges of toxic or corrosive waste are left largely to individual POTWs because of the variability of waste streams. The regulations require discharges of trucked or hauled waste to be made only at specific discharge points designated by POTWs. POTWs are required to use permits or an equivalent mechanism to control discharges by significant industrial users, who must file semiannual reports on their discharges. See Hogeland, EPA's Pretreatment Regulation Amendments: Forcing Enforcement, 20 Envtl. Rep. 889 (1990).

5. In a 1991 report to Congress, EPA reaffirmed its faith in the pretreatment program, which it found had reduced discharges of metals by 95 percent and discharges of toxic organics by 40 to 75 percent. The report noted that data from the Toxic Release Inventory indicated that at least 680 million pounds of toxics were discharged to 1,700 POTWs in 1988. While the report found that two-thirds of POTWs had not established local limits for dischargers, it maintained that the flexibility afforded to POTWs by the program was necessary because of wide variations in local circumstances. EPA, Report to Congress on the National Pretreatment Program (1991). The growth of new industries that generate new types of pollutants, such as the rapid rise of the semiconductor industry during the 1990s, poses a particular challenge for the pretreatment program. EPA, EPA's National Pretreatment Program, 1973-2003: Thirty Years of Protecting the Environment (2004). Yet many new contaminants passing through POTWs may be the product of waste generated by households. A study released in 2002 by the U.S. Geological Survey found that of 139 streams analyzed in 30 states 80 percent had some contamination from antibiotics, steroids, synthetic hormones, and other commonly used pharmaceutical drugs. Pharmaceuticals, Hormones, and Other Organic Wastewater Contaminants in U.S. Streams 1999-2000: A National Reconnaissance, 36 Envtl. Sci. & Tech. 1202 (2002).

6. POTWs discharging into marine waters may obtain waivers from treatment requirements under section 301(h) of the Clean Water Act. More than 50 POTWs have obtained such waivers, which EPA may approve only with the concurrence of the state in which the POTW is located. EPA issued regulations governing the section 301(h) waiver process in August 1994. 59 Fed. Reg. 40,642 (1994).

WATER POLLUTION CONTROL: A PATHFINDER

An excellent review of the early history of water pollution control efforts in the U.S. is William L. Andreen, The Evolution of Water Pollution Control in the United States—State, Local, and Federal Efforts, 1789-1972: Part I, 22 Stan. Envtl. L.J. 145 (2003), and Part II, 23 Stan. Envtl. L.J. 215 (2003). The Federal Water Pollution Control Act, now known as the Clean Water Act, at 33 U.S.C. §§1251-1387, was enacted in 1972 and substantially amended in 1977, 1981, and

1987. Other federal laws for controlling water pollution are outlined on page 592. The U.S. Environmental Protection Agency's regulations implementing the Clean Water Act are codified at 40 C.F.R. pts. 100-140. Effluent guidelines and standards and general pretreatment regulations are located at 40 C.F.R. pts. 400-471. EPA's regulations governing the issuance of permits under section 404 of the Act can be found at 40 C.F.R. pts. 230-233; the regulations governing the U.S. Army Corps of Engineers' section 404 permit program are found at 33 C.F.R. pts. 323-331. These CFR sections are available online through the National Archives and Records Administration's website, which includes a searchable version of the Code of Federal Regulations (*http://www.gpoaccess.gov/cfr/index.html*) and an electronic version of the CFR ("e-CFR") updated continuously, which can be found at *http://www.gpoaccess.gov/ecfr.*

EPA's Office of Water (OW) is responsible for implementing the Clean Water Act. OW's website is located at *http://www.epa.gov/ow.* A web page describing EPA's regulatory docket for water programs is located at *http://www.epa.gov/ow/docket.html.* The goals EPA seeks to achieve through its National Water Program are described at *http://www.epa.gov/ow/programs/goals.html.* EPA's efforts to encourage action to control nonpoint source pollution are described at *http://www.epa.gov/owow/nps/.* The activities of the Agency's Office of Wastewater Management are explained at *http://www.epa.gov/owm/.*

The EPA Water Office's website features a Watershed Information Network, which allows users to "Surf Your Watershed" to obtain information about the watershed in which they live. It includes a national watershed atlas, which can be found at *http://www.epa.gov/wateratlas,* a search function for locating watersheds by zip code, city, river, county or state (*http://www.cfpub.epa.gov/surf/locate/index.cfm*), an index of watershed indicators for assessing the health of individual watersheds, and an "Adopt Your Watershed" program at *http://www.epa.gov/adopt.* EPA operates a toll-free Wetlands Helpline that provides information about wetlands issues and regulatory requirements concerning development in wetlands areas. The Wetlands Helpline can be reached by phoning (800) 832-7828. The EPA also has a webpage with links to agency policy and technical documents concerning its administration of the section 404 permit program that can be accessed at *http://www.epa.gov/owow/wetlands/guidance.*

D.   WATER QUALITY-BASED CONTROLS: THE REGULATORY "SAFETY NET"?

The enactment of the Clean Water Act in 1972 reflected a fundamental shift away from a water quality-based approach to pollution control toward an approach that emphasized technology-based effluent limitations. This shift was a result of a broad consensus that previous water quality-based control efforts had been a dismal failure. Congress recognized that ambient water quality standards were ineffective because of "the character of the standards themselves, which focused on the tolerable effects rather than the preventable causes of water pollution," EPA v. California State Water Resources Board, 426 U.S. 200, 202 (1976). To ensure that reductions were required in pollutant discharges, Congress required the use of certain technology-based levels of control regardless of the conditions of the receiving waters, as illustrated by Weyerhaeuser v. Costle, 590 F.2d 1011 (D.C. Cir. 1978).

Despite the Act's new emphasis on a technology-based approach, Congress did not entirely abandon water quality-based controls; rather, it retained them as a "safety net" to back up the technology-based controls on which the Act primarily relies. Section 301(b)(1)(C) requires that NPDES permits include any more stringent limits that are necessary to ensure compliance with water quality standards the states and qualifying tribes must adopt pursuant to section 303. To implement this requirement, section 303(d) directs states to identify waters with insufficient controls and to calculate limits on pollutant loadings necessary for such waters to achieve water quality standards with a margin of safety. As discussed below, these provisions are becoming quite important as gains from technology-based reductions diminish.

Section 302 provides another vehicle for water quality-based controls by dictating that they be used to prevent discharges from interfering with "attainment or maintenance" of desired levels of water quality. EPA has not used this provision because it also authorizes modifications of effluent limits if a discharger demonstrates that there is no reasonable relationship between their costs and benefits. §302(b)(2)(A).

1. Water Quality Standards

Water quality standards have two components: (1) identification of the designated uses of a water body and (2) water quality criteria designed to protect the designated use. "Designated uses" represent the purposes for which each water segment is to be protected (e.g., public water supplies, propagation of fish and wildlife, recreational purposes, agriculture). "Water quality criteria" reflect judgments concerning the degree of protection from individual pollutants that is necessary to attain designated uses. When combined with designated uses, water quality criteria yield what are called "water quality standards," limits on ambient concentrations of pollutants in particular classes of waters. States and tribes must review and revise their water quality standards every three years (a "triennial review") and they must submit such standards to EPA for review and approval. §303(c). EPA can modify state or tribal standards that fail to meet the requirements of the Act. §303(c)(4).

A. Designated Uses and Antidegradation

While states and tribes have some flexibility in establishing designated uses for water segments, section 303(c)(2)(A) directs them in vague terms to "protect the public health or welfare, enhance the quality of water and serve the purposes" of the Act. States and tribes are directed to consider the use and value of their waters "for public water supplies, propagation of fish and wildlife, recreational purposes, and agricultural, industrial, and other purposes," including navigation. This ambiguous language has been interpreted by EPA to require at a minimum that water quality standards meet the "fishable/swimmable" goal of section 101(a)(2) unless that would result in "substantial and widespread economic and social impact." EPA also has required states and tribes to establish antidegradation policies designed to protect existing uses of water segments and to prevent deterioration of waters that exceed the purity necessary to meet the fishable/swimmable goal unless "necessary to accommodate important economic or social development." 40 C.F.R. §131.12(a)(2).

B. WATER QUALITY CRITERIA

States and tribes must adopt water quality criteria that specify maximum ambient levels of pollutants that will ensure that waters can be used for their designated purposes. EPA is directed by section 304(a) of the Act to develop water quality criteria, which can be used as a point of reference for states promulgating their own criteria. EPA's regulations do not specify for what pollutants criteria must be adopted by the states and tribes. Rather, they simply require that sufficient criteria be adopted "to protect the designated use."

The section 304(a) criteria are scientific recommendations that EPA develops for states to consider in adopting regulatory criteria under section 303(c). EPA's initial approach to issuing criteria was to conduct reviews of the scientific literature, which resulted in a series of water quality criteria documents, known as the 1968 "Green Book," the 1973 "Blue Book," and the 1976 "Red Book." The Agency subsequently adopted more formal procedures for developing water quality criteria, and it promulgated guidelines for developing criteria to protect aquatic life and human health when it published criteria for 64 toxic pollutants in November 1980. 45 Fed. Reg. 79,318. Additional criteria were adopted later, as summarized in the 1986 "Gold Book," called Quality Criteria for Water 1986. By 1999, EPA had established water quality criteria for more than 100 pollutants. Criteria to protect aquatic life have been published for 31 chemicals; criteria to protect human health have been published for 100 chemicals.

States were slow to promulgate water quality standards, despite issuance of EPA criteria. Most states failed to promulgate numerical standards for toxics or adopted standards far more lenient than those recommended by EPA's criteria. The Reagan administration contributed to the problem by expressing the view that EPA's criteria were scientifically flawed and should not be relied on by states.

In light of the uneven record of the states in adopting water quality criteria, the 1987 Amendments added a requirement that states adopt criteria for toxic pollutants "the discharge or presence of which in the affected waters could reasonably be expected to interfere with those designated uses adopted by the State." §303(c)(2)(B). Because of the difficulty in determining what levels of pollutants are safe for attaining designated uses, some states had adopted "narrative criteria" (e.g., "free from toxicity") that do not specify numerical limits on the ambient concentration of pollutants but that could form the basis for whole effluent toxicity testing. In the absence of numeric criteria for specific chemicals, however, it is difficult to employ water quality standards to impose additional limitations on discharges to a water body. The 1987 Amendments addressed this problem by requiring that numerical criteria be adopted for toxic pollutants, section 303(c)(2)(B), and they expressly endorsed the use of biological assessment criteria when numerical criteria are not available.

EPA has issued regulations requiring permit writers to translate state water quality standards that contain narrative criteria into chemical-specific effluent limits for permitees. The EPA regulations give permit writers three options: (1) use a calculated numeric water quality criterion derived from proposed state numeric criteria or other state policy interpreting the narrative criteria, (2) use EPA's recommended numeric criteria, or (3) rely on limits on the discharge of other pollutants found in the source's effluent ("indicator parameters"). These regulations were upheld in American Paper Institute, Inc. v. EPA, 996 F.2d 346 (D.C. Cir. 1993). The court stated that they "provide an eminently reasonable means of effectuating the intent of the previously adopted narrative criteria as well as Congress's own intent, made explicit in section 301 of the CWA, that *all* state water quality standards be enforced through meaningful limitations in individual NPDES permits." Id. at 351.

Some states have adopted water quality standards that are far more lenient than recommended by EPA's criteria. For example, EPA's 1984 criteria document for dioxin recommends that the concentration of dioxin be no greater than .0013 parts per quadrillion (ppq) in water bodies used as sources of drinking water or edible fish. Yet Virginia and Maryland adopted water quality standards limiting dioxin concentrations to 1.2 ppq, a level nearly 1,000 times more lenient than recommended by EPA's criteria. After EPA approved the standards, environmental groups brought suit. In Natural Resources Defense Council v. EPA, 16 F.3d 1395 (4th Cir. 1993), the court held that EPA could approve such standards so long as they were scientifically defensible and protective of designated uses, even though they were based on assumptions different from those employed by EPA in assessing the toxicity of dioxin. The court emphasized that states have the primary role in establishing water quality standards and that EPA's decision to approve them should be upheld if there is a rational basis for it in the record. The court also held that the availability of new data does not obligate EPA to update its water quality criteria guidance documents, and that such documents are not subject to judicial review under the Administrative Procedure Act because they do not represent final agency action.

Thus, even though new data indicated that EPA had greatly underestimated dioxin's tendency to bioconcentrate in fish (by factors ranging from 4 to 30 times), the court held that EPA had not acted improperly in allowing Virginia and Maryland to use even lower estimates of dioxin's potency and risk. Citing the complexity and uncertainty of the science, the court concluded that it would not second-guess EPA's decision. The court acknowledged that the 1.2 ppq water quality standard adopted by Virginia and Maryland could tolerate cancer risks as high as 1 in 10,000, while EPA's criteria were designed to tolerate risks only as great as 1 in 10 million. The court held that EPA had acted properly in approving the Virginia and Maryland standards, even though section 303(c)(3) of the CWA requires the EPA administrator to determine whether a state water quality standard "meets the requirements" of the Act.

NOTES AND QUESTIONS

1. The environmental groups in NRDC v. EPA argued that Virginia's water quality standard for dioxin was inadequate to protect groups of native Americans living near a Virginia paper mill who consume large quantities of fish.

If subsistence fishers tend to be from low-income and minority communities, does EPA's approach of basing its criteria on *average* fish consumption across the population raise environmental justice concerns? President Clinton's environmental justice executive order (Executive Order 12,898) directs all federal agencies, "whenever practicable and appropriate," to "collect, maintain, and analyze information on the consumption patterns of populations who principally rely on fish and/or wildlife for subsistence." The order directs agencies to "communicate to the public the risks of those consumption patterns." It also instructs agencies to incorporate consideration of "differential patterns of consumption of natural resources among minority populations and low-income populations" in their agency-wide environmental justice strategies. Could this require EPA to revise its water quality criteria for dioxin?

2. The Fourth Circuit rejected the argument that the dioxin standards should be stricter in order to protect recreational and subsistence fishers who consume much higher quantities of fish than the national average used in calculating the dioxin criteria. One approach for protecting subsistence users of contaminated fish has been to post warnings advising against consumption of certain types of fish. However, such warnings often are ignored. See Steinberg, Anglers Ignore Hudson Warnings, N.Y. Times, Sept. 3, 1994, at 24 (survey of fishermen by a New York environmental group found that more than 35 percent ate more fish than recommended).

3. EPA's review of the state dioxin water quality standards was based only on consideration of human health effects. Are there any regulations that could be used to restrict dioxin discharges more stringently in order to protect aquatic organisms and wildlife?

4. Tremendous uncertainty surrounds efforts to assess the effects on humans and aquatic organisms of a bewildering mix of toxic water pollutants. Can uncertainty be used to justify dramatically different water quality standards in different states?

Water Quality Criteria: Sources of Scientific Uncertainty

Consider the following sources of uncertainty concerning the effects of water pollutants on humans and aquatic organisms. Only a small fraction of the tens of thousands of commonly used chemicals have been tested for toxicity to aquatic organisms. Most testing has focused on acute toxicity because it is faster and easier to perform such tests. Thus, our knowledge of chronic effects is quite limited even though they may be more serious than acute effects.

Pollutants have different impacts on different organisms. Scientists typically select surrogate species of aquatic organisms, usually a crustacean, a fish, and an alga, for use in testing. But we know very little concerning the relative sensitivity of the hundreds of significant species of aquatic organisms in relation to surrogate species. Aquatic toxicity testing traditionally has had gross lethality as its end-point of concern, rather than sublethal effects of toxics on the growth and development of aquatic organisms. Such testing may make scientists reasonably confident that they know what dose of a given chemical will kill half of the species within a given period of time (the LD50, or lethal dose for 50 percent of the test organisms), but it does not necessarily reveal much about the full range of effects of chemicals on actual ecosystems. Moreover, tests of specific substances on isolated species do not reflect actual conditions in a water body where organisms encounter complex mixtures of chemical compounds and are affected by ecosystem processes as well as interactions with other organisms.

Water quality criteria are based on concern for protecting human health or aquatic life from concentrations of pollutants in the water. Yet scientists have discovered that concentrations of pollutants on a water body's surface, or microlayer, often are very different from concentrations below. As a result, compliance with water quality criteria in the water column may not be sufficient to protect the health of aquatic organisms, particularly those for whom the microlayer is unusually important. Also, many toxic pollutants accumulate in sediments in concentrations different from those in the water. They may become resuspended in the water column when sediments are disturbed, and they may have severe impacts on benthic organisms. While there is voluminous research on contamination of aquatic sediments, EPA has not promulgated any sediment quality criteria, though some states have begun to do so. See Marcus, Managing Contaminated Sediments in Aquatic Environments: Identification, Regulation, and Remediation, 21 Envtl. L. Rep. 10020 (1991). EPA instead is developing a national inventory of sites of sediment contamination and has pledged to consider the problem when developing effluent guidelines for industries that are significant contributors to it. 59 Fed. Reg. 44,880 (1994).

There also are practical obstacles to implementing water quality-based approaches, including difficulties in detecting and measuring reliably the presence of certain substances in environmental media and the absence of low-cost screening techniques for scanning large numbers of samples. It can be difficult to measure with precision levels of individual pollutants in effluent discharges; it is even more difficult to determine how pollutant flows mix with receiving waters in order to assess the impact of individual discharges on overall water quality.

These factors greatly complicate the task of implementing water quality-based approaches to regulation. While scientists are working to develop improved toxicity testing procedures (the development of biomarkers that focus on cellular and biological responses in aquatic organisms eventually may enable scientists to develop a better early warning system), they simply are unable, given current knowledge, to predict reliably the impact of specific contaminants on specific aquatic resources. Uncertainty seems destined to dominate debates over the significance of changes in water quality for years to come.

2. The Impact of Water Quality Standards on Permit Limits

For water quality standards to be effective in preventing pollution, they must be translated into effective discharge limits. Section 301(b)(1)(c) of the Clean Water Act provides that NPDES permits must include limits that will ensure that water quality standards are not violated. In the sections that follow we consider various means by which water quality standards can affect permit limits. These include: (1) the application of water quality standards to discharges that contribute to interstate water pollution, (2) individual control strategies for toxics under section 304(1), (3) section 401(a) certifications, and (4) the establishment of total maximum daily loadings (TMDLs) of pollutants under section 303(d).

A.   APPLICATION OF WATER QUALITY STANDARDS TO INTERSTATE POLLUTION

When water pollutants cross the boundaries of states or Indian reservations they may affect the ability of downstream states or tribes to meet their own water quality standards. In the case below, Oklahoma argued that discharges from an Arkansas wastewater treatment plant should not be permitted because they would degrade water quality in the upper Illinois River in Oklahoma in violation of Oklahoma's water quality standards. Oklahoma had designated the upper Illinois River as a scenic river. The portion of the river downstream from the Arkansas border is used primarily for recreational boating and fishing. It is a particularly popular site for canoeing and rafting.

|| *Arkansas v. Oklahoma* ||
|| 503 U.S. 91 (1992) ||

JUSTICE STEVENS delivered the opinion for a unanimous Court.

I

In 1985, the City of Fayetteville, Arkansas, applied to the EPA, seeking a permit for the City's new sewage treatment plant under the National Pollution Discharge Elimination System (NPDES). After the appropriate procedures, the EPA, pursuant to §402(a)(1) of the Act, 33 U.S.C. §1342(a)(1), issued a permit authorizing the plant to discharge up to half of its effluent (to a limit of 6.1 million gallons per day) into an unnamed stream in northwestern Arkansas. That flow passes through a series of three creeks for about 17 miles, and then enters the Illinois River at a point 22 miles upstream from the Arkansas-Oklahoma Border.

The permit imposed specific limitations on the quantity, content, and character of the discharge and also included a number of special conditions, including a provision that if a study then underway indicated that more stringent limitations were necessary to ensure compliance with Oklahoma's water quality standards, the permit would be modified to incorporate those limits.

Respondents challenged this permit before the EPA, alleging, inter alia, that the discharge violated the Oklahoma water quality standards. Those standards provide that "no degradation [of water quality] shall be allowed" in the upper Illinois River, including the portion of the River immediately downstream from the state line.

Following a hearing, the Administrative Law Judge (ALJ) concluded that the Oklahoma standards would not be implicated unless the contested discharge had something more than a "mere de minimis impact" on the State's waters. He found that the discharge would not have an "undue impact" on Oklahoma's waters and, accordingly, affirmed the issuance of the permit.

On a petition for review, the EPA's Chief Judicial Officer first ruled that §301(b)(1)(C) of the Clean Water Act requires an NPDES permit to impose any effluent limitations necessary to comply with applicable state water quality standards. He then held that the Act and EPA regulations offered greater protection for the downstream state than the ALJ's "undue impact" standard suggested. He explained the proper standard as follows:

> [A] mere theoretical impairment of Oklahoma's water quality standards—i.e., an infinitesimal impairment predicted through modeling but not expected to be actually detectable or measurable—should not by itself block the issuance of the permit. In this case, the permit should be upheld if the record shows by a preponderance of the evidence that the authorized discharges would not cause an actual *detectable* violation of Oklahoma's water quality standards. Id., at 117a (emphasis in original).

On remand, the ALJ made detailed findings of fact and concluded that the City had satisfied the standard set forth by the Chief Judicial Officer. Specifically, the ALJ found that there would be no detectable violation of any of the components of Oklahoma's water quality standards. The Chief Judicial Officer sustained the issuance of the permit.

Both the petitioners (collectively Arkansas) and the respondents in this litigation sought judicial review. Arkansas argued that the Clean Water Act did not require an Arkansas point source to comply with Oklahoma's water quality standards. Oklahoma challenged the EPA's determination that the Fayetteville discharge would not produce a detectable violation of the Oklahoma standards.

The Court of Appeals did not accept either of these arguments. The court agreed with the EPA that the statute required compliance with Oklahoma's water quality standards, see 908 F.2d 595, 602-615 (CA10 1990), and did not disagree with the Agency's determination that the discharges from the Fayetteville plant would not produce a detectable violation of those standards. Id., at 631-633. Nevertheless, relying on a theory that neither party had advanced, the Court of Appeals reversed the Agency's issuance of the Fayetteville permit. The court first ruled that the statute requires that "where a proposed source would discharge effluents that would contribute to conditions currently constituting a violation of applicable water quality standards, such [a] proposed source may not be permitted." Id., at 620. Then the court found that the Illinois River in Oklahoma was already degraded, that the Fayetteville effluent would reach the Illinois River in Oklahoma, and that that effluent could "be expected to contribute to the ongoing deterioration of the scenic [Illinois R]iver" in Oklahoma even though it would not detectably affect the River's water quality. . . .

IV

The parties have argued three analytically distinct questions concerning the interpretation of the Clean Water Act. First, does the Act require the EPA, in crafting and issuing a permit to a point source in one State, to apply the water quality standards of downstream States? Second, even if the Act does not *require* as much, does the Agency have the statutory authority to mandate such compliance? Third, does the Act provide, as the Court of Appeals held, that once a body of water fails to meet water quality standards no discharge that yields effluent that reach[es] the degraded waters will be permitted?

In this case, it is neither necessary nor prudent for us to resolve the first of these questions. In issuing the Fayetteville permit, the EPA assumed it was obligated by both the Act and its own regulations to ensure that the Fayetteville discharge would not violate Oklahoma's standards. As we discuss below, this assumption was permissible and reasonable and therefore there is no need for us to address whether the Act requires as much. Moreover, much of the analysis and argument in the briefs of the parties relies on statutory provisions that govern not only federal permits issued pursuant to §§401(a) and 402(a), but also state permits issued under §402(b). It seems unwise to evaluate those arguments in a case such as this one, which only involves a federal permit.

Our decision not to determine at this time the scope of the Agency's statutory *obligations* does not affect our resolution of the second question, which concerns the Agency's statutory *authority*. Even if the Clean Water Act itself does not require the Fayetteville discharge to comply with Oklahoma's water quality standards, the statute clearly does not limit the EPA's authority to mandate such compliance.

Since 1973, EPA regulations have provided that an NPDES permit shall not be issued "[w]hen the imposition of conditions cannot ensure compliance with the applicable water quality requirements of all affected States." 40 CFR §122.4(d)(1991); see also 38 Fed. Reg. 13533 (1973); 40 CFR §122.44(d)(1991). Those regulations—relied upon by the EPA in the issuance of the Fayetteville permit—constitute a reasonable exercise of the Agency's statutory authority.

Congress has vested in the Administrator broad discretion to establish conditions for NPDES permits. Section 402(a)(2) provides that for EPA-issued permits "[t]he Administrator shall prescribe conditions for such permits to assure compliance with the requirements of [§402(a)(1)] and *such other requirements as he deems appropriate.*" 33 U.S.C. §1342(a)(2) (emphasis supplied). Similarly, Congress preserved for the Administrator broad authority to oversee state permit programs:

> No permit shall issue . . . if the Administrator . . . objects in writing to the issuance of such permit as being outside the guidelines and requirements of this chapter.

33 U.S.C. §1342(d)(2).

The regulations relied on by the EPA were a perfectly reasonable exercise of the Agency's statutory discretion. The application of state water quality standards in the interstate context is wholly consistent with the Act's broad purpose, "to restore and maintain the chemical, physical, and biological integrity of the Nation's waters." 33 U.S.C. §1251(a). Moreover, as noted above, §301(b)(1)(C) expressly identifies the achievement of state water quality standards as one of the Act's central objectives. The Agency's regulations conditioning NPDES permits are a well-tailored means of achieving this goal.

Notwithstanding this apparent reasonableness, Arkansas argues that our description in [International Paper Co. v.] Ouellette [479 U.S. 481 (1987)] of the role of affected States in the permit process and our characterization of the affected States' position as "subordinate," see 479 U.S., at 490-491, indicates that the EPA's application of the Oklahoma standards was error. We disagree. Our statement in *Ouellette* concerned only an affected State's input into the permit process; that input is clearly limited by the plain language of §402(b). Limits on an affected State's direct participation in permitting decisions, however, do not in any way constrain the *EPA's* authority to require a point source to comply with downstream water quality standards.

Arkansas also argues that regulations requiring compliance with downstream standards are at odds with the legislative history of the Act and with the statutory scheme established by the Act. Although we agree with Arkansas that the Act's legislative history indicates that Congress intended to grant the Administrator discretion in his oversight of the issuance of NPDES permits, we find nothing in that history to indicate that Congress intended to preclude the EPA from establishing a general requirement that such permits be conditioned to ensure compliance with downstream water quality standards.

Similarly, we agree with Arkansas that in the Clean Water Act Congress struck a careful balance among competing policies and interests, but do not find the EPA regulations concerning the application of downstream water quality standards at all incompatible with that balance. Congress, in crafting the Act, protected certain sovereign interests of the States; for example, §510 allows States to adopt more demanding pollution-control standards than those established under the Act. Arkansas emphasizes that §510 preserves such state authority only as it is applied to the waters of the regulating State. Even assuming Arkansas' construction of §510 is correct, cf. id., at 493, that section only concerns *state* authority and does not constrain the *EPA's* authority to promulgate reasonable regulations requiring point sources in one State to comply with water quality standards in downstream States.

For these reasons, we find the EPA's requirement that the Fayetteville discharge comply with Oklahoma's water quality standards to be a reasonable exercise of the Agency's substantial statutory discretion. Cf. Chevron U.S.A., Inc. v. Natural Resources Defense Council, Inc., 467 U.S. 837, 842-845 (1984).

V

The Court of Appeals construed the Clean Water Act to prohibit any discharge of effluent that would reach waters already in violation of existing water quality standards. We find nothing in the Act to support this reading.

The interpretation of the statute adopted by the court had not been advanced by any party during the agency or court proceedings. Moreover, the Court of Appeals candidly acknowledged that its theory "has apparently never before been addressed by a federal court." 908 F.2d, at 620, n.39. The only statutory provision the court cited to support its legal analysis was §402(h), see id., at 633, which merely authorizes the EPA (or a state permit program) to prohibit a publicly owned treatment plant that is violating a condition of its NPDES permit from accepting any additional pollutants for treatment until the ongoing violation has been corrected. See 33 U.S.C. §1342(h).

Although the Act contains several provisions directing compliance with state water quality standards, see, e.g., 33 U.S.C. §1311(b)(1)(C), the parties have pointed to nothing that mandates a complete ban on discharges into a waterway that is in violation of those standards. The statute does, however, contain provisions designed to remedy existing water quality violations and to allocate the burden of reducing undesirable discharges between existing sources and new sources. See, e.g., 33 U.S.C. §1313(d). Thus, rather than establishing the categorical ban announced by the Court of Appeals—which might frustrate the construction of new plants that would improve existing conditions—the ("Clean Water Act vests in the EPA and States broad authority to develop long-range, area-wide programs to alleviate and eliminate existing pollution. See, e.g., 33 U.S.C. §1288(b)(2).

To the extent that the Court of Appeals relied on its interpretation of the Act to reverse the EPA's permitting decision, that reliance was misplaced.

VI

The Court of Appeals also concluded that the EPA's issuance of the Fayetteville permit was arbitrary and capricious because the Agency misinterpreted Oklahoma's water quality standards. The primary difference between the court's and the Agency's interpretation of the standards derives from the court's construction of the Act. Contrary to the EPA's interpretation of the Oklahoma standards, the Court of Appeals read those standards as containing the same categorical ban on new discharges that the court had found in the Clean Water Act itself. Although we do not believe the text of the Oklahoma standards supports the court's reading (indeed, we note that Oklahoma itself had not advanced that interpretation in its briefs in the Court of Appeals), we reject it for a more fundamental reason—namely, that the Court of Appeals exceeded the legitimate scope of judicial review of an agency adjudication. . . .

As discussed above, EPA regulations require an NPDES permit to comply "with the applicable water quality requirements of all affected States." 40 CFR §122.4(d)(1991). This regulation effectively incorporates into federal law those state law standards the Agency reasonably determines to be applicable. In such a situation, then, state water quality standards—promulgated by the States with substantial guidance from the EPA and approved by the Agency—are part of the federal law of water pollution control.

Two features of the body of law governing water pollution support this conclusion. First, as discussed more thoroughly above, we have long recognized that interstate water pollution is controlled by *federal* law. Recognizing that the system of federally approved state standards as applied in the interstate context constitutes federal law is wholly consistent with this principle. Second, treating state standards in interstate controversies as federal law accords with the Act's purpose of authorizing the EPA to create and manage a uniform system of interstate water pollution regulation.

Because we recognize that, at least insofar as they affect the issuance of a permit in another State, the Oklahoma standards have a federal character, the EPA's reasonable, consistently held interpretation of those standards is entitled to substantial deference. In this case, the Chief Judicial Officer ruled that the Oklahoma standards—which require that there be "no degradation" of the upper Illinois River—would only be violated if the discharge effected an "actually detectable or measurable" change in water quality.

This interpretation of the Oklahoma standards is certainly reasonable and consistent with the purposes and principles of the Clean Water Act. As the Chief Judicial Officer noted, "unless there is some method for measuring compliance, there is no way to ensure compliance." Moreover, this interpretation of the Oklahoma standards makes eminent sense in the interstate context: If every discharge that had some theoretical impact on a downstream State were interpreted as "degrading" the downstream waters, downstream States might wield an effective veto over upstream discharges.

The EPA's application of those standards in this case was also sound. On remand, the ALJ scrutinized the record and made explicit factual findings regarding four primary measures of water quality under the Oklahoma standards: eutrophication, aesthetics, dissolved oxygen, and metals. In each case, the ALJ found that the Fayetteville discharge would not lead to a detectable change in water quality. He therefore concluded that the Fayetteville discharge would not violate the Oklahoma water quality standards. Because we agree with the Agency's Chief Judicial Officer that these findings are supported by substantial evidence, we conclude that the Court of Appeals should have affirmed both the EPA's construction of the regulations and the issuance of the Fayetteville permit. . . .

In sum, the Court of Appeals made a policy choice that it was not authorized to make. Arguably, as that court suggested, it might be wise to prohibit any discharge into the Illinois River, even if that discharge would have no adverse impact on water quality. But it was surely not arbitrary for the EPA to conclude—given the benefits to the River from the increased flow of relatively clean water and the benefits achieved in Arkansas by allowing the new plant to operate as designed—that allowing the discharge would be even wiser. It is not our role, or that of the Court of Appeals, to decide which policy choice is the better one, for it is clear that Congress has entrusted such decisions to the Environmental Protection Agency.

NOTES AND QUESTIONS

1. Does the Court's decision effectively make EPA the umpire of interstate water pollution disputes? EPA issued the permit challenged in this case only because Arkansas had not been delegated the authority to operate the NPDES program. If Arkansas had been delegated such authority and had issued the permit, how, if at all, would Oklahoma's ability to challenge the permit have been affected?

2. The Court declined to decide whether EPA was required to apply the water quality standards of the downstream state, holding only that it was permissible for EPA to do so. Suppose that in another case an upstream state's discharges did cause "an actually detectable or measurable change in water quality" in violation of a downstream state's standards. Could EPA legally issue a permit for such discharges?

3. How did Arkansas interpret *Ouellette*? How does the Court distinguish it from the instant case? Could Oklahoma file a common law nuisance action against the Arkansas plant? In light of *Ouellette*, what law would apply to such an action?

4. Arkansas argued that it would be chaotic to require dischargers to comply with the water quality standards of all downstream states because some rivers flow through numerous states (e.g., the Mississippi). Is this a valid concern? Could a downstream state effectively dictate the terms of NPDES permits in upstream states by adopting very stringent water quality standards? What checks exist to prevent downstream states from adopting unreasonably stringent water quality standards?

5. What would Oklahoma need to show in order to convince EPA to deny issuance of the permit? In light of the Court's decision, do the existing violations of Oklahoma's water quality standards have any significance for dischargers in upstream states?

6. As the Court notes, section 510 of the Clean Water Act expressly preserves the right of states to adopt and enforce more stringent standards than those required by federal law. While section 518 of the Act provides that Indian tribes may be treated by EPA as states for the purposes of certain enumerated sections of the Act, section 510 is not one of the sections expressly referenced by section 518. Nonetheless in City of Albuquerque v. Browner, 97 F.3d 415 (10th

Cir. 1996), the Tenth Circuit upheld EPA's decision to allow a tribe to impose a more stringent water quality standard on a portion of the Rio Grande River downstream from the city of Albuquerque.

The Iselta Pueblo had designated the use of the water segment as "Primary Contact Ceremonial" because it was used by tribal members for ceremonial immersions. The court held that this could be used to restrict discharges by the upstream city. The court explained that "Congress' failure to incorporate [§510] into §518 does not prevent Indian tribes from exercising their inherent sovereign power to impose standards or limits that are more stringent than those imposed by the federal government." 97 F.3d at 423. The court noted that in Arkansas v. Oklahoma the Supreme Court had explained that section 510 "only concerns *state* authority and does not constrain EPA's authority," 503 U.S. at 107 (emphasis in original). It concluded that section 510 did not implicitly constrain tribes sovereign authority and that EPA's construction of the Act as permitting tribes to establish water quality standards more stringent than the federal minimum "is permissible because it is in accord with powers inherent in Indian tribal sovereignty." Id. See also Flathead Reservation v. EPA, 137 F.3d 1135 (9th Cir. 1998) (upholding regulation allowing tribes to apply water quality standards to non-Indian irrigators owning land within tribal reservation).

B.   INDIVIDUAL CONTROL STRATEGIES FOR TOXIC POLLUTANTS

Having largely abandoned the water quality-based approach to pollution control in 1972, Congress in 1987 sought to resuscitate it as a supplementary mechanism for controlling toxic water pollutants. The 1987 Amendments added section 304(l) to the Clean Water Act, which directs EPA and the states to identify waters with toxic problems and to impose new controls on sources of discharges to them. Recognizing that eventual compliance with BAT standards would be insufficient to meet water quality standards for toxics in some waters, Congress required states to identify such waters and to develop "individual control strategies" for reducing toxic discharges to them.

Section 304(l)(1) required all states to submit three lists of waters to EPA: (A) waters that "cannot reasonably be anticipated to attain or maintain (i) water quality standards for such waters . . . due to toxic pollutants" (the A(i) list), "or (ii) that water quality which shall assure protection of public health, public water supplies, agricultural and industrial uses, and the protection and propagation of a balanced population of shellfish, fish and wildlife, and allow recreational activities in and on the water" (the A(ii) list), and (B) waters not expected to meet water quality standards even after application of BAT due entirely or substantially to toxic pollution from point sources (the B list). Note that the A(i) list is considerably broader than the B list because it apparently includes waters not expected to meet water quality standards due to toxic pollution from nonpoint sources. The A(ii) list is the broadest because it includes even some waters that comply with state water quality standards if they are not expected to meet the water quality goals of the Act.

For each water segment "included on such lists," states are required to determine "the specific point sources discharging any such toxic pollutant which is believed to be preventing or impairing such water quality and the amount of each such toxic pollutant discharged by each such source," §304(l)(1)(C). Although EPA initially interpreted this requirement as applicable only to waters on the B list, in Natural Resources Defense Council v. EPA, 915 F.2d 1314, 1319 (9th Cir. 1990), the Ninth Circuit held that the reference to "lists" made it applicable to waters on any of the three lists. Thus, states must identify point sources contributing to waters whose impairment is not primarily a product of point source pollution. The court reserved judgment on the question of whether individual control strategies had to be applied to waters on each of these lists.

Section 304(l)(1)(D) requires each state to develop "an individual control strategy which . . . will produce a reduction in the discharge of toxic pollutants from point sources identified by the State, . . . which reduction is sufficient, in combination with existing controls on point and nonpoint sources of pollution, to achieve the applicable water quality standard as soon as possible, but not later than 3 years after the date of the establishment of such strategy." §304(l)(1)(D). "The effect of the individual control strategies is simply to expedite the imposition of water-quality-based limitations on polluters—limitations which otherwise would have had to be imposed when the polluters' NPDES permits expired." Natural Resources Defense Council v. EPA, 915 F.2d 1314, 1319 (9th Cir. 1990). Because the states were given until June 1989 to submit their lists to EPA, the control strategies were supposed to achieve water quality standards by June 1992.

Implementation of section 304(l)'s water quality-based "regulatory safety net" has been hampered by the same informational and conceptual obstacles that traditionally have bedeviled such approaches to pollution control. Monitoring data are sparse, and few states have adopted comprehensive water quality criteria for toxics. Many state standards for toxics are expressed in narrative, rather than numerical, form and are difficult to translate into individual controls. Section 303(c)(2) requires states to adopt numerical water quality criteria for all priority pollutants that could reasonably be expected to interfere with the state's designated uses for which EPA has published water quality criteria under section 304(a). By February 1990, only six states had established criteria for toxic pollutants fully acceptable to EPA. By November 1991, EPA determined that 35 states had complied with §303(c)(2). The agency ultimately issued its own numeric criteria for 98 toxic pollutants in 14 states. 57 Fed. Reg. 60,848 (1992).

States varied considerably in the thoroughness of their section 304(l) lists of affected waters and dischargers. In the initial lists submitted in February 1989 some states listed dozens of affected water segments while others listed none. (The number of dischargers included in the states' lists ranged from zero to 180.) Much of the variation in state responses stemmed from differences in the quantity and quality of toxics monitoring data as well as differences in the thoroughness with which existing data sources were reviewed. Few states have adequate toxics monitoring programs; some responded to perceived data inadequacies with a "what-you-don't-know-won't-hurt-you" approach, incorporating only a few waters or dischargers for which the data were clearest. Many failed to consult additional data sources including the Toxics Release Inventory established by the Emergency Planning and Community Right-to-Know Act. Although EPA had encouraged states to include waters affected by any toxic pollutant, rather than just the 126 priority pollutants, few states did so. Yet Connecticut found that nearly one-half of the facilities causing toxic pollution problems in the state's waters were discharging nonpriority pollutants such as biocides, water conditioning agents, and oxidative treatment chemicals. Surface Water "Toxic Hot Spots" Program Criticized as Inadequate at Senate Hearing, 20 Envtl. Rep. 466 (1989).

In June 1989 EPA released a list of 595 water segments and 879 dischargers that the states, supplemented by EPA, had determined to be subject to the requirements of section 304(*l*). Id. Several environmental and citizen groups petitioned EPA to add certain water segments and dischargers to the lists. Petitions by Environmental Groups Could Add Many Industries to 304(*l*) List, 20 Envtl. Rep. 627 (1989). EPA advised the states that it interprets the section 304(*l*) requirements to be part of a continuing process and that the section 304(*l*) lists should be reviewed and updated periodically as additional data about toxic pollution become available. Some states disagree, arguing that the statutory language indicates that it should be a one-time process.

EPA's regulations provide that an individual control strategy (ICS) should be incorporated into a final NPDES permit and be supported by documentation indicating that the permit's effluent limits are sufficient to meet applicable water quality standards. 40 C.F.R. §123.46(c). EPA is required to approve or disapprove ICSs submitted by states. If EPA disapproves a state's control strategy, or if the state fails to submit one, EPA must develop and implement its own control strategy. While section 509(b)(1) makes EPA's promulgation of any individual control strategy reviewable in the United States Courts of Appeals, several circuits have held that it does not authorize such review of EPA decisions to *approve* state ICSs. Borough of St. Marys v. EPA, 945 F.2d 67 (3d Cir. 1991); Roll Coater, Inc. v. Reilly, 932 F.2d 668 (7th Cir. 1991); Boise Cascade Corp. v. EPA, 942 F.2d 1427 (9th Cir. 1991); Lake Cumberland Trust, Inc. v. EPA, 954 F.2d 1218 (6th Cir. 1992); see also Hecla Mining Co. v. EPA, 12 F.3d 164 (9th Cir. 1993) (EPA's inclusion of additional waters on §304(*l*) list not subject to judicial review).

C.   State Water Quality Certification under Section 401

As discussed in Arkansas v. Oklahoma, section 401(a)(1) of the Clean Water Act requires applicants for a federal license or permit to conduct any activity that "may result in any discharge into navigable waters" to provide the licensing or permitting authority with a certification from the state in which the discharge will occur that the discharge will comply with various provisions of the Act. Section 401(d) provides that such certifications "shall set forth any effluent limitations and other limitations, and monitoring requirements necessary to assure that" the applicant complies with the Act "and with any other appropriate requirement of State law set forth in" the certification, which then becomes a condition of the federal permit. Section 401 has been considered a "sleeping giant" of the Clean Water Act because of the potentially broad scope of the conditions it enables states to impose. In the case below, the Supreme Court considered whether a state could condition a section 401 certification for a FERC license to construct a hydroelectric dam on the imposition of minimum stream flow rates.

|| *PUD No. 1 of Jefferson County v.*
Washington Department of Ecology
511 U.S. 700 (1994) ||

Justice O'Connor delivered the opinion of the Court. . . .

II

Petitioners propose to build the Elkhorn Hydroelectric Project on the Dosewallips River. If constructed as presently planned, the facility would be located just outside the Olympic National Park on federally owned land within the Olympic National Forest. The project would divert water from a 1.2-mile reach of the River (the bypass reach), run the water through turbines to generate electricity and then return the water to the River below the bypass reach. Under the Federal Power Act (FPA), 41 Stat. 1063, as amended, 16 U.S.C. §791 et seq., the Federal Energy Regulatory Commission has authority to license new hydroelectric facilities. As a result, the petitioners must get a FERC license to build or operate the Elkhorn Project. Because a federal license is required, and because the project may result in discharges into the Dosewallips River, petitioners are also required to obtain State certification of the project pursuant to §401 of the Clean Water Act, 33 U.S.C. §1341.

The water flow in the bypass reach, which is currently undiminished by appropriation, ranges seasonally between 149 and 738 cubic feet per second (cfs). The Dosewallips supports two species of salmon, Coho and Chinook, as well as Steelhead trout. As originally proposed, the project was to include a diversion dam which would completely block the river and channel approximately 75 percent of the River's water into a tunnel alongside the streambed. About 25 percent of the water would remain in the bypass reach, but would be returned to the original riverbed through sluice gates or a fish ladder. Depending on the season, this would leave a residual minimum flow of between 65 and 155 cfs in the River. Respondent undertook a study to determine the minimum stream flows necessary to protect the salmon and steelhead fisheries in the bypass reach. On June 11, 1986, respondent issued a §401 water quality certification imposing a variety of conditions on the project, including a minimum stream-flow requirement of between 100 and 200 cfs depending on the season.

A state administrative appeals board determined that the minimum flow requirement was intended to enhance, not merely maintain, the fishery, and that the certification condition therefore exceeded respondent's authority under state law. On appeal, the state Superior Court concluded that respondent could require compliance with the minimum flow conditions. The Superior Court also found that respondent had imposed the minimum flow requirement to protect and preserve the fishery, not to improve it, and that this requirement was authorized by state law.

The Washington Supreme Court held that the antidegradation provisions of the State's water quality standards require the imposition of minimum stream flows. 849 P.2d 646, 650 (1993). The court also found that §401(d), which allows States to impose conditions based upon several enumerated sections of the Clean Water Act and "any other appropriate requirement of State law," 33 U.S.C. §1341(d), authorized the stream flow condition. Relying on this language and the broad purposes of the Clean Water Act, the court concluded that §401(d) confers on States power to "consider all state action related to water quality in imposing conditions on section 401 certificates." 849 P.2d, at 652. We granted certiorari to resolve a conflict among the state courts of last resort. See 849 P.2d 646 (1993); Georgia Pacific Corp. v. Dept. of Environmental Conservation, 628 A.2d 944 (1992) (table); Power Authority of New York v. Williams, 457 N.E.2d 726 (1983).

III

The principal dispute in this case concerns whether the minimum stream flow requirement that the State imposed on the Elkhorn project is a permissible condition of a §401 certification under the Clean Water Act. To resolve this dispute we must first determine the scope of the State's authority under §401. We must then determine whether the limitation at issue here, the requirement that petitioners maintain minimum stream flows, falls within the scope of that authority.

A

There is no dispute that petitioners were required to obtain a certification from the State pursuant to §401. Petitioners concede that, at a minimum, the project will result in two possible discharges—the release of dredged and fill material during the construction of the project, and the discharge of water at the end of the tailrace after the water has been used to generate electricity. Petitioners contend, however, that the minimum stream flow requirement imposed by the State was unrelated to these specific discharges, and that as a consequence, the State lacked the authority under §401 to condition its certification on maintenance of stream flows sufficient to protect the Dosewallips fishery.

If §401 consisted solely of subsection (a), which refers to a state certification that a "discharge" will comply with certain provisions of the Act, petitioners' assessment of the scope of the State's certification authority would have considerable force. Section 401, however, also contains subsection (d), which expands the State's authority to impose conditions on the certification of a project. Section 401(d) provides that any certification shall set forth "any effluent limitations and other limitations . . . necessary to assure that *any applicant*" will comply with various provisions of the Act and appropriate state law requirements. 33 U.S.C. §1341(d) (emphasis added). The language of this subsection contradicts petitioners' claim that the State may only impose water quality limitations specifically tied to a "discharge." The text refers to the compliance of the applicant, not the discharge. Section 401(d) thus allows the State to impose "other limitations" on the project in general to assure compliance with various provisions of the Clean Water Act and with "any other appropriate requirement of State law." Although the dissent asserts that this interpretation of §401(d) renders §401(a)(1) superfluous, we see no such anomaly. Section 401(a)(1) identifies the category of activities subject to certification—namely those with discharges. And §401(d) is most reasonably read as authorizing additional conditions and limitations on the activity as a whole once the threshold condition, the existence of a discharge, is satisfied.

Our view of the statute is consistent with EPA's regulations implementing §401. The regulations expressly interpret §401 as requiring the State to find that "there is a reasonable assurance that the *activity* will be conducted in a manner which will not violate applicable water quality standards." 40 CFR §121.2(a)(3)(1992) (emphasis added). See also EPA, Wetlands and 401 Certification 23 (Apr. 1989) ("In 401(d), the Congress has given the States the authority to place any conditions on a water quality certification that are necessary to assure that the applicant will comply with effluent limitations, water quality standards, . . . and with 'any other appropriate requirement of

State Law.'"). EPA's conclusion that *activities*—not merely discharges—must comply with state water quality standards is a reasonable interpretation of §401, and is entitled to deference. See, e.g., Arkansas v. Oklahoma, 503 U.S. 91, 110 (1992); Chevron U.S.A., Inc. v. Natural Resources Defense Council, Inc., 467 U.S. 837 (1984).

Although §401(d) authorizes the State to place restrictions on the activity as a whole, that authority is not unbounded. The State can only ensure that the project complies with "any applicable effluent limitations and other limitations, under [33 U.S.C. §§1311, 1312]" or certain other provisions of the Act, "and with any other appropriate requirement of State law." 33 U.S.C. §1341(d). The State asserts that the minimum stream flow requirement was imposed to ensure compliance with the state water quality standards adopted pursuant to §303 of the Clean Water Act, 33 U.S.C. §1313.

We agree with the State that ensuring compliance with §303 is a proper function of the §401 certification. Although §303 is not one of the statutory provisions listed in §401(d), the statute allows states to impose limitations to ensure compliance with §301 of the Act, 33 U.S.C. §1311. Section 301 in turn incorporates §303 by reference. See 33 U.S.C. §1311(b)(1)(C); see also H. R. Conf. Rep. No. 95-830, p. 96 (1977) ("Section 303 is always included by reference where section 301 is listed"). As a consequence, state water quality standards adopted pursuant to §303 are among the "other limitations" with which a State may ensure compliance through the §401 certification process. This interpretation is consistent with EPA's view of the statute. See 40 CFR §121.2(a)(3)(1992); EPA, Wetlands and 401 Certification, supra. Moreover, limitations to assure compliance with state water quality standards are also permitted by §401(d)'s reference to "any other appropriate requirement of State law." We do not speculate on what additional state laws, if any, might be incorporated by this language.[3] But at a minimum, limitations imposed pursuant to state water quality standards adopted pursuant to §303 are "appropriate" requirements of state law. Indeed, petitioners appear to agree that the State's authority under §401 includes limitations designed to ensure compliance with state water quality standards.

B

Having concluded that, pursuant to §401, States may condition certification upon any limitations necessary to ensure compliance with state water quality standards or any other "appropriate requirement of State law," we consider whether the minimum flow condition is such a limitation. Under §303, state water quality standards must "consist of the designated uses of the navigable waters involved and the water quality criteria for such waters based upon such

---

3. The dissent asserts that §301 is concerned solely with discharges, not broader water quality standards. Infra, 8 n. 2. Although §301 does make certain discharges unlawful, see 33 U.S.C. §1311(a), it also contains a broad enabling provision which requires states to take certain actions, to wit: "In order to carry out the objective of this chapter [viz. the chemical, physical, and biological integrity of the Nation's water] there shall be achieved . . . not later than July 1, 1977, any more stringent limitation, including those necessary to meet water quality standards . . . established pursuant to any State law or regulations." 33 U.S.C. §1311(b)(1)(C). This provision of §301 expressly refers to state water quality standards, and is not limited to discharges.

uses." 33 U.S.C. §1313(c)(2)(A). In imposing the minimum stream flow requirement, the State determined that construction and operation of the project as
planned would be inconsistent with one of the designated uses of Class AA water,
namely "[s]almonid [and other fish] migration, rearing, spawning, and harvesting." The designated use of the River as a fish habitat directly reflects the Clean
Water Act's goal of maintaining the "chemical, physical, and biological integrity
of the Nation's waters." 33 U.S.C. §1251(a). Indeed, the Act defines pollution as
"the man-made or man-induced alteration of the chemical, physical, biological,
and radiological integrity of water." §1362(19). Moreover, the Act expressly
requires that, in adopting water quality standards, the State must take into consideration the use of waters for "propagation of fish and wildlife." 33 U.S.C.
§1313(c)(2)(A).

Petitioners assert, however, that §303 requires the State to protect designated uses solely through implementation of specific "criteria." According to
petitioners, the State may not require them to operate their dam in a manner
consistent with a designated "use"; instead, say petitioners, under §303 the State
may only require that the project comply with specific numerical "criteria."

We disagree with petitioners' interpretation of the language of
§303(c)(2)(A). Under the statute, a water quality standard must "consist of
the designated uses of the navigable waters involved *and* the water quality criteria
for such waters based upon such uses." 33 U.S.C. §1313(c)(2)(A) (emphasis
added). The text makes it plain that water quality standards contain two components. We think the language of §303 is most naturally read to require that a
project be consistent with *both* components, namely the designated use *and* the
water quality criteria. Accordingly, under the literal terms of the statute, a project that does not comply with a designated use of the water does not comply with
the applicable water quality standards.

Consequently, pursuant to §401(d) the State may require that a permit
applicant comply with both the designated uses and the water quality criteria of
the state standards. In granting certification pursuant to §401(d), the State
"shall set forth any ... limitations ... necessary to assure that [the applicant]
will comply with any ... limitations under [§303] ... and with any other appropriate requirement of State law." A certification requirement that an applicant
operate the project consistently with state water quality standards—i.e., consistently with the designated uses of the water body and the water quality criteria—
is both a "limitation" to assure "compliance with ... limitations" imposed
under §303, and an "appropriate" requirement of State law.

EPA has not interpreted §303 to require the States to protect designated
uses exclusively through enforcement of numerical criteria. In its regulations
governing state water quality standards, EPA defines criteria as "*elements* of
State water quality standards expressed as constituent concentrations, levels,
or narrative statements, representing a quality of water that supports a particular
use." §40 CFR 131.3(b)(1992) (emphasis added). The regulations further provide that "when criteria are met, water quality will *generally* protect the designated
use." Ibid, (emphasis added). Thus, the EPA regulations implicitly recognize that
in some circumstances, criteria alone are insufficient to protect a designated use.

Petitioners also appear to argue that use requirements are too open-ended,
and that the Act only contemplates enforcement of the more specific and objective "criteria." But this argument is belied by the open-ended nature of the
criteria themselves. As the Solicitor General points out, even "criteria" are
often expressed in broad, narrative terms, such as "there shall be no discharge

of toxic pollutants in toxic amounts." See American Paper Institute, Inc. v. EPA, 996 F.2d 346, 349 (CADC 1993). In fact, under the Clean Water Act, only one class of criteria, those governing "toxic pollutants listed pursuant to section 13l7(a)(1)," need be rendered in numerical form. See 33 U.S.C. §1313(c)(2)(B); 40 CFR §131.11(b)(2)(1992).

Washington's Class AA water quality standards are typical in that they contain several open-ended criteria which, like the use designation of the River as a fishery, must be translated into specific limitations for individual projects. For example, the standards state that "[t]oxic, radioactive, or deleterious material concentrations shall be less than those which may affect public health, the natural aquatic environment, or the desirability of the water for any use." WAC 173-201-045(c)(vii). Similarly, the state standards specify that "aesthetic values shall not be impaired by the presence of materials or their effects, excluding those of natural origin, which offend the senses of sight, smell, touch, or taste." 173-201-045(c)(viii). We think petitioners' attempt to distinguish between uses and criteria loses much of its force in light of the fact that the Act permits enforcement of broad, narrative criteria based on, for example, "aesthetics."

Petitioners further argue that enforcement of water quality standards through use designations renders the water quality criteria component of the standards irrelevant. We see no anomaly, however, in the State's reliance on both use designations and criteria to protect water quality. The specific numerical limitations embodied in the criteria are a convenient enforcement mechanism for identifying minimum water conditions which will generally achieve the requisite water quality. And, in most circumstances, satisfying the criteria will, as EPA recognizes, be sufficient to maintain the designated use. See 40 CFR §131.3(b)(1992). Water quality standards, however, apply to an entire class of water, a class which contains numerous individual water bodies. For example, in the State of Washington, the Class AA water quality standard applies to 81 specified fresh surface waters, as well as to all "surface waters lying within the mountainous regions of the state assigned to national parks, national forests, and/or wilderness areas," all "lakes and their feeder streams within the state," and all "unclassified surface waters that are tributaries to Class AA waters." WAC 173-201-070. While enforcement of criteria will in general protect the uses of these diverse waters, a complementary requirement that activities also comport with designated uses enables the States to ensure that each activity—even if not foreseen by the criteria—will be consistent with the specific uses and attributes of a particular body of water.

Under petitioners' interpretation of the statute, however, if a particular criterion, such as turbidity, were missing from the list contained in an individual state water quality standard, or even if an existing turbidity criterion were insufficient to protect a particular species of fish in a particular river, the State would nonetheless be forced to allow activities inconsistent with the existing or designated uses. We think petitioners' reading leads to an unreasonable interpretation of the Act. The criteria components of state water quality standards attempt to identify, for all the water bodies in a given class, water quality requirements generally sufficient to protect designated uses. These criteria, however, cannot reasonably be expected to anticipate all the water quality issues arising from every activity which can affect the State's hundreds of individual water bodies. Requiring the States to enforce only the criteria component of their water quality standards would in essence require the States to study to a level of great specificity each individual surface water to ensure that the criteria applicable to that water are sufficiently detailed and individualized to fully protect the water's designated uses. Given that there is no textual support for imposing this requirement, we are loath to attribute to Congress an intent to impose this heavy regulatory burden on the States.

The State also justified its minimum stream flow as necessary to implement the "antidegradation policy" of §303, 33 U.S.C. §1313(d)(4)(B). When the Clean Water Act was enacted in 1972, the water quality standards of all 50 States had antidegradation provisions. These provisions were required by federal law. See U.S. Dept. of Interior, Federal Water Pollution Control Administration, Compendium of Department of Interior Statements on Non-degradation of Interstate Waters 1-2 (Aug. 1968); see also Hines, A Decade of Nondegradation Policy in Congress and the Courts: The Erratic Pursuit of Clean Air and Clean Water, 62 Iowa L. Rev. 643, 658-660 (1977). By providing in 1972 that existing state water quality standards would remain in force until revised, the Clean Water Act ensured that the States would continue their antidegradation programs. See 33 U.S.C. §1313(a). EPA has consistently required that revised state standards incorporate an antidegradation policy. And, in 1987, Congress ex-plicitly recognized the existence of an "antidegradation policy established under [§303]." §1313(d)(4)(B).

EPA has promulgated regulations implementing §303's antidegradation policy, a phrase that is not defined elsewhere in the Act. These regulations require States to "develop and adopt a statewide antidegradation policy and identify the methods for implementing such policy." 40 CFR §131.12 (1992). These "implementation methods shall, at a minimum, be consistent with the . . . existing instream water uses and the level of water quality necessary to protect the existing uses shall be maintained and protected." Ibid. EPA has explained that under its antidegradation regulation, "no activity is allowable . . . which could partially or completely eliminate any existing use." EPA, Questions and Answers re: Antidegradation 3 (1985). Thus, States must implement their antidegradation policy in a manner "consistent" with existing uses of the stream. The State of Washington's antidegradation policy in turn provides that "existing beneficial uses shall be maintained and protected and no further degradation which would interfere with or become injurious to existing beneficial uses will be allowed." WAC 173-201-035(8)(a). The State concluded that the reduced streamflows would have just the effect prohibited by this policy. The Solicitor General, representing EPA, asserts, and we agree, that the State's minimum stream flow condition is a proper application of the state and federal antidegradation regulations, as it ensures that an "existing instream water use" will be "maintained and protected." 40 CFR §131.12(a)(1)(1992).

Petitioners also assert more generally that the Clean Water Act is only concerned with water "quality," and does not allow the regulation of water "quantity." This is an artificial distinction. In many cases, water quantity is closely related to water quality; a sufficient lowering of the water quantity in a body of water could destroy all of its designated uses, be it for drinking water, recreation, navigation or, as here, as a fishery. In any event, there is recognition in the Clean Water Act itself that reduced stream flow, i.e., diminishment of water quantity, can constitute water pollution. First, the Act's definition of pollution as "the man-made or man-induced alteration of the chemical, physical, biological, and radiological integrity of water" encompasses the effects of reduced water quantity. 33 U.S.C. §1362(19). This broad conception of pollution—one which expressly evinces Congress' concern with the physical and biological integrity of water—refutes petitioners' assertion that the Act draws a sharp distinction between the regulation of water "quantity" and water "quality." Moreover, §304 of the Act expressly recognizes that water "pollution" may result from "changes in the movement, flow, or circulation of any navigable waters . . . including changes caused by the construction of dams." 33 U.S.C. §1314(f). This concern with the flowage effects of dams and other diversions is also embodied in the EPA regulations, which expressly require existing dams to be operated to attain designated uses. 40 CFR §131.10(g)(4). . . .

In summary, we hold that the State may include minimum stream flow requirements in a certification issued pursuant to §401 of the Clean Water Act insofar as necessary to enforce a designated use contained in a state water quality standard. The judgment of the Supreme Court of Washington, accordingly, is affirmed.

[In his concurring opinion, JUSTIVE STEVENS emphasized that this was "an easy case" because the Clean Water Act "explicitly recognizes States' ability to impose stricter standards than federal law requires."]

JUSTICE THOMAS, with whom JUSTICE SCALIA joins, dissenting.

. . . The terms of §401(a)(1) make clear that the purpose of the certification process is to ensure that discharges from a project will meet the requirements of the CWA. . . .

The minimum stream flow condition imposed by respondents in this case has no relation to any possible "discharge" that might "result" from petitioners' proposed project. The term "discharge" is not defined in the CWA, but its plain and ordinary meaning suggests "a flowing or issuing out," or "something that is emitted." Webster's Ninth New Collegiate Dictionary 360 (1991). Cf. 33 U.S.C. §1362(16) ("The term 'discharge' when used without qualification includes a discharge of a pollutant, and a discharge of pollutants"). A minimum stream flow requirement, by contrast, is a limitation on the amount of water the project can take in or divert from the river. That is, a minimum stream flow requirement is a limitation on intake—the opposite of discharge. Imposition of such a requirement would thus appear to be beyond a State's authority as it is defined by §401(a)(1).

. . . If, as the Court asserts, §401(d) permits States to impose conditions unrelated to discharges in §401 certifications, Congress' careful focus on discharges in §401(a)(1)—the provision that describes the scope and function of the certification process—was wasted effort. The power to set conditions that are unrelated to discharges is, of course, nothing but a conditional power to deny certification for reasons unrelated to discharges. Permitting States to impose conditions unrelated to discharges, then, effectively eliminates the constraints of §401(a)(1).

Subsections 401(a)(1) and (d) can easily be reconciled to avoid this problem. To ascertain the nature of the conditions permissible under §401(d), §401 must be read as a whole. See United Savings Assn. of Texas v. Timbers of Inwood Forest Associates, Ltd., 484 U.S. 365, 371 (1988) (statutory interpretation is a "holistic endeavor"). As noted above, §401(a)(1) limits a State's authority in the certification process to addressing concerns related to discharges and to ensuring that any discharge resulting from a project will comply with specified provisions of the Act. It is reasonable to infer that the conditions a State is permitted to impose on certification must relate to the very purpose the certification process is designed to serve. Thus, while §401(d) permits a State to place conditions on a certification to ensure compliance of the "applicant," those conditions must still be related to discharges. In my view, this interpretation best harmonizes the subsections of §401. Indeed, any broader interpretation of §401(d) would permit that subsection to swallow §401(a)(1)....

The Court states that, "at a minimum, limitations imposed pursuant to state water quality standards adopted pursuant to §303 are 'appropriate' requirements of state law" under §401(d).[2] A water quality standard promulgated pursuant to §303 must "consist of the designated uses of the navigable waters involved and the water quality criteria for such waters based upon such uses." 33 U.S.C. §1313(c)(2)(A). The Court asserts that this language "is most naturally read to require that a project be consistent with both components, namely the designated use and the water quality criteria." In the Court's view, then, the "use" of a body of water is independently enforceable through §401(d) without reference to the corresponding criteria.

The Court's reading strikes me as contrary to common sense. It is difficult to see how compliance with a "use" of a body of water could be enforced without reference to the corresponding criteria. In this case, for example, the applicable "use" is contained in the following regulation: "Characteristic uses shall include, but not be limited to . . . [s]almonid migration, rearing, spawning, and harvesting." Wash. Admin. Code (WAC) 173-201-045(1)(b)(iii)(1990). The corresponding criteria, by contrast, include measurable factors such as quantities of fecal coliform organisms and dissolved gases in the water. WAC 173-201-045(1)(c)(i) and (ii).[3] Although the Act does not further address (at least not expressly) the link between "uses" and "criteria," the regulations promulgated under §303 make clear that a "use" is an aspirational goal to be attained through compliance with corresponding "criteria." Those regulations suggest that "uses" are to be "achieved and protected," and that "water quality criteria" are to be adopted to "protect the designated uses." 40 CFR §§131.10(a), 131.11(a)(1)(1993).

The problematic consequences of decoupling "uses" and "criteria" become clear once the Court's interpretation of §303 is read in the context of §401. In the Court's view, a State may condition the §401 certification "upon *any limitations* necessary to ensure compliance" with the "uses of the water body" (emphasis added). Under the Court's interpretation, then, state environmental agencies may pursue, through §401, their water goals in any way they choose; the conditions imposed on certifications need not relate to discharges, nor to water quality criteria, nor to any objective or quantifiable standard, so long as they tend to make the water more suitable for the uses the State has chosen. In short, once a State is allowed to impose conditions on §401 certifications to protect "uses" in the abstract, §401(d) is limitless.

To illustrate, while respondents in this case focused only on the "use" of the Dosewallips River as a fish habitat, this particular river has a number of other "characteristic uses," including "recreation (primary contact recreation, sport

---

2. In the Court's view, §303 water quality standards come into play under §401(d) either as "appropriate" requirements of state law, or through §301 of the Act, which, according to the Court, "incorporates §303 by reference." The Court notes that through §303, "the statute allows states to impose limitations to ensure compliance with §301 of the Act." Yet §301 makes unlawful only "the [unauthorized] *discharge* of any pollutant by any person." 33 U.S.C. §1311(a). Thus, the Court's reliance on §301 as a source of authority to impose conditions unrelated to discharges is misplaced.

3. Respondents concede that petitioners' project "will likely not violate any of Washington's water quality criteria." Brief for Respondents 24.

fishing, boating, and aesthetic enjoyment)." WAC 173-201-045(1)(b)(v). Under the Court's interpretation, respondents could have imposed any number of conditions related to recreation, including conditions that have little relation to water quality. In Town of Summersville, 60 FERC 161,291, p. 61,990 (1992), for instance, the state agency required the applicant to "construct . . . access roads and paths, low water stepping stone bridges, . . . a boat launching facility . . . , and a residence and storage building." These conditions presumably would be sustained under the approach the Court adopts today.[4] In the end, it is difficult to conceive of a condition that would fall outside a State's §401(d) authority under the Court's approach.

NOTES AND QUESTIONS

1. In his dissent, Justice Thomas argues that section 401(d) should not be interpreted to allow states to impose conditions unrelated to discharges. Why does Justice Thomas think that a minimum stream flow requirement is unrelated to a pollutant discharge? Why does the Court majority deem the minimum stream flow requirement an appropriate requirement? Does the majority view this requirement as unrelated to pollutant discharges? How does the majority's view in this regard differ from that of Justice Thomas?

2. Justice O'Connor's opinion for the Court states that while "§401(d) authorizes the State to place restrictions on the activity as a whole, that authority is not unbounded." Yet, in his dissent, Justice Thomas argues that the majority's decision "places no meaningful limitations on a State's authority under §401 to impose conditions on certification." What limits, if any, does the Court place on a state's ability to impose conditions on a section 401 certification? How meaningful are they?

3. As noted in the opinions above, Washington state had not established any specific stream flow water quality criteria. Yet the Court majority holds that section 401(d) can be used to protect designated uses (here the protection of fish habitat) independent of specific criteria. In the majority's view, what is the relationship between designated uses and water quality criteria? How does this view differ from that of Justice Thomas in his dissent?

4. The *PUD No. 1* decision was hailed as a victory for states that could enable them to rouse the "sleeping giant" of the Clean Water Act to impose broad environmental conditions on federally licensed activities. However, in North Carolina v. FERC, 112 F.3d 1175 (D.C. Cir. 1997), the D.C. Circuit limited section 401's reach by adopting a narrow interpretation of its applicability. At issue was an amendment to a federal hydropower license that would authorize construction of an intake structure to withdraw 60 million gallons of water a day from a lake on the North Carolina/Virginia border. FERC argued that section 401 did not apply because the project would *withdraw* water from the lake rather than *discharging* it into navigable waters. North Carolina, joined by EPA and 39 other states, argued that section 401 did apply because the withdrawal of water from the lake would alter the nature of the discharges from the

---

4. Indeed, as the §401 certification stated in this case, the flow levels imposed by respondents are "in excess of those required to maintain water quality in the bypass region" and therefore conditions not related to water quality must, in the Court's view, be permitted.

hydropower project. However, the court sided with FERC, holding that a "decrease in the volume of water passing through the dam turbines cannot be considered a 'discharge' as that term is defined in the CWA." 112 F.3d at 1188. The court concluded that "the word 'discharge' contemplates the addition, not the withdrawal, of a substance or substances." 112 F.3d at 1187. In dissent, Judge Wald argued that "if a State must consent before a new discharge is introduced into its waters, then a change in that discharge must require a new consent." 112 F.3d at 1196. She maintained that the notion that a discharge required the addition of a substance was inconsistent with the Supreme Court's decision in *PUD No. 1*. The majority maintained that *PUD No. 1* did not "define a discharge and in no way indicated that an alteration of a discharge was sufficient to invoke the certification requirement of Section 401(a)(1)." Id.

5. In Oregon Natural Desert Ass'n v. Dombeck, 172 F.3d 1092 (9th Cir. 1998), the Ninth Circuit reversed a district court decision that had required a section 401 certification as a condition to the grant of a grazing permit by the U.S. Forest Service. Rejecting the argument that the term "discharge" in section 401 could encompass pollution from nonpoint sources like runoff from grazing, the court held that section 401 applies only to activities that cause point source discharges. The court distinguished *PUD No. 1* by finding that it did not broaden the meaning of "discharge" because "[a]ll parties conceded that the construction of the dam would result in discharges from both the release of dredge and fill material and the release of water through the dam's tailrace," conveyances that involve point sources.

6. The Federal Energy Regulatory Commission issues long-term licenses for hydroelectric projects. Because the licenses for many large hydroelectric projects are expiring in coming years, the Court's decision in *PUD No. 1* offers states a significant tool for using section 401 to protect water quality. In S.D. Warren v. Maine Board of Environmental Protection, 126 S. Ct. 1843 (2006), the U.S. Supreme Court upheld the application of section 401 to a FERC hydropower relicensing proceeding. The Court held that the meaning of "discharge" in section 401 is somewhat broader than the meaning of discharge in section 301 (the section of the Act that triggers the sections 402 and 404 permitting requirements). The Court noted that, unlike section 301, section 401 does not refer to a discharge *of pollutants* and that section 502(16) provides that the "term 'discharge' when used without qualification *includes* a discharge of a pollutant, and a discharge of pollutants, indicating that it may cover more than just activities that add pollutants to navigable waters (emphasis supplied)."

D.   TOTAL MAXIMUM DAILY LOADINGS (TMDLs)

Section 303(d)(1)(A) of the Clean Water Act requires states to identify those waters for which effluent limitations for nontoxic pollutants are not stringent enough to achieve water quality standards. States then are required by section 303(d)(1)(C) to establish the total maximum daily loadings (TMDLs) of these pollutants "at a level necessary to implement the applicable water quality standards" subject to EPA review and approval. TMDLs define the maximum amount of a pollutant that can be discharged into the water segment without violating the water quality standard. By including estimates of pollutant loadings from all sources, including nonpoint sources and natural background levels, TMDLs are supposed to permit a comprehensive assessment of what reductions are necessary to achieve water quality standards.

Interest in TMDLs grew rapidly as gains from technology-based effluent limits were being exhausted. EPA repeatedly has been held to have a duty to establish TMDLs for states that fail to meet their obligations under section 303(d). Scott v. City of Hammond, 741 F.2d 992 (7th Cir. 1984). In Alaska Center for the Environment v. Reilly, 762 F. Supp. 1422 (W.D. Wash. 1991), aff'd, 20 F.3d 981 (9th Cir. 1994), an environmental group sued to require EPA to issue federal TMDLs for Alaska. While Alaska's biennial section 305(b) reports had included several hundred water segments as "impaired" or "threatened" by pollution, in 11 years the state had not submitted a single TMDL to EPA for review and approval. Finding that the state's failure to act was the constructive equivalent of a submission that no TMDLs were necessary, the court held that EPA had a nondiscretionary duty to promulgate TMDLs in the face of state inaction. While EPA and the state subsequently agreed to assess eight water segments, the court ultimately ordered EPA to develop a long-term "schedule for the establishment of TMDLs for all waters designated as water quality limited." Alaska Center for the Environment v. Reilly, 796 F. Supp. 1374, 1381 (W.D. Wash. 1992). The court's decision was affirmed in Alaska Center for the Environment v. Browner, 20 F.3d 981 (9th Cir. 1994).

TMDLs have become the true "sleeping giant" of the Clean Water Act. As Oliver Houck notes, as a result of "the remarkable resurrection of a long-dormant provision of the Clean Water Act, Section 303(d)," TMDLs are "now taking the field and forcing a showdown on the last water quality frontier, non-point source pollution." Houck, TMDLs IV: The Final Frontier, 29 Envtl. L. Rep. 10469, 10471 (1999). As of 2002 EPA was under court order to establish TMDLs in 22 states; litigation seeking similar orders was pending in 5 other states. This wave of TMDL litigation by citizen groups forced EPA to develop a draft TMDL Implementation Strategy, which it issued in November 1996. EPA then convened a federal advisory committee to "provide consensus recommendations" on the TMDL program. The advisory committee's final report was issued in July 1998. EPA proposed revisions to its TMDL regulations in August 1999, 64 Fed. Reg. 46,011 (1999), and it adopted final regulations in July 2000, 65 Fed. Reg. 43,586 (2000). EPA's regulations require states to develop lists of impaired waters using all existing and readily available water quality data and to set priorities and a schedule for issuing TMDLs. TMDLs are to be established for all impaired waters within ten years of listing, though states can get a five-year extension of this deadline if meeting it is impracticable. States must develop implementation plans, subject to EPA review and approval. If states fail to act, EPA is required to establish its own TMDLs for them. The Bush administration has delayed the effective date of the TMDL regulations in order to give it an opportunity to reconsider them.

The most contentious issue involving TMDLs is the question whether section 303(d)'s TMDL requirements apply to nonpoint sources. Agricultural interests, joined by the U.S. Forest Service, have been vocal opponents of including nonpoint sources in load allocations within TMDLs. They argue that section 319, discussed on page 704, should be the exclusive remedy for nonpoint source pollution because Congress addressed nonpoint sources specifically in section 319 but remained silent about them in section 303(d). EPA has long argued that section 303(d) covers nonpoint sources because its text does not exclude from its requirements waters impaired by nonpoint sources. In the case below the U.S. Court of Appeals for the Ninth Circuit addressed the question whether EPA has the authority under section 303(d) of the Clean Water Act to set total maximum daily loadings (TMDLs) for all navigable waters impaired by pollution, including those whose impairment is due to nonpoint sources. After EPA disapproved California's 301(d)(1) list because it omitted sixteen water segments that were impaired only by nonpoint sources, EPA promulgated its own list including these segments. For one of them, the Garcia River, EPA subsequently established a TMDL requiring a 60 percent reduction in sediment loadings. After California sought to comply with the TMDL by restricting activities, such as logging, that generate sediment runoff, a number of farm organizations sued. The decision below is a product of that litigation.

|| *Pronsolino v. Nastri* ||
|| 291 F.3d 1123 (9th Cir. 2002) ||

Berzon, Circuit Judge.

The United States Environmental Protection Agency ("EPA") required California to identify the Garcia River as a water body with insufficient pollution controls and, as required for waters so identified, to set so-called "total maximum daily loads" ("TMDLs")—the significance of which we explain later—for pollution entering the river. Appellants challenge the EPA's authority under the Clean Water Act ("CWA" or the "Act") 303(d), 33 U.S.C. 1313(d), to apply the pertinent identification and TMDL requirements to the Garcia River. The district court rejected this challenge, and we do as well.

CWA 303(d) requires the states to identify and compile a list of waters for which certain "effluent limitations" "are not stringent enough" to implement the applicable water quality standards for such waters. 303(d)(1)(A). Effluent limitations pertain only to point sources of pollution; point sources of pollution are those from a discrete conveyance, such as a pipe or tunnel. Nonpoint sources of pollution are non-discrete sources; sediment run-off from timber harvesting, for example, derives from a nonpoint source. The Garcia River is polluted only by nonpoint sources. Therefore, neither the effluent limitations referenced in 303(d) nor any other effluent limitations apply to the pollutants entering the Garcia River.

The precise statutory question before us is whether the phrase "are not stringent enough" triggers the identification requirement both for waters as to which effluent limitations apply but do not suffice to attain water quality standards and for waters as to which effluent limitations do not apply at all to the pollution sources impairing the water. . . .

I. STATUTORY BACKGROUND

. . . [T]he CWA uses distinctly different methods to control pollution released from point sources and that traceable to nonpoint sources. The Act directly mandates technological controls to limit the pollution point sources may discharge into a body of water. On the other hand, the Act "provides no direct mechanism to control nonpoint source pollution but rather uses the 'threat and promise' of federal grants to the states to accomplish this task," thereby "recogniz[ing], preserv[ing], and protect[ing] the primary responsibilities and rights of States to prevent, reduce, and eliminate pollution, [and] to plan the development and use . . . of land and water resources. . . ." 101(b).

B. Structure of CWA 303

1. Water Quality Standards

Section 303 is central to the Act's carrot-and-stick approach to attaining acceptable water quality without direct federal regulation of nonpoint sources of pollution. Entitled "Water Quality Standards and Implementation Plans," the provision begins by spelling out the statutory requirements for water quality standards: "Water quality standards" specify a water body's "designated uses" and "water quality criteria," taking into account the water's "use and value for public water supplies, propagation of fish and wildlife, recreational purposes, and agricultural, industrial, and other purposes. . . ." 303(c)(2). The states are required to set water quality standards for all waters within their boundaries regardless of the sources of the pollution entering the waters. If a state does not set water quality standards, or if the EPA determines that the state's standards do not meet the requirements of the Act, the EPA promulgates standards for the state. 303(b), (c)(3)-(4).

2. Section 303(d): "Identification of Areas with Insufficient Controls; Maximum Daily Load"

Section 303(d)(1)(A) requires each state to identify as "areas with insufficient controls" "those waters within its boundaries for which the effluent limitations required by section [301(b)(1)(A)] and section [301(b)(1)(B)] of this title are not stringent enough to implement any water quality standard applicable to such waters." Id. The CWA defines "effluent limitations" as restrictions on pollutants "discharged from point sources." CWA 502(11). Section 301(b)(1)(A) mandates application of the "best practicable control technology" effluent limitations for most point source discharges, while 301(b)(1)(B) mandates application of effluent limitations adopted specifically for secondary treatment at publicly owned treatment works. 301(b)(1).

For waters identified pursuant to 303(d)(1)(A) (the "303(d)(1) list"), the states must establish the "total maximum daily load" ("TMDL") for pollutants identified by the EPA as suitable for TMDL calculation. 303(d)(1)(C). "A TMDL defines the specified maximum amount of a pollutant which can be discharged or 'loaded' into the waters at issue from all combined sources." Dioxin/Organochlorine Center v. Clarke, 57 F.3d 1517, 1520 (9th Cir. 1995). The TMDL "shall be established at a level necessary to implement the applicable water quality standards. . . ." 303(d)(1)(C).

Section 303(d)(2), in turn, requires each state to submit its 303(d)(1) list and TMDLs to the EPA for its approval or disapproval. If the EPA approves the list and TMDLs, the state must incorporate the list and TMDLs into its "continuing planning process," the requirements for which are set forth in 303(e). 303(d)(2). If the EPA disapproves either the 303(d)(1) list or any TMDLs, the EPA must itself put together the missing document or documents. Id. The state then incorporates any EPA-set list or TMDL into the state's continuing planning process. Id.

Each state must also identify all waters not placed on its 303(d)(1) list (the "303(d)(3) list") and "estimate" TMDLs for pollutants in those waters. 303(d)(3). There is no requirement that the EPA approve the 303(d)(3) lists or the TMDLs estimated for those waters. Id.

The EPA in regulations has made more concrete the statutory requirements. Those regulations, in summary, define "water quality limited segment[s]"—those waters that must be included on the 303(d)(1) list—as "[a]ny segment where it is known that water quality does not meet applicable water quality standards, and/or is not expected to meet applicable water quality standards, even after the application of the technology-based effluent limitations required by sections 301(b) and 306[, 33 U.S.C. 1316]." 40 C.F.R. 130.2(j)(2000). The regulations then divide TMDLs into two types: "load allocations," for nonpoint source pollution, and "wasteload allocations," for point source pollution. 130.2(g)-(i). Under the regulations, states must identify those waters on the 303(d)(1) lists as "still requiring TMDLs" if any required effluent limitation or other pollution control requirement (including those for nonpoint source pollution) will not bring the water into compliance with water quality standards. 130.7(b)(2000).

3.   Continuing Planning Process

The final pertinent section of 303, 303(e), requiring each state to have a "continuing planning process," gives some operational force to the prior information-gathering provisions. The EPA may approve a state's continuing planning process only if it "will result in plans for all navigable waters within such State" that include, inter alia, effluent limitations, TMDLs, areawide waste management plans for nonpoint sources of pollution, and plans for "adequate implementation, including schedules of compliance, for revised or new water quality standards." 303(e)(3).

The upshot of this intricate scheme is that the CWA leaves to the states the responsibility of developing plans to achieve water quality standards if the statutorily-mandated point source controls will not alone suffice, while providing federal funding to aid in the implementation of the state plans. See *Dombeck*, 172 F.3d at 1097; 303(e); see also 319(h), 33 U.S.C. 1329(h) (providing for grants to states to combat nonpoint source pollution). TMDLs are primarily informational tools that allow the states to proceed from the identification of waters requiring additional planning to the required plans. See Alaska Center for the Environment v. Browner, 20 F.3d 981, 984-85 (9th Cir. 1994). As such, TMDLs serve as a link in an implementation chain that includes federally-regulated point source controls, state or local plans for point and nonpoint source pollution reduction, and assessment of the impact of such measures on water quality, all to the end of attaining water quality goals for the nation's waters.

[The Court then discussed the factual and procedural posture of the case noting that the plaintiffs challenged the EPA's authority to impose TMDLs on rivers polluted only by nonpoint sources of pollution and sought a determination of whether the Act authorized the Garcia River TMDL.]

III.   ANALYSIS

A.   Deference to the EPA

[The court then rejected the plaintiffs' claims that EPA's position was not consistent with the Agency's current regulations and that the Agency had not been consistent in its interpretation of the statute. The court conceded that until the 1990s "the EPA did not actively police the requirement that states include on their 303(d)(1) lists waters polluted only by nonpoint source pollution." But it viewed this as reflecting "a more general regulatory failure to enforce the 303(d) requirements, not a failure with regard only to waters impaired by nonpoint sources."]

B. Plain Meaning and Structural Issues

1. The Competing Interpretations

Section 303(d)(1)(A) requires listing and calculation of TMDLs for "those waters within [the state's] boundaries for which the effluent limitations required by section [301(b)(1)(A)] and section [301(b)(1)(B)] of this title *are not stringent enough to implement any water quality standard* applicable to such waters." 303(d) (emphasis added). The precise statutory question before us is whether, as the Pronsolinos maintain, the term "not stringent enough to implement . . . water quality standard[s]" as used in 303(d)(1)(A) must be interpreted to mean both that application of effluent limitations will not achieve water quality standards and that the waters at issue are subject to effluent limitations. As only waters with point source pollution are subject to effluent limitations, such an interpretation would exclude from the 303(d)(1) listing and TMDL requirements waters impaired only by nonpoint sources of pollution.

The EPA, as noted, interprets "not stringent enough to implement . . . water quality standard[s]" to mean "not adequate" or "not sufficient . . . to implement any water quality standard," and does not read the statute as implicitly containing a limitation to waters initially covered by effluent limitations. According to the EPA, if the use of effluent limitations will not implement applicable water quality standards, the water falls within 303(d)(1)(A) regardless of whether it is point or nonpoint sources, or a combination of the two, that continue to pollute the water.

2. The Language and Structure of 303(d)

Whether or not the appellants' suggested interpretation is entirely implausible, it is at least considerably weaker than the EPA's competing construction. The Pronsolinos' version necessarily relies upon: (1) understanding "stringent enough" to mean "strict enough" rather than "thorough going enough" or "adequate" or "sufficient"; and (2) reading the phrase "not stringent enough" in isolation, rather than with reference to the stated goal of implementing "any water quality standard applicable to such waters." Where the answer to the question "not stringent enough for what?" is "to implement any [applicable] water quality standard," the meaning of "stringent" should be determined by looking forward to the broad goal to be attained, not backwards at the inadequate effluent limitations. One might comment, for example, about a teacher that her standards requiring good spelling were not stringent enough to assure good writing, as her students still used bad grammar and poor logic. Based on the language of the contested phrase alone, then, the more sensible conclusion is that the 303(d)(1) list must contain any waters for which the particular effluent limitations will not be adequate to attain the statute's water quality goals.

Placing the phrase in its statutory context supports this conclusion. Section 303(d) begins with the requirement that each state "identify those waters within its boundaries. . . ." 303(d)(1)(A). So the statute's starting point for the listing project is a compilation of each and every navigable water within the state. Then, only those waters that will attain water quality standards after application of the new point source technology are excluded from the 303(d)(1) list, leaving all those waters for which that technology will not "implement any water quality standard applicable to such waters." 303(d)(1)(A); see American Wildlands v. Browner, 260 F.3d 1192, 1194 (10th Cir. 2001) ("[E]ach state is required to identify all of the waters within its borders not meeting water quality standards and establish [TMDLs] for those waters.") (Citing 303(d)); *Pronsolino,* 91 F. Supp. 2d at 1347. The alternative construction, in contrast, would begin with a subset of all the state's waterways, those that have point sources subject to effluent limitations, and would result in a list containing only a subset of that subset—those waters as to which the applicable effluent limitations are not adequate to attain water quality standards.

The Pronsolinos' contention to the contrary notwithstanding, no such odd reading of the statute is necessary in order to give meaning to the phrase "for which the effluent limitations required by section [301(b)(1)(A)] and section [301(b)(1)(B)] . . . are not stringent enough." The EPA interprets 303(d)(1)(A) to require the identification of any waters not meeting water quality standards only if specified effluent limitations would not achieve those standards. 40 C.F.R. 130.2(j). If the pertinent effluent limitations would, if implemented, achieve the water quality standards but are not in place yet, there need be no listing and no TMDL calculation. Id.

So construed, the meaning of the statute is different than it would be were the language recast to state only that "Each State shall identify those waters within its boundaries . . . [not meeting] any water quality standard applicable to such waters." Under the EPA's construction, the reference to effluent limitations reflects Congress' intent that the EPA focus initially on implementing effluent limitations and only later avert its attention to water quality standards. See e.g., 1 Legislative History 171 ("The Administrator should assign secondary priority to the extent limited manpower and funding may require a choice between a water quality standards process and early and effective implementation of the effluent limitation-permit program." (statement of Sen. Muskie, principal author of the CWA and the Chair of the Senate's Public Works Committee)); see also Environmental Def. Fund, Inc. v. Costle, 657 F.2d 275, 279 (D.C. Cir. 1981) (The 1972 CWA "assigned secondary priority to the [water quality] standards and placed primary emphasis upon both a point source discharge permit program and federal technology-based effluent limitations. . . .").

Given all these language considerations, it is not surprising that the only time this court addressed the reach of 303(d)(1)(A), it rejected a reading of 303(d)(1)(A) similar to the one the Pronsolinos now proffer. In *Dioxin,* 57 F.3d at 1526-27, the plaintiffs argued that the phrase "not stringent enough" prohibited the EPA from listing under 303(d)(1)(A) and establishing TMDLs for toxic pollutants, until after the implementation and proven failure of 301(b)(1)(A) "best practicable technology" effluent limitations. Toxic pollutants, however, are not subject to "best practicable technology" controls, but to more demanding "best available technology," precisely because of their toxicity. Id.

The court in *Dioxin* held that the EPA acted within its statutory authority in setting TMDLs for toxic pollutants, even though the effluent limitations referenced by 303(d)(1)(A) did not apply to those pollutants. Id. at 1528. The court explained that, since best practical technology effluent limitations do not apply to toxic pollutants, those limitations are, as a matter of law, "not stringent enough" to achieve water quality standards. Id. In other words, *Dioxin* read 303(d)(1)(A) as applying to all waters in the state, not only to the subset covered by certain kinds of effluent controls, and it understood "not stringent enough" to mean "not adequate for" or "inapplicable to."

Nothing in 303(d)(1)(A) distinguishes the treatment of point sources and nonpoint sources as such; the only reference is to the "effluent limitations required by" 301(b)(1). So if the effluent limitations required by 301(b)(1) are "as a matter of law" "not stringent enough" to achieve the applicable water quality standards for waters impaired by point sources not subject to those requirements, then they are also "not stringent enough" to achieve applicable water quality standards for other waters not subject to those requirements, in this instance because they are impacted only by nonpoint sources. Additionally, the *Dioxin* court, applying *Chevron* deference, upheld the EPA's interpretation of 303(d) "as requiring TMDLs where existing pollution controls will not lead to attainment of water standards," id. at 1527; see also 40 C.F.R. 130.7(b), a holding that directly encompasses waters polluted only by nonpoint sources.

3. The Statutory Scheme as a Whole

The Pronsolinos' objection to this view of 303(d), and of *Dioxin*, is, in essence, that the CWA as a whole distinguishes between the regulatory schemes applicable to point and nonpoint sources, so we must assume such a distinction in applying 303(d)(1)(A) and (C). We would hesitate in any case to read into a discrete statutory provision something that is not there because it is contained elsewhere in the statute. But here, the premise is wrong: There is no such general division throughout the CWA.

Point sources are treated differently from nonpoint sources for many purposes under the statute, but not all. In particular, there is no such distinction with regard to the basic purpose for which the 303(d) list and TMDLs are compiled, the eventual attainment of state-defined water quality standards. Water quality standards reflect a state's designated uses for a water body and do not depend in anyway upon the source of pollution. See 303(a)-(c).

Nor is there any other basis for inferring from the structure of the Act an implicit limitation in 303(d)(1)(A) and (C). . . . True, there are, as the Pronsolinos point out, two sections of the statute as amended, 208 and 319, that set requirements exclusively for nonpoint sources of pollution. But the structural inference we are asked to draw from those specialized sections—that no other provisions of the Act set requirements for waters polluted by nonpoint sources— simply does not follow. Absent some irreconcilable contradiction between the requirements contained in 208 and 319, on the one hand, and the listing and TMDL requirements of 303 (d), on the other, both apply.

There is no such contradiction. . . .

There is one final aspect of the Act's structure that bears consideration because it supports the EPA's interpretation of 303(d): The list required by 303(d)(1)(A) requires that waters be listed if they are impaired by a combination of point sources and nonpoint sources; the language admits of no other reading. Section 303(d)(1)(C), in turn, directs that TMDLs "shall be established at a level necessary *to implement* the applicable water quality standards. . . . " Id. (emphasis added). So, at least in blended waters, TMDLs must be calculated with regard to nonpoint sources of pollution; otherwise, it would be impossible "to implement the applicable water quality standards," which do not differentiate sources of pollution. This court has so recognized. *Browner,* 20 F.3d at 985 ("Congress and the EPA have already determined that establishing TMDLs is an effective tool for achieving water quality standards in waters impacted by nonpoint source pollution.").

Nothing in the statutory structure—or purpose—suggests that Congress meant to distinguish, as to 303(d)(1) lists and TMDLs, between waters with one insignificant point source and substantial nonpoint source pollution and waters with only nonpoint source pollution. Such a distinction would, for no apparent reason, require the states or the EPA to monitor waters to determine whether a point source had been added or removed, and to adjust the 303(d)(1) list and establish TMDLs accordingly. There is no statutory basis for concluding that Congress intended such an irrational regime.

Looking at the statute as a whole, we conclude that the EPA's interpretation of 303(d) is not only entirely reasonable but considerably more convincing than the one offered by the plaintiffs in this case.

C.   Federalism Concerns

The Pronsolinos finally contend that, by establishing TMDLs for waters impaired only by nonpoint source pollution, the EPA has upset the balance of federal-state control established in the CWA by intruding into the states' traditional control over land use. See Solid Waste Agency of Northern Cook County v. United States Army Corps of Eng'rs, 531 U.S. 159, 172-73 (2001). That is not the case.

The Garcia River TMDL identifies the maximum load of pollutants that can enter the Garcia River from certain broad categories of nonpoint sources if the river is to attain water quality standards. It does not specify the load of pollutants that may be received from particular parcels of land or describe what measures the state should take to implement the TMDL. Instead, the TMDL expressly recognizes that "implementation and monitoring" "are state responsibilities" and notes that, for this reason, the EPA did not include implementation or monitoring plans within the TMDL. EPA, Garcia River Sediment Total Maximum Daily Load 43 (Mar. 16, 1998).

Moreover, 303(e) requires—separately from the 303(d)(1) listing and TMDL requirements—that each state include in its continuing planning process "adequate implementation, including schedules of compliance, for revised or new water quality standards" "for all navigable waters within such State." 303(e)(3). The Garcia River TMDL thus serves as an informational tool for the creation of the state's implementation plan, independently—and explicitly—required by Congress.

California chose both if and how it would implement the Garcia River TMDL. States must implement TMDLs only to the extent that they seek to avoid losing federal grant money; there is no pertinent statutory provision otherwise requiring implementation of 303 plans or providing for their enforcement. See CWA 309, 33 U.S.C. 1319; CWA 505, 33 U.S.C. 1365.

Finally, it is worth noting that the arguments that the Pronsolinos raise here would apply equally to nonpoint source pollution controls for blended waters. Yet, as discussed above, Congress definitely required that the states or the EPA establish TMDLs for all pollutants in waters on 303(d)(1) lists, including blended waters.

We conclude that the Pronsolinos' federalism basis for reading 303 against its own words and structure is unfounded.

IV. CONCLUSION

For all the reasons we have surveyed, the CWA is best read to include in the 303(d)(1) listing and TMDLs requirements waters impaired only by nonpoint sources of pollution. Moreover, to the extent the statute is ambiguous—which is not very much—the substantial deference we owe the EPA's interpretation, under either *Chevron* or *Skidmore*, requires that we uphold the agency's more than reasonable interpretation. We therefore hold that the EPA did not exceed its statutory authority in identifying the Garcia River pursuant to 303(d)(1)(A) and establishing the Garcia River TMDL, even though the river is polluted only by nonpoint sources of pollution.

NOTES AND QUESTIONS

1. Even if EPA can require states to adopt TMDLs for waters polluted only by nonpoint sources, what authority, if any, does the agency have under the CWA to require states to implement and enforce controls on nonpoint sources? In the absence of direct federal controls over nonpoint source pollution, how can the Agency effectively ensure attainment of water quality standards in water segments impaired by nonpoint sources?

2. As the court notes, EPA failed entirely to implement the provisions of section 303(d) and the TMDL program until the 1990s. What do you think accounts for EPA's failure to do so?

3. Translating a TMDL into permit limits for individual dischargers is scientifically and politically difficult. To estimate the impact of specific discharges on water quality under varying flow conditions, states apply dilution factors and mixing zones that vary wildly, often reflecting political rather than scientific judgments. Houck, The Regulation of Toxic Pollutants Under the Clean Water Act, 21 Envtl. L. Rep. 10,528, 10,546 (1991). Moreover, while "EPA has unhelpfully offered several alternative methods for making TMDL allocations, ranging from even to uneven percentage reductions among sources," these do not "even begin to resolve the [political] difficulties of whether a state regulatory agency wishes to place its head into the jaws of a public utility, a chemical plant, or local farmer" in establishing permit limits. Id.

4. The political difficulties of allocating pollutant loads among dischargers are compounded when interstate pollution is involved. In some cases, EPA has worked with states to establish TMDLs for water bodies subject to interstate discharges. To ensure that uniform standards applied to pollutants in New York Harbor, EPA proposed TMDLs for copper, lead, mercury, and nickel that would affect dischargers in both New York and New Jersey. 59 Fed. Reg. 41,293 (1994). At the request of the states of Oregon, Washington, and Idaho,

EPA issued a TMDL for dioxin discharges into the Columbia River. Despite challenges from both industry and environmental groups, EPA's action was upheld in Dioxin/Organochlorine Center v. Clarke, 57 F.3d 1517 (9th Cir. 1995).

5. Oliver Houck has written a series of articles providing a comprehensive review of the history of water quality-based standards under the Clean Water Act from 1972 to the present, Houck, TMDLs: The Resurrection of Water Quality Standards-Based Regulation Under the Clean Water Act, 27 Envtl. L. Rep. 10,329 (July 1997), and their recent resurrection due to an explosion of litigation over TMDLs, Houck, TMDLs, Are We There Yet? The Long Road Toward Water Quality-Based Regulation Under the Clean Water Act. 27 Envtl. L. Rep. 10,391, 10,401 (1997); TMDLs IV: The Final Frontier, 29 Envtl. L. Rep. 10,469 (1999). Houck notes that given the large number of water segments that may not meet applicable water quality standards, the difficulty of obtaining data necessary to support load calculations and the overall cost of developing and implementing TMDLs (perhaps as much as "$1 million per study and an order of magnitude times that amount more for implementation"), the TMDL process may again remind us of the virtues of the Act's technology-based effluent limits.

WATER POLLUTION CONTROL:
A PROBLEM EXERCISE

For nearly 60 years a gun manufacturer has owned a skeet shooting club on a point overlooking a river. It is estimated that 4 million pounds of lead shot and 11 million pounds of clay targets have fallen into the river from the club's 12 shooting ranges. Neither the gun manufacturer nor the club (nor any of the club's patrons) has ever had an NPDES permit authorizing them to discharge lead shot or clay targets into the river. Sediment samples taken from the riverbed have found high levels (up to 640,000 parts per million) of lead, a priority toxic pollutant under the Clean Water Act, and tests on shellfish and waterfowl in the area have found elevated levels of lead in their tissues and blood that the U.S. Fish and Wildlife Service believes to be acutely toxic.

Question One. Has the club or any of its patrons violated the Clean Water Act by discharging pollutants into surface waters without an NPDES permit? See §§502(12), 502(14), and Romero-Barcelo v. Brown, 643 F.2d 835 (1st Cir. 1981), rev'd on other grounds sub nom. Weinberger v. Romero-Barcelo, 456 U.S. 305 (1982). What, if anything, would you advise the club to do to ensure that neither it nor its patrons violates the law?

Question Two. Suppose that an NPDES permit were required in these circumstances, and that an existing, industry-wide effluent standard has been promulgated for the firearms manufacturing industry. Should this standard be incorporated into the club's permit? Could the club obtain a variance from this standard? How? What alternative limits could be incorporated into the club's permit to reduce lead contamination of the river?

Question Three. Suppose that the state has adopted water quality criteria for lead to protect aquatic life and human health based on measurements of the presence of lead in the water column. If levels of lead in the water column are higher than permissible under these criteria, how, if at all, could section 303(d) or section 304(*l*) of the Clean Water Act be used to place additional restrictions on the club's discharges?

Question Four.   Suppose that, despite the high concentration of lead in the sediment, lead levels in the water column do not exceed the criteria, although benthic organisms have accumulated dangerous levels of lead, apparently due to feeding on material in the sediment. Could the state be required to adopt sediment quality criteria under section 303(c)(2)(B)?

Question Five.   If lead levels in the river violate the existing water quality standard for lead, can a foundry in another state located upstream from the club obtain an NPDES permit to discharge lead into the same river?

E.   WETLANDS PROTECTION AND THE SECTION 404 PERMIT PROGRAM

While they can be areas of great beauty, to the untrained eye wetlands often appear as undesirable swamps that could only be improved by development. They were long viewed as "wastelands, sources of mosquitos and impediments to development and travel," J. Kusler, Our National Wetland Heritage 1 (1983), whose draining and filling was a sign of progress, often subsidized by government. See Leovy v. United States, 177 U.S. 621, 636 (1900) ("[T]he police power is never more legitimately exercised than in removing such nuisances."). Scientists now realize that wetlands are among the most vital and productive of all ecosystems. They provide enormously valuable "ecosystem services," including flood control, as was widely recognized in the wake of Hurricane Katrina, whose catastrophic effects in September 2005 were compounded due to the previous loss of vast areas of coastal wetlands in Louisiana and Mississippi. Wetlands also "are the primary pollution control systems of the nation's waters," removing "heavy metals at efficiencies ranging from twenty to one hundred percent" and "up to ninety-five percent of phosphorus, nutrients, and conventional pollutants." Houck & Rolland, Federalism in Wetlands Regulation: A Consideration of Delegation of Clean Water Act Section 404 and Related Programs to the States, 54 Md. L. Rev. 1242, 1245 (1995). Wetlands serve as feeding and breeding grounds for fish and waterfowl. They are a particularly critical link in the ecological chain, even though their environmental importance is not reflected in their market price.

Wetlands also can be attractive sites for development, due in part to humans' love for proximity to water. Development pressures have destroyed a precious part of the nation's ecological heritage. Scientists estimate that more than half (53 percent) of the wetlands in the original 48 states have been destroyed, with total wetland acreage there declining from an estimated 215 million acres to only about 100 million acres today. EPA, Wetlands Fact Sheet 11 (1995). Wetlands remain under relentless assault. Nearly 300,000 acres are disappearing each year, due largely to agricultural and urban development.

1.   The Structure of the Section 404 Program

The most visible (and controversial) wetlands protection program is a product of section 404 of the Clean Water Act. When it adopted the FWPCA in 1972, Congress established a separate permit program, in addition to the NPDES, to govern discharges of dredge and fill material. Section 404 of the Act, whose importance was not immediately appreciated, requires all dischargers of dredge and fill to the waters of the United States to obtain a permit from the U.S. Army Corps of Engineers. The Corps administers the section 404 permit program in cooperation with EPA.

The scope of the waters subject to federal regulation under section 404 is discussed in this chapter on pages 599-616. The definition of dredge and fill material determines whether a permit must be obtained from the Corps under section 404 or from EPA under section 402 of the Clean Water Act, which covers all discharges of pollutants from point sources. The section 404 permit program covers discharges of dredge and fill materials. The former are defined by EPA and the Corps as "material that is excavated or dredged from the waters of the United States." 40 C.F.R. §232.2(g); 33 C.F.R. §323.2(c). Material not excavated from such waters is subject to the section 404 permit program if it is used as fill material. The Corps defines "fill material" as "material used for the primary purpose of replacing an aquatic area with dry land or of changing the bottom elevation of a water body," 33 C.F.R. §323.2(k), while EPA considers any pollutant that has such an effect to be fill. 40 C.F.R. §232.2(i).

Note that the language of section 404 only refers to discharges of dredge and fill material. As a result, there has been considerable uncertainty concerning whether section 404 covers activities that destroy wetlands through ditching, channelization, or excavation. In Avoyelles Sportsmen's League v. Marsh, 715 F.2d 897 (5th Cir. 1983), the Fifth Circuit held that mechanized landclearing activities require a section 404 permit when they redeposit soil in wetland areas. But in Save Our Community v. EPA, 971 F.2d 1155 (5th Cir. 1992), the same court held that drainage of a wetland does not require a section 404 permit unless there is a discharge of some kind.

In 1977 Congress added section 404(e) to the Clean Water Act to authorize the Corps to "issue general permits on a state, regional or nationwide basis for categories of activities that are substantially similar in nature and cause only minimal adverse effects on the environment." These general permits have five-year terms. In 1982, the Corps established 26 nationwide permits. While many of these authorize routine and relatively noncontroversial activities (such as the placement of navigation aids and surveying activities), NWP 26 was the focus of great controversy. Promulgated by the Corps over EPA's objections, it authorized the filling of so-called isolated waters and "headwaters," which resulted in the destruction of large wetlands areas. In 1984, NWP 26 was revised to limit its application to projects of less than ten acres and in 1996 it was revised to limit its application to projects disturbing less than three acres of wetlands. In March 2000, NWP 26 was modified to reduce the acreage of wetlands that may be disturbed without obtaining an individual permit from three acres to one-half acre and to require predischarge notification to the Corps of any activity that will destroy more than one-tenth of an acre of wetlands. 65 Fed. Reg. 12,818 (2000).

The section 404 program has been controversial because it extends the reach of federal regulation more broadly and in a manner that potentially affects more individuals than virtually any other environmental law. However, the potentially expansive reach of section 404 has been tempered in significant ways. Section 404(f)(1) exempts discharges from normal farming, forestry, and ranching operations. Section 404(f)(2) qualifies this exemption by refusing to extend it to activities designed to convert a wetland "into a use to which it was not previously subject." Thus, discharges from the draining or filling of a wetland in order to convert it into additional farmland have been held not to be exempt from section 404's permit requirement even if undertaken by a farming operation. United States v. Bruce, 41 F.3d 117 (3d Cir. 1994). In the *Borden Ranch* case discussed on pages 623-624 of this book, the Ninth Circuit rejected the argument that deep ripping to drain a wetland qualified for the section 404(f) exemption for discharges from normal farming activities because the developer was trying to convert the wetlands to a use to which they were not previously subject. Borden Ranch Partnership v. U.S. Army Corps of Engineers, 261 F.3d 810 (9th Cir. 2001), affirmed by an equally divided Court, 537 U.S. 99 (2002). Wetlands that were drained and converted to cropland prior to enactment of the Swampbuster provisions of the Food Security Act in December 1985 have been exempted from section 404 by regulation. This removed 53 million acres of land from coverage under section 404 even in areas where wetlands vegetation would return to the land if cropping ceased.

A Note on Wetlands Identification and Delineation

Identifying what areas are wetlands for purposes of section 404 has been difficult and controversial. In 1977, EPA and the Corps adopted identical regulatory definitions of wetlands: "Wetlands are those areas that are inundated or saturated by surface or groundwater at a frequency and duration sufficient to support, and that under normal circumstances do support, a prevalence of vegetation typically adapted for life in saturated soil conditions." 33 C.F.R. §328.3(b) (Corps) and 40 C.F.R. §230.3(t) (EPA).

Despite using the same regulatory definition, for years each agency followed different procedures for identifying and delineating wetlands. In 1987, the Corps issued its own Wetlands Delineation Manual which required that the presence of three conditions be demonstrated for an area to be considered a wetland—wetlands hydrology, wetlands vegetation, and wetlands soil conditions. To provide more uniform standards for wetlands delineation, an interagency task force from EPA, the Corps, the Soil Conservation Service, and the Fish and Wildlife Service jointly published the Federal Manual for Identifying and Delineating Jurisdictional Wetlands in 1989. While focusing on the same three conditions as the Corps' 1987 Manual, the 1989 Manual permitted the presence of the requisite hydrology or soil conditions to be inferred, in certain circumstances, from the presence of certain vegetation.

After agriculture and oil interests protested that the 1989 Manual would enlarge the scope of the section 404 program, in August 1991 the Bush administration proposed a new approach to delineation that would drastically reduce the wetlands acreage subject to protection. Scientists who field tested the proposed 1991 revisions denounced them as "without scientific basis" and reported that they would drastically reduce the coverage of the section 404 program. EPA ultimately announced that it would use the Corps' 1987 Manual, pending completion of a study of wetlands delineation by the National Academy of Sciences (NAS).

In May 1995, the NAS Committee on Characterization of Wetlands released its report. National Research Council, Wetlands: Characteristics and Boundaries (1995). While the report generally confirmed the scientific soundness of delineation practices in the 1987 and 1989 manuals, it recommended that a single delineation manual be adopted and that one federal agency be given lead responsibility for wetlands regulation. The report defines a wetland as "an ecosystem that depends on constant or recurrent, shallow inundation or saturation at or near the surface of the substrate." It recommends that wetlands delineation continue to be based on consideration of hydrology, soil characteristics, and the presence of hydrophytic vegetation.

To provide greater predictability to the section 404 permit process, EPA and the Corps have been working with states to conduct advance identification projects that render advisory determinations concerning what areas are wetlands and their suitability for the discharge of dredged or fill material.

2.   The Section 404 Permit Process

The permit process established by section 404 has produced bitter confrontations between developers and environmental groups, each of whom has been highly critical of the process. Development interests argue that the process is too cumbersome and takes too long. Environmentalists argue that the Corps has been far too lenient in granting permits to development interests and that EPA has been too willing to defer to the Corps.

Under EPA guidelines for issuing section 404 permits, permit applicants must demonstrate that (1) there is no "practicable alternative to the proposed discharge" which would be less damaging to the aquatic environment, (2) the proposed activity will not "cause or contribute to significant degradation of the waters of the United States," (3) "appropriate and practicable steps have been taken which will minimize potential adverse impacts of the discharge on the aquatic ecosystem," and (4) the proposed discharge will not violate state water quality standards, toxic effluent standards, the Endangered Species Act or regulations to protect marine sanctuaries under the Marine Mammal Protection Act. 40 C.F.R. §230.10.

Decisions concerning permit applications under section 404 turn largely on an analysis of alternatives to a proposed project. Alternatives analysis is a central feature of several environmental laws, most notably section 102 of the National Environmental Policy Act (NEPA), which requires the preparation of environmental impact statements on major federal actions; section 4(f) of the Department of Transportation Act, which prohibits the construction of federal highways in parklands unless there is no "feasible and prudent alternative"; and section 7 of the Endangered Species Act, which prohibits federal actions that threaten endangered species unless a special committee finds that there are no alternatives, the benefits of the proposal outweigh the benefits from alternatives, and the action is of regional or national significance. NEPA is discussed in Chapter 8 and the Endangered Species Act is discussed in Chapter 9.

The section 404(b)(1) guidelines provide that "no discharge of dredged or fill material shall be permitted if there is a practicable alternative . . . which would have less adverse impact on the aquatic ecosystem. . . ." 40 C.F.R. §230.10(a). The guidelines define an alternative as "practicable" if it is "available" and "capable of being done after taking into consideration cost, existing technology, and logistics in light of overall project purposes." Thus, the guidelines employ a kind of feasibility-limited approach to regulation that is supposed to tolerate environmental damage only if no alternative is available.

If alternatives are available, the permit is to be denied without further inquiry into the suitability of the site and the environmental impact of the discharge.

The guidelines are designed to place a heavy burden on developers who seek approval to locate in wetland areas projects that do not "require access or proximity" to the water. For such non-water-dependent projects, the guidelines presume that a less damaging alternative is available "unless clearly demonstrated otherwise." The developer bears the burden of proving that no alternative is available, which under the guidelines includes demonstrating that no other property could "reasonably" be obtained to fulfill the "basic purpose of the proposed activity." 40 C.F.R. §230.10(a)(2).

How the purposes of a project are defined has a major effect on analysis of the availability of alternatives under section 404. For example, in National Wildlife Federation v. Whistler, 27 F.3d 1341 (8th Cir. 1994), a developer sought a section 404 permit to open an old river channel to provide boat access for a planned housing development near the Missouri River. By defining the project's purpose to be the provision of boat access, the Corps found the project to be water-dependent and concluded that no other alternative was practicable to achieve the project's purpose. After the Corps granted the permit, an environmental group and an adjacent properly owner sued. While plaintiffs argued that the Corps failed to consider the alternative of having residents of the development use a nearby public boat ramp, the court deferred to the Corps' judgment and upheld issuance of the permit. The court distinguished several cases upholding denials of section 404 permits for riverside residential developments by noting that the development in the instant case was on upland property and would have been built even if the Corps denied the permit to provide boat access.

In Bersani v. Robichaud, 850 F.2d 36 (2d Cir. 1988), the Second Circuit addressed the question whether the "availability" of alternative property should be assessed at a project's inception or at the time of permit application. EPA had vetoed the issuance of a section 404 permit for a shopping mall because a non-wetland site subsequently purchased by another developer had been available when the permit applicant entered the market and purchased the wetlands property. A panel of the Second Circuit, by a 2-1 vote, upheld EPA's veto and the "market entry" theory on which it was premised. The court noted that the purpose of the practicable alternatives analysis required by the section 404(b)(1) guidelines is "to create an incentive for developers to avoid choosing wetlands when they could choose an alternative upland site." If this analysis were applied at the time of permit application, rather than at the time of site selection, "it would remove the incentive for a developer to search for an alternative site at the time such an incentive is needed, i.e., at the time it is making the decision to select a particular site." 850 F.2d at 44. In dissent, Judge Pratt argued that EPA's "market entry theory in effect taints a particular developer with respect to a particular site, while ignoring the crucial question of whether the site itself should be preserved." He explained that "developer A would be denied a permit on a specific site because when he entered the market alternatives were available, but latecomer developer B, who entered the market after those alternatives had become unavailable, would be entitled to a permit for developing the same site." 850 F.2d at 48 (Pratt, J., dissenting).

The developer who sought the section 404 permit in *Bersani* had rejected an alternative, upland site because of poor road access and strong community resistance to previous development efforts there. A consultant hired by the Corps' regional office had reported that it was feasible to develop either site but that "from a commercial standpoint only one mall could survive in the area." 850 F.2d at 42. The developer whose permit was vetoed subsequently entered into a joint venture with the owner of the other site and built a shopping mall there that opened in September 1989.

NOTES AND QUESTIONS

1. In National Wildlife Federation v. Whistler, why was the project for which a section 404 permit was sought deemed to be "water-dependent"? If the developer had sought to build the housing development in a wetlands area, would the project have been considered water-dependent? Should it make any difference whether the housing development would be built even without water access and, if so, what effect should this have on the permit decision?

2. Measures to mitigate wetlands losses by enhancing degraded areas or creating new wetlands have become an important aspect of the section 404 permit process. The developer seeking boat access for the planned housing development in National Wildlife Federation v. Whistler, 27 F.3d 1341 (8th Cir. 1994), had agreed to a mitigation plan that would enhance an existing 20-acre wetlands area by providing it with year-round water and saturated soil conditions. In upholding issuance of the permit, the Eighth Circuit emphasized the Corps' finding that, due to the mitigation measures, the project would result in little or no net loss of wetlands. Id. at 1346. In *Bersani,* the developer had promised to turn an abandoned gravel pit into new wetlands that would be larger than the wetlands destroyed by the project. While the Corps maintained that this mitigation measure meant that the non-wetlands site no longer was a less damaging alternative, EPA refused to accept this conclusion. In 1990, EPA and the Corps entered into a Memorandum of Agreement on Mitigation requiring that proposed discharges respond to potential wetlands losses in the following sequence: (1) by avoiding them, (2) by minimizing them, and (3) by compensating for unavoidable adverse effects. Mitigation measures have been controversial. Environmentalists maintain that they have made it too easy to get a section 404 permit when practicable alternatives exist and that the destruction of natural wetlands almost always outweighs the gains from artificial enhancement measures that sometimes fail altogether.

3. What impact will *Bersani*'s "market theory" approach to determining availability have on developers' future choices of sites for non-water-dependent activities? How would you respond to Judge Pratt's criticism of the market entry theory? Is he right that another developer who had not previously entered the market subsequently could use the market entry theory to obtain a section 404 permit for developing the identical site? Or would EPA require an applicant to show that no practicable alternative existed both when it could have entered the market and when it applied for the permit?

4. The Corps has been criticized in the past for giving disproportionate weight to the interests of developers when performing alternatives analysis. For example, the Corps frequently found that alternatives that substantially reduce a developer's profit are not practicable (citing the section 404(b)(1) regulations' directive to consider "cost") without considering the magnitude of environmental losses. See Comment, *Bersani* v. EPA: Toward a Plausible Interpretation of the

§404(b)(1) Guidelines for Evaluating Permit Applications for Wetland Development, 15 Colum. J. Envtl. L. 99, 104 (1990). The Corps initially subsumed its section 404(b)(1) review within the "public interest" review the Corps had performed under the old Rivers and Harbors Act, which emphasized nonenvironmental values. 33 C.F.R. §320.4(a)(1). See Houck, Hard Choices: The Analysis of Alternatives Under Section 404 of the Clean Water Act and Similar Environmental Laws, 60 U. Colo. L. Rev. 773, 779 (1989). However, after a lawsuit by environmentalists, National Wildlife Federation v. Marsh, 14 E.L.R. 20262, 20264 (D.D.C. 1984), the Corps agreed that EPA's section 404(b)(1) guidelines take precedence and a permit may not be issued if it would not comply with the guidelines.

5. In April 1989, the Corps of Engineers issued interim guidance described by Professor Houck as "one of the most astonishing about-faces in the history of federal environmental law." Houck, above, at 795. The guidance, issued in the context of an application to develop a waterfront resort in Louisiana called Plantation Landing, acknowledges that section 404 is designed to discourage development in wetlands. It establishes that cost savings alone cannot justify a permit, because development in wetlands usually is less expensive, and that the relative size of adverse impacts also cannot justify a permit, since the Act is designed to avoid cumulative losses.

6. Professor Houck recommends abandoning the alternatives test and restricting permits in wetland areas to water-dependent activities—activities that must be located there, such as a pier. He would allow only two exceptions: the first for the rare circumstance in which a wetland location is less harmful than an upland alternative as provided in section 404(b)(1), the second for discharges demonstrating "fundamentally different factors" that justify a finding that the applicant is in effect water-dependent. See Houck, above, at 829-830.

"No Net Loss," Mitigation Banking, and the Future of Wetlands Protection

The goal of "no net loss" of wetlands, initially proposed in 1988 by the National Wetlands Policy Forum, has been endorsed as national policy by the past three administrations. Even if regulatory programs to prevent wetland losses are strengthened, no net loss can only be achieved if aggressive restoration efforts are pursued. A National Research Council panel recommended in 1991 an ambitious program to restore 10 million acres of wetlands by the year 2010. Noting that mitigation projects have often failed when undertaken by developers, the panel recommended that a National Aquatic Ecosystem Restoration Trust Fund be established to fund restoration efforts by federal and state agencies. The agencies would offer financial incentives to private landowners to restore wetlands in cooperation with volunteer efforts. The panel also recommended that restoration efforts be undertaken for 2 million acres of polluted lakes and 400,000 miles of rivers and streams. Stevens, Panel Urges Big Wetlands Restoration Project, N.Y. Times, Dec. 12, 1991, at B16.

In August 1993, the Clinton administration unveiled its program for protecting wetlands. White House Office of Environmental Policy, Protecting America's Wetlands: A Fair, Flexible and Effective Approach (1993). While endorsing the goal of no net loss of wetlands, the program emphasized measures to increase the flexibility and fairness of the section 404 permit process by including new deadlines for permit decisions and by creating a new administrative appeal process. The Clinton plan rejected the concept of categorizing wetlands based on assessment of their functional value, on the grounds that it would be unworkable, inordinately costly, and could lead to approval of wetland losses for projects that could easily be pursued elsewhere.

The Clinton wetlands program endorsed mitigation banking and emphasized giving state and local governments greater responsibility for wetlands protection. A wetlands mitigation bank is a wetland area that has been restored, created, or enhanced and then set aside to compensate for future losses of wetlands from development activities. Developers needing to mitigate wetlands losses can purchase credits from a mitigation bank rather than restoring or creating wetlands in the vicinity of the development site. Mitigation banking is now being tried in some states. In Florida, sales of credits generated by wetlands restoration totaled $8 million in the first six months of the program, with prices ranging as high as $42,000 an acre. Firms seeking to acquire credits by restoring wetlands were seeking approval for credits covering 125,000 acres. Binkley, Builders Snap Up Wetland Credits, But Concerns Rise Over Regulation, Wall St. J. (Fla. ed.), Aug. 30, 1995, at F1.

Environmentalists criticize mitigation banking by arguing that it "encourages: (1) off site mitigation that cannot replace many wetlands values which are site specific; (2) an excess of certain kinds of wetlands, such as marshes and shrub wetlands, because they are easier and cheaper to create than other wetlands types; and (3) issuance of fill permits based on wetlands creation when avoidance and minimization alternatives exist." Blumm, The Clinton Wetlands Plan 9 J. Land Use & Envtl. L. 203, 227 (1994). Data indicating that only a small percentage of compensatory mitigation projects by developers have succeeded in creating functional wetlands have contributed to environmentalists' skepticism, while leading others to conclude that a bank run by governmental agencies would be a preferable alternative. Malakoff, Restored Wetlands Flunk Real-World Test, 280 Science 371 (1998).

Efforts to transfer greater responsibility for wetlands protection to state and local governments have also been met by skepticism from the environmental community. As Michael Blumm notes, because development benefits tend to be more localized than the benefits wetlands generate, federal regulation almost always will be more effective. Id. at 229. While agreeing that the federal interest in wetlands protection is stronger than variable state interests, Oliver Houck and Michael Rolland argue that with proper funding and clearer goals, states could be enlisted to improve wetlands protections. They note that the few states with delegated section 404 programs "exercise significantly more control over smaller permit applications than the federal system, activities that largely escape federal review and cause a continuing wetlands hemorrhage." Houck & Rolland, Federalism in Wetlands Regulation: A Consideration of Delegation of Clean Water Act Section 404 and Related Programs to the States, 54 Md. L. Rev. 1242 (1995).

In April 2004 President George W. Bush endorsed the goal of going beyond "no net loss" toward a policy goal of annually *increasing* the amount of wetlands acreage in the United States. Environmental groups have been skeptical of this goal, which the administration has indicated could be accomplished through greater use of wetlands restoration programs administered by the U.S. Fish and Wildlife Service and through greater use of conservation incentives in the Farm Bill.

F.   FUTURE DIRECTIONS IN WATER POLLUTION CONTROL: NONPOINT SOURCE CONTROLS, WATERSHED PROTECTION, AND EFFLUENT TRADING

Despite significant progress in controlling pollution from point sources, serious water quality problems remain due in large part to pollution from non-point sources. Nonpoint sources include urban and cropland runoff; animal wastes; discharges from storm sewers, construction sites, and mining and logging operations; and atmospheric deposition. Pollution from these sources causes severe water quality problems, accounting for nearly all the sediment and the vast majority of nitrogen and phosphorus reaching the nation's surface waters. Beginning in 1997, massive fish kills caused by outbreaks of *Pfiesteria piscidia* focused attention on runoff from chicken farms as a source of harmful nutrients. In 1999 Hurricane Floyd swept vast quantities of animal wastes into surface waters, causing serious public health problems in North Carolina.

Wholly apart from these headline-grabbing incidents, EPA and most states have identified nonpoint sources as the primary reason that water quality is insufficient to support designated uses. Runoff of manure from animal feeding operations (AFOs), which produce 130 times more waste than humans generate each year, is responsible for 20 percent of "impaired river miles," about 35,000 miles in 22 states. Blount, Henderson & Cline, The New Nonpoint Source Battleground: Concentrated Animal Feeding Operations, 14 Nat. Res. & Envt. 42 (Summer 1999). It is estimated that 54 percent of all nitrogen emitted by power plants and motor vehicles ends up in watersheds or coastal estuaries.

The importance of nonpoint sources to water pollution problems has been recognized for decades. Yet nonpoint sources have largely escaped federal regulation because of political, administrative, and technical difficulties. Recall that EPA initially deemed it infeasible to regulate pollution generated by runoff even when conveyed through a point source. The agency argued that it could not "instruct each individual farmer on his farming practices." Natural Resources Defense Council v. Costle, 568 F.2d 1369, 1380 (D.C. Cir. 1977). Considerable progress has been made since then in understanding how improved land use management practices can reduce nonpoint source pollution. But progress in controlling nonpoint sources has been slow in part because land use controls face fierce political resistance, as explored in more detail in Chapter 7.

1.   Federal Efforts to Control Nonpoint Source Pollution

When it created the Clean Water Act's NPDES permit program in 1972, Congress confined the program to point sources, though it included any "concentrated animal feeding operation . . . from which pollutants are or may be discharged" within the definition of "point source" in section 502(14). Permits issued to concentrated animal feeding operations (CAFOs), defined as those that contain more than 1,000 "animal units" and whose discharges are not limited to a 25-year, 24-hour storm event, were to have limits based on the permit writer's "best professional judgment" relating to manure management practices. Yet less than 10,000 of the nation's 1.1 million farms were subjected to the NPDES permit program. C.F. Runge, Environmental Protection from Farm to Market, in Thinking Ecologically 61 (M. Chertow & D. Esty eds., 1997).

Aside from treating CAFOs as point sources, the Clean Water Act did not directly regulate sources of runoff. Instead it relied on a largely ineffective planning process established by section 208. This section requires states to develop "areawide waste treatment management plans" that were to include a process for identifying nonpoint sources and establishing feasible control measures. Plans prepared under section 208 were to be submitted to EPA in return for receiving federal financial assistance for the planning process. Decisions concerning NPDES permits and section 404 permits are supposed to be consistent with the section 208 plans. In 1977, Congress added section 208(j), which authorized the Department of Agriculture to share the costs of "best management practices" adopted by farmers to control nonpoint pollution. This program was not widely embraced by farmers.

The section 208 planning process is widely viewed as a failure. While more than 200 plans were prepared under section 208, they accomplished very little for reasons that included lack of incentives to link planning to implementation and "the basic resistance of local governments to federal efforts to dictate planning structures and results, however flexibly those programs are designed." Adler, Addressing Barriers to Watershed Protection, 25 Envtl. L. 973, 1044 (1995). Federal funding for the section 208 program, which had been at less than half of authorized levels, was discontinued in 1981.

When it amended the Clean Water Act in 1987, Congress expressly declared that "it is the national policy that programs for the control of nonpoint sources of pollution be developed and implemented in an expeditious manner" in order to enable the goals of the Act to be met. §101(a)(7). To control urban runoff, Congress mandated that controls on municipal and industrial storm sewers be strengthened by requiring EPA to bring storm-water discharges into the NPDES permit program pursuant to section 402(p). Storm sewer permits are to prohibit non-storm-water discharges into storm sewers and to include "controls to reduce the discharge of pollutants to the maximum extent practicable."

Congress also added section 319 to the Clean Water Act in the 1987 Amendments. Section 319 requires states to prepare "state assessment reports" that identify waters that cannot reasonably be expected to meet water quality standards because of nonpoint pollution. These reports are to identify significant sources of nonpoint pollution for each affected water segment. §319(a)(1). States are to develop "management programs" that include identification and implementation of best management practices to control significant sources of nonpoint pollution. These programs are to contain schedules for implementation of best management practices, certification that sufficient state authority exists to implement the program, and identification of sources of financial support.

States were to submit their assessment reports and management programs to EPA for review and approval. States with approved programs are eligible for federal financial assistance to implement their programs. By 1992, EPA had approved assessment reports for all states and management programs for 44 states. EPA, Managing Nonpoint Pollution: Final Report to Congress on Section 319 (1992).

The 1987 Amendments generated early enthusiasm for the section 319 program by authorizing $400 million for grants to state programs. However, only a small portion of these funds actually were appropriated, and only

$40 million in grants was distributed during the next three years. Noting that 47 States already had some kind of program for addressing nonpoint sources, Oliver Houck predicted that "[a]t best, the new federal funding will encourage more specificity in these plans. More likely, it will produce a second round of paperwork comparable to that generated in the early 1970s by the hauntingly similar section 208 program." Houck, Ending the War: A Strategy to Save America's Coastal Zone, 47 Md. L. Rev. 358, 377 (1988). This prediction may have been accurate as section 319 has not made great strides in controlling pollution from nonpoint sources. Professor Robert Adler notes that EPA "elected not to play hardball" in approving state plans and did not insist that states adopt regulatory programs to control nonpoint sources. Adler, Addressing Barriers to Watershed Protection, 25 Envtl. L. 973, 1045 n.427 (1995).

In 1990 Congress continued to encourage states to adopt nonpoint source control programs when it added section 1455b to the Coastal Zone Management Act. 16 U.S.C. §1455b. This amendment requires states with federally approved coastal zone management programs to develop a Coastal Nonpoint Pollution Control Program subject to review and approval by EPA and NOAA. While the addition of yet another planning requirement to federal law is not in itself of any great significance, section 1455b of the CZMA requires far more specificity in nonpoint source management planning than ever before. States must identify land uses that contribute to degradation of threatened or impaired coastal waters and critical areas adjacent to them and provide for the implementation of additional management measures to achieve water quality standards. "Management measures" are defined in section 1455b(g)(5) as "economically achievable measures for the control of" nonpoint sources "which reflect the greatest degree of pollutant reduction achievable through the application of the best available nonpoint pollution control practices, technologies, processes, siting criteria, operating methods, or other alternatives."

The state programs must conform to guidance EPA and NOAA issued in 1993. Minimum requirements for the guidance are outlined in section 1455b(g)(2), which reflects an effort to require as much specificity as possible in the description of control measures, regulatory targets, pollutants to be controlled, costs, effects of controls, and monitoring. However, once again, Congress failed to put its money where its mouth was. While EPA estimated that the cost of adopting nonpoint source control measures as recommended in the guidance documents would range from $390 to $590 million, only $50 million in grant money was made available to the states through EPA, and less than $2 million was made available from NOAA.

2.   Toward a Watershed Approach to Pollution Control

Because today's most serious water pollution problems tend to be diffuse in origin and involve all the parts of an interconnected ecosystem, federal policy has shifted emphasis toward community- and watershed-based environmental protection and ecosystem management policies. These programs involve efforts to involve all levels of government and nongovernmental organizations in hydrologically defined drainage basins—watersheds—to develop coordinated strategies for addressing pollution problems that transcend political boundaries.

In February 1998 EPA and the USDA jointly announced a "Clean Water Action Plan" that sought to organize efforts to protect water quality around a "watershed approach." Declaring the watershed approach "the key to the future" of water pollution control, the plan proposed a new collaborative effort by federal, state, tribal, and local governments and the private sector to restore and protect watersheds. The plan proposed to involve these groups in preparing unified watershed assessments and restoration action strategies that will be eligible for special federal funding. It notes that a watershed focus would help "strike the best balance among efforts to control point source pollution and polluted runoff," as well as identifying "the most cost-effective pollution control strategies to meet clean water goals." C. Browner & D. Glickman, Clean Water Action Plan: Restoring and Protecting America's Waters iii (1998).

Although watershed management may sound like a new idea, the concept actually has a long history. See Adler, Addressing Barriers to Watershed Protection, 25 Envtl. L. 973, 1003 (1995). Robert Adler notes that after the outright rejection of early basinwide planning proposals, the watershed concept was abducted "to justify mission-oriented water development programs, as reflected in statutes such as the Reclamation Act, the Federal Power Act, and federal navigation and flood control laws." Id. at 1013. While the new generation of environmental statutes are not designed with a watershed approach in mind, several regional efforts have employed this concept, such as the Chesapeake Bay Program, the Great Lakes Program, and the National Estuary Program.

Whereas previous efforts to use federal financial assistance to encourage states to adopt controls on nonpoint source pollution have not been a notable success, the Clean Water Action Plan's watershed approach may facilitate emissions trading between point and nonpoint sources of water pollution. Emissions trading is part of the Bush administration's strategy for reducing the costs of pollution control. EPA developed a policy promoting effluent trading within watersheds. EPA, Effluent Trading in Watersheds Policy Statement, 61 Fed. Reg. 4,994 (1996). The policy endorses effluent trading as an innovative means for developing solutions to water quality problems that will yield economic, environmental, and social benefits. The program is being implemented on a voluntary basis under existing law, which may involve directing permit writers to allow effluent trades as part of the NPDES permit system. For example, POTWs discharging into North Carolina's Tar Pamlico Basin have engaged in point/nonpoint discharge trades through a program that permits them to pay into a state fund supporting implementation of best management practices on farmlands.

Under the administration of President George W. Bush EPA has continued to emphasize a watershed-based approach to controlling pollution and to encourage effluent trading schemes. In January 2003 EPA published its Water Quality Trading Policy, which encourages effluent trading to reduce nutrient and sediment loads. The agency published draft guidance on how watershed-based NPDES permitting can be implemented in August 2003. 68 Fed. Reg. 51,011 (2003). In November 2004 EPA issued detailed guidance on how effluent trading may be used to improve water quality more efficiently. EPA, Water Quality Trading Assessment Handbook (2004).

NOTES AND QUESTIONS

1. Why have the various federal programs that address nonpoint pollution not been more successful in controlling the problem? Is it a product of their largely nonregulatory approach, which seeks to encourage states voluntarily to

adopt control measures? Is the problem primarily one of inadequate state resources to invest in control measures or is it a lack of technical information concerning what control measures actually work?

2. Are nonpoint sources so numerous and diverse that a regulatory program is simply infeasible? While there are hundreds of thousands of farmers, the Soil Conservation Service (SCS) has an army of 13,000 employees who are charged with providing technical advice and support to them. The SCS and others maintain that only a voluntary approach will induce change in agricultural practices because farmers resist any program that smacks of regulation. Note that the FSA's requirements apply to farmers who wish to continue to receive federal subsidies. Could this be a sufficient "carrot" to permit the SCS to implement an aggressive "best management practices" program?

3. The 1987 Amendments to the Clean Water Act were enacted over President Reagan's veto. In the message accompanying his unsuccessful veto, the president decried them as potentially "the ultimate whip hand for Federal regulators." Do you agree? Examine the provisions of section 402(p) for controlling urban nonpoint pollution and the provisions of section 319 for controlling nonpoint pollution generally. To what extent do these impose pollution control requirements enforceable by citizen suit? Past efforts to control nonpoint sources sought to create incentives for state action, without much effect. How do the provisions of section 319 differ from those of section 208?

4. Airborne pollution is another significant source of water pollution in some areas. For example, according to some studies airborne sources may amount to one-fourth or more of pollutants going into the Chesapeake Bay. Tripp & Oppenheimer, Restoration of the Chesapeake Bay: A Multi-State Institutional Challenge, 47 Md. L. Rev. 425 (1988). Is there any existing authority for imposing more stringent requirements on air polluters in order to protect water quality?

5. The Environmental Law Institute has prepared a comprehensive review of state controls on nonpoint sources of water pollution. ELI, Enforceable State Mechanisms for the Control of Nonpoint Source Water Pollution (1997) and Almanac of Enforceable State Laws to Control Nonpoint Source Water Pollution (1998). The reports find that nearly all states have statutory authority to control discharges that can be shown to result in water pollution and that in about half the states this authority is not limited to point sources. While state erosion and sediment control laws could be significant vehicles for controlling nonpoint source pollution, most exempt agricultural activities. The reports review several ways in which states have contrived to make best management practices enforceable or to link them to other enforcement mechanisms. They conclude that there is a diverse array of tools that states can apply to fill in regulatory gaps left by federal programs.

=7=

Land Use Regulation and Regulatory Takings

> Land use is the forgotten agenda of the environmental movement. In the past twenty-five years, the nation's many environmental laws addressed one problem at a time—air or water pollution, endangered species, waste disposal—and they have done it primarily through prohibitive policies that restrict private behavior. Although their achievements have been significant, such policies seem to offer diminishing returns. Environmental progress in the next generation will increasingly depend on stemming the environmental costs of current land use patterns.
>
> —*John Turner and Jason Rylander**

Although federal law rarely regulates private real estate directly, federal policies have had dramatic effects on land use patterns. The nation's energy, transportation, and housing policies have reshaped the development of urban and rural areas, often with disastrous environmental consequences. Yet regulation of land use generally remains the fiercely guarded province of local levels of government.

As the environmental consequences of unplanned growth and urban sprawl become more evident, land use management has become a prominent part of the environmental agenda. Efforts to develop programs to improve land use management are now being made at all levels of government. The catastrophic damage caused by Hurricane Katrina to the Gulf Coast in 2005 has renewed debate over what the proper federal role should be in regulation of land use.

After examining how land use patterns affect the environment, this chapter reviews federal and state programs to control land use. It discusses state growth management initiatives and the political obstacles they face. The chapter traces the history of regulatory takings doctrine and it explores why taking claims now seem to be raised whenever land use is regulated more stringently. It concludes by examining how environmental problems are challenging traditional conceptions of property rights.

---

*Land Use: The Forgotten Agenda, in Thinking Ecologically 61 (M. Chertow & D. Esty eds., 1997).

A.   LAND USE AND THE ENVIRONMENT

The environmental consequences of how humans use land have been a public concern since 1864, when George Perkins Marsh published the first edition of his classic work Man and Nature; or, Physical Geography as Modified by Human Action. Popularized by the second edition of his book, renamed The Earth as Modified by Human Action, Marsh's warnings concerning the environmental effects of development were influential in boosting the late-nineteenth-century campaign to establish national parks. Today nearly one-third of the land area of the United States remains under federal ownership, much of it protected as national parks, national monuments, or wilderness areas. See pages 713-715.

How land is managed has an immense impact on environmental conditions in all media. Land use patterns influence the severity of water and air pollution problems, the health of wetlands and other ecosystems, and the overall quality and aesthetic flavor of human life. Dramatic changes have occurred in land use patterns in the United States, producing enormous environmental consequences. Residential development in rural areas now consumes much prime farmland, complicating watershed management strategies. As growing populations have fled central cities for suburban venues, the depressing consequences of urban sprawl, traffic congestion, and pollution problems have awakened many communities to the need for more intelligent planning and growth management policies. The following excerpt describes how public policies have influenced land use patterns and the environmental consequences of these changes.

> ### Turner & Rylander, Land Use:
> ### The Forgotten Agenda,
> ### in Thinking Ecologically
> ### (M. Chertow & D. Esty eds., 1997)

Our land use patterns affect the environment in many ways. Most notably, development pressures have significant impacts on habitat. Even where forests and wetlands are preserved, new housing and commercial developments pave over open spaces, alter water courses and runoff flows, and rearrange scenic vistas. Our land use choices also impact air quality. For example, vehicle miles traveled by California's sprawling population have increased more than 200 percent in the past two decades as a consequence of distant suburbanization, exacerbating an already well-known smog problem in the region. Mass transit, which is only viable at relatively high population densities, becomes increasingly impractical as people spread out across the land. . . .

Unfortunately, government policies have historically exacerbated trends toward separation and expansion. Land use planning in the United States has traditionally been the task of local officials who have used property zoning regulation and building codes as their principal tools. Zoning, a twentieth-century invention, was originally intended to protect property owners from their neighbors, to ward off economic, social, or environmental damage inflicted by adjacent land use. Although zoning has sometimes served these needs well, local planners have increasingly used zoning regulations to separate arbitrarily residential and commercial uses of land. As a result, the integration of shops and housing, narrow streets, and dense development that attracts admiring visitors to historic urban areas such as Georgetown in Washington, D.C., is prohibited by most local codes. Yet such multi-use urban development patterns offer residents more choices in type of housing, better access and convenience, less segregation by income and class, and a greater sense of community at far less infrastructure cost. As a whole, the United States' land regulatory system is a failure. It is a policy of directed chaos—multiple programs and policies designed to address usually worthwhile goals but implemented in too small an area without regard to the health of the region and oblivious to their unintended consequences. As Aldo Leopold noted, "To build a better motor we tap the uttermost powers of the human brain; to build a better country-side we throw dice." . . .

Transportation and housing policies have been major contributors to America's wasteful land use patterns. Transportation policies, designed almost exclusively for the automobile, greatly exacerbated suburban sprawl. Thousands of miles of trolley lines were abandoned or paved over to accommodate the car. The Interstate Highway Act of 1956 authorized construction of some forty-one thousand miles of new highways leading from cities to the hinterlands, and where the roads went, development followed. Business and suburban development flocked to the off-ramps of the new roads, but such growth came at the expense of cities and open space. The linkage between transportation and land use was rarely made, and national development patterns reflect that disconnect.

Federal housing policies also contributed to the growth of suburbia and the segregation of housing by class and race. In the decade following World War II, nearly half the houses built in the United States were financed with Federal Housing Administration (FHA) and Veterans Administration assistance. These programs boosted a construction industry floundering after the Great Depression and improved the U.S. stock of housing. But FHA-backed mortgages were only available for new homes—primarily single-family, detached houses on inexpensive suburban land. The agency did not support loans to repair, remodel, and upgrade older houses in the cities that might have provided affordable housing for growing minority and immigrant populations. Cities reaped few of the benefits of the postwar development boom. . . .

We are beginning to understand what we have lost. Despite tremendous technological advances, we have produced housing developments that demean rather than inspire our citizenry. We have built mile after mile of ugliness— cookie-cutter houses, subdivisions devoid of character, congested streets, commercial strips that assault the eye with garish signs and neon lights—all at the expense of townscapes, city cores, open space, productive farmland, and wildlife habitat. The costs of sprawl are not only aesthetic. The decline of cities and segregation of communities that result from land use decisions impose tremendous burdens on society. Local governments are increasingly aware that scattered large-lot zoning does little to protect habitat and often does not generate enough tax revenue to pay for municipal services. And the environmental costs of poor land use practices are rarely factored into local decisions. . . .

Although many people recoil from the thought of a federal land use policy, the reality is that the United States does have such a policy, albeit one that exists not by design but by default, arising from an uncoordinated collection of overlapping and often conflicting mandates and programs. Transportation policies, farm programs, disaster relief, water and sewer support, wetlands and endangered species laws, public housing and financial lending programs combine to create a de facto national land use plan.

NOTES AND QUESTIONS

1. To what extent are the problems identified by Turner and Rylander the unintended consequences of policies adopted to pursue other laudable goals? Are they caused by inadequate planning or deliberate decisions to tolerate certain forms of environmental and aesthetic degradation in return for other benefits?

2. Because authority over land use decisions generally is concentrated in local levels of government, development decisions in one jurisdiction have a great potential to generate externalities that affect conditions in other jurisdictions. To what extent can this problem be solved by creating regional entities and making them responsible for coordinating land use planning?

3. A study released by the Brookings Institution in July 2001 reports that land development in the United States is significantly outstripping population growth. Approximately 25 million acres of agricultural lands and open space have been developed between 1982 and 1997 due to the expansion of metropolitan areas, according to the report entitled "Who Sprawls Most? How Growth Patterns Differ Across the United States." All but 17 of the nation's 281 metropolitan areas are experiencing declines in population density, with the western states the only part of the United States bucking this trend. Atlanta has suffered some of the worst sprawl, growing 81.5 percent in area during the 15 years, while the city's population grew by 60.8 percent. The Pittsburgh metropolitan area's developed surface area grew by 42.6 percent even though its population declined by 8 percent. Toledo increased in area by 30 percent while its population grew by only 0.3 percent. Peter Grant, Sprawl Thins Populations of Older Suburbs, Wall St. J., July 9, 2001.

4. In late August 2005 Hurricane Katrina ripped through the Gulf Coast, submerging vast areas of New Orleans, killing more than 1,800 people, and causing more than $75 billion in property damage, making it the costliest hurricane in U.S. history. As debate rages over how to rebuild the area and to prepare for future hurricanes, it is widely acknowledged that destruction of coastal wetlands and poor land use management policies contributed greatly to the scope of the disaster. This has given greater impetus to those who argue that the federal government should play a greater role in land use planning, as former Interior Secretary Bruce Babbitt has argued in his book, Cities in the Wilderness. Babbitt, Cities in the Wilderness (2005). See Neal Peirce, Katrina's Harsh Land-Use Lesson, Seattle Times, Oct. 24, 2005. Considerable information concerning the legal and policy implications of Hurricane Katrina can be found at the website "Disasters and the Law: Katrina and Beyond," maintained by the University of California-Berkeley Law Library at *http://128.32.29.133/disasters.php*.

B.   FEDERAL REGULATION OF LAND USE

The federal government plays an important role in land use management in two areas. First, federal agencies are responsible for managing lands owned by the federal government, which comprise one-third of the land area of the United States. Under the Property Clause of Article IV, Section 3 of the Constitution, Congress has broad authority to control the management and disposition of federal property. The laws governing federal management of public lands and the resources they contain cover an immense field that is worthy of separate study. They are briefly introduced below in subsection B1. While the federal government generally does not directly regulate lands held by private parties, federal policies have a profound effect on the management and use of private lands. These policies are outlined in subsection B2.

1. Federal Management of Public Lands

The role the federal government should play in managing public lands is a subject of continuing controversy. For the first century of the republic the dominant federal role was to transfer public lands to private parties to encourage settlement and development. The focus of public land management has now shifted. Most laws encouraging disposal of public lands have been repealed—one can no longer "homestead" on the public domain. The result is that one-third of the nation's land is now held permanently in federal ownership. Some of these public lands are protected for their natural, cultural, or scenic values—as parks, wilderness areas, or wildlife refuges. Most are entrusted to the stewardship of the Bureau of Land Management (BLM) and the Forest Service under broad mandates to manage for "multiple uses" that "will best meet the needs of the American public." Multiple Use, Sustained Yield Act, 16 U.S.C. §531(a). See the Federal Land Policy and Management Act of 1976 (FLPMA), 43 U.S.C. §§1701 et seq.; and the National Forest Management Act of 1976, 16 U.S.C. §§1600 et seq. See generally Wilkinson and Anderson, Land and Resource Planning in the National Forests, 64 Or. L. Rev. 1 (1985). That mandate has been a recipe for controversy. See Huffman, Public Lands Management in an Age of Deregulation and Privatization, 10 Pub. Land L. Rev. 29 (1989). The laws governing management of public lands are outlined in the following Pathfinder.

PUBLIC LAND AND NATURAL
RESOURCES LAW: A PATHFINDER

Public Land Management Systems. Public lands are managed in four systems: general public lands, managed by the Bureau of Land Management (BLM); National Forests, managed by the U.S. Forest Service; National Wildlife Refuges, managed by the U.S. Fish and Wildlife Service; and National Parks, managed by the National Park Service. Wilderness areas, governed by the Wilderness Act of 1964, may be designated on lands in any of the four systems.

Multiple Use. Congress has mandated that most public lands, including the 340 million acres managed by BLM and the 191 million acres in the National Forests (except for wilderness areas), be managed for "multiple use" as defined in the Federal Land Policy and Management Act (FLPMA) for BLM lands and the National Forest Management Act (NFMA) for the National Forests. Despite elaborate planning and public participation requirements, "multiple-use" management has been vulnerable to local politics, with land managers often emphasizing economic uses—grazing, logging, and mineral development—over wildlife and wilderness values. Congress also has often undercut the FLPMA and NFMA by, for example, forbidding BLM from raising grazing fees or by specifying the "annual cut" that must be allowed in the National Forests.

Dominant Use. For one class of lands—the National Wildlife Refuges—Congress has placed a thumb on the balance, establishing as a dominant use the conservation of wildlife. Other uses, such as grazing or motorboating, are allowed on a refuge only if "compatible" with the purposes for which the refuge was established. The National Wildlife Refuge System now includes 492 units totaling 88 million acres. Sixteen of these refuges, accounting for 77 million acres, are in Alaska and were created or expanded in the Alaska National Interest Lands Conservation Act of 1980.

Preservation. Two classes of federal lands enjoy almost absolute protection—the National Parks and the National Wilderness Areas. Congress in 1916 created the National Park Service and charged it with management of what today are 350 natural, historic, and recreational preserves covering 80 million acres. "The Park Service's mission is to conserve the scenery and the natural and historic objects and wildlife therein and to provide for the enjoyment of the same in such manner and by such means as will leave them unimpaired for the enjoyment of future generations." 16 U.S.C. §1. Wilderness Areas must be managed under the Wilderness Act to preserve their "primeval character and influence" and "natural condition" with motorized equipment, permanent roads, and commercial activity generally prohibited. 16 U.S.C. §1131(c).

Public Resources. The Mining Law of 1872 guarantees citizens a right to discover, develop, and patent hardrock mineral deposits on any public lands, unless the lands have been expressly withdrawn from mineral entry. Other minerals are subject to lease by the government, principally under the Mineral Leasing Act of 1920 and, offshore, under the Outer Continental Shelf Lands Act of 1953. Congress has also acted to protect important wildlife resources through measures such as the Migratory Bird Treaty Act, the Marine Mammal Protection Act, and other laws.

Fierce conflicts over management of public resources are nothing new. In the early twentieth century a proposal to dam the Hetch Hetchy Valley, a wilderness preserve near Yosemite National Park, to provide water and power for the city of San Francisco, spawned a bitter national battle that raged for more than six years, leaving John Muir and President Theodore Roosevelt, who once had camped together in Yosemite, on opposite sides of the dispute. This episode is described in Roderick Nash, Wilderness and the American Mind 161 (1982). More contemporary versions of these battles include the debate over oil drilling in the Arctic National Wildlife Refuge, described in Chapter 1, and controversies over protection of the spotted owl and endangered salmon species in the Pacific Northwest.

What has changed about today's controversies is the emergence of concern for ecosystem management and protection of biodiversity. As the inadequacies of an eleventh hour, species-by-species approach to conservation have become more apparent, efforts to reorient public policy toward more forward-looking and comprehensive approaches have gained momentum. These efforts have spawned new initiatives for managing public resources to promote environmental values and to preserve biodiversity.

Environmentalists argue that federal resource management policies have caused substantial environmental damage while subsidizing private mining, timber, and grazing interests. A particularly egregious example is the Mining Act of 1872, which gives private parties the right to develop and extract hardrock mineral deposits from public lands without payment of royalties. Twenty-acre tracts of public land on which such minerals are found may be acquired by private interests for $5, even if the land is worth millions. More than 3 million acres of public land have been patented in this manner, including land later converted to ski resorts, condominiums, and golf courses.

While the Clinton administration vowed to reform federal resource management policies by charging royalties for mineral extraction and raising fees for grazing on public lands, these efforts were fiercely resisted. Both houses of Congress passed different versions of mining reform legislation in 1993, but a conference committee was unable to agree on an acceptable compromise. A moratorium on the patenting of claims under the Mining Act of 1872 was imposed, effective September 30, 1994. Support for the moratorium was fueled by the revelation that a Canadian company had used the Act to purchase 1,949 acres of federal land that may contain $10 billion worth of gold for the princely sum of $8,965. Kenworthy, Solid-Gold U.S. Bargain for Canadian Mining Firm, Int'l Herald Trib., Apr. 18, 1994, at 3. In February 1995, the Bureau of Land Management (BLM) adopted new regulations governing grazing on public lands. 60 Fed. Reg. 9894 (1995). These regulations, which allow the BLM to alter authorized uses of rangeland to adjust to environmental conditions when permits are renewed, were upheld in Public Lands Council v. Babbitt, 145 F.3d 154 (10th Cir. 1998).

Federal timber policies have been the focus of similar criticism. Some economists estimate that the government loses up to $200 million per year on timber sales from the national forests. McNeil, How Most of the Public Forests Are Sold to Loggers at a Loss, N.Y. Times, Nov. 3, 1991, at D2. They maintain that most Forest Service land is in areas unsuited for timber harvesting but that "publicly owned trees are cut because the Forest Service sells them so cheaply that loggers would be foolish to say no." The government "builds roads, pays rangers, absorbs the risks of fires and insects, then sells at a loss." Id. The Forest Service argues that its timber sales are profitable, though its calculations have been criticized for ignoring significant categories of costs while amortizing logging roads over unrealistically long periods (e.g., 1,800 years for a road in the Chugach National Forest in Alaska, "as if the current Italian Government was still paying for the Appian Way"). Id.

Economists recommend that federal subsidies be replaced with a policy of charging market prices for minerals, timber, and grazing rights on public lands. Others argue that governments can never manage resources effectively and that the only way to ensure protection of the commons is to privatize public land. Communities dependent on public resources argue that federal subsidies are necessary to preserve jobs, as illustrated by the controversy over protection of the northern spotted owl and the old-growth forests of the Pacific Northwest.

2. Federal Programs Affecting Private Land Use

Regulation of lands owned by private parties has traditionally been a function of local government. However, in the early 1970s, Congress came close to enacting a national land use regulation program. Legislation proposed by President Nixon that would have required all states to establish land use control programs as a condition for receiving federal funds for highway, airport, and recreation projects passed the Senate. However, it failed to win enactment in the House due to strong opposition from local interests who opposed federal involvement in land use decisions. The resistance to federal involvement in land use issues was illustrated by the political backlash against EPA's efforts to mandate land use controls in federal implementation plans to combat air pollution. Responding to this fallout, Congress expressly prohibited EPA from imposing land use controls (such as parking surcharges, reductions in the number of parking spaces, and controls on the location of facilities that attract motor vehicles) when it amended the Clean Air Act in 1977.

Despite political resistance to a federal regulatory role, federal policies have an enormous influence over the nation's land use patterns. Federal programs with overlapping and often conflicting mandates, including programs for farm aid, highway construction, disaster relief, environmental protection, and public housing, help shape patterns of development and their attendant environmental consequences. As discussed in Chapter 8, the National Environmental Policy Act requires that environmental effects be considered before any major federal action likely to have significant environmental effects is taken. This legislation provides a vehicle for incorporating environmental concerns into the decision-making processes of federal agencies.

Few federal laws directly regulate land use. As discussed in Chapter 6, section 404 of the Clean Water Act has evolved into a major program for protecting wetlands, but its jurisdictional trigger requires the discharge of dredged or fill material into navigable waters. As a result of the Supreme Court's *SWANCC* decision, page 604, the jurisdictional reach of section 404 has been narrowed and there is some uncertainty over its precise boundaries.

One federal statute that directly regulates land use is the Surface Mining Control and Reclamation Act (SMCRA), 30 U.S.C. §§1201-1328. Enacted by Congress in 1977, this Act prohibits strip mining in areas where it is deemed to be too damaging to the environment. The Act is administered by the Office of Surface Mining in the Department of the Interior. It was upheld by the U.S. Supreme Court in Hodel v. Virginia Surface Mining & Reclamation Association, Inc., 452 U.S. 264 (1981), despite arguments that it violated states' Tenth Amendment rights by interfering with their traditional police power to regulate land use. The Act creates a fund financed by per-tonnage fees on coal producers, which funds efforts by states and tribes to reclaim abandoned mine land through federally approved reclamation projects.

Other federal environmental statutes influence land use patterns without directly regulating them. As discussed in Chapter 4, CERCLA's liability scheme for recovering the costs of remediating releases of hazardous substances has complicated efforts to redevelop contaminated industrial properties. This has spurred EPA to develop a program for encouraging development of "brownfields" by providing potential developers with assurances concerning future liability. As discussed in Chapter 6, the Clean Water Act has provided federal funds to states to encourage land use planning to prevent nonpoint source pollution.

The Coastal Zone Management Act encourages states to adopt plans to preserve coastal areas, and it directs federal agencies to respect these plans by ensuring that they act in a manner consistent with them. The Coastal Barrier Resources Act denies federal financial aid for developments in sensitive coastal areas.

The federal Endangered Species Act (ESA) is affecting development decisions in certain parts of the country due to its prohibition on "taking" any member of a species on the endangered species list. As discussed in Chapter 9, this prohibition encompasses habitat modifications that may harm endangered species unless an incidental take permit has been issued pursuant to an approved habitat conservation plan. The development of habitat conservation plans has helped spawn considerable land use planning in areas where endangered species are found.

For example, in southern California, an unusual partnership of five counties, 59 local governments, federal and state officials, and private landowners is involved in the Natural Community Conservation Planning Program (NCCP) to preserve southern coastal sage scrub habitat, which is home for the California gnatcatcher and nearly 100 other potentially threatened or endangered species. The program has created a 37,000-acre nature reserve through a series of phased land dedications while creating clear ground rules to channel future development to areas that are less sensitive environmentally. The goal of the program is to enhance the long-term stability of multi-species wildlife and plant communities while accommodating development in rapidly growing urban areas. See *www.dfg.ca.gov/nccp/*.

The U.S. Fish and Wildlife Service (FWS) has established a "Partners for Wildlife" program to encourage private landowners to preserve potential habitat for endangered species. In the past, the Endangered Species Act created perverse incentives for landowners to destroy such habitat for fear that the discovery of an endangered species could restrict future development prospects. FWS's program provides assurance to landowners that further development restrictions will not be imposed on their property if they preserve potential wildlife habitat.

The federal environmental laws also influence transportation and construction projects that have a major effect on future land use and development patterns. Section 176(c) of the Clean Air Act requires that local transportation planning conform to state implementation plans (SIPs) for meeting the national ambient air quality standards (NAAQSs). In the 1990 Clean Air Act Amendments, Congress substantially strengthened these conformity requirements by specifying in more detail what was required to satisfy them and by integrating Clean Air Act standards with the transportation planning process prescribed by the Urban Mass Transportation Act. The latter requires each urban area with more than 50,000 people to create a metropolitan planning organization (MPO) to develop regional transportation plans. The Clean Air Act's section 176(c) prohibits federal agencies from approving or funding any transportation plan, program, or project that has not been found to conform with the applicable SIP for meeting national air quality standards. These provisions have been taken seriously by the courts. In Environmental Defense Fund v. EPA, 167 F.3d 641 (D.C. Cir. 1999), the D.C. Circuit invalidated EPA's conformity regulations because they would have permitted federal funding of projects that had not been demonstrated to conform to currently approved SIPs. While Congress has disavowed the notion that the Clean Air Act infringes on "the existing authority of counties and cities to plan or control land use," CAA section 131, a dissenting judge described the conformity amendments of the Clean Air Act as "a congressional effort to micromanage local transportation planning," 167 F.3d at 652 (Williams, J., dissenting). For a discussion of efforts to integrate transportation and land use planning with environmental concerns, see Kenne, Transportation Conformity and Land-Use Planning: Understanding the Inconsistencies, 30 U. Rich. L. Rev. 1135 (1996).

In an effort to make federal highway programs more responsive to environmental concerns, Congress enacted the Intermodal Surface Transportation Efficiency Act (ISTEA), 49 U.S.C. §5501, in 1991. ISTEA requires transportation planners to give greater consideration to environmental concerns and to consider alternatives to highway construction, including mass transit projects. The law directs states to spend $1 billion of their annual $20 billion in federal highway funds on air pollution control projects, and it creates a $400 million environmental enhancement fund to be used for acquiring scenic easements, building bike paths, or for historic preservation. Reauthorized in 1998 as the Transportation Equity Act for the 21st Century (TEA-21), the legislation gives increased authority to regional planning bodies to determine how federal transportation funds are spent, and it increases states' flexibility to use highway funds for alternative projects to reduce traffic congestion. TEA-21's Congestion Mitigation and Air Quality program authorizes the Department of Transportation to spend $1.4 billion annually on alternative transit projects to improve air quality. The law also extends a federal tax break to employers who subsidize their employees' use of mass transit, a benefit previously available only to those who subsidized employee parking.

Many other federal programs affect private land use decisions. Federal disaster relief programs have been criticized for promoting excessive development in floodplain areas, which have been estimated to constitute nearly 180 million acres, or more than 7 percent of the land area of the United States. The Great Flood of 1993 in the upper Mississippi and Missouri River basins revived concerns that the establishment of an extensive system of levees and dikes along these rivers had exacerbated flooding by reducing natural floodplain areas. Efforts to protect some communities from flooding actually have worsened localized damage to others, although a report by the Interagency Floodplain Management Review Committee in 1994 found that federal flood control programs have worked overall by substantially reducing damages from flooding.

In the aftermath of the 1993 floods, the federal government provided funds to relocate or elevate more than 12,000 flood-damaged properties and incentives to restore as wetlands some lands that were enrolled in the Emergency Wetlands Reserve Program. Congress revised the National Flood Insurance Program in 1994 to make people who choose to live in floodplains bear a greater share of the risk. Congress prohibited post-disaster federal support to those who could purchase flood insurance but who fail to do so, and it incorporated protection of the natural functions of floodplains into the program's rating system, reducing insurance premiums in communities with good floodplain management programs.

Federal farm programs also have become more sensitive to the environmental consequences of land use management. The Food Security Act of 1985 (FSA), 16 U.S.C. §§3811-3813, required farmers on highly erodible lands to adopt conservation plans employing "best management practices" to control runoff and to implement those plans by 1995 on penalty of loss of federal farm subsidies. Because of the importance of such subsidies, this provision has been described as "so severe as to make the plans tantamount to a regulatory requirement." Rosenthal, Going with the Flow: USDA's Dubious Commitment to Water Quality, 5 Envtl. Forum 15, 16 (Sept.-Oct. 1988). The FSA also denied federal farm subsidies to those who plant on wetlands converted to cropland after December 23, 1985.

Another provision of the 1985 farm bill created a Conservation Reserve Program that provides subsidies to farmers who remove land from agricultural production to restore it to a natural state. Approximately 36 million acres of habitat were enrolled in this program during its first decade at a cost of $1.6 billion per year. Stevens, U.S. Effort to Return Farm Land to Natural State Wins Praise, N.Y. Times, Jan. 10, 1995, at C4. Wildlife experts believe that the program helped reverse a sharp decline in duck populations in North America. The Soil Conservation Service reported that these and other programs helped slow soil erosion, which has declined from 3.1 billion tons of soil per year in 1982 to 2.1 billion tons in 1992. Associated Press, Farm-Related Erosion Slows in Last Decade, Aug. 13, 1994, at E17. The most comprehensive assessment yet undertaken of the environmental and economic costs of soil erosion estimated that it costs nearly $44 billion per year in direct damage to farmland and indirect damage to waterways, public health, and infrastructure. Pimentel et al., Environmental and Economic Costs of Soil Erosion and Conservation Benefits, 267 Science 1117 (1995).

Recognizing the importance of land use, transportation, and development decisions to environmental quality, the Clinton administration announced an interagency "smart growth" initiative in 1998. Called "Building Livable Communities for the 21st Century," the administration's plan sought to provide financial assistance to state and local governments to support efforts to preserve green space, ease traffic congestion, and pursue regional "smart growth" strategies. Among the elements included in the program were proposals for $9.5 billion in bond authority (Better America Bonds) to be used by communities for environmental projects, an increase in funding for public transit, and funds to promote local partnerships to design regional "smart growth" strategies. For a review of federal programs that help promote smart growth and improve land use management decisions see Ward, Brown & Lieb, National Incentives for Smart Growth Communities, 13 Nat. Resources & Envt. 325 (Summer 1998).

NOTES AND QUESTIONS

1. When lobbying on behalf of the Nixon administration's proposal for national land use legislation, Russell Train, who then was the chairman of the Council on Environmental Quality, testified that land use is "the single most important element affecting the quality of our environment which remains substantially unaddressed as a matter of national policy." Diamond, Land Use: Environmental Orphan, Envtl. Forum, Jan./Feb. 1993, at 31, 32. Is Train's assessment still accurate today? In his memoirs Train observes that Nixon's proposed National Land Use Policy Act "was an idea that was probably ahead of its time, and in retrospect it is surprising that the legislation got as far as it did, including passage in the Senate twice." Train, Politics, Pollution and Pandas: An Environmental Memoir 109 (2003). He credits White House aide John Ehrlichman as a major champion of the legislation and concludes that his departure from the White House as a result of the Watergate scandal doomed its

prospects for enactment. Train argues that the concept behind the legislation "badly needs revisiting" because local land use decisions have significant consequences for the environment and local governments lack both the broader perspective and financial resources necessary to deal with development pressures. Id.

2. Should Congress enact national land use legislation? What advantages and disadvantages would a federal regulatory program have? See Do We Need a Federal Land Act?, Envtl. Forum, Jan./Feb. 1993 at 28. In light of the welter of different federal laws and programs that influence land use decisions, it has been argued that "rationalization of current federal land-use controls may result in less regulation rather than more." Diamond, Land Use: Environmental Orphan, Envtl. Forum, Jan./Feb. 1993, at 31, 32. Do you agree?

3. Private initiatives to preserve land for environmental purposes have assumed greater importance in recent years. The Nature Conservancy, a private organization with more than 1 million members, purchases land for nature preservation throughout the world. The group manages 1,400 private nature reserves, including 14.5 million acres of habitat in the United States and 83.5 million acres in other countries. See *http://nature.org*.

4. Federal policy has sought to encourage the use of private land trusts and conservation easements to preserve open space and farmland. Pursuant to the 1996 Farm Bill, matching grants of $18 million were made in 1998 to assist state and local agricultural conservation easement programs. Rodegerdts, Land Trusts and Agricultural Conservation Easements, 13 Nat. Resources & Envt. 336, 337 (1998). The Taxpayer Relief Act of 1997 creates a 40 percent federal estate tax exemption for land near metropolitan areas covered by easements that preclude commercial or residential development.

5. Experience with implementation of the Food Security Act of 1985 illustrates how difficult it can be to effect change in mission-oriented agencies. The U.S. Department of Agriculture and the Soil Conservation Service (SCS) failed to implement aggressively the environmental measures in the FSA because to a large extent their traditional missions have been at odds with environmental goals. The General Accounting Office noted in a 1990 report that "[t]he conflict is especially true for USDA because some of its most significant programs and activities involve—and even promote—activities that can lead to increased nonpoint source pollution," including farm commodity price supports and timber harvesting programs. GAO, Greater EPA Leadership Needed to Reduce Nonpoint Source Pollution 15 (1990). What could be done to make these agencies more sympathetic to environmental concerns?

LAND USE REGULATION: A PATHFINDER

Land use regulation in the United States traditionally has been the province of local governments using *zoning ordinances and building codes* as their principal regulatory tools. Several states have enacted comprehensive *growth management* or *critical area protection legislation* in recent years. States with some form of statewide growth management legislation include Florida, Georgia, Maine, Maryland, New Jersey, Oregon, Rhode Island, Vermont, and Washington.

A broad array of *federal laws* affect land use patterns, including federal transportation policies, farm programs, flood insurance, disaster relief, lending, and public housing programs. Some federal laws directly encourage state and local land use planning. The *Coastal Zone Management Act (CZMA)* provides federal financial assistance to states who develop approved plans for managing coastal areas and it requires federal agencies to act in a manner consistent with the plans. The *Intermodal Surface Transportation Efficiency Act (ISTEA)* requires state and local governments to use metropolitan planning organizations to develop comprehensive transportation plans and it requires that transportation projects receiving federal funds conform to these plans. The *National Environmental Policy Act (NEPA)* requires federal agencies to prepare environmental impact statements (EISs) before undertaking actions likely to have significant environmental effects.

A few federal statutes directly regulate activities involving land use. The *Surface Mining Control and Reclamation Act (SMCRA)* requires owners of surface mining operations to restore land after mining operations and it creates a fund to assist states and tribes to reclaim abandoned mine land through federally approved reclamation projects. The *Endangered Species Act (ESA)* requires developers to have approved habitat conservation plans before they can undertake actions that may result in an incidental "take" of protected species. The *Clean Water Act*, which requires developers to have a permit before they discharge dredge or fill materials in the waters of the United States, restricts development in wetlands areas.

Reports on land use policy include the report of the Task Force on Land Use and Urban Growth, *The Use of Land: A Citizen's Policy Guide to Urban Growth*, published in 1973, and the report of the Sustainable Use of Land Project, *Land Use in America*, published in 1996.

A broad coalition of groups, called the *Smart Growth Network*, maintains a website providing information on smart growth initiatives at *www.smartgrowth.org*. Information about developments in land use regulation may be obtained from *Community Rights Counsel* at *www.communityrights.org/*. Information concerning the property rights movement can be obtained from *Defenders of Property Rights* at *http://www.yourpropertyrights.org*.

C.   LAND USE REGULATION BY STATE AND LOCAL GOVERNMENTS

Land use regulation has evolved from the initial municipal zoning ordinances, first adopted by American cities early in the twentieth century, to ambitious statewide programs that seek to manage growth to conform to long-range development plans. While zoning was designed to segregate incompatible land uses, a host of new growth management tools now seek to create economic incentives to improve land use management. These include clustered development or open space zoning, urban growth boundaries, conservation easements, land trusts, tax incentives, transferable development rights (TDRs), and state "smart growth" policies.

As voters become increasingly aware of the environmental and social costs of sprawl, land use regulation has become increasingly popular at the polls. In the November 1998 elections, voters approved more than $7.5 billion in new state and local initiatives to promote land conservation, forest protection, and growth management programs. P. Myers, Livability at the Ballot Box: State and Local Referenda on Parks, Conservation, and Smarter Growth, Election Day 1998 (1999). In their "state of the state" addresses that year, 32 governors identified "smart growth," open space preservation, or urban revitalization as important policy goals. President's Council on Sustainable Development, Towards a Sustainable America 61 (1999). Concern over urban sprawl appears to be a worldwide phenomenon as cities throughout the developed world are now undertaking initiatives to encourage urban revitalization. P. Newman & J. Kenworthy, Sustainability and Cities: Overcoming Automobile Dependence (1999). Given the high stakes involved in land use decisions, it is not surprising that virtually every one of the tools now used by government to regulate land use has been the subject of legal and political challenges. The materials that follow review state authority to regulate land use, some of the practical and political problems faced by state growth management initiatives, and the question whether land use regulation constitutes a taking of private property for public use for which just compensation must be paid by government.

1. Zoning and State Authority to Regulate Land Use

The first comprehensive municipal zoning ordinance was adopted by New York City in 1916. Six years later an Ohio municipality, the Village of Euclid, adopted a comprehensive zoning plan. A real estate company that owned 68 acres of vacant land that had been zoned residential challenged the constitutionality of the zoning ordinance. The company alleged that it had held the land for years in anticipation of selling and developing it for industrial uses for which it would have a market value of $10,000 per acre, but that the residential zoning would reduce the property's market value to less than $2,500 per acre. In the case that follows, the U.S. Supreme Court made a landmark ruling rejecting due process and equal protection challenges to the constitutionality of zoning.

|| *Village of Euclid v. Ambler Realty Co.* ||
272 U.S. 365 (1926)

Mr. Justice Sutherland delivered the opinion of the Court.

Building zone laws are of modern origin. They began in this country about twenty-five years ago. Until recent years, urban life was comparatively simple; but with the great increase and concentration of population, problems have developed, and constantly are developing, which require, and will continue to require, additional restrictions in respect of the use and occupation of private lands in urban communities. Regulations, the wisdom, necessity, and validity of which, as applied to existing conditions, are so apparent that they are now uniformly sustained, a century ago, or even half a century ago, probably would have been rejected as arbitrary and oppressive. Such regulations are sustained, under the complex conditions of our day, for reasons analogous to those which justify traffic regulations, which, before the advent of automobiles and rapid transit street railways, would have been condemned as fatally arbitrary and unreasonable. And in this there is no inconsistency, for while the meaning of constitutional guarantees never varies, the scope of their application must expand or contract to meet the new and different conditions which are constantly coming within the field of their operation. In a changing world, it is impossible that it should be otherwise. But although a degree of elasticity is thus imparted, not to the *meaning*, but to the *application* of constitutional principles, statutes and ordinances, which, after giving due weight to the new conditions, are found clearly not to conform to the Constitution, of course, must fall.

The ordinance now under review, and all similar laws and regulations, must find their justification in some aspect of the police power, asserted for the public welfare. The line which in this field separates the legitimate from the illegitimate assumption of power is not capable of precise delimitation. It varies with circumstances and conditions. A regulatory zoning ordinance, which would be clearly valid as applied to the great cities, might be clearly invalid as applied to rural communities. In solving doubts, the maxim *sic utere tuo ut alienum non laedas*, which lies at the foundation of so much of the common law of nuisances, ordinarily will furnish a fairly helpful clue. And the law of nuisances, likewise, may be consulted, not for the purpose of controlling, but for the helpful aid of its analogies in the process of ascertaining the scope of, the power. Thus the question whether the power exists to forbid the erection of a building of a particular kind or for a particular use, like the question whether a particular thing is a nuisance, is to be determined, not by an abstract consideration of the building or of the thing considered apart, but by considering it in connection with the circumstances and the locality. Sturgis v. Bridgeman, L.R. 11 Ch. 852, 865. A nuisance may be merely a right thing in the wrong place—like a pig in the parlor instead of the barnyard. If the validity of the legislative classification for zoning purposes be fairly debatable, the legislative judgment must be allowed to control.

There is no serious difference of opinion in respect of the validity of laws and regulations fixing the heights of buildings within reasonable limits, the character of materials and methods of construction, and the adjoining area which must be left open, in order to minimize the danger of fire or collapse, the evils of over-crowding, and the like, and excluding from residential sections offensive trades, industries and structures likely to create nuisances. . . .

We find no difficulty in sustaining restriction of the kind thus far reviewed. The serious question in the case arises over the provisions of the ordinance excluding from residential districts, apartment houses, business houses, retail stores and shops, and other like establishments. This question involves the validity of what is really the crux of the more recent zoning legislation, namely, the creation and maintenance of residential districts, from which business and trade of every sort, including hotels and apartment houses, are excluded. Upon that question, this Court has not thus far spoken. . . .

The matter of zoning has received much attention at the hands of commissions and experts, and the results of their investigations have been set forth in comprehensive reports. These reports, which bear every evidence of painstaking consideration, concur in the view that the segregation of residential, business, and industrial buildings will make it easier to provide fire apparatus suitable for the character and intensity of the development in each section; that it will increase the safety and security of home life; greatly tend to prevent street accidents, especially to children, by reducing the traffic and resulting confusion in residential sections; decrease noise and other conditions which produce or intensify nervous disorders; preserve a more favorable environment in which to rear children, etc. With particular reference to apartment houses, it is pointed out that the development of detached house sections is greatly retarded by the coming of apartment houses, which has sometimes resulted in destroying the entire section for private house purposes; that in such sections very often the apartment house is a mere parasite, constructed in order to take advantage of the open spaces and attractive surroundings created by the residential character of the district. Moreover, the coming of one apartment house is followed by others, interfering by their height and bulk with the free circulation of air and monopolizing the rays of the sun which otherwise would fall upon the smaller homes, and bringing, as their necessary accompaniments, the disturbing noises incident to increased traffic and business, and the occupation, by means of moving and parked automobiles, of larger portions of the streets, thus detracting from their safety and depriving children of the privilege of quiet and open spaces for play, enjoyed by those in more favored localities—until, finally, the residential character of the neighborhood and its desirability as a place of detached residences are utterly destroyed. Under these circumstances, apartment houses, which in a different environment would be not only entirely unobjectionable but highly desirable, come very near to being nuisances.

If these reasons, thus summarized, do not demonstrate the wisdom or sound policy in all respects of those restrictions which we have indicated are pertinent to the inquiry, at least, the reasons are sufficiently cogent to preclude us from saying as it must be said before the ordinance can be declared unconstitutional, that such provisions are clearly arbitrary and unreasonable, having no substantial relation to the public health, safety, morals, or general welfare.

NOTES AND QUESTIONS

1. Under the Court's approach, what must be demonstrated in order for a zoning ordinance to be held to have exceeded the state's police power authority? Who has the burden of proof: the party seeking to challenge the validity of a zoning ordinance or the municipality adopting it?

2. Following the *Euclid* decision, the use of zoning by municipalities spread rapidly. By 1930, nearly a thousand cities with more than two-thirds of the nation's urban population had adopted zoning ordinances. C. Haar & M. Wolf, Land-Use Planning 189 (1989).

3. The basic framework established by the *Euclid* decision has proven to be remarkably durable. Professor Michael Allan Wolf identifies three elements of the decision that "have remained inviolate, despite years of experimentation and variation" with land use regulation:

> First, the Court prescribed a flexible approach in the legislative implementation and judicial review of public land use planning devices. Second, the Court endorsed careful, expert-based planning, eschewing the haphazard vagaries of the market. Third, the Court approved the transfer, from individual to collective ownership, of development rights above a level often labeled "reasonable return." [Wolf, *Euclid* at Threescore Years and Ten: Is This the Twilight of Environmental and Land-Use Regulation? 30 U. Rich. L. Rev. 961, 963-964 (1996).]

4. Are there limits to the kinds of land uses that the police power properly may be used to exclude? Justice Sutherland suggests that some of the land uses excluded by the zoning ordinance would "come very near to being nuisances" in residential areas. Can only nuisance-like land uses be excluded through zoning? What is the relationship between nuisance law and zoning? See Wolf, Fruits of the "Impenetrable Jungle": Navigating the Boundary Between Land-Use Planning and Environmental Law, 50 J. Urban & Contemp. L. 5 (1996). Zoning has been used to exclude minorities and the poor from certain neighborhoods, as the New Jersey Supreme Court recognized when striking down zoning that prevented construction of low-income housing. Southern Burlington County NAACP v. Township of Mt. Laurel, 336 A.2d 713 (N.J. 1975). The zoning ordinance at issue in *Village of Euclid* initially was invalidated by the trial court because of its potentially discriminatory impacts on minorities and the poor. Village of Euclid v. Ambler Realty Co., 297 F. 307 (N.D. Ohio 1924), rev'd, 272 U.S. 365 (1926).

"Public Use" and the *Kelo* Decision

In June 2005 the U.S. Supreme Court decided a case interpreting the Fifth Amendment Takings Clause's "public use" requirement. In Kelo v. City of New London, 125 S. Ct. 2655 (2005), the Court considered whether the city of New London, Connecticut could use its powers of eminent domain to acquire private, residential property for an economic development area adjacent to the site of the Pfizer Corporation's new global research facility. The city sought to acquire the property to enable a nonprofit private economic development corporation to develop a project including parks, a marina support facility, and privately owned buildings. In the trial court plaintiffs obtained an injunction by arguing that their property was not being acquired for public use in violation of the Fifth Amendment's Takings Clause that requires the payment of compensation for private property acquired for public use. However, the Connecticut Supreme Court reversed, holding that economic development can be a public use and that the acquisition of the property was primarily intended to benefit the public interest, rather than private entities. Kelo v. City of New London, 843 A.2d 500 (2004).

The private landowners in the *Kelo* case hoped that the court would be influenced by the Michigan Supreme Court's July 2004 reversal of its famous *Poletown* decision (Poletown Neighborhood Council v. Detroit, 304 N.W.2d 455 (1981)), which had upheld condemnation of private land to build a plant for the General Motors Corporation. In County of Wayne v. Hathcock, 684 N.W.2d 765 (Mich. 2004), the Michigan Supreme Court held that a county's efforts to use its powers of eminent domain to take private property for a 1,300-acre business and technology park violated the Takings Clause of the Michigan Constitution because the transfer of condemned properties to private parties did not constitute a "public use." While finding ample evidence that the project would benefit the public by providing jobs and reinvigorating the local economy, the court ruled that the transfer of the condemned property to private parties violated the state constitution's Takings Clause because it was not in accordance with three principles governing "public use." The court held that transfer of condemned property to a private entity can satisfy the public use requirement only upon three conditions: "(1) Where 'public necessity of the extreme sort' requires collective action [citing private railroads, canals, or highways]; (2) where the property remains subject to public oversight after the transfer to a private entity; and (3) where the property is selected because of 'facts of independent public significance,' rather than the interests of the private entity to which the property is eventually transferred." 684 N.W.2d at 783. Because the language of the Michigan constitution's Takings Clause is nearly identical to that of the Fifth Amendment to the United States Constitution, this decision may be influential in takings cases outside of Michigan.

However, in *Kelo* the U.S. Supreme Court ruled 5-4 that economic development could be considered a "public purpose" for which states properly could exercise their powers of eminent domain. The Court majority concluded that while the state could not take private land simply to confer a private benefit on a particular private party, economic development projects could satisfy the Fifth Amendment's "public use" requirement if they had a "public purpose." The Court stated that the judiciary should defer to legislative judgments that economic development projects will provide appreciable benefits to a community. Noting that promotion of economic development is a traditional and long-accepted government function, the Court concluded that there is no principled way to distinguish it from other public purposes. Thus, it rejected the landowners' proposal to require the government to show that there is a reasonable certainty that the expected public benefits actually will accrue.

Because it pertains to physical takings for economic development projects, the *Kelo* decision itself is unlikely to have any direct effect on regulatory takings claims involving environmental regulations. However, it has generated a surprisingly strong outcry from the property rights movement, which is using it to crusade for new legislative limits on state acquisition of private property. The House of Representatives adopted a resolution deploring the Court's decision by a vote of 365 to 33 and it voted 231 to 189 to prohibit the use of federal funds "to enforce the judgment of the Supreme Court" in the case. Several states also are considering legislation to limit the use of eminent domain for economic development projects involving private parties. Kenneth R. Harney, Eminent Domain Ruling Has Strong Repercussions, Wash. Post, July 23, 2005, at F1. While *Kelo* did not change existing law, see Testimony of Thomas A. Merrill, U.S. Senate Committee on the Judiciary, Sept. 20, 2005, property rights groups are seeking to harness the negative public reaction to it to promote legislation to require government to compensate landowners whose property values are diminished by environmental regulations.

2.   State Growth Management and Critical Area Protection Programs

Despite a strong tradition of local control over land use decisions, several states have created programs to manage development and to protect environmentally sensitive areas. These laws generally give state-level entities greater authority over land use decisions, premised on the notion that local interests may not have adequate incentives to take into account larger state interests when making development decisions. When the American Law Institute adopted a Model Land Development Code in 1976 that included critical area protection legislation, some states already had established programs to protect critical areas.

In 1972, California voters approved Proposition 20, the "Coastal Conservation Initiative," which created a state Coastal Commission and required it to adopt a coastal protection plan. The California Coastal Plan, adopted in 1975, served as the basis for the 1976 California Coastal Act, which created one of the nation's strictest critical area protection programs. The Act restricts development along the state's 1,100-mile coastline by requiring a permit for any development in the coastal zone. Permits may be approved only if a development conforms with state coastal policies and local coastal protection plans (LCPs) that the Act required all cities and counties in the coastal zone to prepare. The LCPs must be reviewed and approved by the Coastal Commission, which also has the authority to issue permits and to review permits issued by local authorities. The Commission also reviews federal projects for consistency with the state's Coastal Management Program pursuant to the federal Coastal Zone Management Act.

Maryland has a comprehensive critical area protection program, adopted in 1984 to protect the Chesapeake Bay. Maryland's Critical Areas Act created a state Critical Area Commission and required it to adopt strict criteria to control development in a 1,000-foot buffer zone around the Bay. Following the adoption of the criteria, Maryland counties in the critical area were required to develop comprehensive plans that had to be reviewed and approved by the Commission. These plans are to ensure that local land use decisions will conform with the statewide criteria.

When natural resources transcend state boundaries, efforts to protect them require coordination between neighboring states. Maryland's critical areas program was a product of the state's participation in the Chesapeake Bay Program, a collaborative effort to protect and restore the Chesapeake by EPA and the state governments in the Bay's watershed. To protect Lake Tahoe, which is located in the Sierra Nevada range on the border between California and Nevada, the two states formed an interstate compact. The compact, ratified by Congress in 1969, created the Tahoe Regional Planning Agency (TRPA), the first bi-state regional environmental planning agency in the nation. In 1980 the Compact was amended to require the TRPA to adopt a plan prohibiting any development that would exceed the "environmental threshold carrying capacity" of the area, defined by reference to "standards for air quality, water quality, soil conservation, vegetation preservation and noise."

The TRPA's initial long-range regional plan, adopted in April 1984, was challenged in court as inadequate to protect the environment. Faced with a court-ordered moratorium on new building in the area, the TRPA adopted a new Regional Plan in 1987. The plan includes a complex system for rating the suitability of undeveloped land for development. No additional development is permitted on property located in certain areas that carry runoff into the watershed (called "stream environment zones"). However, owners of such property automatically receive certain transferable development rights (TDRs) that can be sold or used to qualify to develop property in a more suitable location. The idea behind using TDRs, which were promoted initially by John Costonis, Costonis, Development Rights Transfer: An Exploratory Essay, 83 Yale L.J. 75 (1973), is that owners of property located in areas where development is not desired will be compensated for the impact of the development restriction by acquiring valuable rights that can be transferred to owners of property in areas where development is permissible. More than 100 jurisdictions now incorporate TDRs in their land use control schemes.

Statewide land use planning legislation has been adopted by Florida, Oregon, New Jersey, Maine, Rhode Island, and Vermont. These programs generally require that local land use decisions conform to statewide land use plans. The most far-reaching statewide growth management program was adopted by Oregon in 1973. Liberty, Oregon's Comprehensive Growth Management Program: An Implementation Review and Lessons for Other States, 22 Envtl. L. Rep. 10367 (1992). The Oregon program created a citizen commission, the Land Conservation and Development Commission (LCDC), and charged it with the task of adopting statewide planning goals. The LCDC adopted 14 statewide planning goals and five additional goals applicable to the Oregon coast and Willamette River. All Oregon cities and counties were required to adopt comprehensive land use plans to implement the statewide goals, and the LCDC could require revisions in these plans to ensure consistency with the goals. City, county, and regional land use decisions could be appealed to the Oregon Land Use Board of Appeals to ensure consistency with the plans and goals.

The Oregon program required every city to establish an Urban Growth Boundary (UGB) encompassing the city's urban core and sufficient land to accommodate development during the 20- or 50-year planning period. Future urban growth is to be directed inside the UGB, with urban uses generally prohibited outside it. Aside from a few areas where rural development occurred prior to adoption of the program, virtually all private land outside the UGBs is zoned for farming, ranching, or forestry. Land zoned for exclusive farm use (EFU) is strictly regulated to prohibit the construction of residences and other structures unrelated to farming activities.

One of the most thoughtful participants in the Oregon planning process has been Robert Liberty, executive director of 1000 Friends of Oregon, a nonprofit citizens group concerned with growth management. In the article that follows he assesses how Oregon's program has worked and the lessons that it provides for other jurisdictions.

‖ *Liberty, Planned Growth: The Oregon Model* ‖
13 Nat. Resources & Envt. 315 (Summer 1998)

After LCDC adopted the Goals, every city and county began the laborious process of implementing them for all the land within their boundaries. These plans were to be carried out by the standard array of local land use regulations, such as zoning ordinances and maps and subdivision controls.

LCDC and the department spent their first decade reviewing local plans and regulations to determine their consistency with the Goals. This process, at the local and state level, involved open hearings where interested parties could offer comment or present views on whether the plan and regulations complied with the Goals. . . .

The process of reviewing and revising local plans and regulations was far more arduous than anticipated. Many counties had to revise and resubmit their plans and regulations to LCDC three or four times. Parts of many plans approved by the LCDC were overturned on appeal. The last local plan and regulations were approved by LCDC in 1986, thirteen years after S.B. 100 passed. The last appeal from an LCDC order of approval was not settled and acted upon by the local government until the early 1990s.

This highly formal and public process of analyzing and reviewing plans, with clear opportunities for appeal, is a key feature of the Oregon program and accounts for both its success and continuing controversy. . . .

Have Oregon's UGBs worked to stop sprawl? Research shows that the market believes in UGBs. In the Portland area, newspaper reports indicate that when land is brought inside the Portland metropolitan UGB the value increases tenfold.

The distribution of growth between urban land inside UGBs and the rural lands outside UGBs is another important measure of the effectiveness of UGBs. Obviously, if a large share of total population growth is occurring outside UGBs, even though most Oregonians live in urban areas, then UGBs have failed.

In Deschutes County, a rapidly growing county in Central Oregon making the transition from a logging and ranching town to destination resort and retirement community, more than one-half of all residential units built between 1985 and 1989 were built outside the county's three UGBs. At the other end of the scale was the performance inside the Portland Metropolitan UGB, which contains twenty-four cities and about 40 percent of the state's population. During the study period (1985-1989) fully 95 percent of all residential units and nearly 99 percent of the new subdivision lots were created inside the Metropolitan UGBs. . . .

Some interstate comparisons show that UGBs are countering the half-century national trend of falling urban densities. For example, in 1960 the density of the bistate (Oregon and Washington) metropolitan Portland area was 3,412 people per square mile and the density of metropolitan Atlanta was 3,122 people per square mile. In 1990 the density of the Oregon part of the Portland metro area rose to 3,734 people per square mile while Atlanta's had dropped to 1,898 per square mile. In 1994, the Oregon portion of the Portland metropolitan area reached a density of 3,885 people per square mile. . . .

The land in EFU or forest zones under the Oregon planning program is impressive. As of 1986, there were 16,035,830 acres (over 25,000 square miles) in EFU zones. This figure compares favorably with the modest acreage protected in other states through purchase of development right programs or agricultural districting. . . .

However, the amount of land in farm use zoning is meaningless if the zones, or the officials administering them, allow substantial residential development. Available information shows that a steady, but relatively modest, rate of new homes and parcels is being approved each year. Between 1988 and 1994 Oregon counties approved about 720 new houses and 500 new parcels (including 1,459 of 20 acres or less) each year on the 16 million acres in EFU zones. Computer mapping shows that in the EFU zone in Washington County, Oregon, just west of the Portland metropolitan UGB, [housing density] rose from one house for every 39 acres in 1975 to one house for every 33 acres in 1994. . . .

This and other data permits a conclusion that the farm land preservation element of Oregon's planning program has: (1) halted urbanization inside EFU zones (i.e., shopping malls, subdivisions, and more broadly, urban densities of more than 1,000 people per square mile); (2) made a big difference in some parts of the state in slowing low-density residential development and land divisions in farm and ranching areas; but (3) has not completely stopped building of new housing in any area and in some areas there has been substantial hobby-farm, rural homesite development. . . .

A few simple but important lessons are evident in this review of the Oregon planning program. . . . First, the program should address and reconcile a diversity of interests and objectives for the use and conservation of land. This is good politics and good policy. Second, because implementing a new planning framework takes many years, special steps must be taken immediately to govern development during the long implementation period to avoid continuing in the old direction. Third, broad public participation in adoption, implementation, and execution of a new planning framework may add to the length and contentiousness of the effort but more than justifies these costs by improving the quality of decisionmaking and allowing the public to acquire an understanding of why the effort is worthwhile.

NOTES AND QUESTIONS

1. While Liberty now appears pleased with the results of the Oregon growth management program, he found the long and tortuous process of implementing it frustrating. Writing in 1988, Liberty provided some interesting insights into the political difficulties of implementing state land use controls. Liberty, The Oregon Planning Experience: Repeating the Success and Avoiding the Mistakes, 1 Md. Policy Studies 45 (1988). After initial favorable publicity focusing on the benefits of land use controls, press coverage became less favorable as news stories focused on how the program restricted particular individuals' development plans. The initial enthusiasm many administrators had shown for the program diminished in the face of "endlessly repeated cries of outrage over the loss of purely local control over land use decisions," even though the failure of local control had widely been acknowledged as making the legislation necessary. Id.

2. Land use controls affect property values. Restrictions on development increase the value of developed properties. A study of Maryland's Critical Areas Act found that development restrictions increased the prices of homes in the Chesapeake Bay critical area by 46 to 62 percent for shorefront properties and 14 to 27 percent for other homes in the area. Parsons, The Effect of Coastal Land Use Restrictions on Housing Prices: A Repeat Sale Analysis, 22 J. Envtl. Econ. & Mgmt. 25 (1992). Even undeveloped property may benefit from government programs that preserve environmental amenities in the area. Beaton & Pollock, Economic Impact of Growth Management Policies Surrounding the Chesapeake Bay, 68 Land Econ. 434 (1992); Beaton, Living by the Shore: The Impact of Zoning on Housing Costs, 1 Md. Policy Studies 57 (1988). Owners of undeveloped property who can successfully lobby to relax regulations can garner windfall gains. As a result, pressure to relax land use regulations is seemingly relentless. Opponents of Oregon's program tried to repeal key elements of it through ballot initiatives in 1976, 1978, and 1982. All three efforts were defeated by statewide margins of 10 to 20 percentage points.

3. Growth management advocates distrustful of elected officials are now promoting measures to reduce the discretion of administrators to permit development projects. In the November 1998 election, voters in Ventura County, California, approved a package of the most restrictive land use management measures ever adopted in southern California. The initiatives require cities to establish urban growth boundaries (UGBs), and they prohibit agricultural and rural lands outside UGBs from being rezoned for development until the year 2020. Booth, "Slow Growth" on Fast Track in Southern California, Wash. Post, Nov. 27, 1998, at A3. Farmers in Ventura County were vociferous opponents of the initiatives (one described them as having "nothing to do with preserving farmland" but rather "a no-growth measure, sponsored and supported by you all who have just moved here and want us to pull up the drawbridge and stop growing"). Why do you think

farmers opposed the initiatives? (Hint: Prime farmland in the county reportedly sells for $30,000 per acre, but the price rises to $150,000 per acre when it is rezoned for commercial or residential purposes.) Id.

4. Some states have sought to protect certain land uses through programs that are non-regulatory in character by using financial incentives to induce landowners to participate. For example, 15 states now have farmland preservation programs that use public funds to purchase development rights to ensure that land is kept in agricultural use. These programs have protected 420,000 acres of farmland through conservation easements at a cost of $730 million, or approximately $1,750 per acre. Council on Environmental Quality, 1996 Report, at 120 (1998).

5. In 1997, Maryland adopted "smart growth" legislation that seeks to concentrate development in existing population centers, while protecting sensitive resource areas. The law adopts a somewhat different approach than Oregon's program. Rather than prohibiting urban development outside UGBs, the program seeks to discourage it by simply denying all state assistance for projects that are not in areas determined to be suitable for future growth. See Frece & Leahy-Fucheck, Smart Growth and Neighborhood Conservation, 13 Nat. Resources & Envt. 319 (Summer 1998). The concept behind the program is that government resources promoting growth should be concentrated in areas where the infrastructure already exists to support it. The program provides tax incentives to developers who rehabilitate certified heritage structures. For a discussion of the use of historic preservation programs to reduce urban sprawl, see Schowalter, Reuse, Restore, Recycle: Historic Preservation as an Alternative to Sprawl, 29 Envtl. L. Rep. 10,418 (1999).

6. In November 2004 Oregon voters dealt a potentially serious blow to the state's growth management program by approving a voter initiative called "Measure 37" by a margin of 60 to 40 percent. The measure provides that state or local governments must provide compensation to landowners or forego enforcement of land use restrictions that reduce the fair market value of property owned by anyone whose family owned the property before the regulations were adopted. The measure does not apply to regulations that restrict activities that are a public nuisance or that protect public health and safety, though it specifies that the measure is to be construed narrowly in favor of providing compensation. Many supporters of the measure who own farmland that would be more valuable if residential development is permitted are hoping that the state will simply forego enforcement of its existing land use regulations. Oregon Governor Ted Kulongoski is hoping that the state will be able to provide compensation rather than waiving regulations. See John Pendergrass, Oregon Voters Strike at Land Use Regs, 22 Envtl. Forum 6 (Jan./Feb. 2005). A Circuit Court decision invalidating the ballot measure was reversed by the Supreme Court of Oregon in February 2006. MacPherson v. Dep't of Administrative Services, 340 Or. 117 (2006).

D. LAND USE CONTROLS AND REGULATORY TAKINGS

The Fifth Amendment of the U.S. Constitution provides that "private property [shall not] be taken for public use, without just compensation."

Virtually every form of land use regulation that affects property values has been challenged as a "taking" of private property rights for which government is constitutionally required to provide compensation. While judicial interpretations of the Takings Clause have followed a tortuous and often confusing course, the U.S. Supreme Court and the Federal Court of Claims have been more sympathetic to regulatory takings claims in recent years.

1. The Evolution of Regulatory Takings Doctrine

The original understanding of the scope of the Takings Clause appears to have been more limited than subsequent judicial interpretations of it. There is evidence indicating that the framers of the Constitution envisioned the Takings Clause as applying only to actual physical invasions of property. Note, The Origins and Original Significance of the Just Compensation Clause, 94 Yale L.J. 694 (1985). In early cases, government actions that caused a physical invasion of property were considered takings, Pumpelly v. Green Bay Co., 80 U.S. 166 (1871) (construction of dam that flooded private property), while regulations that severely affected the value of property were not. Mugler v. Kansas, 123 U.S. 623 (1887) (compensation not required to brewery owners for ban on production and sale of alcoholic beverages), Hadacheck v. Sebastian, 239 U.S. 394 (1915) (upholding ordinance banning use of brick kilns in neighborhood where brick manufacturer operates).

The notion that regulation could constitute a taking if it destroyed the value of property even if it did not involve a direct physical invasion was endorsed by the Supreme Court in Pennsylvania Coal Co. v. Mahon, 260 U.S. 393 (1922). A statute prohibiting the mining of coal in a manner that could cause the subsidence of homes on the surface was held to be a taking because it effectively abolished the value of underlying mineral rights. Justice Holmes declared that "while property may be regulated to a certain extent, if regulation goes too far it will be recognized as a taking." 260 U.S. at 415. While noting that "[g]overnment hardly could go on if to some extent values incident to property could not be diminished without paying for every such change in general law," Holmes argued that this sort of damage to a private residence was not the kind of public nuisance that must yield to the state's police power. In dissent, Justice Brandeis argued that the regulation was not a taking, but rather "merely the prohibition of a noxious use."

Six years after deciding *Pennsylvania Coal,* the Supreme Court upheld a Virginia law that had been used to require that a tree on private land be destroyed in order to prevent the spread of infection to trees owned by others. In Miller v. Schoene, 276 U.S. 272 (1928), the Supreme Court stated that "[w]here the public interest is involved, preferment of that interest over the property interest of the individual, to the extent even of its destruction, is one of the distinguishing characteristics of every exercise of the police power which affects property." 276 U.S. at 279-280. This decision, which did not even cite *Pennsylvania Coal,* suggests that even regulations that result in the destruction of property will not be viewed as takings if they are designed to protect against at least some kinds of harm.

The growth of national regulatory programs to protect the environment in the early 1970s raised concerns that regulatory takings problems would occur with more frequency. In 1973 the Council on Environmental Quality (CEQ) devoted an entire chapter of its fourth annual report to the takings problem. CEQ argued that conceptions of property rights were changing in the wake of society's increased environmental consciousness. Council on Environmental Quality, Envtl. Quality 149-150 (1973). Land was now being viewed as a scarce resource that society had an interest in protecting for future generations.

This notion was reflected in a decision by the Wisconsin Supreme Court in Just v. Marinette County, 201 N.W.2d 761 (1972). In *Just*, property owners challenged a wetlands protection law that barred them from building on lake-front property. The court rejected the takings claim, holding that it was not reasonable for the property owners to expect to build in a wetland. Noting that the property could be used for harvesting wild crops, hunting, and fishing, the court observed that "[t]his is not a case where an owner is prevented from using his land for natural and indigenous uses. . . . The changing of wetlands and swamps to the damage of the general public by upsetting the natural environment and the natural relationship is not a reasonable use of that land which is protected from police power regulation." Id. at 768.

The Supreme Court has had a difficult time articulating a principled method for determining when regulation "goes too far" and constitutes a taking. In the case that follows, the Court conceded that it had been unable to develop any single formula for defining a regulatory taking. The case involved a challenge to New York City's historic landmark preservation law because it prohibited a railroad from building a 55-story office building above Grand Central Terminal, a landmark designated under the law. Under the legislation, owners of historic structures who were denied permission to build received transferable development rights (TDRs) that could be sold to permit development elsewhere.

Penn Central Transportation Co. v. City of New York
438 U.S. 104 (1978)

Mr. Justice Brennan delivered the opinion of the Court.

Before considering appellants' specific contentions, it will be useful to review the factors that have shaped the jurisprudence of the Fifth Amendment injunction "nor shall private property be taken for public use, without just compensation." The question of what constitutes a "taking" for purposes of the Fifth Amendment has proved to be a problem of considerable difficulty. While this Court has recognized that the Fifth Amendment's guarantee . . . [is] designed to bar Government from forcing some people alone to bear public burdens which, in all fairness and justice, should be borne by the public as a whole, Armstrong v. United States, 364 U.S. 40, 49 (1960), this Court, quite simply, has been unable to develop any "set formula" for determining when "justice and fairness" require that economic injuries caused by public action be compensated by the government, rather than remain disproportionately concentrated on a few persons. See Goldblatt v. Hempstead, 369 U.S. 590, 594 (1962). Indeed, we have frequently observed that whether a particular restriction will be rendered invalid by the government's failure to pay for any losses proximately caused by it depends largely "upon the particular circumstances [in that] case." United States v. Central Eureka Mining Co., 357 U.S. 155, 168 (1958); see United States v. Caltex, Inc., 344 U.S. 149, 156 (1952).

In engaging in these essentially ad hoc, factual inquiries, the Court's decisions have identified several factors that have particular significance. The economic impact of the regulation on the claimant and, particularly, the extent to which the regulation has interfered with distinct investment-backed expectations are, of course, relevant considerations. See Goldblatt v. Hempstead, supra at 594. So, too, is the character of the governmental action. A "taking" may more readily be found when the interference with property can be characterized as a physical invasion by government, see, e.g., United States v. Causby, 328 U.S. 256 (1946), than when interference arises from some public program adjusting the benefits and burdens of economic life to promote the common good.

"Government hardly could go on if, to some extent, values incident to property could not be diminished without paying for every such change in the general law," Pennsylvania Coal Co. v. Mahon, 260 U.S. 393, 413 (1922), and this Court has accordingly recognized, in a wide variety of contexts, that government may execute laws or programs that adversely affect recognized economic values. Exercises of the taxing power are one obvious example. A second are the decisions in which this Court has dismissed "taking" challenges on the ground that, while the challenged government action caused economic harm, it did not interfere with interests that were sufficiently bound up with the reasonable expectations of the claimant to constitute "property" for Fifth Amendment purposes. See, e.g., United States v. Willow River Power Co., 324 U.S. 499 (1945) (interest in high-water level of river for runoff for tailwaters to maintain power head is not property); United States v. Chandler-Dunbar Water Power Co., 229 U.S. 53 (1913) (no property interest can exist in navigable waters); see also Demorest v. City Bank Co., 321 U.S. 36 (1944); Muhlker v. Harlem R. Co., 197 U.S. 544 (1905); Sax, Takings and the Police Power, 74 Yale L.J. 36, 62 (1964).

More importantly for the present case, in instances in which a state tribunal reasonably concluded that "the health, safety, morals, or general welfare" would be promoted by prohibiting particular contemplated uses of land, this Court has upheld land use regulations that destroyed or adversely affected recognized real property interests. See Nectow v. Cambridge, 277 U.S. 183, 188 (1928). Zoning laws are, of course, the classic example, see Euclid v. Ambler Realty Co., 272 U.S. 365 (1026) (prohibition of industrial use); Gorieb v. Fox, 274 U.S. 603, 608 (1927) (requirement that portions of parcels be left unbuilt); Welch v. Swasey, 214 U.S. 91 (1909) (height restriction), which have been viewed as permissible governmental action even when prohibiting the most beneficial use of the property. See Goldblatt v. Hempstead, supra at 592-593, and cases cited; see also Eastlake v. Forest City Enterprises, Inc., 426 U.S. 668, 674 n. 8 (1976). . . .

In contending that the New York City law has "taken" their property in violation of the Fifth and Fourteenth Amendments, appellants make a series of arguments, which, while tailored to the facts of this case, essentially urge that any substantial restriction imposed pursuant to a landmark law must be accompanied by just compensation if it is to be constitutional. . . .

They first observe that the airspace above the Terminal is a valuable property interest, citing United States v. Causby, supra. They urge that the Landmarks Law has deprived them of any gainful use of their "air rights" above the Terminal and that, irrespective of the value of the remainder of their parcel, the city has "taken" their right to this superjacent airspace, thus entitling them to "just compensation" measured by the fair market value of these air rights.

Apart from our own disagreement with appellants' characterization of the effect of the New York City law, the submission that appellants may establish a "taking" simply by showing that they have been denied the ability to exploit a property interest that they heretofore had believed was available for development is quite simply untenable. Were this the rule, this Court would have erred not only in upholding laws restricting the development of air rights, see Welch v. Swasey, supra, but also in approving those prohibiting both the subjacent, see Goldblatt v. Hempstead, 369 U.S. 590 (1962), and the lateral, see Gorieb v. Fox, 274 U.S. 603 (1927), development of particular parcels. "Taking" jurisprudence does not divide a single parcel into discrete segments and attempt to determine whether rights in a particular segment have been entirely abrogated. In deciding whether a particular governmental action has effected a taking, this Court focuses rather both on the character of the action and on the nature and extent of the interference with rights in the parcel as a whole—here, the city tax block designated as the "landmark site."

Secondly, appellants, focusing on the character and impact of the New York City law, argue that it effects a "taking" because its operation has significantly diminished the value of the Terminal site. Appellants concede that the decisions sustaining other land use regulations, which, like the New York City law, are reasonably related to the promotion of the general welfare, uniformly reject the proposition that diminution in property value, standing alone, can establish a "taking," see Euclid v. Ambler Realty Co., 272 U.S. 365 (1926) (75% diminution in value caused by zoning law); Hadacheck v. Sebastian, 239 U.S. 394 (1915) ($87\frac{1}{2}$% diminution in value); cf. Eastlake v. Forest City Enterprises, Inc., 426 U.S. at 674 n. 8, and that the "taking" issue in these contexts is resolved by focusing on the uses the regulations permit. . . .

Stated baldly, appellants' position appears to be that the only means of ensuring that selected owners are not singled out to endure financial hardship for no reason is to hold that any restriction imposed on individual landmarks pursuant to the New York City scheme is a "taking" requiring the payment of "just compensation." Agreement with this argument would, of course, invalidate not just New York City's law, but all comparable landmark legislation in the Nation. We find no merit in it. . . .

Rejection of appellants' broad arguments is not, however, the end of our inquiry, for all we thus far have established is that the New York City law is not rendered invalid by its failure to provide "just compensation" whenever a landmark owner is restricted in the exploitation of property interests, such as air rights, to a greater extent than provided for under applicable zoning laws. We now must consider whether the interference with appellants' property is of such a magnitude that "there must be an exercise of eminent domain and compensation to sustain [it]." Pennsylvania Coal Co. v. Mahon, 260 U.S. at 413. That inquiry may be narrowed to the question of the severity of the impact of the law on appellants' parcel, and its resolution, in turn, requires a careful assessment of the impact of the regulation on the Terminal site.

Unlike the governmental acts in *Goldblatt, Miller, Causby, Griggs,* and *Hadacheck,* the New York City law does not interfere in any way with the present uses of the Terminal. Its designation as a landmark not only permits, but contemplates, that appellants may continue to use the property precisely as it has been used for the past 65 years: as a railroad terminal containing office space and concessions. So the law does not interfere with what must be regarded as Penn Central's primary expectation concerning the use of the parcel. More importantly, on this record, we must regard the New York City law as permitting Penn Central not only to profit from the Terminal but also to obtain a "reasonable return" on its investment.

Appellants, moreover, exaggerate the effect of the law on their ability to make use of the air rights above the Terminal in two respects. First, it simply cannot be maintained, on this record, that appellants have been prohibited from occupying any portion of the airspace above the Terminal. While the Commission's actions in denying applications to construct an office building in excess of 50 stories above the Terminal may indicate that it will refuse to issue a certificate of appropriateness for any comparably sized structure, nothing the Commission has said or done suggests an intention to prohibit any construction above the Terminal. The Commission's report emphasized that whether any construction would be allowed depended upon whether the proposed addition "would harmonize in scale, material, and character with [the Terminal]." Record 2251. Since appellants have not sought approval for the construction of a smaller structure, we do not know that appellants will be denied any use of any portion of the airspace above the Terminal.

Second, to the extent appellants have been denied the right to build above the Terminal, it is not literally accurate to say that they have been denied all use of even those preexisting air rights. Their ability to use these rights has not been abrogated; they are made transferable to at least eight parcels in the vicinity of the Terminal, one or two of which have been found suitable for the construction of new office buildings. Although appellants and others have argued that New York City's transferable development rights program is far from ideal, the New York courts here supportably found that, at least in the case of the Terminal, the rights afforded are valuable. While these rights may well not have constituted "just compensation" if a "taking" had occurred, the rights nevertheless undoubtedly mitigate whatever financial burdens the law has imposed on appellants and, for that reason, are to be taken into account in considering the impact of regulation. Cf. Goldblatt v. Hempstead, 369 U.S. at 594 n. 3.

On this record, we conclude that the application of New York City's Landmarks Law has not effected a "taking" of appellants' property. The restrictions imposed are substantially related to the promotion of the general welfare, and not only permit reasonable beneficial use of the landmark site, but also afford appellants opportunities further to enhance not only the Terminal site proper but also other properties.

Affirmed.

NOTES AND QUESTIONS

1. Justice Rehnquist dissented in an opinion joined by Chief Justice Burger and Justice Stevens. Rehnquist argued that the historic landmark law unfairly singled out one-tenth of 1 percent of all buildings in New York City without providing them the "reciprocity of advantage" that zoning ordinances provide because zoning typically is applied to all property in a designated area. 438 U.S. at 138-140 (Rehnquist, J. dissenting). The Court majority rejected the notion that Penn Central had been singled out, noting that the law was part of "a comprehensive plan to preserve structures of historic or aesthetic interest wherever they might be found in the city," and that it had been applied to 400 structures and 31 historic districts. 438 U.S. at 132.

2. Penn Central had argued that historic landmark preservation "is inevitably arbitrary, or at least subjective, because it is basically a matter of taste," Reply Brief for Appellants 22, thus unavoidably singling out individual

landowners for disparate and unfair treatment. The Court rejected this argument. Noting that Penn Central had failed to challenge the designation of Grand Central Terminal as a landmark, the Court stated that "there is no basis whatsoever for a conclusion that courts will have any greater difficulty identifying arbitrary or discriminatory action in the context of landmark regulation than in the context of classic zoning or indeed in any other context." 438 U.S. at 133.

3. What impact, if any, should the provision of TDRs have on takings claims? While the Court did not decide whether TDRs could constitute just compensation, it suggested that their existence was one factor to consider in weighing whether the regulation unreasonably burdened Penn Central. The company owned several nearby properties, at least eight of which were eligible to use the TDRs.

4. In the years following *Penn Central*, the Court continued to follow the categorical rule that permanent physical invasions of property constituted takings no matter how small the invasion. Loretto v. Teleprompter Manhattan CATV Corp., 458 U.S. 419 (1982) (requirement that landlord must permit installation of cable TV access facilities on roof of building is a taking). But the court continued to be reluctant to define under what circumstances a land use regulation so diminished the value of property as to constitute a taking. In a series of decisions, the Court avoided directly confronting this question by holding that plaintiffs had to apply for variances and exhaust state remedies before a takings claim would be ripe for review. Agins v. Tiburon, 447 U.S. 255 (1980); McDonald, Sommer & Prates v. County of Yolo, 477 U.S. 340 (1986). In *Agins* the Court suggested that regulatory action "effects a taking" if it "does not substantially advance legitimate state interests," 447 U.S. at 260, implying a kind of means-ends test for takings apparently derived from due process precedents. When the Court again confronted the regulatory takings question more directly, it was sharply divided.

2. *The Modern Revival of Regulatory Takings Jurisprudence*

Takings jurisprudence remained unsettled as courts acquiesced in states' efforts to subject plaintiffs raising takings claims to lengthy procedural gauntlets. California courts limited the remedy for a taking to invalidation of the regulation, refusing to allow monetary relief. A major shift in takings jurisprudence was signaled in 1987 when the Supreme Court finally confronted regulatory takings claims in three cases decided during the same term. A sharply divided Court rejected one takings claim, remanded another, and upheld a third.

In Keystone Bituminous Coal v. DeBenedictis, 480 U.S. 470 (1987), the Court held, by a 5-4 margin on facts virtually identical to those of *Pennsylvania Coal*, that a law restricting the exercise of mineral rights was not a taking because it was designed to protect public health and safety by preventing subsidence of surface areas. The Court noted that the law responded to what was perceived to be a significant threat to public welfare. It distinguished *Pennsylvania Coal* by noting that there was no basis for finding that the law made it impossible for the company to profitably engage in its business or that it had unduly interfered with investment-backed expectations.

In First English Evangelical Lutheran Church v. County of Los Angeles, 482 U.S. 304 (1987), the Court reviewed a decision that summarily dismissed an inverse condemnation case raising a takings claim on the ground that the only remedy available under California law for a taking was invalidation of the regulation effecting a taking. The plaintiff was a church prohibited from rebuilding a summer camp for handicapped children by a regulation barring rebuilding in a floodplain. The Court held that while invalidation of an ordinance could make any taking a temporary one, the Constitution "requires that the government pay the landowner for the value of the use of the land during this period." 482 U.S. at 319. The Court remanded the case to the state courts to consider whether the ordinance constituted a taking. On remand, the California Court of Appeals had little trouble finding that no taking was involved because the regulation prevented harm to public health and safety. First English Evangelical Lutheran Church v. County of Los Angeles, 210 Cal. App. 3d 1353 (1989).

The third takings case decided by the U.S. Supreme Court, Nollan v. California Coastal Commission, 483 U.S. 825 (1987), challenged a decision by the California Coastal Commission. James and Marilyn Nollan, who had agreed to purchase beachfront property located between two public beach areas, wanted to replace a small bungalow (used as a guest house until it had fallen into disrepair) with a three-bedroom house. They applied for a coastal development permit from the Coastal Commission. The Commission agreed to grant the permit conditioned on the Nollans' granting the public an easement to pass along a portion of their property between the two public beaches. Maintaining that this condition constituted a taking, the Nollans challenged it in court. In a decision authored by Justice Scalia, the Court agreed.

The Court noted that the easement was tantamount to the kind of permanent physical occupation of property that normally would be a categorical taking. However, it observed that if the permit condition "serves the same legitimate police-power purpose as a refusal to issue the permit," 483 U.S. at 836, it would not be a taking unless a refusal to issue the permit would be a taking. The Court then examined whether the permit condition "substantially advances legitimate state interests." The Commission argued that the permit condition was reasonably related to the public burden created by the Nollans' new house because it would create a "psychological barrier" to beach access and interfere with "visual access" to the beach. However, the Court concluded that it was "quite impossible to understand how a requirement that people already on public beaches be able to walk across the Nollans' property reduces any obstacles to viewing the beach created by the new house." 483 U.S. at 838. While the Commission could have required the Nollans to provide a viewing platform to provide visual access to the beach, Justice Scalia stated that the physical access requirement "utterly fails to further the end" advanced by the Commission. Thus the Court held that the permit condition was unconstitutional because it did not serve the same governmental purpose as the development ban.

The three takings cases decided by the Court in 1987 spawned considerably more litigation challenging land use regulations as takings. With encouragement from a more receptive Supreme Court, takings claims were asserted against a wide variety of regulations. Some courts found that certain land use regulations resulted in regulatory takings, basing their findings on a more liberal application of the diminution-in-value approach and a more restrictive view of the public nuisance exemption.

In Whitney Benefits, Inc. v. United States, 926 F.2d 1169 (Fed. Cir.), cert. denied, 502 U.S. 952 (1991), the Federal Circuit found that a ban on the mining of alluvial valley floors imposed by the Surface Mining Control and Reclamation Act constituted a taking because it deprived two mining companies of all economic use of their coal deposits. Noting that the Act permitted other companies to mine coal, the court found that it could not fit within the nuisance exception and awarded more than $140 million in compensation to the two companies. The Supreme Court denied the government's request for review, which had been premised on the argument that the companies never had been denied a mining permit and could have exchanged the land for other federal land with minerals that could have been mined.

Although it denied review in *Whitney Benefits*, the Supreme Court agreed to review a decision by South Carolina's highest court, which had rejected a takings challenge to regulations that prohibited a landowner from building a home on undeveloped beachfront property. The Court issued the following decision.

Lucas v. South Carolina Coastal Council
505 U.S. 1003 (1992)

JUSTICE SCALIA delivered the opinion of the Court, in which REHNQUIST, C.J., and WHITE, O'CONNOR, and THOMAS, J.J., joined.

In 1986, petitioner David H. Lucas paid $975,000 for two residential lots on the Isle of Palms in Charleston County, South Carolina, on which he intended to build single-family homes. In 1988, however, the South Carolina Legislature enacted the Beachfront Management Act (Act), which had the direct effect of barring petitioner from erecting any permanent habitable structures on his two parcels. A state trial court found that this prohibition rendered Lucas' parcels "valueless." This case requires us to decide whether the Act's dramatic: effect on the economic value of Lucas' lots accomplished a taking of private property under the Fifth and Fourteenth Amendments requiring the payment of "just compensation." . . .

III

A

Prior to Justice Holmes' exposition in Pennsylvania Coal Co. v. Mahon, 260 U.S. 393 (1922), it was generally thought that the Takings Clause reached only a "direct appropriation" of property, Legal Tender Cases, 12 Wall. 457, 551 (1871), or the functional equivalent of a "practical ouster of [the owner's] possession." Transportation Co. v. Chicago, 99 U.S. 635, 642 (1879). Justice Holmes recognized in *Mahon*, however, that if the protection against physical appropriations of private property was to be meaningfully enforced, the government's power to redefine the range of interests included in the ownership of property was necessarily constrained by constitutional limits. If, instead, the uses of private property were subject to unbridled, uncompensated qualification under the police power, "the natural tendency of human nature [would be] to extend the qualification more and more until at last private property disappeared." These considerations gave birth in that case to the oft-cited maxim that, "while property may be regulated to a certain extent, if regulation goes too far it will be recognized as a taking."

Nevertheless, our decision in *Mahon* offered little insight into when, and under what circumstances, a given regulation would be seen as going "too far" for purposes of the Fifth Amendment. In 70-odd years of succeeding "regulatory takings" jurisprudence, we have generally eschewed any "set formula" for determining how far is too far, preferring to "engag[e] in . . . essentially ad hoc, factual inquiries," Penn Central Transportation Co. v. New York City, 438 U.S. 104 (1978). We have, however, described at least two discrete categories of regulatory action as compensable without case-specific inquiry into the public interest advanced in support of the restraint. The first encompasses regulations that compel the property owner to suffer a physical "invasion" of his property. In general (at least with regard to permanent invasions), no matter how minute the intrusion, and no matter how weighty the public purpose behind it, we have required compensation. For example, in Loretto v. Teleprompter Manhattan CATV Corp., 458 U.S. 419 (1982), we determined that New York's law requiring landlords to allow television cable companies to emplace cable facilities in their apartment buildings constituted a taking, id., at 435-440, even though the facilities occupied at most only $1\frac{1}{2}$ cubic feet of the landlords' property.

The second situation in which we have held categorical treatment appropriate is where regulation denies all economically beneficial or productive use of land. See *Agins*, 447 U.S., at 260. As we have said on numerous occasions, the Fifth Amendment is violated when land-use regulation "does not substantially advance legitimate state interests *or denies an owner economically viable use of his land.*" *Agins*, supra, at 260 (emphasis added).[7]

We have never set forth the justification for this rule. Perhaps it is simply, as Justice Brennan suggested, that total deprivation of beneficial use is, from the landowner's point of view, the equivalent of a physical appropriation. See San Diego Gas & Electric Co. v. San Diego, 450 U.S., at 652 (Brennan, J., dissenting). "For what is the land but the profits thereof?" 1 E. Coke, Institutes ch. 1, §1 (1st Am. ed. 1812). Surely, at least, in the extraordinary circumstance when *no* productive or economically beneficial use of land is permitted, it is less realistic to indulge our usual assumption that the legislature is simply "adjusting the benefits and burdens of economic life," in a manner that secures an "average reciprocity

---

7. Regrettably, the rhetorical force of our "deprivation of all economically feasible use" rule is greater than its precision, since the rule does not make clear the "property interest" against which the loss of value is to be measured. When, for example, a regulation requires a developer to leave 90% of a rural tract in its natural state, it is unclear whether we would analyze the situation as one in which the owner has been deprived of all economically beneficial use of the burdened portion of the tract, or as one in which the owner has suffered a mere diminution in value of the tract as a whole. Unsurprisingly, this uncertainty regarding the composition of the denominator in our "deprivation" fraction has produced inconsistent pronouncements by the Court. Compare Pennsylvania Coal Co. v. Mahon, 260 U.S. 393, 414 (1922) (law restricting subsurface extraction of coal held to effect a taking), with Keystone Bituminous Coal Assn. v. DeBenedictis, 480 U.S. 470, 497-502 (1987) (nearly identical law held not to effect a taking); see also id., at 515-520 (Rehnquist, C.J., dissenting). The answer to this difficult question may lie in how the owner's reasonable expectations have been shaped by the State's law of property—i.e., whether and to what degree the State's law has accorded legal recognition and protection to the particular interest in land with respect to which the takings claimant alleges a diminution in (or elimination of) value. In any event, we avoid this difficulty in the present case, since the "interest in land" that Lucas has pleaded (a fee simple interest) is an estate with a rich tradition of protection at common law, and since the South Carolina Court of Common Pleas found that the Beachfront Management Act left each of Lucas' beachfront lots without economic value.

of advantage" to everyone concerned. And the functional basis for permitting the government, by regulation, to affect property values without compensation—that "Government hardly could go on if to some extent values incident to property could not be diminished without paying for every such change in the general law,"—does not apply to the relatively rare situations where the government has deprived a landowner of all economically beneficial uses.

On the other side of the balance, affirmatively supporting a compensation requirement, is the fact that regulations that leave the owner of land without economically beneficial or productive options for its use—typically, as here, by requiring land to be left substantially in its natural state—carry with them a heightened risk that private property is being pressed into some form of public service under the guise of mitigating serious public harm. . . .

We think, in short, that there are good reasons for our frequently expressed belief that when the owner of real property has been called upon to sacrifice *all* economically beneficial uses in the name of the common good, that is, to leave his property economically idle, he has suffered a taking.[8]

B

The trial court found Lucas' two beachfront lots to have been rendered valueless by respondent's enforcement of the coastal-zone construction ban. Under Lucas' theory of the case, which rested upon our "no economically viable use" statements, that finding entitled him to compensation. Lucas believed it unnecessary to take issue with either the purposes behind the Beachfront Management Act, or the means chosen by the South Carolina Legislature to effectuate those purposes. The South Carolina Supreme Court, however, thought otherwise. In its view, the Beachfront Management Act was no ordinary enactment, but involved an exercise of South Carolina's "police powers" to mitigate the harm to the public interest that petitioner's use of his land might occasion. By neglecting to dispute the findings enumerated in the Act or otherwise to challenge the legislature's purposes, petitioner "conceded that the beach/dune area of South Carolina's shores is an extremely valuable public resource; that the erection of new construction, inter alia, contributes to the erosion and destruction of this public resource; and that discouraging new construction in close proximity to the beach/dune area is necessary to prevent a great public

---

8. Justice Stevens criticizes the "deprivation of all economically beneficial use" rule as "wholly arbitrary," in that "[the] landowner whose property is diminished in value 95% recovers nothing," while the landowner who suffers a complete elimination of value "recovers the land's full value." Post, at 4. This analysis errs in its assumption that the landowner whose deprivation is one step short of complete is not entitled to compensation. Such an owner might not be able to claim the benefit of our categorical formulation, but, as we have acknowledged time and again, "the economic impact of the regulation on the claimant and . . . the extent to which the regulation has interfered with distinct investment-backed expectations" are keenly relevant to takings analysis generally. Penn Central Transportation Co. v. New York City, 438 U.S. 104, 124 (1978). It is true that in at least *some* cases the landowner with 95% loss will get nothing, while the landowner with total loss will recover in full. But that occasional result is no more strange than the gross disparity between the landowner whose premises are taken for a highway (who recovers in full) and the landowner whose property is reduced to 5% of its former value by the highway (who recovers nothing). Takings law is full of these "all-or-nothing" situations.

harm." In the court's view, these concessions brought petitioner's challenge within a long line of this Court's cases sustaining against Due Process and Takings Clause challenges the State's use of its "police powers" to enjoin a property owner from activities akin to public nuisances. See Mugler v. Kansas, 123 U.S. 623 (1887) (law prohibiting manufacture of alcoholic beverages); Hadacheck v. Sebastian, 239 U.S. 394 (1915) (law barring operation of brick mill in residential area); Miller v. Schoene, 276 U.S. 272 (1928) (order to destroy diseased cedar trees to prevent infection of nearby orchards); Goldblatt v. Hempstead, 369 U.S. 590 (1962) (law effectively preventing continued operation of quarry in residential area).

It is correct that many of our prior opinions have suggested that "harmful or noxious uses" of property may be proscribed by government regulation without the requirement of compensation. For a number of reasons, however, we think the South Carolina Supreme Court was too quick to conclude that that principle decides the present case. The "harmful or noxious uses" principle was the Court's early attempt to describe in theoretical terms why government may, consistent with the Takings Clause, affect property values by regulation without incurring an obligation to compensate—a reality we nowadays acknowledge explicitly with respect to the full scope of the State's police power. . . .

"Harmful or noxious use" analysis was, in other words, simply the progenitor of our more contemporary statements that "'land-use regulation does not effect a taking if it substantially advances legitimate state interests.'" *Nollan*, supra, at 834 (quoting *Agins*).

The transition from our early focus on control of "noxious" uses to our contemporary understanding of the broad realm within which government may regulate without compensation was an easy one, since the distinction between "harm-preventing" and "benefit-conferring" regulation is often in the eye of the beholder. It is quite possible, for example, to describe in *either* fashion the ecological, economic, and aesthetic concerns that inspired the South Carolina legislature in the present case. One could say that imposing a servitude on Lucas' land is necessary in order to prevent his use of it from "harming" South Carolina's ecological resources; or, instead, in order to achieve the "benefits" of an ecological preserve. . . . Whether one or the other of the competing characterizations will come to one's lips in a particular case depends primarily upon one's evaluation of the worth of competing uses of real estate. . . . [12]

[N]oxious-use logic cannot serve as a touchstone to distinguish regulatory "takings"—which require compensation—from regulatory deprivations that do not require compensation. A fortiori, the legislature's recitation of a noxious-use justification cannot be the basis for departing from our categorical rule that total regulatory takings must be compensated. If it were, departure would virtually always be allowed. The South Carolina Supreme Court's approach would essentially nullify *Mahon*'s affirmation of limits to the noncompensable exercise of the police power. Our cases provide no support for this: None of them that employed the logic of "harmful use" prevention to sustain a regulation involved an allegation that the regulation wholly eliminated the value of the claimant's land.

---

12. In Justice Blackmun's view, even with respect to regulations that deprive an owner of all developmental or economically beneficial land uses, the test for required compensation is whether the legislature has recited a harm-preventing justification for its action. Since such a justification can be formulated in practically every case, this amounts to a test of whether the legislature has a stupid staff. We think the Takings Clause requires courts to do more than insist upon artful harm-preventing characterizations.

Where the State seeks to sustain regulation that deprives land of all economically beneficial use, we think it may resist compensation only if the logically antecedent inquiry into the nature of the owner's estate shows that the proscribed use interests were not part of his title to begin with. This accords, we think, with our "takings" jurisprudence, which has traditionally been guided by the understandings of our citizens regarding the content of, and the State's power over, the "bundle of rights" that they acquire when they obtain title to property. It seems to us that the property owner necessarily expects the uses of his property to be restricted, from time to time, by various measures newly enacted by the State in legitimate exercise of its police powers; "as long recognized, some values are enjoyed under an implied limitation and must yield to the police power." *Pennsylvania Coal Co. v. Mahon*, 260 U.S., at 413. And in the case of personal property, by reason of the State's traditionally high degree of control over commercial dealings, he ought to be aware of the possibility that new regulation might even render his property economically worthless (at least if the property's only economically productive use is sale or manufacture for sale), see Andrus v. Allard, 444 U.S. 51, 66-67 (1979) (prohibition on sale of eagle feathers). In the case of land, however, we think the notion pressed by the Council that title is somehow held subject to the "implied limitation" that the State may subsequently eliminate all economically valuable use is inconsistent with the historical compact recorded in the Takings Clause that has become part of our constitutional culture. . . .

Where "permanent physical occupation" of land is concerned, we have refused to allow the government to decree it anew (without compensation), no matter how weighty the asserted "public interests" involved, Loretto v. Teleprompter Manhattan CATV Corp., 458 U.S., at 426—though we assuredly would permit the government to assert a permanent easement that was a preexisting limitation upon the landowner's title. We believe similar treatment must be accorded confiscatory regulation, i.e., regulations that prohibit all economically beneficial use of land: Any limitation so severe cannot be newly legislated or decreed (without compensation), but must inhere in the title itself, in the restrictions that background principles of the State's law of property and nuisance already place upon land ownership. A law or decree with such an effect must, in other words, do no more than duplicate the result that could have been achieved in the courts—by adjacent landowners (or other uniquely affected persons) under the State's law of private nuisance, or by the State under its complementary power to abate nuisances that affect the public generally, or otherwise.

On this analysis, the owner of a lake bed, for example, would not be entitled to compensation when he is denied the requisite permit to engage in a landfilling operation that would have the effect of flooding others' land. Nor the corporate owner of a nuclear generating plant, when it is directed to remove all improvements from its land upon discovery that the plant sits astride an earthquake fault. Such regulatory action may well have the effect of eliminating the land's only economically productive use, but it does not proscribe a proactive use that was previously permissible under relevant property and nuisance principles. The use of these properties for what are now expressly prohibited purposes was *always* unlawful, and (subject to other constitutional limitations) it was open to the State at any point to make the implication of those background principles of nuisance and property law explicit. . . . When, however, a regulation that declares "off-limits" all economically productive or beneficial uses of land goes beyond what the relevant background principles would dictate, compensation must be paid to sustain it.

The "total taking" inquiry we require today will ordinarily entail (as the application of state nuisance law ordinarily entails) analysis of, among other things, the degree of harm to public lands and resources, or adjacent private property, posed by the claimant's proposed activities, see, e.g., Restatement (Second) of Torts §§826, 827, the social value of the claimant's activities and their suitability to the locality in question, see, e.g., id., §§828(a) and (b), 831, and the relative ease with which the alleged harm can be avoided through measures taken by the claimant and the government (or adjacent private landowners) alike, see, e.g., id., §§827(e), 828(c), 830. The fact that a particular use has long been engaged in by similarly situated owners ordinarily imports a lack of any common-law prohibition (though changed circumstances or new knowledge may make what was previously permissible no longer so, see Restatement (Second) of Torts, supra, §827, comment g). So also does the fact that other landowners, similarly situated, are permitted to continue the use denied to the claimant.

It seems unlikely that common-law principles would have prevented the erection of any habitable or productive improvements on petitioner's land; they rarely support prohibition of the "essential use" of land. The question, however, is one of state law to be dealt with on remand. We emphasize that to win its case South Carolina must do more than proffer the legislature's declaration that the uses Lucas desires are inconsistent with the public interest, or the conclusory assertion that they violate a common-law maxim such as *sic utere tuo ut alienum non laedas*. As we have said, a "State, by *ipse dixit*, may not transform private property into public property without compensation. . . ." Webb's Fabulous Pharmacies, Inc. v. Beckwith. Instead, as it would be required to do if it sought to restrain Lucas in a common-law action for public nuisance, South Carolina must identify background principles of nuisance and property law that prohibit the uses he now intends in the circumstances in which the property is presently found. Only on this showing can the State fairly claim that, in proscribing all such beneficial uses, the Beachfront Management Act is taking nothing. . . .[18]

The judgment is reversed and the case remanded for proceedings not inconsistent with this opinion.

JUSTICE KENNEDY, concurring in the judgment.
 . . . The South Carolina Court of Common Pleas found that petitioner's real property has been rendered valueless by the State's regulation. The finding appears to presume that the property has no significant market value or resale potential. This is a curious finding, and I share the reservations of some of my colleagues about a finding that a beachfront lot loses all value because of a development restriction. . . . While the Supreme Court of South Carolina on remand need not consider the case subject to this constraint; we must accept the finding as entered below. See Oklahoma City v. Tuttle, 471 U.S. 808, 816 (1985). Accepting

---

18. Justice Blackmun decries our reliance on background nuisance principles at least in part because he believes those principles to be as manipulable as we find the "harm prevention"/"benefit conferral" dichotomy. There is no doubt some leeway in a court's interpretation of what existing state law permits—but not remotely as much, we think, as in a legislative crafting of the reasons for its confiscatory regulation. We stress that an affirmative decree eliminating all economically beneficial uses may be defended only if an *objectively reasonable application* of relevant precedents would exclude those beneficial uses in the circumstances in which the land is presently found.

the finding as entered, it follows that petitioner is entitled to invoke the line of cases discussing regulations that deprive real property of all economic value. See *Agins.*

The finding of no value must be considered under the Takings Clause by reference to the owner's reasonable, investment-backed expectations. . . .

There is an inherent tendency towards circularity in this synthesis, of course; for if the owner's reasonable expectations are shaped by what courts allow as a proper exercise of governmental authority, property tends to become what courts say it is. Some circularity must be tolerated in these matters, however, as it is in other spheres. E.g., Katz v. United States, 389 U.S. 347 (1967) (Fourth Amendment protections defined by reasonable expectations of privacy). The definition, moreover, is not circular in its entirety. The expectations protected by the Constitution are based on objective rules and customs that can be understood as reasonable by all parties involved.

In my view, reasonable expectations must be understood in light of the whole of our legal tradition. The common law of nuisance is too narrow a confine for the exercise of regulatory power in a complex and interdependent society. The State should not be prevented from enacting new regulatory initiatives in response to changing conditions, and courts must consider all reasonable expectations whatever their source. The Takings Clause does not require a static body of state property law; it protects private expectations to ensure private investment. I agree with the Court that nuisance prevention accords with the most common expectations of property owners who face regulation, but I do not believe this can be the sole source of state authority to impose severe restrictions. Coastal property may present such unique concerns for a fragile land system that the State can go further in regulating its development and use than the common law of nuisance might otherwise permit.

The Supreme Court of South Carolina erred, in my view, by reciting the general purposes for which the state regulations were enacted without a determination that they were in accord with the owner's reasonable expectations and therefore sufficient to support a severe restriction on specific parcels of property. The promotion of tourism, for instance, ought not to suffice to deprive specific property of all value without a corresponding duty to compensate. Furthermore, the means as well as the ends of regulation must accord with the owner's reasonable expectations. Here, the State did not act until after the property had been zoned for individual lot development and most other parcels had been improved, throwing the whole burden of the regulation on the remaining lots. This too must be measured in the balance. See *Mahon.*

JUSTICE BLACKMUN, dissenting. . . .

. . . If the state legislature is correct that the prohibition on building in front of the setback line prevents serious harm, then, under this Court's prior cases, the Act is constitutional. "Long ago it was recognized that all property in this country is held under the implied obligation that the owner's use of it shall not be injurious to the community, and the Takings Clause did not transform that principle to one that requires compensation whenever the State asserts its power to enforce it." *Keystone,* 480 U.S. at 491-492 (1987). The Court consistently has upheld regulations imposed to arrest a significant threat to the common welfare, whatever their economic effect on the owner. See, e.g., *Goldblatt; Euclid v. Ambler Realty Co.,* 272 U.S. 365 (1926); *Gorieb v. Fox,* 274 U.S. 603, 608 (1927); *Mugler v. Kansas,* 123 U.S. 623 (1887). . . .

This Court repeatedly has recognized the ability of government, in certain circumstances, to regulate property without compensation no matter how adverse the financial effect on the owner may be. More than a century ago, the Court explicitly upheld the right of States to prohibit uses of property injurious to public health, safety, or welfare without paying compensation: "A prohibition simply upon the use of property for purposes that are declared, by valid legislation, to be injurious to the health, morals, or safety of the community, cannot, in any just sense, be deemed a taking or an appropriation of property." Mugler v. Kansas. On this basis, the Court upheld an ordinance effectively prohibiting operation of a previously lawful brewery, although the "establishments will become of no value as property." Id.

Mugler was only the beginning in a long line of cases. . . .

Ultimately even the Court cannot embrace the full implications of its per se rule: It eventually agrees that there cannot be a categorical rule for a taking based on economic value that wholly disregards the public need asserted. Instead, the Court decides that it will permit a State to regulate all economic value only if the State prohibits uses that would not be permitted under "background principles of nuisance and property law."

Until today, the Court explicitly had rejected the contention that the government's power to act without paying compensation turns on whether the prohibited activity is a common-law nuisance. The brewery closed in *Mugler* itself was not a common-law nuisance, and the Court specifically stated that it was the role of the legislature to determine what measures would be appropriate for the protection of public health and safety. In upholding the state action in *Miller [v. Schoene]*, the Court found it unnecessary to "weigh with nicety the question whether the infected cedars constitute a nuisance according to common law; or whether they may be so declared by statute." Instead the Court has relied in the past, as the South Carolina Court has done here, on legislative judgments of what constitutes a harm.

The Court rejects the notion that the State always can prohibit uses it deems a harm to the public without granting compensation because "the distinction between 'harm-preventing' and 'benefit-conferring' regulation is often in the eye of the beholder." Since the characterization will depend "primarily upon one's evaluation of the worth of competing uses of real estate," the Court decides a legislative judgment of this kind no longer can provide the desired "objective, value-free basis" for upholding a regulation. The Court, however, fails to explain how its proposed common law alternative escapes the same trap.

The threshold inquiry for imposition of the Court's new rule, "deprivation of all economically valuable use," itself cannot be determined objectively. As the Court admits, whether the owner has been deprived of all economic value of his property will depend on how "property" is defined. The "composition of the denominator in our 'deprivation' fraction," is the dispositive inquiry. Yet there is no "objective" way to define what that denominator should be. "We have long understood that any land-use regulation can be characterized as the 'total' deprivation of an aptly defined entitlement. . . . Alternatively, the same regulation can always be characterized as a mere partial withdrawal from full, unencumbered ownership of the landholding affected by the regulation. . . ." Michelman, Takings, 1987, 88 Colum. L. Rev. 1600, 1614 (1988).

The Court's decision in *Keystone Bituminous Coal* illustrates this principle perfectly. In *Keystone*, the Court determined that the "support estate" was "merely a part of the entire bundle of rights possessed by the owner." Thus, the Court concluded that the support estate's destruction merely eliminated one segment of the total property. Ibid. The dissent, however, characterized the support estate as a distinct property interest that was wholly destroyed. The Court could agree on no "value-free basis" to resolve this dispute.

Even more perplexing, however, is the Court's reliance on common-law principles of nuisance in its quest for a value-free takings jurisprudence. In determining what is a nuisance at common law, state courts make exactly the decision that the Court finds so troubling when made by the South Carolina General Assembly today: they determine whether the use is harmful. Common-law public and private nuisance law is simply a determination whether a particular use causes harm. See Prosser, Private Action for Public Nuisance, 52 Va. L. Rev. 997, 997 (1966) (*"Nuisance* is a French word which means nothing more than harm"). There is nothing magical in the reasoning of judges long dead. They determined a harm in the same way as state judges and legislatures do today. If judges in the 18th and 19th centuries can distinguish a harm from a benefit, why not judges in the 20th century, and if judges can, why not legislators? There simply is no reason to believe that new interpretations of the hoary common-law nuisance doctrine will be particularly "objective" or "value-free." Once one abandons the level of generality of *sic utere tuo ut alienum non laedas*, one searches in vain, I think, for anything resembling a principle in the common law of nuisance. . . .

I dissent.

[The separate dissent by JUSTICE STEVENS is omitted.]

[JUSTICE SOUTER filed a statement stating that he would dismiss the writ of certiorari as improvidently granted on the ground that the trial court's conclusion that Lucas' land was totally deprived of value was extremely questionable viewing the record as a whole. In his view, this deprived the Court of the ability to clarify the meaning of "total taking," and thus so impaired the ability of the Court to proceed that it should dismiss.]

NOTES AND QUESTIONS

1. **Total Takings.** Justice Blackmun chides the majority for, among other things, articulating a rule of law applicable only in "extraordinary circumstances." These circumstances, namely, a statute's totally depriving property of value, rendering it "valueless," had never arisen in a Supreme Court decision before. In announcing a categorical approach to a certain class of takings cases, what precisely is the Court's definition of that category? Does Justice Scalia's reference to "beneficial or *productive* options" imply that complete destruction of the property's value may not be required for an action to fall within this category?

2. **Other-Than-Total Takings.** What formulation of takings doctrine does *Lucas* suggest is to be applied to regulatory situations that fall outside this category of severe limitations on property rights? Responding to an observation by Justice Stevens that it is anomalous that someone who loses 95 percent of a property's value is entitled to no compensation, Justice Scalia in note 8 states that it is erroneous to assume that a "landowner whose deprivation is one step short of complete is not entitled to compensation." He notes that "[s]uch an

owner might not be able to claim the benefit of our categorical formulation," but he suggests that *Penn Central*'s "interfere[nce] with distinct investment-backed expectations" analysis might be "keenly relevant."

Insofar as Justice Scalia's opinion provides any clues about the jurisprudence outside the total takings category, it is truly delphic. Indeed, it is possible to read part of it as *relaxing* takings doctrine in cases of total takings. After quoting a portion of Justice Brennan's opinion in *Penn Central*, in which the Court refused to subject New York City's landmark preservation law to more severe scrutiny because it confers a benefit on society instead of preventing a harm to society (a nuisance), Justice Scalia writes that "harmful or noxious use" analysis was simply a progenitor of the Court's contemporary statements that "land-use regulation does not effect a taking if it substantially advances legitimate state interests," quoting from his own opinion in *Nollan* (which quotes from *Agins*). If that remark is to be taken literally, it means that a substantial connection to a legitimate state interest *always* saves a regulation from the requirement of compensation regardless of the extent of private deprivation or interference with reasonable investment-backed expectations. It would thus seem to be at least a partial rejection of the three-factor formulation of takings doctrine enunciated in *Penn Central* itself, pursuant to which the takings question turned on the character of the governmental action, its interference with reasonable investment-backed expectations, and the economic impact of the action. Most analysts have interpreted this to mean that each of these factors is relevant in all takings analyses, save for those few areas where categorical analysis takes over (permanent physical occupations, *Teleprompter*, and total takings, *Lucas*).

3. **Deprivation of Value and the "Nuisance Exception."** Without saying so explicitly, Justice Scalia's opinion adopts major portions of Chief Justice Rehnquist's dissents in several important prior cases, especially *Penn Central* and *Keystone Bituminous Coal*, thus indicating that the majority coalition on the Court has indeed shifted to a new, more property-protecting, position. In each of these earlier decisions, the Chief Justice had urged that the so-called nuisance exception to the requirement to compensate for taking private property was narrower than that suggested by the Court majorities. In his view, the Court had become too lax in accepting government arguments that regulation was necessary to prevent a harm to the public, to the degree that the concept of harm prevention had become practically coterminous with the police power, insofar as anything that the government did under the police power to promote the public health, welfare, and morals could be articulated as a regulation preventing harm to the public health, welfare, and morals. He suggested that common law nuisance principles were the appropriate delimiters of the "nuisance exception."

The second objection the Chief Justice made in these two cases was to disagree with the premise that successfully invoking the nuisance exception meant that compensation never had to be paid. "Though nuisance regulations have been sustained despite a substantial reduction in value," he said in *Keystone*, "we have not accepted the proposition that the State may completely extinguish a property interest or prohibit all use without providing compensation."

It was this second objection of the Chief Justice's, coupled with the changed composition of the Court, that supplied Lucas' litigation strategy: In his brief, Lucas insisted that a person who has been deprived of all economically viable use of land is *always* entitled to compensation, whether or not the state is regulating a common law nuisance. This explains why he did not challenge the state's purposes in enacting the coastal zone protection legislation—debating the validity or nature of those purposes was irrelevant to his theory of the case.

In a significant amicus brief in *support* of Lucas written by Richard Epstein, the Institute for Justice rejected Lucas' theory and stressed the first of Justice Rehnquist's arguments: The "nuisance exception" had to be limited to traditional common law nuisances. Professor Epstein's theory was that compensation must be paid whenever government takes *any* "private property," unless it can justify the regulation as an exercise of common law nuisance principles. The extent of diminution is irrelevant; partial takings are as unconstitutional as total takings.

Justice Scalia's opinion for the *Lucas* majority is an interesting variation on these arguments. He announces that regulations that deprive owners of "all economically beneficial use of land" are a special category as to which the government must pay compensation unless it shows a justification under background principles of nuisance and property law, a category slightly larger than that proposed by Professor Epstein. He also agrees with Epstein's position and Chief Justice Rehnquist's earlier opinions by taking the crucial issue of characterizing the government's purpose out of the hands of the legislature and placing it in the hands of the courts. In permitting a showing of consistency with background nuisance principles to obviate compensation, Justice Scalia's opinion appears to diverge from the Chief Justice's earlier views, which were that total deprivation always required compensation. However, it may be that the Chief Justice concluded that as a matter of actual application, nuisance principles will never, or almost never, justify total deprivations, and thus that he was not shifting ground too much in signing onto Justice Scalia's opinion.

4. **The Remand in *Lucas*.** Because the case had not been litigated on the theory adopted by the Supreme Court, it was remanded for further proceedings. On remand, the lawyers for South Carolina Coastal Council believed that they would not be precluded from litigating the issue of valuelessness, and were confident that Lucas would not be owed compensation. They also hoped that the coastal zone construction restrictions could satisfy the nuisance test laid down by the Court. Justice Stevens' omitted opinion stressed his belief that such restrictions may satisfy the majority's formulation, noting that the 29 deaths and more than $6 billion in property damage suffered in South Carolina from the effects of Hurricane Hugo in 1989—effects the state argues would have been mitigated if fewer coastal properties were developed—provide a substantial harm-prevention justification, which may pass muster. However, a change in membership had occurred on the South Carolina Supreme Court since it first decided *Lucas*, and on remand the court brushed aside the arguments of the Coastal Council. Without discussing whether Lucas had been deprived of all the value of his property, the court stated in conclusory fashion:

> Coastal Council has not persuaded us that any common law basis exists by which it could restrain Lucas' desired use of his land; nor has our research uncovered any such common law principle. We hold that the sole issue on remand from this Court to the circuit level is a determination of the actual damages Lucas has sustained as the result of his being temporarily deprived of the use of his property. [Lucas v. South Carolina Coastal Council, 424 S.E.2d 484, 486 (S.C. 1992).]

In 1993, the South Carolina Coastal Council agreed to grant Lucas conditional approval to build on his property. Nevertheless, he pursued a temporary takings claim in state court. In July 1993, the Coastal Council settled the litigation by agreeing to purchase Lucas' land for $850,000 plus $725,000 for interest, attorneys' fees, and costs, for a total settlement of $1,575,000. In February 1994 the state resold Lucas' lots. In the fall of 1994 a house was built on the western lot. Two years later, severe coastal erosion undermined the house built on the Lucas lot and an adjacent home. Sand bags, sand scraping, and beach nourishment were used to protect the structures. The beach is now recovering, but homeowners are seeking to overturn the state's ban on the use of new hard erosion control devices. See Jones et al., *Lucas v. South Carolina Coastal Council*, Revisited, in Proceedings of the 22nd Annual Conference, Association of State Floodplain Managers 138 (1998). See also Notes 1 and 2 on pages 793-794, infra.

5. **Less-Than-Total Takings after *Lucas*.** While *Lucas* is, by its terms, limited to enunciating the doctrine applicable to total takings, lower courts may well combine Justice Scalia's general logic with Justice Stevens' mocking of the distinction between 100 percent and 95 percent deprivation as arbitrary, to apply the same analysis outside the category. If that occurs, takings doctrine will be creeping toward Professor Epstein's position. Epstein, however, is not so confident. He believes that *Lucas* "appears to have adopted a powerful 'hands off' attitude to all forms of partial restriction on land use—a subject that dwarfs the importance of the peculiar circumstances of *Lucas*, the total wipeout of all land uses." Epstein, Yee v. City of Escondido: The Supreme Court Strikes Out Again, 26 Loyola L.A. L. Rev. 3 (1992). Epstein despairs that "the inexorable flow of decided cases under the Takings Clause has been ever more supportive of big government and ever less respectful to the place of private property in our government regime." Id. at 22.

6. **Evolving Conceptions of Property Rights and Environmental Harm.** Recall from Chapter 2 that one of the motivations for legislation in the area of environmental degradation has been a dissatisfaction with the capacity of the common law to mediate between individual property rights and emerging environmental harm in a manner that adequately respects modern concerns about environmental quality. The 1973 CEQ report emphasized the need for changing our understanding of what constitutes "reasonable use" of private property in light of environmental considerations. Does the majority opinion in *Lucas* inhibit the ability of legislatures legitimately to adjust private and public rights and responsibilities to accommodate changing conceptions of "reasonable use"?

Justice Scalia at least recognizes that common law notions of reasonable use must adjust to changed circumstances. He states that "[t]he fact that a particular use has long been engaged in by similarly situated owners ordinarily imports a lack of any common-law prohibition (though changed circumstances or new knowledge may make what was previously permissible no longer so, see Restatement (Second) of Torts, §827, comment g)." 505 U.S. at 1025. Comment g notes that changes in the character of a locality over time may make a particular land use "wholly unsuited to that locality twenty years later." It does not discuss the possibility that new scientific understanding (e.g., concerning the impact of development on nonpoint source pollution) might justify a finding that an activity long thought to be unobjectionable (e.g., building a home in a critical area) creates a nuisance.

Are only common law notions of harm worthy of the Court's respect? In his concurrence, Justice Kennedy states that "[t]he State should not be prevented from enacting new regulatory initiatives in response to changing conditions, and courts must consider all reasonable expectations whatever their source. The Takings Clause does not require a static body of state property law."

505 U.S. at 1035 (Kennedy, J., concurring). How does this view differ from Justice Scalia's? What regulatory initiatives would Justice Kennedy be more inclined to uphold?

7. **Burdens of Proof of Environmental Harm.** Justice Scalia's fondness for common law principles of nuisance seems to be founded on the notion that legislators are not to be trusted to make honest legislative findings of environmental harm. In footnote 12 he observes that since a "harm-preventing justification . . . can be formulated in practically every case, this amounts to a test of whether the legislature has a stupid staff." 505 U.S. at 1026 n.12. Justice Kennedy seems willing to give legislators more leeway, though he does not think they acted properly in *Lucas*. After *Lucas*, under what circumstances could legislative findings that development in a critical area would create a nuisance avoid takings problems like those encountered by South Carolina's Beachfront Management Act?

8. **Real Property, Personal Property, and Investor Expectations.** Real estate is not the only kind of property whose value may be profoundly altered by government policy decisions. Investors bold enough to place their entire investment portfolios in interest rate options could easily lose everything if they guess wrong about the Federal Reserve Board's future policies. Yet such investors clearly are not entitled to compensation even though government action adjusting interest rates effectively can destroy the value of their property. Why then is real property entitled to special constitutional protection not afforded personal property? Justice Scalia appears to rely on investor expectations as the justification for this distinction. He states that "in the case of personal property, by reason of the State's traditionally high degree of control over commercial dealings, [the investor] ought to be aware of the possibility that new regulation might even render his property economically worthless." 505 U.S. at 1027-1028. If investor expectations are the key to takings analysis, is a state free to change its conception of property law to alter what expectations concerning the risk of future regulation are reasonable? Richard Epstein argues that a major problem with *Lucas* is the Court's "failure to explain the relationship between expectations and entitlements" and that society should seek to determine what set of entitlements maximizes social welfare. Epstein, Lucas v. South Carolina Coastal Council: A Tangled Web of Expectations, 45 Stan. L. Rev. 1369, 1371 (1993).

9. How would Just v. Marinette County be decided under the *Lucas* rationale? Joseph Sax argues that *Lucas* may "be viewed as the Court's long-delayed answer" to *Just*. In his view, Justice Scalia "recognizes the emerging view of land as part of an ecosystem, rather than as purely private property," but sought to send a "clear message" limiting its application: "States may not regulate land use solely by requiring landowners to maintain their property in its natural state as part of a functioning ecosystem, even though those natural functions may be important to the ecosystem." Sax, Property Rights and the Economy of Nature: Understanding *Lucas v. South Carolina Coastal Council*, 45 Stan. L. Rev. 1433, 1438 (1993).

10. Considerable additional background information on the *Lucas* case is provided in Carol M. Rose, The Story of Lucas: Environmental Land Use Regulation Between Developers and the Deep Blue Sea, in Environmental Law Stories 237 (Lazarus & Houck eds., 2005). Information concerning what the papers of the late Justice Harry A. Blackmun reveal about the Court's deliberations in *Lucas* and the takings decisions that preceded it is provided in Robert V. Percival, Environmental Law in the Supreme Court: Highlights from the Blackmun Papers, 35 Envtl. L. Rep. 10637, 10651-10657 (2005).

The Impact of Post-Regulation Acquisition
of Property: The *Palazzolo* Case

While *Lucas* spawned a new wave of regulatory takings litigation, few property owners have been able to make successful takings claims because regulation usually cannot be shown to deprive real estate of all its economic value. See, e.g., Florida Rock Industries, Inc. v. United States, 18 F.3d 1560 (Fed. Cir. 1994) (vacating a judgment finding that a 95 percent reduction in property value constituted a regulatory taking); but see Loveladies Harbor, Inc. v. United States, 28 F.3d 1171 (Fed. Cir. 1994) (finding a taking by considering the relevant parcel to be only the portion of the property for which a permit was denied). Another frequent reason for dismissal of regulatory takings claims has been because the property was acquired after it already had become subject to regulation. For example, in Creppel v. United States, 41 F.3d 627 (Fed. Cir. 1994), the Federal Circuit declared that because claimants need to show interference with "investment-backed expectations," in its view takings doctrine "limits recovery to owners who can demonstrate that they bought their property in reliance on the nonexistence of the challenged regulation." As the court explained: "One who buys with knowledge of a restraint assumes the risk of economic loss. In such a case, the owner presumably paid a discounted price for the property. Compensating him for a 'taking' would confer a windfall." 41 F.3d at 632. See also Good v. United States, 189 F.3d 1355 (Fed. Cir. 1999) (owner who acquired property after the enactment of Section 404 of the Clean Water Act could not have had a reasonable expectation that he would obtain approval to fill ten acres of wetlands).

In June 2001, the U.S. Supreme Court rejected the notion that post-regulation acquisition of property serves as an automatic bar to regulatory takings claims. In the case below, the Court, by a 5 to 4 vote, reversed a decision by the Supreme Court of Rhode Island that had rejected a regulatory takings claim on this ground. The petitioner in the case, Anthony Palazzolo, owned waterfront property, almost all of which had been designated by the state as coastal wetlands that could not be developed without a permit due to enactment of a state coastal protection law in 1971. Palazzolo, whose company had purchased the property in 1959, acquired individual title to the property in 1978 by operation of law after the company's corporate charter was revoked for non-payment of taxes. After two of Palazzolo's development proposals for the property were rejected by state authorities, he filed an inverse condemnation action in state court, alleging a regulatory taking. The Rhode Island Supreme Court affirmed the trial court's rejection of Palazzolo's takings claims. The court held that the claims were not ripe, that they were barred by Palazzolo's post-regulation acquisition of the property, and that they failed to meet the *Lucas* test because the upland portion of the property retained $200,000 in development value. Palazzolo obtained review of this judgment by the U.S. Supreme Court, which rendered the decision below.

|| *Palazzolo v. Rhode Island* ||
|| **533 U.S. 606 (2001)** ||

JUSTICE KENNEDY delivered the opinion of the Court.

II

. . . Since [Pennsylvania Coal Co. v.] Mahon, [260 U.S. 393 (1922)], we have given some, but not too specific, guidance to courts confronted with deciding whether a particular government action goes too far and effects a regulatory taking. First, we have observed, with certain qualifications, that a regulation which "denies all economically beneficial or productive use of land" will require compensation under the Takings Clause. *Lucas*, 505 U.S., at 1015; see also id., at 1035 (Kennedy, J., concurring); Agins v. City of Tiburon, 447 U.S. 255, 261 (1980). Where a regulation places limitations on land that fall short of eliminating all economically beneficial use, a taking nonetheless may have occurred, depending on a complex of factors including the regulation's economic effect on the landowner, the extent to which the regulation interferes with reasonable investment-backed expectations, and the character of the government action. *Penn Central*, supra, at 124. These inquiries are informed by the purpose of the Takings Clause, which is to prevent the government from "forcing some people alone to bear public burdens which, in all fairness and justice, should be borne by the public as a whole." Armstrong v. United States, 364 U.S. 40, 49 (1960).

Petitioner seeks compensation under these principles. At the outset, however, we face the two threshold considerations invoked by the state court to bar the claim: ripeness, and acquisition which postdates the regulation.

A

[The Court then rejected the Rhode Island Supreme Court's conclusion that Palazzolo's taking claim was not ripe for review. After reviewing its decision in Williamson County Regional Planning Comm'n v. Hamilton Bank of Johnson City, 473 U.S. 172 (1985), and Suitum v. Tahoe Regional Planning Agency, 520 U.S. 725 (1997), the Court explained:]

These cases stand for the important principle that a landowner may not establish a taking before a land-use authority has the opportunity, using its own reasonable procedures, to decide and explain the reach of a challenged regulation. Under our ripeness rules a takings claim based on a law or regulation which is alleged to go too far in burdening property depends upon the land-owner's first having followed reasonable and necessary steps to allow regulatory agencies to exercise their full discretion in considering development plans for the property, including the opportunity to grant any variances or waivers allowed by law. As a general rule, until these ordinary processes have been followed the extent of the restriction on property is not known and a regulatory taking has not yet been established. See *Suitum*, supra, at 736, and n. 10 (noting difficulty of demonstrating that "mere enactment" of regulations restricting land use effects a taking). Government authorities, of course, may not burden property by imposition of repetitive or unfair land-use procedures in order to avoid a final decision. Monterey v. Del Monte Dunes at Monterey, Ltd., 526 U.S. 687 (1999).

With respect to the wetlands on petitioner's property, the Council's decisions make plain that the agency interpreted its regulations to bar petitioner from engaging in any filling or development activity on the wetlands, a fact reinforced by the Attorney General's forthright responses to our questioning during oral argument in this case. The rulings of the Council interpreting the regulations at issue, and the briefs, arguments, and candid statements by counsel for both sides, leave no doubt on this point: On the wetlands there can be no fill for any ordinary land use. There can be no fill for its own sake; no fill for a beach club, either rustic or upscale; no fill for a subdivision; no fill for any likely or foreseeable use. And with no fill there can be no structures and no development on the wetlands. Further permit applications were not necessary to establish this point.

As noted above, however, not all of petitioner's parcel constitutes protected wetlands. The trial court accepted uncontested testimony that an upland site located at the eastern end of the property would have an estimated value of $200,000 if developed. While Council approval is required to develop upland property which lies within 200 feet of protected waters, see CRMP §100.1(A), the strict "compelling public purpose" test does not govern proposed land uses on property in this classification, see id., §110, Table 1A, §120. Council officials testified at trial, moreover, that they would have allowed petitioner to build a residence on the upland parcel. . . . So there is no genuine ambiguity in the record as to the extent of permitted development on petitioner's property, either on the wetlands or the uplands. . . .

B

We turn to the second asserted basis for declining to address petitioner's takings claim on the merits. When the Council promulgated its wetlands regulations, the disputed parcel was owned not by petitioner but by the corporation of which he was sole shareholder. When title was transferred to petitioner by operation of law, the wetlands regulations were in force. The state court held the postregulation acquisition of title was fatal to the claim for deprivation of all economic use, 746 A.2d, at 716, and to the *Penn Central* claim, id., at 717. While the first holding was couched in terms of background principles of state property law, see *Lucas*, 505 U.S., at 1015, and the second in terms of petitioner's reasonable investment-backed expectations, see *Penn Central*, 438 U.S., at 124, the two holdings together amount to a single, sweeping, rule: A purchaser or a successive title holder like petitioner is deemed to have notice of an earlier-enacted restriction and is barred from claiming that it effects a taking.

The theory underlying the argument that post-enactment purchasers cannot challenge a regulation under the Takings Clause seems to run on these lines: Property rights are created by the State. See, e.g., Phillips v. Washington Legal Foundation, 524 U.S. 156, 163 (1998). So, the argument goes, by prospective legislation the State can shape and define property rights and reasonable investment-backed expectations, and subsequent owners cannot claim any injury from lost value. After all, they purchased or took title with notice of the limitation.

The State may not put so potent a Hobbesian stick into the Lockean bundle. The right to improve property, of course, is subject to the reasonable exercise of state authority, including the enforcement of valid zoning and land-use restrictions. See *Pennsylvania Coal Co.*, 260 U.S., at 413 ("Government hardly could go on if to some extent values incident to property could not be diminished without paying for every such change in the general law"). The Takings Clause, however, in certain circumstances allows a landowner to assert that a particular exercise of the State's regulatory power is so unreasonable or onerous as to compel compensation. Just as a prospective enactment, such as a new zoning ordinance, can limit the value of land without effecting a taking because it can be understood as reasonable by all concerned, other enactments are unreasonable and do not become less so through passage of time or title. Were we to accept the State's rule, the postenactment transfer of title would absolve the State of its obligation to defend any action restricting land use, no matter how extreme or unreasonable. A State would be allowed, in effect, to put an expiration date on the Takings Clause. This ought not to be the rule. Future generations, too, have a right to challenge unreasonable limitations on the use and value of land.

Nor does the justification of notice take into account the effect on owners at the time of enactment, who are prejudiced as well. Should an owner attempt to challenge a new regulation, but not survive the process of ripening his or her claim (which, as this case demonstrates, will often take years), under the proposed rule the right to compensation may not be asserted by an heir or successor, and so may not be asserted at all. The State's rule would work a critical alteration to the nature of property, as the newly regulated landowner is stripped of the ability to transfer the interest which was possessed prior to the regulation. The State may not by this means secure a windfall for itself. See Webb's Fabulous Pharmacies, Inc. v. Beckwith, 449 U.S. 155, 164 (1980) ("[A] State, by *ipse dixit*, may not transform private property into public property without compensation"); cf. Ellickson, Property in Land, 102 Yale L.J. 1315, 1368-1369 (1993) (right to transfer interest in land is a defining characteristic of the fee simple estate). The proposed rule is, furthermore, capricious in effect. The young owner contrasted with the older owner, the owner with the resources to hold contrasted with the owner with the need to sell, would be in different positions. The Takings Clause is not so quixotic. A blanket rule that purchasers with notice have no compensation right when a claim becomes ripe is too blunt an instrument to accord with the duty to compensate for what is taken.

Direct condemnation, by invocation of the State's power of eminent domain, presents different considerations than cases alleging a taking based on a burdensome regulation. In a direct condemnation action, or when a State has physically invaded the property without filing suit, the fact and extent of the taking are known. In such an instance, it is a general rule of the law of eminent domain that any award goes to the owner at the time of the taking, and that the right to compensation is not passed to a subsequent purchaser. See Danforth v. United States, 308 U.S. 271, 284 (1939); 2 Sackman, Eminent Domain, at §5.01 [5][d][i] ("It is well settled that when there is a taking of property by eminent domain in compliance with the law, it is the owner of the property *at the time of the taking* who is entitled to compensation"). A challenge to the application of a land-use regulation, by contrast, does not mature until ripeness requirements have been satisfied, under principles we have discussed; until this point an inverse condemnation claim alleging a regulatory taking cannot be maintained. It would be illogical, and unfair, to bar a regulatory takings claim because of the post-enactment transfer of ownership where the steps necessary to make the claim ripe were not taken, or could not have been taken, by a previous owner.

There is controlling precedent for our conclusion. Nollan v. California Coastal Comm'n, 483 U.S. 825 (1987), presented the question whether it was consistent with the Takings Clause for a state regulatory agency to require ocean-front landowners to provide lateral beach access to the public as the condition for a development permit. The principal dissenting opinion observed it was a policy of the California Coastal Commission to require the condition, and that the Nollans who purchased their home after the policy went into effect, were "on notice that new developments would be approved only if provisions were made for lateral beach access." Id., at 860 (Brennan, J., dissenting). A majority of the Court rejected the proposition. "So long as the Commission could not have deprived the prior owners of the easement without compensating them," the Court reasoned, "the prior owners must be understood to have transferred their full property rights in conveying the lot." Id., at 834, n.2.

It is argued that *Nollan*'s holding was limited by the later decision in Lucas v. South Carolina Coastal Council, 505 U.S. 1003 (1992). In *Lucas* the Court observed that a landowner's ability to recover for a government deprivation of all economically beneficial use of property is not absolute but instead is confined by limitations on the use of land which "inhere in the title itself." Id., at 1029. This is so, the Court reasoned, because the landowner is constrained by those "restrictions that background principles of the State's law of property and nuisance already place upon land ownership." Id., at 1029. It is asserted here that *Lucas* stands for the proposition that any new regulation, once enacted, becomes a background principle of property law which cannot be challenged by those who acquire title after the enactment.

We have no occasion to consider the precise circumstances when a legislative enactment can be deemed a background principle of state law or whether those circumstances are present here. It suffices to say that a regulation that otherwise would be unconstitutional absent compensation is not transformed into a background principle of the State's law by mere virtue of the passage of title. This relative standard would be incompatible with our description of the concept in *Lucas*, which is explained in terms of those common, shared understandings of permissible limitations derived from a State's legal tradition, see *Lucas*, supra, at 1029-1030. A regulation or common-law rule cannot be a background principle for some owners but not for others. The determination whether an existing, general law can limit all economic use of property must turn on objective factors, such as the nature of the land use proscribed. See *Lucas*, supra, at 1030. ("The 'total taking' inquiry we require today will ordinarily entail . . . analysis of, among other things, the degree of harm to public lands and resources, or adjacent private property, posed by the claimant's proposed activities.") A law does not become a background principle for subsequent owners by enactment itself. *Lucas* did not overrule our holding in *Nollan*, which, as we have noted, is based on essential Takings Clause principles.

For reasons we discuss next, the state court will not find it necessary to explore these matters on remand in connection with the claim that all economic use was deprived; it must address, however, the merits of petitioner's claim under *Penn Central*. That claim is not barred by the mere fact that title was acquired after the effective date of the state-imposed restriction.

III

As the case is ripe, and as the date of transfer of title does not bar petitioner's takings claim, we have before us the alternative ground relied upon by the Rhode Island Supreme Court in ruling upon the merits of the takings claims. It held that all economically beneficial use was not deprived because the uplands portion of the property can still be improved. On this point, we agree with the court's decision. Petitioner accepts the Council's contention and the state trial court's finding that his parcel retains $200,000 in development value under the State's wetlands regulations. He asserts, nonetheless, that he has suffered a total taking and contends the Council cannot sidestep the holding in *Lucas* "by the simple expedient of leaving a landowner a few crumbs of value." Brief for Petitioner 37.

Assuming a taking is otherwise established, a State may not evade the duty to compensate on the premise that the landowner is left with a token interest. This is not the situation of the landowner in this case, however. A regulation permitting a landowner to build a substantial residence on an 18-acre parcel does not leave the property "economically idle." *Lucas,* supra, at 1019.

In his brief submitted to us petitioner attempts to revive this part of his claim by refraining it. He argues, for the first time, that the upland parcel is distinct from the wetlands portions, so he should be permitted to assert a deprivation limited to the latter. This contention asks us to examine the difficult, persisting question of what is the proper denominator in the takings fraction. See Michelman, Property, Utility, and Fairness: Comments on the Ethical Foundations of "Just Compensation Law," 80 Harv. L. Rev. 1165, 1192 (1967). Some of our cases indicate that the extent of deprivation effected by a regulatory action is measured against the value of the parcel as a whole, see, e.g., Keystone Bituminous Coal Assn. v. DeBenedictis, 480 U.S. 470, 497 (1987); but we have at times expressed discomfort with the logic of this rule, see *Lucas,* supra, at 1016-1017, n. 7, a sentiment echoed by some commentators, see, e.g., Epstein, Takings: Descent and Resurrection, 1987 Sup. Ct. Rev. 1, 16-17 (1987); Fee, Unearthing the Denominator in Regulatory Takings Claims, 61 U. Chi. L. Rev. 1535 (1994). Whatever the merits of these criticisms, we will not explore the point here. Petitioner did not press the argument in the state courts, and the issue was not presented in the petition for certiorari. The case comes to us on the premise that petitioner's entire parcel serves as the basis for his takings claim, and, so framed, the total deprivation argument fails. . . .

For the reasons we have discussed, the State Supreme Court erred in finding petitioner's claims were unripe and in ruling that acquisition of title after the effective date of the regulations barred the takings claims. The court did not err in finding that petitioner failed to establish a deprivation of all economic value, for it is undisputed that the parcel retains significant worth for construction of a residence. The claims under the *Penn Central* analysis were not examined, and for this purpose the case should be remanded.

The judgment of the Rhode Island Supreme Court is affirmed in part and reversed in part, and the case is remanded for further proceedings not inconsistent with this opinion.

JUSTICE O'CONNOR, concurring.

I join the opinion of the Court but with my understanding of how the issues discussed in Part II-B of the opinion must be considered on remand.

Part II-B of the Court's opinion addresses the circumstance, present in this case, where a takings claimant has acquired title to the regulated property after the enactment of the regulation at issue. As the Court holds, the Rhode Island Supreme Court erred in effectively adopting the sweeping rule that the preacquisition enactment of the use restriction *ipso facto* defeats any takings claim based on that use restriction. Accordingly, the Court holds that petitioner's claim under Penn Central Transp. Co. v. City of New York, 438 U.S. 104 (1978), "is not barred by the mere fact that title was acquired after the effective date of the state-imposed restriction."

The more difficult question is what role the temporal relationship between regulatory enactment and title acquisition plays in a proper *Penn Central* analysis. Today's holding does not mean that the timing of the regulation's enactment relative to the acquisition of title is immaterial to the *Penn Central* analysis. Indeed, it would be just as much error to expunge this consideration from the takings inquiry as it would be to accord it exclusive significance. Our polestar instead remains the principles set forth in *Penn Central* itself and our other cases that govern partial regulatory takings. Under these cases, interference with investment-backed expectations is one of a number of factors that a court must examine. Further, the regulatory regime in place at the time the claimant acquires the property at issue helps to shape the reasonableness of those expectations.

The Fifth Amendment forbids the taking of private property for public use without just compensation. We have recognized that this constitutional guarantee is "'designed to bar Government from forcing some people alone to bear public burdens which, in all fairness and justice, should be borne by the public as a whole.'" *Penn Central*, supra, at 123-124 (quoting Armstrong v. United States, 364 U.S. 40, 49 (1960)). The concepts of "fairness and justice" that underlie the Takings Clause, of course, are less than fully determinate. Accordingly, we have eschewed "any 'set formula' for determining when 'justice and fairness' require that economic injuries caused by public action be compensated by the government, rather than remain disproportionately concentrated on a few persons." *Penn Central*, supra, at 124 (quoting Goldblatt v. Hempstead, 369 U.S. 590, 594 (1962)). The outcome instead "depends largely 'upon the particular circumstances [in that] case.'" *Penn Central*, supra, at 124 (quoting United States v. Central Eureka Mining Co., 357 U.S. 155, 168 (1958)).

We have "identified several factors that have particular significance" in these "essentially ad hoc, factual inquiries." *Penn Central*, 438 U.S., at 124. Two such factors are "[t]he economic impact of the regulation on the claimant and, particularly, the extent to which the regulation has interfered with distinct investment-backed expectations." Ibid. Another is "the character of the governmental action." Ibid. The purposes served, as well as the effects produced, by a particular regulation inform the takings analysis. Id., at 127 ("[A] use restriction on real property may constitute a 'taking' if not reasonably necessary to the effectuation of a substantial public purpose, [citations omitted], or perhaps if it has an unduly harsh impact upon the owner's use of the property"); see also Yee v. Escondido, 503 U.S. 519, 523 (1992) (Regulatory takings cases "necessarily entai[l] complex factual assessments of the purposes and economic effects of government actions"). *Penn Central* does not supply mathematically precise variables, but instead provides important guideposts that lead to the ultimate determination whether just compensation is required.

The Rhode Island Supreme Court concluded that, because the wetlands regulations predated petitioner's acquisition of the property at issue, petitioner lacked reasonable investment-backed expectations and hence lacked a viable takings claim. 746 A.2d 707, 717 (2000). The court erred in elevating what it believed to be "[petitioner's] lack of reasonable investment-backed expectations" to "dispositive" status. Ibid. Investment-backed expectations, though important, are not talismanic under *Penn Central*. Evaluation of the degree of interference with investment-backed expectations instead is *one* factor that points toward the answer to the question whether the application of a particular regulation to particular property "goes too far." Pennsylvania Coal Co. v. Mahon, 260 U.S. 393, 415 (1922).

Further, the state of regulatory affairs at the time of acquisition is not the only factor that may determine the extent of investment-backed expectations. For example, the nature and extent of permitted development under the regulatory regime vis-à-vis the development sought by the claimant may also shape legitimate expectations without vesting any kind of development right in the property owner. We also have never held that a takings claim is defeated simply on account of the lack of a personal financial investment by a postenactment acquirer of property, such as a donee, heir, or devisee. Cf. Hodel v. Irving, 481 U.S. 704, 714-718 (1987). Courts instead must attend to those circumstances which are probative of what fairness requires in a given case.

If investment-backed expectations are given exclusive significance in the *Penn Central* analysis and existing regulations dictate the reasonableness of those expectations in every instance, then the State wields far too much power to redefine property rights upon passage of title. On the other hand, if existing regulations do nothing to inform the analysis, then some property owners may reap windfalls and an important indicium of fairness is lost. As I understand it, our decision today does not remove the regulatory backdrop against which an owner takes title to property from the purview of the *Penn Central* inquiry. It simply restores balance to that inquiry. Courts properly consider the effect of existing regulations under the rubric of investment-backed expectations in determining whether a compensable taking has occurred. As before, the salience of these facts cannot be reduced to any "set formula." *Penn Central*, 438 U.S., at 124. The temptation to adopt what amount to *per se* rules in either direction must be resisted. The Takings Clause requires careful examination and weighing of all the relevant circumstances in this context. The court below therefore must consider on remand the array of relevant factors under *Penn Central* before deciding whether any compensation is due.

JUSTICE SCALIA, concurring.

I write separately to make clear that my understanding of how the issues discussed in Part II-B of the Court's opinion must be considered on remand is not Justice O'Connor's.

The principle that underlies her separate concurrence is that it may in some (unspecified) circumstances be "[un]fai[r]," and produce unacceptable "windfalls," to allow a subsequent purchaser to nullify an unconstitutional partial taking (though, inexplicably, not an unconstitutional total taking) by the government. The polar horrible, presumably, is the situation in which a sharp real estate developer, realizing (or indeed, simply gambling on) the unconstitutional excessiveness of a development restriction that a naive land-owner assumes to be valid, purchases property at what it would be worth subject to the restriction, and then develops it to its full value (or resells it at its full value) after getting the unconstitutional restriction invalidated.

This can, I suppose, be called a windfall—though it is not much different from the windfalls that occur every day at stock exchanges or antique auctions, where the knowledgeable (or the venturesome) profit at the expense of the ignorant (or the risk averse). There is something to be said (though in my view not much) for pursuing abstract "fairness" by requiring part or all of that windfall to be returned to the naive original owner, who presumably is the "rightful" owner of it. But there is nothing to be said for giving it instead to the *government*—which not only did not lose something it owned, but is both the *cause* of the miscarriage of "fairness" and the only one of the three parties involved in the miscarriage (government, naive original owner, and sharp real estate developer) which *acted unlawfully*—indeed *unconstitutionally.* Justice O'Connor would eliminate the windfall by giving the malefactor the benefit of its malefaction. It is rather like eliminating the windfall that accrued to a purchaser who bought property at a bargain rate from a thief clothed with the indicia of title, by making him turn over the "unjust" profit *to the thief.*

In my view, the fact that a restriction existed at the time the purchaser took title (other than a restriction forming part of the "background principles of the State's law of property and nuisance," Lucas v. South Carolina Coastal Council, 505 U.S. 1003, 1029 (1992)) should have no bearing upon the determination of whether the restriction is so substantial as to constitute a taking. The "investment-backed expectations" that the law will take into account do not include the assumed validity of a restriction that in fact deprives property of so much of its value as to be unconstitutional. Which is to say that a *Penn Central* taking, see Penn Central Transp. Co. v. City of New York, 438 U.S. 104 (1978), no less than a total taking, is not absolved by the transfer of title.

[Justice Stevens, in an opinion concurring in part and dissenting in part, agreed with the majority only that the case was ripe for review. Citing Justice Kennedy's concurrence in *Lucas,* Stevens concluded that "even a newly adopted regulation that diminishes the value of property does not produce a significant Takings Clause issue if it (1) is generally applicable and (2) is directed at preventing a substantial public harm." He deemed it "quite likely that a regulation prohibiting the filling of wetlands meets those criteria." Stevens maintained that Palazzolo had no standing to make a takings claim because he was not the owner of the property at the time the regulations were adopted. "If the regulations are invalid, either because improper procedures were followed when they were adopted, or because they have somehow gone 'too far,' Pennsylvania Coal Co. v. Mahon, 260 U.S. 393, 415 (1922), petitioner may seek to enjoin their enforcement, but he has no right to recover compensation for the value of property taken from someone else."]

[Justice Ginsburg, joined by Justice Souter and Justice Breyer dissented. They argued that Palazzolo's takings claim was not ripe for review because the record was ambiguous concerning the extent of permissible development on Palazzolo's land. In a footnote citing Justice O'Connor's concurring opinion, they expressed agreement with the notion "that transfer of title can impair a takings claim."]

[Justice Breyer filed a separate dissent in which he agreed with Justice O'Connor "that the simple fact that a piece of property has changed hands (for example, by inheritance) does not always and *automatically* bar a takings claim." Justice Breyer stated that "without in any way suggesting that Palazzolo has any valid takings claim, I believe his postregulatory acquisition of the property (through automatic operation of law) by itself should not prove dispositive." However, he observed that reasonable investment-backed expectations ordinarily "will diminish in force and significance—rapidly and dramatically—as property changes hands over time," a factor that can be taken into account under *Penn Central* to prevent takings doctrine from rewarding strategic property transfers.]

NOTES AND QUESTIONS

1. Although the Court in *Palazzolo* did not hold that Rhode Island's actions constituted a regulatory taking, its decision that post-regulation transfer of title does not automatically bar takings claims could spawn an avalanche of new takings litigation. Under what circumstances can property owners now premise takings claims on regulations that predate their acquisition of title? Will such claims be limited to owners like Palazzolo who acquired the property by operation of law from those who owned the property when the regulations were adopted? Will they be limited to owners who acquired the property from parties who were unable to litigate taking claims to final judgment? Or will all subsequent purchasers be able to assert takings claims?

2. What justifications does the Court offer for its holding? Isn't the Court right that if takings claims may only be asserted by those who own property at the time of regulatory transitions, these owners still are disadvantaged by their inability to transfer their full pre-regulation interests in land? Is Justice Kennedy right when he asserts that states effectively could "put an expiration date on the Takings Clause" if post-enactment transfer of title bars takings claims?

3. In his partial dissent, Justice Stevens argued that only owners of property at the time regulations were adopted had standing to challenge the regulations as regulatory takings. He argued that "[i]f the existence of valid land-use regulations does not limit the title that the first postenactment purchaser of the property inherits, then there is no reason why such regulations should limit the rights of the second, the third, or the thirtieth purchaser." Is he right? Is there any temporal limit on the ability of subsequent purchasers to bring takings claims?

4. How should *Palazzolo* be decided on remand? The Court remanded the case for reconsideration of Palazzolo's takings claim under the *Penn Central* test. *Penn Central*, page 733, focuses on the economic effect of regulation on the landowner, the extent of interference with reasonable investment-backed expectations, and the character of the government action. What relevance, if any, should it have for this analysis that Palazzolo acquired the property in his individual capacity only after the state regulations limiting development in wetlands areas were adopted? Compare Justice O'Connor's concurrence with that of Justice Scalia. Justice O'Connor maintains that post-regulation acquisition of property is one factor to consider in assessing the reasonableness of investment-backed expectations under *Penn Central*. Justice Scalia vehemently disagrees. He argues that it would be better for litigious subsequent purchasers to reap "windfalls" from landowners who naively accept unreasonable regulations than to reward the government for acting as a "thief." Who is right?

5. Suppose that David Lucas, the plaintiff in Lucas v. South Carolina Coastal Council, had sold his undeveloped South Carolina property for a token sum rather than pursuing his takings claim. Could the purchaser have successfully challenged the Coastal Council's development restrictions as a regulatory taking prior to *Palazzolo*? Could he do so now if he was not allowed to build?

6. Has *Palazzolo* moved the focus of regulatory takings jurisprudence toward the reasonableness of land use regulation rather than the reasonableness

of developer expectations? In his majority opinion Justice Kennedy notes that some regulations are simply "unreasonable and do not become less so through passage of time or title." He notes that it made no difference in Nollan v. California Coastal Commission, page 738, that the Nollans purchased their home after the Coastal Commission had adopted a requirement that oceanfront landowners provide lateral beach access to the public as a condition for obtaining development permits. How should the reasonableness of land use regulation be assessed when considering regulatory takings claims? *Nollan* involved a regulatory exaction of a physical easement. Could *Palazzolo* presage extension to regulatory takings claims of the kind of "rough proportionality" analysis used to assess the reasonableness of regulatory exactions?

7. Citing *Lucas*, Justice Kennedy suggests that what is reasonable "is explained in terms of those common, shared understandings of permissible limitations derived from a State's legal tradition." What factors should govern assessments of the reasonableness of regulations that respond to new information or changed circumstances? Recall Justice Kennedy's discussion of this issue in *Lucas*, page 745. Have Kennedy's views changed?

Are Development Moratoria Temporary Takings? The *Tahoe-Sierra* Decision

In May 1997 the U.S. Supreme Court reversed the Ninth Circuit's dismissal on ripeness grounds of a takings challenge to regulations issued by the Tahoe Regional Planning Agency (TRPA). Suitum v. Tahoe Regional Planning Agency, 520 U.S. 735 (1997). The Court concluded that a landowner's claim that regulations effected a regulatory taking by denying her the right to develop her own property in return for receiving transferable development rights (TDRs) that could be used elsewhere, was not rendered unripe because she had failed to try to sell the TDRs. In April 2002, the U.S. Supreme Court rejected a claim that a temporary moratorium on land development adopted by the TRPA constituted a *per se*, temporary taking under *Lucas*. As noted above, the Tahoe Regional Planning Compact sought to protect Lake Tahoe by creating the TRPA to regulate development around the lake. While formulating its initial land use regulations, the TRPA imposed a temporary moratorium on most residential and all commercial construction on environmentally sensitive land near streams and wetlands. The moratorium, which first became effective on August 24, 1981, was to last only until the new land use regulations became effective. However, their effective date ultimately was postponed from 1984 to 1987 as a result of lawsuits challenging the regulations. A group of 450 landowners ultimately brought suit, claiming that the moratorium constituted a *per se* temporary taking of their property rights.

The Ninth Circuit rejected the property owners' temporary takings claim, though five judges dissented from a denial of rehearing en banc, arguing that the decision conflicted with First English Evangelical Lutheran Church v. County of Los Angeles, page 737. The U.S. Supreme Court granted review. Before the Supreme Court the Tahoe Regional Planning Agency was represented by John Roberts, a lawyer then in private practice who later became a judge on the U.S. Court of Appeals for the District of Columbia Circuit and subsequently the Chief Justice of the United States. In April 2002 the Supreme Court issued the following decision.

Tahoe-Sierra Preservation Council, Inc. v. Tahoe Regional Planning Agency
535 U.S. 302 (2002)

STEVENS, J., delivered the opinion of the Court, in which O'CONNOR, KENNEDY, SOUTER, GINSBURG, and BREYER, JJ., joined.

The question presented is whether a moratorium on development imposed during the process of devising a comprehensive land-use plan constitutes a per se taking of property requiring compensation under the Takings Clause of the United States Constitution. This case actually involves two moratoria ordered by respondent Tahoe Regional Planning Agency (TRPA) to maintain the status quo while studying the impact of development on Lake Tahoe and designing a strategy for environmentally sound growth. The first, Ordinance 81-5, was effective from August 24, 1981, until August 26, 1983, whereas the second more restrictive Resolution 83-21 was in effect from August 27, 1983, until April 25, 1984. As a result of these two directives, virtually all development on a substantial portion of the property subject to TRPA's jurisdiction was prohibited for a period of 32 months. [Litigation challenging the 1984 regulations then resulted in an injunction postponing their effective date until 1987.]

III

Petitioners make only a facial attack on Ordinance 81-5 and Resolution 83-21. They contend that the mere enactment of a temporary regulation that, while in effect, denies a property owner all viable economic use of her property gives rise to an unqualified constitutional obligation to compensate her for the value of its use during that period. Hence, they "face an uphill battle," Keystone Bituminous Coal Assn. v. DeBenedictis, 480 U.S. 470, 495 (1987), that is made especially steep by their desire for a categorical rule requiring compensation whenever the government imposes such a moratorium on development. Under their proposed rule, there is no need to evaluate the landowners' investment-backed expectations, the actual impact of the regulation on any individual, the importance of the public interest served by the regulation, or the reasons for imposing the temporary restriction. For petitioners, it is enough that a regulation imposes a temporary deprivation—no matter how brief—of all economically viable use to trigger a *per se* rule that a taking has occurred. Petitioners assert that our opinions in *First English* and *Lucas* have already endorsed their view, and that it is a logical application of the principle that the Takings Clause was "designed to bar Government from forcing some people alone to bear burdens which, in all fairness and justice, should be borne by the public as a whole." Armstrong v. United States, 364 U.S. 40, 49 (1960).

We shall first explain why our cases do not support their proposed categorical rule—indeed, fairly read, they implicitly reject it. Next, we shall explain why the *Armstrong* principle requires rejection of that rule as well as the less extreme position advanced by petitioners at oral argument. In our view the answer to the abstract question whether a temporary moratorium effects a taking is neither "yes, always" nor "no, never"; the answer depends upon the particular circumstances of the case. Resisting "[t]he temptation to adopt what amount to per se rules in either direction," Palazzolo v. Rhode Island, 533 U.S. 606, 636

(2001) (O'Connor, J., concurring), we conclude that the circumstances in this case are best analyzed within the *Penn Central* framework.

IV

The text of the Fifth Amendment itself provides a basis for drawing a distinction between physical takings and regulatory takings. Its plain language requires the payment of compensation whenever the government acquires private property for a public purpose, whether the acquisition is the result of a condemnation proceeding or a physical appropriation. But the Constitution contains no comparable reference to regulations that prohibit a property owner from making certain uses of her private property. Our jurisprudence involving condemnations and physical takings is as old as the Republic and, for the most part, involves the straightforward application of *per se* rules. Our regulatory takings jurisprudence, in contrast, is of more recent vintage and is characterized by "essentially ad hoc, factual inquiries," *Penn Central*, 438 U.S., at 124, designed to allow "careful examination and weighing of all the relevant circumstances." *Palazzolo*, 533 U.S., at 636 (O'Connor, J., concurring). . . .

. . . *First English* was certainly a significant decision, and nothing that we say today qualifies its holding. Nonetheless, it is important to recognize that we did not address in that case the quite different and logically prior question whether the temporary regulation at issue had in fact constituted a taking.

In *First English*, the Court unambiguously and repeatedly characterized the issue to be decided as a "compensation question" or a "remedial question." Id., at 311 ("The disposition of the case on these grounds isolates the remedial question for our consideration"); see also id., at 313, 318. And the Court's statement of its holding was equally unambiguous: "We merely hold that where the government's activities *have already worked a taking* of all use of property, no subsequent action by the government can relieve it of the duty to provide compensation for the period during which the taking was effective." Id., at 321 (emphasis added). In fact, *First English* expressly disavowed any ruling on the merits of the takings issue because the California courts had decided the remedial question on the assumption that a taking had been alleged. Id., at 312-313 ("We reject appellee's suggestion that . . . we must independently evaluate the adequacy of the complaint and resolve the takings claim on the merits before we can reach the remedial question"). After our remand, the California courts concluded that there had not been a taking, First English Evangelical Church of Glendale v. County of Los Angeles, 210 Cal. App. 3d 1353, 258 Cal. Rptr. 893 (1989), and we declined review of that decision, 493 U.S. 1056 (1990).

To the extent that the Court in *First English* referenced the antecedent takings question, we identified two reasons why a regulation temporarily denying an owner all use of her property might not constitute a taking. First, we recognized that "the county might avoid the conclusion that a compensable taking had occurred by establishing that the denial of all use was insulated as a part of the State's authority to enact safety regulations." 482 U.S., at 313. Second, we limited our holding "to the facts presented" and recognized "the quite different questions that would arise in the case of normal delays in obtaining building permits, changes in zoning ordinances, variances, and the like which [were] not before us." Id., at 321. Thus, our decision in *First English* surely did not approve, and implicitly rejected, the categorical submission that petitioners are now advocating.

Similarly, our decision in *Lucas* is not dispositive of the question presented. Although *Lucas* endorsed and applied a categorical rule, it was not the one that petitioners propose. Lucas purchased two residential lots in 1988 for $975,000. These lots were rendered "valueless" by a statute enacted two years later. The trial court found that a taking had occurred and ordered compensation of $1,232,387.50, representing the value of the fee simple estate, plus interest. As the statute read at the time of the trial, it effected a taking that "was unconditional and permanent." 505 U.S., at 1012. While the State's appeal was pending, the statute was amended to authorize exceptions that might have allowed Lucas to obtain a building permit. Despite the fact that the amendment gave the State Supreme Court the opportunity to dispose of the appeal on ripeness grounds, it resolved the merits of the permanent takings claim and reversed. Since "Lucas had no reason to proceed on a 'temporary taking' theory at trial," we decided the case on the permanent taking theory that both the trial court and the State Supreme Court had addressed. Ibid.

The categorical rule that we applied in *Lucas* states that compensation is required when a regulation deprives an owner of "*all* economically beneficial uses" of his land. Id., at 1019. Under that rule, a statute that "wholly eliminated the value" of Lucas' fee simple title clearly qualified as a taking. But our holding was limited to "the extraordinary circumstance when *no* productive or economically beneficial use of land is permitted." Id., at 1017. The emphasis on the word "no" in the text of the opinion was, in effect, reiterated in a footnote explaining that the categorical rule would not apply if the diminution in value were 95 percent instead of 100 percent. Id., at 1019, n. 8. Anything less than a "complete elimination of value," or a "total loss," the Court acknowledged, would require the kind of analysis applied in *Penn Central. Lucas*, 505 U.S., at 1019-1020, n. 8.

Certainly, our holding that the permanent "obliteration of the value" of a fee simple estate constitutes a categorical taking does not answer the question whether a regulation prohibiting any economic use of land for a 32-month period has the same legal effect. Petitioners seek to bring this case under the rule announced in *Lucas* by arguing that we can effectively sever a 32-month segment from the remainder of each landowner's fee simple estate, and then ask whether that segment has been taken in its entirety by the moratoria. Of course, defining the property interest taken in terms of the very regulation being challenged is circular. With property so divided, every delay would become a total ban; the moratorium and the normal permit process alike would constitute categorical takings. Petitioners' "conceptual severance" argument is unavailing because it ignores *Penn Central*'s admonition that in regulatory takings cases we must focus on "the parcel as a whole." 438 U.S., at 130-131. We have consistently rejected such an approach to the "denominator" question. See *Keystone*, 480 U.S., at 497. See also, Concrete Pipe & Products of Cal., Inc. v. Construction Laborers Pension Trust for Southern Cal., 508 U.S. 602, 644 (1993) ("To the extent that any portion of property is taken, that portion is always taken in its entirety; the relevant question, however, is whether the property taken is all, or only a portion of, the parcel in question"). Thus, the District Court erred when it disaggregated petitioners' property into temporal segments corresponding to the regulations at issue and then analyzed whether petitioners were deprived of all economically viable use during each period. 34 F. Supp. 2d, at 1242-1245. The starting point for the court's analysis should have been to ask whether there was a total taking of the entire parcel; if not, then *Penn Central* was the proper framework.

An interest in real property is defined by the metes and bounds that describe its geographic dimensions and the term of years that describes the temporal aspect of the owner's interest. See Restatement of Property §§7-9 (1936). Both dimensions must be considered if the interest is to be viewed in its entirety. Hence, a permanent deprivation of the owner's use of the entire area is a taking of "the parcel as a whole," whereas a temporary restriction that merely causes a diminution in value is not. Logically, a fee simple estate cannot be rendered valueless by a temporary prohibition on economic use, because the property will recover value as soon as the prohibition is lifted. Cf. Agins v. City of Tiburon, 447 U.S., at 263, n. 9 ("Even if the appellants' ability to sell their property was limited during the pendency of the condemnation proceeding, the appellants were free to sell or develop their property when the proceedings ended. Mere fluctuations in value during the process of governmental decision-making, absent extraordinary delay, are 'incidents of ownership. They cannot be considered as a "taking" in the constitutional sense'") (quoting Danforth v. United States, 308 U.S. 271, 285 (1939)).

Neither *Lucas,* nor *First English,* nor any of our other regulatory takings cases compels us to accept petitioners' categorical submission. In fact, these cases make clear that the categorical rule in *Lucas* was carved out for the "extraordinary case" in which a regulation permanently deprives property of all value; the default rule remains that, in the regulatory taking context, we require a more fact specific inquiry. Nevertheless, we will consider whether the interest in protecting individual property owners from bearing public burdens "which, in all fairness and justice, should be borne by the public as a whole," Armstrong v. United States, 364 U.S., at 49, justifies creating a new rule for these circumstances.

V

Considerations of "fairness and justice" arguably could support the conclusion that TRPA's moratoria were takings of petitioners' property based on any of seven different theories. . . .

With respect to these theories, the ultimate constitutional question is whether the concepts of "fairness and justice" that underlie the Takings Clause will be better served by one of these categorical rules or by a *Penn Central* inquiry into all of the relevant circumstances in particular cases. From that perspective, the extreme categorical rule that any deprivation of all economic use, no matter how brief, constitutes a compensable taking surely cannot be sustained. Petitioners' broad submission would apply to numerous "normal delays in obtaining building permits, changes in zoning ordinances, variances, and the like," 482 U.S., at 321, as well as to orders temporarily prohibiting access to crime scenes, businesses that violate health codes, fire-damaged buildings, or other areas that we cannot now foresee. Such a rule would undoubtedly require changes in numerous practices that have long been considered permissible exercises of the police power. As Justice Holmes warned in *Mahon,* "[g]overnment hardly could go on if to some extent values incident to property could not be diminished without paying for every such change in the general law." 260 U.S., at 413. A rule that required compensation for every delay in the use of property would render routine government processes prohibitively expensive or encourage hasty decisionmaking. Such an important change in the law should be the product of legislative rulemaking rather than adjudication.

More importantly, for reasons set out at some length by Justice O'Connor in her concurring opinion in Palazzolo v. Rhode Island, 533 U.S., at 636 (2001), we are persuaded that the better approach to claims that a regulation has effected a temporary taking "requires careful examination and weighing of all the relevant circumstances." . . .

In rejecting petitioners' *per se* rule, we do not hold that the temporary nature of a land-use restriction precludes finding that it effects a taking; we simply recognize that it should not be given exclusive significance one way or the other.

A narrower rule that excluded the normal delays associated with processing permits, or that covered only delays of more than a year, would certainly have a less severe impact on prevailing practices, but it would still impose serious financial constraints on the planning process. Unlike the "extraordinary circumstance" in which the government deprives a property owner of all economic use, *Lucas*, 505 U.S., at 1017, moratoria like Ordinance 81-5 and Resolution 83-21 are used widely among land-use planners to preserve the status quo while formulating a more permanent development strategy. In fact, the consensus in the planning community appears to be that moratoria, or "interim development controls" as they are often called, are an essential tool of successful development. Yet even the weak version of petitioners' categorical rule would treat these interim measures as takings regardless of the good faith of the planners, the reasonable expectations of the landowners, or the actual impact of the moratorium on property values.

The interest in facilitating informed decisionmaking by regulatory agencies counsels against adopting a *per se* rule that would impose such severe costs on their deliberations. Otherwise, the financial constraints of compensating property owners during a moratorium may force officials to rush through the planning process or to abandon the practice altogether. To the extent that communities are forced to abandon using moratoria, landowners will have incentives to develop their property quickly before a comprehensive plan can be enacted, thereby fostering inefficient and ill-conceived growth. A finding in the 1980 Compact itself, which presumably was endorsed by all three legislative bodies that participated in its enactment, attests to the importance of that concern. 94 Stat. 3243 ("The legislatures of the States of California and Nevada find that in order to make effective the regional plan as revised by the agency, it is necessary to halt temporarily works of development in the region which might otherwise absorb the entire capability of the region for further development or direct it out of harmony with the ultimate plan"). . . .

We would create a perverse system of incentives were we to hold that landowners must wait for a taking claim to ripen so that planners can make well-reasoned decisions while, at the same time, holding that those planners must compensate landowners for the delay.

Indeed, the interest in protecting the decisional process is even stronger when an agency is developing a regional plan than when it is considering a permit for a single parcel. In the proceedings involving the Lake Tahoe Basin, for example, the moratoria enabled TRPA to obtain the benefit of comments and criticisms from interested parties, such as the petitioners, during its deliberations. Since a categorical rule tied to the length of deliberations would likely create added pressure on decisionmakers to reach a quick resolution of land-use questions, it would only serve to disadvantage those landowners and interest groups who are not as organized or familiar with the planning process. Moreover, with a temporary ban on development there is a lesser risk that individual landowners will be "singled out" to bear a special burden that should be shared by the public as a whole. Nollan v. California Coastal Comm'n, 483 U.S. 825, 835 (1987). At least with a moratorium there is a clear "reciprocity of advantage," *Mahon,* 260 U.S., at 415, because it protects the interests of all affected landowners against immediate construction that might be inconsistent with the provisions of the plan that is ultimately adopted. "While each of us is burdened somewhat by such restrictions, we, in turn, benefit greatly from the restrictions that are placed on others." *Keystone,* 480 U.S., at 491. In fact, there is reason to believe property values often will continue to increase despite a moratorium. See, e.g., Growth Properties, Inc. v. Klingbeil Holding Co., 419 F. Supp. 212, 218 (D. Md. 1976) (noting that land values could be expected to increase 20 percent during a 5-year moratorium on development). Cf. Forest Properties, Inc. v. United States, 177 F.3d 1360, 1367 (C.A. Fed. 1999) (record showed that market value of the entire parcel increased despite denial of permit to fill and develop lake-bottom property). Such an increase makes sense in this context because property values throughout the Basin can be expected to reflect the added assurance that Lake Tahoe will remain in its pristine state. Since in some cases a 1-year moratorium may not impose a burden at all, we should not adopt a rule that assumes moratoria always force individuals to bear a special burden that should be shared by the public as a whole.

It may well be true that any moratorium that lasts for more than one year should be viewed with special skepticism. But given the fact that the District Court found that the 32 months required by TRPA to formulate the 1984 Regional Plan was not unreasonable, we could not possibly conclude that every delay of over one year is constitutionally unacceptable. Formulating a general rule of this kind is a suitable task for state legislatures. In our view, the duration of the restriction is one of the important factors that a court must consider in the appraisal of a regulatory takings claim, but with respect to that factor as with respect to other factors, the "temptation to adopt what amount to *per se* rules in either direction must be resisted." *Palazzolo,* 533 U.S., at 636 (O'Connor, J., concurring). There may be moratoria that last longer than one year which interfere with reasonable investment-backed expectations, but as the District Court's opinion illustrates, petitioners' proposed rule is simply "too blunt an instrument," for identifying those cases. Id., at 628. We conclude, therefore, that the interest in "fairness and justice" will be best served by relying on the familiar *Penn Central* approach when deciding cases like this, rather than by attempting to craft a new categorical rule.

CHIEF JUSTICE REHNQUIST, with whom JUSTICE SCALIA and JUSTICE THOMAS join, dissenting.

For over half a decade petitioners were prohibited from building homes, or any other structures, on their land. Because the Takings Clause requires the government to pay compensation when it deprives owners of all economically viable use of their land, see Lucas v. South Carolina Coastal Council, 505 U.S. 1003 (1992), and because a ban on all development lasting almost six years does not resemble any traditional land-use planning device, I dissent. . . .

II

. . . *Lucas* reaffirmed our "frequently expressed" view that "when the owner of real property has been called upon to sacrifice *all* economically beneficial uses in the name of the common good, that is, to leave his property economically idle, he has suffered a taking." 505 U.S., at 1019. See also Agins v. City of Tiburon, 447 U.S. 255, 258-259 (1980). The District Court in this case held that the ordinances and resolutions in effect between August 24, 1981, and April 25, 1984, "did in fact deny the plaintiffs all economically viable use of their land." 34 F. Supp. 2d 1226, 1245 (D. Nev. 1999). The Court of Appeals did not overturn this finding. And the 1984 injunction, issued because the environmental thresholds issued by respondent did not permit the development of single-family residences, forced petitioners to leave their land economically idle for at least another three years. The Court does not dispute that petitioners were forced to leave their land economically idle during this period. But the Court refuses to apply *Lucas* on the ground that the deprivation was "temporary."

Neither the Takings Clause nor our case law supports such a distinction. For one thing, a distinction between "temporary" and "permanent" prohibitions is tenuous. The "temporary" prohibition in this case that the Court finds is not a taking lasted almost six years. The "permanent" prohibition that the Court held to be a taking in *Lucas* lasted less than two years. See 505 U.S., at 1011-1012. The "permanent" prohibition in *Lucas* lasted less than two years because the law, as it often does, changed. The South Carolina Legislature in 1990 decided to amend the 1988 Beachfront Management Act to allow the issuance of "'special permits' for the construction or reconstruction of habitable structures seaward of the baseline." Id., at 1011-1012. Land-use regulations are not irrevocable. And the government can even abandon condemned land. See United States v. Dow, 357 U.S. 17, 26 (1958). Under the Court's decision today, the takings question turns entirely on the initial label given a regulation, a label that is often without much meaning. There is every incentive for government to simply label any prohibition on development "temporary," or to fix a set number of years. As in this case, this initial designation does not preclude the government from repeatedly extending the "temporary" prohibition into a long-term ban on all development. The Court now holds that such a designation by the government is conclusive even though in fact the moratorium greatly exceeds the time initially specified. Apparently, the Court would not view even a 10-year moratorium as a taking under *Lucas* because the moratorium is not "permanent."

Our opinion in First English Evangelical Lutheran Church of Glendale v. County of Los Angeles, 482 U.S. 304 (1987), rejects any distinction between temporary and permanent takings when a landowner is deprived of all economically beneficial use of his land. *First English* stated that "temporary takings which, as here, deny a landowner all use of his property, are not different in kind from permanent takings, for which the Constitution clearly requires compensation." Id., at 318. Because of *First English*'s rule that "temporary deprivations of use are compensable under the Takings Clause," the Court in *Lucas* found nothing problematic about the later developments that potentially made the ban on development temporary. 505 U.S., at 1011-1012 (citing *First English*, supra); see also 505 U.S., at 1033 (Kennedy, J., concurring) ("It is well established that temporary takings are as protected by the Constitution as are permanent ones." (citing *First English*, supra, at 318)).

More fundamentally, even if a practical distinction between temporary and permanent deprivations were plausible, to treat the two differently in terms of takings law would be at odds with the justification for the *Lucas* rule. The *Lucas* rule is derived from the fact that a "total deprivation of use is, from the landowner's point of view, the equivalent of a physical appropriation." 505 U.S., at

1017. The regulation in *Lucas* was the "practical equivalence" of a long-term physical appropriation, i.e., a condemnation, so the Fifth Amendment required compensation. The "practical equivalence," from the landowner's point of view, of a "temporary" ban on all economic use is a forced leasehold. For example, assume the following situation: Respondent is contemplating the creation of a National Park around Lake Tahoe to preserve its scenic beauty. Respondent decides to take a 6-year leasehold over petitioners' property, during which any human activity on the land would be prohibited, in order to prevent any further destruction to the area while it was deciding whether to request that the area be designated a National Park.

Surely that leasehold would require compensation. In a series of World War II-era cases in which the Government had condemned leasehold interests in order to support the war effort, the Government conceded that it was required to pay compensation for the leasehold interest. See United States v. Petty Motor Co., 327 U.S. 372 (1946); United States v. General Motors Corp., 323 U.S. 373, 376 (1945). From petitioners' standpoint, what happened in this case is no different than if the government had taken a 6-year lease of their property. The Court ignores this "practical equivalence" between respondent's deprivation and the deprivation resulting from a leasehold. In so doing, the Court allows the government to "do by regulation what it cannot do through eminent domain—i.e., take private property without paying for it." 228 F.3d 998, 999 (C.A. 9 2000) (Kozinski, J., dissenting from denial of rehearing en banc). . . .

III

The Court worries that applying *Lucas* here compels finding that an array of traditional, short-term, land-use planning devices are takings. But since the beginning of our regulatory takings jurisprudence, we have recognized that property rights "are enjoyed under an implied limitation." *Mahon*, supra, at 413. Thus, in *Lucas*, after holding that the regulation prohibiting all economically beneficial use of the coastal land came within our categorical takings rule, we nonetheless inquired into whether such a result "inhere[d] in the title itself, in the restrictions that background principles of the State's law of property and nuisance already place upon land ownership." 505 U.S., at 1029. Because the regulation at issue in *Lucas* purported to be permanent, or at least long term, we concluded that the only implied limitation of state property law that could achieve a similar long-term deprivation of all economic use would be something "achieved in the courts—by adjacent landowners (or other uniquely affected persons) under the State's law of private nuisance, or by the State under its complementary power to abate nuisances that affect the public generally, or otherwise." Ibid.

When a regulation merely delays a final land use decision, we have recognized that there are other background principles of state property law that prevent the delay from being deemed a taking. We thus noted in *First English* that our discussion of temporary takings did not apply "in the case of normal delays in obtaining building permits, changes in zoning ordinances, variances, and the like." 482 U.S., at 321. We reiterated this last Term: "The right to improve property, of course, is subject to the reasonable exercise of state authority, including the enforcement of valid zoning and land-use restrictions." Palazzolo v. Rhode Island, 533 U.S. 606, 627 (2001). Zoning regulations existed as far back as colonial Boston, see Treanor, The Original Understanding of the Takings Clause and the Political Process, 95 Colum. L. Rev. 782, 789 (1995), and New York City enacted the first comprehensive zoning ordinance in 1916, see 1 Anderson's American Law of Zoning §3.07, p. 92 (K. Young rev. 4th ed. 1995). Thus, the short-term delays attendant to zoning and permit regimes are a long-standing feature of state property law and part of a landowner's reasonable investment-backed expectations. See *Lucas*, supra, at 1034 (Kennedy, J., concurring in judgment).

But a moratorium prohibiting all economic use for a period of six years is not one of the longstanding, implied limitations of state property law. Moratoria are "interim controls on the use of land that seek to maintain the status quo with respect to land development in an area by either 'freezing' existing land uses or by allowing the issuance of building permits for only certain land uses that would not be inconsistent with a contemplated zoning plan or zoning change." 1 E. Ziegler, Rathkopf's The Law of Zoning and Planning §13:3, p. 13-6 (4th ed. 2000). Typical moratoria thus prohibit only certain categories of development, such as fast-food restaurants, see Schafer v. New Orleans, 743 F.2d 1086 (C.A. 5 1984), or adult businesses, see Renton v. Playtime Theatres, Inc., 475 U.S. 41, 106 S. Ct. 925, 89 L. Ed. 2d 29 (1986), or all commercial development, see Arnold Bernhard & Co. v. Planning & Zoning Comm'n, 194 Conn. 152, 479 A.2d 801 (1984). Such moratoria do not implicate *Lucas* because they do not deprive landowners of all economically beneficial use of their land. As for moratoria that prohibit all development, these do not have the lineage of permit and zoning requirements and thus it is less certain that property is acquired under the "implied limitation" of a moratorium prohibiting all development. Moreover, unlike a permit system in which it is expected that a project will be approved so long as certain conditions are satisfied, a moratorium that prohibits all uses is by definition contemplating a new land-use plan that would prohibit all uses. . . .

Because the prohibition on development of nearly six years in this case cannot be said to resemble any "implied limitation" of state property law, it is a taking that requires compensation.

NOTES AND QUESTIONS

1. Justice Stevens rejects the notion that because the government must pay just compensation for a temporary physical taking, it also should be required to pay when a temporary moratorium on development is imposed. He concludes that although physical takings jurisprudence involves the straightforward application of *per se* rules, regulatory takings jurisprudence generally calls for the kind of "ad hoc, factual inquiries" that the Court employed in *Penn Central.* How persuasive is his effort to distinguish between temporary physical and temporary regulatory takings? Has the Court effectively held that there cannot be any such thing as a *per se,* temporary regulatory taking?

2. Like its *Palazzolo* decision, the Court's *Tahoe-Sierra* decision appears to have diminished the importance of *Lucas* while reinforcing the importance of *Penn Central.* While rejecting the notion that a lengthy moratorium on development can be a *per se* regulatory taking, the *Tahoe-Sierra* Court indicates that the landowners could have raised a takings claim under *Penn Central*'s ad hoc approach, a strategy that the landowners eschewed in the lower courts. While

not ruling out the possibility that some moratoria could be deemed a regulatory taking under *Penn Central*, Justice Stevens indicates that this determination would require careful examination of all relevant circumstances, including the length of the moratorium, its purpose, how broadly it was applied, the landowners' reasonable expectations and the moratorium's actual impact on property values. How likely do you think it is that the landowners could have recovered under the *Penn Central* test?

3. How persuasive are Justice Stevens's efforts to distinguish *First English*? In *First English* the Supreme Court decided that invalidation of a regulation does not automatically defeat a takings claim because even temporary takings require payment of just compensation. But it did not address the question whether a regulation intended to be temporary from the start could be deemed to be a taking requiring payment of just compensation. Thus, Justice Stevens views *First English* as addressing only the question of how compensation should be measured once a regulatory taking has been established. But if there is no such thing as a *per se* regulatory taking, under what circumstances would *First English* be applied?

4. Consider the policy arguments made by the majority and the dissenters. Justice Stevens argues that moratoria are an essential tool of successful land use planning and that application of a *per se* takings rule to them would jeopardize responsible planning. Chief Justice Rehnquist argues in favor of finding a *per se* regulatory taking because TRPA's moratoria effectively barred all development for nearly six years, which he maintains would far exceed the length of time any reasonable moratorium could be authorized under background principles of state property law. If a temporary moratorium on development cannot give rise to a *per se* takings claim, can government entities insulate themselves from takings claims simply by pretending that regulations they adopt are temporary and that they ultimately will be revised?

5. After nearly two decades of litigation, challenges to land use controls adopted by the Tahoe Regional Planning Agency (TRPA) during the 1980s appear to have finally come to an end. Following the Court's decision in *Tahoe-Sierra*, the U.S. Court of Appeals for the Ninth Circuit on remand dismissed the remaining challenges to the TRPA's actions. Tahoe Sierra Preservation Council, Inc. v. Tahoe Regional Planning Agency, 322 F.3d 1064 (9th Cir. 2003). The court held that most of the claims were barred by the doctrine of res judicata. "After eighteen years of litigation, ten years of which has been devoted to adjudicating harm allegedly done by the 1987 Plan and its implementation, the final judgments of [the earlier litigation] should finally rest in peace." The plaintiffs declined to seek further Supreme Court review of the Ninth Circuit's decision.

3. Regulatory Exactions

Regulators sometimes condition approvals of development projects on the developer's agreement to do something to provide benefits to the public. As discussed earlier, in Nollan v. California Coastal Commission, 483 U.S. 825 (1987), a state coastal commission had sought to condition a permit to build in a coastal area on landowners granting the public an easement over a portion of their beachfront property. However, the Supreme Court held that because the permit condition was not reasonably related to the project's environmental effects (interference with visual access to the beach), the condition represented a taking. The Supreme Court revisited the question of when regulatory exactions become takings in the case below.

Dolan v. City of Tigard
512 U.S. 374 (1994)

CHIEF JUSTICE REHNQUIST delivered the opinion of the Court.

.... Petitioner Florence Dolan owns a plumbing and electric supply store located on Main Street in the Central Business District of the city. The store covers approximately 9,700 square feet on the eastern side of a 1.67-acre parcel, which includes a gravel parking lot. Fanno Creek flows through the southwestern corner of the lot and along its western boundary. The year-round flow of the creek renders the area within the creek's 100-year floodplain virtually unusable for commercial development. The city's comprehensive plan includes the Fanno Creek floodplain as part of the city's greenway system.

Petitioner applied to the city for a permit to redevelop the site. Her proposed plans called for nearly doubling the size of the store to 17,600 square feet, and paving a 39-space parking lot. The existing store, located on the opposite side of the parcel, would be razed in sections as construction progressed on the new building. In the second phase of the project, petitioner proposed to build an additional structure on the northeast side of the site for complementary businesses and to provide more parking. The proposed expansion and intensified use are consistent with the city's zoning scheme in the Central Business District. [Community Development Code] CDC §18.66.030.

The City Planning Commission granted petitioner's permit application subject to conditions imposed by the city's CDC. The CDC establishes the following standard for site development review approval:

> Where landfill and/or development is allowed within and adjacent to the 100-year floodplain, the city shall require the dedication of sufficient open land area for greenway adjoining and within the floodplain. This area shall include portions at a suitable elevation for the construction of a pedestrian/bicycle pathway within the floodplain in accordance with the adopted pedestrian/bicycle plan. [CDC §18.120-180.A.8.]

Thus, the Commission required that petitioner dedicate the portion of her property lying within the 100-year floodplain for improvement of a storm drainage system along Fanno Creek and that she dedicate an additional 15-foot strip of land adjacent to the floodplain as a pedestrian/bicycle pathway. The dedication required by that condition encompasses approximately 7,000 square feet, or roughly 10 percent of the property. In accordance with city practice, petitioner could rely on the dedicated property to meet the 15 percent open space and landscaping requirement mandated by the city's zoning scheme. The city would bear the cost of maintaining a landscaped buffer between the dedicated area and the new store. ....

The Commission made a series of findings concerning the relationship between the dedicated conditions and the projected impacts of petitioner's project. First, the Commission noted that "[i]t is reasonable to assume that customers and employees of the future uses of this site could utilize a pedestrian/bicycle pathway adjacent to this development for their transportation and recreational needs." City of Tigard Planning Commission Final Order No. 91-09 PC. The Commission noted that the site plan has provided for bicycle parking in a rack in front of the proposed building and "[i]t is reasonable to expect that some of the users of the bicycle parking provided for by the site plan will use the pathway adjacent to Fanno Creek if it is constructed." Ibid. In addition, the Commission found that creation of a convenient, safe pedestrian/bicycle pathway system as an alternative means of transportation "could offset some of the traffic demand on [nearby] streets and lessen the increase in traffic congestion." Ibid.

The Commission went on to note that the required floodplain dedication would be reasonably related to petitioner's request to intensify the use of the site given the increase in the impervious surface. The Commission stated that the "anticipated increased storm water flow from the subject property to an already strained creek and drainage basin can only add to the public need to manage the stream channel and floodplain for drainage purposes." Based on this anticipated increased storm water flow, the Commission concluded that "the requirement of dedication of the floodplain area on the site is related to the applicant's plan to intensify development on the site." The Tigard City Council approved the Commission's final order, subject to one minor modification; the City Council reassigned the responsibility for surveying and marking the floodplain area from petitioner to the city's engineering department.

[Arguing that the city's dedication requirements constituted an uncompensated taking of private property, Dolan challenged the Commission's order in the state courts. Because it found that both the pedestrian/bicycle pathway and storm drainage dedication requirements were reasonably related to the impact of the development, the Oregon Supreme Court rejected Dolan's claim.]

II

The Takings Clause of the Fifth Amendment of the United States Constitution, made applicable to the States through the Fourteenth Amendment, Chicago, B. & Q.R. Co. v. Chicago, 166 U.S. 226, 239 (1897), provides: "[N]or shall private property be taken for public use, without just compensation." One of the principal purposes of the Takings Clause is "to bar Government from forcing some people alone to bear public burdens which, in all fairness and justice, should be borne by the public as a whole." Armstrong v. United States, 364 U.S. 40, 49 (1960). Without question, had the city simply required petitioner to dedicate a strip of land along Fanno Creek for public use, rather than conditioning the grant of her permit to redevelop her property on such a dedication, a taking would have occurred. Nollan, supra, 483 U.S., at 831. Such public access would deprive petitioner of the right to exclude others, "one of the most essential sticks in the bundle of rights that are commonly characterized as property." Kaiser Aetna v. United States, 444 U.S. 164, 176 (1979).

On the other side of the ledger, the authority of state and local governments to engage in land use planning has been sustained against constitutional challenge as long ago as our decision in Euclid v. Ambler Realty Co., 272 U.S. 365 (1926). "Government hardly could go on if to some extent values incident to property could not be diminished without paying for every such change in the general law." Pennsylvania Coal Co. v. Mahon, 260 U.S. 393, 413 (1922). A land use regulation does not effect a taking if it "substantially advance[s] legitimate state interests" and does not "den[y] an owner economically viable use of his land." Agins v. Tiburon, 447 U.S. 225, 260 (1980).

The sort of land use regulations discussed in the cases just cited, however, differ in two relevant particulars from the present case. First, they involved essentially legislative determinations classifying entire areas of the city, whereas here the city made an adjudicative decision to condition petitioner's application for a building permit on an individual parcel. Second, the conditions imposed were not simply a limitation on the use petitioner might make of her own parcel, but a requirement that she deed portions of the property to the city. In *Nollan*, supra, we held that governmental authority to exact such a condition was circumscribed by the Fifth and Fourteenth Amendments. Under the well-settled doctrine of "unconstitutional conditions," the government may not require a person to give up a constitutional right—here the right to receive just compensation when property is taken for a public use—in exchange for a discretionary benefit conferred by the government where the property sought has little or no relationship to the benefit. See Perry v. Sindermann, 408 U.S. 593 (1972); Pickering v. Board of Ed. of Township High School Dist., 391 U.S. 563, 568 (1968).

Petitioner contends that the city has forced her to choose between the building permit and her right under the Fifth Amendment to just compensation for the public easements. Petitioner does not quarrel with the city's authority to exact some forms of dedication as a condition for the grant of a building permit, but challenges the showing made by the city to justify these exactions. She argues that the city has identified "no special benefits" conferred on her, and has not identified any "special burdens" created by her new store that would justify the particular dedications required from her which are not required from the public at large.

III

In evaluating petitioner's claim, we must first determine whether the "essential nexus" exists between the "legitimate state interest" and the permit condition exacted by the city. *Nollan*, 483 U.S., at 837. If we find that a nexus exists, we must then decide the required degree of connection between the exactions and the projected impact of the proposed development. We were not required to reach this question in *Nollan*, because we concluded that the connection did not meet even the loosest standard. 483 U.S., at 838. Here, however, we must decide this question.

A

We addressed the essential nexus question in *Nollan*. The California Coastal Commission demanded a lateral public easement across the Nollan's beachfront lot in exchange for a permit to demolish an existing bungalow and replace it with a three-bedroom house. 483 U.S., at 828. The public easement was designed to connect two public beaches that were separated by the Nollan's property. The Coastal Commission had asserted that the public easement condition was imposed to promote the legitimate state interest of diminishing the "blockage of the view of the ocean" caused by construction of the larger house.

We agreed that the Coastal Commission's concern with protecting visual access to the ocean constituted a legitimate public interest. Id., at 835. We also agreed that the permit condition would have been constitutional "even if it consisted of the requirement that the Nollans provide a viewing spot on their property for passersby with whose sighting of the ocean their new house would interfere." Id., at 836. We resolved, however, that the Coastal Commission's regulatory authority was set completely adrift from its constitutional moorings when it claimed that a nexus existed between visual access to the ocean and a permit condition requiring lateral public access along the Nollan's beachfront lot. Id., at 837. How enhancing the public's ability to "traverse to and along the shorefront" served the same governmental purpose of "visual access to the ocean" from the roadway was beyond our ability to countenance. The absence of a nexus left the Coastal Commission in the position of simply trying to obtain an easement through gimmickry, which converted a valid regulation of land use into "an out-and-out plan of extortion." Ibid., quoting J.E.D. Associates, Inc. v. Atkinson, 432 A.2d 12, 14-15 (N.H. 1981).

No such gimmicks are associated with the permit conditions imposed by the city in this case. Undoubtedly, the prevention of flooding along Fanno Creek and the reduction of traffic congestion in the Central Business District qualify as the type of legitimate public purposes we have upheld. *Agins*, supra, at 260-262. It seems equally obvious that a nexus exists between preventing flooding along Fanno Creek and limiting development within the creek's 100-year floodplain. Petitioner proposes to double the size of her retail store and to pave her now-gravel parking lot, thereby expanding the impervious surface on the property and increasing the amount of storm water run-off into Fanno Creek.

The same may be said for the city's attempt to reduce traffic congestion by providing for alternative means of transportation. In theory, a pedestrian/ bicycle pathway provides a useful alternative means of transportation for workers and shoppers: "Pedestrians and bicyclists occupying dedicated spaces for walking and/or bicycling . . . remove potential vehicles from streets, resulting in an overall improvement in total transportation system flow." A. Nelson, Public Provision of Pedestrian and Bicycle Access Ways: Public Policy Rationale and the Nature of Private Benefits 11, Center for Planning Development, Georgia Institute of Technology, Working Paper Series (Jan. 1994). See also Intermodal Surface Transportation Efficiency Act of 1991, Pub. L. 102-240, 105 Stat. 1914 (recognizing pedestrian and bicycle facilities as necessary components of any strategy to reduce traffic congestion).

B

The second part of our analysis requires us to determine whether the degree of the exactions demanded by the city's permit conditions bear the required relationship to the projected impact of petitioner's proposed development. *Nollan*, supra, at 834, quoting *Penn Central*, 438 U.S. 104, 127 (1978) ("[A] use restriction may constitute a taking if not reasonably necessary to the effectuation of a substantial government purpose"). Here the Oregon Supreme Court deferred to what it termed the "city's unchallenged factual findings" supporting the dedication conditions and found them to be reasonably related to the impact of the expansion of petitioner's business. 854 P.2d, at 443.

The city required that petitioner dedicate "to the city as Greenway all portions of the site that fall within the existing 100-year flood plain [of Fanno Creek] and all property 15 feet above [the floodplain] boundary." In addition, the city demanded that the retail store be designed so as not to intrude into the greenway area. The city relies on the Commission's rather tentative findings that increased storm water flow from petitioner's property "can only add to the public need to manage the [floodplain] for drainage purposes" to support its conclusion that the "requirement of dedication of the floodplain area on the site is related to the applicant's plan to intensify development on the site." City of Tigard Planning Commission Final Order No. 91-09 PC.

The city made the following specific findings relevant to the pedestrian/ bicycle pathway:

> In addition, the proposed expanded use of this site is anticipated to generate additional vehicular traffic thereby increasing congestion on nearby collector and arterial streets. Creation of a convenient, safe pedestrian/bicycle pathway system as an alternative means of transportation could offset some of the traffic demand on these nearby streets and lessen the increase in traffic congestion. [Id.]

The question for us is whether these findings are constitutionally sufficient to justify the conditions imposed by the city on petitioner's building permit. Since state courts have been dealing with this question a good deal longer than we have, we turn to representative decisions made by them.

In some States, very generalized statements as to the necessary connection between the required dedication and the proposed development seem to suffice. See, e.g., Billings Properties, Inc. v. Yellowstone County, 394 P.2d 182 (Mont. 1964); Jenad, Inc. v. Scarsdale, 218 N.E.2d 673 (N.Y. 1966). We think this standard is too lax to adequately protect petitioner's right to just compensation if her property is taken for a public purpose.

Other state courts require a very exacting correspondence, described as the "specific and uniquely attributable" test. The Supreme Court of Illinois first developed this test in Pioneer Trust &: Savings Bank v. Mount Prospect, 176 N.E.2d 799, 802 (Ill. 1961). Under this standard, if the local government cannot demonstrate that its exaction is directly proportional to the specifically created need, the exaction becomes "a veiled exercise of the power of eminent domain and a confiscation of private property behind the defense of police regulations." Id., at 802. We do not think the Federal Constitution requires such exacting scrutiny, given the nature of the interests involved.

A number of state courts have taken an intermediate position, requiring the municipality to show a "reasonable relationship" between the required dedication and the impact of the proposed development. Typical is the Supreme Court of Nebraska's opinion in Simpson v. North Platte, 292 N.W.2d 297, 301 (Neb. 1980), where that court stated:

> The distinction, therefore, which must be made between an appropriate exercise of the police power and an improper exercise of eminent domain is whether the requirement has some reasonable relationship or nexus to the use to which the property is being made or is merely being used as an excuse for taking property simply because at that particular moment the landowner is asking the city for some license or permit.

Thus, the court held that a city may not require a property owner to dedicate private property for some future public use as a condition of obtaining a building permit when such future use is not "occasioned by the construction sought to be permitted." Id., at 302.

Some form of the reasonable relationship test has been adopted in many other jurisdictions. . . .

We think the "reasonable relationship" test adopted by a majority of the state courts is closer to the federal constitutional norm than either of those previously discussed. But we do not adopt it as such, partly because the term "reasonable relationship" seems confusingly similar to the term "rational basis" which describes the minimal level of scrutiny under the Equal Protection Clause of the Fourteenth Amendment. We think a term such as "rough proportionality" best encapsulates what we hold to be the requirement of the Fifth Amendment. No precise mathematical calculation is required, but the city must make some sort of individualized determination that the required dedication is related both in nature and extent to the impact of the proposed development. . . .

It is axiomatic that increasing the amount of impervious surface will increase the quantity and rate of storm water flow from petitioner's property. Record, Doc. No. F, ch. 4, p. 4-29. Therefore, keeping the floodplain open and free from development would likely confine the pressures on Fanno Creek created by petitioner's development. In fact, because petitioner's property lies within the Central Business District, the Community Development Code already required that petitioner leave 15 percent of it as open space and the undeveloped floodplain would have nearly satisfied that requirement. But the city demanded more—it not only wanted petitioner not to build in the floodplain, but it also wanted petitioner's property along Fanno Creek for its Greenway system. The city has never said why a public greenway, as opposed to a private one, was required in the interest of flood control.

The difference to petitioner, of course, is the loss of her ability to exclude others. As we have noted, this right to exclude others is "one of the most essential sticks in the bundle of rights that are commonly characterized as property." *Kaiser Aetna*, 444 U.S., at 176. It is difficult to see why recreational visitors trampling along petitioner's floodplain easement are sufficiently related to the city's legitimate interest in reducing flooding problems along Fanno Creek, and the city has not attempted to make any individualized determination to support this part of its request.

The city contends that recreational easement along the Greenway is only ancillary to the city's chief purpose in controlling flood hazards. It further asserts that unlike the residential property at issue in *Nollan*, petitioner's property is commercial in character and, therefore, her right to exclude others is compromised. United States v. Orito, 413 U.S. 139, 142 (1973) ("The Constitution extends special safeguards to the privacy of the home"). The city maintains that "there is nothing to suggest that preventing [petitioner] from prohibiting [the easements] will unreasonably impair the value of [her] property as a [retail store]." PruneYard Shopping Center v. Robins, 447 U.S. 74, 83 (1980).

Admittedly, petitioner wants to build a bigger store to attract members of the public to her property. She also wants, however, to be able to control the time and manner in which they enter. The recreational easement on the Greenway is different in character from the exercise of state-protected rights of free expression and petition that we permitted in *PruneYard*. In *PruneYard*, we held that a major private shopping center that attracted more than 25,000 daily patrons had to provide access to persons exercising their state constitutional rights to distribute pamphlets and ask passersby to sign their petitions. Id., at 85. We based our decision, in part, on the fact that the shopping center "may restrict expressive activity by adopting time, place, and manner regulations that will minimize any interference with its commercial functions." Id., at 83. By contrast, the city wants to impose a permanent recreational easement upon petitioner's property that borders Fanno Creek. Petitioner would lose all rights to regulate the time in which the public entered onto the Greenway, regardless of any interference it might pose with her retail store. Her right to exclude would not be regulated, it would be eviscerated.

If petitioner's proposed development had somehow encroached on existing greenway space in the city, it would have been reasonable to require petitioner to provide some alternative greenway space for the public either on her property or elsewhere. See *Nollan*, 483 U.S., at 836 ("Although such a requirement, constituting a permanent grant of continuous access to the property, would have to be considered a taking if it were not attached to a development permit, the Commission's assumed power to forbid construction of the house in order to protect the public's view of the beach must surely include the power to condition construction upon some concession by the owner, even a concession of property rights, that serves the same end"). But that is not the case here. We conclude that the findings upon which the city relies do not show the required reasonable relationship between the floodplain easement and the petitioner's proposed new building.

With respect to the pedestrian/bicycle pathway, we have no doubt that the city was correct in finding that the larger retail sales facility proposed by petitioner will increase traffic on the streets of the Central Business District. The city estimates that the proposed development would generate roughly 435 additional trips per day. Dedications for streets, sidewalks, and other public ways are generally reasonable exactions to avoid excessive congestion from a proposed property use. But on the record before us, the city has not met its burden of demonstrating that the additional number of vehicle and bicycle trips generated by the petitioner's development reasonably relate to the city's requirement for a dedication of the pedestrian/bicycle pathway easement. The city simply found that the creation of the pathway "could offset some of the traffic demand . . . and lessen the increase in traffic congestion."

As Justice Peterson of the Supreme Court of Oregon explained in his dissenting opinion, however, "the findings of fact that the bicycle pathway system 'could offset some of the traffic demand' is a far cry from a finding that the bicycle pathway system *will*, or is *likely to*, offset some of the traffic demand." 854 P.2d, at 447 (emphasis in original). No precise mathematical calculation is required, but the city must make some effort to quantify its findings in support of the dedication for the pedestrian/bicycle pathway beyond the conclusory statement that it could offset some of the traffic demand generated. . . .

JUSTICE STEVENS, with whom JUSTICE BLACKMUN and JUSTICE GINSBURG join, dissenting. . . .

Certain propositions are not in dispute. The enlargement of the Tigard unit in Dolan's chain of hardware stores will have an adverse impact on the city's legitimate and substantial interests in controlling drainage in Fanno Creek and minimizing traffic congestion in Tigard's business district. That impact is sufficient to justify an outright denial of her application for approval of the expansion. The city has nevertheless agreed to grant Dolan's application if she will comply with two conditions, each of which admittedly will mitigate the adverse effects of her proposed development. The disputed question is whether the city has violated the Fourteenth Amendment to the Federal Constitution by refusing to allow Dolan's planned construction to proceed unless those conditions are met.

The Court is correct in concluding that the city may not attach arbitrary conditions to a building permit or to a variance even when it can rightfully deny the application outright. I also agree that state court decisions dealing with ordinances that govern municipal development plans provide useful guidance in a case of this kind. Yet the Court's description of the doctrinal underpinnings of its decision, the phrasing of its fledgling test of "rough proportionality," and the application of that test to this case run contrary to the traditional treatment of these cases and break considerable and unpropitious new ground. . . .

. . . The Court's assurances that its "rough proportionality" test leaves ample room for cities to pursue the "commendable task of land use planning"—even twice avowing that "no precise mathematical calculation is required"—are wanting given the result that test compels here. Under the Court's approach, a city must not only "quantify its findings," and make "individualized determinations" with respect to the nature and the extent of the relationship between the conditions and the impact, but also demonstrate "proportionality." The correct inquiry should instead concentrate on whether the required nexus is present and venture beyond considerations of a condition's nature or germaneness only if the developer establishes that a concededly germane condition is so grossly disproportionate to the proposed development's adverse effects that it manifests motives other than land use regulation on the part of the city. The heightened requirement the Court imposes on cities is even more unjustified when all the tools needed to resolve the questions presented by this case can be garnered from our existing case law.

Applying its new standard, the Court finds two defects in the city's case. First, while the record would adequately support a requirement that Dolan maintain the portion of the floodplain on her property as undeveloped open space, it does not support the additional requirement that the floodplain be dedicated to the city. Second, while the city adequately established the traffic increase that the proposed development would generate, it failed to quantify the offsetting decrease in automobile traffic that the bike path will produce. Even under the Court's new rule, both defects are, at most, nothing more than harmless error.

In her objections to the floodplain condition, Dolan made no effort to demonstrate that the dedication of that portion of her property would be any more onerous than a simple prohibition against any development on that portion of her property. Given the commercial character of both the existing and the proposed use of the property as a retail store, it seems likely that potential customers "trampling along petitioner's floodplain," are more valuable than a useless parcel of vacant land. Moreover, the duty to pay taxes and the responsibility for potential tort liability may well make ownership of the fee interest in useless land a liability rather than an asset. That may explain why Dolan never conceded that she could be prevented from building on the floodplain. The City Attorney also pointed out that absent a dedication, property owners would be required to "build on their own land" and "with their own money" a storage facility for the water runoff. Dolan apparently "did have that option," but chose not to seek it. If Dolan might have been entitled to a variance confining the city's condition in a manner this Court would accept, her failure to seek that narrower form of relief at any stage of the state administrative and judicial proceedings clearly should preclude that relief in this Court now.

The Court's rejection of the bike path condition amounts to nothing more than a play on words. Everyone agrees that the bike path "could" offset some of the increased traffic flow that the larger store will generate, but the findings do not unequivocally state that it *will* do so, or tell us just how many cyclists will replace motorists. Predictions on such matters are inherently nothing more than estimates. Certainly the assumption that there will be an offsetting benefit here is entirely reasonable and should suffice whether it amounts to 100 percent, 35 percent, or only 5 percent of the increase in automobile traffic that would otherwise occur. If the Court proposes to have the federal judiciary micromanage state decisions of this kind, it is indeed extending its welcome mat to a significant new class of litigants. Although there is no reason to believe that state courts have failed to rise to the task, property owners have surely found a new friend today.

. . . In our changing world one thing is certain: uncertainly will characterize predictions about the impact of new urban developments on the risks of floods, earthquakes, traffic congestion, or environmental harms. When there is doubt concerning the magnitude of those impacts, the public interest in averting them must outweigh the private interest of the commercial entrepreneur. If the government can demonstrate that the conditions it has imposed in a land-use permit are rational, impartial, and conducive to fulfilling the aims of a valid land-use plan, a strong presumption of validity should attach to those conditions. The burden of demonstrating that those conditions have unreasonably impaired the economic value of the proposed improvement belongs squarely on the shoulders of the party challenging the state action's constitutionality. That allocation of burdens has served us well in the past. The Court has stumbled badly today by reversing it.

I respectfully dissent.

JUSTICE SOUTER, dissenting.

I cannot agree that the application of *Nollan* is a sound one here, since it appears that the Court has placed the burden of producing evidence of relationship on the city, despite the usual rule in cases involving the police power that the government is presumed to have acted constitutionally. Having thus assigned the burden, the Court concludes that the City loses based on one word ("could" instead of "would"), and despite the fact that this record shows the connection the Court looks for. Dolan has put forward no evidence that the burden of granting a dedication for the bicycle path is unrelated in kind to the anticipated increase in traffic congestion, nor, if there exists a requirement that the relationship be related in degree, has Dolan shown that the exaction fails any such test. The city, by contrast, calculated the increased traffic flow that would result from Dolan's proposed development to be 435 trips per day, and its Comprehensive Plan, applied here, relied on studies showing the link between alternative modes of transportation, including bicycle paths, and reduced street traffic congestion. City of Tigard's Comprehensive Plan ("Bicycle and pedestrian pathway systems will result in some reduction of automobile trips within the community"). *Nollan*, therefore, is satisfied, and on that assumption the city's conditions should not be held to fail a further rough proportionality test or any other that might be devised to give meaning to the constitutional limits.

NOTES AND QUESTIONS

1. Unlike the situation in *Nollan*, the Court majority has no difficulty finding that an "essential nexus" exists between the legitimate state interests in preventing flooding and alleviating traffic congestion and the state's attempt to exact dedications of land for storm drainage and a bike pathway. Why then did the exactions fail to satisfy constitutional muster? What would the city have to do under the Court's decision to justify the exactions it sought? How detailed would the city's findings have to be in order to justify the exactions?

2. What test does the Court enunciate for determining whether the degree of exactions demanded bears the constitutionally required relationship to the projected impact of development? How does the Court derive this test? Who bears the burden of proof on this issue—the city or the developer? What test does Justice Stevens propose in dissent? How would it differ from the majority's test?

3. Suppose the city simply had denied the permit request without seeking any exaction. Would the permit denial give rise to any kind of takings claim? If instead of asking Dolan to dedicate her property to public use the city had simply imposed a zoning ordinance requiring that a certain percentage of a lot be maintained as a greenway buffer, would there have been any constitutional problem?

4. Does the Court's decision call into question the constitutionality of charging developers impact fees to help compensate for the increased demand for municipal services caused by development? After issuing the *Dolan* decision, the Court vacated and remanded a California decision requiring a developer to pay mitigation fees for the right to build condominiums on what formerly had been a tennis club. Ehrlich v. Culver City, 19 Cal. Rptr. 2d 468 (1993). The developer was required to pay a $280,000 fee for the loss of public recreational facilities, $30,000 as a park fee, and $33,220 for public art. On remand, the California Supreme Court held that *Dolan*'s "rough proportionality" requirement applied to nonpossessory exactions, including monetary fees. While it upheld the propriety of charging an impact fee for loss of recreational facilities, it found insufficient evidence to support the $280,000 fee. Ehrlich v. Culver City, 50 Cal. Rptr. 2d 242 (1996). The court upheld a requirement that the developer provide public art because it found that this was the type of aesthetic control well within authority of city to impose. How should a court determine whether an impact fee satisfies the "rough proportionality" test?

5. Following the Supreme Court's decision in *Dolan*, Mrs. Dolan again sought permission to expand her hardware store. After further litigation in the state courts, the city eventually agreed to pay Mrs. Dolan $1.5 million to compensate her for a "temporary taking" and to grant her a permit to expand the business. 28 Envtl. Rep. 1474 (1997). In return Mrs. Dolan agreed to give the city the easement it had sought for the bicycle path and the flood control project. Today a new and much larger hardware store occupies the property abutting a bike path crossing over Fanno Creek. (See photo on casebook website.)

6. Can the due process clause be used to challenge regulations? In Eastern Enterprises v. Apfel, 524 U.S. 498 (1998), the Court struck down a requirement in the Coal Industry Retiree Health Benefit Act of 1992, mandating that the former owner of a coal mine make large financial contributions to a pension fund for retired coal miners. Four justices held that the requirement constituted a taking because it placed a severe, disproportionate, and retroactive burden on the company. Justice Kennedy joined the four in invalidating the requirement,

but on due process grounds, while refusing to adopt the takings rationale. Kennedy argued that the requirement could not constitute a taking, even though it "imposes a staggering financial burden" on the company, because it "regulates the former mine owner without regard to property." He explained that the Act "does not operate upon or alter an identified property interest and it is not applicable to or measured by a property interest." 524 U.S., at 540 (Kennedy, J., concurring in the judgment). For an argument that *Eastern Enterprises* renders the retroactive application of CERCLA liability to generators unconstitutional, see L. Salibra II, *Eastern Enterprises v. Apfel* and the Retroactive Application of CERCLA, 29 Envtl. L. Rep. 10695 (1999).

7. How far does *Dolan*'s "rough proportionality" requirement extend? In another takings case that established the propriety of submitting to juries regulatory takings claims brought against cities in federal court, City of Monterey v. Del Monte Dunes at Monterey, Ltd., 526 U.S. 687 (1999), the Court did clarify that *Dolan*'s "rough proportionality test" applied only to decisions to condition the approval of development on the dedication of private property to public use. Thus the Court has confined this requirement to cases involving regulatory exactions. See J. Echeverria, Revving the Engines in Neutral: *City of Monterey v. Del Monte Dunes at Monterey, Ltd.*, 29 Envtl. L. Rep. 10682 (1999).

8. Property rights groups have sought legislation to require the government to pay landowners compensation when regulations reduce the value of property in circumstances that would not satisfy the requirements of the Takings Clause. Although they have not succeeded in winning enactment of such legislation at the federal level, more than two dozen states have adopted some form of state "takings" legislation. These laws take three basic forms: (1) assessment ("look before you leap") laws that require some form of pre-regulation assessment of the prospective impact of regulation on private property rights, (2) compensation laws that require the government to pay property owners when regulation reduces the value of their property by a certain percentage, and (3) conflict resolution laws that establish some procedure that can be used by aggrieved property owners to negotiate solutions to disputes. Assessment laws have been the most popular. For a review of experience with state takings legislation prepared for the Competitive Enterprise Institute, see K. Dodd, And Justice for All: The State Experience with Property Rights Legislation (Oct. 1998).

9. In May 2005, the U.S. Supreme Court repudiated the notion that government regulation of private property effects a taking if it "does not substantially advance legitimate state interests." The "substantially advance" test had worked its way into regulatory takings doctrine largely through repetition in several takings cases of a phrase that first appeared in the Court's decision in Agins v. City of Tiburon, 447 U.S. 255 (1980). The case that precipitated this change involved the question whether a Hawaii law effects a regulatory taking by limiting the rent that oil companies can charge dealers who lease company-owned service stations. After hearing evidence that the law would not have the economic effects intended by the state, a federal district court ruled that the law constituted a regulatory taking because it did not substantially advance the legitimate state purpose of lowering consumer gasoline prices. On appeal, the U.S. Court of Appeals for the Ninth Circuit affirmed. Chevron, U.S.A., Inc. v. Bronster, 363 F.3d 846 (9th Cir. 2004). In the decision below, the U.S. Supreme Court unanimously reversed the Ninth Circuit's decision. Writing for the Court, Justice O'Connor acknowledged the strange provenance of the "substantially advance" test. ("On occasion, a would-be doctrinal rule or test finds its way into our case law

through simple repetition of a phrase—however fortuitously coined.") Recognizing that this test was essentially a due process concept, the Court repudiated it as an element of takings doctrine. Although the *Lingle* decision did not involve a takings challenge to an environmental regulation, the following excerpt from Justice O'Connor's opinion for the Court provides an excellent summary of the current state of takings doctrine that may be very helpful to students seeking to understand its application in environmental contexts.

‖ *Lingle v. Chevron, U.S.A., Inc.* ‖
544 U.S. 528 (2005)

JUSTICE O'CONNOR delivered the opinion of the Court.

. . . Our precedents stake out two categories of regulatory action that generally will be deemed per se takings for Fifth Amendment purposes. First, where government requires an owner to suffer a permanent physical invasion of her property—however minor—it must provide just compensation. See Loretto v. Teleprompter Manhattan CATV Corp., 458 U.S. 419 (1982) (state law requiring landlords to permit cable companies to install cable facilities in apartment buildings effected a taking). A second categorical rule applies to regulations that completely deprive an owner of "*all* economically beneficial us[e]" of her property. *Lucas*, 505 U.S., at 1019 (emphasis in original). We held in *Lucas* that the government must pay just compensation for such "total regulatory takings," except to the extent that "background principles of nuisance and property law" independently restrict the owner's intended use of the property. Id., at 1026-1032.

Outside these two relatively narrow categories (and the special context of land-use exactions discussed below), regulatory takings challenges are governed by the standards set forth in Penn Central Transp. Co. v. New York City, 438 U.S. 104 (1978). The Court in *Penn Central* acknowledged that it had hitherto been "unable to develop any 'set formula'" for evaluating regulatory takings claims, but identified "several factors that have particular significance." Id., at 124. Primary among those factors are "[t]he economic impact of the regulation on the claimant and, particularly, the extent to which the regulation has interfered with distinct investment-backed expectations." Ibid. In addition, the "character of the governmental action"—for instance whether it amounts to a physical invasion or instead merely affects property interests through "some public program adjusting the benefits and burdens of economic life to promote the common good"—may be relevant in discerning whether a taking has occurred. Ibid. The Penn Central factors—though each has given rise to vexing subsidiary questions—have served as the principal guidelines for resolving regulatory takings claims that do not fall within the physical takings or *Lucas* rules. See, e.g., Palazzolo v. Rhode Island, 533 U.S. 606, 617-618 (2001); id., at 632-634 (O'Connor, J., concurring).

Although our regulatory takings jurisprudence cannot be characterized as unified, these three inquiries (reflected in *Loretto, Lucas,* and *Penn Central*) share a common touchstone. Each aims to identify regulatory actions that are functionally equivalent to the classic taking in which government directly appropriates private property or ousts the owner from his domain. Accordingly, each of these tests focuses directly upon the severity of the burden that government imposes upon private property rights. The Court has held that physical takings require compensation because of the unique burden they impose: A permanent physical invasion, however minimal the economic cost it entails, eviscerates the owner's right to exclude others from entering and using her property—perhaps the most fundamental of all property interests. In the *Lucas* context, of course, the complete elimination of a property's value is the determinative factor. See *Lucas*, supra, at 1017 (positing that "total deprivation of beneficial use is, from the landowner's point of view, the equivalent of a physical appropriation"). And the *Penn Central* inquiry turns in large part, albeit not exclusively, upon the magnitude of a regulation's economic impact and the degree to which it interferes with legitimate property interests. . . .

In stark contrast to the three regulatory takings tests discussed above, the "substantially advances" inquiry reveals nothing about the magnitude or character of the burden a particular regulation imposes upon private property rights. Nor does it provide any information about how any regulatory burden is distributed among property owners. In consequence, this test does not help to identify those regulations whose effects are functionally comparable to government appropriation or invasion of private property; it is tethered neither to the text of the Takings Clause nor to the basic justification for allowing regulatory actions to be challenged under the Clause. . . .

[Justice O'Connor then discusses the implications of the Court's jettisoning the "substantial advance test" for cases involving regulatory exactions.] It might be argued that this formula played a role in our decisions in Nollan v. California Coastal Comm'n, 483 U.S. 825 (1987), and Dolan v. City of Tigard, 512 U.S. 374 (1994). But while the Court drew upon the language of *Agins* in these cases, it did not apply the "substantially advances" test that is the subject of today's decision. Both *Nollan* and *Dolan* involved Fifth Amendment takings challenges to adjudicative land-use exactions—specifically, government demands that a landowner dedicate an easement allowing public access to her property as a condition of obtaining a development permit. See *Dolan*, supra, at 379-380 (permit to expand a store and parking lot conditioned on the dedication of a portion of the relevant property for a "greenway," including a bike/pedestrian path); *Nollan*, supra, at 828 (permit to build a larger residence on beachfront property conditioned on dedication of an easement allowing the public to traverse a strip of the property between the owner's seawall and the mean high-tide line).

In each case, the Court began with the premise that, had the government simply appropriated the easement in question, this would have been a per se physical taking. *Dolan*, supra, at 384; *Nollan*, supra, at 831-832. The question was whether the government could, without paying the compensation that would otherwise be required upon effecting such a taking, demand the easement as a condition for granting a development permit the government was entitled to deny. The Court in *Nollan* answered in the affirmative, provided that the exaction would substantially advance the same government interest that would furnish a valid ground for denial of the permit. 483 U.S., at 834-837. The Court further refined this requirement in *Dolan*, holding that an adjudicative exaction requiring dedication of private property must also be "'rough[ly] proportiona[l]' . . . both in nature and extent to the impact of the proposed development." 512 U.S., at 391; see also *Del Monte Dunes*, supra, at 702 (emphasizing that we have not extended this standard "beyond the special context of [such] exactions").

Although *Nollan* and *Dolan* quoted *Agins*' language, the rule those decisions established is entirely distinct from the "substantially advances" test we address today. Whereas the "substantially advances" inquiry before us now is unconcerned with the degree or type of burden a regulation places upon property, *Nollan* and *Dolan* both involved dedications of property so onerous that, outside the exactions context, they would be deemed per se physical takings. In neither case did the Court question whether the exaction would substantially advance some legitimate state interest. Rather, the issue was whether the exactions substantially advanced the same interests that land-use authorities asserted would allow them to deny the permit altogether. As the Court explained in *Dolan*, these cases involve a special application of the "doctrine of 'unconstitutional conditions,'" which provides that "the government may not require a person to give up a constitutional right—here the right to receive just compensation when property is taken for a public use—in exchange for a discretionary benefit conferred by the government where the benefit has little or no relationship to the property." 512 U.S., at 385. That is worlds apart from a rule that says a regulation affecting property constitutes a taking on its face solely because it does not substantially advance a legitimate government interest. In short, *Nollan* and *Dolan* cannot be characterized as applying the "substantially advances" test we address today, and our decision should not be read to disturb these precedents.

Twenty-five years ago, the Court posited that a regulation of private property "effects a taking if [it] does not substantially advance [a] legitimate state interes[t]." *Agins*, supra, at 260. The lower courts in this case took that statement to its logical conclusion, and in so doing, revealed its imprecision. Today we correct course. We hold that the "substantially advances" formula is not a valid takings test, and indeed conclude that it has no proper place in our takings jurisprudence. In so doing, we reaffirm that a plaintiff seeking to challenge a government regulation as an uncompensated taking of private property may proceed under one of the other theories discussed above—by alleging a "physical" taking, a *Lucas*-type "total regulatory taking," a *Penn Central* taking, or a land-use exaction violating the standards set forth in *Nollan* and *Dolan*. Because Chevron argued only a "substantially advances" theory in support of its takings claim, it was not entitled to summary judgment on that claim. Accordingly, we reverse the judgment of the Ninth Circuit and remand the case for further proceedings consistent with this opinion.

NOTES AND QUESTIONS

1. While repudiating the "substantially advances" test as an element of regulatory takings doctrine, Justice O'Connor's majority opinion attempts to distinguish it from the foundations of the "rough proportionality" requirement for regulatory exactions established in *Nollan* and *Dolan*. How successful is she in doing so? As she acknowledges, both *Nollan* and *Dolan* cited *Agins*' now-repudiated "substantially advances" language in justifying their conclusion that the regulatory exaction sought was unconstitutional. What impact, if any, will the *Lingle* decision have on regulatory exactions?

2. Justice O'Connor's summary of the state of regulatory takings doctrine describes *Lucas* as establishing a "relatively narrow" category of regulatory takings when a regulation completely deprives the property owner of all "economically beneficial use" of real estate. While many regulations have been challenged as creating a *Lucas*-type "total wipeout," courts have routinely rejected such claims by finding that the land subject to regulation retains some economic value. As a result the *Penn Central* test appears to have become

the primary touchstone for evaluating regulatory takings claims. Is it fair to conclude that the Rehnquist Court's revival of regulatory takings doctrine has not had much direct effect on environmental regulation? While few judgments have been rendered requiring compensation for regulatory takings, could the Court's revival of regulatory takings doctrine have helped deter regulators from overreaching for fear of incurring liability for a taking?

PROBLEM EXERCISE: ENVIRONMENTAL REMEDIATION AND THE TAKINGS CLAUSE

A developer owns a 100-acre tract of undeveloped land located near a licensed waste disposal site. After it is discovered that toxic wastes from the nearby disposal site are leaching into groundwater and heavily contaminating it, the site is placed on Superfund's National Priorities List for cleanup. Operating under authority granted by CERCLA, EPA seeks the developer's permission to install groundwater monitoring wells on the developer's property. EPA claims it needs the wells to monitor the movement of a plume of toxic chemicals moving through the aquifer from the waste disposal site. After the developer denies EPA permission, EPA issues an access order mandating that it be allowed to install the wells. Over a three-year period, EPA installs 20 groundwater monitoring wells on a 50-foot by 50-foot square portion of the developer's undeveloped land. To use the wells for monitoring purposes, government officials periodically enter the property through a 16-foot wide access corridor. Monitoring data show that a plume of toxic contaminants is flowing directly under the developer's property. After years of expensive remediation efforts, the contamination is removed. The government closes the monitoring wells and terminates its access order 12 years after it first was issued.

The developer then sues the federal government seeking compensation under the Takings Clause. The developer argues that the government's actions constituted a physical taking of the portion of his property on which the wells were installed and a regulatory taking of the balance of the property. The developer argues that the government's actions constituted a total taking because the access order authorized virtually unlimited governmental activity on the portions of the property on which the wells were installed and it made balance of the property unmarketable for nearly 12 years by creating a false impression that the property was contaminated.

The government denies that it owes the developer any compensation for a taking. The government claims it was necessary to place the groundwater monitoring wells on the developer's property in order to respond to a public nuisance and that the developer ultimately benefited from its monitoring and cleanup efforts. The government argues that its actions saved the developer the expense of investigating, characterizing, and remediating contamination beneath his property. If the property was unmarketable, it was a result of the contamination and not the presence of the monitoring wells. The property is now available for development. The government notes that the part used for the monitoring wells could easily become part of a parking lot or landscaped area without reducing the size of any future development. The developer denies that he received any benefits from the government's actions cleaning up the contaminated groundwater because he never planned to use the groundwater when he ultimately developed the property.

Question One.   Has the government taken the developer's property for purposes of the Takings Clause? If so, what kind of taking has occurred—total or partial, physical or regulatory, temporary or permanent?

Question Two.   What difference, if any, does it make for purposes of taking analysis that the government believes its actions were necessary to respond to a public nuisance? Would it make any difference if the government itself had caused the contamination?

Question Three.   What difference, if any, does it make for purposes of takings analysis that the government has now terminated its access order and closed the monitoring wells?

Question Four.   If a taking has occurred, should the developer receive any compensation and, if so, how should it be calculated? See Hendler v. United States, 175 F.3d 1374 (Fed. Cir. 1999).

4.   *Regulatory Takings and Competing Conceptions of Property Rights*

Takings disputes raise fundamental questions concerning the meaning of property and the relationship between individuals and the state in our constitutional system. With the rise of environmental concerns and the growth of the regulatory state, property scholars have engaged in a vigorous debate over the nature and origins of property rights. See C.M. Rose, What Government Can Do for Property (and Vice Versa), in The Fundamental Interrelationships Between Government and Property 209 (1999) (contrasting the Lockean "bottom-up" view that human beings invent property prior to government with Bentham's "top-down" vision that property is simply a basis for expectations that are secured by government). As national regulatory programs to protect the environment rose to prominence, Joseph Sax and others articulated a new vision of property rights that emphasized the subordination of private rights to public trusts in commonly held natural resources. Sax, The Public Trust Doctrine in Natural Resources Law: Effective Judicial Intervention, 68 Mich. L. Rev. 471 (1970). Importing notions from Roman law and English and American cases holding that the government held certain natural resources in trust for the public, see Illinois Central Railroad Co. v. Illinois, 146 U.S. 387 (1892), Professor Sax argued that the public trust doctrine should be used to vindicate the evolving public interest in environmental protection. See Rose, Joseph Sax and the Idea of the Public Trust, 25 Ecology L.Q. 351 (1998). In *Illinois Central Railroad* the Supreme Court invalidated the Illinois legislature's grant of the entire Chicago lakefront to a private railroad by holding that the lakefront was subject to a public trust that barred the state from selling it to private parties. For a detailed analysis of the history of this case and its implications for the public trust doctrine see Joseph D. Kearney & Thomas A. Merrill, The Origins of the American Public Trust Doctrine: What Really Happened in *Illinois Central*, 71 U. Chi. L. Rev. 799 (2004).

While the public trust concept has remained vague, it challenges the notion that regulations preventing private parties from using their land in ways that harm important environmental resources constitute takings. Sax, Takings, Private Property and Public Rights, 81 Yale L.J. 149 (1971). Another challenge arises from what has been described as the "narrative of natural use." Freyfogle, Owning the Land: Four Contemporary Narratives, 13 J. Land Use &

Envtl. L. 279 (1998). This was the concept articulated by the Wisconsin Supreme Court in Just v. Marinette County, 201 N.W.2d 761 (1972), when it stated that "[a]n owner of land has no absolute and unlimited right to change the essential natural character of his land so as to use it for a purpose for which it was unsuited in its natural state and which injures the rights of others." Professor Freyfogle argues that, while this narrative description of the meaning of ownership is perhaps the simplest of all, despite uncertainties concerning the meaning of what is truly natural, nature itself cannot practicably serve as the source of rules in a democratic society.

Richard Epstein takes sharp exception to *Just* and argues that compensation should be required for a broad array of government actions that reduce the economic value of private property. R. Epstein, Takings (1985). Yet, Epstein does not appear to be suggesting that government conversely should recoup *increases* in property values that are the products of its activities. Professor Epstein appears to reject the application of the nuisance exception in cases of nonpoint source pollution by arguing that land use controls do not redress a physical invasion of the property of another, but rather pollution of one's own property. Id. at 123.

These competing conceptions of property rights reflect evolving (and diverging) notions of fairness as well as changes in our understanding of how environmental harm is caused. Lord Holt's ancient maxim that "every man must so use his own as not to damnify another" acquires new meaning once it is understood that actions long recognized as core aspects of property rights (e.g., the building of a home) may contribute to severe environmental damage by exacerbating nonpoint source pollution. Yet environmentalists who decry the unfairness of involuntary exposure to risk also should be concerned about the fairness of visiting disproportionate economic losses on any individual in the name of environmental protection. The CEQ's observation nearly two decades ago remains accurate today:

> [D]espite the criticisms that have been aimed at various judicial formulations, it may well be that no single formula is either possible or desirable. In the final analysis, all such formulae seem to be attempts to extrapolate from what is at base an ethical judgment about the fairness of alternative means of distributing the costs of protecting certain land-related values that yield positive net benefits to society. In most cases that judgment has traditionally suggested that the proper balance between the interests of private landowners and the public is maintained by requiring compensation when land use regulations do not leave the landowner with any "reasonable" use of his property. Increasingly, as new concepts of property have become more firmly established and recognition of the value of land as a scarce resource has mounted, the definition of reasonable use has changed. [CEQ, Environmental Quality 150 (1973).]

Reconciling notions of fairness to individuals with the need to prevent formerly commonplace activities from contributing to serious environmental problems remains an important challenge facing environmental law.

Takings issues invariably arise at times of regulatory transition: when new laws are adopted that regulate land uses, when new regulations are promulgated to implement previously enacted laws, or when new information becomes available, or circumstances change, that results in property not previously thought to be subject to regulation to be so encumbered. There are many options available for making regulatory transitions less burdensome, as outlined by Carol Rose,

Property Rights and Responsibilities, in Thinking Ecologically: The Next Generation of Environmental Policy 49 (M. Chertow & D. Esty eds., 1997). Some of these include: phasing in new regulations during specified transitional periods, offering partial or temporary variances in cases of special hardships, and phasing out or restructuring counterproductive subsidies instead of restricting private uses of land.

Another strategy for defusing takings problems is to improve the information base upon which investment-backed expectations are founded. Some changes in land use patterns are the foreseeable product of existing forces. Sea levels currently are rising and coastal erosion is increasing, phenomena that scientists are forecasting will continue with major implications for coastal property regimes. Many states allow owners of coastal property to construct erosion barriers that protect their property while contributing to intensified erosion of nearby unprotected lands. The following excerpt explores strategies for responding to sea level rise and their implications for current conceptions of property rights. The author, the project manager for sea level rise at EPA's Office of Policy, proposes the use of "rolling easements," a concept borrowed from the common law of Texas that requires human activities to yield the right of way to naturally migrating shorelines.

James G. Titus, Rising Seas, Coastal Erosion, and the Takings Clause: How to Save Wetlands and Beaches Without Hurting Property Owners
57 Md. L. Rev. 1279 (1998)

In the next century, the majority of America's publicly owned tidal shorelines could be replaced by a wall, not because anyone decided that this should happen but because no one decided that it should not. Throughout the United States, housing developments are being built just inland of the marshes, swamps, muddy shores, and sandy beaches that collectively comprise the "public trust tidelands." Because sea level is rising and most shores are eroding, the water will eventually reach these houses unless either the houses are moved or somehow the sea is held back.

The most common response has been to build a wall near the boundary between the private dry land and the public tidelands, saving the former but allowing the latter to erode away. Most states tacitly reward riparian owners who build these walls with sole custody of what had been the public shore, by allowing the owners to exclude the public from the area inland from the wall, where there would have been a public beach or wetland had the wall not been built. In Maryland alone, more than 300 miles of tidal shoreline have been armored in the last twenty years. This trend will accelerate if the greenhouse effect increases the rate of sea level rise. . . .

For example, a four-foot rise in sea level would inundate 7,000 square miles of dry land in the contiguous United States—an area the size of Massachusetts. Although the sea is most likely to rise one foot every fifty years for the next few centuries, it could rise at twice that rate—or more. . . .

We should not, however, paint all coasts with a single brush, because America has two types of coast: the ocean and the bay. Along the ocean, sandy public beaches dominate. Recognizing these beaches to be their "crown jewels," coastal communities and states protect them with a variety of policies that seem likely to ensure their survival in all but a few locations.

Farther inland lies the hidden coast that comprises eighty percent of our tidal shorelines. Part sand, part mud, and part vegetated wetland, these shores have diverse uses. Unlike the open ocean coast, our bay shores are gradually being replaced with walls of steel, stone, concrete, and wood (hereinafter "bulkheads"). Where once a fisherman could walk on the public beach, there is no beach. In order to walk along the bulkheads that replaced it, the fisherman must trespass in the backyards of the property owners who built them. Unlike the ocean resorts, where every block has a road leading to the beach, bayfront developments usually provide no access to the shore. Environmental regulations provide only temporary relief, having been designed as if shorelines and sea level were stable. Effective strategies for saving our natural shores apply to the open ocean—but not to the hidden bay.

Why do we treat the ocean and bay coasts differently? Virtually every state has made the policy decision to keep its ocean beaches and not to privatize ocean shores that are currently open to the public. Yet, policy makers have not addressed the loss of natural shores along the hidden coast. The rising sea has placed riparian owners' rights to protect their homes on a collision course with the public's ownership of the intertidal wetlands and beaches. Some of the shore has been given away, and more will be given away as wetlands and beaches erode.

Should we not decide which portions of our bay shores will remain public and in a natural condition? Ironically, land use planning has provided state and local governments with a process for ensuring that some of the privately owned farms and forests remain as open space. Coastal states, however, have no process for deciding how much of the publicly owned shore should remain in its natural condition, or even in public hands.

[There are] land use planning options by which coastal states might retain some of their public trust tidelands in perpetuity—no matter how much the sea rises—at least in areas that have not yet been developed. A key assumption of this analysis is that policies should protect coastal property values. Any policy that fails to do so is likely to be unfair and inefficient and to engender a well-deserved opposition sufficient to prevent implementation on the scale necessary to have a lasting effect. This analysis also assumes a preference for policies that rely on the free market (where possible) and that deal rationally with our inability to say how much the sea will rise. . . .

[There are] three ways to protect tidelands: (1) prevent development in vulnerable areas seaward of a "setback line," (2) defer action, and (3) create rolling easements, which allow development but prohibit property owners from holding back the sea. . . .

Setbacks have been employed along bay shores to limit pollution runoff and along ocean coasts to keep homes from being built in areas that are vulnerable to erosion or storms. In undeveloped areas where all the low land is within a few hundred feet of the shore, preventing or restricting development may be the best way to retain the tidelands. But purchasing an area the size of Massachusetts would be expensive, and regulations to prevent development in such a large area would be inefficient, unfair, and politically infeasible. Moreover, the need to draw a setback line on the map poses two practical difficulties: (1) sea level rise is uncertain and, therefore, defining the appropriate setback line would be difficult; and (2) eventually the shore would retreat to any setback that is established, unless development was prevented in an area much larger than the land that is at risk in the next century. Deferring action will not save the tidelands unless politicians in the future are willing to buy or order the abandonment of this same land after it is developed.

Rolling easements seem more likely to succeed on a broad scale. They do not require particular lines to be drawn on a map, and their impact on current property values would generally be less than one percent. Governments could afford to compensate riparian owners, but even a failure to compensate them would impose only a minor burden. Developers who deny that the sea will rise would view the policy as costing them nothing. Unlike setbacks, rolling easements allow landowners to decide how best to use their property between now and whenever the land finally erodes. Nevertheless, enforcement may be politically difficult. A combination of density restrictions, setbacks, and rolling easements would probably be more successful than relying on any single option.

Would these policies require compensation under the Takings Clause of the Fifth Amendment? [We may assume] that property owners have the right to build a home and protect it from the sea. In areas where the land has already been subdivided, development would often be the only economically productive use of the land. In such cases, preventing development would require compensation. In areas that have not been subdivided, however, preexisting land uses may be profitable. In these cases, preventing development may not require compensation. Deferring action and subsequently requiring people to abandon their homes would involve a taking if the homeowner is willing and able to protect the shore, assuming a right to hold back the sea. Rolling easements, by contrast, would probably not require compensation, given their trivial impact on property values and the several decades that would pass before they had any actual effect.

[Yet I believe that] shorefront owners do not have a right to hold back the sea. For over a thousand years, the "law of erosion" has held that the boundary between public and private land migrates inland as the shore erodes, and there is no right to increase one's land at the expense of a neighbor. Granted, it does not automatically follow that there is no right to prevent a reduction in one's land at the expense of a neighbor, but the theoretical justifications are the same.

Another ancient principle of property law, the public trust doctrine, provides independent support for this view. Although some portions of this doctrine are controversial, no one disputes the rule that a state does not lose ownership of the shore unless it intends to do so. It follows that the state is never required to allow bulkheads that privatize the shoreline. Thus, rolling easements are a codification of the expectations that generally prevailed under the common law. This logic might apply to deferred action, but not if states waive their property interests by telling property owners that they have a right to hold back the sea.

. . . [T]he low cost of rolling easements allows government to bypass the taking's issue by simply purchasing the easements from current landowners. This option is also available to developers and conservancy groups, and may be feasible even in areas that are already developed.

[The following are] recommendations for moving the issue forward. Local master plans should explicitly indicate which areas will retain natural shorelines. State legislatures should authorize tideland planning studies that recommend how much of the shore should be given away. Conservancies and developers should challenge governments by taking initiatives on their own. The federal government may also have a role in its status as a coastal property owner.

Because land use is a state and local responsibility, [we do not need] a federal regulatory solution to this problem. The federal government has had a paramount role in efforts to stop people from destroying coastal wetlands, because those wetlands are generally found within the ebb and flow of our coastal waters, where the federal government has always had jurisdiction. The survival of our coastal wetlands as the sea level rises, however, depends on how people use land that is currently dry and, as such, outside federal jurisdiction. Nevertheless, those who administer, interpret, or comply with coastal wetland protection laws should stop ignoring the fact that the sea level is rising. Everything that these laws have accomplished will be for naught if the government fails to develop a strategy for allowing wetlands to migrate inland—eventually the wetlands that these laws are protecting will all be under water.

The time has come for Americans to decide how much of our natural shoreline we intend to retain. If we wait until all our coastal areas have been developed before we confront this problem, the solutions will be more expensive, less likely to succeed, and more likely to force a showdown between environmentalists and landowners—a showdown that can be avoided by acting now when decades of lead time make it possible for cooler heads to prevail.

NOTES AND QUESTIONS

1. The setback line approach is what the South Carolina Coastal Council attempted to implement, which gave rise to the *Lucas* litigation. Titus mentions two problems with it—the difficulty of defining an appropriate setback line given the uncertainties of forecasting future erosion and the fact that shoreline eventually will retreat to any setback unless it is set extremely far back. Developments on the Isle of Palms after the *Lucas* litigation illustrate these difficulties. The ocean shoreline along the Isle has continued to fluctuate dramatically as a result of inlet shoal migration and attachment. When South Carolina adopted its Beachfront Management Act in 1988, the shoreline at Beachwood East, where Lucas' lots were located, was at its most-seaward known location in the previous 47 years. Yet by 1997, nine years later, it had shifted 200 feet landward. At nearby Summer Dunes Lane the shoreline went from 230 feet seaward of the setback line in 1993 to 60 feet *landward* of it in 1997, a shift of 290 feet in four years. See Jones et al., *Lucas v. South Carolina Coastal Council,* Revisited, in Proceedings of the 22nd Annual Conference, Association of State Floodplain Managers 138 (1998).

2. South Carolina does not allow the use of new hard erosion control devices to protect coastal properties from erosion. In the fall of 1994 a house was constructed on one of the lots formerly owned by Lucas. Two years later beach erosion undermined a dozen homes on the Isle of Palms, including the home built on Lucas' lot and three other nearby homes on Summer Dunes Lane, which had been built behind the most landward shoreline of the past 40 years. Id. The property owners sued the state of South Carolina, seeking to overturn a decision denying them permits to use 31-ton sandbags to protect their homes. While the state allows the use of 5-gallon sandbags in emergencies, the plaintiffs argued that even the placement of 20,000 of these bags on the beach had been insufficient to protect their properties from erosion. Ellison Smith, attorney for the landowners, argued that no possible societal interest could be served by allowing houses to fall

into the ocean. Mary Shahid, attorney for the state Office of Ocean and Coastal Resources management, responded that the "societal interest is to protect the beaches for the public of South Carolina." Langley, Panel Sack Sandbag Request, Charleston Post & Courier, Sept. 12, 1998. The Coastal Zone Management Panel voted 9-1 to uphold a decision by an administrative law judge denying the permits on the ground that the Beachfront Management Act does not allow new hard erosion control devices.

3. Titus proposes several alternatives for implementing the use of "rolling easements." One approach is simply to prohibit the construction of bulkheads or other structures that interfere with naturally migrating shorelines. 57 Md. L. Rev. at 1313. Another approach is to have the government purchase an easement that would allow it to take possession of privately owned coastal land whenever the sea rises by a certain amount. Titus estimates that the nationwide cost of protecting tidelands with rolling easements purchased by the government would range between $373 million and $1.17 billion. Id. at 1398. Other alternatives would be to require that deeds to coastal property specify that the boundary between publicly owned tidelands and privately owned dryland migrates inland to the natural high water mark regardless of any human activities that artificially prevent water from intruding, or by enacting a statute providing that all coastal land is subject to a rolling easement. Id. at 1313.

4. Does coastal property pose unique problems that warrant greater state intervention? In his opinion concurring in the judgment in *Lucas*, page 744, Justice Kennedy expressed the belief that nuisance prevention cannot be "the sole source of state authority to impose severe restrictions" on development of property. He then noted that "[c]oastal property may present such unique concerns for a fragile land system that the State can go further in regulating its development and use than the common law of nuisance might otherwise permit." 505 U.S. at 1035 (Kennedy, J., concurring in the judgment).

5. Changing conceptions of property rights also are reflected in the adoption of "right-to-farm" legislation by several states. Responding to conflicts spawned by the migration to rural areas of suburbanites who are unaccustomed to the smell of agricultural operations, these laws seek to insulate working farms from nuisance liability. For example, an Iowa right-to-farm law allowed counties to designate certain areas as "agricultural areas." Farm operations located in such areas "shall not be found to be a nuisance regardless of the established date of operation or expansion of the agricultural activities of the farm" so long as they are not operated negligently. Iowa Code §352.11(1). This legislation was struck down in Bormann v. Board of Supervisors for Kossuth County, 584 N.W.2d 309 (1998). The Iowa Supreme Court held that the law exceeded the legislature's authority and violated both the federal and state constitutions because it essentially gave farmers the right to take easements over their neighbor's property by engaging in activities that would interfere with the use or enjoyment of nonagricultural property.

6. Former EPA Administrator William K. Reilly argues that a "primary reason for failure to manage our lands rationally is the continuing lack of consensus about the proper reach of government and public authority in constraining the behavior of private landowners." Reilly, Across the Barricades, in Land Use in America 188 (1996). Some have argued that new forms of collaborative governance may be necessary to resolve these conflicts. What alternative mechanisms can you envision for defusing conflicts between property rights and environmental protection?

=8=

Environmental Impact Assessment

NEPA requires that an agency must—to the *fullest* extent possible under its other statutory obligations—consider alternatives to its actions which would reduce environmental damage. That principle establishes that consideration of environmental matters must be more than a *pro forma* ritual. Clearly, it is pointless to "consider" environmental costs without also seriously considering action to avoid them. Such a full exercise of substantive discretion is required at every important, appropriate, and nonduplicative stage of an agency's proceedings.

—*Judge J. Skelly Wright**

The National Environmental Policy Act (NEPA) of 1969, the statute that launched the "environmental decade" of the 1970s, has been hailed as one of the nation's most important environmental laws. It has also been condemned with equal vigor on grounds that it imposes costly, dilatory, and pointless paper-shuffling requirements on federal agencies and, indirectly, on private parties. NEPA famously requires federal agencies to produce environmental impact statements (EISs) prior to undertaking "major Federal actions significantly affecting the quality of the human environment." It requires little else, and therein lies both its singular genius and its fatal flaw.

—*Bradley C. Karkkainen***

Originating in the United States with the enactment of the National Environmental Policy Act of 1969 (NEPA), environmental impact assessment (EIA) requirements have become the most widely emulated form of environmental regulation in the world today. More than 80 countries and 25 states have adopted some form of environmental assessment requirement. CEQ, The National Environmental Policy Act: A Study of Its Effectiveness After Twenty-five Years (1997). In some countries, EIA requirements serve as the framework for the nation's system of environmental regulation. Global institutions such as the World Bank have adopted EIA requirements for projects they fund throughout the world. This chapter focuses on NEPA and the process of environmental impact assessment in the United States.

---

*Calvert Cliffs Coordinating Committee v. U.S. Atomic Energy Commission, 448 F.2d 1109 (D.C. Cir. 1971).

**Toward a Smarter NEPA: Monitoring and Managing Government's Environmental Performance, 102 Colum. L. Rev. 903, 904 (2002).

A.   THE NATIONAL ENVIRONMENTAL POLICY ACT: AN OVERVIEW

On January 1, 1970, President Richard Nixon inaugurated what would come to be known as "the environmental decade" by signing into law the National Environmental Policy Act (Pub. L. 91-190, codified at 42 U.S.C. §§4321-4370a). The Act, usually referred to as "NEPA," set forth broad principles and goals for the nation's environmental policy. It established as "the continuing policy of the Federal Government . . . to use all practicable means and measures . . . to create and maintain conditions under which man and nature can exist in productive harmony, and fulfill the social, economic and other requirements of present and future generations of Americans." §101(a), 42 U.S.C. §4331 (a).

NEPA adopted an unusual strategy to pursue this ambitious goal. Rather than erecting an elaborate regulatory scheme applicable to business and industry, NEPA instead mandated a significant change in the decision-making procedures used by federal agencies. The Act requires all federal agencies to consider the likely environmental effects of their activities. Specifically, section 102 of NEPA requires that all federal agencies

> include in every recommendation or report on proposals for legislation and other major federal actions significantly affecting the quality of the human environment, a detailed statement by the responsible official on—
>
> (i) the environmental impact of the proposed action, (ii) any adverse environmental effects which cannot be avoided should the proposal be implemented, (iii) alternatives to the proposed action, (iv) the relationship between local short-term uses of man's environment and the maintenance and enhancement of long-term productivity, and (v) any irreversible and irretrievable commitments of resources which would be involved in the proposed action should it be implemented. [42 U.S.C. §4332(C).]

The remarkably simple structure of NEPA is outlined below.

STRUCTURE OF THE NATIONAL ENVIRONMENTAL POLICY ACT

§101 establishes as the continuing policy of the Federal Government the use of all practicable means to create and maintain conditions under which man and nature can exist in productive harmony.

§102(2)(C) requires all federal agencies to prepare an environmental impact statement (EIS) on major federal actions significantly affecting the quality of the environment. The EIS must include a detailed statement of environmental impacts, alternatives to the proposed action and any irretrievable commitments of resources involved.

§102(2)(E) requires all federal agencies to study alternatives to actions involving unresolved resource conflicts.

§201 requires the President to submit to Congress an annual Environmental Quality Report. (The report for the year 1997 was the last report issued due to enactment of the Federal Reports Elimination and Sunset Act, Pub. L. 104-66.)

§202 establishes a three-member Council on Environmental Quality (CEQ) in the Executive Office of the President.

§204 outlines duties and functions of CEQ including annual reporting on the condition of the environment, information gathering, and review and appraisal of federal programs and activities.

Reviewing federal agency actions for compliance with NEPA, the courts quickly established that section 102's obligations were substantial. The "detailed statement" required (known as an "environmental impact statement," or EIS) has become, through judicial and administrative interpretations, an often massive undertaking. While federal regulations provide that an EIS generally should not exceed 150 pages in length, many are far longer. The EIS on an offshore oil lease sale is likely to be several hundred pages, while the EIS for licensing of a nuclear power plant may reach several thousand.

Each federal agency is made responsible for implementing NEPA, but Congress also created a central agency, the Council on Environmental Quality (CEQ), to coordinate agencies' compliance with NEPA. CEQ developed guidelines for NEPA implementation and, in 1978, armed with an executive order from President Carter, CEQ promulgated regulations on NEPA implementation that are binding on all federal agencies. 40 C.F.R. pt. 1500. These regulations, which reflect much of the case law that had developed under the statute, are the first recourse for analysis of any NEPA problem. They spell out many of the details of the NEPA process, and they receive considerable deference from the courts.

The principal arbiters of NEPA's requirements, however, have been the federal courts. Hundreds of judicial decisions have examined and elaborated on NEPA's requirements. The most influential early decision interpreting the duties NEPA imposes on federal agencies was the product of a challenge to the way the Atomic Energy Commission (AEC) had construed the Act.

During the late 1960s the AEC aggressively encouraged electric utilities to build nuclear power plants. In 1968 the Baltimore Gas and Electric Company began construction of a nuclear power plant at Calvert Cliffs, Maryland, along the western shore of the Chesapeake Bay, just a year after announcing the project. Environmentalists opposing the plant formed a group called the Calvert Cliffs Coordinating Committee. The group was particularly concerned about the effect of thermal discharges and radiological emissions from the plant on the Chesapeake Bay.

After NEPA was enacted in 1970, the AEC issued regulations requiring permit applicants to prepare an environmental report to accompany their applications. However, the AEC took the position that it did not have to consider the report unless parties raised specific challenges to it during the licensing process. In the case below the Calvert Cliffs Coordinating Committee argued that the AEC's regulations violated NEPA because they did not require the agency independently to assess environmental impacts.

Calvert Cliffs Coordinating Committee v. United States Atomic Energy Commission
449 F.2d 1109 (D.C. Cir. 1971)

J. SKELLY WRIGHT, Circuit Judge:

These cases are only the beginning of what promises to become a flood of new litigation—litigation seeking judicial assistance in protecting our natural environment. Several recently enacted statutes attest to the commitment of the Government to control, at long last, the destructive engine of material "progress." But it remains to be seen whether the promise of this legislation will become a reality. Therein lies the judicial role. In these cases, we must for the first time interpret the broadest and perhaps most important of the recent statutes: the National Environmental Policy Act of 1969 (NEPA). We must assess claims that one of the agencies charged with its administration has failed to live up to the congressional mandate. Our duty, in short, is to see that important legislative purposes, heralded in the halls of Congress, are not lost or misdirected in the vast hallways of the federal bureaucracy.

NEPA, like so much other reform legislation of the last 40 years, is cast in terms of a general mandate and broad delegation of authority to new and old administrative agencies. It takes the major step of requiring all federal agencies to consider values of environmental preservation in their spheres of activity, and it prescribes certain procedural measures to ensure that those values are in fact fully respected. Petitioners argue that rules recently adopted by the Atomic Energy Commission to govern consideration of environmental matters fail to satisfy the rigor demanded by NEPA. The Commission, on the other hand, contends that the vagueness of the NEPA mandate and delegation leaves much room for discretion and that the rules challenged by petitioners fall well within the broad scope of the Act. . . .

I

We begin our analysis with an examination of NEPA's structure and approach and of the Atomic Energy Commission rules which are said to conflict with the requirements of the Act. The relevant portion of NEPA is Title I, consisting of five sections. Section 101 sets forth the Act's basic substantive policy: that the federal government "use all practicable means and measures" to protect environmental values. Congress did not establish environmental protection as an exclusive goal; rather, it desired a reordering of priorities, so that environmental costs and benefits will assume their proper place along with other considerations. In Section 101(b), imposing an explicit duty on federal officials, the Act provides that "it is the continuing responsibility of the Federal Government to use all practicable means, consistent with other essential considerations of national policy," to avoid environmental degradation, preserve "historic, cultural, and natural" resources, and promote "the widest range of beneficial uses of the environment without . . . undesirable and unintended consequences."

Thus the general substantive policy of the Act is a flexible one. It leaves room for a responsible exercise of discretion and may not require particular substantive results in particular problematic instances. However, the Act also contains very important "procedural" provisions—provisions which are designed to see that all federal agencies do in fact exercise the substantive discretion given them. These provisions are not highly flexible. Indeed, they establish a strict standard of compliance. . . .

. . . Section 102(2)(C) requires that responsible officials of all agencies prepare a "detailed statement" covering the impact of particular actions on the environment, the environmental costs which might be avoided, and alternative measures which might alter the cost-benefit equation. The apparent purpose of the "detailed statement" is to aid in the agencies' own decision-making process and to advise other interested agencies and the public of the environmental consequences of planned federal action. Beyond the "detailed statement," Section [102(2)(E)] requires all agencies specifically to "study, develop, and describe appropriate alternatives to recommended courses of action in any proposal which involves unresolved conflicts concerning alternative uses of available resources." This requirement, like the "detailed statement" requirement, seeks to ensure that each agency decisionmaker has before him and takes into proper account all possible approaches to a particular project (including total abandonment of the project) which would alter the environmental impact and the cost-benefit balance. Only in that fashion is it likely that the most intelligent, optimally beneficial decision will ultimately be made. Moreover, by compelling a formal "detailed statement" and a description of alternatives, NEPA provides evidence that the mandated decisionmaking process has in fact taken place and, most importantly, allows those removed from the initial process to evaluate and balance the factors on their own.

Of course, all of these Section 102 duties are qualified by the phrase "to the fullest extent possible." We must stress as forcefully as possible that this language does not provide an escape hatch for foot-dragging agencies; it does not make NEPA's procedural requirements somehow "discretionary." Congress did not intend the Act to be such a paper tiger. Indeed, the requirement of environmental consideration "to the fullest extent possible" sets a high standard for the agencies, a standard which must be rigorously enforced by the reviewing courts. . . .

. . . [T]he Section 102 duties are not inherently flexible. They must be complied with to the fullest extent, unless there is a clear conflict of *statutory* authority. Considerations of administrative difficulty, delay, or economic cost will not suffice to strip the section of its fundamental importance.

We conclude, then, that Section 102 of NEPA mandates a particular sort of careful and informed decisionmaking process and creates judicially enforceable duties. The reviewing courts probably cannot reverse a substantive decision on its merits, under Section 101, unless it be shown that the actual balance of costs and benefits that was struck was arbitrary or clearly gave insufficient weight to environmental values. But if the decision was reached procedurally without individualized consideration and balancing of environmental factors— conducted fully and in good faith—it is the responsibility of the courts to reverse. As one District Court has said of Section 102 requirements: "It is hard to imagine a clearer or stronger mandate to the Courts."

In the cases before us now, we do not have to review a particular decision by the Atomic Energy Commission granting a construction permit or an operating license. Rather, we must review the Commission's recently promulgated rules which govern consideration of environmental values in all such individual decisions. The rules were devised strictly in order to comply with the NEPA procedural requirements—but petitioners argue that they fall far short of the congressional mandate. [The rules provided that an applicant seeking permission to build and operate a nuclear power plant must prepare an "environmental report" assessing the likely impacts of the facility and possible alternatives. On the basis of the report, Commission staff would then prepare its own "detailed statement." The report and the detailed statement would accompany the application through the review process. However, they would not be considered by the licensing board (which decides the application), or received into evidence, unless environmental issues were raised by a party to the proceeding.] . . .

The question here is whether the Commission is correct in thinking that its NEPA responsibilities may "be carried out in toto outside the hearing process"—whether it is enough that environmental data and evaluations merely "accompany" an application through the review process, but receive no consideration whatever from the hearing board.

We believe that the Commission's crabbed interpretation of NEPA makes a mockery of the Act. What possible purpose could there be in the Section 102(2)(C) requirement (that the "detailed statement" accompany proposals through agency review processes) if "accompany" means no more than physical proximity—mandating no more than the physical act of passing certain folders and papers, unopened, to reviewing officials along with other folders and papers? What possible purpose could there be in requiring the "detailed statement" to be before hearing boards, if the boards are free to ignore entirely the contents of the statement? NEPA was meant to do more than regulate the flow of papers in the federal bureaucracy. The word "accompany" in Section 102(2)(C) must not be read so narrowly as to make the Act ludicrous. It must, rather, be read to indicate a congressional intent that environmental factors, as compiled in the "detailed statement," be *considered* through agency review processes.

Beyond Section 102(2)(C), NEPA requires that agencies consider the environmental impact of their actions "to the fullest extent possible." The Act is addressed to agencies as a whole, not only to their professional staffs. Compliance to the *"fullest"* possible extent would seem to demand that environmental issues be considered at every important stage in the decisionmaking process concerning a particular action—at every stage where an overall balancing of environmental and nonenvironmental factors is appropriate and where alterations might be made in the proposed action to minimize environmental costs. . . .

NEPA mandates a case-by-case balancing judgment on the part of federal agencies. In each individual case, the particular economic and technical benefits of planned action must be assessed and then weighed against the environmental costs; alternatives must be considered which would affect the balance of values. The magnitude of possible benefits and possible costs may lie anywhere on a broad spectrum. Much will depend on the particular magnitudes involved in particular cases. In some cases, the benefits will be great enough to justify a certain quantum of environmental costs; in other cases, they will not be so great and the proposed action may have to be abandoned or significantly altered so as to bring the benefits and costs into a proper balance. The point of the individualized balancing analysis is to ensure that, with possible alterations, the optimally beneficial action is finally taken.

Certification by another agency that its own environmental standards are satisfied involves an entirely different kind of judgment. Such agencies, without overall responsibility for the particular federal action in question, attend only to one aspect of the problem: the magnitude of certain environmental costs. They simply determine whether those costs exceed an allowable amount. Their certification does not mean that they found no environmental damage whatever. In fact, there may be significant environmental damage (e.g., water pollution), but not quite enough to violate applicable (e.g., water quality) standards. Certifying agencies do not attempt to weigh that damage against the opposing benefits. Thus the balancing analysis remains to be done. It may be that the environmental costs, though passing prescribed standards, are nonetheless great enough to outweigh the particular economic and technical benefits involved in the planned action. The only agency in a position to make such a judgment is the agency with overall responsibility for the proposed federal action—the agency to which NEPA is specifically directed. . . .

NEPA requires that an agency must—to the *fullest* extent possible under its other statutory obligations—consider alternatives to its actions which would reduce environmental damage. That principle establishes that consideration of environmental matters must be more than a *pro forma* ritual. Clearly, it is pointless to "consider" environmental costs without also seriously considering action to avoid them. Such a full exercise of substantive discretion is required at every important, appropriate, and nonduplicative stage of an agency's proceedings.

NOTES AND QUESTIONS

1. The AEC had argued that NEPA should be interpreted to create "flexible" duties. How did the court respond to this argument? What must the AEC do to comply with NEPA as a result of this decision?

2. The AEC argued that it need not consider air and water pollution caused by a proposed plant because those effects already are subject to EPA regulation. Is that position unreasonable? Is it supported by NEPA? Why does the court reject it? How would such a rule affect the review envisioned by the court? Does the court's formulation make NEPA review redundant of reviews under other environmental laws?

3. The *Calvert Cliffs* decision is important because it established that NEPA creates judicially enforceable duties. What standard of compliance does the court establish? How much consideration must agencies give to environmental impacts? At what stages of the decision making process must they be considered?

4. Fascinating background information on the enactment of NEPA and the *Calvert Cliffs* litigation is provided by Dan Tarlock in "The Story of *Calvert Cliffs*: A Court Construes the National Environmental Policy Act to Create a Powerful Cause of Action," in Environmental Law Stories 77 (Lazarus & Houck eds., 2005). Tarlock notes that the decision halted licensing of all nuclear power plants for 18 months and forced fundamental changes in the AEC licensing process. It "cemented the principle that the potential adverse environmental impacts and available alternatives of a wide range of government sponsored and licensed activities should be rigorously assessed in advance of the activities." Id. at 102. The result has been the development of what Tarlock refers to as "a 'common law' of impact assessment." Id. This has "democratized NEPA and environmental protection generally" by forcing agencies to open up their decision-making processes to citizen involvement in an effort to forestall subsequent challenges to agency EISs.

5. Another important issue raised by Judge Wright in *Calvert Cliffs* is whether NEPA imposes enforceable *substantive* obligations on federal agencies.

What does Judge Wright say about that in his opinion? The issue was addressed by the Supreme Court several years later in the following case, which it decided summarily without hearing oral argument.

Strycker's Bay Neighborhood Council, Inc. v. Karlen
444 U.S. 223 (1980)

[Plaintiffs sought to enjoin construction of a low-income housing project on the Upper West Side of Manhattan. They challenged the approval of the project by the U.S. Department of Housing and Urban Development (HUD). After the district court upheld HUD's decision, the Second Circuit reversed, holding that NEPA required consideration of alternatives to the proposed project, even though NEPA did *not* require preparation of an EIS. Following the Second Circuit's decisions, the case was remanded to HUD.]

PER CURIAM.

On remand, HUD prepared a lengthy report entitled Special Environmental Clearance (1977). After marshaling the data, the report asserted that, "while the choice of Site 30 for development as a 100 percent low-income project has raised valid questions about the potential social environmental impacts involved, the problems associated with the impact on social fabric and community structures are not considered so serious as to require that this component be rated as unacceptable." Special Environmental Clearance Report 42. The last portion of the report incorporated a study wherein the [New York City Planning] Commission evaluated nine alternative locations for the project and found none of them acceptable. While HUD's report conceded that this study may not have considered all possible alternatives, it credited the Commission's conclusion that any relocation of the units would entail an unacceptable delay of two years or more. According to HUD, "[m]easured against the environmental costs associated with the minimum two-year delay, the benefits seem insufficient to justify a mandated substitution of sites." Id., at 54.

After soliciting the parties' comments on HUD's report, the District Court again entered judgment in favor of petitioners. See Trinity Episcopal School Corp. v. Harris, 445 F. Supp. 204 (1978). The court was "impressed with [HUD's analysis] as being thorough and exhaustive," id., at 209-210, and found that "HUD's consideration of the alternatives was neither arbitrary nor capricious"; on the contrary, "[i]t was done in good faith and in full accordance with the law." Id. at 220.

On appeal, the Second Circuit vacated and remanded again. Karlen v. Harris, 590 F.2d 39 (1978). The appellate court focused upon that part of HUD's report where the agency considered and rejected alternative sites, and in particular upon HUD's reliance on the delay such a relocation would entail. The Court of Appeals purported to recognize that its role in reviewing HUD's decision was defined by the Administrative Procedure Act (APA), 5 U.S.C. §706(2)(A), which provides that agency actions should be set aside if found to be "arbitrary, capricious, an abuse of discretion, or otherwise not in accordance with law. . . ." Additionally, however, the Court of Appeals looked to "[t]he provisions of NEPA" for "the substantive standards necessary to review the merits of agency decisions. . . ." 590 F.2d, at 43. The Court of Appeals conceded that HUD had "given 'consideration' to alternatives" to redesignating the site. Id., at 44. Nevertheless, the court believed that " 'consideration' is not an end in itself." Ibid. Concentrating on HUD's finding that development of an alternative location would entail an unacceptable delay, the appellate court held that such delay could not be "an overriding factor" in HUD's decision to proceed with the development. Ibid. According to the court, when HUD considers such projects, "environmental factors, such as crowding low-income housing into a concentrated area, should be given determinative weight." Ibid. The Court of Appeals therefore remanded the case to the District Court, instructing HUD to attack the shortage of low-income housing in a manner that would avoid the "concentration" of such housing on Site 30. Id., at 45.

In Vermont Yankee Nuclear Power Corp. v. NRDC, 435 U.S. 519, 558 (1978), we stated that NEPA, while establishing "significant substantive goals for the Nation," imposes upon agencies duties that are "essentially procedural." As we stressed in that case, NEPA was designed "to insure a fully informed and well-considered decision," but not necessarily "a decision the judges of the Court of Appeals or of this Court would have reached had they been members of the decisionmaking unit of the agency." Ibid. *Vermont Yankee* cuts sharply against the Court of Appeals' conclusion that an agency, in selecting a course of action, must elevate environmental concerns over other appropriate considerations. On the contrary, once an agency has made a decision subject to NEPA's procedural requirements, the only role for a court is to insure that the agency has considered the environmental consequences; it cannot "interject itself within the area of discretion of the executive as to the choice of the action to be taken." Kleppe v. Sierra Club, 437 U.S. 390, 410, n.21 (1976). See also FPC v. Transcontinental Gas Pipe Line Corp., 423 U.S. 326 (1976).

In the present litigation there is no doubt that HUD considered the environmental consequences of its decision to redesignate the proposed site for low-income housing. NEPA requires no more. The petitions for certiorari are granted, and the judgment of the Court of Appeals is therefore reversed.

MR. JUSTICE MARSHALL, dissenting.

The issue raised by these cases is far more difficult than the *per curiam* opinion suggests. . . .

The issue before the Court of Appeals . . . was whether HUD was free under NEPA to reject an alternative acknowledged to be environmentally preferable solely on the ground that any change in sites would cause delay. This was hardly a "peripheral issue" in the case. Whether NEPA, which sets forth "significant substantive goals," Vermont Yankee Nuclear Power Corp. v. NRDC, supra, at 558, permits a projected 2-year time difference to be controlling over environmental superiority is by no means clear. Resolution of the issue, however, is certainly within the normal scope of review of agency action to determine if it is arbitrary, capricious, or an abuse of discretion. The question whether HUD can make delay the paramount concern over environmental superiority is essentially a restatement of the question whether HUD in considering the environmental consequences of its proposed action gave those consequences a "hard look," which is exactly the proper question for the reviewing court to ask. Kleppe v. Sierra Club, supra, at 410, n.21.

The issue of whether the Secretary's decision was arbitrary or capricious is sufficiently difficult and important to merit plenary consideration in this Court.

Further, I do not subscribe to the Court's apparent suggestion that *Vermont Yankee* limits the reviewing court to the essentially mindless task of determining whether an agency "considered" environmental factors even if that agency may have effectively decided to ignore those factors in reaching its conclusion. Indeed, I cannot believe that the Court would adhere to that position in a different factual setting. Our cases establish that the arbitrary-or-capricious standard prescribes a "searching and careful" judicial inquiry designed to ensure that the agency has not exercised its discretion in an unreasonable manner. *Citizens to Preserve Overton Park, Inc. v. Volpe*, 401 U.S. 402, 416 (1971). Believing that today's summary reversal represents a departure from that principle, I respectfully dissent.

NOTES AND QUESTIONS

1. In *Strycker's Bay*, the Supreme Court states that "once an agency has made a decision subject to NEPA's procedural requirements, the only role for a court is to insure that the agency has considered the environmental consequences." If an agency has "considered" environmental consequences in an EIS, can it then give *no* weight to those factors in its final decision? Consider Justice Marshall's argument in dissent. Consider also Judge Wright's suggestion in *Calvert Cliffs* that a court could "reverse a substantive decision on its merits, under Section 101, [if] the actual balance of costs and benefits that was struck was arbitrary or clearly gave insufficient weight to environmental values." Does the Supreme Court reject that interpretation in *Strycker's Bay*? What "weight" had the Second Circuit required HUD to give to environmental values?

2. *Strycker's Bay* confirms the triumph of process over substance in the NEPA context. As Dan Tarlock notes, "the formulation of affirmative environmental policies—the original purpose for enacting the statute—has become increasingly divorced from the EIS process." Judge Wright in *Calvert Cliffs* had "assumed that the agency would assemble the relevant environmental information and then use this information to make a reasoned choice, balancing between environmental and non-environmental values." But "[i]nstead of forcing agencies to prefer more environmentally sustainable options, . . . an agency need only seriously consider environmental values by displaying adverse impacts and agonizing a bit over the consequences of the proposed decision." A. Dan Tarlock, "The Story of *Calvert Cliffs*: A Court Construes the National Environmental Policy Act to Create a Powerful Cause of Action," in Environmental Law Stories 102 (Lazarus & Houck eds., 2005). As a result, Tarlock argues, the EIS has become like a corporate filing with the Securities and Exchange Commission.

3. The papers of the late Justice Thurgood Marshall reveal that then—Justice Rehnquist authored the per curiam opinion in *Strycker's Bay*, and that it was approved by the Court with remarkable speed and virtually no debate. Five Justices joined the draft per curiam opinion the day after it was first circulated; the other two joined the very next day. Percival, Environmental Law in the Supreme Court: Highlights from the Marshall Papers, 23 Envtl. L. Rep. 10606, 10611 (1993).

4. Two major sets of issues arise frequently in NEPA litigation: (1) questions concerning the circumstances under which agencies are required to prepare EISs, and (2) questions concerning the adequacy of the EIS. In cases where an agency has not prepared an EIS, courts must determine whether an EIS is

required and, if not, whether the agency has complied with NEPA's other requirements. Where the agency has prepared an EIS, judicial review often focuses on the adequacy of that document. We consider these two fundamental sets of questions in turn.

B. UNDER WHAT CIRCUMSTANCES MUST AN ENVIRONMENTAL IMPACT STATEMENT BE PREPARED?

The threshold for the EIS requirement is set out in the statute: An EIS must be prepared for "proposals for legislation and other major Federal actions significantly affecting the quality of the human environment." To determine the scope and timing of NEPA's obligations, the courts have parsed these statutory words and looked to the congressional purposes that lie behind them. To define the boundaries of the inquiry, courts have focused on the first clause: There must be a "proposal" either for "legislation" or for "major Federal action." Within these boundaries the crucial question then becomes whether the action's effects on the "human environment" will be "significant."

1. *"Proposals for Legislation and Other Major Federal Actions"*

By its terms, NEPA applies both to proposals for "legislation" and to proposals for "other major Federal actions." The lion's share of litigation has centered around the application of NEPA to the latter. Before examining what constitutes "major federal action," we consider why the legislative EIS requirement has rarely been enforced.

A. *"PROPOSALS FOR LEGISLATION"*

Even though NEPA's EIS requirement applies to agency "proposals for legislation," legislative EISs rarely have been performed. Although CEQ initially took the position that section 102(2)(C)'s requirements applied to an appropriations request, the council reversed itself when it issued regulations implementing NEPA in 1978. Stating that CEQ's regulations are due "substantial deference," the Supreme Court held in Andrus v. Sierra Club, 442 U.S. 347 (1979), that agencies' requests to Congress for appropriations are not "proposals for legislation" within the meaning of NEPA's EIS requirement.

Legislative EIS issues resurfaced when the Bush administration refused to prepare an EIS for the North American Free Trade Agreement (NAFTA). In 1990, the United States, Mexico, and Canada initiated negotiations on NAFTA, which would significantly reduce trade barriers between the three countries. While it is widely believed that trade liberalization can have significant environmental consequences (see Chapter 11, pages 1074-1078), the Office of the U.S. Trade Representative (USTR) announced that it would not prepare an EIS for any trade agreement that would be submitted to Congress for approval. Public Citizen then filed suit seeking to compel the USTR to prepare an EIS for NAFTA.

Because NEPA does not have its own citizen suit provision, Public Citizen relied on the APA's judicial review provisions, 5 U.S.C. §702. After losing in the district court on the ground that it lacked standing, Public Citizen appealed to the D.C. Circuit, which held that it lacked jurisdiction to hear the suit because the negotiations had not yet been concluded, which meant that there was no final agency action for purposes of the Administrative Procedure Act (APA). Public Citizen v. Office of the U.S. Trade Representative, 970 F.2d 916 (D.C. Cir. 1992).

After two years of negotiations, agreement on NAFTA was reached and signed on December 17, 1992. Public Citizen again filed suit. This time the district court granted Public Citizen's motion for summary judgment and ordered the USTR to prepare an EIS. The government filed an emergency appeal to the D.C. Circuit, which reversed in Public Citizen v. U.S. Trade Representative, 5 F.3d 549 (D.C. Cir. 1993).

The D.C. Circuit held that the failure to prepare an EIS for NAFTA was not judicially reviewable because it is the *President* and not USTR, who ultimately is responsible for submitting NAFTA to Congress for approval. Thus, the only "final action" was that of the President, who, unlike USTR, is not an agency whose actions are subject to review under the APA. The court relied on Franklin v. Massachusetts, 505 U.S. 788 (1992), which held that the method used by the Secretary of Commerce in the 1990 census to determine apportionment of congressional representatives was not judicially reviewable because the only final action affecting plaintiffs under the statute was the President's transmittal of the apportionment to Congress. Public Citizen attempted to distinguish *Franklin* by arguing that the EIS requirement is an independent statutory obligation of the USTR, but the court found that unpersuasive because preparation of the census report also was an independent statutory obligation of the Secretary of Commerce. Responding to the argument that this would be the "death knell" for judicial review of compliance with legislative EIS requirements, the court stated that its decision was "limited to those cases in which the President has final constitutional or statutory responsibility for the final step necessary for the agency action directly to affect the parties." 5 F.3d at 552. In a concurring opinion, Judge Randolph opined that *Franklin*'s "direct effects" requirement should be viewed as the "death knell" of judicial review for failure to prepare a legislative EIS because "it is difficult to see how the act of proposing legislation could generate direct effects on parties, or anyone else for that matter." 5 F.3d at 553 (Randolph, J., concurring).

In 1994, after the Clinton administration completed participation in the Uruguay Round of negotiations on the General Agreement on Tariffs and Trade (GATT), Public Citizen again sued USTR for failing to prepare an EIS. The district court promptly dismissed the case, holding that it was controlled by the D.C. Circuit's decision in the NAFTA litigation. Public Citizen v. Kantor, 864 F. Supp. 208 (D.D.C. 1994).

Congress ultimately approved both NAFTA and U.S. entry into the World Trade Organization (WTO), which was created by the Uruguay Round of GATT negotiations. As discussed in Chapter 10, one condition for U.S. approval of NAFTA was the successful negotiation of side agreements governing environmental and labor concerns. The WTO, which is not subject to such side agreements, has been heavily criticized as insufficiently sympathetic to environmental concerns.

In November 1999, on the eve of the WTO meetings in Seattle, President Clinton announced that he was issuing an executive order requiring that "environmental reviews" be conducted for future trade agreements. Executive Order 13,141 directs the U.S. Trade Representative to prepare an "environmental review" for three types of trade agreements: comprehensive multilateral trade rounds, bilateral or plurilateral free trade agreements, and major new trade agreements in natural resource sectors. While it does not specify how extensive the review is to be, or how it compares with an EIS, the executive order states that the focus of environmental reviews generally "will be impacts in the United States," though "global and transboundary impacts" can be examined when "appropriate and prudent." Where practicable, the reviews are to be made available in draft form for public comment. The executive order states that it does not create any new rights or responsibilities enforceable in court.

IMPLEMENTING NEPA: A PATHFINDER

The National Environmental Policy Act (NEPA) is codified at 42 U.S.C. §§4321-4370e. The Council on Environmental Quality (CEQ), part of the Executive Office of the President, is responsible for coordinating agency compliance with NEPA and for preparing the annual Environmental Quality Report, which the President submits to Congress. CEQ regulations governing compliance with NEPA are the most helpful elaboration of NEPA's requirements; they can be found at 40 C.F.R. pts. 1500-1517. Each federal agency also has regulations specifying their procedures for complying with NEPA.

CEQ also maintains a very helpful homepage located at *http://www.whitehouse.gov/ceq* that provides considerable information about NEPA. CEQ's webpage contains a service known as NEPAnet, at *http://ceq.eh.doe.gov/nepa/nepanet.htm*, which provides links to NEPA regulations, agency NEPA websites, guidance documents, CEQ's annual reports, and other NEPA information. CEQ's annual reports contain summaries of important judicial decisions involving NEPA decided during the previous year, statistics on NEPA litigation and environmental impact statements (EISs) prepared by agencies, and considerable data on environmental conditions and trends. The U.S. Geological Survey maintains an Environmental Impact Analysis Data Links webpage, which is located at *http://water.usgs.gov/eap/env_data.html*. This provides links to diverse data sets useful in preparing and assessing EISs.

CEQ's study, The National Environmental Policy Act: A Study of Its Effectiveness After Twenty-five Years (Jan. 1997), provides a detailed critique of how well NEPA has worked. The report, which is available on CEQ's webpage, contains a useful bibliography. For a report describing how NEPA's requirements have been eroded and attacked in recent years, see Robert G. Dreher, NEPA Under Siege: The Political Assault on the National Environmental Policy Act (2005). The House Committee on Resources has prepared its own critique of NEPA. Task Force on Improving the National Environmental Policy Act and Task Force on Updating the National Environmental Policy Act, Initial Findings and Draft Recommendations, Dec. 21, 2005.

B.   "MAJOR FEDERAL ACTION"

It is now well-settled that the term "major Federal action" is not confined to projects that the federal government is funding or carrying out. The courts have found that the term also includes private projects that require federal approval as well as federal programs, policies, and rules. The case law is summarized in the CEQ Regulations contained in 40 C.F.R. §1508.18. These regulations define "major Federal action" to include "actions with effects that may be major and which are potentially subject to Federal control and responsibility." Id. The CEQ regulations specify that such action may include a failure to act by responsible officials if that failure would be reviewable under the Administrative Procedure Act or other applicable law as agency action.

Under CEQ's interpretation, major federal actions include "projects and programs entirely or partly financed, assisted, conducted, regulated, or approved by federal agencies" as well as "new or revised agency rules, regulations, plans, policies, or procedures." Id. Enforcement actions taken by federal agencies are not included within CEQ's definition of major federal action. The CEQ regulations note that federal actions generally fall within one of the following categories:

(1) Adoption of official policy, such as rules, regulations, and interpretations adopted pursuant to the Administrative Procedure Act, 5 U.S.C. §§551 et seq.; treaties and international conventions or agreements; formal documents establishing an agency's policies which will result in or substantially alter agency programs.

(2) Adoption of formal plans, such as official documents prepared or approved by federal agencies which guide or prescribe alternative uses of federal resources, upon which future agency actions will be based.

(3) Adoption of programs, such as a group of concerted actions to implement a specific policy or plan; systematic and connected agency decisions allocating agency resources to implement a specific statutory program or executive directive.

(4) Approval of specific projects, such as construction or management activities located in a defined geographic area. Projects include actions approved by permit or other regulatory decision as well as federal and federally assisted activities. (40 C.F.R. §1508.18(b).)

Difficult questions about the extent of NEPA's application to a private project arise when only a small but integral part of the project requires federal approval. This occasionally occurs in cases involving "segmentation" of a highway project. In those cases, courts have held that, in approving a proposed highway project, the Federal Highway Administration must consider the effects of possible future highway construction that will be made possible by the instant proposal, unless the proposed segment has "logical termini" and "independent utility." See, e.g., Lange v. Brinegar, 625 F.2d 812 (9th Cir. 1980); Swain v. Brinegar, 542 F.2d 364 (7th Cir. 1976). A somewhat similar issue arose in Winnebago Tribe of Nebraska v. Ray, 621 F.2d 269 (8th Cir. 1980). In that case an Indian tribe argued that because construction of a proposed power line required a permit from the Army Corps of Engineers to cross the Missouri River, the Corps was required to prepare an EIS covering the impact of the entire transmission line. The Eighth Circuit rejected this argument and held that the Corps could restrict its consideration to the impact on the area in and around the navigable waters in determining whether the action required an EIS.

In Ross v. Federal Highway Administration, 162 F.3d 1046 (10th Cir. 1998), the Tenth Circuit upheld a district court decision that a state could not avoid application of NEPA simply by deciding not to use federal funds when it commenced construction of a segment of a highway construction project that affected spiritual sites and property of a Native American tribe. Faced with a ruling that it needed to prepare a supplemental EIS for the project, the Kansas Department of Transportation had asked the Federal Highway Administration to segment the project into four parts. It then began construction of the eastern leg of the project without federal funds. Plaintiffs succeeded in stopping the project by convincing a federal district court that the entire project was a major federal action subject to NEPA because Congress had designated it a federal demonstration project for which $10 million in federal funds could not be segmented.

In 1992, the federal government agreed to settle litigation it had brought against the Southern Florida Water Management District and the Florida Department of Environmental Regulation for contaminating a national wildlife refuge and a national park in the Everglades. The agreement required the state to undertake remedial action to address the contamination and to restore the Everglades. In United States v. Southern Florida Water Management District, 28 F.3d 1563 (11th Cir. 1994), the Eleventh Circuit reversed a district court ruling that an EIS was required because of the federal government's participation in negotiating and implementing the settlement agreement. The Eleventh Circuit explained that a settlement "to compel a nonfederal party to undertake its legal responsibility does not convert the proposed state remedial measures into federal responsibilities for NEPA purposes." 28 F.3d at 1572. The court noted that NEPA obligations may arise in the future if federal agencies get involved in funding the restoration or issuing permits for activities undertaken to implement the settlement. But it concluded that the mere fact that the federal government was involved in reaching the settlement was insufficient to trigger NEPA's requirements.

In other cases, there is a question whether any *action* has been taken by the federal agency. Prior to 1990, the U.S. Forest Service used herbicides to control vegetation in the Lake States National Forests. In 1990, however, the Forest Service decided not to use herbicides. In Minnesota Pesticide Information and Education, Inc. v. Espy, 29 F.3d 442 (8th Cir. 1994), the Eighth Circuit held that the Forest Service was not required to prepare an EIS for deciding not to use herbicides. The court explained that "[t]his is not a decision to do something; rather it is a decision to *not* do something (namely, apply herbicides), which does not trigger NEPA's requirements that an EIS be prepared." 29 F.3d at 443 (emphasis in original). The court explained that until the Forest Service actually decides upon an alternative method for controlling vegetation, "it has effectively elected a course of temporary inaction" to which NEPA does not apply.

In New Jersey Department of Environmental Protection v. Long Island Power Authority, 30 F.3d 403 (3d Cir. 1994), New Jersey sought an injunction to prevent the shipment of partially irradiated nuclear fuel through New Jersey coastal waters until an EIS had been performed. The Third Circuit held that the fact that the Coast Guard had been informed of the shipment but failed to object to it did not constitute major federal action because the Coast Guard was not required to approve the shipment. However, in Citizens Awareness Network, Inc. v. Nuclear Regulatory Commission, 59 F.3d 284 (1st Cir. 1995), the First

Circuit rejected the NRC's claim that it had not engaged in "major federal action" because it was passively monitoring a utility's activities decommissioning a nuclear power plant. The court noted that although the NRC had not specifically approved the utility's decommissioning plan, it had authorized the release of funds set aside by licensees to finance decommissioning activities and it had advised the utility that it could proceed with decommissioning, which itself is an activity that requires preparation of an EIS.

C.   PROBLEMS OF TIMING AND SCOPE

The most difficult and persistent questions in determining whether there is a "proposal for . . . major Federal action" have been the appropriate timing and scope of the review that NEPA requires. As several cases have illustrated, these two questions are bound up together.

The interplay of timing and scope is perhaps most pronounced in federal resource management programs. Thorough review in an EIS may serve useful functions at several stages in the development and implementation of such a program. Choosing the proper time and scope for EIS review thus requires hard choices: Should the agency prepare an EIS for its formulation of national policy so that it may consider the environmental consequences of the fundamental policy choices made at that stage? Should it prepare an EIS for each region of the country before the national program is implemented, so that the particular characteristics, needs, and problems of the region can be considered? Should it prepare an EIS for each action taken in implementing the program in the field (each timber sale, grazing lease, or mining permit approved), so that it can evaluate environmental consequences on the basis of the concrete information that only becomes available when one has a proposal for specific action at a specific site? Should it prepare an EIS at every one of these stages, at the risk of drowning itself, and the public, in paper?

In the case that follows, the Sierra Club argued that the Department of the Interior could not allow further development of federal coal reserves in a four-state area of the Northern Great Plains without preparing a comprehensive EIS on the entire region. Interior had conducted three studies of potential coal development in the region and had prepared a national "Coal Programmatic EIS" for the Department's coal leasing program throughout the country. The D.C. Circuit held that four factors should govern when a programmatic EIS must be commenced: (1) the likelihood and imminence of a program's coming to fruition, (2) the extent of information available on the effects of a program, (3) the extent to which irretrievable resource commitments are being made, and (4) the potential severity of environmental effects. After finding that factors (2) and (4) already made an EIS ripe, the court remanded the case to Interior, which obtained Supreme Court review in the case that follows.

|| *Kleppe v. Sierra Club* ||
|| **427 U.S. 390 (1976)** ||

MR. JUSTICE POWELL delivered the opinion of the Court.

The major issue remains the one with which the suit began: whether NEPA requires petitioners to prepare an environmental impact statement on the entire Northern Great Plains region. Petitioners, arguing the negative, rely squarely upon the facts of the case and the language of §102(2)(C) of NEPA. We find their reliance well placed.

. . . [Section] 102(2)(C) requires an impact statement "in every recommendation or report on proposals for legislation and other major Federal actions significantly affecting the quality of the human environment." Since no one has suggested that petitioners have proposed legislation on respondents' region, the controlling phrase in this section of the Act, for this case, is "major Federal actions." Respondents can prevail only if there has been a report or recommendation on a proposal for major federal action with respect to the Northern Great Plains region. . . . [T]he relevant facts show[] there has been none; instead, all proposals are for actions of either local or national scope. The local actions are the decisions by the various petitioners to issue a lease, approve a mining plan, issue a right-of-way permit, or take other action to allow private activity at some point within the region identified by respondents. Several Courts of Appeals have held that an impact statement must be included in the report of recommendation on a proposal for such action if the private activity to be permitted is one "significantly affecting the quality of the human environment" within the meaning of §102(2)(C). The petitioners do not dispute this requirement in this case, and indeed have prepared impact statements on several proposed actions of this type in the Northern Great Plains during the course of this litigation. Similarly, the federal petitioners agreed at oral argument that §102(2)(C) required the Coal Programmatic EIS that was prepared in tandem with the new national coal-leasing program and included as part of the final report on the proposal for adoption of that program. Their admission is well made, for the new leasing program is a coherent plan of national scope, and its adoption surely has significant environmental consequences.

But there is no evidence in the record of an action or a proposal for an action of regional scope. The District Court, in fact, expressly found that there was no existing or proposed plan or program on the part of the Federal Government for the regional development of the area described in respondents' complaint. It found also that the three studies initiated by the Department in areas either included within or inclusive of respondents' region—that is, the Montana-Wyoming Aqueducts Study, the North Central Power Study, and the NGPRP [Northern Great Plains Resources Program]—were not parts of any plan or program to develop or encourage development of the Northern Great Plains. That court found no evidence that the individual coal development projects undertaken or proposed by private industry and public utilities in that part of the country are integrated into a plan or otherwise interrelated. These findings were not disturbed by the Court of Appeals, and they remain fully supported by the record in this Court. . . .

IV

. . . Even had the record justified a finding that a regional program was contemplated by the petitioners, the legal conclusion drawn by the Court of Appeals cannot be squared with the Act. The court recognized that the mere "contemplation" of certain action is not sufficient to require an impact statement. But it believed the statute nevertheless empowers a court to require the preparation of an impact statement to begin at some point prior to the formal recommendation or report on a proposal. The Court of Appeals accordingly devised its own four-part "balancing" test for determining when, during the contemplation of a plan or other type of federal action, an agency must begin a statement. . . .

The Court's reasoning and action find no support in the language or legislative history of NEPA. The statute clearly states when an impact statement is required and mentions nothing about a balancing of factors. Rather, as we noted last Term, under the first sentence of §102(2)(C) the moment at which an agency must have a final statement ready "is the time at which it makes a recommendation or report on a *proposal* for federal action." Aberdeen & Rockfish R. Co. v. SCRAP, 422 U.S. 289, 320 (1975) (*SCRAP II*) (emphasis in original). The procedural duty imposed upon agencies by this section is quite precise, and the role of the courts in enforcing that duty is similarly precise. A court has no authority to depart from the statutory language and, by a balancing of court-devised factors, determines a point during the germination process of a potential proposal at which an impact statement *should be prepared*. Such an assertion of judicial authority would leave the agencies uncertain as to their procedural duties under NEPA, would invite judicial involvement in the day-to-day decisionmaking process of the agencies, and would invite litigation. As the contemplation of a project and the accompanying study thereof do not necessarily result in a proposal for major federal action, it may be assumed that the balancing process devised by the Court of Appeals also would result in the preparation of a good many unnecessary impact statements. . . .

V

Our discussion thus far has been addressed primarily to the decision of the Court of Appeals. It remains, however, to consider the contention now urged by respondents. They have not attempted to support the Court of Appeals' decision. Instead, respondents renew an argument they appear to have made to the Court of Appeals, but which that court did not reach. Respondents insist that, even without a comprehensive federal plan for the development of the Northern Great Plains, a "regional" impact statement nevertheless is required on all coal-related projects in the region because they are intimately related. . . .

. . . [Section] 102(2)(C) may require a comprehensive impact statement in certain situations where several proposed actions are pending at the same time. NEPA announced a national policy of environmental protection and placed a responsibility upon the Federal Government to further specific environmental goals by "all practicable means, consistent with other essential considerations of national policy." §101(b), 42 U.S.C. §4331(b). Section 102(2)(C) is one of the "action-forcing" provisions intended as a directive to "all agencies to assure consideration of the environmental impact of their actions in decisionmaking." Conference Report on NEPA, 115 Cong. Rec. 40416 (1969). By requiring an impact statement Congress intended to assure such consideration during the development of a proposal or—as in this case—during the formulation of a position on a proposal submitted by private parties. A comprehensive impact statement may be necessary in some cases for an agency to meet this duty. Thus, when several proposals for coal-related actions that will have cumulative or synergistic environmental impact upon a region are pending concurrently before an agency, their environmental consequences must be considered together. Only through comprehensive consideration of pending proposals can the agency evaluate different courses of action.

Agreement to this extent with respondents' premise, however, does not require acceptance of their conclusion that all proposed coal-related actions in the Northern Great Plains region are so "related" as to require their analysis in a single comprehensive impact statement. . . .

. . . Cumulative environmental impacts are, indeed, what require a comprehensive impact statement. But determination of the extent and effect of these factors, and particularly identification of the geographic area within which they may occur, is a task assigned to the special competency of the appropriate agencies. Petitioners dispute respondents' contentions that the interrelationship of environmental impacts is regionwide and, as respondents own submissions indicate, petitioners appear to have determined that the appropriate scope of comprehensive statements should be based on basins, drainage areas, and other factors. We cannot say that petitioners' choices are arbitrary. Even if environmental interrelationships could be shown conclusively to extend across basins and drainage areas, practical considerations of feasibility might well necessitate restricting the scope of comprehensive statements.

In sum, respondents' contention as to the relationships between all proposed coal-related projects in the Northern Great Plains region does not require that petitioners prepare one comprehensive impact statement covering all before proceeding to approve specific pending applications. As we already determined that there exists no proposal for regionwide action that could require a regional impact statement, the judgment of the Court of Appeals must be reversed, and the judgment of the District Court reinstated and affirmed. . . .

MR. JUSTICE MARSHALL, with whom MR. JUSTICE BRENNAN joins, concurring in part and dissenting in part.

While I agree with much of the Court's opinion, I must dissent from Part IV, which holds that the federal courts may not remedy violations of the National Environmental Policy Act of 1969 (NEPA), 83 Stat. 852, 42 U.S.C. §4321 et seq.—no matter how blatant—until it is too late for an adequate remedy to be formulated. As the Court today recognizes, NEPA contemplates agency consideration of environmental factors throughout the decisionmaking process. Since NEPA's enactment, however, litigation has been brought primarily at the end of that process—challenging agency decisions to act made without adequate; environmental impact statements or without any statements at all. In such situations, the courts have had to content themselves with the largely unsatisfactory remedy of enjoining the proposed federal action and ordering the preparation of an adequate impact statement. This remedy is insufficient because, except by deterrence, it does nothing to further early consideration of environmental factors. And, as with all after-the-fact remedies, a remand for preparation of an impact statement after the basic decision to act has been made invites post hoc rationalizations, cf. Citizens to Preserve Overton Park v. Volpe, 401 U.S. 402, 419-420 (1971), rather than the candid and balanced environmental assessments envisioned by NEPA. Moreover, the remedy is wasteful of resources and time, causing fully developed plans for action to be laid aside while an impact statement is prepared.

Nonetheless, until this lawsuit, such belated remedies were all the federal courts had had the opportunity to impose under NEPA. In this case, confronted with a situation in which, according to respondents' allegations, federal agencies were violating NEPA prior to their basic decision to act, the Court of Appeals for the District of Columbia Circuit seized the opportunity to devise a different and effective remedy. It recognized a narrow class of cases—essentially those where both the likelihood of eventual agency action and the danger posed by non-preparation of an environmental impact statement were great—in which it would allow judicial intervention prior to the time at which an impact statement must be ready. The Court today loses sight of the inadequacy of other remedies and the narrowness of the category constructed by the Court of Appeals, and construes NEPA so as to preclude a court from ever intervening prior to a formal agency proposal. This decision, which unnecessarily limits the ability of the federal courts to effectuate the intent of NEPA, is mandated neither by the statute nor by the various equitable considerations upon which the Court relies.

NOTES AND QUESTIONS

1. What environmental reviews had the Secretary undertaken or agreed to undertake? Why did the Sierra Club want more?

2. Consider the question of *timing*. The majority seem to agree that an EIS must be completed by the time of the agency's "recommendation or report on a proposal" for action. What is the debate? What earlier obligations has the Court of Appeals imposed on the agencies? Why does Justice Marshall believe the lower court's approach is necessary? Why did the Sierra Club abandon this approach on appeal?

3. The majority in *Kleppe* relied largely on the interpretation of the statutory term "proposal" in deciding the timing of NEPA's obligations. Two years after *Kleppe*, CEQ defined "proposal" in its regulations as existing "at that stage in the development of an action when an agency subject to the Act has a goal and is actively preparing to make a decision on one or more alternative means of accomplishing that goal and the effects can be meaningfully evaluated." 40 C.F.R. §1508.23. The CEQ reaffirmed that preparation of an EIS should be completed in time for inclusion in any recommendation or report on the proposal. Does this CEQ regulation depart from the Supreme Court's decision in *Kleppe*? The CEQ also issued more general guidance on the issue of "timing," which is contained in 40 C.F.R. §1502.5.

4. CEQ's regulations direct that when "emergency circumstances make it necessary to take an action with significant environmental impact without observing the provisions of these regulations, the Federal agency taking the action should consult with the Council about alternative arrangements." 40 C.F.R. §1506.11. Only "actions necessary to control the immediate impacts of the emergency" can be exempted from NEPA review. In October 1993, CEQ approved a proposal by the Department of Energy to permit an emergency shipment of 144 spent nuclear fuel rods to enter the United States from Belgium without preparing an EIS. Under the Reduced Enrichment for Research and Test Reactors program, the U.S. government has sought to promote nuclear nonproliferation by agreeing to reclaim used nuclear fuel provided by it to foreign countries if they agree to stop using weapons-grade uranium. Legal challenges to the emergency shipment were rejected in South Carolina ex rel. Campbell v. O'Leary, 64 F.3d 892 (4th Cir. 1995). Noting that an elaborate EIS was being prepared for the full program of shipping 24,000 spent fuel rods back to the United States, the Fourth Circuit concluded that it

was not necessary to complete the EIS prior to receiving an urgent shipment of the first fuel rods. The court held that this "segmented" shipment in itself would not have a significant effect on the environment because the fuel rods would be stored in existing and approved facilities, unlike the massive shipments to follow which will require construction of a new storage facility. 64 F.3d at 898-899. CEQ also used its emergency authority in 1998 to allow the Forest Service to sell dead and dying timber on 22,000 acres of national forests in Texas following a massive windstorm. The Forest Service sought approval to prevent an immediate fire hazard for adjacent private lands, while agreeing to analyze the cumulative effects of the sales in a subsequent environmental assessment concerning future sales.

5. Consider also the question of *scope.* In *Kleppe*, the Sierra Club argued that an EIS must be prepared for actions that are "intimately related." Did the Supreme Court reject this interpretation? What would the Sierra Club have to show to persuade a court to compel preparation of a regional EIS? What difficulties does that showing pose for environmental plaintiffs? Might the Sierra Club fare better under the CEQ's post-*Kleppe* regulations contained in 40 C.F.R. §1508.25? These regulations direct agencies to determine the scope of EISs by considering three types of actions (connected actions, cumulative actions, and similar actions), three types of alternatives, and three types of impacts (direct, indirect, and cumulative). Consider the impact and application of these regulations in the following cases.

Thomas v. Peterson
753 F.2d 754 (9th Cir. 1985)

[The Forest Service planned construction of a gravel road to service timber harvesting in an area known as "Jersey Jack." The Service concluded that the road would not have "significant" effects on the environment and therefore approved construction without preparing an EIS. The Service subsequently approved two timber sales in the area, also without preparing an EIS. Conservation groups brought this action to enjoin construction of the road, alleging violations of the National Forest Management Act, the Endangered Species Act, and NEPA.]

Before WRIGHT, SNEED, and ALARCON, Circuit Judges.
SNEED, Circuit Judge.

THE NEPA CLAIM

The central question that plaintiff's NEPA claim presents is whether the road and the timber sales are sufficiently related so as to require combined treatment in a single EIS that covers the cumulative effects of the road and the sales. If so, the Forest Service has proceeded improperly. An EIS must be prepared and considered by the Forest Service before the road can be approved. If not, the Forest Service may go ahead with the road, and later consider the environmental impacts of the timber sales.

Section 102(2)(C) of NEPA requires an EIS for "major Federal actions significantly affecting the quality of the human environment." 42 U.S.C.

§4332(2)(C) (1982). While it is true that administrative agencies must be given considerable discretion in defining the scope of environmental impact statements, see Kleppe v. Sierra Club, 427 U.S. 390, 412-415 (1976), there are situations in which an agency is required to consider several related actions in a single EIS, see id. at 409-410. Not to require this would permit dividing a project into multiple "actions," each of which individually has an insignificant environmental impact, but which collectively have a substantial impact.

Since the Supreme Court decided the *Kleppe* case, the Council on Environmental Quality (CEQ) has issued regulations that define the circumstances under which multiple related actions must be covered by a single EIS. The regulations are made binding on federal administrative agencies by Executive Order. See Exec. Order No. 11991, 3 C.F.R. 1977 Comp. 123 (1978); Andrus v. Sierra Club, 442 U.S. 347, 357-358 (1979). The CEQ regulations and this court's precedents both require the Forest Service to prepare an EIS analyzing the combined environmental impacts of the road and the timber sales.

A.   CEQ Regulations

1.   Connected Actions

The CEQ regulations require "connected actions" to be considered together in a single EIS. See 40 C.F.R. §1508.25(a)(1) (1984). "Connected actions" are defined as actions that "(i) Automatically trigger other actions which may require environmental impact statements, (ii) Cannot or will not proceed unless other actions are taken previously or simultaneously, (iii) Are interdependent parts of a larger action and depend on the larger action for their justification." Id.

The construction of the road and the sale of the timber in the Jersey Jack area meet the second and third, as well as perhaps the first, of these criteria. It is clear that the timber sales cannot proceed without the road, and the road would not be built but for the contemplated timber sales. This much is revealed by the Forest Service's characterization of the road as a "logging road," and by the first page of the environmental assessment for the road, which states that "[t]he need for a transportation route in the assessment area is to access the timber lands to be developed over the next twenty years." Moreover, the environmental assessment for the road rejected a "no action" alternative because that alternative would not provide the needed timber access. The Forest Service's cost-benefit analysis of the road considered the timber to be the benefit of the road, and while the Service has stated that the road will yield other benefits, it does not claim that such other benefits would justify the road in the absence of the timber sales. Finally, the close interdependence of the road and the timber sales is indicated by an August 1981 letter in the record from the Regional Forester to the Forest Supervisor. It states, "We understand that sales in the immediate future will be dependent on the early completion of portions of the Jersey Jack Road. It would be advisable to divide the road into segments and establish separate completion dates for those portions to be used for those sales."

We conclude, therefore, that the road construction and the contemplated timber sales are inextricably intertwined, and that they are "connected actions" within the meaning of the CEQ regulations.

2.   Cumulative Actions

The CEQ regulations also require that "cumulative actions" be considered together in a single EIS. 40 C.F.R. §1508.25(a)(2). "Cumulative actions" are defined as actions "which when viewed with other proposed actions have cumulatively significant impacts." Id. The record in this case contains considerable evidence to suggest that the road and the timber sales will have cumulatively significant impacts. The U.S. Fish & Wildlife Service, the Environmental Protection Agency, and the Idaho Department of Fish & Game have asserted that the road and the timber sales will have significant cumulative effects that should be considered in an EIS. The primary cumulative effects, according to these agencies, are the deposit of sediments in the Salmon River to the detriment of that river's population of salmon and steelhead trout, and the destruction of critical habitat for the endangered Rocky Mountain Gray Wolf. These agencies have criticized the Forest Service for not producing an EIS that considers the cumulative impacts of the Jersey Jack road and the timber sales. For example, the Fish & Wildlife Service has written, "Separate documentation of related and cumulative potential impacts may be leading to aquatic habitat degradation unaccounted for in individual EA's (i.e., undocumented cumulative effects). . . . Lack of an overall effort to document cumulative impacts could be having present and future detrimental effects on wolf recovery potential." These comments are sufficient to raise "substantial questions" as to whether the road and the timber sales will have significant cumulative environmental effects. Therefore, on this basis also, the Forest Service is required to prepare an EIS analyzing such effects. . . .

C.   Timing of the EIS

The Forest Service argues that the cumulative environmental effects of the road and the timber sales will be adequately analyzed and considered in the EA's and/or EIS's that it will prepare on the individual timber sales. The EA or EIS on each action, it contends, will document the cumulative impacts of that, action and all previous actions.

We believe that consideration of cumulative impacts after the road has already been approved is insufficient to fulfill the mandate of NEPA. A central purpose of an EIS is to force the consideration of environmental impacts in the decision-making process. That purpose requires that the NEPA process be integrated with agency planning "at the earliest possible time," 40 C.F.R. §1501.2, and the purpose cannot be fully served if consideration of the cumulative effects of successive, interdependent steps is delayed until the first step has already been taken.

The location, the timing, or other aspects of the timber sales, or even the decision whether to sell any timber at all, affects the location, routing, construction techniques, and other aspects of the road, or even the need for its construction. But the consideration of cumulative impacts will serve little purpose if the road has already been built. Building the road swings the balance decidedly in favor of timber sales even if such sales would have been disfavored had road and sales been considered together before the road was built. Only by selling timber can the bulk of the expense of building the road be recovered. Not to sell timber after building the road constitutes the "irrational" result that *Trout Unlimited*'s standard is intended to avoid [Trout Unlimited v. Morion, 509 F.2d 1276 (9th Cir. 1974)]. Therefore, the cumulative environmental impacts of the road and the timber sales must be assessed before the road is approved. The Forest Service argues that the sales are too uncertain and too far in the future for their impacts to be analyzed along with that of the road. This comes close to saying that building the road now is itself irrational. We decline to accept that conclusion. Rather, we believe that if the sales are sufficiently certain to justify construction of the road, then they are sufficiently certain for their environmental impacts to be analyzed along with those of the road. Cf. City of Davis v. Coleman, 521 F.2d 661, 667-676 (9th Cir. 1975) (EIS for a road must analyze the impacts of industrial development that the road is designed to accommodate). Where agency actions are sufficiently related so as to be "connected" within the meaning of the CEQ regulations, the agency may not escape compliance with the regulations by proceeding with one action while characterizing the others as remote or speculative.

NOTES AND QUESTIONS

1. Is the Ninth Circuit's decision in *Thomas* consistent with the Supreme Court's decision in *Kleppe*? How have the CEQ's post-*Kleppe* regulations changed the analysis of timing and scope?

2. Consideration of cumulative impacts played a major role in lengthy litigation over construction of one of three dams in southern Oregon's Rogue River basin. In Oregon Natural Resources Council v. Marsh, 832 F.2d 1489 (9th Cir. 1987), the court held that the Army Corps of Engineers had violated NEPA by failing to consider the cumulative impact of all three dams in an EIS for construction of the Elk Creek Dam. Although the court's decision eventually was reversed on other grounds by the Supreme Court, Marsh v. Oregon Natural Resources Council, 490 U.S. 360 (1989), the Ninth Circuit subsequently held that the Corps' supplemental EIS again had failed to consider adequately cumulative impacts. Oregon Natural Resources Council v. Marsh, 52 F.3d 1485 (9th Cir. 1995). The court stated that it was not sufficient for the EIS to discuss cumulative impacts only in the context of two specific water quality factors—temperature and turbidity—when they could be significant with respect to other environmental factors as well.

3. CEQ's regulations define "cumulative impact" to be "the impact on the environment which results from the incremental impact of the action when added to other past, present, and reasonably foreseeable future actions regardless of what agency (Federal or non-Federal) or person undertakes such other actions." 40 C.F.R. §1508.7. Does this require agencies to consider the impacts that private acts on private lands could have when analyzing cumulative impacts? In Resources Limited, Inc. v. Robertson, 35 F.3d 1300, 1306 (9th Cir. 1993), the court held that it does. In Sierra Club v. U.S. Forest Service, 46 F.3d 835 (8th Cir. 1995), the court rejected claims that an environmental assessment prepared by the Forest Service did not give sufficient consideration to cumulative impacts from private acts on nearby private lands and to the effect of previous timber sales on habitat fragmentation.

|| *Sierra Club v. Peterson* ||
|| **717 F.2d 1409 (D.C. Cir. 1983)** ||

Before WRIGHT and SCALIA, Circuit Judges, and MACKINNON, Senior Circuit Judge. MACKINNON, Senior Circuit Judge:

In proceedings in the district court, the Sierra Club challenged the decision by the United States Forest Service (Forest Service) and the Department of the Interior (Department) to issue oil and gas leases on lands within the Targhee and Bridger-Teton National Forests of Idaho and Wyoming. The plaintiff alleged that the leasing program violated the National Environmental Policy Act (NEPA), 42 U.S.C. §4321 et seq. (1976), because no Environmental Impact Statement (EIS) was prepared prior to the action. On cross-motion for summary judgment the district court upheld the decision to issue the leases without preparing an EIS. . . .

In 1980, the Forest Service received applications for oil and gas leases in the Palisades Further Planning Area. After conducting an Environmental Assessment (EA), the Forest Service recommended granting the lease applications, but with various stipulations attached to the leases. Because the Forest Service determined that issuance of the leases with the recommended stipulations would not result in significant adverse impacts to the environment, it decided that, with respect to the *entire* area, no Environmental Impact Statement was required at the leasing stage.

The leasing program approved by the Forest Service divides the land within the Palisades Further Planning Area into two categories—"highly environmentally sensitive" lands and non-highly environmentally sensitive lands. The stipulations attached to each lease are determined by the particular character of the land. All of the leases for the Palisades contain "standard" and "special" stipulations. These stipulations require the lessee to obtain approval from the Interior Department before undertaking any surface disturbing activity on the lease, but do not authorize the Department to *preclude* any activities which the lessee might propose. The Department can only impose conditions upon the lessee's use of the leased land.

In addition, a No Surface Occupancy Stipulation (NSO Stipulation) is attached to the leases for lands designated as "highly environmentally sensitive." This NSO Stipulation *precludes* surface occupancy unless and until such activity is specifically approved by the Forest Service.

For leases *without* a[n NSO] Stipulation, the lessee must file an application for a permit to drill prior to initiating exploratory drilling activities. The application must contain a surface use and operating plan which details the proposed operations including access roads, well site locations, and other planned facilities. On land leased without a[n NSO] Stipulation the Department *cannot* deny the permit to drill; it can only impose "reasonable" conditions which are designed to mitigate the environmental impacts of the drilling operations. [Eighty percent of the leases issued in the Palisades contained NSO stipulations. The Sierra Club appealed the district court's judgment only with respect to those lands leased without an NSO stipulation.] . . .

III

The National Environmental Policy Act (NEPA) requires preparation of an Environmental Impact Statement whenever a proposed major federal action will significantly affect the quality of the human environment. 42 U.S.C. §4332(2)(C) (1976). To determine the nature of the environmental impact from a proposed action and whether an EIS will be required, federal agencies prepare an environmental assessment. 40 C.F.R. §1501.4(b) & (c) (1982). If on the basis of the Environmental Assessment the agency finds that the proposed action will produce "no significant impact" on the environment, then an EIS need not be prepared. Id. at §1501.4(e).

An agency's finding of "no significant impact" and consequent decision not to prepare an EIS can only be overturned if the decision was arbitrary, capricious, or an abuse of discretion. Judicial review of an agency's finding of "no significant impact" is not, however, merely perfunctory as the court must insure that the agency took a "hard look" at the environmental consequences of its decision.

Cases in this circuit have employed a four-part test to scrutinize an agency's finding of "no significant impact." The court ascertains

(1) whether the agency took a "hard look" at the problem;
(2) whether the agency identified the relevant areas of environmental concern;
(3) as to the problems studied and identified, whether the agency made a convincing case that the impact was insignificant; and
(4) if there was an impact of true significance, whether the agency convincingly established that changes in the project sufficiently reduced it to a minimum.

Applying the foregoing test to this agency decision, we are satisfied that the agency has taken the requisite "hard look" and has "identified the relevant areas of environmental concern." However, in our opinion, the finding that "no significant impact" will occur as a result of granting leases *without* an NSO Stipulation is not supportable on this record.

The finding of "no significant impact" is premised upon the conclusion that the lease stipulations will prevent any significant environmental impacts until a site-specific plan for exploration and development is submitted by the lessee. At that time, the federal appellees explain, an appropriate environmental analysis, either an Environmental Assessment or an EIS, will be prepared. In bifurcating its environmental analysis, however, the agency has taken a foreshortened view of the impacts which could result from the act of *leasing*. The agency has essentially assumed that leasing is a discrete transition which will not result in any "physical or biological impacts." The Environmental Assessment concludes

that there will be no significant adverse effects on the human environment due to oil and gas lease issuance. Therefore, no environmental impact statement will be prepared. The determination was based upon consideration of the following factors . . . (a) few issued leases result in active exploration operations and still fewer result in discovery or production of oil or gas; (b) the act of issuing a lease involves no physical or biological impacts; (c) the cumulative environmental effect of lease issuance on an area-wide basis is very small; (d) effects of lease activities once permitted will be mitigated to protect areas of critical environmental concern by appropriate stipulations including no-surface occupancy; (e) if unacceptable environmental impacts cannot be corrected, activities will not be permitted; and (f) the action will not have a significant effect on the human environment.

The conclusion that no significant impact will occur is improperly based on a prophecy that exploration activity on these lands will be insignificant and generally fruitless.

While it may well be true that the majority of these leases will never reach the drilling stage and that the environmental impacts of exploration are dependent upon the nature of the activity, nevertheless NEPA requires that federal agencies determine at the outset whether their major actions can result in "significant" environmental impacts. Here, the Forest Service concluded that any impacts which might result from the act of leasing would either be insignificant or, if significant, could be mitigated by exercising the controls provided in the lease stipulations.

Even assuming, arguendo, that all lease stipulations are fully enforceable, once the land is leased the Department no longer has the authority to *preclude* surface disturbing activities even if the environmental impact of such activity is significant. The Department can only impose "mitigation" measures upon a lessee who pursues surface disturbing exploration and/or drilling activities. None of the stipulations expressly provides that the Department or the Forest Service can *prevent* a lessee from conducting surface disturbing activities. Thus, with respect to the smaller area with which we are here concerned, the decision to allow surface disturbing activities has been made at the *leasing stage* and, under NEPA, this is the point at which the environmental impacts of such activities must be evaluated.

NEPA requires an agency to evaluate the environmental effects of its action at the point of commitment. The purpose of an EIS is to insure that the agency considers all possible courses of action and assesses the environmental consequences of each proposed action. The EIS is a decisionmaking tool intended to "insure that . . . environmental amenities and values may be given appropriate consideration in decisionmaking. . . ." 42 U.S.C. §4332(2)(B). Therefore, the appropriate time for preparing an EIS is *prior* to a decision, when the decision-maker retains a maximum range of options. Environmental Defense Fund v. Andrus, 596 F.2d 848, 852-853 (9th Cir. 1979). Accord, Port of Astoria v. Hodel, 595 F.2d 467, 478 (9th Cir. 1979) (NEPA requires that an EIS be prepared "at an early stage when alternative courses of action are still possible . . ."); Scientists' Inst. for Public Information, Inc. v. Atomic Energy Comm'n, 481 F.2d 1079, 1094 (D.C. Cir. 1973) (In determining *when* to prepare an EIS the agency must ascertain to what extent its decision embodies an "irretrievable commitment" of resources which precludes the exercise of future "options."). An EIS is required when the "critical agency decision" is made which results in "irreversible and irretrievable commitments of resources" to an action which will affect the environment. On the facts of this case, that "critical time," insofar as lands leased without a[n] NSO Stipulation are concerned, occurred at the point of leasing.

Notwithstanding the assurance that a later site-specific environmental analysis will be made, in issuing these leases the Department made an irrevocable commitment to allow *some* surface disturbing activities, including drilling and roadbuilding. While theoretically the proposed two-stage environmental analysis may be acceptable, in this situation the Department has not complied with NEPA because it has sanctioned activities which have the potential for disturbing the environment without fully assessing the possible environmental consequences.

The Department asserts that it cannot accurately evaluate the consequences of drilling and other surface disturbing activities until site-specific plans are submitted. If, however, the Department is in fact concerned that it cannot foresee and evaluate the environmental consequences of leasing without site-specific proposals, then it may delay preparation of an EIS provided that it reserves both the authority to *preclude* all activities pending submission of site-specific proposals and the authority to *prevent* proposed activities if the environmental consequences are unacceptable. If the Department chooses not to retain the authority to *preclude* all surface disturbing activities, then an EIS assessing the full environmental consequences of leasing must be prepared at the point of commitment—when the leases are issued. The Department can decide, in the first instance, by which route it will proceed.

NOTES AND QUESTIONS

1. In Sierra Club v. Peterson, the court focuses its review on the Forest Service's determination that the effects of its action will not be "significant." We will discuss that question later. For now, consider the question of timing: Why must the Forest Service prepare an EIS at the leasing stage? The Forest Service had argued that preparation of an EIS should not be required at this stage because "any impacts which might result from the act of leasing would either be insignificant or, if significant, could be mitigated by exercising the controls provided in the lease stipulations." Why does that argument fail? What could the Forest Service do differently in future leasing decisions to avoid the EIS requirement?

2. In Conner v. Burford, 605 F. Supp. 107 (D. Mont. 1985), aff'd in part and rev'd in part, 848 F.2d 1441 (9th Cir. 1988), cert. denied, 489 U.S. 1012 (1989), the plaintiffs pressed the question whether the Forest Service could ignore the possible impacts of oil exploration, development, and production when deciding to issue leases with no surface occupancy (NSO) stipulations. At issue was a Forest Service decision to lease 1.3 million acres of the Gallatin and Flathead National Forests in Montana. Placing NSO stipulations in more than 500 of the 700 leases to be issued, the Forest Service issued a "finding of no significant impact" for the sale, arguing that "the sale of an NSO lease has *no* effect on the environment, let alone a significant one." 848 F.2d at 1447 (emphasis in original). The District Court held that the Forest Service had violated NEPA:

> To use the NSO stipulation as a mechanism to avoid an EIS when issuing numerous leases on potential wilderness areas circumvents the spirit of NEPA. Subsequent site-specific analysis, prompted by a proposal from a lessee of one tract, may result in a finding of no significant environmental impact. Obviously, a comprehensive analysis of cumulative impacts of several oil and gas development activities must be done before any single activity can proceed. Otherwise, a piecemeal invasion of the forests would occur, followed by realization of a significant and irreversible impact. [605 F. Supp. at 108-109.]

On appeal, the Ninth Circuit reversed. The court held that NEPA would apply to subsequent decisions to remove an NSO stipulation and that "piecemeal invasion of the forests will be avoided because . . . government evaluation of surface-disturbing activity on NSO leases must include consideration of the potential for further connected development and cumulative impacts from all oil and gas development activities pursuant to the federal leases." 848 F.2d at 1448. Is that reasoning persuasive? Is lease-by-lease review a good substitute for comprehensive review of the entire 1.3-million-acre sale? If the Forest Service is reviewing one lease at a time, what is the likely form of its review—full environmental impact statement, or environmental assessment? If the Service considers the potential cumulative impacts of related development in reviewing a single lease, what options does it have to address those impacts? How would its options be different if it were reviewing the entire sale?

3. The Makah Indian Tribe in Washington state has been seeking approval to hunt the California gray whale, following its removal from the endangered species list. Supported by the National Oceanic and Atmospheric Administration (NOAA) and the National Marine Fisheries Service (NMFS), the Makah obtained approval to resume limited whale hunting from the International Whaling Commission (IWC) under the "aboriginal subsistence" exception to the IWC's global whaling ban. Opponents of the hunt filed a lawsuit alleging that NOAA and the NMFS had violated NEPA by failing to conduct an environmental assessment before agreeing with the Makah to seek approval for resumed whale hunting. Alerted to a possible NEPA lawsuit, NOAA and the NMFS had quickly prepared an environmental assessment (EA) making a "finding of no significant impact" (FONSI), which had been released the day before the IWC meeting. After a district court dismissed the lawsuit, the plaintiffs appealed to the U.S. Court of Appeals for the Ninth Circuit, which reversed. Metcalf v. Daley, 214 F.3d 1135 (2001). The court concluded that NOAA and the NMFS "did not engage the NEPA process 'at the earliest possible time,'" It observed that the agencies "should not have fully committed to support the Makah whaling proposal before preparing the EA because doing so probably influenced their evaluation of the environmental impact of the proposal." Writing in dissent, Judge Kleinfeld argued that EAs and EISs "are unlikely to persuade agency personnel, who initiated a project, to change their minds." He maintained that their value "comes mostly after the agency has settled on a policy choice" because "[t]he process of preparing them mobilizes groups that may generate political pressure sufficient to defeat the executive initiative." 214 F.3d at 1150-1151.

4. Following the Metcalf v. Daley decision, NOAA and the NMFS prepared a new EA. When the new EA was released in July 2001, it again found no significant environmental impact from the Makah hunt. After the agencies approved renewed whaling by the tribe, animal rights groups filed suit, alleging violations of NEPA and the Marine Mammal Protection Act. These claims were rejected by a trial court, but upheld on appeal in Anderson v. Evans, 314 F.3d 1006 (2002). Rejecting the FONSI, the court held that an EIS should be prepared not because the impact on the entire California gray whale population will be significant, but because of the potential significance of the impact on the resident whale population in the local area.

2.   "Significantly Affecting the Quality of the Human Environment"

The crucial threshold question for NEPA's EIS requirement is whether a proposed action is likely to significantly affect the quality of the human environment. It is this question that is typically the focus of an agency's analysis of its obligations under NEPA. And it is this question that is most troublesome for the courts in enforcing those obligations. This is illustrated by the following early case, which involved the question whether an EIS had to be prepared for the construction of a jail and related facilities as an annex to the federal courthouse in Manhattan. After residents and businesses in the surrounding area filed suit under NEPA, a federal district court held that no EIS was required because the project would not significantly affect the quality of the environment.

The Second Circuit affirmed as to an office building that was part of the project but reversed with respect to the detention center. Hanly v. Mitchell, 460 F.2d 640 (2d Cir. 1972) (*Hanly I*). The court required the General Services Administration (GSA) to evaluate more fully the effects of the detention center (e.g., the possibility of disturbances that would cause noise, the impact of an outpatient treatment center on crime in the neighborhood, and possible traffic and parking problems) before determining that an EIS was unnecessary. On remand, GSA prepared a 25-page "Assessment of the Environmental Impact" that considered these factors in more detail. On the basis of this assessment GSA decided that the detention center would not have a significant effect on the environment. After the district court denied an injunction, the case was again appealed to the Second Circuit, which issued the decision that follows.

Hanly v. Kleindienst
471 F.2d 823 (2d Cir. 1972)

Before FRIENDLY, Chief Judge, and MANSFIELD and TIMBERS, Circuit Judges. MANSFIELD, Circuit Judge: . . .

. . . [W]e believe that the appropriate criterion in the present case is the "arbitrary, capricious" standard established by the Administrative Procedure Act, since the meaning of the term "significantly" as used in §102(2)(C) of NEPA can be isolated as a question of law. . . .

Upon attempting, according to the foregoing standard, to interpret the amorphous term "significantly," as it is used in §102(2)(C), we are faced with the fact that almost every major federal action, no matter how limited in scope, has *some* adverse effect on the human environment. It is equally clear that an action which is environmentally important to one neighbor may be of no consequence to another. Congress could have decided that every major federal action must therefore be the subject of a detailed impact statement prepared according to the procedure prescribed by §102(2)(C). By adding the word "significantly," however, it demonstrated that before the agency in charge triggered that procedure, it should conclude that a greater environmental impact would result than from "any major federal action." Yet the limits of the key term have not been adequately defined by Congress or by guidelines issued by the CEQ and other responsible federal agencies vested with broad discretionary powers under NEPA. Congress apparently was willing to depend principally upon the agency's good faith determination as to what conduct would be sufficiently serious from an ecological standpoint to require use of the full-scale procedure.

Guidelines issued by the CEQ, which are echoed in rules for implementation published by the Public Buildings Service, the branch of GSA concerned with the construction of the MCC, suggest that a formal impact statement should be prepared with respect to "proposed actions, the environmental impact of which is likely to be highly controversial." See Council on Environmental Quality, Statements on Proposed Federal Actions Affecting the Environment, Guidelines §5(b), 36 Fed. Reg. 7724 (April 23, 1971). However, the term "controversial" apparently refers to cases where a substantial dispute exists as to the size, nature, or effect of the major federal action rather than to the existence of opposition to a use, the effect of which is relatively undisputed. This court in *Hanly I,* for instance, did not require a formal impact statement with respect to the office building portion of the Annex despite the existence of neighborhood opposition to it. The suggestion that "controversial" must be equated with neighborhood opposition has also been rejected by others.

In the absence of any Congressional or administrative interpretation of the term, we are persuaded that in deciding whether a major federal action will "significantly" affect the quality of the human environment the agency in charge, although vested with broad discretion, should normally be required to review the proposed action in the light of at least two relevant factors: (1) the extent to which the action will cause adverse environmental effects in excess of those created by existing uses in the area affected by it, and (2) the absolute quantitative adverse environmental effects of the action itself, including the cumulative harm that results from its contribution to existing adverse conditions or uses in the affected area. Where conduct conforms to existing uses, its adverse consequences will usually be less significant than when it represents a radical change. Absent some showing that an entire neighborhood is in the process of redevelopment, its existing environment, though frequently below an ideal standard, represents a norm that cannot be ignored. For instance, one more highway in an area honeycombed with roads usually has less of an adverse impact than if it were constructed through a roadless public park. See, e.g., Citizens to Preserve Overton Park v. Volpe, 401 U.S. 402 (1971).

Although the existing environment of the area which is the site of a major federal action constitutes one criterion to be considered, it must be recognized that even a slight increase in adverse conditions that form an existing environmental milieu may sometimes threaten harm that is significant. One more factory polluting air and water in an area zoned for industrial use may represent the straw that breaks the back of the environmental camel. Hence the absolute, as well as comparative, effects of a major federal action must be considered. . . .

. . . . Rather than encourage agencies to dispense with impact statements, we believe that application of the foregoing objective standards, coupled with compliance with minimum procedural requirements (specified below), which are designed to assure consideration of relevant facts, will lead agencies in doubtful cases (so-called "grey" areas) to obtain impact statements rather than to risk the delay and expense of protracted litigation. . . .

Appellants further contend that they have never been given an opportunity to discuss the MCC with any governmental agency prior to GSA's submission of its Assessment, which raises the question whether the agency acted "without observance of procedure required by law," see Citizens to Preserve Overton Park v. Volpe, 401 U.S. 402. We do not share the Government's view that the procedural mandates of §102(A), (B), and (D) and 42 U.S.C. §4332(2)(A), (B), and (D), apply only to actions found by the agency itself to have a significant environmental effect. While these sections are somewhat opaque, they are not expressly limited to "major Federal actions significantly affecting the quality of the human environment." Indeed if they were so limited §102(D), which requires the agency to develop appropriate alternatives to the recommended course of action, would be duplicative since §102(C), which does apply to actions "significantly affecting" the environment, specifies that the detailed impact statement must deal with "alternatives to the proposed action." 42 U.S.C. §4332(2)(C)(iii). However, in our view the Assessment does, in fact, satisfy the requirement of §102(2)(A) that an interdisciplinary approach taking into account the "natural and social sciences and the environmental design arts" be used. The GSA has retained architects familiar with the design requirements of the Civic Center and consulted with the Office of Lower Manhattan Development in an effort to harmonize the MCC with the Civic Center. The Assessment scrupulously takes into account the aesthetics and the tangible factors involved in the designing and planning of the MCC. Furthermore, we find that §102(2)(D) was complied with insofar as the GSA specifically considered the alternatives to continuing operation at the present facility at West Street and evaluated the selected site as compared with other specified possibilities. Although the assessment of the alternative sites was not as intensive as we might hope, its failure to analyze them in further detail does not warrant reversal.

A more serious question is raised by the GSA's failure to comply with §102(2)(B), which requires the agency to "identify and develop methods and procedures . . . which will insure that presently unquantified environmental amenities and values may be given appropriate consideration in decisionmaking along with economic and technical considerations." 42 U.S.C. §4332(2)(B). Since an agency, in making a threshold determination as to the "significance" of an action, is called upon to review in a general fashion the same factors that would be studied in depth for preparation of a detailed environmental impact statement, §102(2)(B) requires that some rudimentary procedures be designed to assure a fair and informed preliminary decision. Otherwise the agency, lacking essential information, might frustrate the purpose of NEPA by a threshold determination that an impact statement is unnecessary. Furthermore, an adequate record serves to preclude later changes in use without consideration of their environmental significance as required by NEPA.

Where a proposed major federal action may affect the sensibilities of a neighborhood, the prudent course would be for the agency in charge, before making a threshold decision, to give notice to the community of the contemplated action and to accept all pertinent information proffered by concerned citizens with respect to it. Furthermore, in line with the procedure usually followed in zoning disputes, particularly where emotions are likely to be aroused by fears, or rumors of misinformation, a public hearing serves the dual purpose of enabling the agency to obtain all relevant data and to satisfy the community that its views are being considered. However, neither NEPA nor any other federal statute mandates the specific type of procedure to be followed by federal agencies. . . .

Notwithstanding the absence of statutory or administrative provisions on the subject, this court has already held in *Hanly I* at 647 that federal agencies must "affirmatively develop a reviewable environmental record . . . even for purposes of a threshold section 102(2)(C) determination." We now go further and hold that before a preliminary or threshold determination of significance is made the responsible agency must give notice to the public of the proposed major federal action and an opportunity to submit relevant facts which might bear upon the agency's threshold decision. We do not suggest that a full-fledged formal hearing must be provided before each such determination is made, although it should be apparent that in many cases such a hearing would be advisable for reasons already indicated. The necessity for a hearing will depend greatly upon the circumstances surrounding the particular proposed action and upon the likelihood that a hearing will be more effective than other methods in developing relevant information and an understanding of the proposed action. The precise procedural steps to be adopted are better left to the agency, which should be in a better position than the court to determine whether solution of the problems faced with respect to a specific major federal action can better be achieved through a hearing or by informal acceptance of relevant data. . . .

FRIENDLY, Chief Judge (dissenting):

The learned opinion of my brother Mansfield gives these plaintiffs . . . both too little and too much. It gives too little because it raises the floor of what constitutes "major Federal actions significantly affecting the quality of the human environment," 42 U.S.C. §4332(2)(C), higher than I believe Congress intended. It gives too much because it requires that before making a threshold determination that no impact statement is demanded, the agency must go through procedures which I think are needed only when an impact statement must be made. The upshot is that a threshold determination that a proposal does not constitute major Federal action significantly affecting the quality of the human environment becomes a kind of mini-impact statement. The preparation of such a statement under the conditions laid down by the majority is unduly burdensome when the action is truly minor or insignificant. On the other hand, there is a danger that if the threshold determination is this elaborate, it may come to replace the impact statement in the grey area between actions which, though "major" in a monetary sense, are obviously insignificant (such as the construction of the proposed office building) and actions that are obviously significant (such as the construction of an atomic power plant). We would better serve the purposes of Congress by keeping the threshold low enough to insure that impact statements are prepared for actions in this grey area and thus to permit the determination that no statement is required to be made quite informally in cases of true insignificance. . . .

It is not readily conceivable that Congress meant to allow agencies to avoid [the EIS] requirement by reading "significant" to mean only "important," "momentous," or the like. One of the purposes of the impact statement is to insure that the relevant environmental data are before the agency and considered by it prior to the decision to commit Federal resources to the project; the statute must not be construed so as to allow the agency to make its decision in a doubtful case without the relevant data or a detailed study of it. This is particularly clear because of the absence from the statute of any procedural requirement upon an agency in making the threshold determination that an impact statement is not demanded, although the majority has managed to contrive one. What Congress was trying to say was "You don't need to make an impact statement, with the consequent expense and delay, when there is no sensible reason for making one." I thus agree with Judge J. Skelly Wright's view that "a statement is required whenever the action *arguably* will have an adverse environmental impact," Students Challenging Regulatory Agency Procedures (S.C.R.A.P.) v. United States, 346 F. Supp. 189, 201 (D.D.C. 1972) (three-judge court) (emphasis in original), prob. juris. noted, 409 U.S. 1073, with the qualification, doubtless intended, that the matter must be *fairly* arguable. . . .

[The CEQ Guidelines] provide that "if there is *potential* that the environment may be significantly affected, the statement is to be prepared." Guidelines §5(b), 36 Fed. Reg. 7724 (1971) (emphasis added). And they state further, in a remark highly relevant to this case:

> Proposed actions, the environmental impact of which is likely to be highly controversial, should be covered in all cases.

Id. This Guideline has been expressly adopted by the GSA in its own regulations, GSA Public Buildings Service Order 1095.1A, Attachment B, §1(a)(5) (Dec. 2, 1971). With respect, I see no basis for reading this as limited to cases where there is a dispute over what the environmental effects actually will be. Rather, I would think it clear that this includes action which the agency should know is likely to arouse intense opposition, even if the actual environmental impact is readily apparent. Apart from the former being the natural meaning of the words, the CEQ may well have had in mind that when action having some environmental impact "is likely to be highly controversial," an agency assessment that the action does not constitute major Federal action significantly affecting the environment is almost certain to evoke challenge in the courts. The CEQ could well have believed that rather than to incur the delay incident to such a suit, and the further delay if a court sustains the challenge—both vividly illustrated in this case where nearly two years have elapsed since the initial assessment that an impact statement was not required and a further remand is being directed—the agency would do better to prepare an impact statement in the first instance. In addition to possibly providing new information making reconsideration or modification of the project appropriate, such a policy has the added benefits of allowing opponents to blow off steam and giving them a sense that their objections have been considered—an important purpose of NEPA, as it is of the British statutory inquiry. . . .

. . . The energies my brothers would require GSA to devote to still a third assessment designed to show that an impact statement is not needed would better be devoted to making one.

I would reverse and direct the issuance of an injunction until a reasonable period after the making of an impact statement.

NOTES AND QUESTIONS

1. As the court's debate in *Hanly* makes clear, the threshold determination required by NEPA presents difficult questions of both substance and procedure: What does "significantly" mean and how should significance be determined? What answers does the majority provide to these questions? How helpful are its formulations? Does Judge Friendly offer a more workable approach?

2. In another portion of his dissent, Judge Friendly notes that the "action agencies" that are responsible for implementation of NEPA often have "missions" (such as highway or jail construction) that NEPA only serves to impede. Should this influence the degree of deference courts afford to these agencies' interpretation of NEPA?

3. The amorphous and subjective character of the "significance" test continues to plague the agencies and the courts, as discussed below. However, there is much stronger consensus today on the procedure by which this determination must be made.

A.   PROCEDURE FOR DETERMINING WHETHER OR NOT TO PREPARE AN EIS

In the *Hanly* litigation and other early cases, the courts demanded that agencies "affirmatively develop a reviewable environmental record" to support the determinations that their actions would not "significantly affect the quality of the human environment." This "reviewable environmental record" has become what is now called an "environmental assessment." The CEQ regulations reflect these decisions in setting out the process by which agencies determine whether an EIS is required. Section 1501.4 of the CEQ regulations directs agencies to determine whether the proposal is one that "(1) [n]ormally requires an environmental impact statement, or (2) [n]ormally does not require either an environmental impact statement or an environmental assessment (categorical exclusion)." Actions in the first category presumptively require preparation of an EIS; actions in the second category presumptively do not. If the proposed action falls in neither of these two categories, agencies are directed to prepare an environmental assessment and to make the determination of whether or not to prepare an EIS on the basis of the results of that assessment. If an agency determines on the basis of the environmental assessment not to prepare an EIS, the agency must make the finding of no significant impact available to the affected public as specified in §1506.6 of the CEQ regulations. In cases where the proposed action is without precedent or is very similar to one that normally requires preparation of an EIS, the CEQ regulations direct the agency to make a proposed finding of no significant impact available for public review for 30 days before the agency makes its final determination whether or not to prepare an EIS.

The CEQ regulations specify that an environmental assessment should include "brief discussions of the need for the proposal, of alternatives as required by section 102(2)(E), of the environmental impacts of the proposed action and alternatives, and a listing of agencies and persons consulted," in short, a kind of mini-EIS. 40 C.F.R. §1508.9. Under the CEQ regulations the "environmental assessment" serves two purposes. First, it provides the basis for the agency's determination whether to prepare an EIS. Second, when the agency concludes that an EIS is not required, the environmental assessment is the vehicle for the agency's compliance with NEPA's other requirements. Most important, in many cases, under section 102(2)(E), an agency must study alternatives to the proposed action, whether or not it is required to prepare an EIS.

B. DETERMINING THE "SIGNIFICANCE" OF ACTION

In its 1978 regulations, the CEQ made its own attempt to elaborate on how to interpret the term "significantly" in NEPA. 40 C.F.R. §1508.27. The CEQ advised that "significantly" as used in NEPA requires consideration of both context and intensity:

> *(a) Context.* This means that the significance of an action must be analyzed in several contexts such as society as a whole (human, national), the affected region, the affected interests, and the locality. Significance varies with the setting of the proposed action. For instance, in the case of a site-specific action, significance would usually depend upon the effects in the locale rather than in the world as a whole. Both short- and long-term effects are relevant.
>
> *(b) Intensity.* This refers to the severity of impact. Responsible officials must bear in mind that more than one agency may make decisions about partial aspects of a major action. The following should be considered in evaluating intensity:
>
> (1) Impact that may be both beneficial and adverse. A significant effect may exist even if the Federal agency believes that on balance the effect will be beneficial.
>
> (2) The degree to which the proposed action affects public health or safety.
>
> (3) Unique characteristics of the geographic area such as proximity to historic or cultural resources, parklands, prime farmlands, wetlands, wild and scenic rivers, or ecologically critical areas.

(4) The degree to which the effects on the quality of the human environment are likely to be highly controversial.

(5) The degree to which the possible effects on the human environment are highly uncertain or involve unique or unknown risks.

(6) The degree to which the action may establish a precedent for future actions with significant effects or represents a decision in principle about a future consideration.

(7) Whether the action is related to other actions with individually insignificant but cumulatively significant impacts. Significance exists if it is reasonable to anticipate a cumulatively significant impact on the environment. Significance cannot be avoided by terming an action temporary or by breaking it down into small component parts.

(8) The degree to which the action may adversely affect districts, sites, highways, structures, or objects listed in or eligible for listing in the National Register of Historic Places or may cause loss or destruction of significant scientific, cultural, or historical resources.

(9) The degree to which the action may adversely affect an endangered or threatened species or its habitat that has been determined to be critical under the Endangered Species Act of 1973.

(10) Whether the action threatens a violation of Federal, State, or local law or requirements imposed for the protection of the environment. [43 Fed. Reg. 56,005 (1978); 44 Fed. Reg. 874 (1979).]

In Anderson v. Evans, 314 F.2d 1006 (9th Cir. 2002), the Ninth Circuit cited factors 4, 5 and 6 of the intensity regulations in holding that an EIS must be prepared before the Makah Tribe can be granted permission to whale. Although conceding that the Tribe's hunting will not have a significant impact on the overall California gray whale population, the court noted that the likely impact of the hunt on the resident "whale population in the local area where the Tribe wants to hunt" is a matter of "hot dispute" surrounded by considerable uncertainty. 314 F.2d at 1018. It also concluded that the EIS should consider the precedential effect of allowing the Tribe to hunt whales because it could undermine efforts to keep the International Whaling Commission's aboriginal subsistence exception narrowly confined.

Factors 3, 4 and 5 of the intensity regulations were cited by the Ninth Circuit when it required the National Park Service (NPS) to prepare an EIS for its plan to permit more cruise ships to operate in Glacier Bay National Park in Alaska. In National Parks & Conservation Association v. Babbitt, 241 F.3d 722 (9th Cir. 2001), the court emphasized the unique characteristics of Glacier Bay, the substantial controversy surrounding the potential effects of increased vessel traffic, and the great uncertainty surrounding those effects. It rejected the Park Service's argument that an EIS need not be prepared because future mitigation measures could prevent the additional vessel traffic from adversely affecting humpback whales, endangered Steller sea lions, and air and water quality in the park. The court noted that there was "a paucity of analytical data to support the Park Service's conclusion that the mitigation measures would be adequate in light of the potential environmental harms."

NOTES AND QUESTIONS

1. The rise of the environmental justice movement has increased public attention to the disparate impact of environmental problems on poor and minority communities. As discussed in Chapter 1, President Clinton's Executive Order 12,898 directs each federal agency to identify and address disproportionate "adverse human health or environmental effects of its programs, policies, and

activities on minority and low-income populations." In December 1997 CEQ issued guidance to agencies concerning how to comply with the executive order. CEQ Environmental Justice: Guidance Under the National Environmental Policy Act (1997). CEQ takes the position that the executive order does not change NEPA law, but that it should stimulate agencies to give greater consideration to human health or ecological impacts on minority populations, low-income populations, and Indian tribes, and to alternatives that would accommodate environmental justice concerns. The Nuclear Regulatory Commission's Atomic Safety and Licensing Board has ruled that environmental justice concerns must be considered in environmental impact statements prepared for licensing proceedings. The Board required Nuclear Regulatory Commission staff to revise an EIS to give greater consideration to the effects of siting a uranium enrichment plant in a poor and minority community. In re Louisiana Energy Services, L.P. (May 1, 1997).

2. While the circuits initially split over the question of what standard of review should be applied to a decision not to prepare an EIS, the Supreme Court appears to have resolved the debate in Marsh v. Oregon Natural Resources Council, discussed at pages 849-851. The Court adopted the "arbitrary and capricious" standard of review for decisions not to prepare a supplemental EIS. The Court emphasized, however, that "courts should not automatically defer to the agency's express reliance on an interest in finality without carefully reviewing the record and satisfying themselves that the agency has made a reasoned decision based on its evaluation of the significance—or lack of significance—of the new information." 490 U.S. at 378. Based on this statement, the Ninth Circuit has held that when disputes over whether or not to prepare a supplemental EIS involve "predominately legal questions" rather than "factual or technical matters," the reasonableness standard of review should be applied instead of the arbitrary and capricious standard. Alaska Wilderness Recreation & Tourism Ass'n v. Morrison, 67 F.3d 723, 727 (9th Cir. 1995). The Supreme Court's decision in Marsh v. Oregon Natural Resources Council has been interpreted to extend to reviews of *all* agency decisions not to prepare an EIS. Greenpeace Action v. Franklin, 14 F.3d 1324 (9th Cir. 1992); Village of Los Ranchos de Albuquerque v. Marsh, 956 F.2d 970 (10th Cir. 1992) (en banc).

3. In Idaho v. ICC, 35 F.3d 585 (D.C. Cir. 1994), the D.C. Circuit held that the Interstate Commerce Commission had violated NEPA by failing to prepare an EIS before conditionally approving a proposal to abandon a portion of a railroad line. Even though it authorized salvage activities along a heavily contaminated track bed, the ICC had claimed that its decision would not significantly affect the environment because it required the railroad to consult with federal and state environmental agencies about the environmental effects of salvage operations. Citing its decision in *Calvert Cliffs*, p. 798, the D.C. Circuit held that "[a]n agency cannot delegate its NEPA responsibilities in this manner," 35 F.3d at 595. The court concluded that the agency must take its own "hard look" at the environmental effects of its action, and cannot abdicate its NEPA responsibilities in favor of a regulated party.

C. What "Effects" Must Be Considered

In determining whether the effects of an action are "significant," one must, of course, make some judgments about what "effects" must be considered. NEPA demands consideration of effects "on the human environment." The CEQ Regulation defining "effects," 40 C.F.R. §1508.8, provides the following explanation:

> Effects and impacts as used in these regulations are synonymous. Effects includes ecological (such as the effects on natural resources and on the components, structures, and functioning of affected ecosystems), aesthetic, historic, cultural, economic, social, or health, whether direct, indirect, or cumulative. Effects may also include those resulting from actions which may have both beneficial and detrimental effects, even if on balance the agency believes that the effect will be beneficial.

The question of what "effects" are cognizable under NEPA was addressed by the Supreme Court in Metropolitan Edison Co. v. People Against Nuclear Energy (*PANE*), 460 U.S. 766 (1983). In *PANE*, the Court held that NEPA did not require agencies to evaluate the risk that restart of a nuclear power plant that is a companion to the damaged Three Mile Island reactor would harm the psychological health of the surrounding community. The Court concluded that regardless of the gravity of the harm alleged, NEPA does not apply unless the harm has a sufficiently close connection to the physical environment. The question of how direct the causal connection must be between the action under consideration and the environmental effects to be assessed was addressed by the Court in the case that follows.

|| *Dept. of Transportation v. Public Citizen* ||
|| **541 U.S. 752 (2004)** ||

JUSTICE THOMAS delivered the opinion of the Court.

In this case, we confront the question whether the National Environmental Policy Act of 1969 (NEPA) and the Clean Air Act (CAA) require the Federal Motor Carrier Safety Administration (FMCSA) to evaluate the environmental effects of cross-border operations of Mexican-domiciled motor carriers, where FMCSA's promulgation of certain regulations would allow such cross-border operations to occur. Because FMCSA lacks discretion to prevent these cross-border operations, we conclude that these statutes impose no such requirement on FMCSA.

I

[The Court discusses NEPA and notes that] "NEPA itself does not mandate particular results" in order to accomplish [its] ends. Robertson v. Methow Valley Citizens Council, 490 U.S. 332, 350 (1989). Rather, NEPA imposes only procedural requirements on federal agencies with a particular focus on requiring agencies to undertake analyses of the environmental impact of their proposals and actions. . . .

FMCSA, an agency within the Department of Transportation (DOT), is responsible for motor carrier safety and registration. See 49 U.S.C. §113(f). FMCSA has a variety of statutory mandates, including "ensur[ing]" safety, §31136, establishing minimum levels of financial responsibility for motor carriers, §31139, and prescribing federal standards for safety inspections of commercial motor vehicles, §31142. Importantly, FMCSA has only limited discretion regarding motor vehicle carrier registration: It must grant registration to all domestic or foreign motor carriers that are "willing and able to comply with" the applicable safety, fitness, and financial-responsibility requirements. §13902(a)(1). FMCSA has no statutory authority to impose or enforce emissions controls or to establish environmental requirements unrelated to motor carrier safety.

[The Court notes that in 1982 Congress authorized the President to extend a 2-year moratorium it had imposed on new Mexican motor carriers operating in the interior of the United States, authority he exercised. After an international arbitration panel ruled in February 2001 that the moratorium violated the North American Free Trade Agreement (NAFTA), President Bush declared his intention to lift it as soon as the FMCSA promulgated new regulations for such carriers, which it proposed in May 2001. In December 2001, Congress enacted section 350 of the Department of Transportation and Related Agencies Appropriations Act that barred the processing of applications by Mexican motor carriers to operate in the United States until the FMCSA adopted specific application and safety-monitoring regulations for them.]

In January 2002, acting pursuant to NEPA's mandates, FMCSA issued a programmatic [environmental assessment] EA for the proposed Application and Safety Monitoring Rules. . . . Because FMCSA concluded that the entry of the Mexican trucks was not an "effect" of its regulations, it did not consider any environmental impact that might be caused by the increased presence of Mexican trucks within the United States.

The particular environmental effects on which the EA focused, then, were those likely to arise from the increase in the number of roadside inspections of Mexican trucks and buses due to the proposed regulations. The EA concluded that these effects (such as a slight increase in emissions, noise from the trucks, and possible danger to passing motorists) were minor and could be addressed and avoided in the inspections process itself. The EA also noted that the increase of inspection-related emissions would be at least partially offset by the fact that the safety requirements would reduce the number of Mexican trucks operating in the United States. Due to these calculations, the EA concluded that the issuance of the proposed regulations would have no significant impact on the environment, and hence FMCSA, on the same day as it released the EA, issued a [finding of no significant impact] FONSI [and thus declined to prepare an environmental impact statement (EIS)].

[After the FMCSA issued its regulations in March 2002, respondents sued, arguing that the regulations were promulgated in violation of NEPA and the CAA.] The Court of Appeals agreed with respondents, granted the petitions, and set aside the rules. 316 F.3d 1002 (CA 9 2003).

The Court of Appeals concluded that the EA was deficient because it failed to give adequate consideration to the overall environmental impact of lifting the moratorium on the cross-border operation of Mexican motor carriers. According to the Court of Appeals, FMCSA was required to consider the environmental effects of the entry of Mexican trucks because "the President's rescission of the moratorium was 'reasonably foreseeable' at the time the EA was prepared and the decision not to prepare an EIS was made." Id., at 1022 (quoting 40 CFR §§1508.7, 1508.8(b) (2003)). Due to this perceived deficiency, the Court of Appeals remanded the case for preparation of a full EIS. . . .

II

. . . Under NEPA, an agency is required to provide an EIS only if it will be undertaking a "major Federal actio[n]," which "significantly affect[s] the quality of the human environment." 42 U.S.C. §4332(2)(C). Under applicable CEQ regulations, "[m]ajor Federal action" is defined to "includ[e] actions with effects that may be major and which are potentially subject to Federal control and responsibility." 40 CFR §1508.18 (2003). "Effects" is defined to "include: (a) Direct effects, which are caused by the action and occur at the same time and place," and "(b) Indirect effects, which are caused by the action and are later in time or farther removed in distance, but are still reasonably foreseeable." §1508.8. Thus, the relevant question is whether the increase in cross-border operations of Mexican motor carriers, with the correlative release of emissions by Mexican trucks, is an "effect" of FMCSA's issuance of the Application and Safety Monitoring Rules; if not, FMCSA's failure to address these effects in its EA did not violate NEPA, and so FMCSA's issuance of a FONSI cannot be arbitrary and capricious.

[The Court then determined that the respondents had waived any challenge to the EA premised on its failure to consider possible alternatives to the proposed rule because they had not raised such alternatives in their comments during the rulemaking]. . . . With this point aside, respondents have only one complaint with respect to the EA: It did not take into account the environmental effects of increased cross-border operations of Mexican motor carriers. Respondents' argument that FMCSA was required to consider these effects is simple. Under §350, FMCSA is barred from expending any funds to process or review any applications by Mexican motor carriers until FMCSA implemented a variety of specific application and safety-monitoring requirements for Mexican carriers. This expenditure bar makes it impossible for any Mexican motor carrier to receive authorization to operate within the United States until FMCSA issued the regulations challenged here. The promulgation of the regulations, the argument goes, would "caus[e]" the entry of Mexican trucks (and hence also cause any emissions such trucks would produce), and the entry of the trucks is "reasonably foreseeable." 40 CFR §1508.8 (2003). Thus, the argument concludes, under the relevant CEQ regulations, FMCSA must take these emissions into account in its EA when evaluating whether to produce an EIS.

Respondents' argument, however, overlooks a critical feature of this case: FMCSA has no ability to countermand the President's lifting of the moratorium or otherwise categorically to exclude Mexican motor carriers from operating within the United States. To be sure, §350 did restrict the ability of FMCSA to authorize cross-border operations of Mexican motor carriers, but Congress did not otherwise modify FMCSA's statutory mandates. In particular, FMCSA remains subject to the mandate of 49 U.S.C. §13902(a)(1), that FMCSA "*shall* register a person to provide transportation . . . as a motor carrier if [it] finds that the person is willing and able to comply with" the safety and financial responsibility requirements established by the Department of Transportation. (Emphasis added.) Under FMCSA's entirely reasonable reading of this provision, it must certify any motor carrier that can show that it is willing and able to comply with the various substantive requirements for safety and financial responsibility contained in DOT regulations; only the moratorium prevented it from doing so for Mexican motor carriers before 2001. App. 51-55. Thus, upon the lifting of the moratorium, if FMCSA refused to authorize a Mexican motor carrier for cross-border services, where the Mexican motor carrier was willing and able to comply with the various substantive safety and financial responsibilities rules, it would violate §13902(a)(1).

If it were truly impossible for FMCSA to comply with both §350 and §13902(a)(1), then we would be presented with an irreconcilable conflict of laws. As the later enacted provision, §350 would quite possibly win out. But FMCSA can easily satisfy both mandates: It can issue the application and safety inspection rules required by §350, and start processing applications by Mexican motor carriers and authorize those that satisfy §13902(a)(1)'s conditions. Without a conflict, then, FMCSA must comply with all of its statutory mandates.

Respondents must rest, then, on a particularly unyielding variation of "but for" causation, where an agency's action is considered a cause of an environmental effect even when the agency has no authority to prevent the effect. However, a "but for" causal relationship is insufficient to make an agency responsible for a particular effect under NEPA and the relevant regulations. As this Court held in Metropolitan Edison Co. v. People Against Nuclear Energy, 460 U.S. 766, 774 (1983), NEPA requires "a reasonably close causal relationship" between the environmental effect and the alleged cause. The Court analogized this requirement to the "familiar doctrine of proximate cause from tort law." Ibid. In particular, "courts must look to the underlying policies or legislative intent in order to draw a manageable line between those causal changes that may make an actor responsible for an effect and those that do not." Id., at 774, n. 7. See also W. Keeton, D. Dobbs, R. Keeton & D. Owen, Prosser and Keeton on Law of Torts 264, 274-275 (5th ed. 1984) (proximate cause analysis turns on policy considerations and considerations of the "legal responsibility" of actors).

Also, inherent in NEPA and its implementing regulations is a "rule of reason," which ensures that agencies determine whether and to what extent to prepare an EIS based on the usefulness of any new potential information to the decisionmaking process. See Marsh, 490 U.S., at 373-374. Where the preparation of an EIS would serve "no purpose" in light of NEPA's regulatory scheme as a whole, no rule of reason worthy of that title would require an agency to prepare an EIS.

In these circumstances, the underlying policies behind NEPA and Congress' intent, as informed by the "rule of reason," make clear that the causal connection between FMCSA's issuance of the proposed regulations and the entry of the Mexican trucks is insufficient to make FMCSA responsible under NEPA to consider the environmental effects of the entry. The NEPA EIS requirement serves two purposes. First, "[i]t ensures that the agency, in reaching its decision, will have available, and will carefully consider, detailed information concerning significant environmental impacts." Robertson, 490 U.S., at 349. Second, it "guarantees that the relevant information will be made available to the larger audience that may also play a role in both the decisionmaking process and the implementation of that decision." Ibid. Requiring FMCSA to consider the environmental effects of the entry of Mexican trucks would fulfil neither of these statutory purposes. Since FMCSA has no ability categorically to prevent the cross-border operations of Mexican motor carriers, the environmental impact of the cross-border operations would have no effect on FMCSA's decisionmaking—FMCSA simply lacks the power to act on whatever information might be contained in the EIS.

Similarly, the informational purpose is not served. The "informational role" of an EIS is to "giv[e] the public the assurance that the agency 'has indeed considered environmental concerns in its decisionmaking process,' Baltimore Gas & Electric Co. [v. Natural Resources Defense Council, Inc., 462 U.S. 87, 97 437 (1983)], and, perhaps more significantly, provid[e] a springboard for public comment" in the agency decisionmaking process itself, ibid. The purpose here is to ensure that the "larger audience," ibid., can provide input as necessary to the agency making the relevant decisions. See 40 CFR §1500.1(c) (2003) ("NEPA's purpose is not to generate paperwork—even excellent paperwork—but to foster excellent action. The NEPA process is intended to help public officials make decisions that are based on understanding of environmental consequences, and take actions that protect, restore, and enhance the environment"); §1502.1 ("The primary purpose of an environmental impact statement is to serve as an action-forcing device to insure that the policies and goals defined in the Act are infused into the ongoing programs and actions of the Federal Government"). But here, the "larger audience" can have no impact on FMCSA's decisionmaking, since, as just noted, FMCSA simply could not act on whatever input this "larger audience" could provide.

It would not, therefore, satisfy NEPA's "rule of reason" to require an agency to prepare a full EIS due to the environmental impact of an action it could not refuse to perform. Put another way, the legally relevant cause of the entry of the Mexican trucks is not FMCSA's action, but instead the actions of the President in lifting the moratorium and those of Congress in granting the President this authority while simultaneously limiting FMCSA's discretion.

Consideration of the CEQ's "cumulative impact" regulation does not change this analysis. An agency is required to evaluate the "[c]umulative impact" of its action, which is defined as "the impact on the environment which results from the incremental impact of the action when added to other past, present, and reasonably foreseeable future actions regardless of what agency (Federal or non-Federal) or person undertakes such other actions." §1508.7. The "cumulative impact" regulation required FMCSA to consider the "incremental impact" of the safety rules themselves, in the context of the President's lifting of the moratorium and other relevant circumstances. But this is exactly what FMCSA did in its EA. FMCSA appropriately and reasonably examined the incremental impact of its safety rules assuming the President's modification of the moratorium (and, hence, assuming the increase in cross-border operations of Mexican motor carriers). The "cumulative impact" regulation does not require FMCSA to treat the lifting of the moratorium itself, or consequences from the lifting of the moratorium, as an effect of its promulgation of its Application and Safety Monitoring Rules.

We hold that where an agency has no ability to prevent a certain effect due to its limited statutory authority over the relevant actions, the agency cannot be considered a legally relevant "cause" of the effect. Hence, under NEPA and the implementing CEQ regulations, the agency need not consider these effects in its EA when determining whether its action is a "major Federal action." Because the President, not FMCSA, could authorize (or not authorize) cross-border operations from Mexican motor carriers, and because FMCSA has no discretion to prevent the entry of Mexican trucks, its EA did not need to consider the environmental effects arising from the entry.

NOTES AND QUESTIONS

1. This decision is yet another in a long line of Supreme Court cases construing NEPA's requirements narrowly. In Natural Resources Defense Council, Inc. v. Morton, 458 F.2d 827 (D.C. Cir. 1972), the D.C. Circuit had held that NEPA

requires an agency to consider even some alternatives that it did not have the power to adopt on its own. Does DOT v. Public Citizen overrule this decision?

2. Does DOT v. Public Citizen provide any insight into how the Court views the purposes of NEPA? Is it fair to say that the Court does not consider one of NEPA's purposes to be informing other agencies who may be able to control adverse environmental effects identified in the EIS?

3. The Court in *Public Citizen* also held that the FMCSA did not violate the Clean Air Act by failing to determine that emissions from the cross-border operation of Mexican trucks would be in conformity with existing air quality standards because the FMCSA was powerless to stop the emissions.

4. In *Hanly*, the majority was uncertain "whether psychological and socio-logical effects upon neighbors constitute the type of factors that may be consid-ered in making a determination [whether or not to perform an EIS] since they do not lend themselves to measurement." 471 F.2d at 833. Judge Friendly dis-agreed in his dissent, noting that NEPA speaks of "the overall welfare and development of man," 42 U.S.C. §4331(a), and requires federal agencies to act to "assure for all Americans safe, healthful, productive and esthetically and culturally pleasing surroundings." Id. §4331(b)(2). Is his view consistent with the Supreme Court's decision in *PANE*?

5. Is an EIS required for federal actions likely to have a significant *positive* effect on the environment? In Pacific Legal Foundation v. Andrus, 657 F.2d 829 (6th Cir. 1981), the Sixth Circuit held that decisions to list species as threatened or endangered under the Endangered Species Act (ESA) were exempt from NEPA. At the urging of CEQ, 48 Fed. Reg. 49,244 (1983), the Secretary of Interior announced in 1983 that the Department would no longer prepare EISs in con-nection with listing determinations made under section 4 of the ESA. In Douglas County v. Babbitt, 48 F.3d 1495 (9th Cir. 1995), cert. denied, 516 U.S. 1042 (1996), the Ninth Circuit held that decisions to designate critical habitat for an endangered species were not subject to NEPA because neither an EA nor an EIS is "necessary for federal actions that conserve the environment." 48 F.3d at 1505.

PROBLEM EXERCISE: SHOULD THE FCC PREPARE AN EIS ASSESSING THE CUMULATIVE IMPACT OF CELLPHONE TOWER CONSTRUCTION?

Construction of cellular, radio, television, and microwave communications towers in the United States has been growing at a rapid rate, estimated at 6 to 8 percent annually. As of September 2000, the Federal Communications Com-mission's Antenna Structure Registry included more than 74,000 towers, with 45,000 towers rising more than 199 feet above ground level.

In 2001, a pair of environmental groups—Friends of the Earth and the Forest Conservation Council—petitioned the Federal Communcations Commis-sion (FCC) to deny dozens of applications by telecommunications companies to build cellphone towers. The environmental groups argue that the FCC should not be allowed to approve any more applications to build new cellphone towers until it conducts an EIS that assesses the cumulative environmental effects of tower construction. The Commission requires companies to submit environ-mental impact studies with each application to build a new tower, but the environmental groups argue that none of these studies consider the commulative environmental effects of the hundreds of cellphone towers that are erected each year with the FCC's approval. Yochi J. Dreazen, Cellular Towers Get Static From Environmentalists, Wall St. J., July 23, 2001, at B1.

It has been well known since the nineteenth century that tall, lighted structures can pose significant hazards to birds, particularly to the 350 species of night-migrating birds. Cellular telephone towers usually are about 250 feet tall and the Federal Aviation Administration requires all towers more than 199 feet to display lights for aviation safety. The U.S. Fish and Wildlife Service (FWS) estimates that 4 to 5 million birds are killed every year as a result of collisions with communications towers. In addition to the millions of bird deaths that occur each year, environmental groups note that tower construction can damage wetlands and other environmentally sensitive areas. Towers also raise aesthetic concerns and there is considerable controversy over the potential health effects of the electromagnetic radiation they give off.

The telecommunications industry argues that estimates of bird deaths caused by towers are too high. Far more birds (hundreds of millions per year) are killed by collisions with windows and buildings, and pesticides probably kill another 65 million birds annually. David Malakoff, Faulty Towers, Audubon Magazine, Sept. 2001. The companies also argue that there is no conclusive data establishing that radiation emanating from cellphone towers causes health problems.

In November 1999, Jamie Clark, then the director of the FWS asked the chairman of the FCC to consider the cumulative environmental effects of cell-phone tower construction. Clark noted that the towers were being built "with almost no environmental oversight by the FCC." The FCC refused to prepare a cumulative impact study. In September 2000 the FWS developed "Interim Guidelines for Recommendation on Communications Tower Siting, Construction, Operation and Decommissioning" to help mitigate the risks of birds colliding with towers. In 2003 the FCC issued a notice of inquiry soliciting empirical data on the effects of cellphone towers on migratory birds.

It could take more than a year to prepare an environmental impact statement of the cumulative effects of cellphone tower construction at a time when the telecommunications industry is rushing to offer new high-speed mobile access to the Internet. The industry argues that it already is struggling to keep up with surging consumer demand for wireless services and that construction delays caused by environmental reviews could be devastating. Each month's delay in approving construction of a cellphone tower is estimated to cost a company $300,000 per tower in lost revenue. Id.

Question One.   How should the FCC rule on the petition by the environmental goups? Should the Commission consider the economic consequences of delaying cellphone tower construction when deciding whether or not to prepare an EIS of cumulative effects? Is the fact that far more birds are killed by other causes relevant to the decision?

Question Two.   If the FCC refuses to prepare an EIS, what are the chances that the environmental groups can bring a successful lawsuit challenging the Commission's decision?

C.   IS THE EIS ADEQUATE?

When an agency has prepared an EIS for its proposed action, the focus of judicial review naturally shifts to the adequacy of that document. The CEQ

Regulations describe the basic structure and content of the EIS. 40 C.F.R. §1502.10-1502.18. Each EIS must include: a summary (to facilitate public review); an explanation of the purpose of and need for the proposed action; a description and comparative assessment of alternatives; a description of the environment that will be affected by the action; and an analysis of the environmental consequences of the proposal and alternatives. Id. Litigation centers on the adequacy of the agency's assessment of alternatives and the scope and detail of its analysis of environmental consequences.

1. Alternatives

NEPA requires that agencies assess and consider alternatives to proposed actions. These requirements are contained both in section 102(2)(C)(iii)'s description of the elements of an environmental impact statement ("a detailed statement by the responsible official on ... alternatives to the proposed action") and in what is now section 102(2)(E)'s independent requirement that agencies must "study, develop, and describe appropriate alternatives to recommended courses of action in any proposal which involves unresolved conflicts concerning alternative uses of available resources."

Analysis of alternatives is arguably the most important part of NEPA. The question of the adequacy of an agency's assessment of alternatives arose in the early stages of the litigation that culminated in the Strycker's Bay v. Karlen decision discussed on page 802. In Trinity Episcopal School Corp. v. Romney, 523 F.2d 88 (2d Cir. 1975), plaintiffs challenged the decision by the Department of Housing and Urban Development (HUD) to fund construction of low-income public housing on a site in New York City. They argued that HUD was required by NEPA to do more than simply accept the New York City Housing Authority's unsupported conclusion that there were no alternative sites for the public housing project because of the scarcity of land. The Second Circuit agreed. It held that what is now section 102(2)(E) required HUD to study alternatives to the project even though HUD was not obliged to prepare an EIS subject to section 102(2)(C)(iii). On remand, HUD prepared a study of alternatives, but rejected them all. HUD's decision was challenged again, culminating in the Strycker's Bay decision by the Supreme Court.

The Supreme Court previously had an opportunity to interpret directly NEPA's requirement for analysis of alternatives in Vermont Yankee Nuclear Power Corp. v. NRDC, a different portion of which is discussed in Chapter 2 on page 159. Recall that the case involved an Atomic Energy Commission licensing proceeding (a function now performed by the Nuclear Regulatory Commission) for a nuclear power plant being built by Consumers Power. Under the Commission's licensing procedures, when a utility applied for a permit to construct a nuclear power plant, Commission staff were responsible for preparing draft and final environmental impact statements. A public adjudicatory hearing was then held by the Atomic Safety and Licensing Board. In Vermont Yankee the Court considered whether NEPA required the Commission to reopen the proceeding to consider energy conservation measures as an alternative to construction of the plant. In the late 1960s and early 1970s environmentalists had opposed the construction of nuclear power plants on the grounds that they were unsafe and unneeded. Following the energy crises of the early 1970s, environmentalists increasingly turned to arguments that energy conservation measures could supply the equivalent power more cheaply. After the D.C. Circuit held that the Commission was required to address the conservation alternative, the Supreme Court granted review.

	Vermont Yankee Nuclear	
	Power Corp. v. NRDC	
	435 U.S. 519 (1978)	

MR. JUSTICE REHNQUIST delivered the opinion of the Court. . . .

With respect to the permit to Consumers Power, the court first held that the environmental impact statement for construction of the Midland reactors was fatally defective for failure to examine energy conservation as an alternative to a plant of this size. . . .

The Court of Appeals ruled that the Commission's "threshold test" for the presentation of energy conservation contentions was inconsistent with NEPA's basic mandate to the Commission. The Commission, the court reasoned, is something more than an umpire who sits back and resolves adversary contentions at the hearing stage. And when an intervenor's comments "bring 'sufficient attention to the issue to stimulate the Commission's consideration of it,' " the Commission must "undertake its own preliminary investigation of the proffered alternative sufficient to reach a rational judgment whether it is worthy of detailed consideration in the EIS. Moreover, the Commission must explain the basis for each conclusion that further consideration of a suggested alternative is unwarranted." 547 F.2d, at 628, quoting from Indiana & Michigan Electric Co. v. FPC, 502 F.2d 336, 339 (1974), cert. denied, 420 U.S. 946 (1975).

While the court's rationale is not entirely unappealing as an abstract proposition, as applied to this case we think it basically misconceives not only the scope of the agency's statutory responsibility, but also the nature of the administrative process, the thrust of the agency's decision, and the type of issues the intervenors were trying to raise.

There is little doubt that under the Atomic Energy Act of 1954, state public utility commissions or similar bodies are empowered to make the initial decision regarding the need for power. 42 U.S.C. §2021(k). The Commission's prime area of concern in the licensing context, on the other hand, is national security, public health, and safety. §§2132, 2133, 2201. And it is clear that the need, as that term is conventionally used, for the power was thoroughly explored in the hearings. Even the Federal Power Commission, which regulates sales in interstate commerce, 16 U.S.C. §824 et seq. (1976 ed.), agreed with Consumers Power's analysis of projected need.

NEPA, of course, has altered slightly the statutory balance, requiring "a detailed statement by the responsible official on . . . alternatives to the proposed action." 42 U.S.C. §4332(C). But, as should be obvious even upon a moment's reflection, the term "alternatives" is not self-defining. To make an impact statement something more than an exercise in frivolous boilerplate the concept of alternatives must be bounded by some notion of feasibility. As the Court of Appeals for the District of Columbia Circuit has itself recognized:

> There is reason for concluding that NEPA was not meant to require detailed discussion of the environmental effects of "alternatives" put forward in

comments when these effects cannot be readily ascertained and the alternatives are deemed only remote and speculative possibilities, in view of basic changes required in statutes and policies of other agencies—making them available, if at all, only after protracted debate and litigation not meaningfully compatible with the time-frame of the needs to which the underlying proposal is addressed. National Resources Defense Council v. Morton, 458 F.2d 827, 837-838 (1972).

Common sense also teaches us that the "detailed statement of alternatives" cannot be found wanting simply because the agency failed to include every alternative device and thought conceivable by the mind of man. Time and resources are simply too limited to hold that an impact statement fails because the agency failed to ferret out every possible alternative, regardless of how uncommon or unknown that alternative may have been at the time the project was approved. With these principles in mind we now turn to the notion of "energy conservation," an alternative the omission of which was thought by the Court of Appeals to have been "forcefully pointed out by [intervenor] Saginaw in its comments on the draft EIS." Again, as the Commission pointed out, "the phrase 'energy conservation' has a deceptively simple ring in this context. Taken literally, the phrase suggests a virtually limitless range of possible actions and developments that might, in one way or another, ultimately reduce projected demands for electricity from a particular proposed plant." Moreover, as a practical matter, it is hard to dispute the observation that it is largely the events of recent years that have emphasized not only the need but also a large variety of alternatives for energy conservation. Prior to the drastic oil shortages incurred by the United States in 1973, there was little serious thought in most government circles of energy conservation alternatives. Indeed, the Council on Environmental Quality did not promulgate regulations which even remotely suggested the need to consider energy conservation in impact statements until August 1, 1973. See 40 CFR §1500.8(a)(4) (1977); 38 Fed. Reg. 20554 (1973). And even then the guidelines were not made applicable to draft and final statements filed with the Council before January 28, 1974. Id., at 20557, 21265. The Federal Power Commission likewise did not require consideration of energy conservation in applications to build hydroelectric facilities until June 19, 1973. 18 CFR pt. 2, App. A., §8.2 (1977); 38 Fed. Reg. 15946, 15949 (1973). And these regulations were not made retroactive either. Id., at 15946. All this occurred over a year and a half after the draft environmental statement for Midland had been prepared, and over a year after the final environmental statement had been prepared and the hearings completed.

We think these facts amply demonstrate that the concept of "alternatives" is an evolving one, requiring the agency to explore more or fewer alternatives as they become better known and understood. This was well understood by the Commission, which, unlike the Court of Appeals, recognized that the Licensing Board's decision had to be judged by the information then available to it. And judged in that light we have little doubt the Board's actions were well within the proper bounds of its statutory authority. Not only did the record before the agency give every indication that the project was actually needed, but also there was nothing before the Board to indicate to the contrary.

We also think the court's criticism of the Commission's "threshold test" displays a lack of understanding of the historical setting within which the agency action took place and of the nature of the test itself. In the first place, while it is true that NEPA places upon an agency the obligation to consider every significant aspect of the environmental impact of a proposed action, it is still incumbent upon intervenors who wish to participate to structure their participation so that it is meaningful, so that it alerts the agency to the intervenors' position and contentions. This is especially true when the intervenors are requesting the agency to embark upon an exploration of uncharted territory, as was the question of energy conservation in the late 1960s and early 1970s.

> [C]omments must be significant enough to step over a threshold requirement of materiality before any lack of agency response or consideration becomes of concern. The comment cannot merely state that a particular mistake was made . . . ; it must show why the mistake was of possible significance in the results. . . . Portland Cement Assn. v. Ruckelshaus, 486 F.2d 375, 394 (1973), cert. denied sub nom. Portland Cement Corp. v. Administrator, EPA, 417 U.S. 921 (1974).

Indeed, administrative proceedings should not be a game or a forum to engage in unjustified obstructionism by making cryptic and obscure reference to matters that "ought to be" considered and then, after failing to do more to bring the matter to the agency's attention, seeking to have that agency determination vacated on the ground that the agency failed to consider matters "forcefully presented." In fact, here the agency continually invited further clarification of Saginaw's contentions. Even without such clarification it indicated a willingness to receive evidence on the matters. But not only did Saginaw decline to further focus its contentions, it virtually declined to participate, indicating that it had "no conventional findings of fact to set forth" and that it had not "chosen to search the record and respond to this proceeding by submitting citations of matter which we believe were proved or disproved."

We also think the court seriously mischaracterized the Commission's "threshold test" as placing "heavy substantive burdens . . . on intervenors, . . ." 547 F.2d, at 627, and n.11. On the contrary, the Commission explicitly stated:

> We do not equate this burden with the civil litigation concept of a prima facie case, an unduly heavy burden in this setting. But the showing should be sufficient to require reasonable minds to inquire further. App. 344 n.27.

We think this sort of agency procedure well within the agency's discretion.

. . . Nuclear energy may some day be a cheap, safe source of power or it may not. But Congress has made a choice to at least try nuclear energy, establishing a reasonable review process in which courts are to play only a limited role. The fundamental policy questions appropriately resolved in Congress and in the state legislatures are *not* subject to reexamination in the federal courts under the guise of judicial review of agency action. Time may prove wrong the decision to develop nuclear energy, but it is Congress or the States with their appropriate agencies which must eventually make that judgment. In the meantime courts should perform their appointed function. NEPA does set forth significant substantive goals for the Nation, but its mandate to the agencies is essentially procedural. See 42 U.S.C. §4332. It is to insure a fully informed and well-considered decision, not necessarily a decision the judges of the Court of Appeals or of this Court would have reached had they been members of the decisionmaking unit of the agency. Administrative decisions should be set aside in this context, as in every other, only for substantial procedural or substantive reasons as mandated by statute, not simply because the court is unhappy with the result reached. And a single alleged oversight on a peripheral issue, urged by parties who never fully cooperated or indeed raised the issue below, must not be made the basis for overturning a decision properly made after an otherwise exhaustive proceeding.

NOTES AND QUESTIONS

1. What does *Vermont Yankee* tell us about the scope of the agency's duty to consider alternatives? What duty had the Commission conceded? Why does the Court refuse to require it to consider the alternatives suggested by intervenor Saginaw? What should Saginaw have done differently? Was their basic problem a failure to present their arguments to the Commission in a timely fashion, a failure to present sufficiently extensive evidence to bolster their arguments, or both?

2. The Court observes that "the concept of 'alternatives' is an evolving one, requiring the agency to explore more or fewer alternatives as they become better known and understood." What result do you think the Court would reach if the licensing proceeding occurred today and the Commission refused to consider energy conservation as an alternative to construction of the plant?

3. How obvious must an alternative be before it must be considered in an EIS? Can an agency be required to consider alternatives that employ technology that, while not currently available, could be developed in the future?

4. In some cases the number of possible alternatives is virtually infinite. In such situations, the courts have required that agencies consider an array of alternatives that represents the range of possibilities. The Ninth Circuit addressed this problem in California v. Block, 690 F.2d 735 (9th Cir. 1982). The U.S. Forest Service had prepared an EIS on a national management plan for 62 million acres of "roadless areas" in the National Forest System. The Forest Service project, called the "Roadless Area Review and Evaluation II" (RARE II), inventoried all roadless areas and allocated them among three planning categories: wilderness, nonwilderness, and further planning. For the final EIS, the Forest Service used an elaborate set of decision criteria to develop 11 alternative allocations. These included 3 extremes (all wilderness, no wilderness, and no action), which served only as points of reference and were not seriously considered. Of the 8 alternatives given serious consideration *none* allocated more than 33 percent of the roadless area to wilderness. The State of California challenged the EIS, arguing that the Forest Service had violated NEPA by unreasonably restricting the range of alternatives considered. The Ninth Circuit agreed, holding that while the Service's "decision criteria" were diverse, the resulting alternatives were not. The Forest Service was required to consider an alternative that allocated more than a third of the acreage to wilderness.

5. In Resources Limited, Inc. v. Robertson, 35 F.3d 1300 (9th Cir. 1993), the Ninth Circuit rejected a challenge to the adequacy of the analysis of alternatives in a forest-wide EIS prepared for a national forest land and resource management plan. While the plaintiffs argued that the Forest Service failed to consider timber harvest levels that were substantially lower than existing harvest levels, the court noted that 5 of the 17 alternatives considered included harvest levels more than 18 percent lower than existing levels. While no alternative in the plan allocated less than 75 percent of the harvest to cutting of even-aged trees, the court noted that there were relatively few stands of trees available that

were suitable for uneven-aged cutting. "Alternatives that are unlikely to be implemented need not be considered," the court concluded. 35 F.3d at 1307. Is this decision consistent with California v. Block discussed in note 4?

6. In its regulation on the "scope" of an EIS, CEQ requires agencies to consider three types of alternatives: (1) no action, (2) other reasonable courses of action, and (3) mitigation measures not already included in the proposed action. 40 C.F.R. §1508.25. The CEQ Regulations refer to this analysis of alternatives as "the heart of the environmental impact statement," which is designed to define the issues sharply and to provide "a clear basis for choice among options by the decisionmaker and the public." See 40 C.F.R. §1502.14.

7. In *Vermont Yankee*, Justice Rehnquist eschews Judge Wright's suggestion in *Calvert Cliffs* that NEPA imposes substantive obligations enforceable in court. He notes that "NEPA does set forth significant substantive goals for the Nation, but its mandate to the agencies is essentially procedural." Lynton Caldwell criticizes this as a "crabbed interpretation of NEPA" because it views the substantive mandate of section 101(b) as "largely rhetorical, imposing no mandate upon the agencies cognizable by the courts." Caldwell, NEPA Revisited: A Call for a Constitutional Amendment, 6 Envtl. Forum 18 (Nov.-Dec. 1989). Yet the question whether an agency has adequately complied with NEPA's procedural requirements often requires courts to perform some assessment of the quality of an agency's analysis, as explored below.

2. *Analysis*

Each EIS must include a detailed assessment of the environmental consequences of the proposed action and the alternatives. The CEQ Regulations, 40 C.F.R. §1502.16, specify that this assessment must include discussions of:

(a) Direct effects and their significance.

(b) Indirect effects and their significance.

(c) Possible conflicts between the proposed action and the objectives of Federal, regional, State, and local (and, in the case of a reservation, Indian tribe) land use plans, policies, and controls for the area concerned.

(d) The environmental effects of alternatives, including the proposed action. . . .

(e) Energy requirements and conservation potential of various alternatives and mitigation measures.

(f) Natural or depletable resource requirements and conservation potential of various alternatives and mitigation measures.

(g) Urban quality, historic and cultural resources, and the design of the built environment, including the reuse and conservation potential of various alternatives and mitigation measures.

(h) Means to mitigate adverse environmental impacts. [43 Fed. Reg. 55,996 (1978); 44 Fed. Reg. 873 (1979).]

Plaintiffs have identified a nearly infinite variety of flaws in agencies' analyses of "environmental consequences." We consider here three of the most important areas of attack: the quality of the analysis, problems in scope and timing, and assessment of unknown or uncertain effects.

A. QUALITY OF THE ANALYSIS IN AN EIS

As one might expect, courts often are reluctant to judge the quality of analysis in an EIS. In a few cases, however, plaintiffs have been able to demonstrate shortcomings sufficient to persuade a court that an EIS is inadequate. For example, in Sierra Club v. United States Army Corps of Engineers, 701 F.2d 1011 (2d Cir. 1983), plaintiffs challenging plans to construct the Westway, a superhighway that would run along the west side of Manhattan, argued that the final EIS was deficient because it characterized an area of the Hudson River that the project would fill as a "biological wasteland," despite data indicating the presence of a juvenile striped bass population there. EPA, the National Marine Fisheries Service, and the Fish and Wildlife Service all had objected to the EIS and to the Corps' decision to issue a permit to fill the area. Despite a new study finding that fish populations were much richer than previously thought, no supplemental EIS was prepared. After holding a trial that heard extensive testimony concerning how the EIS was prepared, a federal district court enjoined the project pending preparation of a supplemental EIS. The court's decision was appealed to the Second Circuit, which rendered the following decision.

	Sierra Club v. United States	
	Army Corps of Engineers	
	701 F.2d 1011 (2d Cir. 1983)	

KEARSE, Circuit Judge:

A. NEPA

As the Supreme Court has stated repeatedly, although NEPA established "'significant substantive goals for the Nation,' the balancing of the substantive environmental issues is consigned to the judgement of the executive agencies involved, and the judicially reviewable duties that are imposed on the agencies are 'essentially procedural.'" Strycker's Bay Neighborhood Council, Inc. v. Karlen, 444 U.S. 223, 227 (1980) (quoting Vermont Yankee Nuclear Power Corp. v. Natural Resources Defense Council, Inc., 435 U.S. 519, 558 (1978) ("*Vermont Yankee*")). "The only role for a court is to insure that the agency has taken a 'hard look' at environmental consequences; it cannot 'interject itself within the area of discretion of the executive as to the choice of the action to be taken.'" Kleppe v. Sierra Club, 427 U.S. 390, 410 n.21 (1976) (quoting Natural Resources Defense Council, Inc. v. Morton, 458 F.2d 827, 838 (D.C. Cir. 1972)).

The primary function of an environmental impact statement under NEPA is "'to insure a fully informed and well-considered decision,' [although] not necessarily 'a decision the judges of the Court of Appeals or of this Court would have reached had they been members of the decisionmaking unit of the agency.'" Strycker's Bay Neighborhood Council, Inc. v. Karlen, supra, 444 U.S. at 227 (quoting *Vermont Yankee*, supra, 435 U.S. at 558). In order to fulfill its role, the EIS must set forth sufficient information for the general public to make an informed evaluation and for the decisionmaker to "consider fully the environmental factors involved and to make a reasoned decision after balancing the risks of harm to the environment against the benefits to be derived from the proposed action." County of Suffolk v. Secretary of Interior, 562 F.2d 1368, 1375 (2d Cir. 1977), cert. denied, 434 U.S. 1064 (1978). In so doing, the EIS insures the integrity of the process of decision by giving assurance that stubborn problems or serious criticisms have not been "swept under the rug." Silva v. Lynn, 482 F.2d 1282, 1285 (1st Cir. 1973). The "'detailed statement'" required by §102(2)(C) of NEPA thus "is the outward sign that environmental values and consequences have been considered during the planning stage of agency actions." Andrus v. Sierra Club, 442 U.S. 347, 350 (1979).

Given the role of the EIS and the narrow scope of permissible judicial review, the court may not rule an EIS inadequate if the agency has made an adequate compilation of relevant information, has analyzed it reasonably, has not ignored pertinent data, and has made disclosures to the public. . . .

In the present case the district court's rulings on the merits of plaintiffs' NEPA claims were consonant with the proper scope of its review and the proper view of the obligations imposed on FHWA and the Corps. With respect to the fisheries issues, the court found, inter alia, that the FEIS contained false statements depicting the interpier region as "biologically impoverished" and as a "biological wasteland," when in fact the interpier area in winter harbored a concentration of juvenile striped bass. The court found that the FEIS statements regarding aquatic impact had not been compiled in "objective good faith." Notwithstanding NYSDOT's contention that "the FEIS set forth the relevant facts that were known about the interpier area and the surrounding Hudson estuary at the time it was prepared . . . ," the court's findings to the contrary are amply supported by the record.

For example, after the DEIS was issued, the Project received critical comments regarding fisheries impact from Fisheries Service, Wildlife Service, and EPA to the effect that the fish life had been underestimated and that the information provided was inadequate. Although the FEIS purported to respond to these comments, no new studies were performed, no additional information was collected, no further inquiry was made, and the FEIS essentially reiterated or adopted the statements in the DEIS. Employees of the Project and FHWA testified that they knew before getting any data from the Lawler study that the Project's 1973 sampling had been faulty in both timing and technique and that these flaws were the reason the earlier study had revealed virtually no fish in the interpier area. Yet the Water Report, prepared in the wake of comments to the DEIS and appended to the FEIS, simply relied on the 1973 data. Bridwell, who was responsible for the preparation of the FEIS's fisheries discussion, testified that he was aware that the Water Report had not attempted to make any thorough or investigative inquiry into the existence of fish in the interpier area. He stated that the Water Report had attempted to verify only the existing literature on fish life in that area. It is not clear that even this academic study was performed: the Water Report neither identified any existing literature on the subject nor stated that there was no such literature; Bridwell himself was unaware of whether any literature existed. The evidence at trial suggested that there was no literature upon which the Report could have based its conclusion that the interpier area was biologically impoverished. . . .

In short, we concur in the district court's view that the FEIS did not reasonably adequately compile relevant information with respect to fisheries impact. The evidence as to the cavalier manner in which the Project had reached its conclusion that the interpier area was a biological wasteland, and as to FHWA's failure to make an independent evaluation or to react in any way to sister agencies' pointed comments that the draft EIS did not provide adequate information for a reasoned assessment of impact on fisheries, easily supports the district court's findings (1) that the FEIS's fisheries conclusions lacked a "substantial basis in fact," and (2) that a decisionmaker relying on the January 1977 EIS could not have fully considered and balanced the environmental factors. In the circumstances, we agree that FHWA's issuance of the FEIS, and the Corps' reliance on the FEIS, violated NEPA. . . .

The principal relief ordered by the district court was an injunction against any further Westway activities affecting the bed or waters of the Hudson River unless and until a supplemental EIS has been prepared by the Corps containing adequate and accurate information with respect to the fisheries issues. . . . [W]e regard this relief as well within the proper scope of the district court's discretion in the circumstances of the present case.

. . . [T]he record revealed that the authors of the FEIS had not made an adequate compilation of fisheries data, had not compiled information in objective good faith, had paid no heed to the experts' warnings that they lacked needed information, and hence had reached the erroneous conclusion that the interpier area was a biological wasteland. This baseless and erroneous factual conclusion then became a false premise in the decisionmakers' evaluations of the overall environmental impact of Westway and their balancing of the expected benefits of the proposed action against the risks of harm to the environment. Thus, the January 1977 EIS provided no valid "outward sign that environmental values and consequences [had] been considered" with respect to fisheries issues, Andrus v. Sierra Club, supra, 442 U.S. at 350, and hence furnished no assurance that the Westway approvals had been given on a reasoned basis.

Enforcement of NEPA requires that the responsible agencies be compelled to prepare a new EIS on those issues, based on adequately compiled information, analyzed in a reasonable fashion. Only if such a document is forthcoming can the public be appropriately informed and have any confidence that the decisionmakers have in fact considered the relevant factors and not merely swept difficult problems under the rug. Accordingly, we uphold the district court's requirement that before Westway landfill may proceed, FHWA or the Corps must prepare a new EIS on fisheries issues. Whether the new statement be called an amended EIS or a supplemental EIS, as in the judgments below, NEPA requires no less.

Our ruling on this point is not, however, an expansive one. We do not intend to suggest that inaccuracies in an EIS will always, or even usually, warrant a court's ordering the preparation of a supplemental EIS. Had the January 1977 EIS contained a reasoned analysis of fisheries data reasonably adequately compiled, and merely drawn an erroneous factual conclusion, we would not believe it proper to order FHWA or the Corps to prepare a SEIS. See Hanly v. Kleindienst, 471 F.2d 823 (2d Cir. 1972), cert. denied, 412 U.S. 908 (1973). Or had reasonable investigative efforts resulted in less accurate data than later became available, the determination as to whether the later data warranted preparation of a SEIS, see 33 C.F.R. §230.11(b) (1981); see also 33 C.F.R. §209.410(g)(1) (1977); would be a matter committed to the discretion of the responsible agencies, not to the judgment of the court.

Nor do we express any view as to whether the decisionmakers' overall evaluation of the benefits and detriments of Westway was "wrong." We hold simply that a decision made in reliance on false information, developed without an effort in objective good faith to obtain accurate information, cannot be accepted as a "reasoned" decision.

NOTES AND QUESTIONS

1. Note the deferential standard of review the Second Circuit applies in assessing the adequacy of an EIS. It states that "the court may not rule an EIS inadequate if the agency has made an adequate compilation of relevant information, has analyzed it reasonably, has not ignored pertinent data, and has made disclosures to the public." 701 F.2d at 1029. The court also indicates that inaccuracies in an EIS or reliance on data less accurate than that which subsequently becomes available will not routinely be enough to require preparation of a supplemental EIS. What did the court find most persuasive in convincing it that the EIS in this case was inadequate and must be supplemented? Is there anything that FHWA or the Corps could have done differently to avoid having to prepare a supplemental EIS?

2. Despite NEPA's largely procedural thrust, this decision illustrates the substantial impact a successful NEPA challenge can have. Largely as a result of the injunction obtained in this case, the massive Westway highway project was abandoned. Nearly two decades later, a more modest plan to replace the West Side Highway with a new boulevard is still in the planning stages.

3. Disputes over the adequacy of an EIS often turn on the scope of environmental effects it addresses. President Clinton's Executive Order 12,898 requires federal agencies to identify and to address disproportionate effects of their actions on minority and low-income populations. Must such effects be considered in preparing EISs? In October 1994, EPA objected to an EIS prepared by the Nuclear Regulatory Commission (NRC) because it concluded that locating a uranium enrichment facility near a low-income, minority community in Louisiana would not raise environmental justice concerns. While the EIS incorporated demographic information about the parish where the facility would be located, EPA argued that it failed to analyze the demographic characteristics of the population in the immediate vicinity of the site and that it ignored the cumulative nature of the environmental burdens imposed on the community. The NRC's Atomic Safety and Licensing Board ultimately decided that the EIS was inadequate because it had not analyzed the impacts on two low-income and minority communities of closing the only road linking them together. While the EIS had calculated how much additional gasoline would be used driving between the two communities if the road were relocated, a large percentage of the communities' population is too poor to own motor vehicles. "Adding 0.38 miles to the distance between the Forest Grove and Center Springs communities may be a mere 'inconvenience' to those who drive," the Board observed. "Yet permanently adding that distance to the one- or two-mile walk between these communities for those who must regularly make the trip on foot may be more than a 'very small impact,' especially if they are old, ill, or otherwise infirm." In re Louisiana Energy Services, L.P (May 1, 1997).

4. In 1990, a group of Wisconsin environmentalists and botanists launched an effort to use NEPA to improve the quality of the scientific analysis used by the Forest Service (FS). They sued the FS in an effort to require it to employ an ecosystems approach incorporating advanced principles of conservation biology

to provide for diversity of plant and animal communities when making forest management decisions. The plaintiffs argued that the FS should consider the relationships between differing landscape patterns and among various habitats rather than measuring vegetative diversity solely through analysis of the number of plants and animals and the variety of species in a given area. Because the size of a habitat tends to affect its chances of survival, the botanists argued that the FS should reserve larger, unfragmented tracts of forest rather than smaller, fragmented parcels. Despite presenting testimony from 13 highly distinguished scientists, the plaintiffs lost in the district court. The court found that "the agency's choice of methodology is entitled to considerable deference" and that the FS had not acted arbitrarily or capriciously. Sierra Club v. Marita, 845 F. Supp. 1317 (E.D. Wis. 1994). The botanists then took their case to the Seventh Circuit, which affirmed. Sierra Club v. Marita, 46 F.3d 606 (1995). The court noted that CEQ's regulations require agencies to insure the "scientific integrity" of their analyses, to use "high quality" science, and to integrate the natural and social sciences. However, the court found nothing in NEPA, the National Forest Management Act, or implementing regulations that dictates that the FS analyze diversity using any particular approach. Noting that the FS had considered, but rejected, using principles of conservation biology because of their uncertain application, the Seventh Circuit found that it had not acted arbitrarily or capriciously. The court refused to undertake a more detailed inquiry into the reliability of the Service's methodology under Daubert v. Merrell Dow Pharmaceuticals, Inc., 509 U.S. 579 (1993), finding that "forcing an agency to make such a showing as a general rule is intrusive, undeferential, and not required." 46 F.3d at 622. The court concluded that "[t]he Service is entitled to use its own methodology, unless it is irrational," 46 F.3d at 621, and it upheld the agency's choice.

5. When new information becomes available after an EIS is completed, questions inevitably are raised concerning the obligation of agencies to supplement their EISs. The Supreme Court, in the case that follows, addressed that question and the question of what standard of review should be applied by courts reviewing decisions not to supplement EISs.

Marsh v. Oregon Natural Resources Council
490 U.S. 360 (1989)

JUSTICE STEVENS delivered the opinion for a unanimous Court.

[The Army Corps of Engineers had completed an environmental impact statement for a three-dam project in Oregon's Rogue River Basin in 1971. In 1980 the Corps released its Final Environmental Impact Statement Supplement No. 1, but it subsequently refused to prepare a second supplemental EIS to review information developed after 1980. Plaintiffs argued that the Corps was required to prepare a second supplemental EIS because two memoranda prepared after 1980—one by biologists with Oregon's Department of Fish and Wildlife and another by the U.S. Soil Conservation Service—indicated that the project would have greater adverse impacts on the environment than previously thought. The district court rejected this claim, but the Ninth Circuit reversed, holding that the two documents revealed significant new information that the Corps had failed to evaluate with sufficient care.]

The subject of post-decision supplemental environmental impact statements is not expressly addressed in NEPA. Preparation of such statements, however, is at times necessary to satisfy the Act's "action-forcing" purpose. NEPA does not work by mandating that agencies achieve particular substantive environmental results. Rather, NEPA promotes its sweeping commitment to "prevent or eliminate damage to the environment and biosphere" by focusing government and public attention on the environmental effects of proposed agency action. 42 U.S.C. §4321. By so focusing agency attention, NEPA ensures that the agency will not act on incomplete information, only to regret its decision after it is too late to correct. Similarly, the broad dissemination of information mandated by NEPA permits the public and other government agencies to react to the effects of a proposed action at a meaningful time. It would be incongruous with this approach to environmental protection, and with the Act's manifest concern with preventing uninformed action, for the blinders to adverse environmental effects, once unequivocally removed, to be restored prior to the completion of agency action simply because the relevant proposal has received initial approval. As we explained in TVA v. Hill, 437 U.S. 153, 188, n.34 (1978), although "it would make sense to hold NEPA inapplicable at some point in the life of a project, because the agency would no longer have a meaningful opportunity to *weigh* the benefits of the project versus the detrimental effects on the environment," up to that point, "NEPA cases have generally required agencies to file environmental impact statements when the remaining governmental action would be environmentally 'significant.' "

This reading of the statute is supported by Council on Environmental Quality (CEQ) and Corps regulations, both of which make plain that at times supplementation is required. The CEQ regulations, which we have held are entitled to substantial deference, impose a duty on all federal agencies to prepare supplements to either draft or final EIS's if there "are significant new circumstances or information relevant to environmental concerns and bearing on the proposed action or its impacts." Similarly, the Corps' own NEPA implementing regulations require the preparation of a supplemental EIS if "new significant impact information, criteria or circumstances relevant to environmental considerations impact on the recommended plan or proposed action." . . .

. . . [A]n agency need not supplement an EIS every time new information comes to light after the EIS is finalized. To require otherwise would render agency decisionmaking intractable, always awaiting updated information only to find the new information outdated by the time a decision is made. On the other hand, and as [the Government] concede[s], NEPA does require that agencies take a "hard look" at the environmental effects of their planned action, even after a proposal has received initial approval. See Brief for Petitioners 36. Application of the "rule of reason" thus turns on the value of the new information to the still pending decisionmaking process. In this respect the decision whether to prepare a supplemental EIS is similar to the decision whether to prepare an EIS in the first instance: If there remains "major Federal actio[n]" to occur, and if the new information is sufficient to show that the remaining action will "affec[t] the quality of the human environment" in a significant manner or to a significant extent not already considered, a supplemental EIS must be prepared. Cf. 42 U.S.C. §4332(2)(C).

The parties disagree, however, on the standard that should be applied by a court that is asked to review the agency's decision. [The Government] argue[s] that the reviewing court need only decide whether the agency decision was "arbitrary and capricious," whereas respondents argue that the reviewing court must make its own determination of reasonableness to ascertain whether the agency action complied with the law. . . .

The question presented for review in this case is a classic example of a factual dispute the resolution of which implicates substantial agency expertise. Respondents' claim that the Corps' decision not to file a second supplemental EIS should be set aside, primarily rests on the contentions that the new information undermines conclusions contained in the FEISS [Final Environmental Impact Statement Supplement No. 1], that the conclusions contained in the ODFW memorandum and the SCS survey are accurate, and that the Corps' expert review of the new information was incomplete, inconclusive, or inaccurate. The dispute thus does not turn on the meaning of the term "significant" or on an application of this legal standard to settled facts. Rather, resolution of this dispute involves primarily issues of fact. Because analysis of the relevant documents "requires a high level of technical expertise," we must defer to "the informed discretion of the responsible federal agencies." Kleppe v. Sierra Club, 427 U.S. 390, 412 (1976). Under these circumstances, we cannot accept respondents' supposition that review is of a legal question and that the Corps' decision "deserves no deference." Accordingly, as long as the Corps' decision not to supplement the FEISS was not "arbitrary or capricious," it should not be set aside.

. . . When specialists express conflicting views, an agency must have discretion to rely on the reasonable opinions of its own qualified experts even if, as an original matter, a court might find contrary views more persuasive. On the other hand, in the context of reviewing a decision not to supplement an EIS, courts should not automatically defer to the agency's express reliance on an interest in finality without carefully reviewing the record and satisfying themselves that the agency has made a reasoned decision based on its evaluation of the significance—or lack of significance—of the new information. A contrary approach would not simply render judicial review generally meaningless, but would be contrary to the demand that courts ensure that agency decisions are founded on a reasoned evaluation "of the relevant factors."

[Applying the standard of review outlined above, the Supreme Court reversed the Ninth Circuit and held that the Corps was not required to prepare a supplemental EIS.]

NOTES AND QUESTIONS

1. In light of the Court's decision, at what point can an agency simply refuse to consider new information? When an EIS has been completed? When a project has been approved? When construction has begun? When construction is completed?

2. In Alaska Wilderness Recreation and Tourism Association v. Morrison, 67 F.3d 723 (9th Cir. 1995), the Ninth Circuit required the Forest Service to prepare a supplemental EIS for timber sales in the Tongass National Forest as a result of Congress's enactment of the Tongass Timber Reform Act (TTRA). The TTRA repealed a requirement that 4.5 billion board feet of timber be supplied from the Tongass National Forest and restricted harvest of old-growth timber. Previous EISs for the Forest Plans that governed timber sales in the area had routinely rejected alternatives that did not supply enough timber to meet the terms of 50-year contracts between the Forest Service and two paper companies.

After the Forest Service canceled one of the contracts, the Ninth Circuit held that the contract cancellation required preparation of a supplemental EIS because it "opened for consideration alternatives which could not be freely reviewed when the . . . contract was in force." 67 F.3d at 730.

B. TIMING AND SCOPE REVISITED

Courts hearing challenges to EISs are often asked to review the agency's judgments about the appropriate timing and scope of its analysis. They generally have responded by emphasizing that the proper scope of an EIS varies with the nature of the proposed action and that its timing depends on how close the agency is to reaching a critical stage of the decision-making process. For example, in California v. Block, 690 F.2d 753 (9th Cir. 1982), discussed on p. 843, the State of California argued that the EIS prepared for the Forest Service's national management plan for roadless areas had failed to examine adequately site-specific impacts. The Forest Service argued that a programmatic EIS describing the first step in a multi-stage national project need not include detailed examination of the kinds of site-specific impacts normally considered in EISs for more narrowly focused projects. Noting that the "detail that NEPA requires in an EIS depends upon the nature and scope of the proposed action," the Ninth Circuit concluded that the "critical inquiry . . . is not whether the project's site-specific impact should be evaluated in detail, but when. . . ." 690 F.2d at 761. Thus, the court concluded that when preparing a programmatic EIS, "site-specific impacts need not be fully evaluated until a 'critical decision' has been made to act on site development." Id.

Applying this standard, the Ninth Circuit focused on the impact of the designation of areas as wilderness or non-wilderness. The Forest Service argued that a non-wilderness designation meant only that an area will not be considered now for inclusion in the wilderness system and that separate EISs would be prepared when specific development proposals are made concerning specific areas. The Ninth Circuit, however, found that the Forest Service had made a "critical decision" to commit these areas to non-wilderness use because the non-wilderness designation meant that the areas would not be managed as wilderness for at least the next 10 to 15 years. Thus, it held that the EIS must contain detailed site-specific analysis of the program's environmental consequences.

The Forest Service then argued that it had adequately assessed the site-specific impacts of its action by relying on two-page computer printouts for each area in the RARE II inventory. These contained information on the location and acreage of the area, its basic land-form type, its ecosystem type, the number of wilderness-associated wildlife species in the area, and a numerical rating of the area's wilderness attributes. The numerical ratings were obtained by using the Wilderness Attribute Rating System (WARS). This system employed worksheets containing a series of check boxes to indicate generic qualities of the site, and then a small space for comments, described as follows by the district court:

> The comments are of a brief and very general nature. For example, one comment under the "opportunity for solitude" attribute merely stated "good topographical variation." The type of land features or vegetation present in this area is undisclosed. Major features of an area are reduced to highly generalized descriptions such as "mountain" or "river." One can hypothesize how the Grand Canyon might be rated: "Canyon with river, little vegetation." [California v. Bergland, 483 F. Supp. 465, 486 n. 22 (E.D. Cal. 1980.)]

The Ninth Circuit rejected the Forest Service's argument that any deficiencies in the EIS could be remedied simply by considering the WARS worksheets to be part of the final EIS. The court recognized that preparation of site-specific analyses for the RARE II decision would be a mammoth undertaking. However, it concluded that "[h]aving decided to allocate simultaneously millions of acres of land to nonwilderness use, the Forest Service may not rely upon forecasting difficulties or the task's magnitude to excuse the absence of a reasonably thorough site-specific analysis of the decision's environmental consequences." 690 F.2d at 765.

NOTES AND QUESTIONS

1. The court in California v. Block demanded that the programmatic EIS prepared by the Forest Service include detailed analysis of every one of the hundreds of areas affected. Is that a realistic demand? If you were advising the Forest Service, what strategy would you suggest for their NEPA compliance?

2. Consider the following approach, from the CEQ Regulations:

§1508.28 Tiering

"Tiering" refers to the coverage of general matters in broader environmental impact statements (such as national program or policy statements) with subsequent narrower statements or environmental analyses (such as regional or basinwide program statements or ultimately site-specific statements) incorporating by reference the general discussions and concentrating solely on the issues specific to the statement subsequently prepared. Tiering is appropriate when the sequence of statements or analyses is:

(a) From a program, plan, or policy environmental impact statement to a program, plan, or policy statement or analysis of lesser scope or to a site-specific statement or analysis.

(b) From an environmental impact statement on a specific action at an early stage (such as need and site selection) to a supplement (which is preferred) or a subsequent statement or analysis at a later stage (such as environmental mitigation). Tiering in such cases is appropriate when it helps the lead agency to focus on the issues which are ripe for decision and exclude from consideration issues already decided or not yet ripe.

3. The successful use of tiered analysis is illustrated by an important case that was decided by the Sixth Circuit. Because there is no federal repository available yet for the storage of spent nuclear fuel, most nuclear power plants have been storing their waste in liquid pools within their containment vessels. Many are running out of this on-site storage capacity and could be forced to shut down if no extra storage space becomes available. To respond to this problem, the Nuclear Regulatory Commission (NRC) approved the use of a new cask for dry storage of high-level radioactive waste at nuclear power plants. Citing CEQ's tiering regulations, the Sixth Circuit held that the Nuclear Regulatory Commission (NRC) had not violated NEPA by failing to prepare an EIS before approving the use of the cask. Kelley v. Selin, 42 F.3d 1501 (6th Cir. 1995). Even though use of the new casks will enable utilities to expand significantly their capacity to store radioactive waste on-site, the court held that an EIS was not required because the NRC had conducted tiered analysis before approving the cask. Prior to approving use of the new cask, the NRC had prepared an environmental assessment (EA) finding that the new technology

would have no significant impact on the environment. This finding was based in large part on the fact that EISs already had been prepared for each power plant that would use the cask at the time the plant was licensed by the NRC. While plaintiffs argued that site-specific EAs should have been prepared, the court held that the NRC had properly relied on the prior site-specific EISs prepared for each plant as well as on the NRC's previous generic analyses of the safety of on-site storage of radioactive waste.

4. Many of the principles of timing and scope that are articulated in *Kleppe, Thomas,* and Sierra Club v. Peterson are relevant to assessment of the adequacy of an EIS.

C.   ANALYSIS IN UNCERTAINTY

One of the most heated controversies concerning NEPA in recent years has been the debate over what agencies must do to assess adequately effects that are highly uncertain. In Sierra Club v. Sigler, 695 F.2d 957 (5th Cir. 1983), the Fifth Circuit considered an EIS for an oil distribution center and deepwater port in Galveston Bay. The Sierra Club argued that the Army Corps of Engineers should consider the possible effect on the Bay of a total cargo loss by a supertanker using the new port. While all agreed a total cargo loss could occur, there was considerable uncertainty about its likelihood and consequences. The court therefore required the Corps to prepare a "worst-case analysis" to assess the effects of such an accident.

In Save Our Ecosystems v. Clark, 747 F.2d 1240 (9th Cir. 1984), the Ninth Circuit considered the application of NEPA to decisions by the Bureau of Land Management (BLM) and the Forest Service to apply pesticides on lands subject to their jurisdiction. BLM and the Forest Service argued that they did not need to consider the risks associated with pesticide use as long as the pesticides had been approved for such use by the EPA. The court rejected this argument, emphasizing that the licensing of pesticides does not "reflect a conclusion that a pesticide is safe under *any* condition." Noting uncertainty about whether the pesticides were likely to cause cancer, the court held that the agencies must prepare a "worst-case analysis" to assess those risks—the agencies must estimate what the effects of pesticide use would be if the pesticides were in fact carcinogenic.

In response to *Save Our Ecosystems* and similar decisions from other courts, CEQ acted to curtail the worst-case-analysis requirement. In 1986, the CEQ rescinded a "worst-case" regulation it had adopted in 1978 and replaced it with the following revised regulation:

§1502.22 Incomplete or Unavailable Information

When an agency is evaluating reasonably foreseeable significant adverse effects on the human environment in an environmental impact statement and there is incomplete or unavailable information, the agency shall always make clear that such information is lacking.

(a) If the incomplete information relevant to reasonably foreseeable significant adverse impacts is essential to a reasoned choice among alternatives and the overall costs of obtaining it are not exorbitant, the agency shall include the information in the environmental impact statement.

(b) If the information relevant to reasonably foreseeable significant adverse impacts cannot be obtained because the overall costs of obtaining it are exorbitant or the means to obtain it are not known, the agency shall include within the environmental impact statement:

(1) A statement that such information is incomplete or unavailable;

(2) a statement of the relevance of the incomplete or unavailable information to evaluating reasonably foreseeable significant adverse impacts on the human environment;

(3) a summary of existing credible scientific evidence which is relevant to evaluating the reasonably foreseeable significant adverse impacts on the human environment; and

(4) the agency's evaluation of such impacts based upon theoretical approaches or research methods generally accepted in the scientific community. For the purposes of this section, "reasonably foreseeable" includes impacts which have catastrophic consequences, even if their probability of occurrence is low, provided that the analysis of the impacts is supported by credible scientific evidence, is not based on pure conjecture, and is within the rule of reason.

(c) The amended regulation will be applicable to all environmental impact statements for which a Notice of Intent (40 CFR 1508.22) is published in the Federal Register on or after May 27, 1986. For environmental impact statements in progress, agencies may choose to comply with the requirements of either the original or amended regulation. [51 Fed. Reg. 15,625 (1986).]

NOTES AND QUESTIONS

1. Would this new regulation change the result in *Sigler* or in *Save Our Ecosystems*? Would the Corps still have to consider the effects of a total cargo loss by a supertanker? Would BLM be required to assume the pesticide is carcinogenic? Should the NRC assess the environmental consequences of highly uncertain terrorist attacks when it licenses facilities handling nuclear material? See Problem Exercise below.

2. In Robertson v. Methow Valley Citizens Council, 490 U.S. 332 (1989), a companion case to Marsh v. Oregon Natural Resources Council, the Supreme Court reversed a decision by the Ninth Circuit holding that NEPA requires the use of worst-case analysis despite the new CEQ regulations. The Supreme Court rejected the Ninth Circuit's conclusion that the rescinded CEQ regulations were "merely a codification of prior NEPA case law." Noting that the regulations had been amended only after "considerable criticism" of the worst-case-analysis requirement, the Court held that the new regulations were entitled to "substantial deference." 490 U.S. at 356.

PROBLEM EXERCISE: SHOULD EISs FOR NUCLEAR FACILITIES CONSIDER THE RISKS OF TERRORIST ATTACKS?

Does NEPA require the Nuclear Regulatory Commission (NRC) to prepare environmental impact statements (EISs) analyzing the risks of terrorist attacks on nuclear facilities? Two months before the September 11th attacks, a North Carolina group, NC WARN, decried the NRC's failure to assess such risks when approving Carolina Power & Light's expansion of on-site storage for high-level radioactive waste. The group cited "testimony by Ahmed Ressam, the terrorist convicted of trying to import explosives for the purpose of bombing Los Angeles International Airport, who said a terrorist training camp linked to

Osama bin Laden considers power plants as primary targets." NC Warn, CP&L Opens Third Pool at Harris Nuclear Plant, July 12, 2001.

Despite heightened concerns after 9/11 that terrorists will target nuclear facilities, the NRC decided in December 2002 that NEPA does not require it to assess the risks of terrorist attacks on facilities it licenses. The Commission maintains that it has no legal "responsibility under NEPA to consider intentional malevolent acts." In the Matter of Duke Energy Corp. (CLI-02-06). It explained:

> An environmental impact statement is not the appropriate format in which to address the challenges of terrorism. We reached this conclusion for a number of interlocking reasons: (1) the likelihood and nature of postulated terrorist attack are speculative and not 'proximately caused' by an NRC licensing decision; (2) the risk of a terrorist attack cannot be meaningfully determined; (3) NEPA does not require a 'worst case' analysis and such an analysis would not enhance the agency's decision-making process; and (4) a terrorism review is incompatible with the public character of the NEPA process. [Id.]

The NRC reversed a ruling by the Atomic Safety and Licensing Board that EISs had to consider the risks of terrorist attacks on nuclear facilities because they are "reasonably foreseeable" in the post-9/11 era. In the Matter of Duke Cogema Stone & Webster (CLI-02-24). The NRC also claims that it "cannot make publicly available the kind of information necessary for a more than *superficial* NEPA review." In the Matter of Dominion Nuclear Connecticut, Inc. (CLI-02-27).

NRC regulations require licensees to be able to defend their facilities against a commando attack by skilled attackers with automatic weapons, hand-carried explosive and incapacitating agents, and with the assistance of an "insider" and use of a 4-wheel drive vehicle. In periodic mock exercises nearly half the plants failed to repel such attacks. Although nuclear power plants were not designed to withstand an intentional attack from a large commercial airliner, the Commission is undertaking a detailed engineering analysis of the consequences of such an attack.

Question One.   Does NEPA require the NRC to prepare EISs assessing the risks of terrorist attacks on nuclear facilities when it makes licensing decisions? What is the relevance for this issue of Robertson v. Methow Valley's holding (see page 855) that NEPA does not require "worst-case analysis"?

Question Two.   Even if the risks of a terrorist attack are speculative and uncertain, is that a sufficient justification for not including them in an EIS? See Limerick Ecology Action v. NRC, 869 F.2d 719, 744, 754 (3d Cir. 1989). When it challenged licensing of a spent nuclear fuel storage facility on an Indian reservation, the state of Utah argued that the NRC needed to assess the environmental consequences of a terrorist attack on the facility, even if it could not predict its likelihood. Do you agree? Citing City of New York v. U.S. Dep't of Transportation, 715 F.2d 732 (2d Cir. 1982), which held that assessment of the risks of nuclear waste shipments need not consider sabotage, the NRC maintains that it has the discretion to refuse to consider "high-consequence, low-probability events." Is the risk of a terrorist attack on a nuclear facility such an event?

Question Three.   In addressing whether environmental consequences were sufficiently foreseeable to warrant assessment in an EIS, the court in Sierra Club v. Marsh, 976 F.2d 763, 767 (1st Cir. 1985), defined "reasonable foreseeability" under NEPA to mean that an "impact is sufficiently likely to occur that a person of ordinary prudence would take it in to account in reaching a decision." Under this definition, is the risk of a terrorist attack on a nuclear facility "reasonably foreseeable"?

Question Four.   NRC regulations provide that operators of nuclear power plants need not defend against attacks by "enemies of the United States." 10 C.F.R. §50.13. The NRC maintains that this regulation supports its conclusion that the licensing of facilities that may pose attractive targets for terrorists is "too far removed" from the environmental consequences of such terrorism to warrant NEPA review. Should this relieve the NRC of responsibility for assessing terrorism risks?

Question Five.   The NRC maintains that after 9/11 "an overriding government priority is to avoid disclosing to terrorists themselves precisely where and how nuclear facilities might be most vulnerable and what steps have been taken to lessen terrorists' chance of success." In the Matter of Private Fuel Storage (CLI-02-25). Should these concerns preclude preparation of EISs that assess the environmental consequences of terrorist attacks? See Weinberger v. Catholic Action of Hawaii, 454 U.S. 139 (1981) (storage of nuclear weapons may trigger NEPA's EIS requirement even if the EIS cannot be disclosed for national security reasons).

D.   EPILOGUE: HOW WELL DOES NEPA WORK?

Critics of environmental regulation are arguing that NEPA is outdated and flawed and needs "reform," while environmentalists maintain that it is an essential bulwark in our regulatory infrastructure. How effective has NEPA been? NEPA clearly has provided environmental lawyers with a strategic tool that has been used at times to slow down and sometimes stop development projects. For a list of some natural areas, including Mineral King, that have been spared from development largely as a result of NEPA lawsuits, see Turner, The Legal Eagles, Amicus J. 25, 30 (Winter 1988). In the wake of Hurricane Katrina's devastation of New Orleans, NEPA litigation was blamed by some for having blocked construction of a massive hurricane barrier, David Schoenbrod, The Lawsuit That Sank New Orleans, Wall St. J., Sept. 27, 2005, a strange criticism of NEPA since *compliance* with the statute would not have stopped the project, which ultimately floundered for a variety of other reasons.

A more important question may be how frequently the requirement that agencies "consider" environmental effects has resulted in more environmentally responsible actions by agencies. Serge Taylor's classic study of NEPA, Making Bureaucracies Think: The Environmental Impact Statement Strategy of Administrative Reform (1984), found that when agencies allow environmental analysts to explore a wide range of alternatives, all projects tend to benefit from relatively inexpensive mitigation measures. When concerned outsiders with access to the courts also get involved, some of the worst projects—those with "the greatest environmental costs and little political support"—are eliminated. Id. at 251. Consider the following assessment of NEPA's impact from a former deputy general counsel of EPA.

‖ Robert Dreher, NEPA Under Siege (2005) ‖

In its thirty-five year history, the National Environmental Policy Act has been extraordinarily successful in accomplishing its goals.

First, NEPA has unquestionably improved the quality of federal agency decision-making in terms of its sensitivity to environmental concerns. Examples are legion in which proposed federal actions that would have had serious environmental consequences were dramatically improved, or even in some instances abandoned, as a result of the NEPA process.

To cite just a few instances:

- In the early 1990s, mounting problems with obsolete nuclear reactors at its Savannah River site put the Department of Energy under pressure to build enormously expensive new reactors to produce tritium, a key constituent of nuclear warheads. A programmatic EIS allowed DOE to evaluate alternative technologies, including using a particle accelerator or existing commercial reactors, leading ultimately to cancellation of the tritium production reactors. Admiral James Watkins, then Secretary of Energy, testified before the House Armed Services Committee: "Looking back on it, thank God for NEPA because there were so many pressures to make a selection for a technology that it might have been forced upon us and that would have been wrong for the country."
- The NEPA process led to improvements in a land management plan for the Los Alamos National Laboratory that averted a potentially serious release of radiation when the sensitive nuclear laboratory was swept by wildfire in May 2000. The laboratory's initial management plan did not address the risk of wildfire, but other federal agencies alerted the Los Alamos staff to that risk in comments on the draft EIS accompanying the plan. The laboratory prepared a fire contingency plan, cut back trees and underbrush around its buildings, and replaced wooden pallets holding drums of radioactive waste with aluminum. Those preparations turned out to be invaluable when a major wildfire swept Los Alamos the following year, damaging many buildings but not triggering a significant release of radiation.
- In 1997, the Federal Energy Regulatory Commission was considering issuance of a license for construction of a major new hydropower dam on the Penobscot River in Maine. The EIS disclosed that the proposed Basin Mills Dam would undermine long-standing federal, state and tribal efforts to restore wild Atlantic salmon populations to the Penobscot River. FERC received strong comments in opposition to the project from federal and state fishery managers and the Penobscot Indian Nation, among others, and concluded that the public interest was best served by denial of the license.
- The ivory-billed woodpecker, recently rediscovered, to great public celebration, in the swamplands of Arkansas, owes its survival in large part to NEPA. In 1971, shortly after NEPA's enactment, the Army Corps of Engineers advanced a proposal to dredge and channelize the Cache River for flood control, threatening the vast tracts of bottomland hardwood wetlands in the river basin on which the woodpecker and many other species of wildlife depended. Environmentalists challenged the adequacy of the Corps's NEPA analysis in court, pointing out that the Corps had failed to evaluate alternatives to its massive dredging program that would cause less damage to wetland habitat. The court enjoined the Corps from proceeding until it fully considered alternatives, and public outcry subsequently led to the abandonment of the

dredging project and the creation of the national wildlife refuge where the ivory-billed woodpecker was recently sighted.

- A massive timber sale proposed for the Gifford Pinchot National Forest in Oregon, stalled by controversy over impacts on sensitive forest habitat, was entirely rethought as a result of the NEPA process. A coalition of environmentalists, the timber industry, labor representatives and local citizens worked together to develop a plan to use timber harvesting to restore the forest's natural ecosystem. Instead of clearcuts, the new proposal focuses on thinning dense stands of Douglas fir (the result of previous clearcutting) to recreate a more natural, diverse forest structure, while still yielding 5.2 million board feet of commercial timber. The citizen alternative was adopted by the Forest Service and implemented without appeals or litigation. A local resident involved in the process says: "It's a win, win, win."

- In Michigan, communities concerned about the impacts of a proposed new four-lane freeway successfully used the NEPA process to force the state highway agency to consider alternatives for expanding and improving an existing highway, avoiding the largest wetland loss in Michigan's history and saving taxpayers $1.5 billion. Similarly, a proposed freeway in Kentucky's scenic bluegrass region was redesigned to protect historic, aesthetic and natural values thanks to public input and legal action during the NEPA planning process. The National Trust for Historic Preservation acclaimed the Paris Pike as a project that "celebrates the spirit of place instead of obliterating it."

These and other similar examples only begin to tell the story of NEPA's success, however. NEPA's most significant effect has been to deter federal agencies from bringing forward proposed projects that could not withstand public examination and debate. Prior to NEPA, federal agencies could embark on massive dam- or road-building projects, for example, without public consultation and with virtually no advance notice. As a result, family farms, valuable habitat, and sometimes whole communities were destroyed without the opportunity for full and fair debate. Today, many similar projects that could not survive such a debate simply never get off the drawing boards.

More broadly, NEPA has had pervasive effects on the conduct and thinking of federal administrative agencies. Congress's directive that federal agencies use an "interdisciplinary approach" in decision-making affecting the environment, together with the Act's requirement that agencies conduct detailed environmental analyses of major actions, has required federal agencies to add biologists, geologists, landscape architects, archeologists, and environmental planners to their staffs. These new employees brought new perspectives and sensitivities to agencies that formerly had relatively narrow, mission-oriented cultures. NEPA's requirement that agencies consult with federal and state agencies with special environmental expertise also has helped broaden agency awareness of environmental values.

Equally important, NEPA has succeeded in expanding public engagement in government decision-making, improving the quality of agency decisions and fulfilling principles of democratic governance that are central to our society. Today, citizens take it as a given that major governmental actions that could affect their lives and their communities will be subject to searching public examination and discussion. As CEQ concluded in a report commemorating NEPA's 25th anniversary, "NEPA's most enduring legacy is as a framework for collaboration between federal agencies and those who will bear the environmental, social, and economic impacts of their decisions." CEQ noted that "agencies today are more likely to consider the views of those who live and work in the surrounding community and others during the decision-making process." As a result, "Federal agencies today are better informed about and more responsible for the consequences of their actions than they were before NEPA was passed." . . .

In sum, NEPA functions as a critical tool for democratic government decision-making, establishing an orderly, clear framework for involving the public in major decisions affecting their lives and communities.

NOTES AND QUESTIONS

1. As Dreher notes, on NEPA's 25th anniversary, CEQ conducted a study of the statute's effectiveness. CEQ, The National Environmental Policy Act: A Study of Its Effectiveness After Twenty-five Years (1997). The agency concluded that the statute had achieved considerable success, though falling far short of its goals. On the plus side, the study found that NEPA "has made agencies take a hard look at the potential environmental consequences of their actions, and it has brought the public into the agency decisionmaking process like no other statute." Id. at iii. However, the study also found that some agencies "act as if the detailed statement called for in the statute is an end in itself, rather than a tool to enhance and improve decision-making." It also observed that "agencies sometimes engage in consultation only after a decision has—for all practical purposes—been made." This leads agencies to seek "litigation-proof" documents without adequately examining a full range of alternatives. The study also noted concerns about "the length of NEPA processes, the extensive detail of NEPA analyses, and the sometimes confusing overlay of other laws and regulations." Id.

2. A more modest inquiry is whether NEPA assures a reliable assessment of a project's likely effects. Because NEPA entrusts the assessment of impacts to agencies that typically are project proponents, the quality of EISs often depends on the strength of outside pressures. Recall the controversy discussed in Chapter 1 concerning the report by the Fish and Wildlife Service that the environmental impact of oil development in Prudhoe Bay had been greatly underestimated. Some have suggested that projects approved under NEPA should be monitored so that unanticipated environmental consequences can be assessed and mitigated. Others have proposed that EISs be prepared by an independent agency without a vested interest in the results, as is done in some of the many countries that now require EISs. Professor Bradley Karkkainen notes that agencies seeking to avoid NEPA litigation "often substitute quantity for quality, producing large, costly and uninformative documents" while making findings of no significant impact that are premised on mitigation measures that NEPA cannot enforce." Bradley C. Karkkainen, Toward a Smarter NEPA: Monitoring and Managing Government's Environmental Performance, 102 Colum. L. Rev. 903 (2002). He argues that NEPA should be retooled to require "follow-up monitoring, adaptive mitigation, and an environmental management systems-oriented approach." Id.

3. In April 2002, the Council on Environmental Quality announced the formation of a "NEPA Task Force" charged with focusing on "modernizing the NEPA process." The Bush administration has been highly critical of NEPA and it has pushed to exempt from NEPA some military activities and certain decisions

concerning public forest management. In December 2002, CEQ issued "Guidance for Environmental Assessments of Forest Health Projects" that seeks to develop model EAs for "fuels reduction and fire-adapted ecosystem restoration projects" to make it easier to comply with NEPA. In December 2002, the Departments of Agriculture and Interior announced two new categorical exclusions from NEPA reviews for forest thinning, rehabilitation, and stabilization projects and hazardous fuels reduction activities.

4. The House Committee on Resources has prepared its own critique of NEPA. Task Force on Improving the National Environmental Policy Act and Task Force on Updating the National Environmental Policy Act, Initial Findings and Draft Recommendations, Dec. 21, 2005. Among the many recommendations in the draft report are: establishing mandatory deadlines for completing NEPA documents and imposing page limits on them, allowing state environmental reviews to satisfy NEPA requirements, and adding a citizen suit provision to NEPA with time limits on when lawsuits may be filed.

=9=

‖ *Preservation of Biodiversity* ‖

It may seem curious to some that the survival of a relatively small number of three-inch fish among all the countless millions of species extant would require the permanent halting of a virtually completed dam for which Congress has expended more than $100 million . . . We conclude, however, that the explicit provisions of the Endangered Species Act require precisely that result.

—*Chief Justice Burger for the Court in TVA v. Hill (1978)*

Losing species means losing the potential to solve some of humanity's most intractable problems, including hunger and disease. The Endangered Species Act is more than just a law—it is the ultimate safety net in our life support system. As Earth has changed and as science has progressed since the Endangered Species Act was authorized in 1973, the ESA has served our nation well, largely because of its flexibility and its solid foundation in science. It is crucial to maintain these fundamental principles. The challenges of effective implementation of the Act should not be interpreted to require substantive rewriting of this valuable, well-functioning piece of legislation.

—*A Letter from 5,738 Biologists to the U.S. Senate Concerning Science in the Endangered Species Act (March 2006)**

For nearly a century, Congress has been concerned about the need to protect certain species in danger of extinction. But it was only in the last forty years that comprehensive regulatory programs to protect endangered species were developed. Beginning with modest legislation in 1966, Congress in 1973 adopted strict regulatory legislation, the Endangered Species Act. This law and an international convention (the Convention on International Trade in Endangered Species of Wild Fauna and Flora) created a comprehensive program that "restricts the taking of species in danger of extinction or likely to become so, regulates trade in them, provides authority to acquire habitat needed for their survival, and mandates that federal agencies consider the impacts of their activities on these species." M. Bean, The Evolution of National Wildlife Law 193 (3d ed. 1997).

More recently, protection of endangered species has come to be seen in its larger context—the conservation of biological diversity. The international Convention on Biological Diversity, signed at the Rio Earth Summit in 1992, defines biodiversity as "the variability among living organisms from all sources, including terrestrial, marine, and other aquatic ecosystems and the ecological

---

*Available at *http://lawprofessors.typepad.com/environmental_law/files/Biologists_Letter_full_list_whitecover.pdf*

complexes of which they are a part; this includes diversity within species, between species, and of ecosystems." As this definition indicates, "biological diversity" includes not only the diversity of species, but also genetic diversity— the variation among individuals of the same species—and the diversity of eco-systems, or natural communities. It also includes the ecological and evolutionary processes on which those systems depend, such as predation, mutation, and decay.

With this broader understanding, the conservation of biological diversity poses a fundamental challenge, implicating, for example, climate change, toxic chemicals, and land use. But the Endangered Species Act (ESA) is the corner-stone of U.S. efforts to conserve biological diversity. It is a mechanism for saving species, the diversity within them, and the natural systems on which they depend. It is, ultimately, the safety net when broader efforts fail. Before turning to that statute, however, it is worth considering the moral, economic, and political groundings of the conservation of species.

A.   WHY SHOULD WE PRESERVE BIODIVERSITY?

In Chapter 1 we considered some of the intellectual and cultural roots of environmental protection. These issues come to the fore in debates about the extinction of species. Aesthetic concerns and moral principles are often invoked in support of conservation, but conservation may also be justified by narrower concerns for human health and economic well-being. Some of these arguments are set forth in the following excerpt from the writings of Edward O. Wilson, prominent biologist and eloquent champion of biodiversity.

E.O. Wilson, Biophilia
121 (1984)

The current rate [of species extinction] is still the greatest in recent geo-logical history. It is also much higher than the rate of production of new species by ongoing evolution, so that the net result is a steep decline in the world's standing diversity. Whole categories of organisms that emerged over the past ten million years, among them the familiar condors, rhinoceros, manatees, and gorillas, are close to the end. For most of their species, the last individuals to exist in the wild state could well be those living there today. It is a grave error to dismiss the hemorrhaging as a "Darwinian" process, in which species autono-mously come and go and man is just the latest burden on the environment. Human destructiveness is something new under the sun. Perhaps it is matched by the giant meteorites thought to smash into the Earth and darken the atmo-sphere every hundred million years or so (the last one apparently arrived 65 million years ago and contributed to the extinction of the dinosaurs). But even that interval is ten thousand times longer than the entire history of civili-zation. In our own brief lifetime, humanity will suffer an incomparable loss in aesthetic value, practical benefits from biological research, and worldwide biological stability. Deep mines of biological diversity will have been dug out and carelessly discarded in the course of environmental exploitation, without our even knowing fully what they contained.

By economic measure alone, the diversity of species is one of Earth's most important resources. It is also the least utilized. We have come to depend completely on less than 1 percent of living species for our existence, with the remainder waiting untested and fallow. In the course of history, according to estimates recently made by Norman Myers, people have utilized about 7,000 kinds of plants for food, with emphasis on wheat, rye, maize, and about a dozen other highly domesticated species. Yet at least 75,000 exist that are edible, and many of these are superior to the crop plants in use. The strongest of all arguments from surface ethics is a logical conclusion about this unrealized potential: The more the living world is explored and utilized, the greater will be the efficiency and reliability of the particular species chosen for economic use. Among the potential star species are these:

The winged bean (*Psophocarpus tetragonolobus*) of New Guinea has been called a one-species supermarket. It contains more protein than cassava and potato and possesses an overall nutritional value equal to that of soybean. It is among the most rapidly growing of all plants, reaching a height of fifteen feet within a few weeks. The entire plant can be eaten, tubers, seeds, leaves, flowers, stems, and all, both raw and ground into flour. A coffee-like beverage can be made from the liquefied extract. The species has already been used to improve the diet in fifty tropical countries, and a special institute has been set up in Sri Lanka to study and promote it more thoroughly.

The wax gourd (*Benincasa hispida*) of tropical Asia grows an inch every three hours over a course of four days, permitting multiple crops to be raised each year. The fruit attains a size of up to 1 by 6 feet and a weight of 80 pounds. Its crisp white flesh can be eaten at any stage, as a cooked vegetable, a base for soup, or a dessert when mixed with syrup.

The Babussa palm (*Orbigyna martiana*) is a wild tree of the Amazon rain forest known locally as the "vegetable cow." The individual fruits, which resemble small coconuts, occur in bunches of up to 600 with a collective weight of 200 pounds. Some 70 percent of the kernel mass is composed of a colorless oil, used for margarine, shortening, fatty acids, toilet soap, and detergents. A stand of 500 trees on one hectare (2.5 acres) can produce 125 barrels of oil per year. After the oil has been extracted, the remaining seedcake, which is about one-fourth protein, serves as excellent animal fodder.

Even with limited programs of research, biologists have compiled an impressive list of such candidate organisms in the technical literature. The vast majority of wild plants and animals are not known well enough (certainly many have not yet been discovered) even to guess at those with the greatest economic potential. Nor is it possible to imagine all the uses to which each species can be put. Consider the case of the natural food sweeteners. Several species of plants have been identified whose chemical products can replace conventional sugar with negligible calories and no known side effects. The katemfe (*Thaumatococcus danielli*) of the West African forests contains two proteins that are 1,600 times sweeter than sucrose and is now widely marketed in Great Britain and Japan. It is outstripped by the well-named serendipity berry (*Dioscoreophyllum cumminsii*), another West African native whose fruit produces a substance 3,000 times sweeter than sucrose.

Natural products have been called the sleeping giants of the pharmaceutical industry. One in every ten plant species contains compounds with some anticancer activity. Among the leading successes from the screening conducted so far is the rosy periwinkle, a native of the West Indies. It is the very paradigm of a previously minor species, with pretty five-petaled blossoms but otherwise rather ordinary in appearance, a roadside casual, the kind of inconspicuous flowering plant that might otherwise have been unknowingly consigned to extinction by the growth of sugarcane plantations and parking lots. But it also happens to produce two alkaloids, vincristine and vinblastine, that achieve 80 percent remission from Hodgkin's disease, a cancer of the lymphatic system, as well as 99 percent remission from acute lymphocytic leukemia. Annual sales of the two drugs reached $100 million in 1980.

A second wild species responsible for a medical breakthrough is the Indian serpentine root (*Rauwolfia serpentind*). It produces reserpine, a principal source of tranquilizers used to relieve schizophrenia as well as hypertension, the generalized condition predisposing patients to stroke, heart malfunction, and kidney failure.

The natural products of plants and animals are a select group in a literal sense. They represent the defense mechanisms and growth regulators produced by evolution during uncounted generations, in which only organisms with the most potent chemicals survived to the present time. Placebos and cheap substitutes were eliminated at an early stage. Nature has done much of our work for us, making it far more efficient for the medical researcher to experiment with extracts of living tissue than to pull chemicals at random off the laboratory shelf. Very few pharmaceuticals have been invented from a knowledge of the first principles of chemistry and medicine. Most have their origin in the study of wild species and were discovered by the rapid screening of large numbers of natural products.

For the same reason, technical advances utilizing natural products have been achieved in many categories of industry and agriculture. Among the most important have been the development of phytoleum, new plant fuels to replace petroleum; waxes and oils produced from indefinitely renewing sources at more economical rates than previously thought possible; novel kinds of fibers for paper manufacture; fast-growing siliceous plants, such as bamboo and elephant grass, for economical dwellings; superior methods of nitrogen fixation and soil reclamation; and magic-bullet techniques of pest control, by which microorganisms and parasites are set loose to find and attack target species without danger to the remainder of the ecosystem. Even the most conservative extrapolation indicates that many more such discoveries will result from only a modest continuing research effort.

NOTES AND QUESTIONS

1. Why should we care about the extinction of species? What reasons does Wilson articulate? What other reasons are there? Recall the discussion in Chapter 1 of competing values and the different approaches economics and ecology employ in conceptualizing environmental problems. In what respects do arguments concerning the importance of biodiversity reflect an economic perspective? For an attempt to identify the various reasons why biodiversity is valuable to humans, even apart from purely utilitarian values, see S. Kellert, Biological Diversity and Human Society (1996).

2. The Endangered Species Act (ESA) refers to the "esthetic, ecological, educational, historical, recreational, and scientific value" of species in danger of

or threatened with extinction. §2(a)(3), 16 U.S.C. §1531(a)(3). Surely not all species have the same value to mankind, as the ESA implicitly recognizes by excluding from its protections insect pests determined to "present an overwhelming and overriding risk to man." Why then should all disappearing species be entitled to the same level of protection? From an economic perspective, wouldn't it make more sense to vary the level of protection on the basis of some assessment of the value of the species to mankind? How could such an assessment be done given our present knowledge?

3. To what extent does uncertainty justify strict protection for endangered species? We have studied in detail less than one one-hundredth of 1 percent of all species. If we know so little about the characteristics of species that are fast disappearing, is it reasonable to assume that what we are losing includes some valuable resources? Is biodiversity inherently valuable because it is impossible to know what we are losing as species disappear?

4. In his 1992 book The Diversity of Life, Wilson reports that his most conservative estimate of the current rate of species loss is 27,000 per year, the equivalent of 74 per day and three per hour. E. O. Wilson, The Diversity of Life 280 (1992). This estimate includes only the loss of species that is caused by destruction of natural habitat, and not that which is the product of exotic species replacement or endangerment from pollution.

5. It is estimated that the world contains 13 to 14 million species, but only 1.75 million of them have even been described. Terrestrial vertebrates and higher plants are the best known groups, though population trends data are available only for a few groups. CEQ, 1997 Report of the Council on Environmental Quality 70-71 (1999). Of the 20,439 species native to the United States for which sufficient data are available to make a status assessment, nearly one-third are in some danger of extinction. The Nature Conservancy, Priorities for Conservation, 1997 Annual Report Card for U.S. Plant and Animal Species (1997).

6. An example of the pharmaceutical use of rare plants is the development of a drug called Taxol to treat breast cancer and ovarian cancer. The drug originally was made only from material found in the bark and needles of the rare Pacific yew tree. Environmentalists initially were concerned that this discovery threatened to decimate the yew population since it took six 100-year-old yews to make enough Taxol to treat a single patient. However, having developed an understanding of how Taxol production occurs within the yew tree, researchers were able to synthesize the drug using much smaller quantities of yew bark. Scientists also discovered that the drug could be extracted from the leaves of a tree found widely in the Himalayas, *Taxus baccata*, without killing the tree. In December 1994, the FDA approved a new, semi-synthetic version of Taxol that uses the Himalayan tree rather than the rare Pacific yew. New Version of Taxol Is Approved by FDA, N.Y. Times, Dec. 13, 1994, at C6.

7. Experiments conducted by conservation biologists have demonstrated that more biologically diverse communities have more productive ecosystem processes. This finding is a product of research conducted at a facility in England called the "Ecotron." The Ecotron has 16 environmental chambers that were used in an elaborate experiment to replicate terrestrial communities that differ only in their biodiversity. Naeem et al., Declining Biodiversity Can Alter the Performance of Ecosystems, 368 Nature 734 (1994). The study suggests that reduced biodiversity will indeed adversely affect the performance of ecosystems. Similar results were obtained in a large-scale field study of prairie plants,

which found that the more species a plot of experimental prairie had, the more bio-mass it produced and the better it retained nitrogen. Yoon, Ecosystem's Productivity Rises With Diversity of Its Species, N.Y. Times, March 5, 1996, at C4.

B.   THE ENDANGERED SPECIES ACT: AN OVERVIEW

The most significant legislation for preserving biodiversity has been the Endangered Species Act of 1973. The major provisions of the Endangered Species Act are outlined below. The Act protects species that are listed (under section 4) as either "endangered species" or "threatened species" by the Secretary (of Interior for terrestrial and freshwater species or of Commerce for marine species).

MAJOR PROVISIONS OF THE ENDANGERED SPECIES ACT

Section 3: Definitions
§3(6) defines "endangered species" as "any species which is in danger of extinction throughout all or a significant portion of its range."
§3(20) defines "threatened species" as "any species which is likely to become an endangered species within the foreseeable future throughout all or a significant portion of its range."

Section 4: Listing Endangered and Threatened Species
§4(a) requires the Secretary to determine whether any species is "endangered" or "threatened" and to designate critical habitat of such species.
§4(b) provides that the listing determination is to be based solely on "best scientific and commercial data available" and that the designation of critical habitat is to be based on the "best scientific data available . . . taking into consideration the economic impact, and any other relevant impact, of specifying any particular area as critical habitat."
§4(b)(3) provides that citizens may petition to force listing determination.
§4(f) requires the Secretary to develop and implement recovery plans for endangered and threatened species unless he finds they will not promote conservation of the species.

Section 7: Review of Federal Actions
§7(a)(1) requires all federal agencies to carry out programs to conserve endangered and threatened species.
§7(a)(2) provides that all federal agencies must insure, in consultation with the Secretary, that their actions are "not likely to jeopardize the continued existence of any endangered species or threatened species or result in the destruction or adverse modification" of such species' critical habitat.

---

§§7(e)-(h) provide that if action is barred by a "jeopardy" determination, its proponent may seek exemption from the Cabinet-level "Endangered Species Committee."

Section 9: Prohibitions

§9(a) prohibits sale, import, export, or transport of any species listed as endangered.

§§9(a)(1)(B) & (C) make it unlawful to "take" (broadly defined by section 3(19) to cover harassing, harming, killing, capturing, or collecting) any endangered *animal* species.

§9(a)(2)(B) prohibits removal or damage of endangered *plants* on federal lands or anywhere else if in knowing violation of state law.

§9 states that these prohibitions generally apply to threatened species, except as the Secretary has specified otherwise, and they apply to any "person," including any corporation or government entity.

Section 10: Habitat Conservation Plans

§10(a) authorizes the issuance of permits allowing the incidental taking of endangered species to parties with an approved habitat conservation plan to minimize and mitigate the impacts of such a taking where the taking will not appreciably reduce the likelihood of the survival and recovery of the species in the wild.

Section 11: Enforcement and Citizen Suits

§§11(a) & (b) provide civil and criminal penalties for violations of the Act.

§11(g) authorizes citizen suits against any person alleged to be in violation of the Act and against the Secretary for failure to perform any nondiscretionary duty.

While threatened species are to be protected by regulations "necessary and advisable to provide for the conservation of such species," in general, threatened species have been extended the same protections accorded species listed as endangered. Specific protections are provided in sections 7 and 9 of the Act. Section 7 of the Act requires all federal agencies to "insure that any action authorized, funded, or carried out" by them "is not likely to jeopardize the continued existence of any endangered species or threatened species or result in the destruction or adverse modification of [critical] habitat of such species," 16 U.S.C. §1536. Section 9 of the Act regulates private conduct by making it illegal for *any* person to sell, import, export, or transport any plant or animal species listed as endangered. Endangered fish or wildlife are given even greater protection by section 9(a)(1), which makes it illegal for anyone to "take" them. "Take" is broadly defined to mean "to harass, harm, pursue, hunt, shoot, wound, kill, trap, capture, or collect, or to attempt to engage in any such conduct." Section 9(a)(2)(B) makes it illegal to remove or damage endangered plants from federal lands or from any other property if it is done in knowing violation of any state law or regulation including state criminal trespass law.

In the remaining sections of this chapter, we consider the three key sections of the statute: section 4, section 7, and section 9. Any study of the Endangered Species Act must begin, however, with one of the most celebrated cases in environmental law—TVA v. Hill, 437 U.S. 153 (1978)—in which the Supreme Court resoundingly affirmed the sweeping protections that this statute provides to species on the brink of extinction.

The Tennessee Valley Authority (TVA) is a federal agency established as part of New Deal efforts to promote economic development in a poor region of the southeastern United States. The TVA sought to bring cheap electric power to the region by constructing coal-fired power plants and building dams to generate hydroelectric power. By the 1960s, public support for the TVA had eroded as rising environmental concern confronted an agency relentlessly pursuing the construction of dams on virtually every major waterway in Tennessee. The Tellico Dam Project was launched in the early 1960s to dam the Little Tennessee River in order to create a reservoir that would slightly increase the hydropower capacity of the nearby Fort Loudon Dam. Using fanciful economic projections that "downplayed costs and inflated benefits in just about every way imaginable," the TVA obtained congressional approval for a project that would fail any objective cost-benefit scrutiny. Holly Doremus, The Story of TVA v. Hill: A Narrow Escape for a Broad Law, in Environmental Law Stories 109, 116 (Lazarus & Houck eds., 2005).

Construction of the Tellico Dam commenced in March 1967 on one of the last remaining stretches of free-flowing river in southeastern Tennessee, an area of great natural beauty rich in historical sites sacred to the Cherokee Indian Tribe. The project was halted temporarily in 1972 when the Environmental Defense Fund obtained an injunction requiring the TVA to prepare an environmental impact statement to comply with the newly enacted National Environmental Policy Act (NEPA). Environmental Defense Fund v. TVA, 468 F.2d 1164 (6th Cir. 1972). After the EIS was prepared, the injunction was dissolved in 1973. The litigation that resulted in the decision below involved a renewed effort to halt the project by using the newly enacted Endangered Species Act.

TVA v. Hill
437 U.S. 153 (1978)

Mr. Chief Justice Burger delivered the opinion of the Court.

The Little Tennessee River originates in the mountains of northern Georgia and flows through the national forest lands of North Carolina into Tennessee, where it converges with the Big Tennessee River near Knoxville. The lower 33 miles of the Little Tennessee takes the river's clear, free-flowing waters through an area of great natural beauty. . . .

In this area of the Little Tennessee River the Tennessee Valley Authority, a wholly owned public corporation of the United States, began constructing the Tellico Dam and Reservoir Project in 1967, shortly after Congress appropriated initial funds for its development. . . . When fully operational, the dam would impound water covering some 16,500 acres—much of which represents valuable and productive farmland—thereby converting the river's shallow, fast-flowing waters into a deep reservoir over 30 miles in length.

The Tellico Dam has never opened, however, despite the fact that construction has been virtually completed and the dam is essentially ready for operation. Although Congress has appropriated monies for Tellico every year since 1967, progress was delayed, and ultimately stopped, by a tangle of lawsuits and administrative proceedings. After unsuccessfully urging TVA to consider alternatives to damming the Little Tennessee, local citizens and national conservation groups brought suit in the District Court, claiming that the project did not conform to the requirements of the National Environmental Policy Act of 1969 (NEPA), 42 U.S.C. §4331 et seq. After finding TVA to be in violation of NEPA, the District Court enjoined the dam's completion pending the filing of an appropriate environmental impact statement. The injunction remained in effect until late 1973, when the District Court concluded that TVA's final environmental impact statement for Tellico was in compliance with the law.

A few months prior to the District Court's decision dissolving the NEPA injunction, a discovery was made in the waters of the Little Tennessee which would profoundly affect the Tellico Project. Exploring the area around Coytee Springs, which is about seven miles from the mouth of the river, a University of Tennessee ichthyologist, Dr. David A. Etnier, found a previously unknown species of perch, the snail darter, or *Percina (Imostoma) tanasi.* This three-inch, tannish-colored fish, whose numbers are estimated to be in the range of 10,000 to 15,000, would soon engage the attention of environmentalists, the TVA, the Department of the Interior, the Congress of the United States, and ultimately the federal courts, as a new and additional basis to halt construction of the dam.

Until recently the finding of a new species of animal life would hardly generate a cause celebre. This is particularly so in the case of darters, of which there are approximately 130 known species, 8 to 10 of these having been identified only in the last five years. The moving force behind the snail darter's sudden fame came some four months after its discovery, when the Congress passed the Endangered Species Act of 1973, 16 U.S.C. §1531 et seq. (1976) ("Act"). This legislation, among other things, authorizes the Secretary of the Interior to declare species of animal life "endangered" and to identify the "critical habitat" of these creatures. . . .

In January 1975, the respondents in this case and others petitioned the Secretary of the Interior to list the snail darter as an endangered species. After receiving comments from various interested parties, including TVA and the State of Tennessee, the Secretary formally listed the snail darter as an endangered species on October 8, 1975. 40 Fed. Reg. 47505-47506; see 50 C.F.R. §17.11(i) (1976). In so acting, it was noted that "the snail darter is a living entity which is genetically distinct and reproductively isolated from other fishes." 40 Fed. Reg., at 47505. More important for the purposes of this case, the Secretary determined that the snail darter apparently lives only in that portion of the Little Tennessee River which would be completely inundated by the reservoir created as a consequence of the Tellico Dam's completion. Id., at 47506. The Secretary went on to explain the significance of the dam to the habitat of the snail darter.

> [T]he snail darter occurs only in the swifter portions of shoals over clean gravel substrate in cool, low-turbidity water. Food of the snail darter is almost exclusively snails which require a clean gravel substrate for their survival. *The proposed impoundment of water behind the proposed Tellico Dam would result in total destruction of the snail darter's habitat.* Ibid. (Emphasis added.)

Subsequent to this determination, the Secretary declared the area of the Little Tennessee which would be affected by the Tellico Dam to be the "critical habitat" of the snail darter. 41 Fed. Reg. 13926-13928; see 50 CFR §17.81. Using these determinations as a predicate, and notwithstanding the near completion of the dam, the Secretary declared that pursuant to §7 of the Act, "all Federal agencies must take such action as is necessary to insure that actions authorized, funded, or carried out by them do not result in the destruction or modification of this critical habitat area." 41 Fed. Reg., at 13928; 50 CFR, at §17.81(b). This notice, of course, was pointedly directed at TVA and clearly aimed at halting completion or operation of the dam. . . .

In February 1976, pursuant to §11(g) of the Endangered Species Act, 16 U.S.C. §1540(g), respondents filed the case now under review, seeking to enjoin completion of the dam and impoundment of the reservoir on the ground that those actions would violate the Act by directly causing the extinction of the species *Percina (Imostoma) tanasi*. The District Court denied respondents' request for a preliminary injunction and set the matter for trial. . . .

Trial was held in the District Court on April 29 and 30, 1976, and on May 25, 1976, the court entered its memorandum opinion and order denying respondents their requested relief and dismissing the complaint. The District Court found that closure of the dam and the consequent impoundment of the reservoir would "result in the adverse modification, if not complete destruction, of the snail darter's critical habitat," making it "highly probable" that "the continued existence of the snail darter" would be "jeopardize[d]." [Hill v. Tennessee Valley Authority,] 419 F. Supp. 753, 757 (E.D. Tenn. [1976]). Despite these findings, the District Court declined to embrace the plaintiffs' position on the merits: that once a federal project was shown to jeopardize an endangered species, a court of equity is compelled to issue an injunction restraining violation of the Endangered Species Act. . . .

Thereafter, in the Court of Appeals, respondents argued that the District Court had abused its discretion by not issuing an injunction in the face of "a blatant statutory violation." [Hill v. Tennessee Valley Authority,] 549 F.2d 1064, 1069 (6th Cir. 1977). The Court of Appeals agreed, and on January 31, 1977, it reversed, remanding "with instructions that a permanent injunction issue halting all activities incident to the Tellico Project which may destroy or modify the critical habitat of the snail darter." Id. at 1075. The Court of Appeals directed that the injunction "remain in effect until Congress, by appropriate legislation, exempts Tellico from compliance with the Act or the snail darter has been deleted from the list of endangered species or its critical habitat materially redefined." Ibid. . . .

One would be hard pressed to find a statutory provision whose terms were any plainer than those in §7 of the Endangered Species Act. Its very words affirmatively command all federal agencies "to *insure* that actions *authorized, funded,* or *carried out* by them do not *jeopardize* the continued existence" of an endangered species or "*result* in the destruction or modification of habitat of such species. . . ." 16 U.S.C. §1536. (Emphasis added.) This language admits of no exception. Nonetheless, petitioner urges, as do the dissenters, that the Act cannot reasonably be interpreted as applying to a federal project which was well under way when Congress passed the Endangered Species Act of 1973. To sustain that position, however, we would be forced to ignore the ordinary meaning of plain language. It has not been shown, for example, how TVA can close the gates of the Tellico Dam without "carrying out" an action that has been "authorized" and "funded" by a federal agency. Nor can we understand how such action will *"insure"* that the snail darter's habitat is not disrupted. Accepting the Secretary's determinations, as we must, it is clear that TVA's proposed operation of the dam will have precisely the opposite effect, namely the *eradication* of an endangered species.

Concededly, this view of the Act will produce results requiring the sacrifice of the anticipated benefits of the project and of many millions of dollars in public funds. But examination of the language, history, and structure of the legislation under review here indicates beyond doubt that Congress intended endangered species to be afforded the highest of priorities. . . .

The legislative proceedings in 1973 are, in fact, replete with expressions of concern over the risk that might lie in the loss of *any* endangered species.

. . . Congress was concerned about the *unknown* uses that endangered species might have and about the *unforeseeable* place such creatures may have in the chain of life on this planet. . . .

. . . The plain intent of Congress in enacting this statute was to halt and reverse the trend toward species extinction, whatever the cost. This is reflected not only in the stated policies of the Act, but in literally every section of the statute. All persons, including federal agencies, are specifically instructed not to "take" endangered species, meaning that no one is "to harass, harm,[30] pursue, hunt, shoot, wound, kill, trap, capture, or collect" such life forms. 16 U.S.C. §§1532(14), 1538(a)(1)(B) (1976 ed.). . . . The pointed omission of the type of qualifying language previously included in endangered species legislation reveals a conscious decision by Congress to give endangered species priority over the "primary missions" of federal agencies.

One might dispute the applicability of [this argument] to the Tellico Dam by saying that in this case the burden on the public through the loss of millions of unrecoverable dollars would greatly outweigh the loss of the snail darter. But neither the Endangered Species Act nor Art. III of the Constitution provides federal courts with authority to make such fine utilitarian calculations. On the contrary, the plain language of the Act, buttressed by its legislative history, shows clearly that Congress viewed the value of endangered species as "incalculable." Quite obviously, it would be difficult for a court to balance the loss of a sum certain—even $100 million—against a congressionally declared "incalculable" value, even assuming we had the power to engage in such a weighing process, which we emphatically do not. . . .

Having determined that there is an irreconcilable conflict between operation of the Tellico Dam and the explicit provisions of §7 of the Endangered Species Act, we must now consider what remedy, if any, is appropriate. It is correct, of course, that a federal judge sitting as a chancellor is not mechanically obligated to grant an injunction for every violation of law. This Court made plain in Hecht Co. v. Bowles, 321 U.S. 321, 329 (1944), that "[a] grant of *jurisdiction* to issue compliance orders hardly suggests an absolute duty to do so under any and all circumstances." As a general matter it may be said that "[s]ince all or almost

---

30. We do not understand how TVA intends to operate Tellico Dam without "harming" the snail darter. The Secretary of the Interior has defined the term "harm" to mean "an act or omission which actually injures or kills wildlife, including acts which annoy it to such an extent as to significantly disrupt essential behavioral patterns, which include, but are not limited to, breeding, feeding or sheltering; *significant environmental modification or degradation which has such effects is included within the meaning of 'harm.'*" 50 CFR 17.3 (1976) (emphasis added).

all equitable remedies are discretionary, the balancing of equities and hardships is appropriate in almost any case as a guide to the chancellor's discretion." D. Dobbs, Remedies 52 (1973). . . .

But these principles take a court only so far. Our system of government is, after all, a tripartite one, with each Branch having certain defined functions delegated to it by the Constitution. While "[i]t is emphatically the province and duty of the judicial department to say what the law is," Marbury v. Madison, 5 U.S. 137 (1803), it is equally—and emphatically—the exclusive province of the Congress not only to formulate legislative policies and mandate programs and projects, but also to establish their relative priority for the Nation. Once Congress, exercising its delegated powers, has decided the order of priorities in a given area, it is for the Executive to administer the laws and for the courts to enforce them when enforcement is sought.

Here we are urged to view the Endangered Species Act "reasonably," and hence shape a remedy "that accords with some modicum of common sense and the public weal." But is that our function? We have no expert knowledge on the subject of endangered species, much less do we have a mandate from the people to strike a balance of equities on the side of the Tellico Dam. Congress has spoken in the plainest of words, making it abundantly clear that the balance has been struck in favor of affording endangered species the highest of priorities, thereby adopting a policy which it described as "institutionalized caution." . . .

We agree with the Court of Appeals that in our constitutional system the commitment to the separation of powers is too fundamental for us to pre-empt congressional action by judicially decreeing what accords with "common sense and the public weal." Our Constitution vests such responsibilities in the political branches.

Affirmed.

NOTES AND QUESTIONS

1. TVA v. Hill is one of the clearest instances of judicial repudiation of the kind of balancing approaches favored by the economics perspective. The majority opinion relies in part on committee reports expressing the view that biodiversity's genetic legacy is of "literally incalculable" value. Is the majority's rationale for refusing to balance the equities the notion that Congress already has done so? Or is the Court simply agreeing with Congress that such balancing cannot be done because it is impossible to calculate the value of genetic diversity?

2. Proponents of the project had argued that, even if completion of the dam would violate the Endangered Species Act, the judiciary should exercise its equitable discretion to decline to issue an injunction. Why did the Supreme Court instead order that an injunction be issued? Does the Court's decision imply that courts *must* enjoin all actions that violate the Act? If an injunction had not been issued in this case, would the finding of an ESA violation have any practical impact? Are courts required to enjoin violations of other environmental laws? See Weinberger v. Romero-Barcelo, 456 U.S. 305 (1982) (Clean Water Act does not foreclose the exercise of equitable discretion to decline to enjoin violation). What type of judicial relief should be provided when agencies violate procedural requirements, for example, by failing to perform a study or to consult with a certain agency?

3. The papers of the late Justice Thurgood Marshall reveal that the Supreme Court came close to approving completion of the Tellico Dam without even hearing oral argument. When the Court first met to consider whether to review the case, five of the Court's nine justices (Chief Justice Burger and Justices White, Powell, Blackmun, and Rehnquist) favored reversal while the other four justices voted not to review the case. Justice Rehnquist circulated a per curiam opinion summarily reversing the court below, but the five justices could not agree on the rationale for reversal. After vigorous draft dissents were circulated by Justices Stevens and Stewart (who were joined by Justices Brennan and Marshall), the court agreed to hear oral argument. Chief Justice Burger, who initially had argued that continued appropriations for the dam had implicitly amended ESA, and Justice White ultimately changed their minds and voted with the four other justices to uphold the lower court, transforming a prospective 5-4 defeat for the snail darter into a 6-3 victory. Percival, Environmental Law in the Supreme Court: Highlights from the Marshall Papers, 23 Envtl. L. Rep. 10,606, 10,610-10,611 (1993). Justices Powell and Blackmun dissented on the ground that the Act should be interpreted to apply only prospectively and not to actions that are virtually complete when an endangered species is discovered. In a separate dissent, Justice Rehnquist, who had favored summary reversal, argued that the district court's refusal to issue an injunction should be upheld because it was not an abuse of discretion.

4. After the snail darter was discovered, what steps did the plaintiffs have to take before they could invoke the Endangered Species Act? What "action" did they seek to enjoin?

5. Following the Supreme Court's decision, Congress acted swiftly to amend the Endangered Species Act. Section 7 of the Act was extensively amended in 1978, 1979, and 1982. "From an original two sentences, the provision has been expanded to occupy nearly 10 pages of statutory text and now includes detailed procedures for its implementation, new federal duties, and a complex procedure for exempting qualified activities from its commands." M. Bean, The Evolution of National Wildlife Law 355 (2d ed. 1983). While these amendments qualified some of the duties imposed by section 7, "they remain stringent and highly protective" and section 7's "essential command remains intact." Id.

6. As amended, section 7 now includes a process for granting exemptions from its "no jeopardy" rule. Section 7 establishes a process for convening a committee of high-ranking government officials, known as the "God Squad" because of their power to decide the fate of species. The committee is authorized to grant any exemption if it determines that: (1) there are no reasonable and prudent alternatives to the federal action, (2) the action is in the public interest on a regional or national basis, and (3) the benefits of the action clearly outweigh the benefits of alternatives that do not jeopardize preservation of the species. In January 1979 a "God Squad" was convened for the first time to consider the Tellico Dam project. The Committee unanimously refused an exemption for the dam because it determined that there were reasonable alternatives to the project and that the project's benefits did not clearly outweigh the benefits of the alternatives. As the chairman of the President's Council of Economic Advisers explained: "The interesting phenomenon is that here is a project that is 95 percent complete, and if one takes just the cost of finishing it against the benefits and does it properly, it doesn't pay, which says something about the original design." Transcript of Meeting of Endangered Species

Committee, Jan. 23, 1979, quoted in Holly Doremus, The Story of TVA v. Hill: A Narrow Escape for a Broad Law, in Environmental Law Stories 109, 133 (Lazarus & Houck eds., 2005). Since the Committee process was authorized, it has been used only four times, and the "God Squad" has never successfully granted a wholesale exemption from the Act.

7. In TVA v. Hill the Supreme Court rejected the argument that continued congressional appropriations for the Tellico Dam reflected an intent to exempt it from ESA because courts disfavor "repeals by implication." Had the Court instead accepted this argument, what would the consequences have been for application of the ESA to federally funded projects? Congressional proponents of the dam, led by Senate Minority Leader Howard Baker from Tennessee, rammed through an appropriations rider in 1980 that expressly authorized completion of the dam notwithstanding the provisions of the ESA.

> [T]he pork barrel proponents, in forty-two seconds, in an empty House chamber, were able to slip a rider onto an appropriations bill, repealing all protective laws as they applied to Tellico and ordering the reservoir's completion. Despite a half-hearted veto threat by President Carter and a last-minute constitutionally-based lawsuit brought by the Cherokee Indians, the TVA was ultimately able to finish the dam, close the gates, and flood the valley on November 28, 1979. [Plater, In the Wake of the Snail Darter: An Environmental Law Paradigm and Its Consequences, 19 U. Mich. J.L. Ref. 805, 813-814 (1986).]

While completion of the dam destroyed the last significant population of snail darters, small relict populations have been discovered elsewhere.

8. The Tellico Dam is not the only project that Congress has exempted from compliance with ESA. In 1988, Congress specifically authorized the University of Arizona to construct three telescopes at a particular location on Arizona's Mt. Graham even though it had been determined that the project, which was on national forest land, was likely to jeopardize the continued existence of the endangered Mt. Graham red squirrel. However, after the first two telescopes were built, the university sought to build the third telescope at a different location on a nearby peak. This plan was approved by the Forest Service without consultation with the Fish and Wildlife Service pursuant to section 7 of ESA. After opponents of the project brought suit, the Ninth Circuit found that Congress had not exempted construction at the new location from compliance with ESA. Mount Graham Coalition v. Thomas, 53 F.3d 970 (9th Cir. 1995). Thus, the court held that the Forest Service must comply with ESA section 7 prior to authorizing construction of the third telescope at another location.

C. FEDERAL AUTHORITY TO PRESERVE BIODIVERSITY

The Rehnquist Court's efforts to revive constitutional limitations on federal power have raised questions concerning the constitutional limits of federal authority under the Endangered Species Act. In the two cases that follow, plaintiffs, citing United States v. Lopez, 514 U.S. 549 (1995), argued that Congress did not have the constitutional authority under its power to regulate interstate commerce to protect certain endangered species found only within a single state. In the first case the D.C. Circuit considered a challenge to

Congress's constitutional authority to protect an endangered species of fly (the Delhi Sands Flower-Loving Fly, see Figure 9.1). The fly is located entirely within an eight-mile radius in two California counties. Plaintiffs argued on *Lopez* grounds that Congress did not have the power under the Commerce Clause to protect the fly's habitat because it did not bear a sufficient relationship to interstate commerce.

National Association of Home Builders v. Babbitt
130 F.3d 1041 (D.C. Cir. 1997)

WALD, Circuit Judge:

... This dispute arose when the Fish and Wildlife Service ("FWS") placed the [Delhi Sands Flower-Loving] Fly, an insect that is native to the San Bernardino area of California, on the endangered species list. The listing of the Fly, the habitat of which is located entirely within an eight mile radius in southwestern San Bernardino County and northwestern Riverside County, California, forced San Bernardino County to alter plans to construct a new hospital on a recently purchased site that the FWS had determined contained Fly habitat. The FWS

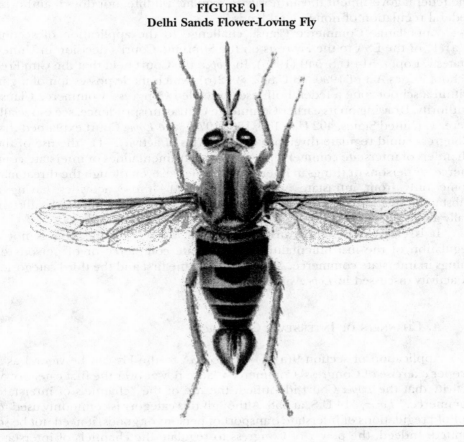

FIGURE 9.1
Delhi Sands Flower-Loving Fly

and San Bernardino County agreed on a plan that would allow the County to build the hospital and a power plant in the area designated as Fly habitat in return for modification of the construction plans and purchase and set aside of nearby land as Fly habitat. In November 1995, FWS issued a permit to allow construction of the power plant. During the same month, however, the County notified the FWS that it planned to redesign a nearby intersection to improve emergency vehicle access to the hospital. The FWS informed the County that expansion of the intersection as planned would likely lead to a "taking" of the Fly in violation of ESA section 9(a). After brief unsuccessful negotiations between the County and FWS, the County filed suit in district court challenging the application of section 9(a)(1) to the Fly. . . .

Appellants challenge the application of section 9(a)(1) of the ESA, which makes it unlawful for any person to "take any [endangered or threatened] species within the United States or the territorial sea of the United States," 16 U.S.C. §1538(a)(1), to the Delhi Sands Flower-Loving Fly. See also Babbitt v. Sweet Home Chapter of Communities for a Greater Oregon, 515 U.S. 687 (1995) (upholding agency's interpretation of the term "take" to include significant habitat degradation). Appellants argue that the federal government does not have the authority to regulate the use of non-federal lands in order to protect the Fly, which is found only within a single state. Indeed, they claim that "the Constitution of the United States does not grant the federal government the authority to regulate wildlife, nor does it authorize federal regulation of non-federal lands." . . .

Appellants' Commerce Clause challenge to the application of section 9(a)(1) of the ESA to the Fly rests on the Supreme Court's decision in United States v. Lopez, 514 U.S. 549 (1995). In *Lopez*, the Court held that the Gun-Free School Zones Act of 1990, 18 U.S.C. §922(q), which made possession of a gun within a school zone a federal offense, exceeded Congress' Commerce Clause authority. Drawing on its earlier Commerce Clause jurisprudence, see especially Perez v. United States, 402 U.S. 146, 150 (1971), the *Lopez* Court explained that Congress could regulate three broad categories of activity: (1) "the use of the channels of interstate commerce," (2) "the instrumentalities of interstate commerce, or persons or things in interstate commerce, even though the threat may come only from intrastate activities," and (3) "those activities having a substantial relation to interstate commerce . . . i.e., those activities that substantially affect interstate commerce." *Lopez*, 514 U.S. at 558-59. . . .

It is clear that, in this instance, section 9(a)(1) of the ESA is not a regulation of the instrumentalities of interstate commerce or of persons or things in interstate commerce. As a result, only the first and the third categories of activity discussed in *Lopez* will be examined . . .

A. CHANNELS OF INTERSTATE COMMERCE

Application of section 9(a)(1) of the ESA to the Fly can be viewed as a proper exercise of Congress' Commerce Clause power over the first category of activity that the *Lopez* Court identified: the use of the "channels of interstate commerce." *Lopez*, 514 U.S. at 558. Although this category is commonly used to uphold regulations of interstate transport of persons or goods, it need not be so limited. Indeed, the power of Congress to regulate the channels of interstate commerce provides a justification for section 9(a)(1) of the ESA for two reasons. First, the prohibition against takings of an endangered species is necessary to enable the government to control the transport of the endangered species in interstate commerce. Second, the prohibition on takings of endangered animals falls under Congress' authority "to keep the channels of interstate commerce free from immoral and injurious uses." Id. (quoting Heart of Atlanta Motel Inc. v. United States, 379 U.S. 241, 256 (1964)).

. . . In *Heart of Atlanta*, the Supreme Court upheld a prohibition on racial discrimination in places of public accommodation serving interstate travelers against a Commerce Clause challenge. The Court explained that "the authority of Congress to keep the channels of interstate commerce free from immoral and injurious uses has been frequently sustained, and is no longer open to question." Id. at 256 (citation omitted) (quoted in *Lopez*, 514 U.S. at 558). It does not matter if the activities that are regulated are of a "purely local character," the Court elaborated, "if it is interstate commerce that feels the pinch, it does not matter how local the operation which applies the squeeze." Id. at 258. . . .

B. SUBSTANTIALLY AFFECTS INTERSTATE COMMERCE

The takings clause in the ESA can also be viewed as a regulation of the third category of activity that Congress may regulate under its commerce power. According to *Lopez*, the test of whether section 9(a)(1) of the ESA is within this category of activity "requires an analysis of whether the regulated activity 'substantially affects' interstate commerce." 514 U.S. at 559. A class of activities can substantially affect interstate commerce regardless of whether the activity at issue—in this case the taking of endangered species—is commercial or non-commercial. As the *Lopez* Court, quoting Wickard v. Filburn, 317 U.S. 111 (1942), noted:

> "Even if appellee's activity be local and though it may not be regarded as commerce, it may still, whatever its nature, be reached by Congress if it exerts a substantial economic effect on interstate commerce, and this irrespective of whether such effect is what might at some earlier time have been defined as 'direct' or 'indirect.'"

Lopez, 514 U.S. at 556 (quoting *Wickard*, 317 U.S. at 125).[7]

The Committee Reports on the ESA reveal that one of the primary reasons that Congress sought to protect endangered species from "takings" was the importance of the continuing availability of a wide variety of species to interstate commerce. . . .

This legislative history distinguishes the ESA from the statute at issue in *Lopez*. In *Lopez*, the Court noted that "as part of our independent evaluation of constitutionality under the Commerce Clause we of course consider legislative findings, and indeed even congressional committee findings regarding effect on

---

7. Indeed, the case at hand is in many ways directly analogous to *Wickard*. In both cases, the appellee's activity, growing wheat for personal consumption and taking endangered species, is local and is not "regarded as commerce." Wickard, 317 U.S. at 125. However, in both cases, the activity exerts a substantial economic effect on interstate commerce—by affecting the quantity of wheat in one case, and by affecting the quantity of species in the other.

interstate commerce." 514 U.S. at 562. The *Lopez* Court found, however, that there were no "congressional findings [that] would enable [it] to evaluate the legislative judgment that the activity in question substantially affected interstate commerce." Id. at 563. In this case, in contrast, the committee reports on the ESA discuss the value of preserving genetic diversity and the potential for future commerce related to that diversity. . . .

Congress could rationally conclude that the intrastate activity regulated by section 9 of the ESA substantially affects interstate commerce for two primary reasons. First, the provision prevents the destruction of biodiversity and thereby protects the current and future interstate commerce that relies upon it. Second, the provision controls adverse effects of interstate competition. . . .

1. Biodiversity

Approximately 521 of the 1,082 species in the United States currently designated as threatened or endangered are found in only one state. The elimination of all or even some of these endangered species would have a staggering effect on biodiversity—defined as the presence of a large number of species of animals and plants—in the United States and, thereby, on the current and future interstate commerce that relies on the availability of a diverse array of species.

The variety of plants and animals in this country are, in a sense, a natural resource that commercial actors can use to produce marketable products. In the most narrow view of economic value, endangered plants and animals are valuable as sources of medicine and genes. Fifty percent of the most frequently prescribed medicines are derived from wild plant and animal species. Such medicines were estimated in 1983 to be worth over $15 billion a year. In addition, the genetic material of wild species of plants and animals is inbred into domestic crops and animals to improve their commercial value and productivity. As Amici Curiae explained: "Fortifying the genetic diversity of U.S. crops played a large part in the explosive growth in farm production since the 1930s, accounting for at least one-half of the doubling in yields of rice, soybeans, wheat, and sugarcane, and a three-fold increase in corn and potatoes. Genetic diversity provided by wild plants also protects domestic crops from disease and pest damage." Id. at 12. Similar genetic engineering can be used with animals. For instance, it is not beyond the realm of possibility that the genes of a wild pollinator species like the Fly might be inbred with the honeybee, which currently pollinates most major U.S. crops, to produce a pollinator that is more disease resistant.

Each time a species becomes extinct, the pool of wild species diminishes. This, in turn, has a substantial effect on interstate commerce by diminishing a natural resource that could otherwise be used for present and future commercial purposes. Unlike most other natural resources, however, the full value of the variety of plant and animal life that currently exists is uncertain. Plants and animals that are lost through extinction undoubtedly have economic uses that are, in some cases, as yet unknown but which could prove vitally important in the future. A species whose worth is still unmeasured has what economists call an "option value"—the value of the possibility that a future discovery will make useful a species that is currently thought of as useless. See Bryan Nolan, Commodity, Amenity, and Morality: The Limits of Quantification in Valuing Biodiversity, in Biodiversity, 200, 202 (Edward O. Wilson ed., 1988). To allow even a single species whose value is not currently apparent to become extinct therefore deprives the economy of the option value of that species. Because our current knowledge of each species and its possible uses is limited, it is impossible to calculate the exact impact that the loss of the option value of a single species might have on interstate commerce. See Alan Randall, What Mainstream Economists Have to Say about the Value of Biodiversity, in Biodiversity, supra, at 217. In the aggregate, however, we can be certain that the extinction of species and the attendant decline in biodiversity will have a real and predictable effect on interstate commerce. . . .

2.   *Destructive Interstate Competition*

The taking of the Fly and other endangered animals can also be regulated by Congress as an activity that substantially affects interstate commerce because it is the product of destructive interstate competition. It is a principle deeply rooted in Commerce Clause jurisprudence that Congress is empowered to act to prevent destructive interstate competition. As the Supreme Court explained in Model v. Virginia Surface Mining & Reclamation Ass'n, 452 U.S. 264 (1981) ("Hodel v. Virginia"), a case that the *Lopez* Court cited repeatedly, "prevention of . . . destructive interstate competition is a traditional role for congressional action under the Commerce Clause." . . .

The parallels between Hodel v. Virginia and the case at hand are obvious. The ESA and the Surface Mining Act both regulate activities—destruction of endangered species and destruction of the natural landscape—that are carried out entirely within a state and which are not themselves commercial in character. The activities, however, may be regulated because they have destructive effects, on environmental quality in one case and on the availability of a variety of species in the other, that are likely to affect more than one state. In each case, moreover, interstate competition provides incentives to states to adopt lower standards to gain an advantage vis-à-vis other states: In Hodel v. Virginia, 452 U.S. 264, the states were motivated to adopt lower environmental standards to improve the competitiveness of their coal production facilities, and in this case, the states are motivated to adopt lower standards of endangered species protection in order to attract development. . . .

KAREN LECRAFT HENDERSON, Circuit Judge, concurring:

I agree with Judge Wald's conclusion that the "taking" prohibition in section 9(a)(1) of the Endangered Species Act (ESA) constitutes a valid exercise of the Congress' authority to regulate interstate commerce under the Commerce Clause. I cannot, however, agree entirely with either of her grounds for reaching the result and instead arrive by a different route.

Judge Wald first asserts that section 9(a)(1) is a proper regulation of the "channels of commerce." In support she cites decisions upholding regulation of commercially marketable goods, such as machine guns and lumber, and public accommodations. In each case, the object of regulation was necessarily connected to movement of persons or things interstate and could therefore be characterized as regulation of the channels of commerce. Not so with an endangered species, as the facts here graphically demonstrate. The Delhi Sands Flower-Loving Flies the Department of the Interior seeks to protect are (along with many other species no doubt) entirely intrastate creatures. They do not move among states either on their own or through human agency. As a result, like the Gun-Free School Zones Act in *Lopez*, the statutory protection of the flies "is not a regulation of the use of the channels of interstate commerce." 514 U.S. at 558.

Judge Wald also justifies the protection of endangered species on the ground that the loss of biodiversity "substantially affects" interstate commerce because of the resulting loss of potential medical or economic benefit. Yet her opinion acknowledges that it is "impossible to calculate the exact impact" of the economic loss of an endangered species. As far as I can tell, it is equally impossible to ascertain that there will be any such impact at all. It may well be that no species endangered now or in the future will have any of the economic value proposed. Given that possibility, I do not see how we can say that the protection of an endangered species has any effect on interstate commerce (much less a substantial one) by virtue of an uncertain potential medical or economic value. Nevertheless, I believe that the loss of biodiversity itself has a substantial effect on our ecosystem and likewise on interstate commerce. In addition, I would uphold section 9(a)(1) as applied here because the Department's protection of the flies regulates and substantially affects commercial development activity which is plainly interstate.

First, I agree with Judge Wald that biodiversity is important to our understanding of ESA and its relation to interstate commerce. . . . The effect of a species' continued existence on the health of other species within the ecosystem seems to be generally recognized among scientists. Some studies show, for example, that the mere presence of diverse species within an ecosystem (biodiversity) by itself contributes to the ecosystem's fecundity. See Yvonne Baskin, Ecologists Dare to Ask: How Much Does Diversity Matter? 264 Science 202 (1994). The Congress recognized the interconnection of the various species and the ecosystems when it declared that the "essential purpose" of ESA, which protects endangered species, is in fact "to protect the ecosystem upon which we and other species depend." H.R. Rep. No. 93-412, at 10 (1973). Given the interconnectedness of species and ecosystems, it is reasonable to conclude that the extinction of one species affects others and their ecosystems and that the protection of a purely intrastate species (like the Delhi Sands Flower-Loving Fly) will therefore substantially affect land and objects that are involved in interstate commerce. There is, therefore, "a rational basis" for concluding that the "taking" of endangered species "substantially affects" interstate commerce so that section 9(a)(1) is within the Congress' Commerce Clause authority.

The interstate effect of a taking is particularly obvious here given the nature of the taking the County proposes. In enacting ESA, the Congress expressed an intent to protect not only endangered species but also the habitats that they, and we, occupy. See H.R. Rep. No. 93-412, at 10 (1973) (identifying ESA's "essential purpose" as "to protect the ecosystem upon which we and other species depend"). At the same time, the Congress expressly found that "economic growth and development untempered by adequate concern and conservation" was the cause for "various species of fish, wildlife, and plants in the United States hav[ing] been rendered extinct." 16 U.S.C. §1531(a)(1). It is plain, then, that at the time it passed ESA the Congress contemplated protecting endangered species through regulation of land and its development, which is precisely what the Department has attempted to do here. Such regulation, apart from the characteristics or range of the specific endangered species involved, has a plain and substantial effect on interstate commerce. In this case the regulation relates to both the proposed redesigned traffic intersection and the hospital it is intended to serve, each of which has an obvious connection with interstate commerce. Insofar as application of section 9(a)(1) of ESA here acts to regulate commercial development of the land inhabited by the endangered species, "it may . . . be reached by Congress" because "it asserts a substantial economic effect on interstate commerce."

SENTELLE, Circuit Judge, dissenting:

This case concerns the efforts of San Bernardino County, California ("the County"), to construct a hospital and supporting infrastructure for its citizens and other humans. Unfortunately, those efforts discomfit an insect—the Delhi Sands Flower-Loving Fly. According to the parties in this case, there are fewer than 300 breeding individuals of this species, all located within forty square miles in southern California. These flies live as larvae for nearly two years under Delhi Sands, a particular type of grit, apparently found only in those forty square miles of southern California, after which they emerge to feed and breed for two weeks before dying.

In 1982, the County began considering construction of a $470 million "state-of-the-art," "earthquake-proof" hospital complex. The day before ground breaking was scheduled to occur in 1993, the U.S. Fish and Wildlife Service ("Service") of the Department of the Interior ("Interior") added the fly to the endangered species list and notified the County that construction of the hospital, on County land using County funds, would harm a colony of six to eight flies and would therefore violate federal law. To prevent being prosecuted by the Service, County officials were forced to move the hospital complex 250 feet northward and to set aside 8 acres of land for the fly, delaying construction for a year and costing County taxpayers around $3.5 million. The Service also imposed a variety of other stringent requirements, including preservation of a flight corridor for the insect which today prevents improvements to a traffic intersection necessary to allow emergency access and avoid "virtual gridlock" when the hospital opens. At one point, the Service threatened to require shutting down the eight-lane San Bernardino Freeway (US 10, one of the most heavily traveled in southern California) for two months every year (I am not making this up). It did later drop this demand. . . .

The Department of Interior asserts that section 9(a)(1)(B) of the ESA, and specifically its use of that section to prohibit activities in southern California which might disturb a fly existing only in southern California, are constitutional under the Commerce Clause. U.S. Const. Art. I, §8, cl. 3. That clause empowers Congress to "regulate commerce with foreign nations, and among the several states, and with the Indian tribes." This brings the next question: Can Congress under the Interstate Commerce Clause regulate the killing of flies, which is not commerce, in southern California, which is not interstate? Because I think the answer is "no," I cannot join my colleagues' decision to affirm the district court's conclusion that it can. . . .

Judge Wald first asserts that the action taken by the Service under section 9(a)(1)(B) is a constitutional regulation of "the use of the 'channels of interstate commerce.'" (quoting *Lopez*, 514 U.S. at 558). The short disposition of this argument is to say it does not command a majority even without me. Judge Henderson rejects it out of hand, noting, correctly, that all authority offered by Judge Wald in support of the channels-of-commerce rationale upheld regulation "necessarily connected to movement of persons or things inter-state. . . ." As Judge Henderson goes on to note, neither the whole of the endangered species, nor any of the individuals comprising it, travel interstate. The Delhi Sands Flower-Loving Fly is an inveterate stay-at-home, a purely intra-state creature. The Gun-Free School Zones Act, stricken as unconstitutional by the Supreme Court in *Lopez*, involved purely local possession of firearms, objects which do move in interstate commerce, presumably through its channels. The Supreme Court without difficulty determined that that section was "not a regulation of the use of the channels of interstate commerce." Neither is this. It does not purport to be.

. . . Judge Wald's supporting analysis of . . . *Heart of Atlanta* is far off the mark.

As Judge Wald notes, . . . *Heart of Atlanta* concerned congressional efforts to "rid the channels of interstate commerce of injurious uses." But . . . prevent-ing habitat destruction contributes nothing to the goal of eliminating the fly, or any other endangered species, from the channels of commerce. The fact that activities like the construction of a hospital might involve articles that have traveled across state lines cannot justify federal regulation of the incidental local effects of every local activity in which those articles are employed. Judge Wald seems to be trying to extend Congress' power over the channels of com-merce to allow direct federal regulation of any local effects caused by any activity using those channels of commerce. She focuses not on the fly in the channels of commerce, but everything else moving in the channels of commerce that may affect the fly. But this improperly inverts the third prong of *Lopez* and extends it without limit. Under Judge Wald's theory, instead of being limited to activities that *substantially affect* commerce, Congress may also regulate anything that is *affected* by commerce. . . .

None of the rationales offered by my colleagues pass . . . examination. Judge Wald offers two possible explanations as to why the challenged regulatory activity falls within category (3). First, she puts forth the "biodiversity" rationale. Under this rationale, she argues that the extinction of a species, and the concomitant diminution of the pool of wild species, "has a substantial effect on interstate commerce by diminishing a natural resource that could otherwise be used for present and future commercial purposes." As I understand her argument, because of some undetermined and indeed undeterminable possi-bility that the fly might produce something at some undefined and undeter-mined future time which might have some undefined and undeterminable medical value, which in turn might affect interstate commerce at that imagined future point, Congress can today regulate anything which might advance the pace at which the endangered species becomes extinct. Judge Henderson rejects this rationale, noting cogently that our colleague admits "that it is 'impossible to calculate the exact impact' of the economic loss of an endangered species." Judge Henderson further notes that "it is equally impossible to ascertain that there will be any such impact at all." Id. She then reasons, and I agree, that we cannot then "say that the protection of an endangered species has any effect on interstate commerce (much less a substantial one) by virtue of an uncertain potential medical or economic value." Id.

. . . [T]he rationale offered by Judge Wald to support this intrastate appli-cation of a statute unlimited by either of the other two subsidiary inquiries has no logical stopping point. As Judge Henderson suggests, the rationale dependent upon the purely speculative future impact of an action with no demonstrable impact at all cannot be said to "have any effect on interstate commerce (much less a substantial one). . . ." If it could, then I do not see how Congress could be prohibited from regulating any action that might conceivably affect the number or continued existence of any item whatsoever. A creative and imaginative court can certainly speculate on the possibility that any object cited in any locality no matter how intrastate or isolated might some day have a medical, scientific, or economic value which could then propel it into interstate commerce. There is no stopping point. If we uphold this statute under Judge Wald's first rationale, we have indeed not only ignored *Lopez* but made the Commerce Clause into what Judge Kozinski suggested: the "hey-you-can-do-whatever-you-feel-like clause."

Though Judge Henderson rejects Judge Wald's "biodiversity" rationale, she relies on a related justification of her own, which is to me indistinguishable in any meaningful way from that of Judge Wald. As I understand her rationale, it depends on "the interconnectedness of species and ecosystems," which she deems sufficient for us "to conclude that the extinction of one species affects others and their ecosystems and that the protection of a purely intrastate species [concededly including the Delhi Sands Flower-Loving Fly] will therefore substantially affect land and objects that are involved in interstate commerce." I see this as no less of a stretch than Judge Wald's rationale. First, the Commerce Clause empowers Congress "to regulate commerce" not "ecosystems." The Framers of the Constitution extended that power to Congress, concededly without knowing the word "ecosystems," but certainly knowing as much about the dependence of humans on other species and each of them on the land as any ecologist today. An ecosystem is an ecosystem, and commerce is commerce. . . .

In addition to their biodiversity/ecosystem justifications, each of my colleagues offers a second rationale for justifying Interior's actions under the third category of *Lopez* regulation. Judge Wald asserts that "the taking of the Fly and other endangered animals can also be regulated by Congress as an activity that substantially affects interstate commerce because it is the product of destructive interstate competition." I am not at all certain what that means in relation to the application of the ESA to the building of a hospital and supporting infrastructure in a single intrastate location. She relies on Hodel v. Virginia, 452 U.S. 264 (1981), Hodel v. Indiana, 452 U.S. 314 (1981), and United States v. Darby, 312 U.S. 100 (1940). Although she asserts "striking parallels" between those cases and the present one, I see no parallel at all. In each of those cases, Congress regulated arguably intrastate commercial activities, specifically mining and lumber production for interstate commerce.

Finally, Judge Henderson would justify the challenged section on the basis that "in enacting the ESA, the Congress expressed an intent to protect not only endangered species, but also the habitats that they, and we, occupy." I see no legally significant distinction between this justification and her "ecosystems" justification. The Commerce Clause empowers Congress to regulate "commerce," not habitat. People and animals lived in habitats at the time of the adoption of the Constitution, and we live in habitats now. Because the power to regulate habitats was "not delegated to the United States by the Constitution, nor prohibited by it to the states," that power is "reserved to the states respectively, or to the people." U.S. Const. Amend. X. For the reasons outlined with reference to the ecosystem justification, the habitat justification fails as well.

NOTES AND QUESTIONS

1. Which of the rationales offered for finding that Congress has power under the commerce clause to protect endangered species is most persuasive? How do the various rationales for justifying federal regulatory authority compare with the reasons for conserving biodiversity offered in the excerpt from E.O. Wilson above? Emphasizing potential future commercial uses of endangered species has political appeal; in the aftermath of *Lopez* is such a strategy now necessary to justify congressional authority to protect them?

2. Endangered species are less likely to have large populations that cross state lines than are healthy species. Does Congress therefore have greater authority to protect thriving species populations than endangered ones?

3. Not all endangered insects are entitled to protection under the ESA. Congress specifically excluded from the statutory definition of "endangered species" any "species of the Class Insecta determined by the Secretary to constitute a pest whose protection under the provisions of this chapter would present an overwhelming and overriding risk to man." ESA §3(6), 16 U.S.C. §1532(6). Can you imagine any circumstances under which an insect that "is in danger of extinction throughout all or a significant portion of its range" ever could "present an overwhelming and overriding risk to man?"

4. Despite Judge Sentelle's vigorous dissent, the U.S. Supreme Court refused to review the D.C. Circuit's decision. Controversy over the fly continues. The fly's habitat—1,200 fragmented acres of dunes—lies in an area subject to intense development pressures due to rapid population growth. Developable land in the area is valued at $60,000 to $100,000 per acre. The fly reportedly continues to block development projects, including an effort by the city of Fontana, California, to develop a 218-acre area for commercial, retail, and residential purposes. See Endangered Fly Stalls Some California Projects, N.Y. Times, Dec. 1, 2002, at 28. Local politicians are lobbying to have the ESA amended or to convene the God Squad to exempt projects that will harm the fly. Congressman Ken Calvert, whose district includes the fly's habitat argues that it is "more than likely" that the fly "will become extinct anyway and all of the time, money and effort [to protect it] will be for naught." Id.

5. In the case that follows, the Fourth Circuit heard a constitutional challenge to the authority of Congress to prohibit private action that would harm an experimental population of endangered red wolves. In an effort to prevent extinction of the wolves, the government had captured surviving members of the species, pursuant to section 10(j) of the ESA, bred them in captivity and then reintroduced them into wildlife refuges in North Carolina and Tennessee. Of the 75 wolves believed to be in the wild, it was estimated that approximately 41 wandered off the refuges onto private land. The lawsuit challenged the government's efforts to protect the wolves when found on private land.

Gibbs v. Babbitt
214 F.3d 483 (4th Cir. 2000)

WILKINSON, Chief Judge:

This case raises a challenge to 50 C.F.R. §17.84(c), a regulation governing the experimental populations of red wolves reintroduced into North Carolina and Tennessee pursuant to section 10(j). The FWS has extended the takings prohibitions of section 9(a)(1) to the experimental red wolf populations with certain exceptions. See 50 C.F.R. §17.84(c) (1998). As noted above, the taking provision of section 9(a)(1) prevents landowners from harassing, harming, pursuing, hunting, shooting, wounding, killing, trapping, capturing, or collecting any endangered species. See 16 U.S.C. §1532(19). However, in order to insure that other agencies and the public would accept the proposed reintroduction, the FWS relaxed the taking standards for wolves found on private land under its authority over experimental populations.

Section 17.84(c) allows a person to take red wolves on private land "[p]rovided that such taking is not intentional or willful, or is in defense of that person's own life or the lives of others." Id. §17.84(c)(4)(i). Private landowners may also take red wolves on their property "when the wolves are in the act of killing livestock or pets, Provided that freshly wounded or killed livestock or pets are evident." Id. §17.84(c)(4)(iii). A landowner may also "harass red wolves found on his or her property . . . Provided that all such harassment is by methods that are not lethal or injurious to the red wolf." Id. §17.84(c)(4)(iv). Finally, landowners may take red wolves after efforts by Service personnel to capture such animals have been abandoned, and such taking has been approved in writing. Id. §17.84(c)(4)(v). All of these exceptions to the taking prohibition are subject to a 24-hour reporting requirement. Id. §17.84(c)(4).

C

Appellants Charles Gibbs, Richard Mann, Hyde County, and Washington County filed the instant action challenging the federal government's authority to protect red wolves on private land. They seek a declaration that the anti-taking regulation, 50 C.F.R. §17.84(c), as applied to the red wolves occupying private land in eastern North Carolina, exceeds Congress's power under the interstate Commerce Clause, U.S. Const, art. I, §8, cl. 3 ("Congress shall have Power . . . To regulate Commerce . . . among the several States . . ."). Appellants also seek an injunction against continued enforcement of the anti-taking regulation on non-federal land. Appellants claim that the red wolves have proven to be a "menace to citizens and animals in the Counties." They further allege that because of the federal regulatory protections surrounding the wolves, North Carolinians cannot effectively defend their property.

On cross-motions for summary judgment, the United States District Court for the Eastern District of North Carolina held that Congress's power to regulate interstate commerce includes the power to regulate conduct that might harm red wolves on private land. See Gibbs v. Babbitt, 31 F. Supp. 2d 531 (E.D.N.C. 1998). The district court found that the red wolves are "things in interstate commerce" because they have moved across state lines and their movement is followed by "tourists, academics, and scientists." Id. at 535. The court also found that the tourism they generate substantially affects interstate commerce. See id. The private landowners and North Carolina Counties now appeal.

II

We consider this case under the framework articulated by the Supreme Court in United States v. Lopez, 514 U.S. 549 (1995), and United States v.

Morrison, 120 S. Ct. 1740 (2000), aff'g Brzonkala v. Virginia Polytechnic Institute and State University, 169 F.3d 820 (4th Cir. 1999). While Congress's power to pass laws under the Commerce Clause has been interpreted broadly, both *Lopez* and *Morrison* reestablish that the commerce power contains "judicially enforceable outer limits." See *Lopez*, 514 U.S. at 566; *Morrison*, 120 S. Ct. at 1748-49 . . .

The *Lopez* Court recognized three broad categories of activity that Congress may regulate under its commerce power. 514 U.S. at 558. "First, Congress may regulate the use of the channels of interstate commerce. Second, Congress is empowered to regulate and protect the instrumentalities of interstate commerce, or persons or things in interstate commerce, even though the threat may come only from intrastate activities. Finally, Congress' commerce authority includes the power to regulate those activities having a substantial relation to interstate commerce, i.e., those activities that substantially affect interstate commerce." Id. at 558-59 (citations omitted).

Section 17.84(c) is "not a regulation of the use of the channels of interstate commerce, nor is it an attempt to prohibit the interstate transportation of a commodity through the channels of commerce." *Lopez*, 514 U.S. at 559. The term "channel of interstate commerce" refers to, inter alia, "navigable rivers, lakes, and canals of the United States; the interstate railroad track system; the interstate highway system; . . . interstate telephone and telegraph lines; air traffic routes; television and radio broadcast frequencies." United States v. Miles, 122 F.3d 235, 245 (5th Cir. 1997). This regulation of red wolf takings on private land does not target the movement of wolves or wolf products in the channels of interstate commerce.

This case also does not implicate *Lopez*'s second prong, which protects things in interstate commerce. Although the Service has transported the red wolves interstate for the purposes of study and the reintroduction programs, this is not sufficient to make the red wolf a "thing" in interstate commerce. See, e.g., *Lopez*, 514 U.S. at 559 (rejecting application of prong two to Gun-Free School Zones Act, despite the fact that the regulated guns likely traveled through interstate commerce); National Assoc. of Home Builders v. Babbitt, 130 F.3d 1041, 1046 (D.C. Cir. 1997) ("*NAHB*") (rejecting notion that Delhi Sands Flower-Loving Fly was a "thing" in interstate commerce). Therefore, if 50 C.F.R. §17.84(c) is within the commerce power, it must be sustained under the third prong of *Lopez*.

Under the third *Lopez* test, regulations have been upheld when the regulated activities "arise out of or are connected with a commercial transaction, which viewed in the aggregate, substantially affects interstate commerce." *Lopez*, 514 U.S. at 561. In *Morrison*, the Supreme Court noted, "In every case where we have sustained federal regulation under *Wickard*'s aggregation principle, the regulated activity was of an apparent commercial character." Morrison, 120 S. Ct. at 1750 n. 4. The Court in *Lopez* likewise placed great emphasis on the "commercial concerns that are central to the Commerce Clause." *Lopez*, 514 U.S. at 583 (Kennedy, J., concurring); see also Hoffman v. Hunt, 126 F.3d 575, 586-87 (4th Cir. 1997) (nothing the importance of the distinction between "the regulation of, on the one hand, those activities that are commercial or economic in nature . . . and, on the other hand, those activities that are not").

Although the connection to economic or commercial activity plays a central role in whether a regulation will be upheld under the Commerce Clause, economic activity must be understood in broad terms. Indeed, a cramped view of commerce would cripple a foremost federal power and in so doing would eviscerate national authority. The *Lopez* Court's characterization of the regulation of homegrown wheat in Wickard v. Filburn, 317 U.S. 111 (1942), as a case involving economic activity makes clear the breadth of this concept. The Court explained that "[e]ven *Wickard*, which is perhaps the most far reaching example of Commerce Clause authority over intrastate activity, involved economic activity in a way that the possession of a gun in a school zone does not." *Lopez*, 514 U.S. at 560; accord *Morrison*, 120 S. Ct. at 1749-50. See also *Brzonkala*, 169 F.3d at 835 (explaining that the Court has a "relatively broad understanding of such [economic] activity"). In fact, our understanding of commerce may not be limited to its "18th-century" forms. See *Lopez*, 514 U.S. at 574 (Kennedy, J., concurring). While we must enforce meaningful limits on the commerce power, we must also be mindful of the "Court's relatively generous conception of economic activity." *Brzonkala*, 169 F.3d at 835. . . .

With these basic principles in mind, we consider appellants' challenge to §17.84(c).

III

Appellants argue that the federal government cannot limit the taking of red wolves on private land because this activity cannot be squared with any of the three categories that Congress may regulate under its commerce power. Appellants assert that 50 C.F.R. §17.84(c) is therefore beyond the reach of congressional authority under the Commerce Clause.

We disagree. It was reasonable for Congress and the Fish and Wildlife Service to conclude that §17.84(c) regulates economic activity. The taking of red wolves implicates a variety of commercial activities and is closely connected to several interstate markets. The regulation in question is also an integral part of the overall federal scheme to protect, preserve, and rehabilitate endangered species, thereby conserving valuable wildlife resources important to the welfare of our country. Invalidating this provision would call into question the historic power of the federal government to preserve scarce resources in one locality for the future benefit of all Americans.

A

To fall within Congress's commerce power, this regulation must have a "substantial relation to interstate commerce"—it must "substantially affect interstate commerce." *Lopez*, 514 U.S. at 559. The Supreme Court recently emphasized that "in those cases where we have sustained federal regulation of intrastate activity based upon the activity's substantial effects on interstate commerce, the activity in question has been some sort of economic endeavor." *Morrison*, 120 S. Ct. at 1750-51. Intrastate activities may be subject to federal regulation if they have a "meaningful connection with [a] particular, identifiable economic enterprise or transaction." *Brzonkala*, 169 F.3d at 834. We therefore must consider whether the taking of red wolves on private land is "in any sense of the phrase, economic activity." *Morrison*, 120 S. Ct. at 1751-52.

Unlike the Violence Against Women Act (VAWA) in *Morrison* and the Gun-Free School Zones Act (GFSZA) in *Lopez*, §17.84(c) regulates what is in a meaningful sense economic activity. The Court in *Morrison* explained that both the VAWA and the GFSZA involved activity that was noneconomic and only tenuously linked to interstate commerce. 120 S. Ct. at 1749-52. Yet the taking of a red wolf on private land is unlike gender-motivated violence or guns near schools. The protection of commercial and economic assets is a primary reason for taking the wolves. Farmers and ranchers take wolves mainly because they are concerned that the animals pose a risk to commercially valuable livestock and crops. Indeed, appellants' arguments focus quite explicitly on these economic concerns—they want freer rein to protect their property and investments in the land. See Appellants' Br. at 10 ("In the face of these threats [from red wolves], North Carolinians cannot effectively defend their property."); id. at 12.

The relationship between red wolf takings and interstate commerce is quite direct—with no red wolves, there will be no red wolf related tourism, no scientific research, and no commercial trade in pelts. We need not "pile inference upon inference," *Lopez*, 514 U.S. at 567, to reach this conclusion. While a beleaguered species may not presently have the economic impact of a large commercial enterprise, its eradication nonetheless would have a substantial effect on interstate commerce. And through preservation the impact of an endangered species on commerce will only increase.

Because the taking of red wolves can be seen as economic activity in the sense considered by *Lopez* and *Morrison*, the individual takings may be aggregated for the purpose of Commerce Clause analysis. See *Morrison*, 120 S. Ct. at 1750 n. 4. While the taking of one red wolf on private land may not be "substantial," the takings of red wolves in the aggregate have a sufficient impact on interstate commerce to uphold this regulation. This is especially so where, as here, the regulation is but one part of the broader scheme of endangered species legislation.

Further, §17.84(c) is closely connected to a variety of interstate economic activities. Whether the impact of red wolf takings on any one of these activities qualifies as a substantial effect on interstate commerce is something we need not address. We have no doubt that the effect of the takings on these varied activities in combination qualifies as a substantial one. The first nexus between the challenged regulation and interstate commerce is tourism. The red wolves are part of a $29.2 billion national wildlife-related recreational industry that involves tourism and interstate travel. See *Heart of Atlanta Motel*, 379 U.S. at 256 (finding it is well-established that "[c]ommerce among the States . . . consists of intercourse and traffic between their citizens" (internal quotation marks omitted)). Many tourists travel to North Carolina from throughout the country for "howling events"—evenings of listening to wolf howls accompanied by educational programs. These howlings are a regular occurrence at the Alligator River National Wildlife Refuge. According to a study conducted by Dr. William E. Rosen of Cornell University, the recovery of the red wolf and increased visitor activities could result in a significant regional economic impact. See William E. Rosen, Red Wolf Recovery in Northeastern North Carolina and the Great Smoky Mountains National Park: Public Attitudes and Economic Impacts (unpublished, Joint Appendix at 633). Rosen estimates that northeastern North Carolina could see an increase of between $39.61 and $183.65 million per year in tourism-related activities, and that the Great Smoky Mountains National Park could see an increase of between $132.09 and $354.50 million per year. This is hardly a trivial impact on interstate commerce. Appellants understandably seek to criticize the Rosen study, but concede that the howling events attract interstate tourism and that red wolf program volunteers come from all around the country.

While there are no formal congressional findings that the ESA affects interstate commerce, such findings are neither necessary nor sufficient to sustain a statute or regulation. In *Lopez*, the Court said that "Congress normally is not required to make formal findings as to the substantial burdens that an activity has on interstate commerce." 514 U.S. at 562; see also Perez v. United States, 402 U.S. 146, 156 (1971) (particularized findings are not necessary for Congress to legislate). Further, in *Morrison*, the Court emphasized in the face of voluminous congressional findings that "the existence of congressional findings is not sufficient, by itself, to sustain the constitutionality of Commerce Clause legislation." 120 S. Ct. at 1752. In evaluating whether there is a rational basis for the promulgation of a statute or regulation under the commerce power, we often consider congressional committee findings. See *Lopez*, 514 U.S. at 562. Here, Congress has provided numerous sources of informal findings. Committee reports and legislative debates have emphasized the importance of endangered species to interstate commerce. We independently evaluate the constitutionality of this regulation, but we also take account of congressional judgment and the judgment of the agency designated to implement the statute.

Appellants argue that the tourism rationale relates only to howling events on national park land or wildlife refuges because people do not travel to private land. They reason that without tourism on private land the regulated activity does not substantially affect interstate commerce. Yet this argument misses the mark. Since reintroduction, red wolves have strayed from federal lands onto private lands. Indeed, wolves are known to be "great wanderers." See 60 Fed. Reg. 18,940, 18,943 (1995). In 1998, it was estimated that 41 of the 75 wolves in the wild now live on private land. Because so many members of this threatened species wander on private land, the regulation of takings on private land is essential to the entire program of reintroduction and eventual restoration of the species. Such regulation is necessary to conserve enough red wolves to sustain tourism. Appellants in fact seem unmindful of the history of endangered species regulation. The Endangered Species Acts of 1966 and 1969 initially targeted conservation efforts only on federal lands, but they met with limited success. See Note, Evolution of Wildlife Legislation in the United States: An Analysis of the Legal Efforts to Protect Endangered Species and the Prospects for the Future, 5 Geo. Int'l Envtl. L. Rev. 441, 449-53 (1993). The Endangered Species Act of 1973 was motivated in part by the need to extend takings regulation beyond the limited confines of federal land. See id. at 556. The prohibition of takings on private land was critical to the overall success of the ESA in halting and reversing the near extinction of numerous species. See 16 U.S.C. §1538(a)(1). The success of many commercial enterprises depends on some regulation of activity on private land, and interstate tourism is no exception.

Tourism, however, is not the only interstate commercial activity affected by the taking of red wolves. The regulation of red wolf takings is also closely connected to a second interstate market—scientific research. Scientific research generates jobs. It also deepens our knowledge of the world in which we live. The red wolf reintroduction program has already generated numerous scientific studies. For example, the red wolf is used as a model for other carnivore reintroductions. See Donald E. Moore III & Roland Smith, The Red Wolf as a Model for Carnivore Reintroductions, 62 Symp. Zool. Soc. Lond. 263 (1990). Scientists have also studied how the red wolf affects small mammal populations and how the wolves interact with the ecosystem as a whole. See, e.g., Bryan T. Kelly,

Alligator River National Wildlife Refuge Red Wolf (Canis Rufus) Scat Analysis: Preliminary Analyses of Mammalian Prey Consumed by Year, Season, Pack, Sex, and Age (April 1994) (unpublished, Joint Appendix at 942). By studying the effects of red wolves on the ecosystem, scientists learn about the interdependence of plants and animals, as well as how other threatened species may be reintroduced in the future. Scientific research can also reveal other uses for animals—for instance, approximately 50 percent of all modern medicines are derived from wild plants or animals. See Norman Myers, A Wealth of Wild Species: Storehouse for Human Welfare 4 (1983). Protection of the red wolves on private land thus encourages further research that may have inestimable future value, both for scientific knowledge as well as for commercial development of the red wolf.

The anti-taking regulation is also connected to a third market—the possibility of a renewed trade in fur pelts. Wolves have historically been hunted for their pelts. See Stanley P. Young & Edward A. Goldman, The Wolves of North America I, 165-70 (1964). Congress had the renewal of trade in mind when it enacted the ESA. The Senate Report noted that the protection of an endangered species "may permit the regeneration of that species to a level where controlled exploitation of that species can be resumed. In such a case businessmen may profit from the trading and marketing of that species for an indefinite number of years, where otherwise it would have been completely eliminated from commercial channels." S. Rep. No. 91-526, at 3 (1969), reprinted in 1969 U.S.C.C.A.N. 1413, 1415. The American alligator is a case in point. In 1975, the American alligator was nearing extinction and listed as endangered, but by 1987 conservation efforts restored the species. Now there is a vigorous trade in alligator hides. See Catharine L. Krieps, Sustainable Use of Endangered Species Under CITES: Is it a Sustainable Alternative?, 17 U. Pa. J. Int'l Econ. L. 461, 479-80 (1996) (explaining that many environmentalists are now encouraging the purchase of alligator products to create an incentive for protecting alligators and their habitats). Although alligator hides have more recently been a part of interstate commercial trade and red wolves were sold for their pelts primarily in the nineteenth century, this temporal difference is beside the point. It is not for the judiciary to move from species to species, opining that species A possesses great commercial potential, but species B does not. Assessing the relative scientific value and commercial impact of alligators and red wolves is for Congress and the FWS, informed as they are by biologists, economists, and others whose expertise is best delivered to the political branches, not the courts.

Finally, the taking of red wolves is connected to interstate markets for agricultural products and livestock. For instance, appellant landowners find red wolves a menace because they threaten livestock and other animals of economic: and commercial value. By restricting the taking of red wolves, §17.84(c) is said to impede economic development and commercial activities such as ranching and farming. This effect on commerce, however, still qualifies as a legitimate subject for regulation. It is well-settled under Commerce Clause cases that a regulation can involve the promotion or the restriction of commercial enterprises and development. Indeed, "[t]he motive and purpose of a regulation of interstate commerce are matters for the legislative judgment." United States v. Darby, 312 U.S. 100, 115 (1941). We recognize that "Congress can regulate interstate commerce for any lawful motive." United States v. Soderna, 82 F.3d 1370, 1374 (7th Cir. 1996). The regulation here targets takings that are economically motivated—farmers take wolves to protect valuable livestock and crops. It is for Congress, not the courts, to balance economic effects—namely whether the negative effects on interstate commerce from red wolf predation are outweighed by the benefits to commerce from a restoration of this species. To say that courts are ill-suited for this act of empirical and political judgment is an understatement. . . .

Section 17.84(c) aims to reverse threatened extinction and conserve the red wolf for both current and future use in interstate commerce. Congress is entitled to make the judgment that conservation is potentially valuable, even if that value cannot be presently ascertained. The Supreme Court has held that the congressional decision to maintain abandoned railroad track is reasonable "even if no future rail use for it is currently foreseeable." Preseault v. ICC, 494 U.S. 1, 19 (1990). The Court reasoned that "[g]iven the long tradition of congressional regulation of railroad abandonments, that is a judgment that Congress is entitled to make." Id. (citations omitted). Similarly, Congress has long been involved in the regulation of scarce and vital natural resources. The full payoff of conservation in the form of tourism, research, and trade may not be foreseeable. Yet it is reasonable for Congress to decide that conservation of species will one day produce a substantial commercial benefit to this country and that failure to preserve a species will result in permanent, though unascertainable, commercial loss. . . .

The protection of the red wolf on both federal and private land substantially affects interstate commerce through tourism, trade, scientific research, and other potential economic activities. To overturn this regulation would start courts down the road to second-guessing all kinds of legislative judgments. There is a "rational basis" as defined by *Lopez* for sustaining this regulation. We therefore hold that the anti-taking provision at issue here involves regulable economic and commercial activity as understood by current Commerce Clause jurisprudence.

B

This regulation is also sustainable as "an essential part of a larger regulation of economic activity, in which the regulatory scheme could be undercut unless the intrastate activity were regulated." *Lopez*, 514 U.S. at 561. The Supreme Court in Hodel v. Indiana stated: "A complex regulatory program . . . can survive a Commerce Clause challenge without a showing that every single facet of the program is independently and directly related to a valid congressional goal. It is enough that the challenged provisions are an integral part of the regulatory program and that the regulatory scheme when considered as a whole satisfies this test." 452 U.S. 314, 329 n. 17 (1981). . . .

Once a species has been designated as endangered, there are by definition only a few remaining animals. . . . It would be perverse indeed if a species nearing extinction were found to be beyond Congress's power to protect while abundant species were subject to full federal regulatory power. Yet under appellants' theory, the more endangered the species, the less authority Congress has to regulate the taking of it. According to this view, endangered species would lie beyond congressional protection because there are too few animals left to make a commercial difference. Such reasoning would eviscerate the comprehensive federal scheme for conserving endangered species and turn congressional judgment on its head. . . .

IV

A

It is imperative to set forth at the outset the historic roles of federal and state authority in this area. The regulated activity at issue here does not involve an "area of traditional state concern," one to which "States lay claim by right of history and expertise." *Lopez*, 514 U.S. at 580, 583 (Kennedy, J., concurring). . . .

In contrast to gender-motivated violence or guns in school yards, the conservation of scarce natural resources is an appropriate and well-recognized area of federal regulation. The federal government has been involved in a variety of conservation efforts since the beginning of this century. In 1900, Congress passed the Lacey Act, which provided penalties for the taking of wildlife in violation of state laws. See Act of May 25, 1900, ch. 553, 31 Stat. 187 (codified as amended 16 U.S.C. §701 (1994)). The Migratory Bird Treaty Act of 1918 forbade all takings of numerous bird species and explicitly preempted state laws. See 16 U.S.C. §§703-12. Furthermore, Congress has regulated wildlife on non-federal property through numerous statutes, including the Bald Eagle Protection Act of 1940, which prohibits, inter alia, the taking, possession, selling, or exporting of bald eagles or any of their parts. See 16 U.S.C. §§668-668d (1994). Similarly, the Marine Mammal Protection Act of 1972 regulates the taking of marine mammals and restricts the importing of marine mammals and their products through an elaborate system of permits. See 16 U.S.C. §§1361-1421h (1994 & Supp. III 1997). The Magnuson Fishery Conservation and Management Act of 1976 provides national standards for fishery conservation and management along with an elaborate system of enforcement. See 16 U.S.C. §§1801-83 (1994 & Supp. III 1997).

The Supreme Court has repeatedly upheld these statutes and the conservation efforts of Congress with regard to a variety of animal species. In Missouri v. Holland, the Court upheld the Migratory Bird Treaty Act as a necessary and proper means of executing Congress's treaty power. The conservation of endangered wildlife, Justice Holmes stated, was a "matter[] of the sharpest exigency for national well being." 252 U.S. 416, 432-33 (1920). In 1977, the Supreme Court held that Congress had the power under the Commerce Clause to grant federal fishing licenses for use in state waters, thereby preempting conflicting state laws. See Douglas v. Seacoast Products, Inc., 431 U.S. 265 (1977). Later in Andrus v. Allard, the Court emphasized that the "assumption that the national commerce power does not reach migratory wildlife is clearly flawed." 444 U.S. 51, 63 n. 19 (1979). . . .

D

. . . The rationale for this regulation thus stops far short of conferring upon Congress a broad police power. It is instead appellants' arguments for invalidating this regulation that go too far. If the federal government cannot regulate the taking of an endangered or threatened species on private land, its conservation and preservation efforts would be limited to only federal lands. A ruling to this effect would place in peril the entire federal regulatory scheme for wildlife and natural resource conservation.

LUTTIG, Circuit Judge, dissenting:

. . . The killing of even all 41 of the estimated red wolves that live on private property in North Carolina would not constitute an economic activity of the kind held by the Court in *Lopez* and in *Morrison* to be of central concern to the Commerce Clause, if it could be said to constitute an economic activity at all. *Morrison*, 120 S. Ct. at 1750 ("[A] fair reading *of Lopez* shows that the noneconomic, criminal nature of the conduct at issue was central to our decision in that case."). It is for this reason that the majority's attempted aggregation is impermissible: "While we need not adopt a categorical rule against aggregating the effects of any noneconomic activity in order to decide these cases, thus far in our Nation's history our cases have upheld Commerce Clause regulation of intrastate activity only where that activity is economic in nature." 120 S. Ct. at 1751 (citations omitted). But even assuming that such is an economic activity, it certainly is not an activity that has a substantial effect on interstate commerce. The number of inferences (not even to mention the amount of speculation) necessary to discern in this activity a substantial effect on interstate commerce is exponentially greater than the number necessary in *Lopez* to show a substantial effect on interstate commerce from the sale of guns near schools or in *Morrison* to show a substantial effect on interstate commerce from domestic assault. The number (and the speculation) is even greater than that necessary in Wickard v. Filburn, 317 U.S. 111 (1942). And, it bears reminding, the regulated activity in *Lopez* and *Wickard* at least was in some sense economic in character.

. . . I would invalidate this particular agency regulation under *Lopez*, *Morrison*, and *Brzonkala*, and instead recognize as the aberration that action of invalidation, rather than the opinions in *Lopez*, *Morrison*, and *Brzonkala*, as does the majority. Compare *Morrison*, 120 S. Ct. at 1773-74 (Souter, J., dissenting) (similarly to majority, characterizing *Lopez* and *Morrison*, and by implication *Brzonkala*, as aberrational vis-à-vis the sixty years of jurisprudence predating *Lopez* and predicting that *Lopez* and *Morrison* will not be "enduring law"); see also *Morrison*, 120 S. Ct. at 1777-78 (Breyer, J., dissenting) ("And even were I to accept *Lopez* as an accurate statement of the law, which I do not. . . ."). I would do so without any fear whatsoever that such "would place in peril the entire federal regulatory scheme for wildlife and natural resource conservation," ante at 504, as the majority over-rhetorically predicts would result from the invalidation of this lone regulation. No more so than in *Brzonkala* will "[m]aintaining the integrity of the enumerated powers" by invalidating this single regulation "mean that statutes will topple like falling dominos." *Brzonkala*, 169 F.3d at 897 (Wilkinson, J., concurring).

While it could be lost in a reading of the majority opinion, we do not address here Congress' power over either the channels or instrumentalities of interstate commerce. We do not address activity that is interstate in character. We do not address in this case a statute or a regulation with an express interstate commerce jurisdictional requirement, which would all but ensure constitutional validity. We do not have before us an activity that has obvious economic character and impact, such as is typically the case with non-wildlife natural resources, and even with other wildlife resources. We are not even presented with an activity as to which a plausible case of future economic character and impact can be made.

To the contrary, we are confronted here with an administrative agency regulation of an activity that implicates but a handful of animals, if even that, in one small region of one state. An activity that not only has no current economic character, but one that concededly has had no economic character for well over a century now. An activity that has no foreseeable economic character at all, except upon the baldest (though admittedly most humorous) of speculation that the red wolf pelt trade will once again emerge as a centerpiece of our Nation's economy. And, importantly, an activity that Congress could plainly regulate under its spending power and under its power over federal lands, regardless. . . .

Accordingly, I would faithfully apply in this case the Supreme Court's landmark decisions in *Lopez* and *Morrison,* as I would in any other case. The affirmative reach and the negative limits of the Commerce Clause do not wax and wane depending upon the subject matter of the particular legislation under challenge.

NOTES AND QUESTIONS

1. Why does the majority believe that the regulations challenged in this case regulate "economic activity"? Would the case have come out differently if the regulations had not been considered to regulate economic activity?

2. In justifying federal power to protect the red wolves, the court majority emphasizes that they "are part of a $29.2 billion national wildlife-related recreational industry that involves tourism and interstate travel," that they attract scientific researchers, and that their protection is essential if a pelt trade is ever to be revived. Does this imply that Congress has lesser power to protect a non-charismatic endangered species that does not attract tourists or researchers to cross state lines and that is of less obvious commercial value?

3. In his majority opinion, Chief Judge Wilkinson notes that the federal government has a long history of regulation of wildlife to protect migratory species. Thus, he rejects the argument that the Endangered Species Act impermissibly infringes on what has traditionally been a state function. The federal government does not have nearly as long a history of involvement in regulating pollution than it does in protecting wildlife. Does this mean that Congress has less power to regulate pollution than it has to protect endangered species?

4. Although the U.S. Supreme Court refused to review the *Gibbs* decision, constitutional challenges to federal authority to enforce the Endangered Species Act (ESA) have continued, and they continue to be unsuccessful. In March 2003 the U.S. Court of Appeals for the Fifth Circuit upheld the ESA's prohibition on taking endangered species as applied to six species of invertebrates found only in caves in two counties in Texas. The court concluded that most of the activities the ESA seeks to prohibit to protect species are commercial in nature, thus allowing Wickard v. Filburn cumulative effects aggregation for purposes of assessing how substantial an activity's effects on interstate commerce are. It explained that the "ESA is an economic regulatory scheme; the regulation of intrastate takes of the Cave Species is an essential part of it. Therefore, Cave Species takes may be aggregated with all other ESA takes" and "such aggregation substantially affects interstate commerce." GDF Realty Investments, Ltd. v. Norton, 326 F.3d 622, 640-641 (5th Cir. 2003). In a concurring opinion, Judge Dennis noted that the ESA is "a comprehensive program for the conservation of endangered and threatened species and the ecosystems upon which they depend." As a result, he concluded that "Congress has the authority to make

a rational determination to conserve such non-commercial, intrastate species as an essential or integral part of the comprehensive ESA program that regulates activities having a substantial impact on interstate commerce." 326 F.3d at 641 (Dennis, J., concurring).

5. In February 2004 the U.S. Court of Appeals for the Fifth Circuit denied rehearing en banc in GDF Realty v. Norton over the dissents of six judges. In a dissent from the denial of rehearing en banc, Judge Edith Jones argued: "For the sake of species of 1/8-inch-long cave bugs, which lack any known value in commerce, much less interstate commerce, the panel crafted a constitutionally limitless theory of federal protection." Distinguishing Gibbs v. Babbitt (see page 886), the dissent argued that "many ESA-prohibited takings of endangered species may be regulated, and even aggregated, under *Lopez* and *Morrison* because they involve commercial or commercially-related activities like hunting, tourism and scientific research." But the dissent maintained that "there is no link . . . between Cave Species takes and any sort of commerce, whether tourism, scientific research, or agricultural markets."

6. In April 2003 the D.C. Circuit rejected a developer's challenge to the constitutionality of the ESA's protection of the arroyo southwestern toad, holding that the case was governed by the Delhi Sands Flower-Loving Fly case (NAHB v. Babbitt, pages 877-885). The court rejected the developer's argument that Morrison v. United States (see page 113) had undermined NAHB v. Babbitt. The court stated that the regulated activity for purposes of Commerce Clause analysis was the developer's planned commercial housing development, rather than the toad, and that the ESA was designed in large part to preserve the commercial benefits of biodiversity. Rancho Viejo, LLC, v. Norton, 323 F.3d 1062 (D.C. Cir. 2003). In a concurring opinion, Chief Judge Douglas Ginsburg sought to qualify the court's holding by questioning whether a lone hiker could be prohibited from taking an endangered species in a non-commercial context. "Our rationale is that, with respect to a species that is not an article in interstate commerce and does not affect interstate commerce, a take can be regulated if—but only if—the take itself substantially affects interstate commerce. Just as important, however, the lone hiker in the woods, or the homeowner who moves dirt in order to landscape his property, though he takes the toad, does not affect interstate commerce." 323 F.3d at 1080 (Ginsburg, C.J., concurring).

7. In July 2003, the D.C. Circuit denied a rehearing en banc in the *Rancho Viejo* case over the dissents of two of the nine judges. 334 F.3d 1158. Judge David Sentelle argued in dissent that "protecting a toad from a land owner pinning a fence on its own property" is not the kind of commercial activity that could be regulated under Congress's power to regulate interstate commerce. Then-Judge and now Chief Justice John Roberts also dissented. He argued that by focusing on "whether the challenged regulation substantially affects interstate commerce, rather than whether the activity being regulated does so," the panel had adopted a rationale inconsistent with that employed by the Fifth Circuit in the *GDF Realty* case. "The panel's approach in this case leads to the result that regulating the taking of a hapless toad that, for reasons of its own, lives its entire life in California constitutes regulating 'Commerce . . . among the several States.' " While conceding that the panel's decision was consistent with National Association of Home Builders v. Babbitt, 130 F.3d 1041 (D.C. Cir. 1997) (see page 877), he argued that it was inconsistent with the rationale of GDF Realty and that en banc review "would also afford the opportunity to consider

alternative grounds for sustaining application of the Act that may be more consistent with Supreme Court precedent."

8. During Senate confirmation hearings on his nomination to be Chief Justice on September 13, 1995, Judge John Roberts emphasized that in the *Rancho Viejo* case he had not joined Judge Sentelle's dissent questioning the constitutionality of the Endangered Species Act. Roberts explained that his "opinion did not conclude that there was no authority under the commerce clause" to protect the endangered toad and that he had wanted *Rancho Viejo* reheard en banc in order to explore "other ways of sustaining this act that don't implicate the concern that has caused the [Fifth Circuit in *GDF Realty*] to question our approach." When GDF Realty sought Supreme Court review of the Fifth Circuit's decision, the Court held the petition for review in abeyance pending its decision in Gonzales v. Raich, a case challenging federal power to prohibit the cultivation and use of marijuana in states that have authorized its use for medical purposes.

9. In June 2005, the Supreme Court decided Gonzales v. Raich, 125 S. Ct. 2195 (2005). The Court upheld federal authority to prohibit the cultivation and use of marijuana for medical purposes. In an opinion by Justice Stevens that was joined by four other Justices, the Court held that Congress had a rational basis for concluding that the personal cultivation and use of marijuana would substantially affect interstate commerce because failure to regulate intrastate cultivation and use would leave a gaping hole in the comprehensive federal scheme for regulating illicit drugs. The Court majority emphasized that Congress clearly acted rationally in deciding that regulation of intrastate cultivation and use of marijuana was an essential part of the larger regulatory scheme. Justice Scalia, who did not join the majority opinion, filed a separate opinion concurring in the judgment. Scalia argued that Congress's authority to regulate intrastate activities that substantially affect interstate commerce derives from the Necessary and Proper Clause. "Where necessary to make a regulation of interstate commerce effective, Congress may regulate even those intrastate activities that do not themselves substantially affect interstate commerce," Scalia stated.

One week after it decided Gonzales v. Raich, the Supreme Court denied review in the *GDF Realty* case, which it had held pending its decision concerning federal authority to prohibit cultivation and use of medical marijuana. This may indicate that the Court believes that there is no constitutional problem with applying the Endangered Species Act to species who are so endangered that their destruction would not itself substantially affect interstate commerce because, like intrastate use of marijuana, regulation is necessary to effectuate a broader regulatory scheme. 125 S. Ct. 2898 (2005).

D. WHICH SPECIES ARE PROTECTED: SECTION 4

As TVA v. Hill makes clear, the Endangered Species Act provides potentially powerful protections. These protections, however, extend only to species that have been *listed* as "endangered" or "threatened" by the Secretary of the Interior (or, for certain marine species, the Secretary of Commerce). The determination to list a species, governed by section 4, is thus the key to the entire statute.

TVA v. Hill also clearly illustrates that the determination to list a species also carries potentially enormous consequences. In the wake of the Supreme

Court's decision, Congress amended the Act in 1978, imposing elaborate procedures and strict deadlines on the Secretary's listing determinations. See generally M. Bean, The Evolution of National Wildlife Law 334-341 (2d ed. 1983). These new requirements paralyzed the listing process. Published listing proposals for approximately 2,000 species were withdrawn because the Secretary could not meet the new deadlines. Id. at 335. Then, in 1981, OMB insisted that every listing proposal be subject to a "regulatory impact analysis" to assess its economic implications. Listings ceased almost entirely. In the first year of the Reagan administration, only two species made it through the process and onto the endangered species list: an orchid in Texas and the Hay Springs amphipod, a crustacean found only in the National Zoo in Washington, D.C.

In 1982, Congress moved to resurrect the listing process. It streamlined section 4, stripping away procedural requirements that it had added four years before and narrowing the Secretary's discretion. These new provisions were intended to ensure that listing decisions are based solely on scientific evidence concerning species' prospects for survival, to the exclusion of all other factors.

Listing decisions are enormously important because they trigger the requirement to designate critical habitat, and they are necessary to afford listed species the protections against federal actions that jeopardize them, and against private or public actions that "take" them. Fearful of the potential economic consequences of these protections, the Secretaries of Interior (responsible for listing terrestrial and freshwater species) and of Commerce (responsible for listing marine species) made listing decisions only with great reluctance. After enactment of the 1982 amendments, the pace of listings improved somewhat, but by 1988 nearly 1,000 species found to be eligible for listing were awaiting approval, more than 3,000 other species remained candidates for listing, while only about 50 species per year actually were being listed. Houck, The Endangered Species Act and its Implementation by the U.S. Departments of Interior and Commerce, 64 U. Colo. L. Rev. 277, 284-285 (1993).

Two strategies for avoiding listings were to determine that listing is "warranted but precluded" by the press of other listing proposals, or to conclude that other efforts to minimize harm to a species were likely to prevent extinction. For example, in 1988 the Fish and Wildlife Service denied petitions to list the northern spotted owl even though it found that "substantial data were available to indicate that the petitioned action may be warranted." Unlike the snail darter whose only habitat was thought to be in the vicinity of the Tellico Dam, the northern spotted owl roams over wide areas of old-growth forest. Scientists estimated that 1,000 acres of old-growth forest might be necessary to sustain one pair of such owls. Thus, the Fish and Wildlife Service was well aware that a listing decision could necessitate designating millions of acres of old-growth forest as critical habitat for the owl. Faced with potentially enormous economic consequences for the timber industry, the Service declined to add the owl to the endangered species list. This decision was overturned in Northern Spotted Owl v. Model, 716 F. Supp. 479 (W.D. Wash. 1988), which held that the decision not to list the northern spotted owl was arbitrary and capricious and contrary to law. The court noted that the Fish and Wildlife Service's documents did not contain any expert analysis supporting the decision not to list and that "the expert opinion is entirely to the contrary." This decision ultimately resulted in the owl being declared a threatened species, creating a major controversy in the Pacific Northwest.

The *Northern Spotted Owl* case is only one of several holding that the Fish and Wildlife Service (FWS) or the National Marine Fisheries Service (NMFS) have improperly declined to list a species as threatened or endangered. In Oregon Natural Resources Council v. Daley, 6 F. Supp. 2d 1139 (D. Or. 1998), a court rejected a decision by the NMFS not to list the Oregon coast coho salmon as threatened. The court rejected the notion that the state's pledge of voluntary future conservation efforts should be considered in the listing decision as well as the rationale that a two-year time horizon was adequate for projecting the future fate of the fish. In Defenders of Wildlife v. Norton, 258 F.3d 1136 (9th Cir. 2001), the Ninth Circuit upheld a challenge to the Secretary of Interior's decision not to designate the flat-tailed horned lizard as a threatened species. The court rejected the government's argument that the threat of extinction of the species on private land did not warrant a listing because the species could survive on public land if protected through a voluntary conservation agreement. The court interpreted the statutory trigger for listing to mean that "a species can be extinct 'throughout . . . a significant portion of its range' if there are major geographical areas in which it is no longer viable but once was." Thus, it concluded that the Secretary of Interior "must at least explain her conclusion that the area in which the species can no longer live [on private land] is not a 'significant portion of its range.'" Quoting Aldo Leopold's Sand County Almanac, the court observed that "[t]he text of the ESA and its subsequent application seems to have been guided by the following maxim: 'There seems to be a tacit assumption that if grizzlies survive in Canada and Alaska, that is good enough. It is not good enough for me. . . . Relegating grizzlies to Alaska is about like relegating happiness to heaven; one may never get there.'" Aldo Leopold, A Sand County Almanac 277 (1966). 258 F.3d at 1145 n.10. The court also concluded that the Secretary had improperly relied upon a conservation agreement whose benefits were unclear in determining that the species was not threatened. Compare Selkirk Conservation Alliance v. Forsgren, 336 F.3d 944 (9th Cir. 2003) (holding that it was proper for the Fish and Wildlife Service to rely on an agreement with a private timber company as the grounds for making a finding of "no jeopardy" with respect to grizzly bears).

As of April 2006, there were 1,869 listed species. Of these, 1,121 were animal species (923 of these were listed as endangered and 198 as threatened) and 748 were plants (600 of these were listed as endangered and 148 as threatened). A total of 1,300 listed species were found in the United States (including 555 animals and 745 plants). States with the most listed species included Hawaii (317), California (308), Alabama (117), and Florida (112). See Figure 9.2.

Section 4 requires that when the Secretary lists a species as endangered or threatened, he or she must also designate the species' "critical habitat," to the extent that the critical habitat can be determined, and designation is prudent. These provisions were intended to ensure that listing decisions were not held up by uncertainty about critical habitat. They also provide enforceable standards. Indeed, when the FWS ultimately decided to list the northern spotted owl as "threatened," but declined to designate critical habitat, claiming inadequate information, the court held that critical habitat designation may be deferred only in "extraordinary circumstances," and ordered the Secretary to propose a

FIGURE 9.2

Listed Species Range by State/Territory as of Fri Apr 7 01:00:07 MDT 2006

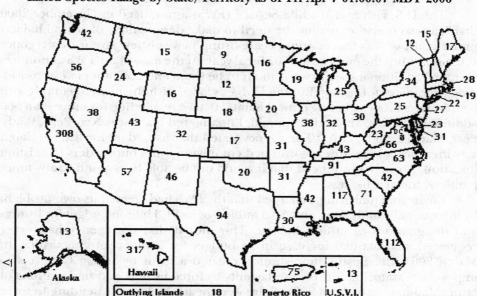

designation within 60 days. Northern Spotted Owl v. Lujan, 758 F. Supp. 621 (W.D. Wash. 1991). In 1992, the Secretary designated nearly 7 million acres in 190 areas as critical habitat for the owl. Since then there has been a virtual moratorium on designation of critical habitat. Only a few marine animals have had critical habitat designated since 1992. As a result, critical habitat designations have not been made for nearly 90 percent of all listed species. Wiygul & Weiner, Critical Habitat Destruction, 16 Envtl. Forum, May/June 1999 at 13. In May 2003, Interior Secretary Gale Norton announced that the Bush administration was suspending designation of critical habitat for endangered species. The administration is proposing that Congress remove the ESA's requirement for designating critical habitat and replace it with a new process. In the 2004 National Defense Authorization bill, Pub. L. 108-136, 117 Stat. 1392, Congress exempted land on military installations from designation as critical habitat if the Secretary of Interior determines that the military has prepared an integrated natural resources plan that benefits the species for which critical habitat otherwise would have been designated.

Decisions not to designate critical habitat have come under fire in the courts. In Conservation Council for Hawaii v. Babbitt, 2 F. Supp. 2d 1280 (D. Haw. 1998), a court rejected the Fish and Wildlife Service's rationale for declining to designate critical habitat for 245 plant species. The FWS had argued that a critical habitat designation would increase threats posed to the plants by collectors and would have little benefit because the plants were found mostly on private, rather than federal, lands. After another court rejected the conclusion that critical habitat should not be designated for the endangered cactus ferruginous pygmy owl because it would increase threats from bird-watchers, more than 730,000 acres were designated as critical habitat for the species in Arizona. 63 Fed. Reg. 71820 (1998).

Species Listing Determinations: Resource Constraints

The U.S. Fish and Wildlife Service (FWS) announced in November 2000 that it was so overwhelmed by the need to make designations of critical habitat under court orders that it would cease listing new species, save for emergency situations, until the end of the 2001 fiscal year. At the time of the FWS announcement, 39 additional species were about to be listed and 236 others were considered candidates for listing. But the FWS was faced with the need to comply with court orders for designating critical habitat that were pending for more than 300 additional species. Michael Grunwald, Endangered List Faces New Peril, Wash. Post, Mar. 12, 2001, at A1. The agency stated that its budget for listing-related activities was being entirely consumed complying with court orders in existing litigation. Thus, it announced that it would not be able to respond to any more petitions for new listings.

Environmental groups charged that the FWS had created its own problem by intentionally budgeting only $6.3 million of its $1.3 billion budget for listings and designations of critical habitat. They noted that the agency had never requested a substantial increase in its budget for listing-related activities. In March 2001, the Bush administration created a furor by asking Congress to impose a moratorium on private lawsuits to force listings and designations of critical habitat. As of April 2001, there were nearly 80 lawsuits pending to force species listing, and notices of intent to sue had been served in 95 additional cases. The Species Litigation Act, Wall St. J., April 20, 2001, at A14. While Congress rejected the proposed moratorium, former Secretary of Interior Bruce Babbitt supported the Bush administration's claim that the listing process had placed impossible demands on federal agencies.

On August 28, 2001, the FWS reached agreement with three environmental organizations to expedite the listing of 29 endangered species most in need of immediate protection in return for deferring by six months the designation of critical habitat for species already listed. By deferring the deadlines for critical habitat designations that were the products of prior lawsuits, the settlement freed up $600,000 that the FWS agreed to redirect to expedite the listing decisions. Center for Biological Diversity, Historic Agreement Reached to Protect 29 Imperiled Species from Coast to Coast, *www.biologicaldiversity.org/swcbd/activist/ESA/settlement.html.* While this agreement was hailed as a breakthrough, see, e.g., A Victory for Endangered Species, N.Y. Times, Sept. 3, 2001; the basic problem of insufficient resources for species listing and critical habitat designation remains. FWS estimates that it will need at least $120 million simply to process the current backlog it faces.

To help protect species that are candidates for listing, but for which the government lacks resources to pursue a listing at present, the concept of Candidate Conservation Agreements (CCAs) has been established. These are formal agreements between the Fish and Wildlife Service and those who make a voluntary commitment to actions that will remove or reduce the threats facing a candidate species. Most of these agreements have been reached with other federal agencies, state or local units of government, or conservation organizations. If they are successful in reducing the threat faced by the species, a listing decision may be avoided. The use of Candidate Conservation Agreements with Assurances is a means of providing nonfederal landowners with a commitment that the government will not impose additional restrictions on the development of the property over and above those the landowner voluntarily agrees to undertake as part of the CCA.

PROTECTION OF BIODIVERSITY: A PATHFINDER

The Endangered Species Act (ESA) is codified at 16 U.S.C. §§1531-1544. It is administered by the Secretaries of Interior, whose Fish and Wildlife Service (FWS) has responsibility for protecting endangered plants, fish and wildlife, and the Secretary of Commerce, whose National Marine Fisheries Service (NMFS) has the responsibility for protecting marine life. These two agencies have jointly promulgated regulations to govern implementation of the Act; they appear at 50 C.F.R. pt. 402. The official list of endangered and threatened species can be found in 50 C.F.R. pt. 17.

The U.S. Fish and Wildlife Service maintains an endangered species webpage, which is located at *http://endangered.fws.gov/index.html*. This page contains a list of the species on the endangered species list, maps of their locations, news concerning biodiversity protection, information about the operation of the ESA and agencies' policies for promoting biodiversity, and detailed statistics concerning listed species and their status. The FWS and NMFS have jointly published an Endangered Species Habitat Conservation Planning Handbook (1996) which provides landowners with guidance concerning application of the ESA and how to develop habitat conservation plans to qualify for incidental take permits under §10 of the ESA.

The most definitive treatise on the ESA and other wildlife protection statutes is Michael Bean's The Evolution of National Wildlife Law (3d ed. 1997), published by Praeger. Among the best scientific introductions to the biodiversity protection issues are E.O. Wilson's Biodiversity (1986), published by National Academy Press, and the Diversity of Life (1992), published by Harvard University Press. Current biodiversity scholarship is contained in the journals Conservation Biology and BioScience.

E.   REVIEW OF FEDERAL ACTIONS: SECTION 7

The most important protection accorded endangered and threatened species is contained in section 7, the provision made famous by TVA v. Hill. As that case explained, section 7 provides for review of all federal actions that may affect endangered species and section 7(a)(2) prohibits those actions that are found to "jeopardize" the existence of any such species. These include not only activities undertaken directly by federal agencies, but also nonfederal actions that involve federal authorization or assistance, such as activities that require federal permits, are funded by federal agencies, or are undertaken by private parties on public lands. Section 7(a)(1) directs agencies to use their authorities to further the purposes of ESA by carrying out affirmative programs to conserve listed species. The following case explains the "consultation" process that section 7 establishes and the authorities that section provides.

Thomas v. Peterson
753 F.2d 754 (9th Cir. 1985)

Before WRIGHT, SNEED, and ALARCON, Circuit Judges. SNEED, Circuit Judge:

Plaintiffs sought to enjoin construction of a timber road in a former National Forest roadless area. The District Court granted summary judgment in favor of defendant R. Max Peterson, Chief of the Forest Service, and plaintiffs appealed. We affirm in part, reverse in part, and remand for further proceedings consistent with this opinion. . . .

THE ENDANGERED SPECIES ACT CLAIM

The plaintiffs' third claim concerns the Forest Service's alleged failure to comply with the Endangered Species Act (ESA) in considering the effects of the road and timber sales on the endangered Rocky Mountain Gray Wolf.

The ESA contains both substantive and procedural provisions. Substantively, the Act prohibits the taking or importation of endangered species, see 16 U.S.C. §1538, and requires federal agencies to ensure that their actions are not "likely to jeopardize the continued existence of any endangered species or threatened species or result in the destruction or adverse modification" of critical habitat of such species, see 16 U.S.C. §1536(a)(2).

The Act prescribes a three-step process to ensure compliance with its substantive provisions by federal agencies. Each of the first two steps serves a screening function to determine if the successive steps are required. The steps are:

> (1) An agency proposing to take an action must inquire of the Fish & Wildlife Service (F & WS) whether any threatened or endangered species "may be present" in the area of the proposed action. See 16 U.S.C. §1536(c)(1).
> (2) If the answer is affirmative, the agency must prepare a "biological assessment" to determine whether such species "is likely to be affected" by the action. Id. The biological assessment may be part of an environmental impact statement or environmental assessment. Id.
> (3) If the assessment determines that a threatened or endangered species "is likely to be affected," the agency must formally consult with the F & WS. Id. §1536(a)(2). The formal consultation results in a "biological opinion" issued by the F & WS. See id. §1536(b). If the biological opinion concludes that the proposed action would jeopardize the species or destroy or adversely modify critical habitat, see id. §1536(a)(2), then the action may not go forward unless the F & WS can suggest an alternative that avoids such jeopardization, destruction, or adverse modification. Id. §1536(b)(3)(A). If the opinion concludes that the action will not violate the Act, the F & WS may still require measures to minimize its impact. Id. §1536(b)(4)(ii)-(iii).

Plaintiffs first allege that, with respect to the Jersey Jack road, the Forest Service did not undertake step (1), a formal request to the F & WS. The district court found that to be the case, but concluded that the procedural violation was insignificant because the Forest Service was already aware that wolves may be present in the area. The court therefore refused to enjoin the construction of the road. Plaintiffs insist, based on TVA v. Hill, 437 U.S. 153 (1978), that an injunction is mandatory once any ESA violation is found. Defendants respond, citing Village of False Pass v. Clark, 733 F.2d 605 (9th Cir. 1984), that *TVA* applies only to substantive violations of the ESA, and that a court has discretion to deny an injunction when it finds a procedural violation to be de minimis.

We need not reach this issue. The Forest Service's failure goes beyond the technical violation cited by the district court, and is not de minimis.

Once an agency is aware that an endangered species may be present in the area of its proposed action, the ESA requires it to prepare a biological assessment to determine whether the proposed action "is likely to affect" the species and therefore requires formal consultation with the F & WS. See supra. The Forest Service did not prepare such an assessment prior to its decision to build the Jersey Jack road. Without a biological assessment, it cannot be determined whether the proposed project will result in a violation of the ESA's substantive provisions. A failure to prepare a biological assessment for a project in an area in which it has been determined that an endangered species may be present cannot be considered a de minimis violation of the ESA.

The district court found that the Forest Service had "undertaken sufficient study and action to further the purposes of the ESA," Memorandum Decision at 1149, E.R. 103. Its finding was based on affidavits submitted by the Forest Service for the litigation. See Memorandum Decision at 1148, E.R. 99. These do not constitute a substitute for the preparation of the biological assessment required by the ESA.

. . . The procedural requirements of the ESA are analogous to those of NEPA: under NEPA, agencies are required to evaluate the environmental impact of federal projects "significantly affecting the quality of the human environment," 42 U.S.C. §4332(2)(C); under the ESA, agencies are required to assess the effect on endangered species of projects in areas where such species may be present. 16 U.S.C. §1536(c). A failure to prepare a biological assessment is comparable to a failure to prepare an environmental impact statement. . . .

The Forest Service argues that the procedural requirements of the ESA should be enforced less stringently than those of NEPA because, unlike NEPA, the ESA also contains substantive provisions. We acknowledge that the ESA's substantive provisions distinguish it from NEPA, but the distinction acts the other way. If anything, the strict substantive provisions of the ESA justify *more* stringent enforcement of its procedural requirements, because the procedural requirements are designed to ensure compliance with the substantive provisions. The ESA's procedural requirements call for a systematic determination of the effects of a federal project on endangered species. If a project is allowed to proceed without substantial compliance with those procedural requirements, there can be no assurance that a violation of the ESA's substantive provisions will not result. The latter, of course, is impermissible. See TVA v. Hill, 437 U.S. 153.

The district court, citing Palila v. Hawaii Dept. of Land and Natural Resources, 639 F.2d 495 (9th Cir. 1981), held that "[a] party asserting a violation of the Endangered Species Act has the burden of showing the proposed action would have some prohibited effect on an endangered species or its critical habitat," and found that the plaintiffs in this case had not met that burden. Memorandum Decision at 1149, E.R. 102. This is a misapplication of *Palila.* That case concerned the ESA's prohibition of the "taking" of an endangered species,

16 U.S.C. §1538(a)(1)(B), not the ESA's procedural requirements. Quite naturally, the court in *Palila* found that a plaintiff, in order to establish a violation of the "taking" provision, must show that such a "taking" has occurred. See 639 F.2d at 497. The holding does not apply to violations of the ESA's procedural requirements. A plaintiff's burden in establishing a procedural violation is to show that the circumstances triggering the procedural requirement exist, and that the required procedures have not been followed. The plaintiffs in this case have clearly met that burden.

. . . Congress has assigned to the agencies and to the Fish & Wildlife Service the responsibility for evaluation of the impact of agency actions on endangered species, and has prescribed procedures for such evaluation. Only by following the procedures can proper evaluation be made. It is not the responsibility of the plaintiffs to prove, nor the function of the courts to judge, the effect of a proposed action on an endangered species when proper procedures have not been followed. Cf. City of Davis v. Coleman, 521 F.2d 661, 667 (9th Cir. 1975) (under NEPA, agency, not plaintiff, is responsible for investigating the environmental effects of a proposed action).

We therefore hold that the district court erred in declining to enjoin construction of the Jersey Jack road pending compliance with the ESA.

Affirmed in part, reversed in part, and remanded.

NOTES AND QUESTIONS

1. The ESA imposes a graduated review requirement somewhat reminiscent of NEPA's hierarchy of categorical exclusion, environmental assessment, and environmental impact statement. Recall that under NEPA, the proponent of an action makes each determination about what review NEPA requires. How is ESA different? How are the key determinations made? Who finally determines whether an action may go forward?

2. The Secretary of Interior, who is responsible for protecting freshwater and terrestrial species, has delegated his responsibilities under ESA to FWS. The Secretary of Commerce, who is responsible for protecting most marine species, has delegated his responsibilities under ESA to the National Marine Fisheries Service (NMFS).

3. A study of the consultation process by the World Wildlife Fund found that nearly 100,000 section 7 consultations were undertaken between the FWS and other federal agencies during a five-year period. Approximately 95,000 of these were rapid, informal consultations, many of which occurred by telephone, and resulted in no delay or modification of a project. A total of 2,719 formal consultations occurred with 2,367 (87 percent) resulting in "no jeopardy" opinions. Only 352 "jeopardy" opinions were issued, and more than one-third of these involved only two proposed projects. Only 54 projects were terminated during the five-year period. Thus, only 0.3 percent of all consultations resulted in jeopardy opinions, and the vast majority of these projects were able to proceed after adopting "reasonable and prudent" alternatives identified by FWS in its opinion. World Wildlife Fund, Talk Is Cheaper Than We Think: The Consultation Process Under the Endangered Species Act (1994).

4. After reviewing many of the jeopardy findings, Oliver Houck concludes that "the great majority of them allowed projects to go forward with only

minimal harm-avoiding conditions, such as 'don't dredge while the eagles are nesting,' speed limit signs in manatee waters, and a wider median strip in a federal highway routed through wolf habitat to enable wolves to pause safely while crossing." Houck, Reflections on the Endangered Species Act, 25 Envtl. L. Rep. 689, 692 (1995). Describing a variety of strategies employed by the Department of Interior to avoid jeopardy findings, Professor Houck concludes that the agency is "doing everything possible within law, and beyond, to limit the effect of protection under section 7(a)(2)." Houck, The Endangered Species Act and Its Implementation by the U.S. Departments of Interior and Commerce, 64 U. Colo. L. Rev. 277, 326 (1993).

5. A dramatic decline in the stocks of salmon in the Pacific Northwest has resulted in the addition of several salmon species to the endangered species list. As a result, federal and state agencies in the area have struggled to develop plans for protecting the salmon. In Pacific Rivers Council v. Thomas, 30 F.3d 1050 (9th Cir. 1994), the Ninth Circuit required a district court to enjoin all federal logging, grazing, and road construction projects in two national forests pending consultations between the Forest Service and NMFS concerning efforts to protect the Snake River Salmon. The intersection of section 7's consultation requirements and the high degree of federal involvement in resource management in the Pacific Northwest has had profound consequences because it has subjected many policies to systematic biological scrutiny for the first time, including fish hatchery practices, harvest management, and habitat management. This has created the "prospect of designing a restoration program that would address all major sources of salmon mortality, including public land and water use decisionmaking, not just hydropower." Michael C. Blumm & Greg D. Corbin, Salmon and the Endangered Species Act: Lessons from the Columbia Basin, 74 Wash. L. Rev. 519, 589 (1999). Based on their review of the consequences of the salmon listings in the Pacific Northwest, Blumm and Corbin conclude that "contrary to some claims, the effect of ESA consultation is hardly draconian, and in fact is quite sensitive to economic considerations." Id. at 549. They note that the absence of a statutory definition of jeopardy has enabled the NMFS to accept "fairly modest probabilities for species recovery" and that key measures to protect salmon provided in NMFS's biological opinions (such as a reservoir drawdown) have not been implemented because of concern over their economic impact. Id. at 593-597. Federal officials are continuing to develop plans for protecting the endangered salmon.

6. In April 2001, a decision to stop the flow of federal irrigation water in California's Klamath River Basin to protect endangered salmon and suckerfish spawned harsh protests by farmers and ranchers who forceably reopened the irrigation canal. After a new and highly controversial biological opinion was issued by the National Marine Fisheries Service, the Bush administration ordered the irrigation flows restored. In September 2002, 33,000 wild salmon suddenly died in a massive fish kill in the Klamath River. While federal officials deemed the cause of the fish kill a mystery, scientists from the Califonia Department of Fish and Game released a report in January 2003 that attributed the fish kill to the federal diversions of water for irrigation.

7. The determination whether an action is likely to "jeopardize" a listed species must be based on "the best scientific and commercial data available." What is the "best . . . available"? That is the issue in the next case.

Roosevelt Campobello International Park Commission v. EPA
684 F.2d 1041 (1st Cir. 1982)

COFFIN, Chief Judge.

Pittston proposes to construct an oil refinery and marine terminal in Eastport, Maine, a relatively pristine area of great natural beauty near the Canadian border. The area is known for being the foggiest on the East Coast, experiencing some 750-1,000 hours of fog a year; daily tides approximate 20 feet. The plan contemplates that crude oil shipments will arrive several times a week in supertankers, or Very Large Crude Carriers (VLCCs), as long as four football fields, or slightly less than a quarter of a mile. The tankers will travel through Canadian waters around the northern tip of Campobello Island, where the Roosevelt Campobello International Park is located, see 16 U.S.C. §1101 et seq., down Head Harbor Passage to a refinery near Eastport where they will be turned and berthed. Numerous barges and small tankers will carry the refined product from Eastport to destination markets in the Northeast.

The protracted procedural history of this case begins in April 1973, when Pittston applied to the Maine Board of Environmental Protection (BEP) for permission to locate the refinery in Eastport. After public hearings, the BEP approved the proposal under the Maine Site Location of Development Law, 38 M.R.S.A. §481 et seq., subject to a number of pre-construction and pre-operation conditions designed primarily to reduce the risk of oil spills. Pittston subsequently filed an application with EPA to obtain an NPDES permit, and submitted an Environmental Assessment Report to aid EPA in its duty to prepare an Environmental Impact Statement (EIS) pursuant to NEPA. EPA promulgated a draft EIS recommending issuance of the permit as conditioned by the Maine BEP, held a joint public hearing with the Army Corps of Engineers in Eastport, and received approximately 600 responses during a public comment period. In September 1977, the Maine Department of Environmental Protection certified, under §401(a)(1) of the Clean Water Act, 33 U.S.C. §1341(a)(1), that the proposed discharge would satisfy the appropriate requirements of state and federal law. In June 1978, the final EIS was issued, again recommending that the permit be issued pursuant to the BEP conditions.

Several months later, the National Marine Fisheries Service (NMFS) of the Department of Commerce and the Fish and Wildlife Service (FWS) of the Department of Interior initiated consultations with EPA concerning the proposed refinery's impact on endangered species—the right and humpback whales, and the northern bald eagle, respectively—under §7 of the Endangered Species Act (ESA), 16 U.S.C. §1536. In November, the NMFS issued a threshold determination that there were insufficient data to conclude that the project was not likely to jeopardize the continued existence of the endangered whales. In December, the FWS concluded that the project was likely to jeopardize the bald eagle. In light of these opinions and of the value of the natural resources in the Eastport area as noted in the EIS, EPA's Region I issued a notice of determination to deny Pittston's application for an NPDES permit in January 1979. Pittston thereafter sought an adjudicatory hearing and administrative review of this decision. . . .

The adjudicatory hearing took place over five weeks in January and February of 1980. More than fifty witnesses testified and were cross-examined; several hundred exhibits were introduced. In January 1981, the ALJ

[Administrative Law Judge] rendered EPA's Initial Decision, overturning EPA Region I and ordering that the NPDES permit issue. He concluded that the EIS was adequate to comply with NEPA, and that no supplemental EIS was necessary; that the risk of oil spills was "minute" and that the refinery was therefore not likely to jeopardize any endangered species; and that the conditions imposed by the Maine BEP, and assumed by the EIS, were not required to be conditions of the federal permit. Petitioners subsequently sought review before the EPA Administrator, and also moved to reopen the record to admit a recent study showing an increased number of endangered whales in the Eastport region. Both motions were denied, and in September 1981 EPA Region I issued the NPDES permit to the Pittston Company. Petitioners now seek review in this court pursuant to §509(b)(1)(F) of the Clean Water Act, 33 U.S.C. . . .

The obligation imposed on EPA by section 7(a)(2) of the ESA, 16 U.S.C. §1536(a)(2) is to "insure that any action authorized, funded, or carried out . . . is not likely to jeopardize the continued existence of any endangered species." An action would "jeopardize" the species if it "reasonably would be expected to reduce the reproduction, numbers, or distribution of a listed species to such an extent as to appreciably reduce the likelihood of the survival and recovery of that species in the wild." 50 C.F.R. §404.02 (1980). . . .

An agency's duty to consult with the Secretary of Commerce or Interior, depending on the particular endangered species, does not divest it of discretion to make a final decision that "it has taken all necessary action to insure that its actions will not jeopardize the continued existence of an endangered species." National Wildlife Federation v. Coleman, 529 F.2d 359, 371 (5th Cir. 1976). The consultation process, however, is not merely a procedural requirement. Not only is a biological opinion required of the Secretary of Commerce or Interior, "detailing how the agency action affects the species or its critical habitat," 16 U.S.C. §1536(b), but the 1979 Amendments to ESA require that in fulfilling its consultation duty and in insuring the absence of likelihood of jeopardy "each agency shall use the best scientific and commercial data available." 16 U.S.C. §1536(a)(2). Moreover, the legislative history emphasizes that "[c]ourts have given substantial weight to these biological opinions as evidence of an agency's compliance" with the Act, that "[t]he Amendment would not alter this state of the law or lessen in any way an agency's obligation" under §7, and that a federal agency which "proceeds with [an] action in the face of inadequate knowledge or information . . . does so with the risk that it has not satisfied the standard of" §7(a)(2). H. Conf. Rep. at 12, reprinted in 1979 U.S. Code Cong. & Ad. News at 2576. See also H.R. Rep. No. 95-1625, 95th Cong., 2d Sess. 12, reprinted in 1978 U.S. Code Cong. & Ad. News 9453, 9462.

In reviewing an agency's decision after consultation our task is "to ascertain whether 'the decision was based on a consideration of the relevant factors and whether there has been a clear error of judgment.'" National Wildlife Federation v. Coleman, 529 F.2d at 372 (quoting Citizens to Preserve Overton Park, Inc. v. Volpe, 401 U.S. 402, 416 (1971)). We must also inquire into whether the ALJ "followed the necessary procedural requirements." Overton Park, 401 U.S. at 417. . . .

The ALJ's conclusion that the risk of a major oil spill was minute was based primarily on three items of evidence. First, the ALJ relied heavily on assurances from the Coast Guard which, after reviewing the testimony of Pittston's witnesses before the BEP and other data, wrote EPA on March 28, 1977, that the channel in Head Harbor Passage was "adequate for safe navigation by 250,000 DWT tankers" if four conditions were met. These conditions were

(1) that the channel passage area depths, configurations and current data shown on nautical charts and surveys be confirmed by hydrographic survey;
(2) provision for a navigation system wherein the existence and movement of all traffic in the area could be monitored, communicated with and scheduled;
(3) provision for means to control movement of tankers in the event of steering and/or propulsion failure during transit; and
(4) development and strict adherence to an operating procedure for tanker passage.

In response to a request by the Council on Environmental Quality that the Coast Guard assist Pittston in carrying out "real time simulation" studies in order to ascertain the precise conditions for safe navigation prior to granting the permit, Rear Admiral Fugaro of the Coast Guard responded in August 1977 that it could not divert scarce resources until "final clearance had been granted for construction of a refinery . . . [so that] no possibility exists that these efforts may be wasted." . . .

Second, the ALJ found confirmation of the Coast Guard's assurance in the computer simulation studies of Dr. Eda, who concluded that a loaded 250,000 DWT tanker could maintain a trajectory close to a desired track in Head Harbor Passage without tug assistance in a 60-knot wind. . . .

Also cited with approval by the ALJ was a second study by Frederick R. Harris, Inc. premised on provision for a more adequate turning basin for the VLCCs than an earlier study which had approved the project subject to severe restrictions and "a high order of seamanship and prudence." This study, the ALJ found, deemed the proposed approach "satisfactory for the type and size of vessels specified providing navigational aids are installed, and providing recommended operational procedures were followed." These included tug assistance from entry into channel, lighted buoys and radar reflectors, an electronic guidance system involving land-based radar and electronic range finders, confining berthing and deberthing to slack tide, limiting Head Harbor transit to daylight or clearly moonlit hours, proscribing entrance to the Passage if visibility is less than a mile, and barring tankers awaiting a berth from anchoring in Eastport waters.

Finally, the ALJ made rather minute review of testimony concerning prevailing currents and cross-currents, fog, wind, and duration of oil spill effects, concluding in general that currents were not excessive for shipping, that the expected presence of fog was not so great as to bar shipping during most of the time, that winds were in general within tolerable limits, and that the effects of large known oil spills had not been long lasting over a period of years.

We have set forth in some detail and full strength all of the strands of the decision of the ALJ because we conclude that, in light of EPA's duty to insure that the project is unlikely to jeopardize endangered whales or eagles, the ALJ's failure to require, at a minimum, that "real time simulation" studies be done to assure the low risk of an oil spill prior to granting the permit violated his duty to "use the best scientific . . . data available." Given the Supreme Court's statement that the ESA is designed to prevent the loss of any endangered species, "regardless of the cost," TVA v. Hill, 437 U.S. at 188 n.34, we cannot see how the permit can issue when real time simulation studies, which EPA, the State of Maine, and the Coast Guard all view as being necessary to a final determination of safety, are to be delayed until the Coast Guard has adequate funds to undertake them.

NOTES AND QUESTIONS

1. In *Roosevelt Campobello*, why did section 7 apply to a private construction project? What species were involved? Who decides whether the proposed project is "likely to jeopardize" those species? What process does the Act prescribe for that determination? The Act requires use of the "best data available." What is the basis for the court's determination that the data considered were inadequate? What does "available" mean under the court's interpretation?

2. As several courts have indicated, the ESA's requirement that the agencies use the best available data does not require the agency to conduct new research, but rather only to seek out and consider existing scientific information. Heartwood, Inc. v. U.S. Forest Service, 380 F.3d 428, 436 (9th Cir. 2004).

3. The question of how to develop the best scientific data available has been a source of continuing controversy. Among the events triggering the current controversy over protection of endangered salmon in the Pacific Northwest was a court's rejection of a "no jeopardy" determination by the NMFS in its 1993 biological opinion on the effects of hydroelectric operations on salmon. The NMFS had premised its "no jeopardy" finding on the grounds that the salmon would experience improved survival over a base period of 1986-1990 and that salmon populations would stabilize within 15 years. The court found that the selection of a baseline period of 1986-1990 was not biologically sound because it involved years of drought and low salmon runs and that the NMFS had not employed the "best available" scientific information because it had ignored the views of scientists from states and tribes. Idaho Dep't of Fish & Game v. National Marine Fisheries Service, 850 F. Supp. 886 (D. Or. 1994). In September 1999, another NMFS "no jeopardy" determination was struck down because the agency had not assessed compliance at the project or site level and had failed to consider the short-term impacts of timber sales on endangered salmon. The court held that the agency's approach virtually guaranteed that no timber sale ever would be found to jeopardize salmon despite overwhelming evidence of ongoing degradation of their habitat. Pacific Coast Federation of Fishermen's Association v. National Marine Fisheries Service, 71 F. Supp. 2d 1063 (W.D. Wash. 1999).

4. Criticism of the science employed in connection with salmon recovery planning has led to the creation of an independent group of scientists to advise the agencies. Following the *Idaho Dep't of Fish & Game* decision, the NMFS's next biological opinion on the effects of hydroelectric operations on salmon established a process called the Plan for Analyzing and Testing Hypotheses (PATH). PATH uses a working group of 25 scientists from federal and state agencies, Indian tribes, and academia, who advise the agency on options for species recovery. Michael C. Blumm & Greg D. Corbin, Salmon and the Endangered Species Act: Lessons from the Columbia Basin, 74 Wash. L. Rev. 519, 558 (1999).

5. In implementing section 7, agencies and courts have focused on the "no jeopardy" proscription of section 7(a)(2). But section 7 proclaims a broader, more affirmative mandate, as outlined in the next case.

	Carson-Truckee Water Conservancy	
	District v. Clark	
	741 F.2d 257 (9th Cir. 1984)	

Before DUNIWAY, Senior Circuit Judge, PREGERSON, and NORRIS, Circuit Judges.
PREGERSON, Circuit Judge:

The Carson-Truckee Water Conservancy District and Sierra Pacific Power Company (appellants) sought a declaratory judgment that the Secretary of the Interior (Secretary) violated the Washoe Project Act, 43 U.S.C.A. §§614-614d (West 1964) and related reclamation laws in refusing to sell water from the Stampede Dam and Reservoir on the Little Truckee River for municipal and industrial (M & I) use in Reno and Sparks. In addition, Nevada sought a determination that the Secretary was required to obtain a permit from the Nevada State Engineer to operate the Stampede Dam in California. The Pyramid Lake Paiute Tribe of Indians (Tribe) intervened in support of the Secretary. We affirm in part and vacate in part.

FACTUAL BACKGROUND AND DISTRICT COURT DECISIONS

. . . The Little Truckee River flows into the Truckee River, which then flows from California into Nevada and into Pyramid Lake. Stampede Dam is located on the Little Truckee in California. The Secretary now operates Stampede Dam in a way that conserves two species of fish, the cui-ui fish and Lahontan cutthroat trout, that are protected under the Endangered Species Act (ESA), 16 U.S.C. §§1531-1543 (1982). Appellants concede that the Secretary's obligations under ESA supersede his obligations under the Washoe Project Act and related federal reclamation laws. Appellants, however, challenge the extent of the Secretary's obligations under ESA. . . .

[The District Court held that the Secretary is required to sell water from Stampede Dam not needed to fulfill his trust obligations to the Tribe and his obligations under ESA, that ESA required the Secretary to give priority to conserving the cui-ui fish and Lahontan cutthroat trout as long as they were endangered and threatened, and that the Secretary's finding that there was no excess water to sell after fulfilling those statutory obligations was not arbitrary. The appellants challenged the court's interpretation of the ESA.]

Appellants urge a reading of ESA that would lead to a result at odds with the statute's clearly stated objectives. Appellants contend that the Secretary's authority is defined solely by ESA §7(a)(2), 16 U.S.C. §1536(a)(2). Thus, they argue that the Secretary is authorized only to take actions that avoid "jeopardizing" the continued existence of a species. Appellants contend that the Secretary may not do more than that.

In addition to its §7(a)(2) "jeopardy" provision, however, ESA also directs the Secretary to conserve threatened and endangered species to the extent that they are no longer threatened or endangered. Appellants, relying solely on §7(a)(2), would have us ignore the other sections of ESA directly applicable here and relied on by the district court. *Carson-Truckee II*, 549 F. Supp. at 708-710. ESA §2(b), (c), & §3(3), 16 U.S.C. §1531(b), (c), & §1532(3). ESA §7(a)(1), moreover, specifically directs that the Secretary "shall" use programs administered by him to further the conservation purposes of ESA. 16 U.S.C.

§1536(a)(1). Those sections, as the district court found, direct that the Secretary actively pursue a species conservation policy. See also Tennessee Valley Authority v. Hill, 437 U.S. 153, 184 (1978) (ESA requires the Secretary to give highest priority to the preservation of endangered species; Congress intended to "halt *and reverse* the trend toward species extinction, whatever the cost." (emphasis added)).

The purpose of ESA §7(a)(2) is to ensure that the federal government does not undertake actions, such as building a dam or highway, that incidentally jeopardize the existence of endangered or threatened species. See TVA v. Hill, 437 U.S. 153 for an example of §7(a)(2)'s application. Contrary to appellants' contention, ESA §7(a)(2) is inapplicable here because the Secretary has not undertaken a project that threatens an endangered species. Instead, following the mandate of ESA §7(a)(1), §2(b), (c), & §3(3), 16 U.S.C. §1536(a)(1), §1531(c), (b), & §1532(3), the Secretary actively seeks to conserve endangered species. Thus, the district court properly applied ESA §2(b), (c), §3(3) rather than ESA §7(a)(2) to this case.

Applying the proper code sections to this case, the Secretary's decision is well justified. The Washoe Project Act anticipates but does not require the Secretary to sell water to recover project construction costs. See supra 741 F.2d at 260-261. ESA, on the other hand, directs the Secretary to use programs under his control for conservation purposes where threatened or endangered species are involved. Following this directive, the Secretary here decided to conserve the fish and not to sell the project's water. Given these circumstances, the ESA supports the Secretary's decision to give priority to the fish until such time as they no longer need ESA's protection.

NOTES AND QUESTIONS

1. How did the court find authority for the Secretary of the Interior to allocate water to the conservation of these endangered fish? Does he have an enforceable duty to do so? What duty or authority do *other* federal agencies have to take such actions?

2. In September 1994, 12 federal agencies entered into a Memorandum of Understanding with the U.S. Fish and Wildlife Service (FWS) and the National Marine Fisheries Service (NMFS) to coordinate their species conservation efforts on the nearly 600 million acres of land and water resources they are responsible for managing. Professor J.B. Ruhl argues that this agreement provides a promising avenue for transforming section 7(a)(1)'s directive that agencies carry out programs to conserve endangered species into a powerful tool to promote species conservation. Ruhl, Section 7(a)(1) of the "New" Endangered Species Act: Rediscovering and Redefining the Untapped Power of Federal Agencies' Duty to Conserve Species, 25 Envtl. L. Rep. 1107 (1995).

3. Professor Ruhl describes the *Carson-Truckee* decision as an example of using section 7(a)(1) as a shield to defend prior agency action. He maintains that section 7(a)(1) also creates a duty to conserve that could be used "as a sword requiring a federal agency to maximize use of *significant* conservation measures in its action selection and [to] justify any departure from full attention to species conservation with relevant factors," such as countervailing statutory directives. Cf. Florida Key Deer v. Stickney, 864 F. Supp. 1222 (S.D. Fla. 1994) (agency failure to consider effects on endangered species of issuing new flood insurance

policies in last remaining habitat of endangered deer violates section 7(a)(1));
Platte River Whooping Crane Critical Habitat Maintenance Trust v. FERC, 962
F.2d 27 (D.C. Cir. 1992) (section 7(a)(1) does not require FERC to evaluate the
need for conditioning annual licensing of hydroelectric projects on measures to
protect wildlife). Professor Ruhl also suggests that section 7(a)(1) could be used
"as a prod" to require "each federal agency to implement all species conservation measures that are within the scope of the agency's authority, but which do
not necessarily depend for their initiation or effect on the agency proposing
or taking an action pursuant to the agency's primary mission authorities."
Id. at 1137.

4. In Sierra Club v. Glickman, 156 F.3d 606 (5th Cir. 1998), the Fifth
Circuit interpreted section 7(a)(1) as imposing "an affirmative duty on each
federal agency to conserve each of the [species listed under section 4]." Id. at
616. Thus, it upheld a district court decision that the U.S. Department of
Agriculture, which funded irrigation programs using the Edwards Aquifer in
Texas, had violated section 7(a)(1) by failing to consult with the U.S. Fish
and Wildlife Service and to develop programs to conserve endangered
species dependent upon springs fed by the aquifer. The court rejected
the notion that section 7(a)(1)'s obligations were too vague to be judicially
reviewable.

5. Federal agencies have begun to use the section 7 consultation process
to develop more creative approaches to species protection. For example, the
Department of Interior has joined with Colorado, Utah, and Wyoming to establish a Recovery Implementation Program for Endangered Fish Species in the
Upper Colorado River Basin. Rather than attempting simply to halt the decline
of listed species, the program is pursuing their full recovery over a 15-year
period. The recovery program is managed by an implementation committee
consisting of representatives of three federal agencies, the three states, water-
development interests, and environmentalists. See Evans, A "Recovery" Partnership for the Upper Colorado River to Meet ESA §7 Needs, 8 Nat. Resources &
Envt. 24 (Summer 1993). In 1994, the federal government reached agreement
with California on a long-term cooperative management program for the San
Francisco Bay–Delta area to protect endangered species in the area. See Tarlock,
Biodiversity Federalism, 54 Md. L. Rev. 1315, 1349-1351 (1995).

6. In American Forest and Paper Ass'n v. U.S. EPA, 137 F.3d 291 (5th Cir.
1998), the Fifth Circuit held that EPA could not require, as a condition for
delegating operation of the Clean Water Act's NPDES permitting program to
Louisiana, that the state consult with the U.S. Fish and Wildlife Service (FWS)
and the National Marine Fisheries Service (NMFS) before issuing permits.
Although Louisiana had consented to the arrangement, which allowed EPA
to exercise its authority to veto permits if the federal agencies found that they
threatened endangered species, a trade association of forest and paper products firms sued EPA to challenge it. The Fifth Circuit held that the arrangement exceeded EPA's authority because the Clean Water Act did not
specifically enumerate protection of endangered species as a ground for
denying delegation to a state. While acknowledging that ESA section 7(a)(2)
requires EPA to consult with FWS or NMFS before undertaking action that
may jeopardize species, the court held that the section confers no substantive
powers on the agency to condition delegations of NPDES permitting authority. Five months after the Fifth Circuit's decision, the Tenth Circuit dismissed
a virtually identical lawsuit challenging EPA's conditioning of an NPDES

delegation to Oklahoma on the ground that the plaintiff, American Forest and Paper Association, lacked standing to challenge the arrangement. American Forest & Paper Association v. U.S. EPA, 154 F.3d 1155 (10th Cir. 1998). EPA has agreed to consult with the FWS and NMFS before approving TMDLs under the Clean Water Act. Does EPA have the authority to do so in light of the Fifth Circuit's decision?

F.   PROTECTION AGAINST PRIVATE ACTION: SECTION 9

By its terms, section 7 applies only to federal actions. The Endangered Species Act also provides listed species some protection against private actions. Section 9 prohibits any "person" (including any corporation or other private entity, and any government agency) from taking, selling, importing, or exporting any protected species. 16 U.S.C. §1532(13). These provisions are designed to stop the trade in live animals, skins, and other parts that threatens the existence of many species, such as parrots, alligators, and elephants. But section 9 provides even broader restrictions on private action because of the prohibition on takings. As noted in TVA v. Hill, the term "take" is defined by section 3(19) of the Act to mean: "to harass, harm, pursue, hunt, shoot, wound, kill, trap, capture, or collect, or to attempt to engage in any such conduct."

In Palila v. Hawaii Department of Land and Natural Resources, 639 F.2d 495 (9th Cir. 1981), the Ninth Circuit affirmed a district court decision requiring Hawaiian officials to remove feral sheep and goats from the critical habitat of an endangered bird. These animals, which had been placed on the island by state officials to promote sport hunting, were found to be harming mamane trees. The endangered Palila, a bird found only in a small area on the upper slopes of Mauna Kea on the island of Hawaii, depends on mamane trees for food. Noting that "'[h]arm' is defined to include activity that results in significant environmental modification or degradation of the endangered animal's habitat," the Ninth Circuit held that the state violated section 9 of ESA by "maintaining feral sheep and goats in the critical habitat . . . since it was shown that the Palila was endangered by the activity."

Following the *Palila I* decision, the Secretary of Interior in 1981 sought to clarify the "take" prohibition in section 9 of the ESA by defining "harm" as:

> an act which actually kills or injures wildlife. Such act may include significant habitat modification or degradation where it actually kills or injures wildlife by significantly impairing essential behavioral patterns, including breeding, feeding, or sheltering. [50 C.F.R. §17.3 (1985).]

This definition became the focus of new litigation over the Palila bird in 1986. Having removed the feral sheep and goats, Hawaiian officials were still trying to maintain a mouflon (wild) sheep population for sport hunting on the island. Based on new research showing that the mouflon sheep also harmed the mamane trees, the Sierra Club filed suit to have the mouflon sheep removed.

When the district court decided *Palila I* in 1979, it was estimated that only 1,400 to 1,600 Palila remained. By 1986, approximately 2,200 Palila were on the island. Noting that the Palila population had grown since *Palila I*, state officials argued that there was no evidence that the mouflon sheep actually were harming the bird. However, the state's own experts conceded that the mouflon sheep, by eating the mamane, were degrading the mamane forest and suppressing its regeneration, and that continued degradation could drive the Palila into extinction because they depend on the mamane for food. The state argued that this indirect effect on the Palila was only a "potential" injury not encompassed within the Secretary's redefinition of "harm." The district court rejected this defense.

In *Palila II* (Palila v. Hawaii Department of Land and Natural Resources, 649 F. Supp. 1070 (D. Haw. 1986)), the court held that a finding of "harm" did not require a showing of death to individual members of a species, but rather only "an adverse impact on the protected species." Thus, the district court concluded that "harm" did not require a decline in population numbers. Instead, it held that "[i]f the habitat modification prevents the population from recovering, then this causes injury to the species and should be actionable under section 9." 649 F. Supp. at 1077. The court ordered the removal of the mouflon sheep on the grounds that their presence injured the Palila by decreasing its food and nesting sites.

State officials appealed the district court's decision to the Ninth Circuit, In affirming the district court, the Ninth Circuit stated: "We do not reach the issue of whether harm includes habitat degradation that merely retards recovery. The district court's (and the Secretary's) interpretation of harm as including habitat destruction that could result in extinction, and findings to that effect are enough to sustain an order for the removal of the mouflon sheep." Palila v. Hawaii Dep't of Land & Natural Resources, 852 F.2d 1106, 1110 (9th Cir. 1988).

NOTES AND QUESTIONS

1. The *Palila* litigation was filed by the Sierra Club Legal Defense Fund and the Hawaii Audubon Society. When they filed their initial lawsuit in January 1978, they named as the lead plaintiff "Palila (*Psittirostra bailleui*), an endangered species." The opening sentence of the district court's initial opinion reads: "Palila (*Psittirostra bailleui*) seeks the protection of this Court from harm caused by feral sheep and goats." Environmental philosopher Rod Nash notes that "[f]or the first time in American legal history a non-human became a plaintiff in court. Moreover, the bird won!" Nash, The Rights of Nature 177 (1989).

2. What result would you expect if the *Palila* case arose on private land? On federal land? In Sierra Club v. Yeutter, 926 F.2d 429 (5th Cir. 1991), the Fifth Circuit held that the Forest Service had violated section 9 by authorizing clear-cutting in forests that were habitat for the endangered red-cockaded woodpecker, finding that the practice "resulted in significant habitat modification" that had "caused and accelerated the decline in the species." 926 F.2d at 438. In Defenders of Wildlife v. EPA, 882 F.2d 1294 (8th Cir. 1989), the Eighth Circuit held that EPA had violated section 9 when it registered pesticides containing strychnine. The court found that endangered species had been poisoned by the pesticides, which could not have been used without the EPA registration.

Private Actions, Incidental Takings, and Habitat Conservation Plans

Section 9 of ESA is particularly significant because it applies to private as well as governmental action. The great majority of endangered species are found on private land or adjacent waterways and a substantial number of them occur entirely on such land. Bean, The Endangered Species Act and Private Land: Four Lessons Learned From the Past Quarter Century, 28 Envtl. L. Rep. 10701 (1998). Section 9's prohibition of "taking" applies broadly to proscribe even takings that are incidental to other activities. By contrast, section 7 has provided some flexibility for incidental takings. If an agency action and the resulting incidental taking are not likely to jeopardize the continued existence of the species and the impact of the taking will be minimized, section 7(b)(4) authorizes the Secretary to provide the agency with a written statement authorizing the taking. See Defenders of Wildlife v. EPA, 882 F.2d 1294, 1300 (8th Cir. 1989).

During its first decade, ESA provided no similar flexibility for private actions. Any private action that would incidentally harm a protected animal was subject to criminal sanctions. In 1982, Congress responded to this inconsistency by adding section 10(a) to ESA. This section authorizes the Secretary to permit "incidental" takings associated with private action if the actor prepares a habitat conservation plan (HCP) to minimize the impact of the taking and assures that it "will not appreciably reduce the likelihood of the survival and recovery of the species in the wild." §10(a)(2)(B)(iv). Congress intended for section 10 to apply the same basic standard that had been applied to permit incidental takings under section 7(a)(2).

When Congress adopted section 10 (a) it had a specific model in mind—an HCP being prepared for the development of San Bruno Mountain, the last bastion of the mission blue butterfly and San Bruno elfin butterfly. The San Bruno HCP was the product of lengthy negotiations among the landowner, developer, conservationists, and local governments. It produced a plan to permanently protect 87 percent of the butterfly habitat, while authorizing limited housing development on the remaining 13 percent. To provide continued funding to support habitat management and long-term enforcement of the plan, assessments were made on units within the development. By itself, construction of the housing development was estimated to reduce the species' chances of survival by 2 to 5 percent. However, this was more than offset by the effect of the HCP, which removed exotic vegetation, controlled recreational use, and provided for active habitat management, thus enhancing the butterflies' overall prospects for survival.

Because FWS had never enforced section 9 against incidental takings, there was little initial incentive for anyone to seek a permit. Thus, it was hardly surprising that in the first decade only about two dozen HCPs were approved. But with FWS showing more interest in enforcement, many more HCPs are now being developed. The prospect of enforcement also spurred a significant legal challenge to the Secretary's interpretation that section 9's "take" prohibition includes "significant habitat modification or degradation where it actually kills or injures wildlife." This challenge ultimately produced the following decision.

	Babbitt v. Sweet Home Chapter of	
	Communities for a Great Oregon	
	515 U.S. 687 (1995)	

JUSTICE STEVENS delivered the opinion of the Court.

. . . Respondents in this action are small landowners, logging companies, and families dependent on the forest products industries in the Pacific Northwest and in the Southeast, and organizations that represent their interests. They brought this declaratory judgment action against petitioners, the Secretary of the Interior and the Director of the Fish and Wildlife Service, in the United States District Court for the District of Columbia to challenge the statutory validity of the Secretary's regulation defining "harm," particularly the inclusion of habitat modification and degradation in the definition. Respondents challenged the regulation on its face. Their complaint alleged that application of the "harm" regulation to the red-cockaded woodpecker, an endangered species, and the northern spotted owl, a threatened species, had injured them economically. . . .

Because this case was decided on motions for summary judgment, we may appropriately make certain factual assumptions in order to frame the legal issue. First, we assume respondents have no desire to harm either the red-cockaded woodpecker or the spotted owl; they merely wish to continue logging activities that would be entirely proper if not prohibited by the ESA. On the other hand, we must assume *arguendo* that those activities will have the effect, even though unintended, of detrimentally changing the natural habitat of both listed species and that, as a consequence, members of those species will be killed or injured. Under respondents' view of the law, the Secretary's only means of forestalling that grave result—even when the actor knows it is certain to occur—is to use his §5 authority to purchase the lands on which the survival of the species depends. The Secretary, on the other hand, submits that the §9 prohibition on takings, which Congress defined to include "harm," places on respondents a duty to avoid harm that habitat alteration will cause the birds unless respondents first obtain a permit pursuant to §10.

The text of the Act provides three reasons for concluding that the Secretary's interpretation is reasonable. First, an ordinary understanding of the word "harm" supports it. The dictionary definition of the verb form of "harm" is "to cause hurt or damage to: injure." Webster's Third New International Dictionary 1034 (1966). In the context of the ESA, that definition naturally encompasses habitat modification that results in actual injury or death to members of an endangered or threatened species. Respondents argue that the Secretary should have limited the purview of "harm" to direct applications of force against protected species, but the dictionary definition does not include the word "directly" or suggest in any way that only direct or willful action that leads to injury constitutes "harm." Moreover, unless the statutory term "harm" encompasses indirect as well as direct injuries, the word has no meaning that does not duplicate the meaning of other words that §3 uses to define "take." A reluctance to treat statutory terms as surplusage supports the reasonableness of the Secretary's interpretation. See, e.g., Mackey v. Lanier Collection Agency & Service, Inc., 486 U.S. 825, 837 (1988).

Second, the broad purpose of the ESA supports the Secretary's decision to extend protection against activities that cause the precise harms Congress enacted the statute to avoid. In TVA v. Hill, 437 U.S. 153 (1978), we described the Act as "the most comprehensive legislation for the preservation of endangered species ever enacted by any nation." Id., at 180. Whereas predecessor statutes enacted in 1966 and 1969 had not contained any sweeping prohibition against the taking of endangered species except on federal lands, see id., at 175, the 1973 Act applied to all land in the United States and to the Nation's territorial seas. As stated in §2 of the Act, among its central purposes is "to provide a means whereby the ecosystems upon which endangered species and threatened species depend may be conserved. . . ." 16 U.S.C. §1531 (b).

In *Hill*, we construed §7 as precluding the completion of the Tellico Dam because of its predicted impact on the survival of the snail darter. See 437 U.S., at 193. Both our holding and the language in our opinion stressed the importance of the statutory policy. "The plain intent of Congress in enacting this statute," we recognized, "was to halt and reverse the trend toward species extinction, whatever the cost. This is reflected not only in the stated policies of the Act, but in literally every section of the statute." Id., at 184. Although the §9 "take" prohibition was not at issue in *Hill*, we took note of that prohibition, placing particular emphasis on the Secretary's inclusion of habitat modification in his definition of "harm." In light of that provision for habitat protection, we could "not understand how TVA intends to operate Tellico Dam without 'harming' the snail darter." Id., at 184, n. 30. Congress' intent to provide comprehensive protection for endangered and threatened species supports the permissibility of the Secretary's "harm" regulation.

Respondents advance strong arguments that activities that cause minimal or unforeseeable harm will not violate the Act as construed in the "harm" regulation. Respondents, however, present a facial challenge to the regulation. Thus, they ask us to invalidate the Secretary's understanding of "harm" in every circumstance, even when an actor knows that an activity, such as draining a pond, would actually result in the extinction of a listed species by destroying its habitat. Given Congress' clear expression of the ESA's broad purpose to protect endangered and threatened wildlife, the Secretary's definition of "harm" is reasonable.

Third, the fact that Congress in 1982 authorized the Secretary to issue permits for takings that §9(a)(1)(B) would otherwise prohibit, "if such taking is incidental to, and not the purpose of, the carrying out of an otherwise lawful activity," 16 U.S.C. §1539(a)(1)(B), strongly suggests that Congress understood §9(a)(1)(B) to prohibit indirect as well as deliberate takings. The permit process requires the applicant to prepare a "conservation plan" that specifies how he intends to "minimize and mitigate" the "impact" of his activity on endangered and threatened species, 16 U.S.C. §1539(a)(2)(A), making clear that Congress had in mind foreseeable rather than merely accidental effects on listed species. No one could seriously request an "incidental" take permit to avert §9 liability for direct, deliberate action against a member of an endangered or threatened species, but respondents would read "harm" so narrowly that the permit procedure would have little more than that absurd purpose. "When Congress acts to amend a statute, we presume it intends its amendment to have real and substantial effect." Stone v. INS, 514 U.S. 386, 397 (1995). Congress' addition of the §10 permit provision supports the Secretary's conclusion that activities not intended to harm an endangered species, such as habitat modification, may constitute unlawful takings under the ESA unless the Secretary permits them.

The Court of Appeals made three errors in asserting that "harm" must refer to a direct application of force because the words around it do.[15] First, the court's premise was flawed. Several of the words that accompany "harm" in the §3 definition of "take," especially "harrass," "pursue," "wound," and "kill," refer to actions or effects that do not require direct applications of force. Second, to the extent the court read a requirement of intent or purpose into the words used to define "take," it ignored §9's express provision that a "knowing" action is enough to violate the Act. Third, the court employed *noscitur a sociis* to give "harm" essentially the same function as other words in the definition, thereby denying it independent meaning. The canon, to the contrary, counsels that a word "gathers meaning from the words around it." Jarecki v. G. D. Searle & Co., 367 U.S. 303, 307 (1961). The statutory context of "harm" suggests that Congress meant that term to serve a particular function in the ESA, consistent with but distinct from the functions of the other verbs used to define "take." The Secretary's interpretation of "harm" to include indirectly injuring endangered animals through habitat modification permissibly interprets "harm" to have "a character of its own not to be submerged by its association." Russell Motor Car Co. v. United States, 261 U.S. 514, 519 (1923). . . .

We need not decide whether the statutory definition of "take" compels the Secretary's interpretation of "harm," because our conclusions that Congress did not unambiguously manifest its intent to adopt respondents' view and that the Secretary's interpretation is reasonable suffice to decide this case. See generally Chevron U.S.A. Inc. v. Natural Resources Defense Council, Inc., 467 U.S. 837 (1984). The latitude the ESA gives the Secretary in enforcing the statute, together with the degree of regulatory expertise necessary to its enforcement, establishes that we owe some degree of deference to the Secretary's reasonable interpretation. See Breyer, Judicial Review of Questions of Law and Policy, 38 Admin. L. Rev. 363, 373 (1986). . . .

JUSTICE O'CONNOR, concurring.

My agreement with the Court is founded on two understandings. First, the challenged regulation is limited to significant habitat modification that causes actual, as opposed to hypothetical or speculative, death or injury to identifiable protected animals. Second, even setting aside difficult questions of scienter, the regulation's application is limited by ordinary principles of proximate causation, which introduce notions of foreseeability. These limitations, in my view, call into question Palila v. Hawaii Dept. of Land and Natural Resources, 852 F.2d 1106 (9th Cir. 1988) (*Palila II*), and with it, many of the applications derided by the dissent. Because there is no need to strike a regulation on a facial challenge out of concern that it is susceptible of erroneous application, however, and because

---

15. The dissent makes no effort to defend the Court of Appeals' reading of the statutory definition as requiring a direct application of force. Instead, it tries to impose on §9 a limitation of liability to "affirmative conduct intentionally directed against a particular animal or animals." Under the dissent's interpretation of the Act, a developer could drain a pond, knowing that the act would extinguish an endangered species of turtles, without even proposing a conservation plan or applying for a permit under §9(a)(1)(B); unless the developer was motivated by a desire "to get at a turtle," no statutory taking could occur. Because such conduct would not constitute a taking at common law, the dissent would shield it from §9 liability, even though the words "kill" and "harm" in the statutory definition could apply to such deliberate conduct. We cannot accept that limitation. In any event, our reasons for rejecting the Court of Appeals' interpretation apply as well to the dissent's novel construction.

there are many habitat-related circumstances in which the regulation might validly apply, I join the opinion of the Court.

In my view, the regulation is limited by its terms to actions that actually kill or injure individual animals. Justice Scalia disagrees, arguing that the harm regulation "encompasses injury inflicted, not only upon individual animals, but upon populations of the protected species." At one level, I could not reasonably quarrel with this observation; death to an individual animal always reduces the size of the population in which it lives, and in that sense, "injures" that population. But by its insight, the dissent means something else. Building upon the regulation's use of the word "breeding," Justice Scalia suggests that the regulation facially bars significant habitat modification that actually kills or injures *hypothetical* animals (or, perhaps more aptly, causes potential additions to the population not to come into being). Because "impairment of breeding does not 'injure' living creatures," Justice Scalia reasons, the regulation *must* contemplate application to "a *population* of animals which would otherwise have maintained or increased its numbers."

I disagree. As an initial matter, I do not find it as easy as Justice Scalia does to dismiss the notion that significant impairment of breeding injures living creatures. To raze the last remaining ground on which the piping plover currently breeds, thereby making it impossible for any piping plovers to reproduce, would obviously injure the population (causing the species' extinction in a generation). But by completely preventing breeding, it would also injure the individual living bird, in the same way that sterilizing the creature injures the individual living bird. To "injure" is, among other things, "to impair." Webster's Ninth New Collegiate Dictionary 623 (1983). One need not subscribe to theories of "psychic harm" to recognize that to make it impossible for an animal to reproduce is to impair its most essential physical functions and to render that animal, and its genetic material, biologically obsolete. This, in my view, is actual injury. . . .

By the dissent's reckoning, the regulation at issue here, in conjunction with 16 U.S.C. §1540(1), imposes liability for any habitat-modifying conduct that ultimately results in the death of a protected animal, "regardless of whether that result is intended or even foreseeable, and no matter how long the chain of causality between modification and injury." Even if §1540(1) does create a strict liability regime (a question we need not decide at this juncture), I see no indication that Congress, in enacting that section, intended to dispense with ordinary principles of proximate causation. Strict liability means liability without regard to fault; it does not normally mean liability for every consequence, however remote, of one's conduct. See generally W. Keeton, D. Dobbs, R. Keeton, and D. Owen, Prosser and Keeton on Law of Torts 559-560 (5th ed. 1984) (describing "practical necessity for the restriction of liability within some reasonable bounds" in the strict liability context). I would not lightly assume that Congress, in enacting a strict liability statute that is silent on the causation question, has dispensed with this well-entrenched principle. In the absence of congressional abrogation of traditional principles of causation, then, private parties should be held liable under §1540(1) only if their habitat-modifying actions proximately cause death or injury to protected animals. Cf. Benefiel v. Exxon Corp., 959 F.2d 805, 807-808 (9th Cir. 1992) (in enacting the Trans-Alaska Pipeline Authorization Act, which provides for strict liability for damages that are the result of discharges, Congress did not intend to abrogate common-law principles of proximate cause to reach "remote and derivative" consequences); New York v. Shore Realty Corp., 759 F.2d 1032, 1044, and n. 17 (2d Cir. 1985) (noting that "traditional tort law has often imposed strict liability while recognizing a causation defense," but that, in enacting CERCLA, Congress "specifically rejected including a causation requirement"). The regulation, of course, does not contradict the presumption or notion that ordinary principles of causation apply here. Indeed, by use of the word "actually," the regulation clearly rejects speculative or conjectural effects, and thus itself invokes principles of proximate causation.

Proximate causation is not a concept susceptible of precise definition. See Keeton, supra, at 280-281. It is easy enough, of course, to identify the extremes. The farmer whose fertilizer is lifted by a tornado from tilled fields and deposited miles away in a wildlife refuge cannot, by any stretch of the term, be considered the proximate cause of death or injury to protected species occasioned thereby. At the same time, the landowner who drains a pond on his property, killing endangered fish in the process, would likely satisfy any formulation of the principle. We have recently said that proximate causation "normally eliminates the bizarre," Jerome B. Grubart, Inc. v. Great Lakes Dredge & Dock Co., 513 U.S. 527, 536 (1995), and have noted its "functionally equivalent" alternative characterizations in terms of foreseeability, see Milwaukee & St. Paul R. Co. v. Kellogg, 94 U.S. 469, 475 (1877) ("natural and probable consequence"), and duty, see Palsgraf v. Long Island R. Co., 162 N.E., 99 (1928); Consolidated Rail Corp. v. Gottshall, 512 U.S. 532, 546 (1994). Proximate causation depends to a great extent on considerations of the fairness of imposing liability for remote consequences. The task of determining whether proximate causation exists in the limitless fact patterns sure to arise is best left to lower courts. But I note, at the least, that proximate cause principles inject a foreseeability element into the statute, and hence, the regulation, that would appear to alleviate some of the problems noted by the dissent. See, e.g., infra (describing "a farmer who tills his field and causes erosion that makes silt run into a nearby river which depletes oxygen and thereby [injures] protected fish").

In my view, then, the "harm" regulation applies where significant habitat modification, by impairing essential behaviors, proximately (foreseeably) causes actual death or injury to identifiable animals that are protected under the Endangered Species Act. Pursuant to my interpretation, *Palila II*—under which the Court of Appeals held that a state agency committed a "taking" by permitting feral sheep to eat mamane-naio seedlings that, when full-grown, might have fed and sheltered endangered palila—was wrongly decided according to the regulation's own terms. Destruction of the seedlings did not proximately cause actual death or injury to identifiable birds; it merely prevented the regeneration of forest land not currently inhabited by actual birds. . . .

JUSTICE SCALIA, with whom THE CHIEF JUSTICE and JUSTICE THOMAS join, dissenting.

The Court's holding that the hunting and killing prohibition incidentally preserves habitat on private lands imposes unfairness to the point of financial ruin—not just upon the rich, but upon the simplest farmer who finds his land conscripted to national zoological use. I respectfully dissent. . . .

The regulation has three features which, for reasons I shall discuss at length below, do not comport with the statute. First, it interprets the statute to prohibit habitat modification that is no more than the cause-in-fact of death or injury to wildlife. Any "significant habitat modification" that in fact produces that result by "impairing essential behavioral patterns" is made unlawful, regardless of whether that result is intended or even foreseeable, and no matter how long the chain of causality between modification and injury. See, e.g., Palila v. Hawaii Dept. of Land and Natural Resources (*Palila II*), 852 F.2d 1106, 1108-1109 (9th Cir. 1988) (sheep grazing constituted "taking" of palila birds, since although sheep do not destroy full-grown mamane trees, they do destroy mamane seedlings, which will not grow to full-grown trees, on which the palila feeds and nests). See also Davison, Alteration of Wildlife Habitat as a Prohibited Taking under the Endangered Species Act, 10 J. Land Use & Envtl. L. 155, 190 (1995) (regulation requires only causation-in-fact).

Second, the regulation does not require an "act": the Secretary's officially stated position is that an omission will do. The previous version of the regulation made this explicit. See 40 Fed. Reg. 44,412, 44,416 (1975) ("'Harm' in the definition of 'take' in the Act means an act or omission which actually kills or injures wildlife . . ."). When the regulation was modified in 1981 the phrase "or omission" was taken out, but only because (as the final publication of the rule advised) "the [Fish and Wildlife] Service feels that 'act' is inclusive of either commissions or omissions which would be prohibited by section [1538(a)(1)(B)]." 46 Fed. Reg. 54,748, 54,750 (1981). In its brief here the Government agrees that the regulation covers omissions, see Brief for Petitioners 47 (although it argues that "an 'omission' constitutes an 'act' . . . only if there is a legal duty to act"), ibid.

The third and most important unlawful feature of the regulation is that it encompasses injury inflicted, not only upon individual animals, but upon populations of the protected species. "Injury" in the regulation includes "significantly impairing essential behavioral patterns, including *breeding*," 50 CFR §17.3 (1994) (emphasis added). Impairment of breeding does not "injure" living creatures; it prevents them from propagating, thus "injuring" a *population* of animals which would otherwise have maintained or increased its numbers. What the face of the regulation shows, the Secretary's official pronouncements confirm. The Final Redefinition of "Harm" accompanying publication of the regulation said that "harm" is not limited to "direct physical injury to an individual member of the wildlife species," 46 Fed. Reg. 54,748 (1981), and refers to "injury to a *population*," id., at 54,749 (emphasis added).

None of these three features of the regulation can be found in the statutory provisions supposed to authorize it. The term "harm" in §1532(19) has no legal force of its own. An indictment or civil complaint that charged the defendant with "harming" an animal protected under the Act would be dismissed as defective, for the only operative term in the statute is to "take." If "take" were not elsewhere defined in the Act, none could dispute what it means, for the term is as old as the law itself. To "take," when applied to wild animals, means to reduce those animals, by killing or capturing, to human control. See, e.g., 11 Oxford English Dictionary (1933) ("Take . . . To catch, capture (a wild beast, bird, fish, etc.)"); Webster's New International Dictionary of the English Language (2d ed. 1949) (take defined as "to catch or capture by trapping, snaring, etc., or as prey"); Geer v. Connecticut, 161 U.S. 519, 523 (1896) ("All the animals which can be taken upon the earth, in the sea, or in the air, that is to say, wild animals, belong to those who take them") (quoting the Digest of Justinian); 2 W. Blackstone, Commentaries 411 (1766) ("Every man . . . has an equal right of pursuing and taking to his own use all such creatures as are *ferae naturae*"). This is just the sense in which "take" is used elsewhere in federal legislation and treaty. See, e.g., Migratory Bird Treaty Act, 16 U.S.C. §703 (1988 ed., Supp. V) (no person may "pursue, hunt, take, capture, kill, [or] attempt to take, capture, or kill" any migratory bird); Agreement on the Conservation of Polar Bears, Nov. 15, 1973, Art. I, 27 U.S.T. 3918, 3921, T.I.A.S. No. 8409 (defining "taking" as "hunting, killing and capturing"). And that meaning fits neatly with the rest of §1538(a)(1), which makes it unlawful not only to take protected species, but also to import or export them (§1538(a)(1)(A)); to possess, sell, deliver, carry, transport, or ship any taken species (§1538(a)(1)(D)); and to transport, sell, or offer to sell them in interstate or foreign commerce (§§1538(a)(1)(E), (F)). The taking prohibition, in other words, is only part of the regulatory plan of §1538(a)(1), which covers all the stages of the process by which protected wildlife is reduced to man's dominion and made the object of profit. It is obvious that "take" in this sense—a term of art deeply embedded in the statutory and common law concerning wildlife— describes a class of acts (not omissions) done directly and intentionally (not indirectly and by accident) to particular animals (not populations of animals). . . .

[T]he Court's contention that "harm" in the narrow sense adds nothing to the other words underestimates the ingenuity of our own species in a way that Congress did not. To feed an animal poison, to spray it with mace, to chop down the very tree in which it is nesting, or even to destroy its entire habitat in order to take it (as by draining a pond to get at a turtle), might neither wound nor kill, but would directly and intentionally harm. . . .

[T]he Court seeks support from a provision which was added to the Act in 1982, the year after the Secretary promulgated the current regulation. The provision states:

> The Secretary may permit, under such terms and conditions as he shall prescribe— . . . "any taking otherwise prohibited by section 1538(a)(1)(B) . . . if such taking is incidental to, and not the purpose of, the carrying out of an otherwise lawful activity." [16 U.S.C. §1539(a)(1)(B).]

This provision does not, of course, implicate our doctrine that reenactment of a statutory provision ratifies an extant judicial or administrative interpretation, for neither the taking prohibition in §1538(a)(1)(B) nor the definition in §1532(19) was reenacted. See Central Bank of Denver, N.A. v. First Interstate Bank of Denver, N.A., 511 U.S. 164, 185 (1994). The Court claims, however, that the provision "strongly suggests that Congress understood [§1538(a)(1)(B)] to prohibit indirect as well as deliberate takings.". . . . That would be a valid inference if habitat modification were the only substantial "otherwise lawful activity" that might incidentally and nonpurposefully cause a prohibited "taking." Of course it is not. This provision applies to the many otherwise lawful takings that incidentally take a protected species—as when fishing for unprotected salmon also takes an endangered species of salmon, see Pacific Northwest Generating Cooperative v. Brown, 38 F.3d 1058, 1067 (9th Cir. 1994). Congress has referred to such "incidental takings" in other statutes as well—for example, a statute referring to "the incidental taking of . . . sea turtles in the course of . . . harvesting [shrimp]" and to the "rate of incidental taking of sea turtles by United States vessels in the course of such harvesting," 103 Stat. 1038 §609(b)(2), note following 16 U.S.C. §1537 (1988 ed., Supp. V); and a statute referring to "the incidental taking of marine mammals in the course of commercial fishing operations," 108 Stat. 546, §118(a). The Court shows that it misunderstands the question when it says that "no one could seriously request an 'incidental' take permit to avert . . . liability for direct, deliberate action *against a member of an endangered or threatened species.*" Ante, at 2414 (emphasis added). That is not an *incidental* take at all. . . .

[T]he Court and the concurrence suggest that the regulation should be read to contain a requirement of proximate causation or foreseeability, principally *because the statute does*—and "nothing in the regulation purports to weaken those requirements [of the statute]." I quite agree that the statute contains such a limitation, because the verbs of purpose in §1538(a)(1)(B) denote action directed at animals. *But the Court has rejected that reading.* The critical premise on which it has upheld the regulation is that, despite the weight of the other words in §1538(a)(1)(B), "the statutory term 'harm' encompasses indirect as well as direct injuries," ante. Consequently, unless there is some strange category of causation that is indirect and yet also proximate, the Court has already rejected its own basis for finding a proximate-cause limitation in the regulation. In fact "proximate" causation simply *means* "direct" causation. The only other reason given for finding a proximate-cause limitation in the regulation is that "by use of the word 'actually,' the regulation clearly rejects speculative or conjectural effects, and thus itself *invokes* principles of proximate causation." *Non sequitur*, of course. That the injury must be "actual" as opposed to "potential" simply says nothing at all about the length or foreseeability of the causal chain between the habitat modification and the "actual" injury. It is thus true and irrelevant that "the Secretary did not need to include 'actually' to connote 'but for' causation," ante, at 2414 n. 13; "actually" defines the requisite *injury*, not the requisite *causality*. The regulation says (it is worth repeating) that "harm" means (1) an act which (2) actually kills or injures wildlife. If that does not dispense with a proximate-cause requirement, I do not know what language would. And changing the regulation by judicial invention, even to achieve compliance with the statute, is not permissible. . . .

But since the Court is reading the regulation and the statute incorrectly in other respects, it may as well introduce this novelty as well—law a la carte. As I understand the regulation that the Court has created and held consistent with the statute that it has also created, habitat modification can constitute a "taking," but only if it results in the killing or harming of *individual animals,* and only if that consequence is the direct result of the modification. This means that the destruction of privately owned habitat that is essential, not for the feeding or nesting, but for the *breeding,* of butterflies, would not violate the Act, since it would not harm or kill any living butterfly. I, too, think it would not violate the Act—not for the utterly unsupported reason that habitat modifications fall outside the regulation if they happen not to kill or injure a living animal, but for the textual reason that only action directed at living animals constitutes a "take."

NOTES AND QUESTIONS

1. In light of *Sweet Home,* what activities are prohibited by section 9? The Court upheld the Secretary of Interior's definition of "harm" prohibited by section 9 as including "significant habitat modification or degradation where it actually kills or injures wildlife. . . ." It rejected both the D.C. Circuit's

interpretation that section 9 applies only to the direct application of force to endangered species and Justice Scalia's argument that it prohibits only "affirmative conduct intentionally directed against a particular animal or animals." In a portion of his dissent not reproduced above, Justice Scalia argued that any other interpretation could make many "routine private activities," such as farming, construction, and logging violations of section 9 "when they fortuitously injure protected wildlife, no matter how remote the chain of causation and no matter how difficult to foresee (or to disprove) the 'injury' may be (e.g., an 'impairment' of breeding)." 515 U.S. at 721-722 (Scalia, J., dissenting). Justice O'Connor took issue with this claim in her concurring opinion by arguing that normal principles of proximate cause would limit liability. While none of the other Justices in the majority joined Justice O'Connor's opinion, in a footnote to his majority opinion Justice Stevens indicated that he saw no reason why section 9 "should not be read to incorporate ordinary requirements of proximate causation and foreseeability." 515 U.S. at 701 n.15.

2. How can landowners know what habitat modifications are prohibited by section 9? Should the government issue species-by-species guidelines or regulations that specify what habitat modifications are likely to harm which species? The U.S. Fish and Wildlife Service has established such guidelines for a few species. For example, they specify that a landowner located within a quarter mile of any active red-cockaded woodpecker colony may harvest timber without harming the bird so long as at least 60 acres of pine trees 10 inches or more in diameter with a total basal area of 3,000 square feet are left. U.S. Fish & Wildlife Service, Draft Red-Cockaded Woodpecker Procedures Manual for Private Lands. (Oct. 1992). If a landowner challenges the agency's judgment concerning whether certain actions will injure members of a particular species, should the guidelines be entitled to any deference?

3. In the wake of *Sweet Home,* what must the government prove to establish a violation of section 9? Does the government have to prove that a habitat modification actually caused death or injury to specific members of an endangered species? Can it still obtain an injunction to block activities that it fears will cause such harm even before the harm has become evident? In Marbeled Murrelet v. Babbitt, 83 F.3d 1060 (9th Cir. 1996), the Ninth Circuit rejected a timber company's argument that *Sweet Home* required proof of actual past injury to an endangered species before an injunction could be issued to prevent logging that would modify the habitat of an endangered bird. The court held that a "reasonably certain threat of imminent harm to a protected species is sufficient for issuance of an injunction under section 9 of the ESA," 83 F.3d at 1066, and that "habitat modification which significantly impairs the breeding and sheltering of a protected species amounts to 'harm' under the ESA." Id. at 1067. The court found that evidence that approximately 100 endangered birds had been detected in the area throughout their breeding season for three consecutive years, coupled with expert testimony that logging would impair breeding and increase attacks on the birds by predators, was sufficient evidence of future harm to sustain an injunction. In another case the Ninth Circuit upheld a district court's rejection of an environmental group's request to enjoin construction of a high school complex on 60 acres of a 90-acre parcel of land used by endangered pygmy owls. The district judge found that the owls used only the 30 acres of the parcel that would remain undeveloped and fenced off. He noted that the Fish and Wildlife Service did not believe the school construction would harm the owls and that expert testimony offered by

the parties on this issue was inconclusive. Defenders of Wildlife v. Bernal, 204 F.3d 920 (9th Cir. 2000).

When the federal government sought to enjoin logging of a 94-acre tract of old growth forest because a pair of northern spotted owls nested a little more than a mile away, a district court required the government to produce radio-telemetry or other data showing that the owls actually used the tract in question. After giving the government a year to gather data to support its case, the court ultimately lifted its preliminary injunction after deciding that the government had failed to meet its burden of proving that the timber harvest would harm the endangered owls. The court concluded that evidence that the male owl of the pair had foraged on part of the 94-acre tract of old growth forest was insufficient to prove a prospective take in light of the pair's home range of 3,600 acres and its high rate of reproduction. United States v. West Coast Forest Resources, Ltd., 2000 WL 298707 (D. Or. 2000). Evidence that a single endangered piping plover had been found dead in the tire tracks of an off-road vehicle (ORV) was deemed sufficient evidence of harm to grant federal authorities an order requiring a town to prohibit driving of ORVs on a beach where the endangered bird was nesting. United States v. Town of Plymouth, 6 F. Supp. 2d 81 (D. Mass. 1998). Compare Cold Mountain v. Garber, 375 F.3d 884 (9th Cir. 2004) (rejecting studies offered to prove that helicopter hazing harms buffalo).

4. Despite the government's victory in *Sweet Home*, section 9 has not had a sufficiently broad sweep to prevent many forms of habitat modification that are among the most significant causes of species endangerment. These include the decline of natural fires as a landscape shaping device (due to fire suppression efforts or roads that serve as barriers to the spread of fire), habitat fragmentation that causes "edge effects" by opening up formerly safe habitat to predation by other animals, and the introduction of non-native species that threaten naturally occurring ones. Michael J. Bean, The Endangered Species Act and Private Land: Four Lessons Learned From the Past Quarter Century, 28 Envtl. L. Rep. 10701, 10705 (1998). Invasive species encroachment is now considered one of the most significant threats to native ecosystems. To combat this threat, Congress passed the Nonindigenous Aquatic Nuisance Prevention and Control Act of 1990, Pub. L. 101-636, which creates a task force to develop and implement a program to control and to prevent the introduction and dispersal of such species. In February 1999, President Clinton issued Executive Order 13,112 directing all federal agencies to prevent and control introductions of invasive species.

5. The *Palila* case is still the only one to find a taking as a result of a failure to remove a non-native species. Ironically, as a result of the removal of the feral sheep and goats, highly flammable, non-native grasses have now proliferated in the palila's habitat, posing a new and different threat to the bird. Id. at 10,705. Is *Palila II* still good law? In her concurring opinion, Justice O'Connor expressed the view that the case had been "wrongly decided." Do you agree? Noting that none of the other Justices had joined Justice O'Connor's opinion, the Ninth Circuit in Seattle Audubon Society v. Moseley, 80 F.3d 1401 (9th Cir. 1996) stated that "five Justices affirmed *Palila* in all respects." Id. at 1405. Do you agree with this assessment of *Sweet Home*'s impact on *Palila*?

6. The population of grizzly bears in the lower 48 states has declined from more than 50,000 to less than 1,000 who live in small, isolated populations. Because researchers have found that "bears and roads don't mix," managers of national forests have been under pressure to close roads in areas of endangered bear habitat. Kenworthy, Wrestling with a Bear of a Problem in the

Western Wilderness, Wash. Post, Nov. 21, 1994, at A3. In National Wildlife Federation v. Burlington Northern Railroad, 23 F.3d 1508 (9th Cir. 1994), a railroad's accidental spillage of corn along tracks running through bear habitat that led to seven grizzlies being struck and killed by trains was held to be a taking in violation of §9. However, the court refused to issue an injunction in light of the extensive efforts made by the railroad to avoid similar incidents that had helped ensure that no grizzlies had been hit by trains in more than three years.

7. Can state or local agencies that license activities that harm endangered species be held liable for a section 9 taking? In Strahan v. Coxe, 127 F.3d 155 (1st Cir. 1997), the First Circuit held the state of Massachusetts could be held liable for the incidental taking of right whales that became entangled in commercial fishermen's gillnets and lobster pots because the state licensed their use in areas where the whales breed. The court rejected the argument that this was tantamount to holding state motor vehicle regulators liable for all crimes committed by automobile users by noting that such crimes required a "conscious and independent decision" to disregard the law while "the state has licensed commercial fishing operations to use gillnets and lobster pots in specifically the manner that is likely to result in a violation" of section 9 of the ESA. 127 F.3d at 164. In a subsequent case the First Circuit refused to hold the U.S. Coast Guard liable for takings by non-Coast Guard vessels that it licenses on the ground that the agency had no discretion to deny the permits. Strahan v. Linnon, 1998 WL 1085817 (1st Cir. 1998).

8. Some have argued that section 9 of the ESA can be counterproductive by encouraging landowners to make their property inhospitable to endangered species in order to avoid restrictions on development. See Michael J. Bean, The Endangered Species Act and Private Land: Four Lessons Learned from the Past Quarter Century, 28 Envtl. L. Rep. 10,701, 10,706 (1998) (arguing that an exaggerated fear of land use restrictions has prompted preemptive land management practices), but cf. Jeffrey J. Rachlinski, Protecting Endangered Species Without Regulating Private Landowners: The Case of Endangered Plants, 8 Cornell J.L. & Pub. Pol'y 1, 7 (1998) (arguing that situations in which the ESA's land use restriction do more harm than good are probably rare). Responding to these concerns, the federal government has pursued initiatives to encourage landowners to use land management practices that would benefit endangered species largely by making creative use of section 10's provisions for incidental take permits to landowners who implement approved habitat conservation plans (HCPs). Beginning in 1994, the Interior Department has followed a "no surprises" policy assuring participants in HCPs that if the measures in the plan to mitigate the impact of development proved inadequate, the government would bear the risk. This program was adopted as a rule in 1998, 63 Fed. Reg. 8859 (1998). Since 1995 the government also has promoted a "safe harbors" program that allows landowners essentially to "freeze" their responsibilities to a species under the ESA at current levels in return for an agreement to create, enhance, or restore habitat for that species. The program seeks to ensure that landowners who successfully attract additional members of an endangered species to their land will not be "rewarded" with additional restrictions on development. It is implemented through section 10 habitat conservation plans approved by the Fish and Wildlife Service (FWS). For example, in Texas the coastal prairie habitat of the endangered Attwater's prairie chicken has been restored by ranchers under a safe harbor agreement and in South Carolina owners of 84,000

acres of land have pledged to enroll in a program to protect the red-cockaded woodpecker. See Bean, *supra*, at 10,707.

9. The "no surprises" and "safe harbors" programs have been criticized by some environmentalists who argue that they weaken the protections of the ESA by limiting the options available to government authorities in the event that unforeseen circumstances arise. However, Michael Bean argues that while the addition of section 10 to the ESA in 1982 "appeared to weaken the Act by creating a new exception to its nearly absolute prohibition against taking," it actually did the opposite because it gave the FWS "its first practical means of influencing what private landowners did on their lands." Michael J. Bean, The Endangered Species Act and Private Land: Four Lessons Learned From the Past Quarter Century, 28 Envtl. L. Rep. 10,701, 10,708 (1998). He notes that HCPs "can be the vehicles for restoring former habitat, protecting existing but unoccupied habitat, reconnecting fragmented habitats, ensuring active management to replicate the effects of prior natural disturbances, controlling non-native species, and doing a host of other essential things that the taking prohibition has never been able to compel." Id. As of April 2006, a total of 446 major HCPs had been issued covering 30 million acres of land and protecting more than 200 endangered or threatened species. Further information about habitat conservation plans and the "no surprises" program can be found at *http://www.fws.gov/endangered/hcp/NOSURPR.HTM.*

10. Section 9 provides lesser protection for endangered plants than for endangered wildlife. Consider the following report.

Ignoring Pleas of Environmentalists, Kansas Man Digs Up Virgin Prairie
N.Y. Times, Nov. 23, 1990, at B18

The largest remaining stretch of virgin prairie in northeast Kansas disappeared under the plow this week after futile attempts by the Nature Conservancy and local environmentalists to buy it. The plowing of the 80-acre Elkins Prairie was first noticed soon after sunrise on Sunday, and the news quickly spread to a community group that had worked for two years to preserve the land, one of the few remaining unspoiled pieces of the 200 million acres of tall grass prairie that once covered North America.

Environmentalists hurried to the site and pleaded with the landowner to stop his tractor. The Douglas County Commission called an emergency meeting and after negotiating half the night offered to pay the landowner $6,000 an acre within six months, the equivalent of what developers had recently paid for nearby land. But the owner, Jack Graham, rejected the offer and resumed plowing. By late Monday, only a small strip of virgin prairie remained.

"It's heart-wrenching," said Joyce Wolf, leader of a group that had hoped to buy the land for an environmental education area. "He has stolen a resource from a community." Mr. Graham, a 39-year-old businessman who bought the land five years ago, declined to comment on his action. His lawyer, Thomas Murray, said Mr. Graham and his family "simply wanted to make their property more productive," but he would not elaborate.

Only about 2 percent of the original tall-grass prairie in North America remains, and Craig Freeman, coordinator of the state's Natural Heritage

Program, said the Elkins stretch, about a mile outside this booming college town, was a particularly fine example of the complex prairie ecosystem. It was home to 150 species of plants, including two threatened species, Mead's milkweed and the western prairie fringed orchid. . . .

Last year the Nature Conservancy, a national land preservation organization, offered to buy the Elkins Prairie for $3,500 an acre within a year, Ms. Wolf said, a bid that had unintended consequences. The organization's failure to offer a higher price, Mr. Murray said, convinced the Grahams that the land was not as environmentally important as many Lawrence residents believed. The Kansas director of the conservancy, Alan Pollom, defended the offer, saying it was based on an appraisal. "We can't unjustifiably enrich someone using the funds of a nonprofit organization," he said. . . .

"We had hoped to use the Elkins Prairie to teach generations of young people what this countryside looked like before we tore it up into sections and fenced lines and blacktopped roads," said Stan Herd, an artist known for creating large images by planting and plowing farmland. "This was a tiny speck of our heritage, and it's gone."

Throughout the day on Monday, people gathered on a corner across the busy two-lane highway from the Elkins Prairie, talking as they watched the tractor work its way back and forth across the land. "I question the wisdom of plowing up good prairie, but I would defend his right to do it," said Larry Warren, a farmer and neighbor. "It's his land; it's his prerogative."

But Buzz Hoagland, a biology professor at the University of Kansas, argued that individuals have a responsibility to preserve the environment, even at the expense of their own profits. "It took a couple of million years for this land to evolve to the state it is in today, and it took 48 hours to destroy it," Dr. Hoagland said. "One of the things that bothers me the most is that we get up in arms over destruction of the rain forest, when the natural habitats in North America have been all but eliminated. We don't seem to get upset about the destroying of the things in our own backyard."

NOTES AND QUESTIONS

1. Why does the Endangered Species Act provide less protection to plants than to other endangered species? Although it does not directly affect private landowners' use of their property, it can restrict their activities in certain situations, such as when federal permits (e.g., a Clean Water Act section 404 permit to develop wetlands) are needed for activities that may harm listed plants. In those circumstances section 7 of the ESA would prohibit issuance of a permit if it would jeopardize the continued existence of a listed plant or adversely affect land designated as critical habitat. See Jeffrey J. Rachlinski, Protecting Endangered Species Without Regulation Private Landowners: The Case of Endangered Plants, 8 Cornell J.L. & Pub. Pol'y 1, 9 (1998).

2. The article notes that the Elkins Prairie was the home to 150 species of plants, including two threatened species, Mead's milkweed and the western prairie fringed orchid. If threatened plants are entitled to essentially the same protections under the Endangered Species Act as are endangered plants, did Mr. Graham act legally when he plowed up the virgin prairie? Why or why not?

3. Suppose that a local Earth First! group had gotten wind of Mr. Graham's plans to plow up the virgin prairie. They decide to sneak onto the Elkins Prairie

in the middle of the night to dig up as many Mead's milkweeds and western prairie fringed orchids as possible and to transplant them elsewhere. Would such actions violate section 9 of the Endangered Species Act?

4. Does the local environmentalists' unwillingness to pay the price Mr. Graham wanted for the Elkins Prairie demonstrate that it was not worth preserving? Do you agree with Mr. Warren that because the land belonged to Mr. Graham it was his prerogative to plow it under, or with Dr. Hoagland's argument that individuals have a responsibility to preserve the environment even at the expense of their own profits?

PROBLEM EXERCISE: THE ENDANGERED SPECIES ACT

The Four Seasons motel is located on private land in the center of the town of East Yellowstone, which is just outside Yellowstone National Park and in the heart of grizzly bear territory. The fine restaurant of this motel is surrounded by picture windows that overlook its grounds. On one edge of this panorama the motel has placed an open dumpster, where it disposes of all the waste from its kitchen. The dumpster is illuminated by a spotlight.

Garbage is an easy source of food for grizzly bears, and an open dumpster will quickly draw grizzlies away from their usual foraging. So it is no surprise that grizzly bears frequent the dumpster at the Four Seasons motel. Indeed, the bears have become a major attraction for the motel.

Garbage is not known to be harmful to grizzly bears. But the principal cause of grizzly bear mortality is confrontations with humans, and when bears are drawn into town on a regular basis it is likely that a human confrontation will eventually occur. For this reason, the Audubon Society has asked the Four Seasons motel to take the simple measures necessary to ensure that bears cannot get into its dumpster. The motel has refused.

The grizzly bear is listed as a threatened species in Yellowstone and the surrounding area. Can Audubon establish that the Four Seasons motel is violating the Endangered Species Act? What should their theory be?

G. NEW APPROACHES TO BIODIVERSITY PROTECTION

As the inadequacies of an eleventh hour, species-by-species approach to conservation have become more apparent, efforts to reorient public policy toward more forward-looking and comprehensive approaches have gained momentum. These efforts have spawned new initiatives for managing public resources to promote environmental values and to preserve biodiversity. One such effort was the Northwest Forest Plan, an outgrowth of the controversy over efforts to protect the endangered northern spotted owl.

1. The Northwest Forest Plan: An Ecosystem Approach

The ancient forests of the Pacific Northwest sustain rich biological communities that are complex and distinctive ecosystems. In addition to their aesthetic value, old-growth forests are critical and irreplaceable reservoirs of biological diversity. Containing 500-year-old evergreens towering more than 300 feet, the Northwest's old-growth forests are the habitat of the rare northern spotted owl, which became both the symbol of the forest's ecological values and a lightning rod for controversy. Scientists estimate that thousands of acres of old-growth forest are necessary to provide an adequate food supply for one pair of these beautiful birds. As logging reduced the habitat of the owl, its numbers dwindled to fewer than 3,000 pairs and its continued survival is now in jeopardy.

When it became apparent the spotted owl was a "threatened" species, an Interagency Scientific Committee (ISC) was established by the Forest Service, Bureau of Land Management (BLM), the Fish and Wildlife Service, and the National Park Service to develop a habitat conservation strategy for the spotted owl. On April 2, 1990, the ISC issued its Report of the Interagency Scientific Committee to Address the Conservation of the Northern Spotted Owl, A Conservation Strategy for the Northern Spotted Owl (1990). The report concluded that "the owl is imperiled over significant portions of its range because of continuing losses of habitat from logging and natural disturbances" and that "delay in implementing a conservation strategy cannot be justified on the basis of inadequate knowledge." On June 22, 1990, the owl was formally listed as a threatened species under the Endangered Species Act. 55 Fed. Reg. 26,114 (1990).

In January 1992, the Fish and Wildlife Service proposed a habitat conservation plan for the spotted owl that would restrict logging on 6.9 million acres of land owned by the federal government. The Service predicted that its plan would cost 20,700 jobs in the timber industry, based on a model assuming 10.3 jobs lost per million board feet of unsold timber. Timber industry representatives denounced the plan as "a legal lynching of an entire region by an out-of-control federal agency." Logging Limits Proposed on 7 Million Acres, N.Y. Times, Jan. 10, 1992, at A12.

BLM refused to adopt the guidelines recommended by the ISC. Faced with a preliminary determination that several of its proposed sales might jeopardize the continued existence of the spotted owl, BLM refused to enter consultations with the Fish and Wildlife Service, the usual process for finding alternatives that could avoid jeopardy. Rather, in September 1991, BLM asked the Secretary of Interior to convene the "God Squad" established by section 7(e) of the Endangered Species Act so that it could seek an exemption from the Act's restrictions as applied to 44 sales of old-growth timber. The Secretary approved the request to convene the panel.

The hearing convened in January 1992. On May 15, 1992, the Committee issued its decision. By a 5-2 vote, the Committee granted BLM an exemption for 13 of the 44 proposed sales.

In June 1992, the Sierra Club Legal Defense Fund and ten other environmental organizations filed suit in the U.S. Court of Appeals for the Ninth Circuit, challenging the God Squad's decision. The lawsuit claimed that BLM failed to show (1) that the sales were of regional or national significance, (2) that there were no alternatives with lesser effects on the spotted owl, (3) that the benefits of the sales clearly outweighed the costs of more protective alternatives, and (4) that the public interest supported proceeding with the sales. After the Clinton administration informed the court that it did not wish to go forward with the timber sales exempted by the God Squad, the government agreed to vacate the God Squad's decision, and the Ninth Circuit dismissed the Sierra Club's lawsuit as moot.

In an effort to resolve the spotted owl controversy, President Clinton convened a forest conference in Portland on April 2, 1993, to hear the views of environmental leaders, timber industry representatives, the public, and government officials. On July 1, 1993, President Clinton unveiled a plan to reduce sales of public timber to 1.2 billion board feet per year (approximately one-third of previous levels) while providing more than $1 billion in economic assistance to displaced loggers. The plan, called the "Pacific (or Northwest) Forest Plan" includes a system of interconnected reserves of old-growth forest, stream buffers to protect aquatic species, and new rules for timber harvests outside the core reserves that will require logging operations to be more selective.

In December 1994, the Northwest Forest Plan was approved by Judge Dwyer in Seattle Audubon Society v. Lyons, 871 F. Supp. 1291 (W.D. Wash. 1994). He noted that the plan was "the result of a massive effort by the executive branch of the federal government to meet the legal and scientific needs of forest management." 871 F. Supp. at 1303. Praising the government for "unprecedented thoroughness in doing this complex and difficult job," the judge rejected all challenges to the record of decision and final supplemental EIS for the forest management plan. He expressly endorsed the use of an ecosystem approach to management of old-growth forest habitat. Indeed, the judge observed that "[g]iven the current condition of the forests, there is no way the agencies could comply with the environmental laws *without* planning on an ecosystem basis." 871 F. Supp. at 1311 (emphasis in original). However, he cautioned that "any more logging sales than the plan contemplates would probably violate the laws." Thus, he warned that its continued legality "will depend upon future events and conditions." Id. at 1300. This decision was affirmed in Seattle Audubon Society v. Moseley, 80 F.3d 1401 (9th Cir. 1996).

Then-Secretary of the Interior Bruce Babbitt stated that the Northwest Forest Plan "represents, in my judgment, the beginning of an entirely new chapter in American resource history" by "deploy[ing] science in search for a model of sustainable forestry." Bruce Babbitt, Science: Opening the Next Chapter of Conservation History, 267 Science 1954 (1995).

While praising the Northwest Forest Plan, Professor Oliver Houck cautions that policies promoted as "ecosystem management" can be used to provide cover for "politics with a strong flavor of law-avoidance." Houck, On the Law of Biodiversity and Ecosystem Management, 81 Minn. L. Rev. 869, 975 (1997). He notes that the U.S. Forest Service, which has an explicit statutory directive to protect biodiversity in section 6(g)(3)(B) of the National Forest Management Act, 16 U.S.C. 1604(g)(3)(B), has used "ecosystem management" as a vehicle for backing away from forest planning focused explicitly on biodiversity. Id. at 923-929. Houck prefers approaches like the Northwest Forest Plan that use indicator species to develop objective, numerical requirements tied to express species recovery goals. He also cites the interim strategy for managing anadromous fish habitats developed by the NMFS and BLM in 1993 that required the creation of specific buffer zones around streams designated as Riparian Habitat Conservation Areas. Timber harvests were prohibited in these areas and other development activity was discouraged in order to achieve specific water quality objectives to protect endangered salmon. Id. at 934-935.

As a result of the listing of several species of salmon on the endangered species list, the National Marine Fisheries Service (NMFS) has issued biological opinions on the effect of the Northwest Forest Plan on endangered salmon. Blumm and Corbin note that the courts may not scrutinize land management consultation plans very strictly due to their level of generality, but that they have shown that they will not allow specific projects to proceed based solely on the assumption that protections promised in the Northwest Forest Plan will be implemented. Blumm & Corbin, Salmon and the Endangered Species Act: Lessons from the Columbia Basin, 74 Wash. L. Rev. 519, 580-582 (1999).

In August 1999, Judge Dwyer ruled that the Forest Service and the BLM had violated the terms of the Northwest Forest Plan by failing to conduct certain wildlife surveys mandated by the Plan before timber sales can be approved. Oregon Natural Resources Council Action v. U.S. Forest Service, 59 F. Supp. 2d 1085 (W.D. Wash. 1999). While the judge rejected a claim by environmentalists that a supplemental EIS should be prepared because environmental conditions had deteriorated more than anticipated, he granted a preliminary injunction halting sales of 100 million board feet of old-growth timber.

In August 2002 President George W. Bush announced a "Healthy Forests" Initiative designed "to prevent the damage caused by catastrophic wildfires by reducing unnecessary regulatory obstacles that hinder active forest management." Arguing that forest fires have been made more catastrophic due to failure to harvest dead trees and brush, the administration's plan seeks to reduce environmental reviews of certain operations in the national forests. The Bush administration argues that the "1994 Northwest Forest Plan, which was designed to produce a healthy and sustainable forest economy while providing needed habitat protection, has failed to live up to its promise due to costly delays and unnecessary litigation." It has pledged to "work with all interested parties, including Congress, to resolve the legal and procedural problems that have undermined the promise of the Northwest Forest Plan."

2. Reauthorizing the Endangered Species Act

Because the costs of species protection measures are far more visible and immediate than are the diffuse, long-term benefits of preserving biodiversity, efforts to relax the provisions of the ESA continue. Arguments by opponents of the ESA resemble those made by loggers protesting outside the "God Squad" hearings on the spotted owl, who carried signs reading "Loggers Pay Taxes, Owls Do Not" and "We Need Jobs, Not Birds." Egan, Politics Reign at Spotted Owl Hearing, N.Y. Times, Jan. 9, 1992, at A14. A BLM lawyer at the hearings argued that it is immoral to favor animals over humans and that current policy "is far more likely to result in homeless people rather than homeless owls." Id. Alaska Congressman Don Young argues that protection of the spotted owl is a product of "imperfect 'feel good' legislation [that causes] a comfortable urbanized population to be spared the costs of their compulsions" while imposing these costs on others. Young, The Survival of the Fittest, 1990 Envtl. Forum, 34 (July-Aug. 1990).

Congressman Young and others argue that ESA should be amended to compensate private interests affected by the Act, to remove protections for certain species deemed not worth saving, and to require that listing decisions be based on a balancing of the costs and benefits of listing. Michael Bean, an attorney with the Environmental Defense Fund, replies that uncertainty makes it impossible to incorporate such approaches into the Endangered Species Act. Bean, We Don't Know the Benefits Side of the Equation, 7 Envtl. Forum 30 (July-Aug. 1990).

Public opinion polls show strong support for the Endangered Species Act even when the spotted owl controversy was in the news. A poll released in 1992 showed that voters supported the Act by 66 percent to 11 percent. When asked to choose between protecting species or saving jobs and businesses, species protection won out by a margin of 48 percent to 29 percent. Sawhill, Saving Endangered Species Doesn't Endanger Economy, Wall St. J., Feb. 20, 1992, at A15.

In an effort to win public support for proposals to relax the ESA, its critics argue that it has not been successful and thus needs "fixing." The National Research Council (NRC) has published a report evaluating experience under the ESA. NRC, Science and the Endangered Species Act (1995). The report, which had been commissioned by Congress, found that "the ESA is based on sound scientific principles." Id. at 4. Noting that the Earth is experiencing a major mass extinction of species, the report concluded that "[t]he major cause of the current extinction is human activity," unlike the other five mass extinctions of the past 500 million years. Id. at 5. While finding it "difficult to quantify the effectiveness of the act in preventing species extinction," the report concluded that "there is no doubt that it has prevented the extinction of some species and slowed the declines of others." Id. at 4. The NRC recommended that critical habitat for the survival of threatened or endangered species be designated immediately upon listing, rather than waiting for years after listing. It also endorsed the notion of protecting distinct subpopulations of species and it found no scientific reason for providing lesser protection for plants than for animals.

On September 29, 2005, the U.S. House of Representatives approved a bill that would make substantial changes in the ESA. Called the "Threatened and Endangered Species Recovery Act of 2006," the bill was championed by Congressman Richard Pombo, the Republican chairman of the House Resources Committee. It passed the House by a vote of 229-193 after an environmentally more sensitive substitute was defeated by a vote of 206-216. Under the bill, which is believed to be unlikely to win Senate approval, private landowners may request a written determination of whether a proposed use of their property would violate section 9 of the ESA. If no such determination is issued within 180 days, the proposed use is to be deemed to comply with the ESA. If a determination is made that the proposed use would violate section 9, the legislation requires the government to compensate the landowner based on the fair market value of the foregone use. One unusual provision in the bill is a requirement that customers of federal power projects receive a line-item on their bills for ESA compliance costs.

Supporters of the ESA deny that it has been a failure. They credit it with playing a substantial role in the dramatic recovery of many species, such as the bald eagle and the whooping crane, and they emphasize that programs like "SafeHarbors" and Candidate Conservation Agreements have helped reduce compliance burdens and provided private landowners with incentives to engage in voluntary actions to preserve biodiversity.

In 2003, on the thirtieth anniversary of enactment of the ESA, a coalition of environmental groups released a set of thirty success stories of species that have been protected by the ESA. These facts sheets are available online at http://www.stopextinction.org/site/c.epIQKXOBJsG/b.913259/k.9D77/ESA_Celebrates_30_Years_of_Species_Protection_with_30_Success_Stories.htm.

In March 2006, a group of 5,738 biologists signed a letter to the U.S. Senate "Concerning Science in the Endangered Species Act." The biologists praised the ESA and criticized proposals to weaken its protections. They observed that:

> [L]ess than one percent of listed species have gone extinct since 1973, while 10 percent of candidate species still waiting to be listed have suffered that fate. In addition to the hundreds of species that the Act has protected from extinction, listing has contributed to population increases or the stabilization of populations for at least 35 percent of listed species, and perhaps significantly more, as well as the recovery of such signature species as the peregrine falcon. While complete recovery has been realized for just two percent of species listed, given the precarious state of most species when listed, this represents significant progress. [Letter from 5,738 Biologists to the U.S. Senate Concerning Science in the Endangered Species Act, March 2006, available online at http://www. lawprofessors.typepad.com/environmental_law/files/Biologists_Letter_full_ list_whitecover.pdf]

The biologists stressed the importance of the ESA's emphasis on "best available science" and they criticized efforts to mandate the use of non-scientific factors to delay or block listing decisions, designations of critical habitat or implementation of species recovery plans.

=10=

‖ *Environmental Enforcement* ‖

Unfortunately, our system of public environmental enforcement is more fragile and overwhelmed than most people realize. Annual enforcement accomplishment reports praise government's effectiveness in enforcing the law. But, there is less than meets the eye to claims that the law is being effectively enforced. Despite the many enforcement success stories reported by the government, the number of violations overwhelm the enforcement capacity of both the federal and state governments.

—*David R. Hodas**

What's it to you?

—*Antonin Scalia***

If regulation is to achieve its goals, it must induce compliance. Thus it is critical that the environmental laws include enforcement provisions that create incentives for compliance. While the environmental statutes provide broad enforcement authorities, compliance problems have been widespread. A survey of corporate counsel found that two-thirds admitted that their companies recently had violated the environmental laws. Lavelle, Environmental Vise: Law, Compliance, Nat'l L.J., Aug. 30, 1993, at S1. Most of the lawyers surveyed asserted that it was not possible to achieve full compliance with the environmental laws because of their cost, complexity, or the uncertainty that surrounds how they are interpreted. Yet virtually all believed that environmental regulation is becoming more stringent throughout the world, and nearly 70 percent agreed that greater attention to environmental concerns would enhance the long-term profitability of their companies.

Many factors contribute to environmental enforcement problems. The vast number and diversity of regulatory targets make compliance monitoring difficult. Often, regulations are poorly designed from an enforcement perspective. Some judges still view regulatory violations as technical matters if they do not clearly cause substantial harm. Enforcement resources are limited and the procedural protections afforded defendants increase with the stringency of potential penalties. When government agencies, which have included some of the most notorious polluters, break the environmental laws, they often do not face credible enforcement sanctions.

This chapter explores how environmental laws are enforced by governmental authorities and citizens. It begins by focusing on how compliance with

---

* Enforcement of Environmental Law in a Triangular Federal System: Can Three Not Be a Crowd When Enforcement Authority Is Shared by the United States, the States, and their Citizens? 54 Md. L. Rev. 1552, 1558-1559 (1995).

** The Doctrine of Standing as an Essential Element of Separation of Powers, 17 Suffolk Univ. L. Rev. 881, 882 (1983).

environmental regulations is monitored and the controversy over policies providing incentives to encourage voluntary self-audits. The chapter then explores criminal enforcement of the environmental laws and the debate over what *mens rea* is required before criminal sanctions can be imposed on violators. Standing and citizen access to the courts is discussed next, followed by a discussion of the role of citizen suits in enforcing the laws. The chapter concludes by focusing on problems that arise when enforcement actions are brought against government agencies.

A.   MONITORING AND DETECTING VIOLATIONS

Serious enforcement difficulties can be avoided if regulatory programs are designed to facilitate compliance monitoring. Establishing objective means for measuring and monitoring compliance can be enormously difficult given the vast number, variety, and complexity of pollutants and dischargers subject to environmental regulation. The Clean Water Act regulates more than 350,000 point sources discharging hundreds of different pollutants. Yet the Act's permit provisions have become a model for other enforcement programs, including the Clean Air Act's new national permit program. Permits embody a written record of the controls applicable to each source that can be compared with the results of monitoring to determine if violations have occurred.

Determining whether or not a discharger is in compliance with permit limits is not as easy as one might think. Inspectors cannot simply walk into any plant, insert "some perfectly accurate meter into the waste-water or smoke stack emission stream," and obtain "a constant rate-of-discharge result that could be expressed equally well in any time unit, from per second to per year." C. Russell, W. Harrington & W. Vaughan, Enforcing Pollution Control Laws 10 (1986). Inspectors first have to gain access to a plant, which usually involves announcing inspections in advance, giving the plant operator an opportunity to conceal violations. Sampling is costly and time-consuming and may yield results with large margins of error.

> [E]ven when the source is trying to comply with the permit terms it will have fluctuating discharges. These fluctuations may have both periodic elements due to production patterns, boiler soot-blowing, or other routine causes as well as random components ultimately traceable to human or machine failure, fluctuations in ambient conditions such as temperature, or random startup and shut-down decisions. Thus, the stream being measured is not constant, and measurements at one time can be applied only to broader compliance questions through statistical inference with associated probabilities of errors of two types—that a violation will be found where none exists or that true violations will be missed. To further complicate matters, the measurement instruments have their own errors that must be accounted for in the inference procedure. The perfect instrument does not exist. [Id.]

Faced with these difficulties, environmental enforcement authorities rely heavily on self-monitoring and self-reporting requirements to detect violations. The pollution control statutes generally authorize EPA to impose monitoring, recordkeeping, and reporting requirements (e.g., CWA §308(a)(A), CAA §114) on dischargers. Under the Clean Water Act, dischargers of water pollutants are required to monitor their discharges on a regular basis and to file discharge monitoring reports (DMRs) that are available to the public. When self-reported violations are included in DMRs, it is relatively easy for regulatory authorities or citizen groups to bring successful enforcement actions. Recognizing the danger that sources will not report adverse monitoring data truthfully, regulatory authorities prosecute reporting violations with vigor. When false reporting or tampering with monitoring data has been discovered, criminal prosecutions often follow. To make it possible to uncover false reports, the environmental laws generally give enforcement officials the right to conduct inspections. However, EPA needs a warrant before it can inspect a business without the consent of the owner. Marshall v. Barlow's, Inc., 436 U.S. 307 (1978).

Although it is not widely known, most of the major federal environmental statutes have provisions that protect employees who report violations by their employers. These provisions prohibit an employer from discharging or discriminating against any employee who reports environmental violations (e.g., CWA §507, CAA §322, OSHA §660(c), RCRA §7001, CERCLA §110, SDWA §1450(i), TSCA §23). Regulations implementing these statutes appear at 29 C.F.R. §§24.1 et seq. Whistle-blowers may seek a hearing before an administrative law judge in the Department of Labor who may award them back pay, reinstatement, or other relief, subject to judicial review and civil judicial enforcement. These provisions have not been used extensively. Robert Devore of the Department of Labor reported that between 1983 and 1991, 490 whistle-blower complaints were heard by the Department; 92 employees won judgments, which totaled $822,900. Most cases involved the provisions of section 210 of the Energy Reorganization Act, which protects workers at nuclear power plants.

When it amended the Clean Air Act in 1990, Congress sought to help enforcement authorities acquire evidence of violations by adding a bounty provision in section 113(f) of the Act. This authorizes EPA to pay a reward of up to $10,000 to anyone who provides information that leads to a criminal conviction or civil penalty under the Act. Bounty provisions also are included in CERCLA section 109(d) and the Act to Prevent Pollution from Ships. The latter generated a $250,000 reward for tourists on a cruise ship who videotaped the ship's illegal waste disposal at sea, resulting in a $500,000 fine against the Princess Cruise Line.

In the 1990 Clean Air Act Amendments, Congress also sought to make it procedurally much easier to enforce the requirements of the Act. The original Clean Air Act had made it very difficult to prove violations. Prosecutors had to show that an individual source had acted in a manner that violated the applicable state implementation plan (SIP), which was very difficult, particularly since it was hard even to identify what SIP requirements were applicable to a specific source. To correct this problem, the 1990 Amendments established a federal operating permit system in Title V of the Clean Air Act, modeled in part on the Clean Water Act's NPDES permit program.

To make it easier to enforce the new Title V permits, Congress required major sources of air pollution to improve their emissions monitoring and reporting. To improve monitoring, utilities subject to Title IV of the Clean Air Act must install continuous emissions monitoring systems or their equivalent. CAA §412(a), 42 U.S.C. §7651k(a). Tampering with monitoring equipment may result in criminal prosecutions when detected. See, e.g., Schneider, Coal Company Admits Safety Test Fraud, N.Y. Times, Jan. 19, 1991, at A14 (since 1980, six mining companies have been convicted for tampering with devices that monitor levels of coal dust in mines). Congress has directed EPA in section 412(d) of the Clean Air Act to issue regulations specifying the consequences of breakdowns in monitoring equipment. To provide an incentive for utilities to keep monitors operating properly (and to prevent them from turning off monitors to conceal high levels of emissions), EPA adopted a rule that assumes that emissions are at a higher level "the longer the gap in recorded data and/or the lower the annual monitor availability. . . ." 58 Fed. Reg. 3,590, 3,635 (1993). Maximum emissions levels are assumed for any outage from a continuous emissions monitor (CEM) that has not achieved at least 90 percent availability in the prior year, while average values are assumed for outages of less than 24 hours from CEMs that have been available more than 95 percent of the time.

Enforcement officials recognize that even effective emissions monitoring will not guarantee full compliance with all environmental regulations. Given the large number of entities subject to regulation, the diversity of the regulated community, and limited government enforcement resources, efforts to promote voluntary compliance are essential. Thus, enforcement officials are encouraging firms to perform voluntary self-audits to discover and correct environmental violations.

In response to concerns that self-audits could generate information that would make it easier to prosecute companies, several states have enacted laws making the results of such audits privileged information. In July 1993, Oregon became the first state to adopt a law creating a qualified "environmental self-audit privilege." The law provides that environmental audits will be protected from disclosure in criminal prosecutions if violations discovered in the audit are promptly corrected, unless the privilege is asserted for a fraudulent purpose or the prosecution can establish a compelling need for the information. By April 1996, 18 states had enacted audit privilege statutes. Cushman, Many States Give Polluting Firms New Protections, N.Y. Times, Apr. 7, 1996, at A1. The state laws have followed two principal models: (1) the "privilege-only" model, adopted in Oregon and five other states, which bars environmental audits and related documents from being used as evidence in civil or criminal proceedings, and (2) the "privilege and immunity" model, adopted in Colorado and 11 other states, which provides immunity from any type of penalty in addition to making the audit privileged. Van Cleve & Holman, Promise and Reality in the Enforcement of the Amended Clean Air Act—Part II: Federal Enforceability and Environmental Auditing, 27 Envtl. L. Rep. 10,151, 10,161 (1997). There are some variations on the privilege and immunity model. In Colorado, the legislation creates a presumption of immunity from all penalties for violations found during "self-evaluations" which are voluntarily disclosed and addressed within a reasonable time. The presumption of immunity can be rebutted only if an enforcement agency proves that the disclosure was not voluntary. The Texas law requires companies that wish to qualify for immunity to provide public notice of their intent to conduct a self-audit. During the first year of experience with the law, 239 companies in Texas gave notice of their intent to audit. Id.

While opposing legislation to create audit privileges, EPA and the Justice Department have sought to encourage voluntary self-auditing. In 1991, the Justice Department issued guidelines providing that self-auditing and voluntary disclosure of environmental violations would be considered important mitigating factors when prosecutorial discretion is exercised and at sentencing. Spurred in part by the proliferation of state privilege legislation, EPA began in 1994 to explore whether additional incentives were needed to encourage self-auditing. While developing its policy on self-auditing, EPA noted that a survey conducted by Price Waterhouse in 1995 found that half of corporate respondents would expand their environmental auditing efforts if penalties were reduced for violations voluntarily discovered and corrected. 60 Fed. Reg. 66,711 (1995).

After conducting several public meetings and receiving extensive public comment on an interim policy, EPA adopted a final policy statement in December 1995. The policy seeks to encourage firms voluntarily to discover, disclose, and correct environmental violations by reducing civil penalties for such violations and by agreeing not to pursue criminal prosecutions for them if certain conditions are met. In April 2000, EPA made minor revisions to its incentives for self-policing policy. An excerpt from EPA's policy, as revised, is reproduced below.

EPA, *Final Policy Statement on Incentives for Self-Policing of Violations*
65 Fed. Reg. 19,618 (2000)

C. INCENTIVES FOR SELF-POLICING

1. No Gravity-Based Penalties

If a regulated entity establishes that it satisfies all of the conditions of Section D of this Policy, EPA will not seek gravity-based penalties for violations of Federal environmental requirements discovered and disclosed by the entity.

2. Reduction of Gravity-Based Penalties by 75%

If a regulated entity establishes that it satisfies all of the conditions of Section D of this Policy except for D(1)—systematic discovery—EPA will reduce by 75% gravity-based penalties for violations of Federal environmental requirements discovered and disclosed by the entity.

3. No Recommendation for Criminal Prosecution

(a) If a regulated entity establishes that it satisfies at least conditions D(2) through D(9) of this Policy, EPA will not recommend to the U.S. Department of Justice or other prosecuting authority that criminal charges be brought against the disclosing entity, as long as EPA determines that the violation is not part of a pattern or practice that demonstrates or involves:

(i) A prevalent management philosophy or practice that conceals or condones environmental violations; or

(ii) High-level corporate officials' or managers' conscious involvement in, or willfull blindness to, violations of Federal environmental law;

(b) Whether or not EPA recommends the regulated entity for criminal prosecution under this section, the Agency may recommend for prosecution the criminal acts of individual managers or employees under existing policies guiding the exercise of enforcement discretion.

4.   No Routine Request for Environmental Audit Reports

EPA will neither request nor use an environmental audit report to initiate a civil or criminal investigation of an entity. For example, EPA will not request an environmental audit report in routine inspections. If the Agency has independent reason to believe that a violation has occurred, however, EPA may seek any information relevant to identifying violations or determining liability or extent of harm.

D.   CONDITIONS

1.   Systematic Discovery

The violation was discovered through:
(a) An environmental audit; or
(b) A compliance management system reflecting the regulated entity's due diligence in preventing, detecting, and correcting violations. The regulated entity must provide accurate and complete documentation to the Agency as to how its compliance management system meets the criteria for due diligence outlined in section B and how the regulated entity discovered the violation through its compliance management system. EPA may require the regulated entity to make publicly available a description of its compliance management system.

2.   Voluntary Discovery

The violation was discovered voluntarily and not through a legally mandated monitoring or sampling requirement prescribed by statute, regulation, permit, judicial or administrative order, or consent agreement. For example, the Policy does not apply to:
(a) Emissions violations detected through a continuous emissions monitor (or alternative monitor established in a permit) where any such monitoring is required;
(b) Violations of National Pollutant Discharge Elimination System (NPDES) discharge limits detected through required sampling or monitoring; or
(c) Violations discovered through a compliance audit required to be performed by the terms of a consent order or settlement agreement, unless the audit is a component of agreement terms to implement a comprehensive environmental management system.

3.   Prompt Disclosure

The regulated entity fully discloses the specific violation in writing to EPA within 21 days (or within such shorter time as may be required by law) after the entity discovered that the violation has, or may have, occurred. The time at which the entity discovers that a violation has, or may have, occurred begins when any officer, director, employee or agent of the facility has an objectively reasonable basis for believing that a violation has, or may have, occurred.

4. Discovery and Disclosure Independent of Government or Third-Party Plaintiff

(a) The regulated entity discovers and discloses the potential violation to EPA prior to:

(i) The commencement of a Federal, State or local agency inspection or investigation, or the issuance by such agency of an information request to the regulated entity (where EPA determines that the facility did not know that it was under civil investigation, and EPA determines that the entity is otherwise acting in good faith, the Agency may exercise its discretion to reduce or waive civil penalties in accordance with this Policy);

(ii) Notice of a citizen suit;

(iii) The filing of a complaint by a third party;

(iv) The reporting of the violation to EPA (or other government agency) by a "whistleblower" employee, rather than by one authorized to speak on behalf of the regulated entity; or

(v) imminent discovery of the violation by a regulatory agency.

(b) For entities that own or operate multiple facilities, the fact that one facility is already the subject of an investigation, inspection, information request or third-party complaint does not preclude the Agency from exercising its discretion to make the Audit Policy available for violations self-discovered at other facilities owned or operated by the same regulated entity.

5. Correction and Remediation

The regulated entity corrects the violation within 60 calendar days from the date of discovery, certifies in writing that the violation has been corrected, and takes appropriate measures as determined by EPA to remedy any environmental or human harm due to the violation. EPA retains the authority to order an entity to correct a violation within a specific time period shorter than 60 days whenever correction in such shorter period of time is feasible and necessary to protect public health and the environment adequately. If more than 60 days will be needed to correct the violation, the regulated entity must so notify EPA in writing before the 60-day period has passed. Where appropriate, to satisfy conditions D(5) and D(6), EPA may require a regulated entity to enter into a publicly available written agreement, administrative consent order or judicial consent decree as a condition of obtaining relief under the Audit Policy, particularly where compliance or remedial measures are complex or a lengthy schedule for attaining and maintaining compliance or remediating harm is required.

6. Prevent Recurrence

The regulated entity agrees in writing to take steps to prevent a recurrence of the violation. Such steps may include improvements to its environmental auditing or compliance management system.

7.   No Repeat Violations

The specific violation (or a closely related violation) has not occurred previously within the past three years at the same facility, and has not occurred within the past five years as part of a pattern at multiple facilities owned or operated by the same entity. For the purposes of this section, a violation is:

(a) Any violation of Federal, State or local environmental law identified in a judicial or administrative order, consent agreement or order, complaint, or notice of violation, conviction or plea agreement; or

(b) Any act or omission for which the regulated entity has previously received penalty mitigation from EPA or a State or local agency.

8.   Other Violations Excluded

The violation is not one which (a) resulted in serious actual harm, or may have presented an imminent and substantial endangerment, to human health or the environment, or (b) violates the specific terms of any judicial or administrative order, or consent agreement.

9.   Cooperation

The regulated entity cooperates as requested by EPA and provides such information as is necessary and requested by EPA to determine applicability of this Policy.

E.   Economic Benefit

EPA retains its full discretion to recover any economic benefit gained as a result of noncompliance to preserve a "level playing field" in which violators do not gain a competitive advantage over regulated entities that do comply. EPA may forgive the entire penalty for violations that meet conditions D(1) through D(9) and, in the Agency's opinion, do not merit any penalty due to the insignificant amount of any economic benefit.

F.   Effect on State Law, Regulation or Policy

EPA will work closely with States to encourage their adoption and implementation of policies that reflect the incentives and conditions outlined in this Policy. EPA remains firmly opposed to statutory environmental audit privileges that shield evidence of environmental violations and undermine the public's right to know, as well as to blanket immunities, particularly immunities for violations that reflect criminal conduct, present serious threats or actual harm to health and the environment, allow noncomplying companies to gain an economic advantage over their competitors, or reflect a repeated failure to comply with Federal law. EPA will work with States to address any provisions of State audit privilege or immunity laws that are inconsistent with this Policy and that may prevent a timely and appropriate response to significant environmental violations. The Agency reserves its rights to take necessary actions to protect public health or the environment by enforcing against any violations of Federal law.

NOTES AND QUTESTIONS

1. Why does EPA's policy distinguish between violations discovered through an environmental audit or compliance management system that reflects due diligence and all other violations? What are the consequences of this distinction with respect to EPA's willingness to reduce penalties?

2. Several environmental laws require regulated entities to self-report information that may include data indicating that a firm violated the law. EPA's initial interim self-audit policy statement did not allow disclosures of violations required to be reported by statute, regulation, or permit to qualify for penalty reductions. 60 Fed. Reg. 16,875, 16,877 (1995). However, after complaints that this would severely limit incentives for self-policing, EPA adopted a somewhat different approach. EPA concluded that the "final policy generally applies to any violation that is voluntarily discovered, regardless of whether the violation is required to be reported." 60 Fed. Reg. 66,706, 66,708 (1995). But the final policy states that violations identified through legally required monitoring will not be considered to have been voluntarily discovered. Would Exxon's notification to the Coast Guard that the *Exxon Valdez* was spilling enormous quantities of oil in Prince William Sound constitute "voluntary discovery" under EPA's policy? Could it qualify Exxon for a reduction of gravity-based penalties for the oil spill?

3. By August 1999, a total of 430 companies had reported environmental violations at 1,788 facilities in order to qualify for reduced penalties under EPA's self-audit policy. Relief had been granted to 164 companies at 540 facilities where violations were disclosed and corrected. EPA, Enforcement and Compliance Assurance FY1998 Accomplishments Report, 4 (1999). Most of the companies were not required to pay penalties. Herman, It Takes a Partnership, 14 Envtl. Forum 26, 31 (May/June 1997). EPA reported in January 2002 that during fiscal year 2001 a total of 364 companies agreed to conduct self-audits and to correct environmental violations at 1,754 facilities in exchange for a waiver or significant reduction in penalties from EPA. While many industry groups have been critical of EPA's policy for not going far enough to create incentives for self-auditing, others have greeted it with cautious optimism. Banks, EPA's New Enforcement Policy: At Last, a Reliable Roadmap to Civil Penalty Mitigation for Self-Disclosed Violations, 26 Envtl. L. Rep. 10227 (1996).

4. EPA's policy offers to waive all or 75 percent of "gravity-based penalties," which the agency defines as "that portion of a penalty over and above the economic benefit," 60 Fed. Reg. 66,711 (1995). Why does EPA insist on retaining the discretion to recover a defendant's economic gain from noncompliance? Will this insistence tend to encourage or discourage prompt discovery and correction of violations? When it revised its initial incentives for self-policing policy in April 2000, EPA also adopted a Final Policy on Compliance Incentives for Small Business. 65 Fed. Reg. 19,630. The most significant aspect of EPA's policy for encouraging compliance by small businesses is that it provides that EPA will forgo all penalties—including recovery of the economic benefit of violations—for small businesses that make a "good faith" effort to comply with regulations either through conducting environmental audits or receiving on-site compliance assistance. Small businesses are defined as companies with 100 or fewer employees on a companywide basis. Why would EPA be willing to forgo recovery of the economic benefit of violations when small businesses are the violators?

5. During its 1996 session, a state legislature considered a bill that would grant immunity for environmental violations discovered during an environmental

audit if they are voluntarily disclosed and corrected. The bill defined voluntary disclosure to mean a written disclosure that occurs prior to: (1) discovery or knowledge of the violation by the state environmental agency, (2) the initiation of an enforcement action by the state or EPA, or (3) the regulated entity's actual knowledge that the discovery of the violation by a regulatory agency or a third party is imminent. How is this legislation different from EPA's policy? Which would do more to encourage prompt disclosure and correction of violations, EPA's policy or the proposed state law?

6. EPA has expressed concern that some legislation undermines the ability of states to operate their delegated federal programs effectively. Citizen groups in several states have petitioned EPA to withdraw delegation of federal authority on the ground that the privilege and immunity laws prevent their states from enforcing federal requirements adequately. EPA has taken the position that state laws barring penalties for violations would not be applicable in federal enforcement actions. Fear of federal program withdrawal reportedly influenced at least one state to allow its privilege and immunity law to lapse. Some states have considered adopting audit laws that are expressly modeled on EPA's self-audit policy to ensure compliance with federal requirements.

7. California uses a stick, rather than a carrot, to encourage corporate disclosure of safety hazards. California's Corporate Criminal Liability Act, Cal. Penal Code §387, requires corporate managers to notify their employees and state authorities in writing when they become aware of "a serious concealed danger" in a workplace. Failure to disclose such hazards is a felony punishable by up to three years in prison and a fine of up to $1 million. What effect is this law likely to have on corporate enthusiasm for self-audits of workplace hazards?

8. When it adopted the 1990 Clean Air Act Amendments, Congress rejected a proposal to preclude prosecutions for violations discovered and corrected following environmental audits. Opponents feared that such immunity could be abused to insulate corporations from sanctions for serious violations. Proposals for even broader immunity now regularly surface in Congress. During the Clinton administration EPA and the Justice Department strongly opposed enactment of such immunity or the creation of a federal self-audit privilege. They argued that immunity would severely undermine compliance incentives and that an audit privilege would permit companies to use self-audits as dumping grounds for incriminating information to shield against its use in subsequent prosecutions. They also argued that audit privilege legislation will further complicate enforcement cases by creating endless litigation over questions of privilege. They maintained that there is no need for such legislation since there has been no federal or state case in which a criminal prosecution was premised on the results of a self-audit voluntarily disclosed to the government.

9. A study conducted by the National Conference of State Legislatures surveyed environmental compliance officials at 988 manufacturing facilities in more than 30 states. The study found that more than 75 percent of the facilities performed compliance audits, but that there was no statistically significant difference in auditing rates between facilities in states with laws or policies to encourage auditing and those in states without them. Most facilities did not disclose violations discovered during an audit and there was no significant difference in disclosure rates between states with audit laws or policies and states without them. Steven A. Herman, NCSL Study Finds That State Environmental Audit Laws Have No Impact on Company Self Auditing and Disclosure of Violations, 13 Nat'l Envtl. Enf. J. 18 (Dec. 1998/Jan. 1999).

10. In December 1998, EPA and the National Pork Producers Council (NPPC) announced an unusual agreement to create a Clean Water Act Compliance Assurance Program (CAP). 63 Fed. Reg. 69,627 (1998). The agreement establishes an independent environmental auditing program run by the NPPC, an industry trade association. Producers who register for the program are audited by an NPPC assessment team which submits its findings to the producer and then a final report to EPA. If the producer reports violations to EPA under the agreement, it is then allowed to enter into a pre-negotiated consent agreement with stipulated penalties (ranging from $250 to $1,000 for violations quickly corrected and from $2,500 to $10,000 for violations that take longer to correct). Violations already known to EPA or a state prior to the assessment are excluded from the program and EPA retains the right to sue for injunctive relief if a violation is causing harm to public health or the environment. See Schwartz, Quarles & Steen, Encouraging Self-Auditing within the Pork Industry: The Nationwide Clean Water Act Enforcement Agreement for Agriculture's First Industry-Wide Environmental Auditing Program, 29 Envtl. L. Rep. 10,395 (1999).

B. ENFORCEMENT AUTHORITIES AND POLICIES

Even when violations of environmental regulations are discovered, enforcement can be time-consuming and expensive and its outcome uncertain. Defendants enjoy procedural protections that can make it costly for authorities to discharge their burden of proving violations. To facilitate enforcement, the environmental laws provide a wide menu of enforcement options—criminal, civil, and administrative—whose procedural requirements vary in stringency with the severity of potential sanctions. They also authorize citizens to sue violators when government authorities have failed to take enforcement action.

After the initial generation of federal environmental laws were enacted, officials seeking to enforce the new laws frequently encountered courts who were reluctant to impose substantial sanctions on those who violated environmental regulations. Some judges viewed regulatory violations as technical matters that should not be considered serious offenses, particularly if they were not clearly linked to substantial environmental damage. Over time, as public understanding of the purposes of environmental regulation has improved and as Congress has increased the potential penalties for regulatory violations, this attitude has diminished somewhat. However, considerable controversy remains concerning which of two competing approaches to environmental enforcement should be emphasized by government officials.

Deterrence-based enforcement seeks to ensure compliance by emphasizing the consequences of noncompliance. It seeks to ensure that those who violate environmental regulations will incur penalties substantial enough to deter future violations. Although this approach was emphasized by federal officials during the Clinton administration, many state officials and the Bush administration favor a more conciliatory, cooperation-oriented approach to enforcement. This approach is premised in part on the notion that companies will voluntarily comply with regulations if government officials help them understand what is necessary for compliance without threatening them with substantial penalties for violations. For a discussion of these two competing visions of environmental enforcement, see Clifford Rechtschaffen, Competing Visions: EPA and the States Battle for the Future of Environmental Enforcement, 30 Envtl. L. Rep. 10,803 (2000).

1. Enforcement Authorities

The enforcement provisions of the Clean Water Act, which are typical of those found in the major federal environmental laws, are outlined below. As these provisions illustrate, the statutes provide a broad range of penalties for violators. Criminal violations can result in imprisonment and heavy fines. Civil suits can result in injunctive relief and substantial monetary penalties. Lesser monetary penalties may be imposed administratively. In addition, violators may be barred from receiving federal contracts or loans.

ENFORCEMENT PROVISIONS OF THE CLEAN WATER ACT

§308 authorizes monitoring and reporting requirements and inspections by authorities.

§309(a) authorizes issuance of administrative compliance orders.

§309(b) authorizes civil enforcement actions for injunctive relief.

§309(c) provides criminal penalties for negligent violations (fines of $2,500 to $25,000 per day and up to 1 year in prison), knowing violations (fines of $5,000 to $50,000 per day of violation and up to 3 years in prison with doubled penalties for repeat violations), knowing endangerment of another (fines of up to $250,000 and 15 years in prison), and false statements (fines of up to $10,000 and 2 years in prison).

§309(d) provides civil penalties of up to $25,000 per day for each violation.

§309(e) & (f) require EPA to join states as defendants in suits against municipalities and authorizes suits against treatment works and dischargers for violations of pretreatment regulations.

§309(g) authorizes administrative penalties (up to $10,000 per violation with a $25,000 maximum for violations heard without an adjudicatory hearing—"Class I penalties"—and up to $10,000 per day with a $125,000 maximum for violations subject to adjudicatory hearings—"Class II penalties") and gives citizens the right to comment on them.

§402(h) authorizes a ban on new sewer hookups to publicly owned treatment works violating their discharge permits.

§504 authorizes EPA to sue to restrain any source contributing to pollution "presenting an imminent or substantial endangerment" to public health or welfare.

> §505 authorizes citizen suits for injunctive relief and civil penalties against any person violating an effluent standard or order and provides for awards of attorneys' fees to prevailing parties.
>
> §508 gives EPA authority to blacklist violators, barring them from all federal contracts and loans.

Virtually every time it has reauthorized the major environmental statutes, Congress has expanded and strengthened their enforcement authorities. For example, when the Clean Water Act was amended in 1987, Congress substantially increased the maximum civil and criminal penalties for violations and it gave EPA administrative enforcement authority under the Act for the first time. In 1990 Congress added even stronger enforcement provisions to the Clean Air Act. See CAA §113.

Because judicial enforcement actions generally are more formal and more expensive, environmental authorities usually go to court only to prosecute the most egregious violations. A former assistant attorney general responsible for environmental enforcement has noted, "[t]he simple truth is that we cannot bring . . . even a significant number of these [enforcement] actions to court." Dinkins, Shall We Fight or Will We Finish: Environmental Dispute Resolution in a Litigious Society, 14 Envtl. L. Rep. 10,398 (1984). While defendants do not have a constitutional right to a jury trial in suits that seek exclusively equitable relief, the Supreme Court has held that the Seventh Amendment's right to a jury trial applies in suits for civil penalties under the environmental laws. Tull v. United States, 481 U.S. 412 (1987). Trials are expensive and time-consuming; thus, more than 95 percent of environmental enforcement cases are resolved through settlements. Settlements often include negotiated penalties incorporated into consent decrees approved by a court.

Resources devoted to criminal enforcement efforts increased substantially during the 1990s. After enactment of the Pollution Prosecution Act of 1990, EPA expanded its criminal enforcement program. Under the administration of President George W. Bush the number of criminal prosecutions for environmental violations has declined substantially, though certain industries, such as cruise ship lines, have been targeted for criminal enforcement actions. During fiscal year 2004, EPA conducted 425 criminal investigations and brought criminal charges against 293 defendants. A total of $47 million in criminal fines and restitution were imposed. Prison sentences totaling 77 years were imposed on persons convicted of environmental crimes. Most criminal prosecutions over the years have been for violations of the Clean Water Act and RCRA.

The vast majority of environmental enforcement actions never see the courthouse door. More than 95 percent are handled through administrative enforcement procedures, which are procedurally simpler but provide less stringent penalties. Administrative enforcement actions may involve the issuance of administrative orders and the assessment of civil penalties. Most environmental statutes authorize EPA to issue administrative orders (see, e.g., CAA §113(a), CWA §309(g), RCRA §3008(a)), which give officials flexibility to specify remedial action that must be taken by a certain date. If, after notice and an opportunity for a hearing, the action specified in the administrative order is not taken, environmental authorities can go to court to seek its enforcement. The environmental laws also authorize EPA to assess administrative civil penalties, which may be contested in hearings before an administrative law judge whose decisions are subject to judicial review based on the administrative record. Nearly all administrative cases ultimately are settled; fewer than 5 percent proceed to hearings before an administrative law judge. To hear appeals of administrative enforcement decisions, EPA has created a permanent, three-person Environmental Appeals Board.

Minor violations also can be handled by sending a notice of violation, which requires the recipient to correct a technical violation without assessing a penalty. Notices of violation may be used by federal enforcement officials to give state authorities operating delegated programs an opportunity to take enforcement action prior to the initiation of federal enforcement proceedings. The 1990 Clean Air Act Amendments also authorize EPA to issue field citations, akin to traffic tickets but with penalties of up to $5,000 per day of violation. CAA §113(d)(3).

2. *Penalty Policies*

Environmental officials have used their enforcement authorities to encourage companies to incorporate compliance concerns into management structures. Enforcement settlements now often feature agreements by violators to conduct environmental audits to help prevent future violations. Defendants also are agreeing to implement pollution prevention programs or to undertake supplemental environmental projects. A total of $65 million was committed by companies to fund supplemental environmental projects during fiscal year 2003.

Enforcement officials also have acted to improve the deterrent effect of enforcement actions by publicizing enforcement actions more widely and by increasing penalties. EPA's Policy on Civil Penalties is designed to ensure that penalties imposed on violators are sufficient to recoup the economic benefit of violations and to encourage future compliance. Under this policy, civil penalties are calculated based on the economic benefit of delayed compliance (as calculated by a computer program developed by EPA staff), the gravity of the offense (based on its actual and potential impact on public health and the environment, and its effect on EPA's ability to perform its regulatory functions), the wilfulness of the offense, and the violator's past compliance and cooperation with enforcement authorities. Debarment of violators from government contracts also can be used as a sanction.

An illustration of how courts have used EPA's civil penalties policy to determine the size of a monetary penalty is provided by the following decision. This case involved a successful citizen suit against an oil company for discharging produced water (water generated during drilling operations that becomes contaminated with chemicals) into Galveston Bay without a permit. After finding that produced water was a "pollutant" whose discharge without a permit violated the Clean Water Act (CWA), the court considered how great a penalty to assess for the violation.

Sierra Club v. Cedar Point Oil Co.
73 F.3d 546 (5th Cir. 1996)

The CWA directs district courts to assess civil penalties for violations of the CWA. 33 U.S.C. §1319(d). Specifically, the statute states that violators "shall be subject to a civil penalty not to exceed $25,000 per day for each violation." Id. Aside from this maximum amount, the statute guides the court's discretion in setting the penalty as follows:

> In determining the amount of a civil penalty the court shall consider the seriousness of the violation or violations, the economic benefit (if any) resulting from the violation, any history of such violations, any good-faith efforts to comply with the applicable requirements, the economic impact of the penalty on the violator, and such other matters as justice may require.

Id. The Eleventh Circuit has taken these statutory directives and developed a procedural framework for calculating penalties under the CWA. [Atlantic States Legal Found., Inc. v.] *Tyson Foods,* [Inc.] 897 F.2d [1128], 1142 [(11th Cir. 1990)]. First, the court is to calculate the maximum penalty that could be assessed against the violator. Id. Using that maximum as a starting point, the court should then determine if the penalty should be reduced from the maximum by reference to the statutory factors. Id.

The district court followed the *Tyson Foods* framework in this case. The parties had stipulated that there were 797 days of unpermitted discharge of produced water prior to trial. The judgment was entered twelve days later, during which time the discharge presumably continued. Accordingly, the court multiplied the statutory figure of $25,000 per day by 809 days of unpermitted discharge to arrive [at] a maximum penalty of $20,225,000.

The district court then made findings of fact with respect to the statutory factors. First, the court found that the violation was moderately serious because of the effect of the discharge on benthic organisms and the lack of monitoring and reporting with respect to the discharge. Second, the court found that the economic benefit to Cedar Point from the violation was $186,070, which the court determined was the amount that Cedar Point saved by not disposing of its produced water in a reinjection well. Third, the court found that Cedar Point had been violating the CWA since it began operating state well 1876. Fourth, the court found that Cedar Point had not demonstrated good faith in attempting to comply with the CWA. In this regard, the court noted that, although Cedar Point had attempted to obtain a NPDES permit for its discharge, it had not explored other ways to comply with the CWA. Finally, the court reviewed Cedar Point's financial position and expected future profits from the Cedar Point field and determined that Cedar Point could at least afford a penalty equal to the economic benefit attained from the violation.

In weighing these facts and calculating the penalty, the district court held that the maximum penalty of $20,225,000 was inappropriate. The court determined, however, that the penalty should at a minimum recapture the savings realized by Cedar Point because of the violation. Although the court's findings with respect to the other statutory factors were also not favorable to Cedar Point, the court apparently chose not to accord these factors any weight because it did not increase the penalty beyond what it found to be the economic benefit to Cedar Point. Accordingly, the court assessed a penalty of $186,070. . . .

. . . [W]e do not think that the district court abused its discretion in assessing a penalty in an amount that reflected only the economic benefit to Cedar Point. The Supreme Court has described the process of weighing the statutory factors in calculating civil penalties under the CWA as "highly discretionary" with the trial court. Tull v. United States, 481 U.S. 412, 427 (1987). It is clear from the district court's Memorandum Opinion that it considered all of the statutory factors before settling on an amount based only on economic benefit. Considering that the court could have imposed a penalty as high as $20,225,000, this appears to be a fair and just result. As such we perceive no abuse of discretion. Therefore, we affirm the district court's assessment of a penalty in the amount of $186,070 for Cedar Point's violation of the CWA.

NOTES AND QUTESTIONS

1. The civil penalty applied in this case was designed to recoup only the economic benefit of the violation. Should the district court have imposed a higher penalty in light of the other factors it considered? If civil penalties routinely were assessed in a manner that only recouped the economic gain enjoyed by the violator, what incentive would they provide for companies to comply on their own? If Cedar Point had discovered the violation, voluntarily disclosed it to EPA, and corrected it prior to receiving notice of the citizen's suit, would their penalty have been as great under EPA's self-audit policy?

2. Why should a violator's economic circumstances be taken into account when determining the size of civil penalties? Does this imply that firms that are marginally profitable need not fear substantial civil penalties for violating the Clean Water Act?

3. After receiving the Sierra Club's statutorily required notice of intent to file a citizen suit, Cedar Point filed suit against the Sierra Club and EPA, alleging that they were conspiring to deprive it of unspecified constitutional rights and seeking an injunction barring the citizen suit. Cedar Point's lawsuit was dismissed. A month later, Cedar Point filed a counterclaim against the Sierra Club's citizen suit alleging abuse of process and seeking compensatory damages for emotional distress allegedly suffered by its officers and directors and $10 million in punitive damages. This counterclaim also was dismissed.

4. As the court notes, section 309(d) of the Clean Water Act specifies five factors that courts should consider in determining the amount of a civil penalty, as well as "such other matters as justice may require." What other matters can you identify that would be relevant considerations for courts to use in determining the amount of civil penalties under this broad directive?

5. Should the maximum penalty for violations be based on the number of violations, the number of days of noncompliance, or some combination of both? The Clean Water Act provides for a civil penalty "not to exceed $25,000 per day for each violation." 33 U.S.C. §1319(d). The trial court in *Cedar Point* had computed the maximum penalty by multiplying the number of days on which violations occurred by the statutory figure of $25,000 per day. In Chesapeake Bay Foundation v. Gwaltney of Smithfield, Ltd., 791 F.2d 304 (4th Cir. 1986), reversed on other grounds, 484 U.S. 49 (1987), the Fourth Circuit stated that "where a violation is defined in terms of a time period longer than a day, the maximum penalty assessable for that violation should be defined in terms of the number of days in that time period." Id. at 314. The court declined to reach the separate question of "whether multiple violations attributable to a single day may give rise to a maximum penalty in excess of [the penalty amount] for that day." Id. at 308. The latter issue was addressed in United States v. Smithfield Foods, Inc., 191 F.3d 516 (4th Cir. 1999), where the court stated that "[I]f the

maximum penalty that could be levied against a violator on a single day was $25,000, no matter how many different Permit effluent limitations were violated, the permittee would have a strong disincentive to comply with the other permit limitations." Id. at 527-528. Thus, the court treated each permit violation "as a separate and distinct infraction for purposes of penalty calculation." Id. at 528. This approach also was followed in Borden Ranch Partnership v. U.S. Army Corps of Engineers, 261 F.3d 810 (9th Cir. 2001), aff'd by an equally divided Court, 537 U.S. 99 (2002), which upheld a penalty for violating section 404 of the Clean Water Act that had been calculated based on the number of unpermitted passes by a deep ripper through wetlands rather than the number of days on which the ripping occurred.

6. Should the amount of warning a company received prior to violating an environmental law be a factor taken into account in determining the size of a civil penalty? If a company mistakenly believes that it is in compliance, can it be fined when it later discovers that EPA interprets the regulations differently? In General Electric Co. v. EPA, 53 F.3d 1324 (D.C. Cir. 1995), the D.C. Circuit set aside a $25,000 fine against a company for violating TSCA regulations because EPA did not provide the company with fair warning of its interpretation of regulations that were unclear. The court upheld EPA's interpretation of regulations that required the immediate incineration of solvents used in extracting PCBs. However, the court found that it would violate due process for the company to be fined without fair warning that EPA interpreted the regulations to prohibit distillation and recycling of a portion of the solvents prior to their ultimate incineration. "In the absence of notice—for example, where the regulation is not sufficiently clear to warn a party about what is expected of it—an agency may not deprive a party of property by imposing civil or criminal liability." 53 F.3d at 1328-1329. The court noted that "in many cases the agency's pre-enforcement efforts to bring about compliance will provide adequate notice," such as when a regulated entity is informed that it needs to obtain a permit. "If, by reviewing the regulations and other public statements issued by the agency, a regulated party acting in good faith would be able to identify with 'ascertainable certainty' the standard with which the agency expects parties to conform, then the agency has fairly notified a petitioner of the agency's interpretation." Id. at 1329.

7. Federal law now requires EPA to update the maximum civil penalties it may levy in enforcement actions to keep up with inflation. In February 2004, EPA adopted a Civil Monetary Penalty Inflation Adjustment Rule, 69 Fed. Reg. 7,121 (Feb. 13, 2004). The rule, which was authorized by the Federal Civil Penalties Inflation Adjustment Act of 1990, as amended by the Debt Collection Improvement Act of 1996, increases the maximum amount of civil penalties that the Agency may collect from environmental violators to take inflation into account. For example, fines that formerly could be as great as $27,500 now can be as much as $32,500.

3. The Federal-State Enforcement Relationship

The environmental laws authorize EPA to delegate to states responsibility for administering and enforcing the federal clean water, clean air, and hazardous waste programs. To qualify for program delegation, states must satisfy EPA that they can operate the programs in a manner that meets all federal requirements. EPA retains supervisory authority over the states' operation of the programs. If states operating delegated federal programs fail to meet minimum federal standards, EPA has the authority to withdraw the delegation, but this authority is virtually never exercised because the Agency is loathe to take over operation of state programs without receiving additional resources. The EPA also has generally had the authority to take enforcement action on its own when it does not believe that states have adequately addressed certain violations. This "overfiling" authority was contested in the case below.

Harmon Industries v. Browner
191 F.3d 894 (8th Cir. 1999)

HANSEN, Circuit Judge:

I.　FACTS AND PROCEDURAL BACKGROUND

Harmon Industries operates a plant in Grain Valley, Missouri, which it utilizes to assemble circuit boards for railroad control and safety equipment. In November 1987, Harmon's personnel manager discovered that maintenance workers at Harmon routinely discarded volatile solvent residue behind Harmon's Grain Valley plant. This practice apparently began in 1973 and continued until November 1987. Harmon's management was unaware of its employees' practices until the personnel manager filed his report in November 1987. Following the report, Harmon ceased its disposal activities and voluntarily contacted the Missouri Department of Natural Resources (MDNR). The MDNR investigated and concluded that Harmon's past disposal practices did not pose a threat to either human health or the environment. The MDNR and Harmon created a plan whereby Harmon would clean up the disposal area. Harmon implemented the cleanup plan. While Harmon was cooperating with the MDNR, the EPA initiated an administrative enforcement action against Harmon in which the federal agency sought $2,343,706 in penalties. Meanwhile, Harmon and the MDNR continued to establish a voluntary compliance plan. In harmonizing the details of the plan, Harmon asked the MDNR not to impose civil penalties. Harmon based its request in part on the fact that it voluntarily self-reported the environmental violations and cooperated fully with the MDNR.

On March 5, 1993, while the EPA's administrative enforcement action was pending, a Missouri state court judge approved a consent decree entered into by the MDNR and Harmon. In the decree, MDNR acknowledged full accord and satisfaction and released Harmon from any claim for monetary penalties. MDNR based its decision to release Harmon on the fact that the company promptly self-reported its violation and cooperated in all aspects of the investigation. After the filing of the consent decree, Harmon litigated the EPA claim before an administrative law judge (ALJ). The ALJ found that a civil penalty against Harmon was appropriate in this case. The ALJ rejected the EPA's request for a penalty in excess of $2 million but the ALJ did impose a civil fine of $586,716 against Harmon. A three-person Environmental Appeals Board panel affirmed the ALJ's monetary penalty. Harmon filed a complaint challenging the EPA's decision in federal district court on June 6, 1997. In its August 25, 1998, summary judgment order, the district court found that the EPA's decision to impose civil penalties violated the Resource Conservation and Recovery Act and contravened principles of res judicata. See Harmon Indus., Inc. v. Browner, 19 F. Supp. 2d 988 (W.D. Mo. 1998). The EPA appeals to this court.

II. Discussion

A. *The Permissibility of Overfiling*

When reviewing a federal agency's interpretation of a federal statute, a federal court must defer to the agency's interpretation only if it finds that the agency's interpretation is consistent with the plain language of the statute or represents a reasonable interpretation of an ambiguous statute. See Chevron U.S.A., Inc. v. Natural Resources Defense Council, Inc., 467 U.S. 837, 842-45 (1984). We review de novo a district court's findings and conclusions regarding the correctness of an agency's statutory interpretations. See Moore v. Custis, 736 F.2d 1260, 1262 (8th Cir. 1984).

The Resource Conservation and Recovery Act (RCRA), 42 U.S.C. §6901-6992K (1994), permits states to apply to the EPA for authorization to administer and enforce a hazardous waste program. See 42 U.S.C. §6926(b). If authorization is granted, the state's program then operates "in lieu of the federal government's hazardous waste program." Id. The EPA authorization also allows states to issue and enforce permits for the treatment, storage, and disposal of hazardous wastes. Id. "Any action taken by a State under a hazardous waste program authorized under [the RCRA] [has] the same force and effect as action taken by the [EPA] under this subchapter." 42 U.S.C. §6926(d). Once authorization is granted by the EPA, it cannot be rescinded unless the EPA finds that (1) the state program is not equivalent to the federal program, (2) the state program is not consistent with federal or state programs in other states, or (3) the state program is failing to provide adequate enforcement of compliance in accordance with the requirements of federal law. See 42 U.S.C. §6926(b). Before withdrawing a state's authorization to administer a hazardous waste program, the EPA must hold a public hearing and allow the state a reasonable period of time to correct the perceived deficiency. See 42 U.S.C. §6926(e).

Missouri, like many other states, is authorized to administer and enforce a hazardous waste program pursuant to the RCRA. Despite having authorized a state to act, the EPA frequently files its own enforcement actions against suspected environmental violators even after the commencement of a state-initiated enforcement action. See Bryan S. Miller, Harmonizing RCRA's Enforcement Provisions: RCRA Overfiling in Light of Harmon Industries v. Browner, 5 Environmental Law. 585 (1999). The EPA's process of duplicating enforcement actions is known as overfiling. See id. The permissibility of over-filing apparently is a question of first impression in the federal circuit courts. See Harmon, 19 F. Supp. 2d at 995. After examining this apparent issue of first impression, the district court concluded that the plain language of section 6926(b) dictates that the state program operate "in lieu" of the federal program and with the "same force and effect" as EPA action. Accordingly, the district court found that, in this case, the RCRA precludes the EPA from assessing its own penalty against Harmon. See id.

The EPA contends that the district court's interpretation runs contrary to the plain language of the RCRA. Specifically, the EPA cites section 6928 of the RCRA, which states that:

> (1) Except as provided in paragraph (2), whenever on the basis of any information the [EPA] determines that any person has violated or is in violation of any requirement of this subchapter, the [EPA] may issue an order assessing a civil penalty for any past or current violation, requiring compliance immediately or within a specified time period, or both, or the [EPA] may commence a civil action in the United States district court in the district in which the violation occurred for appropriate relief, including a temporary or permanent injunction.
>
> (2) In the case of a violation of any requirement of [the RCRA] where such violation occurs in a State which is authorized to carry out a hazardous waste program under section 6926 of this title, the [EPA] shall give notice to the State in which such violation has occurred prior to issuing an order or commencing a civil action under this section.

42 U.S.C. §6928(a)(1) and (2).

The EPA argues that the plain language of section 6928 allows the federal agency to initiate an enforcement action against an environmental violator even in states that have received authorization pursuant to the RCRA. The EPA contends that Harmon and the district court misinterpreted the phrases "in lieu of" and "same force and effect" as contained in the RCRA. According to the EPA, the phrase "in lieu of" refers to which regulations are to be enforced in an authorized state rather than who is responsible for enforcing the regulations. The EPA argues that the phrase "same force and effect" refers only to the effect of state issued permits. The EPA contends that the RCRA, taken as a whole, authorizes either the state or the EPA to enforce the state's regulations, which are in compliance with the regulations of the EPA. The only requirement, according to the EPA, is that the EPA notify the state in writing if it intends to initiate an enforcement action against an alleged violator.

Both parties argue that the plain language of the RCRA supports their interpretation of the statute. We also are ever mindful of the long-established plain language rule of statutory interpretation, see Walker v. Dilworth, 2 U.S. (2 Dall.) 257, 259 (1796), as we inquire into the scope of the EPA's enforcement powers under the RCRA. Such an inquiry requires examining the text of the statute as a whole by considering its context, "object, and policy." Pelofsky v. Wallace, 102 F.3d 350, 353 (8th Cir. 1996).

An examination of the statute as a whole supports the district court's interpretation. The RCRA specifically allows states that have received authorization from the federal government to administer and enforce a program that operates "in lieu of" the EPA's regulatory program. 42 U.S.C. §6926(b). While the EPA is correct that the "in lieu of" language refers to the program itself, the administration and enforcement of the program are inexorably intertwined.

The RCRA gives authority to the states to create and implement their own hazardous waste program. The plain "in lieu of" language contained in the RCRA reveals a congressional intent for an authorized state program to supplant the federal hazardous waste program in all respects including enforcement. Congressional intent is evinced within the authorization language of section 6926(b) of the RCRA. Specifically, the statute permits the EPA to repeal a state's authorization if the state's program "does not provide adequate enforcement of compliance with the requirements of" the RCRA. Id. This language indicates that Congress intended to grant states the primary role of enforcing their own hazardous waste program. Such an indication is not undermined, as the EPA suggests, by the language of section 6928. Again, section 6928(a)(1) allows the EPA to initiate enforcement actions against suspected environmental violators, except as provided in section 6928(a)(2). Section 6928(a)(2) permits the EPA to enforce the hazardous waste laws contained in the RCRA if the agency gives written notice to the state. Section 6928(a)(1) and (2), however, must be interpreted within the context of the entire Act. Harmonizing the section 6928(a)(1) and (2) language that allows the EPA to bring an enforcement action in certain circumstances with section 6926(b)'s provision that the EPA has the right to withdraw state authorization if the state's enforcement is inadequate manifests a congressional intent to give the EPA a secondary enforcement right in those cases where a state has been authorized to act that is triggered only after state authorization is rescinded or if the state fails to initiate an enforcement action. Rather than serving as an affirmative grant of federal enforcement power as the EPA suggests, we conclude that the notice requirement of section 6928(a)(2) reinforces the primacy of a state's enforcement rights under RCRA. Taken in the context of the statute as a whole, the notice requirement operates as a means to allow a state the first chance opportunity to initiate the statutorily-permitted enforcement action. If the state fails to initiate any action, then the EPA may institute its own action. Thus, the notice requirement is an indicator of the fact that Congress intended to give states, that are authorized to act, the lead role in enforcement under RCRA.

The "same force and effect" language of section 6926(d) provides additional support for the primacy of states' enforcement rights under the RCRA when the EPA has authorized a state to act in lieu of it. The EPA argues that the "same force and effect" language is limited to state permits because the words appear under a heading that reads: "Effect of State Permit." The EPA contends that the "same force and effect" language indicates only that state-issued permits will have the same force and effect as permits issued by the federal government. The EPA claims that the district court was incorrect when it applied the "same force and effect" language to encompass the statute's enforcement mechanism. We disagree.

Regardless of the title or heading, the plain language of section 6926(d) states that "[a]ny action taken by a State under a hazardous waste program authorized under this section shall have the same force and effect as action taken by the [EPA] under this subchapter." 42 U.S.C. §6926(d). In this context, the meaning of the text is plain and obvious. "Any action" under this provision broadly applies to any action authorized by the subchapter, and this language is not limited to the issuance of permits. The state authorization provision substitutes state action (not excluding enforcement action) for federal action. It would be incongruous to conclude that the RCRA authorizes states to implement and administer a hazardous waste program "in lieu of" the federal program where only the issuance of permits is accorded the same force and effect as an action taken by the federal government. Contrary to the EPA's assertions, the statute specifically provides that a "[s]tate is authorized to carry out [its hazardous waste program] in lieu of the Federal program . . . and to issue and enforce permits." 42 U.S.C. §6926(b). Issuance and enforcement are two of the functions authorized as part of the state's hazardous waste enforcement program under the RCRA. Nothing in the statute suggests that the "same force and effect" language is limited to the issuance of permits but not their enforcement. We believe that if Congress had intended such a peculiar result, it would have stated its preference in a clear and unambiguous manner. Absent such an unambiguous directive, we will apply a common sense meaning to the text of the statute and interpret its provisions in a manner logically consistent with the Act as whole. . . .

There is no support either in the text of the statute or the legislative history for the proposition that the EPA is allowed to duplicate a state's enforcement authority with its own enforcement action. The EPA argues that the statute and legislative history support its contention that it may initiate an enforcement action if it deems the state's enforcement action inadequate. The EPA's argument misses the point. Without question, the EPA can initiate an enforcement action if it deems the state's enforcement action inadequate. Before initiating such an action, however, the EPA must allow the state an opportunity to correct its deficiency and the EPA must withdraw its authorization. See 42 U.S.C. §6926(b) and (e). Consistent with the text of the statute and its legislative history, the EPA also may initiate an enforcement action after providing written notice to the state when the authorized state fails to initiate any enforcement action. See 42 U.S.C. §6928(a)(2); 1976 U.S.C.C.A.N. 6270. The EPA may not, however, simply fill the perceived gaps it sees in a state's enforcement action by initiating a second enforcement action without allowing the state an opportunity to correct the deficiency and then withdrawing the state's authorization.

A contrary interpretation would result in two separate enforcement actions. Such an interpretation, as explained above, would derogate the RCRA's plain language and legislative history. Companies that reach an agreement through negotiations with a state authorized by the EPA to act in its place may find the agreement undermined by a later separate enforcement action by the EPA. While, generally speaking, two separate sovereigns can institute two separate enforcement actions, those actions can cause vastly different and potentially contradictory results. Such a potential schism runs afoul of the principles of comity and federalism so clearly embedded in the text and history of the RCRA. When enacting the RCRA, Congress intended to delegate the primary enforcement of EPA-approved hazardous waste programs to the states. See 1976 U.S.C.C.A.N. 6262, 6270. In fact, as we have noted above, the states' enforcement action has the "same force and effect as an action taken by" the EPA. See 42 U.S.C. §6926(d). In EPA authorized states, the EPA's action is an alternative method of enforcement that is permitted to operate only when certain conditions are satisfied. See 42 U.S.C. §6926(b) and (e); 42 U.S.C. §6928(b). The EPA's interpretation simply is not consistent with the plain language of the statute, its legislative history, or its declared purpose. Hence, it is also an unreasonable interpretation to which we accord no deference. Therefore, we find that the EPA's practice of overfiling, in those states where it has authorized the state to act, oversteps the federal agency's authority under the RCRA.

NOTES AND QUTESTIONS

1. The Tenth Circuit has explicitly rejected *Harmon* and upheld EPA's ability to overfile. In United States v. Power Engineering Co., 303 F.2d 1232 (10th Cir. 2002), the Tenth Circuit systematically rejected every aspect of *Harmon*'s reasoning in holding that EPA could bring an RCRA enforcement

action even when a state pursued its own action for the same violations. The EPA had filed suit against Power Engineering after the state of Colorado refused in its own enforcement action to demand that the company comply with financial assurance regulations to ensure coverage of the cost of remedying the violations. Although the state sought to impose penalties of $1.13 million for the violations, EPA won an order requiring the company to provide more than $2.11 million in financial assurances. The Tenth Circuit first rejected *Harmon*'s conclusion that "the administration and enforcement of the program are inexorably intertwined." The court stated:

> This interpretation fails to account for the placement of "enforcement" and "in lieu of" in separate clauses of section 6926(b), and it does not adequately consider the structure of the statute. Section 6926 addresses the administration and enforcement of state regulations by authorized states, while the federal enforcement of such regulations is addressed in a different part of the statute—section 6928. Given this statutory structure, the EPA's conclusion that administration and enforcement of RCRA are not inexorably intertwined— and that authorization of a state program therefore does not deprive the EPA of its enforcement powers—is not unreasonable.

303 F.3d at 1238.

The Tenth Circuit noted that "the only explicit limitation" on EPA's enforcement authority "is that the EPA must provide prior notice to authorized states." Id. Noting that "[w]ithdrawal of authorization for a state program is an 'extreme' and 'drastic' step that requires the EPA to establish a federal program to replace the cancelled state program," the court concluded that "[n]othing in the text of the statute suggests that such a step is a prerequisite to EPA enforcement or that it is the only remedy for inadequate enforcement." Id. at 1238-1239. The court also rejected the notion that the "same force and effect" language in section 6926(d) indicated an intent to bar separate EPA enforcement. Noting that the provision is part of a section headed "Effect of a State permit," the court said this "suggests that this subsection only intends for state permits to have the 'same force and effect' as federal permits." Thus, "[i]t would be reasonable to conclude that Congress simply intended for section 6926(d) to clarify that recipients of state-issued permits need not obtain a permit from the EPA," preventing "the EPA from denying the effect of a state permit," but not preventing "the EPA from taking action when a violation occurs." Id. at 1239.

2. In United States v. Elias, 269 F.3d 1003 (9th Cir. 2001), the Ninth Circuit rejected an effort to use *Harmon* to challenge one of the largest criminal penalties ever imposed for an environmental violation—a 17-year prison term for a businessman convicted for knowingly endangering an employee while violating RCRA. The businessman, Allan Elias, had ordered an employee to clean out a storage tank containing cyanide without using safety equipment. Overcome by cyanide fumes, the employee suffered brain damage and nearly died. The court rejected the argument that the federal criminal prosecution for violating RCRA was barred by the fact that Idaho had delegated authority from EPA to operate the RCRA program. The Ninth Circuit concluded that nothing in *Harmon* foreclosed EPA's ability to bring criminal charges. The court explained that "under RCRA, the federal government retains both its criminal and its civil enforcement powers . . . even where a state law counterpart exists, for many of these 'counterparts' provide only misdemeanor punishments where federal law prescribes a

felony." The court concluded that "RCRA only contemplates that the federal permitting scheme is supplanted by authorized state ones," meaning that "[w]hat changes, and what is supplanted by state law, is . . . the sovereign from whom generators must obtain the necessary permit originally—in this case, Idaho." 269 F.3d at 1012.

3. *Harmon*'s reasoning also has been found to be inapplicable in the context of the Clean Air Act. In United States v. LTV Steel Co., 118 F. Supp. 2d 827 (N.D. Ohio 2000), a steel company argued that a settlement it had reached with the city of Cleveland should bar EPA from overfiling and imposing penalties on it for violations involving fugitive dust emissions. Distinguishing *Harmon*, the court stated that: "Unlike RCRA, the Clean Air Act contains language in its enforcement section which seems to anticipate overfiling." The court noted that the Clean Air Act expressly provides for considering "payment by the violator of penalties previously assessed for the same violation" in computing penalties under the Act. 118 F. Supp. 2d at 833. The court also rejected the company's claim that res judicata barred the EPA action, noting that EPA and the city were not in privity and were enforcing separate bodies of law.

4. In *Harmon*, company employees had routinely dumped hazardous organic solvents on the ground behind the plant for a period of 14 years, a practice that violated RCRA for the last seven years that it continued. After the company disclosed the violations to state environmental officials, the state officials informed EPA, which requested the state to insist on a substantial monetary penalty. Harmon convinced the state not to impose a penalty in part by contending that it had cost the company more than $800,000 to change its processes to discontinue use of the solvents, while increasing annual operating costs by $125,000. When state authorities declined to seek a penalty, EPA filed its own administrative complaint against Harmon on September 30, 1991, before the state had concluded a consent decree with the company, which ultimately was not approved until March 5, 1993. Ridgway M. Hall, Jr., *Harmon* Limits RCRA Enforcers to One Bite, 29 Envtl. L. Rep. 10,781, 10,782 (1999). Should it make any difference to the question of EPA's authority to overfile that EPA filed its action *before* the state had negotiated the consent decree? Should it matter that EPA first had requested the state to seek a penalty and filed only when the state refused to do so?

5. If Harmon had disclosed the violation to EPA and promptly corrected it, could the company qualify for a reduced civil penalty under EPA's "Incentives for Self-Policing" Policy, discussed in section A above? What would be the minimum penalty that EPA would seek to recover under its penalty policies?

6. In light of the court's decision, what remedies would EPA have if it believes that the state is not adequately enforcing a federal program? How credible is the threat that EPA would withdraw a state's delegated authority to operate a program? A rare example of EPA withdrawing state program authorization occurred in December 2001 when EPA withdrew Maryland's authority to operate the Clean Air Act's Title V permit program. After repeated extensions of deadlines for correcting deficiencies in state permit programs, EPA was sued by the Earthjustice Legal Defense Fund in June 2000. In settlement of the lawsuit EPA agreed not to extend the deadline for any state to correct deficiencies in its Title V permit program beyond December 1, 2001. Maryland missed the deadline because it failed to change state law to grant standing to challenge permit decisions to all parties who would have standing under federal law as required by section 502(b)(6) of the Clean Air Act. Thus, Maryland's Part 70 permit

program was replaced by an EPA Part 71 federal operating permit program effective December 1, 2001. However, this change did not make much practical difference because EPA immediately delegated to Maryland the authority to implement and enforce the Part 71 federal permit program. 66 Fed. Reg. 63,236 (Dec. 5, 2001). While this program is to be implemented and enforced by Maryland, EPA retains final decision-making authority on all permit issues including the issuance or denial of permits and permit terms.

7. In 1998, EPA's inspector general issued a report finding widespread failures to enforce some of the basic requirements of the environmental laws. After auditing enforcement records in several states, the inspector general found that state officials frequently had failed to enforce the laws or to report violations to EPA and that EPA had been lax in supervising state enforcement. Cushman, EPA and State Found to Be Lax on Pollution Law, N.Y. Times, June 7, 1998, at A1. The report found that many major dischargers had expired NPDES permits that had not been reissued, often for periods as long as ten years, and that very few formal enforcement actions were taken against significant dischargers when they violated their permits.

8. Steven A. Herman, EPA's Assistant Administrator for Enforcement and Compliance Assurance at the time *Harmon* was decided, argues that it is important for EPA to have overfiling authority to prevent states from competing for industry through lax enforcement policies. He cites the case of Smithfield Foods as one where "EPA had to step in despite strong opposition both from the company and the state of Virginia." Herman, Environmental Enforcement at the Federal Level, Remarks to the Arizona Association of Industries Environmental Summit, Aug. 13, 1998.

> Smithfield Foods failed to install adequate pollution control equipment or to properly treat its wastewater, resulting in more than 5,000 violations involving pollutants such as phosphorous, ammonia, cyanide, oil, grease, and fecal coliform. Company employees falsified documents and destroyed water quality records. Virginia only took perfunctory actions against the violations, which had major impacts on the Pagan River, the James River, and the Chesapeake Bay. Pursuant to EPA's enforcement action, a federal district court fined Smithfield Foods a record $12.6 million penalty. [Id.]

How will the *Harmon* decision affect EPA's ability to deal with situations like that which occurred at Smithfield Foods? A state legislative audit found "major deficiencies" in Virginia's enforcement policies—in FY 1996 the state collected *only $4,000* in civil penalties for Clean Water Act violations under a long-standing policy that the state *not* seek to recoup the economic benefit of violations. Joint Legislative Audit and Review Commission, Review of the DEQ, 119-120 (1996).

9. The Bush administration is reducing the resources devoted by EPA to enforcement while pledging to increase federal grants to states for enforcement. The administration moved to eliminate 270 enforcement positions in EPA's Office of Enforcement and Compliance Assurance while shifting $25 million in federal grants to states for enforcement activities. A report issued by the General Accounting Office in July 2001 questioned whether this approach would impair the effectiveness of overall enforcement efforts. EPA's Office of Inspector General has found that only a handful of states have aggressive environmental enforcement programs. Eric Pianin, GAO Issues Warning on EPA Enforcement, Wash. Post, Aug. 23, 2001, at A23.

C.   CRIMINAL ENFORCEMENT

While criminal penalties for environmental violations are found in the Refuse Act of 1899, criminal prosecutions only recently have played a significant role in environmental enforcement. Criminal penalties were included in the major federal environmental statutes enacted in the 1970s. As these acts have been reauthorized, Congress has expanded the range of violations for which criminal penalties apply while increasing substantially the size of the penalties. Federal and state authorities also have devoted increased resources to criminal enforcement of the environmental laws. The Pollution Prosecution Act of 1990 quadrupled the number of federal agents investigating environmental crimes. In large cities today many U.S. attorneys' and district attorneys' offices have divisions that specialize in criminal enforcement of the environmental laws.

Virtually all the federal environmental laws now provide criminal penalties for "knowing" or "wilful" violations of environmental regulations. See, e.g., Clean Air Act §113(c); Clean Water Act §309(c); CERCLA §§103(b), (c), and (d)(2); RCRA §§3008(d) and (e); TSCA §§15 and 16; FIFRA §14(b). The Clean Air Act Amendments of 1990 make virtually all knowing violations of any requirement of the Act a felony, including violations of recordkeeping and reporting requirements. Both the Clean Water Act and Clean Air Act also impose criminal penalties for certain negligent acts that violate the statutes. CWA §309(c)(1), Apex Oil Co. v. United States, 530 F.2d 1291 (8th Cir.), cert. denied, 429 U.S. 827 (1976); United States v. Frezzo Brothers, Inc., 703 F.2d 62 (3d Cir.), cert. denied, 464 U.S. 829 (1983); CAA §113(c)(4).

Courts have long drawn a distinction between regulatory statutes to protect public health or safety and common law crimes in addressing what needs to be proved to establish a criminal violation. In United States v. Dotterweich, 320 U.S. 277 (1943) and United States v. Park, 421 U.S. 658 (1975), the Supreme Court indicated that responsible corporate officials can be held criminally liable for violating health or safety regulations without requiring proof of evil intent. As case law interpreting some of the criminal provisions of the environmental laws developed, courts have built on these decisions by allowing juries to infer that acts are "knowing" or "wilful" from evidence demonstrating that a defendant should have known that an act is a violation. See, e.g., United States v. Sellers, 926 F.2d 410 (5th Cir. 1991) ("knowingly" in RCRA does not require knowledge that materials were regulated as hazardous wastes, but rather only that the defendant knew that materials had potential to cause harm); United States v. McDonald & Watson Waste Oil Co., 933 F.2d 35 (1st Cir. 1991); United States v. Buckley, 934 F.2d 84 (6th Cir. 1991).

The environmental laws generally make both corporate officers and employees who make corporate decisions personally liable. United States v. Northeastern Pharmaceutical & Chemical Co., 810 F.2d 726, 745 (8th Cir. 1986). The Clean Water Act and Clean Air Act both expressly provide that "any responsible corporate officer" may be held liable for criminal acts. CWA §309(c)(6); CAA §113(c)(6). Employees can be held criminally liable if they knew or should have known that their employer failed to comply with applicable regulations. United States v. Hong, 242 F.3d 528 (4th Cir. 2001) (CWA); United States v. Johnson & Towers, 741 F.2d 662, 663 (3d Cir. 1984), cert. denied, 469 U.S. 1208 (1985) (RCRA). Even federal contractors have been found criminally liable. In United States v. Dee, 912 F.2d 741 (4th Cir. 1990), three civilian managers at the U.S. Army's Aberdeen Proving Ground were convicted of knowingly managing hazardous wastes without a permit in violation of RCRA.

Criminal penalties are particularly severe for knowing violations that endanger human life. The Clean Water Act provides penalties of up to 15 years in prison and fines of up to $250,000 for violations when a defendant knows "that he thereby places another person in imminent danger of death or serious bodily injury." §309(c)(3). However, in United States v. Borowski, 977 F.2d 27 (1st Cir. 1992), the First Circuit interpreted this "knowing endangerment" provision as applying only to endangerment that occurs *after* a violation has been committed. The court reversed the felony convictions of the owner of a nickel-plating company who violated pretreatment standards by having his employees ladle high quantities of nickel and nitric acid into plating-room sinks from which they flowed untreated into a sewer. This caused the employees to suffer daily nose bleeds, rashes, blisters, and difficulty breathing. Even though the defendant had placed his employees in danger, the court held that a conviction "cannot be premised upon danger that occurs before the pollutant reaches a publicly-owned sewer or treatment works," because the Act was not violated until then. 977 F.2d at 32.

In October 1994, a plant manager and an employee of Durex Industries were sentenced to 27 months in prison for illegal disposal of hazardous waste in violation of RCRA. They placed waste chemicals into a dumpster, where their fumes killed two nine-year-old boys who climbed inside the dumpster. The defendants were acquitted of the more serious offense of knowing endangerment.

Courts continue to wrestle with difficult issues that arise at the intersection between criminal law and environmental law. Conflicts over criminal enforcement of the environmental laws can be viewed in part as the latest battleground in a war between two fundamentally different views on environmental issues, which have been termed "moral outrage" and "cool analysis." The "morally outraged" view environmental standards as establishing a moral obligation, while "cool analysts" view sanctions as simply part of the cost of doing business. The two approaches differ over both the aims to be served by environmental standards and their attitudes toward compliance, as described in Schroeder, Cool Analysis Versus Moral Outrage in the Development of Federal Environmental Criminal Law, 35 Wm. & Mary L. Rev. 251 (1993). Professor Richard Lazarus argues that the sharply divergent characteristics of environmental law and criminal law make assimilation and integration of them an enormous challenge. Lazarus, Meeting the Demands of Integration in the Evolution of Environmental Law: Reforming Environmental Criminal Law, 83 Geo. L.J. 2407 (1995). He notes that: (1) environmental law deals with reducing risks of harm, while criminal laws are concerned with actual harm; (2) proof of causation is far more difficult in environmental cases than for traditional crimes; (3) pollution is inevitable and pervasive; and (4) environmental law is aspirational, dynamic, and inherently complex.

Consider the interface between environmental and criminal laws as you read the case below. It involves prosecution of two managers of a sewage treatment plant for illegal discharges of pollutants in violation of an NPDES permit. The government argued that it was not necessary to prove that the managers knew the discharges exceeded levels allowed in the permit in order to obtain criminal convictions. The panel's decision was so controversial that it generated five votes for a rehearing en banc accompanied by a vigorous dissent, also reproduced below, when that petition was denied.

|| *United States v. Weitzenhoff* ||
   35 F.3d 1275 (9th Cir. 1994)

FLETCHER, Circuit Judge:

Michael H. Weitzenhoff and Thomas W. Mariani, who managed the East Honolulu Community Services Sewage Treatment Plant, appeal their convictions for violations of the Clean Water Act ("CWA"), 33 U.S.C. §§1251 et seq., contending that the district court misconstrued the word "knowingly" under section 1319(c)(2) of the CWA. . . .

FACTS AND PROCEDURAL HISTORY

In 1988 and 1989 Weitzenhoff was the manager and Mariani the assistant manager of the East Honolulu Community Services Sewage Treatment Plant ("the plant"), located not far from Sandy Beach, a popular swimming and surfing beach on Oahu. The plant is designed to treat some 4 million gallons of residential wastewater each day by removing the solids and other harmful pollutants from the sewage so that the resulting effluent can be safely discharged into the ocean. The plant operates under a permit issued pursuant to the National Pollution Discharge Elimination System ("NPDES"), which established the limits on the Total Suspended Solids ("TSS") and Biochemical Oxygen Demand ("BOD")—indicators of the solid and organic matter, respectively, in the effluent discharged at Sandy Beach. During the period in question, the permit limited the discharge of both the TSS and BOD to an average of 976 pounds per day over a 30-day period. It also imposed monitoring and sampling requirements on the plant's management.

The sewage treatment process that was overseen by Weitzenhoff and Mariani . . . [generates a substance] known as waste activated sludge ("WAS"), [that is] pumped to WAS holding tanks. From the holding tanks, the WAS could either be returned to other phases of the treatment process or hauled away to a different sewage treatment facility.

From March 1987 through March 1988, the excess WAS generated by the plant was hauled away to another treatment plant, the Sand Island Facility. In March 1988, certain improvements were made to the East Honolulu plant and the hauling was discontinued. Within a few weeks, however, the plant began experiencing a buildup of excess WAS. Rather than have the excess WAS hauled away as before, however, Weitzenhoff and Mariani instructed two employees at the plant to dispose of it on a regular basis by pumping it from the storage tanks directly into the outfall, that is, directly into the ocean. The WAS thereby bypassed the plant's effluent sampler so that the samples taken and reported to Hawaii's Department of Health ("DOH") and the EPA did not reflect its discharge.

The evidence produced by the government at trial showed that WAS was discharged directly into the ocean from the plant on about 40 separate occasions from April 1988 to June 1989, resulting in some 436,000 pounds of pollutant solids being discharged into the ocean, and that the discharges violated the plant's 30-day average effluent limit under the permit for most of the months during which they occurred. Most of the WAS discharges occurred during the night, and none was reported to the DOH or EPA. DOH inspectors contacted the plant on several occasions in 1988 in response to complaints by lifeguards at

Sandy Beach that sewage was being emitted from the outfall, but Weitzenhoff and Mariani repeatedly denied that there was any problem at the plant. In one letter responding to a DOH inquiry in October 1988, Mariani stated that "the debris that was reported could not have been from the East Honolulu Wastewater Treatment facility, as our records of effluent quality up to this time will substantiate." One of the plant employees who participated in the dumping operation testified that Weitzenhoff instructed him not to say anything about the discharges, because if they all stuck together and did not reveal anything, "they [couldn't] do anything to us."

Following an FBI investigation, Weitzenhoff and Mariani were charged in a thirty-one-count indictment with conspiracy and substantive violations of the Clean Water Act ("CWA"), 33 U.S.C. §§1251 et seq. At trial, Weitzenhoff and Mariani admitted having authorized the discharges, but claimed that their actions were justified under their interpretation of the NPDES permit. The jury found them guilty of six of the thirty-one counts.[1]

Weitzenhoff was sentenced to twenty-one months and Mariani thirty-three months imprisonment. Each filed a timely notice of appeal.

DISCUSSION

A. *Intent Requirement*

Section 1311(a) of the CWA prohibits the discharge of pollutants into navigable waters without an NPDES permit. 33 U.S.C. §1311(a). Section 1319(c)(2) makes it a felony offense to "knowingly violate[ ] section 1311, 1312, 1316, 1317, 1318, 1321(b)(3), 1328, or 1345 . . . , or any permit condition or limitation implementing any of such sections in a permit issued under section 1342."

Prior to trial, the district court construed "knowingly" in section 1319(c)(2) as requiring only that Weitzenhoff and Mariani were aware that they were discharging the pollutants in question, not that they knew they were violating the terms of the statute or permit. According to appellants, the district court erred in its interpretation of the CWA and in instructing the jury that "the government is not required to prove that the defendant knew that his act or omissions were unlawful," as well as in rejecting their proposed

---

1. Weitzenhoff and Mariani were found guilty of count 1, conspiracy to discharge the WAS in violation of the NPDES permit and the Clean Water Act, a violation of 18 U.S.C. §371; count 9, knowingly discharging WAS in violation of the permit between March and October 1988, a violation of 33 U.S.C. §§1311(a) and 1319(c)(2) and 18 U.S.C. §2; count 10, knowingly rendering inaccurate the plant's monitoring method by discharging WAS beyond the plant's effluent sampler during a period in 1988, a violation of 33 U.S.C. §1319(c)(4) and 18 U.S.C. §2; count 22, knowingly making false representations in monthly discharge monitoring reports filed with government regulators by failing to report their discharges of WAS, a violation of 33 U.S.C. §1319(c)(4) and 18 U.S.C. §2; count 30, knowingly discharging WAS in violation of the permit between January and July 1989, a violation of 33 U.S.C. §§1311(a) and 1319(c)(2) and 18 U.S.C. §2; and count 31, knowingly rendering inaccurate the plant's monitoring method by discharging WAS beyond the plant's effluent sampler during a period in 1989, a violation of 33 U.S.C. §1319(c)(4) and 18 U.S.C. §2. On appeal, most of appellants' energies are directed against the section 1319(c)(2) violations, which are premised on the language of the NPDES permit. Section 1319(c)(4) criminalizes the making of false statements in any document or rendering inaccurate of any monitoring device or method required to be maintained under the CWA.

instruction based on the defense that they mistakenly believed their conduct was authorized by the permit. Apparently, no court of appeals has confronted the issue raised by appellants.

We review a question of statutory construction de novo . . .

As with certain other criminal statutes that employ the term "knowingly," it is not apparent from the face of the statute whether "knowingly" means a knowing violation of the law or simply knowing conduct that is violative of the law. We turn, then, to the legislative history of the provision at issue to ascertain what Congress intended.

In 1987, Congress substantially amended the CWA, elevating the penalties for violations of the Act. See H.R. Conf. Rep. No. 1004, 99th Cong., 2d Sess. 138 (1986). Increased penalties were considered necessary to deter would-be polluters. S. Rep. No. 50, 99th Cong., 1st Sess. 29 (1985). With the 1987 amendments, Congress substituted "knowingly" for the earlier intent requirement of "willfully" that appeared in the predecessor to section 1319(c)(2).[4] The Senate report accompanying the legislation explains that the changes in the penalty provisions were to ensure that "criminal liability shall . . . attach to any person who is not in compliance with all applicable Federal, State and local requirements and permits *and causes* a POTW [publicly owned treatment works] to violate any effluent limitation or condition in any permit issued to the treatment works." Id. (emphasis added). Similarly, the report accompanying the House version of the bill, which contained parallel provisions for enhancement of penalties, states that the proposed amendments were to "provide penalties for dischargers or individuals who knowingly or negligently violate *or cause the violation of* certain of the Act's requirements." H.R. Rep. No. 189, 99th Cong., 1st Sess. 29-30 (1985) (emphasis added). Because they speak in terms of "causing" a violation, the congressional explanations of the new penalty provisions strongly suggest that criminal sanctions are to be imposed on an individual who knowingly engages in conduct that results in a permit violation, regardless of whether the polluter is cognizant of the requirements or even the existence of the permit.

Our conclusion that "knowingly" does not refer to the legal violation is fortified by decisions interpreting analogous public welfare statutes. The leading case in this area is United States v. International Minerals & Chem. Corp., 402 U.S. 558 (1971). In *International Minerals,* the Supreme Court construed a statute which made it a crime to "knowingly violate[ ] any . . . regulation" promulgated by the [Interstate Commerce Commission] pursuant to 18 U.S.C. §834(a), a provision authorizing the agency to formulate regulations for the safe transport of corrosive liquids. Id. at 559. The Court held that the term "knowingly" referred to the acts made criminal rather than a violation of the regulation, and that "regulation" was a shorthand designation for the specific acts or omissions contemplated by the act. Id. at 560-562. "Where . . . dangerous or deleterious devices or products or obnoxious waste materials are involved, the probability of regulation is so great that anyone who is aware that he is in possession of them or dealing with them must be presumed to be aware of the regulation." Id. at 565.

---

4. At least two courts held that specific intent was not required for conviction under the earlier version of section 1319, which imposed penalties for "willful or negligent" violations of the CWA without distinction. The current statute imposes harsher penalties for knowing violations than for negligent ones. United States v. Baytank (Houston), Inc., 934 F.2d 599, 618-19 & n.32 (5th Cir. 1991); United States v. Frezzo Bros., Inc., 546 F. Supp. 713, 720-21 (E.D. Pa. 1982), aff'd, 703 F.2d 62 (3d Cir.), cert. denied, 464 U.S. 829 (1983).

This court followed *International Minerals* in United States v. Hoflin, 880 F.2d 1033 (9th Cir. 1989), cert. denied, 493 U.S. 1083 (1990), when it held that knowledge of the absence of a permit is not an element of the offense defined by 42 U.S.C. §6928(d)(2)(A), part of the Resource Conservation and Recovery Act ("RCRA"). Id. at 1039. "There can be little question that RCRA's purposes, like those of the Food and Drug Act, '. . . touch phases of the lives and health of people which, in the circumstances of modern industrialism, are largely beyond self-protection.'" Id. at 1038 (quoting United States v. Dotterweich, 320 U.S. 277, 280 (1943) (construing Food, Drug and Cosmetic Act)); see also United States v. Sherbondy, 865 F.2d 996, 1001-03 (9th Cir. 1988) (use of word "knowingly" in 18 U.S.C. §§922(g) & 924(A)(1)(B), part of Firearms Owners' Protection Act, does not require proof that defendant knew he was violating law).[5] Other courts have also followed *International Minerals* by similarly construing the knowledge requirement in statutes that regulate deleterious devices or obnoxious waste materials. E.g., United States v. Laughlin, 10 F.3d 961, 965-66 (2d Cir. 1993) (§6928(d)(2)(A) of RCRA), cert. denied, 114 S. Ct. 1649 (1994); United States v. Buckley, 934 F.2d 84, 88 (6th Cir. 1991) (pre-1990 version of §7413(c)(1)(C) of the Clean Air Act); United States v. Dee, 912 F.2d 741, 745 (4th Cir. 1990), cert. denied, 499 U.S. 919 (1991) (§6928(d)(2)(A) of RCRA); United States v. Corbin Farm Servs., 444 F. Supp. 510, 519-20 (E.D. Cal.), aff'd, 578 F.2d 259 (9th Cir. 1978) (Federal Insecticide, Fungicide and Rodenticide Act).[6]

Appellants seek to rely on the Supreme Court's decision in Liparota v. United States, 471 U.S. 419 (1985), to support their alternative reading of the intent requirement. *Liparota* concerned 7 U.S.C. §2024(b)(1), which provides that anyone who "knowingly uses, transfers, acquires, alters, or possesses [food stamp] coupons or authorization cards in any manner not authorized by [the statute] or regulations" is subject to a fine or imprisonment. Id. at 420. The Court, noting that the conduct at issue did not constitute a public welfare offense, distinguished the *International Minerals* line of cases and held that

---

5. Weitzenhoff argues that this case is controlled by United States v. Speach, 968 F.2d 795, 796-97 (9th Cir. 1992), in which we held that 42 U.S.C. §6928(d)(1), which imposes criminal liability on parties who "knowingly transport[ ] . . . hazardous waste . . . to a facility which does not have a permit," requires that the transporter know that he acted in violation of the statute. This argument is unavailing because *Speach* recognizes the general rule that public welfare offenses are not to be construed to require proof that the defendant knew he was violating the law in the absence of clear evidence of contrary congressional intent and finds only a narrow exception to this general rule. In *Speach*, we relied on the fact that the defendant was not the permittee but simply the individual who transported waste to the permittee, and, as contrasted to the permittee was not "the person in the best position to know the facility's permit status." Id. at 797. Although we considered it unreasonable to put the defendant at risk for failing to ascertain the permit status of the receiving facility, we recognized that such a risk is not unreasonable when the permittee is also the defendant. Id. In this case, as the permittees, appellants are clearly in the best position to know their own permit status, and are among those persons upon whom the *Speach* court would impose liability.

6. Like the court in *International Minerals*, we construe the language in §1319(c)(2)(A) prohibiting knowing violation of "any permit condition" as a "shorthand designation for specific acts" that violate the CWA. See *International Minerals*, 402 U.S. at 567. In both §1319(c)(2)(A) and the statute in question in *International Minerals*, the penalty provisions were drafted in a general fashion to encompass a wide variety of possible violations of the Acts and the word "knowingly" is used to reflect a requirement that the government prove general intent in order to establish a violation.

the government must prove the defendant knew that his acquisition or possession of food stamps was in a manner unauthorized by statute or regulations. Id. at 432-33.

Subsequent to the filing of the original opinion in this case, the Supreme Court decided two cases which Weitzenhoff contends call our analysis into question. See Ratzlaf v. United States, 114 S. Ct. 655 (1994); Staples v. United States, 114 S. Ct. 1793 (1994). We disagree.

The statute in *Ratzlaf* does not deal with a public welfare offense, but rather with violations of the banking statutes. The Court construed the term "willfully" in the anti-structuring provisions of the Bank Secrecy Act to require both that the defendant knew he was structuring transactions to avoid reporting requirements and that he knew his acts were unlawful. The Court recognized that the money structuring provisions are not directed at conduct which a reasonable person necessarily should know is subject to strict public regulation and that the structuring offense applied to all persons with more than $10,000, many of whom could be engaged in structuring for innocent reasons. *Ratzlaf,* 114 S. Ct. at 660-62. In contrast, parties such as Weitzenhoff are closely regulated and are discharging waste materials that affect public health. The *International Minerals* rationale requires that we impute to these parties knowledge of their operating permit. This was recognized by the Court in *Staples.*

The specific holding in *Staples* was that the government is required to prove that a defendant charged with possession of a machine gun knew that the weapon he possessed had the characteristics that brought it within the statutory definition of a machine gun. But the Court took pains to contrast the gun laws to other regulatory regimes, specifically those regulations that govern the handling of "obnoxious waste materials." See *Staples,* 114 S. Ct. at 1798. It noted that the mere innocent ownership of guns is not a public welfare offense. Id. at 1804. The Court focussed on the long tradition of widespread gun ownership in this country and, recognizing that approximately 50% of American homes contain a firearm, id. at 1801, acknowledged that mere ownership of a gun is not sufficient to place people on notice that the act of owning an unregistered firearm is not innocent under the law.

Staples thus explicitly contrasted the mere possession of guns to public welfare offenses, which include statutes that regulate "dangerous or deleterious devices or products or obnoxious waste materials," id. at 1800, and confirmed the continued vitality of statutes covering public welfare offenses, which "regulate potentially harmful or injurious items" and place a defendant on notice that he is dealing with a device or a substance "that places him in 'responsible relation to a public danger.'" Id. "In such cases Congress intended to place the burden on the defendant to ascertain at his peril whether [his conduct] comes within the inhibition of the statute." Id. at 1798 (citations and internal quotations omitted).

Unlike "guns [which] in general are not 'deleterious devices or products or obnoxious waste materials,' *International Minerals,* supra, . . . that put their owners on notice that they stand 'in responsible relation to a public danger[,]' *Dotterweich,* 320 U.S. at 281," *Staples,* 114 S. Ct. at 1800, the dumping of sewage and other pollutants into our nation's waters is precisely the type of activity that puts the discharger on notice that his acts may pose a public danger. Like other public welfare offenses that regulate the discharge of pollutants into the air, the disposal of hazardous wastes, the undocumented shipping of acids, and the use of pesticides on our food, the improper and excessive discharge of sewage causes cholera, hepatitis, and other serious illnesses, and can have serious repercussions for public health and welfare.[7]

The criminal provisions of the CWA are clearly designed to protect the public at large from the potentially dire consequences of water pollution, see S. Rep. No. 99-50, 99th Cong., 1st Sess. 29 (1985), and as such fall within the category of public welfare legislation. *International Minerals* rather than *Liparota* controls the case at hand. The government did not need to prove that Weitzenhoff and Mariani knew that their acts violated the permit or the CWA. . . .

KLEINFELD, Circuit Judge, with whom Circuit Judges REINHARDT, KOZINSKI, TROTT, and T.G. NELSON join, dissenting from the order rejecting the suggestion for rehearing en banc.

I respectfully dissent from our decision to reject the suggestion for rehearing en banc.

Most of us vote against most such petitions and suggestions even when we think the panel decision is mistaken. We do so because federal courts of appeals decide cases in three judge panels. En banc review is extraordinary, and is generally reserved for conflicting precedent within the circuit which makes application of the law by district courts unduly difficult, and egregious errors in important cases. In my view, this is a case of exceptional importance, for two reasons. First, it impairs a fundamental purpose of criminal justice, sorting out the innocent from the guilty before imposing punishment. Second, it does so in the context of the Clean Water Act. This statute has tremendous sweep. Most statutes permit anything except what is prohibited, but this one prohibits all regulated conduct involving waters and wetlands except what is permitted. 33 U.S.C. §1311(a); United States v. Riverside Bayview Homes, Inc., 474 U.S. 121 (1985). Much more ordinary, innocent, productive activity is regulated by this law than people not versed in environmental law might imagine.

The harm our mistaken decision may do is not necessarily limited to Clean Water Act cases. Dilution of the traditional requirement of a criminal state of mind, and application of the criminal law to innocent conduct, reduces the moral authority of our system of criminal law. If we use prison to achieve social goals regardless of the moral innocence of those we incarcerate, then imprisonment loses its moral opprobrium and our criminal law becomes morally arbitrary.

We have now made felons of a large number of innocent people doing socially valuable work. They are innocent, because the one thing which makes

---

7. In *Staples,* the Court also noted that the penalty attached to a violation of a criminal statute in the past has been a relevant factor in determining whether the statute defines a public welfare offense. The Court recognized that public welfare offenses originally involved statutes that provided only light penalties such as fines or short jail sentences, see 114 S. Ct. at 1802, but that modern statutes now punish public welfare offenses with much more significant terms of imprisonment. E.g., *International Minerals,* 402 U.S. 558 (ten years imprisonment if death or bodily injury results from violation); United States v. Freed, 401 U.S. 601, 609-10 (1971) (five years imprisonment for possession of unregistered grenade); *Hoflin,* 880 F.2d 1033 (two years imprisonment for certain violations of RCRA). While the *Staples* opinion expresses concern with this evolution of enhanced punishments for public welfare offenses, it refrains from holding that public welfare offenses may not be punished as felonies. *Staples,* 114 S. Ct. at 1804 (stating that: the early cases suggest that public welfare offenses might not extend to felonies, but noting that "we need not adopt such a definitive rule of construction to decide this case").

their conduct felonious is something they do not know. It is we, and not Congress, who have made them felons. The statute, read in an ordinary way, does not. If we are fortunate, sewer plant workers around the circuit will continue to perform their vitally important work despite our decision. If they knew they risk three years in prison, some might decide that their pay, though sufficient inducement for processing the public's wastes, is not enough to risk prison for doing their jobs. We have decided that they should go to prison if, unbeknownst to them, their plant discharges exceed permit limits. Likewise for power plant operators who discharge warm water into rivers near their plants, and for all sorts of other dischargers in public and private life. If they know they are discharging into water, have a permit for the discharges, think they are conforming to their permits, but unknowingly violate their permit conditions, into prison they go with the violent criminals.

The statute does not say that. The statute at issue makes it a felony, subject to three years of imprisonment, to "knowingly violate[ ] . . . any permit condition or limitation." 33 U.S.C. §1319(c)(2)(A).[1] . . . In this case, the defendants, sewage plant operators, had a permit to discharge sewage into the ocean, but exceeded the permit limitations. The legal issue for the panel was what knowledge would turn innocently or negligently violating a permit into "knowingly" violating a permit. Were the plant operators felons if they knew they were discharging sewage, but did not know that they were violating their permit? Or did they also have to know they were violating their permit? Ordinary English grammar, common sense, and precedent, all compel the latter construction.

As the panel opinion states the facts, these two defendants were literally "midnight dumpers." They managed a sewer plant and told their employees to dump 436,000 pounds of sewage into the ocean, mostly at night, fouling a nearby beach. Their conduct, as set out in the panel opinion, suggests that they must have known they were violating their National Pollution Discharge Elimination System (NPDES) permit. United States v. Weitzenhoff, 1 F.3d 1523, 1527-28 (9th Cir. 1993). But we cannot decide the case on that basis, because the jury did not. The court instructed the jury that the government did not have to prove the defendants knew their conduct was unlawful, and refused to instruct the jury that a mistaken belief that the discharge was authorized by the permit would be a defense. Because of the way the jury was instructed, its verdict is consistent with the proposition that the defendants honestly and reasonably believed that their NPDES permit authorized the discharges.

This proposition could be true. NPDES permits are often difficult to understand and obey. The EPA had licensed the defendants' plant to discharge 976 pounds of waste per day, or about 409,920 pounds over the fourteen months covered by the indictment, into the ocean. The wrongful conduct was not discharging waste into the ocean. That was socially desirable conduct by which the defendants protected the people of their city from sewage-borne disease and earned their pay. The wrongful conduct was violating the NPDES permit by discharging 26,000 more pounds of waste than the permit authorized during the fourteen months. Whether these defendants were innocent or not, in the sense of knowing that they were exceeding their permit limitation, the panel's holding will make innocence irrelevant in other permit violation cases where the

---

1. A 1987 Amendment raised the crime from a misdemeanor to a felony, and changed the intent requirement from "willfully" to "knowingly." Pub. L. No. 100-4, §312, 101 Stat. 42 (1987).

defendants had no idea that they were exceeding permit limits. The only thing they have to know to be guilty is that they were dumping sewage into the ocean, yet that was a lawful activity expressly authorized by their federal permit.

The statute says "knowingly violates . . . any permit condition or limitation." "Knowingly" is an adverb. It modifies the verb "violates." The object of the verb is "any permit condition or limitation." The word "knowingly" is placed before "violates" to "explain its meaning in the case at hand more clearly." 1 George O. Curme, A Grammar of the English Language 72 (1935). Congress has distinguished those who knowingly violate permit conditions, and are thereby felons, from those who unknowingly violate permit conditions, so are not. The panel reads the statute as though it says "knowingly discharges pollutants." It does not. If we read the statute on the assumption that Congress used the English language in an ordinary way, the state of mind required is knowledge that one is violating a permit condition.

This approach has the virtue of attributing common sense and a rational purpose to Congress. Cf. Longview Fibre Co. v. Rasmussen, 980 F.2d 1307, 1311 (9th Cir. 1992); United States v. Martinez-Cano, 6 F.3d 1400, 1405 (9th Cir. 1993) (dissent). It is one thing to defy a permit limitation, but quite another to violate it without realizing that one is violating it. Congress promulgated a parallel statute making it a misdemeanor "negligently" to violate a permit condition or limitation. 33 U.S.C. §1319(c)(1)(A). If negligent violation is a misdemeanor, why would Congress want to make it a felony to violate the permit without negligence and without even knowing that the discharge exceeded the permit limit? That does not make any sense. It would deter people from working in sewer plants, instead of deterring people from violating permits. All dischargers acting lawfully pursuant to a permit know that they are discharging pollutants. The presence or absence of that knowledge, which is the only mental element determining guilt under the panel's decision, has no bearing on any conduct Congress could have meant to turn into a felony. The only knowledge which could have mattered to Congress, the only knowledge which distinguishes good conduct from bad, is knowledge that the discharge violates the permit. That is what the statute says, "knowingly violates," not "knowingly discharges." There is no sensible reason to doubt that Congress meant what it said and said what it meant.

The panel reaches its surprising result in surprising ways. First, it says that the statute is ambiguous. "As with certain other criminal statutes that employ the term 'knowingly,' it is not apparent from the face of the statute whether 'knowingly' means a knowing violation of the law or simply knowing conduct that is violative of the law." *Weitzenhoff,* 1 F.3d at 1529. As explained above, a grammatical and sensible reading of the statute leaves no room for ambiguity. But for the sake of discussion, suppose that the statute is ambiguous, as the panel says. Then the rule of lenity requires that the construction allowing the defendant more liberty rather than less be applied by the courts. . . .

The panel . . . tries to bolster its construction by categorizing the offense as a "public welfare offense," as though that justified more aggressive criminalization without a plain statutory command. This category is a modernized version of "malum prohibitum." Traditionally the criminal law distinguishes between malum in se, conduct wrong upon principles of natural moral law, and malum prohibitum, conduct not inherently immoral but wrong because prohibited by law. Black's Law Dictionary 1112 (4th ed. 1951). To put this in plain, modern terms, any normal person knows murder, rape, and robbery are wrong, and they would be wrong even in a place with no sovereign and no law. Discharging 6% more pollutants than one's permit allows is wrong only because the law says so. Substitution of the modern term "public welfare offense" for the traditional one, malum prohibitum, allows for confusion by rhetorical suggestion. The new term suggests that other offenses might merely be private in their impact, and therefore less serious. The older set of terms made it clear that murder was more vile than violating a federal regulation. The category of malum prohibitum, or public welfare offenses, makes the rule of lenity especially important, most particularly for felonies, because persons of good conscience may not recognize the wrongfulness of the conduct when they engage in it.

Staples v. United States, 114 S. Ct. 1793 (1994), reminds us that "offenses that require no *mens rea* generally are disfavored. . . ." 114 S. Ct. at 1797. *Mens rea* may be dispensed within public welfare offenses, but the penalty is a "significant consideration in determining whether the statute should be construed as dispensing with *mens rea*." 114 S. Ct. at 1802. . . . If Congress makes a crime a felony, the felony categorization alone is a "factor tending to suggest that Congress did not intend to eliminate a *mens rea* requirement. In such a case, the usual presumption that a defendant must know the facts that make his conduct illegal should apply." 114 S. Ct. at 1804. In the case at bar, "the facts that make his conduct illegal" are the permit violations, not the discharges of pollutants. Discharge of pollutants was licensed by the federal government in the NPDES permit. Under *Staples,* it would be presumed, even if the law did not plainly say so, that the defendant would have to know that he was violating the permit in order to be guilty of the felony. . . .

The panel cites United States v. International Minerals & Chem. Corp., 402 U.S. 558 (1971) . . . in support of its reading. *International Minerals* was a . . . misdemeanor case. Because of the syntactically similar statute at issue in that case, it is the strongest authority for the panel's decision and raises the most serious question for my own analysis. It held that a shipper of sulfuric acid could be convicted of violating a statute applying to those who "knowingly violate[ ]" regulations governing shipments of corrosive liquids, regardless of whether he had knowledge of the regulations. *International Minerals* expressly limits its holding to "dangerous or deleterious devices or products or obnoxious waste materials." 402 U.S. at 565. The Court distinguished materials not obviously subject to regulation:

> Pencils, dental floss, paper clips may also be regulated. But they may be the type of products which might raise substantial due process questions if Congress did not require . . . "*mens rea*" as to each ingredient of the offense. But where, as here . . . , dangerous or deleterious devices or products or obnoxious waste materials are involved, the probability of regulation is so great that anyone who is aware that he is in possession of them or dealing with them must be presumed to be aware of the regulation.

Id. at 564-565. *International Minerals* would have much persuasive force for Weitzenhoff, because of the grammatical similarity of the statute, if (1) the Clean Water Act limited pollutants to "dangerous or deleterious devices or products or obnoxious waste materials"; (2) the crime was only a misdemeanor; and (3) *Staples* had not come down this term. But all three of these conditions are contrary to fact. The pollutants to which the Clean Water Act felony statute applies include many in the "pencils, dental floss, paper clips" category. Hot water, rock, and sand are classified as "pollutants" by the Clean Water Act. See

33 U.S.C. §1362(6). Discharging silt from a stream back into the same stream may amount to discharge of a pollutant. For that matter, so may skipping a stone into a lake. So may a cafeteria worker's pouring hot, stale coffee down the drain. Making these acts a misdemeanor is one thing, but a felony is quite another as *Staples* teaches. . . .

The panel, finally, asserts that as a matter of policy, the Clean Water Act crimes "are clearly designed to protect the public at large from the dire consequences of water pollution." That is true, but the panel does not explain how the public is to be protected by making felons of sewer workers who unknowingly violate their plants' permits. Provision for sanitary sewage disposal is among the most ancient laws of civilization. Deuteronomy 23:12-13. Sewage workers perform essential work of great social value. Probably nothing has prevented more infant mortality, or freed more people from cholera, hepatitis, typhoid fever, and other disease, than the development in the last two centuries of municipal sewer systems. See W.H. Corfield, The Treatment and Utilisation of Sewage 17-27 (1871). Sewage utility workers perform their difficult work in malodorous and dangerous environments. We have now imposed on these vitally important public servants a massive legal risk, unjustified by law or precedent, if they unknowingly violate their permit conditions.

Nor is the risk of prison limited to sewage plant workers. It applies to anyone who discharges pollutants pursuant to a permit, and unknowingly violates the permit. The panel suggests that criminalizing this innocent conduct will protect the public from water pollution. It is at least as likely that the increased criminal risk will raise the cost and reduce the availability of such lawful and essential public services as sewage disposal. We should not deprive individuals of justice, whether the judicial action would serve some desirable policy or not. It is by no means certain that the panel's construction will advance the underlying policy it attributes to Congress. We should apply the words Congress and the President promulgated as law, leaving the difficult policy choices to them.

We undermine the foundation of criminal law when we so vitiate the requirement of a criminal state of knowledge and intention as to make felons of the morally innocent.

NOTES AND QUESTIONS

1. The defendants had argued at trial that their midnight dumping of toxic sludge actually was an effort to restore the treatment plant's biological balance to prevent a complete shutdown of the plant that would have caused far more environmental harm. While the plant's NPDES permit authorized bypasses for "essential maintenance to assure efficient operation" of the plant, the court found that the discharges were not permissible bypasses. 35 F.3d at 1288. The court found that the plant's permit was not unconstitutionally vague, noting that "appellants had adequate notice of the illegality of their dumping" as was indicated

> by the considerable pains they took to conceal their activities. The discharges were effected mainly at night; plant personnel were not to discuss them; and Weitzenhoff and Mariani consistently repeatedly denied the illicit operation when questioned by health authorities. These are not the ways of conscientious managers seeking to safeguard the environment. [Id. at 1289.]

Would the defendants have been more likely to prevail on appeal if they had made no effort whatsoever to conceal their activities?

2. Even the judges dissenting from the denial of a rehearing en banc agreed that the defendants' conduct "suggests that they must have known that they were violating their [NPDES] permit." 35 F.3d at 1294. Why then did the dissenting judges suggest the convictions should be reversed?

3. What is the rationale for not requiring a showing of specific intent to violate regulations when "public welfare" offenses are involved? What type of offenses should be considered public welfare offenses? Do the judges who dissented from denial of a rehearing en banc agree that violating the terms of an NPDES permit should be considered to be a public welfare offense? Do they differ from the majority in their views concerning the seriousness of the violations?

4. In United States v. Ahmad, 101 F.3d 386 (5th Cir. 1996), the Fifth Circuit reversed a criminal conviction under the Clean Water Act of a defendant who claimed at trial that he thought he was discharging water and not gasoline. The court held that the mens rea of knowledge applied to each element of the offense, thus requiring the government to prove that the defendant knew that what he was discharging was a pollutant. The court distinguished *Weitzenhoff* as addressing only whether the language of the Clean Water Act creates a mistake-of-law defense, as opposed to the mistake-of-fact defense raised in *Ahmad*. In United States v. Wilson, 133 F.3d 251 (4th Cir. 1997), a panel of the Fourth Circuit followed the *Ahmad* interpretation of the mens rea required for a criminal conviction under the Clean Water Act. The *Wilson* court rejected the defendant's argument that it should construe the word "knowingly" as requiring that the defendant appreciate the illegality of his acts, finding that such an interpretation would obliterate the distinction between "knowingly" and "willfully." However, the court held that "Congress intended that the defendant have knowledge of each of the elements constituting the proscribed conduct even if he were unaware of their legal significance." Thus it concluded that while a defendant's ignorance of his conduct's illegality does not provide a defense, a defendant can argue a mistake of fact as a defense. As a result, "to establish a felony violation of the Clean Water Act" the government

> must prove: (1) that the defendant knew that he was discharging a substance, eliminating a prosecution for accidental discharges; (2) that the defendant correctly identified the substance he was discharging, not mistaking it for a different, unprohibited substance; (3) that the defendant knew the method or instrumentality used to discharge the pollutants; (4) that the defendant knew the physical characteristics of the property into which the pollutant was discharged that identify it as a wetland, such as the presence of water and water-loving vegetation; (5) that the defendant was aware of the facts establishing the required link between the wetland and waters of the United States; and (6) that the defendant knew he did not have a permit. This last requirement does not require the government to show that the defendant knew that permits were available or required. Rather, it, like the other requirements, preserves the availability of a mistake of fact [defense] if the defendant has something he mistakenly believed to be a permit to make the discharges for which he is being prosecuted. [133 F.3d at 264.]

5. Some have proposed enacting legislation that would bar the imposition of civil or criminal penalties on defendants who "reasonably in good faith determined" that they were in compliance with an environmental regulation. What effect would such legislation have on enforcement efforts? In General

Electric Company v. EPA, 53 F.3d 1324 (D.C. Cir. 1995), discussed on page 953, the D.C. Circuit barred the imposition of civil penalties on defendants who did not have "fair warning" of EPA's interpretation of regulations. The court held that "[w]here, as here, the regulations and other policy statements are unclear, where the petitioner's interpretation is reasonable, and where the agency itself struggles to provide a definitive reading of the regulatory requirements, a regulated party is not 'on notice' of the agency's ultimate interpretation of the regulations, and may not be punished." 53 F.3d at 1333-1334. Does the availability of this defense make the use of a general intent standard for proving environmental felonies less troublesome?

6. Professor Richard Lazarus argues the public welfare rationale for dispensing with specific intent requirements, as represented by the *International Minerals* decision, should not be applied reflexively to environmental felonies. Lazarus, Meeting the Demands of Integration in the Evolution of Environmental Law: Reforming Environmental Criminal Law, 83 Geo. L.J. 2407 (1995). He notes that *International Minerals*, which involved a misdemeanor, did not hold that persons dealing with hazardous materials *must* be presumed to be aware of the applicable regulations, but rather only that Congress could choose to assume such knowledge without violating due process. Lazarus observes that in many environmental law contexts it is not the case that regulations are readily discernible or that regulated entities are part of a specialized, highly regulated activity, factors that would make dispensing with specific intent requirements more palatable. Lazarus' arguments were challenged by the Assistant and Deputy Assistant Attorneys General for the Environment and Natural Resources Division in Schiffer & Simon, The Reality of Prosecuting Environmental Criminals: A Response to Professor Lazarus, 83 Geo. L.J. 2531 (1995). They maintain that adopting a specific intent or "willfulness" requirement would make convictions impossible under the following circumstances:

(1)   A trucker dumps hundreds of drums of flammable, explosive, and toxic wastes in fields and vacant lots in a rural area. He knows that they are dangerous, but he has no knowledge of the laws that regulate the handling of such wastes.

(2)   A ship owner loads hazardous wastes as ballast and dumps those wastes at sea at a place unknown to authorities. He knows of the legal restrictions on dumping, but neither harm nor threat of harm can be determined reliably after the fact.

(3)   A laboratory that was paid to analyze environmental samples instead simply disposes of the samples and provides clients with fictitious results that always show that the clients are in compliance with their permits. Given those assurances, the clients take no steps to remove contaminants from their wastestreams. No one can reconstruct what contaminants were actually released to the environment or what harm was caused. [Id.]

Do you agree that requiring proof that the defendant knew the regulations were being violated would make prosecution impossible in these situations? Would this imply that environmental law needs to criminalize even some conduct that is nonculpable in order to make it possible to convict certain truly culpable individuals?

7. The debate over the proper intent standard for environmental felonies reflects concerns about how much discretion prosecutors have and how well

they exercise that discretion. Assistant Attorney General Lois Schiffer argues that there already are sufficient legal protections to prevent abuses of prosecutorial discretion, citing the rule of lenity and the doctrine that "an honest mistake regarding facts that would otherwise make . . . conduct criminal . . . negates the intent required for a felony conviction under the environmental laws." Id. at 2535. In addition, prosecutorial discretion is subject to policy guidance.

In January 1994, EPA issued a guidance document on criminal enforcement entitled The Exercise of Investigative Discretion. The publication directs agency investigators to focus on the "most significant and egregious violators" of the environmental laws based on the environmental consequences of the violations and the culpability of the conduct that generated them. Criteria for assessing the culpability of conduct include a history of repeat violations, evidence of deliberate misconduct, efforts to conceal violations, and operations conducted without permits or other regulatory documentation. For an argument that EPA has not done a good job of targeting only the most serious violations, see Gaynor & Bartman, Specific Intent Standard for Environmental Crimes: An Idea Whose Time Has Come, 25 Envtl. Rep. 2206 (1995). Citing potential abuses of prosecutorial discretion, Gaynor and Bartman maintain that the environmental laws should be amended to require that specific intent be proven before convictions can be obtained. EPA's guidance on criminal case selection suggests that cases involving neither culpable conduct nor significant harm ordinarily should not be prosecuted as criminal cases.

8. Staples v. United States, 511 U.S. 600 (1994), involved a statute which made it a felony to possess an unregistered "firearm." The statute defined "firearm" to include a fully automatic gun, which would fire more than one bullet on a single pull of the trigger, but not a semiautomatic. The defendant possessed a fully automatic gun, but testified that he did not know it would fire more than one bullet with a single trigger pull. The trial judge had instructed the jury that his ignorance did not matter, so long as the government proved he possessed "a dangerous device of a type as would alert one to the likelihood of regulation." But the Supreme Court held this to be error, explaining that, unlike hand grenades, semiautomatics are innocently possessed by many people and that the mere knowledge that guns are dangerous and regulated is not enough to require their owners to ascertain regulatory compliance at the risk of a felony conviction.

> Congress might see fit to criminalize the violation of certain regulations concerning automobiles, and thus might make it a crime to operate a vehicle without a properly functioning emission control system. But we probably would hesitate to conclude on the basis of silence that Congress intended a prison term to apply to a car owner whose vehicle's emissions levels, wholly unbeknownst to him, began to exceed legal limits between regular inspection dates. [511 U.S. at 614.]

9. Despite the impassioned dissent of five judges from the denial of a rehearing en banc, the Supreme Court refused to review *Weitzenhoff*. The Second Circuit reached a similar result in United States v. Hopkins, 53 F.3d 533 (2d Cir. 1995), which the Supreme Court also declined to review. In *Hopkins,* the court held that deliberate and conscious avoidance of knowledge could satisfy the mens rea requirement of section 309(c)(2) of the Clean Water Act. The court upheld the conviction of a corporate official who had his employees manipulate samples of wastewater discharges to keep them within permit limits, while insisting that he not be told of the results. Hopkins was found guilty of

tampering with a wastewater monitoring device and falsifying discharge monitoring reports in violation of the Clean Water Act. Testimony at trial showed that he routinely discarded monitoring samples that indicated permit violations and diluted others until they did not show violations. Citing *Weitzenhoff,* the Second Circuit held that the government was required to prove that the defendant "knew the nature of his acts and performed them intentionally, but was not required to prove that he knew that those acts violated the CWA, or any particular provision of that law, or the regulatory permit. . . ." 53 F.3d at 541.

D.   STANDING AND CITIZEN ACCESS TO THE COURTS

The public also can play a significant role in enforcement. The environmental laws generally authorize citizen suits against government agencies that fail to implement the laws and against anyone who violates them. Before examining the citizen suit provisions, we consider what persons have a sufficient stake in a controversy to have standing to sue, which was addressed in the following classic case.

Sierra Club v. Morton
405 U.S. 727 (1972)

MR. JUSTICE STEWART delivered the opinion of the Court.

The Mineral King Valley is an area of great natural beauty nestled in the Sierra Nevada Mountains in Tulare County, California, adjacent to Sequoia National Park. It has been part of the Sequoia National Forest since 1926, and is designated as a national game refuge by special Act of Congress. Though once the site of extensive mining activity, Mineral King is now used almost exclusively for recreational purposes. Its relative inaccessibility and lack of development have limited the number of visitors each year, and at the same time have preserved the valley's quality as a quasi-wilderness area largely uncluttered by the products of civilization.

The United States Forest Service, which is entrusted with the maintenance and administration of national forests, began in the late 1940s to give consideration to Mineral King as a potential site for recreational development. Prodded by a rapidly increasing demand for skiing facilities, the Forest Service published a prospectus in 1965, inviting bids from private developers for the construction and operation of a ski resort that would also serve as a summer recreation area. The proposal of Walt Disney Enterprises, Inc., was chosen from those of six bidders, and Disney received a three-year permit to conduct surveys and explorations in the valley in connection with its preparation of a complete master plan for the resort.

The final Disney plan, approved by the Forest Service in January 1969, outlines a $35 million complex of motels, restaurants, swimming pools, parking lots, and other structures designed to accommodate 14,000 visitors daily. This complex is to be constructed on 80 acres of the valley floor under a 30-year use permit from the Forest Service. Other facilities, including ski lifts, ski trails, a cog-assisted railway, and utility installations, are to be constructed on the mountain slopes and in other parts of the valley under a revocable special-use permit. To provide access to the resort, the State of California proposes to construct a highway 20 miles in length. A section of this road would traverse Sequoia National Park, as would a proposed high-voltage power line needed to provide electricity for the resort. Both the highway and the power line require the approval of the Department of the Interior, which is entrusted with the preservation and maintenance of the national parks.

Representatives of the Sierra Club, who favor maintaining Mineral King largely in its present state, followed the progress of recreational planning for the valley with close attention and increasing dismay. They unsuccessfully sought a public hearing on the proposed development in 1965, and in subsequent correspondence with officials of the Forest Service and the Department of the Interior, they expressed the Club's objections to Disney's plan as a whole and to particular features included in it. In June 1969 the Club filed the present suit in the United States District Court for the Northern District of California, seeking a declaratory judgment that various aspects of the proposed development contravene federal laws and regulations governing the preservation of national parks, forests, and game refuges, and also seeking preliminary and permanent injunctions restraining the federal officials involved from granting their approval or issuing permits in connection with the Mineral King project. The petitioner Sierra Club sued as a membership corporation with "a special interest in the conservation and the sound maintenance of the national parks, game refuges and forests of the country," and invoked the judicial-review provisions of the Administrative Procedure Act, 5 U.S.C. §701 et seq.

After two days of hearings, the District Court granted the requested preliminary injunction. It rejected the respondents' challenge to the Sierra Club's standing to sue, and determined that the hearing had raised questions "concerning possible excess of statutory authority, sufficiently substantial and serious to justify a preliminary injunction. . . ." The respondents appealed, and the Court of Appeals for the Ninth Circuit reversed. 433 F.2d 24. With respect to the petitioner's standing, the court noted that there was "no allegation in the complaint that members of the Sierra Club would be affected by the actions of [the respondents] other than the fact that the actions are personally displeasing or distasteful to them," id., at 33, and concluded:

> We do not believe such club concern without a showing of more direct interest can constitute standing in the legal sense sufficient to challenge the exercise of responsibilities on behalf of all the citizens by two cabinet level officials of the government acting under Congressional and Constitutional authority. Id., at 30.

Alternatively, the Court of Appeals held that the Sierra Club had not made an adequate showing of irreparable injury and likelihood of success on the merits to justify issuance of a preliminary injunction. The court thus vacated the injunction. The Sierra Club filed a petition for a writ of certiorari which we granted, 401 U.S. 907, to review the questions of federal law presented.

The first question presented is whether the Sierra Club has alleged facts that entitle it to obtain judicial review of the challenged action. Whether a party has a sufficient stake in an otherwise justiciable controversy to obtain judicial resolution of that controversy is what has traditionally been referred to as the question of standing to sue. Where the party does not rely on any specific statute authorizing invocation of the judicial process, the question of standing depends upon whether the party has alleged such a "personal stake in the outcome of the controversy," Baker v. Carr, 369 U.S. 186, 204, as to ensure that "the dispute sought to be adjudicated will be presented in an adversary context and in a form historically viewed as capable of judicial resolution." Flast v. Cohen, 392 U.S. 83, 101. Where, however, Congress has authorized public officials to perform certain functions according to law, and has provided by statute for judicial review of those actions under certain circumstances, the inquiry as to standing must begin with a determination of whether the statute in question authorizes review at the behest of the plaintiff.

The Sierra Club relies upon §10 of the Administrative Procedure Act (APA), 5 U.S.C. §702, which provides:

> A person suffering legal wrong because of agency action, or adversely affected or aggrieved by agency action within the meaning of a relevant statute, is entitled to judicial review thereof.

Early decisions under this statute interpreted the language as adopting the various formulations of "legal interest" and "legal wrong" then prevailing as constitutional requirements of standing. But, in Data Processing Service v. Camp, 397 U.S. 150, and Barlow v. Collins, 397 U.S. 159, decided the same day, we held more broadly that persons had standing to obtain judicial review of federal agency action under §10 of the APA where they had alleged that the challenged action had caused them "injury in fact," and where the alleged injury was to an interest "arguably within the zone of interests to be protected or regulated" by the statutes that the agencies were claimed to have violated.

In *Data Processing,* the injury claimed by the petitioners consisted of harm to their competitive position in the computer-servicing market through a ruling by the Comptroller of the Currency that national banks might perform data-processing services for their customers. In *Barlow,* the petitioners were tenant farmers who claimed that certain regulations of the Secretary of Agriculture adversely affected their economic position vis-à-vis their landlords. These palpable economic injuries have long been recognized as sufficient to lay the basis for standing, with or without a specific statutory provision for judicial review. Thus, neither *Data Processing* nor *Barlow* addressed itself to the question, which has arisen with increasing frequency in federal courts in recent years, as to what must be alleged by persons who claim injury of a noneconomic nature to interests that are widely shared. That question is presented in this case.

The injury alleged by the Sierra Club will be incurred entirely by reason of the change in the uses to which Mineral King will be put, and the attendant change in the aesthetics and ecology of the area. Thus, in referring to the road to be built through Sequoia National Park, the complaint alleged that the development "would destroy or otherwise adversely affect the scenery, natural and historic objects and wildlife of the park and would impair the enjoyment of the park for future generations." We do not question that the type of harm may amount to an "injury in fact" sufficient to lay the basis for standing under §10 of the APA. Aesthetic and environmental well-being, like economic well-being, are important ingredients of the quality of life in our society, and the fact that particular environmental interests are shared by the many rather than the few does not make them less deserving of legal protection through the judicial process. But the "injury in fact" test requires more than an injury to a cognizable interest. It requires that the party seeking review be himself among the injured.

The impact of the proposed changes in the environment of Mineral King will not fall indiscriminately upon every citizen. The alleged injury will be felt directly only by those who use Mineral King and Sequoia National Park, and for whom the aesthetic and recreational values of the area will be lessened by the highway and ski resort. The Sierra Club failed to allege that it or its members would be affected in any of their activities or pastimes by the Disney development. Nowhere in the pleadings or affidavits did the Club state that its members use Mineral King for any purpose, much less that they use it in any way that would be significantly affected by the proposed actions of the respondents. . . .

The trend of cases arising under the APA and other statutes authorizing judicial review of federal agency action has been toward recognizing that injuries other than economic harm are sufficient to bring a person within the meaning of the statutory language, and toward discarding the notion that an injury that is widely shared is ipso facto not an injury sufficient to provide the basis for judicial review. We noted this development with approval in *Data Processing*, 397 U.S., at 154, in saying that the interest alleged to have been injured "may reflect 'aesthetic, conservational, and recreational' as well as economic values." But broadening the categories of injury that may be alleged in support of standing is a different matter from abandoning the requirement that the party seeking review must himself have suffered an injury.

Some courts have indicated a willingness to take this latter step by conferring standing upon organizations that have demonstrated "an organizational interest in the problem" of environmental or consumer protection. Environmental Defense Fund v. Hardin, 428 F.2d 1093, 1097. It is clear that an organization whose members are injured may represent those members in a proceeding for judicial review. See, e.g., NAACP v. Button, 371 U.S. 415, 428. But a mere "interest in a problem," no matter how longstanding the interest and no matter how qualified the organization is in evaluating the problem, is not sufficient by itself to render the organization "adversely affected" or "aggrieved" within the meaning of the APA. The Sierra Club is a large and long-established organization, with a historic commitment to the cause of protecting our Nation's natural heritage from man's depredations. But if a "special interest" in this subject were enough to entitle the Sierra Club to commence this litigation, there would appear to be no objective basis upon which to disallow a suit by any other bona fide "special interest" organization, however small or short-lived. And if any group with a bona fide "special interest" could initiate such litigation, it is difficult to perceive why any individual citizen with the same bona fide special interest would not also be entitled to do so.

The requirement that a party seeking review must allege facts showing that he is himself adversely affected does not insulate executive action from judicial review, nor does it prevent any public interests from being protected through the judicial process. It does serve as at least a rough attempt to put the decision as to whether review will be sought in the hands of those who have a direct stake in the outcome. That goal would be undermined were we to construe the APA to authorize judicial review at the behest of organizations or individuals who seek to do no more than vindicate their own value preferences through the judicial process. The principle that the Sierra Club would have us establish in this case would do just that.

As we conclude that the Court of Appeals was correct in its holding that the Sierra Club lacked standing to maintain this action, we do not reach any other questions presented in the petition, and we intimate no view on the merits of the complaint. The judgment is affirmed.

MR. JUSTICE POWELL and MR. JUSTICE REHNQUIST took no part in the consideration or decision of this case.

MR. JUSTICE DOUGLAS, dissenting.

I share the view of my Brother Blackmun and would reverse the judgment below.

The critical question of "standing" would be simplified and also put neatly in focus if we fashioned a federal rule that allowed environmental issues to be litigated before federal agencies or federal courts in the name of the inanimate object about to be despoiled, defaced, or invaded by roads and bulldozers and where injury is the subject of public outrage. Contemporary public concern for protecting nature's ecological equilibrium should lead to the conferral of standing upon environmental objects to sue for their own preservation. See Stone, Should Trees Have Standing?—Toward Legal Rights for Natural Objects, 45 S. Cal. L. Rev. 450 (1972). This suit would therefore be more properly labeled as Mineral King v. Morton.

Inanimate objects are sometimes parties in litigation. A ship has a legal personality, a fiction found useful for maritime purposes. The corporation sole—a creature of ecclesiastical law—is an acceptable adversary and large fortunes ride on its cases. The ordinary corporation is a "person" for purposes of the adjudicatory processes, whether it represents proprietary, spiritual, aesthetic, or charitable causes.

So it should be as respects valleys, alpine meadows, rivers, lakes, estuaries, beaches, ridges, groves of trees, swampland, or even air that feels the destructive pressures of modern technology and modern life. The river, for example, is the living symbol of all the life it sustains or nourishes—fish, aquatic insects, water ouzels, otter, fisher, deer, elk, bear, and all other animals, including man, who are dependent on it or who enjoy it for its sight, its sound, or its life. The river as plaintiff speaks for the ecological unit of life that is part of it. Those people who have a meaningful relation to that body of water—whether it be a fisherman, a canoeist, a zoologist, or a logger—must be able to speak for the values which the river represents and which are threatened with destruction. . . .

The voice of the inanimate object, therefore, should not be stilled. That does not mean that the judiciary takes over the managerial functions from the federal agency. It merely means that before these priceless bits of Americana (such as a valley, an alpine meadow, a river, or a lake) are forever lost or are so transformed as to be reduced to the eventual rubble of our urban environment, the voice of the existing beneficiaries of these environmental wonders should be heard.

NOTES AND QUESTIONS

1. The Sierra Club's complaint contained the following allegations concerning the Club's interest in the dispute:

Plaintiff Sierra Club is a non-profit corporation organized and operating under the laws of the State of California, with its principal place of business in San Francisco, California since 1892. Membership of the club is approximately

78,000 nationally, with approximately 27,000 members residing in the San Francisco Bay Area. For many years the Sierra Club by its activities and conduct has exhibited a special interest in the conservation and the sound maintenance of the national parks, game refuges and forests of the country, regularly serving as a responsible representative of persons similarly situated. One of the principal purposes of the Sierra Club is to protect and conserve the national resources of the Sierra Nevada Mountains. Its interests would be vitally affected by the acts hereinafter described and would be aggrieved by those acts of the defendants as hereinafter more fully appears.

Why was this allegation insufficient to establish the Sierra Club's standing? What would they have had to allege concerning their interests and activities in order to have had standing to bring their action?

2. The government argued before the Supreme Court that if the Sierra Club had standing on the basis of their allegation, then "anyone who asserts an interest in a controversy has standing." Do you agree?

3. While Sierra Club v. Morton was before the Supreme Court, the Wilderness Society and other environmental groups filed an amicus brief that described in more detail the specific nature of the Sierra Club's interest in Mineral King. It recited the Club's long efforts to include the area in Sequoia National Park, that the Club regularly conducted camping trips in the area, and that its individual members used the area for recreational purposes and would be damaged by its development. In its reply brief, however, the Sierra Club expressly declined to rely on this as a basis for standing. Why, do you think, did they refuse to do so?

The papers of the late Justice Thurgood Marshall indicate that the Court was well aware that the Sierra Club's use of Mineral King was more direct than reflected in the complaint's allegations. Justice Brennan sought to have the Court dismiss the case as improvidently granted because the Club's members did actually use the area. While he was unsuccessful in this effort, Justice Stewart did agree to modify the majority opinion one week before it was released to add a crucial footnote specifying that the Sierra Club was free to amend its complaint on remand. Percival, Environmental Law in the Supreme Court: Highlights from the Marshall Papers, 23 Envtl. L. Rep. 10,606, 10,620 (1993).

4. Although he did not join in Justice Douglas' very personal dissent, Justice Blackmun also dissented. Noting that the case involved "significant aspects of a wide, growing, and disturbing problem, that is, the nation's and the world's deteriorating environment," Justice Blackmun questioned whether the law must "be so rigid and our procedure so inflexible that we render ourselves helpless when the existing methods and the traditional concepts . . . do not prove to be entirely adequate for new issues." Both Justice Douglas and Justice Blackmun felt so strongly about their dissents that they took the unusual step of reading them from the bench when the decision was announced.

5. A great deal of additional, and fascinating, background information about the history of Mineral King and Sierra Club v. Morton is provided in Turner, Who Speaks for the Future?, 1990 Sierra 30 (July-Aug. 1990), an article that includes extensive photographs of the Mineral King area. The article reports that the area is known as Mineral King because of a brief silver mining boom that in 1879 led 300 miners into the area. The boom went bust by 1882, but it left a sufficient residue of development to keep the area from being included in Sequoia National Park when the park was created in 1890. In 1908, John Muir and the Sierra Club launched a major campaign to expand

Sequoia National Park to include Mineral King. After a lengthy struggle, Mineral King was again left out of the park when the park was doubled in size in 1926, although Mineral King did become part of the Sequoia National Game Refuge.

Ironically, the Board of Directors of the Sierra Club had endorsed the development of a ski resort in the area in 1949 when the Forest Service first called for bids to develop a small hotel and two ski lifts. (The area has spectacular natural attractions for skiers—"high bowls that border the valley on three sides, deep powder snow, spectacular views.") No bids were forthcoming then because of the high cost of making the remote area accessible to skiers. After the Forest Service issued a new request for bids in 1965, the Disney plan was selected. The Disney plan was for a development ten times larger and more expensive than contemplated in the Forest Service's request for bids. The Sierra Club decided to oppose the project only after a year of rancorous internal debate. When the Club asked for a public hearing, the Forest Service replied that no hearing was necessary because one had been held more than a decade earlier. Why did the government choose to challenge the Club's standing rather than focusing its defense on the substance of the case? Was this a wise strategy?

6. The Supreme Court's recognition that injury to aesthetic and environmental values may be sufficient to confer standing even if the injury is shared by many remains the case's most significant legacy. While the Court ruled against the Sierra Club on the standing issue, it noted in a footnote that the decision did not bar the Sierra Club from seeking to amend its complaint when the case returned to the district court. On remand, the Sierra Club amended its complaint to allege that its members used the area and it added as coplaintiffs nine individuals who regularly visited Mineral King and a group that owns property nearby. The Club also added a new claim that the National Environmental Policy Act, which had been enacted after the original lawsuit had been filed, required the preparation of an environmental impact statement (EIS). The draft EIS was released in January 1975. By then Mineral King had become a national environmental *cause celebre.* When the final EIS was released in 1976, the Mineral King project had essentially died a natural death. The EIS found severe environmental impacts from the proposed development and recommended that the project be scaled down significantly. The ski resort was never built. The Sierra Club's lawsuit eventually was dismissed without prejudice in 1977. Mineral King was made part of Sequoia National Park in October 1978. It remains spectacularly beautiful and largely off the beaten path today. The narrow, winding road into the secluded canyon has not been improved and trailers and RVs are prohibited from tackling its 639 curves, which are a challenge to motorists.

Standing Doctrine in Environmental Cases after *Sierra Club v. Morton*

Sierra Club confirmed a shift in standing logic. Previously, standing doctrine in effect conceived of the government as being just like a private party, and standing could be determined by the following test. Hypothetically substitute "Jones" for the government agency as defendant in the case. If the complaint stated a cause of action in tort, or for breach of contract, or for violation of a property right against Jones, the plaintiff had standing. This became known as the "legal wrong" test of standing. The government agency could then invoke its alleged statutory authority for the action, and thus the issue of the validity of the statute or the propriety of the action under the statute would be joined.

This legal wrong test, which has also been termed a "private law" model of standing, was modified somewhat as the regulatory state expanded. The Supreme Court began to acknowledge standing in situations where specific statutory language suggested that Congress had intended to give additional parties the right to sue. For instance, in FCC v. Sanders Brothers Radio Station, 309 U.S. 470 (1940), the Court permitted a competitor of an FCC licensee to sue on the basis of the competitor's alleged economic injury, even though the common law did not protect against competitively caused economic loss, because the Federal Communications Act allows anyone "aggrieved or whose interests are adversely affected" to seek judicial review, 47 U.S.C. §402(b)(6), and the competitor had suffered a traditionally recognized type of injury, economic damage.

When the Administrative Procedure Act was passed in 1946, it provided that "a person suffering legal wrong because of agency action, or adversely affected or aggrieved by agency action within the meaning of a relevant statute, is entitled to judicial review thereof." 5 U.S.C. §702. In his influential manual on the APA, the attorney general stated that this language codified then-existing law.

In the 1960s, lower courts pushed standing doctrine to the limits of section 702, largely under the influence of citizen and environmental groups—the presumed beneficiaries of many of the statutes Congress had enacted—who were dissatisfied with agency interpretations and actions. The details of these doctrinal developments are told in Stewart, The Reformation of American Administrative Law, 88 Harv. L. Rev. 1669 (1975), and Sunstein, Standing and the Privatization of Public Law, 88 Colum. L. Rev. 1432 (1988).

Sierra Club and contemporary cases seemed to recognize a general right of citizens to challenge government action as long as they had suffered "injury in fact" and raised claims "arguably" within the "zone of interests" that Congress sought to protect. *Sierra Club* was followed in the Court's next term by United States v. Students Challenging Regulatory Agency Proceedings, 412 U.S. 669 (1973) (*SCRAP*). Plaintiffs were law students challenging the ICC's approval of a freight rate they alleged would discourage the use of recycled materials. As injury-in-fact, they alleged that the rate change would lead to increased litter, as well as an increase in consumption of natural resources, in the forests, parks, and mountain areas around Washington, D.C., which the students used for hiking, fishing, and backpacking. Although the Court thought this an "attenuated line of causation," it held the plaintiffs' allegations sufficient for standing.

SCRAP was a high-water mark for environmental standing. Although it has never overruled *SCRAP*, the Court has issued decisions suggesting that it has drawn back from it. This is especially so in one recurring pattern of cases in which the plaintiff's injury is not directly caused by the complained-of agency action, but is mediated by the actions of third parties. In such cases, the Court has expressed concern over whether a ruling in the plaintiff's favor will actually redress the plaintiff's injury; otherwise, it has said, "exercise of its power . . . would be gratuitous and thus inconsistent with the Art. III limitation" limiting federal jurisdiction to "cases and controversies." Simon v. Eastern Kentucky Welfare Rights Organization, 426 U.S. 26, 38 (1976) (*EKWRO*).

In *EKWRO*, the Court denied the standing of a representative of indigent patients to challenge an IRS rule allowing hospitals to retain charitable tax-exempt status regardless of their treatment of indigent patients—allegedly in violation of federal law. The decision to treat such patients was made by the hospital board of directors; plaintiffs had not convincingly shown that the change in tax policy would lead to the directors' decision to change hospital treatment policy.

In Allen v. Wright, 468 U.S. 737 (1984), plaintiffs, representatives of minority children, challenged tax-exempt treatment of discriminatory private schools, alleging that this treatment interfered with desegregation of public schools by siphoning white students away from the public school system. The Court denied standing, finding "[t]he links in the chain of causation between the challenged Government conduct and the asserted injury are far too weak for the chain as a whole to sustain respondents' standing."

In recent years, the Court has articulated the requirements of standing as consisting of four parts. To have standing to sue, a plaintiff must allege:

1. that the challenged action will cause plaintiff some actual or threatened injury-in-fact;
2. that the injury is fairly traceable to the challenged action;
3. that the injury is redressable by judicial action; and
4. that the injury is to an interest arguably within the zone of interests to be protected by the statute alleged to have been violated.

It has also stated that the first three requirements are constitutional, based on Art. III, while the fourth is "prudential," and thus can be altered by Congress. (Congress could, for example, grant standing to everyone in the world who satisfied the first three requirements, thus eliminating the fourth part entirely.) See, e.g., Valley Forge Christian College v. Americans United for Separation of Church and State, 454 U.S. 464 (1982).

Organizations have standing to assert the interests of their members so long as (1) the members themselves would have standing to sue and (2) the interests the organization seeks to protect are "germane to the organization's purposes." Automobile Workers v. Brock, 477 U.S. 274 (1986).

In a 1983 law review article that was little noticed at the time, then-Circuit Judge Antonin Scalia argued that standing doctrine was a "critical and inseparable element" of separation of powers principles that should be more rigidly interpreted by the courts to reduce judicial intrusion into the operations of the other branches. Scalia, The Doctrine of Standing as an Essential Element of the Separation of Powers, 1983 Suffolk Univ. L. Rev. 881 (1983). What is remarkable about this article is not only how well it foreshadowed subsequent standing decisions Justice Scalia authored for the Supreme Court, but also its express hostility toward suits on behalf of environmental interests. Scalia argued that judges who enforce environmental laws are "likely (despite the best of intentions) to be enforcing the political prejudices of their own class." He explains that "[t]heir greatest success in such an enterprise—ensuring strict enforcement of the environmental laws . . . met with approval in the classrooms of Cambridge and New Haven, but not in the factories of Detroit and the mines of West Virginia." Id. at 896-897. Quoting the language of Judge J. Skelly Wright in the *Culvert Cliffs* decision (see Chapter 8 at 798), he asks:

"Does what I have said mean that, so long as no minority interests are affected, 'important legislative purposes, heralded in the halls of Congress, [can be] lost or misdirected in the vast hallways of the federal bureaucracy?' Of *course* it does—and a good thing, too. Where no peculiar harm to particular individuals or minorities is in question, lots of once-heralded programs ought to get lost or misdirected, in vast hallways or elsewhere. . . . The ability to lose or misdirect laws can be said to be one of the prime engines of social change, and the prohibition against such carelessness is (believe it or not) profoundly conservative. Sunday blue laws, for example, were widely unenforced long before they were widely repealed—and had the first not been possible the second might never have occurred." Id. at 897 (emphasis in original).

The first major standing decision authored by Justice Scalia addressed the question of how specific the allegations of a user of public lands have to be in order to establish standing. In Lujan v. National Wildlife Federation, 497 U.S. 871 (1990), the National Wildlife Federation (NWF) challenged decisions by the Bureau of Land Management (BLM) to lift protective restrictions on 180 million acres of public land. NWF alleged that BLM had violated both the Federal Land Policy and Management Act (FLPMA) and the National Environmental Policy Act (NEPA). After years of preliminary skirmishing that included entry of a preliminary injunction, the trial court ultimately dismissed the lawsuit on the ground that NWF lacked standing.

NWF had submitted affidavits from two of its members, one of whom stated that she used and enjoyed federal lands, "particularly those in the vicinity of South Pass-Green Mountain, Wyoming," an area of some two million acres. Noting that only 4,500 acres of this land were affected by BLM's decisions, the district court determined the affidavits insufficiently specific to allege "use and enjoyment." After the D.C. Circuit reversed the trial court, the Supreme Court granted review.

In a majority opinion authored by Justice Scalia, the Court held that NWF had not made sufficient allegations to establish standing to challenge BLM's actions. He concluded that "averments which state only that one of respondent's members uses unspecified portions of an immense tract of territory, on some portions of which mining activity has occurred," were insufficiently specific. Justice Scalia also concluded that NWF could not challenge BLM's "land withdrawal review program" as a whole because it consisted of decisions about more than 1,200 discrete tracts of land that would not be ripe for judicial review until specific actions had been taken with respect to individual tracts.

The Supreme Court revisited environmental standing issues in the case below. The case involved a challenge to the Secretary of Interior's decision that the Endangered Species Act does not require other federal agencies to consult with the department when their activities may destroy critical habitat for endangered species outside the United States. Defenders of Wildlife sued the Secretary of Interior. The group tried to establish standing by offering affidavits from two of its members, as discussed in the following decision.

Lujan v. Defenders of Wildlife
504 U.S. 555 (1992)

JUSTICE SCALIA delivered the opinion of the Court.

This case involves a challenge to a rule promulgated by the Secretary of the Interior interpreting §7 of the Endangered Species Act of 1973 (ESA), 87 Stat. 892, as amended, 16 U.S.C. §1536, in such fashion as to render it applicable only to actions within the United States or on the high seas. [Section 7 of the ESA requires all federal agencies, in consultation with the Secretary of the Interior, to insure that their actions do not jeopardize the continued existence of any endangered species.] The preliminary issue, and the only one we reach, is whether the respondents here, plaintiffs below, have standing to seek judicial review of the rule. . . .

III

. . . Respondents had not made the requisite demonstration of (at least) injury and redressability.

A

Respondents' claim to injury is that the lack of consultation with respect to certain funded activities abroad "increas[es] the rate of extinction of endangered and threatened species." Complaint para. 5. Of course, the desire to use or observe an animal species, even for purely aesthetic purposes, is undeniably a cognizable interest for purpose of standing. See, e.g., Sierra Club v. Morton, 405 U.S., at 734. "But the 'injury in fact' test requires more than an injury to a cognizable interest. It requires that the party seeking review be himself among the injured." Id. at 734-735. To survive the Secretary's summary judgment motion, respondents had to submit affidavits or other evidence showing, through specific facts, not only that listed species were in fact being threatened by funded activities abroad, but also that one or more of respondents' members would thereby be "directly" affected apart from their "'special interest' in th[e] subject." Id. at 735, 739.

With respect to this aspect of the case, the Court of Appeals focused on the affidavits of two Defenders' members—Joyce Kelly and Amy Skilbred. Ms. Kelly stated that she traveled to Egypt in 1986 and "observed the traditional habitat of the endangered Nile crocodile there and intend[s] to do so again, and hope[s] to observe the crocodile directly," and that she "will suffer harm in fact as a result of [the] American . . . role . . . in overseeing the rehabilitation of the Aswan High Dam on the Nile . . . and [in] developing . . . Egypt's . . . Master Water Plan." Ms. Skilbred averred that she traveled to Sri Lanka in 1981 and "observed th[e] habitat" of "endangered species such as the Asian elephant and the leopard" at what is now the site of the Mahaweli Project funded by the Agency for International Development (AID), although she "was unable to see any of the endangered species"; "this development project," she continued, "will seriously reduce endangered, threatened, and endemic species habitat including areas that I visited . . . [, which] may severely shorten the future of these species"; that threat, she concluded, harmed her because she "intend[s] to return to Sri Lanka in the future and hope[s] to be more fortunate in spotting at least the endangered elephant and leopard." When Ms. Skilbred was asked at a subsequent deposition if and when she had any plans to return to Sri Lanka, she reiterated that "I intend to go back to Sri Lanka," but confessed that she had no current plans: "I don't know [when]. There is a civil war going on right now. I don't know. Not next year, I will say. In the future."

We shall assume for the sake of argument that these affidavits contain facts showing that certain agency-funded projects threaten listed species—though that is questionable. They plainly contain no facts, however, showing how damage to the species will produce "imminent" injury to Mss. Kelly and Skilbred. That the women "had visited" the areas of the projects before the projects commenced proves nothing. As we have said in a related context, "[p]ast exposure to illegal conduct does not in itself show a present case or controversy regarding injunctive relief . . . if unaccompanied by any continuing, present adverse effects." *Lyons,* 461 U.S., at 102 (quoting O'Shea v. Littleton, 414 U.S. 488, 495-496 (1974)). And the affiants' profession of an "inten[t]" to return to the places they had visited before—where they will presumably, this time, be deprived of the opportunity to observe animals of the endangered species—is simply not enough. Such "some day" intentions—without any description of concrete plans, or indeed even any specification of *when* the some day will be—do not support a finding of the "actual or imminent" injury that our cases require.[2]

Besides relying upon the Kelly and Skilbred affidavits, respondents propose a series of novel standing theories. The first, inelegantly styled "ecosystem nexus," proposes that any person who uses *any part* of a "contiguous ecosystem" adversely affected by a funded activity has standing even if the activity is located a great distance away. This approach, as the Court of Appeals correctly observed, is inconsistent with our opinion in [Lujan v.] *National Wildlife Federation* which held that a plaintiff claiming injury from environmental damage must use the area affected by the challenged activity and not an area roughly "in the vicinity" of it. 497 U.S., at 887-889; see also *Sierra Club,* 405 U.S., at 735. It makes no difference that the general-purpose section of the ESA states that the Act was intended in part "to provide a means whereby the ecosystems upon which endangered species and threatened species depend may be conserved," 16 U.S.C. §1531(b). To say that the Act protects ecosystems is not to say that the Act creates (if it were possible) rights of action in persons who have not been injured in fact, that is, persons who use portions of an ecosystem not perceptibly affected by the unlawful action in question.

Respondents' other theories are called, alas, the "animal nexus" approach, whereby anyone who has an interest in studying or seeing the endangered animals anywhere on the globe has standing; and the "vocational nexus" approach, under which anyone with a professional interest in such animals can sue. Under these theories, anyone who goes to see Asian elephants in the Bronx Zoo, and anyone who is a keeper of Asian elephants in the Bronx Zoo, has standing to sue because the Director of AID did not consult with the Secretary regarding the AID-funded project in Sri Lanka. This is beyond all reason. Standing is not "an ingenious academic exercise in the conceivable," United States v. Students Challenging Regulatory Agency Procedures (SCRAP), 412 U.S. 669, 688 (1973), but as we have said requires, at the summary judgment stage, a factual showing of perceptible harm. It is clear that the person who observes or works with a particular animal threatened by a federal decision is facing perceptible

---

2. . . . [T]here is certainly no reason in principle to demand evidence that third persons will take the action exposing the plaintiff to harm, while *presuming* that the plaintiff himself will do so. Our insistence upon these established requirements of standing does not mean that we would, as the dissent contends, "demand . . . detailed descriptions" of damages, such as a "nightly schedule of attempted activities" from plaintiffs alleging loss of consortium. That case and the others posited by the dissent all involve *actual* harm; the existence of standing is clear, though the precise extent of harm remains to be determined at trial. Where there is no actual harm, however, its imminence (though not its precise extent) must be established.

harm, since the very subject of his interest will no longer exist. It is even plausible—though it goes to the outermost limit of plausibility—to think that a person who observes or works with animals of a particular species in the very area of the world where that species is threatened by a federal decision is facing such harm, since some animals that might have been the subject of his interest will no longer exist, see Japan Whaling Assn. v. American Cetacean Soc., 478 U.S. 221, 231, n.4 (1986). It goes beyond the limit, however, and into pure speculation and fantasy, to say that anyone who observes or works with an endangered species, anywhere in the world, is appreciably harmed by a single project affecting some portion of that species with which he has no more specific connection.[3] . . .

IV

The Court of Appeals found that respondents had standing for an additional reason: because they had suffered a "procedural injury." The so-called "citizen-suit" provision of the ESA provides, in pertinent part, that "any person may commence a civil suit on his own behalf (A) to enjoin any person, including the United States and any other governmental instrumentality or agency . . . who is alleged to be in violation of any provision of this chapter." 16 U.S.C. §1540(g). The court held that, because §7(a)(2) requires interagency consultation, the citizen-suit provision creates a "procedural righ[t]" to consultation in all "persons"—so that *anyone* can file suit in federal court to challenge the Secretary's (or presumably any other official's) failure to follow the assertedly correct consultative procedure, notwithstanding their inability to allege any discrete injury flowing from that failure. To understand the remarkable nature of this holding one must be clear about what it does *not* rest upon: This is not a case where plaintiffs are seeking to enforce a procedural requirement the disregard of which could impair a separate concrete interest of theirs (e.g., the procedural requirement for a hearing prior to denial of their license application, or the procedural requirement for an environmental impact statement before a federal facility is constructed next door to them).[7] Nor is it simply a case where concrete injury has been suffered by many persons, as in mass fraud or

---

3. . . . It cannot be that a person with an interest in an animal automatically has standing to enjoin federal threats to that species of animal, anywhere in the world. Were that the case, the plaintiff in *Sierra Club,* for example, could have avoided the necessity of establishing anyone's use of Mineral King by merely identifying one of its members interested in an endangered species of flora or fauna at that location. Justice Blackmun's accusation that a special rule is being crafted for "environmental claims" is correct, but *he* is the craftsman. . . .

7. There is this much truth to the assertion that "procedural rights" are special: The person who has been accorded a procedural right to protect his concrete interests can assert that right without meeting all the normal standards for redressability and immediacy. Thus, under our case-law, one living adjacent to the site for proposed construction of a federally licensed dam has standing to challenge the licensing agency's failure to prepare an Environmental Impact Statement, even though he cannot establish with any certainty that the Statement will cause the license to be withheld or altered, and even though the dam will not be completed for many years. (That is why we do not rely, in the present case, upon the Government's argument that, *even if* the other agencies were obliged to consult with the Secretary, they might not have followed his advice.) What respondents' "procedural rights" argument seeks, however, is quite different from this: standing for persons who have no concrete interests affected—persons who live (and propose to live) at the other end of the country from the dam.

mass tort situations. Nor, finally, is it the unusual case in which Congress has created a concrete private interest in the outcome of a suit against a private party for the government's benefit, by providing a cash bounty for the victorious plaintiff. Rather, the court held that the injury-in-fact requirement had been satisfied by congressional conferral upon *all* persons of an abstract, self-contained, noninstrumental "right" to have the Executive observe the procedures required by law. We reject this view.[8]

We have consistently held that a plaintiff raising only a generally available grievance about government—claiming only harm to his and every citizen's interest in proper application of the Constitution and laws, and seeking relief that no more directly and tangibly benefits him than it does the public at large—does not state an Article III case or controversy. . . .

JUSTICE KENNEDY, with whom JUSTICE SOUTER joins, concurring in part and concurring in the judgment.

Although I agree with the essential parts of the Court's analysis, I write separately to make several observations.

I agree with the Court's conclusion in Part III-A that, on the record before us, respondents have failed to demonstrate that they themselves are "among the injured." Sierra Club v. Morton, 405 U.S. 727, 735 (1972). . . .

While it may seem trivial to require that Mss. Kelly and Skilbred acquire airline tickets to the project sites or announce a date certain upon which they will return, this is not a case where it is reasonable to assume that the affiants will be using the sites on a regular basis, see Sierra Club v. Morton, supra, at 735, n.8, nor do the affiants claim to have visited the sites since the projects commenced. With respect to the Court's discussion of respondents' "ecosystem nexus," "animal nexus," and "vocational nexus" theories, I agree that on this record respondents' showing is insufficient to establish standing on any of these bases. I am not willing to foreclose the possibility, however, that in different circumstances a nexus theory similar to those proffered here might support a claim to standing. See Japan Whaling Assn. v. American Cetacean Soc., 478 U.S. 221, 231, n.4 (1986) ("respondents . . . undoubtedly have alleged a sufficient 'injury in fact' in that the whale watching and studying of their members will be adversely affected by continued whale harvesting"). . . .

I also join Part IV of the Court's opinion with the following observations. As government programs and policies become more complex and far-reaching, we must be sensitive to the articulation of new rights of action that do not have clear analogs in our common-law tradition. Modern litigation has progressed far from

---

8. . . . We do *not* hold that an individual cannot enforce procedural rights; he assuredly can, so long as the procedures in question are designed to protect some threatened concrete interest of his that is the ultimate basis of his standing. . . . The dissent is unable to cite a single case in which we actually found standing solely on the basis of "procedural right" unconnected to the plaintiff's own concrete harm. Its suggestion that we did so in *Japan Whaling Association,* supra, and Robertson v. Methow Valley Citizens Council, 490 U.S. 332 (1989), is not supported by the facts. In the former case, we found that the environmental organizations had standing because the "whale watching and studying of their members would be adversely affected by continued whale harvesting," see 478 U.S., at 230-231, n.4; and in the latter we did not so much as mention standing, for the very good reason that the plaintiff was a citizen's council for the area in which the challenged construction was to occur, so that its members would obviously be concretely affected, see Methow Valley Citizens Council v. Regional Forester, 833 F.2d 810, 812-813 (9th Cir. 1987).

the paradigm of Marbury suing Madison to get his commission, Marbury v. Madison, 1 Cranch 137 (1803), or Ogden seeking an injunction to halt Gibbons' steamboat operations. Gibbons v. Ogden, 9 Wheat. 1 (1824). In my view, Congress has the power to define injuries and articulate chains of causation that will give rise to a case or controversy where none existed before, and I do not read the Court's opinion to suggest a contrary view. See Warth v. Seldin, 422 U.S. 490, 500 (1975). In exercising this power, however, Congress must at the very least identify the injury it seeks to vindicate and relate the injury to the class of persons entitled to bring suit. The citizen-suit provision of the Endangered Species Act does not meet these minimal requirements, because while the statute purports to confer a right on "any person . . . to enjoin . . . the United States and any other governmental instrumentality or agency . . . who is alleged to be in violation of any provision of this chapter," it does not of its own force establish that there is an injury in "any person" by virtue of any "violation." 16 U.S.C. §1540(g)(1)(A). . . .

JUSTICE STEVENS, concurring in the judgment.

Because I am not persuaded that Congress intended the consultation requirement in §7(a)(2) of the Endangered Species Act of 1973 (ESA), 16 U.S.C. §1536(a)(2), to apply to activities in foreign countries, I concur in the judgment of reversal. I do not, however, agree with the Court's conclusion that respondents lack standing because the threatened injury to their interest in protecting the environment and studying endangered species is not "imminent." . . .

In my opinion a person who has visited the critical habitat of an endangered species, has a professional interest in preserving the species and its habitat, and intends to revisit them in the future has standing to challenge agency action that threatens their destruction. Congress has found that a wide variety of endangered species of fish, wildlife, and plants are of "aesthetic, ecological, educational, historical, recreational, and scientific value to the Nation and its people." 16 U.S.C. §1531(a)(3). Given that finding, we have no license to demean the importance of the interest that particular individuals may have in observing any species or its habitat, whether those individuals are motivated by aesthetic enjoyment, an interest in professional research, or an economic interest in preservation of the species. Indeed, this Court has often held that injuries to such interests are sufficient to confer standing, and the Court reiterates that holding today.

The Court nevertheless concludes that respondents have not suffered "injury in fact" because they have not shown that the harm to the endangered species will produce "imminent" injury to them. I disagree. An injury to an individual's interest in studying or enjoying a species and its natural habitat occurs when someone (whether it be the government or a private party) takes action that harms that species and habitat. In my judgment, therefore, the "imminence" of such an injury should be measured by the timing and likelihood of the threatened environmental harm, rather than—as the Court seems to suggest—by the time that might elapse between the present and the time when the individuals would visit the area if no such injury should occur. . . .

[W]e have denied standing to plaintiffs whose likelihood of suffering any concrete adverse effect from the challenged action was speculative. In this case, however, the likelihood that respondents will be injured by the destruction of the endangered species is not speculative. If respondents are genuinely interested in the preservation of the endangered species and intend to study or observe these animals in the future, their injury will occur as soon as the animals are destroyed. Thus the only potential source of "speculation" in this case is whether respondents' intent to study or observe the animals is genuine.[2] In my view, Joyce Kelly and Amy Skilbred have introduced sufficient evidence to negate petitioner's contention that their claims of injury are "speculative" or "conjectural." As Justice Blackmun explains, a reasonable finder of fact could conclude, from their past visits, their professional backgrounds, and their affidavits and deposition testimony, that Ms. Kelly and Ms. Skilbred will return to the project sites and, consequently, will be injured by the destruction of the endangered species and critical habitat. . . .

JUSTICE BLACKMUN, with whom JUSTICE O'CONNOR joins, dissenting.
    . . . I think a reasonable finder of fact could conclude from the information in the affidavits and deposition testimony that either Kelly or Skilbred will soon return to the project sites, thereby satisfying the "actual or imminent" injury standard. . . . Contrary to the Court's contention that Kelly's and Skilbred's past visits "prove[] nothing," the fact of their past visits could demonstrate to a reasonable factfinder that Kelly and Skilbred have the requisite resources and personal interest in the preservation of the species endangered by the Aswan and Mahaweli projects to make good on their intention to return again. . . . Similarly, Kelly's and Skilbred's professional backgrounds in wildlife preservation also make it likely—at least far more likely than for the average citizen—that they would choose to visit these areas of the world where species are vanishing.
    By requiring a "description of concrete plans" or "specification of *when* the some day [for a return visit] will be," the Court, in my view, demands what is likely an empty formality. No substantial barriers prevent Kelly or Skilbred from simply purchasing plane tickets to return to the Aswan and Mahaweli projects. This case differs from other cases in which the imminence of harm turned largely on the affirmative actions of third parties beyond a plaintiff's control. To be sure, a plaintiff's unilateral control over his or her exposure to harm does not *necessarily* render the harm non-speculative. Nevertheless, it suggests that a finder of fact would be far more likely to conclude the harm is actual or imminent, especially if given an opportunity to hear testimony and determine credibility.
    I fear the Court's demand for detailed descriptions of future conduct will do little to weed out those who are genuinely harmed from those who are not. More likely, it will resurrect a code-pleading formalism in federal court summary judgment practice, as federal courts, newly doubting their jurisdiction, will demand more and more particularized showings of future harm. Just to survive summary judgment, for example, a property owner claiming a decline in the value of his property from governmental action might have to specify the exact

---

2. . . . [R]espondents would not be injured by the challenged projects if they had not visited the sites or studied the threatened species and habitat. But, as discussed above, respondents did visit the sites; moreover, they have expressed an intent to do so again. This intent to revisit the area is significant evidence tending to confirm the genuine character of respondents' interest, but I am not at all sure that an intent to revisit would be indispensable in every case. The interest that confers standing in a case of this kind is comparable, though by no means equivalent, to the interest in a relationship among family members that can be immediately harmed by the death of an absent member, regardless of when, if ever, a family reunion is planned to occur. Thus, if the facts of this case had shown repeated and regular visits by the respondents, proof of an intent to revisit might well be superfluous.

date he intends to sell his property and show that there is a market for the property, lest it be surmised he might not sell again. A nurse turned down for a job on grounds of her race had better be prepared to show on what date she was prepared to start work, that she had arranged daycare for her child, and that she would not have accepted work at another hospital instead. And a Federal Torts Claims Act plaintiff alleging loss of consortium should make sure to furnish this Court with a "description of concrete plans" for her nightly schedule of attempted activities.

The Court also concludes that injury is lacking, because respondents' allegations of "ecosystem nexus" failed to demonstrate sufficient proximity to the site of the environmental harm. To support that conclusion, the Court mischaracterizes our decision in Lujan v. National Wildlife Federation, 497 U.S. 871 (1990), as establishing a general rule that "a plaintiff claiming injury from environmental damage must use the area affected by the challenged activity." In *National Wildlife Federation,* the Court required specific geographical proximity because of the particular type of harm alleged in that case: harm to the plaintiff's visual enjoyment of nature from mining activities. One cannot suffer from the sight of a ruined landscape without being close enough to see the sites actually being mined. Many environmental injuries, however, cause harm distant from the area immediately affected by the challenged action. Environmental destruction may affect animals traveling over vast geographical ranges, see, e.g., Japan Whaling Assn. v. American Cetacean Soc., 478 U.S. 221 (1986) (harm to American whale watchers from Japanese whaling activities), or rivers running long geographical courses, see, e.g., Arkansas v. Oklahoma, 503 U.S. 91 (1992) (harm to Oklahoma residents from wastewater treatment plant 39 miles from border). It cannot seriously be contended that a litigant's failure to use the precise or exact site where animals are slaughtered or where toxic waste is dumped into a river means he or she cannot show injury.

The Court also rejects respondents' claim of vocational or professional injury. The Court says that it is "beyond all reason" that a zoo "keeper" of Asian elephants would have standing to contest his government's participation in the eradication of all the Asian elephants in another part of the world. I am unable to see how the distant location of the destruction necessarily (for purposes of ruling at summary judgment) mitigates the harm to the elephant keeper. If there is no more access to a future supply of the animal that sustains a keeper's livelihood, surely there is harm.

I have difficulty imagining this Court applying its rigid principles of geographic formalism anywhere outside the context of environmental claims. As I understand it, environmental plaintiffs are under no special constitutional standing disabilities. Like other plaintiffs, they need show only that the action they challenge has injured them, without necessarily showing they happened to be physically near the location of the alleged wrong. . . .

The Court concludes that any "procedural injury" suffered by respondents is insufficient to confer standing. It rejects the view that the "injury-in-fact requirement . . . [is] satisfied by congressional conferral upon *all* persons of an abstract, self-contained, noninstrumental 'right' to have the Executive observe the procedures required by law." Whatever the Court might mean with that very broad language, it cannot be saying that "procedural injuries" *as a class* are necessarily insufficient for purposes of Article III standing.

Most governmental conduct can be classified as "procedural." Many injuries caused by governmental conduct, therefore, are categorizable at some level of generality as "procedural" injuries. Yet, these injuries are not categorically beyond the pale of redress by the federal courts. When the Government, for example, "procedurally" issues a pollution permit, those affected by the permittee's pollutants are not without standing to sue. Only later cases will tell just what the Court means by its intimation that "procedural" injuries are not constitutionally cognizable injuries. In the meantime, I have the greatest of sympathy for the courts across the country that will struggle to understand the Court's standardless exposition of this concept today.

The Court expresses concern that allowing judicial enforcement of "agencies' observance of a particular, statutorily prescribed procedure" would "transfer from the President to the courts the Chief Executive's most important constitutional duty, to 'take Care that the Laws be faithfully executed,' Art. II, sec. 3." In fact, the principal effect of foreclosing judicial enforcement of such procedures is to transfer power into the hands of the Executive at the expense—not of the courts—but of Congress, from which that power originates and emanates. . . .

It is to be hoped that over time the Court will acknowledge that some classes of procedural duties are so enmeshed with the prevention of a substantive, concrete harm that an individual plaintiff may be able to demonstrate a sufficient likelihood of injury just through the breach of that procedural duty. For example, in the context of the NEPA requirement of environmental-impact statements, this Court has acknowledged "it is now well settled that NEPA itself does not mandate particular results [and] simply prescribes the necessary process," but "*these procedures are almost certain to affect the agency's substantive decision.*" Robertson v. Methow Valley Citizens Council, 490 U.S., 332, 350 (1989) (emphasis added). This acknowledgement of an inextricable link between procedural and substantive harm does not reflect improper appellate factfinding. It reflects nothing more than the proper deference owed to the judgment of a coordinate branch—Congress—that certain procedures are directly tied to protection against a substantive harm. . . .

NOTES AND QUESTIONS

1. Does Justice Scalia's majority opinion change in any way the nature of the injury that may be asserted by environmentalists to qualify for standing? Is injury to aesthetic values, as recognized in Sierra Club v. Morton, still a cognizable interest for purposes of standing? How do Justice Scalia and Justice Blackmun differ in their views concerning what plaintiffs must demonstrate about the imminence of harm in order to establish standing?

2. In order for a plaintiff to qualify for standing, how close must the connection be in space and time between the action challenged in a lawsuit and the plaintiff's asserted injury? Does the closeness of the geographic nexus required for standing vary with the type of harm alleged? How do Justice Scalia and Justice Blackmun differ in their interpretation of Lujan v. National Wildlife Federation? Why does the majority reject the ecosystem, animal, and vocational nexus theories offered by *Defenders*? Note that two members of the majority, Justices Kennedy and Souter, indicate in their concurrence that they are more sympathetic to these theories than the majority and that it may be possible to establish standing using similar nexus claims in different circumstances. Eight years later, Justices Kennedy and Souter joined five other justices in endorsing a

more liberal view of standing in citizen enforcement suits in Friends of the Earth v. Laidlaw Environmental Services, Inc., 528 U.S. 167 (2000), a case discussed below on page 1017.

3. Justice Kennedy states that "Congress has the power to define injuries and articulate chains of causation that will give rise to a case or controversy where none existed before. . . ." Does this mean that Congress can affect who has standing to sue by making legislative determinations of what constitutes injury and who is harmed by certain actions? Cass Sunstein argues that when Congress creates a right of action enabling people to sue over "destruction of environmental assets, it is really giving people a kind of property right in a certain state of affairs. Invasion of the property right is the relevant injury." Sunstein, What's Standing After *Lujan*? Of Citizen Suits, "Injuries," and Article III, 91 Mich. L. Rev. 163, 191 (1992). Can Congress create procedural rights whose injury can give rise to standing? Could it give anyone bringing a citizen enforcement action a financial stake in the outcome of the suit sufficient to confer standing simply by authorizing monetary rewards for successful plaintiffs?

4. What types of "procedural injury" does Justice Scalia recognize could give rise to standing? How does he attempt to distinguish the kind of procedural injury plaintiffs allege from the kind that he believes could give rise to standing? Why must Justice Scalia concede (in footnote 7 of his opinion) that in certain circumstances some "procedural rights" can be asserted "without meeting the normal standards for redressability and immediacy"?

5. The papers of the late Justice Harry Blackmun reveal that Justice Scalia's initial draft opinion sought to elevate the prudential bar on standing to redress generalized grievances to one of constitutional status. Scalia had argued that only particularized grievances were sufficiently concrete to meet the constitutional requirement of injury-in-fact. Justice Souter strenuously objected to this in a memo to Justice Scalia on May 28, 1992. "I doubt anyone would lack standing to sue on the basis of a concrete injury that everyone else has suffered; Congress might, for instance, grant everyone standing to challenge government action that would rip open the ozone layer and expose all Americans to unhealthy doses of radiation. Yet the repeated references to a particularity requirement, which might be taken as conceptually independent of a concreteness requirement, draw that conclusion into doubt." After Justice Kennedy endorsed Justice Souter's view, Justice Scalia removed the offending language from his draft opinion. Robert V. Percival, Environmental Law in the Supreme Court: Highlights from the Blackmun Papers, 35 Envtl. L. Rep. 10,637, 10,659 (2005).

6. In another portion of this opinion, Justice Scalia suggests that separation-of-powers principles limit the constitutional authority of Congress to open the courts to citizen enforcement suits. "To permit Congress to convert the undifferentiated public interest in executive officers' compliance with the law into an 'individual right' vindicable in the courts is to permit Congress to transfer from the President to the courts the Chief Executive's most important constitutional duty, to 'take Care that the Laws be faithfully executed.'" Does this call into question the constitutionality of the citizen suit provisions of the environmental laws? See Sunstein, supra, at 165-166, 221. Professor Sunstein asks, "[I]f a court could set aside executive action at the behest of plaintiffs with a plane ticket, why does the Take Care Clause forbid it from doing so at the behest of plaintiffs without a ticket?" Id. at 213.

7. Justices Kennedy and Souter suggest that plaintiffs in *Defenders* could have established standing with relatively little extra effort by making specific

travel plans. In his concurring opinion, Justice Kennedy concedes that "it may seem trivial to require that [the plaintiff's members] acquire airline tickets to the project site or announce a date certain upon which they will return." Because their votes were crucial to the majority in *Defenders,* does this statement suggest that the decision will have relatively little impact on environmental litigation, aside from encouraging environmentalists to get to know their travel agents better? What purpose is served by requiring plaintiffs to buy plane tickets? Is Justice Blackmun right that "the Court's demand for detailed descriptions of future conduct . . . will do little to weed out those who are genuinely harmed from those who are not"?

8. In the aftermath of *Defenders,* courts continued to wrestle with issues of standing in cases challenging regulatory decisions by government agencies. Some courts explicitly rejected arguments that *National Wildlife Federation* and *Defenders* wrought significant changes in standing doctrine imposing stricter burdens on plaintiffs to demonstrate injury-in-fact. In Seattle Audubon Society v. Espy, 998 F.2d 669 (9th Cir. 1993), the Ninth Circuit held that an Audubon Society chapter had standing to challenge the Forest Service's failure to prepare a management plan for critical habitat of the spotted owl. The court distinguished *Defenders* because the members of the local Audubon chapter lived near the affected forests and visited them regularly, 998 F.2d at 702-703, and it reaffirmed the validity of its pre-*Defenders* decision in Idaho Conservation League v. Mumma, 956 F.2d 1508 (9th Cir. 1992). In *Idaho Conservation League,* the court had upheld the standing of a conservation group to challenge a decision not to designate more than 100,000 acres of public land as wilderness. The court held that the group's allegation that it uses specific roadless areas which might be developed was sufficient to establish standing, noting that the plaintiffs in *National Wildlife Federation* had only alleged that they visited lands "in the vicinity of" those subject to the challenged action. 956 F.2d at 1515. See also Resources Limited, Inc. v. Robertson, 35 F.3d 1300 (9th Cir. 1994).

9. Other decisions distinguished *Defenders* because environmental plaintiffs alleged that they actually live near, visit, or study the animals they seek to protect. In Didrickson v. U.S. Dep't of Interior, 982 F.2d 1332 (9th Cir. 1992), a group called Friends of the Sea Otter (FSO) was found to have standing to challenge a regulation authorizing limited taking of sea otters because the group's Alaska members "have declared that they have observed, enjoyed and studied sea otters in specific areas in Alaska." Id. at 1340. In Idaho Farm Bureau v. Babbitt, 58 F.3d 1392 (9th Cir. 1995), two conservation groups were held to have standing to appeal a decision to delist the endangered Bruneau Hot Springs Snail because their members visit the area in which the snail is found and "maintain a factual and scientific understanding" of the snail and its habitat. Id. at 1399.

10. Could an animal welfare organization establish standing to challenge decisions affecting an endangered species of wildlife by having their members "adopt" particular members of the species by sending them a picture of the animal in return for a contribution? See Humane Society v. Babbitt, 46 F.3d 93 (D.C. Cir. 1995) (suggesting in dicta that even a deeply felt emotional attachment to Lota, an endangered Asian elephant, could not suffice to establish injury-in-fact).

11. In a decision with echoes of the ripeness rationale invoked in Lujan v. National Wildlife Federation, the Supreme Court in 1998 held that a Sierra Club lawsuit challenging a land and resource management plan for Ohio's Wayne National Forest was not ripe for judicial review. The Court held that the Sierra

Club had not suffered "practical harm" as a result of the Plan, which authorized logging on 126,000 acres of a national forest in Ohio, because site-specific environmental assessments still had to be performed before logging of any specific tracts could commence. However, the Court did note that "a person with standing who is impaired by a failure to comply with the NEPA procedure may complain of that failure at the time the failure takes place, for the claim can never get riper." Ohio Forestry Ass'n v. Sierra Club, 523 U.S. 726 (1998). Does this decision indicate that environmental plaintiffs who seek to challenge logging in national forests must wait until specific tracts of land they use are about to be cut?

The Zone of Interests Test and Standing for Business Interests

In several cases, the courts have used the "zone of interests" prong of standing doctrine to reject efforts by industry groups to use the environmental statutes to their benefit. For example, efforts by a group of ranchers to pursue alleged procedural violations of NEPA and the National Forest Management Act in order to block reductions in grazing levels were rejected in Nevada Land Action Association v. U.S. Forest Service, 8 F.3d 713 (9th Cir. 1993). The court found that the ranchers lacked standing because "[t]he purpose of NEPA is to protect the environment, not the economic interests of those adversely affected by agency decisions." 8 F.3d at 716. While the ranchers argued that their members "have an economic interest in maintaining the forest resources and therefore in protecting the environment," the court noted that they did "not allege that the increased grazing levels [they] seek would benefit the natural environment, and there seems to be substantial evidence to the contrary." In Portland Audubon Society v. Hodel, 866 F.2d 302 (9th Cir. 1989), a timber industry group was held not to have standing to intervene in an NEPA lawsuit because the group's economic interests had no direct relation to the interests protected by the statute. In Competitive Enterprise Institute v. National Highway Safety Administration, 901 F.2d 107 (D.C. Cir. 1990), the D.C. Circuit held that a nonprofit group representing business interests fell within the zone of interests protected by the Energy Policy and Conservation Act by alleging that fuel-economy standards adversely affect the safety of vehicle occupants. However, the court held that the group did not fall within the zone of interests protected by NEPA.

In Bennett v. Plenert, 63 F.3d 915 (9th Cir. 1995), ranch operators and irrigation districts who used water for commercial and recreational purposes were found not to have standing to challenge a decision to maintain a minimum water level in two public reservoirs to protect species of fish on the endangered species list. The court held that "only plaintiffs who allege an interest in the *preservation* of endangered species fall within the zone of interests protected by the ESA." 63 F.3d at 919 (emphasis in original). The Supreme Court reversed this decision in Bennett v. Spear, 520 U.S. 154 (1997). The Court held that because the ESA's citizen suit provision used the expansive language "any person may commence a civil suit," it expanded the zone of interests entitled to sue under the Act to embrace even business interests alleging "overenforcement" of environmental restrictions. The Court found that the irrigation districts could sue the director of the Fish and Wildlife Service and the Secretary of the Interior for failure to perform nondiscretionary duties under §4 of the ESA to use "the best scientific data available" and to consider "the economic impact" when "specifying any particular area as critical habitat" for an endangered species. While finding that the districts' claim of a §7 violation did not involve a nondiscretionary duty subject to citizen suit under the ESA, the Court held that it was actionable under the Administrative Procedure Act. The Court emphasized that the zone of interests test was to be determined "not by reference to the overall purpose of the Act in question (here, species preservation), but by reference to the particular provision of law upon which the plaintiff relies." Thus, even though the irrigation districts obviously did not care about species preservation, the Court held them entitled to sue because it construed the "obvious purpose" of the "best data" requirement to be "to avoid needless economic dislocations produced by agency officials zealously but unintelligently pursuing their environmental objectives." The government had argued that the mere preparation of a biological opinion did not constitute final agency action affecting the plaintiffs' allocations of water. However, the Court rejected this argument and upheld the districts' right to sue by finding that because the opinion specified what actions lawfully could incidentally take endangered species, it "has direct and appreciable legal consequences."

E. CITIZEN SUITS

As noted above, the environmental laws do not leave enforcement entirely in the hands of government. Recognizing that federal agencies had a long history of unresponsiveness to environmental concerns, Congress sought to enlist citizens in the tasks of ensuring that the laws were implemented and enforced properly. It did so by authorizing citizen suits, a major innovation first incorporated in the Clean Air Act Amendments of 1970, 42 U.S.C. §7604, and included in virtually all the major environmental laws Congress subsequently adopted. See, e.g., CWA §505, ESA §11(g), RCRA §7002, TSCA §18, CERCLA §310.

1. Citizen Suit Provisions in the APA and the Federal Environmental Laws

The federal environmental laws generally authorize private parties to bring three types of lawsuits. The first allows citizens to act as "private attorney generals" to supplement government enforcement against those who violate environmental regulations. We refer to these as citizen enforcement actions. These provisions generally authorize "any person" to commence an action against "any person" alleged to be in violation of the laws. They require citizens to notify the alleged violator and federal and state authorities prior to filing suit. Sixty days' notice usually is required, although the amount of notice can vary for certain violations (e.g., section 505(b) of the Clean Water Act authorizes suits alleging violations of NSPS requirements or toxic effluent standards to be brought immediately after notice, as does section 7002(b)(1)(A) of RCRA for violations of RCRA subtitle C). The citizen suit provisions usually specify that if federal or state authorities are diligently prosecuting an action to require compliance, filing of a citizen suit is barred, though citizens are authorized to intervene in federal enforcement actions as of right (e.g., CWA §505(b)(1)(B), CAA §304(b)(1)(B)).

While federal agencies and officials are among the "persons" who can be sued for violating environmental regulations, the statutes also generally authorize suits to force officials to perform their mandatory duties. For example, the Clean Water Act provides that the EPA administrator may be sued by citizens "where there is alleged a failure of the Administrator to perform any act or duty . . . which is not discretionary," 33 U.S.C. §1365(a)(1)(2). (The citizen suit provisions in the other statutes contain virtually identical language.) Suits such as these typically challenge an agency's failure to meet a statutory deadline to take some action. When they do, they generally are called "deadline suits." This type of litigation has been an important action-forcing device to ensure that regulations implementing the environmental statutes are issued.

The federal environmental laws also generally include judicial review provisions that authorize citizen suits to review the legality of agency actions. These provisions supplement the judicial review provisions of the Administrative Procedure Act, 5 U.S.C. §§701-706, by specifying additional procedural requirements, such as those contained in section 307(b) of the Clean Air Act (requiring that petitions for review of nationally applicable regulations must be filed in the U.S. Court of Appeals for the D.C. Circuit within 60 days of promulgation).

If an agency has failed to issue regulations by a deadline imposed by statute, a citizen suit generally may be brought to force the agency to issue the regulations. Cases seeking to force agencies to take other actions often turn on whether the courts view the agency as having a non-discretionary duty to take such actions.

For example, in June 2004, the U.S. Supreme Court decided an important case challenging the failure of the Bureau of Land Management (BLM) to enforce laws governing management of public lands. The case arose when the Southern Utah Wilderness Alliance and other environmental groups sued the BLM in 1999, alleging that the agency had violated the Federal Land Policy Management Act (FLPMA) and the National Environmental Policy Act (NEPA) by failing to control off-road vehicle use on federal lands classified as wilderness study areas. The plaintiffs argued that BLM had failed to carry out its non-discretionary duty to prevent impairment of wilderness study areas for suitability as wilderness and to undertake certain actions identified in its own land management plans as necessary to protect those areas, such as inventorying existing trails, closing areas to off-road vehicle (ORV) use, and monitoring such use. After the district court held that the claims were not reviewable under Section 706(1) of the APA, the plaintiffs appealed to the Tenth Circuit, which reversed. The Tenth Circuit (Southern Utah Wilderness Alliance v. Norton, 301 F.3d 1217 (10th Cir. 2003)) held that the FLPMA imposed a mandatory, non-discretionary duty upon the Secretary of Interior and that breach of that duty was subject to review under Section 706(1) of the APA. The U.S. then sought and obtained review of the Tenth Circuit's decision by the U.S. Supreme Court, which issued the decision below.

|| ***Norton v. Southern Utah Wilderness Alliance*** ||
|| **542 U.S. 55 (2004)** ||

JUSTICE SCALIA delivered the opinion of the Court.

In this case, we must decide whether the authority of a federal court under the Administrative Procedure Act (APA) to "compel agency action unlawfully withheld or unreasonably delayed," 5 U.S.C. §706(1), extends to the review of the United States Bureau of Land Management's stewardship of public lands under certain statutory provisions and its own planning documents. . . .

All three claims at issue here involve assertions that BLM failed to take action with respect to [off-road vehicle] or ORV use that it was required to take. Failures to act are sometimes remediable under the APA, but not always. We begin by considering what limits the APA places upon judicial review of agency inaction.

The APA authorizes suit by "[a] person suffering legal wrong because of agency action, or adversely affected or aggrieved by agency action within the meaning of a relevant statute." 5 U.S.C. §702. Where no other statute provides a private right of action, the "agency action" complained of must be "*final* agency action." §704 (emphasis added). "Agency action" is defined in §551(13) to include "the whole or a part of an agency rule, order, license, sanction, relief, or the equivalent or denial thereof, *or failure to act.*" (Emphasis added.) The APA provides relief for a failure to act in §706(1): "The reviewing court shall . . . compel agency action unlawfully withheld or unreasonably delayed."

Sections 702, 704, and 706(1) all insist upon an "agency action," either as the action complained of (in §§702 and 704) or as the action to be compelled (in §706(1)). The definition of that term begins with a list of five categories of decisions made or outcomes implemented by an agency—"agency rule, order, license, sanction [or] relief." §551(13). All of those categories involve circumscribed, discrete agency actions, as their definitions make clear: "an agency statement of . . . future effect designed to implement, interpret, or prescribe law or policy" (rule); "a final disposition . . . in a matter other than rule making" (order); a "permit . . . or other form of permission" (license); a "prohibition . . . or taking [of] other compulsory or restrictive action" (sanction); or a "grant of money, assistance, license, authority," etc., or "recognition of a claim, right, immunity," etc., or "taking of other action on the application or petition of, and beneficial to, a person" (relief). §§551(4), (6), (8), (10), (11).

The terms following those five categories of agency action are not defined in the APA: "or the equivalent or denial thereof, or failure to act." §551(13). But an "equivalent . . . thereof" must also be discrete (or it would not be equivalent), and a "denial thereof" must be the denial of a discrete listed action (and perhaps denial of a discrete equivalent).

The final term in the definition, "failure to act," is in our view properly understood as a failure to take an agency action—that is, a failure to take one of the agency actions (including their equivalents) earlier defined in §551(13). Moreover, even without this equation of "act" with "agency action" the interpretive canon of ejusdem generis would attribute to the last item ("failure to act") the same characteristic of discreteness shared by all the preceding items. See, e.g., Washington State Dept. of Social and Health Servs. v. Guardianship Estate of Keffeler, 537 U.S. 371, 384-385 (2003). A "failure to act" is not the same thing as a "denial." The latter is the agency's act of saying no to a request; the former is simply the omission of an action without formally rejecting a request—for example, the failure to promulgate a rule or take some decision by a statutory deadline. The important point is that a "failure to act" is properly understood to be limited, as are the other items in §551(13), to a discrete action.

A second point central to the analysis of the present case is that the only agency action that can be compelled under the APA is action legally required.

This limitation appears in §706(1)'s authorization for courts to "compel agency action unlawfully withheld."[1] In this regard the APA carried forward the traditional practice prior to its passage, when judicial review was achieved through use of the so-called prerogative writs—principally writs of mandamus under the All Writs Act, now codified at 28 U.S.C. §1651(a). The mandamus remedy was normally limited to enforcement of "a specific, unequivocal command," ICC v. New York, N.H. & H.R. Co., 287 U.S. 178, 204 (1932), the ordering of a "'precise, definite act . . . about which [an official] had no discretion whatever,'" United States ex rel. Dunlap v. Black, 128 U.S. 40, 46 (1888) (quoting Kendall v. United States ex rel. Stokes, 12 Pet. 524, 613 (1838)). As described in the Attorney General's Manual on the APA, a document whose reasoning we have often found persuasive, §706(1) empowers a court only to compel an agency "to perform a ministerial or non-discretionary act," or "to take action upon a matter, without directing *how* it shall act." Attorney General's Manual on the Administrative Procedure Act 108 (1947) (emphasis added).

Thus, a claim under §706(1) can proceed only where a plaintiff asserts that an agency failed to take a discrete agency action that it is required to take. These limitations rule out several kinds of challenges. The limitation to discrete agency action precludes the kind of broad programmatic attack we rejected in Lujan v. National Wildlife Federation, 497 U.S. 871 (1990). There we considered a challenge to BLM's land withdrawal review program, couched as unlawful agency "action" that the plaintiffs wished to have "set aside" under §706(2). Id., at 879. We concluded that the program was not an "agency action":

> "[R]espondent cannot seek *wholesale* improvement of this program by court decree, rather than in the offices of the Department or the halls of Congress, where programmatic improvements are normally made. Under the terms of the APA, respondent must direct its attack against some particular 'agency action' that causes it harm." Id., at 891 (emphasis in original).

The plaintiffs in National Wildlife Federation would have fared no better if they had characterized the agency's alleged "failure to revise land use plans in proper fashion" and "failure to consider multiple use," ibid., in terms of "agency action unlawfully withheld" under §706(1), rather than agency action "not in accordance with law" under §706(2).

The limitation to required agency action rules out judicial direction of even discrete agency action that is not demanded by law (which includes, of course, agency regulations that have the force of law). Thus, when an agency is compelled by law to act within a certain time period, but the manner of its action is left to the agency's discretion, a court can compel the agency to act, but has no power to specify what the action must be. For example, 47 U.S.C. §251(d)(1), which required the Federal Communications Commission "to establish regulations to implement" interconnection requirements "[w]ithin 6 months" of the date of enactment of the Telecommunications Act of 1996, would have supported a judicial decree under the APA requiring the prompt issuance of regulations, but not a judicial decree setting forth the content of those regulations.

---

1. Of course §706(1) also authorizes courts to "compel agency action . . . unreasonably delayed"—but a delay cannot be unreasonable with respect to action that is not required.

III

A

With these principles in mind, we turn to SUWA's first claim, that by permitting ORV use in certain WSAs, BLM violated its mandate to "continue to manage [WSAs] . . . in a manner so as not to impair the suitability of such areas for preservation as wilderness," 43 U.S.C. §1782(c). SUWA relies not only upon §1782(c) but also upon a provision of BLM's Interim Management Policy for Lands Under Wilderness Review, which interprets the nonimpairment mandate to require BLM to manage WSAs so as to prevent them from being "degraded so far, compared with the area's values for other purposes, as to significantly constrain the Congress's prerogative to either designate [it] as wilderness or release it for other uses." App. 65.

Section 1782(c) is mandatory as to the object to be achieved, but it leaves BLM a great deal of discretion in deciding how to achieve it. It assuredly does not mandate, with the clarity necessary to support judicial action under §706(1), the total exclusion of ORV use.

SUWA argues that §1782 does contain a categorical imperative, namely the command to comply with the nonimpairment mandate. It contends that a federal court could simply enter a general order compelling compliance with that mandate, without suggesting any particular manner of compliance. It relies upon the language from the Attorney General's Manual quoted earlier, that a court can "take action upon a matter, without directing how [the agency] shall act," and upon language in a case cited by the Manual noting that "mandamus will lie . . . even though the act required involves the exercise of judgment and discretion." Safeway Stores v. Brown, 138 F. 2d 278, 280 (Emerg. Ct. App. 1943). The action referred to in these excerpts, however, is discrete agency action, as we have discussed above. General deficiencies in compliance, unlike the failure to issue a ruling that was discussed in *Safeway Stores*, lack the specificity requisite for agency action.

The principal purpose of the APA limitations we have discussed—and of the traditional limitations upon mandamus from which they were derived—is to protect agencies from undue judicial interference with their lawful discretion, and to avoid judicial entanglement in abstract policy disagreements which courts lack both expertise and information to resolve. If courts were empowered to enter general orders compelling compliance with broad statutory mandates, they would necessarily be empowered, as well, to determine whether compliance was achieved—which would mean that it would ultimately become the task of the supervising court, rather than the agency, to work out compliance with the broad statutory mandate, injecting the judge into day-to-day agency management. To take just a few examples from federal resources management, a plaintiff might allege that the Secretary had failed to "manage wild free-roaming horses and burros in a manner that is designed to achieve and maintain a thriving natural ecological balance," or to "manage the [New Orleans Jazz National] [H]istorical [P]ark in such a manner as will preserve and perpetuate knowledge and understanding of the history of jazz," or to "manage the [Steens Mountain] Cooperative Management and Protection Area for the benefit of present and future generations." 16 U.S.C. §§1333(a), 410bbb-2(a)(1), 460nnn-12(b). The prospect of pervasive oversight by federal courts over the manner and pace of agency compliance with such congressional directives is not contemplated by the APA.

B

SUWA's second claim is that BLM failed to comply with certain provisions in its land use plans, thus contravening the requirement that "[t]he Secretary shall manage the public lands . . . in accordance with the land use plans . . . when they are available." 43 U.S.C. §1732(a); see also 43 CFR §1610.5-3(a) (2003) ("All future resource management authorizations and actions . . . and subsequent more detailed or specific planning, shall conform to the approved plan"). The relevant count in SUWA's second amended complaint alleged that BLM had violated a variety of commitments in its land use plans, but over the course of the litigation these have been reduced to two, one relating to the 1991 resource management plan for the San Rafael area, and the other to various aspects of the 1990 ORV implementation plan for the Henry Mountains area.

The actions contemplated by the first of these alleged commitments (completion of a route designation plan in the San Rafael area), and by one aspect of the second (creation of "use supervision files" for designated areas in the Henry Mountains area) have already been completed, and these claims are therefore moot. There remains the claim, with respect to the Henry Mountains plan, that "in light of damage from ORVs in the Factory Butte area," a sub-area of Henry Mountains open to ORV use, "the [plan] obligated BLM to conduct an intensive ORV monitoring program." Brief for SUWA 7-8. This claim is based upon the plan's statement that the Factory Butte area "will be monitored and closed if warranted." App. 140. SUWA does not contest BLM's assertion in the court below that informal monitoring has taken place for some years, see Brief for Appellee Secretary of Interior et al. in No. 01-4009 (CA10), p. 23, but it demands continuing implementation of a monitoring program. By this it apparently means to insist upon adherence to the plan's general discussion of "Use Supervision and Monitoring" in designated areas, App. 148-149, which (in addition to calling for the use supervision files that have already been created) provides that "[r]esource damage will be documented and recommendations made for corrective action," "[m]onitoring in open areas will focus on determining damage which may necessitate a change in designation," and "emphasis on use supervision will be placed on [limited and closed areas]." Id., at 149. SUWA acknowledges that a monitoring program has recently been commenced. Brief for SUWA 12. In light, however, of the continuing action that existence of a "program" contemplates, and in light of BLM's contention that the program cannot be compelled under §706(1), this claim cannot be considered moot.

The statutory directive that BLM manage "in accordance with" land use plans, and the regulatory requirement that authorizations and actions "conform to" those plans, prevent BLM from taking actions inconsistent with the provisions of a land use plan. Unless and until the plan is amended, such actions can be set aside as contrary to law pursuant to 5 U.S.C. §706(2). The claim presently under discussion, however, would have us go further, and conclude that a statement in a plan that BLM "will" take this, that, or the other action, is a binding commitment that can be compelled under §706(1). In our view it is not—at least absent clear indication of binding commitment in the terms of the plan.

FLPMA describes land use plans as tools by which "present and future use is *projected*." 43 U.S.C. §1701(a)(2) (emphasis added). The implementing regulations make clear that land use plans are a preliminary step in the overall process of managing public lands—"designed to guide and control future management actions and the development of subsequent, more detailed and limited scope plans for resources and uses." 43 CFR §1601.0-2 (2003). The statute and regulations confirm that a land use plan is not ordinarily the medium for affirmative decisions that implement the agency's "project[ions]." Title 43 U.S.C. §1712(e) provides that "[t]he Secretary may issue management decisions to implement land use plans"—the decisions, that is, are distinct from the plan itself. Picking up the same theme, the regulation defining a land use plan declares that a plan "is not a final implementation decision on actions which require further specific plans, process steps, or decisions under specific provisions of law and regulations." 43 CFR §1601.0-5(k) (2003). The BLM's Land Use Planning Handbook specifies that land use plans are normally not used to make site-specific implementation decisions. See Handbook II-2.

Plans also receive a different agency review process from implementation decisions. Appeal to the Department's Board of Land Appeals is available for "a specific action being proposed to implement some portion of a resource management plan or amendment." 43 CFR §1610.5-3(b). However, the Board, which reviews "decisions rendered by Departmental officials relating to . . . [t]he use and disposition of public lands and their resources," §4.1(b)(3)(i), does not review the approval of a plan, since it regards a plan as a policy determination, not an implementation decision. See, e.g., Wilderness Society, 109 I.B.L.A. 175, 178 (1989); Wilderness Society, 90 I.B.L.A. 221, 224 (1986); see also Handbook II-2, IV-3. Plans are protested to the BLM director, not appealed.

The San Rafael plan provides an apt illustration of the immense scope of projected activity that a land use plan can embrace. Over 100 pages in length, it presents a comprehensive management framework for 1.5 million acres of BLM-administered land. Twenty categories of resource management are separately discussed, including mineral extraction, wilderness protection, livestock grazing, preservation of cultural resources, and recreation. The plan lays out an ambitious agenda for the preparation of additional, more detailed plans and specific next steps for implementation. Its introduction notes that "[a]n [ORV] implementation plan is scheduled to be prepared within 1 year following approval of the [San Rafael plan]." San Rafael Plan 9. Similarly "scheduled for preparation" are activity plans for certain environmentally sensitive areas, "along with allotment management plans, habitat management plans, a fire management plan, recreation management plans . . . , cultural resource management plans for selected sites, watershed activity plans, and the wild and scenic river management plan." Ibid. The projected schedule set forth in the plan shows "[a]nticipated [i]mplementation" of some future plans within one year, others within three years, and still others, such as certain recreation and cultural resource management plans, at a pace of "one study per fiscal year." Id., at 95-102.

Quite unlike a specific statutory command requiring an agency to promulgate regulations by a certain date, a land use plan is generally a statement of priorities; it guides and constrains actions, but does not (at least in the usual case) prescribe them. It would be unreasonable to think that either Congress or the agency intended otherwise, since land use plans nationwide would commit the agency to actions far in the future, for which funds have not yet been appropriated. Some plans make explicit that implementation of their programmatic content is subject to budgetary constraints. See Brief for Petitioners 42-43, and n. 18 (quoting from such plans). While the Henry Mountains plan does not contain such a specification, we think it must reasonably be implied. A statement by BLM about what it plans to do, at some point, provided it has the funds and there are not more pressing priorities, cannot be plucked out of context and made a basis for suit under §706(1).

Of course, an action called for in a plan may be compelled when the plan merely reiterates duties the agency is already obligated to perform, or perhaps when language in the plan itself creates a commitment binding on the agency. But allowing general enforcement of plan terms would lead to pervasive interference with BLM's own ordering of priorities. For example, a judicial decree compelling immediate preparation of all of the detailed plans called for in the San Rafael plan would divert BLM's energies from other projects throughout the country that are in fact more pressing. And while such a decree might please the environmental plaintiffs in the present case, it would ultimately operate to the detriment of sound environmental management. Its predictable consequence would be much vaguer plans from BLM in the future—making coordination with other agencies more difficult, and depriving the public of important information concerning the agency's long-range intentions.

We therefore hold that the Henry Mountains plan's statements to the effect that BLM will conduct "use supervision and monitoring" in designated areas—like other "will do" projections of agency action set forth in land use plans—are not a legally binding commitment enforceable under §706(1). That being so, we find it unnecessary to consider whether the action envisioned by the statements is sufficiently discrete to be amenable to compulsion under the APA.[5]

NOTES AND QUESTIONS

1. In light of the Court's decision, what, if anything, can private parties do to force BLM to prevent impairment of wilderness study areas for suitability as wilderness?

2. When citizen suits are brought to force agencies to issue regulations by a statutory deadline that has expired, there usually is no question concerning whether the agency has failed to perform a non-discretionary duty because the deadline clearly establishes such a duty. However, the relief a court can provide usually is only a court order directing the regulations to be issued by some new deadline. Courts may not dictate the content of the regulations, though they subsequently may review whether the regulations are consistent with the agency's statutory authority.

3. In addition to lawsuits against agencies that fail to perform mandatory duties, the citizen suit provisions of the environmental laws also generally authorize private parties to sue violators of the laws and the regulations issued pursuant to them. The next section considers efforts by defendants to defeat such citizen suits.

2. Citizen Enforcement Actions and the Gwaltney Problem

While action-forcing litigation against EPA played a major role in the development of environmental law during the 1970s, citizen enforcement

---

5. We express no view as to whether a court could, under §706(1), enforce a duty to monitor ORV use imposed by a BLM regulation, see 43 CFR §8342.3 (2003). That question is not before us.

actions against private parties who violated environmental regulations were rarely filed during this period. This changed in 1982 due to concern over a dramatic decline in governmental enforcement efforts during the early years of the Reagan administration. The Natural Resources Defense Council (NRDC) initiated a national project to use citizen suits to fill the enforcement void.

The citizen suit project focused on enforcement of the Clean Water Act because it was easy to prove violations. Dischargers are required to file discharge monitoring reports (DMRs), which are available to the public and can serve as prima facie evidence of NPDES permit violations. Joined by local environmental groups, NRDC systematically scrutinized DMRs and sent 60-day notice letters to dischargers who reported violations of permit limits. Notice letters were then followed by citizen suits. As a result of this project, the total number of citizen suits brought under the Clean Water Act increased from 6 in 1981 to 62 in 1983, surpassing the 56 Clean Water Act cases referred by EPA to the Justice Department for prosecution that year. Miller, Private Enforcement of Federal Pollution Control Laws, 14 Envtl. L. Rep. 10,407, 10,424 (1984).

Based on self-reported violations contained in the DMRs, citizen suits became relatively easy to win, particularly after several courts rejected efforts to create new defenses to such suits (including claims that discharge monitoring reports prepared by defendants were too unreliable to serve as the basis for violations or that they violated the Fifth Amendment privilege against self-incrimination). After complaints from dischargers (the general counsel of the Chemical Manufacturers Association complained that his members would have contested permit provisions more aggressively if they had known that their permits were going to be enforced), EPA commissioned a comprehensive study of citizen suits in 1984. The study found that citizen suits generally had been operating in a manner consistent with the goals of the environmental statutes by both stimulating and supplementing government enforcement. Environmental Law Institute, Citizen Suits: An Analysis of Citizen Enforcement Actions Under EPA-Administered Statutes (1984). The study found no evidence that citizen suits had interfered with government enforcement efforts or that they had focused on trivial violations. More recent studies of the impact of citizen suit provisions in the environmental laws were presented in April 2003 at a symposium at Widener University School of Law. The symposium on "Environmental Citizen Suits at Thirtysomething: A Celebration & Summit" featured leading figures in the citizen suit movement who discussed its history and current status. The symposium proceedings have been published in two parts beginning at 10 Widener L. Rev. 1 (2004).

After courts rejected repeated efforts by dischargers in the early 1980s to create new defenses to citizen suits, defendants finally stumbled on a more successful strategy when they focused on the language of section 505 of the Clean Water Act, which authorizes suits against any person "alleged to be in violation" of the Act. Defendants argued that because this phrase used the present tense, it must mean that to prevail a citizen plaintiff had to prove that dischargers were in violation of the Act at the moment the suit was filed rather than simply relying on past monitoring reports. This argument received a mixed reception in the U.S. Courts of Appeals, culminating in the following Supreme Court decision.

Gwaltney of Smithfield Ltd. v.
Chesapeake Bay Foundation
484 U.S. 49 (1987)

JUSTICE MARSHALL delivered the opinion of the Court.

In this case, we must decide whether §505(a) of the Clean Water Act, 33 U.S.C. §1365(a), confers federal jurisdiction over citizen suits for wholly past violations. . . .

The holder of a federal NPDES permit is subject to enforcement action by the Administrator for failure to comply with the conditions of the permit. The Administrator's enforcement arsenal includes administrative, civil, and criminal sanctions. §1319. The holder of a state NPDES permit is subject to both federal and state enforcement action for failure to comply. §§1319, 1342(b)(7). In the absence of federal or state enforcement, private citizens may commence civil actions against any person "alleged to be in violation of" the conditions of either a federal or state NPDES permit. §1365(a)(1). If the citizen prevails in such an action, the court may order injunctive relief and/or impose civil penalties payable to the United States Treasury. §1365(a).

The Commonwealth of Virginia established a federally approved state NPDES program administered by the Virginia State Water Control Board (Board). Va. Code §§62.1-44 et seq. (1950). In 1974, the Board issued a NPDES permit to ITT-Gwaltney authorizing the discharge of seven pollutants from the company's meat-packing plant on the Pagan River in Smithfield, Virginia. The permit, which was reissued in 1979 and modified in 1980, established effluent limitations, monitoring requirements, and other conditions of discharge. In 1981, petitioner Gwaltney of Smithfield acquired the assets of ITT-Gwaltney and assumed obligations under the permit.

Between 1981 and 1984, petitioner repeatedly violated the conditions of the permit by exceeding effluent limitations on five of the seven pollutants covered. These violations are chronicled in the Discharge Monitoring Reports (DMRs) that the permit required petitioner to maintain. The most substantial of the violations concerned the pollutants fecal coliform, chlorine, and total Kjeldahl nitrogen (TKN). Between October 27, 1981, and August 30, 1984, petitioner violated its TKN limitation 87 times, its chlorine limitation 34 times, and its fecal coliform limitation 31 times. Petitioner installed new equipment to improve its chlorination system in March 1982, and its last reported chlorine violation occurred in October 1982. The new chlorination system also helped to control the discharge of fecal coliform, and the last recorded fecal coliform violation occurred in February 1984. Petitioner installed an upgraded waste-water treatment system in October 1983, and its last reported TKN violation occurred on May 15, 1984.

Respondents Chesapeake Bay Foundation and Natural Resources Defense Council, two nonprofit corporations dedicated to the protection of natural resources, sent notice in February 1984, to Gwaltney, the Administrator of EPA, and the Virginia State Water Control Board, indicating respondents' intention to commence a citizen suit under the Act based on petitioner's violations of its permit conditions. Respondents proceeded to file this suit in June 1984, alleging that petitioner "has violated . . . [and] will continue to violate its NPDES permit." Respondents requested that the District Court provide declaratory and injunctive relief, impose civil penalties, and award attorney's fees and costs. The District Court granted partial summary judgment for respondents in August 1984, declaring Gwaltney "to have violated and to be in violation" of the Act. The District Court then held a trial to determine the appropriate remedy.

Before the District Court reached a decision, Gwaltney moved in May 1985 for dismissal of the action for want of subject-matter jurisdiction under the Act. Gwaltney argued that the language of §505(a), which permits private citizens to bring suit against any person "alleged to be in violation" of the Act, requires that a defendant be violating the Act at the time of suit. Gwaltney urged the District Court to adopt the analysis of the Fifth Circuit in Hamker v. Diamond Shamrock Chemical Co., 756 F.2d 392 (1985), which held that "a complaint brought under [§505] must allege a violation occurring at the time the complaint is filed." Id., at 395. Gwaltney contended that because its last recorded violation occurred several weeks before respondents filed their complaint, the District Court lacked subject-matter jurisdiction over respondents' action.

The District Court rejected Gwaltney's argument concluding that §505 authorizes citizens to bring enforcement actions on the basis of wholly past violations. . . .

The Court of Appeals affirmed, expressly rejecting the Fifth Circuit's approach in *Hamker* and holding that §505 "can be read to comprehend unlawful conduct that occurred only prior to the filing of a lawsuit as well as unlawful conduct that continues into the present." 791 F.2d 304, 309 (4th Cir. 1986). . . .

The Court of Appeals concluded that the "to be in violation" language of §505 is ambiguous, whereas petitioner asserts that it plainly precludes the construction adopted below. We must agree with the Court of Appeals that §505 is not a provision in which Congress' limpid prose puts an end to all dispute. But to acknowledge ambiguity is not to conclude that all interpretations are equally plausible. The most natural reading of "to be in violation" is a requirement that citizen-plaintiffs allege a state of either continuous or intermittent violation— that is, a reasonable likelihood that a past polluter will continue to pollute in the future. Congress could have phrased its requirement in language that looked to the past ("to have violated"), but it did not choose this readily available option.

Respondents urge that the choice of the phrase "to be in violation," rather than phrasing more clearly directed to the past, is a "careless accident," the result of a "debatable lapse of syntactical precision." But the prospective orientation of that phrase could not have escaped Congress' attention. Congress used identical language in the citizen suit provisions of several other environmental statutes that authorize only prospective relief. See, e.g., Clean Air Act, 42 U.S.C. §7604; Resource Conservation and Recovery Act of 1976, 42 U.S.C. §6972 (1982 ed. and Supp. III); Toxic Substances Control Act, 15 U.S.C. §2619 (1982 ed. and Supp. IV). Moreover, Congress has demonstrated in yet other statutory provisions that it knows how to avoid this prospective implication by using language that explicitly targets wholly past violations. . . .

Our reading of the "to be in violation" language of §505(a) is bolstered by the language and structure of the rest of the citizen suit provisions in §505 of the Act. These provisions together make plain that the interest of the citizen-plaintiff is primarily forward-looking.

One of the most striking indicia of the prospective orientation of the citizen suit is the pervasive use of the present tense throughout §505. A citizen suit may be brought only for violation of a permit limitation "which is in effect" under the Act. 33 U.S.C. §1365(f). Citizen-plaintiffs must give notice to the alleged violator, the Administrator of EPA, and the State in which the alleged violation "occurs." §1365(b)(1)(A). A Governor of a State may sue as a citizen when the Administrator fails to enforce an effluent limitation "the violation of which is occurring in another State and is causing an adverse effect on the public health or welfare in his State." §1365(h). The most telling use of the present tense is in the definition of "citizen" as "a person . . . having an interest which is or may be adversely affected" by the defendant's violations of the Act. §1365(g). This definition makes plain what the undeviating use of the present tense strongly suggests: the harm sought to be addressed by the citizen suit lies in the present or the future, not in the past.

Any other conclusion would render incomprehensible §505's notice provision, which requires citizens to give 60 days notice of their intent to sue to the alleged violator as well as to the Administrator and the State. §1365(b)(1)(A). If the Administrator or the State commences enforcement action within that 60 day period, the citizen suit is barred, presumably because governmental action has rendered it unnecessary. §1365(b)(1)(B). It follows logically that the purpose of notice to the alleged violator is to give it an opportunity to bring itself into complete compliance with the Act and thus likewise render unnecessary a citizen suit. If we assume, as respondents urge, that citizen suits may target wholly past violations, the requirement of notice to the alleged violator becomes gratuitous. Indeed, respondents, in propounding their interpretation of the Act, can think of no reason for Congress to require such notice other than that "it seemed right" to inform an alleged violator that it was about to be sued.

Adopting respondents' interpretation of §505's jurisdictional grant would create a second and even more disturbing anomaly. The bar on citizen suits when governmental enforcement action is under way suggests that the citizen suit is meant to supplement rather than to supplant governmental action. The legislative history of the Act reinforces this view of the role of the citizen suit. The Senate Report noted that "[t]he Committee intends the great volume of enforcement actions [to] be brought by the State," and that citizen suits are proper only "if the Federal, State, and local agencies fail to exercise their enforcement responsibility." S. Rep. No. 92-414, p. 64 (1971), reprinted in 2 A Legislative History of the Water Pollution Control Act Amendments of 1972, p. 1482 (1973) (hereinafter Leg. Hist.). Permitting citizen suits for wholly past violations of the Act could undermine the supplementary role envisioned for the citizen suit. This danger is best illustrated by an example. Suppose that the Administrator identified a violator of the Act and issued a compliance order under §309(a). Suppose further that the Administrator agreed not to assess or otherwise seek civil penalties on the condition that the violator take some extreme corrective action, such as to install particularly effective but expensive machinery, that it otherwise would not be obliged to take. If citizens could file suit, months or years later, in order to seek the civil penalties that the Administrator chose to forgo, then the Administrator's discretion to enforce the Act in the public interest would be curtailed considerably. The same might be said of the discretion of state enforcement authorities. Respondents' interpretation of the scope of the citizen suit would change the nature of the citizens' role from interstitial to potentially intrusive. We cannot agree that Congress intended such a result. . . .

Our conclusion that §505 does not permit citizen suits for wholly past violations does not necessarily dispose of this lawsuit, as both lower courts recognized. The District Court found persuasive the fact that "[respondents'] allegation in the complaint, that Gwaltney was continuing to violate its NPDES permit when plaintiffs filed suits, appears to have been made fully in good faith." 611 F. Supp., at 1549, n.8. On this basis, the District Court explicitly held, albeit in a footnote, that "even if Gwaltney were correct that a district court has no jurisdiction over citizen suits based entirely on unlawful conduct that occurred entirely in the past, the Court would still have jurisdiction here." Ibid. The Court of Appeals acknowledged, also in a footnote, that "[a] very sound argument can be made that [respondents'] allegations of continuing violations were made in good faith," 791 F.2d, at 308, n.9, but expressly declined to rule on this alternative holding. Because we agree that §505 confers jurisdiction over citizen suits when the citizen-plaintiffs make a good-faith allegation of continuous or intermittent violation, we remand the case to the Court of Appeals for further consideration.

Petitioner argues that citizen-plaintiffs must prove their allegations of ongoing noncompliance before jurisdiction attaches under §505. We cannot agree. The statute does not require that a defendant "be in violation" of the Act at the commencement of suit; rather, the statute requires that a defendant be "*alleged* to be in violation." Petitioner's construction of the Act reads the word "alleged" out of §505. As petitioner itself is quick to note in other contexts, there is no reason to believe that Congress' drafting of §505 was sloppy or haphazard. We agree with the Solicitor General that "Congress's use of the phrase 'alleged to be in violation' reflects a conscious sensitivity to the practical difficulties of detecting and proving chronic episodic violations of environmental standards." Our acknowledgment that Congress intended a good-faith allegation to suffice for jurisdictional purposes, however, does not give litigants license to flood the courts with suits premised on baseless allegations. Rule 11 of the Federal Rules of Civil Procedure, which requires pleadings to be based on a good-faith belief, formed after reasonable inquiry, that they are "well grounded in fact," adequately protects defendants from frivolous allegations.

Petitioner contends that failure to require proof of allegations under §505 would permit plaintiffs whose allegations of ongoing violation are reasonable but untrue to maintain suit in federal court even though they lack constitutional standing. Petitioner reasons that if a defendant is in complete compliance with the Act at the time of suit, plaintiffs have suffered no injury remediable by the citizen suit provisions of the Act. Petitioner, however, fails to recognize that our standing cases uniformly recognize that allegations of injury are sufficient to invoke the jurisdiction of the court. In Warth v. Seldin, 422 U.S. 490, 501 (1975), for example, we made clear that a suit will not be dismissed for lack of standing if there are sufficient "allegations of fact"—not proof—in the complaint or supporting affidavits. This is not to say, however, that such allegations may not be challenged. In United States v. SCRAP, 412 U.S. 669, 689 (1973), we noted that if the plaintiffs' "allegations [of standing] were in fact untrue, then the [defendants] should have moved for summary judgment on the standing issue and demonstrated to the District Court that the allegations were sham and raised no genuine issue of fact." If the defendant fails to make such a showing after the plaintiff offers evidence to support the allegation, the case proceeds to trial on the merits, where the plaintiff must prove the allegations in order to prevail. But the Constitution does not require that the plaintiff offer this proof as a threshold matter in order to invoke the District Court's jurisdiction.

Petitioner also worries that our construction of §505 would permit citizen-plaintiffs, if their allegations of ongoing noncompliance become false at some later point in the litigation because the defendant begins to comply with the Act, to continue nonetheless to press their suit to conclusion. According to petitioner, such a result would contravene both the prospective purpose of the citizen suit provisions and the "case or controversy" requirement of Article III. Longstanding principles of mootness, however, prevent the maintenance of suit when "there is no reasonable expectation that the wrong will be repeated." United States v. W.T. Grant Co., 345 U.S. 629, 633 (1953) (quoting United States v. Aluminum Co. of America, 148 F.2d 416, 448 (2d Cir. 1945)). In seeking to have a case dismissed as moot, however, the defendant's burden "is a heavy one." 345 U.S., at 633. The defendant must demonstrate that it is "*absolutely clear* that the alleged wrongful behavior could not reasonably be expected to recur." United States v. Phosphate Export Assn., Inc., 393 U.S. 199, 203 (1968) (emphasis added). Mootness doctrine thus protects defendants from the maintenance of suit under the Clean Water Act based solely on violations wholly unconnected to any present or future wrongdoing, while it also protects plaintiffs from defendants who seek to evade sanction by predictable "protestations of repentance and reform." United States v. Oregon State Medical Society, 343 U.S. 326, 333 (1952).

Because the court below erroneously concluded that respondents could maintain an action based on wholly past violations of the Act, it declined to decide whether respondents' complaint contained a good-faith allegation of ongoing violation by petitioner. We therefore remand the case for consideration of this question. The judgment of the Court of Appeals is vacated, and the case is remanded for further proceedings consistent with this opinion.

NOTES AND QUESTIONS

1. After *Gwaltney*, under what circumstances can a citizen suit be maintained in light of the "in violation" language of section 505? What must a plaintiff allege about the violation in order to be authorized to sue? Can a plaintiff be required to prove at trial that this allegation is true?

2. The Court's decision is premised on the notion that citizen suits can only be used to address present or future harms. Is Justice Marshall correct that "any other conclusion would render incomprehensible" the 60-day notice requirement? Could a notice requirement be useful even if citizen suits could be brought against wholly past violations?

3. As noted above, the Clean Water Act had been the most popular vehicle for citizen suits because it was easy to prove that a violation had occurred using defendants' own discharge monitoring reports (DMRs). After *Gwaltney*, citizens must be prepared to prove the likelihood of ongoing violations. What constitutes an "ongoing" or "continuing" violation? Can a citizen prove an ongoing violation solely by reference to the DMRs? The Court did not accept Gwaltney's argument that the "in violation" language required plaintiffs to prove that the violation was occurring at the moment suit was filed. In a concurring opinion Justice Scalia noted that neither a "good or lucky day" nor "the dubious state in which a past effluent problem is not recurring at the moment but the cause of that problem has not been completely and clearly eradicated" was sufficient to place a discharger in a state of compliance. Can a one-shot discharge be considered an "ongoing" violation if its harmful effects still linger?

4. How did Justice Marshall answer the question of what happens if a good-faith allegation of a continuing violation proves to be untrue? In his concurrence Justice Scalia argued that if a violation had been corrected the plaintiff

would not have standing because there would be "no remediable injury in fact that could support the suit"? Is this correct? After a defendant has voluntarily corrected a violation is it really no longer possible to provide judicial redress? Wouldn't the possibility of a subsequent penalty provide some redress, by deterring future violations and reducing the likelihood that the past violation would ever be repeated? Has the Supreme Court construed the purpose of citizen suits too narrowly as abatement rather than deterrence, thus undermining efforts to use citizen suits to encourage pollution prevention?

5. Does *Gwaltney* make it possible for defendants to defeat any citizen suit for readily correctable violations? If so, will citizen suits only be able to deter violations that are the most difficult for defendants to avoid? The result in *Gwaltney* is a particularly ironic contrast to the Justice Department's 1970 policy for suits under the Refuse Act, which encouraged suits "to punish or prevent significant discharges which are either accidental or infrequent, but which are not of a continuing nature resulting from the ordinary operations of a manufacturing plant." United States Department of Justice, Guidelines for Litigation Under the Refuse Act §11 (1970). Can *Gwaltney* be reconciled with this policy?

6. The Court rejected the Chesapeake Bay Foundation's explanation that the phrase "to be in violation" was a "careless accident" by observing that Congress used identical language in the citizen suit provisions contained in other environmental laws. Yet isn't it reasonable to assume that Congress simply borrowed the same language whenever it wanted to include a citizen suit provision in subsequent legislation, thus buttressing CBF's argument?

The Congressional Response to *Gwaltney*

Gwaltney's impact was broad because the "to be in violation" language also appeared in the citizen suit provisions of other federal environmental statutes. However, Congress eventually was more careful in its choice of words. The citizen suit provision included in the Emergency Planning and Community Right-to-Know Act, EPCRA §326, 42 U.S.C. §11046, authorizes any person to sue an owner or operator of a facility "for *failure to do*" any of four enumerated requirements (e.g., submitting a toxic chemical release form required by section 313). When Congress amended the Clean Air Act in 1990 it replaced the language "alleged to be in violation" with the phrase "alleged to have violated (if there is evidence that the alleged violation has been repeated) or to be in violation." CAA §304(2)(1), 42 U.S.C. §7604(a)(1) (1993). Similar amendments have been proposed as Congress considers reauthorization of other statutes.

How should these provisions be interpreted? Do they authorize citizen suits for wholly past violations? See Atlantic States Legal Found. v. United Musical Instrument, Inc., 61 F.3d 473 (6th Cir. 1995) (EPCRA precludes citizen suits seeking civil penalties for violation cured after receipt of citizen-suit notice letter but before suit filed). Note that both section 326 of EPCRA and section 304 of the CAA retain the 60-day notice requirement that the Court found to be a striking sign of section 505's "prospective orientation." Do these amendments reflect a larger pattern of greater congressional specificity in response to narrow interpretations of public law by the Supreme Court? See Eskridge, Overriding Supreme Court Statutory Interpretation Decisions, 101 Yale L.J. 331 (1991).

The *Gwaltney* Remand

On remand, the Fourth Circuit interpreted the *Gwaltney* decision to authorize citizens to file suit based on "a good faith allegation of ongoing violation" but to require proof of such a violation at trial. Chesapeake Bay Foundation v. Gwaltney of Smithfield, Ltd., 844 F.2d 170 (4th Cir. 1988). The court noted that this could be accomplished either "(1) by proving violations that continue on or after the date the complaint is filed, or (2) by adducing evidence from which a reasonable trier of fact could find a continuing likelihood of a recurrence in intermittent or sporadic violations." The district court then reinstated the entire judgment. The judge found that although the violations had not continued, when the suit was filed "there existed a very real danger and likelihood of further violation" because witnesses had expressed doubt that the upgraded wastewater treatment system would cure all nitrogen discharge violations. Chesapeake Bay Foundation v. Gwaltney of Smithfield, Ltd., 688 F. Supp. 1078, 1079 (E.D. Va. 1988). Gwaltney then appealed once again to the Fourth Circuit.

The Fourth Circuit affirmed the district court's conclusion that a penalty could be imposed even though the violations did not recur and rejected Gwaltney's claims of mootness and lack of standing. Chesapeake Bay Foundation v. Gwaltney of Smithfield, Ltd., 890 F.2d 690 (4th Cir. 1989). The court held that the plaintiffs did not lack standing because judicial redress could be provided to them through the deterrent effect of civil penalties. The court held that the case was not moot, regardless of subsequent events, because there was an ongoing violation when the suit was filed and "a suit seeking penalties is intrinsically incapable of being rendered moot by the polluter's corrective actions." 890 F.2d at 696. However, the court held that "for purposes both of determining ongoing violations and of assessing penalties" it must consider separately each permit parameter alleged to have been violated. 890 F.2d at 698. The court affirmed the $289,822 penalty for nitrogen (TKN) discharge violations by holding that even though the last violation occurred prior to filing of the lawsuit a "reasonable trier of fact could find a continuing likelihood of a recurrence in intermittent or sporadic violations" of the permit's TKN limits. But the court reversed the $995,500 penalty for chlorine violations. Gwaltney's subsequent compliance problems are discussed on page 961. See also U.S. v. Smithfield Foods, Inc., 23 Wm. & Mary Envtl. L. & Pol'y Rev. 381 (1999).

Citizen Suits in the Aftermath of *Gwaltney*

Questions raised by *Gwaltney* have been addressed by the lower federal courts in numerous subsequent cases as defendants have sought to block citizen suits. The post-*Gwaltney* cases generally indicate that: (1) determinations concerning whether or not a violation is ongoing are to be made as of the time the complaint is filed, Atlantic States Legal Found., Inc. v. Tyson Foods, Inc., 897 F.2d 1128 (11th Cir. 1990); (2) a violation is not ongoing if remedial measures ensure that there is no reasonable prospect for recurrence, Chesapeake Bay Found. v. Gwaltney of Smithfield, Ltd., 844 F.2d 170 (4th Cir. 1988) (*Gwaltney II*); (3) plaintiffs need only make a good-faith allegation of an ongoing violation in order to be able to file suit, Sierra Club v. Union Oil of California,

853 F.2d 667 (9th Cir. 1988), but they must be able to prove it to prevail at trial, *Gwaltney II*; Carr v. Alta Verde Indus., 924 F.2d 558 (5th Cir. 1991); and (4) courts are divided on whether a parameter-by-parameter assessment of violations must be made in determining whether a violation is ongoing, but ongoing violations can be established either by showing that violations continued on or after the filing of a complaint or by producing evidence from which a reasonable trier of fact could find a continuing likelihood that intermittent or sporadic violations would occur. Compare *Gwaltney II* with Natural Resources Defense Council v. Texaco, 2 F.3d 493 (3d Cir. 1993); see also Connecticut Coastal Fishermen's Ass'n v. Remington Arms Co., 989 F.2d 1305 (2d Cir. 1993).

Another question that arose after *Gwaltney* is whether a violator may effectively escape liability by completing remedial action after the complaint is filed but before judgment is rendered. Discussions of mootness in *Gwaltney*, in the context of the jurisdictional issue, suggested to some courts that the main purpose of citizen suits was to abate existing violations and therefore subsequent compliance may "moot out" the pending action. For example, in Atlantic States Legal Found. v. Tyson Foods, Inc., 897 F.2d 1128 (11th Cir. 1990), a district court had stayed proceedings in a citizen suit to give a defendant time to come into compliance and then dismissed the suit as moot. Plaintiffs appealed and the Eleventh Circuit reversed, holding that claims for civil penalties were not mooted by post-complaint compliance. See also Atlantic States Legal Found. v. Stroh Die Casting Co., 116 F.3d 814 (7th Cir. 1997). In Steel Company v. Citizens for a Better Environment, 523 U.S. 83 (1998), the Supreme Court held that pre-complaint corrective action could defeat a citizen plaintiff's standing in an EPCRA enforcement action, see page 1016. Relying on this decision, the Fourth Circuit held that post-complaint corrective action rendered a citizen suit moot. Friends of the Earth v. Laidlaw Environmental Services, 149 F.3d 303 (4th Cir. 1998). However, as discussed below (see pages 1017-1023), the Supreme Court reversed the Fourth Circuit and held that post-complaint corrective action does not defeat standing because civil penalties can benefit plaintiffs by deterring future violations. Friends of the Earth v. Laidlaw Environmental Services, 528 U.S. 167 (2000).

3. Standing in Citizen Enforcement Actions

Prior to the Supreme Court's decision in Friends of the Earth v. Laidlaw Environmental Services, 528 U.S. 167 (2000), the lower courts were wrestling with questions raised by a string of Supreme Court decisions restricting citizen standing. Some of the most vexing questions arose in citizen enforcement actions against private parties who violated environmental regulations. Many environmental statutes also contain provisions requiring regulated parties to report their own discharges of pollutants. Indeed, it is the periodic self-reporting of discharges that has provided the basis for most of the citizen suits under the Clean Water Act, because it is a fairly straightforward task to compare the discharges allowable under a point source's permit to the actual discharges reported on the source's discharge monitoring reports (DMRs) to determine whether a violation has occurred. In the wake of the court's standing decisions, what are the standing restrictions, if any, on the ability of a citizen to sue a point source for failure to report discharges, or failure to report them accurately? A second standing question concerns what standing restrictions, if any, are imposed on citizens' ability to sue for a violation of the permit itself. Is it sufficient to allege and prove that a source discharged pollutants unlawfully—that is, in excess of the amounts allowed under its permit—or is something more required?

As to the second question, several courts of appeals initially held that standing requires some showing of harm to the ecosystem, e.g., Friends of the Earth v. Gaston Copper Recycling Corp., 179 F.3d 107 (4th Cir. 1999), reversed, 204 F.3d 149 (4th Cir. 2000) (en banc); Public Interest Research Group of New Jersey v. Magnesium Elektron, Inc., 123 F.3d 111 (3rd Cir. 1997) (*MEI*). The plaintiffs in *MEI* had secured a judgment in the district court of $2.625 million in civil penalties plus attorney's fees, after proving numerous discharges by MEI into the Wickecheoke Creek in excess of defendant's NPDES permit. At the penalty phase of the trial, defendant's limnologist had testified without rebuttal that MEI's discharges had caused no harm to the Creek's ecosystem.

On appeal, the Third Circuit held that the plaintiff lacked standing. Plaintiffs' affidavits had stated that named individuals hiked, walked, studied nature, swam, and fished in the Delaware River and Raritan Canal, into which the Wickecheoke flows. They further stated that their enjoyment of these activities was lessened to the extent they knew of MEI's unlawful discharges, and one swore that she avoided eating fish caught in the Delaware River out of concern for contamination. By a 2-1 vote, the court majority, which included future Supreme Court Justice Samuel Alito, held that these allegations were insufficient to support standing. The majority wrote that "knowledge that MEI exceeded the effluent limits set by its NPDES permit does not, by itself demonstrate injury or threat of injury." 123 F.3d at 120. In the court's view, plaintiffs constituted only "concerned bystanders," indistinguishable from environmentalists in Colorado or California who felt strongly about MEI's violations. Plaintiffs' reducing their recreational and other uses of the waterway "cannot support the injury prong of standing when a court also concludes that a polluter's violations of an effluent standard has not harmed the affected waterway and that it, in fact, poses no threat to that waterway." Id. at 121.

In *Gaston Copper,* individuals also sued for NPDES violations, including the owner of a 67-acre lake in which he and his family fish and swim, located four miles downstream from defendant's plant. The lake owner swore that he fishes less frequently and lets his grandchildren swim in the lake only once each summer, out of concern over defendant's discharges. 179 F.3d at 110. The panel majority, over a vigorous dissent by Judge J. Harvie Wilkinson, held this insufficient for standing because plaintiff had introduced no evidence that defendant's discharges had an "adverse effect" on the lake. Id. at 113. Judge Wilkinson would have recognized that the plaintiff was within the acknowledged discharge area of the plant. "Whether we characterize the harm as the actual pollution to the waterway, [plaintiff's] reasonable fear or concern, or Gaston Copper's threat to the waterway is 'unimportant,' " he wrote. Id. at 117.

MEI also addressed when plaintiffs could sue directly on the basis of reporting or monitoring violations. In a footnote, the court said that a plaintiff who had not suffered injury in fact as the court had defined it might sometimes still be able to sue a defendant solely for its failure to monintor and report if the plaintiff or some other individual had previously suffered injuries from some prior discharges. That history could give rise to reasonable decisions to forego using the river when a defendant subsequently fails to report its discharges, which "might" constitute the type of injury necessary to support standing. 125 F.3d at 124, n.9. Plaintiffs' bare desire for accurate reporting information from defendant, however, even when accompanied by decreased use of the river, was insufficient in the case itself, because plaintiff had failed to show the discharges had had any effect on the river, and the uncontradicted evidence was that defendant's discharges had not "caused the type of injury feared by [plaintiffs]." Id. at 124.

One federal statute, the Emergency Planning and Community Right-to-Know Act (EPCRA), is unique in that the only duties it imposes on regulated parties are duties to report toxic emissions. One issue that courts have faced in EPCRA litigation is whether citizens can sue under its citizen suit provision for failures to report that companies cure after they receive the required notice from the citizen plaintiffs of an intent to sue. In part this is a question of whether specific wording of the EPCRA citizen suit provision is materially distinguishable from the citizen suit provision in the Clean Water Act, under which the Supreme Court has ruled suit cannot be brought for wholly past violations. See the discussion of Gwaltney v. Chesapeake Bay Foundation, page 1007. After the Seventh Circuit ruled that citizens could sue under EPCRA based on such wholly past violations, this created a conflict with a prior decision by the Sixth Circuit, see page 1012, which the Supreme Court agreed to review.

In Steel Company v. Citizens for a Better Environment, 523 U.S. 83 (1998), the Court held that plaintiffs lacked standing to sue for reporting violations that the defendant had cured between its receipt of the plaintiffs' notice of intention to sue and the date that the plaintiffs filed their case in federal court. The Court did not reach the statutory issue.

The *Steel Company* plaintiffs had alleged an interest in having accurate discharge information so that they could react appropriately to it in various ways, such as working on emergency preparedness plans or working to achieve further reductions in neighborhood discharges. The Court expressly did not reach the question of whether the defendant's "failure to provide EPCRA information in a timely fashion and the lingering effects of that failure" gives rise to a concrete injury satisfying injury in fact, because it held in any event that the complaint failed the redressability prong of the standing requirement. 523 U.S. at 105.

The plaintiffs had requested a number of remedies, including "any further relief as the court deems appropriate," but the Court concluded that none of them could redress the plaintiffs injury of failing to have access to timely EPCRA reports that had now been filed. Declatory relief was "worthless to respondent [and] . . . to all the world," in a case in which the defendant had conceded its wrongdoing. Civil penalties failed because they are payable to the United States Treasury, and consequently served to remediate not the plaintiffs' particular injury, but rather the "undifferentiated public interest" in faithful execution of EPCRA. In response to Justice Stevens dissenting opinion stating "it is enough that respondent will be gratified by seeing petitioner punished for its infractions and that the punishment will deter the risk of future harm," Justice Scalia wrote that "such a principle would make the redressability requirement vanish." The request for costs of investigating and prosecuting the case was insufficient because the plaintiff could not "achieve standing to litigate a substantive issue by bringing suit for the cost of bringing suit." Id. at 107.

The last specific remedies sought were authority to inspect defendant's plant and records, and an order directing defendant to provide plaintiff copies of compliance reports filed with EPA in the future. Such forward-looking relief, the Court wrote, "cannot conceivably remedy any past wrong but is aimed at deterring petitioner from violating EPCRA in the future. The latter objective can of course be 'remedial' for Article III purposes, when threatened injury is one of the gravamens of the complaint. If respondent had alleged a continuing violation or the imminence of a future violation, the injunctive relief requested would remedy that alleged harm. But there is no such allegation here—and on the facts of the case, there seems to be no basis for it." Id. at 108.

Shortly after *Steel Company,* the Supreme Court decided Federal Election Commission v. Akins, 524 U.S. 11 (1998), in which it upheld the standing of a group of voters to sue a federal agency for failing to require a lobbying group to register and disclose certain information. The Court held that the plaintiffs' inability to obtain information required to be disclosed by statute constituted sufficient injury-in-fact to give them standing. The Court distinguished this case from its traditional prudential ban on taxpayer standing by noting that a federal statute specifically gave the plaintiffs a right to receive the information they sought.

The next major standing controversy decided by the Court arose as a result of a decision by the U.S. Court of Appeals for the Fourth Circuit in Friends of the Earth v. Laidlaw Environmental Services, 149 F.3d 303 (4th Cir. 1998). Citing the doctrine that a plaintiff must satisfy all the elements of standing throughout the course of a litigation, the Fourth Circuit dismissed a suit against a company whose wastewater treatment plant in Roebuck, South Carolina had nearly 900 violations of its NPDES discharge permit. Occasional violations continued after the complaint was filed in 1992, but the last recorded violation occurred two years prior to the entry of the district court judgment in 1997. Interpreting *Steel Company* to say that a plaintiff lacks standing to challenge wholly past violations when the only available remedies fail that opinion's redressability standard, the Fourth Circuit reversed an award by the district court of $405,880 in civil penalties plus attorneys' fees. On writ of certiorari, the Supreme Court reversed in the following decision.

|| *Friends of the Earth v.*
Laidlaw Environmental Services
528 U.S. 167 (2000) ||

JUSTICE GINSBURG delivered the opinion of the Court.

This case presents an important question concerning the operation of the citizen-suit provisions of the Clean Water Act. Congress authorized the federal district courts to entertain Clean Water Act suits initiated by "a person or persons having an interest which is or may be adversely affected." To impel future compliance with the Act, a district court may prescribe injunctive relief in such a suit; additionally or alternatively, the court may impose civil penalties payable to the United States Treasury. In the Clean Water Act citizen suit now before us, the District Court determined that injunctive relief was inappropriate because the defendant, after the institution of the litigation, achieved substantial compliance with the terms of its discharge permit. The court did, however, assess a civil penalty of $405,800. The "total deterrent effect" of the penalty would be adequate to forestall future violations, the court reasoned, taking into account that the defendant "will be required to reimburse plaintiffs for a significant amount of legal fees and has, itself, incurred significant legal expenses."

The Court of Appeals vacated the District Court's order. The case became moot, the appellate court declared, once the defendant fully complied with the terms of its permit and the plaintiff failed to appeal the denial of equitable relief. . . .

We reverse the judgment of the Court of Appeals. The appellate court erred in concluding that a citizen suitor's claim for civil penalties must be dismissed as moot when the defendant, albeit after commencement of the litigation, has come into compliance. In directing dismissal of the suit on grounds of mootness, the Court of Appeals incorrectly conflated our case law on initial standing to bring suit, see, e.g., Steel Co. v. Citizens for Better Environment, with our case law on post-commencement mootness, see, e.g., City of Mesquite v. Aladdin's Castle, Inc., 455 U.S. 283 (1982). A defendant's voluntary cessation of allegedly unlawful conduct ordinarily does not suffice to moot a case. The Court of Appeals also misperceived the remedial potential of civil penalties. Such penalties may serve, as an alternative to an injunction, to deter future violations and thereby redress the injuries that prompted a citizen suitor to commence litigation.

I

B

[Between 1987 and 1995, Laidlaw violated its NPDES permit nearly 500 times by discharging greater than permitted quantities of mercury into the North Tyger River. After FOE filed suit in June 12, 1992, more exceedances occurred, the last reported one taking place on January, 1995, "long after the complaint was filed but about two years before judgment was rendered."]

On January 22, 1997, the District Court issued its judgment. It found that Laidlaw had gained a total economic benefit of $1,092,581 as a result of its extended period of noncompliance with the mercury discharge limit in its permit. The court concluded, however, that a civil penalty of $405,800 was adequate in light of the guiding factors listed in 33 U.S.C. §1319(d). In particular, the District Court stated that the lesser penalty was appropriate taking into account the judgment's "total deterrent effect." In reaching this determination, the court "considered that Laidlaw will be required to reimburse plaintiffs for a significant amount of legal fees." The court declined to grant FOE's request for injunctive relief, stating that an injunction was inappropriate because "Laidlaw has been in substantial compliance with all parameters in its NPDES permit since at least August 1992."

FOE appealed the District Court's civil penalty judgment, arguing that the penalty was inadequate, but did not appeal the denial of declaratory or injunctive relief. Laidlaw cross-appealed, arguing, among other things, that FOE lacked standing to bring the suit. . . . The United States . . . participate[d] as amicus curiae in support of FOE.

[The Court of Appeals reversed.]

We granted certiorari, 525 U.S. 1176 (1999), to resolve the inconsistency between the Fourth Circuit's decision in this case and the decisions of several other Courts of Appeals, which have held that a defendant's compliance with its permit after the commencement of litigation does not moot claims for civil penalties under the Act.

II

A

. . . Laidlaw contends first that FOE lacked standing from the outset even to seek injunctive relief, because the plaintiff organizations failed to show that any of their members had sustained or faced the threat of any "injury in fact" from Laidlaw's activities. In support of this contention Laidlaw points to the District Court's finding, made in the course of setting the penalty amount, that there had been "no demonstrated proof of harm to the environment" from Laidlaw's mercury discharge violations. 956 F. Supp., at 602; see ibid. ("[T]he NPDES permit violations at issue in this citizen suit did not result in any health risk or environmental harm.").

The relevant showing for purposes of Article III standing, however, is not injury to the environment but injury to the plaintiff. To insist upon the former rather than the latter as part of the standing inquiry . . . is to raise the standing hurdle higher than the necessary showing for success on the merits in an action alleging noncompliance with an NPDES permit. Focusing properly on injury to the plaintiff, the District Court found that FOE had demonstrated sufficient injury to establish standing. For example, FOE member Kenneth Lee Curtis averred in affidavits that he lived a half-mile from Laidlaw's facility; that he occasionally drove over the North Tyger River, and that it looked and smelled polluted; and that he would like to fish, camp, swim, and picnic in and near the river between 3 and 15 miles downstream from the facility, as he did when he was a teenager, but would not do so because he was concerned that the water was polluted by Laidlaw's discharges. Curtis reaffirmed these statements in extensive deposition testimony. For example, he testified that he would like to fish in the river at a specific spot he used as a boy, but that he would not do so now because of his concerns about Laidlaw's discharges.

Other members presented evidence to similar effect. . . .

These sworn statements, as the District Court determined, adequately documented injury in fact. We have held that environmental plaintiffs adequately allege injury in fact when they aver that they use the affected area and are persons "for whom the aesthetic and recreational values of the area will be lessened" by the challenged activity. Sierra Club v. Morton. See also *Defenders of Wildlife* ("Of course, the desire to use or observe an animal species, even for purely aesthetic purposes, is undeniably a cognizable interest for purposes of standing."). . . .

In contrast [to *Lujan v. National Wildlife Federation*] the affidavits and testimony presented by FOE in this case assert that Laidlaw's discharges, and the affiant members' reasonable concerns about the effects of those discharges, directly affected those affiants' recreational, aesthetic, and economic interests. These submissions present dispositively more than the mere "general averments" and "conclusory allegations" found inadequate in *National Wildlife Federation*. Nor can the affiants' conditional statements—that they would use the nearby North Tyger River for recreation if Laidlaw were not discharging pollutants into it—be equated with the speculative "'some day' intentions" to visit endangered species halfway around the world that we held insufficient to show injury in fact in *Defenders of Wildlife.*

Los Angeles v. Lyons . . . does not weigh against standing in this case. In *Lyons,* we held that a plaintiff lacked standing to seek an injunction against the enforcement of a police chokehold policy because he could not credibly allege that he faced a realistic threat from the policy. In the footnote from *Lyons* cited by the dissent, we noted that "[t]he reasonableness of Lyons' fear is dependent upon the likelihood of a recurrence of the allegedly unlawful conduct," and that his "subjective apprehensions" that such a recurrence would even take place were not enough to support standing. Here, in contrast, it is undisputed that Laidlaw's unlawful conduct—discharging pollutants in excess of permit limits—was occurring at the time the complaint was filed. Under *Lyons,* then, the only "subjective" issue here is "[t]he reasonableness of [the] fear" that led the affiants to respond to the concededly ongoing conduct by refraining from use of the North Tyger River and surrounding areas. Unlike the dissent, we see nothing "improbable" about the proposition that a company's continuous and pervasive illegal discharges of pollutants into a river would cause nearby residents to curtail their recreational use of that waterway and would subject them to other economic and aesthetic harms. The proposition is entirely reasonable, the District Court found it was true in this case, and that is enough for injury in fact.

Laidlaw argues next that even if FOE has standing to seek injunctive relief, it lacked standing to seek civil penalties. Here the asserted defect is not injury but redressability. Civil penalties offer no redress to private plaintiffs, Laidlaw argues, because they are paid to the government, and therefore a citizen plaintiff can never have standing to seek them. . . .

[I]t is wrong to maintain that citizen plaintiffs facing ongoing violations never have standing to seek civil penalties.

We have recognized on numerous occasions that "all civil penalties have some deterrent effect." More specifically, Congress has found that civil penalties in Clean Water Act cases do more than promote immediate compliance by limiting the defendant's economic incentive to delay its attainment of permit limits; they also deter future violations. This congressional determination warrants judicial attention and respect. "The legislative history of the Act reveals that Congress wanted the district court to consider the need for retribution and deterrence, in addition to restitution, when it imposed civil penalties. . . . [The district court may] seek to deter future violations by basing the penalty on its economic impact." Tull v. United States, 481 U.S. 412 (1987).

It can scarcely be doubted that, for a plaintiff who is injured or faces the threat of future injury due to illegal conduct ongoing at the time of the suit, a sanction that effectively abates that conduct and prevents its recurrence provides a form of redress. Civil penalties can fit that description. To the extent that they encourage defendants to discontinue current violations and deter them from committing future ones, they afford redress to citizen plaintiffs who are injured or threatened with injury as a consequence of ongoing unlawful conduct. . . .

We recognize that there may be a point at which the deterrent effect of a claim for civil penalties becomes so insubstantial or so remote that it cannot support citizen standing. . . .

In this case we need not explore the outer limits of the principle that civil penalties provide sufficient deterrence to support redressability. Here, the civil penalties sought by FOE carried with them a deterrent effect that made it likely, as opposed to merely speculative, that the penalties would redress FOE's injuries by abating current violations and preventing future ones—as the District Court reasonably found when it assessed a penalty of $405,800.

Laidlaw contends that the reasoning of our decision in *Steel Co.* directs the conclusion that citizen plaintiffs have no standing to seek civil penalties under the Act. We disagree. *Steel Co.* established that citizen suitors lack standing to seek civil penalties for violations that have been abated by the time of the suit. We specifically noted in that case that there was no allegation in the complaint of any continuing or imminent violation, and that no basis for such an allegation appeared to exist. [S]ee also *Gwaltney* ("the harm sought to be addressed by the citizen suit lies in the present or the future, not in the past"). In short, *Steel Co.* held that private plaintiffs, unlike the Federal Government, may not sue to assess penalties for wholly past violations, but our decision in that case did not reach the issue of standing to seek penalties for violations that are ongoing at the time of the complaint and that could continue into the future if undeterred.

B

Satisfied that FOE had standing under Article III to bring this action, we turn to the question of mootness.

The only conceivable basis for a finding of mootness in this case is Laidlaw's voluntary conduct—either its achievement by August 1992 of substantial compliance with its NPDES permit or its more recent shutdown of the Roebuck facility. It is well settled that "a defendant's voluntary cessation of a challenged practice does not deprive a federal court of its power to determine the legality of the practice." City of Mesquite, 455 U.S., at 289. "[I]f it did, the courts would be compelled to leave [t]he defendant . . . free to return to his old ways." In accordance with this principle, the standard we have announced for determining whether a case has been mooted by the defendant's voluntary conduct is stringent: "A case might become moot if subsequent events made it absolutely clear that the allegedly wrongful behavior could not reasonably be expected to recur." The "heavy burden of persua[ding]" the court that the challenged conduct cannot reasonably be expected to start up again lies with the party asserting mootness.

The Court of Appeals justified its mootness disposition by reference to *Steel Co.*, which held that citizen plaintiffs lack standing to seek civil penalties for wholly past violations. In relying on *Steel Co.*, the Court of Appeals confused mootness with standing. The confusion is understandable, given this Court's repeated statements that the doctrine of mootness can be described as "the doctrine of standing set in a time frame: The requisite personal interest that must exist at the commencement of the litigation (standing) must continue throughout its existence (mootness)." Arizonans for Official English, 520 U.S., at 68.

Careful reflection on the long-recognized exceptions to mootness, however, reveals that the description of mootness as "standing set in a time frame" is not comprehensive. As just noted, a defendant claiming that its voluntary compliance moots a case bears the formidable burden of showing that it is absolutely clear the allegedly wrongful behavior could not reasonably be expected to recur. By contrast, in a lawsuit brought to force compliance, it is the plaintiff's burden to establish standing by demonstrating that, if unchecked by the litigation, the defendant's allegedly wrongful behavior will likely occur or continue, and that the "threatened injury [is] certainly impending." Thus, in *Lyons,* as already noted, we held that a plaintiff lacked initial standing to seek an injunction against the enforcement of a police chokehold policy because he could not credibly allege that he faced a realistic threat arising from the policy. Elsewhere in the opinion, however, we noted that a citywide moratorium on police chokeholds—an action that surely diminished the already slim likelihood that any particular individual would be choked by police—would not have mooted an otherwise valid claim for injunctive relief, because the moratorium by its terms was not permanent. The plain lesson of these cases is that there are circumstances in which the prospect that a defendant will engage in (or resume) harmful conduct may be too speculative to support standing, but not too speculative to overcome mootness. . . .

Standing doctrine functions to ensure, among other things, that the scarce resources of the federal courts are devoted to those disputes in which the parties have a concrete stake. In contrast, by the time mootness is an issue, the case has been brought and litigated, often (as here) for years. To abandon the case at an advanced stage may prove more wasteful than frugal. This argument from sunk costs does not license courts to retain jurisdiction over cases in which one or both parties have settled or a plaintiff pursuing a nonsurviving claim has died. . . . But the argument surely highlights an important difference between the two doctrines. . . .

For the reasons stated, the judgment of the United States Court of Appeals for the Fourth Circuit is reversed, and the case is remanded for further proceedings consistent with this opinion.

NOTES AND QUESTIONS

1. Laidlaw closed its facility after the Fourth Circuit rendered its decisions, and argued that this fact had rendered the case moot in any event. In another portion of the opinion, the Court noted that either this fact or "Laidlaw's earlier achievement of substantial compliance with its permit requirements, might moot the case, but—we once more reiterate—only if one or the other of these events made it absolutely clear that Laidlaw's permit violations could not reasonably be expected to recur." Because the effects of these events were disputed facts, the case was remanded for further consideration of them. In a concurring opinion Justice Stevens argued that post-judgment conduct could never invalidate an award of civil penalties.

2. Suppose Laidlaw had brought itself into substantial compliance prior to the filing of the suit. Would *Steel Company* then apply, with the result that FOE would have lacked standing?

3. What effect will the *Steel Company* and *Laidlaw* decisions have on incentives to comply? Will *Steel Company* give companies greater incentives not to comply until they receive 60-day notice letters? Will *Laidlaw* make the delivery of the 60-day notice letters a more powerful tool for stimulating compliance since putative defendants now know they can defeat citizen suits only by coming into compliance before lawsuits are filed? On the other hand, does the result in *Laidlaw* reduce the incentives for defendant to cure discharge situations once the suit has been filed, because they know that doing so will not provide them with a basis for having the case dismissed?

4. Would amendments to environmental statutes such as EPCRA and CWA that allowed citizens to keep some portion of any monetary award levied, as a bounty for their vindicating the public interest, obviate the obstacle to standing created by *Steel Company*?

5. Justice Scalia, joined by Justice Thomas, decried the Court's decision as having "grave implications for democratic governance." Justice Kennedy concurred separately to note that the question whether a delegation of executive power to private parties to exact public fines is consistent with Article II had not been raised. In another standing case, the Supreme Court ruled that private plaintiffs had standing to seek *qui tarn* recoveries on behalf of the federal government under the False Claims Act from defendants alleged to have defrauded the government. Vermont Agency of Natural Resources v. United States ex rel. Stevens, 529 U.S. 765 (2000). Writing for the Court, Justice Scalia concluded that injury in fact to the United States conferred standing on private relators to bring *qui tarn* actions under the False Claims Act because relators stood in the shoes of the federal government. However, the Court also held that Congress had not intended to subject states to liability under the False Claims Act because states did not clearly fit within the definition of "person" for purposes of the Act. In a footnote, Justice Scalia sought to keep alive the question whether citizen suits violated principles of separation of powers by noting that the Court expressed "no view on the question whether *qui tarn* suits violate Article II" on the ground that it had not been raised by the petitioner.

6. As a result of *Laidlaw,* the Fourth Circuit sitting en banc unanimously reversed the *Gaston Copper* panel decision, discussed on page 1015, that had dismissed a citizen suit for lack of standing. Friends of the Earth, Inc. v. Gaston Copper Recycling Corp., 204 F.3d 149 (4th Cir. 2000) (en banc). *Laidlaw* has made it easier for citizen groups to establish standing in environmental enforcement suits, although it has not guaranteed that their standing will be upheld. See, e.g., Central and South West Services v. EPA, 220 F.3d 683 (5th Cir. 2000) (dismissing Sierra Club's challenge to EPA regulations allowing disposal of PCB bulk product waste for failure of individual members who filed affidavits to demonstrate through objective evidence that PCBs from local landfill could leach into their town's water supply as they feared); Friends for Ferrell Parkway, LLC v. Stasko, 282 F.3d 315 (4th Cir. 2002); Puerto Rico Campers' Ass'n v. Puerto Rico Aqueduct & Sewer Authority, 219 F. Supp. 2d 201 (D.P.R. 2002) (association had standing to sue sewer authority for violations by one wastewater treatment plant, but not another because the affidavits by members reflect concern over the possible effects of contamination of beaches but not of the river into which the latter plant discharges, thus failing to meet the "mild burden" to establish standing under *Laidlaw*).

7. Additional background information on the *Laidlaw* litigation can be found in William W. Buzbee, The Story of *Laidlaw*: Standing and Citizen Enforcement, in Environmental Law Stories 201 (Lazarus & Houck eds., 2005). Professor Buzbee notes that despite the lengthy litigation and the Court's decision in their favor, the plaintiffs' law firm did not receive an attorneys' fee award due to the bankruptcy of the defendant.

8. As a tribute to the Court's *Laidlaw* decision, Professor Craig N. Johnston of Lewis & Clark has composed lyrics for a song to be sung to the tune of Eric Clapton's "Layla," the passionate anthem Clapton wrote about the woman who later became his wife (the song first appeared on the album "Layla and Other

Assorted Love Songs" released December 1970 by Clapton's group Derek and the Dominos). As you read the lyrics below, reprinted by permission of Professor Johnston, recall that *Laidlaw* was decided by a 7-2 vote with only Justices Antonin Scalia and Clarence Thomas (C.T. in the lyrics) dissenting.

Laidlaw

What do we do when we get sued now
If the Court's not on our side?
If we can't rely on standing constraints
Do they expect us to comply?

Laidlaw!
What are these non-use injuries?
Laidlaw!
Based on subjectivity
Laidlaw!
Antonin, please ease our worried minds.

Defenders gave us consolation
And *Steel Co.* made us paint the town.
But like fools, we put our faith in you.
You and C.T. got voted down.

Laidlaw!
What about these penalties?
Laidlaw!
Where's the redressability?
Laidlaw!
Antonin, please ease our worried minds.

Let's make the best of the situation.
Article II's our last resort.
Please don't say we'll never find a way
To keep these plaintiffs out of court.

Laidlaw!
What was it Sandra didn't see?
Laidlaw!
Where were the Chief and Kennedy?
Laidlaw!
Antonin, please ease our worried minds.

Laidlaw!
We miss the old majority.
Laidlaw!
How can we pay these penalties?
Laidlaw!
Antonin, please ease our worried minds.

Lyrics by Professor Craig N. Johnston.

4. Government Preclusion of Citizen Suits

As noted above, citizen suits may be precluded if federal or state authorities have commenced and are "diligently prosecuting" their own civil or criminal enforcement action against the alleged violator. CWA §505(b)(1)(B), CAA §304(b)(1)(B). These provisions seek to prevent citizen suits from infringing on the exercise of enforcement discretion by federal and state authorities.

Courts have wrestled with the question whether a properly commenced citizen suit may continue after the defendant reaches a settlement agreement with government officials. In Atlantic States Legal Foundation v. Eastman Kodak Co., 933 F.2d 124 (2d Cir. 1991), the Second Circuit held that as long as the settlement reasonably assures that the violations alleged in the citizen suit have ceased and will not recur, then the citizen suit cannot proceed even though the state did not initiate enforcement proceedings during the 60-day statutory notice period. However, the court held that plaintiffs could seek an attorneys' fees recovery because they had motivated the settlement agreement. In EPA v. City of Green Forest, 921 F.2d 1394 (8th Cir. 1990), the Eighth Circuit reached a similar decision, holding that a consent decree filed by EPA after a properly commenced citizen suit could bar the citizen action. Even though the plaintiffs had been precluded from participating in the consent decree negotiations, the court noted that their role as private attorneys general was fully served by the EPA. While noting that "there may be some cases in which it would be appropriate to let a citizens' action go forward in the wake of a subsequently filed government enforcement action," the court emphasized that EPA must be afforded a preeminent role in enforcing CWA violations. 921 F.2d at 1404. Other courts have stressed that the government enforcement cannot bar a previously filed citizen suit unless it addresses the claims made in the citizen suit. See Hudson River Fishermen's Ass'n v. County of Westchester, 686 F. Supp. 1044 (S.D.N.Y. 1988).

Prior to the 1987 Amendments, the language of the Clean Water Act's citizen suit provision provided that the only government enforcement action that barred a citizen suit was "a civil or criminal action in a court of the United States," §505(b)(1)(B). Administrative enforcement actions were not held to bar citizen suits because they were limited to small penalties assessed in proceedings in which citizens could not intervene. Friends of the Earth v. Consolidated Rail Corp., 768 F.2d 57 (2d Cir. 1985). When it gave EPA administrative enforcement authority in the 1987 Amendments, Congress added a provision precluding citizens from obtaining civil penalties in citizen suits if EPA had filed an administrative enforcement action or if "a State has commenced and is diligently prosecuting an action under a State law comparable to [§309(g)]." §309(g)(6)(A). However, Congress required that citizens be given an opportunity to comment on proposed administrative penalties, §309(g)(4)(A), and to seek a hearing, §309(g)(4)(B), and judicial review to contest penalty assessments, §309(g)(8). In light of these provisions, courts have wrestled with how to determine the comparability of state administrative enforcement proceedings.

In North & South Rivers Watershed Association v. Town of Scituate, 949 F.2d 552 (1st Cir. 1992), the First Circuit held that a state administrative order which did not impose civil penalties barred a citizen suit even though the state did not have delegated authority to operate the NPDES program and even though state law provided no notice to citizens of agency orders or penalty proceedings. See also Arkansas Wildlife Fed'n v. ICI Americas, Inc., 29 F.3d 376 (8th Cir. 1994) ("[T]he comparability requirement may be satisfied so long as the state law contains comparable penalty provisions which the state is authorized to enforce, has the same overall enforcement goals as the federal

CWA, provides interested citizens a meaningful opportunity to participate at significant stages of the decision-making process, and adequately safeguards their interests."). The *Scituate* decision is criticized in Hodas, Enforcement of Environmental Law in a Triangular Federal System: Can Three Not Be a Crowd When Enforcement Authority Is Shared by the United States, the States, and Their Citizens?, 54 Md. L. Rev. 1552, 1633-1645 (1995). Professor Hodas maintains that this decision reflects "a compliance theory of enforcement" founded on the notion that "bringing an individual defendant into compliance is more important than sanctioning that violator with civil penalties sufficiently large to deter others." Id. at 1633. Other courts have held that citizen suits seeking civil penalties are not barred by administrative compliance orders that do not seek penalties. Washington Public Interest Research Group v. Pendleton Woolen Mills, 11 F.3d 883 (9th Cir. 1993).

Section 304(b)(1)(B) of the Clean Air Act bars citizen suits when EPA or a state is "diligently prosecuting a civil action in a court of the United States or a state." The Fifth Circuit has held that in light of this provision's clear reference to courts, state administrative enforcement actions do not bar citizen enforcement actions under the Clean Air Act. Texans United for a Safe Economy Education Fund v. Crown Central Petroleum Corp., 207 F.3d 789 (5th Cir. 2000).

While EPA's policy has been not to initiate preemptive enforcement actions in response to citizen-suit notice letters, several states have been aggressively preempting citizen suits at the behest of defendants. See Hodas, 54 Md. L. Rev. at 1648-1651. For example, in *Laidlaw* the defendant asked the state of South Carolina to file suit against it in order to bar the citizen suit by Friends of the Earth (FOE). The company drafted the complaint against itself and even paid the filing fee for the state. On the day before FOE's 60-day notice period was to expire, the company announced a settlement with the state in which it agreed to pay a $100,000 civil penalty and to make "every effort" to comply with its permit obligations. However, the district court found that the settlement did not bar FOE's citizen suit because it did not constitute the kind of "diligent prosecution" required by §505(b)(1)(B). Friends of the Earth, Inc. v. Laidlaw Environmental Services, 528 U.S. 167, 176-177 (2000).

5. *Permit Shields*

An important issue that emerged in CWA enforcement actions was the question whether NPDES permits insulate dischargers from liability for discharges of pollutants not specifically regulated by their permits. In the case below, a public interest group filed a citizen suit after discovering that a company's TRI report included surface water discharges of pollutants not covered by the company's NPDES permit. The trial court agreed with the defendant that the CWA does not prohibit discharges of pollutants by a permittee that do not violate specific limits established in the permit. The court stated that although §301(a) of the Act generally prohibits unpermitted discharges, "the statutory and regulatory scheme of the Act takes enforcement actions against permit holders *outside* that general prohibition." Atlantic States Legal Found. v. Eastman Kodak Co., 809 F. Supp. 1040, 1047 (W.D.N.Y. 1992). The decision was appealed to the Second Circuit, which reached the following decision.

Atlantic States Legal Foundation, Inc. v. Eastman Kodak Co.
12 F.3d 353 (2d Cir. 1994)

Before: WINTER, MCLAUGHLIN, and JACOBS, Circuit Judges. WINTER, Circuit Judge:

This appeal raises the issue of whether private groups may bring a citizen suit pursuant to Section 505 of the Federal Water Pollution Control Act (commonly known as the Clean Water Act), 33 U.S.C. §1365, to stop the discharge of pollutants not listed in a valid permit issued pursuant to the Clean Water Act ("CWA" or "the Act"), 33 U.S.C. §1342 (1988). . . .

BACKGROUND

Appellee Eastman Kodak Company ("Kodak") operates an industrial facility in Rochester, New York, that discharges wastewater into the Genesee River and Paddy Hill Creek under a State Pollutant Discharge Elimination System ("SPDES") permit issued pursuant to 33 U.S.C. §1342. Appellant Atlantic States Legal Foundation, Inc. ("Atlantic States") is a not-for-profit environmental group based in Syracuse, New York.

Kodak operates a wastewater treatment plant at its Rochester facility to purify waste produced in the manufacture of photographic supplies and other laboratory chemicals. The purification plant employs a variety of technical processes to filter harmful pollutants before discharge into the Genesee River at the King's Landing discharge point (designated Outfall 001) pursuant to its SPDES permit.

Kodak first received a federal permit in 1975. At that time, the pertinent regulatory scheme was the National Pollutant Discharge Elimination System ("NPDES") that was administered directly by the federal Environmental Protection Agency ("EPA"). Subsequently, 33 U.S.C. §1342(b), (c) delegated authority to the states to establish their own programs in place of the EPA's. As a result, Kodak applied in July 1979 to renew its permit to the New York State Department of Environmental Conservation ("DEC"). The DEC declined to act on Kodak's renewal application, and Kodak's NPDES permit remained in effect. As part of the pending application for an SPDES permit, in April 1982 Kodak provided the DEC with a Form 2C describing estimated discharges of 164 substances from each of its outfalls. Kodak also submitted an Industrial Chemical Survey ("ICS") disclosing the amounts of certain chemicals used in Kodak's facility and whether they might appear in the plant's wastewater. Although the ICS originally requested information on 144 substances, including some broad classes such as "unspecified metals," the DEC restricted the inquiry to chemicals used in excess of specified minimum levels.

On the basis of these disclosures, DEC issued Kodak an SPDES permit, number 000-1643, effective November 1, 1984, establishing specific effluent limitations for approximately 25 pollutants. The permit also included "action levels"[2] for five other pollutants as well as for three of the pollutants for which it had established effluent limits. DEC further required Kodak to conduct a semi-annual

---

2. If the action level is exceeded, the permittee must undertake a "short-term, high-intensity monitoring program." If levels higher than the action levels are confirmed, the permit is reopened for consideration of revised action levels or effluent limits.

scan of "EPA Volatile, Acid and Base/Neutral Fractions and PCB's priority pollutants on a 24-hr, composite sample." In May 1989, Kodak applied to renew the
SPDES permit submitting a new Form 2C and ICS, but the 1984 permit will
continue to remain in effect until DEC issues a final determination. . . .

On November 14, 1991, Atlantic States filed the complaint in the instant
matter. The complaint alleged that Kodak had violated Sections 301 and 402 of
the Clean Water Act, 33 U.S.C. §§1311, 1342, by discharging large quantities of
pollutants not listed in its SPDES permit.[4] . . .

After discovery, Atlantic States moved for partial summary judgment as to
Kodak's liability in relation to the post-April 1, 1990 discharge of one or more of
16 of the 27 pollutants listed in the complaint. The 16 pollutants are all listed as
toxic chemicals under Section 313(c) of the Emergency Planning and Community Right-to-Know Act, 42 U.S.C. §11023(c). Atlantic States argued that General
Provision 1(b) of the SPDES permit and Section 301 of the CWA, 33 U.S.C.
§1311, prohibit absolutely the discharge of any pollutant not specifically authorized under Kodak's SPDES permit.

On December 28, 1992, the district court denied Atlantic States' motion
for partial summary judgment, granted Kodak's cross-motion for summary judgment, and dismissed the case. Atlantic States Legal Found., Inc. v. Eastman
Kodak Co., 809 F. Supp. 1040 (W.D.N.Y. 1992). Atlantic States appealed from
the judgment entered on that order. . . .

A.   *"Standards and Limitations" of the Clean Water Act*

Atlantic States argues first that the plain language of Section 301 of the
CWA, 33 U.S.C. §1311, prohibits the discharge of any pollutants not expressly
permitted. With regard to this claim, therefore, Atlantic States' standing to bring
this action turns on the merits of the action itself.

Section 301(a) reads: "Except as in compliance with this section and
sections 1312, 1316, 1317, 1328, 1342, and 1344 of this title, the discharge of
any pollutant by any person shall be unlawful." This prohibition is tempered,
however, by a self-referential host of exceptions that allow the discharge of
many pollutants once a polluter has complied with the regulatory program
of the CWA. The exception relevant to the instant matter is contained in
Section 402, which outlines the NPDES, 33 U.S.C. §1342(a), and specifies
the requirements for suspending the national system with the submission of
an approved state program, 33 U.S.C. §1342(b), (c). Section 402(k) contains
the so-called "shield provision," 33 U.S.C. §1342(k), which defines compliance
with an NPDES or SPDES permit as compliance with Section 301 for the purposes of the CWA's enforcement provisions. The Supreme Court has noted that
"The purpose of [Section 402 (k)] seems to be . . . to relieve [permit holders]
of having to litigate in an enforcement action the question whether their permits are sufficiently strict." E.I. du Pont de Nemours & Co. v. Train, 430 U.S.
112 (1977).

---

4. Specifically, the complaint alleged that Kodak had discharged "282,744 pounds
of unpermitted pollutants in 1987, 308,537 pounds in 1988, 321,456 pounds in 1989[,]
and 290,121 pounds in 1990," and that Atlantic States believed that Kodak continued to
discharge such pollutants.

Atlantic States' view of the regulatory framework stands that scheme on its head. Atlantic States treats permits as establishing limited permission for the discharge of identified pollutants and a prohibition on the discharge of unidentified pollutants. Viewing the regulatory scheme as a whole, however, it is clear that the permit is intended to identify and limit the most harmful pollutants while leaving the control of the vast number of other pollutants to disclosure requirements. Once within the NPDES or SPDES scheme, therefore, polluters may discharge pollutants not specifically listed in their permits so long as they comply with the appropriate reporting requirements and abide by any new limitations when imposed on such pollutants.[8]

The EPA lists tens of thousands of different chemical substances in the Toxic Substances Control Act Chemical Substance Inventory pursuant to 15 U.S.C. §2607(b) (1988). However, the EPA does not demand even information regarding each of the many thousand chemical substances potentially present in a manufacturer's wastewater because "it is impossible to identify and rationally limit every chemical or compound present in a discharge of pollutants." Memorandum from EPA Deputy Assistant Administrator for Water Enforcement Jeffrey G. Miller to Regional Enforcement Director, Region V, at 2 (Apr. 28, 1976). "Compliance with such a permit would be impossible and anybody seeking to harass a permittee need only analyze that permittee's discharge until determining the presence of a substance not identified in the permit." Id. Indeed, Atlantic States conceded at oral argument that even plain water might be considered a "pollutant" under its view of the Act.

The EPA has never acted in any way to suggest that Atlantic States' absolutist and wholly impractical view of the legal effect of a permit is valid. In fact, the EPA's actions and policy statements have frequently contemplated discharges of pollutants not listed under an NPDES or SPDES permit. It has addressed such discharges by amending the permit to list and limit a pollutant when necessary to safeguard the environment without considering pre-amendment discharges to be violations calling for enforcement under the CWA. 33 U.S.C. §§1319, 1365. The EPA thus stated in its comments on proposed 40 C.F.R. §122.68(a), which applied the "application-based" limits approach to implementation of the CWA reporting scheme,

> There is still some possibility . . . that a [NPDES or SPDES] permittee may discharge a large amount of a pollutant not limited in its permit, and EPA will not be able to take enforcement action against the permittee as long as the permittee complies with the notification requirements [pursuant to the CWA].

45 Fed. Reg. 33,516, 33,523 (1980). The EPA's statement went on to note that this possibility constituted a "regulatory gap," and that, "the final regulations control discharges only of the pollutants listed in the [NPDES or SPDES] permit

---

8. The cases Atlantic States cites are therefore inapposite because each involves either a failure to correctly disclose accurately the discharge of pollutants and thus comply with regulation or a failure to secure the requisite NPDES or SPDES permit. Atlantic States Legal Found., Inc. v. Reynolds Metals Co., 31 Env't Rep. Cas. (BNA) 1156, 1158 (N.D.N.Y. 1990) (failing to "apply proper detection"); United States v. Tom-Kat Development, Inc., 614 F. Supp. 613 (D. Alaska 1985) (failing to obtain permit); Kitlutsisti v. ARCO Alaska, Inc., 592 F. Supp. 832 (D. Alaska 1984) (failing to obtain permit), vacated on other grounds, 782 F.2d 800 (9th Cir. 1986); Love v. New York State Dep't of Envt'l Conservation, 429 F. Supp. 832 (S.D.N.Y. 1981) (failing to obtain proper permit).

application, which consist primarily of the listed toxic pollutants and designated hazardous substances." Id. In a clarification of EPA policy on Section 304, 33 U.S.C. §1314, and water quality-based effluent limitations, an EPA official recently stated that:

> EPA did not intend to require water quality-based permit limitations on all pollutants contained in a discharge. . . . The proper interpretation of the regulations is that developing water quality-based limitations is a step-by-step process. . . . Water quality-based limits are established where the permitting authority reasonably anticipates the discharge of pollutants by the permittee at levels that have the reasonable potential to cause or contribute to an excursion above any state water quality criterion. . . .

Memorandum from Director, Office of Wastewater Enforcement and Compliance to Water Management Division Directors, Regions I-X, at 2-3 (Aug. 14, 1992).

The EPA is the federal agency entrusted with administration and enforcement of the CWA. 33 U.S.C. §1251(d). As such, EPA's reasonable interpretations of the Act are due deferential treatment in the courts. Chevron, U.S.A., Inc. v. Natural Resources Defense Council, 467 U.S. 837, 844 (1984). . . . Because the EPA's implementation of the CWA is entirely reasonable, we defer to it. . . .

CONCLUSION

For the reasons stated above, we affirm the order of the district court granting summary judgment to Kodak.

NOTES AND QUESTIONS

1. Does the court's decision mean that a discharger with an NPDES permit legally can discharge any material not specifically restricted in its permit? What, if anything, would prevent a discharger from dramatically changing the nature of its discharges once it has been granted an NPDES permit?

2. How did the court and Atlantic States differ in their interpretations of the effect of the language of section 301 providing that "the discharge of any pollutant by any person shall be unlawful" except as in compliance with other provisions of the Clean Water Act? The court's decision, its interpretation of the statutory language, and EPA's history of implementation of the permit provisions of the Clean Water Act are criticized in Axline and McGinley, Universal Statutes and Planetary Programs: How EPA Has Diluted the Clean Water Act, 8 J. Envtl. L. & Litig. 253 (1993).

3. The court suggests that its interpretation of the Clean Water Act is justified because it would be impossible for EPA to identify and to regulate every one of the thousands of chemicals that are discharged by industrial facilities. Is it true that compliance with the Act would be impossible if the court accepted Atlantic States' view that the discharge of unidentified pollutants is prohibited?

4. How realistic is the fear expressed by EPA that if Atlantic States' view was accepted, "anybody seeking to harass a permittee need only analyze that permittee's discharge until determining the presence of a substance not identified in the permit"? How difficult would it be for citizen groups to sample and analyze discharges and to prove that pollutants are being discharged that are

unauthorized in a permit? If citizens were successful in proving such discharges, wouldn't permittees seek to have these discharges specifically addressed in their permits?

5. Does the court's decision preclude EPA from bringing an enforcement action against a permittee for discharges not addressed in an NPDES permit? In at least one other case a court has allowed the federal government to take enforcement action against discharges not regulated in an NPDES permit. United States v. Ketchikan Pulp Co., Civ. No. A92-587 (D. Alaska 1993).

6. In October 1994, Kodak agreed to pay a $5 million fine and to spend more than $60 million as a result of violations of federal hazardous waste laws at the plant targeted in Atlantic States' citizen suit. McKinley, Kodak Fined $5 Million for Toxic Chemical Leaks, N.Y. Times, Oct. 8, 1994, at 29.

7. In Northwest Environmental Advocates v. Portland, 56 F.3d 979 (9th Cir. 1995), the Ninth Circuit held that a citizen group could maintain an action against Portland, Oregon, for violations of water quality standards due to discharges from combined sewer overflow (CSO) outfalls even though the CSOs were not separately listed in the city's NPDES permit. Despite EPA's approval of the permit, the court held that because it was illegal for the permit not to establish technology-based effluent limits for the CSOs, the permit should be interpreted as covering those outfalls.

8. Implementation of the permit provisions of the Clean Air Act Amendments of 1990 eventually may produce a new wave of citizen suits. Section 504 of the Clean Air Act mandates new monitoring and reporting requirements that will facilitate citizen suits for permit violations. The 1990 Amendments specifically authorize the imposition of "appropriate civil penalties" in citizen suits, §304(a), and they direct that such penalties either be deposited into a special fund "to finance air compliance and enforcement activities," §304(g)(1), or "be used in beneficial mitigation projects" (limited to $100,000 per action) consistent with the Act to "enhance the public health or the environment." §304(g)(2).

PROBLEM EXERCISE: CITIZEN ENFORCEMENT OF THE CLEAN WATER ACT

On August 22, a volunteer for a local environmental group you represent informs you that a fish kill has been discovered in a nearby stream 500 yards downriver from an outfall pipe at a manufacturing plant. The plant has an NPDES permit issued by the state that limits the amount of phosphorus, nitrogen, and total suspended solids in discharges from its outfall. A friend who works at the plant subsequently informs you in confidence that an accident occurred at the plant on August 15 that caused a large quantity of toxic chemicals to spill into a holding tank. He tells you that similar accidents have occurred twice before during the five years he has worked at the plant. Although your friend does not know what happened to the chemicals, he notes that when he checked the holding tank on August 24, he discovered that it had been emptied.

On November 15, the environmental group checks with the state environmental agency to review the discharge monitoring report (DMR) the plant was required to file for August. After discovering that the plant failed to file a DMR for August, the environmental group asks you to file a citizen suit on their behalf. On November 25, you send a letter to the owner of the plant, the state environmental agency, and EPA informing them that you plan to file a citizen suit against the plant owner for failure to file a DMR for August and for discharging pollutants in violation of the plant's permit.

On March 25, you file a citizen suit against the owner of the plant, alleging that he has violated the Act by failing to file a DMR and by discharging pollutants in violation of the plant's NPDES permit. On April 7, the plant owner belatedly submits to the state environmental agency a DMR reporting no violations of the plant's permit during August.

Question One. Suppose that defense counsel, citing *Gwaltney,* files motions to dismiss and for summary judgment arguing that there is no ongoing violation because the missing DMR has now been filed, that the case is now moot, and that you lack standing since there is no relief available that would redress any injury to you. How would you respond? Is your case likely to survive the motion to dismiss? Would the result be different if the company filed the missing DMR the day before you filed your citizen suit?

Question Two. Suppose that after your lawsuit is filed the state environmental agency assesses a $1,000 administrative penalty against the owner of the plant for failing to file a DMR in timely fashion. The owner agrees to pay the penalty in return for the state's agreement not to pursue further investigation into the fish kill. Although you are outraged by what you perceive to be a sweet heart settlement, state law does not permit you to challenge it in court. Defense counsel renews his motion to dismiss, arguing that the penalty should bar your citizen suit because it is now moot and that you lack standing since there is no relief available that would redress your alleged injury. How would you respond? Who is likely to prevail on this issue? Would it make any difference if the administrative settlement included a pledge by the company not to violate its permit terms in the future? Would it make any difference if the state had commenced its administrative enforcement action on March 20? See section 309(g)(6). Is there any way to challenge the administrative settlement outside of state court? See sections 309(g)(4) and (6).

Question Three. Your friend who works at the plant reports that the employee responsible for preparing DMRs was told by the plant manager that the plant would be closed and he would lose his job if the company lost the citizen suit. Your friend is reluctant to testify at trial because he is certain he would be fired. Without your friend's testimony it will be impossible to link the plant to the fish kill. What protection is available to your friend under section 507 of the Clean Water Act?

Question Four. Suppose that the court reserves judgment on the motion to dismiss and the case proceeds to trial. With Perry Mason as your co-counsel, you succeed in having the employee responsible for preparing the DMR break down on the stand and confess that he falsified it to cover up deliberate discharge of the toxics. Under section 309 of the Clean Water Act, what is the potential criminal liability of the following persons for the filing of the false DMR or the deliberate discharge of the toxics: (1) the employee who prepared the DMR, (2) the plant manager, and (3) the owner of the company?

Question Five. Citing its tough policy of not tolerating violations of the environmental laws by its employees, the company then fires the employee who broke down on the stand and blames him for any violations. Is he entitled to protection under section 507? See section 507(d). If plant employees do not testify, what is the likely outcome of your citizen suit? If you win, what relief can the court grant and what penalties can be imposed on the company?

Question Six. Suppose the company is acquired by another firm pledging to "clean up" the plant in the wake of the adverse publicity concerning environmental violations. The acquiring firm had itself been in trouble with environmental officials for numerous violations of the Clean Water Act three years before. It hires an outside consultant to conduct an environmental audit at the plant. The audit discovers that for years plant employees routinely have been discarding vials containing toxic chemicals into a portion of the river upstream from the outfall pipe, which now has become a biological wasteland as a result of these discharges. This practice has saved the firm approximately $2 million in disposal costs. If the new firm promptly discloses these activities to the authorities and orders its employees to stop the practice, can it take advantage of EPA's self-auditing policy to seek a penalty reduction? Will the policy protect the workers against criminal liability? Should any penalty be imposed on the firm and, if so, how large should it be?

6. The Eleventh Amendment and Citizen Suits against States

In Seminole Tribe v. Florida, 517 U.S. 44 (1996), the Supreme Court revived the Eleventh Amendment by holding that Congress does not have authority to abrogate a state's Eleventh Amendment immunity from suit by private citizens under the Indian Commerce Clause. The 5-4 decision, featuring the same lineup of Justices as in United States v. Lopez, 514 U.S. 549 (1995), also overruled Pennsylvania v. Union Gas Company, 491 U.S. 1 (1989), which had held that the Interstate Commerce Clause gave Congress the power to abrogate states' Eleventh Amendment immunity for purposes of authorizing private cost-recovery actions against states under CERCLA.

The most significant impact of Seminole Tribe on environmental law enforcement may well be with respect to CERCLA liability itself, where states will no longer be liable for costs of removal or remediation in contribution actions by private parties. Because Eleventh Amendment immunity has not been extended to counties, municipalities, or other sub-state governmental units unless "the state treasury is vulnerable," Hess v. Port Auth. Trans-Hudson Corp., 513 U.S. 30 (1994), the CERCLA liability of such governmental units is not affected by Seminole Tribe. The decision does not preclude actions by federal authorities or citizen suits authorized by Congress for prospective injunctive enforcement of environmental laws, under the holding in Ex Parte Young, 209 U.S. 123 (1908).

The logic of Seminole Tribe's limitation on congressional authority to authorize citizen suits against states extends to environmental statutes other than CERCLA, insofar as those statutes are predicated on the Commerce Clause. However, while most of those statutes authorize civil penalties against states that violate the laws (see, e.g., 33 U.S.C. §§1362(5), 1365(a)(1), declaring that states are "persons" for purposes of the citizen suit provisions of the CWA, and making civil penalties available in such cases), monetary awards against states have played a relatively insignificant role in citizen enforcement actions. But see Cronin & Kennedy, Jr., Losing Our Day in Court, N.Y. Times, Apr. 4, 1996, at A25 (describing citizen suit against state prison for unlawful discharges of sewage). Seminole Tribe also leaves unaffected current doctrines governing liability of state officials acting in their individual capacities. See generally Wright v. Smith, 21 F.3d 496, 501 (2d. Cir. 1994) (reviewing categories of behavior that may render a state official individually liable, including direct participation, failure to remedy a subordinate's wrongdoing, creation of a policy or custom condoning wrongdoing, gross negligence, or deliberate indifference in supervising subordinates who commit wrongdoing).

In Bragg v. West Virginia Coal Association, 248 F.3d 275 (4th Cir. 2001), the Fourth Circuit held that a citizen suit seeking an injunction against West Virginia officials for violating the Clean Water Act and the Surface Mining Control and Reclamation Act (SMCRA) when issuing permits for mountain top mining practices was barred by the Eleventh Amendment. The court held that West Virginia did not waive its Eleventh Amendment immunity by participating in the SMCRA program, which grants "exclusive jurisdiction" to states with federally approved programs for regulating surface mining. The court refused to allow a citizen suit for prospective injunctive relief against the state director of the surface mining program under the *Ex parte Young* exception because it found that it was not necessary to "vindicate the supreme authority of federal law." Noting that under West Virginia law citizens could bring enforcement actions in state court, the Fourth Circuit declared that "[b]ecause West Virginia courts are open to such suits, the federal interest in maintaining the State's compliance with its own program may be fulfilled via suit in that forum, in a manner that does not offend the dignity of the State."

In Federal Maritime Commission v. South Carolina State Ports Authority, 535 U.S. 743 (2002), the Supreme Court held that state sovereign immunity bars the Federal Maritime Commission from adjudicating a private party's complaint against a nonconsenting state agency. Acknowledging that the text of the Eleventh Amendment did not support this result, the Court rested it on the importance of affording "States the dignity that is consistent with their status as sovereign entities." *Federal Maritime* could undermine implementation of the whistle-blower protection provisions of the environmental laws when whistle-blowers are state agency employees, as Justice Breyer pointed out in his dissent in the decision. See, e.g., Rhode Island Department of Environmental Management v. United States, 286 F.3d 27 (1st Cir. 2002).

F.   ENFORCEMENT AGAINST FEDERAL FACILITIES

Federal facilities have been some of the most notorious violators of the environmental laws. Although most federal environmental legislation is the product of concern over the inadequacy of decentralized regulatory approaches, federal environmental laws rely heavily on state authorities to administer and enforce the national programs. Enforcement against federal facilities has been particularly problematic.

Many of the environmental laws specify that their provisions are applicable to facilities owned or operated by federal agencies. For example, section 313(a) of the Clean Water Act provides that the federal government, its officers, agents, and employees "shall be subject to, and comply with, all Federal, State, interstate, and local requirements, administrative authority, and process and sanctions respecting the control and abatement of water pollution in the same manner, and to the same extent as any nongovernmental entity including the payment of reasonable service charges." Section 6001 of RCRA has virtually identical language. But federal agencies are not necessarily subject to the same sanctions as other violators of the environmental laws. Section 313(a) of the CWA provides that "the United States shall be liable only for those civil penalties arising under Federal law or imposed by a State or local court to enforce an order or the process of such court." RCRA section 6001 initially waived only federal immunity from sanctions for the enforcement of injunctive relief. EPA generally had been precluded from taking direct enforcement action against sister federal agencies, while states had been handicapped in recovering penalties from federal agencies due to narrow interpretations of waivers of sovereign immunity in the environmental laws. Congress amended RCRA in 1992 to make federal violators liable for civil penalties and to authorize EPA enforcement actions against them.

In 1990 the Congressional Budget Office found that the federal government was spending more money trying to bring its own facilities into compliance with the environmental laws than in administering the laws. CBO, Federal Liabilities Under Hazardous Waste Laws (May 1990). However, insufficient funding for environmental compliance and the absence of effective enforcement have contributed to serious compliance problems at some facilities owned or operated by federal agencies. In July 1988, the U.S. Department of Energy estimated that environmental cleanup at federal nuclear weapons facilities could cost between $66 to $100 billion. Department of Energy, Environmental, Safety, and Health Report for the Department of Energy Defense Complex (July 1, 1988). At the time, 32 federal land disposal facilities were on EPA's list of significant noncompliers with RCRA.

In United States v. Dee, 912 F.2d 741 (4th Cir. 1990), federal employees were convicted of criminal violations of RCRA for the first time. The defendants were engineers working for the United States Army who were convicted for knowing violations of RCRA's TSD standards. The Fourth Circuit rejected the argument that sovereign immunity barred the prosecution, stating that while "federal officers enjoy a degree of immunity for a particular sphere of official actions, there is no general immunity from criminal prosecution." Criminal prosecution of federal officials was one of the few effective sanctions for noncompliance when states were not permitted to impose civil penalties on federal facilities. However, there are substantial barriers to states' conducting criminal prosecutions for violators at federal facilities, including the fact that most crimes at such facilities occur on federal land. Smith, Shields for the King's Men: Official Immunity and Other Obstacles to Effective Prosecution of Federal Officials for Environmental Crimes, 16 Colum. J. Envtl. L. 1 (1991).

Justice Department officials argued that states should not be able to impose civil penalties for environmental violations by federal agencies because it would be a convenient means for states to line their coffers at federal expense while disrupting federal priorities for environmental compliance.

In Department of Energy v. Ohio, 503 U.S. 607 (1992), the Supreme Court held that federal agencies are immune from civil penalties for violations of the Clean Water Act and RCRA. Emphasizing that waivers of sovereign immunity must be unequivocal, the Court held that federal agencies are liable only for fines designed to induce them to comply with judicial orders to modify their behavior prospectively, and not for fines imposed as penalties for past violations. In dissent, Justice White complained that the Court's decision "deprives the States of a powerful weapon in combatting federal agencies that persist in despoiling the environment." 503 U.S. at 630.

The Supreme Court's decision was overridden in large part when Congress enacted the Federal Facility Compliance Act of 1992 (FFCA), Pub. L. No. 102-386 (1992), which President Bush signed into law on October 6, 1992. The FFCA expressly waives the federal government's immunity from civil penalties for violations of RCRA. The legislation that became the FFCA had actually passed both houses of Congress during the previous session in 1991, prior to the Supreme Court's DOE v. Ohio decision, which served as a catalyst for convening a conference committee and achieving final passage of the legislation.

The FFCA amended section 6001 of RCRA to waive federal sovereign immunity for civil or administrative penalties or fines, regardless of whether they are "punitive or coercive in nature or are imposed for isolated, intermittent, or continuing violations." This effectively overrode the Supreme Court's unanimous holding in DOE v. Ohio that the previous version of section 6001 did not waive federal sovereign immunity for punitive penalties. The FFCA also amended the definition of "person" in section 1004(15) of RCRA to "include each department, agency, and instrumentality of the United States," thus effectively overriding the Court's holding that federal facilities are immune from civil penalties under RCRA's citizen suit provision. However, the FFCA did not address the Court's holdings with respect to waivers of sovereign immunity in the Clean Water Act.

Opponents of the legislation had maintained that states could abuse their civil penalty authority to line their coffers at federal expense. In response to this concern, the legislation required that all funds collected by states for violations by federal agencies be used "only for projects designed to improve or protect the environment or to defray the costs of environmental protection or enforcement." While the term "environmental protection" is not defined in the FFCA, supporters of the Act maintained that it should be construed broadly to include wetlands protection and preservation of open space as well as pollution control. States with preexisting laws or constitutional provisions that bar earmarking of funds collected in enforcement actions are exempted from this limitation.

The Federal Facility Compliance Act also included provisions to force DOE to develop a plan for cleaning up the enormous quantities of mixed radioactive and hazardous waste it had generated. The Secretary of Energy was required to provide a comprehensive state-by-state inventory of the sources and amounts of such wastes to EPA and to the governor of each state where DOE stores or generates mixed wastes. This inventory had to include estimates of the amount of each type of mixed waste that DOE expected to generate at each of its facilities during the next five years and information concerning the technology available for treating such wastes. DOE was required to submit a detailed description of its plans for treating mixed wastes and for identifying and developing treatment technologies for wastes for which no treatment technology exists. EPA or states with delegated RCRA program authority had to review and approve the plans, which were then to be incorporated in administrative orders requiring compliance.

To improve EPA enforcement, the Act also amended section 3007(c) of RCRA to require EPA annually to inspect each federal facility used for the treatment, storage, or disposal of hazardous waste even in states authorized to administer the RCRA program. The 1984 Hazardous and Solid Waste Amendments had previously required such inspections only in states without delegated program authority. EPA was to be reimbursed for the costs of such inspections by the federal agency that owns or operates each facility. The initial EPA inspection had to include groundwater monitoring unless it had been performed during the year prior to enactment.

A particularly significant provision in FFCA authorized EPA to bring administrative enforcement actions against other federal agencies. While EPA had maintained that it had such authority under RCRA, the Justice Department maintained that it would violate constitutional principles of separation of powers for EPA to issue administrative orders against another executive agency, a position undermined by Morrison v. Olson, 487 U.S. 654, 695-696 (1988). The conference report describes the Act's express endorsement of EPA administrative enforcement actions against federal facilities as an effort "to reaffirm the original intent" of RCRA. 138 Cong. Rec. H8865 (Sept. 22, 1992 daily ed.). The report states that EPA should use its section 3008(a) administrative order authority against federal facilities for the same types of violations for which it is used against private parties. EPA had complained that other federal agencies were reluctant to negotiate compliance agreements with it because EPA had no credible threat of enforcement leverage to use against them in the absence of such an agreement. With this new authority, EPA will be able to move more rapidly to penalize recalcitrant agencies. FFCA requires that EPA give the defendant agency an opportunity to confer with the EPA administrator before any administrative order can become final.

The U.S. Court of Appeals for the Eleventh Circuit has held unconstitutional EPA's effort to use an administrative compliance order to impose sanctions on the Tennessee Valley Authority (TVA) for alleged violations of the new source review (NSR) provisions of the Clean Air Act. EPA alleged that projects the TVA characterized as routine maintenance and repair of its coal-fired power plants actually constituted major modifications that required the utility to obtain preconstruction permits imposing more stringent emissions limits. Rather than suing the TVA, another federal agency, in federal court, the EPA issued an administrative compliance order (ACO) against it pursuant to CAA section 113(a), 42 U.S.C. §7413(a). After the TVA conferred with EPA, as permitted under the Act, the EPA repeatedly modified the ACO and then directed the agency's Environmental Appeals Board (EAB) to informally adjudicate whether TVA had violated the CAA. After the EAB decided that the TVA had violated the Act, TVA sought review of this decision in the U.S. Court of Appeals.

In January, 2002, a panel of the Eleventh Circuit issued a decision finding that it had jurisdiction after rejecting the Department of Justice's arguments that the private utilities lacked standing and that there can be no justiciable controversy because the TVA and EPA are both federal agencies. In June 2003, the Eleventh Circuit reversed course and determined that it had no jurisdiction to review the EAB's decision. The court determined that ACOs did not constitute final agency action because it would be unconstitutional for EPA to be able to impose severe civil and criminal penalties for violating them without any adjudication or meaningful judicial review preceding their issuance. Tennessee Valley Authority v. Whitman, 336 F.3d 1236 (11th Cir. 2003). The court concluded that "EPA must prove the existence of a CAA violation in district court; until then, TVA is free to ignore the ACO without risking the imposition of penalties for noncompliance with its terms." 335 F.3d at 1239-1240. Because EPA already is pursuing civil suits against the private utilities involved in its NSR enforcement action, the impact of this decision is likely to be limited. It does not call into question EPA's administrative penalty authority under

§113(d) because this requires the use of formal adjudicatory procedures to determine whether a violation has occurred.

While the FFCA effectively overruled the RCRA portion of the holding in Department of Energy v. Ohio, the scope of the congressional waiver of sovereign immunity is even broader than the penalties at issue in that decision. Because the federal government is now subject "to the full range of available enforcement tools . . . to penalize isolated, intermittent or continuing violations as well as to coerce future compliance," the legislation also effectively precludes assertion by federal defendants of a *Gwaltney* defense in citizen suits alleging violations of RCRA. As the conference report explains:

> By subjecting the federal government to penalties and fines for isolated, intermittent, or continuing violations, the waiver also makes it clear that the federal government may be penalized for any violation of federal, state, interstate or local law, whether a single or repeated occurrence, notwithstanding the holding of the Supreme Court in Gwaltney of Smithfield, Ltd. v. Chesapeake Bay Foundation, Inc., 484 U.S. 49 (1987). [Id.]

While the enactment of FFCA overruled the holding of Department of Energy v. Ohio with respect to RCRA, federal facilities may remain immune from civil penalties for violation of the Clean Water Act because the latter are not addressed by the FFCA. For a pessimistic assessment of the effectiveness of the FFCA, see Kassen, The Inadequacies of Congressional Attempts to Legislate Federal Facility Compliance With Environmental Requirements, 54 Md. L. Rev. 1475 (1995).

The Ninth Circuit has upheld the right of states to seek penalties in state court from a federal agency for violating the Clean Air Act. After a California state air quality management district sought penalties in state court for Clean Air Act violations at an Air Force base, the Air Force removed the case to federal court. While the federal district court found the Air Force to be immune from penalties under the Clean Air Act, the Ninth Circuit reversed and ordered the case returned to state court. The Ninth Circuit held that the Clean Air Act specifically preserves the right of state and local governments to seek penalties from federal agencies in state court for violations of state and local air quality regulations. California ex rel. Sacramento Metropolitan Air Quality Management District v. United States, 215 F.3d 1005 (9th Cir. 2000).

=11=

Protection of the Global Environment

The continued poverty of the majority of the planet's inhabitants and excessive consumption by the minority are the two major causes of environmental degradation. The present course is unsustainable and postponing action is no longer an option.

—*Global Environment Outlook 2000**

We have entered a new era of public policy, defined by a growing number of concerns that straddle national borders. . . . [I]t poses a dual challenge. One is the need to transform international cooperation from its traditional place as "external affairs" into policy-making applicable to most, if not all, domestic issue areas. The second challenge is to develop the concepts and instruments needed to overcome problems of collective action. In particular this will require actions to "internalize externalities"—to deal with potentially contagious phenomena at the source, before they spill across borders.

—*Inge Kaul, Isabelle Grunberg & Marc Stern***

Perhaps the most stunning recent development in environmental policy has been the rapid rise of international concern for the environment. Environmental problems increasingly are viewed as transcending national borders and, in some cases, posing major risks to the health of the planet that could cause worldwide economic and social dislocation. The globalization of environmental concern is having a profound impact on international trade and diplomacy, stimulating the development of new international legal regimes that are assuming an increasingly important role in environmental policy.

The globalization of environmental problems is a product of many factors, including rapid worldwide population growth, the expanding scale of international economic activity, and improvements in scientific understanding of humankind's impact on earth's ecosystems. The world's population, estimated to be 6.1 billion people in 2002, is expected to rise to 9.3 billion by the year 2050 with virtually all population growth occurring in less developed countries. United Nations, World Population Prospects: The 2000 Revision (2001). As global economic activity continues to expand dramatically over the next several decades, the nations of the world will become even more interdependent, both economically and ecologically. Global environmental problems are what the World Commission on Environment and Development has termed

---

*Report of the United Nations Environment Programme, Sept. 15, 1999.

**Global Public Goods: International Cooperation in the 21st Century XXV (1999).

"interlocking crises," troubles spawned by the ecological impact of human activity and the scramble to meet the basic needs of a rapidly growing world population.

The link between poverty and environmental degradation is now widely recognized. It is estimated that 1.2 billion people do not have access to safe drinking water and that nearly 2.5 billion people lack proper toilets or sewage disposal systems. More than 5 million people die annually from water-borne diseases. Providing these people with basic human needs without taxing emerging limits on earth systems will require the creative application of technology, policy, and resources.

The process of "internationalizing" environmental law has continued even as domestic environmental laws have been subject to some rethinking. In 1970, the UN listed 52 environment-related treaties; by 1999 the number was 215. L. Brown, N. Lenssen & H. Kane, Vital Signs 1995 90-91 (1995); D. Roodman, Building a Sustainable Society, in State of the World 1999 177 (L. Bronn, C. Flowin & H. French eds., 1999); see also H. French, Partnership for the Planet (1995). By one estimate there are now more than 1,000 international legal instruments with at least one important environmental provision. Weiss & Jacobson, Getting Countries to Comply with International Agreements, Environment, July/Aug. 1999 at 17.

The importance of international forums is not limited to formal diplomatic negotiations. Environmental activists have found that even multinational oil companies and seemingly intransigent governments sometimes can be forced to change plans in response to protests, media coverage, and consumer boycotts. Hertsgaard, Are the French Headed for a Meltdown? Wash. Post, Sept. 3, 1995, at C5. The steady growth in international trade also has caused some industries to support voluntary environmental standards to provide a common baseline to apply even in countries with weak environmental laws. White, Sustainability and the Accountable Corporation, Environment, Oct. 1999 at 30-43.

After introducing international environmental law, this chapter explores a range of issues from ozone depletion and global warming to international trade and development policies. It emphasizes that international law is developed, implemented, and enforced very differently than U.S. law. The need to build consensus among states with vastly different cultures and resources presents great challenges to international law. However, there also are similarities as both legal regimes need to overcome scientific uncertainty and to balance short-term economic considerations with long-term environmental values. The growing role of nongovernmental organizations (NGOs) in a sphere traditionally dominated by states also offers interesting parallels to the importance of citizen participation in U.S. environmental law. The special problems of compliance and enforcement of international agreements are addressed in section E.

A.   INTRODUCTION TO INTERNATIONAL ENVIRONMENTAL LAW

Unlike domestic law, where common law, legislation, and constitutional provisions provide a relatively clear framework for the operation of environmental regulation, international law depends largely on negotiations and political relationships to define the rights and responsibilities of sovereign states. For the most part, international law operates with "little procedural hierarchy" and does not give any court or agency an "accepted primacy over another." M. Janis, An Introduction to International Law 8 (4th ed. 2003). Litigation and adjudication are rare. International law is "soft law" that is largely the product of international diplomacy and custom and whose enforcement depends less on "legal" sanctions than on "moral" suasion or fear of diplomatic retribution. Id. at 3.

INTERNATIONAL ENVIRONMENTAL LAW: A PATHFINDER

Treaties to which the United States is a party are published by the U.S. State Department in United States Treaties and Other International Agreements (UST). Prior to the appearance of the bound volumes of UST, slips of such treaties were published by the U.S. Government Printing Office (GPO) as Treaties and Other International Acts (TIAS). Treaties can be shepardized through Shepard's United States Citations: Statutes. The GPO also issues an annual publication, Treaties in Force: A List of Treaties and Other International Agreements of the United States. Many international documents can be accessed through the Electronic Information System for International Law at *http://www.eisil.org*.

Valuable *periodicals* include the Bureau of National Affairs' weekly International Environment Reporter, the monthly Department of State Bulletin, which reports on developments in international relations and is accessible through NEXIS, Environment magazine, and the European Environmental Review. A comprehensive, up-to-date compendium of documents relevant to public and private international law (including treaties to which the United States is not a party) can be found in the American Society of International Law's bimonthly publication, ILM: International Legal Materials, which is accessible through LEXIS. The Worldwatch Institute also publishes a bimonthly magazine entitled Worldwatch. Newsletters include UNEP News, published by the U.N. Environment Programme, and the OECD Observer.

The Worldwatch Institute publishes an annual State of the World report that reviews environmental trends, as does the World Resources Institute. The World Wildlife Fund's International Atlas of the Environment also provides valuable data on international environmental conditions. Greenpeace and the World Wildlife Fund are among the largest *environmental groups* active in the international arena. The Center for International Environmental Law in Washington and the Foundation for International Environmental Law and Development in London specialize in this area.

Useful textbooks include E. Brown Weis, S. McCaffrey, D. Magraw, P. Szasz & R. Lutz, International Environmental Law and Policy (1998) and D. Hunter, J. Salzman & D. Zaelke, International Environmental Law and Policy (2002).

Many valuable on-line sources for international environmental documents and information have become available, and new sources appear regularly. See generally Hunter, Salzman & Zaelke, supra at 1507-1521. The Climate Convention secretariat has a website with access to the most recent documents and information on the status of national ratification (*http://unfccc.int*). Web pages are also available for the World Bank and many United Nations agencies. The Earth Negotiations Bulletin (ENB), produced in Canada by the International Institute for Sustainable Development, provides daily journalistic summaries of developments at the most important international environmental negotiations. It has a website at *http:// www.iisd.ca/ linkages.* The American Society for International Law (ASIL) maintains an excellent webpage listing electronic resources in international environmental law at *www.asil.org/resource/env1.htm.* The webpage for the Hunter, Salzman and Zaelke textbook, located at *www.wcl.american.edu/pub/iel/index.html,* also is quite useful.

The clearest and most significant source of international environmental law is agreements between sovereign states. International treaties or conventions are akin to contracts in that they derive their legal force from the consent of the parties. Bilateral agreements to address cross-boundary environmental problems long have been popular. For example, the Boundary Waters Treaty of 1909 between the United States and Canada served as the basis for the *Trail Smelter* decision, and the Migratory Bird Treaty of 1916 between the same nations gave rise to the Supreme Court decision in Missouri v. Holland, 252 U.S. 416 (1920). While President Theodore Roosevelt's attempt to convene a world conference on conservation of natural resources failed in 1909, multilateral agreements, like the Montreal Protocol on Substances that Deplete the Ozone Layer, have now become an important means for addressing global environmental problems. The United States is a party to approximately one-third of these agreements, many of which have influenced the practices of nonsignatories. J. Sebenius, Grafting a Winning Coalition, in Greenhouse Warming: Negotiating a Global Regime 69, 70-71 (1991). For example, the United States has announced that it will abide by the provisions of the Biosafety Protocol to the Convention on Biological Diversity despite its failure to ratify the convention.

In the absence of express agreements between sovereigns, international law also can be derived from customary practices observed by nations in the course of their international relations, which give rise to reliance interests. The domestic practices of most or all states also can be a source for deriving general principles of international law. The assumption is that rules observed by nearly all sovereigns are sufficiently fundamental to be deemed a component of international law. M. Janis, An Introduction to International Law 5-6 (4th ed. 2003).

Like domestic common law, international law has rarely dealt effectively with transboundary pollution problems. The *Trail Smelter* arbitration in 1935 relied on common law nuisance principles, recognized in Missouri v. Illinois and Georgia v. Tennessee Copper, see Chapter 2, to hold a Canadian smelter liable for damage caused in the United States. The decision, however, is virtually the only case involving adjudication of a transboundary pollution dispute, and its precedential value is limited because it was founded on unusual stipulations and a bilateral agreement establishing procedures for resolving such disputes.

Developments in the Law—International Environment Law, 104 Harv. L. Rev. 1484, 1500-1501 (1991). See also the International Court of Justice decision on the Gabcikovo dam controversy, p. 1048. In addition to the problem of proving causal injury that has plagued the common law, there is no systematic set of legal procedures governing most international pollution disputes.

1. *The UN Conferences*

Efforts to develop general principles for resolving transboundary pollution disputes and for combating other international environmental problems have proceeded in both regional and global intergovernmental organizations (IGOs). In 1972, the United Nations convened the first Conference on the Human Environment in Stockholm. The 133 nations who were represented at the conference approved the Stockholm Declaration on Human Environment, which outlined international environmental rights and responsibilities in strong, but highly general, language. Principle I of the Stockholm Declaration provides that "Man has the fundamental right to freedom, equality and adequate conditions of life, in an environment of quality that permits a life of dignity and well-being." The Declaration states that governments have a responsibility to protect and improve the environment for both present and future generations. While it recognizes that nations have "the sovereign right to exploit their own resources pursuant to their own environmental policies," it declares that they also have "the responsibility to ensure that activities within their jurisdiction or control do not cause damage to the environment of other States or of areas beyond the limits of national jurisdiction." Stockholm Declaration on the Human Environment, Principle 21.

Although it left the development of more specific principles of international environmental law to future negotiation, the Stockholm Conference was a landmark event. It launched a process of international collaboration on environmental policy and led to creation of the United Nations Environment Programme (UNEP). International cooperation intensified after a follow-up conference in Nairobi, UNEP's headquarters, in 1982. The Nairobi Conference led to the creation of the World Commission on Environment and Development. In 1987, the Commission issued a report, entitled Our Common Future, which proposed that the UN develop an international convention outlining new environmental rights and responsibilities for all nations based on principles of sustainable development. Noting that no effective mechanism exists for settling international environmental disputes through binding procedures, the Commission proposed that new procedures be established to facilitate resolution of disputes parties are unable to resolve through negotiation.

UNEP's activities, and the Stockholm and Nairobi conferences, have helped to promote international environmental agreements, such as the Montreal Protocol, that address specific environmental problems. Petsonk, The Role of the United Nations Environment Programme (UNEP) in the Development of International Environmental Law, 5 Am. U. J. Int'l L. 351 (1990). The process initiated with the 1972 Stockholm Conference continued with the 1992 United Nations Conference on Environment and Development in Rio de Janeiro. The Earth Summit, as the Rio meeting was called, was an event of unprecedented size and complexity, an Olympics of international environmental negotiation larger than any previous international summit.

The 178 nations that attended approved a declaration of environmental principles called the Rio Declaration and adopted treaties that addressed global warming and the loss of biological diversity, as well as a nonbinding declaration of forest conservation principles. The most ambitious document, Agenda 21, which was also nonbinding, addressed in 800 pages almost every aspect of environment and development.

The agreements reached at the Earth Summit are comprised mainly of broadly worded principles with little force from the perspective of an American lawyer. For assessments of the Rio Declaration, see Wirth, The Rio Declaration on Environment and Development; Two Steps Forward and One Back, or Vice-Versa? 30 Ga. L. Rev. 599 (1995); M. Grubb et al., Earth Summit Agreements: A Guide and Assessment (1993); J. Nanda, International Environmental Law and Policy 103-131 (1994). Excerpts from the Rio Declaration appear below.

> ## United Nations Conference on Environment and Development, Declaration of Principles
> ### (1992)

The Conference on Environment and Development, ...

Recognizing the integral and interdependent nature of the earth, our home,

Proclaims that:

Principle 1. Human beings are at the center of concerns for sustainable development. They are entitled to a healthy and productive life in harmony with nature.

Principle 2. States have, in accordance with the Charter of the United Nations and the principles of international law, the sovereign right to exploit their own resources pursuant to their own environmental and developmental policies, and the responsibility to insure that activities within their jurisdiction or control do not cause damage to the environment of other states or of areas beyond the limits of national jurisdiction.

Principle 3. The right to development must be fulfilled so as to equitably meet developmental and environmental needs of present and future generations.

Principle 4. In order to achieve sustainable development, environmental protection shall constitute an integral part of the development process and cannot be considered in isolation from it. . . .

Principle 7. States shall cooperate in a spirit of global partnership to conserve, protect and restore the health and integrity of the Earth's ecosystem. In view of the different contributions to global environmental degradation, states have common but differentiated responsibilities. The developed countries acknowledge the responsibility that they bear in the international pursuit of sustainable development in view of the pressures their societies place on the global environment and of the technologies and financial resources they command.

Principle 8. To achieve sustainable development and a higher quality of life for all people, states should reduce and eliminate unsustainable patterns of production and consumption and promote appropriate demographic policies. . . .

Principle 13. States shall develop national law regarding liability and compensation for the victims of pollution and other environmental damage. States shall also cooperate in an expeditious and more determined manner to develop further international law regarding liability and compensation for adverse effects of environmental damage caused by activities within their jurisdiction or control to areas beyond their jurisdiction.

Principle 14. States should effectively cooperate to discourage or prevent the relocation and transfer to other states of any activities and substances that cause severe environmental degradation or are found to be harmful to human health.

Principle 15. In order to protect the environment, the precautionary approach shall be widely applied to states according to their capabilities. Where there are threats of serious or irreversible damage, lack of full scientific certainty shall not be used as a reason for postponing cost-effective measures to prevent environmental degradation.

Principle 16. National authorities should endeavor to promote the internalization of environmental costs and the use of economic instruments, taking into account the approach that the polluter should, in principle, bear the cost of pollution, with due regard to the public interest and without distorting international trade and investment.

NOTES AND QUESTIONS

1. What is the value of the UNCED Declaration? Does it articulate any new substantive principles of international environmental law? Does it create any new rights or provide any new remedies for addressing international environmental problems?

2. In language virtually identical to the 1972 Stockholm Declaration, the UNCED Declaration reaffirms each nation's right to exploit its own resources and its responsibility to prevent extraterritorial damage. How much guidance does the Declaration provide concerning how to balance the competing values implicated by environmental protection? Compare the Declaration's treatment of these issues with that of U.S. environmental law.

3. Tensions between developing countries and the industrialized world are reflected throughout the UNCED Declaration and have continued to be a central theme of negotiations on biodiversity, climate change, trade, and other international environmental issues. Other portions of the Declaration declare eradication of poverty to be "an indispensible requirement for sustainable development" and state that the needs of developing countries "shall be given special priority." Noting that environmental "[s]tandards applied by some countries may be inappropriate and of unwarranted economic and social cost to other countries," it recommends that further measures to address "transboundary or global environmental problems should, as far as possible, be based on an international consensus." Why is a provision on consensus-based approaches included in a set of principles on environment and development?

The World Summit on Sustainable Development

The World Summit on Sustainable Development (WSSD) met in Johannesburg, South Africa, in late August and early September 2002 to provide a ten-year review of progress since the Rio Conference. The mandate for the WSSD was a decision by the UN General Assembly in December 2000 to convene a review of progress since UNCED. In form and appearance, the WSSD shared much in common with the Earth Summit. The official attendance included over 21,000 participants from 191 countries, and several sites were employed over a wide area separating the political events from those of business and civil society. However, there were no new treaties or major agreements; eighty-two heads of state attended (compared with over 100 in 1992), but President Bush was among those who did not. The choice of South Africa was viewed as politically important in emphasizing the need for greater emphasis on African development and the linkages between poverty alleviation and sustainable development.

In contrast with 1992, the focus was primarily on more effective implementation of existing agreements rather than negotiation of new ones, an inherently more difficult task. "If Rio was a coming-of-age party for environmental issues on the global stage, Johannesburg was more like a mid-life birthday party, where the optimism of youth has been tempered by the realities of hard-won experience." H. French, World Summit Briefs, *www.worldwatch.org/worldsummit/briefs/20021022.html* (Oct. 15, 2002). For documents and links to related UN activities, see the website of the U.N. Department of Economic and Social Affairs, Division for Sustainable Development at *www.un.org/esa/sustdev/index.html.*

Several features of the meeting are worthy of note when compared with 1992. One was the much greater participation of non-state actors in the negotiation process. The level and character of private sector participation was also much greater than in 1992, when the concept of a shared interest between business and the environment was relatively new. See generally Hanneberg, From Rio to Johannesburg, Tomorrow, Aug. 2002, at 8-13. More than 100 CEOs and corporate heads attended. Numerous companies had exhibits making the case for their environmental concern and accomplishments, generating praise in some quarters and worries about growing corporate influence on the UN from others.

A second development since Rio was the understanding that sustainable development requires a broader understanding of the links between poverty and environmental degradation. "Unlike Agenda 21, the Plan of Implementation recognizes poverty as a running theme, linked to its multiple dimensions, from access to energy, water and sanitation, to the equitable sharing of the benefits of biodiversity." Summary of the World Summit on Sustainable Development, Earth Negotiations Bulletin, *www.iisd.ca/linkages/2002/wssd* (vol. 22, no. 51), Sept. 6, 2002. These issues were also given greater salience by the location of the meeting in Africa. A separate section was also included for the first time on globalization.

Finally, the WSSD process highlighted the need to include finance, development, and environmental ministries in an integrated approach to sustainable development. More ministers attended from non-environment ministries, and the need for synergy across political boundaries (linking the WSSD to a previous meeting on finance and forthcoming meetings on trade) was a frequent theme.

NOTES AND QUESTIONS

1. Has the summit model been exhausted by overuse and the added cost and complexity associated with increasing security concerns? Such events seem generally to have become less newsworthy in and of themselves, and the

availability of the Internet arguably reduces the need for bringing people together for information sharing. On the other hand, the periodic pressure to report on progress and debate emerging trends is difficult to replicate other than through an international summit.

2. Those concerned with developing more effective institutions of global environmental governance are debating several issues. See, e.g., Eileen Claussen, Global Environmental Governance: Issues for the New U.S. Administration, 43 Environment 29 (Jan./Feb. 2001). These include the following: How and to what extent should existing institutions of environmental governance be restructured or replaced? How can coordination between them be improved? Should a World Environmental Organization, on a par with the WTO, be created, or will more decentralized approaches, built on emerging models of collaborative governance, offer more promise of success? Should new patterns of international governance and political authority be developed, and, if so, how can they be reconciled with traditional notions of state sovereignty? Can truly enforceable international environmental obligations be created? International human rights law has evolved to alter older concepts of state sovereignty; how should international environmental law evolve? See also Maria Ivanova, Can the Anchor Hold? Rethinking the United Nations Environment Programme for the 21st Century (Yale FES Report No. 7, 2005).

3. Gus Speth, a founder of the Natural Resources Defense Council, Administrator of the UN Development Programme, and now Dean of the Yale School of Forestry and Environmental Studies, argues that a legalistic approach to global environmental problems was understandable, but with few exceptions has proven to be woefully inadequate. He cites numerous deficiencies: The UN agencies charged with oversight of these issues "are among the weakest multilateral organizations"; the negotiation processes "give maximum leverage to any country with an interest in protecting the status quo"; the diplomats in international negotiations lack "a shared political culture" that might facilitate agreement; and discussions are typically unable to overcome perceptions of "environment versus economy" and "North versus South." The UN conferences were in his view part of this faulty paradigm, producing a global agenda that "emerged and moved forward thanks primarily to a relatively small international leadership community" and produced outcomes "forged top-down at the international level." Consequently, he concludes, these processes "underscore the weak political base on which our concern for the global environment has rested." Speth concludes that "[i]n light of these barriers to progress, it is a wonder that any progress was made." James Gustave Speth, Red Sky at Morning (2004). If a legal approach has lost its way, what is the alternative? We return to this question at the end of the chapter.

2. International Adjudication of Environmental Disputes

Most international disputes that are adjudicated are decided by domestic, rather than international, courts. M. Janis, An Introduction to International Law 7 (2003). While some international tribunals have been established (e.g., the International Court of Justice (ICJ), the European Court of Justice, and the European Court of Human Rights), sovereign states are reluctant to accede legal responsibility to a foreign tribunal. Proposals to create an international body with authority to enforce standards of environmental conduct have been opposed by nations fearful of encroachments on their sovereignty. Hunter, Salzman & Zaelke, International Environmental Law and Policy 417-422 (1998). Arrangements for adjudicating transboundary environmental disputes through new regional legal structures eventually may prove more effective, although progress toward a strong European environmental program has so far been mixed. See Visch, Implementation and Enforcement of EC Environmental Law, 7 Geo. Intl. Envt'l L. Rev. 377 (1995); Helfer & Slaughter, Toward a Theory of Effective Supranational Adjudication, 107 Yale L.J. 273 (1997).

In 1997, the International Court of Justice (ICJ) released a rare decision on a dispute between Hungary and Slovakia over whether a dam construction project on their borders should be abandoned on environmental grounds. Following the collapse of communism, Hungary withdrew from the massive project that it had been building jointly with Czechoslovakia, pursuant to a 1977 treaty. On January 1, 1993 Czechoslovakia split into the Czech Republic and Slovakia. After Slovakia continued to pursue the project, Hungary sought relief in the ICJ. The Court's decision, which found fault with both parties and urged further negotiations to resolve the dispute, discussed the effect of new international environmental norms.

> ### International Court of Justice, Case Concerning the Gabcíkovo-Nagymaros Project (Hungary/Slovakia)
> #### 25 September 1997

111. Finally, the Court will address Hungary's claim that it was entitled to terminate the 1977 Treaty because new requirements of international law for the protection of the environment precluded performance of the Treaty.

112. Neither of the Parties contended that new peremptory norms of environmental law had emerged since the conclusion of the 1977 Treaty, and the Court will consequently not be required to examine the scope of Article 64 of the Vienna Convention on the Law of Treaties. On the other hand, the Court wishes to point out that newly developed norms of environmental law are relevant for the implementation of the Treaty and that the parties could, by agreement, incorporate them through the application of Articles 15, 19 and 20 of the Treaty. These articles do not contain specific obligations of performance but require the parties, in carrying out their obligations to ensure that the quality of water in the Danube is not impaired and that nature is protected, to take new environmental norms into consideration when agreeing upon the means to be specified in the Joint Contractual Plan.

By inserting these evolving provisions in the Treaty, the parties recognized the potential necessity to adapt the Project. Consequently, the Treaty is not static, and is open to adapt to emerging norms of international law. By means of Articles 15 and 19, new environmental norms can be incorporated in the Joint Contractual Plan.

The responsibility to do this was a joint responsibility. The obligations contained in Articles 15, 19 and 20 are, by definition, general and have to be transformed into specific obligations of performance through a process of consultation and negotiation. Their implementation thus requires a mutual willingness to discuss in good faith actual and potential environmental risks.

It is all the more important to do this because as the Court recalled in its Advisory Opinion on the *Legality of the Threat or Use of Nuclear Weapons,* "the environment is not an abstraction but represents the living space, the quality of life and the very health of human beings, including generations unborn" (I.C.J. Reports 1996, para. 29; see also paragraph 53 above).

The awareness of the vulnerability of the environment and the recognition that environmental risks have to be assessed on a continuous basis have become much stronger in the years since the Treaty's conclusion. These new concerns have enhanced the relevance of Articles 15, 19 and 20.

113. The Court recognizes that both Parties agree on the need to take environmental concerns seriously and to take the required precautionary measures, but they fundamentally disagree on the consequences this has for the joint Project. In such a case, third-party involvement may be helpful and instrumental in finding a solution, provided each of the Parties is flexible in its position. . . .

140. It is clear that the Project's impact upon, and its implications for, the environment are of necessity a key issue. The numerous scientific reports which have been presented to the Court by the Parties—even if their conclusions are often contradictory—provide abundant evidence that this impact and these implications are considerable.

In order to evaluate the environmental risks, current standards must be taken into consideration. This is not only allowed by the wording of Articles 15 and 19, but even prescribed, to the extent that these articles impose a continuing—and thus necessarily evolving—obligation on the parties to maintain the quality of the water of the Danube and to protect nature.

The Court is mindful that, in the field of environmental protection, vigilance and prevention are required on account of the often irreversible character of damage to the environment and of the limitations inherent in the very mechanism of reparation of this type of damage.

Throughout the ages, mankind has, for economic and other reasons, constantly interfered with nature. In the past, this was often done without consideration of the effects upon the environment. Owing to new scientific insights and to a growing awareness of the risks for mankind—for present and future generations—of pursuit of such interventions at an unconsidered and unabated pace, new norms and standards have been developed, set forth in a great number of instruments during the last two decades. Such new norms have to be taken into consideration, and such new standards given proper weight, not only when States contemplate new activities but also when continuing with activities begun in the past. This need to reconcile economic development with protection of the environment is aptly expressed in the concept of sustainable development.

For the purposes of the present case, this means that the Parties together should look afresh at the effects on the environment of the operation of the Gabcíkovo power plant. In particular they must find a satisfactory solution for the volume of water to be released into the old bed of the Danube and into the side-arms on both sides of the river.

NOTES AND QUESTIONS

1. Because it found some fault on both sides while failing to direct specifically what must be done to resolve the dispute, the decision by the ICJ in this

case was widely viewed as not resolving the controversy. Does the decision illustrate that international diplomacy remains more important than international "law" as a vehicle for resolving disputes between nations?

2. A separate opinion by ICJ Vice-President Weeramantry concluded that sustainable development is a principle with "normative value" crucial to the determination of the case.

B. PROTECTION OF THE GLOBAL ATMOSPHERE

The discovery that air pollutants are causing long-term, and potentially irreversible, damage to the global atmosphere has been a powerful catalyst for the development of international environmental law. Unlike transboundary pollution that primarily affects countries downwind or downriver, pollution of the Earth's atmosphere threatens serious damage to the entire planet. Mounting evidence of damage to this global commons has forced the countries of the world to join together in unprecedented efforts to develop international environmental controls.

Ozone depletion and global warming are the two principal problems caused by pollution of the global atmosphere. The discovery in 1985 of a hole in the Earth's ozone layer over Antarctica stimulated intense intergovernmental negotiations. These negotiations culminated in a remarkable diplomatic achievement, the signing of the Montreal Protocol on Substances that Deplete the Ozone Layer in September 1987.

The Montreal Protocol's innovative approach for implementing global, technology-forcing regulation in the face of widely disparate national interests and considerable scientific and technological uncertainty has become a model for the development of international environmental controls. The sections that follow explore the complex process that led to the Montreal Protocol and efforts to use it as a model for developing an effective international response to global warming.

1. Ozone Depletion

High in the Earth's stratosphere is a layer of ozone, an unstable compound of three oxygen atoms, that is essential to the health of the planet. Because ozone absorbs certain wavelengths of ultraviolet radiation, it protects the Earth from excessive radiation that otherwise would cause millions of skin cancer deaths, widespread blindness, and other serious health problems, as well as severe damage to plants and animals.

A. SCIENTIFIC WARNINGS

In 1974, two scientists from the University of California, Sherwood Rowland and Mario Molina, published a paper suggesting that the ozone layer could be threatened with destruction from a family of chemicals once hailed as a miracle of modern science. Chlorofluorocarbons (CFCs), chemicals used in a wide variety of industrial applications including aerosol propellants, foam blowing, air conditioning, and solvents, were discovered in the 1920s but only used widely beginning in the 1950s. Ironically, much of their attraction stemmed from their lack of other environmental risks—they are not toxic or flammable, and they have excellent insulating, cooling, and cleaning properties. Weisskopf, CFCs: Rise and Fall of Chemical "Miracle," Wash. Post, Apr. 10, 1988, at A1.

The remarkable stability of CFCs allows them to remain in the atmosphere for up to a century or more, unlike conventional air pollutants, which are broken down in a period of hours or days. Thus, Rowland and Molina hypothesized that CFCs would reach the upper atmosphere, where they could be broken apart by the intense energy of the sun, releasing chlorine. The chlorine would then act as a catalyst, converting ozone (O_3) to oxygen, destroying the Earth's protective ozone shield.

In the mid-1970s, the United States accounted for almost one-half of global CFC use, the majority of it used as propellants for aerosol sprays. As publicity focused on potential harm to the ozone layer, American consumers stopped buying aerosol sprays (including those without CFCs); in less than two years the market for products with such sprays dropped by two-thirds without any government regulation. R. Benedick, Ozone Diplomacy: New Directions in Safeguarding the Planet 31 (1991) (hereinafter Ozone Diplomacy); S. Anderson, K. Sharma & K. Brown, Protecting the Ozone Layer: The United Nations History (2002). The United States banned most aerosol propellant uses of CFCs in 1978, but few other nations followed suit.

Pressure for companies in the United States to develop alternatives to CFCs continued to build following a further warning of the threat to the ozone layer from the National Academy of Sciences in 1979. But this pressure evaporated in the early 1980s after equivocal research results and the Reagan administration's deregulation campaign resulted in the announcement that the United States would no longer support international controls. Convinced that further regulation was unlikely, U.S. companies shelved research to develop CFC substitutes.

In 1983, after William Ruckelshaus had succeeded Anne Gorsuch Burford as EPA administrator, the United States reversed its position and supported international controls. Not surprisingly, the United States advocated a policy based on what it had already done, that is, a worldwide ban on aerosol propellant uses of CFCs. The European governments, in turn, advocated a ban on construction of new capacity—a policy in effect in the European Community and without adverse economic consequences due to substantial excess CFC production capacity. Leaders of European industry and government "felt that the Americans had been panicked into 'over-hasty measures.' . . ." R. Benedick, Ozone Diplomacy 33 (1991). Finding agreement on regulation impossible, the parties in March 1985 approved the Vienna Convention to Protect the Ozone Layer, which established a framework to govern future scientific cooperation and negotiations.

While a major international research effort under the auspices of the World Meteorological Organization and UNEP was under way, scientists with the British Antarctic Survey published startling findings in May 1985. Based on measurements of springtime levels of ozone in the stratosphere over Halley Bay, Antarctica, they found that seasonal ozone loss had sharply accelerated to the point where a "hole" of greatly diminished ozone levels in the stratosphere had grown to cover an area the size of the United States. These findings were so astonishing that the scientists had delayed publication of them for three years while double-checking their accuracy. Because this discovery indicated that the ozone layer was in far greater jeopardy than previously thought, it spurred more detailed investigations and intensified international negotiations. In 1987, the Airborne Antarctic Ozone Experiment, using high-altitude airplanes, ground monitors, and satellites, launched studies that eventually found even greater ozone loss and linked it to the presence of human-made chemicals in the stratosphere. See CFCs and Stratospheric Ozone, 19 Ambio (Oct. 1990) (special issue).

B.   THE MONTREAL PROTOCOL

Even before international research could confirm the role of CFCs in ozone depletion, the discovery of the ozone "hole" had demonstrated the vulnerability of the ozone layer. This contributed to a heightened sense of urgency that spurred international negotiations based on the framework established by the Vienna Convention. Four negotiating sessions, beginning in Geneva in December 1986, culminated in the signing of the Montreal Protocol on Substances that Deplete the Ozone Layer in September 1987. The Protocol called for a freeze on production and consumption of CFCs and halons at 1986 levels, followed by a 50 percent reduction in CFC use by industrialized countries over a ten-year period. While developing countries were allowed to increase CFC consumption for ten years, trade restrictions were imposed on imports to, and exports from, nonparties to the Protocol.

The Protocol represented a remarkable diplomatic achievement given the obstacles to agreement on international environmental controls. First, the science of ozone depletion was highly uncertain throughout the entire negotiation process. S. Roan, The Ozone Crisis (1989). Year-to-year measurements of global ozone had shown no statistically significant changes. Estimates of eventual ozone loss—anticipated to occur decades later—actually had *declined* from about 18 percent in 1979 to only 3 percent in 1983. Despite the discovery of the ozone "hole," scientists were unable to link it precisely to CFCs until after the Protocol was completed (some environmentalists even had sought to delay negotiations in hopes that better evidence would become available). R. Benedick, Ozone Diplomacy 9-20 (1991).

To further challenge negotiators, CFCs had high economic value and powerful advocates in industry who argued that reasonable substitutes were unavailable for many applications. Public concern was evident in the United States, but some Europeans were skeptical of U.S. motives. At the outset of the negotiations, the United States, which already had taken unilateral action against aerosols, was virtually the only major country actively seeking CFC reductions. Moreover, developing countries maintained that it would be unfair to restrict their access to a technology that had contributed to development of the industrialized world. Finally, the concept of damage to the ozone layer was not easily translated into identifiable risks except for skin cancer, a relatively manageable disease that afflicts only a subset of the population. Id.; Mathews, Introduction and Overview, in Greenhouse Warming: Negotiating a Global Regime (J. Mathews ed., 1991).

Gus Speth cites four factors arguably most responsible for the successful conclusion of the Montreal Protocol:

- The problem was successfully defined in the public mind in terms of cancer and other serious public health threats;
- The proponents succeeded in making the "precautionary principle" the decision rule, as opposed to waiting for certainty;

- The issue was given a major boost by the discovery of the ozone hole, which effectively focused media and public attention; and
- The NGOs and other advocates of regulation were more effectively organized and out-hustled the opposition.

Speth at 182, citing Grundmann, The Strange Success of the Montreal Protocol, 10 Int'l Envtl. Aff. 197 (1998).

Two issues in the evolution of the Protocol merit particular attention:

1. The Role of Science. Richard Benedick does not attribute the success of the negotiations to the discovery of the ozone hole because its cause had not been established when the Protocol was signed. Others disagree, arguing that the ozone hole led to media and public interest that in turn influenced political perceptions. Benedick notes that close collaboration and communication between scientists and government officials played an important role in overcoming obstacles to agreement at several stages of the negotiations. R. Benedick, Ozone Diplomacy 78-79 (1991). Scientists played an important role not only in the formulation of national policy but also as an informal transnational network outside government control.

2. Technology Forcing and the Role of Industry. The response of industry to the Protocol is remarkable as an example of technology forcing. As late as the spring of 1986, CFC producers were aggressively insisting that substitutes were not feasible and that regulation would be ruinous for many industries. Miller, Cleaning the Air While Filling Corporate Coffers: Technology Forcing and Economic Growth, 1990 N.Y.U. Ann. Survey Am. L. 69 (1991). After the Protocol was signed, substitutes for CFCs were announced at an astonishing rate, and their projected costs declined steadily. By mid-1989, industry accepted the feasibility of a complete phaseout of CFCs, and EPA estimated that a total phaseout would cost less than it had projected for a 50 percent reduction only two years earlier. While chemical companies produced substitutes, about half the market went to not-in-kind alternatives or process changes, rather than proprietary chemicals. Some CFC substitutes were found to offer superior performance. Pollack, Moving Fast to Protect the Ozone Layer, N.Y. Times, May 15, 1991, at D1. OTA, Environmental Policy Tools: A User's Guide (1995); Barrett, Montreal v. Kyoto: International Cooperation and the Global Environment, in Global Public Goods 192-219 (I. Kaul, I. Grunberg & M. Stern eds., 1999).

C.   Accelerating the Phaseout

In March 1988, the Ozone Trends Panel, a team of more than 100 scientists from 10 countries, released the results of 16 months of research using newly developed methodology to analyze all previous measurements of the ozone layer. The Panel's alarming findings showed that significant ozone depletion already had occurred over heavily populated areas of the northern hemisphere, that a "large, sudden, and unexpected" decline in ozone levels had occurred over Antarctica, and that an ozone "hole" might soon be found over the Arctic and mid-latitudes of the northern hemisphere. The Panel was able to conclusively link CFCs and halons to ozone depletion for the first time. Kerr, Stratospheric Ozone Is Decreasing, 239 Science 1489 (1988).

In June 1990, under the Protocol review provisions described by Benedick, the parties met in London to consider measures to strengthen the Protocol.

There were two priorities: agreement on faster, more comprehensive emission reductions, and participation from the major developing nations to avoid increased use by nonparties. The latter was problematic as the major developing nations, especially India and China, were quick to point out that roughly 90 percent of the world's CFCs had been used by nations with less than a quarter of the world's population.

Negotiating a phaseout of CFCs proved easier than working out an agreement with developing countries. The European Community, now fully converted, sought the most rapid timetable for emission reductions. The final agreement provided for the total elimination of CFC production and use by 2000, with scheduled interim reductions by 1993, 1995 and 1997. Separate reduction schedules were established for halons and other ozone-depleting chemicals. Developing countries were again extended an additional ten-year grace period and the possibility of continued use of halons if "necessary to satisfy essential uses for which no adequate alternatives are available." Restrictions on hydrochlorofluorocarbons (HCFCs), chemicals with about .02 of the ozone-depleting potential of CFCs due to shorter atmospheric lifetimes, were debated but left for future consideration. See generally Bryk, The Montreal Protocol and Recent Development to Protect the Ozone Layer, 15 Harv. Envtl. L. Rev. 275 (1991).

The participation of developing nations quickly became primarily a question of money. The parties agreed to establish a multilateral fund with an initial commitment of $240 million. The fund is managed by a secretariat and governed by a 14-nation council equally divided between donors and recipient nations. The processing of applications, design of projects, and distribution of funds is handled primarily by the World Bank and UN Development Programme. See the website of the Multilateral Fund for the Implementation of the Montreal Protocol at *www.multilateralfund.org.*

As evidence accumulated that ozone depletion had progressed much further than expected, concern grew that even the accelerated phaseout agreed to in London might be inadequate. The European Community responded by further accelerating its own phaseout of CFCs, shortening the deadline by three years to 1997. EPA bested the EC's new timetable by a year when it announced in February 1992 that it would require the phaseout to be completed in the United States by 1996. This continued acceleration of the phaseout was driven largely by two factors: scientific data revealing even greater damage to the ozone layer, and the discovery that the phaseout would be far less costly than initially anticipated.

U.S. production of ozone-depleting substances has varied over time— surging until environmental concerns were raised in the mid-1970s, falling sharply, and then increasing again until the Montreal Protocol's restrictions took effect. Their ultimate phasedown was accomplished through use of a market-based approach to regulation. Rather than attempting to determine what emissions reductions each of the five U.S. producers of CFCs were capable of achieving, EPA gave each company tradeable permits for CFC production based on its 1986 production level. As the annual supply of permits declined to comply with the Protocol, companies could ensure that reductions were achieved in the most efficient manner by buying and selling the diminishing pool of CFC production rights.

To create further incentives for finding substitutes for ozone-depleting compounds, Congress imposed an escalating tax on such substances that in 1990 more than doubled, and in 1995 more than tripled, the pre-regulation price of CFCs. The powerful price signal created by this tax helped reduce dramatically consumption of ozone-depleting compounds. Indeed, CFC production fell so much faster than anticipated that the tax raised only half of the $6 billion it had been expected to raise between 1990 and the end of 1995.

NOTES AND QUESTIONS

1. What lessons can be learned from the acceleration of the Montreal Protocol's phaseout? A World Resources Institute review of the experience suggests some themes: (1) it is crucial to establish environmental goals in a manner that permits adjustments to reflect new scientific information; (2) market-based approaches to regulation can help government and industry implement regulatory policy with greater flexibility and at lower cost; (3) industries "can find ways to innovate and gain competitive advantages in response to environmental challenges." Cook, Marking a Milestone in Ozone Protection: Learning from the CFC Phase-Out 12-13 (1996). Jessica Mathews observes that "CFCs seemed irreplaceable only because there had never been a reason to look for substitutes." She notes that "[o]nce there was a need to replace them, a modest economic incentive (in this case a tax) and enough time to develop alternatives, innovation bloomed." Mathews, Clean Sweeps: Two Success Stories for the Environment, Wash. Post, Dec. 18, 1995, at A23.

2. Retail prices of CFCs skyrocketed with regulation and continuing demand, particularly for car air conditioners in all models prior to 1993. The federal tax created powerful incentives to develop substitutes, but it also made noncompliance more profitable. A large black market developed as CFCs purchased abroad, sometimes falsely labeled recycled, were smuggled into the United States to avoid the $5.35 per pound federal tax. Halpert, Freon Smugglers Find Big Market, N.Y Times, Apr. 30, 1995, at A1; "Focus Report," Global Envtl. Change Rep., Mar. 12, 1999 at 1. As production of CFCs in the developing countries is gradually eliminated—a process well along by mid-1999—this problem should correspondingly diminish.

3. One exception to the record of technical and economic success in replacing ozone-depleting chemicals has been a continuing debate about the use of methyl bromide, a gas widely used for pest eradication in the storage and shipping of grain as well as for production of berries and other high-value food crops. Beginning in 2003, the United States requested "essential use" exemptions under provisions of the Montreal Protocol to use about 21 million pounds in 2005, an increase relative to 2003, and to keep millions of pounds of the chemical in production until at least 2008. The Department of Agriculture also announced that either methyl bromide fumigation or blasting with high heat will be required for shipping products to the United States in wood containers. The shift in U.S. policy was criticized by both environmentalists and chemical companies that invested in producing substitutes for ozone-depleting compounds—including DuPont, which invented CFCs. A DuPont official noted, "The companies that stepped up and did the right thing are penalized for it." Former EPA Administrator William Reilly noted, "Asbestos, lead, PCBs—all of those were efficient products and all played an important role in the economy at the time and were a source of significant revenues to manufacturers and were convenient to consumers. And we phased out every one. This is not unprecedented." Rebecca Adams, Ozone v. Food Supply, A Chemical Dilemma, CQ Weekly, Sept. 5, 2005.

2.   Global Climate Change

Many scientists believe that, as a result of the buildup of carbon dioxide and other gases in the atmosphere, the Earth is on the verge of unprecedented global climate change. If predictions of a worldwide temperature increase of 3-8° Fahrenheit by the middle of the twenty-first century prove accurate, many fear widespread disruption of the Earth's ecosystems, a rise in sea level, increased drought, and potentially vast environmental and economic damage.

A.   SCIENCE AND THE "GREENHOUSE EFFECT"

The "greenhouse effect" at the root of global warming is very much a part of the evolution of climate and life on Earth. As Figure 11.1 indicates, carbon dioxide (CO_2) is known to have been present at a concentration of about 280 ppm in the atmosphere in the mid-eighteenth century prior to the industrial revolution. Since then its concentration has increased by about 30 percent to approximately 360 ppm by 1997. Roughly half of that increase has occurred since 1970. Council on Environmental Quality, Environmental Quality—1997 Report 194 (1999). Carbon dioxide, CFCs, and methane are the most significant gases that have an effect crudely comparable to that of the glass in a greenhouse—they allow visible light to pass through the atmosphere. Heat radiated from the Earth is transmitted in a different form, as infrared rays, and much of it is trapped by these gases, resulting in a net warming effect.

Measurements of ice cores show much higher concentrations of carbon dioxide and much warmer temperatures today than in previous epochs. Further physical proof of the greenhouse effect is provided by study of other planets: Mars, with virtually no atmosphere, is a frozen wasteland, while Venus, with an atmosphere largely comprised of carbon dioxide, is as hot as an oven. Schneider, The Greenhouse Effect: Science and Policy, 243 Science 771 (1989).

FIGURE 11.1
Atmospheric Concentrations of Carbon Dioxide, 1764-1998

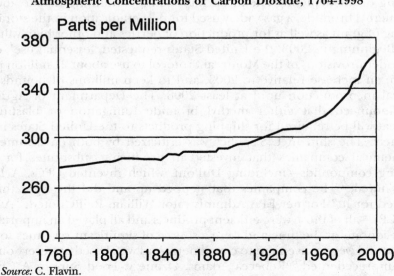

Source: C. Flavin.

While the greenhouse effect is a part of nature, the rapid increase in the atmospheric concentrations of greenhouse gases is directly caused by human-kind's activities. The combustion of fossil fuels releases carbon dioxide; coal releases almost twice as much per unit of energy as natural gas, while oil is about halfway in between. Since trees store carbon dioxide as they grow, cutting and burning of trees (as is occurring on a vast scale in tropical rain forests) releases carbon dioxide while simultaneously reducing the amount of carbon dioxide being removed from the atmosphere by forests. Other significant greenhouse gases include methane and nitrous oxides, both of which are emitted by the use of fossil fuels and also from agriculture and other human activities. A new source of concern is the realization that some alternatives to CFCs are potent greenhouse gases.

The problem of controlling emissions of greenhouse gases is exacerbated by their distribution. Western industrialized countries accounted for over two-thirds of CFC use in the mid-1980s but only about 40 percent of greenhouse gas emissions. The use of fossil fuels is increasing far more rapidly in developing countries than in industrialized nations. Developing countries are projected to account for more than 50 percent of carbon emissions from fossil fuels in a few decades. The countries that are the largest sources of carbon emissions from fossil fuels are indicated in Figures 11.2 and 11.3.

The magnitude and pace of global warming are difficult to predict for many of the same reasons weather forecasts remain unreliable—localized climate is a chaotic system, subject to sudden and unanticipated changes. Moreover, year-to-year variations in temperatures can mask long-term trends. Despite a growing consensus that some global warming will occur, there also is great uncertainty concerning the severity of its consequences. Some of the more likely effects include a gradual rise in sea level accompanied by flooding of coastlines and loss of wetlands, localized damage to agriculture and forests, and species loss. Warmer temperatures could exacerbate air pollution, increase the severity of tropical storms, and change the world in other, unexpected ways. See Woodwell, The Effects of Global Warming, in J. Leggett, Global Warming: The Greenpeace Report 116-132 (1990); J. Smith & D. Tirpak, The Effects of Climate Change on the United States (1990); K. Fredrick & P. Gleick, Water and Global Climate Change (1999); David Suzulei Foundation, Taking Our Breath Away (1998).

FIGURE 11.2
Carbon Emissions by Country, 2000

Rank	Country	Total Emissions (million tons)	Emissions per Person GNP (tons)	Emissions Growth 1990-2000 (percent)
1.	United States	5,762	20.2	17.9
2.	China	3,473	2.7	39.3
3.	Russia	1,540	10.6	−32.1
4.	Japan	1,225	9.6	12.3
5.	India	1,008	1.0	63.7
6.	Germany	837	10.2	−15.2
7.	UK	558	9.5	−3.3
8.	Canada	521	16.9	22.1

Source: World Resources Institute.

FIGURE 11.3
Carbon Emissions from Fossil Fuel Burning, by Economic Region, 1950-1998

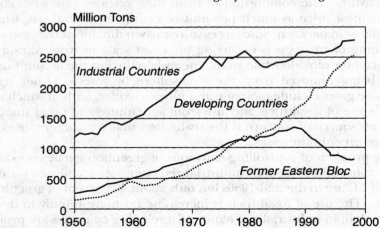

Source: ORNL, BP.

In an effort to reach international consensus on climate change, two UN agencies, the World Meteorological Organization and UNEP, organized an Intergovernmental Panel on Climate Change (IPCC) in 1988. The IPCC is composed of nearly 2,500 independent scientists from more than 100 countries who are charged with reviewing and summarizing what is known about climate change. Its reports are reviewed and approved by governments.

In 1990, the IPCC released its first report summarizing the scientific knowledge about climate change. The report found that it is "certain" that "there is a natural greenhouse effect which already keeps the Earth warmer than it would otherwise be" and that "emissions resulting from human activities are substantially increasing the atmospheric concentrations of the greenhouse gases." IPCC, Scientific Assessment xi (1990). The report "calculated with confidence" that global mean temperatures would increase at a rate of about 0.3° per decade and that global mean sea levels would rise about 6 cm per decade during the next century under a "business-as-usual scenario" in which emissions continue to rise steadily.

The IPCC issued its first major reassessment of the state of science concerning climate change in 1995. The report's most widely quoted finding was that "the balance of evidence suggests that there is a discernible human influence on global climate." In February 2001, the IPCC issued another reassessment warning that the magnitude of global warming will be even greater than previously thought. Intergovernmental Panel on Climate Change, Third Assessment Report (2001). The IPCC report concluded that average global temperatures will rise by between 2.5 and 10.4 degrees Fahrenheit by 2100, a 60 percent increase over the level forecast just six years ago. The IPCC found that there is new and stronger evidence that most of the warming observed over the last 50 years is attributable to human activities, which will continue to change the composition of the atmosphere throughout the twenty-first century.

Following the issuance of the IPCC report, the Bush administration asked the National Academy of Sciences (NAS) to perform its own assessment of the state of scientific knowledge concerning climate change. On June 6, 2001, the NAS's National Research Council released its report, Climate Change

Science: An Analysis of Some Key Questions. The report, prepared by a committee of eleven of the nation's leading climate scientists, confirmed the findings of the IPCC and concluded that global warming could well have "serious adverse societal and ecological impacts by the end of this century." The report agreed that the climatic changes observed during the past several decades are most likely due to human activities, although the committee could not rule out the possibility that the climate's natural variability could be responsible for a significant portion of the trend. The NRC agreed that human-induced warming and sea level rise are expected to continue through the twenty-first century and beyond, although current predictions of the magnitude and rate of future warming "should be regarded as tentative and subject to future adjustments (either upward or downward)." The following is an excerpt of some of the NRC's key conclusions.

National Research Council, Climate Change Science: An Analysis of Some Key Questions
(2001)

• *Are greenhouse gases causing climate change?*

The IPCC's conclusion that most of the observed warming of the last 50 years is likely to have been due to the increase in greenhouse gas concentrations accurately reflects the current thinking of the scientific community on this issue. The stated degree of confidence in the IPCC assessment is higher today than it was ten, or even five years ago, but uncertainty remains because of (1) the level of natural variability inherent in the climate system on time scales of decades to centuries, (2) the questionable ability of models to accurately simulate natural variability on those long time scales, and (3) the degree of confidence that can be placed on reconstructions of global mean temperature over the past millennium based on proxy evidence. Despite the uncertainties, there is general agreement that the observed warming is real and particularly strong within the past twenty years. Whether it is consistent with the change that would be expected in response to human activities is dependent upon what assumptions one makes about the time history of atmospheric concentrations of the various forcing agents, particularly aerosols.

• *By how much will temperatures change over the next 100 years and where?*

Climate change simulations for the period of 1990 to 2100 based on the IPCC emissions scenarios yield a globally-averaged surface temperature increase by the end of the century of 1.4 to 5.8° C (2.5 to 10.4° F) relative to 1990. The wide range of uncertainty in these estimates reflects both the different assumptions about future concentrations of greenhouse gases and aerosols in the various scenarios considered by the IPCC and the differing climate sensitivities of the various climate models used in the simulations. The range of climate sensitivities implied by these predictions is generally consistent with previously reported values.

The predicted warming is larger over higher latitudes than over low latitudes, especially during winter and spring, and larger over land than over sea. Rainfall rates and the frequency of heavy precipitation events are predicted to increase, particularly over the higher latitudes. Higher evaporation rates would accelerate the drying of soils following rain events, resulting in lower relative humidities and higher daytime temperatures, especially during the warm season. The likelihood that this effect could prove important is greatest in semi-arid regions, such as the U.S. Great Plains. These predictions in the IPCC report are consistent with current understanding of the processes that control local climate. . . .

- *What will be the consequences of global warming (e.g., extreme weather, health effects) of increases of various magnitude?*

In the near term, agriculture and forestry are likely to benefit from carbon dioxide fertilization and an increased water efficiency of some plants at higher atmospheric CO_2 concentrations. The optimal climate for crops may change, requiring significant regional adaptations. Some models project an increased tendency toward drought over semi-arid regions, such as the U.S. Great Plains. Hydrological impacts could be significant over the western United States, where much of the water supply is dependent on the amount of snow pack and the timing of the spring runoff. Increased rainfall rates could impact pollution runoff and flood control. With higher sea level, coastal regions could be subject to increased wind and flood damage even if tropical storms do not change in intensity. A significant warming also could have far reaching implications for ecosystems. The costs and risks involved are difficult to quantify at this point and are, in any case, beyond the scope of this brief report.

Health outcomes in response to climate change are the subject of intense debate. Climate is one of a number of factors influencing the incidence of infectious disease. Cold-related stress would decline in a warmer climate, while heat stress and smog induced respiratory illnesses in major urban areas would increase, if no adaptation occurred. Over much of the United States, adverse health outcomes would likely be mitigated by a strong public health system, relatively high levels of public awareness, and a high standard of living.

Global warming could well have serious adverse societal and ecological impacts by the end of this century, especially if globally-averaged temperature increases approach the upper end of the IPCC projections. Even in the more conservative scenarios, the models project temperatures and sea-levels that continue to increase well beyond the end of this century, suggesting that assessments that examine only the next 100 years may well underestimate the magnitude of the eventual impacts.

- *Has science determined whether there is a "safe" level of concentration of greenhouse gases?*

The question of whether there exists a "safe" level of concentration of greenhouse gases cannot be answered directly because it would require a value judgment of what constitutes an acceptable risk to human welfare and ecosystems in various parts of the world, as well as a more quantitative assessment of the risks and costs associated with the various impacts of global warming. In general, however, risk increases with increases in both the rate and the magnitude of climate change.

Climate Science: The Continuing Debate

The next IPCC Assessment Report is scheduled to be released in 2007. In the interim, the scientific debate on the causes and risks associated with the ongoing buildup of greenhouse gas emissions continues. The intense skepticism of climate change in some circles was captured in a novel by Michael Crichton, State of Fear, in which the villains are eco-terrorists seeking to create the appearance of natural disasters in order to enhance public belief in climate change. (The novel also includes extensive footnotes to scientific journals, a lengthy annotated bibliography, and a summary of the author's views in an effort to add credibility to its aggressive skepticism toward climate change.) Although not a scientist, Crichton was given opportunities to express his views before the Senate Environment and Public Works Committee as well as on national television. The concern that public discussion of climate change might be biased by politically motivated interventions was fueled by reports in 2005 showing that a Bush administration official with a background in the petroleum industry had edited a summary report on climate change to emphasize doubts. Revkin, Bush Aide Edited Climate Reports, N.Y. Times, June 8, 2005, at 1. The journalistic tendency to report both sides of every issue without noting the extent to which one "side" is actually the vast majority of scientific opinion led one group of climate scientists to establish a website with the purpose of presenting neutral scientific information: *www.realclimate.org*.

On the other hand, the unusual number and severity of hurricanes in 2005 led Time magazine to query whether climate change might be responsible. As hurricanes derive their energy from ocean temperatures, this linkage has some logic but as yet is not agreed upon by scientists. Research by Kerry Emanuel, an atmospheric physicist at MIT, concludes that the total power released by storms has increased dramatically in recent decades. This is consistent with warming in the tropical oceans, although not proof of cause and effect. R. Monastersky, "Stronger Hurricanes? Researchers Debate Whether Global Warming Will Make Storms More Destructive," Chronicle of Higher Education, Sept. 8, 2005. For a review of research on this topic, see the website of the Pew Climate Center, *www.pewclimate.org*. Other recent research found a striking parallel between the pattern of ocean warming with actual measurements since the 1960s, a development they argue cannot be explained by any natural temperature variations. R. Monastersky, "Researchers Present What They Call Conclusive Evidence of Global Warming from Greenhouse Gases," Chronicle of Higher Education, Feb. 18, 2005.

Another striking empirical development supporting climate change has been a steady decline in summer Arctic sea ice, which climate models now predict will disappear in coming decades with untold consequences. Revkin, "No Escape: Thaw Gains Momentum," N.Y. Times, Oct. 25, 2005. The magnitude of changes in the Arctic has been of particular scientific concern as summarized in an 1800-page international consensus report Impacts of a Warming Arctic, released in November 2004.

Whether or not related to climate change, Hurricane Katrina demonstrated the wide reach and economic impact of weather-related natural disasters. Insurance losses are expected to amount to $40 billion or more, with total costs many times greater. Proposals for rebuilding New Orleans and surrounding areas are also likely to have costs in the tens of billions. Indirect costs included a substantial rise in national natural gas and oil prices due to the shutdown in regional production. Midwest farmers dependent on Mississippi River barges for export of corn and soybeans estimated their losses at $2 billion. "Alarm Growing on Storm's Cost for Agriculture," N.Y. Times, Sept. 8, 2005. The succession of natural disasters was particularly worrisome for insurance companies, who may have to rewrite policies and increase premiums. "A New Worry for Insurers," Washington Post, Oct. 5, 2005, at D1. See also Center for Health and the Global Environment, Climate Change Futures: Health, Ecological and Economic Dimensions (2005).

The IPCC process has become an important precedent for building international scientific consensus on other international environmental issues. The Millenium Ecosystem Assessment was initiated in 2001 to assess the consequences of ongoing changes in the ecosystem (including climate change) for human well-being. The final report, Living Beyond Our Means: Natural Assets and Human Well-Being, was released in March 2005. Preparation of the report involved more than 1300 scientists from 95 countries. The Report documents the unprecedented rate of change in the Earth's natural systems. For example, more land has been converted to crop land since WW II than in the previous two centuries, and more than 20 percent of coral reefs and 35 percent of mangroves have been lost in the last several decades. As much as 30 percent of all bird, mammal, and amphibian species are now threatened with extinction. The Report outlines a broad range of response measures including policies, business leadership, and local action that can reverse these trends. The report is available on-line at *www.millenniumassessment.org.*

B. LEGAL AND POLICY RESPONSES TO GLOBAL WARMING AND CLIMATE CHANGE

As noted above, substantial uncertainties surround assessments of global warming, including its timing, pace, magnitude, and distribution of impacts. Faced with a problem that involves both high risk and high uncertainty, how should society respond? The understandable political response is to avoid policies with costs or consequences that risk offending powerful economic interests (compare the evolution of acid rain policy) while seeking further information. See, e.g., letter to the editor from Senators Hagel and Murkowski, High Costs of Kyoto, Wash. Post, Jan. 29, 2000, at A17. However, Jessica Mathews argues that this is akin to driving a car over unknown terrain without headlights and refusing to slow down as it gets darker because nothing has been hit yet. She maintains that the United States should act as it did during the Cold War when it adopted defense policies designed to provide insurance against dangers of uncertain but potentially catastrophic magnitude. "There are too many unknowns for rigorous economic analysis," she notes, the risks are not reversible, and the uncertainties will not soon be removed. Mathews, Science, Uncertainty and Common Sense, Wash. Post, Nov. 3, 1991, at C7. To these difficult analytical issues must also be added the reality of differences in national political priorities and economic interests. Compare Richard Benedick's analysis of the Montreal Protocol. Would the absence of U.S. leadership inevitably be a fatal obstacle to achieving an effective international agreement?

An international response to the global warming problem began with a UN General Assembly resolution in December 1988 declaring climate change a "common concern of mankind" and calling for global action to combat the problem. In 1989, the European Community stated its support for an international agreement on global warming. At the end of 1990, the General Assembly adopted a resolution entitled Protection of Global Climate for Present and Future Generations of Mankind that established a process for negotiating an international framework convention on climate change. In response, the UN Secretary General established an ad hoc secretariat in Geneva with the goal of signing an agreement in time for the 1992 Rio Conference on Environment and Development. During the contentious negotiations that followed, most European nations pushed for "targets and timetables" while the United States insisted on a more cautious approach. Abramson, Global Warming Treaty Talks Bog Down, L.A. Times, Feb. 29, 1992, at A22. However, agreement was reached in time for signing in Rio.

In June 1992, the United States and more than 150 governments attending the Rio Earth Summit signed a Framework Convention on Climate Change. The Convention was ratified by the U.S. Senate in October 1992 and entered into force on March 21, 1994, 90 days after having been ratified by 50 signatures. The Framework Convention endorsed the principle of stabilizing emissions of greenhouse gases in order to prevent dangerous interference with the global climate system. However, it did not establish any specific numeric limits or time-tables for reducing emissions.

In subsequent negotiations, the parties to the Climate Convention ultimately agreed to establish an ad hoc process for negotiating a protocol or other legal instrument to set quantified limits and emissions reduction objectives, but only for developed countries, for the years 2005, 2010, and 2020. This agreement, subsequently coined "the Berlin Mandate," took on added importance as U.S. opposition to further action to limit emissions focused on the absence of developing country commitments.

KYOTO PROTOCOL TO THE CONVENTION ON CLIMATE CHANGE

The evolution of the Climate Convention took another major step with the conclusion of the Third Conference of the Parties in Kyoto, Japan, in December 1997. The major industrialized nations (those listed in Annex 1 of the Convention) agreed to accept new obligations to reduce their greenhouse gas emissions that, if met, would result in an average reduction of 5 percent relative to 1990 levels in the period 2008 to 2012. Nations negotiated differing obligations reflecting differing circumstances—reductions of 6 percent by Japan, 7 percent by the United States, and 8 percent by the European Union. Several nations were allowed increased emissions, including Australia, Iceland, and Norway. Developing nations rejected any new commitments and only reluctantly agreed in principle to allow emission trading between Annex 1 nations.

The negotiation of a 5 percent reduction followed months of uncertainty concerning the U.S. position. The European Union had come out for a 15 percent reduction relative to 1990 levels in the spring, while Japan announced support for roughly a 5 percent reduction in October. President Clinton waited until October 22, only five weeks before the meetings, to announce that the

United States supported a return to 1990 emission levels averaged over the period 2008 to 2012. The United States also wanted strong provisions for trading to reduce costs and some expression of willingness to constrain emissions by developing nations. The latter requirement was a response to Senate Resolution 98 adopted 95 to 0 only a few months before, which directed the President to sign a climate treaty that includes new commitments to limit greenhouse gas emissions only if it also "mandates new specific scheduled commitments to limit or reduce greenhouse gas emissions for Developing Country Parties within the same compliance period." On the politics of the U.S. position, see generally Begley, "Too Much Hot Air," Newsweek, Oct. 20, 1997.

The U.S. position was widely criticized by other nations as inadequate. In response, the administration emphasized that its proposal would require about a 30 percent reduction relative to the increase in emissions that was expected in the absence of government intervention. They also argued that the U.S. position included more gases than the EU, which focused on carbon dioxide, narrowing the effective difference between the two proposals. The Parties thus came to Kyoto with very divergent positions and very little opportunity for serious negotiation prior to the event. See Stevens, "Greenhouse Gas Issue: Haggling Over Fairness," N.Y. Times, Nov. 30, 1997.

Many of the most important issues, including national commitments and the acceptability of trading, remained for resolution in the final hours. At a point when gridlock seemed insurmountable, Vice President Gore arrived and announced that he had instructed the U.S. delegation to be more flexible.

The meetings were scheduled to conclude on December 10th but went on through the night and into the next day. In the middle of the night China and India announced opposition to trading provisions deemed essential by the United States, leading to dramatic warnings by the Chair that the agreement could still blow up. After a short break, a compromise was reached allowing for trading in principle but leaving the details for further negotiation at the next Conference of the Parties. Eventually coffee and food ran out, the heat was turned off, and movers arrived to begin preparations for another meeting scheduled shortly thereafter. Many participants had to leave without the final text in order to catch flights. Press reports frequently referred to the final hours as "negotiation by exhaustion."

The U.S. effort to obtain some expression by the largest developing nations of their willingness to constrain their emissions at some future time was completely unsuccessful. The G-7 and China consistently referred to the principles agreed to in Berlin at the first Conference of the Parties (COP), which included a promise that nonAnnex 1 nations would not be subject to any new obligations in the next treaty. New Zealand introduced a proposed compromise that would have triggered negotiation of post-2015 restraints on the growth in non-Annex 1 emissions if Annex 1 nations first fulfilled their commitments to reduce emissions. This and other efforts produced a chorus of loud rejections from developing nations. As a consequence, several Senate Republicans immediately pronounced the Protocol "dead on arrival."

The Protocol became effective on February 16, 2005, as a result of ratification by the Russian Federation and without the United States. The text of the Protocol is available at the website of the UN Framework Convention on Climate Change at *www.unfccc.int.* While implementation of the Kyoto Protocol was formally initiated by the Russian agreement to ratify in February 2005, many observers continue to believe that a smaller forum with participation limited to the largest GHG emitters may be more effective. For that reason, there was some hope generated by the G8 Summit at Gleneagles in July 2005. The meeting was joined by representatives of China, India, Brazil, Mexico, and South Africa, as well as the heads of the International Energy Agency, United Nations, World Bank, and WTO. The joint statement included recognition that climate change is happening and that human activity is contributing to it. While broadly stated, the parties agreed on a new dialog between the G8 nations and major developing nations to promote clean energy technologies. The World Bank agreed to take on a direct role in promoting this dialog, which could become the first formal basis for engaging major developing country economies in discussing strategies for reducing the growth in their GHG emissions. See Gleneagles Summit Documents at *www.g8.gov.uk.*

Arguably the most innovative and controversial feature of the Kyoto Protocol is the Clean Development Mechanism (CDM) authorized by Article 12. Environmentalists have divided in their view of the CDM, with some embracing the opportunity for more efficient reductions while others worry about the potential for creating loopholes and removing incentives for technological innovation. What lessons might be taken from the U.S. experience with emissions trading? Given the potential for investment that it represents, why has rapid implementation of the CDM not been fully embraced by the developing countries? See generally United Nations Development Programme, Issues and Options: The Clean Development Mechanism (1998). Michael Grubb describes the CDM as "a leap into *terra incognita* that is unlikely to work simply as a way to distribute abatement efforts globally at least cost." M. Grubb, C. Vrolijk & D. Brack, The Kyoto Protocol: A Guide and Assessment 245 (1999). One problem is that the most cost-effective projects are the ones most likely to be undertaken even in the absence of the CDM. He argues that there will be "powerful tensions over the basic objectives" because while Japan and the United States want to minimize global costs, developing countries want to maximize resource and technology transfer flows without interfering with foreign aid. Eastern European countries "will have an interest in minimizing use of the CDM overall." Id. Grubb concludes that "the defining purpose of the CDM should be to help direct foreign corporate investment toward goals of sustainable development, in its many forms and interpretations according in part to national preference." Id. at 247. In this respect the CDM is a natural private sector complement to the Global Environment Facility, discussed on page 1112.

Carbon trading under the Protocol has numerous specific requirements and is overseen by an Executive Board, resulting in complex and sometimes controversial issues of eligibility and verification. For an overview and up-to-date information on Board decisions, see *www.unfccc.int.* However, the concept of carbon trading assumes numerous forms including an Emission Trading Scheme (ETS) adopted by the EU effective in 2005, a voluntary trading system administered by the Chicago Climate Exchange, and an evolving regional trading system for the northeastern United States initiated by the State of New York.

Carbon trading grew rapidly in 2004 and 2005 due to the combined influence of the ratification of the Kyoto Protocol and the implementation of the ETS. Buyers include private and public entities in Europe and Japan. The supply of credits has been concentrated in a few countries, including India, Brazil, and Chile with very limited transactions in poorer or smaller countries and Africa (why might this be so?). By volume, the largest source of emission reduction credits is projects abating non-CO_2 emissions, ironically much of it destruction of chemicals introduced as refrigerants as alternatives to CFCs. Projects based on the capture and burning of methane and N_2O from landfills and animal waste are also frequent. In both cases, the value reflects the fact that these gases have a much greater global warming impact than does CO_2. In contrast, investments in renewable energy and energy efficiency have accounted for less than a fifth of the total market. International Emissions Trading Association, State and Trends of the Carbon Market 2005. Current trends imply a very large shortfall in emission reductions, insufficient supply of CDM and JI projects, and large price increases. Carbon Market Analyst, Sept. 12, 2005. The biggest short-term question is what happens after 2012, since without further agreements or regulation carbon credits will have no value subsequent to that date.

Carbon trading continues to generate substantial interest because of the potential to lower the costs of reducing greenhouse gas emissions, provide developing countries with a stream of revenue and potentially investments in clean technologies, and more generally to provide a source of financing for projects that contribute to sustainable development. However, there is also a concern that on the one hand the certification and verification process is too cumbersome and expensive, severely constraining the market, while on the other hand, hoped-for contributions to sustainable development have yet to materialize as projects are overly geographically concentrated and primarily limited to destruction of chemicals and burning of landfill gases—projects without substantial sustainable development benefits.

NOTES AND QUESTIONS

1. According to the Energy Information Administration, U.S. emissions of carbon dioxide increased from 1,337 tons in 1990 to 1,559 tons in 2001, and based on current trends and policies will increase to 2,237 tons in 2025. See Annual Energy Outlook 2003, available at the EIA website, *www.eia.doe.gov*. This growth is continuing, despite an expected decline in the carbon intensity of the economy. It reflects the influence of relatively low energy prices, the trend to less fuel efficient vehicles, and the increased share of electric power generation from fossil energy. Are there risks to the U.S. economy and to U.S. companies in continuing in a direction so contrary to other developed nations, now that the Kyoto Protocol is ratified. Professor Bodansky argues that the answer depends on whether the United States decides to implement stringent domestic requirements, independent of the Protocol. See Bodansky, Working Paper: Implications for U.S. Companies of Kyoto's Entry into Force with the United States (2002) (available at *www.pewclimate.org/events/bodansky.cfm*).

2. **State Initiatives to Control Emissions of Greenhouse Gases.** While the Bush administration continues to oppose efforts to regulate emissions of greenhouse gases that contribute to global warming, several states have taken the initiative to do so. A group of nine northeastern states—New York, New Jersey, Delaware, Connecticut, Rhode Island, Massachusetts, Vermont, New Hampshire, and Maine—have formed the Regional Greenhouse Gas Initiative (RGGI) to develop a regional strategy for controlling emissions of greenhouse gases. The RGGI plans to develop a cap-and-trade program that will restrict greenhouse gas emissions in these nine states while incorporating an emissions trading system to more efficiently control them.

In September 2004 California's Air Resources Board (CARB) approved the first standard to require reductions in emissions of carbon dioxide from new cars and light trucks. The standard, which will take effect beginning in 2009, requires a 30 percent reduction in these emissions by the 2016 model year. It implements California legislation enacted in July 2002 that directed the CARB to adopt regulations that achieve the maximum feasible and cost-effective reduction of greenhouse gas emissions from motor vehicles. Because California is the largest market for motor vehicles in the United States, with nearly 1.7 million new cars and light trucks being purchased every year, the regulation is enormously significant. Roughly one-third of all carbon dioxide emissions in the United States (and 56 percent in California) come from the transportation sector.

On December 7, 2004, the Alliance of Automobile Manufacturers, a trade association representing nine of the largest automobile manufacturers in the United States, Germany, and Japan, filed suit in federal district court in California to challenge the legality of the standard. The auto manufacturers claim that it is a disguised effort to regulate fuel economy that conflicts with existing fuel economy standards promulgated by the National Highway Traffic Safety Administration (NHTSA). In February 2005, Honda Motors surprisingly endorsed tougher U.S. fuel economy standards in a move widely viewed as a gesture to environmental groups angered by the company's decision to join the lawsuit against the California standards. Shore, Enlightenment, Envtl. Forum, Sept./Oct. 2002, at 19-25; Thinking Globally, Acting Locally, 7 Global Change, Summer 2002, at 2-2; Rabe, Greenhouse and Statehouse: The Evolving State Government Role in Climate Change (Pew Center on Global Climate Change, 2002); Pew Center on Global Climate Change, Climate Change Activities in the United States 2004 Update. To what extent can state and local action substitute for the absence of national policy?

3. A growing number of lawsuits raise questions of regulatory authority to address global warming and issues of responsibility for its consequences: (i) Connecticut v. American Electric Power, discussed in Chapter 2, is a nuisance suit filed by eight states and the City of New York against six large electric utilities seeking injunctive relief to restrict their carbon dioxide emissions (see page 1012); (ii) A 2-1 decision by the D.C. Circuit in 2005 in Massachusetts v. EPA, rejected efforts by several states seeking to require EPA to regulate emissions of greenhouse gases. This case is discussed in Chapter 5 (see page 482); (iii) Two environmental groups joined by the cities of Boulder and Oakland filed suit under NEPA to require the Overseas Private Investment Corporation (OPIC) to assess their contribution to global warming when insuring fossil fuel projects. A federal district court rejected a motion to dismiss in August 2005. For documents see *www.climatelawsuit.org*; (iv) Another potential source of litigation is based on requirements for disclosure of material risk under securities regulations. A group of large investors organized the Carbon Disclosure Project to request large companies to analyze and report their emissions. See information at *www.socialfunds.com* and *www.ceres.org*; R. Repetto, Protecting Investors and the Environment through Financial Disclosure (2003); (v) The Inuit Circumpolar Conference, a federation of native tribes in the Arctic region encompassing the United States, Canada, Russia, and Greenland, is preparing a claim based on violation of their human rights as a petition to the Inter-American Commission of Human Rights. See *http://www.ciel.org/Climate/Climate_Inuit.html*. What prospects for success do plaintiffs have in each of these actions? See Grossman, Warming Up to a Not So Radical Idea: Tort-Based Climate Change Litigation, 28 Colum.

J. Envtl. L. 1 (2003); Healy & Tapick, Climate Change: It's Not Just a Policy Issue for Corporate Counsel—It's a Legal Problem, 29 Colum. J. Envtl. L. 89 (2004). How might the increasing prevalence of such litigation influence strategic decisions by corporations? In his novel, State of Fear, Michael Crichton describes environmental litigation brought knowingly without any prospect of success— the litigation team disbands almost immediately after the press conference to announce the suit—solely as a means of supporting the fund-raising efforts of the environmental group. How realistic do you consider his scenario?

4. **Economic Models of Climate Change.** Resistance to regulating GHG emissions is based on the assumption that doing so to any significant degree necessarily implies large costs to the economy. There is no disagreement that large reductions in GHG emissions will require substantial changes in the sources and uses of energy, but there is considerable controversy with respect to the costs associated with making these changes. While the limitations of models used for predicting climate change from greenhouse gas emissions have been widely noted (and even described at length in a novel—Michael Crichton's State of Fear), there has been much less discussion of the comparable uncertainties and inaccuracies associated with economic models, and the confidence that should be ascribed to predictions of economic doom associated with policies to reduce emissions.

After reviewing the range of economic analyses of the impact of moderate greenhouse gas reductions on the United States, economist Stephen DeCanio concluded that outcomes "depend primarily on modeling assumptions (including definition of the system boundaries, i.e., whether environmental benefits are included in the analysis)." Stephen DeCanio, Economic Models of Climate Change 150 (2003). Most studies failed to incorporate the full range of means for mitigating costs, including tax shifts (utilizing carbon revenues to offset less efficient taxes), international allowance trading, and some opportunity for investment in carbon sinks (expanding forests to increase the uptake of carbon). In the long run, the most fundamental determinant of reductions costs is the rate of technological changes in measures to reduce emissions (e.g., renewable energy and energy efficiency improvements), assuming that policy instruments can accelerate this process lowers costs and can even result in net economic gains. The link between policies and technological progress cannot be accurately predicted and is one of the critical assumptions noted by DeCanio. See also Goulder, Induced Technological Change and Climate Policy (Pew Center on Global Climate Change 2004).

The rapid rise in oil prices from 2004 to mid-2005 illustrates the difficulty predicting adverse impacts on the economy. Oil prices increased more than a dollar a gallon in a period of months, a larger and more rapid rise than implied by proposals for carbon taxes (equivalent in effect to a carbon tax of about $400/ton). See review of studies in M. Toman ed., Climate Change Economics and Policy (2001). The U.S. economy continued its relatively robust growth, demonstrating the limitation of economic models even with respect to short-term changes in energy prices. The issues are much more complex in making long-term forecasts, as technological options and the range of consumer responses becomes much greater.

5. **Legislative Debate.** The Climate Stewardship Act proposed by Senators McCain and Lieberman was defeated by the margin of 43-55 in October 2003 in the first Senate debate on global warming since 1998. The bill was modeled on the acid rain trading program and would have required a reduction in carbon

dioxide levels to 2000 levels (as opposed to the much lower 1990 baseline used in the Kyoto Protocol) by 2010. The proposal would apply to the electricity generation, transportation, industrial, and commercial sectors, estimated to account for about 85 percent of U.S. emissions. To reduce the costs of compliance, a central feature was proposed reliance on a system of allowances and trading comparable to the acid rain program but considerably more complex reflecting the larger number of emitters, the potential for international trading, and provision for sequestration. For a description of the bill see *http://www.pewclimate.org/policy_center/analyses/s_139_summary.cfm*.

In an effort to accommodate White House proposals to promote technology-based solutions to global warming, the bill was amended in 2005 to provide for the use of some of the revenues from trading to create incentives for commercialization of alternatives to conventional fossil fuel power generation including solar, wind, and nuclear power. See *http://lieberman.senate.gov/newsroom/release.cfm?id=238307*.

6. Another topic of growing importance is the relationship between climate change policies and air pollution and ozone layer protection. One source of uncertainty in climate modeling is that while the primary greenhouse gas is carbon dioxide, other anthropogenic sources of "radiative forcing" include gases regulated by the Montreal Protocol and black carbon particles released by the incomplete combustion of fossil fuels. Linkages between protecting the ozone layer and global climate system were the subject of a 2005 IPCC report finding that the phaseout of ozone depleting substances has reduced emissions equivalent to about one-fourth of global fossil fuel combustion. On the other hand, some of the substances introduced as substitutes for CFCs are potent greenhouse gases and will increase the rate of warming if not regulated. IPCC & TEAP, Safeguarding the Ozone Layer and the Global Climate System (2005). Another set of linkages with important policy implications has to do with air pollution regulation. To address acid rain from coal, utilities often install controls that use substantial amounts of energy and result in increased carbon dioxide emissions. On the other hand, uncontrolled emissions of black particles from fossil fuel combustion contribute to global warming. James Hansen et al., Efficacy of Climate Forcings, 110 J. Geophysical Resources D18104 (2005).

7. With the ratification of the Kyoto Protocol and the certain absence of U.S. participation, the Convention process must now turn to the question of what happens after 2012, the final year covered by the Protocol. Bringing both the United States and major developing countries into any future control regime is a high priority. One hint of future directions may be the outcome of the 2005 meetings of the leaders of the G8, the seven largest industrialized economies and the Russian Federation, hosted by the United Kingdom in Gleneagles. The meeting included participation by senior officials from China, India, Brazil, Mexico, and South Africa, all large and rapidly growing sources of greenhouse gas emissions. A communiqué of the parties included the following: "We know that, globally, emissions must slow, peak and then decline, moving us toward a low-carbon economy. This will require leadership from the developed world. . . . Our discussions mark the beginning of a new Dialogue between the G8 nations and other countries with significant energy needs, consistent with the aims and principles of the UN Framework Convention on Climate Change. This will explore how best to exchange technology, reduce emissions, and meet our energy needs in a sustainable way, as we implement and build on the Plan of Action." *www.G8.gov.uk*. See generally Bodansky,

Chou & Jorge-Tresolini, International Climate Efforts Beyond 2012: A Survey of Approaches (Pew Center 2004), and Aldy et al., Beyond Kyoto: Advancing the International Effort Against Climate Change (Pew Center, 2003).

RESULTS OF THE MONTREAL CLIMATE CHANGE COP/MOP

Parties to the UNFCCC met in Montreal in December 2005, for the first time as two separate bodies—the Eleventh Conference of the Parties (COP) to the convention, and, following ratification by Russia, the first Meeting of the Parties (MOP) to the Kyoto Protocol. By several measures the meetings were the most significant since Kyoto in 1997 with almost 10,000 attendees, over 40 decisions, and at least modest first steps to open a discussion of the post-2012 climate regime. Several decisions also gave a further boost to the carbon market, making it increasingly likely that a trading system will continue.

The most contentious and momentous discussions in Montreal focused on the process for discussing future commitments. As negotiations approached their climax, the U.S. walked out. The political drama was enhanced by an unscheduled appearance by Bill Clinton shortly thereafter; the former President attacked U.S. concerns about the economic impacts of emissions reductions as "flat wrong" and warned that melting of sea ice could require that future meetings in Canada be held on "a raft somewhere." The eventual agreement required extending the meetings past their scheduled conclusion on a Friday until 6 a.m. the following morning. The decisions provide for a process of "nonbinding" dialogues, consideration of ways to promote climate friendly technologies in developing countries, and the creation of an open-ended ad hoc group to consider further commitments by Annex I Parties beyond 2012.

The meetings also made progress on some important legal and operational issues. One was the approval of the Marrakesh Accords, a set of agreements reached at COP 7 for the implementation of the Kyoto Protocol that had to be, and were, approved again by the Parties to the MOP. A second set of agreements addressed some of the concerns about the logjam of applications and perceived inefficiencies associated with the administration of the CDM. The decision includes measures to improve the CDM Board's transparency and efficiency. Recognizing the need for increased funding to speed processing, the Parties agreed to additional direct contributions and to levy $0.10 to $0.20 per Certified Emissions Reduction for administrative expenses. The decision also requests further work on how to demonstrate additionality and other methodological issues.

Adaptation was another issue that received increasing emphasis at COP 11/MOP 1. The primary decision on this issue was a commitment to a five-year work program, although without clarifying the necessary additional sources of funds. Progress was made although no final decisions were taken with respect to two additional sources of funding for adaptation projects, a Special Climate Change Fund supported by voluntary donor contributions and a Kyoto Protocol Adaptation Fund to be financed by some proceeds from CDM projects.

The potential need for additional technological options to address climate change was highlighted by a special report of the IPCC on carbon capture and storage presented to the Parties. See www.ipcc.ch. With the evidence increasing that reliance on GHG mitigation measures alone may come too little and too late, the technical and economic feasibility of such technologies may be one option. The Bush Administration has also expressed interest in this approach as a potential basis for "zero emissions" generation of electricity of coal, and in December 2005 announced a partnership to build a demonstration plant with carbon sequestration capabilities. Hess, "Incentives Boost Coal Gasification," C&EN, Jan. 16, 2006, at 22-24.

For more detailed written reports on the ministerial debates (high-level segment), see *http://www.iisd.ca/vol12/enb12289e.html* and *http://www.iisd.ca/vol12/enb12290e.html*. Complete webcast records of these speeches are available online at *http://unfccc.streamlogics.com/unfccc/agenda.asp*.

The U.S. also brought a focus on technology to a new Asia Pacific Partnership on Clean Development and Climate, a six country regional initiative which had its inaugural meeting in Australia in January 2006. In addition to the U.S. and Australia—both non-signatories to the Kyoto Protocol and major coal producers—the meetings included China, India, Japan, and Korea. The outcomes reached focused primarily on improving technology for coal combustion and manufacture of aluminum (a very energy intensive process). The meetings were also attended by numerous industry leaders.

The political sensitivity surrounding U.S. climate policy was further highlighted by the revelation in January 2006 that Dr. James Hansen, a prominent NASA climate scientist, had been directed to screen interview requests through the agency's public affairs staff. Government officials defended the requirement as necessary to assure coordination, avoid surprises, and to leave discussion of policy issues to policy makers. In response, Hansen announced he would ignore the restrictions "because public concern is probably the only thing capable of overcoming the special interests that have obfuscated the topic." "Climate Expert Says NASA Tried to Silence Him," N.Y. Times, Jan. 29, 2006.

PROBLEM EXERCISE: LEGAL AND POLICY STRATEGIES TO COMBAT CLIMATE CHANGE

(1) As scientific evidence of human-induced climate change continues to increase, are there legal strategies that might be successfully pursued by environmentalists? Consider the relative benefits and limitations of legal actions based on the following theories:

(a) Environmental groups bring suit on behalf of their members against the Export-Import Bank and Overseas Private Investment Corporation for failing to prepare an environmental impact statement on the effect of their financing of fossil fuel projects on climate change. See *www.climatelawsuit.org/* (press release announcing lawsuit by Friends of the Earth, Greenpeace, and the City of Boulder against the Export-Import Bank and Overseas Private Investment Corporation).

(b) A group of countries injured by sea level rise and other impacts of climate change pursue an action against the United States before the International Court of Justice, or in the alternative, the same countries could ask the UN General Assembly to ask the ICJ for an advisory opinion. Seelye, Global Warming May Bring New Variety of Class Action, N.Y. Times, Sept. 6, 2001.

(c) As parties to the Kyoto Protocol, the EU and Japan petition the WTO seeking the right to impose countervailing duties against goods made in the United States due to the refusal of the United States to ratify the Kyoto

Protocol. Strauss, Suing the United States for Global Warming Emissions: Discussion Paper for In the Red Conference, London, July 10, 2001.

(d) Action brought against coal and oil companies by state attorney's general for health costs and other damages incurred by states. Cortese, As the Earth Warms, Will Companies Pay?, N.Y. Times, Aug. 18, 2002.

Is the value of such litigation solely a function of the chances of success? Consider the views of Professor Esty: "In some circumstances legal actions are evaluated or pursued not with expectations of success in court, but recognizing that a real victory would be in the court of public opinion."

(2) One legislative proposal developed in response to the Kyoto Protocol is to guarantee U.S. companies that they will receive a credit for voluntary reductions in greenhouse gas emissions even if they are undertaken before the Kyoto Protocol is ratified. The basic concept is to create the equivalent of an escrow account for legitimate greenhouse gas reductions voluntarily achieved by U.S. companies in advance of the 2008-2012 compliance period. Under the proposal, participating companies would be guaranteed credits against any subsequently developed regulatory requirements. The intention is to create an incentive for early action without rewarding phantom emission reductions.

The proposal has divided both supporters and opponents of the Kyoto agreement. Some conservatives oppose it because they fear it will succeed in creating momentum to ratify the Protocol, as the value of credits would depend on the agreement taking effect. Environmental opponents include the executive director of Ozone Action, who describes the credit for early reductions proposal as "corporate welfare wrapped in environmentally friendly rhetoric." He likens it to "a doctor only prescribing a cholesterol-lowering pill to a patient with heart disease" instead of "prescribing a low-fat diet and increased exercise."

Should the early reductions legislation be adopted? Even if it is, there is no guarantee that the U.S. Senate will ratify the Kyoto Protocol. If it is uncertain whether the credits ultimately will be worth anything, why would a company choose to reduce emissions unless it already was planning to do so for other reasons? How can it be determined whether an emissions reduction was the result of the credit assurance or something that would have occurred anyway? Even if it is the latter, does the credit for early reduction idea still have any environmental benefits? Why might adoption of the legislation affect prospects for Senate ratification of the Kyoto Protocol?

C.   INTERNATIONAL TRADE AND THE ENVIRONMENT

1.   *Overview*

The accelerating trend toward a global economy has become one of the most noted developments of the past decade. With the collapse of communism as a competing economic system, modern capitalism has been compared to a

> wondrous new machine . . . that plows across field and fencerows with a fierce momentum that is exhilarating to behold and also frightening. As it goes, the machine throws off enormous mows of wealth and bounty while it leaves behind great furrows of wreckage.

> Now imagine that there are skillful hands on board, but no one is at the wheel. In fact, this machine has no wheel nor any internal governor to control the speed and direction. It is sustained by its own forward motion, guided mainly by its own appetites. And it is accelerating. [W. Greider, One World, Ready or Not: The Manic Logic of Global Capitalism 11 (1997).]

The trend toward global economic integration is measured in several ways. One is the growth in global trade. From 1950 to 1997, exports increased 15-fold compared with a 6-fold increase in the size of the world economy; they grew from 6 to 15 percent of the gross world product. L. Brown, M. Renner & B. Harwell eds., Vital Signs 1999 at 68 (1999).

Another measure of economic integration is the growth in foreign direct investment (FDI) and the increasing share going to developing nations.[1] FDI in 1997-1998 was more than seven times the level of the 1970s, about 40 percent in developing countries or countries with economies in transition. This trend has been relatively stable even as other forms of financing dropped dramatically during the Asian fiscal crisis in 1998, and multilateral aid flows dropped by a third in real terms from 1990 to less than $60 billion annually. UNDP, Human Development Report 1999 at 30-31; World Bank, Global Development Finance 47-80 (1999). In contrast with the decline in multilateral aid, annual private capital flows to developing countries have exceeded the Earth Summit's goal of $125 billion in new and additional resources each year since 1992. Schmidheiny & Gentry, Privately Financed Sustainable Development, in Thinking Ecologically 118-119 (M. Chertow & D. Esty eds., 1997).

Not all countries are sharing in the flow of investment dollars. The distribution of investment in developing nations has been extremely uneven, with more than 80 percent going to about 20 countries. Investment is also no guarantee of growth or an improved quality of life; the countries of sub-Saharan Africa maintain a high export-to-GDP ratio, due to an emphasis on exports of primary commodities, but nevertheless have low growth economies. The top fifth of people in the richest countries are the recipients of more than 80 percent of global export trade, while the bottom fifth receive barely 1 percent. More than 100 countries receive less than $100 million per year in FDI. UNDP, Human Development Report 1999 at 30-31; World Bank, Global Development Finance 47-80 (1999).

Another facet of this trend is the increasing concentration of wealth in multinational corporations (MNCs). For many opponents of economic globalization, this perceived shift in power is a central concern. See, e.g., J. Cavanagh & J. Mander, Alternatives to Economic Globalization 49 (2004). The combined value added of MNCs was 7 percent of world GDP in 1997, up from 5 percent in the mid-1980s, and their share of exports reached a third of the world total in 1995. U.S.-based MNCs account for more than a quarter of the country's GDP. Many large corporations now have annual sales greater than the GNP of most

---

1. FDI includes manufacturing plants owned in whole or in part by foreign companies. In recent years this has included a significant amount of investment in the purchase of government assets like a national steel company in Mexico, and with the privatization of utilities, investment in what would previously have been government-funded infrastructure projects such as power plants. Additional private capital flows to developing nations in the form of privately issued debt and portfolio investments in securities. Schmidheiny & Gentry, Privately Financed Sustainable Development, in Thinking Ecologically 118, 120 (M. Chertow & D. Esty eds., 1997).

countries. As mergers between major corporations continue—Daimler-Chrysler, MCI/Worldcom, Exxon and Mobil, AOL/Time Warner—this trend toward concentration is likely to continue. UNDP, Human Development Report 1999 at 31-32.

Many authorities give considerable credit for the rapid expansion of world trade to the successful evolution of the General Agreement on Tariffs and Trade (GATT), first drafted in 1947 and transformed into the World Trade Organization in 1994. The aim of the GATT treaty "is the moderation of national foreign trade policies to ensure, as much as possible, the unencumbered flow of international commerce." M. Janis, An Introduction to International Law 296 (2003). Toward this end, a process is created for parties to challenge, through WTO review, national measures (including environmental regulations) that constitute unjustified nontariff trade barriers. Environmental criticism of the GATT regime has been on both procedural and substantive grounds, reflecting its intentionally narrow focus and insular style. As Professor Esty argues, these characteristics arguably have much to do with the success of the system but need to evolve in response to evolving societal needs. D. Esty, Greening the GATT 52-54 (1994). See also Charnovitz, Participation of Nongovernmental Organizations in the World Trade Organization, 17 U. Pa. J. Int'l Econ. L. 331. These issues are taken up further in the section on the WTO below, pages 1078-1091.

The relationship between these global economic trends and the environment is the subject of active debate. A variety of issues have been raised, but the initial question broadly concerns the environmental consequences of expanding trade and associated measures to open national markets.

Herman Daly, a professor at the University of Maryland who is a pioneer in ecological economics, argues that there is a clear conflict between free trade and national efforts to internalize environmental costs.

> If one nation internalizes environmental and social costs to a high degree, . . . and then enters into free trade with a country that does not force its producers to internalize those costs, then the result will be that firms in the second country will have lower prices and will drive the competing firms in the first country out of business. [Daly, From Adjustment to Sustainable Development: The Obstacle of Free Trade, 15 Loy. L.A. Int'l & Comp. L.J. 33, 36 (1992).]

Daly maintains that environmental externalities have become so important that this conflict should be resolved in favor of "tariffs to protect, not an inefficient industry, but an efficient national policy of internalizing external costs into prices." Id.

Daly holds that international free trade is in fundamental conflict with five important domestic policies: (1) getting prices right (by making it more difficult for a country to use regulation to internalize the external costs of pollution), (2) moving toward a more just distribution of income between labor and capital (by reducing returns to domestic labor), (3) fostering community (by forcing greater labor mobility and further separating ownership from the community as foreign investment occurs), (4) controlling the macroeconomy (by creating huge international payment imbalances), and (5) keeping scale within ecological limits (as more nations seek to live in excess of a sustainable development path by importing carrying capacity from others). Daly, From Adjustment to Sustainable Development: The Obstacle of Free Trade, 15 Loy. L.A. Int'l & Comp. L.J. 33 (1992).

In contrast to Daly, a report prepared by the GATT Secretariat for the Rio Summit not surprisingly adopts the view that trade makes countries richer and less polluting. It also argues in favor of consensual multilateral environmental agreements and environmental aid and technology transfer as an alternative to trade sanctions or other penalties against countries with lax environmental standards. GATT Secretariat, Trade and the Environment (Feb. 1992). See also OTA, Trade and Environment: Conflicts and Opportunities 4-6, 22-24 (1992); and Environmental Imperialism, The Economist, Feb. 15, 1992, at 78. Judge Stephen Williams of the D.C. Circuit speculates that trade liberalization may help the environment by reducing poverty. He cites data suggesting that because "low-income persons tend to buy in much smaller quantities than persons of higher income buying economy-size packages, they impose a heavier per capita load of packaging waste." Public Citizen v. U.S. Trade Representative, 970 F.2d 916, 921 n.6 (D.C. Cir. 1992).

Skepticism about the benefits of trade liberalization appear to be growing as negotiators from the U.S. and other industrialized countries confront the challenges of further reductions in agricultural tariffs and other politically powerful sectors, and evidence mounts that the benefits of economic growth in the developing countries tends to be unevenly distributed. See, e.g., Tired of Globalisation, The Economist, Nov. 3, 2005. However, the case that trade does not—or at least need not—result inevitably in harm to the environment continues to receive general support from economists. See, e.g., Martin Wolf, Why Globalization Works (2004) ("The alleged link between trade liberalization and environmental damage is wholly unsupported by the evidence. What is true, however, is that the management of environmental externalities requires well-targeted measures aimed at making decision makers aware of the costs." Id. at 194; Douglas Irwin, Free Trade Under Fire (2d ed. 2005) ("[F]ree trade and a cleaner environment are not incompatible. Because free trade in itself is not a driving force behind pollution, a policy of free trade rarely detracts from such goals, in many instances may help." Id. at 59.

As the preceding discussion suggests, much of the debate on trade and the environment has been based on theoretical and political perspectives. What has been largely missing to date is empirical evidence evaluating the environmental consequences of free trade policies. A review of the evidence concerning these competing claims is presented in the excerpt that follows.

Frederiksson, Trade, Global Policy, and the Environment: New Evidence and Issues
(1999)

Although many issues in the trade and environment debate are contentious, a consensus appears to be emerging on a few matters. Many participants in the debate now agree that (a) more open trade improves growth and economic welfare, and (b) increased trade and growth without appropriate environmental policies in place may have unwanted effects on the environment. However, in some situations more open trade may also reduce pressure on the environment. This ambiguity occurs because trade policy and trade flows have several conflicting effects on both the environment and resource use. It has proven useful to view the various effects of trade liberalization in three categories: *scale, composition,* and *technique effects.* This is now a standard way of thinking about the problem and a helpful tool for analyzing the issues involved. . . .

Scale Effect

The *scale* effect refers to the fact that more open trade creates greater economic activity, thus raising the demand for inputs such as raw materials, transportation services, and energy. If output is produced and delivered using unchanged technologies, an increase in emissions and resource depletion must follow.

Composition Effect

The *composition* effect stems from changes in the relative size of the economic sectors following a reduction in trade barriers. Lowering trade barriers changes the relative prices between goods produced in different sectors, so that producers and consumers face new trade-offs. Countries tend to specialize production in sectors in which they have a comparative advantage; this tendency becomes more pronounced with freer trade. If the difference between abatement costs and the price of resource extraction is sufficiently large—making environmental regulations more important in the determination of comparative advantage—countries with lax regulations are likely to shift away from relatively clean sectors and specialize in more polluting or resource-dependent sectors, thus damaging the environment.

If, on the other hand, the base for international comparative advantage is differences in the supply of labor and capital or in the efficiency of technologies, then the impact of changing sector composition (in response to trade liberalization) on environmental quality and resource extraction will be ambiguous. . . .

Technique Effect

The *technique* effect refers to changes in production methods that follow trade liberalization. Pollution emissions per unit of output do not necessarily stay constant; final intensity depends on a number of subcomponents:

- Since trade liberalization generates increased income levels, demand for environmental quality is also likely to increase. Assuming that this leads to political pressure for more stringent environmental policies and enforcement, the per-unit pollution load will be lower.
- If investment liberalization also takes place, foreign investment may bring modern technologies which are likely to be cleaner than older versions.
- As the relative price of intermediate inputs changes when tariffs are lowered, the input mix chosen by firms is adjusted; the new mix may be more or less pollution-intensive.
- Governments may begin competing for investment and jobs by setting lower environmental standards—a "race to the bottom." However, if foreign consumers demand goods produced with cleaner methods, international trade could reduce pollution intensities, instead stimulating a "race to the top."
- Closely related to the previous point, incentives for lobby groups to pressure governments for more favorable environmental legislation may shift as a result of liberalization. If the sectoral composition effect

(discussed above) implies a shift into more pollution-intensive sectors, both industry and environmental interests can be expected to intensify their efforts to receive favors from environmental policy-makers—at higher output levels more is at stake, both in terms of profits and environmental degradation.

In sum, the technique effect has an ambiguous effect on pollution and resource extraction, but is generally believed to be positive for environmental quality. In addition, seen from a global perspective, free trade results in a more efficient use of resources; thus fewer raw materials and inputs are used to produce a given amount of output. As noted above, however, the amount of output produced is not constant.

The three main effects described above often have both local and global environmental implications, and their relative importance differs among countries. The final impact of trade liberalization on the environment is therefore ambiguous. A quantification of the relative magnitude of these effects, and their final result, is therefore useful to understand the range of the relative significance of the three effects in different countries.

The country-specific effects point to a need to identify and forecast the effects of existing and future trade and environmental policies—which puts great pressure on policy-making institutions. Sufficient institutional capacity is not always in place to permit environmental problems to be prevented or handled as they arise, underscoring the need for a thorough analysis of future environmental effects as foreign trade continues to open up.

NOTES AND QUESTIONS

1. Fredriksson identifies three avenues by which trade liberalization may affect environmental conditions. To what extent does his analysis support or contradict Daly's views?

2. Can international trade agreements preempt domestic law? See Missouri v. Holland, 252 U.S. 416 (1920) (treaties have supremacy over state law). Could a president effectively repeal a domestic environmental law by agreeing to a treaty that preempts it? See Wirth, A Matchmaker's Challenge: Marrying International Law and American Environmental Law, 32 Va. J. Int'l L. 377 (1992). David Wirth argues that because international law lacks many of domestic law's procedural protections for ensuring public disclosure, scrutiny, and participation in decision making, the trend toward internationalization of environmental law may prove to be a mixed blessing for environmental interests.

3. Can an international agreement expand foreigners' standing to seek redress in the U.S. courts? In Corrosion Proof Fittings v. EPA, 947 F.2d 1201 (5th Cir. 1991), Canadian asbestos producers argued that they had standing to challenge EPA's asbestos ban because GATT gives them the right to challenge another country's environmental standards as de facto trade barriers. Noting that GATT establishes its own procedures for solving trade disputes, the court rejected this argument. The Fifth Circuit held that the Canadians did not fall within the zone of interests protected by U.S. law because TSCA does not require EPA to consider the extraterritorial effect of domestic regulation. The court noted that section 6(c)(1)(D) of TSCA expressly requires EPA to consider "the effect [of a rule] on the *national* economy," 15 U.S.C. §2605(c)(1)(D)

(emphasis supplied), and that "[i]nternational concerns are conspicuously absent from the statute." 947 F.2d at 1209.

4. Should national interest be considered in attempting to determine whether environmental measures are disguised protectionism? A Canadian tax on alcoholic beverages sold in nonrefillable containers when voluntary recycling was permitted for soft drinks disproportionately impacted U.S. beer importers and was challenged under GATT. Crosby, Green Beer: When Is an Environmental Measure a Disguised Restriction on International Trade?, 7 Geo. Int'l Envtl. L. Rev. 537 (1995). The matter was settled by a compromise. Battle Over a Bottle, World Watch, Jan./Feb. 1994, at 9.

5. The Montreal Protocol's restrictions on international trade in CFCs initially were opposed by the EC as a possible violation of GATT. Under the Protocol, parties are prohibited from importing CFCs or halons from nonparties and, beginning in January 1993, developing countries were precluded from exporting them to nonparties. These restrictions were included in the Montreal Protocol after a GATT representative explained that they qualified for exceptions provided in Article XX(b) & (g) for standards "necessary to protect human, animal, or plant life or health" or "relating to the conservation or exhaustion of exhaustible natural resources." Benedick, Ozone Diplomacy 91 (1991). See also Frankel, Climate and Trade: Links Between the Kyoto Protocol and the WTO, 47 Env't 8 (2005).

2. *The GATT and WTO*

The World Trade Organization (WTO) is a product of the Marrakesh Agreement that completed the Uruguay Round of negotiations under the old General Agreement on Tariffs and Trade (GATT) in December 1993. United States membership in the WTO was approved by Congress in December 1994, and the WTO came into being on January 1, 1995. The principles established under GATT still remain the centerpiece of the international trading system, which now has been integrated into a new, unified system under the WTO. Unlike GATT's "contracting parties," the WTO has "Members" who are required to attend the organization's ministerial conferences. The WTO's General Council, which reports to the ministerial conference, is responsible for running the day-to-day business of the WTO. Its subsidiary, the General Council on Trade and Goods administers existing trade agreements, the role GATT used to play. The WTO has dispute settlement provisions that are more developed than GATT's by making the formation of dispute settlement panels and the adoption of their decisions automatic, subject to appeal to an Appellate Body of seven members.

GATT insulates health and environmental regulations from attacks as trade restrictions as long as they "are not applied in a manner which would constitute a means of arbitrary or unjustifiable discrimination between countries where the same conditions prevail, or a disguised restriction on international trade." GATT, art. XX. Thus, trade disputes often turn on whether a regulation discriminates against foreign products. While a GATT panel rejected a challenge to CERCLA's feedstock tax because it applied equally to foreign and domestic chemical products, more difficult issues arise when ostensibly nondiscriminatory measures have a disproportionate impact on imported products, as with the EU's ban on hormone-treated beef and the U.S. effort to ban asbestos, nearly all of which is imported. D. Esty, Greening the GATT (1994).

Conflicts over the trade implications of environmental standards may be avoided when the standards are themselves a product of international agreement. Several existing treaties, such as the Montreal Protocol, which regulates trade in CFCs, impose trade restrictions to protect the environment. The Convention on International Trade in Endangered Species of Wild Fauna and Flora (CITES) has been highly effective because it imposes strict controls on trade in endangered species.

Trade disputes have been spawned by U.S. environmental laws that use trade sanctions to promote environmental protection outside U.S. borders. The most prominent example is the Marine Mammal Protection Act of 1972 (MMPA). Designed to reduce the incidental kill of marine mammals in the course of commercial fishing, the MMPA requires the government to "ban the importation of commercial fish or products from fish which have been caught with commercial fishing technology which results in the incidental kill or incidental serious injury of ocean mammals in excess of United States standards." 16 U.S.C. §1371(a)(2). In order to import yellowfin tuna caught in a certain area of the Pacific Ocean, a country had to demonstrate that the average incidental taking rate (in terms of dolphins killed each time the purse seine nets are set) for its tuna fleet was no more than 1.25 times the average taking rate of U.S. vessels in the same period. While seemingly nondiscriminatory, these regulations spawned international trade disputes because they represented a unilateral effort to promote extraterritorial environmental protection. In 1991, the United States imposed a ban on tuna imports from Mexico and four other countries after environmentalists won a judgment holding that such an embargo was required by the MMPA. Earth Island Institute v. Mosbacher, 929 F.2d 1449 (9th Cir. 1991). Arguing that the embargo was inconsistent with GATT, the Mexican government then asked the GATT Council to convene a panel to hear its complaint. The panel rendered the following decision.

GATT Council, United States— Restrictions on Imports of Tuna: Report of the Panel 1991

[After describing the tuna embargo, the Panel noted that MMPA also provides for an embargo of tuna products from any "intermediary nation" that fails within 90 days to prove that it has acted to ban tuna imports from the target country. Six months after the initial ban, the Pelly Amendment authorized the president to ban imports of all fish and wildlife products from the target country "for such duration as the President determines appropriate and to the extent that such prohibition is sanctioned by the General Agreement on Tariffs and Trade."]

The Panel proceeded to examine whether Article XX(b) or Article XX(g) could justify the MMPA provisions on imports of certain yellowfin tuna and yellowfin tuna products, and the import ban imposed under these provisions. The Panel noted that Article XX provides that:

"Subject to the requirement that such measures are not applied in a manner which would constitute a means of arbitrary or unjustifiable discrimination between countries where the same conditions prevail, or a disguised restriction on international trade, nothing in this Agreement shall be construed to prevent the adoption or enforcement by any contracting party of measures . . .

(b) necessary to protect human, animal or plant life or health; . . .

(g) relating to the conservation of exhaustible natural resources if such measures are made effective in conjunction with restrictions on domestic production or consumption; . . . "

The Panel noted that the United States considered the prohibition of imports of certain yellowfin tuna and certain yellowfin tuna products from Mexico, and the provisions of the MMPA on which this prohibition is based, to be justified by Article XX(b) because they served solely the purpose of protecting dolphin life and health and were "necessary" within the meaning of that provision because, in respect of the protection of dolphin life and health outside its jurisdiction, there was no alternative measure reasonably available to the United States to achieve this objective. Mexico considered that Article XX(b) was not applicable to a measure imposed to protect the life or health of animals outside the jurisdiction of the contracting party taking it and that the import prohibition imposed by the United States was not necessary because alternative means consistent with the General Agreement were available to it to protect dolphin lives or health, namely international co-operation between the countries concerned.

The Panel noted that the basic question raised by these arguments, namely whether Article XX(b) covers measures necessary to protect human, animal or plant life or health outside the jurisdiction of the contracting party taking the measure, is not clearly answered by the text of that provision. It refers to life and health protection generally without expressly limiting that protection to the jurisdiction of the contracting party concerned. The Panel therefore decided to analyze this issue in the light of the drafting history of Article XX(b), the purpose of this provision, and the consequences that the interpretations proposed by the parties would have for the operation of the General Agreement as a whole.

The Panel noted that the proposal for Article XX(b) dated from the Draft Charter of the International Trade Organization (ITO) proposed by the United States, which stated in Article 32, "Nothing in Chapter IV [on commercial policy] of this Charter shall be construed to prevent the adoption or enforcement by any Member of measures . . . (b) necessary to protect human, animal or plant life or health." In the New York Draft of the ITO Charter, the preamble had been revised to read as it does at present, and exception (b) read: "For the purpose of protecting human, animal or plant life or health, if corresponding domestic safeguards under similar conditions exist in the importing country." This added proviso reflected concerns regarding the abuse of sanitary regulations by importing countries. Later, Commission A of the Second Session of the Preparatory Committee in Geneva agreed to drop this proviso as unnecessary. Thus, the record indicates that the concerns of the drafters of Article XX(b) focused on the use of sanitary measures to safeguard life or health of humans, animals, or plants within the jurisdiction of the importing country.

The Panel further noted that Article XX(b) allows each contracting party to set its human, animal or plant life or health standards. The conditions set out in Article XX(b) which limit resort to this exception, namely that the measure taken must be "necessary" and not "constitute a means of arbitrary or unjustifiable discrimination or a disguised restriction on international trade," refer to the trade measure requiring justification under Article XX(b), not, however, to the life or health standard chosen by the contracting party. The Panel recalled the finding of a previous panel that this paragraph of Article XX was intended to allow contracting parties to impose trade restrictive measures inconsistent with the General Agreement to pursue overriding public policy goals to the extent that such inconsistencies were unavoidable. The Panel considered that if the broad interpretation of Article XX(b) suggested by the United States were accepted, each contracting party could unilaterally determine the life or health protection policies from which other contracting parties could not deviate without jeopardizing their rights under the General Agreement. The General Agreement would then no longer constitute a multilateral framework for trade among all contracting parties but would provide legal security only in respect of trade between a limited number of contracting parties with identical internal regulations.

The Panel considered that the United States' measures, even if Article XX(b) were interpreted to permit extrajurisdictional protection of life and health, would not meet the requirement of necessity set out in that provision. The United States had not demonstrated to the Panel—as required of the party invoking an Article XX exception—that it had exhausted all options reasonably available to it to pursue its dolphin protection objectives through measures consistent with the General Agreement, in particular through the negotiation of international cooperative arrangements, which would seem to be desirable in view of the fact that dolphins roam the waters of many states and the high seas. Moreover, even assuming that an import prohibition were the only resort reasonably available to the United States, the particular measure chosen could in the Panel's view not be considered to be necessary within the meaning of Article XX(b). The United States linked the maximum incidental dolphin taking rate which Mexico had to meet during a particular period in order to be able to export tuna to the United States to the taking rate actually recorded for United States fishermen during the same period. Consequently, the Mexican authorities could not know whether, at a given point of time, their policies conformed to the United States' dolphin protection standards. The Panel considered that a limitation on trade based on such unpredictable conditions could not be regarded as necessary to protect the health or life of dolphins.

On the basis of the above considerations, the Panel found that the United States' direct import prohibition imposed on certain yellowfin tuna and certain yellowfin tuna products of Mexico and the provisions of the MMPA under which it is imposed could not be justified under the exception in Article XX(b).

The Panel proceeded to examine whether the prohibition . . . could be justified under the exception in Article XX(g). The Panel noted the United States, in invoking Article XX(g) with respect to its direct import prohibition under the MMPA, had argued that the measures taken under the MMPA are measures primarily aimed at the conservation of dolphin, and that the import restrictions on certain tuna and tuna products under the MMPA are "primarily aimed at rendering effective restrictions on domestic production or consumption" of dolphin. The Panel also noted that Mexico had argued that the United States measures were not justified under the exception in Article XX(g) because, inter alia, this provision could not be applied extrajurisdictionally.

The Panel noted that Article XX(g) required that the measures relating to the conservation of exhaustible natural resources be taken "in conjunction with restrictions on domestic production or consumption." A previous panel had found that a measure could only be considered to have been taken "in conjunction with" production restrictions "if it was primarily aimed at rendering effective these restrictions." A country can effectively control the production or consumption of an exhaustible natural resource only to the extent that the production or consumption is under its jurisdiction. This suggests that Article XX(g) was intended to permit contracting parties to take trade measures primarily aimed at rendering effective restrictions on production or consumption within their jurisdiction.

The Panel further noted that Article XX(g) allows each contracting party to adopt its own conservation policies. The conditions set out in Article XX(g) which limit resort to this exception, namely that the measures taken must be related to the conservation of exhaustible natural resources, and that they not "constitute a means of arbitrary or unjustifiable discrimination . . . or a disguised restriction on international trade" refer to the trade measure requiring justification under Article XX(g), not, however, to the conservation policies adopted by the contracting party. The Panel considered that if the extrajurisdictional interpretation of Article XX(g) suggested by the United States were accepted, each contracting party could unilaterally determine the conservation policies from which other contracting parties could not deviate without jeopardizing their rights under the General Agreement. The considerations that led the Panel to reject an extrajurisdictional application of Article XX(b) therefore apply also to Article XX(g).

The Panel did not consider that the United States measures, even if Article XX(g) could be applied extrajurisdictionally, would meet the conditions set out in that provision. A previous panel found that a measure could be considered as "relating to the conservation of exhaustible natural resources" within the meaning of Article XX(g) only if it was primarily aimed at such conservation. The Panel recalled that the United States linked the maximum incidental dolphin-taking rate which Mexico had to meet during a particular period in order to be able to export tuna to the United States to the taking rate actually recorded for United States fishermen during the same period. Consequently, the Mexican authorities could not know whether, at a given point in time, their conservation policies conformed to the United States conservation standards. The Panel considered that a limitation on trade based on such unpredictable conditions could not be regarded as being primarily aimed at the conservation of dolphins.

On the basis of the above considerations, the Panel found that the United States' direct import prohibition on certain yellowfin tuna products of Mexico directly imported from Mexico, and the provisions of the MMPA under which it is imposed, could not be justified under Article XX(g).

NOTES AND QUESTIONS

1. Does the panel's decision mean that the Article XX(b) exemption extends only to measures designed to protect resources within a nation's boundaries? If other countries choose to harm their own environment, does the United States have a legitimate interest in not trading with them? The UNCED Declaration endorses GATT's approach and states that "[u]nilateral actions to deal with environmental challenges outside the jurisdiction of the importing country should be avoided." Could restrictions designed solely to protect resources in another country ever be justified? What if the harm spills over into the global commons? Are there any circumstances in which import

restrictions validly could be imposed under GATT solely to protect resources in the global commons?

2. The panel found that the United States failed to meet the "necessity" requirement of Article XX(b) because it had not first exhausted all options to pursue dolphin protection consistent with GATT. What other options were open to the United States? Is the panel saying, in effect, that unilateral import restrictions will presumptively be invalid?

3. Why did the panel reject the U.S. claim that the tuna embargo was a valid conservation measure under Article XX(g)? Could the MMPA regulations be amended to satisfy these objections? In the first dispute involving the Canada-U.S. Free Trade Agreement (the precursor to NAFTA), a trade panel found that regulations under Canada's Fisheries Act that required biological sampling of fish prior to export were invalid because their primary goal was not conservation. The panel indicated that regulations restricting trade would be upheld only if their *sole* purpose was conservation and only if there was no available alternative that was less restrictive. McKeith, The Environment and Free Trade, 10 Pac. Basin L.J. 183, 207 (1991).

4. Could this problem be resolved by implementing a "dolphin-safe" labeling scheme, as discussed in Chapter 2? Would such a scheme essentially let U.S. consumers decide whether they are willing to pay more to protect the global commons? In 1990, Congress enacted the Dolphin Consumer Protection Information Act, 16 U.S.C. §1385 (1990), which provides penalties for companies that use "dolphin safe" labels falsely. The GATT tuna panel went on to hold that this legislation was not inconsistent with U.S. obligations under GATT.

5. Hardly any U.S. tuna boats fish in the waters of the eastern tropical Pacific Ocean. If the United States had little or no tuna industry of its own that was competing directly with the Mexican fleet, should this fact make it more likely or less likely that the tuna embargo would be deemed a protectionist measure?

6. How is the methodology used to assess the validity of import restrictions under GATT similar to, or different from, the Supreme Court's formula for assessing the constitutionality of state restrictions on waste imports? Recall Philadelphia v. New Jersey and its progeny. Note the importance of the principle of nondiscrimination for both. Is the Article XX(b) exception for health and safety measures equivalent to the "nuisance exception" to Commerce Clause doctrine? Is GATT's provision for measures to conserve natural resources in Article XX(g) the equivalent of the conservation cases discussed above in Chapter 3?

7. Despite this ruling in its favor, Mexico announced that it would strengthen its dolphin protections by requiring internationally certified observers on all tuna boats and by seeking legislation authorizing prison sentences for violators of its dolphin protection laws.

The *Tuna/Dolphin II* Decision

Although the Mexican government sought to delay enforcing the GATT decision pending negotiations with the United States, a U.S. district court directed that the tuna embargo be broadened, under the provisions of the Pelly Amendment, to prevent "tuna laundering" by 30 countries that purchased tuna from Mexico. Earth Island Institute v. Mosbacher, 785 F. Supp. 826 (N.D. Cal. 1992). The United States then negotiated a compromise to defuse the tuna-dolphin dispute with Mexico. In June 1992, the United States came to an agreement with Mexico, Vanuatu, and Venezuela to ban the practice of setting purse seine nets around schools of tuna swimming with dolphins. The Earth Island Institute, the group that initiated the lawsuit that required the embargo, supported the compromise, Pro-Dolphin Accord Made, N.Y. Times, June 16, 1992, at D9, which was implemented through amendments to the MMPA approved by Congress in October 1992. The International Dolphin Conservation Act of 1992, 16 U.S.C.A. §§952 et seq., authorizes the Secretary of State to negotiate a five-year moratorium on the use of purse seine nets that encircle dolphins or other marine mammals during the harvesting of tuna. The amendments also banned the sale of any tuna product that is not "dolphin safe." Does the ban on the sale of such tuna indicate that the labeling approach was a failure? Does the settlement of the tuna-dolphin dispute indicate that, GATT notwithstanding, for certain countries and certain products trade with the United States is so important that unilateral trade sanctions by the United States can be effective in changing how other countries use the global commons?

Several European nations remained dissatisfied with Mexico's settlement with the United States. They decided to file their own GATT complaint based on their status as "intermediary nations" under MMPA—importers of yellowfin tuna that also export tuna to the United States. Under the Act, these nations must certify that they have not imported products subject to prohibition from import into the United States within the preceding six months. As GATT panel decisions are not binding on subsequent proceedings, the second panel addressed issues similar to those considered in the first. General Agreement on Tariffs and Trade: Dispute Settlement Panel Report on United States Restrictions on Imports of Tuna, 33 I.L.M. 839 (1994).

In its review of Article XX(g), the *Tuna/Dolphin II* panel rejected arguments that the exhaustible natural resource to be conserved could not be located outside the territorial jurisdiction of the country taking the measure. Noting that the text of the provision is silent and the drafting history ambiguous on the location of resources covered, the Panel cited the fact that Article XX(g) has been applied to migratory species of fish in two previous decisions and that no distinction had been made on the basis of where the fish had been caught. The Panel further observed that other measures of Article XX applied to actions occurring outside the territory of the party taking the measure (e.g., Article XX(e) which relates to products of prison labor). Finally, the Panel made reference to general principles of international law that permit states to regulate conduct outside their territory, especially with respect to fishermen and vessels on the high seas.

The United States was, however, again unsuccessful in defending the legality under GATT of measures that required changes in the policies of other countries in order to be effective. Noting that the bias of GATT decisions has been to interpret Article XX exceptions narrowly, the Panel concluded:

> If however Article **XX** were interpreted to permit contracting parties to take trade measures so as to force other contracting parties to change their policies within their jurisdiction, including their conservation policies, the balance of rights and obligations among contracting parties, in particular the right of access to markets, would be seriously impaired. Under such an interpretation the General Agreement could no longer serve as a multilateral framework for trade among contracting parties.

The United States also lost with respect to assertions that the MMPA was justified by Article XX(b) as a measure necessary to protect the life and health of dolphins. Based on the same logic that led to its narrow interpretation of Article XX(g), the Panel concluded that allowing trade embargoes to force other countries to protect living things would also seriously impair the objectives of the General Agreement. In a paragraph labeled Concluding Observations, the Panel added that the importance of sustainable development and efforts to protect dolphins was not in dispute: "The issue was whether, in the pursuit of its environmental objectives, the United States could impose trade embargoes to secure changes in the policies which other contracting parties pursued within their own jurisdiction." Specifically, the Panel had to resolve whether the intent in Article XX was to accord parties the right to impose trade embargoes as a means for promoting conservation. "The Panel had examined this issue in the light of the recognized methods of interpretation and had found that none of them lent any support to the view that such an agreement was reflected in Article XX."

NOTES AND QUESTIONS

1. Unlike the panel in *Tuna/Dolphin I,* the *Tuna/Dolphin II* panel suggests that the resources covered by Article XX(g)'s exemption of measures to conserve exhaustible natural resources do not have to be located within the jurisdiction of the country adopting the conservation measure. Why did the panels reach a different conclusion in this regard?

2. While the United States believed that the embargo on intermediary nations was necessary to prevent "tuna laundering" from undermining the effectiveness of its sanctions, the *Tuna/Dolphin II* panel finds it objectionable because it seeks to encourage other governments to adopt trade policies similar to those of the United States. Can you think of any circumstances under which an embargo on intermediary nations could be upheld in light of the decision in *Tuna/Dolphin II*?

3. In September 1994, another GATT panel upheld key provisions of U.S. fuel economy measures that had been challenged by the European Union (EU) as violative of GATT. General Agreement on Tariffs and Trade: Dispute Settlement Panel Report on United States—Taxes on Automobiles (Sept. 29, 1994). The panel held that U.S. Corporate Average Fuel Economy (CAFE) requirements, a "gas guzzler" tax, and a luxury tax on expensive cars did not discriminate against Mercedes and BMW. However, the panel did strike down one aspect of the regulations—CAFE accounting rules that establish separate "domestic" and "import" fleets for determining overall fuel economy. This panel decision is noteworthy because it may suggest latitude within GATT principles for regulations on imports based on more than differences in their physical characteristics or end uses. The two previous panel decisions finding U.S. regulations on the importation of tuna designed to protect dolphins inconsistent with GATT caused significant concern that nations could not regulate imports based on the manner in which they were produced, a potentially serious obstacle to environmental regulation. (Note that none of these panel decisions has been formally adopted, and that there is no *stare decisis* in GATT or WTO decisions.)

The *Auto Taxes* panel was still concerned that any discrimination due to an environmental regulation be "based on factors directly relating to the product as such." Differential taxes based on fuel economy passed the test, but the CAFE accounting regulations did not. "Thus, the Auto Taxes Panel seems to have expanded the leeway for measures that are closely related to, but do not strictly affect, the product; however, it is impossible to say just how broad or narrow that expansion is." R. Housman et al., The Use of Trade Measures in Select Multilateral Environmental Agreements (paper prepared for the United Nations Environment Programme, 1995). See Lee, Process and Product: Making the Link Between Trade and the Environment, 6 Int'l Envtl. Aff. 320 (1994).

4. The *Auto Taxes* and *Tuna/Dolphin* decisions all concerned the GATT consistency of unilateral legislative acts. The issue might have been very different if presented in conjunction with a bilateral or multilateral environmental agreement. With the increasing number and importance of such agreements, the application of GATT rules to actions taken pursuant to multilateral agreements is of considerable importance. R. Housman et al. argue that *Tuna/Dolphin I* implied that measures operating under the authority of an international agreement would be covered by the Article XX exceptions to the GATT. Id. The *Tuna/Dolphin II* panel employed a three-part test for determining the applicability of Article XX, which subsequently was followed by the *Auto Taxes* panel.

> First, the *policy* upon which the measure is based must fall within the range of policies covered by the relevant article **XX** provisions.
> Second, the *measure* must be either "necessary" to protect human, animal or plant life or health under XX(b), or "related to" the conservation of exhaustible natural resources, and made effective "in conjunction" with restrictions on domestic production or consumption under XX(g).
> Third, the measure must be applied in a manner consistent with the requirements of article XX's preamble; specifically, the measure cannot be applied in a manner that would constitute a means of arbitrary or unjustifiable discrimination between countries where the same conditions prevail or in a manner that would constitute a disguised restriction on international trade.

Measures taken to protect the environment outside of a country's territorial jurisdiction were acceptable to the *Tuna/Dolphin II* panel. However, measures to change the policies of other countries, acting within their own jurisdiction, were not acceptable if such measures would achieve their intended effect only if they were followed by such changes. The *Tuna/Dolphin II* panel stated that such measures would "seriously impair the objectives of the GATT" and, thus, could neither be considered "necessary" as required by the Article XX(b) exception nor "primarily aimed at" legitimate conservation goals as required by Article XX(g). Multilateral environmental agreements that seek to alter the policies of other countries, acting within their own jurisdiction, thus could be vulnerable under the reasoning of the *Tuna/Dolphin II* panel.

Housman et al. argue that both the history of GATT and strong policy arguments support treating multilateral protections differently than unilateral protections. They maintain that "broad-based multilateral protections are the only effective means of addressing problems that spill over borders, affect the global commons, or are global in nature" and that they "serve to harmonize measures within their purview," thus reducing trade barriers. Id.

5. Fears that the WTO could threaten domestic environmental regulations were reinforced in January 1996 when the organization ruled against the United States in response to a complaint by Venezuela. The WTO ruled that a regulation governing reformulated gasoline in the Clean Air Act unfairly discriminated against some foreign refiners because it based standards for domestic refiners on the quality of gasoline they actually produced in 1990, while holding foreign refiners to a standard based on the overall average quality

of gasoline in the United States. Sanger, World Trade Group Orders U.S. to Alter Clean Air Act, N.Y. Times, Jan. 18, 1996, at D1. Because the provision of the Clean Air Act applied in differential fashion only until 1998, the decision itself was not of great concern, but the potential implications of allowing the WTO to authorize trade sanctions against the United States because of its environmental regulations was worrisome to many.

6. The United States has sometimes availed itself of the WTO to attack regulations motivated by environmental concerns, most notably in response to an EU regulation restricting imports of meat products derived from cattle given growth hormones. Because the United States, but not the EU, produces most of its meat with these hormones, the effect fell disproportionately on U.S. beef exports. The United States based its challenge on the Agreement on the Application of Sanitary and Phytosanitary Measures, relying particularly on Article 5.1, which requires that food safety measures be "based on an assessment, as appropriate to the circumstances, of the risks to human, animal or plant life or health, taking into account risk assessment techniques developed by the relevant international organizations."

In reviewing the basis for the EU policy, a WTO appellate body considered the scientific basis for the import restriction and, more particularly, whether the EU had used a risk assessment within the meaning of Article 5.1. The body found against the EU on both counts, noting a lack of scientific evidence supporting the conclusion that use of the hormones is unsafe, even assuming abusive use.

The EU unsuccessfully sought to rely on the precautionary principle as further support for its measures. The United States refused to accept that the precautionary principle represents customary international law and suggested it is more "approach" than "principle." The appellate body found more narrowly that the principle (whether or not accepted) would not change their interpretation of the provisions of the SPS agreement. WTO, EC Measures Concerning Meat and Meat Products (Hormones), WT/DS26/AB/R, Jan. 16, 1998.

The *Shrimp/Turtle* Decision

On April 6, 1998, a World Trade Organization (WTO) dispute settlement panel ruled that U.S. enforcement of §609 of Pub. L. 101-162 was inconsistent with U.S. obligations under the WTO Agreement. This law, enacted in 1989, bans the import of shrimp harvested with technology that may adversely affect sea turtles on the endangered species list. Shrimp fishers in the U.S. are required to use "turtle excluder devices" (TEDs) when trawling for shrimp. These devices prevent sea turtles from drowning when caught in shrimp nets, which had been estimated to kill 150,000 turtles a year. Although the U.S. initially applied section 609 only to countries in the Caribbean/Western Atlantic, the U.S. Court of International Trade ruled in December 1995 that it was illegal to so limit the geographical scope of the import ban. After the U.S. Department of State published guidelines broadening the ban to apply to "all shrimp products harvested in the wild by citizens or vessels of nations which have not been certified" as using turtle-safe harvesting methods, Thailand, Malaysia, India, and Pakistan filed a complaint with the WTO.

The WTO panel's decision focused on Article XX(g) and issues similar to those raised in *Tuna/Dolphin I,* page 1079 above, with the addition of evidence that the law was designed to protect a highly migratory species identified as endangered under the Convention on International Trade in Endangered Species. In defending the law, the U.S. had noted that the law applied equally to American fishers and that the TEDs are both inexpensive and effective. Yet the panel refused to interpret Article XX to permit such measures. The panel stated:

> In our view, if an interpretation of the chapeau of Article XX were to be followed which would allow a Member to adopt measures conditioning access to its market for a given product upon the adoption by the exporting Members of certain policies, including conservation policies, GATT 1994 and the WTO Agreement could no longer serve as a multilateral framework for trade among Members as security and predictability of trade relations under those agreements would be threatened. This follows because, if one WTO Member were allowed to adopt such measures, then other Members would also have the right to adopt similar measures on the same subject but with differing, or even conflicting requirements. If that happened, it would be impossible for exporting Members to comply at the same time with multiple conflicting policy requirements. Indeed, as each of these requirements would necessitate the adoption of a policy applicable not only to export production (such as specific standards applicable only to goods exported to the country requiring them) but also to domestic production, it would be impossible for a country to adopt one of those policies without running the risk of breaching other Members' conflicting policy requirements for the same product and being refused access to these other markets. We note that, in the present case, there would not even be the possibility of adapting one's export production to the respective requirements of the different Members. Market access for goods could become subject to an increasing number of conflicting policy requirements for the same product and this would rapidly lead to the end of the WTO multilateral trading system.

The panel emphasized that it was not dealing with measures undertaken to implement any international agreement and that it did not challenge any nation's right to ban products that it believes are dangerous. It stressed that the key defect of the law was that it "condition[ed] access to the U.S. market for a given product on the adoption by the exporting Member of certain conservation policies." While stating that the U.S. could require "that U.S. norms regarding the characteristics of a given product be met for that product to be allowed on the U.S. market," the panel explained that "requiring that other Members adopt policies comparable to the U.S. policy for their domestic markets and all other markets represents a threat to the WTO multilateral trading system." The panel concluded by recognizing that protection of sea turtles was an important goal, but it stated that the goal could best be pursued by reaching "cooperative agreements on integrated conservation strategies," rather than through trade sanctions.

The U.S. decided to appeal the panel's decision, which had reinforced concerns of environmentalists that the WTO always will rule against the use of trade sanctions to promote environmental goals, no matter how small the restraint on trade.

An appeal produced a similar result, although based on somewhat narrower reasoning. WTO, United States—Import Prohibition of Certain Shrimp and Shrimp Products, WT/DS58/AB/R, Oct. 12, 1998. The Appellate Body emphasized that the application of the law effectively required a regulatory program "essentially the same" as that applied to American vessels. This was unacceptable without taking into account differences in conditions in other territories. In addition, the U.S. scheme excluded imports of shrimp from waters of countries not certified under the regulatory program whether or not caught using methods identical to those required in the United States. Finally, the

United States was found at fault for failing to negotiate seriously with some shrimp-exporting parties and, ironically, for failing to avail itself of potentially relevant mechanisms in international agreements, including several conventions it had failed to ratify.

NOTES AND QUESTIONS

1. Does the *Shrimp/Turtle* decision represent a threat to domestic environmental regulation, or is it largely a product of U.S. failure to apply a legitimate regulation in a manner that does not discriminate against imports from other nations?

2. The U.S. General Accounting Office issued a report in June 2000 that examined the impact of the WTO's dispute settlement procedures on U.S. laws and regulations. GAO, World Trade Organization: U.S. Experience to Date in Dispute Settlement System (June 2000). The report found that as of April 2000 the United States had initiated 25 cases at the WTO and had been a defendant in 17 cases brought against it by other countries. In 13 of the 25 cases initiated by the United States, the United States prevailed in a final WTO dispute settlement ruling; 10 cases were resolved without a rule, and the United States did not prevail in the other 2. Of the 17 cases brought against the U.S., 10 were resolved without a ruling, the U.S. lost 6 cases and prevailed in only 1. A total of 187 complaints had been filed with the WTO during the first five years of its existence, with the United States and the European Union being the most active participants in the system. The GAO concluded "that the United States has gained more than it has lost in the WTO dispute settlement system to date. WTO cases have resulted in a substantial number of changes in foreign trade practices, while their effect on U.S. laws and regulations has been minimal." Id. at 4.

3. Protests against WTO have been cited as evidence of strong grassroots support for efforts to develop a fairer system of world trade and economic development that respects environmental and social justice. The director-general of the World Trade Organization has recognized that "in the absence of environmental protection policies, trade will exacerbate existing environmental problems" and that in some circumstances "trade can itself be the cause of environmental problems." When industrialists, government officials, and other members of the world elite gathered in Davos, Switzerland last January for their annual World Economic Forum, consumer, labor, environmental, and human rights activists gathered in Porto Alegre, Brazil for the first counter forum, called the World Social Forum. This forum highlighted the distributional consequences of policies that fail to consider the social and environmental costs of trade liberalization. Stephen Buckley, Foes Take Moderate Tack on Globalism, Wash. Post, Jan. 27, 2001, at A15.

4. While the *Corrosion Proof Fittings* decision, discussed in Chapter 4, derailed EPA's efforts to ban asbestos in the United States, a growing number of countries throughout the world are enacting asbestos bans. When Spain banned asbestos on July 3, 2001, it became the thirteenth out of fifteen members of the European Union to ban the import and use of the substance. Chile banned asbestos in July 2001 despite a personal plea not to do so by Canadian Prime Minister Jean Chretien. Argentina followed suit in August 2001. Australia, Saudi Arabia, and Brazilian cities and states accounting for 70 percent of Brazil's market also have banned asbestos use. El Salvador banned asbestos in the mid-1980s.

In September 2000, a WTO panel rejected a challenge by Canada to France's 1996 ban on imports of chrysotile asbestos. World Trade Organization, European Communities—Measures Affecting Asbestos and Asbestos-Containing Products (WT/DS135/R, Sept. 18, 2000). Although the panel found that an import ban normally would violate WTO rules promoting free trade, it concluded that a ban on asbestos imports was justified under Article XX(b), the GATT's provision exempting measures necessary to protect life or health. This decision is highly significant because it represents the first time that a measure restricting trade has been upheld on environmental grounds. Throughout the dispute, Canada argued that France's asbestos ban was not based on adequate scientific research and that it was contrary to international trade rules. The Canadian government claimed that chrysotile asbestos is safer than many alternative products, and that it is perfectly safe to use and install if adequate safety measures are taken. France, supported by the European Union, maintained that asbestos kills approximately 2,000 people in France each year. All five scientific experts consulted by the WTO panel agreed that chrysotile asbestos is carcinogenic and dangerous to human health. Canada appealed the panel's decision to the WTO's Appellate Body, which upheld the decision in March 2001. Canada, the world's second largest producer and the largest exporter of chrysotile asbestos, is particularly concerned that this decision could influence countries in other parts of the world to ban asbestos, particularly in developing countries where the industry has been making a push to expand exports.

5. An analysis of the implications of WTO decisions for the environment after the *Shrimp-Turtle* ruling identifies three factors that seem most important to the determination whether environmental measures are being applied in an unacceptably arbitrary manner: the measures must be flexible in allowing how the environmental objective is to be achieved; the enacting state must make good faith efforts to negotiate a multilateral agreement; and there must be reasonable phase-in times for those affected to come into compliance. While noting that numerous questions remain, they conclude: "At the end of the day, though, the new state of trade law in the area of PPMs and ET (extraterritoriality) is a much more balanced and nuanced approach—one that stems directly from the integration of sustainable development into the fabric of WTO law through its preamble." Mann & Porter, The State of Trade and Environmental Law 2003: Implications for Doha & Beyond vii (2003).

6. From the perspective of developing nations, the effort to link environmental objectives with trade is not always welcome. A self-declared group of "third world intellectuals" led by Columbia University professor Jagdish Bagwati has criticized such efforts as selectively biased and inconsistent with the purposes of the WTO. They argue that an unbiased review of the United States might conclude that trade sanctions should be imposed because of its acceptance of juvenile capital punishment, "an egregious violation of the Convention of the Rights of the Child." Similarly, the United States could be challenged for its failure to address recurrent evidence of sweatshops (a human rights violation) or even its inadequate protection of the right of laborers to organize (arguably inconsistent with international labor standards). Their position is that social and environmental concerns should be addressed separately, recognizing only inherently overlapping problems such as the need to define the appropriate role for trade sanctions in multilateral environmental agreements. See Linking Trade to Social Issues Is Challenged, Earth Times, Sept. 16-30, 1999, at 11-12.

7. Douglas Irwin argues that WTO rulings have not weakened U.S. environmental protections. He notes that as of late 2004, "fewer than 10 of the 140 disputes brought before the WTO had dealt with environmental and health issues" and the "few environmental cases have mainly focused on whether the regulation in question has been implemented in a nondiscriminatory way, not whether the regulation is justifiable." Douglas Irwin, Free Trade Under Fire 231 (2005). Irwin draws three lessons from the WTO decisions: (1) world trade rules are not anti-environmental, (2) there are sound reasons for not allowing any and all process regulations because this could open the door to the imposition of standards that developing countries cannot afford, and (3) unilateral trade sanctions are a poor instrument for achieving environmental objectives because keeping foreign goods out of the U.S. market does not solve the underlying problem to which the sanctions are directed.

3.   The North American Free Trade Agreement (NAFTA) and the Environment

Some opponents of global free trade, including Herman Daly, distinguish regional trade agreements as more likely to achieve the benefits of trade based on comparative advantage. On the other hand, the economic disparity between the United States and Mexico has been the source of its own unique environmental concerns. Beginning in 1965, the Mexican government created a free-trade zone in a 60-mile strip along the 2,000-mile border with the United States. In this area, *maquiladoras* owned jointly by U.S. and Mexican companies operate tariff-free, importing raw materials or components and shipping finished products or components back to the United States. More than 2,500 factories operate in this free-trade zone, until relatively recently largely without environmental regulation. See generally P. Johnson & A. Beaulieu, The Environment and NAFTA (1996); Hunter, Salzman & Zaelke, International Environmental Law and Policy 1220-1274 (1998).

The initial proposal to create a North American Free Trade Agreement was opposed by many environmentalists, who feared it would undermine environmental standards in the United States and foster relocation of pollution-intensive industries on the Mexican side of the border, where they could benefit from lax regulation. In response, President Clinton negotiated an environmental side agreement, the North American Agreement on Environmental Cooperation (Sept. 8, 1993), 32 I.L.M. 1480. The side agreement created the North American Commission for Environmental Cooperation (CEC) and endowed it with authority to investigate allegations by citizens that a party is failing to enforce its environmental laws and regulations. Tuchton, The Citizen Petition Process Under NAFTA's Environmental Side Agreement: It's Easy to Use, But Does It Work?, 26 Envtl. L. Rep. 10,018 (1996).

The environmental problems of the border zone were the subject of a separate bilateral agreement that created two new institutions, the Border Environment Cooperation Commission and the North American Development Bank.

NAFTA itself makes only sparce reference to environmental protection measures. Under Article 712.2, each country reserves the right to establish the "appropriate level of protection" for life or health within its territory "notwithstanding any other provision" of NAFTA. However, the countries are directed to "avoid arbitrary or unjustifiable distinctions" in levels of health or environmental protection that would cause "unjustifiable discrimination" against goods from another country or that would "constitute a disguised restriction on trade." For a more detailed analysis of NAFTA's environmental provisions, see Charnovitz, NAFTA: An Analysis of Its Environmental Provisions, 23 Envtl. L. Rep. 10,067 (1993).

The first complaint to the CEC, made by the National Audubon Society and two Mexican groups, cited the deaths of more than 40,000 migratory birds at the Silva Reservoir in central Mexico. The CEC determined that the deaths were caused by exposure to raw sewage and recommended that a new agency be created to monitor the health of wildlife. U.S. environmentalists complained to the CEC about the appropriations rider that lifted legal restrictions on "timber salvage" operations on public lands. This claim was rejected on the ground that it reflected a relaxation of the environmental laws, rather than a failure to enforce them. The CEC concluded that "enactment of legislation which specifically alters the operation of pre-existing environmental law in essence becomes a part of the greater body of laws and statutes on the books." Trade-Environment: NAFTA Environment Commission Disappoints, Inter-Press Service, Dec. 15, 1995.

In 1997 the CEC for the first time directed the United States to respond to a complaint charging it with violating NAFTA by failing to enforce its own environmental laws. The complaint, filed by two citizen groups in the U.S. charged that the U.S. Defense Department violated NEPA by failing to prepare an EIS for its decision to relocate 2,000 new army personnel to a fort in Arizona. A NEPA lawsuit filed by the citizen groups previously had been dismissed because the statute of limitations had expired.

In 1997 the CEC released the results of its investigation into complaints filed in 1996 by three NGOs concerning an alleged failure by Mexican authorities to enforce their environmental laws when approving a new cruise ship pier in Cozumel. Final Factual Record of the Cruise Ship Pier Project in Cozumel, Quintana Roo (1997). The 55-page report summarized the facts concerning the submission, the response of the Mexican government, and other relevant factual information gathered by Secretariat of the CEC. However, the report made no conclusions and provided no remedies, apparently leaving it to the political process in each country to determine the appropriate response.

By June 2001, the CEC had completed its assessment of 19 citizen complaints and had found that only two of these warranted preparation of a public factual record. Twelve additional complaints were under review. There is some evidence that NAFTA has increased environmental awareness in Mexico, contributing to a growing environmental movement there. See Pollution Fight Takes Root in Courtrooms of Mexico, San Jose Mercury News, April 30, 2001, at A11.

Chapter 11 of NAFTA, which is designed to protect foreign investors against arbitrary action by governments, has come under considerable scrutiny as a result of a ruling against Mexico in a case brought by the Metalclad Corporation. Anthony DePalma, NAFTA's Powerful Little Secret, March 11, 2001, at C2. Metalclad alleged that Mexico had effectively expropriated a hazardous waste landfill it was building when local officials in Mexico refused to license the project, despite prior assurances to the company by the Mexican government that it would be allowed to operate. Metalclad then invoked Chapter 11's provisions for convening an arbitral tribunal of the International Centre for the Settlement of Investment Disputes. Mexico argued that the permit denial was the result of a change of plans by Metalclad, which had decided to significantly expand its site despite public opposition. The tribunal awarded Metalclad $16.68 million after finding that the locality had exceeded its authority and that a decree by the region's governor declaring the site a protected natural area was tantamount to expropriation without compensation.

A study by Kevin Gallagher provides some empirical analysis of the environmental consequences of NAFTA, and by analogy, the larger consequences of trade liberalization. His primary finding is that "on a national level, a number of environmental conditions worsened in Mexico despite rising incomes, but not because dirty industry in the United States flocked there. Rather, environmental degradation worsened because the Mexican and U.S. governments did not instate effective environmental policies that would have brought the desired benefits from economic integration." Kevin Gallagher, Free Trade and the Environment 7 (2004). He further concludes:

- While Mexico reached $5,000 GDP per capita in 1985, a level of income associated with environmental improvements by the Kuznets Curve, the country has yet to reach a general turning point and may not "for decades to come." Id. at 8.
- The marginal costs of pollution abatement in the United States are too small to justify relocation to Mexico (the "pollution haven hypothesis"), and the composition of Mexican industry became less pollution-intensive with growth. Id. at 8-9.
- Increases in pollution due to growth in manufacturing exceeded reductions due to declines in pollution intensity, and total criteria air pollution in manufacturing nearly doubled. Id. at 9.
- The impact of transfer of technology (the "technique effect") was evident in the steel and cement industries, which are less polluting than firms in the United States; but in general "the share of those industries in Mexico that are cleaner than their U.S. counterparts has been shrinking by every measure." Id.
- "Since 1993, the year after NAFTA was signed, real spending and plant-level environmental inspections have both fallen by 45 percent. On an international level, the environmental side accords of NAFTA, with some exceptions have done little fill this gap." Id.

Gallagher's work represents an important middle ground in discussions about the environmental consequences of free trade and leads to several important conclusions. First, policies associated with trade liberalization can lead to environmental problems if they are used to justify dismantling or not enforcing domestic environmental regulations as has unfortunately sometimes been the case. Second, effective environmental policies are not likely to discourage foreign investment and can avoid substantial costs from pollution. And third, Mexico and other developing nations require much greater assistance to develop and implement effective environmental policies simultaneously with the development of the laws and institutions required for economic growth. While economists have widely recognized the general importance of laws and institutions as a fundamental condition for economic growth, few recognize the analogous importance of the same for environmental policies.

4.   International Trade in Hazardous Substances

International trade in hazardous substances has exacerbated tensions between developing nations and the industrialized world. As industrialized countries adopt increasingly stringent environmental standards, countries without such standards have become inviting targets for the marketing and disposal of hazardous substances. Three types of activities—exports of hazardous waste, marketing of products banned in industrialized nations, and trade in other hazardous substances—raise environmental concerns explored below.

A. POLICY ISSUES

Exports of hazardous waste from industrialized nations have created international incidents when developing nations have discovered that they were the intended dumping grounds for toxic residue. When 8,000 drums of toxic waste, including 150 tons of PCBs, were dumped in a small Nigerian fishing village by an Italian firm, Nigeria recalled its ambassador to Italy and forced the firm to reclaim the waste. The waste, aboard the *Karin B.,* was then refused by five countries before being returned to Italy. Guinea jailed a Norwegian diplomat after a Norwegian ship dumped toxic waste there. After Panama refused a shipment of incinerator ash on board the *Khian Sea,* the shipper tried to dump it on a Haitian beach but was stopped after unloading 3,000 tons. The *Khian Sea* then roamed the oceans for 18 months, unable to find a willing recipient for its cargo. After visiting five continents and changing its name three times the boat reappeared, without its cargo, which probably was dumped in the Indian Ocean. French, A Most Deadly Trade, World-Watch 11 (July-Aug. 1990).

It is not difficult to understand why increasing quantities of hazardous waste are being exported by industrialized nations. Wendy Grieder of EPA's Office of International Activities notes that some developing countries charge as little as $40 per ton for disposal of wastes that can cost $250 to $300 per ton to dispose of in the United States. Chepesiuk, From Ash to Cash: The International Trade in Toxic Waste, 31, 35 (July-Aug. 1991). While data on the volume of waste exports are sketchy, it is estimated that industrialized nations shipped three million tons of toxic waste to less developed countries between 1986 and 1988, Obstler, Toward a Working Solution to Global Pollution: Importing CERCLA to Regulate the Export of Hazardous Waste, 16 Yale J. Int'l L. 73, 76 (1991), and that the volume of exports was increasing. But see Montgomery, Reassessing the Waste Trade Crisis: What Do We Really Know?, 4 J. Env't & Dev. 1 (1995) (arguing that the data do not support the conclusion that the problem is serious).

The export of hazardous substances also has expanded. As regulation and increased consumer awareness reduced the domestic demand for such substances, producers of hazardous substances intensified marketing efforts in developing countries. Products that are banned in the United States generally can be manufactured for export. For example, the pesticides heptachlor and chlordane, which have been banned by EPA, are currently being manufactured in the United States for export. Several other pesticides that have not been approved by EPA also are manufactured for export. Exports of such pesticides and other hazardous materials place workers at risk in developing countries, where regulatory standards are far less strict than in the United States. U.S. consumers may continue to be exposed to pesticides banned as unreasonably dangerous under FIFRA when residues of such pesticides are present on imported fruits and vegetables, a phenomenon called the "circle of poison." See D. Weir & M. Shapiro, Circle of Poison: Pesticides and People in a Hungry World (1982).

Export markets have been aggressively pursued for products whose use was phased out or discouraged to protect health in the United States. For example, after the United States prohibited use of lead additives in gasoline to prevent lead poisoning, manufacturers of lead additives expanded their sales to developing countries. In 1991 the Ethyl Corporation of Richmond, Virginia, applied for permission to double production of lead additives at a plant in Sarnia, Canada, to facilitate greater exports to South America. Although Canada also has banned lead additives in gasoline, fuel additives manufactured for export are exempt from the 1988 Canadian Environmental Protection Act's prohibition on the export of products banned domestically. Gorrie, Groups Oppose Canada's Export of Lead Additive, Toronto Star, Mar. 25, 1991, at D8. U.S. exports of cigarettes to developing countries have soared, easily offsetting substantial declines in domestic demand. In 1989 smoking in the United States dropped by 5 percent, while U.S. exports of tobacco rose 20 percent. Despite dramatic declines in smoking in the United States, tobacco use has soared by 75 percent worldwide during the past 20 years. The American Medical Association charged that this dramatic increase was a result of U.S. trade policies that ignored the hazards of U.S. products sold abroad. Arguing that the United States has no business dictating how American companies should respond to foreign demand, the U.S. Cigarette Export Association opposed efforts to require foreign-language health warning labels on cigarettes exported from the United States. A.M.A. Assails Nation's Export Policy on Tobacco, N.Y. Times, June 27, 1990, at A12. When Thailand sought to ban cigarette imports, the United States invoked GATT, and the ban was struck down because it did not apply to Thai cigarettes.

Critics of the international trade in hazardous substances argue that it is unfair or immoral for industrialized nations to export risks they are unwilling to bear to poor countries that are ill-prepared to handle them. Because "[m]ost developing countries have neither the technical capability nor the regulatory infrastructure to ensure safe handling and destruction of toxic waste," NRDC representatives argue that exports to such countries are "economically, environmentally, morally, and technically indefensible." Uva & Bloom, Exporting Pollution: The International Waste Trade, 31 Environment 4 (June 1989). Critics argue that the absence of effective controls on hazardous substance exports also promotes environmental damage, poisons relations between industrialized and developing countries, and puts U.S. consumers at risk through the "circle of poison."

Opponents of stricter regulation argue that it is paternalistic for the industrialized world to dictate environmental standards to less developed countries. They argue that it may be more efficient for developing countries to adopt less stringent environmental standards to promote development. In a controversial memorandum, Lawrence Summers, then the World Bank's chief economist, wrote that "the economic logic behind dumping a load of toxic waste in the lowest wage country is impeccable" because lost earnings caused by a given amount of health damage would be lower there. Arguing that "underpopulated countries in Africa are vastly *under*polluted," the memo maintained that cancer risks should be of less concern there because life expectancy already is low. Weisskopf, World Bank Official's Irony Backfires, Wash. Post, Feb. 10, 1992, at A9. Brazil's environmental minister dubbed this reasoning "perfectly logical but totally insane." Cockburn, "Earth Summit" Is in Thrall to the Marketeers, L.A. Times, Mar. 1, 1992, at M5.

B. REGULATION OF INTERNATIONAL TRADE IN HAZARDOUS SUBSTANCES

One approach to the problems raised by international trade in hazardous substances is to emphasize the principle of informed consent in a manner similar to the informational approaches to regulation explored in Chapter 4. This is the approach most existing U.S. laws follow, as indicated in Figure 11.4. Section 3017 of RCRA requires persons seeking to export hazardous waste to notify EPA at least 60 days prior to shipment of the waste. The Secretary of State is then required to notify the government of the intended recipient and those of any countries through which the waste will pass in transit. Waste may not be exported until written consent has been obtained from the recipient's government, and copies of such consent must be attached to a manifest accompanying such shipments. Waste shipped pursuant to a bilateral agreement, such as the existing agreement between the United States and Canada (the largest recipient of U.S. hazardous waste exports), is exempt from the prior notification and consent requirements on the theory that the agreement already constitutes blanket consent to such shipments.

TSCA and FIFRA require that other countries be notified when regulatory action is taken against a chemical substance or when a pesticide's registration is canceled or suspended. Both statutes, however, permit products banned in the United States to be exported. Indeed, they actually insulate products manufactured solely for export from most domestic regulation. Under section 12(a) of TSCA, EPA can only regulate such products if it determines the risks they present *within the United States* are unreasonable, without considering their impact in countries importing them.

Signed in 1989, the Basel Convention on the Control of Transboundary Movement of Hazardous Wastes sought to establish a framework for controlling hazardous waste exports. It banned hazardous waste exports unless the receiving country and any transit countries have consented in writing to such shipments. While the U.S. Senate ratified the Basel Convention in 1992, the U.S. has not become a formal party because Congress has not adopted legislation amending RCRA to conform to Basel requirements. In 1991 African nations signed the Bamako Convention, prohibiting hazardous waste imports into Africa. In 1994 the Basel COP agreed to prohibit exports of hazardous waste from OECD to non-OECD countries. In 1999 the parties to the Basel Convention agreed to impose strict liability on exporting states for damages caused by waste shipments.

Tort Litigation in the United States for Actions Abroad by U.S. Multinationals

One possible strategy for holding multinational companies accountable for damage caused by the export of hazardous substances is tort litigation by foreigners injured due to exposure to such substances. In addition to the usual difficulties of proving causation in toxic tort cases, foreign plaintiffs face other

FIGURE 11.4
Provisions in U.S. Environmental Statutes Addressing International Trade in Hazardous Substances

Statutory Provision	Activities or Substances Covered	Requirements
RCRA §3017	Export of hazardous wastes	Prohibited unless notification is provided and the receiving country agrees to accept the waste or unless shipped in conformance with agreement between the United States and the receiving country
TSCA §12(a)	Chemical substances intended for export and so labeled unless found to present an unreasonable risk of injury to health or the environment within the United States	Exempt from all provisions of TSCA except for recordkeeping and reporting requirements imposed under §8
TSCA §12(b)	Chemical substances intended for export for which a data submission has been required under §4 or §5(b) or for which restrictions have been proposed or promulgated under §5 or §6	Notification of government of importing country of availability of data required to be submitted or of the existence of restrictions
FIFRA §17(a)	Unregistered pesticides produced solely for export to a foreign country	Exempt from most regulation when prepared and packed according to the specifications of a foreign purchaser when accompanied by a signed statement filed by the purchaser acknowledging that the pesticide is not registered in the United States
FIFRA §17(b)	Pesticides whose registration is canceled or suspended	Notification of governments of other countries and of appropriate international agencies of cancellation or suspension of registration

formidable obstacles. American courts may refuse to hear cases brought by plaintiffs injured in foreign countries by invoking the doctrine of *forum non conveniens,* as illustrated by the litigation over the Bhopal tragedy, which was rejected by American courts. In re Union Carbide Corp. Gas Plant Disaster, 809 F.2d 195 (2d Cir. 1987). See Arthaud, Environmental Destruction in the Amazon: Can U.S. Courts Provide a Forum for the Claims of Indigenous Peoples?, 7 Geo. Int'l Envtl L. Rev. 195 (1994). Because American tort law is perceived to be more generous to plaintiffs than the law in most foreign countries, the choice of forum can have a substantial impact on the amount of damages recoverable. In Dow Chemical Co. v. Alfaro, 786 S.W.2d 674 (Tex. 1990), banana workers in Costa Rica claimed that they had been injured by a pesticide that EPA had banned within the United States, but which continues to be produced in the United States for export abroad. The workers brought a tort action in Texas state court against the U.S. company that manufactured the pesticide. After the trial court dismissed the action, the plaintiffs appealed to the Texas Supreme Court. The court's 5-4 decision produced sharp disagreement among the justices, with the majority ruling that the case must be heard in Texas. In a concurring opinion, Justice Doggett explained why:

> Shell Oil Company is a multinational corporation with its world headquarters in Houston, Texas. Dow Chemical Company, though headquartered in Midland, Michigan, conducts extensive operations from its Dow Chemical USA building located in Houston. Dow operates this country's largest chemical manufacturing plant within 60 miles of Houston in Freeport, Texas. The district court where this lawsuit was filed is three blocks away from Shell's world headquarters, One Shell Plaza in downtown Houston.
>
> Shell has stipulated that all of its more than 100,000 documents relating to DBCP are located or will be produced in Houston. Shell's medical and scientific witnesses are in Houston. The majority of Dow's documents and witnesses are located in Michigan, which is far closer to Houston (both in terms of geography and communications linkages) than to Costa Rica. The respondents have agreed to be available in Houston for independent medical examinations, for depositions and for trial. Most of the respondents' treating doctors and co-workers have agreed to testify in Houston. Conversely, Shell and Dow have purportedly refused to make their witnesses available in Costa Rica.
>
> The banana plantation workers allegedly injured by DBCP were employed by an American company on American-owned land and grew Dole bananas for export solely to American tables. The chemical allegedly rendering the workers sterile was researched, formulated, tested, manufactured, labeled and shipped by an American company in the United States to another American company. The decision to manufacture DBCP for distribution and use in the third world was made by these two American companies in their corporate offices in the United States. Yet now Shell and Dow argue that the one part of this equation that should not be American is the legal consequences of their actions. . . .
>
> Comity—deference shown to the interests of the foreign forum—is a consideration best achieved by rejecting forum non conveniens. Comity is not achieved when the United States allows its multinational corporations to adhere to a double standard when operating abroad and subsequently refuses to hold them accountable for those actions. . . .
>
> The doctrine of forum non conveniens is obsolete in a world in which markets are global and in which ecologists have documented the delicate balance of all life on this planet. The parochial perspective embodied in the doctrine of forum non conveniens enables corporations to evade legal control merely because they are transnational. This perspective ignores the reality that actions of our corporations affecting those abroad will also affect Texans.

Although DBCP is banned from use within the United States, it and other similarly banned chemicals have been consumed by Texans eating foods imported from Costa Rica and elsewhere. See D. Weir & M. Schapiro, Circle of Poison 28-30, 77, 82-83 (1981). In the absence of meaningful tort liability in the United States for their actions, some multinational corporations will continue to operate without adequate regard for the human and environmental costs of their actions. This result cannot be allowed to repeat itself for decades to come. [786 S.W.2d at 681, 687, 689.]

In response, Justice Gonzalez argued in dissent:

Under the guise of statutory construction, the court today abolishes the doctrine of forum non conveniens in suits brought pursuant to section 71.032 of the Civil Practice and Remedies Code. This decision makes us one of the few states in the Union without such a procedural tool, and if the legislature fails to reinstate this doctrine, Texas will become an irresistible forum for all mass disaster lawsuits. See generally, Note, Foreign Plaintiffs and Forum Non Conveniens: Going Beyond *Reyno,* 64 Tex. L. Rev. 193 (1985). "Bhopal"-type litigation, with little or no connection to Texas, will *add* to our already crowded dockets, forcing our residents to wait in the corridors of our courthouses while foreign causes of action are tried. I would hold that section 71.031 of the Texas Civil Practice and Remedies Code *does not* confer upon foreign litigants an *absolute right* to bring suit in Texas. Because I believe that trial courts have the inherent power to apply forum non conveniens in appropriate cases, I would provide guidelines and set parameters for its use. I would thus modify the judgment of the court of appeals and remand the cause to the trial court for further proceedings.

This cause of action arose in Costa Rica where certain Costa Rican agricultural workers suffered injuries allegedly as a result of exposure to a pesticide manufactured by the defendants. The injured workers are seeking to enforce in Texas courts claims for personal injuries that occurred in Costa Rica. Several suits involving many of the same plaintiffs and essentially the same defendants have previously been filed in the United States and then dismissed on forum non conveniens grounds. . . .

In conclusion, I have no intent, much less "zeal," to implement social policy as Justice Doggett charges. That is not our role. It is clear that if anybody is trying to advance a particular social policy, it is Justice Doggett. I admire his altruism, and I too sympathize with the plight of the plaintiffs. However, the powers of this court are well-defined, and the sweeping implementations of social welfare policy Justice Doggett seeks to achieve by abolishing the doctrine of forum non conveniens are the exclusive domain of the legislature. [786 S.W.2d at 690, 697.]

NOTES AND QUESTIONS

1. The pesticide DBCP to which the plaintiffs were exposed had been banned in the United States since 1977. The history behind this ban is told in Davis, When Smoke Ran Like Water 195-200 (2002).

2. Do you agree with Justice Doggett's claim that forum non conveniens is an obsolete doctrine in a world of global markets? A court's decision to invoke the doctrine to avoid hearing a case is often determinative of the outcome. In a portion of his concurring opinion not reproduced here, Justice Doggett cited a study that concluded that fewer than 4 percent of cases dismissed by

American courts pursuant to the doctrine of forum non conveniens ever are litigated in foreign courts. Robertson, Forum Non Conveniens in America and England: "A Rather Fantastic Fiction," 103 Law Q. Rev. 398, 419 (1987). After the Bhopal litigation was rejected by courts in the United States, the Supreme Court of India approved a settlement in 1989 that barred all actions against Union Carbide, the owner of the plant involved in the Bhopal tragedy, in return for a payment of $470 million to compensate the victims. Efforts to overturn the settlement have not been successful. More than 3,000 people were killed and more than 100,000 were injured by the gas leak.

3. Should foreign plaintiffs be permitted to forum shop in search of the most favorable court to hear their claims? In his dissent, Justice Gonzalez noted that the plaintiffs in *Alfaro* previously had filed three lawsuits that had been dismissed by courts in other states on forum non conveniens grounds—two in Florida federal courts and one in a federal court in California.

4. Foreigners can be sued in U.S. courts if it is reasonably foreseeable that actions they take outside the United States will cause harm here. See Ohio v. Wyandotte Chemicals Corp., 401 U.S. 493 (1971).

5. It is easy to understand why the Costa Rican plaintiffs preferred a U.S. forum for their claims. Under Costa Rican law they would have been limited to recoveries of no more than $1,500 each. Developments in the Law—International Environmental Law, 104 Harv. L. Rev. 1484, 1618 (1991). The *Alfaro* decision may have opened the door to similar lawsuits on behalf of foreigners allegedly injured by U.S. corporations. In October 1991, a toxic tort suit was filed against a company in Brownsville, Texas, on behalf of a group of more than 60 Mexican children who are deformed or retarded. McClintock, In Matamoros, Residents' Rage at Polluting U.S.-Owned Companies Is Growing, Baltimore Sun, Jan. 19, 1992, at A8.

6. The *Alfaro* case was settled shortly before it was scheduled to go to trial in Texas state court in August 1992. Terms of the settlement were not disclosed, but plaintiffs are thought to have received close to $50 million. One factor leading to the settlement was the plaintiffs' concern that the Texas legislature or supreme court would overturn *Alfaro* and reinstate the forum non conveniens doctrine in Texas. The business community expected a change in the membership of the Texas Supreme Court to reinstate the doctrine. When that did not occur, overturning *Alfaro* through legislation became the business lobby's top priority for the 1993 legislative session. In February 1993, the Texas legislature passed a bill reinstating the forum non conveniens doctrine. The legislation took effect on September 1, 1993. Ironically, after *Alfaro* was decided by the Texas Supreme Court, but before the new legislation was enacted, Exxon moved its corporate headquarters from New York to Texas.

7. The *Alfaro* case was not the end of tort suits against U.S. chemical companies by foreign banana workers exposed to DBCP. In May 1997, Shell, Dow Chemical Co., and Occidental Chemical Corp. settled a class action filed on behalf of 13,000 banana workers in the Philippines, Honduras, Nicaragua, Ecuador, Guatemala, and Costa Rica who allegedly became sterile or suffered other health problems as a result of exposure to DBCP. Although the companies maintained that any harm to the workers was caused by misuse of the pesticide, they agreed to create a $41.5 million fund to compensate the workers. The first payments from the fund were received by the workers in December 1997. Filipino Workers Receive Compensation from Banana Pesticide Settlement Fund, Wall St. J., Dec. 12, 1997, at B9C. Workers who suffered health problems received

between $800 and $5,000, depending on the seriousness of their problems. Workers unable to document health problems, but who could show they were exposed to DBCP were to receive $100 each. While these payments are small by U.S. standards, the average daily wage of a Filipino banana worker is approximately $4.60.

8. Several other lawsuits have been brought against U.S. corporations for alleged environmental torts committed in other countries. In the case below, a resident of Indonesia sued mining companies that allegedly discharged 100,000 tons of tailings per day in several rivers, rendering them unusable for bathing and drinking.

Beanal v. Freeport-McMoran, Inc.
197 F.3d 161 (5th Cir. 1999)

Before KING, Chief Judge, and SMITH and STEWART, Circuit Judges. CARL E. STEWART, Circuit Judge:

This case involves alleged violations of international law committed by domestic corporations conducting mining activities abroad in the Pacific Rim. Freeport-McMoran, Inc., and Freeport-McMoran Copper & Gold, Inc., ("Freeport"), are Delaware corporations with headquarters in New Orleans, Louisiana. Freeport operates the "Grasberg Mine," an open pit copper, gold, and silver mine situated in the Jayawijaya Mountain in Irian Jaya, Indonesia. The mine encompasses approximately 26,400 square kilometers. Beanal is a resident of Tamika, Irian Jaya within the Republic of Indonesia (the "Republic"). He is also the leader of the Amungme Tribal Council of Lambaga Adat Suki Amungme (the "Amungme"). In August 1996, Beanal filed a complaint against Freeport in federal district court in the Eastern District of Louisiana for alleged violations of international law. Beanal invoked jurisdiction under (1) 28 U.S.C. §1332, (2) the Alien Tort Statute, 28 U.S.C. §1350, and (3) the Torture Victim Protection Act of 1991, sec. 1, et seq., 28 U.S.C. §1350 note. In his First Amended Complaint, he alleged that Freeport engaged in environmental abuses, human rights violations, and cultural genocide. Specifically, he alleged that Freeport mining operations had caused harm and injury to the Amungme's environment and habitat. . . . Freeport moved to dismiss Beanal's claims under Fed. R. Civ. Proc. 12(b)(6). The district court in April 1997 issued a thorough forty-nine page Opinion and Order dismissing Beanal's claims without prejudice and with leave to amend. See Beanal v. Freeport-McMoran, 969 F. Supp. 362 (E.D. La. 1997). . . .

Alien Tort Statute

Beanal claims that Freeport engaged in conduct that violated the Alien Tort Statute (the "ATS" or "§1350"). Under §1350:

> The district courts shall have original jurisdiction of any civil action by an alien for a tort only, committed in violation of the law of nations or a treaty of the United States.

Section 1350 confers subject matter jurisdiction when the following conditions are met: (1) an alien sues, (2) for a tort, (3) that was committed in violation of the "law of nations" or a treaty of the United States. See Kadic v. Karadzic, 70 F.3d 232, 238 (2d Cir. 1995). Beanal does not claim that Freeport violated a United States treaty. Thus, the issue before us is whether Beanal states claims upon which relief can be granted for violations under the "law of nations," i.e., international law. . . . The law of nations is defined by customary usage and clearly articulated principles of the international community. One of the means of ascertaining the law of nations is "by consulting the work of jurists writing professedly on public law or by the general usage and practice of nations; or by judicial decisions recognizing and enforcing that law." See Carmichael, 835 F.2d at 113 (citing United States v. Smith, 18 U.S. (5 Wheat.) 153, 160-61, (1820)), see also Kadic, 70 F.3d at 238; Filartiga v. Pena-Irala, 630 F.2d 876, 880 (2d Cir. 1980). Courts "must interpret international law not as it was in 1789, but as it has evolved and exists among the nations of the world today." Kadic, 70 F.3d at 238; Filartiga, 630 F.2d at 881. Although Beanal's claims raise complex issues of international law; nonetheless, the task before us does not require that we resolve them. We are only required to determine whether the pleadings on their face state a claim upon which relief can be granted. . . .

Environmental Torts and Abuses

Beanal argues that Freeport through its mining activities engaged in environmental abuses which violated international law. In his Third Amended Complaint, Beanal alleges the following:

> FREEPORT, in connection with its Grasberg operations, deposits approximately 100,000 tons of tailings per day in the Aghwagaon, Otomona and Akjwa Rivers. Said tailings have diverted the natural flow of the rivers and have rendered the natural waterways of the plaintiff unusable for traditional uses including bathing and drinking. Furthermore, upon information and belief, the heavy metal content of the tailings have and/or will affect the body tissue of the aquatic life in said rivers. Additionally, tailings have blocked the main flow of the Ajkwa River causing overflow of the tailings into lowland rain forest vegetation destroying the same.

Third Amended Complaint P 13.

> FREEPORT in connection with its Grasberg operations has diverted the aforesaid rivers greatly increasing the likelihood of future flooding in Timika, the home of the plaintiff, TOM BEANAL.

Id. P 14.

> FREEPORT, in connection with its Grasberg mining operations has caused or will cause through the course of its operations 3 billion tons of "overburden" to be dumped into the upper Wanagon and Carstensz creating the likely risk of massive landslides directly injurious to the plaintiff. Furthermore, said "overburden" creates acid rock damage which has created acid streams and rendering the Lake Wanagon an "acid lake" extremely high in copper concentrations,

Id. P 15.

However, Freeport argues that Beanal's allegations of environmental torts are not cognizable under the "law of nations" because Beanal fails to show that

Freeport's mining activities violate any universally accepted environmental standards or norms. Furthermore, Freeport argues that it would be improper for a United States tribunal to evaluate another country's environmental practices and policies. The district court conducted a thorough survey of various international law principles, treaties, and declarations and concluded that Beanal failed to articulate environmental torts that were cognizable under international law.

Beanal and the amici refer the court to several sources of international environmental law to show that the alleged environmental abuses caused by Freeport's mining activities are cognizable under international law. Chiefly among these are the Principles of International Environmental Law I: Frameworks, Standards and Implementation 183-18 (Phillip Sands ed., 1995) ("Sands"),[5] and the Rio Declaration on Environment and Development, June 13, 1992, U.N. Doc. A/CONF. 151/5 rev. 1 (1992) (the "Rio Declaration").

Nevertheless, "[i]t is only where the nations of the world have demonstrated that the wrong is of mutual and not merely several, concern, by means of express international accords, that a wrong generally recognized becomes an international law violation in the meaning of the [ATS]." Filartiga, 630 F.2d at 888. Thus, the ATS "applies only to shockingly egregious violations of universally recognized principles of international law." See Zapata v. Quinn, 707 F.2d 691, 692 (2d Cir. 1983) (per curiam). Beanal fails to show that these treaties and agreements enjoy universal acceptance in the international community. The sources of international law cited by Beanal and the amici merely refer to a general sense of environmental responsibility and state abstract rights and liberties devoid of articulable or discernable standards and regulations to identify practices that constitute international environmental abuses or torts. Although the United States has articulable standards embodied in federal statutory law to address environmental violations domestically, see The National Environmental Policy Act (42 U.S.C. §4321 et seq.) and The Endangered Species Act (16 U.S.C. §1532), nonetheless, federal courts should exercise extreme caution when adjudicating environmental claims under international law to insure that environmental policies of the United States do not displace environmental policies of other governments. Furthermore, the argument to abstain from interfering in a sovereign's environmental practices carries persuasive force especially when the alleged environmental torts and abuses occur within the sovereign's borders and do not affect neighboring countries.[6] Therefore, the district court did not err when it concluded that Beanal failed to show in his pleadings that Freeport's mining activities constitute environmental torts or abuses under international law.

---

5. Sands features three environmental law principles: (1) the Polluter Pays Principle; (2) the Precautionary Principle; and (3) the Proximity Principle.

6. Although Beanal cites the Rio Declaration to support his claims of environmental torts and abuses under international law, nonetheless, the express language of the declaration appears to cut against Beanal's claims. Principle 2 on the first page of the Rio Declaration asserts that states have the "sovereign right to exploit their own resources pursuant to their own environmental and developmental policies," but also have "the responsibility to ensure that activities within their jurisdiction or control do not cause damage to the environment or other States or areas beyond the limits of national jurisdiction." Beanal does not allege in his pleadings that Freeport's mining activities in Indonesia have affected environmental conditions in other countries.

NOTES AND QUESTIONS

1. Why does the court reject the notion that the principles outlined in the Rio Declaration provide the kind of universal norms a violation of which could be subject to a remedy under the Alien Tort Statute? For a discussion of the history of the Alien Tort Claims Act and efforts to apply it to remedy environmental abuses see Richard L. Herz, Litigating Environmental Abuses Under the Alien Tort Claims Act: A Practical Assessment, 40 Va. J. Int'l L. 522 (2000). Assuming that the practices Beanal complains about would not have been permissible under the law of the United States, why does the court reject his claim?

2. Would it have made a difference to Beanal's case if he had been able to allege that pollution caused by the mining companies was having an adverse effect on people or property in another country? Why or why not?

3. Following the Fifth Circuit's decision, the very kind of harm feared by plaintiffs in the *Beanal* litigation occurred. The plaintiffs had alleged that overburden dumped by the company's Grasberg mining operation created a risk of landslides that threatened them. On May 4, 2000, a rock-waste containment for the overburden collapsed, causing an adjoining water basin to overflow, killing four workers and spilling waste and water into the Wanagon Valley. Jay Solomon, U.S. Mining Firm, Indonesia at Odds over Latest Spill, Wall St. J., May 8, 2000, at A30. The Indonesian Ministry of Environmental Affairs stated that it had "warned Freeport a long time ago" about the dangers of its waste containment, but that the company had not acted to correct the problem. Id. On May 24, 2000, Freeport agreed not to continue placing overburden in the Wanagon basin and to temporarily limit production at its Grasberg open pit to an average of no more than 200,000 metric tons of ore per day pending completion of studies concerning how to prevent future spills.

4. On June 20, 2001, the Exxon/Mobil Corporation was sued in federal district court in Washington, D.C., by the International Labor Rights Fund, which represents eleven villagers from Aceh, Indonesia. Doe v. Exxon/Mobil Corporation, No. 01-CV-1357 (D.D.C.). The lawsuit seeks to hold Exxon Mobil accountable for human rights abuses by Indonesian soldiers guarding the company's oil facilities in Indonesia. It alleges that the company bought military equipment and paid mercenaries who have assisted Indonesian security forces in efforts to crush dissent by torturing and assaulting villagers. Exxon denies responsibility for the behavior of the Indonesian military and says that it condemns the violation of human rights in any form. In 2006 the court refused to dismiss the case despite a State Department claim that it could have a "seriously adverse impact on significant interests of the United States, including interests related directly to the ongoing struggle against international terrorism."

5. In Jota v. Texaco, Inc., 157 F.3d 153 (2d Cir. 1998), the Second Circuit reversed the dismissal of a lawsuit against a U.S.-based multinational oil company for environmental damage its oil drilling operations caused in the rain forests of Ecuador. The company argues that its operations were approved by the government of Ecuador and that it did not violate any Ecuadoran laws. The plaintiffs argued that the oil company knew that its practices would cause substantial environmental damage and that it never would have operated in that manner in the United States or another developed country. The Second Circuit held that the district court should not have dismissed the lawsuit on grounds of *forum non conveniens* without at least requiring the company to submit to Ecuador's jurisdiction. In Aguinda v. Texaco, Inc., 303 F.3d 470 (2d Cir. 2002), the court

affirmed the subsequent dismissal of this suit on *forum non conveniens* grounds conditioned on Texaco waiving statute of limitations defenses in Ecuador.

6. In Flores v. Southern Peru Copper Corp., 414 F.3d 233 (2d Cir. 2003), the Second Circuit affirmed the dismissal of a lawsuit brought by residents of Peru under the Alien Tort Statute (ATS) against a U.S. company operating a copper smelter in their neighborhood. The court held that the plaintiffs' allegations that uncontrolled emissions from the smelter injured their health and threatened their lives did not rise to the level of a violation of the "law of nations" as required to state a case under the ATS because it only involved "intranational pollution."

7. **Doe v. Unocal Settlement and Sosa v. Alvarez-Machain Decision.** A settlement was announced in December 2004 in an important Alien Tort Statute (ATS) case that had been reargued en banc in the U.S. Court of Appeals for the Ninth Circuit. The case was filed by 15 Burmese villagers as a class action in federal district court against the Unocal Corporation. Unocal is building a 416-mile gas pipeline in the Yadana region of Burma, beginning underwater, continuing on land through the Tenasserim region, and ending at a new power plant in Thailand. The lawsuit alleged that the Unocal Corporation should be held liable for forced labor, murder, rape, and torture inflicted on natives of Burma by the country's military in the course of construction of the pipeline. Unocal argued that it is improving Burmese lives by providing schools, electricity, and new roads, plaintiffs alleged that hundreds of Burmese villagers have been abused by military officials during pipeline construction. The villagers sought damages for past injuries, slave trading practices, and gross human rights violations inflicted upon them and asked the court to stop further pipeline development in the region. After the district court dismissed the lawsuits, the plaintiffs appealed to the Ninth Circuit. A panel of the Ninth Circuit held in September 2002 that Unocal could be found liable under the ATS for aiding and abetting the military's actions if the plaintiffs' allegations were found to be true at trial. In February 2003, the Ninth Circuit vacated the panel's decision and agreed to rehear the case en banc. The case was argued before the en banc court on June 17, 2003, with the U.S. government supporting dismissal of the lawsuits. Doe v. Unocal Corp., Nos. 00-56603, 00-56628, 00-57195, 00-57197 (9th Cir.). Before the Ninth Circuit could issue a decision in the case, the settlement was reached. While the terms of the settlement are confidential, Unocal announced that it "will compensate plaintiffs and provide funds enabling plaintiffs and their representatives to develop programs to improve living conditions, health care and education and protect the rights of people from the pipeline region."

The Ninth Circuit had held off on deciding Doe v. Unocal pending the U.S. Supreme Court's decision in Sosa v. Alvarez-Machain, 542 US. 692 (2004). In *Sosa* the Supreme Court rejected an effort by a Mexican national to recover against the federal government and agents of the U.S. Drug Enforcement Agency for abducting him and forcibly taking him to the United States for trial on charges of murdering a DEA agent, a crime for which he later was acquitted. The Court held that the U.S. government was immune from liability under the "foreign country" exception to the Federal Tort Claims Act. It also held that a single illegal detention of less than one day prior to transferring the Mexican citizen to lawful authorities in the United States did not violate any norm of customary international law that is so well defined as to give rise to a cause of action under the Alien Tort Statute (ATS). The Court's decision narrowed the range of cases that may be brought under the ATS, while not entirely foreclosing them. The Court interpreted the ATS as a jurisdictional statute that creates no new causes of action, but it noted that courts could recognize private causes of action for certain torts in violation of the law of nations. However, it cautioned that courts should exercise caution in allowing such actions by not recognizing claims under federal common law for violations of any international law norm with less definite content and acceptance among civilized nations than those familiar when the ATS was enacted in 1789.

D. INTERNATIONAL DEVELOPMENT POLICY AND THE ENVIRONMENT

Environmentalists have been urging international development policy to shift to a model of "sustainable development" that respects the absorptive and regenerative capacities of ecosystems. Sustainable development is development that occurs on a scale that does not exceed the carrying capacity of the biosphere. While it is difficult to define, the concept has been valuable as a broad goal for shaping environmental policy debates. See The Role of Law in Defining Sustainable Development, 3 Widener L. Symp. J. 1 (1998). Efforts to move development policy toward sustainability have focused on influencing federal agencies and international financial institutions.

1. Multilateral Development Banks

The World Bank made more than $20 billion in loans in FY 2004. While much smaller than private financial flows, the influence of the World Bank and the smaller regional development banks on the financing of international development projects greatly exceeds their direct lending, which serves as a catalyst for attracting funding from other sources. These projects have historically included construction of large dams, clearing of large forest areas, and other activities with major environmental impact. Until the early 1990s, lending was done with minimal environmental review and even less public input.

The multilateral development banks (MDBs) are run by boards of governors composed of representatives from member countries with voting power based on each country's respective financial contribution to the bank. A board of executive directors has substantial delegated authority over significant policy decisions subject to approval of the board of governors. The MDBs are becoming aware of environmental concerns, in part because environmental organizations in the United States and Europe have been able to focus greater public attention on the disparity between environmental requirements in developing countries and those established by European and U.S. law.

With the dramatic increase in private financing directed to developing nations, the role of the World Bank has increasingly been questioned. Countries with open markets and attractive policy environments can obtain private financing on terms as attractive as those from the Bank, and without being subjected to politically sensitive policy dialogues or public scrutiny. Countries without open markets and supportive policies may not be good candidates for Bank loans. In response, the Bank has attempted to demonstrate its continued relevance to global needs in numerous ways, not all necessarily compatible. As reflected in its 1999 Annual Report, the Bank now emphasizes that its core mission is not generalized growth but poverty alleviation. To achieve this goal, more attention is being given to the "software" of development—training, technical assistance, and institution building more often associated with UN agencies. Other priorities include combating corruption, working with NGOs, and in general responding more directly to country priorities (which rarely include climate change and other global environmental concerns). While not the highest priority, environmental issues have also received increased attention. The World Bank's environmental experts rose from a handful in 1990 to more than 300 in 1999, and environment was made the subject of its own department. Summarizing these changes, an article in an environmental newspaper was aptly headlined "The Kinder, Softer, Leaner, Tougher, More Transparent, Environmentally Sensitive, Corruption-Busting World Bank." Earth Times, Sept. 16-30, 1999, at 13 (available at *www.earthtimes.org*). Environmental initiatives at the World Bank are reported annually in the publication Environment Matters, available at the World Bank's website at *www.worldbank.org.*

|| *Seymour & Dubash,*
 World Bank's Environmental
 Reform, Agenda
 Foreign Policy in Focus 1-2 (March 1999) ||

Environmental concerns have been at the leading edge of a movement to reform the World Bank over the past 15 years. The bank has come under fire for financing a series of environmentally damaging projects, including dams on the Narmada River in India, transmigration in Indonesia, and road building into the Brazilian Amazon. These projects have led to a variety of adverse impacts in borrower countries, including deforestation and displacement of indigenous peoples.

In response to criticism voiced by environmental advocates and amplified through the U.S. Congress, the World Bank adopted policies and procedures in the late 1980s and early 1990s to assess and mitigate the adverse environmental impacts of individual projects. These reforms included mandatory environmental assessment procedures and the public disclosure of these assessments in advance of project approval. In addition, the bank's board of executive directors has mandated a series of sector-specific policies to guide World Bank investment in such areas as forestry and energy. For example, the bank's forestry policy prohibits the institution from financing logging in primary tropical forests.

Frustration with the World Bank's lack of vigilance in applying the new policies and procedures led environmental advocates to pursue a second generation of reforms in the early 1990s focusing on increasing the transparency and accountability of lending operations. Again, conditions set by the U.S. Congress were crucial in pressuring bank management to agree to these reforms. As a result, the World Bank must now comply with an information disclosure policy governing the timing and content of documents released to the public. Moreover, the bank's actions are subject to review by an independent inspection panel established to investigate claims of those alleging that they were harmed by the bank's failure to abide by its own policies.

Along with these policy reform efforts, the World Bank has pursued structural changes and investment strategies intended to demonstrate its commitment to environmentally sustainable development. A separate environmental unit created in the 1980s has evolved into a vice-presidency for Environmentally and Socially Sustainable Development (ESSD) in the 1990s. The bank has recruited staff with technical environmental credentials to supplement the institution's professional core, which is overwhelmingly dominated by economists. By the mid-1990s, these staff had begun to develop a portfolio of environment-sector projects, ranging from support for national environmental agencies to investments in national parks. . . .

These achievements have engendered a sense of complacency in official circles—including bank management and member governments—regarding the urgency of the World Bank's environmental reform agenda. In fact, World Bank President Wolfensohn's much touted "Strategic Compact" with the bank's board in 1997 did not feature environmental performance as a priority objective for improvement.

At the same time, the World Bank has evidenced a growing confidence in its ability to provide global leadership on environmental issues. In 1998, President Wolfensohn convened logging industry leaders from around the world to promote a shift to sustainable forestry practice. In the climate change arena, World Bank staffers have proposed a Prototype Carbon Fund, through which the bank would broker investment flows between industrialized and developing countries tied to reducing greenhouse gas emissions. Critics question the bank's legitimacy as an environmental leader, given its own poor performance record, its failure to mainstream environmental objectives into its lending portfolios, and its failure to engage key constituencies in borrower countries. The moment is clearly ripe for a reassessment of the World Bank's environmental reform agenda.

Despite the achievements highlighted above, the World Bank's mitigation-oriented, "do no harm" approach to the environment has had mixed results on its own terms and has failed to transform the institution into an agent of environmentally sustainable development. In fact, many environmental advocates fear that the World Bank is currently in a period of retrenchment from its environmental commitments. As evidence, they cite the disempowerment of environmental staff through recent reorganizations, the watering down of environmental policies through a recent reformatting exercise, and a proposed reconsideration of the bank's forestry policy in 1999. Moreover, they note that the bank's lending portfolio continues to include environmentally destructive projects, particularly in the energy sector.

A decade after the adoption of much-needed environmental policies and procedures, there continue to be significant lapses in the application of policy reforms. A recently published history of the World Bank characterized its environmental reforms as efforts to deflect outside criticism, not as significant changes in the bank's internal incentives or performance. The bank's continuing consideration of a major oil pipeline project in West Africa, despite the opposition of most internal environmental specialists, indicates that lending imperatives tied to traditional models of economic growth continue to outweigh environmental considerations.

The World Bank's project-by-project approach to environmental issues has also failed to address the fundamental choices faced by borrowers in determining which development path to follow. An internal review of the bank's environmental assessment procedures concluded that it has insufficiently considered alternative ways of meeting development goals. As it is, the bank's focus is usually on mitigating the impacts of its original project designs rather than exploring more environmentally sustainable ways of achieving project objectives. For example, environmental assessments of coal-fired power plants focus on technical methods for reducing the emissions of such plants rather than alternative ways of meeting demand for electricity or active management of that demand.

Environmental assessment procedures have not yet been adequately developed or implemented at the ecosystem, sectoral, or economy-wide levels. For example, in 1996 the World Bank failed to consider the likely impacts of rural road improvement on biologically rich forests as part of its transport sector loan to Cameroon. The narrow focus of the bank is also evident in its structural adjustment loans, which, in addition to increasing poverty, often provide incentives that accelerate natural resource exploitation, while forcing governments to cut budgets for social services and environmental protection. The World Bank's Country Assistance Strategies, which provide a framework for policy advice and lending portfolios, tend not to highlight environmental issues or identify possible strategies to address environmental degradation.

Another problem is the tendency of many environmental advocates, both inside and outside the World Bank, to focus disproportionate attention on the merits of specific projects and on addressing international environmental issues such as biodiversity conservation and climate change at the global level. Though these efforts are important, they too often overshadow the need for the bank to address environmental issues more strategically through development of progressive investment portfolios and promotion of policy reform in individual borrower countries. For example, although it is important that the U.S. executive director on the World Bank's board vote against environmentally damaging projects, this is not sufficient to change the "upstream" dynamic that generates such projects in the first place. . . .

Despite promises to mainstream environmental awareness into its overall lending program, the World Bank suffers from a credibility deficit. Its legacy of support for environmentally destructive projects and devastating structural adjustment programs has undermined its legitimacy as a proponent of environmental objectives. This credibility problem is evident in Indonesia, where the bank is attempting to promote forestry sector reform in the context of adjustment lending. Previous loans and grants to the Ministry of Forestry under the Suharto regime, allegations that the bank ignored that regime's corruption, and the inclusion of a Suharto crony in Wolfensohn's meeting of timber industry leaders all make it difficult for the World Bank to be accepted as a sincere proponent of forestry sector reform. Internationally, the bank's credibility as an advocate of climate protection has been undermined by its failure to redirect its own energy and transport sector lending portfolios away from fossil fuels and toward alternative investments in renewables and energy efficiency.

NOTES AND QUESTIONS

1. Although it has declined dramatically relative to total financial flows, multilateral and nationally supported lending to developing countries still exerts significant influence on the economies of most developing nations.

The United States and other industrialized nations provide insurance and guarantees through agencies like the Export-Import Bank to facilitate exports. By some estimates, such policies support about 10 percent of foreign investment in developing nations, including some of the most controversial projects like the Three Gorges Dam in China. Miller, Environmental Policy in the New World Economy, 3 Widener L. Symp. J. 287, 306 (1998). The indirect stimulus to investment created by such programs may be even greater as the presence of multilateral banks and export credit agencies legitimizes projects for other investors.

2. World Bank policy is largely controlled by a 21-member board, on which each country's influence is roughly proportional to its financial contribution. As a consequence, no country or small group of countries has a veto; this effectively insulates the Bank from short-term political intervention, but it also impedes attempts at reform. The Bank was also traditionally very restrictive about disclosures of project and loan information. Although it is not subject to the Freedom of Information Act or similar requirements of U.S. law, the Bank has begun to make itself more accessible to public scrutiny, as noted above. These actions respond in part to environmentalists' criticisms, as articulated in Wirth, Legitimacy, Accountability, and Partnership: A Model for Advocacy on Third World Environmental Issues, 100 Yale L.J. 2645, 2664 (1991); and Rodgers, Looking a Gift Horse in the Mouth: The World Bank and Environmental Accountability, 3 Geo. Int'l Envtl. L. Rev. 457 (1990).

3. In December 1989, the International Development and Finance Act, 103 Stat. 2492 (1989), was enacted by Congress. The Act requires U.S. executive directors of MDBs to refrain from voting in favor of projects with a major effect on the environment unless an environmental assessment has been performed at least 120 days in advance of the vote. This legislation and other amendments to foreign aid laws require the U.S. representatives to the MDBs to promote the hiring of trained environmental staff, to develop and implement management plans to ensure environmental review of projects, to involve citizens' and indigenous peoples' organizations in project planning, and to increase the proportion of lending to environmental projects, including integrated pest management, solar energy, and small-scale mixed farming. 22 U.S.C. §§2621(a), (k). The Agency for International Development (AID) is further directed to analyze environmental impacts of proposed multilateral development loans and, where substantial adverse impacts are found, to ensure a public investigation. 22 U.S.C. §262(m)(2)(A). Since 1989, the World Bank has required that an environmental assessment be prepared for virtually all major projects. World Bank Operational Directive 4.00 (1989). In 1991, the Bank broadened this directive to require consultation with nongovernmental organizations and the public in preparation of such assessments. World Bank Operational Directive 4.01 (1991). See Scott, Making a Bank Turn, 1992 Envtl. Forum 21 (Mar.-Apr. 1992). Are these provisions enforceable through litigation by environmental groups? Do they provide any assurance that the U.S. position will prevail? Critics of these provisions argue that they inject politics into World Bank decision making in violation of Article IV of the Bank's Articles of Agreement, which states that "[o]nly economic considerations shall be relevant" to such decisions.

4. What role, if any, should the World Bank and other MDBs have with respect to climate change? Insofar as developing countries are not obligated to reduce their emissions under the Kyoto Protocol, developing countries may

question the appropriateness of efforts to impose additional costs or otherwise require their response to climate change. On the other hand, the Convention requires all parties to prepare inventories of emissions and to prepare mitigation programs, many developing countries have voluntarily adopted laws and policies to promote clean energy, and lenders as well as recipient countries have reason to identify and modify investments that may be at risk from climate change. The World Bank has also taken an active role in developing the carbon market on behalf of donor governments, and as of 2005 is the largest buyer of carbon credits. Critics also have proposed that the MDBs do more to quantify and report the carbon emissions associated with their investments. Sohn, Nakhooda & Baumert, Mainstreaming Climate Change Considerations at the Multilateral Development Banks (WRI Issue Brief, 2005). The 2005 G8 Communiqué also identified a role for the World Bank in facilitating a dialogue with large developing countries concerning opportunities for emission reductions. In 2004 the World Bank adopted a growth target of 20 percent per year for five years for its investments in renewable energy and energy efficiency improvements. World Bank Group, World Bank Group Progress on Renewable Energy and Energy Efficiency: 1990-2004.

5. A related issue is the appropriate role for environmental analysis and standards when the MDBs facilitate investment through financial intermediaries. As the role of the Banks is less direct, typically providing commercial credit or guarantees to facilitate project finance or the development of domestic financial markets, the extent of their responsibility is one-step removed. In general, environmental standards for such lending have tended to become more stringent. See Curmally, Sohn & Wright, Multilateral Development Bank Lending Through Financial Intermediaries: Environmental and Social Challenges (2005). This influence is also evident in the behavior of many private banks investing in developing countries, a topic discussed below (see pages 1124-1125).

6. In July 2005 James Wolfensohn retired as President of the World Bank Group. Wolfensohn was widely credited with increasing the transparency of Bank operations, expanding the role of the Bank to encompass a much wider range of social, health, and environmental concerns, and actively seeking engagement with civil society. The scope and impact of his efforts continues to be debated. See, e.g., Sebastian Mallaby, The World's Banker (2004). Wolfensohn was succeeded by Paul Wolfowitz, who had been the U.S. Deputy Defense Secretary and a key architect of the Iraq war.

7. The World Bank and other international financial institutions must walk a narrow line in supporting resource development in poor countries with significant financial needs but weak governance, a combination frequently associated with mining and resource extraction in Africa. The World Bank attempted to create a model for transparency and effective oversight of resource revenues, including prohibitions on redirecting funds to military purposes, in support for an oil pipeline through Chad and Cameroon. The loan had to be suspended when the government of Chad openly announced its intention to use funds for purposes contrary to the agreement. Another loan for mining in Ghana was described by Bank managers as "expected to become a demonstration for how to handle environmental, social and community development issues." According to a Bank official, the mining company did not need the loan but wanted the stamp of approval that went with meeting the Bank's environmental and social standards. Duggar, "Loan for Foreign Mining in Ghana Approved," N.Y. Times, Feb. 1, 2006.

2. *The Global Environment Facility*

The Global Environment Facility (GEF) was initially created as a pilot program by the World Bank in November 1990. H. Sjöberg, From Idea to Reality: The Creation of the Global Environment Facility (1994). The GEF seeks to promote multilateral funding for environmentally desirable projects. The Fund, which was established with contributions of more than $1.5 billion, is designed to enhance the attractiveness of investments with environmental benefits that fail to meet traditional lending criteria. Loans are available for projects that address biological diversity, forestry, global warming (including energy efficiency), land degradation and persistent organic pollutants, and ozone depletion (where necessary to supplement the ozone fund).

After completing its initial three-year pilot phase, the GEF was the subject of a detailed and highly critical assessment prepared by an independent evaluation committee to inform decisions about restructuring and further financing. UN Development Programme, UN Environment Programme, and the World Bank, Global Environmental Facility: Independent Evaluation of the Pilot Phase (1994). See also I. Bowles & G. Prickett, Reframing the Green Window: An Analysis of the GEF Pilot Phase Approach to Biodiversity and Global Warming and Recommendations for the Operational Phase (1994); Wells, The Global Environment Facility and Prospects for Biodiversity Conservation, 6 Int'l Envtl. Aff. 69 (1994).

Based on the evaluation, participating governments agreed in March 1994 to restructure the GEF. Twenty-six countries pledged to provide $2 billion for three years. Decisions will now be supervised by a council of 32 nations—18 from recipients and 14 from developed countries. Voting is by a "double majority" system and requires a 60 percent majority of both the participating governments and GEF "shareholders" (with shares awarded in proportion to each country's financial contribution). The future of the GEF grows increasingly important, as it becomes the financial mechanism of choice for implementing environmental agreements including the climate and biodiversity conventions. H. French, Partnership for the Planet 24-28 (1995). H. Sjöberg, Restructuring the Global Environment Facility (1999). In 2002, the donors agreed to further replenish the GEF with an additional $3 billion for four years.

	Horta, In Focus:	
	Global Environment Facility	
	Foreign Policy in Focus 1-3 (Dec. 1998)	

The establishment of the GEF prior to the 1992 United Nations Conference on Environment and Development (UNCED), commonly known as the Rio Earth Summit, effectively preempted alternative proposals for a green fund which some Southern governments were expected to present in Rio. Because they had no role in its creation, many Southern governments now feel ambivalent about the GEF, although they will accept whatever financial resources may be made available through the facility. At the Rio summit, Southern nations were presented with an already established GEF with a $1 billion core fund, which donor governments promised to make available in addition to their ongoing development assistance programs.

The Rio summit produced a global action plan called Agenda 21. This ambitious plan to make development environmentally, socially, and economically sustainable stipulated that Northern nations had to increase their aid flow to the South. According to the plan, the North would provide $141 billion annually in grants and low-interest loans in the 1993-2000 period to foster sustainable development. This aid would, among other things, facilitate the North-South transfer of environmental technologies. But the promise of Agenda 21, though initially hailed as a major advance in international environmental cooperation, has fallen short—mainly because it never received the backing of the United States. Other donor countries, pointing to the failure of the U.S. to take the lead and meet its share of Agenda 21 obligations, have also failed to increase their assistance to the South.

The creation of the GEF prior to the Rio Earth Summit allowed the U.S. and its G-7 partners to define global environmental problems as they perceived them and to establish the limits and scope of their responsibilities in assisting developing countries. Furthermore, the existence of the GEF has proved a convenient way for the G-7 nations to sidestep the more ambitious North-South funding plan outlined in Agenda 21.

Problems with Current U.S. Policy . . .

Numerous problems beset Washington's policy with respect to the GEF. These include the U.S. failure: (1) to pay its assessed contribution, (2) to insist on the implementation of environmental reforms by the World Bank and the GEF's Implementing Agencies (primarily the World Bank), and (3) to ratify the Kyoto Protocol of the UN Biodiversity Conservation Convention and the Kyoto Protocol of the Climate Change Convention.

With support from its German counterparts, the French government launched the GEF proposal as a way of responding to growing domestic pressure to do something about the global environment. With less of a domestic constituency for international environmental efforts, the U.S. government was initially reluctant to accept the Franco-German proposal. The U.S. government knew that making a financial commitment to a new international entity would be fraught with difficulties given congressional reluctance to authorize funding to cover U.S. arrears with the UN. In addition, the administration was aware that any attempt to obtain replenishment funds for international financial institutions like the World Bank would be subject to extensive congressional questioning and delays.

Several key congressional members with seats on important oversight committees together with a few administration officials with years of experience trying to promote environmental reforms in World Bank operations believed that entrusting the World Bank with the management of a fund intended to protect the global environment was tantamount to putting the proverbial fox in charge of the chicken coop. In their view, the World Bank's massive lending to promote the energy sector and forestry without adequate environmental safeguards made the institution part of the problem in both the climate change and biodiversity areas. Consequently, these congressional members and administration officials felt that the World Bank should first demonstrate the ability to implement environmental reforms in its own operations before undertaking new environmental responsibilities.

But the initial U.S. reluctance to support the GEF was quickly overcome. With preparations for the 1992 UNCED event fully under way and more than one hundred heads of state expected at Rio, endorsement of the GEF was a convenient way of demonstrating environmental leadership. Because the size of the contributions of donor governments to the GEF is based on the size of a country's economy—a principle known as "burden-sharing"—the U.S. became the GEF's largest donor followed by Japan and Germany.

Congressional conditions on U.S. funding have helped bring about some reforms in the GEF, such as greater public access to information and broader participation by NGOs in both GEF policy discussions and project implementation. But the accumulation of arrears of the U.S. contribution has hampered determined action on the part of the U.S. to obtain more fundamental reforms. When other donor governments threaten to withhold their funding unless the U.S. pays its share, U.S. credibility is hurt. But to achieve further GEF reforms, Washington will need to fulfill its financial obligations.

The greatest problem thus far has been the failure of the implementing agencies (and especially the World Bank) to meet their promises of mainstreaming global environmental goals into their overall programs. The World Bank's annual lending portfolio of more than $20 billion finances development projects that contribute to the very problems that the GEF seeks to address. What is more, the proposals advocated in the Country Assistance Strategies reports, which are the World Bank's blueprints for its development financing programs in individual borrowing countries, do not reflect any systematic consideration of the environmental implications of these strategies.

An additional problem for U.S. foreign policy—and a major irony—is that the GEF has been adopted, at least on an interim basis, as the financial mechanism for both the UN Biodiversity Conservation and Climate Change conventions (not yet ratified by the U.S.). As such, one of its principal tasks is to assist countries in implementing their obligations under the conventions.

Finally, U.S. foreign policy with regard to the GEF elicits charges of hypocrisy due to U.S. failure to take determined action at home to reduce the use of fossil fuels and to protect its old-growth forests. Meanwhile, the United States uses the GEF to call on other countries to prevent climate change and conserve biodiversity.

NOTES AND QUESTIONS

1. As of March 2005 the GEF had committed over $5 billion for more than 1,500 projects in 151 countries. GEF Annual Report 2004, available at GEF website *www.gefweb.org*. An independent evaluation of the GEF is prepared every four years as an input to the negotiation of the GEF replenishment. The most recent is the Third Overall Performance Study 2005, also available at the GEF website.

2. Financial contributions to the GEF are made on the basis of a burden-sharing formula proportional to GDP, with the United States responsible for a little less than 21 percent of the total. As of October 2005, the United States was in arrears due to its failure to make payments of $140 million. Under the GEF Instrument, other parties were allowed to reduce their payments pro rata such that total resources available to the GEF were further reduced. Trustee Report, Oct. 11, 2005 (GEF/C.27/Inf.3), available at the GEF website.

3. GEF support continues to be an important source of incentives for renewable energy and energy efficiency projects. During 2003-2004, the World Bank implemented $489 million of clean energy projects using $104 million of GEF Funds. Sohn, Nakhooda & Baumert, Mainstreaming Climate Change Considerations at the Multilateral Development Banks (World Resources Institute Issue Brief, 2005).

4. The scope of GEF support for global environmental programs continues to expand beyond the original strategies for climate change mitigation and biodiversity. New programs have been added for adaptation to climate change and rehabilitation of coal-burning power plants, and new commitments have been made to support the Convention to Combat Desertification and the Stockholm Convention on Persistent Organic Pollutants. The demand for GEF resources has thus increased considerably, while donor commitment of resources has increased only modestly. Revised Programming Document for GEF 4 (GEF/R.4/27, Nov. 16, 2005).

E.   COMPLIANCE AND ENFORCEMENT

As in domestic environmental law, success in international law requires more than agreement on a legal framework; it also requires compliance. In an international regime, the question of compliance presents yet another challenge due to the absence of a centralized enforcement regime. How to respond to this challenge has become the subject of a growing body of investigation. "[A]fter an exciting period of treaty-making and institution-building, international environmental lawyers have now turned to the even more difficult task of building compliance with good laws already made and good institutions already in place." M. Janis, An Introduction to International Law 234 (1999).

|| *Weiss & Jacobson,*
 Getting Countries to Comply
 with International Agreements
 Environment (July/Aug. 1999) ||

An essential first step in the analysis is to distinguish between implementation, compliance, and effectiveness. *Implementation* refers to measures that countries take to effectuate international treaties in their domestic law. Most treaties are not self-executing and require national legislation or regulations. *Compliance* goes beyond implementation. It refers to whether countries in fact adhere to the agreement's provisions and to the implementing measures that they have instituted. Some obligations are procedural (such as national reporting); others are substantive (such as reducing or phasing out ozone-depleting substances). Moreover, even if the formal obligations are complied with, there may be a question of compliance with the spirit of the convention. *Effectiveness* is related to compliance, but is not identical. A country may comply with an agreement but the agreement may nonetheless be ineffective at achieving its objectives. . . .

The research confirmed the conventional wisdom that the smaller the number of participants involved, the easier and less expensive it is to regulate and to monitor activity. The striking contrast between the limited number of facilities that produced ozone-depleting substances regulated under the Montreal protocol and the millions of individuals who could engage in illicit trade in endangered species helps to explain why CITES is much more difficult to enforce than the Montreal protocol.

The characteristics of an accord, such as the perceived equity of the obligations, the precision of the obligations, provisions for obtaining scientific and technical advice, monitoring and reporting requirements, implementation and noncompliance procedures, incentives, and sanctions, are important to compliance.

Not surprisingly, for parties to comply with treaties, they must regard the obligations imposed as equitable. The Montreal protocol's differentiated obligations for industrialized and for developing countries as well as the Montreal Protocol Multilateral Fund to help the latter are essential in convincing developing countries to join the protocol. . . .

Although it is difficult to assess whether a country has complied with an agreement when the obligations are imprecise, stating obligations precisely cannot always override factors that run against compliance. For example, even though the CITES obligations are relatively precise, customs officers find it difficult to identify the subtle differences between species, particularly for flora.

National reporting served as the primary means for monitoring compliance in four of the five treaties studied.

Sole reliance on reporting, however, poses problems. Many parties do not fulfill their reporting obligations and may be unwilling to publicize their own shortcomings. Filing reports also is burdensome for governments, especially for smaller developing countries. The locus of the responsibility for preparing the reports may be unclear. Even larger and richer countries sometimes have difficulty fully complying with reporting requirements. . . .

Incentives and sanctions render additional tools. Giving countries financial or other assistance to help them comply with their obligations under the Montreal protocol helped advance compliance. . . .

The International Environment

The international community's increasing attention to international environmental issues, including international environmental accords, is one of the most important factors explaining the acceleration in the trend toward improved implementation and national compliance observed in the late 1980s and early 1990s. . . .

The prominence of environmental issues mobilized the worldwide media, roused public opinion, and energized national and international NGOs and the public to put increased pressure on governments to deal with environmental issues. This enhanced implementation and compliance. . . .

Most importantly, having a "leader" country (or countries) was crucial to the negotiation of particular treaties and to compliance with them. For example, the United States enacted laws dealing with its natural heritage, with endangered species, and with ozone-depleting substances and then took the lead in pressing for international treaties that would deal with the same issues and in negotiating the agreements. It also played a leading role in the negotiation of the London Convention of 1972. Later, as the conventions went into effect (that is, when the required number of states had joined the agreement), the United States and the European Union, because of their economic strength, were in a position to play important roles in promoting treaty compliance.

Factors Involving the Country

Countries are at the center of the compliance process and must take the required actions to fulfill their obligations under the treaties. The performance of the eight countries and the European Union in implementing and complying with the five treaties examined in this study differed substantially mainly because of the countries' varied characteristics. . . .

A country's administrative capacity is crucial to compliance. Strong administrative capacity generally leads to better implementation and compliance. Administrative capacity correlates with gross national product (GNP). . . .

Citizen monitoring is facilitated by democratic governments more than authoritarian ones because the former are normally more transparent. Citizens can bring pressure to bear for improved implementation and compliance. NGOs generally have more freedom to operate under democratic governments. . . .

At the same time, however, democratic governments are normally more responsive to public opinion than authoritarian governments, and public opinion is not always supportive of environmental concerns. Democratic governments allow conflicts about environmental issues to flare, which may lead to less compliance.

Democratization does not necessarily automatically or quickly lead to improved compliance. Democratization in Brazil and in Russia, however, seems to have contributed to improved compliance for certain agreements. . . .

Individuals make a crucial difference in national implementation and compliance. For example, then Brazilian President Fernando Collor played a major role in having Rio de Janeiro selected as the site for UNCED. Brazil's compliance with the five treaties improved during his presidency. . . .

	Zaelke, Stilwell & Young,	
	What Reason Demands:	
	Making Laws Work for	
	Sustainable Development	
	Making Law Work: Environmental	
	Compliance & Sustainable Development	
	(Zaelke, Kaniaru & Kruzikova eds., 2005)	

The efforts of various governments and institutions . . . are helping advance the rule of law and good governance. However, these efforts must be further strengthened by increasing the focus on compliance and enforcement. The need to strengthen enforcement and compliance has received some attention at international meetings, but more is required to convert words into action. Many States still lack a sound foundation for the rule of law, and many judicial and legal systems still function poorly. Despite a growing body of environmental law both at the national and international levels, environmental quality and some important social indicators have been declining around the world. One reason for these trends is the inadequate investment in assuring effective compliance and enforcement, at both the national and international levels. International and national donor agencies should expand their efforts on good governance and rule of law to include an explicit focus on compliance and enforcement.

While the challenges across these levels differ, some notable commonalities exist. Among other things, enhancing compliance requires:

Strengthening the empirical foundations of compliance. Effective policies, including those relating to compliance, must be based on a sound empirical foundation. More empirical research is required about the behavior of different actors—states, firms and individuals—in different circumstances. It has been said of compliance at the national level that, "20 percent of the regulated population will automatically comply with any regulation, 5 percent will attempt to evade it, and the remaining 75 percent will comply as long as they think that the 5 percent will be caught and punished."

Understanding the spectrum of actors in practice, and how to change their behavior, is a key task in conducting empirical research and in enforcing compliance. . . .

Applying new analytical tools. New analytic techniques need to be applied to problems of compliance, including systems approaches, simulation and modeling techniques, configurational comparisons and meta-analyses, case studies, counterfactuals and narratives, and structured stakeholder interviews, all of which provide a toolkit for understanding the broader human-environment interactions.

Strengthening the theoretical foundations of compliance. Empirical data is interpreted and given meaning through theories, and theories generate testable hypotheses. Theories about compliance provide accounts of why different actors comply or do not comply with international and domestic laws. . . . To be effective, policymakers must understand the various theories and when they will be useful, make their own theoretical assumptions explicit, measure these assumptions against the evolving empirical results to ensure they are sound, and make adjustments as required.

Diagnosing specific problems. Reliable empirical data and sound theory can help diagnose underlying problems of non-compliance accurately. Why are some problems harder to address than others? What specifically is the source of non-compliance? Given the limited and fixed budgets of most enforcement and compliance agencies, they need to find the most cost effective means to ensure compliance . . .

Understanding and empowering key actors. When diagnosing problems, policymakers at all levels should take an expansive, system-wide view of the actors in the universe they are attempting to regulate. Several of the more recent theories of compliance tend to recognize that States and firms are not unitary actors, but rather are made up of numerous entities and are influenced by various forces that all contribute to compliance behavior. Actors such as scientists, the media, NGOs, and financial institutions, in addition to the individuals and departments that comprise States and firms, all have important roles to play in promoting compliance, the rule of law, and sustainable development. Policymakers should consider how these actors could best be empowered, in order to most efficiently and effectively generate the desired behavioral changes in the regulated community.

Strengthening the role of civil society. Enhancing compliance requires tools that empower citizens to participate in governance, including through access to justice, with opportunities to apply pressure on and through the judicial and legal systems. The international community is moving in this direction. The Aarhus Convention guarantees the rights of access to information, public participation in decision-making, and access to justice in environmental matters. These rights empower citizens to ensure that environmental laws are properly enforced and complied with, as well as foster norms that complement and support the rule of law and good governance.

Building capacity of regulators and those they regulate. Strengthening efforts to build capacity is essential, to enhance both the ability of those in the regulated community to comply and the knowledge and capability of those seeking to secure compliance—judges, policymakers, and other governmental officials . . . .

Building political will and expanding funding. It is increasingly recognized that the fundamental changes needed to promote the rule of law and sustainable development require the support and commitment of the key decision-makers within the system—whether in government or civil society—and this core group needs to be given enabling assistance to help build the essential internal political will these reforms require. Donor assistance is critical, but so is the will to reform, which must be fostered from within.

Strengthening the norms that complement and support compliance and the rule of law. Efforts to strengthen compliance and the rule of law must be complemented by broader efforts to replace cultures of non-compliance and corruption with cultures of compliance. Institutions built on cultures of non-compliance, like buildings erected on sand, are likely to founder. Consequently, additional efforts must be made to promote social norms that complement and support the rule of law and that support legal and judicial reform. This includes general norms such as the norms of good governance; rule of law; and compliance, obedience, and law-abidingness. More specific environmental norms also should be considered.

NOTES AND QUESTIONS

1. The study of compliance has become a major topic within comparative law. See Victor and Skolnikoff, Translating Intent into Action: Implementing Environmental Commitments, 41 Environment 16 (March 1999); Young, Hitting the Mark, 41 Environment 20 (Oct. 1999); and P. Haas, R. Keohane & M. Levy, eds., Institutions for the Earth: Sources of Effective International Environmental Protection (1993). A robust conclusion from the work to date is the absence of a "smoking gun" in the sense of one mechanism or type of mechanism that will provide an explanation as to why some international environmental agreements are more successful than others. Young, Hitting the Mark, 41 Environment 27-28 (Oct. 1999).

2. The question of compliance should not be viewed as necessarily synonymous with effectiveness in achieving the objectives of an international convention; it is possible to have compliance while failing to achieve larger goals. For example, this may be the case with the Convention on International Trade in Endangered Species (CITES), which has not stopped the extinction of many species due to habitat loss despite high rates of compliance with restrictions on trade. Is the opposite possible; that is, can a Convention achieve its goals without high rates of compliance?

3. Compare the role of citizens as agents for domestic enforcement with the role of citizen organizations in promoting compliance with international agreements. In what ways are they similar, and in what ways do the differ?

Promoting Voluntary Corporate Actions to Improve the Environment

The increasing economic importance of multinational corporations has led to a growing interest in strategies that foster voluntary environmentalism by corporations. One approach seeks to build on the trend toward corporate environmental reports. By one estimate, more than 1,000 companies now produce such reports annually. White, Sustainability and the Accountable Corporation, Environment, Oct. 1999, 30-43. However, these reports so far lack any common scope or content, making comparison and interpretation difficult. The Coalition for Environmentally Responsible Economies (CERES) launched the Global Reporting Initiative in 1997 to address this need. The GRI is an international initiative that includes UN agencies as well as business and environmental interests. It seeks to achieve some standardization and encompasses criteria for sustainability that transcend narrow environmental, health, and safety concerns. A core group of companies is piloting a set of initial principles as the basis for guidelines expected to be available in 2000. If they are used widely by national environmental agencies and financial reporting services, proponents hope such reporting policies could become highly influential in promoting environmental protection wholly apart from national regulations.

Another source of incentives for voluntary improvements in the environmental behavior of private companies is through private standards developed by national and international standard-setting agencies. The growth in trade has added to interest in this approach because trading companies have an interest in standardized measures of the quality of products purchased from foreign suppliers. Much of this effort is coordinated by the International Organization for Standardization (ISO), an international association of standard-setting agencies founded in 1947. See generally ISO 14001 and Beyond: Environmental Management Systems in the Real World (1997); Miller, Environmental Policy in the New World Economy, 3 Widener Symp. L.J. 287, 297-301 (1998); D. Hunter, J. Salzman & D. Zaelke, International Environmental Law and Policy 1396-1409 (1998).

Historically, ISO standards have mostly focused on technical issues of product manufacture and performance (e.g., procedures for measuring the strength or elasticity of a material). However, in the last decade ISO began to develop standards for quality management systems, including internal audit procedures. Compliance with these standards, ISO 9000 and 10011, has become a condition for doing business in many nations, especially in Europe. More and more, compliance must also be certified by an independent third party.

ISO 9000/10011 touched on environmental issues as one element of overall quality control and generated interest in a more formal examination of the potential for an environmental focus. This led to the initiation of an exploratory committee on environmental issues in 1991 and the creation of a Technical Committee (the basic decision-making body) for environmental standards in 1993, TC-207. Standards are being developed in five areas: management systems, audits, labeling, environmental performance evaluation, and life-cycle assessment. Under the ISO numbering system, these standards have been assigned numbers corresponding to the five main subject areas from ISO 14000 through 14060. Saunders, ISO Environmental Management Standardization Efforts (NISTIR Paper Number 5638, Apr. 1995).

For the most part, ISO standards address business practices rather than environmental outcomes. For example, the EMS draft proposal requires companies to identify key environmental issues, establish an environmental policy, set targets, and adopt training and documentation procedures. The proposal addresses products and services as well as facilities and is expected to be adopted widely; Austria was one of the first countries to adopt the draft specifications document as a national standard.

The potential impact on international practices is enormous. On the positive side, such standards may help alleviate concerns about the practices of multinational corporations investing in developing countries by providing a baseline against which to evaluate performance. For instance, firms operating in Mexico but seeking to export will also have strong incentives to be certified and the standards may expedite changes in practice by Mexican companies still unclear about their environmental obligations. Knight, Wells & Pratt, After the Crisis, Envtl. Forum, May/June 1995, at 22-26. East European firms interested in export have also found they must upgrade to meet ISO standards. "East Looks West," Tomorrow, Sept./Oct. 1999, 34.

On the negative side, there are also concerns about the extent and effectiveness of developing country participation because of the cost and technical nature of the standards development process. Environmentalists have also only begun to participate recently and have concerns about reliance on management systems in lieu of regulations on emissions. Companies from the United States worry that the draft standards are based on European models and therefore may be more easily satisfied by foreign competitors. Some also fear that despite their voluntary nature, the ISO standards could be used as the basis for tort liability in the United States where such suits are much more easily maintained than in other nations. For a discussion of the potential influence of international voluntary standards on international environmental law, see generally Roht-Arriaza, Shifting the Point of Regulation: The International Organization for Standardization and Global Law-making on Trade and the Environment, 22 Ecol. L.Q. 479 (1995); Fowler, International Standards for Transnational Corporations, 25 Envtl. L. 1 (1995); Baram, Multinational Corporations, Private Codes and Technology Transfer for Sustainable Development, 24 Envtl. L. 33 (1994).

In addition to being involved in the ISO program, some corporations also are involved in voluntary product certification programs that allow them to approach consumers with independent certification that they engage in best environmental practices in their global operations. For example, all of Chiquita's banana farms have been certified by the Rainforest Alliance as complying with a Better Banana program, a set of environmental and social best practices that involves significant reductions in pesticide use and water pollution and improved waste management practices. In April 2001, officials of the Canadian timber industry agreed with a coalition of environmental groups to protect from logging 1.5 million acres of coastal rainforest in British Columbia. Jim Carlton, Canada, Timber Firms Agree on Rainforest Pact, Wall St. J., April 4, 2001, at A2. The agreement follows successful efforts by environmental groups to get large retailers like Home Depot to agree to phase out selling products using wood from old growth forests. A representative of the Natural Resource Defense Council explained: "The basic goal is for the consumer to ask, 'Where does my wood come from?' " Id. Other environmentalists predicted that the agreement represented "the beginning of the end for old-growth logging." Id.

One consequence of increasing global economic interdependence is that exporters must be sensitive to the demands of importers. The significance of this trend was evident from U.S. participation in negotiation of the Cartagena Protocol on Biosafety to the Convention on Biological Diversity. Although the United States is not a party to the Convention, it could not afford to ignore negotiations on rules applicable to imports of genetically modified foods, seeds, and organisms. Along with 129 other nations, the United States on January 29, 2000 agreed to the first global treaty regulating trade in genetically modified foods and crops. When ratified by 50 countries, the Cartagena Protocol will impose a notice and consent feature: Exporters will be required to obtain permission from an importing country before the first shipment of a living modified organism (seeds, fish, or microbes) intended for release into the environment can occur. To allow for compiling and processing information of such a highly technical nature, the Protocol further provides for the creation of a biosafety clearinghouse to help countries share data. See Pollack, 130 Nations Agree on Safety Rules for Biotech Food, N.Y. Times, Jan. 30, 2000, at A1. Text of the agreement can be found at *www.biodiv.org*.

The United States, Canada, and a few smaller countries resisted agreement on a similar notification system for foodstuffs, insisting that the ability to distinguish such products was impractical and would mire trade in red tape. The issue was therefore postponed for two years, with the understanding that market demand and technology might clarify the issue. The potential for market driven response was illustrated by a large American producer of corn chips that is able to specify that it only will purchase non-genetically modified corn because it contracts for corn directly from farmers. On the other hand, the company lacks similar ability to distinguish the source of oils and other inputs used in making its product. Gillis, New Seed Planted in Genetic Flap, Wash. Post, Feb. 6, 2000, at H1.

Another compromise in the agreement addressed the inclusion of the precautionary principle, allowing for regulation in advance of scientific proof, in contrast with the WTO's requirement for "sufficient scientific evidence." The inclusion of this principle was labeled a significant victory by environmentalists, but the relationship between the two treaties was not clarified.

NOTES AND QUESTIONS

1. The Rio Declaration proclaims that "[p]eace, development and environmental protection are interdependent and indivisible." Rio Declaration, Principle 25. Developing countries argue that a transition to sustainable development will require a massive infusion of aid from the industrialized world. In response to these concerns, Principle 5 of the Rio Declaration states that eradication of poverty is "an indispensable requirement for sustainable development, in order to decrease the disparities in standards of living and better meet the needs of the majority of the people of the world." How much support should developed countries provide to the developing world in making the transition to sustainable development? To what extent should that support be conditioned on developing countries' agreement to pursue specific measures, such as population control efforts?

2. Will concepts of national sovereignty have to change before a truly effective response can be made to global environmental problems? Consider

the example of the Montreal Protocol. To what extent did its signatories give up some national sovereignty to combat a global problem?

3. What impact will voluntary international standards such as ISO 14000 have on global environmental progress? Does the absence of government enforcement mechanisms undermine the potential for voluntary standards to change corporate behavior substantially?

4. The literature on non-regulatory and voluntary means of "greening" business continues to grow. For a review of experience with labeling and certification programs such as the Forest Stewardship program for sustainably harvested hardwoods, see, e.g., B. Cashore, G. Auld & D. Newsom, Governing Through Markets: Forest Certification and the Emergence of Non-State Authority (2004). For a thorough, but generally skeptical, view of voluntary environmental and social initiatives, see D. Vogel, The Market for Virtue (2005). For an analysis of the factors that explain why some corporations are more responsive to environmental concerns than others in the same industry, see J. Diamond, Collapse: How Societies Choose to Fail or Succeed (2004).

PROBLEM EXERCISE: STRUCTURING AN INTERNATIONAL AGREEMENT TO REGULATE PERSISTENT ORGANIC POLLUTANTS (POPs)

A class of chemicals known as organochlorines has been the subject of long-standing environmental concern due to evidence that they cause harm to humans and animals, including disruption of the hormonal system, and adverse effects on immune and reproductive systems. In addition to their toxicity, these chemicals are particularly dangerous because they accumulate in body fat and resist normal cleansing mechanisms. Because of their persistence and mobility in the global environment, the need for international control measures was recognized in a decision of the Governing Council of the United Nations Environment Programme on February 7, 1997, with the objective of reaching agreement on a treaty by late 2000. For documents and other information about these chemicals see *http://www.chem.unep.ch/pops*.

At the initial negotiating session in June 1998, the parties agreed to focus initially on 12 POPs: aldrin, chlordane, DDT, dieldrin, dioxin, endrin, furans, heptachlor, hexachlorobenzene, mirex, PCBs, and toxaphene. Negotiations concentrated on reducing or eliminating the 12 chemicals, and key issues included how to deal with POPs stockpiles, how to eliminate the use of DDT, and how to finance the necessary actions by developing nations.

Question One.   Based on experience with past multilateral environmental agreements, how should the POPs agreement be structured? What features should be incorporated into it to ensure its adoption both by developed and developing countries? What elements are necessary to enhance its chances of being effective in eliminating, or at least minimizing, use of these chemicals?

Question Two.   DDT is still used by 23 nations as an inexpensive and effective measure to control malaria by killing mosquitoes that spread the disease. China and India are the largest users; Mexico has pledged to stop spraying by the year 2007. The American Society of Tropical Medicine and Hygiene argues that malaria deaths will increase dramatically if DDT is phased out. This group is proposing that the treaty allow DDT to be sprayed in small quantities on the interior walls of homes. Arguing that even small amounts of DDT harm the environment, the World Wildlife Fund seeks to have the treaty ban DDT by 2007. Stolberg, DDT, Target of Global Ban, Finds Defenders in Experts on Malaria, N.Y Times, Aug. 29, 1999, at A1. Should DDT be phased out in the treaty and, if so, how rapidly?

Question Three. Many developing countries argue that they cannot afford the cost of alternatives to DDT. Pyrethroids, a leading alternative, are considerably more expensive than DDT. An EPA entomologist estimates that the cost of treating one home with DDT ranges from $1.60 to $8.50, compared with $4.20 to $24.00 for treating the same house with pyrethroids. Id. at 6. How should the treaty deal with this problem?

Question Four. In May 2001, 91 countries, including the United States, signed the Stockholm Convention on Persistent Organic Pollutants. The Convention, which entered into force on May 17, 2004, calls for the immediate elimination of eight POPs—aldrin, chlordane, dieldrin, endrin, heptachlor, hexachlorobenzene, mirex, and toxaphene—as soon as the treaty enters into force 90 days after 50 countries have ratified it. It is predicted that this will take three to four years. The treaty also prohibits the production of PCBs and calls for the phasing out of their remaining uses over time, including their removal from electrical transformers and other equipment by 2025. The treaty also promotes strong actions to minimize releases of by-product POPs, such as dioxins and furans, and actions taken to eliminate these by-products where feasible. President Bush has submitted the treaty to the Senate for ratification. Why do you think the Bush administration enthusiastically supports this treaty?

Question Five. The controversy over proposals to ban DDT was resolved by providing that DDT eventually should be eliminated, but that it could continue to be used for disease vector control by countries that need to use DDT against malaria until affordable alternatives are available to them. The treaty follows the approach supported by the World Health Organization (WHO). Despite DDT's temporary exemption from the POPs ban, it is reported that "[t]he world is losing the war against malaria" which today kills more than a million people annually in Africa alone, because developed countries are refusing to fund the use of DDT in the developed world. Fighting Malaria with DDT, N.Y. Times, Dec. 23, 2002, at A26. How would you respond to this concern? For a discussion of the dramatic reduction in levels of DDT found in humans in the developed world due to the banning of DDT and why this actually makes it difficult to assess its health effects, see Devra Davis, When Smoke Ran Like Water: Tales of Environmental Deception and the Battle Against Pollution 167-172 (2002).

The Equator Principles

Beginning in the early 1990s, project finance has become an increasingly common means of financing large infrastructure projects in developing countries. Typically, such financing is based on the creation of a legally independent company with financing secured solely by project assets (e.g., power plants, mines, and toll roads). Private banks frequently help structure project finance as well as acting as lenders. The size and potential environmental consequences of such projects have made private banks an increasing target for environmental critics. In 2002 several large private banks approached the International Finance Corporation (IFC), the private sector arm of the World Bank, to discuss the Bank's approach to sustainable development. The banks were interested in identifying common standards that would be both practical and credible, and they quickly settled on the World Bank and IFC policies as the most relevant to private practice. On June 4, 2003, a group of ten large banks announced the adoption of the Equator Principles. By November 2005 the list of participating banks and financial institutions had grown to 36, including institutions accounting for a substantial percentage of all privately funded project finance in developing countries. See *www.equator-principles.com*; Esty, Knop & Sesia, The Equator Principles: An Industry Approach to Managing Environmental and Social Risks (Harvard Business School, June 2005).

The Equator Principles commit participating institutions to follow IFC safeguard policies and World Bank Pollution Prevention and Abatement guidelines. The basic approach requires categorization of the risks associated with each project and analysis of mitigation measures. Projects with higher levels of risk are required to have an environmental management plan outlining risk mitigation measures that must be included in the loan agreements; failure to comply means a borrower can be declared in default.

Why have so many banks (particularly large banks) signed on to the Equator Principles? Several factors presumably are at work. One is the need for evaluating environmental risks that may threaten the financial performance of an investment, a potentially serious concern with large infrastructure projects. For example, a large, highly profitable gold mine in Peru has been endangered by public uprisings. Perlez & Bergman, Tangled Strands in Fight Over Peru Gold Mine, N.Y. Times, Oct. 25, 2005. While the banks individually define their environmental review procedures, following practices of public institutions provides added credibility; the fact that the IFC and World Bank use them provides some confidence in their practicality.

The environmentalist reaction to the Equator Principles has been mixed. NGOs are suspicious that private banks will not follow the same disclosure and transparency requirements that apply to the IFC and World Bank, and they also worry that the Principles apply only to project finance and not to the much wider range of corporate lending practices. The Principles also do not include "no-go" zones. The IFC is revising its safeguards, a process criticized by some NGOs worried about the potential for downgrading to satisfy the private banks. See *http://www.ifc.org/policyreview*.

Similar issues have been raised with respect to World Bank funding of commercial banks and with respect to the environmental practices of export credit agencies. Curmally, Sohn & Wright, Multilateral Development Bank Lending Through Financial Intermediaries (WRI Issue Brief 2005); Harmon, Maurer, Sohn & Carbonell, Diverging Paths: What Future for Export Credit Agencies in Development Finance? (2005).

NOTES AND QUESTIONS

1. As consumers become more aware of their influence on corporate behavior, how will companies under pressure from competing interest groups define what constitutes "responsible" behavior? Shell has come under considerable criticism for its activities in producing oil in Nigeria, which includes not only pollution and other environmental concerns but allegations of at least indirect support for government suppression of political dissent. The International Finance Corporation has come under pressure to include conditions related to human rights as an element of its safeguard policies, which will

in turn influence private practice through the Equator Principles. "IFC May Add Human Rights to Lending Criteria," Financial Times, Nov. 4, 2003. The inclusion of issues such as provision of marital benefits to gay couples has complicated this evaluation still further.

2. Promising to "go green" is one thing, being able to deliver and profit is something else. As The Economist notes in an article about General Electric, a focus on environmental services is no guarantee of success. Many companies rushed into this market in the 1980s expected rapid growth. "Alas, by the late 1990s many of these firms had scaled back their investments. The market continued growing but not at the sizzling pace they had originally expected." "A lean, clean, electric machine," The Economist, Dec. 10, 2005, at 79. The risk is particularly notable for companies seeking to pursue new technologies or business strategies, as opposed to investments to reduce waste and improve productivity. In the fall of 2005 GE announced a major commitment to environmental technologies called Ecomagination, supported by a substantial increase in spending on research and a commitment to reduce corporate greenhouse gas emissions in 2012 by 1 percent relative to an otherwise expected increase of 40 percent from levels in 2004. The Economist noted that the targets would require GE to achieve successful product breakthroughs, traditionally not a strength of the company which is better known for efficiency and quality. Ibid.

3. Are the legal obligations of corporations consistent with concepts of social responsibility that go beyond actions that can be clearly justified by enhancements of short-term profitability? Some authorities argue that significant legal changes are needed before companies can safely depart from a pure profit-maximizing norm. Elhauge, Sacrificing Corporate Profits in the Public Interest, N.Y.U. L. Rev. 80 (2005). A coalition of NGOs in the United Kingdom is promoting legal changes that would give directors broader obligations to society as well as shareholders, and similar initiatives are being discussed in the United States. Doane, "The Myth of CSR," Stanford Social Innovation Review, Fall 2005, at 22-29.

4. Multinationals with a large presence in developing countries increasingly find themselves expected to provide basic social services in the absence of effective governments. While corporations may feel ill-equipped to serve this role, they may find that—up to a point—accommodating unmet public needs for health, water, and education is a necessary cost of doing business. Such activities reflect the increasingly complicated role of corporations doing business in resource rich but poor countries. "As Exxon Pursues African Oil, Charity Becomes a Political Issue," Wall St. J., Jan. 10, 2006, at 1.

5. Recall Gus Speth's pessimistic view of the prospects for continued reliance on legal approaches as a means for advancing the global environmental agenda (page 1047). Can you envision realistic alternatives based on motivating greater corporate social responsibility?

=12=

Environmental Progress and Prospects

Early in this century . . . federal sharpshooters hunted wolves for bounty. Today, the federal Fish and Wildlife Service is orchestrating the wolf's revival. Sixty-five years ago the Hoover Dam, rising 70 stories above the bed of the Colorado River, was hailed as the greatest engineering feat in American history. Today, dams are increasingly seen as enemies of the natural order and are actually being dismantled. Only 30 years ago the Hudson River, once among America's most majestic waterways, was little more than a 350-mile sewer stretching from the Adirondacks to Manhattan, choked with untreated municipal waste, industrial chemicals and agricultural runoff. Today, the Hudson pulses with life.

—*New York Times Editorial**

[I]n the four years beginning in 1969, almost overnight in political terms, congressional action transformed what had been mainly state and local housekeeping chores into a national campaign to protect the environment. . . . [Now] the United States has embarked on a much more difficult and politically treacherous environmental campaign— . . . to control many dispersed, often invisible sources of pollution and to conserve ecological resources on private lands. Those decisions—and the ones that will follow—are far more complex than choices made during the past 30 years to control large sources of pollution and conserve ecological resources on public lands, difficult as those were. They create new tension between national goals and state preferences, between public concerns and private property, and between common interest and commercial enterprise.

—*Mary Graham***

This book has provided a whirlwind tour of the complex maze that environmental law has become. Today, four decades after the rise of the modern environmental movement, environmental protection has grown from a national concern to a global imperative. Yet in a very real sense environmental law now stands at the proverbial crossroads. When the 25th anniversary of the first Earth Day was celebrated in 1995, the theme of the National Earth Day Rally was "Don't Turn Back the Clock on Environmental Protection," a sign of how dramatically the political climate in Congress had changed with respect to environmental issues. More than a decade later, Congress remains mired in legislative gridlock on environmental issues, but considerable thought has been given about how to improve environmental law to prepare it to face the next

*A New Way of Living with Nature, Dec. 19, 1999, at 12.
**The Morning After Earth Day: Practical Environmental Politics 4 (1999).

1127

generation of policy challenges. This chapter reviews what environmental law
has accomplished to date and its prospects for future improvement.

A. ENVIRONMENTAL PROGRESS

Clearly, much progress has been made, but it is equally clear that most of the
laws have failed to live up to the lofty expectations that accompanied their
enactment. Looking back to the First Annual Report of the Council on Environmental Quality, one cannot help but be struck by how similar the problems
outlined in the report are to today's environmental concerns. CEQ, Environmental Quality—1970, at 93 (1970). Although the ozone hole had not yet been discovered, the CEQ report devoted an entire chapter to concern that atmospheric
pollution might cause global warming and climate change. New concerns, such as
ozone depletion and radon, have been added to the environmental agenda. But
with the possible exception of noise pollution, none of the environmental concerns outlined by CEQ in 1970 has vanished from the national agenda.

The CEQ was prescient in forecasting not only the significance of the
policy changes launched in 1970, but also that environmental problems were
bound to get worse before they got better. In the opening paragraphs of its first
annual report, CEQ noted that:

> Historians may one day call 1970 the year of the environment. They may not be
> able to say that 1970 actually marked a significant change for the better in the
> quality of life; in the polluting and the fouling of the land, the water, and the air;
> or in health, working conditions, and recreational opportunity. Indeed, they
> are almost certain to see evidence of worsening environmental conditions in
> many parts of the country.
> Yet 1970 marks the beginning of a new emphasis on the environment—a
> turning point, a year when the quality of life has become more than a phrase;
> environment and pollution have become everyday words; and ecology has
> become almost a religion to some of the young. Environmental problems,
> standing for many years on the threshold of national prominence, are now at
> the center of nationwide concern. Action to improve the environment has been
> launched by government at all levels. And private groups, industry, and indivi-
> duals have joined the attack. [CEQ, Environmental Quality—1970, at 5 (1970).]

What progress has been made? What have been the success stories and the
failures, and what can be learned from them to help shape the development of
better policy in the future? Consider the following assessment by the Council on
Environmental Quality.

	Council on Environmental Quality,	
	Environmental Quality,	
	25th Anniversary Report	
	(1996)	

Over the past 25 years, Americans have witnessed remarkable changes in
policy and perspectives about the environment.

It was not so long ago that most environmental problems were thought to
be largely local in nature and to have short-term, benign effects. Even when the

effects were neither short-term nor benign, as in the case of coal mine workers' exposure to coal dust, there was in some quarters a willingness to accept such conditions as an unalterable part of life. In this 25-year period, we have learned that environmental problems can be local, regional, or global in scale, and that many effects are both long-term and life-threatening. Furthermore, we have learned that some environmental problems actually threaten the most fundamental global systems and cycles. In response, we have taken action on numerous fronts. For example, in just 25 years, we have:

- substantially reduced most conventional air and water pollution;
- taken international action to phase out chlorofluorocarbons (CFCs), after learning they could deplete the stratospheric ozone layer;
- made significant progress in reducing children's average blood lead levels, after learning that lead can have devastating impacts on children's intellectual development.

. . . [C]ommand-and-control approaches, with the help of a strong monitoring and enforcement effort, have been successful in controlling large point sources of pollution such as industrial facilities or mass-produced products such as cars. They have been somewhat less successful when the targets are more numerous and diverse and there are many more control options. . . .

Overall, between 1970 and 1994 the combined emissions of the six principal [air] pollutants declined 24 percent. . . . Since passage of the Clean Water Act in 1972, most of the conspicuous water pollution from point sources has been eliminated. More than 57,000 industrial facilities now operate under a pollution control permit. . . . Direct industrial discharges of toxic pollutants are down dramatically since 1972. . . .

Despite the progress that has been made on some fronts, many challenges remain. In some cases, the pressures posed by population growth have been difficult to overcome. Partly as a result of the growth in the number of automobiles on the road, total emissions of nitrogen oxides (NOx) have increased since 1970, which has contributed to a continuing problem with ground-level ozone in many cities. Population and development have played a role in the continuing degradation of coastal zones and estuaries and the wide-scale destruction of critical habitats, though in many cases creative policymaking and careful management can at least partially overcome such conflicts.

In addition, about 40 percent of the nation's rivers, lakes and estuaries still don't meet basic clean water standards; wetlands losses on nonfederal lands were about 70,000-90,000 acres per year during the early 1990s; and localized cases of waterborne disease continue to threaten drinking water safety.

A few problems escaped attention under the early command-and-control approaches. The most notable was non-point source water pollution, such as pesticide and fertilizer runoff from farms and stormwater runoff in urban areas.

A few problems were late-bloomers, including the realization that indoor air pollutants such as environmental tobacco smoke and radon pose significant human health risks.

Finally, there was a growing realization that human activities could be affecting the global environment. In this realm, the emerging issues have included stratospheric ozone depletion, deforestation, declining marine fishery resources in some species and regions, and new evidence that some air emissions were affecting global climate. Since 1972, for example, worldwide generation of carbon dioxide, a common "greenhouse" gas, has increased by 8 percent. Most scientists now believe that such emissions have contributed to an increase in global temperature.

Over the past 25 years a great deal has been learned about environmental problems and strategies to deal with them. Though a number of residual problems remain, the effort was generally successful and has almost certainly provided benefits well in excess of the costs.

NOTES AND QUESTIONS

1. Why has environmental policy been more successful in some areas than in others? In its 1990 report, the Council on Environmental Quality suggests that problems with diverse and widely dispersed sources and problems that emerged slowly have been particularly difficult to control. Council on Environmental Quality, Environmental Quality: Twentieth Annual Report 11 (1990). Is this an accurate assessment of progress to date? What examples of specific problems support or contradict this assessment?

2. Dr. Barry Commoner, an outspoken environmental scientist who has been a persistent critic of the current regulatory system, is far less sanguine about environmental law's accomplishments. He argues that

> changes in the technology of production are the *root cause* of modern environmental pollution. . . . Only in the few instances in which the technology of production has been changed—by eliminating lead from gasoline, mercury from chlorine production, DDT from agriculture, PCB from the electrical industry, and atmospheric nuclear explosions from the military enterprise—has the environment been substantially improved. [B. Commoner, Failure of the Environmental Effort, 18 Envtl. L. Rep. 10195, 10196 (1988).]

Commoner maintains that rather than focusing on defining "acceptable" levels of pollution, the environmental laws should focus on changing production technology to prevent pollutants from being generated. Do you agree that changes in technology are the "root cause" of contemporary environmental problems? Even if this is true, does the solution necessarily require that the government intervene in the production process?

3. Note that the prohibition of lead additives in gasoline and the phaseout of the production of CFCs are two prominent examples cited by CEQ as environmental success stories. To what extent were these initiatives the product of idiosyncratic factors, rather than the result of the routine application of existing laws?

4. As a result of progress in combating some of the more obvious sources of environmental problems, environmental policy now confronts a more diffuse, but important, set of challenges. This shift in the environmental policy agenda may have profound political consequences for our ability to address remaining problems successfully, as Mary Graham explains in the following excerpt.

|| **Mary Graham, The Morning** ||
|| ***After Earth Day (1999)*** ||

The generation of national efforts to protect the environment that followed the celebration of Earth Day in 1970 represents a rare and remarkable achievement in American government: the successful introduction of a new theme into national policy. New themes are unusual in our political system. Sudden change is intentionally minimized by the Constitution's separation of powers and by a legislative structure that encourages the balancing of opposing interests. Yet in the four years beginning in 1969, almost overnight in political terms, congressional action transformed what had been mainly state and local housekeeping chores into a national campaign to protect the environment. Legislation created new public participation in major government and private decisions, new notions of federalism, and new government power over big business.

Those laws also have sparked 30 years of political battles. . . .

As those conflicts continue, the United States has embarked on a much more difficult and politically treacherous environmental campaign—though without the fanfare that accompanied federal efforts in the 1970s. In the last decade, ad hoc responses to novel conflicts have begun to define policies to control many dispersed, often invisible sources of pollution and to conserve ecological resources on private land. Those decisions—and the ones that will follow—are far more complex than choices made during the past 30 years to control large sources of pollution and conserve ecological resources on public lands, difficult as those were. They create new tension between national goals and state preferences, between public concerns and private property, and between common interests and commercial enterprise. . . .

. . . Today's most serious water pollution threats come from chemicals and organic wastes in farmers' fields, commercial developments, city and suburban streets, and homeowners' lawns, driveways, and septic fields, washed by rain into rivers, lakes, and bays. Today's most serious air pollution threats arise from diverse sources inside homes, schools, and workplaces, in part because that is where people spend most of their time. Today's most serious auto pollution problems are caused by emissions from aging or poorly maintained cars, exacerbated by the fact that drivers log in more miles per vehicle each year. Today's most serious problems from especially hazardous air pollutants can be traced to an array of sources: vehicles and motorized equipment, consumer and commercial solvents, dry cleaners and other neighborhood businesses, as well as factories. Today's most serious conservation challenges arise from individual choices in the use of private property: the ways that farmers work their land, ranchers graze their herds, and developers plan subdivisions. In terms of contentious problems, the direction of change is from the visible, concentrated, and well known toward the invisible, diffuse, and unfamiliar.

Such controversies change the political calculus. They are difficult to resolve through national standards, which have been the usual means of translating national priorities into requirements for business or guidelines for the management of public lands. They sometimes fail to elicit broad public support. In the early 1970s people became outraged by the pollution from factory smokestacks that blackened window sills and reduced visibility, and by the pollution from refineries and steel mills that clogged rivers in some urban areas. It is easier to ignore invisible gases from small businesses, emissions from aging automobiles, and chemicals carried away by storm runoff. They are hard to identify and hard to trace to their source. Also, such issues create new and potentially explosive clashes between the public's proven concern with environmental protection and its commitment to other enduring values: protection of private property, encouragement of small businesses and family farms, preservation of local autonomy in land use decisions, and respect for individual choice.

To complicate matters further, the costs and inconvenience of making such adjustments tend to fall directly on more people than has been true of environmental improvements in the past. American businesses pay a high price for pollution control, more than $76 billion a year. In the abstract, voters may understand that ultimately that price is paid by consumers, shareholders, or employees. Yet the impact of those control efforts is rarely discernible to individual buyers, investors, or workers. By contrast, environmental progress that relies on getting people to maintain their cars or improve their septic tanks is experienced directly by millions of people across the country. . . .

In one sense, the growing national concern about these more complex, less visible environmental problems is good news. They are receiving more attention in part because 30 years of national efforts have produced clear successes in controlling many concentrated sources of pollution and in improving balanced management of federal lands. These successes are particularly impressive because they have taken place during a time when economic activity has more than doubled, the nation's population has increased by nearly a third, and vehicle miles traveled have increased 121 percent. . . .

Successes . . . do not mean that factory pollution is a thing of the past. Manufacturers still discharge millions of pounds of pollutants into the air, on land, or into water—legally. To cite one example, in 1995 industry discharged 2.2 billion pounds of chemicals included in the federal Toxics Release Inventory, most of it into the air. Technological change will continue to play a central role in reducing industrial pollution. But that role, too, is being re-cast. Ongoing efforts to capture pollution from smokestacks and drain pipes before it enters the air or water are beginning to be accompanied by longer term efforts to reorganize industrial processes to minimize waste. Such attempts to employ "industrial ecology" borrow a lesson from nature. Interdependent plants and animals use waste from one process as energy for another. New emphasis is on myriad changes that can reduce use of materials, encourage less-polluting forms of energy, or employ discharges as resources.

Big businesses are still caught cheating. . . .

Public lands also remain political battlegrounds. . . . But during a period when the voters' confidence in their public servants has been low, it is worth acknowledging a governmental success—the addition of a new set of values to the American political system, and their influence not just on government and industry practices, but also on reducing pollution and improving conservation.

As less visible and more diffuse problems gain prominence, simple assumptions that formed the foundation for national policy 30 years ago have been replaced with new paradoxes. The framework of the laws enacted between 1969 and 1973 reflected a particular moment in American history. Congress responded to the public's sense of crisis. It responded to voters' enduring trust in its ability to find quick remedies combined with their suspicions that bureaucrats would thwart those efforts. It responded to doubts that state and local governments could or would address pressing problems. And it reflected the public's abiding faith in the capability of big business to find technological solutions to the nation's problems coupled with a deep distrust of its will to use that capability to improve the environment.

A generation later, the political and economic ground has shifted. Basic questions recur and their answers today bear little resemblance to assumptions that have supported national policy for the past 30 years. The public's sense of crisis has been replaced with enduring support for improving pollution control and conservation, but also with a frequent reluctance to pay the public costs of increased protection or to change everyday habits. The federal government's ability to understand and manage environmental problems has increased immeasurably since the early 1970s. But, in practice, possibilities for national action are now constrained by the increasing power of international forces, the declining influence of federal agencies over state and local government actions, an unmanageable workload, and an aging system of laws and regulations sometimes out of sync with new science and new issues. State governments have gained in competence and been given greater responsibilities. But the strength of state programs varies enormously. And states are caught in a funding squeeze between taxpayer revolts and diminishing federal funds. That funding squeeze is especially damaging in less affluent states, where environmental programs may be weaker than in more prosperous states. American companies, once insulated by tariffs and technological superiority, compete in a fast-changing national and international economy. Interestingly, business attitudes toward environmental protection have become more positive as business's economic position has become less secure. But big business also has new reasons to minimize costs, and many smaller businesses and farmers, upon whom much environmental progress depends, lack the resources and incentives to modify their practices.

These changes in public support and in government and business capabilities matter because, under our system of government, approaches to environmental protection, like approaches to other domestic problems, are inevitably collaborative. Federal officials cannot themselves reduce pollution or improve conservation, except on government property. They can make rules, impose penalties, and spend money. But ultimately they rely on the cooperation of state and local governments, businesses, and individuals to produce the results they want. Collaboration becomes more important as public attention turns to environmental problems that are hard to manage with simple national rules. . . .

After a generation, pollution control and conservation have been assimilated into the American political system. As national priorities, they have stood the test of time, and they have weathered political challenges. They have become a permanent part of government and business decisionmaking. But changing times also have revealed new puzzles about the character of public support and the capacity of government and business to address a new generation of environmental problems.

NOTES AND QUESTIONS

1. What factors does Graham think explain the extraordinary congressional response to environmental concerns in the early 1970s? What features of current environmental concerns make them a greater political challenge to address?

2. Graham argues that environmental politics has "matured" as both political parties have accepted the appropriateness of federal environmental programs. However, she does not believe that the days of bitter political battles over environmental regulation are over. Graham notes that business interests, environmental groups, and state and local officials are engaged in pragmatic efforts to "customize" many aspects of federal environmental policy. "The simple structure of uniform standards and deadlines of the 1970s is evolving

into a complex web of requirements and negotiated agreements tailored to suit particular situations." Graham, The Morning After Earth Day 11 (1999).

3. Graham notes that the field of industrial ecology is yielding new insights on how technology can be changed to reduce its environmental impact through process changes that reduce pollution and energy use at the source. For a discussion of how this is being accomplished see Braden R. Allenby, Industrial Ecology: Policy Framework and Implementation (1999). Allenby defines industrial ecology as "the multidisciplinary study of industrial systems and economic activities, and their links to fundamental natural systems." Id. at 12. He explains that it can help provide product or process design teams with a better understanding of the life cycle environmental costs of alternative designs.

4. Graham believes that developing accurate and objectively interpreted environmental information will be crucial to future innovation in environmental policy. While technological changes are creating unprecedented opportunities to expand the potential of informational approaches to regulation, these opportunities have not been fully exploited yet.

B. ENVIRONMENTAL PROSPECTS

Visions of the future world environment are many and varied. Many believe that changes in technology offer the best hope for defusing some of the political difficulties of regulating smaller and more diffuse sources of pollution and for overcoming the daunting global challenges posed by population growth and increasing resource consumption. Consider the following reflections from the editors of the New York Times, discussing the fundamental changes that occurred in humankind's attitude toward nature over the past century and what they may portend for the future of environmental policy.

A New Way of Living with Nature
N.Y. Times, Dec. 19, 1999, at 12

A century that will be remembered for material and scientific progress may also be remembered for something more modest—as a moment when mankind, realizing that the earth's resources were not infinite and perhaps seeking expiation for years of predatory behavior, struck a truce with nature. For the first time since the dawn of the industrial age there was, at least in the West and certainly in America, a rough armistice between the forces of economic growth and the forces of preservation.

The big question on the eve of the next century is whether this armistice will hold. The earth's six billion people will grow to nine billion by 2050, creating new pressures on natural resources, food and habitation. There is also the related question of whether what can loosely be called the environmental ethic, now largely confined to the industrialized world, can be extended to poorer nations that believe it is their turn to industrialize.

America, for example, seems to have settled on a policy of preserving its national forests and adding incrementally to its protected wilderness. By contrast, countries like Brazil, Malaysia and Indonesia are chewing up their forests at a ferocious clip. Similarly, the industrialized West is actively seeking alternatives to the carbon-based fuels that are contributing to potentially disruptive changes in the earth's climate. Yet unless the big developing countries like India and China do likewise, what the West does will make very little difference.

Still, it is worth celebrating the attitudinal changes in this country that have cast nature, once seen as an unruly force needing discipline, in a more congenial light. Early in this century, for example, federal sharpshooters hunted wolves for bounty. Today, the federal Fish and Wildlife Service is orchestrating the wolf's revival. Sixty-five years ago the Hoover Dam, rising 70 stories above the bed of the Colorado River, was hailed as the greatest engineering feat in American history. Today, dams are increasingly seen as enemies of the natural order and are actually being dismantled. Only 30 years ago the Hudson River, once among America's most majestic waterways, was little more than a 350-mile sewer stretching from the Adirondacks to Manhattan, choked with untreated municipal waste, industrial chemicals and agricultural runoff. Today, the Hudson pulses with life.

Wolves, dams, wilderness, forests, lakes, rivers, estuaries—all are seen differently now than they were less than 50 years ago. Of course if reparations were to be made at all, the century now ending was surely the proper time to make them. For it was not until the 20th century that we began to develop the technology that enabled us to destroy nature on a truly grand scale—the implacable machinery that in a heartbeat (measured in millennial time) could foul the air, clear-cut the forests and strip-mine the oceans.

It was thus fitting that this same century would eventually produce a citizens' revolt against environmental degradation. This revolt—symbolized by the first Earth Day in 1970, and defined by the creation of an astonishing body of environmental laws—not only gave the nation the tools with which to heal itself but conferred upon ordinary citizens the indispensable right to take even the government to court if it failed to carry out these laws.

There are many who believe that the technology that got us into trouble will get us out—that fuel cells will replace the internal combustion engine, that microbes will dispose of the waste stream. But of course technology is neutral. What will matter in the future is what has always mattered, namely the values and political will of those at the controls. The truth is, people can accomplish mighty acts of repair. If they can destroy the Everglades with levees and canals, as they did in the 1940's, they can help save the Everglades by replumbing it. If they can decimate the world's swordfish with factory ships, they can replenish the swordfish by keeping those ships in port.

Therein lies one answer to the environmental pessimists who believe that the world is past recovery, that the battle to preserve open spaces and biodiversity is already lost because there are simply too many people coveting too much land and demanding too many resources. What they overlook is that we are not at the same point on the learning curve that we were 70 or even 30 years ago. Having discovered that we can actually change the way nature operates, we have also discovered that with this power comes a sacred obligation to restore what we once nearly ruined.

NOTES AND QUESTIONS

1. Who are the "environmental pessimists" to which the Times editors refer? Do environmental groups fall into this category or is this just a facile

caricature? When they refer to society's "learning curve," do they mean general improvements in environmental technology, changes in the political process that made it more responsive to environmental concerns, or something else?

2. Journalist Gregg Easterbrook charges that environmentalists have been unduly alarmist about the state of the planet. Adopting an approach he calls "ecorealism," Easterbrook maintains that most of the developed world's major environmental problems are nearly solved, as discussed below.

Easterbrook, A Moment on the Earth: The Coming Age of Environmental Optimism
(1995)

Ecological consciousness is a leading force for good in world affairs. Without the imperatives of modern environmentalism—without its three decades of unstinting pressure on government and industry—the Western world today might actually be in the kind of ecological difficulty conventional wisdom assumes it to be in. Instead, the Western world today is on the verge of the greatest ecological renewal that humankind has known; perhaps the greatest that the Earth has known. Environmentalists deserve the credit for this remarkable turn of events.

Yet our political and cultural institutions continue to read from a script of instant doomsday. Environmentalists, who are surely on the right side of history, are increasingly on the wrong side of the present, risking their credibility by proclaiming emergencies that do not exist. What some doctrinaire environmentalists wish were true for reasons of ideology has begun to obscure the view of what is actually true in "the laboratory of nature." It's time we began reading from a new script, one that reconciles the ideals of environmentalism with the observed facts of the natural world. Toward that end [I] advance the following premises:

- That in the Western world pollution will end within our lifetimes, with society almost painlessly adapting a zero-emissions philosophy.
- That several categories of pollution have already ended.
- That the environments of Western countries have been growing cleaner during the very period the public has come to believe they are growing more polluted.
- That First World industrial countries, considered the scourge of the global environment, are by most measures much cleaner than developing nations.
- That most feared environmental catastrophes, such as runaway global warming, are almost certain to be avoided.
- That far from becoming a new source of global discord, environmentalism, which binds nations to a common concern, will be the best thing that's ever happened to international relations.
- That nearly all technical trends are toward new devices and modes of production that are more efficient, use fewer resources, produce less waste, and cause less ecological disruption than technology of the past.
- That there exists no fundamental conflict between the artificial and the natural.

- That artificial forces which today harm nature can be converted into allies of nature in an incredibly short time by natural standards.
- Most important, that humankind, even a growing human population of many billions, can take a constructive place in the natural order.

None of these notions are now common currency. It is possible to find yourself hooted down for proposing them at some public forums. A few years ago at a speech at a Harvard Divinity School conference on environmental affairs I was hissed merely for saying "People are more important than plants and animals." What better barometer is there of how nonsensical doomsday thinking can become?

But that is a passing situation. In the near future the propositions stated above will be widely embraced by society and even by the intelligentsia. Collectively I call these views ecorealism.

Ecorealism will be the next wave of environmental thinking. The core principles of ecorealism are these: that logic, not sentiment, is the best tool for safeguarding nature; that accurate understanding of the actual state of the environment will serve the Earth better than expressions of panic; that in order to form a constructive alliance with nature, men and women must learn to think like nature. . . .

Human sprawl is ubiquitous on planet Earth. Cities both grand and dolorogenic dot six of the seven continents. Autos, trucks, and trains scurry everywhere. Mighty aircraft arc the skies; vessels larger than medieval towns course the seas; chandeliers of technology hang in space. Through human action whole provinces of Earth have been converted from forest or prairie to farms and pasture. Countless rivers have been dammed or diverted. And everywhere are man's machines, from the little motors that power handheld devices to the giant engines known as factories—machines spewing toxic chemicals, respiratory irritants, acids, greenhouse gases, water pollutants, caustic sodas, production slag, agricultural husks, cattle gristle, mineral till, "depleted" uranium, ash, polymer slurries, and products at times hard to distinguish from by-products. In parallel the homes of First World citizens have become little factories in their own right, generating heat or cold, ablaze with lights, pumping out wastes of every variety. . . .

From nature's perspective the picture is surely different. No one could dispute that genus *Homo* affects the Earth more than any other species. Humanity is resourceful and mischievous, assiduously engaged in environmental harm. But is nature really on the run? Several important indexes suggest that it is not.

First, the portion of Earth taken over by humanity is fantastically exaggerated in the popular imagination. The United States is the most growth-obsessed and machine-oriented of cultures. Yet so far only two percent of the U.S. surface area is "built up," according to the U.S. Geological Survey. This figure reflects the concrete footprint of cities, towns, roads, suburbs, homes, offices, factories, airports, and other artificial impositions upon American land. Two percent. If lakes formed by dams are thought of as built-up land, the figure rises to slightly over three percent. The comparable figure for Europe is about eight percent built-up. Europe has been in pursuit of the materialist lifestyle for several centuries longer than the United States. Yet even there only a small portion of the biosphere has been seized by people. North and west of New York City and London and Chicago, south of Paris and Bonn, east of San Francisco and Moscow, in all directions around Atlanta and Denver and Warsaw and Madrid, and in many similar locations worldwide, extensive tracts of habitat that have known only occasional human intervention abut centers of mechanistic human excess. . . .

An important area in which human and natural perceptions differ is the forest. That portion of the world that remains wooded is a fine proxy for whether nature is in decline; for forests, even the tree plantations of the big lumber companies, are primarily temples of nature, not man.

Today most Americans would surely say that forests are in critical condition. Commentary on the 1990s dispute pitting loggers against the spotted owl in the Olympic forests of Oregon and Washington State was, for example, thick with the words "disaster," "destroyed," "ravaged," and "lost forever" in reference to American forests.

Deforestation is without doubt currently taking a toll on forests in many tropical nations. But in most affluent countries, forest cover has not been declining but expanding for at least several decades. The environmentalist's notion of a forest wipeout in progress is in the Western nations the reverse of the natural reality.

Western Europe today has nearly 30 percent more forest area than it had half a century ago, despite the fact that its human population has increased rapidly through that period. In the United States forests reached their nadir in the 1920s, damaged extensively by shoddy logging practices. But as the forestry analyst Roger Sedjo, of the Washington think tank Resources for the Future, has written, sometime around the early 1940s "forest growth nationally came into balance with harvests, and since that time growth has exceeded harvest." The total amount of forest has been expanding in the United States and Western Europe during the postwar era—the very period during which, environmental doctrine says, nature has been put to rout. . . .

At several points in the twentieth century, various environmental problems have seemed to reach a level at which they become irreversible. Forest loss, overuse of bioaccumulative pesticides such as DDT, and stratospheric ozone depletion are three examples. In each case commentators decreed hopelessness. In each case the irreversible problem promptly reversed itself. Forest acres in the developed world are now expanding; DDT was banished and its bioaccumulative effects are nearly gone from the U.S. biosphere; CFCs and other chemicals linked to ozone depletion are already in decline and will go out of production in most countries in 1996, with projections now showing ozone layer replenishment beginning early in the twenty-first century. Yet doctrines of pessimism somehow never get amended as the result of positive experiences.

At this writing two problems widely viewed as irreversible are loss of equatorial rainforests and the artificial greenhouse effect. But what if the developing world executes the same sequence of forest protection seen in the industrial world? A period of unregulated forest loss may be followed by a period of stabilization (deforestation rates have declined sharply in the last three years in Brazil, the country where the problem is worst) and after that a forest recovery. A forestation of tropical woodlands might begin as soon as the early twenty-first century, a split second from now by the natural stopwatch. And what if nations learn to reduce greenhouse emissions through energy efficiency? That is already underway in many countries. Rather than steadily increasing, as commentators consider inevitable, artificial greenhouse gases may begin to decline. Then the specter of global warming will recede as well. . . .

Today we cannot imagine a Western economy based on anything other than a whopping consumption of petroleum. But a century ago no leading intellectual imagined the world running on oil. Just as horses in nineteenth-century cities were certain to yield to some other mode of transportation, what the materialist lifestyle today depends on for its inputs is certain to change repeatedly through the centuries ahead.

Perhaps the most fundamental point of understanding about the biosphere is that it is a living system, not static but continuously reacting with itself and its circumstances. Human society is the same, alive and always in transition. If human society attempted to stand still by continuing to gulp petroleum at its current rate, fiasco would follow. But social change will not come to a halt, freezing current trends in place. Through the last 20 years, Western use of petroleum has begun shifting markedly in the direction of conservation. Such changes are partly driven by prices and government policies. But partly they may be seen as organic self-adaption—society reacting just as nature would to self-correct a resource imbalance.

A Western energy economy based on hydrogen, solar-electric conversion, biomass from vegetation, and similar renewable power is not only not science fiction, it is odds-on to be realized in the lifetimes of some readers of this book. Currently many engineers scoff at the notion that hydrogen and solar-electric conversion will be useful on a commercial scale. But not much more than 100 years ago, gasoline and internal combustion were derided as nonsense. A century ago any sensible economist would have sworn that every dollar of capital in the world would be insufficient to construct the vast infrastructure necessary to create an auto culture: oil fields, refineries, pipelines, ubiquitous gasoline stations, automobile manufacturing facilities, repair shops, and so on. Yet Western society reinvented itself from no cars to all cars in 50 years.

It is well to remember that approaching the turn of the twentieth century, commentators called horse proliferation an "irreversible" peril to society—pasture land would crowd out farms, horse droppings would make cities unlivable, towns would run out of space to bury the horse carcasses, and so on. Just at the moment too many horses seemed an unresolvable environmental threat, the horse population began to drop drastically in response to the arrival of motor carriages. Running out of coal was a common refrain in the 1920s; the U.S. Department of the Interior and the British admiralty, charged with stocking the colliers of the English fleet, were among many authorities to declare coal would soon be gone forever. Within a decade a coal glut began, in response to new coal seam finds occurring at the same time that coal demand fell as the world's infatuation with petroleum commenced. In turn the imminent exhaustion of petroleum was universally decried in the 1970s. Shortly thereafter the price of oil began to plummet.

Here we may proclaim a law of environmental affairs: Whenever all respectable commentators believe a problem cannot be solved, it is about to be solved. Since respectable commentators now consider global warming unstoppable, this law predicts the greenhouse effect is about to become old news. And since respectable commentators now are "sure" that society can never wean itself from fossil fuels, therefore let's predict that the end of the fossil-fuel economy is near at hand.

Though a zero-polluting, renewable-energy economy is not practical at present, no improbable technological leaps are required to bring one into being. Today's fossil-fuel economy is already much closer in structure to a renewable-energy regime than the last century's energy economy was to today's. The Princeton physicists Joan Ogden and Robert Williams have suggested that within a decade or two, cost-effective solar-electric converters will become widely available. Large fields of such devices, placed in deserts where sunshine is intense and there are few living things to disturb, would provide renewable power to separate hydrogen from water. The hydrogen would be piped back to cities for use as a gasoline replacement. In such an energy economy the basic fuel sources would be sunlight and water; the pollution output would be negligible, as hydrogen burns without meaningful air emissions or greenhouse gases. Once an advanced energy economy is realized, petroleum might still be employed as a chemical feedstock and for other uses, but its political and social significance will conclude. Oil by and large will return to its former status of a murky nuisance that sometimes leaks from the ground; historians will come to consider the Oil Age a curiosity of less lasting significance than the Bronze Age. The industrial way of life may be irksome, but on several important fronts like this it is well ahead of the world's feudal cultures in pursuit of ecological transparency. Nature may love the citizens of the Third World but be rooting for the engineers of the First.

NOTES AND QUESTIONS

1. Do you agree with Easterbrook that environmentalists often have exaggerated the true dimensions of the environmental problems we face? If so, what have been the consequences of such "doom and gloom" forecasts?

2. What is the source of Easterbrook's optimism concerning future environmental prospects? Trends already in place? Technological advances? The adaptive capacity of the environment?

3. Not surprisingly, Easterbrook's views generated considerable controversy. Environmentalists maintained that he did not fully appreciate that many of the positive environmental trends he cites are due to hard-fought battles waged by them. As one reviewer writes, "He wants it both ways—to condemn professional enviros and other doomsayers and at the same time to champion nature. This amounts to ecosophistry and ignores the fact that what are often perceived as extreme positions effect moderate, positive gains in any field." Conaway, Mother Nature's Prospects, Wash. Post Book World, Apr. 23, 1995, at 5. Fellow environmental journalist Philip Shabecoff argues that "Easterbrook's ecorealism is constructed out of a tissue of muddy logic, careless dismissal of what in many cases is overwhelming scientific consensus, and confused or caricatured use of facts." Shabecoff, "Feel-Good" Environmentalism, in Is There Cause for "Environmental Optimism"? 29 Envtl. Sci. & Tech. 366, 368 (1995). Scientist Devra Davis maintains that "[i]n his search for glad tidings, Easterbrook confuses a lack of environmental health data with success." She maintains that "Easterbrook tacitly adopts the 'dead body' approach to public health regulation, appearing to side with those who require proof of human harm and discount experimental evidence." Davis, A "Dead-Body" Approach to Health, in Is There Cause for "Environmental Optimism"?, 29 Envtl. Sci. & Tech. 366, 368 (1995).

4. The Environmental Defense Fund (EDF) convinced Easterbrook to print an erratum correcting his charge that EDF had accepted payments from corporations for its advice. EDF prepared what it calls a list of scientific errors it found in Easterbrook's book. The following is an excerpt from their report.

| | *Environmental Defense Fund, A Moment of Truth: Correcting the Scientific Errors in Gregg Easterbrook's* **A Moment on the Earth** *(1995)* | |

INTRODUCTION

In his book *A Moment on the Earth,* Gregg Easterbrook argues that environmentalists "are surely on the right side of history, but increasingly on the wrong side of the present, risking their credibility by proclaiming emergencies that do not exist." Yet his account of environmental issues is replete with errors and misinterpretations of the scientific evidence. This is especially notable in regard to the four chapters that deal with habitat loss, global warming, ozone depletion, and species extinction, probably the four most serious threats to the natural environment, according to a recent report by the Science Advisory Board of the U.S. Environmental Protection Agency.

We believe that the record should be set straight on Easterbrook's critical scientific errors, for the faulty statements in these four chapters substantially undermine his thesis that many environmental problems have been overstated. . . .

In his chapter on global warming, Easterbrook makes many fundamental errors. He continually confuses global, regional, and local temperature trends, which may differ considerably; he mischaracterizes the results of a poll that was undertaken to determine scientists' views on global warming; and he mistakenly asserts that the sea level has not risen significantly, when it has.

Most flagrantly, however, he erroneously claims that the National Academy of Sciences (NAS) and the Intergovernmental Panel on Climate Change (IPCC), the two most respected scientific authorities on the subject, have substantially lowered their projections of future warming due to a doubling of carbon dioxide in the atmosphere, when they have not. . . .

In [the] chapter ["Radiation, Natural"] and elsewhere, Easterbrook attempts to contrast what he calls the "doomsday" approach to environmental problems with his own so-called "eco-realism," ridiculing, for example, the "idea that relatively tiny amounts of CFCs could trigger an unstoppable progression that strips the entire ozone layer, leaving the biosphere defenseless" (*A Moment on the Earth,* p. 535). Yet this is what in essence could well have occurred, with very large depletions developing throughout the world, unleashing potentially disastrous consequences for the biosphere, *if* the decision to aggressively limit the use and production of CFCs had not been made.

Moreover, he places himself against the weight of scientific evidence in claiming that UV radiation may not have risen since the emergence of ozone depletion, and that where radiation increases occur, they may have little or no effect. Along the way, he makes elementary errors in relating the history of the discovery of ozone depletion and even suggests, against medical evidence to the contrary, that increases in UV radiation may not be harmful to human health. . . .

The chapter on the northern spotted owl in *A Moment on the Earth* is so full of scientific errors and inaccurate assumptions that its conclusion—that the threat of extinction faced by the owl is overstated—is essentially worthless.

To his credit, Easterbrook is supportive of the Endangered Species Act and the efforts of environmental groups to save species in general. But in opposing the conclusions of independent biologists that the northern spotted owl faced extinction, Easterbrook neglects to cite the voluminous scientific evidence for this position, as contained in numerous peer-reviewed studies. Most importantly, he neglects to mention the definitive findings of the meeting in December 1993, in Colorado, in which biologists and statisticians from throughout the United States and Europe undertook the single largest population study of a bird of prey, and concluded that the northern spotted owl was indeed in rapid decline. . . .

Easterbrook's arguments in his chapter on endangered species are equally problematic. While disputing the conclusions of natural scientists and wildlife biologists that human activities are causing the planet to experience a loss of species of major proportions throughout the globe, he relies on inaccurate assumptions and faulty reasoning.

Moreover, as in the spotted owl chapter, he fails to grasp the difference between the better counting of existing numbers of species with observed trends that show that many of these species are in decline. This is evident when he wrongly dismisses as contradictory the increasing scientific estimates of the total number of species on Earth, and the consensus of biologists that extinction is proceeding at a rate unprecedented since the close of the age of the dinosaurs. . . .

CONCLUSION

In *A Moment on the Earth*, Gregg Easterbrook attempts to contrast his own supposedly "eco-realistic" views with the views of those he labels environmental "doomsayers." Yet what the book really does is to set Mr. Easterbrook's own opinions against the weight of scientific evidence, consisting of the findings of hundreds of independent climatologists, atmospheric scientists, and wildlife biologists, working in their respective fields throughout the world. While continually dismissing the assessments of these experts as overly pessimistic, he caricatures their positions, and incorrectly characterizes their work as part of a biased environmental "orthodoxy." In the process, he impugns the intelligence, judgment, and impartiality of some of the most esteemed scientists of our time, including Rachel Carson, James Anderson, and E.O. Wilson.

Moreover, he repeatedly criticizes scientists whose dire predictions have not come to pass, without fully acknowledging that their forecasts catalyzed changes in laws and policies that forestalled the predictions themselves.

Though the Environmental Defense Fund celebrates the successes of the past, including the banning of DDT and the restrictions on the use of CFCs, and believes that further achievements are within our grasp, we hold that this will be possible only with a realistic assessment of those environmental problems that still remain, based on the best scientific evidence.

Far from being "eco-realistic," Easterbrook's work betrays an extreme naivete concerning the workings of physical processes and natural ecosystems, resulting in an entirely unwarranted optimism that we will easily solve all of our environmental problems in the near future, if we have not done so already. Perhaps he himself should take to heart the advice he offers up so readily to environmentalists: "Learn science and speak logic. Many lesser creatures will thank you." (*A Moment on the Earth*, p. 647.)

NOTES AND QUESTIONS

1. Were the successes of past policies due in part to public response to "doom and gloom" forecasts by environmentalists? While Easterbrook maintains that ecorealism "is not a philosophy of don't worry, be happy," isn't there a danger that his views will prompt precisely such a response?

2. What forces *are* operating to influence how technology develops? To what extent do existing environmental regulations help or hinder the development of environmentally superior technology? What types of collective action are best suited for stimulating such technological innovation?

3. While population control measures have not been a focus of environmental regulation in the industrialized world, population growth has played a prominent role in competing forecasts concerning the future health of the planet. Warning that population growth would soon overwhelm the Earth's carrying capacity, ecologist Paul Ehrlich attracted national attention in 1968 with his book, The Population Bomb, which forecast mass starvation and mineral shortages. Calling Ehrlich a Malthusian, economist Julian Simon argued in The Ultimate Resource that "[n]atural resources are not finite" because human ingenuity continually finds more efficient ways to use them. In 1980, the two agreed to test their theories by betting $1,000 on whether the prices of five metals—chrome, copper, nickel, tin, and tungsten—would be higher or lower in the year 1990. Ehrlich argued that prices would rise with increased demand for a finite supply of the metals. Simon bet that prices would fall. In 1990, Simon won the bet when the prices of all five metals had declined in real terms due in part to the development of substitutes (such as plastics). The story of the bet is told in Tierney, A Bet on the Planet Earth, N.Y. Times Mag., Dec. 2, 1990, at 52. Tierney notes that Ehrlich, who lost the bet, had been highly popular with the public, while Simon, who won, had few followers.

4. Does the outcome of Ehrlich's bet with Simon prove that Ehrlich's ideas are wrong, or just that he is a poor gambler? Does Simon's argument imply that no action needs to be taken to avert environmental crises or just that we need not get too worried about the future because we can and will act to avert crises? The more people agree with Ehrlich, the more likely it is that society will impose stringent environmental protection measures. Is Simon's optimism more likely to prove correct if more people believe that Ehrlich is right and act to prevent environmental damage? Prior to Simon's death in 1998, Simon and Ehrlich had been sparring over terms for another bet. Ehrlich offered "15 separate bets, totaling $1,000 each, that 15 environmental indicators—things like greenhouse gases, biodiversity, fishery stocks—will get worse over the next decade." Simon rejected the proposal. McCoy, When the Boomster Slams the Doomster, Bet on a New Wager, Wall St. J., June 5, 1995, at A1.

Easterbrook Round II? Bjorn Lomborg's "Skeptical Environmentalist"

A book by Bjorn Lomborg, an associate professor of statistics from Denmark's University of Aarhus, received considerable attention due to its claims that the global environmental movement has vastly overstated the scope of environmental problems. Lomborg's book, The Skeptical

Environmentalist (Cambridge Univ. Press 2001), makes claims remarkably similar to those in Gregg Easterbrook's A Moment on the Earth. Lomborg writes:

> We will not lose our forests; we will not run out of energy, raw materials, or water. We have reduced atmospheric pollution in the cities of the developed world and have good reason to believe that this will also be achieved in the developing world. Our oceans have not been defiled, our rivers have become cleaner and support more life. . . . Nor is waste a particularly big problem. . . . The problem of the ozone layer has been more or less solved. The current outlook on the development of global warming does not indicate a catastrophe. . . . And, finally, our chemical worries and fear of pesticides are misplaced and counterproductive.

Lomborg claims to have been a committed environmentalist until encountering the work of Julian Simon (see notes 3 & 4 above). He bases his argument on analysis of statistical data concerning global environmental trends. Lomborg then charges that the reason this good news is not more widely accepted is that environmental groups have engaged in a pattern and practice of exaggeration and statistical manipulation to mislead the media. Not surprisingly, opponents of environmental regulation were quick to acclaim Lomborg's work. See, e.g., Alex Kozinski, Gore Wars, 100 Mich. L. Rev. 1742 (2002) (book review).

Lomborg's claims provoked a fierce reaction from the environmental community, much as Gregg Easterbrook's "eco-skepticism" launched a similar debate in 1995. In response to criticism, Lomborg has had to acknowledge some errors in his statistical analysis. Critics note that Lomborg's focus on global averages masks more localized environmental trends such as the collapse of particular fisheries and worsening environmental problems in heavily overpopulated urban areas of the developing world. Like Easterbrook, Lomborg also fails to give credit to increased public awareness of environmental problems and the public policies this spawned for much of the progress he cites. Lomborg's replies to his critics are available online at www.lomborg.com. Case Western Law Review published a symposium issue on Lomborg's work that can be found at 53 Case W. Res. L. Rev. 249-495 (2002). Grist Magazine published extensive criticisms of Lomborg's work in its Dec. 12, 2001 issue.

Surprisingly, Lomborg never cites Eastbrook's work, nor does it appear in Lomborg's extensive bibliography. Despite the striking similarity of their theme that environmental conditions are improving more than most environmentalists acknowledge, Easterbrook's work is more nuanced than Lomborg's. Although making the same optimistic claims Lomborg does, Easterbrook recognizes that not all environmental trends are moving in a positive direction, and he gives more credit to environmental regulation as a source of environmental progress. While both decry doom and gloom forecasts by environmentalists, Lomborg puts a different "spin" on his argument. Lomborg claims that fear mongering by environmentalists has led society to put too much emphasis on environmental protection, and he suggests that resources should be shifted to other priorities.

Lomborg's work is criticized in Robert V. Percival, Skeptical Environmentalist or Statistical Spin-Doctor? Bjorn Lomborg and the Relationship Between Environmental Law and Environmental Progress, 53 Case W. Res. L. Rev. 263 (2002). This article notes that while Lomborg observes a correlation between environmental progress and increasing levels of national income, he makes no systematic effort to explore the underlying causes of environmental progress. If rising national incomes correlate with improvements in environmental conditions because the public increasingly demands government action to protect the environment, then Lomborg's work provides scant basis for suggesting that existing environmental protection efforts should be relaxed. It also notes that Lomborg appears to be concerned only with the possibility that exaggerations by environmentalists could cause overregulation, ignoring how frequently industries have made highly exaggerated claims concerning the doom and gloom that would befall our economy if environmental protection measures were adopted. With scant evidence to support him, Lomborg denies the possibility that much of the environmental progress he trumpets is the product of existing environmental protection policies. If the state of the environment is improving because environmental policies are working, this progress provides no basis for Lomborg's claim that environmental protection efforts should be relaxed. As one reviewer has noted, "The ultimate irony is that Lomborg could have presented his mass of data as a tribute to the effectiveness of environmental policy. That he chooses to do the opposite says far more about him than about any claimed objectivity of his statistical analysis." Michael Grubb, Relying on Manna from Heaven?, 294 Science 1285, 1286 (Nov. 9, 2001).

NOTES AND QUESTIONS

1. A vigorous debate over the future of environmental politics has been spawned by environmental advocates who are frustrated with the movement's progress in recent years. In fall 2004 Ted Nordhaus and Michael Shellenberger presented foundation leaders with a paper entitled "The Death of Environmentalism" that argues in favor of focusing the environmental movement's energy on a broader set of progressive causes. Felicity Barringer, Debate Stirs on the Value of Ecopolitics, N.Y. Times, Feb. 6, 2005, at A1. Their paper cites data finding that the percentage of people who believe pollution is necessary to protect jobs rose from 17 percent in 1992 to 29 percent in 2004. Adam Werbach, a former president of the Sierra Club, made a similar argument in a speech entitled "Is Environmentalism Dead?" in December 2004. Carl Pope, executive director of the Sierra Club, vehemently disagrees with this assessment. The text of these speeches and other contributions to this ongoing debate can be viewed at *http://gristmill.grist.org/story/2005/1/13/134030/929.*

2. A mass market thriller, entitled "State of Fear," by popular author Michael Crichton was published in 2005. It portrays environmentalists as fear-mongering wimps eager to create disasters to convince the public that global warming is an imminent peril. While the book is a work of fiction, it includes extensive footnotes and a bibliography intended to convey the impression that the author has discovered the real facts debunking global warming. The result has been described by one reviewer as "pure porn for global warming deniers" and by another as an indication that Crichton "has completely lost all sense of perspective." Bruce Barcott, Not So Hot, New York Times Book Review, Jan. 30, 2005, at 12. Crichton's book is also reviewed in Alan S. Miller, Bad Fiction, Worse Science, Issues in Science and Technology, Winter 2006, at 93. For a response to the book by the Natural Resources Defense Council see "They Don't Call It Science Fiction for Nothing," at *http://www.nrdc.org/globalwarming/fcrichton.asp.* For a response by environmental scientists see "Michael Crichton's State of Confusion," at *http://www.realclimate.org/index.php?p=74.*

3. Several groups have been involved in projects to assess how to improve the environmental protection infrastructure. These groups include the National

Academy of Public Administration (NAPA), the President's Council on Sustainable Development (PCSD), the Next Generation Project of the Yale Center for Environmental Law and Policy, and a group called the Enterprise for the Environment (E4E). These projects, often described as efforts to "rethink" or "reinvent" environmental regulation, have generated several reports. The themes articulated in these reports provide a glimpse of potential future directions for environmental law and policy, as summarized below.

> ## President's Council on Sustainable Development, Towards a Sustainable America
> ### (1999)

There are many convergent themes in the reports, as discussed in the sections below.

The Environmental Protection System, Past and Future

- All of the reports recognize that the current system has brought about a much cleaner environment over the past three decades, largely through application of technology-based regulations on large point sources of pollution and through national standards applicable to various products, processes and substances.
- At the same time, the reports argue that the current system is not well-equipped to address the environmental challenges that remain or that loom on the horizon.
- Several of the reports describe the current system as likely being in a zone of "diminishing returns," where further tightening of technology-based regulations will produce modest environmental improvement at very high cost.
- The reports call for evolution, not revolution. None of the reports call for a dismantling of the current regulatory system; they recommend building on it. The reports recommend modifying and supplementing the existing system, experimenting with new approaches, and carefully evaluating the results. In E4E, the metaphor for this evolution was the use of "stepping stones" to cross a river. The E4E report stated that this evolution would require "experimentation, prudent risk taking, mistakes, learning, adaptation, and a rebuilding of trust." In a similar vein, the Aspen Institute concluded, "The Alternative Path supplements the current regulatory system rather than replacing it. The current system is needed to serve as a benchmark for performance as new methods are tested."

Goals

- Most next generation reports emphasize the need for the nation to set clear, measurable environmental goals to guide the environmental protection system. The PCSD set forth 10 interrelated goals that it felt were essential in guiding the nation toward sustainable development, and it offered suggestions of indicators to measure progress toward each goal. One of the Aspen Institute's 11 broad, underlying principles developed in *The Alternative Path* is: "Environmental protection goals should underlie a new system and be clear and measurable." E4E's vision for the future recommended that an improved environmental protection system "set and pursue clear environmental goals and milestones for the nation, states, localities, and tribes, and use understandable indicators to measure progress."

• None of the next generation reports suggest that environmental goals (or milestones) obviate the need for regulations or nonregulatory policy tools to bring about reductions in pollution or other changes necessary to protect the environment.

Information and Data

• Next generation reports stress the need for greatly improved information and data systems. Information and data relevant to the environmental protection system encompass those related to ambient conditions, emission sources, and risks to human health and ecosystems, as well as measures of Agency resource use and impacts, and broader social and economic impacts.

• The improved environmental protection system called for in next generation reports requires better information and data than does the current system. A system focusing on environmental goals as described above requires better monitoring and tracking of environmental conditions and more sophisticated information systems than traditional technology-based regulations.

• The PCSD, E4E, and NAPA reports contain recommendations to strengthen the base of scientific knowledge; increase its use by decision-makers and the general public; and improve the quality, collection, management, and accessibility of environmental information.

Evolution of the Regulatory System

• Next generation reports call for evolutionary change in the regulatory system, with an emphasis on performance-based standards (rather than technology-based standards) and with regulated entities having more flexibility in meeting these standards while maintaining high standards of accountability.

• This evolution would also include a more integrated, multimedia regulatory structure; more encouragement of pollution prevention; and more streamlined reporting requirements.

• The PCSD's conclusion in this area represented a breakthrough: for the first time, a prominent group of national environmental organizations and business leaders jointly endorsed the

... growing consensus that the existing regulatory system may be greatly improved by moving toward performance-based policies that encourage pollution prevention. Regulations that specify performance standards based on strong protection of health and environment—but without mandating the means of compliance—give companies and communities flexibility to find the most cost-effective way to achieve environmental goals. In return for this flexibility, companies can pursue technological innovation that will result in superior environmental protection at far lower costs. But this flexibility must be coupled with accountability and enforcement to ensure that public health and the environment are safeguarded. [PCSD, Sustainable America 28 (1996).]

- Several next generation reports address the thorny issue of "superior environmental performance," i.e., whether regulators should offer more flexible, cost-saving approaches only if regulated entities provide greater environmental protection than that achieved by current regulations. The conclusions are very similar: superior environmental performance should not be required of each and every improvement to the regulatory system. The PCSD distinguished between general streamlining and improvement of the regulatory system (expected to produce cost savings and/or incremental environmental improvement), and bold experiments in alternatives to the current system that would require superior environmental performance as a condition for a far greater range of flexibility for the regulated entity. This distinction is echoed in *The Alternative Path* and the E4E report.
- Many next generation reports cited the desirability of regulatory approaches that encouraged pollution prevention across all media.
- Many reports emphasize the desirability of improving the collection, organization, and dissemination of information to reduce duplication and streamline reporting requirements while enhancing access to relevant information by regulators and the public at large.

Expanded Set of Policy Tools

Next generation reports call on government to expand the set of policy tools it uses to protect the environment. Examples include greater use of:

- Pollution taxes, often discussed in the context of a revenue-neutral tax shift in which taxes on labor and/or capital would be reduced.
- Pricing of various services that reflects their environmental impacts; e.g., transportation and waste disposal.
- Reform of subsidies that encourage environmental degradation.
- Tradeable permits, such as the Clean Air Act's sulphur dioxide allowance trading system, the RECLAIM program for controlling air pollution in the Los Angeles air basin, various water effluent trading programs, and land-oriented tradeable permits (e.g., wetlands mitigation banking).
- Information disclosure requirements, such as the Toxics Release Inventory and California's Proposition 65.
- Systems of extended product responsibility in which designers, producers, suppliers, users and disposers accept responsibility for environmental effects through all phases of a product's life.

Federal-State Partnerships

- Several next generation reports address the nature of the federal-state partnership in protecting the environment.

- Next generation reports generally embrace the principle that EPA should differentiate its oversight responsibilities based on a state's environmental performance. The PCSD recommended differentiated oversight based on performance: "Federal agencies should develop effective partnerships with state governments to administer environmental regulatory programs. These partnerships should eliminate duplicative activities and greatly reduce federal oversight of state programs that have a proven track record."

Federal Policy Integration

- Next generation reports emphasize the need for better policy integration at the federal level. The policies of many federal departments and agencies have a significant impact on the environment through their influence on the activities of various sectors of the economy. Consistent with this theme, the PCSD report contains sections addressing many of these sectors.
- Several next generation reports recommend environmental concerns be better integrated into federal agencies through revitalization of the National Environmental Policy Act. E4E also cited the need for stronger coordination among agencies in dealing with problems ranging from water quality to endangered species to climate change, and argued that responsibility for this ultimately lies with the president who can choose to empower the Council on Environmental Quality or another White House office to perform the leadership and coordination function.
- Several reports call on Congress to better integrate its fragmented committee structure to improve both its legislative and oversight functions in the area of environmental protection.

Other Themes in Next Generation Reports

Several next generation reports emphasize the key role of private sector stewardship in protecting the environment. The Council recommends adoption of a voluntary system that ensures responsibility for a product's environmental effects by all firms involved in the product's life-cycle. The E4E report contains recommendations including: development [of] better metrics and indicators for stewardship; more extensive private networks of information sharing on pollution prevention and environmental stewardship; and industry adoption of a set of environmental best practices that promote both environmental protection and improved profitably.

NOTES AND QUESTIONS

1. Which of these recommendations do you think is most likely to be adopted? Which are likely to be the most problematic? What policies offer the greatest prospects for substantial improvements in environmental protection?

2. Yale's "Next Generation" project published its vision for the future in a book entitled Thinking Ecologically: The Next Generation of Environmental Policy (M. Chertow & D. Esty eds., 1997). Cautioning that "the devil lies in the details," Dan Esty and Marian Chertow warn that "reforms" in environmental

policy must "not become an excuse for shifting pollution costs onto the public or for inattention to the risk of environmental disasters." Id. at 233. Esty and Chertow sketch their vision for the future by attempting to describe how the world would look in 2020 if policies incorporating the ideas of the "Next Generation" project were implemented.

> ### Daniel C. Esty & Marian R. Chertow,
> ### A Vision for the Future, in
> ### Thinking Ecologically: The Next
> ### Generation of Environmental Policy
> ### (Chertow & Esty eds., 1997)

Our vision is deliberately optimistic, and by no means the most likely. But we think it is useful as an illustration of the changes in day-to-day life that might unfold with the right mix of next-generation policies: . . .

- Environmental policy has become more ecological—comprehensive in focus and attentive to linkages across problems. Systems thinking in the form of both industrial ecology and ecosystem management has emerged as the analytic core of ecological policy. Fragmented regulatory approaches derived from individual laws separately governing air and water pollution and waste management have, over time, been reassembled, omitting some parts, adding others, into a more coherent and unified set of obligations. Similarly, a focus on the integration of human and natural systems, with its broad perspective on the competing needs and desires of the public, gives concreteness to commitments to sustainable development.

- In the land use context, this new policy approach provides a mechanism to address the cumulative impacts of many small harms and thus to ensure that environmental goals are better connected to development decisions. With an emphasis on comprehensive analysis and data-driven decisionmaking, new procedures gauge the air, water, and habitat impacts of proposed land uses. This process supports local priority setting and helps to guarantee that any environmental burdens created are not unfairly imposed on those in the next town, in the next state, or even thousands of miles away. . . .

- While responsibility for some policy matters has been decentralized, the "spirit of regulatory devolution" from the 1990s has given way to a recognition that the diversity of environmental and resource use issues requires a diversity of responses. Some problems are known to be best dealt with at a community or company level; other issues require a national or even global response. Local, state (and Indian tribe), and federal activities are supplemented by multitown, multistate, and multination compacts where the ecosystem scale dictates.

- Environmental rights—the entitlement of every person to be free from pollution harms—have been firmly established, actually reestablished, building on the tradition of nuisance law. The property rights of the public have similarly been clarified, and landowners recognize that they must pay for harms that spill beyond their property boundaries or for any scarce common resources such as air or water that they consume or pollute.

- A carefully structured system of fees for emissions has been established. Payment is required for discharges that cause adverse ecological or public health effects above established thresholds. After a phase-in period that extended twenty years in some sectors, companies from multinational giants to mom-and-pop enterprises pay emissions fees. Similarly, users of public resources such as water and grazing land are charged market prices for their consumption. Even farmers have gotten used to paying full price for their water and "nitrogen-loadings" fees on their fertilizer purchases.

- Individuals, as well, pay for their pollution. Pay-as-you-throw garbage charges have become a universal standard, and the prospect of a flat fee for trash pick-up seems as humorously outdated as unmetered electricity might have in the 1990s. Other "green" fees have also become commonplace: "highway bills" for those commuting on major roads (many of which have now been privatized—improving maintenance and decreasing congestion); electronically collected smog tolls for those driving polluting vehicles in areas with substandard air; and greenhouse gas taxes on gasoline, fuel oil, and natural gas (scaled to reflect the relative climate change impacts of the various fossil fuels).

- Tax-free electric cars have become popular among commuters and most fleet vehicles run on natural gas to reduce the environmental fees they must pay. General Motors, spurred by the changing economics of engine fuels, has a full line of hydrogen-powered vehicles.

- The income tax has been abolished. A consumption tax—with rates determined by annual family purchases—augmented by revenues from pollution fees has replaced it. The new revenue structure encourages savings and investment and simultaneously promotes resource conservation. Equity concerns over the regressive nature of pollution taxes and the fear that poor people will not be able to pay fees such as highway use charges have been addressed through a graduated consumption tax schedule under which the first twenty thousand dollars in purchases for an average household is tax-free.

- Systems thinking has led to a reorganization of federal policymaking. The former Environmental Protection Agency, Department of Energy, Forest Service, Interior Department, National Oceanic and Atmospheric Administration, Food and Drug Administration, and Occupational Safety and Health Administration have been consolidated into a new Public Health, Environment, and Resources Department (PHER, "Fair," as it is called). PHER's central role is evaluating and putting a price on public health and ecological harms.

- PHER's work is supported by a Bureau of Environmental Indicators and Statistics and a reconfigured independent scientific agency, the National Institutes of Health and Environment (NIHE). The NIHE scientists, drawn from a variety of disciplines, have garnered a reputation for anticipating new environmental and health issues, and even a grudging respect from regulated industries for the rigor and transparency of their technical analyses. . . .

- Although the enforcement officials still must pursue a small set of industry laggards, most companies operate under a command-and-covenant system through which their compliance with established environmental performance goals is monitored by independent auditors. Deficiencies are reported to the government and result in enforcement actions.

- In many cases, environmental protection efforts proceed without government involvement. Companies pay close attention to their "resource productivity" and competitive advantages gained through technological innovation. Corporate cost accounting practices have been refined to permit close tracking of all materials and energy flows. The International Organization for Standardization's environmental management guidelines (ISO 14000) from the 1990s have flowered into the ISO 28000 series of substantive product and production process requirements.

- Moving beyond the end-of-pipe pollution controls of the 1970s and even the pollution prevention efforts of the 1990s, businesses now analyze comprehensively the environmental harms and risks created by all of their facilities and throughout the life-cycles of their products. Sophisticated computer models linked to vast impact databases give a methodological rigor to life-cycle analysis that seemed unimaginable in the late twentieth century. Moreover, the systems focus encouraged by industrial ecology-based policies promotes careful corporate consideration of opportunities to reduce environmental impacts across the spectrum of activities of the firm, as well as upstream (with suppliers) and downstream (with customers). . . .

- If a proposed building site contains a wetland or other ecologically important area, the developer instantly learns its "value rank." Although permission to build on red maple swamps or other high-value habitats is severely restricted, construction is permitted on low-value sites after a contribution (commensurate with the value of the habitat loss) is made to a wetlands or "ecosystem conservation" bank. The bank uses the funds to purchase high-value properties for protection and also to restore damaged wetlands as an offset against the habitat loss from new construction.

- Internationally, a half-dozen U.N. agencies and various treaty secretariats with environmental missions have been consolidated into a Global Environmental Organization (GEO). This new, leanly staffed body manages the international response to global-scale problems, provides a mechanism for data and information exchange, coordinates policy with other international bodies such as the World Trade Organization (WTO), and offers dispute settlement services for trans-boundary environmental issues. GLOBE, a group of environmentally interested legislators from around the world, conducts oversight hearings on the GEO's performance.

- The World Bank and other multilateral development banks have been rechartered. They now focus on assistance to the least developed countries (those unable to attract private capital) and on subsidizing the global benefits of environmental investments in projects where a nation-state level benefit-cost analysis would not justify action because the benefits fall outside the country.

- Environmental nongovernmental organizations (NGOs) help to shape and legitimize international environmental policymaking. As part of a rapidly evolving global civil society, the NGOs link local citizens to the otherwise distant governance processes at the world scale, inform the public about policy choices, and ensure a measure of public participation in various international organizations such as the GEO and the WTO.

NOTES AND QUESTIONS

1. Which features of the vision described above would require changes in the federal environmental laws? What changes would have to be made, and to which statutes? How realistic politically is it to expect that such change could be accomplished?

2. To what extent could the changes described above be accomplished without changing the environmental laws? What would be required to bring these changes about?

3. In Chapter 11, we noted the analysis by Gus Speth, who argues that the legal approach to international problems may be an inadequate response. Drawing on work by the World Business Council for Sustainable Development, Speth outlines a scenario called "JAZZ":

> "[P]eople and businesses create a world full of unscripted, voluntary initiatives that are decentralized and improvisational, like jazz. In the JAZZ world, information about business behavior is abundant, and good conduct is enforced by public opinion and consumer decisions. Governments facilitate more than regulate, environmental and consumer groups are very active, and businesses see strategic advantage in doing the right thing."

Speth, Red Sky at Morning 173 (2004). What prospects do you foresee for the JAZZ scenario? How would it affect the role of law in promoting environmental protection?

4. Enactment of the Sarbanes-Oxley Act of 2002 has placed increased attention on disclosure of environmental liabilities by corporations. The Act requires a company's chief executive officer and chief financial officer to certify that the company has an adequate internal management system consisting of "disclosure controls and procedures" encompassing environmental matters required to be reported in filings with the Securities and Exchange Commission (SEC). While the SEC's role in environmental matters has been relatively minor, both environmental groups and advocates for improved corporate governance have been pushing companies to make greater environmental disclosures. In recent years there has been a significant increase in the percentage of large companies voluntarily producing reports on their environmental performance. This trend has been facilitated by the Global Reporting Initiative (GRI) spearheaded by the Coalition for Environmentally Responsible Economies (CERES) and the United Nations Environment Programme (UNEP). See *http://www.globalreporting.org* and *http://www.ceres.org*.

C. SOME CONCLUDING THOUGHTS

Because environmental regulation raises many fundamental policy dilemmas for which there are no clear answers, it is hardly surprising that it has been such a persistent source of controversy. As we saw at the outset of this book, beneath the veneer of consensus on environmental values that permits politicians to declare the environment a "moral issue," lie deep divisions over policy.

The characteristics of modern environmental problems—uncertainty of mechanism and effect, the collective nature of risk, irreversibility, and potentially catastrophic effects—help explain why. While some believe that these challenges are so daunting that environmental protection should become "the central organizing principle for civilization," A. Gore, Earth in the Balance: Ecology and the Human Spirit 269 (1992), others depict environmentalists as power-hungry alarmists bent on destroying jobs. See, e.g., Will, Earth Day's Hidden Agenda, Wash. Post, Apr. 19, 1990, at A27.

These divisions are not simply the product of different interpretations of environmental "facts"; they also turn largely on differences in values concerning how much environmental risk society should tolerate, how that risk should be distributed, and how cautious society should be in the face of uncertainty. The difficulty of resolving such questions of value is reflected in the common law's long struggle between utilitarian and rights-based approaches to environmental problems. This tension persists today, even as public law has taken center stage in environmental protection efforts, in the fierce debate over competing approaches to regulatory policy.

While public law has overcome many of the common law's limitations, it faces difficulties of its own in designing and implementing regulatory policies that will affect human behavior in predictable ways. More than three decades of experience with federal regulation has generated considerable knowledge that can be used to improve future regulatory policy. We have learned that regulation can affect human behavior in unintended and counterproductive ways, but that it also can stimulate technological innovation, expanding our capability to control environmental problems and reducing the costs of such controls. As the limitations of policies that emphasized command-and-control regulation become more evident, environmental law is becoming increasingly receptive to approaches that use economic incentives to affect behavior.

Improved scientific understanding of environmental problems has made us more acutely aware of the limits of our knowledge even as our desire to know more intensifies. We have come to realize that even small changes in human behavior can have an enormous impact on our environment, even if we still cannot trace micro-level impacts with precision. This understanding is contributing to expanded notions of social responsibility embodied in laws that extend liability to parties more remotely connected to environmental damage or that seek to regulate increasingly smaller entities.

As legal responsibility for environmental protection expands, conflicts between environmental regulation and individual autonomy may arise more frequently. In such circumstances, environmentalists may become the cool analysts while their opponents seek to muster moral outrage against perceived threats to their property. Recognition that concern for fairness and respect for individual autonomy are at the root of much environmental regulation should provide some common ground for resolving these controversies as society decides how to control environmental risks and how to distribute the costs of regulation.

Many of the same policy dilemmas that have confronted national environmental policy making are now appearing on a global scale as the international community seeks to develop a coordinated response to global environmental problems. How the world community addresses these issues will have a profound effect not only on what sort of planet we leave our children, but also on the values they will hold and their ability to fulfill their aspirations.

══ APPENDIX A ══

‖ *Glossary* ‖

This glossary and the acronym list in Appendix B are adapted from various EPA publications, including EPA, Terms of Environment (1997). Some of them have been modified by the casebook authors to improve their clarity or accuracy. EPA now maintains a more extensive glossary and acronym list on-line at *www.epa.gov/OCEPAterms/*. The definitions are intended to acquaint you with the basic concepts; they do not represent legal definitions of the terms.

Acid deposition. Particulates and gases deposited onto soil and surface waters after emissions of sulfur and nitrogen compounds are transformed by chemical processes in the atmosphere. The wet forms, popularly called "acid rain," can fall as rain, snow, or fog.

Action level. The level of a pollutant or contaminant that, when detected, triggers a requirement for some form of further action.

Active ingredient. In any pesticide product, the component that kills, or otherwise controls, target pests. Pesticides are regulated primarily on the basis of their active ingredients.

Administrative order. A directive requiring an individual, business, or other entity to take action or to refrain from an activity. It can be enforced in court and may be issued as a result of an administrative complaint ordering payment of a penalty for violations of a statute.

Advanced waste water treatment. Treatment of sewage that goes beyond the secondary or biological water treatment stage by removing nutrients such as phosphorus and nitrogen and a high percentage of suspended solids.

Advisory. A non-regulatory document that communicates risk information to persons.

Airborne particulates. Total suspended particulate matter found in the atmosphere as solid particles or liquid droplets, including windblown dust, emissions from industrial processes, smoke from the burning of wood and coal, and the exhaust of motor vehicles.

Air quality criteria. Documents summarizing what is known about adverse health and welfare effects associated with various levels of air pollution.

Air quality standards. Regulations limiting levels of pollutants in the ambient air that may not be exceeded during a specified time in a defined area.

Anthropogenic. Caused by or relating to the impact of human activity on the environment.

Anti-degradation policy. A policy that restricts activities that would cause air or water quality to deteriorate in areas that currently meet applicable air or water quality standards.

1155

Aquifer.   An underground layer of permeable rock, sand, or gravel containing groundwater that can supply wells and springs.

Asbestos.   A family of fibrous silicate minerals with electrical and thermal insulating properties that can cause lung cancer, mesothelioma, or asbestosis when inhaled.

Asbestosis.   A disease associated with chronic exposure to and inhalation of asbestos fibers that makes breathing progressively more difficult and can lead to death.

Ash.   The mineral content of a product remaining after complete combustion.

Assimilative capacity.   The ability of a body of air or water to receive pollutants without causing significant environmental damage.

Attainment area.   An area where air quality is in compliance with the national ambient air quality standards established under the Clean Air Act. An area may be an attainment area for one pollutant and a nonattainment area for others.

Background level.   The naturally occurring level of a chemical substance found in air, water, or soil in the absence of a source of pollution.

Banking.   A system for recording credits for qualified emissions reductions for later use in bubble, offset, or netting transactions.

BEN.   EPA's computer model for analyzing a violator's economic gain from not complying with the law.

Benthic organism (Benthos).   A form of aquatic plant or animal life that is found on or near the bottom of a stream, lake, or ocean.

Benthic region.   The bottom layer of a body of water.

Best available control technology (BACT).   An emission limitation based on the maximum degree of emission reduction achievable through application of production processes and available methods, systems, and techniques. Use of the BACT concept is allowable on a case-by-case basis for major new or modified emissions sources in attainment areas, and it applies to each regulated pollutant.

Best Demonstrated Available Technology (BDAT).   As identified by EPA, the most effective commercially available means of treating specific types of hazardous waste. The BDATs may change with advances in treatment technologies.

Best Management Practices (BMP).   Methods that have been determined to be the most effective, practical means of preventing or reducing pollution from nonpoint sources.

Bioaccumulative.   The propensity of substances to increase in concentration in living organisms as they are ingested because they are very slowly metabolized or excreted.

Bioassay.   A test used to evaluate the effects of a chemical substance by exposing living organisms (*in vivo*) or isolated tissue (*in vitro*) to it.

Biochemical oxygen demand (BOD).   A measure of the amount of oxygen consumed in the biological processes that break down organic matter in water.

Biodegradable.   Having the ability to break down or decompose rapidly under natural conditions and processes.

Biodiversity.   Refers to the variety and variability among living organisms and the ecological complexes in which they occur. Diversity can be defined as the number of different items and their relative frequencies. For biological diversity, these items are organized at many levels, ranging from complete ecosystems to the biochemical structures that are the molecular basis of heredity. Thus, the term encompasses different ecosystems, species, and genes.

Biological treatment. A treatment technology that uses bacteria to consume waste by breaking down organic materials.

Biomass. All of the living material in a given area; often refers to vegetation. Also called "biota."

Biomonitoring. (1) The use of living organisms to test the effects of effluent discharges. (2) Analysis of blood, urine, and tissues to measure chemical exposure in humans.

Biosphere. The portion of Earth and its atmosphere that can support life.

BOD5. The amount of dissolved oxygen consumed in five days by biological processes breaking down organic matter.

Brownfields. Real estate with some degree of environmental contamination, usually due to previous industrial use, which may deter redevelopment because of fears of environmental liability.

Bubble policy. An EPA policy that allows a plant complex with several facilities to decrease pollution from some facilities while increasing it from others, so long as total results are equal to or better than those required by previous limits. Facilities where this is done are treated as if they exist in a bubble in which total emissions are averaged out.

Cancellation. Refers to revoking the registration of a pesticide under section 6(b) of the Federal Insecticide, Fungicide and Rodenticide Act (FIFRA) if unreasonable adverse effects to the environment and public health develop when a product is used according to widespread and commonly recognized practice, or if its labeling or other material required to be submitted does not comply with FIFRA provisions.

Cap. A layer of clay or other highly impermeable material installed over the top of a closed landfill to prevent entry of rainwater and to minimize production of leachate, or a limit on the total amount of emissions from a group of pollution sources covered by a particular control regime.

Cap and trade. Technique for controlling pollution by setting a limit on the total emissions from a group of sources while allowing the sources to trade emissions allowances to reduce the overall cost of complying with the cap.

Carbon dioxide (CO_2). A colorless, odorless gas that results from fossil-fuel combustion and is normally a part of the ambient air. Increasing levels of carbon dioxide in the atmosphere are contributing to the greenhouse effect,

Carbon monoxide (CO). A colorless, odorless, poisonous gas produced by incomplete fossil fuel combustion.

Carcinogen. Any substance that can cause or contribute to the production of cancer.

Carrying capacity. The amount of use a natural area can sustain without deterioration of its integrity.

Catalytic converter. An air pollution abatement device that removes pollutants from motor vehicle exhaust, either by oxidizing them into carbon dioxide and water or reducing them to nitrogen and oxygen.

Categorical exclusion. A class of actions that does not require preparation of an environmental assessment or environmental impact statement under the National Environmental Policy Act (NEPA) because they are deemed not to have a significant effect on the environment.

Categorical pretreatment standard. A technology-based effluent limitation for an industrial facility that discharges into a municipal sewer system.

Characteristic hazardous waste. A waste deemed hazardous because it exhibits any one of four hazardous characteristics: ignitability, corrosivity, reactivity, or toxicity.

Chlorinated hydrocarbons. A class of compounds consisting of chlorine, hydrogen, and carbon that are very persistent in the environment and that tend to bioaccumulate in living organisms. Examples include polychlorinated and polybrominated biphenyls and pesticides such as DDT, aldrin, dieldrin, heptachlor, chlordane, lindane, endrin, mirex, and toxaphene.

Chlorination. The application of chlorine to drinking water, sewage, or industrial waste to disinfect it or to oxidize undesirable compounds.

Chlorofluorocarbons (CFCs). A family of inert, nontoxic, and easily liquified chemicals formerly used widely in refrigeration, air conditioning, packaging, and insulation or as solvents and aerosol propellants. Because of their stability, CFCs are not destroyed until they drift into the upper atmosphere, where their chlorine components destroy the Earth's protective ozone layer.

Chronic toxicity. The capacity of a substance to cause adverse health effects due to exposure for an extended period of time, usually at least one-tenth of an organism's lifetime.

Clear-cut. The harvesting of all trees in one area at one time, which can contribute to soil erosion and nonpoint source water pollution.

Climate change. Changes in worldwide climate and weather patterns of anthropogenic origin, including changes in precipitation patterns and storm activity, induced by global warming.

Closed-loop recycling. Reclaiming or reusing materials in an enclosed process.

Coastal zone. An area adjacent to a seacoast whose use can affect the sea and coastal ecosystems.

Coefficient of haze. A measurement of atmospheric interference with visibility.

Coliform index. A rating of the purity of water based on a count of fecal bacteria.

Combined sewers. A sewer system that carries both sewage and storm water runoff. Normally its entire flow goes to a waste treatment plant, but during a heavy storm, the storm water volume may be so great as to cause overflows, releasing untreated mixtures of storm water and sewage into receiving waters.

Comment period. Time provided for the public to review and comment on a proposed federal agency action after the proposal is published in the Federal Register.

Community water system. Under the Safe Drinking Water Act, a system for providing the public with water that has at least 15 service connections or that regularly serves at least 25 individuals.

Compliance schedule. An agreement between a regulated entity and a government agency that specifies a schedule of actions to be taken by certain dates to bring the entity into compliance with a regulation.

Concentrated animal feeding operation. Agricultural operations where large numbers of animals are kept and raised in confined situations with feed being brought to the animals rather than the animals grazing or otherwise seeking feed in pastures. These operations are subject to regulation under the Clean Water Act because the animal waste and wastewater they generate can enter water bodies from spills or breaks of waste storage structures (due to accidents or excessive rain), and from non-agricultural application of manure to crop land.

Consent decree. A legal document, approved by a judge, that formalizes an agreement reached to settle litigation between opposing parties.

Conservation biology. An interdisciplinary approach to the problems of biological conservation emphasizing the maintenance of biodiversity at the genetic, species, and ecosystem levels.

Contaminant. Any physical, chemical, biological, or radiological substance or matter that has an adverse effect on air, water, or soil.

Contingency plan. A document outlining a planned course of action to be followed in case of an accident that releases materials that threaten human health or the environment.

Conventional pollutants. Water pollutants other than those listed as toxic or nonconventional. These include suspended solids, fecal coliform, and oxygen-demanding nutrients.

Corrosive. A chemical agent that reacts with the surface of a material, causing it to deteriorate or wear away.

Cost-effectiveness analysis. Analysis that compares alternative means to achieve a given objective in order to determine which is the least costly.

Cost recovery. A legal process by which potentially responsible parties who contributed to contamination at a Superfund site can be required to reimburse the government for money it spent during cleanup actions.

Criteria air pollutants. Six air pollutants for which national ambient air quality standards have been established by EPA: ozone, carbon monoxide, total suspended particulates, sulfur dioxide, lead, and nitrogen oxide. The term derives from the requirement that EPA issue air quality criteria describing the characteristics and potential health and welfare effects of these pollutants.

Critical areas. Environmentally sensitive lands, often located adjacent to shorelines, that may be subject to particular restrictions on development to protect the environment.

Critical habitat. A region where physical and biological features essential to the survival of an endangered or threatened species are found.

Data call-in. A request that pesticide manufacturers provide EPA with test data on the effects of existing pesticides to expedite re-registration or cancellation.

DDT. The first chlorinated hydrocarbon insecticide (chemical name: dichloro-diphenyl-trichloroethane). It has a half-life of 15 years and can collect in fatty tissues of certain animals. EPA banned registration and interstate sale of DDT for virtually all but emergency uses in the United States in 1972 because of its persistence in the environment and accumulation in the food chain.

Decommissioning. Process of closing, dismantling, and rendering safe abandoned nuclear power plants after the end of their operating lives.

Decomposition or degradation. The breakdown of matter by bacteria, enzymes, erosion, and fungi to transform a complex substance into simpler compounds or its constituent elements.

Delegated program. A federal program that a state (or other government entity) has applied for and received authority to administer within its territory, subject to federal supervision.

Delisting. A decision to exclude a waste generated at a particular facility from listing as hazardous under RCRA subtitle C in response to a petition demonstrating that site-specific factors render the waste nonhazardous.

Designated uses. The purposes for which individual water segments are to be protected as identified by state authorities under the Clean Water Act (e.g., cold water fisheries, public water supply, or agriculture).

Dioxin. Any of a family of compounds known chemically as dibenzo-p-dioxins that are a by-product or contaminant of herbicides, paper mill emissions, and combustion processes. Concern about them arises from their persistence and bioaccumulative capacity, their adverse effects on the immune system, and their association with cancer and birth defects in certain animal species.

Direct discharger. A municipal or industrial facility that introduces pollution directly into surface waters.

Dissolved oxygen (DO). The level of oxygen available in water, an important indicator of a water body's ability to support aquatic life.

Dissolved solids. Disintegrated organic and inorganic material contained in water. Excessive amounts make water unfit to drink or use in industrial processes.

Ecological economics. Movement that promotes the integration of economics and ecology into a transdiscipline that promotes sustainable development by properly valuing natural resources and the environmental services they provide.

Ecological impact. The effect that an action or activity has on living organisms and their nonliving (abiotic) environment.

Ecology. Study of the relationship of living things to one another and their environment.

Ecosystem. The interacting system of a biological community and its environmental surroundings.

Ecosystem services. Benefits produced by ecosystems through natural processes including filtration of pollutants, flood control, pollination, nutrient cycling, and other services.

Effluent. Waste material discharged into surface waters.

Effluent limitation. A regulation restricting the quantities, rates, or concentrations of pollutants in wastewater discharges.

Effluent trading. The purchase, sale or exchange of allowances to discharge effluents or runoff into particular watersheds.

Electrostatic precipitator. An air pollution control device that removes particles from the gas stream (smoke) after combustion occurs by imparting an electrical charge to the particles, causing them to adhere to metal plates inside the precipitator.

Eminent domain. Government acquisition of private land for public use, with compensation paid to the landowner.

Emission standard. A regulation limiting the amount of pollutants that legally may be discharged from a source.

Emissions trading. The buying and selling of allowances to emit pollution in order to enable pollutant sources to reduce the cost of pollution control.

Endangered species. An animal, bird, fish, plant, or other species that is in danger of extinction throughout all or a significant portion of its range.

Environment. The sum of all external conditions affecting the life, development, and survival of an organism.

Environmental assessment. A written analysis prepared pursuant to the National Environmental Policy Act to determine whether a federal action would significantly affect the environment and thus require preparation of a more detailed environmental impact statement.

Environmental audit. A systematic assessment of an entity's compliance with applicable environmental requirements which may include evaluation of compliance policies, practices, and controls.

Environmental impact statement. A document the National Environmental Policy Act requires federal agencies to prepare before undertaking major projects or legislative proposals significantly affecting the environment. It provides a detailed assessment of the environmental consequences of the proposed action and it must include an analysis of alternative actions.

Environmental management system. Corporate management system for ensuring compliance with environmental regulations and for incorporating environmental concerns into corporate decisions.

Epidemiology. Study of the health effects of environmental exposures to a substance based on systematic comparisons of the incidence of diseases in population groups that differ primarily in their levels of exposure to the substance.

Estuary. Regions of interaction between rivers and near-shore ocean waters where tidal action and river flow create a mixing of fresh and salt water.

Eutrophication. The process by which shallow bodies of water receive increased amounts of dissolved nutrients such as nitrogen and phosphorus that encourage excessive plant growth and result in oxygen depletion.

Exceedance. Violation of environmental protection standards by exceeding allowable limits or concentration levels.

Extremely hazardous substances. Any of hundreds of chemicals identified by EPA on the basis of their toxicity and listed as extremely hazardous under the Emergency Planning and Community Right-to-Know Act.

Feasibility study. Analysis of the practicability of alternative means for remediating environmental contamination, a study that usually starts as soon as a remedial investigation is under way; together, they are commonly referred to as the "RI/FS."

Filtration. A treatment process for removing solid (particulate) matter from water by passing the water through porous media such as sand or a man-made filter.

Finding of no significant impact. A decision, based upon the results of an environmental assessment, finding that a proposed action would not have a significant impact on the environment and thus would not require preparation of an environmental impact statement.

Flue gas desulfurization. A technology that uses a sorbent, usually lime or limestone, to remove sulfur dioxide from the gases produced by burning fossil fuels.

Fly ash. Noncombustible residual particles from the combustion process carried by flue gas.

Food chain. A sequence of organisms, each of which uses the next lower member of the sequence as a food source.

Fuel economy standard. The Corporate Average Fuel Economy Standard (CAFE), which imposes financial penalties on motor vehicle manufacturers whose vehicles fail to meet certain average levels of fuel economy (as measured in miles per gallon).

Fugitive emissions. Emissions not caught by a capture system.

Fungicide. A pesticide used to control, prevent, or destroy fungi.

General permit. A permit automatically applicable to a class or category of dischargers that does not require processing of individual permit applications.

Global warming. An increase in worldwide temperature due to increased atmospheric concentrations of carbon dioxide and other gases that contribute to the greenhouse effect.

Greenhouse effect. The accumulation of carbon dioxide and other greenhouse gases in the upper atmosphere that allows sunlight to raise the surface temperature of the Earth while preventing the escape of heat.

Greenhouse gas. A gas whose presence in the upper atmosphere contributes to the greenhouse effect by allowing visible light to pass through the atmosphere while preventing heat radiating back from the Earth from escaping. Greenhouse gases from anthropogenic sources include carbon dioxide, nitrous oxide, methane, and CFCs. There also are even larger quantities of naturally occurring greenhouse gases, notably ozone and water vapor, whose concentrations may be affected by interactions with atmospheric pollutants.

Groundwater. The supply of fresh water found beneath the Earth's surface, usually in aquifers, which is often used for supplying wells and springs.

Habitat. The place where a population (e.g., human, animal, plant, microorganism) lives and its surroundings, both living and nonliving.

Habitat conservation plan. A plan for minimizing and mitigating the impact of activities that otherwise would harm endangered species that must be approved as a condition for receiving a permit authorizing activities that would result in the incidental taking of such species pursuant to section 10 of the Endangered Species Act.

Hazard identification. A determination of whether or not a substance is capable of causing some form of adverse effect (e.g., determining if a substance is a carcinogen or reproductive toxin).

Hazardous air pollutants. Air pollutants that may cause death, serious irreversible, or incapacitating reversible illness and that are not covered by ambient air quality standards. Since the 1990 Clean Air Act Amendments these include an initial list of 189 chemicals designated by Congress that is subject to revision by EPA.

Hazardous substance. Any material that poses a threat to human health or the environment. CERCLA makes broad classes of parties strictly liable for the costs of remediating releases of hazardous substances which it broadly defines to include any toxic water pollutant, hazardous waste, hazardous air pollutant, imminently hazardous chemical, or any substance designated by EPA to be reported if a designated quantity of the substance is released into the environment.

Hazardous waste. A solid waste regulated under subtitle C of RCRA because it may pose a substantial present or potential hazard to human health or the environment when improperly managed either because it exhibits at least one of four hazardous characteristics (ignitability, corrosivity, reactivity, or toxicity) or because it has been specifically listed by EPA as hazardous.

Hazard ranking system. The principal screening tool used by EPA to evaluate risks to public health and the environment associated with abandoned or uncontrolled hazardous waste sites. Based on assessment of the potential for hazardous substances to cause harm to human health or the environment, the HRS calculates a score that is the primary factor in deciding if the site should be on the National Priorities List for cleanup under the Superfund program.

Heavy metals. Metallic elements with high atomic weights (for example, mercury, cadmium, and lead), which can damage living things and can be stored in tissues for long periods of time.

Herbicide. A chemical agent designed to control or destroy unwanted vegetation.

High-level radioactive waste. Highly radioactive waste generated by the fuel of a nuclear reactor, found primarily at nuclear power plants. This waste will remain highly radioactive, and thus dangerous, for thousands of years.

Hydrocarbons (HC). Chemical compounds that consist entirely of carbon and hydrogen.

Hydrogeology. Study of geological formations that contain groundwater, with particular emphasis on its fate and transport.

Hydrology. The science dealing with the properties, distribution, and circulation of water.

Ignitable. Capable of burning or causing a fire.

Impoundment. A body of water or sludge confined by a dam, dike, floodgate, or other barrier.

Indicator species. A species whose condition is thought to reflect the health of a larger ecosystem.

Indirect discharger. Commercial or industrial facilities that discharge wastes into local sewers.

Indoor air pollution. Chemical, physical, or biological contaminants in the air inside a home, building, or other habitable structure.

Inert ingredient. Pesticide components such as solvents, carriers, and surfactants that are not active against target pests.

Injection well. A well into which fluids are injected for purposes such as waste disposal, improving the recovery of crude oil, or solution mining.

Injection zone. A geological formation, group of formations, or part of a formation receiving fluids through a well.

Inorganic chemicals. Chemical compounds that do not contain carbon.

Insecticide. An agent that destroys or controls the growth of insects.

Inspection and maintenance. Programs to ensure proper operation of emission control systems on automobiles.

Integrated pest management. Pest control practices that emphasize the use of natural predators to control pests.

Interim status. Regulatory status that allowed treatment, storage, and disposal facilities for hazardous waste to continue to operate temporarily after the enactment of RCRA in 1980 pending denial or issuance of a permit.

Interstitial monitoring.   The continuous surveillance of the space between the walls of an underground storage tank.

Inversion.   An atmospheric condition that occurs when a layer of warm air prevents the rise of cooler air trapped beneath it, causing pollutants that might otherwise be dispersed to become more concentrated.

In vitro.   (1) "In glass"; a test-tube culture. (2) Any laboratory test using living cells taken from an organism.

In vivo.   In the living body of a plant or animal. In vivo tests are those laboratory experiments carried out on whole animals or human volunteers.

Ionizing radiation.   Radiation with enough energy to penetrate matter and eject electrons or protons, producing charged ion pairs.

ISO 14000.   A series of voluntary standards relating to environmental management systems for corporations drafted by the International Organization for Standardization, named "ISO" after the Greek prefix for "equal."

Joint and several liability.   A concept employed in CERCLA and derived from the common law of torts that permits any or all joint tortfeasors to be held for the full amount of damage they cause in the absence of proof of divisibility of the harm.

Land disposal restrictions.   Rules issued under RCRA that require hazardous wastes to be treated before disposal on land to destroy or immobilize hazardous constituents that otherwise might migrate into soil or groundwater.

Landfills.   Sites where wastes are disposed by being buried and covered with soil.

Leachate.   The liquid that results from water collecting contaminants as it trickles through a landfill, which may result in the entry of hazardous substances into surface water, groundwater, or soil.

Leachate collection system.   A system that gathers leachate and pumps it to the surface for treatment.

Leaching.   The process by which soluble constituents are dissolved and carried down through the soil by a percolating fluid.

Lead (Pb).   A heavy metal that exerts toxic effects on the nervous, reproductive, renal, and immune systems, and that is associated with increases in blood pressure.

Liner.   A relatively impermeable barrier, usually of plastic or clay, that is designed to prevent leachate from leaking from a landfill.

Listed hazardous waste.   Waste expressly listed as hazardous under subtitle C of RCRA because it is part of a waste stream that may pose a substantial threat to human health or the environment when managed improperly.

Local emergency planning committee.   A committee appointed by a state's emergency response commission, as required by section 301 of the Emergency Planning and Community Right-to-Know Act, to formulate a comprehensive emergency response plan.

Lowest achievable emission rate (LAER).   Under the Clean Air Act, this is the rate of emissions that reflects (a) the most stringent emission limitation contained in the implementation plan of any state for such source unless the owner or operator of the proposed source demonstrates such limitations are not achievable; or (b) the most stringent emissions limitation achieved in practice, whichever is more stringent.

Low-level radioactive waste. Radioactive wastes generated by hospitals, research laboratories, and certain industries that contain lower levels of radioactivity than those generated by a nuclear reactor.

Major modification. Any nonroutine physical or operational change in a stationary source that will result in a significant net increase in emissions that may subject the source to PSD or new source review requirements under the Clean Air Act.

Major stationary source. Any stationary source that emits or has the potential to emit certain threshold levels of emissions to which PSD and new source requirements of the Clean Air Act are applicable.

Material safety data sheet. A compilation of information OSHA requires certain employers to provide to workers to inform them of the identities of hazardous chemicals, health and physical hazards, exposure limits, and precautions.

Maximum contaminant level (MCL). The maximum permissible level of a contaminant in water delivered to any user of a public water system established pursuant to the Safe Drinking Water Act.

Maximum contaminant level goal (MCLG). The maximum level of a contaminant in water at which no known or anticipated adverse effects on health occur and which includes an adequate margin of safety.

Methane. A greenhouse gas that is colorless, odorless, and flammable which is produced by the decomposition of organic matter.

Metropolitan planning organization. Metropolitan-wide planning organization that is responsible for developing regional transportation plans under the Urban Mass Transportation Act.

Mitigation. Measures taken to reduce the adverse environmental effects of an activity.

Mixing zone. Area in which effluent discharges mix with receiving waters to be diluted prior to assessing compliance with water quality standards.

Mobile source. A source of air pollution that moves, such as cars, trucks, motorcycles, and airplanes.

Modeling. Efforts to predict the fate and transport of pollutants or the environmental effects of human activities by using a mathematical or physical representation of a system to test the effect of changes in system components.

Monitoring. Periodic or continuous surveillance or testing to determine the level of compliance with statutory requirements or to assess pollutant levels in various media or in humans, animals, and other living things.

Monitoring wells. Wells drilled to collect groundwater samples for the purpose of determining the amounts, types, and distribution of contaminants in the groundwater.

Mutagen/Mutagenicity. Any chemical or physical agent capable of causing a permanent genetic change in a cell other than that which occurs during normal growth. Mutagenicity is the capacity of any agent to cause such changes.

National Ambient Air Quality Standards. Uniform, national air quality standards established by EPA that restrict ambient levels of certain pollutants to protect public health (primary standards) or public welfare (secondary standards).

National Contingency Plan. The federal plan that outlines procedures and standards for responding to releases of oil and hazardous substances including responses to sites designated for cleanup under the Superfund program.

National Emissions Standards for Hazardous Air Pollutants. National standards established by EPA that limit emissions of hazardous air pollutants.

National Pollutant Discharge Elimination System. The Clean Water Act's national permit program that regulates the discharge of pollutants into waters of the United States.

National Priorities List. EPA's list of sites identified as priorities for remedial action under CERCLA.

National Response Center. Operations center run by the U.S. Coast Guard and open 24 hours per day that receives notifications of releases of oil and hazardous substances into the environment, evaluates the reports, and notifies the appropriate agency for responding to the releases.

National Response Team. Representatives of various federal agencies who coordinate federal responses to nationally significant incidents of pollution and provide advice and technical assistance to the responding agency or agencies before and during a response action.

Navigable waters. Initially, waters sufficiently deep and wide for navigation but now including waters adjacent to or connected to waters navigable in fact.

New source. Any stationary source built or modified after publication of final or proposed regulations that prescribe a standard of performance intended to apply to that type of emissions source.

New Source Performance Standards. Uniform national EPA air emissions and water effluent standards that limit the amount of pollution allowed from new sources or from existing sources that have been modified.

Nitrate. A form of nitrogen that can exist in the atmosphere or as a dissolved gas in water and that can have harmful effects on humans and animals.

Nitric oxide (NO). A gas formed by the oxidation of nitrogen or ammonia, whose primary source is the combustion pressure in an internal combustion engine. It can change into nitrogen dioxide in the ambient air, contributing to photochemical smog.

Nitrogen dioxide (NO_2). A major component of photochemical smog formed when nitric oxide combines with oxygen in the atmosphere.

Nitrogen oxide (NO_x). A product of combustion by mobile and stationary sources and a major contributor to acid deposition and the formation of ozone in the troposphere.

No Observable Adverse Effect Level (NOAEL). An exposure level at which there are no statistically or biologically significant increases in the frequency or severity of adverse effects between the exposed population and its appropriate control.

Nonattainment area. A geographic area that is not in compliance with the National Ambient Air Quality Standard for a criteria air pollutant under the Clean Air Act.

Nonconventional pollutant. Water pollutants that are not listed as toxic pollutants or conventional pollutants, including color, nitrates, iron, ammonia, and chlorides.

Nonpoint source pollution. Pollution from sources that are diffuse and that do not have any single point of origin or discharge, such as pollutants generally carried off land by runoff.

Nutrient. Any substance assimilated by living things that promotes growth. Contaminant of water resources by excessive inputs of nutrients causes excess algal production.

Oncogenic. Capable of causing tumors, whether benign or malignant.

Opacity. A measure of the amount of light obscured by particulate pollution in the air; clear window glass has a zero opacity, a brick wall has 100 percent opacity.

Open dump. A site where solid waste is disposed of without satisfying the criteria established by EPA under section 4004 of RCRA.

Organic. (1) Derived from or relating to living organisms. (2) In chemistry, any compound containing carbon.

Organic matter. Carbonaceous waste contained in plant or animal matter and originating from domestic or industrial sources.

Organism. Any living thing.

Organophosphates. Relatively nonpersistent insecticides that contain phosphorus.

Organotins. Chemical compounds used to kill bacteria, algae, molluscs, fungi, and insects which are known to be toxic to the immune system.

Outfall. The place where effluent is discharged into receiving waters.

Overburden. The rock and soil cleared away before mining.

Overfiling. Filing of federal enforcement actions in cases where states with delegated enforcement authority either have failed to act or have pursued actions deemed insufficient by federal authorities.

Ozone (O_3). A substance found in the stratosphere and the troposphere. In the stratosphere (the atmospheric layer beginning 7 to 10 miles above the Earth's surface), ozone is a form of oxygen found naturally that provides a protective layer shielding the Earth from ultraviolet radiation. In the troposphere (the layer extending up 7 to 10 miles from the Earth's surface), ozone is a chemical oxidant and a major component of photochemical smog.

Ozone depletion. Destruction of the stratospheric ozone layer caused by the breakdown of certain chlorine- and/or bromine-containing compounds (chlorofluorocarbons or halons), which catalytically destroy ozone molecules.

Particulates. Fine liquid or solid particles found in air, such as dust, smoke, mist, fumes, or smog.

Pathogenic. Capable of causing disease.

Pathogens. Microorganisms (such as bacteria, viruses, or parasites) that can cause disease in other organisms, including humans, animals, and plants.

PCBs. A group of toxic, persistent chemicals (polychlorinated biphenyls) formerly used in electrical transformers and capacitors for insulating purposes and in gas pipeline systems as a lubricant.

Percolation. The movement of water downward and radially through subsurface soil layers, usually continuing downward to groundwater.

Permit. An authorization, license, or equivalent control document issued by a government agency.

Persistence. The length of time a compound, once introduced into the environment, stays there.

Pesticide. A general term for any agent that destroys, injures, inhibits, or prevents the growth of rodents, insects, plants, algae, or fungi.

Pesticide tolerance. The amount of pesticide residue allowed by law to remain in or on a harvested crop.

pH. A measure of the acidity or alkalinity of a liquid or solid material.

Phosphates. Organic compounds of phosphoric acid physiologically important for acid-base balance in the blood. Produced in the environment by decaying organic matter and used as a component of detergents and fertilizers, phosphates have been a major cause of the eutrophication of water bodies by serving as nutrients for algae blooms.

Photochemical oxidants. Air pollutants formed by the action of sunlight on oxides of nitrogen and hydrocarbons.

Photochemical air pollution. Also called photochemical smog, a type of oxidizing pollution characterized by hydrocarbons, nitrogen oxides, and photochemical oxidants. Results from photochemical reactions of sunlight, automobile exhaust, and other oxidant pollutants.

Point source. A stationary location or fixed facility from which pollutants are discharged or emitted such as a pipe, ditch, or smokestack.

Pollutant. Generally, any substance introduced into the environment that adversely affects the usefulness of a resource.

Pollution. Generally, the presence of matter or energy whose nature, location, or quantity produces undesired environmental effects.

Polychlorinated Biphenyls (PCBs). A group of toxic, persistent chemicals used in electrical transformers and capacitors for insulating purposes, and in gas pipeline systems as lubricants, the sale and new use of which were banned in 1979.

Post-closure period. The time period following the shutdown of a waste management facility during which the site must be monitored.

Potentially responsible party. Any individual or company potentially liable under section 107 of CERCLA for the costs of responding to releases of hazardous substances.

Preliminary assessment. The process of collecting and reviewing available information about a known or suspected waste site or release.

Pretreatment. Processes used to reduce, eliminate, or alter the toxicity of pollutants in wastewater from nondomestic sources before it is discharged into a sewer system.

Prevention of significant deterioration. An EPA program in which state or federal permits are required to restrict emissions from new or modified stationary sources in places where air quality is already better than required to meet primary and secondary ambient air quality standards.

Primary waste treatment. The first steps in wastewater treatment which typically use screens and sedimentation tanks to remove most materials that float or will settle.

Project XL. A project, whose acronym stands for Excellence and Leadership, that is designed to provide businesses and state and local governments with greater flexibility in deciding how to meet environmental standards. Participants enter into contracts with EPA that promise greater reductions of pollutant discharges than would be achieved through existing standards.

Prompt letter. Letter from the administrator of OMB's Office of Information and Regulatory Affairs requesting an agency to consider taking some regulatory action.

Publicly owned treatment works. A waste-treatment works owned by a state, unit of local government, or Indian tribe, usually designed to treat domestic wastewaters.

Public water system. Under the Safe Drinking Water Act, a system that provides piped water for human consumption to at least 15 service connections or that regularly serves at least 25 individuals.

Radiation. A general term for radiant energy emitted in the form of particles or electromagnetic waves from radioactive elements, fluorescent substances, or luminous bodies.

Radio Frequency Radiation. Non-ionizing electromagnetic radiation that does not change the structure of atoms but does heat tissue and may cause harmful biological effects. This radiation is emitted by microwaves, radio waves, and low-frequency electromagnetic fields from high-voltage transmission lines.

Radionuclide. Isotopes of elements that spontaneously emit radiation by disintegration (decay) of their unstable nuclei. Can be man-made or naturally occurring.

Radon. A colorless, naturally occurring, radioactive, inert gaseous element formed by decay of radium atoms in soil or rocks.

Reasonably available control technology (RACT). Control technology that is reasonably available and both technologically and economically feasible. Usually it is applied to existing sources of air pollution in nonattainment areas.

Recharge. The process by which water is added to a zone of saturation, usually by percolation from the soil surface, for example, the recharge of an aquifer.

Recharge area. A land area in which water reaches to the zone of saturation from surface infiltration, for example, an area where rainwater soaks through the earth to reach an aquifer.

Recommended maximum contaminant level. The term formerly used for maximum contaminant level goal.

Record of decision. A public document that explains which cleanup alternative(s) will be used at National Priorities List sites.

Recycling. The process of minimizing the generation of waste by recovering usable products that might otherwise become waste. Examples are the recycling of aluminum cans, wastepaper, and bottles.

Reference Dose (RfD). A numerical estimate of a daily oral exposure to the human population, including sensitive subgroups such as children, for which a particular substance is not likely to cause harmful effects during a lifetime.

Registration. Formal listing with EPA of a new pesticide under the Federal Insecticide, Fungicide, and Rodenticide Act so that it can be sold or distributed in intrastate or interstate commerce.

Remedial action. The actual construction or implementation phase of a Superfund site cleanup that follows remedial design.

Remedial design. A stage of the Superfund cleanup process that follows the remedial investigation feasibility study and includes development of engineering drawings and specifications for a site cleanup.

Remedial investigation. An in-depth study designed to gather the data necessary to determine the nature and extent of contamination at a Superfund site, establish criteria for cleaning up the site, identify preliminary alternatives for remedial actions, and support the technical and cost analyses of the alternatives. The remedial investigation is usually done with the feasibility study. Together they are referred to as the "RI/FS."

Removal actions.   Short-term actions taken to address releases of hazardous substances (e.g., removal of chemical drums).

Reportable quantity.   The quantity of a hazardous substance that triggers reporting requirements under CERCLA. If a substance is released in amounts exceeding this quantity, the release must be reported to the National Response Center, state authorities, and community emergency coordinators for areas likely to be affected.

Reregistration.   The reevaluation and relicensing of existing pesticides originally registered prior to the implementation of current scientific and regulatory standards.

Resource recovery.   The process of obtaining matter or energy from materials formerly discarded.

Response action.   A CERCLA-authorized action involving either a removal action or a remedial action.

Restricted use.   A pesticide whose uses have been restricted because it requires special handling due to its toxicity. Restricted-use pesticides may be applied only by trained, certified applicators or those under their direct supervision.

Riparian rights.   Entitlement of a land owner to the water on or bordering his or her property, including the right to prevent diversion or misuse of upstream waters.

Risk assessment.   The process of identifying and characterizing the nature and magnitude of the adverse effects of a substance or activity.

Risk communication.   The exchange of information about the nature and magnitude of health or environmental risks between risk assessors, risk managers, and the general public.

Risk management.   The process of evaluating and selecting among alternative strategies for managing environmental risks.

Rodenticide.   An agent that kills, repels, or controls rodents to prevent the spread of disease and consumption or contamination of food.

Rolling easements.   Legal arrangements that transfer property rights through options, easements, covenants or defeasible estates as shorelines migrate.

Saturated zone.   A subsurface area in which all pores and cracks are filled with water under pressure equal to or greater than that of the atmosphere.

Scrubber.   An air pollution device that uses a spray of water or reactant or a dry process to trap pollutants in emissions.

Secondary treatment.   The second step in most publicly owned waste treatment systems, in which bacteria consume the organic parts of the waste. It is accomplished by bringing together waste, bacteria, and oxygen in trickling filters or in an activated sludge process.

Sedimentation.   Letting solids settle out of wastewater by gravity during waste-water treatment.

Sedimentation tanks.   Holding areas for wastewater where floating wastes are skimmed off and settled solids are removed for disposal.

Sediments.   Soil, sand, and minerals washed from land into water, usually after rain.

Selective catalytic reduction.   A process for reducing emissions of nitrogen oxides from electricity generators.

Service line.   The pipe that carries tap water from the public water main to a building.

Settling tank. A holding area for wastewater where heavier particles sink to the bottom for removal and disposal.

Sewage. The waste and wastewater produced by residential and commercial establishments and discharged into sewers.

Sewage sludge. Waste produced by sewage treatment processes at a publicly owned treatment works, the disposal of which is regulated under the Clean Water Act.

Sewer. A channel or conduit that carries wastewater or stormwater runoff from the source to a treatment plant or receiving stream.

Silviculture. Management of forest land for timber.

Site inspection. The collection of data concerning the extent and severity of hazards posed by a site where hazardous substances have been released to gather information necessary to score the site, using the Hazard Ranking System, and to determine if the site presents an immediate threat that requires prompt removal action.

Siting. The process of choosing a location for a facility.

Sludge. A semisolid residue from any of a number of air or water treatment processes.

Slurry. A watery mixture of insoluble matter that results from some pollution control techniques.

Smart growth. Policies that seek to encourage residential, commercial and industrial development that is environmentally sound and fiscally smart by channeling new development to areas with existing infrastructure.

Smelter. A facility that melts or fuses ore, often with an accompanying chemical change, to separate the metal.

Smog. Air pollution associated with oxidants.

Sole source aquifer. An aquifer that supplies 50 percent or more of the drinking water of an area.

Solid waste. Defined by RCRA to include "any garbage, refuse, sludge from a waste treatment plant, water supply treatment plant, or air pollution control facility and other discarded material, including solid, liquid, semisolid, or contained gaseous materials resulting from industrial, commercial, mining, and agricultural activities."

Solvent. A substance (usually liquid) capable of dissolving or dispersing one or more other substances.

Sorption. The action of soaking up or attracting substances.

Special review. A regulatory process through which existing pesticides suspected of posing unreasonable risk to human health, nontarget organisms, or the environment are referred for review by EPA.

Species. A reproductively isolated aggregate of interbreeding populations of organisms.

Spoil. Dirt or rock that has been removed from its original location, destroying the composition of the soil in the process, as with strip-mining or dredging.

Stabilization. Conversion of the active organic matter in sludge into inert, harmless material.

State emergency response commission. The commission appointed by each governor according to the requirements of the Emergency Planning and Community Right-to-Know Act. The SERCs designate emergency planning districts, appoint local emergency planning committees, and supervise and coordinate their activities.

State implementation plans.   EPA-approved state plans for the establishment, regulation, and enforcement of air pollution standards.

Stationary sources.   Fixed, nonmoving producers of pollution, including power plants and other facilities using industrial combustion processes.

Storm sewer.   A system of pipes that carry only water runoff from building and land surfaces.

Stratosphere.   The uppermost portion of the atmosphere that is 10 to 25 miles above the Earth's surface.

Strip-mining.   A process that uses machines to scrape soil or rock away from mineral deposits just under the Earth's surface.

Sulfur dioxide (SO_2).   A heavy, pungent, colorless, gaseous air pollutant formed primarily by the combustion of fossil fuels, which causes respiratory problems in humans and contributes to acid deposition.

Sump.   A pit or tank that catches liquid runoff for drainage or disposal.

Sump pump.   A mechanism for removing water or wastewater from a sump or wet well.

Superfund.   A trust fund established by the Comprehensive Environmental Response, Compensation, and Liability Act (CERCLA) to help pay for cleanup of hazardous waste sites and for legal action to force those responsible for the sites to clean them up. Also used to refer to the program operated under the legislative authority of CERCLA that carries out EPA response activities.

Surface impoundment.   A facility for the treatment, storage, or disposal of liquid wastes in ponds.

Surface water.   All water naturally open to the atmosphere (rivers, lakes, reservoirs, streams, impoundments, seas, estuaries, and so on) and all springs, wells, or other collectors that are directly influenced by surface water.

Suspended solids.   Small particles of solid pollutants that float on the surface of, or are suspended in, sewage or other liquids.

Sustainable development.   Development that meets the needs of the present without compromising the ability of future generations to meet their own needs.

Synthetic organic chemicals.   Man-made organic chemicals.

Tailings.   Residue of raw materials or waste separated out during the processing of crops or mineral ores.

Technology-based standards.   Emission limits that are established on the basis of what levels of pollution control certain types or levels of technology can achieve.

Teratogen.   A substance that causes malformation or abnormal development of embryos and fetuses.

Tertiary treatment.   Advanced cleaning of wastewater that goes beyond the secondary or biological treatment stage to remove nutrients such as phosphorus and nitrogen and most suspended solids.

Thermal pollution.   Discharge of heat from industrial processes that can affect the environment adversely.

Threshold limit value.   The maximum air concentrations of chemical substances to which it is believed that workers may be exposed on a daily basis without adverse effect.

Threshold planning quantity.   A quantity designated for each chemical on the list of extremely hazardous substances that triggers EPCRA notification to state emergency response commissions.

Tolerances. Permissible residue levels for pesticides in raw agricultural produce and processed foods.

Total maximum daily loading. The maximum amount of a pollutant that can be discharged into a water segment each day by all sources without causing violation of a water quality standard.

Total suspended solids. A measure of the suspended solids in wastewater, effluent, or water bodies.

Toxicity. The degree of danger posed by a substance to living organisms. Acute toxicity involves harmful effects in an organism through a single or short-term exposure. Chronic toxicity is the ability of a substance or mixture of substances to cause harmful effects over an extended period, usually upon repeated or continuous exposure sometimes lasting for the entire life of the exposed organism. Subchronic toxicity is the ability of the substance to cause effects for more than one year but less than the lifetime of the exposed organism.

Toxicology. The study of adverse effects of chemicals on living organisms.

Toxic pollutant. A pollutant that is capable of causing adverse effects on living organisms.

Toxics Release Inventory. The national inventory of the quantities of toxic substances released into different environmental media annually by facilities that manufacture, process, or use (in quantities above a specific amount) chemicals listed under the Emergency Planning and Community Right-to-Know Act.

Transferable development rights. Development rights sometimes allocated to property owners unable to develop a specific property that can be sold or used to qualify to develop another property in a more suitable location.

Treatment, storage, or disposal facility. A site where hazardous wastes are treated, stored, or disposed.

Trichloroethylene (TCE). A stable, low-boiling, colorless liquid, toxic by inhalation. TCE is used as a solvent and as a metal degreasing agent and in other industrial applications.

Troposphere. The lowermost portion of the atmosphere up to 10 kilometers from the Earth's surface, where clouds are formed.

Tundra. A type of ecosystem dominated by lichens, mosses, grasses, and woody plants, which is found at high latitudes (arctic tundra) and high altitudes (alpine tundra).

Turbidity. (1) Haziness in air caused by the presence of particles and pollutants. (2) A similar cloudy condition in water due to suspended silt or organic matter.

Ultraviolet rays. Radiation from the sun to which humans are exposed that can cause skin cancer or other tissue damage.

Underground injection control. The program under the Safe Drinking Water Act that regulates the use of underground injection wells to pump fluids into the ground.

Underground storage tank. A tank located totally or partially underground that is designed to hold gasoline or other petroleum products or chemical solutions.

Unsaturated zone. The area above the water table where the soil pores are not fully saturated, although some water may be present.

Urban growth boundary. Growth management device that seeks to channel future urban growth inside a boundary drawn around an existing urban area generally by prohibiting or discouraging urban development outside the boundary.

Urban runoff. Stormwater from city streets and adjacent domestic or commercial properties that may carry pollutants of various kinds into the sewer systems or receiving waters.

Vaporization. The change of a substance from a liquid to a gas.

Variance. Government permission for a delay or exception in the application of a given law, ordinance, or regulation.

Virus. A minute organism comprised of either one strand of DNA or RNA, which is dependent on nutrients inside cells in order to live and to reproduce intracellularly.

Volatile. Capable of evaporating readily.

Volatile organic compound. An organic compound that participates in atmospheric photochemical reactions.

Waste load allocation. The maximum load of pollutants each discharger of waste is allowed to release into a particular waterway.

Waste minimization. Measures or techniques that reduce the amount of wastes generated during industrial production processes; term also is applied to recycling and other efforts to reduce the amount of waste going into the waste stream.

Wastewater treatment plant. A facility containing a series of tanks, screens, niters, and other processes by which pollutants are removed from water.

Water quality criteria. Specific levels of water quality that, if reached, are expected to render a body of water suitable for certain designated uses.

Water quality standards. State-adopted and EPA-approved ambient standards for water bodies that specify the water quality that must be met to protect designated uses.

Watershed. The land area that drains into a stream or other water body.

Water table. The level of groundwater.

Wetlands. An ecosystem that depends on constant or recurrent shallow inundation or saturation at or near the surface. Wetlands commonly feature hydric soils and hydrophytic vegetation, except where specific factors have removed them or prevented their development.

Xenobiotic. A chemical substance that is not normally a constitutive component of a biological system (i.e., non-naturally occurring man-made substances found in the environment, such as synthetic material solvents or plastics).

Zero-Emission Vehicles. Cars or trucks that will produce no tailpipe emissions of any pollutant throughout their lifetimes. ZEVs presumably will be powered by electricity.

═══ APPENDIX B ═══

‖ *List of Acronyms* ‖

AA Assistant Administrator or Associate Administrator

ACGIH American Council of Government Industrial Hygienists

ACL alternate concentration limit

ADI acceptable daily intake

ADR alternative dispute resolution

AEA Atomic Energy Act

AFO animal feeding operation

AHERA Asbestos Hazard Emergency Response Act

ALJ administrative law judge

ANPR advance notice of proposed rulemaking

ANSI American National Standards Institute

ANWR Arctic National Wildlife Refuge

APA Administrative Procedure Act

ARAR applicable or relevant and appropriate standards, limitations, criteria, and requirements

ATSDR Agency for Toxic Substances and Disease Registry (HHS)

BACT best available control technology

BADT best available demonstrated technology

BART best available retrofit technology

BAT best available technology

BATEA best available treatment economically achievable

BCT best control technology

BDAT best demonstrated achievable technology

BDT best demonstrated technology

BLM Bureau of Land Management

BMPs best management practices

BOD biochemical oxygen demand

BPJ best professional judgment

BPT best practicable technology, or best practicable treatment

BTU British thermal unit

CAA Clean Air Act

CAFE corporate average fuel economy

CAFO concentrated animal feeding operation

CAG Carcinogen Assessment Group

CAIR Clean Air Interstate Rule

CAS Chemical Abstract Service

CASAC Clean Air Scientific Advisory Committee

CBA cost-benefit analysis

CBF Chesapeake Bay Foundation

CBO Congressional Budget Office

CDC Centers for Disease Control (HHS)

CDM Clean Development Mechanism

CEC Commission for Environmental Cooperation

CEQ Council on Environmental Quality

CERCLA Comprehensive Environmental Response, Compensation, and Liability Act of 1980

CERCLIS Comprehensive Environmental Response, Compensation, and Liability Information System

CERES Coalition for Environmentally Responsible Economics

CFCs chlorofluorocarbons
CFR Code of Federal Regulations
CMA Chemical Manufacturers
Association (now the American
Chemistry Council)
COP Conference of the Parties
CPSC Consumer Product Safety
Commission
CRA Congressional Review Act
CRS Congressional Research
Service
CSO combined sewer overflow
CWA Clean Water Act (also known
as FWPCA)
CZMA Coastal Zone Management
Act

DDT dichloro-diphenyl-
trichloroethane
DMR discharge monitoring report
DO dissolved oxygen
DOD Department of Defense
DOE Department of Energy
DOI Department of the Interior
DOJ Department of Justice
DOL Department of Labor
DOT Department of Transportation
DPA Deepwater Ports Act
DSAP data self-auditing program

EA environmental assessment
EC European Commission
EGOS Environmental Council of
the States
ECRA Environmental Cleanup
Responsibility Act (New Jersey)
EDF Environmental Defense Fund
(now Environmental Defense)
EEC European Economic
Commission
E4E Enterprise for the
Environment
EHS extremely hazardous substance
EIS environmental impact statement
EJ environmental justice
ELI Environmental Law Institute
EO executive order
EMF electromagnetic frequency
radiation
EMS environmental management
system

EPA U.S. Environmental Protection
Agency
EPCRA Emergency Planning and
Community Right-to-Know Act
ESA Endangered Species Act
ETS emergency temporary
standard, environmental
tobacco smoke
EU European Union

FACA Federal Advisory Committee
Act
FDA Food and Drug Administration
FDF fundamentally different factors
FERC Federal Energy Regulatory
Commission
FFDCA Federal Food, Drug, and
Cosmetic Act
FHWA Federal Highway
Administration
FIFRA Federal Insecticide,
Fungicide, and Rodenticide Act
FIP federal implementation plan
FLPMA Federal Land Policy and
Management Act
FMCSA Federal Motor Carrier
Safety Administration
FOIA Freedom of Information Act
FONSI finding of no significant
impact
FR Federal Register
FS Forest Service (U.S.)
FTC Federal Trade Commission
FWPCA Federal Water Pollution
Control Act (Clean Water Act)
FWS Fish and Wildlife Service
(U.S.)

GAO Government Accountability
Office
GATT General Agreement on
Tariffs and Trade
GEF Global Environment Facility
GEMI Global Environmental
Management Initiative
GPRA Government Performance
and Results Act

HCP habitat conservation plan
HHS Department of Health and
Human Services

HLRW high-level radioactive waste

HMTA Hazardous Materials Transportation Act

HRS hazard ranking system

HSWA Hazardous and Solid Waste Amendments of 1984

HWIR Hazardous Waste Identification Rule

IARC International Agency for Research on Cancer

ICS individual control strategy

IG inspector general

I/M inspection/maintenance

IPM integrated pest management

IQA Information Quality Act

ISC Interagency Scientific Committee

ISTEA Intermodal Surface Transportation Efficiency Act

JI joint implementation

LAER lowest achievable emission rate

LEV low-emission vehicle

LLRWPA Low Level Radioactive Waste Policy Act

LOEL lowest observed effect level

MACT maximum achievable control technology

MAER maximum allowable emission rate

MCL maximum contaminant level

MCLG maximum contaminant level goal

MDB multilateral development bank

MIR maximum individual risk

MMPA Marine Mammal Protection Act

MMT methylcyclopentadienyl manganese tricarbonyl

MOU memorandum of understanding

MPO metropolitan planning organization

MPRSA Marine Protection, Research, and Sanctuaries Act (Ocean Dumping Act)

MSHA Mine Safety and Health Administration (DOL)

MSW municipal solid waste

MTBE methyl tertiary butyl ether

MTD maximum tolerated dose

NAAEC North American Agreement on Environmental Cooperation

NAAQS national ambient air quality standards

NAFTA North American Free Trade Agreement

NAPA National Academy of Public Administration

NAPAP National Acid Precipitation Assessment Program

NAS National Academy of Sciences

NBAR non-binding allocation of responsibility

NCP National Contingency Plan

NEPA National Environmental Policy Act

NEPPS National Environmental Performance Partnership System

NESHAP national emissions standard for hazardous air pollutants

NFMA National Forests Management Act

NGO nongovernmental organization

NHANES National Health and Nutrition Examination Survey

NHTSA National Highway Traffic Safety Administration

NIEHS National Institute of Environmental Health Sciences

NIH National Institutes of Health

NIMBY not in my backyard

NIOSH National Institute of Occupational Safety and Health

NMFS National Marine Fisheries Service

NO nitric oxide

NO$_2$ nitrogen dioxide

NOAA National Oceanic and Atmospheric Administration

NOAEL no observable adverse effect level

NOx nitrogen oxide

NPDES National Pollutant Discharge Elimination System

NPL National Priority List
NPRM notice of proposed rulemaking
NPS National Park Service
NRC National Research Council, National Response Center, or Nuclear Regulatory Commission
NRDC Natural Resources Defense Council
NSF National Science Foundation
NSO nonferrous smelter orders
NSPS new source performance standards
NSR new source review
NTP National Toxicology Program
NWF National Wildlife Federation
NWPA Nuclear Waste Policy Act

OCS outer continental shelf
OCSLA Outer Continental Shelf Lands Act
OECD Organization for Economic Cooperation and Development
OIRA Office of Information and Regulatory Affairs (OMB)
OMB Office of Management and Budget
OPA 90 Oil Pollution Prevention, Response, Liability, and Compensation Act
ORV off-road vehicle
OSHA Occupational Safety and Health Administration
OSH Act Occupational Safety and Health Act
OSM Office of Surface Mining
OTA Office of Technology Assessment (abolished in 1995)
OTAG Ozone Transport Assessment Group
OTC Ozone Transport Commission
OTR ozone transport region

PA preliminary assessment
PCBs polychlorinated biphenyls
PCSD President's Council on Sustainable Development
PEL permissible exposure limit
PIC prior informed consent

PM2.5 particulate matter smaller than 2.5 micrometers in diameter
PM10 particulate matter (nominally 10m and less)
PM15 particulate matter (nominally 15m and less)
PMN premanufacture notification
POM polycyclic organic matter
POP persistent organic pollutant
POTW publicly owned treatment works
ppm parts per million
PRA Paperwork Reduction Act
PRP potentially responsible party
PSD prevention of significant deterioration
PTE potential to emit
PVC polyvinyl chloride

QA/QC quality assurance/quality control
QRA quantitative risk assessment

RA regulatory analysis, remedial action, or risk assessment
RACM reasonably available control measures
RACT reasonably available control technology
RARG Regulatory Analysis Review Group
RCRA Resource Conservation and Recovery Act
RD remedial design
REACH Registration, Evaluation, and Authorisation of Chemicals (EU)
R&D research and development
RECLAIM Regional Clean Air Incentives Market
RFA Regulatory Flexibility Act
RFDs reference dose values
RGGI Regional Greenhouse Gas Initiative
RTF reasonable further progress
RIA regulatory impact analysis
RI/FS remedial investigation/feasibility study
ROD record of decision

RPAR rebuttable presumption against registration
RQ reportable quantities

SAB Science Advisory Board
SAR structure activity relationship
SARA Superfund Amendments and Reauthorization Act of 1986
SBLRBRA Small Business Liability Relief and Brownfields Revitalization Act
SBREFA Small Business Regulatory Enforcement Fairness Act
SCAQMD South Coast Air Quality Management District (California)
SCR selective catalytic reduction
SCS Soil Conservation Service
SDWA Safe Drinking Water Act
SEPA State Environmental Protection Agency (China)
SERC state emergency response commission
SIP state implementation plan
SMCRA Surface Mining Control and Reclamation Act
SNUR significant new use rule
SO₂ sulfur dioxide
SQG small quantity generator
STEL short-term exposure limit
SUWA Southern Utah Wilderness Alliance
SWDA Solid Waste Disposal Act
SWMU solid waste management unit

TCE trichloroethylene
TCDD dioxin (tetrachlorodibenzo-p-dioxin)
TCDF tetrachlorodibenzofurans

TCLP toxicity characteristic leachate procedure
TCP transportation control plan
TDR transferable development right
TDS total dissolved solids
TEL tetraethyl lead
TKN total kjeldahl nitrogen
TLV threshold limit value
TMDL total maximum daily loading
TQM total quality management
TRI Toxics Release Inventory
TSCA Toxic Substances Control Act
TSD treatment, storage, and disposal facility
TVA Tennessee Valley Authority

UDMH unsymmetrical dimethylhydrazine
UGB urban growth boundary
UIC underground injection control
ULEV ultra low-emission vehicle
UMTRCA Uranium Mill Tailings Radiation Control Act
UN United Nations
UNEP United Nations Environment Programme
UST underground storage tank
UV ultraviolet

VOC volatile organic compound

WCED World Commission on Environment and Development
WHO World Health Organization
WTO World Trade Organization
WSA wilderness study area

ZEV zero-emission vehicle

‖ *Table of Cases* ‖

‖ *Index* ‖